GALE ENCYCLOPEDIA OF

MULTICULTURAL AMERICA

THIRD EDITION

EDITED BY THOMAS RIGGS

GALE ENCYCLOPEDIA OF

MULTICULTURAL AMERICA

ACADIANS–CZECH AMERICANS

EDITED BY THOMAS RIGGS

GALE
CENGAGE Learning·

Detroit • New York • San Francisco • New Haven, Conn • Waterville, Maine • London

© 2014 Gale, Cengage Learning

WCN: 01-100-101

Gale Encyclopedia of Multicultural America

Thomas Riggs, Editor

Project Editor: Marie Toft

Editorial: Jeff Hunter, Carol Schwartz

Technical Assistance: Luann Brennan, Grant Eldridge, Jeffrey Muhr, Rebecca Parks

Rights Acquisition and Management: Sheila Spencer

Composition: Evi Abou-El-Seoud

Manufacturing: Wendy Blurton

Imaging: John Watkins

Product Design: Kristine Julien

Index: Shana Milkie

For product information and technology assistance, contact us at
Gale Customer Support, 1-800-877-4253.
For permission to use material from this text or product,
submit all requests online at **www.cengage.com/permissions**.
Further permissions questions can be emailed to
permissionrequest@cengage.com.

Cover photographs and art reproduced with the following permission:

For Asian business man, © aslysun/Shutterstock.com; for Indian businessman, © Kenneth Man/Shutterstock.com; for young Sephardic Jewish man, © Howard Sandler/Shutterstock.com; for African American female, © Flashon Studio/Shutterstock.com; for Rastafarian male, © Alan Bailey/Shutterstock.com; for Muslim woman (side view), © szefei/Shutterstock.com; for young woman in white t-shirt and jeans, © Vlasov Volodymyr/Shutterstock.com; for Hispanic woman in white blouse, © Warren Goldswaini/Shutterstock.com; for puzzle vector illustration, © VikaSuh/Shutterstock.com.

While every effort has been made to ensure the reliability of the information presented in this publication, Gale, a part of Cengage Learning, does not guarantee the accuracy of the data contained herein. Gale accepts no payment for listing; and inclusion in the publication of any organization, agency, institution, publication, service, or individual does not imply endorsement of the editors or publisher. Errors brought to the attention of the publisher and verified to the satisfaction of the publisher will be corrected in future editions.

Library of Congress Cataloging-in-Publication Data

Gale Encyclopedia of Multicultural America / Thomas Riggs, editor. — 3rd edition.
   pages cm
   Includes bibliographical references and index.
   ISBN 978-0-7876-7550-9 (set : hardcover) — ISBN 978-0-7876-7551-6 (vol. 1 : hardcover) — ISBN 978-0-7876-7552-3 (vol. 2 : hardcover) — ISBN 978-0-7876-7553-0 (vol. 3 : hardcover) — ISBN 978-1-4144-3279-3 (vol. 4 : hardcover)
   1. Cultural pluralism—United States—Encyclopedias. 2. Ethnology—United States—Encyclopedias. 3. Minorities—United States—Encyclopedias. 4. United States—Ethnic relations—Encyclopedias. 5. United States—Race relations—Encyclopedias. I. Riggs, Thomas.
   E184.A1G14 2014
   305.800973—dc23
                                                          2013049273

Gale
27500 Drake Rd.
Farmington Hills, MI, 48331-3535

ISBN-13: 978-0-7876-7550-9 (set)
ISBN-13: 978-0-7876-7551-6 (vol. 1)
ISBN-13: 978-0-7876-7552-3 (vol. 2)
ISBN-13: 978-0-7876-7553-0 (vol. 3)
ISBN-13: 978-1-4144-3279-3 (vol. 4)

This title is also available as an e-book.
ISBN-13: 978-1-4144-3806-1
Contact your Gale, a part of Cengage Learning sales representative for ordering information.

TABLE OF CONTENTS

CONTENTS OF ALL VOLUMES

EDITOR'S NOTE

The third edition of the *Gale Encyclopedia of Multicultural America*—a major revision to the previous editions published in 1995 and 2000—includes 175 entries, each focusing on an immigrant or indigenous group in the United States. Some entries provide historical and cultural overviews of commonly recognized groups, such as Mexican Americans and Japanese Americans, while others discuss much smaller groups—for example, Cape Verdean Americans, Jordanian Americans, and the Ojibwe. The third edition has 23 new entries; the 152 entries from the second edition were thoroughly revised and reorganized, creating up-to-date coverage and a more consistent approach throughout the book. The writing or revision of each entry was reviewed by a scholar with extensive research background in the group.

The structure and content of the *Gale Encyclopedia of Multicultural America* was planned with the help of the project's advisory board. Joe Feagin—professor of sociology at Texas A&M University and a member of the advisory board—revised and updated the encyclopedia's introduction, originally written by Rudolph Vecoli. The introduction provides a broad historical overview of race and ethnicity in the United States, explaining how cultural and legal influences, especially racism, helped shape the experience of indigenous and immigrant groups.

ORGANIZATION

The 175 entries are arranged alphabetically across three volumes. The length of the entries varies from about 4,000 to 20,000 words. All entries share a common structure, providing consistent coverage of the groups and a simple way of comparing basic elements of one entry with another. Birth and death dates are provided for people mentioned in the entries except when dates could not be found or verified. The encyclopedia has more than 400 color images.

Each entry has 14 sections:

Overview: Basic information about the group's origins, homeland, immigration to or migration within the United States, and population and principal areas of settlement.

History of the People: Significant historical events of the group in its original region or country.

Settlement in the United States: For immigrant groups, waves of immigration and notable settlement patterns; for indigenous groups, original area of settlement, as well as migration within North America after the group's contact with Europeans.

Language: Native languages and their influence on the present-day group. Some entries have a section on greetings and popular expressions.

Religion: Religions and religious practices of the group, both in the original country or region and in the United States.

Culture and Assimilation: Traditional beliefs and customs, as well as the status of these traditions in the present-day group; topics include cuisine, dress, dances and songs, holidays, and health care issues and practices. Some entries have a sidebar on proverbs.

Family and Community Life: Topics include family structure and traditions; gender roles; education; dating practices, marriage, and divorce; and relations with other Americans.

Employment and Economic Conditions: Types of jobs commonly done by early immigrants or by indigenous people as they came into contact with European settlers, as well as notable employment trends among later generations of the group.

Politics and Government: Topics include the group's involvement in American politics and government (including voting patterns, significant events, and legislation) and contemporary interest in the parent country.

Notable Individuals: Examples of accomplished members of the group in various fields, with brief summaries.

Media: List of television and radio stations, as well as newspapers and periodicals, that are directed toward the group or provide significant coverage of it.

Organizations and Associations: List of organizations and associations related to the group.

Museums and Research Centers: List of museums and research centers related to the group.

Sources for Additional Study: A bibliography of books and articles about the group, including recent sources.

ACKNOWLEDGMENTS

Many people contributed time, effort, and ideas to the third edition of the *Gale Encyclopedia of Multicultural America*. Marie Toft, senior content project editor at Cengage Gale, served as in-house manager for the project. The quality of the book owes much to her ideas and feedback, as well as to her oversight of the book's production.

We would like to express our appreciation to the advisors, who, in addition to creating the list of new entry topics, helped evaluate the second edition and proposed ideas for producing an improved third edition. We would also like to thank the contributors for their carefully prepared essays and for their efforts to summarize the cultural life of ethnic groups without stereotyping. We are grateful to the many scholars who reviewed entries for accuracy and coverage.

The long process of reorganizing and revising the second-edition entries, as well as preparing the new ones, was overseen by Joseph Campana, project editor, who also helped identify and correspond with the advisors. Anne Healey, senior editor, managed the editing process and was helped by Mary Beth Curran, David Hayes, and Lee Esbenshade, all associate editors. Hannah Soukup, assistant editor, identified and corresponded with the academic reviewers. Other important assistance came from Mariko Fujinaka, managing editor, and Jake Schmitt and Theodore McDermott, assistant editors. The line editors were Robert Anderson, Cheryl Collins, Tony Craine, Gerilee Hunt, Amy Mortensen, Jill Oldham, Kathy Peacock, Donna Polydoros, Natalie Ruppert, and Will Wagner.

Thomas Riggs

 # ADVISORY BOARD

CHAIR

David R. M. Beck
Professor, Department of Native American Studies, University of Montana, Missoula.

ADVISORS

Joe Feagin
Ella C. McFadden Professor, Department of Sociology, Texas A&M University.

Patricia Fernandez-Kelly
Professor, Department of Sociology, Office of Population Research, Princeton University.

David Gerber
University at Buffalo Distinguished Professor Emeritus, Department of History, University at Buffalo, The State University of New York.

Rebecca Stuhr
Coordinator for Humanities Collections, Librarian for Classical Studies and History, University of Pennsylvania Libraries, Member, Ethnic & Multicultural Information Exchange Round Table, American Library Association.

Vladimir F. Wertsman
Retired Chair, Publishing and Multicultural Materials Committee, Ethnic and Multicultural Information Exchange Round Table, American Library Association.

LIST OF ACADEMIC REVIEWERS

HOLLY ACKERMAN

Ph. D. Librarian for Latin American, Iberian, & Latino Studies, Duke University, Durham, North Carolina

DEIRDRE ALMEIDA

Director of the American Indian Studies Program, Eastern Washington University, Cheney

BARBARA WATSON ANDAYA

Professor of Asian Studies, University of Hawai'i, Manoa

BARBARA A. ANDERSON

Ronald Freedman Collegiate Professor of Sociology and Population Studies, University of Michigan, Ann Arbor

JOSEPH ARBENA

Professor Emeritus of History, Clemson University, South Carolina

LAURIE ARNOLD

Director of Native American Studies, Gonzaga University, Spokane, Washington

CHRISTOPHER P. ATWOOD

Associate Professor of Central Eurasian Studies, Indiana University, Bloomington

ANNY BAKALIAN

Associate Director of the Graduate Center, City University of New York

CARINA BANDHAUER

Professor of Sociology, Western Connecticut State University, Danbury, Connecticut

CARL L. BANKSTON III

Professor of Sociology, Tulane University, New Orleans, Louisiana

LAURA BARBAS-RHODEN

Associate Professor of Foreign Languages, Wofford College, Spartanburg, South Carolina

DAVID BECK

Department Chair of the Native American Studies Department and Professor of Native American Studies, University of Montana, Missoula

JOHN BIETER

Associate Professor of History, Boise State University, Idaho

ADRIAN VILIAMI BELL

Visiting Assistant Professor of Anthropology, University of Utah, Salt Lake City

BRIAN BELTON

Ph.D., as well as Senior Lecturer, YMCA George Williams College, London, United Kingdom

SAMIR BITAR

Lecturer of Arabic Language and Cultures, Department of Anthropology, and Assistant Director of Outreach-Central and Southwest Asian Studies Center, University of Montana, Missoula

LASZLO BORHI

Senior Research Fellow, Institute of History Hungarian Academy of Sciences, Budapest, Hungary

GREGORY CAMPBELL

Professor of Anthropology, University of Montana, Missoula

MAURICE CARNEY

Independent scholar, Friends of the Congo, Washington D.C

JUAN MANUEL CASAL

Professor and Chair, Department of History, Universidad de Montevideo, Uruguay

ELIZABETH CHACKO

Associate Professor of Geography and International Affairs and Chair of the Department of Geography, George Washington University, Washington, D.C.

ALLAN CHRISTELOW

Professor of History, Idaho State University, Pocatello

STEPHEN CRISWELL

Associate Professor of English and Native American Studies, University of South Carolina, Lancaster

JAMSHEED CHOKSY

Professor of Iranian and Islamic Studies, Indiana University, Bloomington

RICHMOND CLOW

Professor of Native American Studies, University of Montana, Missoula

STEPHANIE COX

Visiting Assistant Professor of French, Carleton College, Northfield, Minnesota

SHAHYAR DANESHGAR

Senior Lecturer of Central Eurasian Studies, Indiana University, Bloomington

JEAN DENNISON

Assistant Professor of Anthropology, University of North Carolina, Chapel Hill

JOSE R. DEUSTUA

Associate Professor of History, Eastern Illinois University, Charleston, Illinois

MUNROE EAGLES

Program Director of Canadian Studies and Professor of Political Science, State University of New York, Buffalo

SARAH ENGLAND

Associate Professor of Anthropology and Director of Social and Behavioral Sciences, Soka University of America, Alisa Viejo, California

PHYLLIS FAST

Professor of Anthropology, University of Alaska, Anchorage

SUJATHA FERNANDES

Associate Professor of Sociology, Queens College and the Graduate Center of the City University of New York

ANN FIENUP-RIORDAN

Independent scholar, Calista Elders Council, Bethel, Alaska

SEAN FOLEY

Associate Professor of History, Middle Tennessee State University, Murfreesboro

JAMES GIGANTINO

Assistant Professor of History, University of Arkansas, Fayetteville

EDWARD GOBETZ

Professor Emeritus of Sociology, Kent State University, Ohio

STEVEN J. GOLD

Professor of Sociology and Associate Chair in the Department of Sociology, Michigan State University, East Lansing

ANGELA A. GONZALES

Associate Professor of Development Sociology and American Indian Studies, Cornell University, Ithaca, New York

JONATHAN GOSNELL

Associate Professor of French Studies, Smith College, Northampton, Massachusetts

ISHTAR GOVIA

Lecturer of Psychology, University of the West Indies, Mona, Jamaica

YVONNE HADDAD

Professor of the History of Islam and Christian-Muslim Relations, Georgetown University, Washington, D.C.

JEFFREY HADLER

Associate Professor of South and Southeast Asian Studies, University of California, Berkeley

MARILYN HALTER

Professor of History, Institute on Culture, Religion, and World Affairs, Boston University, Brookline, Massachusetts

ANNE PEREZ HATTORI

Professor of History and Chamorro Studies, University of Guam, Mangilao

MICHAEL HITTMAN

Professor of Anthropology, Long Island University, Brooklyn, New York

INEZ HOLLANDER

Lecturer of Dutch Studies, University of California, Berkeley

JON D. HOLTZMAN

Associate Professor of Anthropology, Western Michigan University, Kalamazoo

KATHLEEN HOOD

Publications Director and Events Coordinator, The UCLA Herb Alpert School of Music, Department of Ethnomusicology, University of California, Los Angeles

MAREN HOPKINS

Director of Research, Anthropological Research, LLC, Tucson, Arizona

GUITA HOURANI

Director of the Lebanese Emigration Research Center, Notre Dame University, Kesrwan, Lebanon

SALLY HOWELL

Assistant Professor of History, University of Michigan, Dearborn

TARA INNISS

Lecturer in History, University of the West Indies, Cave Hill Campus, Barbados

ALPHINE JEFFERSON

Professor of History, Randolph-Macon College, Ashland, Virginia

PETER KIVISTO

Richard A. Swanson Professor of Social Thought, Augustana College, Rock Island, Illinois

MICHAEL KOPANIC, JR.

Adjunct Full Professor of History, University of Maryland University College, Adelphi, and Adjunct Associate Professor of History, St. Francis University, Loretto, Pennsylvania

DONALD B. KRAYBILL

Distinguished College Professor and Senior Fellow, Young Center for Anabaptist and

Pietist Studies, Elizabethtown College, Pennsylvania

GARY KUNKELMAN

Senior Lecturer, Professional Writing, Penn State Berks, Wyomissing, Pennsylvania

AL KUSLIKIS

Senior Program Associate for Strategic Initiatives, American Indian Higher Education Consortium, Alexandria, Virginia

WILLIAM LAATSCH

Emeritus Professor of Urban and Regional Studies, University of Wisconsin, Green Bay

BRUCE LA BRACK

Professor Emeritus of Anthropology, University of the Pacific, Stockton, California

SARAH LAMB

Professor of Anthropology, Brandeis University, Waltham, Massachusetts

LAURIE RHONDA LAMBERT

Doctoral candidate in English and American Literature, New York University

JOHN LIE

C. K. Cho Professor, University of California, Berkeley

HUPING LING

Changjiang Scholar Chair Professor and Professor of History, Truman State University, Kirksville, Missouri

JOSEPH LUBIG

Associate Dean for Education, Leadership and Public Service, Northern Michigan University, Marquette

ALEXANDER LUSHNYCKY

President of the Shevchenko Scientific Society Study Center, Elkins Park, Pennsylvania

NEDA MAGHBOULEH

Assistant Professor, Department of Sociology, University of Toronto, Ontario

WILLIAM MEADOWS

Professor of Anthropology, Missouri State University, Springfield

MARIANNE MILLIGAN

Visiting Assistant Professor of Linguistics, Macalester College, Saint Paul, Minnesota

NAEEM MOHAIEMEN

Doctoral student in Anthropology at Columbia University, New York

ALEXANDER MURZAKU

Professor and Chair of World Cultures and Languages, College of Saint Elizabeth, Morristown, New Jersey

GEORGE MUSAMBIRA

Associate Professor of Communication, University of Central Florida, Orlando

GHIRMAI NEGASH

Professor of English & African Literature, Ohio University, Athens

JENNY NELSON

Associate Professor of Media Studies, Ohio University, Athens

RAFAEL NÚÑEZ-CEDEÑO

Coeditor of Probus: International Journal of Latin and Romance Linguistics and Professor Emeritus of Hispanic Studies, University of Illinois, Chicago

GREG O'BRIEN

Associate Professor of History, University of North Carolina, Greensboro

GRANT OLSON

Coordinator of Foreign Language Multimedia Learning Center, Northern Illinois University, DeKalb

THOMAS OWUSU

Professor and Chair of Geography, William Paterson University, Wayne, New Jersey

JODY PAVILACK

Associate Professor of History, University of Montana, Missoula

BARBARA POSADAS

College of Liberal Arts and Sciences Distinguished Professor of History, Northern Illinois University, DeKalb

JASON PRIBILSKY

Associate Professor of Anthropology, Whitman College, Walla Walla, Washington

LaVERN J. RIPPLEY

Professor of German, St. Olaf College, Northfield, Minnesota

MIKA ROINILA

Ph.D., as well as International Baccalaureate Program Coordinator and Fulbright

Specialist, John Adams High School, South Bend, Indiana

WILL ROSCOE

Ph.D., Independent scholar, San Francisco, California

LEONID RUDNYTZKY

Professor and Director of Central and Eastern European Studies Program, La Salle University, Philadelphia

NICHOLAS RUDNYTZKY

Independent scholar and Board member of the St. Sophia Religious Association of Ukrainian Catholics, Elkins Park, Pennsylvania

YONA SABAR

Professor of Hebrew, University of California, Los Angeles

LOUKIA K. SARROUB

Associate Professor of Education, University of Nebraska, Lincoln

RICHARD SATTLER

Adjunct Assistant Professor, University of Montana, Missoula

RICHARD SCAGLION

UCIS Research Professor, University of Pittsburgh, Pennsylvania

HELGA SCHRECKENBERGER

Chair of the Department of German and Russian and Professor of German, University of Vermont, Burlington

BRENDAN SHANAHAN

Doctoral student in North American history, University of California, Berkeley

KEMAL SILAY

Professor of Central Eurasian Studies and Director of the Turkish Studies Program, Indiana University, Bloomington

JEANNE SIMONELLI

Professor of Cultural and Applied Anthropology, Wake Forest University, Winston-Salem, North Carolina

GUNTIS ŠMIDCHENS

Kazickas Family Endowed Professor in Baltic Studies, Associate Professor of Baltic Studies, and Head of Baltic Studies Program, University of Washington, Seattle

MATTHEW SMITH

Senior Lecturer in History, University of the West Indies, Mona, Jamaica

MARY S. SPRUNGER

Professor of History, Eastern Mennonite University, Harrisonburg, Virginia

THOMAS THORNTON

Director for the MSc in Environmental Change and Management, University of Oxford, United Kingdom

ELAISA VAHNIE

Executive Director at the Burmese American Community Institute, Indianapolis, Indiana

DOUGLAS VELTRE

Professor Emeritus of Anthropology, University of Alaska, Anchorage

MILTON VICKERMAN

Associate Professor of Sociology, University of Virginia, Charlottesville

KRINKA VIDAKOVIC-PETROV

Principal Research Fellow, Institute for Literature and Arts, Belgrade, Serbia

BETH VIRTANEN

President, Finnish North American Literature Association

MARTIN VOTRUBA

Director of the Slovak Studies Program, University of Pittsburgh, Pennsylvania

MARY WATERS

M. E. Zukerman Professor of Sociology, Harvard University, Cambridge, Massachusetts

MARVIN WEINBAUM

Professor Emeritus of Political Science, University of Illinois, Urbana-Champaign

BRENT WEISMAN

Professor of Anthropology, University of South Florida, Tampa

THOMAS L. WHIGHAM

Professor of History, University of Georgia, Athens

BRADLEY WOODWORTH

Assistant Professor of History, University of New Haven, West Haven, Connecticut

KRISTIN ELIZABETH YARRIS

Assistant Professor of International Studies and Women's & Gender Studies, University of Oregon, Eugene

XIAOJIAN ZHAO

Professor of Asian American Studies, University of California, Santa Barbara

LIST OF CONTRIBUTORS

NABEEL ABRAHAM

Abraham holds a PhD in anthropology and is a university professor.

JUNE GRANATIR ALEXANDER

Alexander holds a PhD and has been a university professor.

DONALD ALTSCHILLER

Altschiller holds a PhD in library science and works as a university librarian.

DIANE ANDREASSI

Andreassi is a journalist and freelance writer

GREG BACH

Bach holds an MA in classics and is a freelance writer.

CARL L. BANKSTON III

Bankston holds a PhD in sociology and is a university professor.

CRAIG BEEBE

Beebe holds an MA in geography and works in nonprofit communications.

DIANE E. BENSON ("LXEIS")

Benson holds an MFA in creative writing and is a playwright, actor, and director.

BARBARA C. BIGELOW

Bigelow is an author of young adult books and a freelance writer and editor.

D. L. BIRCHFIELD

Birchfield was a university professor and novelist.

BENJAMIN BLOCH

Bloch holds an MFA in creative writing and an MFA in painting.

ELIZABETH BOEHEIM

Boeheim holds an MA in English literature and has been a university instructor.

CAROL BRENNAN

Brennan is a freelance writer with a background in history.

HERBERT J. BRINKS

Brinks was an author and editor and served as a curator at a university library.

K. MARIANNE WARGELIN BROWN

Wargelin Brown holds a PhD in history and is an independent scholar.

SEAN T. BUFFINGTON

Buffington holds an MA and is the president of The University of the Arts.

PHYLLIS J. BURSON

Burson holds a PhD in psychology and works as an independent consultant.

HELEN BUSH CAVER

Caver held a PhD and worked as a university librarian.

CIDA S. CHASE

Chase holds a PhD and is a university professor.

CLARK COLAHAN

Colahan holds a PhD and is a university professor.

ROBERT J. CONLEY

Conley holds an MA in English, is an award-winning novelist, and has served as a university professor.

JANE STEWART COOK

Cook is a freelance writer.

CHRISTINA COOKE

Cooke holds an MFA in creative nonfiction and works as a university instructor and freelance writer.

AMY COOPER

Cooper holds a PhD in anthropology and is a university professor.

PAUL ALAN COX

Cox holds a PhD in biology and is the director of the Institute of Ethnomedicine.

GIANO CROMLEY

Cromley holds an MFA in creative writing and is a university instructor.

KEN CUTHBERTSON

Cuthbertson is a writer, editor, and freelance broadcaster.

ROSETTA SHARP DEAN

Dean is a former school counselor and president of the Sharp-Dean School of Continuing Studies, Inc.

CHAD DUNDAS

Dundas holds an MFA in creative writing and has been a university instructor and freelance writer.

STANLEY E. EASTON

Easton holds a PhD and is a university professor.

TIM EIGO

Eigo holds a law degree and is writer and editor.

LUCIEN ELLINGTON

Ellington holds an EdD and is a university professor.

JESSIE L. EMBRY

Embry holds a PhD in history and is a research professor.

ALLAN ENGLEKIRK

Englekirk holds a PhD in Spanish and is a university professor.

RICHARD ESBENSHADE

Esbenshade holds a PhD in history and has been a university professor and freelance writer.

MARIANNE P. FEDUNKIW

Fedunkiw holds a PhD in strategic communications and is a university instructor and consultant.

DENNIS FEHR

Fehr holds a PhD in art education and is a university professor.

DAISY GARD

Gard is a freelance writer with a background in English literature.

CLINT GARNER

Garner holds an MFA in creative writing and is a freelance writer.

CHRISTOPHER GILES

Giles holds an MA in classics and an MA in history and is a college instructor and administrator.

MARY GILLIS

Gillis holds an MA has worked as a freelance writer and is a painter and sculptor.

EDWARD GOBETZ

Gobetz holds a PhD in sociology and is a retired university professor and former executive director of the Slovenian Research Center of America.

MARK A. GRANQUIST

Granquist holds a PhD and is a university professor.

DEREK GREEN

Green is a freelance writer and editor.

PAULA HAJAR

Hajar holds an EdD and has worked as a university professor and high school teacher.

LORETTA HALL

Hall is a freelance writer and the author of five works of nonfiction.

FRANCESCA HAMPTON

Hampton is a freelance writer and university instructor.

RICHARD C. HANES

Hanes holds a PhD and has served as the Division Chief of Cultural, Paleontological Resources, and Tribal Consultation for the Bureau of Land Management.

SHELDON HANFT

Hanft holds a PhD in history and is a university professor.

RODNEY HARRIS

Harris is a PhD candidate in history.

JOSH HARTEIS

Harteis holds an MA in English literature and is a freelance writer.

KARL HEIL

Heil is a freelance writer.

EVAN HEIMLICH

Heimlich is a freelance writer and university instructor.

ANGELA WASHBURN HEISEY

Heisey is a freelance writer.

MARY A. HESS

Hess is a freelance writer.

LAURIE COLLIER HILLSTROM

Hillstrom is a freelance writer and editor. She has published more than twenty works of history and biography.

MARIA HONG

Hong is a freelance writer and poet and was a Bunting Fellow at Harvard University in 2010-2011.

RON HORTON

Horton holds an MFA in creative writing and has been a high school English instructor and freelance writer.

EDWARD IFKOVIĆ

Ifković is a professor of creative writing and the author of four novels.

ALPHINE W. JEFFERSON

Jefferson holds a PhD in history and is a university professor.

CHARLIE JONES

Jones is a high school librarian.

J. SYDNEY JONES

Jones has worked as a freelance writer and correspondent and has published twelve works of fiction and nonfiction.

JANE JURGENS

Jurgens has been a university instructor.

JIM KAMP

Kamp is a freelance writer and editor.

OSCAR KAWAGLEY

Kawagley held a PhD in social and educational studies and was a university professor.

CLARE KINBERG

Kinberg holds a masters in library and information science and has been a literary journal editor.

KRISTIN KING-RIES

King-Ries holds an MFA in creative writing and has been a university instructor.

VITAUT KIPEL

Kipel held a PhD in mineralogy and an MLS and worked in the Slavic and Baltic Division of the New York Public Library.

JUDSON KNIGHT

Knight holds BIS in international studies, works as a freelance writer, and is co-owner of The Knight Agency, a literary sales and marketing firm.

PAUL S. KOBEL

Kobel is a freelance writer.

DONALD B. KRAYBILL

Kraybill holds a PhD in sociology and is a university professor.

LISA KROGER

Kroger holds a PhD in English literature and has been a university instructor.

KEN KURSON

Kurson is the editor-in-chief of the New York Observer.

ODD S. LOVOLL

Lovoll holds a PhD in U.S. history and is a university professor.

LORNA MABUNDA

Mabunda is a freelance writer.

PAUL ROBERT MAGOCSI

Magocsi holds a PhD in history and is the chair of Ukrainian Studies at the University of Toronto.

MARGUERITE MARÍN

Marín holds a PhD in sociology and is a university professor.

WILLIAM MAXWELL

Maxwell is a freelance writer who has worked as an editor at A Gathering of the Tribes magazine.

THEODORE MCDERMOTT

McDermott holds an MFA in creative writing and has been a university instructor and freelance writer.

JAQUELINE A. MCLEOD

McLeod holds a JD and PhD and is a university professor.

H. BRETT MELENDY

Melendy held a PhD in history and served as university professor and administrator.

MONA MIKHAIL

Mikhail holds a PhD in comparative literature and is a writer, translator, and university professor.

OLIVIA MILLER

Miller is a freelance writer, consultant, and university instructor.

CHRISTINE MOLINARI

Molinari is a freelance writer and editor and an independent researcher.

AARON MOULTON

Moulton holds an MA in Latin American studies. He is a PhD candidate in history and a university instructor.

LLOYD E. MULRAINE

Mulraine holds a DA in English and is a university professor.

JEREMY MUMFORD

Mumford holds a PhD in history and has worked as a university professor.

N. SAMUEL MURRELL

Murrell holds a PhD in biblical and theological studies and is a university professor.

AMY NASH

Nash is a published poet and has worked as a freelance writer and communications manager for Meyer, Scherer, & Rockcastle, Ltd., an architecture firm.

JOHN MARK NIELSEN

Nielsen is the executive director at the Danish Immigrant Museum.

ERNEST E. NORDEN

Norden holds a PhD and is a retired university professor.

SONYA SCHRYER NORRIS

Norris has worked as a freelance writer and website developer.

LOLLY OCKERSTROM

Ockerstrom holds a PhD in English and is a university professor.

KATRINA OKO-ODOI

Oko-Odoi is a PhD candidate in Spanish language literature and a university instructor.

JOHN PACKEL

Packel has worked as a freelance writer and is an associate director at American Express.

TINAZ PAVRI

Pavri holds a PhD in political science and is a university professor.

RICHARD E. PERRIN

Perrin was a university reference librarian.

PETER L. PETERSEN

Petersen holds a PhD in history and is a university professor.

MATTHEW T. PIFER

Pifer holds a PhD in composition and is a university professor.

GEORGE POZETTA

Pozetta held a PhD in history and was a university professor.

NORMAN PRADY

Prady is a freelance writer.

ELIZABETH RHOLETTER PURDY

Purdy is an independent scholar and has published numerous articles on political science and women's issues.

BRENDAN A. RAPPLE

Rapple holds an MBA and PhD and is a university librarian.

MEGAN RATNER

Ratner is a film critic and an associate editor at Bright Lights Film Journal.

WYLENE RHOLETTER

Rholetter holds a PhD in English literature and is a university professor.

LAVERN J. RIPPLEY

Rippley holds a PhD in German studies and is a university professor.

JULIO RODRIGUEZ

Rodriguez is a freelance writer.

PAM ROHLAND

Rohland is a freelance writer.

LORIENE ROY

Roy holds a PhD and MLS and is a university professor.

LAURA C. RUDOLPH

Rudolph is a freelance writer.

ANTHONY RUZICKA

Ruzicka is pursuing an MFA in poetry and has worked as a university instructor.

KWASI SARKODIE-MENSAH

Sarkodie-Mensah holds a PhD, is an author of research guides, and works as a university librarian.

LEO SCHELBERT

Schelbert holds a PhD in history and is a retired university professor.

JACOB SCHMITT

Schmitt holds an MA in English literature and has been a freelance writer.

MARY C. SENGSTOCK

Sengstock holds a PhD in sociology and is a university professor.

ELIZABETH SHOSTAK

Shostak is a freelance writer and editor.

STEFAN SMAGULA

Smagula has written for The Austin Chronicle and Zymurgy magazine and has designed software for Google, Bloomberg L.P., and The Economist. He works as software product designer in Austin, Texas.

HANNAH SOUKUP

Soukup holds an MFA in creative writing.

JANE E. SPEAR

Spear holds an MD and is a freelance writer and copyeditor.

TOVA STABIN

Stabin holds a Masters of Library and Information Science and works as a writer, editor, researcher, and diversity trainer.

BOSILJKA STEVANOVIĆ

Stevanović holds an MS in Library Science and is an independent translator.

SARAH STOECKL

Stoeckl holds a PhD in English literature and is a university instructor and freelance writer.

ANDRIS STRAUMANIS

Straumanis is a freelance writer and editor, as well as a university instructor.

PAMELA STURNER

Sturner is the executive director of the Leopold Leadership Program.

LIZ SWAIN

Swain has worked as a freelance writer and crime reporter and is a staff writer for the San Diego Reader.

MARK SWARTZ

Swartz holds an MA in art history, has served as writer for numerous nonprofits (including the American Hospital Association), and has published two novels.

THOMAS SZENDREY

Szendrey is a freelance writer.

HAROLD TAKOOSHIAN

Takooshian holds a PhD in psychology and is a university professor.

BAATAR TSEND

Tsend is an independent scholar and writer.

FELIX UME UNAEZE

Unaeze is a university librarian.

STEVEN BÉLA VÁRDY

Várdy holds a PhD in history and is a university professor.

GRACE WAITMAN

Waitman is pursuing a PhD in educational psychology. She holds an MA in English literature and has been a university instructor.

DREW WALKER

Walker is a freelance writer.

LING-CHI WANG

Wang holds a PhD and is a social activist and retired university professor.

KEN R. WELLS

Wells is a freelance writer and editor and has published works of young adult science fiction and nonfiction.

VLADIMIR F. WERTSMAN

Wertsman is a member of the American Library Association and the retired chair of the Publishing and Multicultural Materials Committee.

MARY T. WILLIAMS

Williams has worked as a university professor.

ELAINE WINTERS

Winters is a freelance writer, editor, and program facilitator. She has provided professional training for a number of Fortune 500 companies, including Apple, Nokia, and Nortel.

EVELINE YANG

Yang holds an MA in international and public affairs and is a PhD candidate in the Department of Central Eurasian Studies at Indiana University.

ELEANOR YU

Yu is the Supervising Producer at Monumental Mysteries at Optomen Productions.

INTRODUCTION

The term multiculturalism is used to describe a society characterized by a diversity of cultures. Religion, language, customs, traditions, and values are some components of culture, and culture also includes the perspectives through which people perceive and interpret society. A shared culture and common historical experience form the basis for a sense of peoplehood.

Over the course of U.S. history two divergent paths have led to this sense of peoplehood. All groups except indigenous Americans (Native Americans), have entered North America as voluntary or involuntary immigrants. Some of these immigrant groups and their descendants have been oppressed by the dominant group—white Americans that have been for centuries primarily of northern European descent—and were defined as inferior racial groups. A *racial group* is a societal group that people inside or outside that group distinguish as racially inferior or superior, usually on the basis of arbitrarily selected physical characteristics (for example, skin color). Historically whites have rationalized the subordination of other racial groups, viewing them as biologically and culturally inferior, uncivilized, foreign, and less than virtuous. To the present day Asian, African, Native, and Mexican Americans have been regularly "racialized" by the dominant white group. Even some non-British European immigrant groups (for example, Italian Americans) were for a short period of time defined as inferior racial groups, but within a generation or two they were defined as white.

Another term often used for certain distinctive social groups is *ethnic group*. While some social scientists have used it broadly to include racial groups, the more accurate use of the term is a group that is distinguished or set apart, by others or its own members, primarily on the basis of national-origin characteristics and cultural characteristics that are subjectively selected. "Ethnic" is an English word derived from the Greek word *ethnos* (for "nation") and was originally used for European immigrants entering in the early twentieth century. Examples are Polish Americans and Italian Americans, groups with a distinctive national origin and cultural heritage. Both racial groups and ethnic groups are socially constructed under particular historical circumstances and typically have a distinctive sense of peoplehood and cultural history. However, the lengthy historical and contemporary experiences of racial discrimination and subordination differentiate certain groups, such as African Americans and Native Americans, from the experiences and societal status of the ethnic groups of European origin that are now part of the white umbrella racial group.

"Multicultural America," the subject of this encyclopedia, is the product of the interaction of many different indigenous and immigrant peoples over the course of four centuries in what is now the United States. Cultural diversity was characteristic of the continent prior to the coming of European colonists and the Africans they enslaved. The indigenous inhabitants of North America numbered at least 7 million, and perhaps as many as 18 million, in the sixteenth century and were divided into hundreds of indigenous societies with distinctive cultures. Although the numbers of "Indians," as they were named by European colonizers, declined precipitously over the centuries as a result of European genocidal killings and diseases, their population has rebounded over the last century. As members of particular indigenous groups (such as Navajo, Ojibwa, and Choctaw) and as Native Americans, they are very much a part of today's cultural pluralism.

Most North Americans, in contrast, are the descendants of immigrants from other continents. Since the sixteenth century, from the early Spanish settlement at St. Augustine, Florida, the process of repopulating the continent has gone on apace. Several hundred thousand Europeans and Africans were recruited or enslaved and transported across the Atlantic Ocean during the colonial period to what eventually became the United States. The first census of 1790 revealed the racial and national origin diversity that marked the U.S. population. Almost a fifth of Americans were of African ancestry. (The census did not include Native Americans.) A surname analysis of the white population revealed that about 14 percent were Scottish and Scotch-Irish Americans and about 9 percent were German Americans—with smaller percentages of French, Irish, Dutch, Swedish, and Welsh Americans. English Americans comprised about 60 percent of the white population. At the time of its birth in 1776, the United States was already a complex racial and ethnic mosaic, with a wide variety of communities differentiated by the extent of racial oppression and by their national ancestry, culture, language, and religion.

The present United States includes not only the original 13 colonies but lands that were subsequently purchased or conquered by an often imperialistic U.S. government. Through this territorial expansion, other peoples and their lands were brought within the boundaries of the country. These included, in addition to many Native American societies, French, Hawaiian, Inuit, Mexican, and Puerto Rican groups, among others. Since 1790 great population growth, other than by natural increase, has come primarily through three eras of large-scale immigration. Arriving in the first major era of immigration (1841–1890) were almost 15 million newcomers: more than 4 million Germans, 3 million each of Irish and British (English, Scottish, and Welsh), and 1 million Scandinavians. A second major era of immigration (1891–1920) brought an additional 18 million immigrants: almost 4 million from Italy, 3.6 million from Austria-Hungary, and 3 million from Russia. In addition, more than 2 million Canadians immigrated prior to 1920. The following decades, from 1920 to 1945, marked a hiatus in immigration because of restrictive and discriminatory immigration policies, economic depression, and World War II. A modest postwar influx of European refugees was followed by a new era of major immigration resulting from the U.S. government abandoning in 1965 its openly discriminatory immigration policy favoring northern European immigrants. Totaling more than 40 million immigrants from 1965 to 2013—and still in progress—this third major era of immigration has encompassed about 20 million newcomers from Mexico and other parts of Central and South America and the Caribbean, as well as roughly 10 million newcomers from Asia. The rest have come from Canada, Europe, the Middle East, and Africa. While almost all the immigrants in the first two eras originated in Europe, a substantial majority since 1965 have come from Latin America, the Caribbean, Asia, Africa, and the Middle East.

Immigration has introduced a great diversity of racial-ethnic groups and cultures into the United States. The 2000 U.S. Census, the latest national census to report on ancestry, provides an interesting portrait of the complex origins of the people of the United States. Responses to the question "What is your ancestry or ethnic origin?" were tabulated for many groups. The largest ancestry groups reported were, in order of magnitude, German, Irish, African American, and English, all with more than 24 million individuals. Other groups reporting more than 4 million were Mexican, Italian, Polish, French, Native American, Scottish, Dutch, Norwegian, Scotch-Irish, and Swedish, with many other groups reporting more than 1 million each. There is also an array of smaller groups: Hmong, Maltese, Honduran, and Nigerian, among scores of others. Only 7 percent identified themselves simply as "American"—and less than one percent only as "white."

Immigration has contributed to the transformation of the religious character of the United States. The dominant Anglo-Protestantism (itself divided among numerous denominations and sects) of early English colonists was over time reinforced by the arrival of millions of Lutherans, Methodists, and Presbyterians and diluted by the heavy influx of Roman Catholics—first by the Irish and Germans, then by eastern Europeans and Italians, and more recently by Latin Americans. These immigrants have made Roman Catholicism the largest U.S. denomination. Meanwhile, Slavic Christian and Jewish immigrants from central and eastern Europe established Orthodox Christianity and Judaism as major religious bodies. As a consequence of Middle Eastern immigration—and the conversion of many African Americans to Islam—there are currently several million Muslims in the United States. Smaller numbers of Buddhists, Hindus, and followers of other religions have also arrived. In many U.S. cities houses of worship now include mosques and temples, as well as churches and synagogues. Religious pluralism is an important source of U.S. multiculturalism.

The immigration and naturalization policies pursued by a country's central government are revealing about the dominant group's public conception of the country. By determining who to admit to residence and citizenship, the dominant group defines the future racial and ethnic composition of the population. Each of the three great eras of immigration inspired much soul-searching and intense debate, especially in the dominant European American group, over the consequences of immigration for the U.S. future. If the capacity of this society to absorb tens of millions of immigrants over the course of more than 17 decades is impressive, it is also true that U.S. history has been punctuated by major episodes of vicious and violent nativism and xenophobia. With the exception of the British, it is difficult to find an immigrant group that has not been subject to significant racial or ethnic prejudice and discrimination. From early violent conflicts with Native Americans to the enslavement of Africans, Americans of northern European ancestry sought to establish "whiteness" as an essential marker of racial difference and superiority. They crafted a racial framing of society in order to legitimate and rationalize their subordination of numerous racial and ethnic groups. For example, the Naturalization Act (1790), one of the first passed in the new U.S. Congress, specified that citizenship in the United States was available only to an immigrant who was "a free white person." By this dramatic provision not only were African Americans ineligible for naturalization but also future immigrants who were deemed not to be "white." From that time to the present, the greater the likeness of immigrants to the northern European Protestants, the more readily they were welcomed by the dominant group.

There were, however, opposing, liberty-and-justice views held by racially and ethnically oppressed groups, as well as a version of this outlook supported by a minority of the dominant European American group. For example, in the nineteenth century, citing democratic ideals and universal brotherhood, many African Americans and some white Americans advocated the abolition of slavery and the human rights of those freed from slavery.

Since at least the 1880s debates over immigration policy have periodically brought contrasting views of the United States into collision. The ideal of the United States as a shelter and asylum for the oppressed of the world has exerted a powerful influence for a liberal reception of diverse newcomers. Early support for this liberal framing of immigration came from the descendants of early immigrants who were racially or ethnically different from the then dominant British American group. Poet Emma Lazarus's sonnet, which began "Give me your tired, your poor, your huddled masses yearning to breathe free, the wretched refuse of your teeming shore," struck a responsive chord among many Americans and was placed on the Statue of Liberty, a gift to the United States by the people of France. Emma Lazarus (1849-87) herself was the daughter of early Sephardic (Portuguese) Jewish immigrants to the colonies.

Over the centuries many U.S. businesses have depended upon the immigrant workers of Europe, Latin America, and Asia to develop the country's factories, mines, and railroads. Periodically, nonetheless, many white Americans have framed this immigration in negative terms—as posing a threat to societal stability, to their jobs, or U.S. cultural and biological integrity. Historically the strength of organized anti-immigrant movements has waxed and waned with the volume of immigration, as well as with fluctuations in the condition of the U.S. economy. Although the immigrant targets of nativistic attacks have changed over time, a constant theme in the framing of them by the dominant group has been the "danger" posed by "foreigners" to the core U.S. values and institutions.

For example, coming in large numbers from the 1830s to the 1850s, Irish Catholics were viewed as the dependent minions of the Catholic pope and thus as enemies of the Protestant character of the United States. A Protestant crusade against these immigrants culminated in the formation of the "Know-Nothing" Party in the 1850s, whose political battle cry was "America for the Americans!" This anti-Catholicism continued to be a powerful strain of nativism well into the middle of the twentieth century, including during the election and presidency of John F. Kennedy, an Irish Catholic American, in the early 1960s.

Despite frequent episodes of xenophobia, during its first decades of existence, the U.S. government generally welcomed newcomers with minimal regulation. In the 1880s, however, two important laws passed by a Congress controlled by (northern) European American politicians initiated a significant tightening of restrictions on some immigration. The first law established certain health and "moral" standards by excluding criminals, prostitutes, lunatics, idiots, and paupers. The second, the openly racist Chinese Exclusion Act, was the culmination of an anti-Chinese movement among European Americans centered on the West Coast. It denied admission to new Chinese laborers and barred Chinese workers already here from acquiring citizenship. Following the law's enactment, agitation for exclusion of Asian immigrants continued as the new Japanese and other Asian immigrant workers arrived. This European American nativism soon resulted in the blatantly racist provisions of the 1924 Immigration Law, which denied entry to "aliens ineligible for citizenship" (that is, those who were not "white"). It was not until 1950s and 1960s that a combination of international politics and civil rights movements, with their democratic ideals, resulted in the elimination of the more overtly racial restrictions from U.S. immigration and naturalization policies.

In the mid- to late-nineteenth century "scientific racism," which reiterated the superiority of whites of northern European origin, was embraced by many scientists and political leaders as justification for immigration restrictions and growing U.S. imperialism on the continent and overseas. By the late-nineteenth century the second immigration era was quite evident, as large numbers of immigrants from southern and eastern Europe entered the country. Nativists of northern European ancestry campaigned for a literacy test and other measures to restrict the entry of what they termed "inferior" European nationalities (sometimes termed "inferior races"). World War I created a xenophobic climate that prepared the way for the immigration acts of 1921 and 1924. Inspired by nativistic ideas, these laws established a national quota system designed to greatly reduce the number of southern and eastern Europeans entering the United States and to bar Asians. The statutes intentionally sought to maintain the northern European racial-ethnic identity of the country by protecting it from "contamination" from abroad.

Until 1965 the U.S. government pursued a very restrictive immigration policy that kept the country from becoming more diverse racially, ethnically, and religiously. The 1965 Immigration Act finally did away with the discriminatory national origins quotas and opened the country to immigration from throughout the world, establishing preferences for family members of citizens, skilled workers, entrepreneurs, and refugees. One consequence was the third wave of immigration. Since then, the annual volume of authorized immigration has increased steadily to about 1 million arrivals each year, and the majority of these new residents have come from Asia and Latin America.

The cumulative impact of the immigration of tens of millions of non-European immigrants since 1965 has aroused intense concerns, mostly in the dominant white group, regarding the demographic, cultural, and racial future of the United States. The skin color, as well as the languages and cultures, of most of the newcomers and their descendants have again been viewed negatively by many whites. Nativistic white advocates of tighter immigration restriction have warned that if current rates of immigration continue, white Americans will likely be a minority of the U.S. population by 2050.

One particular cause of white anxiety is the number of undocumented immigrants from Mexico (down to about 140,000 per year by 2013). Contrary to popular belief, the majority of undocumented immigrants do not cross the border from Mexico but enter the country with student or tourist visas and stay. Indeed, many are Europeans and Asians. The 1986 Immigration Reform and Control Act (IRCA) sought to solve the problem by extending amnesty for undocumented immigrants under certain conditions, imposing penalties on employers who hired them, and making provision for temporary agricultural migrant workers. Although more than 3 million people qualified for consideration for amnesty, employer sanctions failed for lack of enforcement, and for a time the number of undocumented immigrants did not decrease. Congress subsequently enacted the Immigration Act of 1990, which established a cap on immigrants per year, maintained preferences based on family reunification, and expanded the number of skilled workers admitted. The Illegal Immigration Reform and Immigrant Responsibility Act (IIRIRA), passed in 1996, established yet more regulations restricting legal and undocumented immigration and increased border control agents.

In 2006 Congress passed yet more restrictive legislation, the Secure Fence Act. It mandated the building of a billion-dollar border fence and other expensive surveillance technology and increased border enforcement personnel. Over recent decades the extensive border surveillance procedures have played a role in many of the estimated 5,100 lives lost as undocumented men, women, and children have tried to cross an ever more difficult U.S.-Mexico border—with its intensively policed and often extremely hot and waterless conditions--to improve their dire economic situations. Latin American immigration has continued to be a hotly debated U.S. political issue. Responding to the nativist mood of the country, politicians have advocated yet more restrictive measures to reduce immigration, as well as limiting access to government programs by legal and undocumented immigrants.

Forebodings about an "unprecedented immigrant invasion," however, have been greatly exaggerated. In the early 1900s the rate of immigration (the number of immigrants measured against the total population) was higher than in recent decades. While the number of foreign-born individuals in the United States reached nearly 40 million in 2010, an all-time high, they accounted for only 12.9 percent of the population, compared with 14.7 percent in 1910, giving the United States a smaller percentage of foreign-born individuals than some other contemporary nations. Moreover, in the early twenty-first century, Mexican immigration to the United States has been decreasing significantly, to the point that in 2005-10 there was a net zero migration to United States—that is, as many Mexicans were leaving the United States as were coming in. A persuasive argument has also been made that immigrants contribute much more than they take from the U.S. economy and pay more in taxes than they receive in social services. As in the past, new immigrants are often made the scapegoats for the country's broader economic and political problems.

Difficult questions face analysts of U.S. history. How have these millions of immigrants with such differing backgrounds and cultures been incorporated into the society? What changes have they wrought in the character of United States? The problematical concept of "assimilation" has traditionally been used to try to understand the process through which immigrants have adapted to U.S. society. Assimilation theorists view cultural assimilation (acculturation) as the one-way process whereby newcomers assume U.S. cultural attributes, such as the English language and political values, and social-group assimilation as the process of immigrant incorporation into important social networks (work, residence, and families) of the dominant group. In many cases such adaptation has not come easily. Many immigrants of color have culturally adapted to a significant degree but have experienced only limited incorporation into many mainstream networks and institutions because of persisting white racial bias and discrimination.

Indeed, since they have always wielded great social and political power, white Americans as a group have been able to decide who to include and exclude in the country. "Race" (especially skin color) has been the major barrier to full acceptance into historically white-controlled institutions. Asian and Latino Americans, as well as African Americans and Native Americans, have long been excluded from full integration into major white-dominated institutions. Race, language, religion, and national origin have been impediments to access. Social class has also strongly affected interactions among U.S. racial and ethnic groups. Historically, U.S. society has been highly stratified, with a close congruence between social class and racial or ethnic group. Thus, a high degree of employment and residential segregation has been central to maintaining the United States as a racially segregated society, with white Americans very disproportionately in the powerful upper and upper-middle classes.

The status of women within American society, as well as within particular racial and ethnic groups, has affected the ability of female immigrants to adapt to their new country. Historically, to a greater or lesser extent depending on their group, women have been restricted to traditional gender roles or have had limited freedom to pursue opportunities in the larger society. The density and location of immigrant settlements have also influenced the incorporation of immigrants into the dominant culture and institutions. Concentrated urban settlements and isolated rural settlements, by limiting contacts between immigrants and native-born Americans, tend to inhibit the processes of assimilation.

Historically one important variable is the determination of immigrants themselves whether or not to shed important aspects of their cultures. Through chain migrations, relatives and friends have often regrouped in cities, towns, and the countryside for mutual assistance and to maintain their customary ways in a sometimes hostile and difficult U.S. society. Establishing churches, newspapers, and other institutions, they have built communities and have developed an enlarged sense of peoplehood. Thus, national origin and home cultures have been important in many immigrants' attempts to cope with life in the United States. Theirs is often a selective adaptation, in which they have taken from the dominant U.S. culture what they needed and have kept significant aspects of their home culture that they value. The children and grandchildren of immigrants usually retain less of their ancestral cultures (languages are first to go) and have assumed more attributes of the dominant culture. Still, many have retained, to a greater or lesser degree, a sense of identity with a particular nationality or racial group. These patterns of societal adaptation vary greatly for different groups, historically and in the present. Immigrant groups of color and their descendants have been racialized by the dominant white group and have thus had quite different experiences from immigrants who are part of distinctive national origin groups within a white America. Racialized immigrant groups often use their home culture and its values and perspectives for resources in fighting against the racism and discrimination they face in their everyday lives.

For centuries the core culture of the colonies and early United States was essentially British American in most important aspects, and the immigrants (almost all European until the 1850s) and their offspring had to adapt to that dominant culture. Over time a few aspects of that core culture—such as music, food, and literature—have experienced some significant changes. These aspects of the core culture are today products of syncretism—the melding of different, sometimes discordant elements of the cultures of European and non-European immigrants and their descendants. Multiculturalism today is not a museum of immigrant cultures but rather a complex of the living, multitudinous cultures of the contemporary United States interacting with each other. Nonetheless, most of the central social, political, and economic realities of the U.S. core culture are still very much European American (especially British American) in their institutional structures, normative operation, and folkways. These include the major economic, legal, political, and educational institutions.

The country's ideological heritage includes the ideals of freedom and equality from the American Revolution. Such ideals have often been just abstract principles, especially for the dominant white group, that have been handed down from the eighteenth century to the present. However, subordinated racial and ethnic groups, taking these ideals very seriously, have employed them as weapons to combat economic exploitation and racial and ethnic discrimination. If the United States has been the "promised land" for many immigrants, that promise has been realized, if only in part, after prolonged and collective societal struggles. Through civil rights and labor movements, they have contributed greatly to keeping alive and enlarging the ideals of freedom, equality, and justice. If the

United States has transformed the numerous immigrant and indigenous groups in significant ways, these groups have on occasion significantly transformed the United States.

How has the dominant white American group historically conceived of this polyglot, kaleidoscopic society? Over the centuries two major models of a society comprised of various racial and ethnic groups have competed with each other. The dominant white model long envisioned a society based on racial "caste"— a society constitutionally and legally divided into those who were free and those who were not. Such a societal order existed for about 85 percent of this country's history (until the late 1960s). While the Civil War destroyed slavery, the Jim Crow system of segregation maintained extreme white oppression of black Americans for another hundred years. This model of intensive racial-ethnic oppression was not limited to black-white relationships. The industrial economy created a caste-like structure in much of the North. For a century prior to the progressive "New Deal" era of the 1930s, U.S. power, wealth, and status in the North were concentrated in the hands of a British-American elite, while U.S. workers there, made up largely of European immigrants and their children, were the low-paid serfs of factories, railroads, and farms. In subsequent decades this pattern has shifted as immigrants of color and their children have often filled many of these jobs on farms and in factories in the North and the South. By the 1960s official Jim Crow segregation ended in Southern and border states, and African Americans continued their movement out of the South to the North, which had begun in earnest in the 1930s and 1940s.

Over the centuries, since at least the 1700s, immigrants to this country have been expected by the dominant group to adapt and conform to the British-American ("Anglo-Saxon") core culture. Convinced of their cultural and biological superiority, Americans of British and other northern European descent have pressured Native Americans, African Americans, Latinos, and Asian Americans to modify or abandon their distinctive linguistic and cultural patterns and conform in a more or less one-way adaptive pattern to the dominant culture and folkways. However, even as they have demanded this conformity, European Americans have erected racial barriers that have severely limited egalitarian social intercourse and integration with those they have framed as racially inferior. Indeed, a prime objective of the U.S. public school system has been the one-way "assimilation" of "alien" children to the dominant cultural values and behaviors. The intensity of this pressure can be seen in the successful attacks, mostly white-led, on various programs of bilingual education, especially those involving the Spanish language of many Latin American immigrants and their descendants.

Nonetheless, over the course of U.S. history, and especially since the early 1900s, this intense one-way adaptation model has been countered by variations on a melting pot perspective. The "melting pot" symbolizes the process in which diverse immigrant groups are assimilated into a new "American blend." There have been many variants of this ideology of the melting pot, including the prevailing one in which the European American is still the cook stirring and determining the immigrant ingredients. In all versions the United States is viewed as becoming a distinctive amalgam of varied cultures and peoples emerging from the racial-ethnic crucible. Expressing confidence in the capacity of the country to incorporate diverse newcomers, the melting pot ideology has also provided the rationale for a more liberal approach to immigrants and immigration policy. Even so, this liberal melting pot ideology has periodically come under increasing attacks from anti-immigrant and other nativist groups, even after the progressive changes in U.S. immigration laws in the 1960s.

A third model of immigrant adaptation emerged during World War I in opposition to intensive pressures on immigrants for one-way "Americanization," a model often termed "cultural pluralism." In this model, while sharing a common U.S. citizenship and loyalty, racial and ethnic groups should be able to maintain and foster their particular languages and distinctive cultures. The metaphors employed for the cultural pluralism model have included a symphony orchestra, a flower garden, and a mosaic. All suggest a reconciliation of group diversity with an encompassing harmony and coherence of racial and ethnic groups. During the 1930s, when cultural democracy was more in vogue, pluralist ideas were more popular. Again during the social movements of the

1960s and the 1970s, cultural pluralism attracted a considerable following. By the early twenty-first century, heightened fears, especially among white Americans, that U.S. society is fragmenting and moving away from the dominance of the English language and Euro-American culture have caused many people to reject any type of significant cultural pluralism.

Questions about racial and ethnic matters loom large as the United States moves ever more deeply into the twenty-first century. Its future as a racially and ethnically plural society and socially just society is vigorously debated. Is the United States more diverse today than in the past? Can discriminatory racial and ethnic barriers be finally removed? Can this multiracial society really be made more just and democratic? The old model of one-way conformity to the white-controlled core culture has lost its ideological and symbolic value for a great many Americans who believe we need to implement a more egalitarian societal model. These Americans see the United States as a respectfully multicultural and truly democratic people in the context of a multicultural world.

Suggested Reading On issues of systemic racism and the creation of U.S. racial groups, see Joe R. Feagin, *Systemic Racism: A Theory of Oppression* (2006) and *The White Racial Frame* (2nd edition, 2013). On conventional assimilation theory, see Milton Gordon's *Assimilation in American Life: The Role of Race, Religion, and National Origins* (1964). On recent assimilation theory and applicable data, see Richard Alba, *Blurring the Color Line: The New Chance for a More Integrated America* (2009). For discussion of racial and ethnic group definitions, see Joe R. Feagin and Clairece B. Feagin, *Racial and Ethnic Relations (2011). Harvard Encyclopedia of American Ethnic Groups* (1980), edited by Stephan Thernstrom, is a standard reference work with articles on racial-ethnic themes and specific groups. Roger Daniels's *Coming to America: A History of Immigration and Ethnicity in American Life* (1991) is a comprehensive history. For a comparative history of racial-ethnic groups, see Ronald Takaki's *A Different Mirror: A History of Multicultural America* (1993). A classic work on nativism is John Higham's *Strangers in the Land: Patterns of American Nativism: 1860-1925* (1963). On the British American elite's history, see E. Digby Baltzell's *The Protestant Establishment: Aristocracy and Caste in America* (1964). On contemporary ancestry groups, see Angela Brittingham and G. Patricia de la Cruz, *Ancestry: 2000* (2004).

Rudolph Vecoli
Updated and revised by Joe Feagin

ACADIANS

Evan Heimlich

OVERVIEW

Acadians are the descendants of a group of French-speaking settlers who migrated from coastal France in the late sixteenth century to establish a colony called Acadia in an area that is now Nova Scotia, Prince Edward Island, and New Brunswick (three Maritime Provinces of Canada), as well as part of the state of Maine. Since 1785 Acadians in the United States have lived, for the most part, either along the Canadian border in Maine or in an area of southern Louisiana known as Acadiana. Acadians in Louisiana refer to themselves as Cajuns and far outnumber their counterparts in the Northeast. In Maine, Acadians have settled in modest numbers along the Saint John River in the small towns of Madawaska and Van Buren in the northwestern part of the state and along the Bay of Fundy, in the northeastern part of Maine. In southern Louisiana, Acadiana (or Cajun country), consists of a triangular area that begins in New Orleans in the east, runs due west to the Texas border and up to Lafayette, Louisiana. The region covers about 15,000 square miles (24,000 kilometers), an area slightly larger than the state of Maryland.

Acadian communities in Maine and Cajun communities in the southeastern United States are predominately Roman Catholic, but while the northeastern Acadians are a relatively homogenous group with members tending to marry within their communities, Cajuns are a diverse population of peoples of mixed ancestry, including over a dozen French-speaking immigrant groups. Several Native American tribes also call Acadiana home, including the Attakapas and the Tunica-Biloxi. Since the late 1900s Vietnamese, Laotian, and Cambodian settlers have become part of Acadiana, too. While the Acadians of Canada and Maine primarily farm the land or run small businesses, the Cajuns of Acadiana have, in addition to farming, taken on mining and construction work made available by the oil industry. On the whole, Acadians in Maine are less wealthy and live simpler lives than most New England residents. Likewise, Acadiana is less wealthy than the suburbs of New Orleans and Lafayette.

Acadians prospered under French rule in the Northeast until 1713, when the colony was transferred to the British with the signing of the Treaty of Utrecht at the end of the War of Spanish Succession. They maintained a tenuous relationship with the British for forty years. In 1755 the British expelled over 6,000 Acadians (more than half of the Acadian population), dispersing some among the colonies on the Atlantic seaboard and deporting others to France. This forced migration, known as Le Grand Dérangement, continued until 1763. The Acadians who remained in the Northeast lived as fugitives and began to migrate south, many of them initially settling in the Georgia area. In 1764, 21 Acadian people from four families migrating from Georgia settled in New Orleans. The following year, 600 more Acadians from Georgia joined them, with steady migration continuing for a decade. The Louisiana population spiked again in 1785 when the French government sent nearly 1,600 Acadians previously deported by the British to the new Acadian settlement in the United States. Although Le Grand Dérangement had ended in 1763, Acadians did not begin to recoup their numbers in the Northeast until the 1840s; by then about 3,500 Acadians were living in the Saint John River Valley on both sides of the Canadian border.

Reliable estimates of the Acadian population in Maine and the Cajun population in the Southeast are difficult to ascertain because the U.S. Census Bureau does not offer Acadian or Cajun as ancestry categories when compiling population data. Adding the sum of 2010 population totals for towns in Maine known to be predominately Acadian puts the Acadian population in the state at roughly 30,000. According to the American Community Survey's 2011 estimates, just over 42,000 people in Louisiana and nearly 16,500 people in Texas self-identified as Cajun. However, in 1990, when Cajun was offered as an ancestry category on the U.S. Census, approximately 650,000 Americans claimed Cajun ancestry. Many of the Acadians in Maine continue to live in the towns where they were born; however, since 2000 increasing numbers have taken up residence in other areas of New England. Nevertheless, a significant number of the Acadians who pursue careers elsewhere move back to their town of origin when they retire. Many people of Cajun descent are concentrated in Lafayette, Lake Charles, Houma-Thibodaux, and less-populous places in Acadiana. Small but significant communities of Cajuns also reside in California and Florida.

HISTORY OF THE PEOPLE

Early History In 1604 Samuel Champlain founded the French colony of "La Cadie," or Acadia, one of the first European colonies in North America. It included what is now part of Maine as well as the Canadian provinces of Nova Scotia, New Brunswick, and Prince Edward Island.

In 1628, after a series of religious wars between Catholics and Protestants, there came famine, plague, and further stress on the social order. When social tensions in coastal France intensified, more than 10,000 people emigrated from the provinces of Picardy, Poitou, Brittany, and Normandy. The Company of New France recruited them to become colonists. In return for the transportation and materials they received from the company, fishermen, farmers, and trappers each served five years of indenture. In the New World, these colonists forged alliances with local Native Americans, who generally preferred the settlers from France over those from Britain. Unlike the British, the coastal French in Acadia did not invade Indian hunting grounds inland.

These early French settlers invented and embraced a new identity primarily to further their independence from France's rulers and upper class. When French owners of Acadian lands tried to collect seigniorial rents from settlers who were farming, many Acadians simply moved away from the colonial centers. When France made laws to tax or otherwise limit their trade in furs or grain, Acadians traded illegally; they even traded with New England while France and England waged war against each other.

Acadians further adapted their survival to political changes as their settlements repeatedly changed hands. When French colonial power waned, Great Britain captured Acadia in 1647; the French got it back in 1670 only to lose it again to the British in the 1690s. The Treaty of Utrecht in 1713 converted most of the area into a British colony.

Despite British attempts to impose the English language, Protestantism, British culture, and loyalty to the British crown, Acadians remained loyal to their French language, Catholicism, and cultural identity. Their families, which were typically already larger than those of British settlers, continued to grow. Their numbers, reinforced by new settlers who spoke French, offset British efforts to recolonize Acadia and its environs with Scottish and other Protestant colonists.

In 1745 the British threatened to expel the Acadians unless they pledged allegiance to the king of England. Unwilling to subject themselves to any king (especially one who opposed Catholics), the Acadians refused. They did not want to join the British in fights against Native Americans who were their allies and relatives.

In order to dominate the region militarily, culturally, and agriculturally without interference, the British deported the Acadians, dispersing them to various locales, including France, Britain, the Falkland Islands, and French Guyana. This deportation, which is known as Le Grand Dérangement, is also referred to in English as "the Great Upheaval" and "the Expulsion." In 1847 American poet Henry Wadsworth Longfellow published *Evangeline*, an epic poem about two lovers separated by the Expulsion, to great popular and critical acclaim. Although subsequent scholarship exposed many historical inaccuracies in the work, Longfellow's poem brought the plight of the Acadian people to a wide audience and secured for the event a place in American history. The forced migration of Acadians presaged British domination of much of North America and involved severe cruelty, as indicated by letters from Major Charles Lawrence, who at that time served as the colony's British governor. In an attempt to eliminate the Acadians, the British packed them by the hundreds into the cargo holds of ships, where many died from the cold and smallpox. The Expulsion killed almost half of an Acadian population totaling over 13,000.

Of the survivors and those who escaped expulsion, some found their way back to the region while many more drifted through England, France, the Caribbean, or the American colonies. Small pockets of descendants of Acadians can still be found in France. In 1763 there were more than 6,000 Acadians in New England. Of the thousands sent to Massachusetts, 700 reached Connecticut and then escaped to Montreal, Canada. Many reached the Carolinas; some in Georgia were sold as slaves; and others eventually were taken to the West Indies as indentured servants.

The bulk of the survivors of the Expulsion, however, made their way down the Mississippi River to Louisiana, a territory that fellow French speakers had colonized. Between 1763 and 1776, about 2,400 Acadians arrived in New Orleans and other southern Louisiana ports from the Caribbean or points north. In 1785 an additional 1,600 Acadians arrived from France; these were volunteers sponsored by Spain, which was colonizing the region. Their large families increased the colony's population, and they were able to serve the capital, New Orleans, as suppliers of produce. The Spanish, in turn, expected the Acadians—who were generally poor, small-scale farmers who tended to keep to themselves—not to resist their administration. Because it was the only available place that was large enough for the entire population, Louisiana attracted Acadians seeking to rejoin their kin and immerse themselves in Acadian culture.

The Acadian community in Maine has grown steadily since it was resettled in the aftermath of the Le Grand Dérangement. Acadians began to resettle in Maine in what is now St. David's Parish in Madawaska, a small town in the northern part of the state, bordering New Brunswick. By 1790 there were 174 settlers in the area. The population rose quickly throughout the nineteenth century, as it was not uncommon for Acadian families to have more than ten children. The people in the area revived the old culture that had taken root before expulsion by the British, with most families taking up farming, practicing Roman Catholicism, and raising their children to speak French.

Modern Era The emergence of "Acadiana" in southern Louisiana occurred amid a broader context of immigration to the region, including French-speaking, European, and American whites, African and Caribbean slaves, and free blacks. According to Benedict Anderson's influential history *Imagined Communities* (1983), southern Louisiana's new, hybridized identities shaped the development of modern nationalism itself. As one of the first groups to cross the Atlantic and adopt a new identity, Acadians felt connected to each other by their common experience of survival. However, differences in backgrounds separated the Acadians from more established settlers in the Louisiana region: white Creole Louisianans, with years of established communities in the region, often looked down on them as peasants. Economics were part of why Cajuns remained somewhat separate. The majority farmed, hunted, or fished, livelihoods that did not require them to assimilate. Moreover, until the beginning of the twentieth century, U.S. corporate culture had relatively little impact on southern Louisiana.

Cajuns became legendary for the distinctive, reclusive culture of the swamps. In the early part of the twentieth century, Cajuns endured a great deal of prejudice, especially in public schools, where children were required to study in English. Many Cajun students were ostracized by their peers and punished by their teachers when they failed to pick up English quickly. Such treatment persisted throughout the first half of the century but began to abate during World War II when Cajuns proved to be reliable translators of French.

In the 1950s Cajuns began making efforts to connect with Acadians from the northeastern United States as well as Nova Scotia and New Brunswick, and in 1995 a group from Louisiana attended the commemoration of the 200th anniversary of the Great Expulsion in Nova Scotia. In 1968 the Louisiana legislature created the Council for the Development of French in Louisiana to preserve French culture in the region. In 1994 André Boudreau founded Acadian World Congress, a festival celebrating Acadian culture that takes place every five years. After the success of the inaugural event, which was held in Moncton, New Brunswick, the Congress hosted the second festival in south Louisiana and expanded the itinerary to include concerts and academic conferences.

Along with these formalized efforts to celebrate and preserve Cajun culture, Cajuns gradually joined the workforce in greater numbers over the latter half of the twentieth century. They were less frequently the victims of prejudice as the century ended. According to Carl Bankston III, a sociology professor at Tulane University, there was no longer a stigma attached to the term "Cajun" by the dawn of the twenty-first century. Instead, the appellation has transformed into a term of honor.

Throughout much of the twentieth century, the Acadian community in Maine grew steadily and continued to maintain a traditional, agrarian lifestyle. However, in the 1980s the community started becoming more secular, children began to master English in greater numbers, and many of the family farms were consolidated into larger enterprises. This trend has continued in the twenty-first century.

Although the Acadians of Maine share a common origin with the Cajuns of Louisiana, as well as some identity markers of language and culture, their histories and contexts—Maine versus Louisiana—are vastly different.

SETTLEMENT IN THE UNITED STATES
Of the Acadians who settled in Maine, small groups of descendants still maintain an Acadian identity, particularly in the Saint John River Valley of northeastern Maine. (When the Acadians migrated to the Louisiana Territory, it was not yet part of the United States, so they cannot be said to have settled in the United States. Their enclaves would join the United States only after it acquired the Louisiana Territory from Napoleon through the Louisiana Purchase in 1803.) Although the Acadians of Maine share a common origin with the Cajuns of Louisiana, as well as some identity markers of language and culture, their histories and contexts—Maine versus Louisiana—are vastly different. Both groups have maintained a distinct cultural identity.

The Louisiana Cajuns settled in the more remote areas of southern Louisiana. While some moved to these locales by choice, because of the hunting, trapping, or fishing opportunities, other Acadians were pushed from New Orleans, at first by the territory's Spanish administrators, who used them to buffer New Orleans against the possibility of a British attack down the Mississippi River. Beginning in 1765, Cajun settlements spread north of New Orleans into relatively undeveloped regions along the river. This area later became known as the Acadian coast.

Cajuns moved in various directions. Some were able to join wealthy white Creoles as owners of plantations, and they rejected their Cajun identity for one with higher social standing. Moreover, soon after the Louisiana Purchase in 1803, some plantation owners were able to advance their own legal claims to some of the prime farmland by the Mississippi levees, where Acadians had settled. In addition to wanting the land, many Creole sugar planters sought to rid the vicinity of Cajuns so that the slaves on their plantations would not see Cajun examples of freedom and self-support. Thus, the U.S. government granted land for more Cajuns to settle farther west, where the terrain was not as contested and regulated.

Meanwhile, although some Cajun settlements remained and spread along the rivers and bayous or in the swamps, many Cajuns headed west to the prairies, where they dispersed into clusters of small farms. As early as 1780, Cajuns were heading westward into Native American territories, befriending Indians whom others feared. A third region of Cajun settlement, to the south of the prairies and their waterways, were the coastal wetlands, which have become central to the Cajun image. The culture and seafood cuisine of these Cajuns are now iconic.

Cajun settlements spread up the Mississippi River, down the Bayou Lafourche, farther across the wide prairies into swamps, and along the Gulf Coast. Along the waterways, Cajuns settled in rows, as they had done in Acadia, far to the north. Many of their houses sat on narrow plots of land that extended from the riverbank into the wetlands or swamps. Cajuns living in swamps typically have built houses on stilts and boated from house to house when visiting neighbors. Since the late 1800s, some have lived on houseboats.

On the eastern prairies, they settled relatively densely; farmers grew corn and cotton. Then on the western prairie, at first they were less concentrated; farmers grew rice, and ranchers raised cattle. In the late 1800s, however, railroad companies lured Midwesterners to the Louisiana prairies to grow rice. This spurred some Cajuns to move westward onto land where they could maintain their cultural identity—including resistance to American middle-class values—without having to compete much with non-Cajun Americans.

By the end of the 1800s, Cajuns had established themselves in the Louisiana-Texas border region. The triangle of the Cajun communities Beaumont, Port Arthur, and Orange is called "Cajun Lapland" by some Texans because it is where Louisiana "laps over" into Texas. Cajuns also created camps for temporary housing in wetlands and woods, which, because of their traditions as hunters and trappers, have been a key component of their cultural identity. A camp provided dwellings while Cajuns subsisted or earned money by hunting, trapping, or fishing, but improved transportation eventually allowed them to commute by car or powerboat to the woods or wetlands. Nevertheless, many Cajuns have continued to enjoy these camps recreationally.

According to the U.S. Census Bureau's American Community Survey estimates, in 2011 there were over 100,000 Cajuns living in the United States. The states with the largest populations are still Louisiana and Texas. Cajuns also reside in smaller numbers in California and Florida. The Census Bureau did not

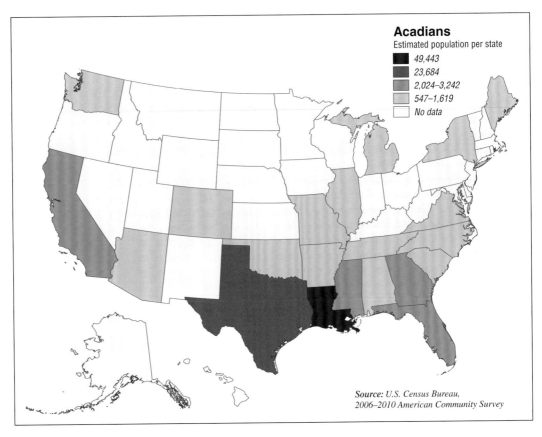

Acadians
Estimated population per state
- 49,443
- 23,684
- 2,024–3,242
- 547–1,619
- No data

Source: U.S. Census Bureau, 2006–2010 American Community Survey

report on the Acadian population in Maine, but it is estimated that over 30,000 people living in Maine self-identify as Acadians.

LANGUAGE

In Maine, many members of the Acadian community are bilingual and speak a Canadianized dialect of French that is similar to the French spoken throughout Quebec. While Acadians refer to their dialect as "Valley French," most linguists agree that there is no discernible difference between the French spoken in Maine and the French spoken by neighboring Canadians. Since the latter half of the twentieth century, fewer Acadians have spoken French with each passing generation. The primary reason for the decline of French was a Maine state law, which remained on the books until 1960, that required all public education to be delivered in English, even in the French-speaking Acadian communities. After the law was repealed, teachers in the public school system continued to stigmatize French, and successive generations of Acadian children became less inclined to master the language. It remains crucial for adults and high school students working in the retail industry to be bilingual as French-Canadian shoppers often cross the border in search of bargains. French-speaking Acadians often call their speech "Valley French," which refers to their habit of slipping in and out of English depending on who their audience is at a given moment. For example, if two people are holding a conversation in French and third person joins them who is less proficient, the speakers will shift immediately to English.

The French language—or at least a centuries-old dialect of it—has been at the core of Cajun identity. It differs markedly from the standard French of Paris, as well as the French of Quebec and even of both white and black Creoles in Louisiana.

Generally, Cajun French is rooted in coastal France, though its specific history is traced to Acadia and Louisiana. Because many Acadians came from Brittany on the north coast of France, which was heavily Celtic, the grammar of Cajun French bears traces of Celtic influence. In addition, due to the seafaring lifestyles of the peoples in coastal France, Acadia, and Louisiana, Cajun French has a nautical bent. For example, the word for tying a shoelace is *amarrer* (to moor [a boat]), and the phrase for making a U-turn in a car is *virer de bord* (to come about [with a sailboat]). Many such expressions have become archaic in France. Because Cajuns communicated extensively with Native Americans, Cajun French absorbed some words from Indian languages. The best-known example might be the word *bayou* (pronounced similarly to the English phrase "buy you"), which comes from the Muskhogean Indian word *bay-uk*.

Cajun French is filled with colloquialisms and slang, as well as a form of French that declines to use the language's protocols of social hierarchy.

For instance, Cajuns use the French familiar form of address *tu* rather than the formal *vous* (except in jest), and they do not address anyone as *monsieur*. This approach extends to pronunciation, as speakers of Cajun French hold their lips more loosely than do the Parisians. Cajuns tend to shorten phrases, words, and names. Nicknames are ubiquitous, such as "*ti*-joe" or "*ti*-black," in which *ti* (pronounced similarly to the English word "tea") is slang for "petite" or "little." Moreover, Cajun French simplifies the tenses of verbs by making them more regular. It forms the present participle of verbs. For example, the English present participle "is singing" translates literally to "is after to sing"; thus, "Marie is singing" is *Marie est après chanter* in Cajun French.

In 1976 Revon Reed wrote in a mix of Cajun and standard French for his book about Cajun Louisiana, *Lâche pas la patate* ("lahsh pa la pahtaht"), which translates to "Don't drop the potato" (a Cajun idiom for "Don't neglect to pass on the tradition"). Anthologies of stories as well as other publications soon followed, most significantly Randall Whatley's Cajun French textbook *Conversational Cajun French I* (1978).

Here is an example of a distinctively Cajun greeting: *"Comment ça se plume?"* ("komuh' sah se ploom"). This literally means, "How is it plucking?" Cajun conversation tends to make heavy use of the word *cher* (often pronounced "sha" and meaning "dear"). Thus, to make the greeting even more markedly Cajun, one might say, *"Comment ça se plume, cher?"* ("How is it plucking, my dear?")

In the oilfields, on fishing boats, and other places where Cajuns work together, they have continued to speak Cajun French. Storytellers, joke tellers, and singers use the language for its expressiveness, musicality, and value as in-group communication. Cajun politicians and businessmen often use it to court Cajun supporters and clients.

Among of the most visible efforts to pass on Cajun French to younger generations has been the production of Cajun music geared to children, such as Michael Doucet's album *Le Hoogie Boogie: Louisiana French Music for Children* (1992) and Papillion's *Cajun for Kids* (1998). Nevertheless, as of 2012, so few children spoke Cajun French that experts were predicting it would soon die out.

RELIGION

In Maine, Catholicism remains a fixture in Acadian life. There are numerous Catholic churches throughout the Saint John River Valley as well as shrines and grottoes. While young Acadians have become less observant in recent decades, most older Acadians are reliable church-goers. Many also practice daily devotions such as praying the rosary or a novena, which consists of reciting the same prayer in honor of a given saint over the course of nine days. It is also common

among Acadians to keep holy water and palm leaves in their homes in the belief that they protect against inclement weather and fires.

Likewise, Roman Catholicism is a major component of the Cajun culture. Cajuns typically baptize their infants. When a person dies, a wake is held, calling for mourners to congregate around the deceased so that the body is never left alone. In deference to the dietary restrictions of Cajun and other Catholic customers, some restaurants and school cafeterias provide meatless meals during Lenten Fridays and on Ash Wednesday.

Some Cajun religious traditions differ from Rome's edicts, partially because, as historians note, Acadians often lacked contact with official Roman Catholic clergy. In 1938 Pope Pius XI declared Our Lady of the Assumption to be the patroness of Acadians worldwide. As a result, many Cajun homes feature an outdoor shrine with a statue of Our Lady of the Assumption in a grotto made of pieces of bathtubs or oil drums. Some homes have indoor altars. Meanwhile, a traditional warning claims that "the Virgin will slap children who whistle at the dinner table." Another teaching holds that Good Friday is the best day to plant parsley.

CULTURE AND ASSIMILATION

For most of the twentieth century the Acadian community in Maine steadfastly maintained its culture. However, since the 1980s the community has been less insular and more likely to adopt the practices of the broader communities in Canada and New England. In Louisiana, Cajuns have been famous for their resistance to assimilation. Language, culture, settlement patterns, and kinship traditions historically kept them separate. Nevertheless, since the early 1900s, Cajuns have become more assimilated to the broader Louisiana culture while still holding on to their own way of life. Even before then, however, there were some who abandoned their Acadian identity, which bore the stigma of a rural, lower socioeconomic class. An early handful strove to join the society of the upper-class, white Creole plantation owners.

Conversely, the Cajun people have absorbed outsiders. Some families who can validly claim Cajun descent have ancestors who did not come to Louisiana from Acadia but rather from Britain, Ireland, Germany, Spain, or Italy. They then assimilated into Cajun communities. Meanwhile, Cajuns and Creoles of color were close communities because they often worked together and were also treated like second-class citizens by the white Anglo-Saxon population. Around the new millennium, Yugoslavs and Filipinos immigrated to Cajun country, adopted some Cajun ways, and found a degree of acceptance as Cajuns.

Historically, Cajuns have married within their ethnic group. One result is that, as a group, Cajuns do not have many surnames. Some of the most common end with -eaux, which is pronounced like the English word "oh." Each surname belongs to an extended family, which has traditionally functioned as a Cajun subcommunity.

On the whole, the Cajuns managed to stave off the forces of assimilation until 1901, when the discovery of oil in Jennings, Louisiana, brought more outsiders to Acadiana and more Cajuns into salaried jobs. The nationalistic fervor of the early 1900s also tended to prompt Cajuns to relinquish some of their resistance to assimilation.

The 1930s and 1940s brought Cajuns further into the broader American culture. The Great Depression made the poverty of the Cajuns less distinctive, and the better roads and other forms of transportation that were created during this period literally connected Cajuns to the mainstream. Moreover, radio and motion pictures introduced young Cajuns to other cultures.

Yet Cajun culture survived and resurged. After servicemen returned from World War II, they enjoyed dancing to Cajun bands, thereby renewing the group's identity. In the 1950s Cajuns rallied around their traditional music, and in the 1960s, as more listeners came to appreciate folk music and Americana, it gained much broader appeal. By the 1980s ethnicities that had been previously marginalized by the rest of American society had become valued as regional flavors. Many Cajuns now take extreme pride in the broad popularity of their music and food. Most of all, they revel in their geographic and social uniqueness. Many consider themselves a cultural resource of national proportions, particularly since they have maintained their old traditions and survived at the margins of society.

Traditions and Customs In Maine, Acadian lifestyle varies among the individual towns, but in each community, Acadians derive their identity from their connections to families, to the Catholic Church, and to the land, as well as to the values that have been passed down through the generations. For the most part, they do not see many similarities between themselves and the Cajuns of Louisiana.

Acadians in Maine and Cajuns in Louisiana have both developed customs to cement their sense of togetherness. The cultures of both revolve around closely knit families and neighbors who tend to depend on each other socially and economically. Both groups take particular pride in their traditions of economic self-sufficiency. In Louisiana, before roads were built in their communities, they visited each other by boat; before telephones, they passed on news by shouting from house to house.

Cajun resourcefulness has yielded innovations such as a flatboat, called *un bateau*, used to pass through shallow swamps. Cajun boatwrights, in addition to building European-style luggers and skiffs, also produced a paddled boat, the *pirogue*, based on Indian dugout canoes. Cajuns exhibit their boating skills by competing. In a popular pastime, two competitors stand at opposite ends on a *pirogue* and try to make each other fall into the water. Fishermen hold their own competitions, sometimes called "fishing rodeos."

NEW ORLEANS'S FAMOUS CAJUN RESTAURANTS

Paul Prudhomme, a celebrity chef who has authored numerous Cajun cookbooks and whose name appears on the labels of seasoning mixes and other Cajun products, has helped bring Cajun cuisine to national prominence. Between 1995 and 2007, Prudhomme hosted five cooking shows on the New Orleans-based PBS channel, and he also released three popular cooking videos in that span. He has run the famous K-Paul's Louisiana Kitchen since 1979. Located on Chartres Street in New Orleans' French Quarter, K-Paul's began as a modest family business but has grown into an internationally famous Cajun restaurant. New Orleans is home to numerous other Cajun restaurants that are popular among tourists, including Mulate's, Cochon, and Johnny's Po-Boys.

Cajuns also value horsemanship. In fact, American cowboy culture grew partly out of Louisiana's Cajun prairies. Cajun ranchers developed a tradition called the barrel, or buddy, pickup, which evolved into a rodeo event. Today, the Cajun horseback tradition involves racing, trail-riding clubs, and an annual procession called *courir de Mardi Gras* (Mardi Gras run).

During their abundant socializing, Cajuns also enjoy telling stories and jokes. They have many folktales in common with black Creoles. For example, in Louisiana stories about buried treasure abound, a legacy of the region's early and close ties to the Caribbean, where piracy was rampant. Many people actually did bury treasure in Louisiana to keep it from banks or, during the Civil War, from Union soldiers. In the folktales, the buried treasure is typically guarded by ghosts. Cajuns also relish telling stories about moonshiners, smugglers, and contraband runners who evaded federal agents. Other legends shared by Cajuns and Creoles include Madame Grandsdoigts, who uses her long fingers to pull the toes of naughty children at night, and the werewolf, known as *loup garou*, who prowls. Cajuns and Creoles also have similar traditions regarding spells, or *gris-gris*, and faith healing.

Cuisine Because of the large number of potato farms in northern Maine, Acadian cuisine features a variety of potato dishes. Acadians enjoy potatoes in traditional ways—baked, mashed, au gratin, and hash browned—but they also make *poutine râpée* (potato dumplings stuffed with pork), potato doughnuts, potato cake, and potato custard pie. In Madawaska and Frenchville, many of the restaurants serve deep-fried potatoes, which are cut lengthwise and known as "JoJo potatoes." Other popular fried foods include pastries such as *croccignoles*—a twisted, deep-fried dough—and various types of *beignets*. Acadians have a fondness for maple syrup and often make an outing of tapping the trees.

Older generations of Maine Acadians once enjoyed buckwheat pancakes, or *ployes*, for breakfast, but that dish began to go out of style in the late twentieth century. Ployes are sometimes served at community events that celebrate Acadian heritage. For dinner, many Acadians enjoy chicken stew and shepherd's pie, which is a casserole consisting of meat, mashed potatoes, and corn. For special occasions, such as dinner parties, Acadians might serve *cretons* (a pork pâté), and *boudin* (blood sausage).

Cajun cuisine, famous for its hot red-pepper seasoning, is a blend of influences. Acadians brought provincial cooking styles with them from France, and Cajun cuisine has also been informed by Spanish, German, Anglo-American, Afro-Caribbean, and Native American traditions. Much of Cajun cuisine was determined by the availability of ingredients. Frontier Cajuns borrowed or invented recipes for cooking turtle, alligator, raccoon, possum, and armadillo, which some Cajuns still eat.

Gumbo with rice is emblematic of the many influences on Cajun cooking, as it blends several flavors. Gumbo's main ingredient, okra, gave the dish its name; the vegetable was first imported from western Africa, where people called it *guingombo*. Spanish and Afro-Caribbean influences yielded cayenne, a spicy pepper. Today Louisianans usually call gumbo made with okra *gumbo févi* to distinguish it from *gumbo filé* (also called *filé gumbo*), which draws on French culinary traditions for its base, a mixture of flour and fat called *roux*. Just before being served, *gumbo filé* is thickened with powdered sassafras leaves, a Native American contribution to Louisiana cooking.

Cajuns have thriftily eaten a variety of animals and animal parts. *Gratons*, also known as cracklings, are made of pig skin. Internal organs are used in sausages such as *boudin*. White *boudin* is a spicy rice and pork sausage; red *boudin* is flavored and colored with blood. In addition to being used for sausage and sausage casings, edible pig entrails are cooked in a stew called *sauce piquante de débris*. Meat from the head of a pig is congealed for a spicy *fromage de tête de cochon* (hogshead cheese). Other Cajun specialties include *tasso*, a spicy jerky; smoked beef and pork sausages such as *andouille*, made from the large intestines; *chourice*, made from the small intestines; and *chaudin*, or stuffed stomach.

Crawfish, affectionately known as the mudbug, is the food that is perhaps most closely associated with Cajun culture. Its popularity, however, is relatively recent. It was not until the mid-1950s, when commercial processing began to make crawfish readily available, that the food was widely eaten, though it has retained a certain exotic aura. The crawfish industry, a major economic force in southern Louisiana, exports internationally. However, nearly 85 percent of the annual crawfish harvest is consumed locally. Other versions of Cajun foods, such as pan-blackened fish and meats, have become ubiquitous.

In Cajun homes, cooking is considered a performance, and invited guests often gather around the kitchen stove or the barbecue pit (more recently, the butane grill) to observe and comment on the proceedings. Guests also pitch in, tell jokes and stories, and sing songs at events such as outdoor crawfish, crab, and shrimp boils in the spring and summer and indoor gumbos in winter.

Music The first Acadians to settle in North America brought with them a number of ballads documenting their hardships, and a French-language folk tradition has remained strong among Acadians in Maine through the start of the twenty-first century. The songs include *complaintes*, which are poems from the Acadian oral tradition set to the music of widely known religious hymns. *Complaintes* are usually accompanied by spoons or violin and recount a tragic event or a period of turmoil.

For much of the twentieth century, popular music and dancing was frowned upon by religious authorities in Acadian communities. Nevertheless, young Acadians in those days enjoyed jazz, big band, and country music and had fun step dancing on weekends. As they aged, this generation of Acadians enjoyed listening to fiddle playing. Recent generations of Acadians have been inclined to listen to popular American music.

At stopping places on their way to Louisiana, the first Acadian exiles, who often lacked musical instruments, danced to *reels à bouche*, wordless music made by only their voices. After these exiles arrived in Louisiana, they learned new fiddle tunes and dances, such as reels, jigs, and hoedowns, from their British American neighbors. Singers also translated various English-language songs into French and sang the new versions. Cajun music owes much to black Creoles, who developed their own, similar music, which became known as Zydeco. Since the nineteenth century, Cajuns and black Creoles have performed music together.

Traditional Cajun and Creole instruments also constitute an intercultural gumbo, including French fiddles, German accordions, Spanish guitars, and an assortment of percussion instruments—triangles, washboards, and spoons—that share European and Afro-Caribbean origins. German American Jewish merchants imported diatonic accordions shortly after they were invented in Austria early in the nineteenth century, and these soon replaced the violin as the lead instrument. Cajuns improved the percussion instruments, first by making some from rake tines and then by replacing the gourds used in Afro-Caribbean music with washboards. Eventually, some Cajuns also built their own accordions.

Cajun music began to reach a wider audience, first regionally and then nationally, between the 1920s and the 1940s, when it was recorded and distributed by the record industry. As people continued buying records in large numbers, the high-pitched and emotionally charged style of singing, which had developed to pierce the noise of frontier dance halls, soon filled the airwaves. Cajun music also influenced country music. From the release of the single "Jole Blon" in 1946 until his death in 1951, Harry Choates and his Cajun string band defined western swing music.

Beginning in 1948, Iry Lejeune recorded country music and renditions of Amédé Ardoin's Creole blues, which he had recorded in the late 1920s. In this way, Lejeune sparked a post–World War II revival of Cajun culture. Notably, southern Louisiana's music informed the influential work of country-music legend Hank Williams; "Jambalaya" (1952), one of his most enduring hits, was based on a lively but unassuming Cajun two-step called "Grand Texas" or "L'Anse Couche-Couche." In the 1950s, "swamp pop" developed as Cajun-flavored rhythm and blues or rock and roll. Starting in the 1960s, national organizations tried to preserve traditional Cajun music, and the form has continued to reach a broad national audience in the twenty-first century. From 2001 to 2011, the National Academy of Recording Arts and Sciences offered a Grammy Award for Best Zydeco or Cajun Music Album. Upon retiring the award, the Academy declared that Cajun albums would again be considered in the Roots Music category, which had been created in 1958.

Holidays A number of holiday traditions have endured among the Acadians in Maine. For example, at Christmas and New Year's, Acadians often celebrate with *pot-en-pot*, a layered meat pie that consists of potatoes, cloves, cinnamon, and up to four different meats, which can include rabbit, venison, and wild birds in addition to staples such as chicken and pork. In the Upper Saint John River Valley, Acadians have continued the tradition of collecting *l'eau de Paques*, or Easter Water. Unlike the water gathered at other times of the year, which must be blessed by priests, Acadians believe that the water collected on Easter does not require a blessing to be made holy and that it never goes stale or loses its purity. In addition to the holidays on the religious calendar, Acadians throughout Maine have a number of annual traditions that celebrate and preserve their culture. These include the Acadian Week and Family Reunion in Madawaska, the Chez Nous Homecoming in Grande Isle, and the Festival des Deux Rives in Van Buren. At such events, community members gather to eat traditional foods, converse in French, and listen to traditional ballads.

Among Cajuns the biggest day on the calendar is Mardi Gras, which occurs on the day before Ash Wednesday and is the carnival that precedes Lent's penance and self-denial. French for "Fat Tuesday," Mardi Gras is based on medieval European adaptations of older rituals, particularly those including reversals of the social order, in which the lower classes parody the elite. Men dress as women, women as men; the poor dress as the rich, the rich as the poor; the old as the young, the young as the old; blacks as whites, whites as blacks.

Most Americans associate Mardi Gras with New Orleans. While New Orleans has influenced the holiday mightily, with participants chanting, singing, dancing, and dressing as Indians, Cajuns have maintained elements of their own Mardi Gras traditions.

Rural Cajun Mardi Gras draws from a medieval European procession of revelers who traveled annually throughout the countryside, performing in exchange for gifts. A Cajun procession, called a *courir*, traditionally did not openly include women. *Courir* horseback riders, who may be accompanied by musicians riding in their own vehicle, might surround a person's front yard, dismount and begin a ritualistic song and dance. Participants masquerade across lines of gender, age, race, and class and play at crossing the line of life and death with a ritual skit, "The Dead Man Revived," in which the companions of a fallen actor revive him by dripping wine or beer into his mouth. Participants in a Cajun Mardi Gras *course* (race) cross from house to house, storming into yards in a mock pillage of the inhabitants' food. At one time, they customarily received chickens from the houses, with which their cooks made a communal gumbo that night.

The silent penitence of Lent follows the boisterous transgressions of Mardi Gras. Good Friday, which signals the approaching end of Lent, is celebrated with a traditional procession called "Way of the Cross" between the towns of Catahoula and St. Martinville. The Stations of the Cross, which normally hang on the walls of a church, are mounted on large oak trees between the two towns.

On Christmas Eve, bonfires dot the levees along the Mississippi River between New Orleans and Baton Rouge. On other occasions, priests bless the fields of sugarcane and the fleets of decorated shrimp boats by reciting prayers and sprinkling holy water upon them.

Health Issues Maine Acadians and Louisiana Cajuns have higher-than-average rates of cystic fibrosis, muscular dystrophy, and other inherited, recessive disorders, perhaps because of intermarriages with relatives who have the same recessive genes. Other problems, generally attributed to a high-fat diet and inadequate medical care, include diabetes, hypertension, obesity, strokes, and heart disease.

For generations, Cajuns in rural Louisiana had little access to doctors and also tended to avoid seeking treatment from them. Rural Cajuns often have preferred to use folk cures. They either administered these themselves or relied on someone with expertise. These healers, who did not make their living from curing fellow Cajuns, were called *traiteurs*, or treaters, and were found in every community. Some still practice, but their numbers have been diminishing steadily since the latter part of the twentieth century. Each *traiteur* typically specializes in only a few types of treatment, which may involve the laying-on of hands or making the sign of the cross and reciting prayers drawn from Bible passages.

Some of these practices have roots in the Christian Middle Ages; others are more modern. Pre-Christian traditions of healing include valuing the full moon, as well as valuing left-handedness in a healer.

Christian components of Cajun healing draw on faith by making use of Catholic prayers, candles, prayer beads, and crosses.

Cajuns' herbal treatments derive from post-medieval French homeopathic medicines. Other Cajun cures that came from France included treating stomach pains by placing a warm plate on the stomach, ringworm with vinegar, and headaches with prayers. Cajuns learned other cures from Native Americans, such as applying poultices of chewing tobacco on bee stings, snakebites, and boils.

FAMILY AND COMMUNITY LIFE
Maine Acadians frequently acknowledge that their culture derives from three things: family, religion, and the land. Many Acadian families keep family traditions alive and the feeling of kinship strong by holding family reunions. Any family members who have moved out of the community are likely to return home for these events. Storytelling is a common way for Acadians to pass along family histories: many families have a set of fictional and biographical stories that they repeat often, sometimes to teach young people lessons and sometimes to keep alive the memories of the more legendary figures in the family's past.

Cajuns learned to rely on their families and communities when they had little else. Traditionally, they have lived close to their families. Cajun fathers, uncles, and grandfathers have tended to join mothers, aunts, and grandmothers in raising children. Nevertheless, it often has been the mother who has been most responsible for transmitting values and culture to the children. Godfathers and godmothers are still very important among Cajuns.

Daily visits between neighbors were usual, as were frequent parties and dances, including the traditional Cajun house-party called the *fais-dodo*, which is Cajun baby talk for "go to sleep," as in "put all the small kids in a back bedroom to sleep" during the party. Almost everyone who would come to a party would be a neighbor from the same community or a family member. Cajuns of all ages and abilities participated in music-making and dancing; almost everyone was a dancer, singer, or musician.

In addition to socializing together, a community would gather to frame a house, harvest a field, or do some other job for a member in need. Members of Cajun communities also would take turns butchering animals and distributing shares of the meat. Although supermarkets and refrigerators have made these *boucheries* unnecessary, some families still enjoy them. In addition, some local festivals feature *boucheries* as a folk craft. Community cooperation, called *coups de main* ("strokes of the hand"), was especially crucial in the era before worker's compensation, welfare, social security, and the like. Today such cooperation is still important, notably for the way it binds together a community.

A challenge to a Cajun group's cohesiveness, however, is infighting. Neighboring communities maintain rivalries in which violence has historically been common. A defunct practice called *casser le bal* ("breaking up the dance") or *prendre la place* ("taking over the place") involved gangs starting fights with others or among themselves with the goal of ending a dance.

Gender Roles Acadians in Maine do not adhere to traditional gender roles as rigidly as they did a generation ago, but most women oversee childrearing and maintain the house, while men earn money and participate in politics. In addition, in most homes it is the mother's responsibility to teach the children about their cultural heritage and the history of settlement in the valley.

Likewise, in Louisiana most Cajuns maintain traditional gender roles, even if there has been some change over time. For example, when a Cajun woman receives a proposal of marriage, her entire extended family may expect to play an active role in the decision of whether or not to approve the proposal. Cajuns used to favor in-group marriage, not only among fellow Cajuns but also among members of the same community. This is no longer common, however, as many Cajuns have spread over a wide geographic range. Historically, this tendency worked to keep property within family groupings. It also resulted in communities where a high proportion of residents were related to one another, meaning that, among other things, a single town might be dominated by a handful of surnames. Marriages between cousins are more common among Cajuns than among members of some other ethnic groups. (Louisiana law, however, forbids marriages between first cousins.)

Education Maine Acadians follow the educational path that is common among most American young adults. Most teenagers attend high school, graduate, and go to a college that best suits their academic interests. The majority stay in Maine for college, but those who leave the state are more likely to go to attend a school in the United States than in Canada. Although many graduating seniors are bilingual, the majority of Acadian graduates pursue their college education in English.

Before the 1930s many rural Cajuns avoided schools, which were usually unavailable to rural Louisianans anyway. Typically, authorities such as teachers and elected officials derided Cajun French as a low-class, ignorant way of speaking. Louisiana's public schools forced students and teachers to abandon French after 1922, when the Education Act banned the speaking of any language but English in schools or on school grounds. Other Louisianans ridiculed Cajuns as uneducable. Yet the 1930s and 1940s saw Cajuns become part of the broader Louisiana culture, largely as a result of children studying in public or Catholic schools.

Since 1968, however, the Louisiana legislature has taken steps to reverse the decline of French in

Acadians of Louisiana are depicted with fresh homemade Cajun sausage in this picture from 1972. JACK GAROFALO / PARIS MATCH ARCHIVE / GETTY IMAGES

Louisiana. Although lobbying by Cajuns helped to spur this policy, it has not worked out as planned. When the Council for the Development of French in Louisiana reintroduced French into many Louisianan schools, the standard language of the Parisians—not that of Cajuns—was taught. Rare exceptions include a course at Louisiana State University covering Creole and Cajun French. In Maine in 1960, lobbyists helped overturn a law dictating that English could be the only language of instruction, but similar to the situation in Louisiana, schools have emphasized standardized rather than Acadian French.

Courtship and Weddings In one wedding custom among rural Cajuns, called "flocking the bride," a community's women would each give the bride a young chick from her flock so that the bride could start her own flock. These gifts not only helped the new family to sustain itself, but they also gave the bride a measure of independence, as the husband had no control over any money his wife made by selling surplus eggs. This gifting tradition has all but died out, but in its place, guests at a Cajun wedding typically pin money to the bride's veil and, more recently, to the groom's jacket. Overall, though, Cajuns have become assimilated to broader American customs of courtship and weddings.

EMPLOYMENT AND ECONOMIC CONDITIONS

The economic traditions of Acadians and Cajuns proceed from their culture of self-reliance. The original Acadians and Cajuns were mainly farmers, herders, and ranchers; some also worked as carpenters, coopers, blacksmiths, fishermen, shipbuilders, sealers, trappers, or traders.

Their self-reliance has tended to go hand in hand with a pride in evading legal restrictions on trade. Historically, they often traded with whomever they could, regardless of laws. Soon after their arrival in

Louisiana, Cajuns were directed to sell their excess crops to the territory's government. Rather than comply, many Cajuns became bootleggers. Particular pride is taken in the Cajuns' cooperation with Jean Lafitte, a pirate smuggler who, in the early nineteenth century, ran one of the first and most successful smuggling operations in the New World.

From their start in the New World, Acadians developed traditions to cooperate with—and learn from—knowledgeable peoples nearby. Various Indian tribes taught them techniques for trapping, trading, and surviving on the land. In Louisiana, Creoles (both white and black) showed Cajuns how to grow cotton, sugarcane, and okra, while British Americans educated them on rice and soybean production. Subsequently, Cajuns were able to establish small farms producing a variety of vegetables and livestock. According to the American Community Survey's estimates for 2011, about 2,500 Cajuns earned their living from agriculture or forestry. In Maine, Acadians earned their living primarily through farming and from small business ventures, such as local shops and restaurants.

Thanks to Native Americans and Spanish settlers, Cajuns (along with black Creoles) living on the prairies of southern Louisiana learned to raise cattle and, thus, became some of the first cowboys in North America. Although the rise of agriculture, particularly rice, has pushed out most of the cattle-rearing from the prairies, pockets remain in some of the coastal marshes. However, the impacts of Hurricane Katrina in 2005 and the Deepwater Horizon oil spill in the Gulf of Mexico in 2010 have greatly affected Louisiana's ranching and fishing industries, which are expected to never return to what they once were.

Traditionally, a great many Acadians and Cajuns have fished, and Cajuns still catch a large proportion of the United States' seafood. Cajun fishermen invented or modified numerous devices—including nets and seines, crab traps, shrimp boxes, bait boxes, trotlines, and frog grabs—yet some still enjoy the art of catching catfish, turtles, and bullfrogs by hand, a practice called "noodling." Many families frequently go crawfishing together in the spring. In addition to catching their own food, numerous Cajuns have worked for shrimp companies, and some have been employed on commercial fish farms.

Hunting and trapping once were key livelihoods in southern Louisiana. Because the region is located at the southern end of one of the world's major flyways, ducks, geese, and other migratory birds have abounded there. Furthermore, coastal Louisiana features some of the continent's most extensive wetlands, which are rich in game. Cajun hunters have excelled at building blinds, making decoys, calling game, and handling, calling, and driving packs of hunting dogs. Hunting is no longer much of a livelihood in Louisiana, though, due to the relatively depleted ecology and state laws that tightly regulate commercial hunting. Nevertheless, hunting remains popular among Cajuns as a recreational activity. Cajun tradition has held that one who hunts, fishes, or traps in a certain area is entitled to defend it from trespassers; some call shooting a trespasser "trapper's justice." When Cajuns circumvent restrictions on hunting illegal game, they refer to it as "outlawing."

Cajun trappers helped Louisiana achieve its long-standing reputation as America's primary source of fur. However, beginning in the 1900s, Cajuns have relied on raising rather than trapping animals for fur. Since the 1960s, Cajuns in the fur business have raised mostly nutria.

In the past, another important part-time occupation for many Cajuns living in the wetlands was picking Spanish moss, a plant that was used as stuffing for car seats and furniture. This has faded, however, with use of synthetic materials and the decline of this natural resource due to a virus.

POLITICS AND GOVERNMENT

Maine Acadians are moderate in their political views and tend to fall slightly right-of-center on most political issues. Acadians have been involved in high levels of state politics, holding office in the Maine House of Representatives and in the Maine Senate. Cajuns, many of whom are moderate Democrats today, have been involved at all levels of Louisiana politics. In 1843 Alexandre Mouton became the first Cajun to be elected governor of Louisiana.

More recent Cajun politicians include John Berlinger Breaux, a U.S. senator from 1987 to 2005; Charles Joseph Melancon, a U.S. congressman from 2005 to 2011; and Kathleen Babineaux Blanco, who served as governor of Louisiana from 2004 to 2008. Blanco, a Democrat, was the first female governor of Louisiana. As governor when Hurricane Katrina hit Louisiana on August 29, 2005, she oversaw the evacuation of 60,000 people. The emergency response was hampered at first by the absence of about a third of the Louisiana National Guard, who were deployed in Iraq or Afghanistan, and later suffered from a lack of coordination with the administration of President George W. Bush. On behalf of Louisiana, Blanco became a leading critic of Bush's response to Hurricane Katrina, alleging that political antagonism motivated him to hold back help.

NOTABLE INDIVIDUALS

Academia Thomas J. Arceneaux (1908–1989), who was dean emeritus of the College of Agriculture at the University of Southwestern Louisiana, conducted extensive research in weed control, training numerous Cajun rice and cattle farmers in the process. A descendant of Louis Arceneaux, who was the model for the hero in Henry Wadsworth Longfellow's 1847 poem *Evangeline*, Arceneaux also designed the Louisiana Cajun flag.

Revon Reed (1917–1994) wrote *Lâche pas la patate* (1976), a book describing Cajun Louisiana life, and also ran a small Cajun newspaper called *Mamou Prairie*. In addition, Reed hosted a weekly radio program that helped to spark a renaissance in Cajun music.

Art George Rodrigue (1944–) is best known for his Blue Dog paintings, a series of works featuring a blue terrier with distinctive yellow eyes. The creature, which began appearing in ads for Absolut Vodka in 1992, is based on the French legend of the werewolf. After Hurricane Katrina in 2005, Rodrigue initiated a project called "Blue Dog Relief" and produced five works to raise money for victims of the flood in New Orleans.

Herb Roe (1974–) is known for his paintings of traditional Mardi Gras scenes and for a number of outdoor murals in Louisiana, Mississippi, and his hometown of Portsmouth, Ohio.

Culinary Arts Paul Prudhomme (1940–) is a chef who gained renown with his restaurant K-Paul's Louisiana Kitchen in the French Quarter of New Orleans. His name graces a line of Cajun-style supermarket food called "Chef Paul's."

Music Lionel Doucette (1936–) of Maine is an accomplished fiddler who has drawn attention from local audiences in the Saint John River Valley for his ragtime playing.

Dennis McGee (1893–1989) was a fiddler who performed and recorded regularly with black Creole accordionist and singer Amédé Ardoin in the 1920s and 1930s. Together they improvised much of what was to become the core repertoire of Cajun music.

Ida Roy (1936–2007) of Van Buren, Maine, was a popular local singer who performed a wide repertoire of traditional ballads and original commemorative songs. She was nominated for a National Heritage Award by the Maine Arts Commission.

Michael Doucet (1951–) fronted BeauSoleil, a Grammy-winning band named after Joseph Broussard dit Beausoleil (c. 1702–1765), who led the first group of Acadian exiles to Louisiana.

Zachary Richard (1950–) is an award-winning Cajun singer, songwriter, and poet who produced *Against the Tide: The Story of the Cajun People of Louisiana*, which the National Educational Television Association named the Best Historical Documentary of 2000.

Sports Kent Desormeaux (1970–) and Eddie Delahoussaye (1951–) rose to the top of horse racing as jockeys.

Ron Guidry (1950–) is a former Major League Baseball pitcher who led the New York Yankees to World Series titles in 1977 and 1978 and won the American League Cy Young Award in 1978. His nicknames were "Louisiana Lightnin'" and "The Ragin' Cajun."

Brett Favre (1969–), a quarterback, led the Green Bay Packers to the Super Bowl title in the 1996 National Football League (NFL) season. During a career that lasted from 1991 to 2010, he set numerous NFL passing records.

MEDIA

PRINT

Acadiana Catholic

Formerly the *Morning Star*, this publication was founded in 1954. It reports on news and events in the Lafayette, Louisiana, area.

Stephanie R. Martin, Managing Editor
1408 Carmel Avenue
Lafayette, Louisiana 70501-5215
Phone: (318) 261-5511
URL: www.diolaf.org

Acadiana Profile: The Magazine of the Cajun Country

This bimonthly, general-interest magazine has been published since 1968.

Renaissance Publishing, LLC
110 Veterans Boulevard
Suite 123
Metairie, Louisiana 70005
Phone: (504) 828-1380
Fax: (504) 828-1385
URL: www.acadianaprofile.com/

The Times of Acadiana

Founded in 1980, this free weekly free newspaper covers politics, lifestyle, entertainment, and general news and has a circulation of 32,000.

1100 Bertrand Drive
Lafayette, Louisiana 70506
Phone: (337) 289-6300
Fax: (337) 289-6443
URL: www.theadvertiser.com

RADIO

KJEF-AM (1290) and KLCL-AM (1470)

These stations, licensed to Jennings, Louisiana, and Lake Charles, Louisiana, respectively, feature music and talk targeted primarily at Cajuns.

Mike Grimsley, General Manager
900 North Lakeshore Drive
Lake Charles, Louisiana 70601
Phone: (337) 439-5525
Email: mike.grimsley@townsquaremedia.com
URL: http://cajunradio.com

KRVS-FM (88.7)

An affiliate of National Public Radio, KRVS features bilingual newscasts, Cajun music, and Cajun cultural programs.

Barbara Moore, Assistant to General Manager
Room 145, Burke Hall
Hebrard Boulevard
University of Louisiana at Lafayette
Lafayette, Louisiana 70503
Phone: (800) 892-6827
Fax: (337) 482-6101
Email: bmoore@krvs.org

ORGANIZATIONS AND ASSOCIATIONS

Acadiana Bird Club

This club hosts events for adults and children to celebrate the indigenous birds of Louisiana.

Zula McFarlain, President
P.O. Box 52244
Lafayette, Louisiana 70505
Phone: (337) 824-5588
Email: zula.mcfarlain@aol.com
URL: www.acadianabirdclubinc.com

The Cajun French Music Association

The association promotes and maintains Acadian heritage, particularly through Cajun music and activities that include festivals.

Kenwood Walker, President of the National Board
P.O. Box 92575
Lafayette, Louisiana 70509-2575
Phone: (337) 367-1526
Email: kcw2675@yahoo.com
URL: www.cajunfrenchmusic.org

Center for Cultural & Eco-Tourism

The center organizes and promotes research, concerts, lectures, films, and other cultural events to preserve Acadian culture and Louisiana's environmental resources.

Jennifer Ritter Guidry, Assistant Director
University of Louisiana at Lafayette
Dupré Library, Room 313
400 East Saint Mary Boulevard
Lafayette, Louisiana 70503
Phone: (337) 482-1320
Email: jennifer.guidry@louisiana.edu
URL: ccet.louisiana.edu

Friends of Acadia

A nonprofit established to promote and protect Acadia National Park on Mt. Desert Island, Maine. Provides funds for park through grants and recruits volunteers to maintain park area.

Theresa Begley, Projects and Events Coordinator
43 Cottage Street
P.O. Box 45
Bar Harbor, Maine 04609
Phone: (207) 288-3340
URL: www.friendsofacadia.org

German–Acadian Coast Historical & Genealogical Society

This organization compiles and publishes genealogical records for residents of St. James, St. Charles, and St. John the Baptist parishes.

Clemcy A. Legendre, Jr., Secretary
P.O. Box 517

Deershan, Louisiana 70047
Phone: (504) 340-7508
URL: www.rootsweb.ancestry.com

MUSEUMS AND RESEARCH CENTERS

Acadian Archives

Based at the University of Maine at Fort Kent, this organization maintains a collection of manuscripts and audio-visual documentation of local Acadian culture. Offers outreach presentations and workshops on Acadian folklore and regional history.

Lise Pelletier, Director
University of Maine at Fort Kent
23 University Drive
Fort Kent, Maine 04743
Phone: (207) 834-7535
Email: lise.m.pelletier@maine.edu
URL: www.umfk.edu/archive

The Center for Acadian and Creole Folklore

Located at the University of Louisiana at Lafayette, the center organizes festivals, special performances, and television and radio programs. It also offers classes and workshops through the Francophone Studies Program in the Department of Modern Languages and sponsors musicians as adjunct professors at the university.

Barry Jean Ancelet, Director
P.O. Box 40831
University of Louisiana at Lafayette
Lafayette, Louisiana 70504
Email: ancelet@louisiana.edu

LARC's Acadian Village

Visitors can see preservations and reconstructions of many nineteenth-century buildings in Lafayette at the LARC's Acadian Village, run by Tulane University's Louisiana Research Collection, or at the Vermilionville Living History and Folk Life Park.

Jeanne Lousao, Assistant Director
200 Greenleaf Drive
Lafayette, Louisiana 70506
Phone: (337) 981-2364
Email: jeanne@acadianvillage.org
URL: www.acadianvillage.org

Madawaska Historical Society

Founded in 1968 to collect and distribute material that illustrates local culture.

Ken Theriault, Jr., Museum Director
393 Main Street
Madawaska, Maine 04756
Email: ktheriault@madawaskahistorical.org
URL: www.madawaskahistorical.org

Vermilionville Living History and Folk Life Park

Rachelle Dugas, Coordinator
300 Fisher Road
Lafayette, Louisiana 70508
Phone: (337) 233-4077
Email: rachelle@vermilionville.org
URL: www.bayouvermiliondistrict.org

SOURCES FOR ADDITIONAL STUDY

Ancelet, Barry; Jay D. Edwards; Glen Pitre, et al. *Cajun Country*. Jackson: University of Mississippi Press, 1991.

Bankston, Carl, and Jacques Henry. "The Silence of the Gators: Cajun Ethnicity and Intergenerational Transmission of Louisiana French." *Journal of Multilingual and Multicultural Development* 19, no. 1 (1998): 1–23.

Bernard, Shane K. *The Cajuns: Americanization of a People*. Jackson: University Press of Mississippi, 2003.

Brasseaux, Ryan A. *Cajun Breakdown: The Emergence of an American-Made Music*. New York: Oxford University Press, 2009.

Chetro-Szivos, John. *Talking Acadian: Communication, Work, and Culture*. New York: YBK Publishers, 2006.

Collins, Charles W. *The Acadians of Madawaska, Maine*. Toronto: University of Toronto Libraries, 2011.

Craig, Béatrice. "Kinship and Migration to the Upper St. John Valley, 1785–1842." *Quebec Studies* 1 (Spring 1983): 151–64.

Griffiths, N. E. S. *From Migrant to Acadian: A North American Border People, 1604–1755*. Montreal: McGill-Queen's University Press, 2004.

Hodson, Christopher. *The Acadian Diaspora: An Eighteenth-Century History*. New York: Oxford University Press, USA, 2012.

Madore, Nelson, and Barry Rodrigue, eds. *Voyages: A Maine Franco-American Reader*. Gardiner, ME: Tilbury House Publishers, 2007.

AFGHAN AMERICANS

Tim Eigo

OVERVIEW

Afghan Americans are immigrants or descendants of people from Afghanistan, a country in southern Asia. Officially the Islamic Republic of Afghanistan, the country is bordered by Turkmenistan, Tajikistan, Uzbekistan, and China to the north, Pakistan to the east and south, and Iran to the west. The terrain alternates between the rugged mountain ranges of the Hindu Kush (making parts of the country virtually inaccessible) and the plains of the North and Southwest. Only 12 percent of Afghanistan is arable. The climate can be harsh, bringing earthquakes, damaging floods, and devastating droughts. Afghanistan's total land area is 251,827 square miles (652,230 square kilometers), which is roughly the size of Texas.

According to the *CIA World Factbook*, the population of Afghanistan was an estimated 30,419,928 in 2012. The last official census was suspended in 1979, when the Soviet Union invaded the country. About 80 percent of the population is Sunni Muslim; 19 percent is Shia Muslim; and 1 percent is some other religion. Afghanistan is ethnically diverse, divided among the Pashtun (42 percent), Tajik (27 percent), Uzbek (9 percent), Aimak (4 percent), Turkmen (3 percent), and Baloch (2 percent). Many Afghans are bilingual. Half the population speaks Afghan, Persian, or Dari. The latter is an official language, as is Pashto, which is spoken by 35 percent of the population. Afghanistan has one of the lowest standards of living in the world, with a per capita income of only $1,000 in 2011. More than a third of the population is unemployed, and 36 percent of Afghans live below the poverty line. Some 79 percent of the workforce is engaged in the agricultural sector, with many Afghans involved in subsistence farming.

Afghans first started settling in the United States in the 1920s and 1930s, beginning with a group of two hundred Pashtuns in 1920. Early Afghan immigrants tended to come from the professional classes, often immigrating as students and never returning home. They settled mostly in California, New York, and Washington, D.C., where large Afghan American communities still exist. Early Afghan immigrants were able to acclimatize well to life in the United States while continuing to preserve their own culture and maintaining strong ties with

Afghanistan. Acclimation has been much more difficult for Afghans who came to the United States as refugees rather than as immigrants seeking improved opportunities.

According to the U.S. Census Bureau's 2011 American Community Survey estimates U.S. residents reported being of Afghan descent. In 2005 the American Community Survey had placed the Afghan American population at 70,063. The states with the largest Afghan American populations were California, Virginia, New York, Maryland, and Texas.

HISTORY OF THE PEOPLE

Early History Some of the earliest stirrings of the nation-state that became Afghanistan occurred in 1747, when lands controlled by the Pashtuns were united under Ahmad Shah Durrani. Durrani established the first independent Pashtun-controlled region in central Asia, becoming known as the "Father of Afghanistan." The British invaded the country in 1839, setting off the three-year Anglo-Afghan War. That year King Shah Shujah was installed as the head of the newly created monarchy. After Afghanistan achieved its independence from Britain in 1919, it endured decades of invasion, war, and internal conflict.

Modern Era In 1953 General Mohammed Daud, the new prime minister, turned to the Soviet Union for both financial and military assistance. A series of social reforms were subsequently instituted. Daud was ousted in 1963, and the following year Afghanistan redefined itself as a constitutional monarchy, adopting a new constitution that laid the groundwork for the eventual creation of a parliamentary democracy. Daud managed to recapture control through a successful coup in 1973, but a communist countercoup followed in 1978 with backing from the Soviet Union. Because it was generally viewed as pro-Russian and anti-Islamic, the countercoup led to widespread uprisings. As a result, more than 400,000 refugees fled to Pakistan, and 600,000 more escaped to Iran. At first the Soviets assisted the Afghan government in suppressing the uprisings, but they chose to invade Afghanistan in 1979. The invasion motivated the United States to supply Afghan rebels with military equipment.

The Soviet invasion generated a new wave of Afghan refugees, who fled to neighboring countries. By 1981 there were some three million Afghans in Pakistan and 250,000 in Iran. By 1985 half the population of Afghanistan had been displaced by war, and by 1991 the number of Afghan refugees had climbed to five million. The Soviet Union withdrew from Afghanistan in 1989, leaving behind a country devastated by decades of war. In 1994 the Taliban seized control of Kabul and imposed strict adherence to Islamic law. Afghan women left Afghanistan in droves, and many immigrated to the United States and Canada. On September 11, 2001, al-Qaeda terrorists with links to the Taliban attacked the United States. The subsequent invasion launched by the administration of President George W. Bush and NATO allies in 2001 ousted the Taliban-led government. By 2004 a new constitution had been ratified, and elections were held in Afghanistan. Hamid Karzai became the first president of Afghanistan ever to be democratically elected, and he headed up efforts to revitalize Afghanistan. He was reelected in 2009.

SETTLEMENT IN THE UNITED STATES

Although early records are vague or nonexistent, the first Afghans to reach U.S. shores probably arrived in the 1920s or 1930s. It is known that a group of two hundred Pashtuns came to the United States in 1920. Owing to the political boundaries in central Asia at that time, however, most were probably residents of British India (which today is in Pakistan). Some were probably Afghan citizens, however. Most Afghan immigrants in the 1930s and 1940s arrived alone or in family groups, and some were married to Europeans. Many of those immigrants were students who came to the United States to study and chose to remain permanently in the United States rather than returning to their homeland.

From 1953 until the early 1970s, about 230 Afghans immigrated to the United States and became American citizens. That number does not reflect those who arrived in the United States to earn a university degree and then returned to Afghanistan, or who visited here for other reasons. From 1973 to 1977, 110 Afghan immigrants were naturalized in the United States.

Although the first Afghan immigrants to arrive in the United States were well educated and professional, more recent immigrants have less education, interact less with other Americans, and are less proficient in English. Since the terrorist attacks of September 11, 2001, many Afghan Americans have experienced a strong sense of isolation within American society.

Large numbers of Afghan refugees began arriving in the United States in 1980 in the wake of the Soviet invasion. Some were officially designated as refugees, while others were granted political asylum. Others arrived through a family reunification program or by illegal entry. About 2,000 to 4,000 Afghans arrived every year until 1989, when the Soviet Union withdrew its troops. Estimates of the number of Afghan refugees in the United States ranged from 45,000 to 75,000.

After 1989 most Afghans arrived in the United States under the family reunification program. In that case, a visa is contingent on the willingness of family members or an organization to guarantee their support for a certain period of time. This process inevitably leads immigrant groups to settle near each other. After a brief stall in 1994, a new wave of Afghan immigrants escaping the Taliban began in 1996, with approximately 1,000 arriving each year until the year 2000. Although the first Afghan immigrants to arrive in the United States were well educated and professional, more recent immigrants have less education, interact less with other Americans, and are less proficient in English. Since the terrorist attacks of September 11, 2001, many Afghan Americans have experienced a strong sense of isolation within American society.

From 1999 the U.S. government began admitting Afghans who had fled to Pakistan by granting them refugee status. Most within this group were well educated, and 2,800 Afghan women arrived in the United States after 1999. About 70 percent of those women were Tajiks, and more than half were doctors, engineers, lawyers, and teachers. At the other end of the spectrum were working-class immigrants who joined the American workforce as sales clerks, office personnel, and service workers. In 2001 about half the female Afghan immigrants had been widowed. In 2006 the U.S. government created a special immigrant visa program to allow Afghans and Iraqis who had worked with the American military at great risk to their lives and safety to enter the United States. However, benefits allotted for these immigrants are often difficult to obtain and expire six months after arrival. Most of these special entrants have been unable to find jobs commensurate with their professional training and job skills. Therefore, they have been forced to work at low-paying jobs, and some have been unable to find work at all.

According to the 2000 U.S. Census, 53,709 Afghan Americans lived in the United States. After the ousting of the Taliban in 2001 and the installation that year of the Western-backed government, the annual number of Afghan immigrants more than doubled; from 2002 to 2011 an average of 2,500 Afghans annually immigrated to the United States (as reported by the Organisation for Economic Co-operation and Development). Many Afghan Americans also returned to Afghanistan to take on major responsibilities in rebuilding the nation. In 2011 the U.S. Census Bureau's American Community Survey (ACS) reported that an estimated 89,040 people of Afghan descent were living in the United States.

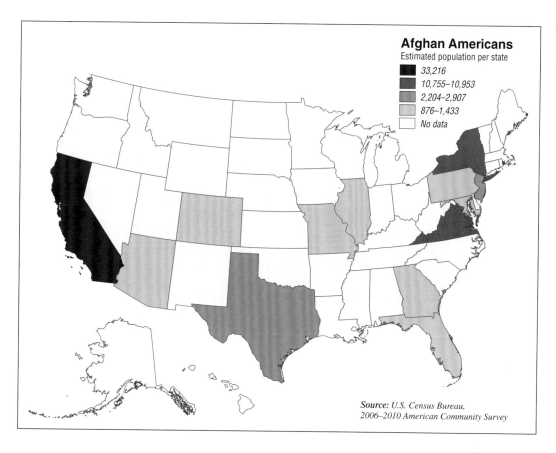

Afghan Americans
Estimated population per state

- 33,216
- 10,755–10,953
- 2,204–2,907
- 876–1,433
- No data

*Source: U.S. Census Bureau,
2006–2010 American Community Survey*

The majority of Afghan immigrants settled in California, New York, and Washington, D.C., and established their own communities. Census figures taken in 2005 indicated that Afghan Americans had spread out to Virginia, Maryland, and Texas. In California the largest Afghan American communities are found in the San Francisco Bay Area and the Los Angeles area. No city is more associated with Afghan Americans than Fremont, California, which is home to the largest concentration of Afghan Americans in the country. According to the ACS estimates, in 2010 there were 2,760 individuals of Afghan descent living in Fremont. The area of "Little Kabul" is filled with Afghan restaurants and shops and regularly hosts events that promote the Afghan culture. The Bay Area, which was home to some 11,400 Afghan Americans in 2010 (ACS estimate), has long been considered a haven for Afghan Americans, providing them with access to mosques, grocery stores, restaurants, and a local radio and television station in their own language. Another 7,500 lived in the Los Angeles area, and 3,200 called San Diego home. The climate, diverse culture, and availability of social programs have drawn many Afghan Americans to California. About 8,900 Afghan Americans lived in the New York City metropolitan area, which includes northern, New Jersey and Long Island. Many Muslim Afghan Americans have found a home in the "Little Afghanistan" section of Queens, New York. A much smaller group of Afghan Jews

has made their home in New York City. Other cities with smaller Afghan American populations include Washington D.C., Baltimore, Dallas-Fort Worth, Chicago, Denver, Boulder, Albany, Philadelphia, Seattle, Atlanta, Phoenix, and Minneapolis-St. Paul.

LANGUAGE

Although a number of dialects are spoken in Afghanistan, there are two related languages spoken throughout the country. Pashto is one of the official languages; the dialect known as Northern Pashto is spoken in some provinces of Pakistan. Pashto speakers have traditionally made up the ruling class of Afghanistan. Dari, which is also an official language, is a variety of Persian. Dari is more often used in the cities and in business. Whereas Pashto speakers make up one ethnic group—the Pashtun—those who speak Dari include many ethnicities from many regions. Both Pashto and Dari are used by educated Afghans, who learn both languages as well as English in school. When teaching general subjects, teachers use the language that is most common to the region in which the school is located.

Dari and Pashto are more similar written than as spoken languages. In written language, both Pashto and Dari use adaptations of the Arabic alphabet. Four additional consonants are added to that alphabet in Dari for sounds unique to Afghanistan. In Pashto those four consonants are added as well as eight additional letters. Other languages spoken in Afghanistan stem from the Turkish language family, including Uzbek, Turkmen, Balochi, Pashai, Nuristani, and Pamiri. Each of these languages is the official language in the area in which the designated group is the majority.

Most Afghan immigrants to the United States speak Dari, Pashto, or Tajik. Many adopt English after their arrival, but certain groups of immigrants struggle to acquire the language. For example, many poorer immigrants, who were illiterate in their home country, find it difficult to learn English. Younger Afghan immigrants continue to demonstrate their ease in learning new languages by becoming adept at English. This facility with language aids the youth in their academic and career prospects, but it can be a double-edged sword; as the member of a family who is most adept at English, a child may be called upon to interact with authority figures outside the family, such as school principals and social service agencies. Although this dialogue may be vital to the family's well-being, it upsets the traditional Afghan family hierarchy and sometimes contributes to the despair of parents who bemoan the loss of traditional family patterns.

Another dilemma faced by Afghan Americans is the combination of English words and phrases when they speak Dari or Pashto to each other. This combination of two languages has made communication among Afghan youth easier, but it has also created a serious problem in communication between children and parents with limited English language skills. According to the 2009–2011 estimates by the American Community Survey, the vast majority of Afghan Americans (89.2 percent) spoke a language other than English at home. However, the majority of those (65.7 percent) also reported that they spoke English "very well." Researchers have found that Afghan Americans tend to use Dari and Pashto in conversations related to intimacy and family life but use English in conversations related to status. Although such language combinations may aid communication when all speakers have similar skill levels in both languages, long-term mixture may dilute Afghan languages among Afghan Americans.

Greetings and Popular Expressions in Dari and Pashto Hello / Peace be with you. *Salaam. / As-Salaamu 'alaykum.*

Welcome. *Khoosh aamadeyn. / Kha raaghlaast.*

How are you? *Chutoor hastee? / Tsenga yee?*

Fine. And you? *Khoob astum. Chutoor asten? / Za Kha yam. Tatsenga?*

What is your name? *Naamet chees? / Staa num tsa deh?*

Do you speak English? *Ingleesee yaad daaree? / Tta pe Inglisee Khabaree kawaley shee?*

Thank you for your help. *Aaz khumeketaan tashakur. / Staa la maraste tsaKha manana.*

AFGHAN PROVERBS

Bae yeak gul bahear namesaewaed.

One flower does not bring spring.

Hach guli ba char mast.

No rose is without thorns.

Yag roz didi dost, degaqre roz didi bridar.

The first day you meet, you are friends; the next day you meet, you are brothers.

Qatrra qattra dary aa mey-sha.

Rivers are made drop by drop.

Dil ba dil roh darad.

Heart to heart, there is a way.

Maahee-ra har waq taz aab biggeree taaaza ast.

Whenever you take fish from water, it is always fresh.

Se che karey agha ba rabey.

What you sow, shall you reap.

RELIGION

Afghanistan is predominantly Muslim, and politics and religion there are interrelated, with religious laws often governing daily life. The majority of the population, 80 percent, is Sunni, the most mainstream branch of Islam. Another 19 percent are Shia Muslims, who are considerably more conservative than Sunnis. The remaining one percent of Afghans tend to be Pashtunwali, Baha'i, Buddhists, Hindus, or Zoroastrians. In a largely inaccessible country such as Afghanistan, the wider Islamic influence was once limited, and a strict adherence to its tenets was not kept. However, the Taliban strictly enforced Islamic law, and religious law continues to play a major role in the legal system and customs of contemporary Afghanistan.

In the United States, many Afghan Americans experience conflicts with American society that can be traced to Islamic traditions, history, and identity. Those conflicts have accelerated greatly since the terrorist attacks of September 11, 2001, and religious discrimination against Muslim Americans has been on the rise as some Americans equate Islam with terrorism and confuse Afghans with al-Qaeda. One of the ironies of this position is that many Afghan Americans who are accused of being terrorists have joined the military to fight "terrorists." Another irony is that many young Afghan Americans identify themselves chiefly as Americans, and many have never even seen Afghanistan.

Muslims avoid alcohol and all pork products. During Ramadan—the month-long period of fasting—eating, drinking, smoking, and sexual activity are forbidden during the day. One difficulty for Afghan American youths is that Islam discourages marriage outside the faith. There is, however, a gender-based disparity in the consequences of these types of marriages. A son who marries a non-Muslim is accepted, because it is assumed that his new wife will convert to Islam. When a daughter marries a non-Muslim, she is often shunned. She is seen as a traitor to her family and her religion.

CULTURE AND ASSIMILATION

Observers have noted that many Afghan immigrants feel a sense of isolation when entering the United States. This is particularly true of those who arrived as political refugees. That sense of isolation accelerated even further after the terrorist attacks of 9/11 because of the Taliban's links to al-Qaeda, the perpetrator of the attacks. In 1994 the Taliban, a Pakistani-sponsored group, took control of Afghanistan, and many Afghans fled the country. In 1999 the American government began granting refugee status to all Afghans entering the United States via Pakistan. The vast majority had no plan to remain permanently in the United States. Instead, they came to find physical safety. Many were trained as professionals in Afghanistan but found work impossible to obtain in the United States due to difficulties with the English language, depleted savings, or lack of a social support. Some Afghan Americans are fighting back by filing lawsuits against those who discriminate against them. One recent incident involved the harassment of four Afghan American sales people who were called "terrorists" by a general manager at a Toyota dealership in Fremont, California, during a staff meeting. They ultimately resigned after being subjected to an extended period of ongoing harassment. In 2012 Fremont Toyota settled the lawsuit for $400,000 and focused national attention on the issue of harassment of Arab Americans in the wake of 9/11.

Afghan immigrants to the United States in the early 1980s tended to be urban professionals, but those who arrived in the late 1980s were often middle-class immigrants who arrived via family reunification. They were followed by Afghans seeking refugee status who tended to have even lower levels of education. Because Afghans receive only an average of nine years of schooling (with females attending for only seven years while males attend for eleven years) and the literacy rate is low (28.1 percent), many new Afghan American immigrants are illiterate in their own language as well as in English. Afghan women's literacy rate is less than 13 percent, so problems were even worse for some female immigrants.

Afghan Americans sometimes define integration into American society in ways that are distinct from those of other immigrants. Among the Afghan American refugee community, integration often means simply earning enough to support their families while maintaining their cultural and traditional beliefs and experiencing some level of stability and satisfaction, usually while isolating themselves within the Afghan American community. As Juliene Lipson and Patricia Omidian note in *Refugees in America* (1996), for many Afghan American refugees integration does not mean assimilation. Although Afghans who have been in the United States for many years are more accustomed to American culture, Lipson and Omidian found little assimilation of Afghans into the American mainstream, no matter how long they had lived in the United States. Because they speak Afghan languages at home, eat Afghan food, listen to Afghan music, and continue to participate in the religion and culture of their homeland, most Afghan families encourage links with Afghanistan. Even among children and teens, for whom assimilation is easiest, many young people have attempted to maintain their Afghan identity while changing only superficially.

Following the events of 9/11, Columbia University's Oral History Research Office began interviewing Afghan Americans, along with other Arab Americans, about their experiences within the context of the Oral History Narrative Memory Project. Individuals interviewed were generally young, extremely literate, and largely secular (rather than practicing Muslims). Most identified themselves as Americans rather than Afghans because they had either been born in the United States or immigrated at an early age and remembered little of life in Afghanistan. Most said they had experienced some level of racism in the post-9/11 environment. Among those interviewed, the sense of being unjustly treated after 9/11 has been particularly strong among those born and/or raised in the United States. Although they decried the attacks, some Afghan Americans felt that it was important for Americans to have a taste of the violence that had become a part of daily life for Afghans living in a country torn apart by both external and internal strife.

As with many immigrants, Afghans tend to settle in areas where there are already a large number of their own ethnic group present. This has occasionally led to increased difficulty with neighboring communities of other ethnicities, especially in places such as California, where resentment toward immigrants has heightened in the wake of 9/11 and the economic downturn of the early twenty-first century. The neighborhoods in which Afghan Americans settle also tend to be less expensive and sometimes more dangerous than those to which they are accustomed. Thus, many of those at most risk, such as the very old and very young, remain inside, contributing to an additional sense of isolation and further hindering acculturation. After 9/11 some job applicants chose to avoid listing education and job experience obtained in Afghanistan on job applications, even at the risk of appearing less qualified.

The strength of the Afghan people in the United States lies in their strong sense of family and tribal loyalty. Although strained by the dispersal of extended families and by financial stresses, that loyalty binds Afghan Americans to their cultural traditions, which have largely been transported unchanged from their homeland. Thus, faced with a difficult situation in Afghanistan, many Afghans chose to enter the United States owing to their strong family connections.

Traditions and Customs Central to the Afghan way of life is storytelling, and many stories are so well known that they can be recited by heart at family and community gatherings. Those stories have been brought to the United States by Afghan immigrants, who tell them to their children and grandchildren. Many young Afghan Americans, particularly those born in the United States, have not always felt connected to popular Afghan tales. However, the experiences of 9/11 aroused many young Afghan Americans' interest in their native culture. On college campuses with large Afghan American student populations, new groups have been organized to promote the Afghan languages and culture, such as the Afghan Student Association of the University of California at Berkeley and the Afghan Student Union at the University of Colorado at Boulder. Within Afghan American homes, most families have kept Afghan traditions alive by speaking only Dari or Pashto, listening to Afghan music, and eating traditional Afghan foods. Organizations such as America's Islamic Heritage Museum and Cultural Center in Washington, D.C., keep Islamic culture and traditions alive through events such as the Afghan American Oral History Night, held in September 2011.

As in all cultures, some of the most renowned Afghan stories are those for children. These stories, usually with a moral lesson, are often about foolish people getting what they deserve. Other sources of narrative enjoyment are tales about the mullah, a respected Islamic leader or teacher. In these stories, the narrator casts the mullah as a wise fool; that is, the one who appears to be foolish but who, later, is shown to be intelligent and full of sage advice.

Heroism plays an important role in Afghan stories, and many such tales are taken from the *Shahnama*, or *The Book of Kings*. In a geographic region that has been fought over, conquered, divided, and reunited, it is not surprising that what defines a hero is subject to debate. For example, one popular story is about a real man who overthrew the Pashtun government in 1929. However, that same man is anything but a hero in a traditional Pashtun tale, which portrays him as a fool.

Love stories are also important to Afghans. In one tale, the young lovers Majnun and Leilah are separated and unable to reunite after they grow older. Disappointed, they each die of grief and sadness.

Arab mythology tells of spirits known as jinn that can change shape and become invisible, and a belief in the jinn is strong among Afghans and Afghan Americans. These spirits are usually considered evil. Protection from jinn is derived from a special amulet worn around the neck. Jinn frequently find their way into Afghan stories.

Cuisine As in many countries of Asia, bread is central to the Afghan diet. Along with rice and dairy products, a flatbread called naan is an important part of most meals. This and other breads may be leavened or unleavened, and the process of cooking naan requires speed and dexterity. Afghan bread typically is cooked inside a round container made of pottery with an opening in the top. The container's bottom is buried in the earth and heated by coals. After forming the dough, the baker slaps it onto the rounded interior of the container, where it adheres and quickly begins cooking, after which it is served immediately. This method is used in many Afghan and Middle Eastern restaurants in the United States today.

Another important element of the Afghan meal is rice, cooked with vegetables or meats. The rice dishes vary from house to house and from occasion to occasion. They range from simple meals to elegant fare cooked with sheep, raisins, almonds, and pistachios. Because Afghanistan is a Muslim country, pork is forbidden. Popular Afghan foods cooked in Afghan American homes include meatballs, sweet pumpkin, handmade noodles, meat dumplings, and sweets such as *halwa*, *jelabi*, and rice pudding.

The usual drink in Afghanistan is tea. Green tea is drunk in the northern regions, and black tea is partaken south of the Hindu Kush mountains. Alcohol, forbidden by Islam, is not drunk.

Clothing Traditionally, an Afghan man wears a long-sleeved shirt that reaches his knees. His trousers are baggy and have a drawstring at the waist. Vests and coats are sometimes worn. In rural areas, the coats are often brightly striped. Turbans are worn by most men. Traditionally, the turban was white, but now a variety of colors are seen. Since the fall of the Taliban, many young Afghan males have become fashion-conscious and have begun to mirror the wardrobes of most young Afghan American males, wearing jeans with T-shirts or sweatshirts and appearing in other Western fashions.

Women in Afghanistan wear pleated trousers under a long dress. Their heads are usually covered. Under the Taliban, the wearing of the burqa, a traditional piece of clothing, was reinstated. The burqa is an ankle-length cloth covering worn by Afghan women that reaches from head to toe, with mesh for the eyes and nose. The burqa had been banned by the government in 1959 as Afghanistan modernized. In the wake of the Taliban's fall, the burqa continued to be worn widely in public. However, in private many Afghan women wear Western-style clothing such as tight jeans and high-heeled boots. Among Afghan American women, most wear Western-style clothes when in public. Although many Afghan American women continued to cover their heads in public, some removed the coverings following the 9/11 attacks because of the animosity of some Americans who linked traditional Afghan clothing with al-Qaeda and terrorism.

Dances and Songs Afghan adults enjoy both songs and dancing. They do not dance with partners, the method more typical in the West. Instead, they dance in circles in a group or dance alone. A favorite pastime among men is to relax in teahouses listening to music and talking.

Traditional Afghan music has been influenced by a number of cultures, including Arab, Persian, Indian, Mongolian, and Chinese. Contemporary Afghan music, which is usually sung in either Dari or Pashto, is more similar to Western music than it is to any Asian music. Traditional instruments include drums, a wind instrument, and a stringed gourd. The males of some tribes still take part in traditional dances that involve swinging swords or guns while engaging in a war dance. For women, belly dancing is part of certain rituals in tribes such as the Durani, and the women wear long colorful dresses and many silver bracelets. The music and dance of Afghanistan have been kept alive for Afghan Americans as many continue to listen to traditional music in their homes and in gatherings with friends and family. Technology enables Afghan Americans to stay in touch with the Afghan pop scene, and websites such as Afghansongs.com provide Afghan Americans with ready access to popular songs and videos. Even though tribal dances are not performed outside the homeland, the Afghan belly dance has been transported to other cultures, including the United States. Although the belly dance is not generally performed in public, numerous videos of it are available via YouTube.

While Afghanistan was under Taliban control, many forms of Afghan music were completely banned, and it became illegal to attend mixed-gender parties. Even though the ousting of the Taliban from their official position has allowed the Afghan music scene to resurface, some repression continues. In 2012, for instance, fifteen males and two females were beheaded by members of the Taliban for attending a mixed-gender party.

In 2010 Afghan journalist Najibullah Quraishi released the documentary *The Dancing Boys of Afghanistan*, which focusing attention on the practice of poor Afghan parents selling their sons to wealthy Afghans for sexual and entertainment purposes. Although the practice is illegal, the law is rarely enforced.

Holidays A countryside filled with farm animals dyed a variety of colors is a sign that the most important annual Afghan holiday, Nowruz, has arrived. Nowruz, the ancient Persian new year celebration, occurs at the beginning of spring and is celebrated on the Spring Equinox each year. An important Nowruz ceremony is the raising of the flag at the tomb of Ali, Muhammad's son-in-law, in the city of Mazar-e-Sharif in northern Afghanistan. Pilgrims travel to touch the staff that was raised, and on the fortieth day after Nowruz, the staff is lowered. At that time, a short-lived species of tulip blooms. The holiday is brightened by the arrival of

AFGHANI PUMPKIN (KADDO BOWRANI)

Ingredients

1 2–2.5 pound sugar pumpkin
2 tablespoons vegetable oil
1 cup sugar
½ teaspoon ground cinnamon
1 cup plain yogurt
2 tablespoons chopped fresh mint
1 clove garlic, crushed
2 tablespoons vegetable oil
2 medium onions, chopped
1 pound lean ground beef
1 clove garlic, crushed
1 cup tomato sauce
½ cup water
1¼ teaspoons ground coriander seed
½ teaspoon ground turmeric
1 teaspoon ground black pepper
1 teaspoon salt

Preparation

Preheat the oven to 350°F.

For pumpkin:

Cut the pumpkin into quarters. Remove seeds and strings, peel the skin, and cut into about 2-inch chunks. Heat 2 tablespoons oil in a skillet over medium high. Brown the pumpkin pieces, turning frequently, until golden brown (about 5 minutes). Transfer pumpkin to a roasting pan. Mix sugar and cinnamon, and sprinkle over pumpkin. Cover with foil and bake for 30 minutes, or until tender. While the pumpkin is baking, make the yogurt sauce and the meat sauce.

Yogurt sauce:

Mix together yogurt, mint, and 1 clove of crushed garlic in a bowl; season to taste with salt & pepper.

Meat sauce:

In a skillet, heat 2 tablespoons of oil and cook the onions until lightly browned. Add ground beef, second clove of garlic, coriander, turmeric, salt, and pepper. Mix well and cook until beef is browned. Add tomato sauce and water and bring to a simmer. Lower heat and cook about 20 minutes, until thickened.

To serve:

Spoon yogurt sauce onto dinner plates, add a portion of the cooked pumpkin, and top with meat sauce.

Serves 4

special foods such as *samanak*, made with wheat and sugar. Sugar is expensive in Afghanistan, and its use indicates a special occasion. Another special dish is *haft*

"Tahmina Comes into Rustam's Chamber," illustration from the *Book of Kings,* by Abu'l-Qasim Manur Firdawsi (c. 934–c. 1020), from Herat, Afghanistan, c.1410. Opaque with gold on paper. ARTHUR M. SACKLER MUSEUM, HARVARD UNIVERSITY ART MUSEUMS, USA / GIFT OF MRS E.C. FORBES, MRS E. SHROEDER & THE A.S. COBURN FUND / THE BRIDGEMAN ART LIBRARY

miwa, a combination of nuts and fruits. While Afghan Americans have always been free to celebrate Nowruz, the practice was banned within Afghanistan during the reign of the Taliban. A religious nation, Afghanistan celebrates most of its holidays by following the Islamic calendar. The holidays include Ramadan, the month of fasting from dawn until dusk, and Eid al-Adha, a sacrifice feast that lasts three days to celebrate the monthlong pilgrimage to Mecca.

Health Care Issues As with all immigrants, Afghan Americans are affected by the conditions of the land they left. Within Afghanistan, children continue to be the most vulnerable of all groups to the conditions of war, poverty, and inadequate access to potable water and good health care. Afghanistan has the highest infant mortality rate in the world (121.63 deaths per 1,000 live births). One in four dies before their fifth birthday, and one in ten are severely malnourished. In 1996 the United Nations found that the capital Kabul had more land mines than any other country in the world, and more than 400,000 Afghan children had been disabled by those mines. Over one million Afghan children suffer from post-traumatic stress disorder. In 2010 there were more than two million orphaned children, and 600,000 Afghan children live on the streets. Many Afghan Americans have demonstrated their willingness to adopt or foster Afghan orphans. According to Passports USA, however, it is impossible for Americans to adopt Afghan orphans because of legal differences in adoption laws of the two countries.

Afghan Americans seeking health care face many of the same problems as other Muslim immigrants. Many Afghan American Muslims are uncomfortable with medical providers of a different sex. They may require that their beds face Mecca, and many are uncomfortable with having parts of their body exposed. Some Afghan Americans adhere to the traditional belief that females require male chaperonage when in public, and this can present problems when Afghan American females are hospitalized. Because health care is often inadequate and inaccessible in Afghanistan, more recent immigrants may be completely unfamiliar with Western medical procedures. Most Afghan American Christians who have become acclimatized to American society experience little difficulty in adjusting to the American health care system, as many of the problems experienced by Afghan Muslim immigrants are related to their religious beliefs. Recent immigrants may experience language barriers, and they may delay seeking help because of the lack of health insurance and the cultural tendency of Afghans to believe that illnesses can be treated by home remedies or through cultural rituals.

Mental health issues related to the trauma of war are common among Afghan Americans, especially more recent arrivals. Dislocation, relocation, and the death of family members and friends all weigh heavily on uprooted people. Post-traumatic stress disorder has frequently been diagnosed in the Afghan American population. In addition, there is evidence of family stress based on changing gender roles in the face of American culture.

Many elderly Afghans who had prepared to enter a period of heightened responsibility and respect enter instead a period of isolation. Their extended families are dispersed, and their immediate family members work long hours to make ends meet. Because they themselves do not speak English, they feel trapped inside their homes. Even parents and youth suffer a sense of loss as they contend with social service agencies and schools. Women, often more willing than men to take jobs below their abilities or former status, must deal with resentment from other family members as they become primary breadwinners.

Among Afghan Americans who have been in the United States for a longer period of time, there are fewer health and mental health problems and more satisfaction with their lives in the United States. Their increasing financial and career stability provides optimism for the newer arrivals.

One problem growing in severity among Afghan Americans is the use and abuse of alcohol. This issue is emerging even though Islam forbids the drinking of alcohol. Alcohol abuse often stems from the traumas and stresses of upheaval and problems with money, jobs, and school. In such a traditionally abstinent group, abuse of alcohol leads to shame and loss of traditional culture.

Death and Burial Rituals Religious practices brought from their homeland play a major role in the funeral rituals of Afghan American Muslims. During the ceremony, passages from the Quran are read, and prayers might be offered asking that God grant long lives to remaining family members. Women are required to sit in a separate room, where services are heard only through a loudspeaker. Funerals frequently become social occasions; as is common at Afghan American social gatherings, food is an important part of the occasion. The meal may be served at the mosque where the funeral takes place or at the home of a family member. Afghan American Christians follow the practices of their own religions, and services have much in common with those of other American funerals.

FAMILY AND COMMUNITY LIFE

To the Afghan people, the most important social unit is not the nation but the family. An Afghan has obligations to his or her immediate and extended families. The head of the family is unequivocally the father (or the grandfather in extended family situations), regardless of social class or education. As economic pressures are brought to bear on Afghan American families, that dynamic has shifted in some cases, at times causing stress. Almost all immigrants in the 1980s and 1990s suffered a severe loss of status with their move to the United States because they were often forced to take on lower-paying jobs, and many could not obtain positions in the fields for which they were trained. Thus, they were required to grow accustomed to what they viewed as a loss of status. Since more recent immigrants tend to come from lower educational and occupational statuses, the change is generally less traumatic for them.

Both family size and dynamics are vastly different in the United States than in Afghanistan. Because in Afghanistan infant mortality is high and many families live off the land, Afghan women give birth to an average of six children. Extended family members often live together in one household, sometimes behind a walled compound. In the United States, families are smaller and more spread out, with grown children often moving to different states. Afghan American women have broken with tradition by entering the workplace, where they are exposed to a range of situations and people. Within some Afghan American families, this exposure creates challenges to the role of the male as responsible for females he feels morally bound to protect. Afghan American young people are exposed to even more outside forces and must walk a fine line in trying to fit in with their peers while continuing to respect the cultural traditions of their families. Because respect for authority figures such as fathers and teachers is inherent in Afghan culture, traditional Afghan American families often have difficulty adjusting to changing familial roles.

> One of the first differences I noticed in America is the size of families. In Afghanistan, even the smallest family has five or six kids. And extended-family members are very close-knit; brothers-and sisters-in-law, aunts and uncles, and grandparents all live together or nearby.
>
> M. Daud Nassery in 1988 in *New Americans: An Oral History: Immigrants and Refugees in the U.S. Today*, by Al Santoli (Viking Penguin, Inc., New York, 1988)

Gender Roles Within Afghanistan, life for women is often dangerous and is considered repressive, by Western standards. Females can be imprisoned at the request of family members or they can be forced to serve as proxies when their husbands commit crimes. Young girls are forced into arranged marriages; if they escape, they often have nowhere to turn. Some Afghans still engage in the practice of *baadh*, in which females are given to other family members to pay off debts. Freedom of movement is severely restricted for Afghan females.

In the United States, Afghan women have proved to be strong, resourceful, and valuable members of their families. Although the father plays the dominant role in the community and extended family, the mother's role should not be overlooked. Researchers have generally found that young Afghan women have adapted to living in the United States better than their male counterparts. Elderly Afghan American women have not done as well. They often feel isolated and lonely at a time of their lives when they could have expected to be secure in the center of a loving extended family. Many Afghan American women have taken on occupations that would have been below their former status in Afghanistan, such as housekeeping. Afghan American women who work outside the home are still expected to clean and cook at home. As in their home country, they also have had to bear the major responsibility of caring for children.

Because marriage and childbearing is considered the primary role for women, single Afghan American women contend with unique stresses. Often Afghan American men perceive their female counterparts as too Westernized to be suitable mates. They may prefer to marry women who live in Afghanistan or Pakistan.

Birth As in many cultures, the birth of a child is cause for celebration in an Afghan household. The birth of a boy leads to an elaborate celebration. It is not until children are three days old that they are named, and an uncle on the father's side of the family chooses the name. At the celebration, the mullah, a respected Islamic leader, whispers into the newborn's ear "*Allah-u-Akbar*," or "God is great," and then whispers the child's new name. He tells the newborn about his or her ancestry and to be a good Muslim and maintain the family honor. In the United States, Afghan American Muslims have continued this practice. A parent or grandparent might whisper in the ear of a newborn, "*A shadu ala ilaha ilalahu wa ashadu anna Muhammadan abdoho wa raswuloh*," which means "I testify that there is no God but God, and I testify that Muhammad is His messenger."

Education Education levels among Afghan Americans vary greatly. Many Afghan immigrants possess college degrees, often earned in the United States, and some have been able to achieve positions of prominence in American society. Other Afghan Americans have not been as fortunate. Many entered the United States in desperate straits, with little or no money, and were forced to take jobs of lower status than those held in their homeland. Many were victims of an inferior Afghan educational system in which most males attended school for eleven years but females for only seven. During the Taliban era, girls were often prevented from attending schools. Schools are underfunded, and teachers are often inadequately trained. With a renewed interest in education during Afghan reconstruction, there is an acute shortage of teachers. The result of the poor educational system is that literacy in Afghanistan is very low, particularly for females.

With female literacy at 12.6 percent, and male literacy at 43.1 percent. and the education system is rudimentary. Originally schooling was available only in mosques and only for boys. It was not until 1903 that the first truly modern school was created in which both religious and secular subjects were taught. The first school for girls was not founded until 1923 in Kabul. In the most Western of Afghan cities, Kabul, the University of Kabul opened in 1946. Even there, however, there were separate faculties for men and women.

A terrible blow befell Afghan schooling in the aftermath of the invasion by the Soviet Union. Before the invasion, it was estimated that there were more than 3,400 schools and more than 83,000 teachers. By the late 1990s only 350 schools existed, with only 2,000 teachers. The method of teaching in those schools was rote memorization. In the late twentieth century, failure to pass to the next grade was common.

Immigrants to the United States in the 1980s and 1990s confronted a daunting economic landscape. After fleeing Afghanistan, even Afghans who had been educated in the United States found themselves unable to find work there. This was often due to poor English skills or outdated training, especially in medicine and engineering. Also significant, however, was the need for many to find work immediately. Often family members required public assistance, and social workers instructed them to choose from the first few jobs offered. As a result, doctors and other trained professionals worked at low-paying, often menial jobs.

Young Afghan Americans confront their own challenges in the American school system. Unlike other immigrants who may have moved to the United States for increased economic or educational opportunities, many more recent Afghan refugees were fleeing war. Those of school age may have spent years in refugee camps, where camp administrators felt that schools were not necessary for "short-term" stays. In American schools, these children often faced the humiliating experience of being placed in classrooms with far younger children. Those placed in English as a Second Language classes, however, proved that like most young immigrants Afghan American children learned more quickly than adult immigrants.

Courtship and Weddings In Afghanistan, 80 percent of all marriages are forced or arranged, and 57 percent involve girls under the age of sixteen. Girls as young as nine or ten may be forced to marry males in their sixties. Those who refuse to marry the partner chosen by their families may be imprisoned. In the United States, Afghan parents may still exercise considerable control over a child's choice of marriage partners. More traditional families often encourage young people to choose a spouse still living in Afghanistan and bring them to the United States. Such practices may result in acquiring a spouse who is uneducated and completely lacking in English-language skills. For that reason, a more common practice is for Afghan Americans to marry within the Afghan American community, although many marry non-Afghans. American-style dating is discouraged among the more traditional Afghan American families, particularly among Muslims, because of the emphasis on chastity for females.

Weddings among Afghan Americans vary according to religious traditions. In most Afghan American weddings, the bride wears an American-style white wedding dress and veil, and the groom wears a suit or tuxedo. However, Afghan music and dancing are the norm, and Afghan food is likely to be served at the reception.

EMPLOYMENT AND ECONOMIC CONDITIONS

Afghan Americans have found occupations in a variety of fields. The growing number of Afghan and Middle Eastern restaurants in the United States is a testimony to their hard work and excellent cuisine. For many Afghan Americans who are college educated, their positions in government, media, and American industry are prestigious. For many other immigrants, the route to economic stability was self-sufficiency. Thus, many exert themselves in sales of ethnic items at flea markets and garage sales. Immigrants to the San Francisco Bay Area have found work in computer components companies. Others, especially first-generation immigrants, work as taxi drivers, babysitters, and convenience store owners and workers. Their children, earning high school diplomas and college degrees, soon move into their own professional careers in ways identical to that of other Americans.

Even in those Afghan American families that have achieved some measure of success and financial stability, there has been a loss of traditions. In families in which virtually every member of the family works, perhaps at more than one job, family connections becomes fragile, and the cultural roles played by each family member begin to disintegrate. This economic necessity extends even to the children in Afghan American families, who often work rather than engage in extracurricular activities or other community or school programs. The need to constantly work in order to survive inevitably contributes to an immigrant community's sense of otherness, its isolation, and its lack of acculturation. Despite these obstacles, changes have come to the Afghan American community, including increases in the rate of home ownership and increased numbers of young people attending postsecondary and professional schools.

POLITICS AND GOVERNMENT

Like other Muslim immigrants, Afghan American immigrants have traditionally been conservative and have expressed support for the Republican Party. However, the terrorist attacks of 9/11 and the subsequent so-called War on Terror launched by President George W. Bush led to outrage among many Muslim groups, who have been increasingly more inclined to support the Democratic Party. The vote of Afghan Americans was considered particularly important in battleground states during the 2012 presidential election.

In 2001 Radio Afghanistan, a listener-supported radio station that operates in the Los Angeles area, found that Afghan American callers were divided in their reactions to the 9/11 attacks and political events in Afghanistan. While some supported the Taliban, others supported the anti-Taliban efforts of the Northern Alliance. Some were opposed to both groups. Whatever their opinions, they all condemned terrorism. The sense of isolation felt by many Afghan Americans continued to grow in the wake of 9/11, and open discrimination proliferated. Many fought back by filing discrimination suits. In August 2012 four Afghan American car salesmen employed by a car dealership in Fremont, California, received $400,000 to settle a discrimination suit they filed after they stated that a general manager called them terrorists during a staff meeting. Fremont is home to the largest group of Afghans living in the United States.

Relations with Afghanistan A factor that strongly influences Afghan Americans' sense of tradition and culture is the maintenance of close ties to family members who still live in Afghanistan. This connection with their former country provides its share of tribulations as well. Because of the many years of bloodshed in Afghanistan, most Afghan Americans were unable to return. The invasion of Afghanistan by the United States and NATO and the ousting of the Taliban in 2001, however, drastically changed the dynamics of the relationship of Afghan Americans to their homeland. The installation of a new government headed by President Hamid Karzai allowed many Afghan Americans to return to Afghanistan to take on a role in rebuilding the country. Back in Afghanistan, Afghan Americans ran for political office, accepted appointments in various bureaucracies, served as linguists, and opened businesses of all kinds. Other Afghan Americans remained in the United States, contenting themselves with sending private donations and helping to raise funds for American relief efforts. The Afghan American diaspora has also been involved with other Afghans in founding a new generation of organizations dedicated to the effort to revitalize Afghanistan by empowering its people. One such organization is Young Women for Change, which was founded in 2011 by Noorjahan Akbar and Anita Haidary for the purpose of motivating Afghan women to become active socially, economically, and politically.

NOTABLE INDIVIDUALS

Academia Mohammed Jamil Hanifi (1935–) is a professor of anthropology who specializes in the study of Afghan culture. He is best known for works that include *Islam and the Transformation of Culture* (1974) and *Historical and Cultural Dictionary of Afghanistan* (1976).

Nake M. Kamrany (1934–) has had a distinguished career as a professor of economics. He is the cofounder of the Center for Afghan Studies at the University of Nebraska and has published more than twenty works about the Afghan economy; his expertise has proved instrumental during the restructuring of Afghanistan.

Anthropology professor Nazif Shahrani, born in Afghanistan, is a specialist in Central Eurasian studies who has remained in the forefront in discussions

One of Afghanistan's most revered singers, Ustad Farida Mahwash (1947–) was exiled after the political turmoil of the 1970s and 80s. She was granted asylum in the U.S. in 1991. Here she is shown in her home in Fremont, California. KATY RADDATZ / SAN FRANCISCO CHRONICLE / CORBIS

of current issues affecting Afghanistan, including "Afghanistan Can Learn from Its Past," a thought-provoking op-ed piece for the *New York Times* (October 14, 2001) written in the wake of the events of 9/11.

Economist Abdul W. Haqiqi (1945–) is one of the many Afghan Americans who returned to Afghanistan after the ousting of the Taliban.

Business California businessman Jawid Siddiq has established himself in the area known as "Little Kabul" in Fremont, California. In 2004 he purchased the only single-screen theater in Fremont. Amid great controversy, he renamed it "The Palace" and recreated it as a venue for movies, dinner theater, and cultural events.

Culinary Arts Afghan Americans have been instrumental in helping exiled Afghans to maintain ties with their own culture by opening Afghan restaurants in areas with large Afghan American populations. Three of the most notable individuals in the field were the siblings of Afghan president Hamid Karzai (1957–). Brothers Quayum Karzai (1956–) and Mahmoud Karzai and sister Fauzia Karzai were all in the restaurant business in the United States before returning to Afghanistan to take part in the rebuilding of Afghanistan.

Film Both director Anwar Hajher and producer Mithaq Kazimi established their reputations with the documentary *16 Days in Afghanistan* (2007), which chronicles the days immediately following the fall of the Taliban.

Another rising figure in the film industry had his career tragically cut short. Jawed Wassel (1959–2001), the writer and director of *FireDancer* (2002), was murdered by his business partner. *FireDancer* was the first Afghan film to ever be under consideration for an Academy Award.

Actress and TV host Azita Ghanizada (1979–) has appeared on a number of popular television shows, including *The Closer, Bones, Ghost Whisperer,* and *How I Met Your Mother.*

Government One of the most prominent Americans of Afghan heritage, Zalmay Khalilzad (1951–), served as the U.S. ambassador to Afghanistan from 2003 to 2005. After serving two years as U.S. ambassador to Iraq, he was designated in 2007 as the permanent U.S. ambassador to the United Nations, where he served until 2009.

Journalism Based in San Francisco, Fariba Nawa (1973–) is one of the best-known Afghan American journalists. She has written extensively on Afghan women and the Afghan drug scene.

Nabil Miskinyar (1948–) operates Ariana Afghanistan International, a television station based in Orange County, California. Journalist Lina Rozbih serves as a correspondent for Voice of America.

Literature The best known of all Afghan American writers is Khaled Hosseini (1965–), author of the best-selling novel *The Kite Runner* (2003), the film adaptation (2007) of which also won critical acclaim. After returning to Afghanistan for the first time since the Soviets invaded in 1979, Hosseini published *A Thousand Splendid Suns* (2007).

Tamin Ansary (1948–) is best known for his memoir *West of Kabul, East of New York*, published in October 2001, when the United States was still reeling from the events of 9/11.

Coeditors Zohra Saed (1975–) and Sahar Muradi (1979–) received recognition for bringing the stories of Afghan American culture to an international audience in *One Story: Thirty Stories: An Anthology of Current Afghan American Literature* (2010), which combines history and literature to tell the stories of Afghan Americans.

Writer and playwright Youssof Kohzad (1935–) is an Afghan American of Tajik descent; in 2000 he immigrated to the United States with his wife, journalist Zakia Kohzad.

Music Popular figures within the Afghan American music scene range from those who date from the 1970s to the present. Singer and songwriter Naim Popal (1954–) is considered one of the most influential figures within the Afghan American music community. Ehsan Aman (1959–) is considered one of the most visible representatives of Afghanistan's Golden Age of Music of the 1970s, before music began to be suppressed by authorities. California-based Haider Salim has remained popular with Afghan American audiences since the 1970s. California is also home to Afghan pop singers Mariam Wafa (1973–) and Jawad Ghaziyar. Afghan American singer-songwriter Zohra Atash and her band, Religious to Damn, blend the sounds of

Middle Eastern music accompanied by the *rubab* and the harmonium to the sounds of contemporary alternative rock. Afghan American rapper J. Mecka is a member of the hip-hop duo D-Clique.

MEDIA

RADIO

Azadi Afghan Radio (WUST-AM 1120)

Omar Samad
2131 Crimmins Lane
Falls Church, Virginia 22043
Phone: (703) 532-0400
Fax: (703) 532-5033
URL: www.azadiradio.org

TELEVISION

Ariana Afghanistan International TV

Primarily serving the Afghan community in the United States, Ariana Afghanistan International TV offers Afghan-related and international news.

15375 Barranca Parkway, Suite 103
Irvine, California 92618
Phone: (949) 825-7400
Fax: (949) 825-7474
URL: www.aa-tv.com

Nooor TV

Considered the foremost Afghan American television station, Nooor TV offers both news and entertainment.

5700 Stoneridge Mall Road
Pleasanton, California 94588-2874
Phone: (925) 577-8060
Fax: (925) 467-1542
Email: info@nooortv.com
URL: http://nooor-tv.com/home/

ORGANIZATIONS AND ASSOCIATIONS

Afghan-American Chamber of Commerce

This organization endeavors to promote business and trade ties between Afghanistan and the United States, with an emphasis on improving the business climate in Afghanistan.

8201 Greensboro Drive, Suite 103
McLean, Virginia 22102
Phone: (703) 442-5005
Fax: (703) 442-5008
Email: info@a-acc.org
URL: http://a-acc.org

Afghans4Tomorrow

Founded by young professionals, the organization is dedicated to rebuilding Afghanistan following decades of occupation and war.

Chloe Breyer, Vice President
4699 Apple Way
Boulder, Colorado 80301

Email: Info@afghans4tomorrow.org
URL: www.afghans4tomorrow.com

Afghanistan Council of the Asia Society

Founded in 1960, the Afghanistan Council seeks to introduce Afghan culture to the United States. Its coverage includes archeology, folklore, handicrafts, politics and history, and performing and visual arts. The Afghanistan Council also aids in producing and distributing educational materials.

725 Park Avenue
New York, New York 10021
Phone: (212) 288-6400
Fax: (212) 517-8315
URL: http://afghanistancouncil.com

Afghanistan Studies Association (ASA)

Organization of scholars, students, and others who seek to extend and develop Afghan studies. The ASA helps in the exchange of information between scholars; identifies and attempts to find funding for research needs; acts as a liaison between universities, governments, and other agencies; and helps scholars from Afghanistan working in the United States.

Charley Reed, Media Relations Coordinator
Center for Afghan Studies
University of Nebraska
Omaha, Nebraska 68182-0227
Phone: (402) 554-2376
Fax: (402) 554-3681
Email: cdreed@unomaha.edu
URL: http://world.unomaha.edu/cas

U.S. Afghan Women's Council

Founded through the cooperation of the American and Afghan governments, the group promotes efforts to improve the lives and status of Afghan women.

Elaine Jones, Executive Director
Georgetown Center for Child and Human Development
3300 Whitehaven Street NW
Washington, D.C. 20057
Phone: (202) 687-5095
Email: USAWC.Georgetown@gmail.com
URL: http://gucchd.georgetown.edu/76315.html

MUSEUMS AND RESEARCH CENTERS

9/11 Oral History Project, Columbia Center for Oral History, Columbia University

Created in the wake of the terrorist attacks of September 11, 2001, the project includes interviews with Afghan Americans about their experiences and reactions to 9/11.

801 Butler Library
535 West 114th Street
New York, New York 10027
Phone: (212) 854-7083
Email: oralhist@libraries.cul.columbia.edu
URL: http://library.columbia.edu/content/libraryweb/indiv/ccoh.html

Center for Afghan Studies

The first center for Afghan Studies created in the United States. Housed at the University of Nebraska, it offers courses in all aspects of Afghan culture as well as language training in Dari.

Charley Reed, Media Relations Coordinator
University of Nebraska
6001 Dodge Street
Omaha, Nebraska 68182
Phone: (402) 554-2129
Email: cdreed@unomaha.edu
URL: http://world.unomaha.edu/cas

SOURCES FOR ADDITIONAL STUDY

Barfield, Thomas. *Afghanistan: A Cultural and Political History.* Princeton, NJ: Princeton University Press, 2012.

Conley, Ellen Alexander. *The Chosen Shore: Stories of Immigrants.* Berkeley: University of California Press, 2004.

Cvetkovich, Ann. "Can the Diaspora Speak? Afghan Americans and the 9/11 Oral History Archive." *Radical History Review* 2011, no. 111 (2011): 90-100.

Daulatzai, Anila. "Acknowledging Afghanistan: Notes and Queries on an Occupation." *Cultural Dynamics* 18, no. 3 (2006): 293-311.

Foster, Laila Merrell. *Afghanistan.* New York: Grolier, 1996.

Lipson, Juliene G., and Patricia A. Omidian. "Afghans." In *Refugees in America in the 1990s: A Reference Handbook*, edited by David W. Haines. Westport, CT: Greenwood Press, 1996.

———. "Health Issues of Afghan Refugees in California," *Western Journal of Medicine* 157 (1992): 271-75.

Marsden, Peter. *The Taliban: War, Religion and the New Order in Afghanistan.* New York: Oxford University Press, 1998.

Rubin, Barnett R. *The Fragmentation of Afghanistan: State Formation & Collapse in the International System.* New Haven, CT: Yale University Press, 1995.

Sultan, Masuda. *My War at Home.* New York: Washington Square Press, 2006.

Vollmann, William T. *An Afghanistan Picture Show.* New York: Farrar, Straus & Giroux, 1992.

AFRICAN AMERICANS

Barbara C. Bigelow

OVERVIEW

African Americans are descendants of people from Africa, many of whose ancestors came to the United States as slaves during the seventeenth through nineteenth centuries. Africa, the second-largest continent, is bisected by the equator and bordered to the west by the Atlantic Ocean and to the east by the Indian Ocean. Africa is essentially a huge plateau divided naturally into two sections: Northern Africa, a Mediterranean region that includes the Sahara Desert, and Sub-Saharan Africa, which is mainly tropical, with rain forests clustered around the equator. Africa contains fifty-four internationally recognized countries, including six islands, that add up to about 11.5 million square miles, or 20 percent of the world's land mass. The entire United States could easily fit into just the northwestern part of the African continent.

Africa is the world's most diverse continent in terms of people and, especially, languages. Its total population was more than one billion in 2011, according to the United Nations, making it the second-most populous continent on Earth. Countless ethnic groups inhabit the land. In 2012 the CIA *World Factbook* estimated that there were more than 250 different ethnic groups in the West African nation of Nigeria alone. As of 2012, an estimated 45 percent of the African population was Christian, approximately 40 percent was Muslim, and around 15 percent followed traditional African religions. Due to a number of factors, Africa continued to be the world's poorest and least-developed continent, according to the UN's Human Development Index in 2011. While many African countries—including Sudan, Angola, and Equatorial Guinea—achieved a steady growth rate of around 5 to 7 percent in the first decade of the twenty-first century, this did not lead to job growth or a reduction in poverty. In addition, the global financial crisis that began in 2007 led to a food-security crisis on the African continent in 2008 that left 100 million more Africans without access to essential nutrition.

Unlike many early New World immigrants who came voluntarily in search of better lives, most Africans who arrived in the Americas between the seventeenth and nineteenth centuries were imported as slaves against their will. More than six million African slaves were brought to the Americas during the eighteenth century alone. The majority of these people were employed as agricultural laborers on large plantations in the Caribbean and South America, though approximately 475,000 of the 12.5 million came to the United States, most to the southern colonies and, later, states. While emigration from Africa fell dramatically after the abolition of the slave trade in the nineteenth century, it rose significantly in the twentieth century, with 1.4 million African immigrants residing in the United States by 2007, according to the Migration Policy Institute. The majority of those immigrants arrived after 1990 as refugees or asylum seekers. The Migration Policy Institute documented that in 2007, the top countries of origin were Nigeria (13.1 percent of all African immigrants), Egypt (9.6 percent), and Ethiopia (9.5 percent).

There were approximately forty-two million African Americans residing in the United States in 2010, according to the U.S. Census, which roughly equates to the population of California. Since African Americans have been living in the United States for centuries, they have largely been absorbed into the broader population. As of 2010, according to the U.S. Census, the majority of African Americans (55 percent) resided in the southern region of the nation. Cities and states where significant numbers of African Americans live include Washington, D.C., New Jersey, New York, and Virginia.

HISTORY OF THE PEOPLE

Early History Some historians consider ancient Africa to be the cradle of human civilization. In *Before the Mayflower*, Lerone Bennett Jr., contends that "the African ancestors of American Blacks were among the major benefactors of the human race. Such evidence ... clearly shows that Africans were on the scene and acting when the human drama opened."

Over the course of a dozen centuries, beginning around 300 CE, a series of three major political states arose in Africa: Ghana, Mali, and Songhay. These agricultural and mining empires began as small kingdoms but eventually established great wealth and control throughout Western Africa and reached into the Middle East.

African societies were marked by varying degrees of political, economic, and social advancement. "Wherever we observe the peoples of Africa," writes John Hope Franklin in *From Slavery to Freedom*, "we find some sort of political organization, even among the so-called stateless. They were not all highly organized kingdoms—to be sure, some were simple, isolated family states—but they all … [established] governments to solve the problems that every community encounters." Social stratification existed, with political power residing in a chief of state or a royal family, depending on the size of the state. People of lower social standing were respected as valued members of the community.

Agriculture and mining have always been key foundations of African economics. Some rural African peoples worked primarily as sheep, cattle, and poultry raisers, and African artisans maintained a steady trade in clothing, baskets, pottery, and metalware, but farming was the way of life for most Africans. While land was owned by individuals, it brought communities together frequently as a result of trade. "Africa was … never a series of isolated self-sufficient communities," writes Franklin. Rather, tribes specialized in various economic endeavors, then traveled and traded their goods and crops with other tribes.

The slave trade in Africa dates almost to biblical times and was already an established industry when European traders entered into the scene in the mid-fifteenth century. Ancient Africans held slaves. They, like many other people in the pre-modern world, regarded prisoners of war as sellable property, or chattel. According to Franklin, though, these slaves "often became trusted associates of their owners and enjoyed virtual freedom." Moreover, in many parts of Africa the children of slaves could never be sold and were often freed by their owners.

West Africans commonly sold their slaves to Arab traders in the Mediterranean, establishing a strong trans-Saharan trade network with North Africa. The slave trade increased significantly when the Portuguese and Spanish, who had established sugar-producing colonies in Latin America, the West Indies, and islands off the coast of Africa, began to trade along the African coast. The Dutch quickly followed, along with a large influx of other European traders in the ensuing decades; they traded for both mineral resources (mainly gold) and salt, as well as for slaves, to feed the hungry labor markets in the New World.

Modern Era Much of Africa had become the domain of European colonial powers by the late nineteenth century. A growing nationalistic movement in the mid-twentieth century, fueled by concepts of freedom and independence learned from African participation in World War II, resulted in the creation of independent nations throughout the continent. By the mid-1990s, even South Africa, a country that had long been gripped by the injustice of apartheid's white supremacist policies, held its first free and fair multiracial elections.

Numerous African nations experienced internal violence in the twentieth century. In 1999 the United Nations disbanded and then re-deployed a peacekeeping force in Angola, a nation that had suffered a long civil war. In 1974, after years of opposition from Angolans, Portugal withdrew as the colonial ruler of Angola and a struggle for power ensued. Although Angola is rich with fertile farming land and oil reserves, it has failed to tap into these resources because of its ongoing internal war. Colonialism left the majority of recently independent African nations without the resources and infrastructure to function on their own, and most former colonial powers still influenced African politics. This phenomenon is often referred to as neo-colonialism.

One of the most lasting impacts of colonialism on African nations is the ethnic strife caused by national boundaries that were arbitrarily drawn by colonial powers. Such artificial borders have created divisions and tensions between rival tribes, leading to many incidents of race-based violence and, on several occasions, genocide. The United Nations continued to seek justice in Rwanda in the wake of the genocide that occurred there in 1994. In 1999 the International Criminal Tribunal for Rwanda charged former Women's Development and Family Welfare Minister Pauline Nyiramasuhuko with rape. She was not personally charged with the crime; rather, Nyiramasuhuko was prosecuted, according to Kingsley Moghalu of the United Nations, "under the concept of command responsibility" for failing to prevent her subordinates from raping women during the 1994 uprising.

Similar ethnic strife emerged in Sudan as a result of the lingering effects of colonialism. Mounting human rights violations in Darfur, Sudan, drew international attention in 2003 when rebel groups mainly representing the non-Arab Sudanese community revolted against the Sudanese government in protest of the perceived mistreatment of their people by authorities. Known as the Darfur Conflict, or Darfur Genocide, it resulted in the deaths of several hundred thousand Sudanese and the displacement of millions into refugee camps. Atrocities and policies of ethnic cleansing have been attributed to both sides of the conflict. Initial peace negotiations began in 2006 but were unsuccessful. A peace agreement was finally signed by the Sudanese government and rebel groups in 2011, but the fighting and unrest continued into 2012. Most human rights organizations blame the Sudanese government for the majority of the violence in Sudan and for its refusal to prosecute the perpetrators of crimes against humanity and unwillingness to cooperate with international humanitarian aid groups.

Acquired Immune Deficiency Syndrome (AIDS) continued to spread death in African countries in the 1990s. AIDS has been a bigger problem in Africa than in many other regions of the world due to various factors, mainly the lack of adequate health care,

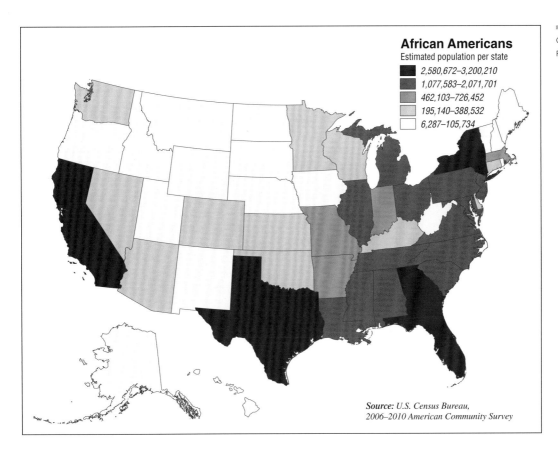

African Americans
Estimated population per state

2,580,672–3,200,210
1,077,583–2,071,701
462,103–726,452
195,140–388,532
6,287–105,734

Source: U.S. Census Bureau,
2006–2010 American Community Survey

including insufficient access to necessary medications such as antiretrovirals, and poor education regarding how to prevent contracting the virus. The combination of these factors has proved deadly for millions of Africans. In Kenya in August 1999, for example, President Daniel Arap Moi announced that AIDS was killing approximately 420 Kenyans each day. In 2011 Sub-Saharan Africa remained the region hardest hit by HIV and AIDS with nearly twenty-four million HIV cases, or 69 percent of the international total. However, the number of new HIV infections in the region decreased dramatically between 1997 and 2011, from 2.6 million to 1.7 million. The main reasons for this improvement include major behavioral changes in the African community as a result of widespread education programs and increased access to life-preserving AIDS treatments.

SETTLEMENT IN THE UNITED STATES

Most Africans transported to the New World as slaves came from West Africa and Southern Africa. These areas, located on the continent's Atlantic side, now consists of more than a dozen modern nations, including Gabon, the Republic of the Congo, Cameroon, Nigeria, Benin, Togo, Ghana, Burkina Faso, the Ivory Coast, Liberia, Sierra Leone, Guinea, Gambia, and Senegal.

Africans are believed to have traveled to the New World with European explorers—especially

the Spanish and the Portuguese—at the turn of the fifteenth century. They served as crew members, servants, and slaves. (Many historians agree that Pedro Alonzo Niño, who accompanied Christopher Columbus on his expedition to the New World, was black; in addition, it has been established that in the early 1500s, blacks journeyed to the Pacific with Spanish explorer Vasco Núñez de Balboa and into Mexico with Cortés.) The early African slave population worked on European coffee, cocoa, tobacco, and sugar plantations in the West Indies, as well as on the farms and in the mines that operated in Europe's South American colonies.

Later, in the seventeenth and eighteenth centuries, the Dutch, French, and English became dominant forces in New World slave trade, and by the early eighteenth century, colonization efforts focused on the North American mainland. In August 1619, the first ship carrying Africans sailed into the harbor at Jamestown, Virginia, beginning the presence of Africans in what would become the United States.

During the early years of colonial society, the population was divided by class rather than race. In fact, many of the first Africans in North America were not slaves but indentured servants. Many black laborers worked alongside whites for a set amount of time before earning their freedom. According to Lerone Bennett, "The available evidence suggests that most of the first generation of African Americans worked out their terms of servitude and were freed." Using the bustling colony of Virginia as an example of prevailing colonial attitudes, Bennett explains that the coastal settlement, in its first several decades of existence, "was defined by what can only be called equality of oppression. ... The colony's power structure made little or no distinction between black and white servants, who were assigned the same tasks and were held in equal contempt."

However, North American landowners began to face a labor crisis in the 1640s. Indians had proven unsatisfactory laborers in earlier colonization efforts, and the indentured servitude system failed to meet increasing colonial labor needs. As Franklin observes in *From Slavery to Freedom*, "Although Africans were in Europe in considerable numbers in the seventeenth century and had been in the New World at least since 1501 ... the colonists and their Old World sponsors were extremely slow in recognizing them as the best possible labor force for the tasks in the New World."

By the second half of the 1600s, however, white colonial landowners began to see slavery as a solution to their economic woes. Thus, the fateful system of forced black labor—achieved through a program of perpetual, involuntary servitude—was set into motion in the colonies. Changing demographics, including a declining mortality rate in the colonies, led white colonists to believe that Africans were strong, inexpensive, and available in seemingly unlimited supplies. In addition, their black skin made them highly visible in the white world, thereby decreasing the likelihood of their escape from bondage. Black enslavement became vital to the American agricultural economy, and racism and subjugation emerged as the means to justify the system. Once the color line was drawn, white servants were separated from their black comrades. Codes to legalize slavery were soon enacted in all of the colonies to control almost every aspect of the slaves' lives, leaving them with virtually no rights or freedoms.

Approximately 12.5 million Africans left their native continent for the New World as part of the slave trade between 1600 and 1850. The process began slowly, with an estimated 300,000 slaves coming to the Americas prior to the seventeenth century, and reached its peak in the eighteenth century with the importation of more than six million Africans.

The more slaves transported to the New World on a single ship, the more money the traders made. Consequently, Africans, chained together in pairs, were crammed by the hundreds onto the ships' decks; lying side by side in rows, they had no room to move and barely enough air to breathe. Their one-way trip, commonly referred to as the Middle Passage, ended in the Americas and the islands of the Caribbean. Between 12 and 40 percent of the slaves shipped from Africa never even completed the Middle Passage: many died of disease or committed suicide by jumping overboard.

By the mid-1700s the majority of Africans in what would become the United States lived in the Southern Atlantic colonies, where the plantation system had a great demand for black labor. Virginia took and maintained the lead in slave ownership with, according to Franklin, more than 120,000 blacks in 1756—about half mainland North America's total enslaved population. Around the same time in South Carolina, blacks outnumbered whites. Slavery also existed in all of the northern colonies, though no plantation economy developed and slaves constituted less than 10 percent of the total population.

By 1790 the black population approached 760,000, and only 8 percent of all blacks in America were free. Even free blacks were bound by many of the same regulations that applied to slaves. The ratification of the U.S. Constitution in 1789 guaranteed equality and "certain inalienable rights" to the white population, but these rights rarely extended to African Americans. Free blacks faced limited employment opportunities and restrictions on their ability to travel, vote, and bear arms.

The invention of the cotton gin in 1793 greatly increased the profitability of cotton production, thereby heightening the demand for slaves to work on plantations in the American South. The slave population in the South rose with the surge in cotton production and with the expansion of plantations along the western portion of the southern frontier. However, not all slaves worked in cotton production. By the middle of the nineteenth century, nearly half a million were working in cities as domestics, skilled artisans, and factory hands, and many more toiled on rice or sugar plantations.

An abolitionist movement—among both blacks and whites—became a potent force in the 1830s. There was growing support for doing away with an institution that violated the basic rights of a human being, and laws had been passed in several countries in the early nineteenth century outlawing slave trading, including in England in 1807 and Spain four years later. In the United States, slavery continued to thrive in the South, despite the abolition of the institution in all northern states by 1804 and Thomas Jefferson's passage of the Act Prohibiting Importation of Slaves in 1807. The growth of abolitionism in the United States was largely a result of the Second Great Awakening, in which religious revivalists argued that slavery was an individual sin and that only emancipation would bring about absolution. Organizations such as the American Anti-Slavery Society garnered increasing support for their cause. African American activists such as former slaves Frederick Douglass and William Wells Brown also provided compelling anti-slavery leadership, although black abolitionists often felt patronized by whites in the movement. Slavery became a bitter point of contention between northern and southern states, and it was one of the main factors that divided the country in the mid-1800s and brought about the Civil War.

By the early nineteenth century, the population of free blacks in the North was growing rapidly, and this swelling community sought a place in American society. While many northerners were more tolerant of blacks than southerners were, free African Americans still faced much discrimination and often struggled to find employment and housing in northern cities. Whites did not accept them into their social circles, and blacks were therefore forced to live and socialize amongst themselves, still treated like second-class citizens. It was in response to this alienation and stigmatization experienced that a philosophy of reverse migration emerged as a solution. The American Colonization Society pushed for the return of blacks to Africa. By the early 1820s, the first wave of black Americans had landed on Africa's western coastal settlement of Liberia; nearly 1,500 blacks were resettled throughout the 1830s. But the idea of repatriation was largely opposed, especially by freed blacks in the North: having been "freed," they were now subjected to racial hatred, legalized discrimination, and political and economic injustice in a white world. They sought equity at home rather than resettlement in Africa as the only acceptable end to more than two centuries of oppression, especially since almost all of them had never been to Africa and, therefore, retained no connection to the continent.

The political and economic turbulence leading to the Civil War intensified racial troubles. Initially, President Abraham Lincoln and many of his allies viewed emancipation as a military necessity rather than a human rights issue. Abolitionists along with Republican allies successfully ratified the Thirteenth Amendment to the Constitution in December 1865, thereby abolishing slavery. The Fourteenth Amendment, adopted in 1868, extended the definition of U.S. citizenship to include African Americans, while the Fifteenth Amendment, adopted in 1870, declared that all male citizens had the right to vote regardless of their race. However, even in the late 1800s and early 1900s, the black population in the United States saw few changes in its social, political, and economic standing.

With no money, land, or livestock, freed slaves were hardly in a position to establish their own farming communities in the South. Thus began the largely exploitative system of tenant farming, more often called sharecropping, which allowed tenants (most of whom were black) to work the farms of landlords (most of whom were white) and earn a percentage of the proceeds from each crop harvested. Unfortunately, the system provided little long-term economic benefits for the tenants, as it trapped them in a cycle of poverty that replicated slavery in many ways.

The Jim Crow era began gradually after the end of Reconstruction in 1876, with state and local governments in the South establishing racial segregation in all public areas. A "separate but equal" status was assigned to African Americans—although this was far from the truth. In 1896 the Supreme Court affirmed in *Plessy v. Ferguson* that it was legal for the government to establish separate public facilities and discriminate according to race. This era was marked by constant acts of racial violence against blacks and the violation of their civil rights, often resulting in the murder or lynching of innocent African Americans. Statistics from the Tuskegee Institute indicate that approximately 4,730 people died from lynchings in the United States between 1882 and 1951, with 3,437 of those being of African descent. However, the actual number is most likely much higher since many lynchings went unreported or undocumented.

With the decline of cotton prices and the increase in industrial production spurred by World War I, African Americans migrated to the North in large numbers beginning in the 1910s and continuing until World War II. Prior to World War I, more than three-quarters of all blacks in the United States lived in the southern states. Between 1910 and 1970, about 6.5 million African Americans migrated to the northern United States.

However, manufacturing jobs in the northern United States decreased in the 1960s. As the need for unskilled industrial laborers fell, urban areas fell into disrepair and saw increased crime rates and poverty. By the early 1970s, a large number of blacks, barred from many of the benefits enjoyed by whites following World War II, were left in urban areas by themselves after whites had fled to more affluent suburbs.

More recent immigrant groups from Africa do not generally consider themselves part of the "African American" community, and those African immigrants of the first few generations continue to remain within their country-of-origin communities. Due to the great cultural, ethnic, and religious diversity of the African continent, most recent African immigrants prize their national identities over their regional identities. According to the Migration Policy Institute, there were large groups of first- and second-generation Ethiopians (134,547), Nigerians (185,787), and Egyptians (136,648) living in the U.S. in 2007.

A 2008 U.S. Census report estimated that by the year 2042, minorities (including people of African, Asian, and Hispanic descent) will make up the majority of the nation's population. While Hispanics account for the biggest bump in the minority population, the shifting demographics will have a strong impact on all minorities, including African Americans. According to the 2010 U.S. Census, approximately 13.5 percent of the U.S. population was black. The 2010 U.S. Census further states that the black population grew by 12 percent from 2000 to 2010, a more rapid rate than the general population (9.7 percent). Blacks will make up about 15 percent of the nation's population by 2050, according to the 2008 U.S. Census report. The growth of the black and Hispanic populations has afforded these groups more political influence than ever.

LANGUAGE

More than a thousand different languages are spoken in Africa, many of which have similar characteristics. The multitudinous languages of Africa are grouped into several large families, including the Niger-Congo family (those spoken mainly in the southern portion of the continent) and the Afro-Asiatic family (spoken in northern Africa, the eastern horn of Africa, and Southwest Asia).

Africa has a long and rich oral tradition. Few languages of the Old World ever took a written form, so literature and history in ancient Africa were passed from generation to generation orally. Beginning in earnest in the fourteenth century, the use of Arabic by educated Muslim blacks was rather extensive, and some oral literature was subsequently reduced to a more permanent written form. Despite this Muslim influence, however, the oral heritage of Africans remained strong, serving not only as an educational device but also as a guide for the administration of government and the conduct of religious ceremonies.

Starting with the arrival of the first Africans in the New World, Anglo-American words were slowly infused into African languages. Successive generations of blacks born in America, as well as Africans transported to mainland North America later in the slave trading era, began to use standard English as their principal language. Over the years, this standard English has been modified by African Americans to encompass their own culture, language, and experience.

The social-change movements of the 1960s gave birth to a number of popular black expressions. Later, in the 1980s and 1990s, the music of hip-hop and rap artists became a culturally significant expression of the trials of black urban life. In her book *Talkin & Testifyin*, linguistic scholar Geneva Smitherman offers this explanation of the formation of a distinctive black English: "In a nutshell: Black Dialect is an Africanized form of English reflecting Black America's linguistic-cultural African heritage and the conditions of servitude, oppression, and life in America. Black Language is Euro-American speech with Afro-American meaning, nuance, tone, and gesture. The Black Idiom is used by 80 to 90 percent of American Blacks, at least some of the time. It has allowed Blacks to create a culture of survival in an alien land, and as a by-product has served to enrich the language of all Americans."

As recounted in *Before the Mayflower*, scholar Lorenzo Turner found linguistic relics of the African past in the syntax, word-formations, and intonations of African Americans. Among these words in general use, especially in the South, are "goober" (peanut), "gumbo" (okra), "ninny" (female breast), "tote" (to carry), and "yam" (sweet potato). Additionally, Turner discovered a number of African-inspired names among African Americans in Chicago, including "Bobo,"

African American-styled gospel music and choirs have had a profound impact on African American culture as well as the larger U.S. cultural landscape. PRESSELECT / ALAMY

meaning one who cannot talk; "Geiji," the name of a language and tribe in Liberia; "Agona," after a country in Ghana; "Ola," a Yoruban word meaning that which saves; and "Zola," meaning to love.

RELIGION

In *From Slavery to Freedom*, John Hope Franklin describes the religion of early Africans as "ancestor worship." Religions varied widely but shared some common elements: they were steeped in ritual, magic, and devotion to the spirits of the dead, and they placed heavy emphasis on the need for a knowledge and an appreciation of the past.

Christianity was first introduced in West Africa by the Portuguese in the sixteenth century. Franklin notes that resistance among the Africans to Christianization stemmed from their association of the religion with the institution of slave trade to the New World. "It was a strange religion, this Christianity," he writes, "which taught equality and brotherhood and at the same time introduced on a large scale the practice of tearing people from their homes and transporting them to a distant land to become slaves." West Africans were also resistant to this new religion because it challenged the tenets of Islam, which had already spread throughout the region. Indeed, Islam has deep roots throughout Africa and has remained one of the dominant religions on the continent through modern times.

In the New World, missionaries continued their efforts to convert Africans to Christianity. As far back as 1700, the Quakers sponsored monthly Friends meetings for blacks. However, an undercurrent of anxiety among a majority of white settlers curbed the formation of free black churches in colonial America: many colonists felt that if blacks were allowed to congregate at separate churches, they would plot dangerous rebellions. By the mid-1700s, black membership in both the Baptist and Methodist churches had increased significantly; few blacks, however, became ordained members of the clergy in these predominantly white sects.

African Americans organized the first independent black congregation—the Silver Bluff Baptist Church—in South Carolina in the early 1770s. Other black congregations sprang up in the first few decades of the 1800s, largely as outgrowths of established white churches. In 1816 Richard Allen, a slave who bought his own freedom, formed the African Methodist Episcopal (AME) Church in Philadelphia in response to an unbending policy of segregated seating in the city's white Methodist church.

An increase in slave uprisings led fearful whites to impose restrictions on the activities of black churches in the 1830s. In the post–Civil War years, however, black Baptist and Methodist ministers exerted a profound influence on their congregations, urging peaceful social and political involvement for the black population as Reconstruction-period policies unfolded.

However, as segregation became a national reality in the 1880s and 1890s, some black churches and ministers began to advocate decidedly separatist solutions to the religious, educational, and economic discrimination that existed in the United States. AME bishop Henry McNeal Turner, a former Civil War chaplain, championed the idea of African migration for blacks with his "Back to Africa" movement in 1895—more than twenty years before the rise of black nationalist leader Marcus Garvey. By the early 1900s, churches were functioning to unite blacks politically.

Organized religion has always been a strong institution among African Americans. In 2007, 87 percent of black Americans belonged to a religious organization, and nearly half attended religious services at least once a week, according to a 2007 survey by the Pew Research Center's Forum on Religion & Public Life. Black congregations reflect the traditional strength of community ties in their continued devotion to social improvement. This is evident in the launching of youth programs, anti-drug crusades, and parochial schools and in ongoing efforts to provide the needy with food, clothing, and shelter.

In 2007, 59 percent of all African Americans belonged to historically black Protestant denominations, including the National Baptist Convention of the U.S.A., Inc., the AME Church, the Christian Methodist Episcopal Church, and the Church of God in Christ, a Pentecostal denomination that cuts across socioeconomic lines. The 1990s saw a steady increase in black membership in the Islamic religion and the Roman Catholic Church as well, although by 2007 membership of blacks in both denominations made up less than 10 percent of the general African American population. (A separate African American Catholic congregation, not sanctioned by the church in Rome, was founded in 1989 by George A. Stallings Jr.) Less-mainstream denominations include Louis Farrakhan's Nation of Islam, based on the black separatist doctrine of Elijah Muhammad. Though faulted by some critics for its seemingly divisive, controversial teachings, the Nation of Islam maintains a fairly sizeable following.

CULTURE AND ASSIMILATION

Black assimilation in the United States continues to be a painful subject in the nation's history. Many historians argue that slavery's legacy of social inequality has persisted in American society—even well more than a century after the post–Civil War emancipation of slaves in the United States.

Legally excluded from the white world, blacks were forced to establish their own social, political, and economic institutions. In the process of building a solid cultural base in the black community, they formed a whole new identity: that of the African American. African Americans recognized their African heritage but also accepted America as home, integrating various white traditions into their own.

In addition, African Americans began to employ the European tactics of petitions, lawsuits, and organized protest to fight for their rights. This movement, which started in the late eighteenth century, involved the formation and utilization of mutual aid societies, independent black churches, lodges and fraternal organizations, and educational and cultural institutions designed to fight oppression.

Traditions and Customs Over the centuries, various aspects of African culture have blended into American society. The complex rhythms of African music, for instance, are evident in the sounds of American blues and jazz. In addition, a growth in the study of American folklore—and the development of American-style folktales—can be linked in part to Africa's long oral tradition. A new interest in the Old World began to surface in the 1970s. In an effort to connect with their African heritage, some black Americans have adopted African names to replace the Anglo names of their ancestors' slaveowners. Increasing numbers of African American men and women are also donning the traditional garb of Africans—including African-inspired jewelry, headwear, and brightly colored, loose-fitting garments called *dashikis*—to show pride in their roots.

A notable spiritual tradition from Africa that has been adopted and transformed by African American culture is Yoruba religion, which originated in Nigeria and parts of Benin and Togo among the Yoruba people. Often referred to as Ifa, followers of this tradition believe in one supreme being who is accessed through *orishas*, or intermediaries between the divine being and humanity. African slave communities throughout the Americas who sought to maintain their religious roots and reconcile them with the reality they faced in the New World developed different adaptations of the Yoruba religion. Often, these traditions combined Yoruba influences with Catholicism, a process referred to as religious syncretism. These include Santeria, practiced in Cuba and the United States; Candomble in Brazil; Voudun (also spelled vudu) in Haiti and the Dominican Republic; and Voodoo in the United States. In *Osun Across the Waters*, Joseph Murphy and Mei-Mei Sanford explain how Yoruba traditions became a "key feature of African-Atlantic strategies of adaptation and resistance to European values and spirituality" under conditions of enslavement and cultural marginalization. While condemned by dominant American society as foolish superstition, Voodoo and other Yoruba traditions are regarded as legitimate religions by their followers and continue to be practiced in the United States today by African Americans and other immigrant communities from the Caribbean, including Cubans and Haitians. The tradition is particularly strong in Louisiana, as well as Miami, Florida, where followers of the orisha Oshun gather every September 8 to make offerings at the shore of Biscayne Bay. In Philadelphia the Odunde festival draws thousands of Oshun devotees every year to worship at the Schuylkill River.

Cuisine Most African nations are essentially agricultural societies. For centuries, a majority of men have worked as farmers and cattle raisers, although some have made their living as fishermen. Planting, sowing, and harvesting crops were women's duties in traditional West African society. The task of cooking also seems to have fallen to women in ancient Africa. They prepared meals such as *fufu*—a traditional dish made of pounded yams and served with soups, stew, roasted meat, and a variety of sauces—over huge open pits.

Africans from many different ethnic groups exchanged their regional recipes freely, leading to the development of a multinational cooking style among blacks in America. During the colonial period, heavy breakfast meals of hoecakes (small cornmeal cakes) and molasses were prepared to fuel the slaves for work from sunup to sundown. Spoonbread, crab cakes, corn pone (corn bread), corn pudding, greens, and succotash—cooked over an open pit or fireplace—became common items in a black cook's repertoire in the late 1700s and the 1800s.

Slaves would often grow their own crops in small gardens by their dwellings in order to supplement the meager food provided to them by their masters. Some slaves would even trade the fruits and vegetables they grew amongst each other, developing their own informal economies. There was very little meat in their diets; when they did eat meat, it was generally pork.

African Americans served as cooks for both the northern and southern armies throughout the Civil War. Because of the scarcity of supplies, the cooks were forced to improvise and invent their own recipes. Some of the dishes that sprang from this period of culinary creativity include jambalaya (herbs and rice cooked with chicken, ham, sausage, shrimp, or oysters), bread pudding, dirty rice, gumbo, and red beans and rice—all of which remain staples of southern cuisine.

The late 1800s and early 1900s saw the establishment of many African American-owned eateries specializing in southern fried chicken, pork chops, fish, potato salad, turkey and dressing, and rice and gravy. In later years, this diet—which grew to include pigs' feet, chitlins (hog intestines), collard greens (a vegetable), and ham hocks—became known as "soul food." This cuisine became popular throughout the United States in the twentieth century, with soul food restaurants popping up from New Orleans, Louisiana, to California.

Food plays a large role in African American traditions, customs, and beliefs. Nothing underscores this point more than New Year's Day, a time of celebration that brings with it new hopes for the coming months. Some of the traditional foods enjoyed on this day are

AFRICAN PROVERBS

A wealth of proverbs from African culture have survived in the U.S. through the generations, such as:

- If you want to know the end, look at the beginning.

- When one door closes, another one opens.

- If we stand tall it is because we stand on the backs of those who came before us.

- Two men in a burning house must not stop to argue.

- Where you sit when you are old shows where you stood in youth.

- You must live within your sacred truth.

- The one who asks questions doesn't lose his way.

- If you plant turnips you will not harvest grapes.

- God makes three requests of his children: do the best you can, where you are, with what you have now.

- You must act as if it is impossible to fail.

black-eyed peas, which represent good fortune; rice, a symbol of prosperity; greens, which stand for money; and fish, which represent the motivation and desire to increase wealth. Traditional southern barbecue, which is enjoyed today by whites and blacks alike, dates to the slavery period when African slaves would prepare whatever animal parts they could find—often from hogs, including ribs and tails, as well as from chickens—over oak and hickory logs on an outdoor grill. Barbecues continue to be an opportunity for African American families to gather together, and the tradition has been adopted by the larger American community and incorporated into national holidays such as Fourth of July.

The cuisine of recent African immigrants varies greatly by national origin, as each culture has its own traditional cuisine. For example, Ethiopian cuisine is similar to Middle Eastern or Cajun food, with pepper spices combined with vegetables such as potatoes and green beans. As with many other African nations, Ethiopian food is traditionally eaten without utensils. Individuals instead use a flatbread-like bread called *injera* to scoop up their food, which often includes beef or lamb. A staple among many African immigrants is *fufu*, a starchy substance that is similar to American mashed potatoes and is accompanied by

dishes such as stews or soups made with palm oil and meat and vegetables that vary depending on the country of origin. Many Africans cook with okra, fish, hot pepper, lentils, and goat or lamb meat.

Holidays Martin Luther King Day is an official national holiday that is celebrated not only by blacks but also by the United States as a whole. It honors the legacy of King, who was one of the leading African American activists during the civil rights movement and was assassinated in 1968. In addition to Christian holidays, other dates on the calendar year hold a special significance for African Americans. For example, on June 19 each year, many blacks celebrate Juneteenth. Although the Emancipation Proclamation, which declared an end to slavery in the Confederacy, took effect on January 1, 1863, the news of slavery's end did not reach the black population in Texas until June 19, 1865. Union General Gordon Granger arrived outside Galveston, Texas, that day to announce the freedom of the state's 250,000 enslaved blacks. Former slaves in Texas and Louisiana held a major celebration that turned into an annual event and spread throughout the nation as free blacks migrated west and north.

From December 26 to January 1, many African Americans observe Kwanzaa (which means "first fruits" in Swahili), a nonreligious holiday that celebrates family, culture, and ancestral ties. This weeklong commemoration was instituted in 1966 by Dr. Maulana Karenga to promote unity and pride among people of African descent.

Kwanzaa comes directly from the tradition of the agricultural people of Africa, who gave thanks for a bountiful harvest at designated times of the year. In this highly symbolic celebration, *mazeo* (crops) represent the historical roots of the holiday and the rewards of collective labor; *mekeka* (a mat) stands for tradition and foundation; *kinara* (a candleholder) represents African forebears; *muhindi* (ears of corn) symbolize a family's children; *zawadi* (gifts) reflect the seeds sown by the children (such as commitments made and kept) and the fruits of the parents' labor; and the *kikombe cha umoja* functions as a unity cup. For each day during the week of Kwanzaa, a particular principle or *nguzo saba* ("n-goo-zoh sah-ba") is observed: day one is *Umoja* ("oo-moe-ja")—unity in family, community, nation, and race; day two is *Kujichagulia* ("coo-gee-cha-goo-lee-ah")—self-determination, independence, and creative thinking; day three is *Ujima* ("oo-gee-mah")—collective work and responsibility to others; day four is *Ujamaa* ("oo-jah-mah")—cooperative economics, as in the formation and support of black businesses and jobs; day five is *Nia* ("nee-ah")—purpose, as in the building and development of black communities; day six is *Kuumba* ("coo-oom-bah")—creativity and beautification of the environment; and day seven is *Imani* ("ee-mah-nee")—faith in God, parents, leaders, and the righteousness and victory of the black struggle.

For African Americans, all of February is set aside not as a holiday but as an observance of black heritage in what is known as Black History Month. Introduced in 1926 by historian Carter G. Woodson and originally called Negro History Week, it is a key tool in the American educational system's growing multicultural movement. Black History Month was designed to foster a better understanding of the role black Americans have played in U.S. history.

Misconceptions and Stereotypes African Americans have struggled against racial stereotypes for centuries. The white slaveholding class rationalized the institution of slavery as a necessary evil: aside from playing an integral part in the nation's agricultural economy, the system was viewed by some as the only way to control a wild, pagan race. In eighteenth- and nineteenth-century America, black people were considered genetically inferior to whites.

The black population has been historically misunderstood by white America. The significance of Old World influences in modern African American life—and an appreciation of the complex structure of traditional African society—went largely unrecognized by the majority of the nation's non-blacks. Even in the latter half of the twentieth century, as more African nations embraced multiparty democracy and underwent massive urban and industrial growth, the distorted image of Africans as uncivilized continued to pervade the consciousness of an alarmingly high percentage of white Americans. As social commentator Ellis Cose explains in a 1994 *Newsweek* article, "Theories of blacks' innate intellectual inadequacy provided much of the rationale for slavery and for Jim Crow [legal discrimination based on race]. They also accomplished something equally pernicious, and continue to do so today: they caused many blacks (if only subconsciously) to doubt their own abilities—and to conform to the stereotype, thereby confirming it."

For decades, these images were perpetuated by the American media. Prime-time television shows of the 1960s and 1970s often featured blacks in demeaning roles—those of servants, drug abusers, common criminals, and all-around threats to white society. During the controversial "blaxploitation" phase in American cinema—a period that saw the release of films such as *Shaft* (1971) and *Super Fly* (1972)—sex, drugs, and violence prevailed on the big screen. Though espoused by some segments of the black artistic community as a legitimate outlet for black radicalism, these films were seen by many critics as alienating devices that glorified urban violence and drove an even greater wedge between blacks and whites. Nevertheless, there was some progress made in television entertainment during the civil rights era, as evidenced by the first scripted interracial kiss on TV, between a white man and a black woman on the series *Star Trek* in 1968.

African American entertainment mogul Bill Cosby is credited with initiating the breakdown of

media stereotypes. His long-running situation comedy *The Cosby Show* (1984–1992)—a groundbreaking program that dominated the ratings—helped to dispel the myths of racial inferiority. The show, featuring a black family of well-educated, professional parents and socially responsible children, served as a model for more enlightened, racially balanced programming. Another watershed moment in black entertainment occurred in 1980 when Robert L. Johnson launched the first black-owned cable television network, Black Entertainment Television (BET), which was also the first network to target the African American community as its primary audience. In the early 2000s, BET continued to be the most prominent cable network for the African American community, despite criticism that it perpetuates certain stereotypes about blacks. The success of actor, director, and producer Tyler Perry has also been reflective of the increasing prominence of African Americans in the entertainment industry. His notorious character Madea—an over-the-top, tough black elderly woman whom he played in drag—pushed the envelope for black cinema by humorously criticizing dominant social values within the African American community. In 2011 *Forbes* named Perry the highest-paid man in the entertainment industry.

These advances have not come without struggles. For example, the fall 1999 television lineup of the four major networks (ABC, NBC, CBS, and Fox) featured only a smattering of black characters. Black leaders called on the networks to rectify the situation, and they immediately responded by crafting black characters. Television shows and movies in the early 2000s finally began to present blacks in a more diverse range of roles and increasingly reflected America's multiracial and multicultural makeup, especially in the portrayals of interracial relationships and the representations of multiracial families. More television roles were created for strong black female characters, such as the black divorcee Renee Perry (Vanessa Williams) in the ABC drama *Desperate Housewives* and the powerful Washington lawyer Olivia Pope (Kerry Washington) in ABC's *Scandal*. An interracial couple—Brad and Jane Williams (Eliza Coupe and Damon Wayans Jr.)—was the subject of the ABC comedy *Happy Endings*. Additionally, more movies emerged featuring interracial romances, including *Save the Last Dance* (2001), about a white teenage girl (Julia Stiles) who falls in love with a young African American man (Sean Patrick Thomas), and *Guess Who* (2005), a comedy about a black woman (Zoe Saldana) who takes her white fiancé (Ashton Kutcher) home to meet her family. More African American actors and actresses received awards and recognition for their performances, including Halle Berry, who became the first black woman to win an Academy Award for Best Actress for her performance in *Monster's Ball* (2001). Other black actors to receive Academy Awards in the early 2000s include Jennifer Hudson (Supporting Actress, *Dreamgirls*

2006), Octavia Spencer (Supporting Actress, *The Help*, 2011) and Forest Whitaker (Best Actor, *The Last King of Scotland*, 2006).

Health Care Issues and Practices African Americans are at a high risk for serious health problems, including cancer, diabetes, and hypertension. Several studies show a direct connection between poor health and the problem of underemployment or unemployment among African Americans. In 2011, according to the U.S. Census Bureau, 28 percent of the black population had an income at or below the poverty level. Illnesses brought on by an improper diet or substandard living conditions are often compounded by a lack of quality medical care—largely a result of inadequate health insurance coverage.

Statistics indicate that African Americans have a greater likelihood of succumbing to many more life-threatening illnesses than white Americans. This grim reality is evident even from birth: in 2008 black babies under one year of age died at more than twice the rate of white babies in the same age group, according to the Centers for Disease Control (CDC) National Vital Statistics Reports. A lack of prenatal care among low-income mothers is believed to be the greatest single factor in the high mortality rate among African American infants.

A 2002 medical survey titled "Cancer Statistics for African Americans" found that black Americans were the racial group most impacted by cancer in the United States, experiencing higher incidence and mortality rates of the disease than whites for many decades. However, there were slight improvements documented since 1992: cancer incidence rates declined by 2.7 percent per year for black men, while they stabilized in African American females. These numbers are linked to the fact that, according to the survey, "most cancers detectable by screening are diagnosed at a later stage and survival rates are lower within each stage of disease in African Americans than in whites." These disparities are at least partially reflective of unequal access to health care as a result of poverty and underemployment or unemployment.

Hypertension, or high blood pressure, strikes a third more African Americans than whites. Although the Public Health Service reports that the hypertension is largely inherited, other factors, such as poor diet and stress, can play key roles in the development of the disorder. A reduction in dietary fat and salt are recommended for all hypertensive patients. African Americans are believed to be particularly sensitive to blood pressure problems brought on by a high-salt diet. This high intake of salt is largely due to the lower-quality diet of many African Americans due to limited resources.

Sickle cell anemia is a serious and painful disorder that occurs almost exclusively in people of African descent. The disease is believed to have been brought to the United States as a result of African immigration, and by the last decade of the twentieth century it had found its way to all corners of the world. In some African nations, 2 to 3 percent of all babies die from the disease. In the United States, one in every 12 African Americans carries the trait; of these, about one in 500 develops the disease. Sickle cell anemia is generally considered to be the most common genetically determined blood disease to affect a single ethnic group. By the early 2000s, researchers had begun to make strides in the treatment and prevention of some of the life-threatening complications associated with sickle cell anemia, including damage to the heart, lungs, immune system, and nervous system.

Although the threats to the health of African Americans are numerous and varied, homicide was the number one killer of young black men in the United States in 2011, according to the CDC. In the early 1990s, the CDC began viewing violence as a disease. The severity of the problem has led the CDC to take an active role in addressing violence as a public health issue.

There were promising changes in the life expectancy of African Americans in the first decade of the twenty-first century. The CDC reported that the life expectancy for black men grew from 68.8 to 70.8 from 2003 to 2008, while it rose from 75.7 to 77.5 in black women during the same period. This began to close the gap in life expectancy between whites and blacks in the United States, reducing it to 5.4 years for men in 2008 from 6.5 years in 2003. Researchers attributed the improvement to advancement in the prevention and treatment of both heart disease and HIV among blacks.

FAMILY AND COMMUNITY LIFE

In *From Slavery to Freedom*, Franklin points out that "the family was the basis of social organization … [and] the foundation even of economic and political life" in early Africa, with descent being traced through the mother. Historians have noted that Africans placed a heavy emphasis on their obligations to their immediate and extended family members and their community as a whole. In addition, according to Franklin, Africans are said to have believed that "the spirits of their forefathers had unlimited power over their lives"; thus, a sense of kinship was especially significant in the Old World.

Slavery exerted an undeniable strain on the traditional African family unit, tearing at the very fiber of family life. In some cases, husbands and wives were sold to different owners, and children born into servitude could be separated—sold—from their mothers on a white man's whim. However, according to Nicholas Lemann in *The Promised Land*, "the mutation in the structure of the black family" that occurred during slavery did not necessarily destroy the black family. Rather, it is the enduring cycle of poverty among African Americans that seems to have had the strongest negative impact on the stability of the family.

As of 2011, the U.S. Bureau of the Census had estimated that 28.1 percent of African Americans lived below the poverty level (with family incomes of less than $14,000). It is this segment of the underclass that defines the term "families in crisis." These people are besieged by poverty and further challenged by an array of cyclical social problems, including high unemployment rates, teenage pregnancy, a preponderance of fatherless households, inadequate housing or homelessness, inferior health care against a backdrop of high health hazards, staggering school dropout rates, and alarming incarceration rates. (According to The Sentencing Project, one out of nine [11.7 percent] African American males between the ages of twenty-five and twenty-nine was in prison in 2007.) Experts predict that temporary assistance alone will not provide long-term solutions to these problems. Without resolutions, impoverished black families are in danger of falling further and further behind. Having been denied fundamental civil rights and economic opportunities for generations, the African American community was unable to build the same type of generational wealth that led to the growing prosperity of whites and other immigrant and ethnic groups in the United States.

In response to perceived inadequacies in black American education, a progressive philosophy known as Afrocentrism developed around 1980. An alternative to the nation's Eurocentric model of education, Afrocentrism places the black student at the center of history, thereby instilling a sense of dignity and pride in black heritage.

Another third of all African American families found themselves in tenuous financial positions in the latter part of the twentieth century, corresponding with the prevailing economic climate of the United States in the late 1980s and early 1990s and further exacerbated by the cuts to many government assistance programs carried out by Ronald Reagan during his presidency. These families faced increasing layoffs or job termination as the nation's once-prosperous industrial base deteriorated and the great business boom of the early 1980s faded. Still, they managed to hold their extended family units together and provide support systems for their children.

The financial crisis that began in 2007 affected minority groups, including African Americans, much more heavily than whites. While white household wealth declined by 16 percent between 2005 and 2009, black households lost 53 percent of their wealth. This was largely due to the effect of foreclosures, which hit minority households harder than whites. The abusive lending practices that helped to spark the housing collapse were rooted in racial discrimination, as minorities were targeted for subprime market lending, which led to huge disparities in foreclosure rates. By 2010 African Americans and Latinos were 47 percent and 45 percent, respectively, more likely than whites to face foreclosure, according to a 2010 article titled "Foreclosures by Race and Ethnicity: The Demographics of a Crisis." The link between race and foreclosure has been made crystal clear. According to a 2011 NPR report, "Making It in the U.S.: More Than Just Hard Work" by Pam Fessler, "Study after study shows that white families are more likely than blacks and Hispanics to enjoy certain economic advantages—even when their incomes are similar."

At the same time, more than 40 percent of African American families were headed by one or two full-time wage earners. This middle- and upper-middle-class segment of the nation's black population includes men and women who are second-, third-, or fourth-generation college graduates—and who have managed to prosper within a system that, according to some observers, continues to breed legalized racism in both subtle and substantive ways.

Education Before the arrival of Europeans to the continent, many African civilizations thrived as powerful empires and kingdoms with sophisticated political, governmental, and educational systems. Notable early African civilizations include the kingdoms of Benin, Mali, and Kongo, as well as the empire of Songhai. Traditional African education was mainly informal and based on preparing youths to be productive tribal members who contributed to community development. Numerous entities participated in the educational and socialization process, including families, kinship and village groups, and the larger regional community. Instruction was primarily disseminated orally through diverse channels, such as legends, songs, stories, and dances, that passed on tribal laws and customs and helped children develop their relationships with the natural environment. Other forms of education were based on practical training in a specific trade, such as fishing, weaving, or woodwork, that often took the form of apprenticeship. Community members who aspired to leadership positions such as that of tribal chief, religious leader, or traditional medicinal expert underwent years of elaborate rituals and training.

As early as the 1620s and 1630s, European missionaries in the United States began efforts to convert Africans to Christianity and provide them with a basic education. Other inroads in the black educational process were made by America's early white colonists. Pennsylvania Quakers (members of a Christian sect known as the Society of Friends) were among the most vocal advocates of social reform and justice for blacks in the eighteenth and nineteenth centuries. Staunch opponents of slavery, the Quakers began organizing educational meetings for people of African heritage in the late 1700s; in 1774 they launched a school for

Civil rights leader James Armstrong (1923–2009) works in his Birmingham, Alabama, barber shop where he cut Dr. Martin Luther King Jr.'s hair. Armstrong participated in the Bloody Sunday march with Dr. King and was arrested six times during various civil rights protests in the 1960s. His children, Dwight and Floyd, were the first African Americans to integrate Graymont Elementary School in Birmingham in 1963. Five days later a bomb killed four girls at the Sixteenth Street Baptist Church. MARIO TAMA / GETTY IMAGES

blacks in Philadelphia. By the mid-1800s the city had become a center for black learning, with public, industrial, charity, and private schools providing educations for more than 2,000 African American students.

After the Civil War and the abolition of slavery, the federal government created the Freedmen's Bureau, which strove to provide educational opportunities to former slaves. Under the Freedmen's Bureau Acts passed by Congress in the 1860s, more than 2,500 schools were established in the South.

Over the next decade or so, several colleges opened for black students, including Fisk University in Nashville, Tennessee, Morehouse College in Atlanta, Georgia, and Howard University in Washington, D.C.. While some blacks had been able to receive college educations in the North prior to the Civil War, the emergence of multiple institutions of higher learning for blacks in the South created new opportunities for the African American community. Religious organizations and government-sponsored land-grant programs played important roles in the establishment and support of many early black institutions of higher learning. By 1900 more than 2,000 black Americans had graduated from college.

The end of the nineteenth century saw a surge in black educational leadership. One of the best-known and most powerful leaders in the black community at this time was educator and activist Booker T. Washington. A graduate of Virginia's Hampton Normal and Agricultural Institute, Washington set up a similar school in Tuskegee, Alabama, in 1881, with a $2,000 grant from the Alabama legislature. Committed to the ideal of economic self-help and independence, his Tuskegee Institute offered teachers' training—as well as industrial and agricultural education—to young black men and women. While Washington championed a more practical form of technical education that stressed job training, another influential black leader, W. E. B. Du Bois, opposed this conservative approach to black advancement. Du Bois argued that black schools should offer a liberal arts curriculum in order to develop an elite group of African American leaders, whom he called the "Talented Tenth."

Activist Mary McLeod Bethune, the most prominent black woman of her era, also had a profound impact on black education at the turn of the twentieth century. In 1904, with less than two dollars

A segregated school in the southern U.S., prior to the Civil Rights era. CARL IWASAKI / TIME & LIFE PICTURES / GETTY IMAGES

in savings and a handful of students, she founded the Daytona Normal and Industrial Institute in Florida. Devoted mainly to the education of African American girls, the Daytona Institute also served as a cornerstone of strength for the entire black community. The school later merged with Cookman's Institute, a Florida-based men's college, to become Bethune-Cookman College.

The achievements of Bethune and dozens of other black educational leaders occurred amid irrefutable adversity. The doctrine of "separate but equal" accommodations for blacks upheld by the U.S. Supreme Court in 1896 in the case of *Plessy v. Ferguson* affected schools directly. It took more than half a century for the *Plessy* decision to be overturned, when in 1954, the Supreme Court handed down its decision in *Brown v. Board of Education of Topeka*, concluding that separating students based on color established a sense of inferiority among African Americans and was counterproductive to promoting civil rights and racial equality.

Brown was a landmark decision that set the tone for further social advancements among African Americans, but its passage failed to guarantee integration and equality in education. Southern states launched a campaign of "Massive Resistance" that slowed the enactment of the *Brown* decision across the United States. Even four decades after *Brown*, true desegregation in American public schools had not been achieved. The school populations in cities such as Detroit, Michigan, Chicago, and Los Angeles remained almost exclusively black, and high school dropout rates in poor, urban, predominantly black districts were often among the highest in the nation—sometimes reaching over 40 percent. This was exacerbated by the flight of whites to suburban school districts.

Not all attempts at school desegregation have failed. The East Harlem school district in New York,

formerly one of the worst in the city, designed such an impressive educational system for its black and Hispanic students that neighboring whites began transferring into the district. Educational experts have suggested that the key to successful, nationwide school integration is the establishment of high-quality educational facilities in segregated urban areas. Superior school systems in segregated cities, they argue, would discourage urban flight—thereby increasing the racial and economic diversity of the population—and bring about a natural end to segregation. Resegregation of many schools became more frequent in the 1990s and early 2000s, largely because of increasingly segregated neighborhoods that populated specific schools. A 2012 article in the *New York Times* reported that this phenomenon was especially severe in New York City and Charlotte, North Carolina. A 2009–2010 report by the *New York Times* found that more than half of the schools in New York City were at least 90 percent black and Hispanic.

As of 2010, studies continued to show that lower percentages of blacks than whites went to college, but there have been some promising trends. The National Center for Education Statistics reported that the percentage of American college students who are racial minorities, including blacks, Hispanics, and Asian/Pacific Islanders, has increased over the past few decades. From 1976 to 2010 the percentage of black students attending college rose from 9 to 14 percent. The percentage of white students during the same period fell from 83 to 61 percent.

In response to perceived inadequacies in black American education, a progressive philosophy known as Afrocentrism developed around 1980. An alternative to the nation's Eurocentric model of education, Afrocentrism places the black student at the center of history, thereby instilling a sense of dignity and pride in black heritage. Proponents of the movement—including its founder, activist and scholar Molefi Kete Asante—feel that the integration of the Afrocentric perspective into the American consciousness will benefit students of all colors in a racially diverse society. In addition, pro-Afrocentric educators believe that empowered black students will be better equipped to succeed in an increasingly complex world.

Another important development in education was the emergence of ethnic studies as a recognized field at the university and high school levels. The National Association for Ethnic Studies explains, "Ethnic Studies grew out of the civil rights movement and the concerns of minority students on college campuses throughout the United States. Campus strikes began in the 1960s driven by the demands of students of color and others in the Third World Liberation Front demanding an increase of students of color, faculty of color, a more comprehensive curriculum that spoke the concerns and needs of marginalized communities of color." Ethnic studies offers an interdisciplinary approach to the subject of ethnicity

An African American college student studies in Santa Monica, California. JOE SOHM / VISIONS OF AMERICA, LLC / ALAMY

on national and international levels and has served as an avenue for many racial minority students, including blacks and Latinos, to learn about their own cultural histories and to better understand the mechanisms of oppression suffered by their communities in the United States. This program faced a conservative backlash in the Tucson, Arizona, school system, which banned the teaching of ethnic studies courses in 2010 for being racially biased. Many scholars and minority activists saw this as a threat to the success of minority students and an attempt to protect the white majority. Similar legislation has appeared in other traditionally conservative states.

Weddings American tradition calls for the bride to have "something old, something new, something borrowed, and something blue" in her possession for luck on her wedding day. While modern African American couples marry in the Western tradition, many are personalizing their weddings with ancestral touches to add to the day's historical and cultural significance.

Among Africans, marriage represents a union of two families, not just the bride and groom. In keeping with West African custom, it is essential for parents and extended family members to welcome a man or woman's future partner and offer emotional support to the couple throughout their marriage. The bonding of the families begins when a man obtains formal permission to marry his prospective bride.

In the true oral tradition, Africans often deliver the news of their upcoming nuptials by word of mouth. Some African American couples have modified

this tradition by having their invitations printed on a scroll, tied with raffia, and then hand-delivered by friends. The ancestral influence on modern ceremonies can also be seen in the accessories worn by the bride and groom. On African shores, the groom wears his bride's earring, and the bride dons an elaborate necklace reserved exclusively for her.

Because enslaved Africans in America were often barred from marrying in a legal ceremony, they created their own marriage rite. It is said that couples joined hands and jumped over a broom together into "the land of matrimony." Many twentieth- and twenty-first-century black American couples reenact "jumping the broom" during their wedding ceremonies or receptions.

Interracial Marriage As late as 1967, anti-miscegenation laws (laws prohibiting the marriage of whites to members of another "race") were still on the books in seventeen states. Many of these laws were written and instituted in the early twentieth century, largely because of lobbying by eugenicists who claimed that the black race was biologically inferior and wanted to preserve the purity of the white race. A notable example of such legislation is Virginia's Racial Integrity Act of 1924, which was championed by two eugenicists, John Powell and Walter Plecker, and aimed to avoid the "mongrelization" of the white race with nonwhite blood. Laws such as this were finally addressed on a national level with the *Loving v. Virginia* U.S. Supreme Court case of 1967, which legalized interracial marriage across the country. The case was filed by an interracial couple in Virginia: the

solidarity in the early 1990s. Many black women—"the culture bearers"—opposed the idea of interracial marriage, opting instead for racial strength and unity through the stabilization of the black family, according to Ruth Holladay in a 1990 *Indianapolis Star* article. This movement seemed to continue, to an extent, in the early 2000s, and was more common in regions where the populations were predominately and historically African American, including Washington, D.C., Virginia, Maryland, and parts of the South. Recent African immigrants are much less likely to wed interracially, preferring to maintain cultural and linguistic ties to the homeland by marrying within their community. It is also common for African immigrant men to return to their home country to find a wife and then bring her to the United States to establish a family.

EMPLOYMENT AND ECONOMIC CONDITIONS

When African Americans left the South in the early 1900s to migrate North, many found jobs in manufacturing, especially in the automobile, tobacco, meatpacking, clothing, steel, and shipping industries. African Americans, then, were hit especially hard by the decline of the nation's manufacturing economy later in the century. In the 1960s, U.S. presidents John F. Kennedy and Lyndon Baines Johnson launched a "war on poverty." Some blacks were able to move out of the ghettos during these years, following the passage of the Civil Rights and Fair Housing Acts, the inauguration of affirmative action policies, and the increase of black workers in government jobs. However, Franklin contends in *From Slavery to Freedom* that the Civil Rights Act of 1964, though "the most far-reaching and comprehensive law in support of racial equality ever enacted by Congress," actually reflected only "the illusion of equality."

Designed to protect blacks against discrimination in voting, education, the use of public facilities, and the administration of federally funded programs, the Civil Rights Act of 1964 led to the establishment of the Equal Employment Opportunity Commission and the institution of affirmative action programs to redress past discrimination against African Americans. Affirmative action measures were initiated in the mid-1960s to improve educational and employment opportunities for minorities. However, opponents of affirmative action have argued that racial quotas breed racial resentment. A strong feeling of "white backlash" accompanied the passage of the Civil Rights Act of 1964; racial tensions sparked violence across the country as blacks tried to move beyond the limits of segregation—economically, politically, and socially—in the latter half of the twentieth century. Still, more than four decades after the act's passage, economic inequities persist in the United States.

The conservative policies of U.S. presidents Ronald Reagan and George H. W. Bush had a strong effect on black advancement in the 1980s and early 1990s. The percentage of Americans living in poverty

black Mildred Jeter Loving and the white Richard Loving. After having driven to Washington, D.C., to get married, the couple was arrested by Virginia law enforcement agents in the middle of the night for violating the state's anti-miscegenation law. Despite *Loving v. Virginia*, many states left anti-miscegenation laws on the books. South Carolina did not remove its ban until 1998, and Alabama had its in place until 2000.

Interracial marriages are now commonplace. The Pew Research Center reported that in 2010 one in twelve married couples in the United States was interracial. About 15 percent of all new marriages in the United States in 2010 were between individuals of different races or ethnicity, which was more than double the rate from 1980 (6.7 percent). Furthermore, the American public's opinion on interracial marriage changed drastically from the 1980s to 2010. The Pew Center reported that nearly two-thirds of Americans (63 percent) said it would be acceptable to them if a member of their own family were to marry someone of another race or ethnicity, compared to only one-third of the public (33 percent) who viewed intermarriage as acceptable in 1986. This decline in social bias is the main reason for the large increase in cross-cultural marriages seen in the United States since the 1980s.

Still, according to the Pew Center, only 9 percent of black women married outside of their race in 2010. A 1994 *Newsweek* magazine article quoted one young black woman as saying that "relationships are complicated enough" without the extra stress of interracial tensions. Conflict in the United States over blackwhite relationships stems from the nation's brutal history of slavery, when white men held all the power in society. Well over a century after the abolition of slavery, America's shameful legacy of racism remains. According to some observers, high rates of abortion, drug abuse, illness, and poverty among African Americans seemed to spark a movement of black

"rose in the 1980s, when the government [cut] back its efforts" to support social programs, according to Nicholas Lemann in the *Washington Post National Weekly Edition* in 1989. Budget cuts and reductions in government assistance made by these Republican administrations drastically reduced black employment opportunities.

The U.S. financial crisis that began in 2007 hit the African American population especially hard. In an executive summary of the Pew Research Center's findings in 2011, Rakesh Kochhar, Richard Fry, and Paul Taylor note that "the bursting of the housing market bubble in 2006 and the recession that followed from late 2007 to mid-2009 took a far greater toll on the wealth of minorities than whites." Between 2005 and 2009, median household wealth fell by 53 percent among blacks, compared to 16 percent among white households.

In November 2012, the U.S. Bureau of Labor Statistics stated that the unemployment rate for African Americans had increased to 14.3 percent, as opposed to 7 percent for whites and 10 percent for Hispanics. Furthermore, unemployment among blacks between the ages of sixteen and nineteen went from 35.4 percent in October 2011 to 40.5 percent in October 2012; in contrast, the white teenage unemployment rate in October 2012 was 20.6 percent. A primary reason for these numbers among blacks is that a large part of the African American population is employed in the public sector, which was hit most severely during the Great Recession.

A 2011 report by the Economic Policy Institute noted that black unemployment in many of the nation's largest metropolitan areas had increased substantially between 2007 and 2011. In 2007 black unemployment hovered around 10 percent in Detroit, Milwaukee, Wisconsin, and Minneapolis, Minnesota, but by 2010 it had jumped to 20 percent or higher in those cities. According to the Economic Policy Institute, unemployment in the nation's capital in 2010 stood at 20.3 percent, markedly higher than the 3.3 percent rate among whites. The outlook for black employment across the nation remained bleak in late 2012, prompting African American activists to call for bolder measures by the government to spur a faster economic recovery.

Nevertheless, a strong black presence is evident in the fields of health care, business, and law, and a new spirit of entrepreneurship is burgeoning among young, upwardly mobile African Americans. Despite such gains, however, a large sector of the black population is trapped in a cycle of poor education, multigenerational poverty, and underemployment, which was only further exacerbated by the Great Recession.

POLITICS AND GOVERNMENT

The abolitionist movement of the 1830s produced a multiracial coalition in the quest for black emancipation and equality. In addition to agitating for civil rights through traditional legal means, the abolitionists took a daring step by operating the legendary Underground Railroad system, a covert network of safe havens that assisted fugitive slaves in their flights to freedom in the North. "Perhaps nothing did more to intensify the strife between North and South, and to emphasize in a most dramatic way the determination of abolitionists to destroy slavery, than the Underground Railroad," Franklin writes in *From Slavery to Freedom*. "It was this organized effort to undermine slavery … that put such a strain on intersectional relations and sent antagonists and protagonists of slavery scurrying headlong into the 1850s determined to have their uncompromising way." Around 50,000 slaves escaped to the northern United States and Canada through the Underground Railroad.

The reality of the black plight was magnified in 1856 with the Supreme Court's decision in the case of *Dred Scott vs. Sandford*, which reinforced the fact that slaves were not legal U.S. citizens and, thus, were not afforded the same rights. A slave named Dred Scott had traveled with his master out of the slave state of Missouri during the 1830s and 1840s. He sued his owner for freedom, arguing that his journeys to free territories made him free. The Supreme Court disagreed, ruling that slaves could not file lawsuits because they lacked the status of a U.S. citizen; in addition, an owner was said to have the right to transport a slave anywhere in U.S. territory without changing the slave's status.

The Union victory in the Civil War and the abolition of slavery under President Lincoln consolidated black political support in the Republican Party. This affiliation lasted until the 1930s, when Democrats under Franklin Delano Roosevelt brought African American voters into the New Deal coalition. Republicans helped elected African American representatives in the Reconstruction era to make significant legislative gains. The Civil Rights Act of 1866 and the Fourteenth Amendment to the Constitution were intended to provide full citizenship—with the corresponding rights and privileges—to all blacks. The Fifteenth Amendment, ratified in 1870, granted black American men the right to vote.

Such measures failed, however, to guarantee blacks the freedom to choose at the ballot box. Poll taxes, literacy tests, and grandfather clauses were established by some state and local governments to deny blacks their right to vote following the establishment of legalized racial segregation with the Supreme Court ruling in *Plessy v. Ferguson*. (The poll tax would not be declared unconstitutional until 1964, with the passage of the Twenty-fourth Amendment.) These legalized forms of oppression presented seemingly insurmountable obstacles to black advancement in the United States.

By the turn of the twentieth century, Booker T. Washington had gained prominence as the chief spokesperson on the state of black America and the issue of racial reconciliation. Recognized throughout the United States as an outstanding black leader and mediator, he advocated accommodationism as the preferred method of attaining black rights. His leading opponent, black historian, militant, and author W. E. B. Du Bois, felt it was necessary to take more aggressive measures in the fight for equality. In 1905 Du Bois spearheaded the Niagara Movement, a radical black intellectual forum that attempted to form a talented black elite capable of leading the larger African American community toward social and economic advancement. Members of the group merged with white progressives in 1910 to form the National Association for the Advancement of Colored People (NAACP). After Washington's death in 1915, the NAACP became a greater force in the struggle for racial reform.

The massive black migration to the North in the 1920s showed that racial tension was no longer just a rural, southern issue. Antiblack attitudes, combined with the desperate economic pressures of the Great Depression, exerted a profound effect on politics nationwide. Roosevelt attracted black voters with his "New Deal" relief and recovery programs in the 1930s. Their belief in Roosevelt's "serious interest in the problem of the black man caused thousands of [African Americans] to change their party allegiance," as Franklin notes in *From Slavery to Freedom*. Housing and employment opportunities started to open up, and blacks began to gain seats in various state legislatures in the 1930s and 1940s.

World War II ushered in an era of unswerving commitment to the fight for civil rights. According to Franklin, the continued "steady migration of [African Americans] to the North and West and their concentration in important industrial communities gave blacks a powerful new voice in political affairs. In cities like Chicago, Detroit, and Cleveland [Ohio] they frequently held the balance of power in close elections, and in certain pivotal states the [black vote] came to be regarded as crucial in national elections." Progress was being made on all fronts by national associations, political organizations, unions, the federal branch of the U.S. government, and the nation's court system.

President Harry S. Truman, who assumed office after the death of Roosevelt in 1945, contributed to black advancement by desegregating the military, establishing fair employment practices in the federal service, and beginning the trend toward integration in public accommodations and housing. His civil rights proposals of the late 1940s came to fruition a decade later during President Dwight Eisenhower's administration. The Civil Rights Act of 1957, also known as the Voting Rights Act of 1957, was the first major piece of civil rights legislation passed by Congress in more than eight decades. It expanded the role of the federal government in civil rights matters and established the U.S. Commission on Civil Rights to monitor the protection of black rights.

However, the commission soon determined that unfair voting practices persisted in the South; blacks were still being denied the right to vote in certain southern districts. Because of these abuses, the Civil Rights Act of 1957 was followed three years later by a second act that offered extra protection to blacks at the polls. In 1965 African Americans finally secured definitive voting rights via the Voting Rights Act, which eliminated literacy tests and safeguarded black rights during the voter registration process.

The postwar agitation for black rights had yielded slow but significant advances in school desegregation and suffrage. These advances were met, however, with bold opposition from some whites. By the mid- to late 1950s, as the black fight for progress gained ground, white resistance continued to mount. Martin Luther King Jr. took the helm of the fledgling civil rights movement—a multiracial effort to eliminate segregation and achieve equality for blacks through nonviolent resistance. The movement began with the boycott of city buses in Montgomery, Alabama, and, by 1960, had broadened in scope, becoming a national crusade for black rights. Over the next decade, civil rights agitators—both black and white—organized economic boycotts of racist businesses and attracted front-page news coverage with black voter registration drives and anti-segregationist demonstrations, marches, and sit-ins. Bolstered by the new era of independence that simultaneously swept through sub-Saharan Africa, the push for African American equality gained international attention.

Around the same time, racial tensions, especially in the South, reached violent levels with the emergence of new white supremacist organizations and an increase in Ku Klux Klan activity. Racially motivated discrimination on all fronts—from housing to employment—rose as southern resistance to the civil rights movement intensified. By the late 1950s, racist hatred had once again degenerated into brutality and bloodshed: blacks connected to the civil rights cause were being murdered, and their white killers were escaping punishment.

In the midst of America's growing racial tragedy, Democrat John F. Kennedy gained the black vote in the 1960 presidential election. His domestic agenda included the expansion of federal action in civil rights cases—especially through the empowerment of the U.S. Department of Justice on voting rights issues and the establishment of the Committee on Equal Employment Opportunity. Civil rights organizations continued their peaceful assaults against barriers to integration, but black frustrations with racial injustice were escalating. The protest movement heated up in 1961, when groups such as the Congress of Racial Equality, the Student Nonviolent Coordinating Committee, and the Southern Christian Leadership Conference organized "freedom rides" that defied segregationist policies on public transportation systems.

Oprah Winfrey waves as she speaks during the "Let Freedom Ring Commemoration and Call to Action" to commemorate the 50th anniversary of the 1963 March on Washington for Jobs and Freedom at the Lincoln Memorial in Washington, D.C. SAUL LOEB / AFP / GETTY IMAGES

"By 1963," writes Franklin, "the Black Revolution was approaching full tide."

Major demonstrations were staged in April 1963, most notably in Birmingham, Alabama, under the leadership of King. Cries for equality met with harsh police action against the black crowds. Two months later, Mississippi's NAACP leader, Medgar Evers, was assassinated. Soon demonstrations were springing up throughout the nation, and Kennedy was contemplating his next move in the fight for black rights.

On August 28, 1963, more 200,000 black and white demonstrators converged at the Lincoln Memorial in Washington, D.C., to push for the passage of a new civil rights bill. This historic rally, called the "March on Washington" and highlighted by King's legendary "I Have a Dream" speech, brought the promise of stronger legislation from the president.

After Kennedy's assassination that November, President Johnson continued his predecessor's civil rights program. The passage of the Civil Rights Act of 1964 sparked violence throughout the country, including turmoil in cities in New York, New Jersey, Pennsylvania, and Illinois. The Ku Klux Klan stepped up its practice of black intimidation with venomous racial slurs, cross burnings, firebombings, and even acts of murder.

The call for racial reform in the South became louder in early 1965. King, who had been honored with the Nobel Peace Prize for his commitment to race relations, commanded the spotlight for his key role in the 1965 Freedom March from Selma to Montgomery in Alabama. However, African Americans were disheartened by the lack of tangible progress in securing black rights. Despite the legislative gains made over two decades, "between 1949 and 1964 the relative participation of [blacks] in the total economic life of the nation declined significantly," as Franklin notes.

Black discontent over economic, employment, and housing discrimination reached frightening proportions in the summer of 1965, with rioting in the Watts section of Los Angeles. This event marked a major change in the tone of the civil rights movement. Nearly a decade of nonviolent resistance had failed to remedy the racial crisis in the United States, particularly regarding the economic advancement of blacks, a disproportionate number of whom still remained below the poverty line. Consequently, a more militant reformist element began to emerge. "Black Power"

African Americans in the southern U.S. celebrate the election of Barack Obama in 2008 as the first black American to be elected to the U.S. presidency. EDSTOCK / ISTOCKPHOTO.COM

became the rallying cry of the middle and late 1960s, and more and more civil rights groups adopted all-black leadership. King's assassination in 1968 only compounded the nation's explosive racial situation. According to Franklin, King's murder symbolized for many blacks "the rejection by white America of their vigorous but peaceful pursuit of equality." The Black Revolution had finally crystallized, and with it came a grave sense of loss and despair within the black community. The new generation of black leaders seemed to champion independence and separatism for blacks rather than integration into white American society.

Fear of black advancement and urban rioting led many whites to shift their allegiance to the Republican Party in the late 1960s. The conservative movement, spearheaded first by Barry Goldwater, united whites who feared competition with blacks and were anxious over the social changes that were underway in the United States. With the exception of Jimmy Carter's term as president from 1977 to 1981, Republicans remained in the White House for the rest of the 1970s and 1980s. The race-based politics employed by Reagan and his allies during this period did lasting damage to many of the social programs

for blacks that had been established during the civil rights and Great Society eras. However, a new era of black activism arose with the election of Democratic Bill Clinton as president in 1992. After a dozen years of conservatism under presidents Reagan and Bush, Clinton was seen as a champion of "the people"—all people. Committed to policies that would cut across the lines of gender, race, and economics, he offered a vision of social reform, urban renewal, and domestic harmony for the United States. Once in office, Clinton appointed African Americans to key posts in his cabinet, and the black population began wielding unprecedented influence in government. For example, the 102nd Congress included twenty-five African American representatives; the elections in 1993 brought black representation in the 103rd Congress up to thirty-eight.

Despite the advancements made by African Americans in politics, as well as in business, gang violence continued to plague African American communities in the 1990s. To foster positive feelings, Nation of Islam leader Louis Farrakhan and civil rights activist Phile Chionesu organized the Million Man March. On October 16, 1995, close to one million African

American men converged on the nation's capital to hear speeches and connect with other socially conscious black men. Reverend Jesse Jackson spoke at the event, as did poet Maya Angelou, Damu Smith of Greenpeace, civil rights icon Rosa Parks, Reverend Joseph Lowery, and other luminaries.

In October 1997, African American women held their own massive march. The Million Woman March attracted hundreds of thousands of African American women to Philadelphia, where they experienced a sense of community and cohesion. The attendees heard speeches and discussed issues such as the rising prison populations, the idea of independent schools for black children, the use of alternative medicines, and the progress of black women in politics and business.

Many milestones in African American politics occurred at the turn of the twenty-first century, including the election of Illinois Democrat Carol Moseley-Braun to the Senate, the first time an African American woman had reached that office. In 2005, in George W. Bush's administration, Condoleezza Rice became the first female African American secretary of state. In 2008 Barack Obama, a black senator from Illinois, made history when he became the first African American president of the United States. For many, his victory marked a turning point in civil rights and African American politics, and this spirit was embodied in his campaign slogan of "Hope and Change." In his speech after being elected, Obama proclaimed, "It's been a long time coming, but tonight, because of what we did on this day, in this election, at this defining moment, change has come to America."

President Obama's first term was dominated by the severe economic effects of the Great Recession that he inherited from his predecessor, George W. Bush. Nevertheless, he passed the Health Care Reform Act (known colloquially as "Obamacare"), which expanded access to medical care and provided subsidies for people who could not afford it; ended the "Don't Ask, Don't Tell" policy regarding gays in the military; bailed out and, in turn, revived the American auto industry; ended the War in Iraq; and facilitated the death of al-Qaeda terrorist leader Osama bin Laden. While Obama faced much criticism throughout his first term, he was elected to a second term in 2012, beating Republican Mitt Romney.

Military As far back as 1702, blacks fought against the French and the Indians in the New World. Virginia and South Carolina allowed African Americans to enlist in the militia, and throughout the eighteenth century, some slaves were able to exchange their military service for freedom. African American soldiers served in the armed forces during the American Revolution, the War of 1812, the Civil War, the Spanish-American War, World I, World War II, the Korean War, the Vietnam War, the Persian Gulf War, peacekeeping ventures in Somalia and Haiti,

and the wars in Iraq and Afghanistan. For nearly two centuries, however, segregation existed in the U.S. military—a shameful testament to the nation's long history of racial discrimination.

On March 5, 1770, prior to the outbreak of the American Revolution, a crowd of angry colonists gathered in the streets of Boston to protest unjust British policies. This colonial rally—which would later be remembered as the Boston Massacre—turned bloody when British soldiers retaliated with gunfire. A black sailor named Crispus Attucks is said to have been the first American to die in the conflict. The death of Attucks symbolizes the cruel irony of the revolutionary cause in America—one that denied equal rights to its African American population.

The American Revolution focused increased attention on the thorny issue of slavery. An underlying fear existed that enslaved blacks would revolt if granted the right to bear arms, so most colonists favored the idea of an all-white militia. Although some blacks fought at the battles of Lexington, Concord, and Bunker Hill in 1775, General George Washington issued a ban on the enlistment of slaves that summer; by November he had extended the ban to all blacks, enslaved or free. However, the Continental Congress—apprehensive about the prospect of black enlistment in the British Army, which offered slaves their freedom in exchange for military service—partially reversed the policy in the next year. An estimated 5,000 blacks eventually served in the colonial army, a much smaller number than that on the British side. Since the colonial army did not offer slaves their freedom, many black soldiers in its ranks were forced to fight against their will.

Integration of the fledgling American Army ended in 1792, when Congress passed a law limiting military service to white men. More than half a century later, blacks were still unable to enlist in the U.S. military.

For African Americans, the Civil War, which began in April 1861, was a war against slavery. However, as Alton Hornsby Jr. points out in *Chronology of African-American History*, "Lincoln's war aims did not include interference with slavery where it already existed." Early in the struggle, states Hornsby, the president felt that a stand "against slavery would drive additional Southern and Border states into the Confederacy," a risk he could not afford to take at a time when the Union seemed dangerously close to dissolving. By mid-1862, though, the need for additional Union Army soldiers became critical. The Emancipation Proclamation, issued by Lincoln in 1863, freed the slaves of the Confederacy. With their new "free" status, blacks were allowed to participate in the Civil War. By the winter of 1864–1865, the Union Army boasted 168 volunteer regiments of black troops, comprising more than 10 percent of its total strength. More than 35,000 blacks died in combat.

Between 300,000 and 400,000 African Americans served in the U.S. armed forces during World War I, but only 10 percent were assigned to combat duty. Blacks were still hampered by segregationist policies that perpetuated an erroneous notion of inferiority among the troops. However, the stellar performances of many black soldiers during the era of the two world wars helped to dispel these stereotypes. In 1940, for example, Benjamin O. Davis Sr. became the first black American to achieve the rank of brigadier general. Over the next decade, his son, U.S. Air Force officer Benjamin O. Davis Jr., distinguished himself as commander of the 99th Fighter Squadron, the 332nd Fighter Group, the 477th Bombardment Group, and the 332nd Fighter Wing.

Several hundred thousand blacks fought for the United States in World War II. Still, according to Franklin, "too many clear signs indicated that the United States was committed to maintaining a white army and a black army, and ironically the combined forces of this army had to be used together somehow to carry on the fight against the powerful threat of fascism and racism in the world."

In an effort to promote equality and opportunity in the American military, President Truman issued Executive Order 9981 on July 26, 1948, banning segregation in the armed forces. Six years later, the U.S. Department of Defense adopted an official policy of full integration, abolishing all-black military units. The late 1950s and early 1960s saw a steady increase in the number of career officers in the U.S. military. By the mid-1990s, close to 40 percent of the American military was black. Yet by 2008, only 19 percent of the military's active-duty enlisted force was black, compared to 13 percent of the country's general population, according to a 2009 CBS News report. Many military analysts attributed this drop in black enlistment to the unpopular Iraq War and a growing mistrust of the Bush administration. Despite these declines however, the percentage of blacks in the military continues to exceed its percentage within the U.S. population. Some social commentators feel that the disproportionately large number of African Americans in the military calls attention to the obstacles young black people face in forging mainstream career paths.

NOTABLE INDIVIDUALS

Education Alain Locke (1886–1954) was a prolific author, historian, educator, and drama critic. A Harvard University graduate and Rhodes Scholar, he taught philosophy at Howard University for thirty-six years and is remembered as a leading figure in the Harlem Renaissance.

Kenneth B. Clark (1914–2005), social scientist and Spingarn medalist, taught psychology for more than three decades at New York's City College. His work, along with that of his wife, Mamie Phipps Clark (1917–1983), on the psychology of segregation played an important part in the Supreme Court's 1954 ruling in *Brown vs. Board of Education*.

Johnnetta B. Cole (1936–), anthropologist and writer, in 1987 became the first African American woman president of Spelman College, the nation's oldest and most esteemed institution of higher learning for black females. Cole went on to serve as the president of Bennett College from 2002 to 2007 and later took a position as the director of the Smithsonian Institution's National Museum of African Art.

Henry Louis Gates Jr. (1950–)—a respected literary scholar and critic, an Alphonse Fletcher University Professor at Harvard University, and the director of the W. E. B. Du Bois Institute for African and African American Research—offered a new perspective on the related roles of black tradition, stereotypes, and the plurality of the American nation in the field of education. He is best known for championing a multicultural approach to learning.

Angela Davis (1944–), a scholar, author, and political activist, was a professor in the History of Consciousness Department and the director of the Feminist Studies Department at the University of California, Santa Cruz, from 1991 to 2008. A long-time advocate of prisoner rights, Davis founded Critical Resistance, an organization that works toward the abolition of the prison-industrial complex.

Gloria Jean Watkins (1952–), generally known by her pen name bell hooks, is a feminist theorist, professor, and activist whose work focuses on the interconnectivity of race, capitalism, and gender. One of the best known of her more than thirty books is *Feminist Theory: From Margin to Center* (1984). Geoffrey Canada (1952–), educational innovator, best known for his Harlem Children's Zone project.

Government Charles Hamilton Houston (1895–1950), attorney and educator, was a brilliant leader in the legal battle to erode segregation in the United States; his student Thurgood Marshall (1908–1993) successfully argued against the constitutionality of segregation in *Brown vs. Board of Education* (1954). A director of the NAACP Legal Defense and Educational Fund for more than two decades, Marshall went on to become a U.S. Supreme Court justice in 1967.

Colin Powell (1937–), career military officer, made his mark on American history as the first black chairman of the Joint Chiefs of Staff, a position he held from 1989 to 1993, and the first black secretary of state, serving under George W. Bush from 2001 to 2005.

Jesse Jackson (1941–), an early follower of Martin Luther King Jr., became a potent force in American politics in his own right. In 1984 and 1988 he campaigned for the Democratic nomination for the U.S. presidency. The founder of Operation PUSH and the National Rainbow Coalition, Jackson was committed to the economic, social, and political advancement of America's dispossessed and disfranchised peoples.

Carol Moseley-Braun (1947–), attorney and politician, won election to the U.S. Senate in 1992, making her the first black woman senator in the

Sweet Emma Barrett and Her Preservation Jazz Band performs in Preservation Hall in New Orleans. NATHAN BENN / ALAMY

nation. She served in that office until 1999 and went on to become U.S. Ambassador to New Zealand until 2001.

Kweisi Mfume (born Frizzell Gray; 1948–), a Democratic U.S. congressman from Maryland former five-term chairman of the powerful Congressional Black Caucus from 1993 to 1994, and Mfume served as the president of the NAACP from 1997 to 2004.

Condoleezza Rice (1954–), an American political scientist and diplomat, became the first female African American secretary of state, serving in the Bush administration from 2005 to 2009.

Barack Obama (1961–) made history by being elected the first black president of the United States in 2008. He was elected to a second term in 2012.

Journalism Frederick Douglass (1818–1875), the famous fugitive slave and abolitionist, recognized the power of the press and used it to paint a graphic portrait of the horrors of slavery. He founded *The North Star*, a black newspaper, in 1847 to expose the realities of the black condition in nineteenth-century America.

John Henry Murphy (1840–1922), a former slave and the founder of the *Baltimore Afro-American*,

was inspired by a desire to represent black causes with honor and integrity.

T. Thomas Fortune (1856–1928), a staunch defender of black rights during the late nineteenth and early twentieth centuries, used his editorial position at various urban newspapers in the North to crusade for an end to racial discrimination.

Robert S. Abbott (1870–1940) was a key figure in the development of black journalism in the twentieth century. The first issue of his *Chicago Defender* went to press in 1905.

Charlayne Hunter-Gault (1942–) broke the color barrier at the University of Georgia, as she and Hamilton Hunter Holmes became the first black undergraduates to enroll in the University. She received her degree in journalism from the formerly segregated institution in 1963. Hunter-Gault was a national correspondent for public television's *MacNeil/Lehrer NewsHour* from 1983 until 1999, earning distinction for her socially conscious brand of investigative reporting.

Michele Norris (1961–), an American radio journalist, served as the host of the National Public Radio

(NPR) news program *All Things Considered* beginning in 2002. She was the first African American female program host for NPR.

Gwendolyn "Gweb" Ifill (1955–), an American journalist, author, and television newscaster, served as the moderator for the 2004 and 2008 vice presidential debates. She worked as a senior correspondent for the *PBS NewsHour* and as the managing editor and a moderator for *Washington Week*, also on PBS.

Literature Langston Hughes (1902–1967) was a major figure of the Harlem Renaissance, a period of intense artistic and intellectual activity centered in New York City's black community during the early 1920s. An author of poetry, long and short fiction, plays, autobiographical works, and nonfiction pieces, Hughes infused his writings with the texture of urban African Americana.

Pulitzer Prize-winning author Alex Haley (1921–1992) traced his African heritage, his ancestors' agonizing journey to the New World, and the brutal system of slavery in the United States in his 1976 best seller *Roots*.

Playwright Lorraine Hansberry (1930–1965), author of the classic play *A Raisin in the Sun* (1959), was the first black recipient of the New York Drama Critics Circle Award.

Bob Kaufman (1925–1986) was the most prominent African American beatnik poet, and he is considered by many to be the finest.

Maya Angelou (1928–), a renowned chronicler of the black American experience, earned national acclaim in 1970 with the publication of the first volume of her autobiography, *I Know Why the Caged Bird Sings*. She presented her moving original verse *On the Pulse of Morning* at the inauguration of U.S. president Bill Clinton in January 1993.

Cultural historian and novelist Toni Morrison (1931–), the author of such works as *The Bluest Eye* (1970), *Tar Baby* (1981), *Beloved* (1987), and *A Mercy* (2008), was awarded the Nobel Prize in Literature in 1993.

Terry McMillan (1951–) emerged in the late 1980s as a powerful new voice on the literary scene. Her 1992 novel *Waiting to Exhale* was a best seller.

Music The blues, an improvisational African American musical form, originated around 1900 in the Mississippi Delta region and left a profound impact on American cultural history. Some of its pioneering figures include legendary cornet player, bandleader, and composer W. C. Handy (1873–1958), often called the "Father of the Blues"; singing marvel Bessie Smith (1898–1937), known as the "Empress of the Blues"; and Muddy Waters (1915–1983), a practitioner of the urban blues strain that evolved in Chicago in the 1940s.

African Americans were also the originators of jazz, a blend of European traditional music, blues, and southern instrumental ragtime that developed in the

South in the 1920s. Key figures in the evolution of jazz include New Orleans horn player and swing master Louis "Satchmo" Armstrong (1900–1971), who had hits such as "Hello, Dolly" (1964) and "What a Wonderful World" (1967); Lionel Hampton (1909–2002), the first jazz musician to popularize vibes; trumpeter Dizzy Gillespie (1917–1993), a chief architect of a modern jazz form called bebop; singer Ella Fitzgerald (1918–1996), a master of improvisation who came to be known as "The First Lady of Song"; innovative and enigmatic trumpeter, composer, and bandleader Miles Davis (1926–1991), who pioneered the genre's avant-garde period in the 1950s and electrified jazz with elements of funk and rock, thereby beginning the fusion movement in the late 1960s; and Melba Liston (1926–1999), a trombonist, an arranger, and the leader of an all-female jazz group in the 1950s and 1960s.

Vocalist, composer, and historian Bernice Johnson Reagon (1942–), founder of the female *a cappella* ensemble Sweet Honey in the Rock, was committed to maintaining Africa's diverse musical heritage.

In the field of classical music, Marian Anderson (1902–1993) was one of the greatest contraltos of all time. She was also a victim of racial prejudice: a star in Europe for years before her American debut, she was actually barred from making an appearance at Constitution Hall by the Daughters of the American Revolution in April of 1939—an incident that prompted First Lady Eleanor Roosevelt to resign from the organization. Shortly thereafter, on Easter Sunday, Anderson sang on the steps of the Lincoln Memorial.

Composer and pianist Margaret Bonds (1913–1972) wrote works that explore the African American experience. Her best-known compositions include the ballet *Migration* (1964), *Spiritual Suite for Piano* (1950s), *Mass, D Minor* (1959), and the songs "The Ballad of the Brown King" (1960) and "The Negro Speaks of Rivers" (1935).

African Americans continue to set trends and break barriers in the music business, especially in pop, rap, blues, and jazz. In addition to the aforementioned people, a partial list of celebrated African American musicians includes guitarist Jimi Hendrix (1942–1970), singer Otis Redding (1941–1967), singer Aretha Franklin (1942–), singer Al Green (1946–), saxophonist John Coltrane (1926–1967), Sly and the Family Stone front man Sylvester "Sly" Stone (1944–), singer-songwriter Phoebe Snow (1952–2011), rap artist Snoop Dogg (1972–), rap artist and record company executive Sean "Puffy" Combs (1969–), pop superstar and cultural icon Michael Jackson (1958–2009), singer Lauryn Hill (1975–), pianist-songwriter Ray Charles (1930–2004), singer Little Richard (1932–), singer Diana Ross (1944–), blues guitarist B. B. King (1925–), rap artist Easy-E (1963–1995), singer Billy Preston (1946–2006), and singer Whitney Houston (1963–2012). The younger generation of musical artists includes R&B singers Alicia Cook (better known as Alicia Keys, 1981–) and John Stephens (John Legend, 1978–), pop singers Beyonce Knowles-Carter (1981–) and Robyn Fenty (Rihanna, 1988–), and rap artists Dwayne Michael Carter Jr. (Lil Wayne, 1982–), Shawn Corey Carter (Jay-Z, 1969–), and Kanye West (1977–).

Performance Dancer and choreographer Katherine Dunham (1909–2006) is known as the mother of Afro-American dance. She is best remembered for blending elements of traditional Caribbean dance with modern African American rhythms and dance forms. Also a noted activist, Dunham went on a forty-seven-day hunger strike in 1992 to protest U.S. policy on Haitian refugees.

Science and Technology Granville T. Woods (1856–1910) was a trailblazer in the fields of electrical and mechanical engineering. His various inventions include a telephone transmitter, an egg incubator, and a railway telegraph.

George Washington Carver (1864–1943) was born into slavery but became a leader in agricultural chemistry and botany. He was one of the most famous African Americans of his era.

Inventor Garrett A. Morgan (1877–1963), a self-educated man, developed the first gas mask and traffic signal.

Ernest Everett Just (1883–1915), recipient of the first Spingarn medal ever given by the NAACP, made important contributions to the studies of marine biology and cell behavior.

Percy Lavon Julien (1889–1975), also a Spingarn medalist, was a maverick in the field of organic chemistry. He created synthesized versions of cortisone (to relieve the pain and inflammation of arthritis) and physostigmine (to reduce the debilitating effects of glaucoma).

Surgeon and scientist Charles Richard Drew (1904–1950) refined techniques of preserving liquid blood plasma.

Samuel L. Kountz (1930–1981), an international leader in transplant surgery, successfully transplanted a kidney from a mother to a daughter—the first operation of its kind between individuals who were not identical twins. He also pioneered anti-rejection therapy in transplant patients.

Benjamin Carson (1951–), a pediatric neurosurgeon, gained international acclaim in 1987 by separating twins who were joined at their heads.

Medical doctor and former astronaut Mae C. Jemison (1957–) made history as the first black woman to serve as a mission specialist for the National Aeronautics and Space Administration (NASA). She was a crew member on a 1992 flight of the Space Shuttle *Endeavour*.

Patricia Bath (1942–), an ophthalmologic surgeon, cofounded the American Institute for the Prevention of Blindness in 1976.

Shirley Ann Jackson (1946–) was the first black woman to earn a doctorate in theoretical physics and to head the United States Nuclear Regulatory Commission. In 2009 President Obama appointed Jackson to serve as an advisor of the President's Council of Advisors on Science and Technology.

Social Issues Harriet Tubman (1820?-1913) was a runaway slave who became a leader in the abolitionist movement. A nurse and spy for the Union Army during the Civil War, she earned distinction as the chief "conductor" of the Underground Railroad, leading an estimated three hundred slaves to freedom in the North.

Attorney, writer, activist, educator, and foreign consul James Weldon Johnson (1871–1938) was an early leader of the NAACP and a strong believer in the need for black unity as the legal fight for civil rights evolved. He composed the black anthem "Lift Every Voice and Sing" in 1900.

Labor and civil rights leader A. Philip Randolph (1889–1979) fought for greater economic opportunity in the black community. A presidential consultant in the 1940s, 1950s, and 1960s and a key organizer of the 1963 "March on Washington," Randolph is perhaps best remembered for his role in establishing the Brotherhood of Sleeping Car Porters, the first black union in the country, in 1925.

Ella Baker (1903–1986), renowned for her organizational and leadership skills, cofounded the Southern Christian Leadership Conference, the Student Nonviolent Coordinating Committee, and the Mississippi Freedom Democratic Party, groups that were at the forefront of the civil rights movement in the United States.

Mississippi native Fannie Lou Hamer (1917–1977) was an impassioned warrior in the fight for black voter rights, black economic advancement, and women's rights.

Rosa Parks (1913–2005) ignited the Montgomery, Alabama, bus boycott in December 1955 when her refusal to give up her seat to a white passenger landed her in jail.

Malcolm X (born Malcolm Little; 1925–1965) advocated a more radical pursuit of equal rights than did Martin Luther King Jr., the champion of nonviolent resistance to racism. A fiery speaker who urged blacks to seize self-determination "by any means necessary," Malcolm X embraced the concept of global unity toward the end of his life and revised his black separatist ideas. In 1965 he was assassinated by members of the Nation of Islam, an organization with which he had severed earlier ties.

Attorney and activist Marian Wright Edelman (1939–) founded the Children's Defense Fund in 1973.

Randall Robinson (1942?–), who served as executive director of the human rights lobbying organization TransAfrica, Inc., played a key role in influencing progressive U.S. foreign policy in South Africa, Somalia, and Haiti.

Sports A second baseman for the Brooklyn Dodgers from 1947 to 1956, Jackie Robinson (1919–1972) is credited with breaking the color barrier in professional baseball.

In 1974 Frank Robinson (1935–), a former National League and American League Most Valuable Player, became the first black manager of a Major League Baseball franchise.

Running back Jim Brown (1936–), a superstar with the Cleveland Browns in the late 1950s and 1960s, helped to change the face of professional football—a sport that for years had been dominated by whites.

The on-court skills and charisma of two of the top National Basketball Association (NBA) players of the 1980s and early 1990s, Los Angeles Lakers forward/guard Earvin "Magic" Johnson (1959–) and Chicago Bulls guard Michael Jordan (1963–), left indelible marks on the game of basketball.

One of the best basketball players ever, Bill Russell (1934–) made further history when he became the first black head coach in NBA history in 1966 with the Boston Celtics.

Track legend Jesse Owens (1913–1980) blasted the notion of Aryan supremacy by winning four gold medals at the 1936 Olympics in Berlin.

Wilma Rudolph (1940–1994) overcame the crippling complications of polio and became the first American woman to win three Olympic gold medals in track and field.

John Carlos (1945–) and Tommie Smith (1944–) won gold and bronze medals, respectively, in the 200-meter dash in the 1968 Olympics. Even more memorably, they gave black power salutes while on the podium during the medal ceremony in protest of racial injustice against blacks in the United States. They were immediately suspended from the U.S. Olympic team, but they now are regarded as heroes.

Olympic boxing gold medalist and longtime heavyweight champion Muhammad Ali (born Cassius Clay; 1942–) remains one of the most widely recognized figures in the sport's history.

Althea Gibson (1927–2003) and Arthur Ashe (1943–1993) both rocked the tennis world with their accomplishments. Gibson, the first black player ever to win at Wimbledon, was a pioneer in the white-dominated game at the dawn of the civil rights era; Ashe, a dedicated activist who fought against racial discrimination in all sports, was the first African American male to triumph at Wimbledon, the U.S. Open, and the Australian Open.

Jackie Joyner-Kersee (1962–), a track and field star and six-time Olympic gold medalist, was voted the greatest female athlete of the twentieth century by *Sports Illustrated* magazine.

Tennis player Serena Williams (1981–) was ranked number one in singles by the Women's Tennis Association several different times and won four Olympic gold medals.

Gymnast Gabrielle "Gabby" Douglas (1995–) won gold medals in both the individual and team all-around competitions in the 2012 Olympics. She was both the first woman of color and the first African American gymnast in Olympic history to become the individual all-around champion.

Stage and Screen Actor Charles Gilpin (1878–1930) is considered to be the dean of early African American theater. In 1921 the former vaudevillian was awarded the NAACP Spingarn Award for his theatrical accomplishments.

Richard B. Harrison (1864–1935) was an esteemed actor who gained national prominence for his portrayal of De Lawd in *Green Pastures*. For three decades, Harrison entertained black audiences with one-man performances of William Shakespeare's *Macbeth* and *Julius Caesar*, as well as with readings of poems by Edgar Allan Poe, Rudyard Kipling, and Paul Laurence Dunbar.

Actor, writer, director, and civil rights activist Ossie Davis (1917–2005) was committed to advancing black pride through his work. He was a groundbreaking figure in American theater, film, and television for over five decades.

Best known for her role as Mammy in *Gone with the Wind* (1939), Hattie McDaniel (1895–1952) won the 1940 Academy Award for Best Supporting Actress. It was the first time an Oscar was awarded to an African American performer.

Actress and writer Anna Deavere Smith (1950–), a bold and intriguing force in American theater, examined issues like racism and justice in original works such as *Fires in the Mirror* (1992) and *Twilight: Los Angeles 1992* (1994).

Actor and dancer Gregory Hines (1946–2003) earned a place among the great African American entertainers. A tap dancer since childhood, Hines acted in numerous plays and movies and received many awards for his efforts. In 1999 Hines starred in his own television sitcom, "The Gregory Hines Show."

Performers such as Bernard Jeffrey McCullough (better known as Bernie Mac, 1957–2008) and Broderick Steven "Steve" Harvey (1957–) put black comedians on the map. Both Mac and Harvey had their own television shows, *The Bernie Mac Show* (2001–2006) and *The Steve Harvey Show* (1996–2002). Harvey's daytime talk show, *Steve Harvey* (2012), was nominated for an Emmy Award in 2013.

Film actress Halle Berry became the first African American woman to win an Academy Award for Best Actress with her performance in *Monster's Ball* (2001).

Visual Arts Sculptor Sargent Johnson (1888–1967), a three-time winner of the prestigious Harmon Foundation medal for outstanding black artist, was heavily influenced by the art forms of Africa.

Romare Bearden (1914–1988) was a highly acclaimed painter, collagist, and photomontagist who depicted the black experience in his work. His images reflect black urban life, music, religion, and the power of the family. A series titled *The Prevalence of Ritual* is among his best-known works.

Jacob Lawrence (1917–2000), a renowned painter, depicted both the history of racial injustice and the promise of racial harmony in America. His works include the *Frederick Douglass* series, the *Harriet Tubman* series, the *Migration of the Negro* series, and *Builders*.

Augusta Savage (1900–1962), a Harlem Renaissance sculptor, was the first black woman to win acceptance in the National Association of Women Painters and Sculptors. *Lift Every Voice and Sing, Black Women*, and *Lenore* are among her notable works.

Multimedia artist and activist Faith Ringgold (1930–) seeks to raise the consciousness of her audience by focusing on themes of racial and gender-based discrimination. Ringgold is known for weaving surrealist elements into her artworks; her storytelling quilt *Tar Beach* inspired a children's book of the same title.

Betye Irene Saar (1926–) is notable for her work in the field of assemblage, in which she transformed stereotyped African American figures from folk culture and advertising into statements of political and social protest.

The work of Kara Walker (1969–) explores race, gender, sexuality, violence and identity. Walker is famous for her room-sized displays of black cut-out paper silhouettes that explore the experience of slavery.

MEDIA

PRINT

African American Review

Founded in 1967 as the *Negro American Literature Forum*, this quarterly publication contains interviews and essays on black American art, literature, and culture.

Nathan L. Grant, Editor
Saint Louis University
Adorjan Hall 317
3800 Lindell Boulevard
St. Louis, Missouri 63108
Phone: (314) 977-3688
Email: ngrant2@slu.edu
URL: http://aar.slu.edu/index.html

New York Amsterdam News

This source was founded in 1909 and is devoted to black community-interest stories.

Elinor Tatum, Editor in Chief
2340 8th Avenue
New York, New York 10027
Phone: (212) 932-7400
Email: amity.paye@amsterdamnews.com
URL: www.amsterdamnews.com

Chicago Daily Defender

Founded in 1905 by Robert S. Abbott as a black weekly newspaper, it is now a daily paper with a black perspective.

Kathy Chaney, Managing Editor
4445 S. MLK Drive.
Chicago, Illinois 60653
Phone: (312) 225-2400
Fax: (312) 225-9231
Email: info@chicagodefender.com
URL: www.chicagodefender.com

Crisis

The official publication of the National Association for the Advancement of Colored People, this monthly magazine, founded in 1910, features articles on civil rights issues.

Jabari Asim, Editor in Chief
4805 Mt. Hope Drive
Baltimore, Maryland 21215
Phone: (410) 580-5137
URL: www.thecrisismagazine.com

Ebony and Jet

Both of these publications are part of the family of Johnson Publications, which was established in the 1940s by entrepreneur John H. Johnson. *Ebony*, a monthly magazine, and *Jet*, a newsweekly, cover African Americans in politics, business, and the arts.

Ebony—

Amy D. Barnett, Editor in Chief

Jet—

Mitzi Miller, Editor in Chief
Johnson Publishing Co., Inc.
820 South Michigan Avenue
Chicago, Illinois 60605
Phone: (312) 322-9200
Fax: (312) 322-1082
URL: www.ebony.com

Essence

First published in 1970, this monthly magazine targets a black female audience.

Constance C. R. White, Editor
Essence Communications, Inc.
135 West 50th Street
4th Floor
New York, New York 10020
Phone: (212) 522-1212
Fax: (212) 921-5173

RADIO

WESL (1490 AM)

Founded in 1934, this station has a gospel format.

Chuck Spearman
8049 Litzsinger Road
St. Louis, Missouri 63144
Phone: (314) 436-7424

Fax: (206) 600-6539
Email: Chuckspearman14@aol.com
URL: www.weslradio.com

WBLS (107.5 FM)

Founded in 1941, WBLS has an urban/contemporary format, playing primarily R&B.

Charles M. Warfield, Jr., President and CEO
395 Hudson Street
7th Floor
New York, New York 10014
Phone: (212) 447-1000
Fax: (212) 447-5211
Email: info@wbls.com
URL: www.wbls.com

TELEVISION

Black Entertainment Television (BET)

The first cable network devoted exclusively to black programming, BET airs news, public affairs, and talk shows, as well as television magazines, sports updates, concerts, videos, and syndicated series.

Debra L. Lee, President and Chief Executive Officer
1235 West Street NE
Washington, D.C. 20018-1211
Phone: (202) 608-2000
URL: www.bet.com

WWJ-TV Channel 62, Detroit

This groundbreaking black-owned television station first went on the air September 29, 1975. It began as an independent network and became a CBS affiliate in 1994.

Kris Kelly, Community Affairs Manager
26905 West 11 Mile Road
Southfield, Michigan 48033
Phone: (248) 355-7000
Email: kgkelly@cbs.com
URL: http://detroit.cbslocal.com

ORGANIZATIONS AND ASSOCIATIONS

Black Filmmaker Foundation (BFF)

This organization was founded in 1978 to support and promote independently produced film and video work for African American artists.

Warrington Hudlin, President
11 West 42nd Street
9th Floor
New York, New York 10036
Phone: (212) 253-1690

NAACP Legal Defense and Educational Fund (LDF)

A nonprofit organization founded in 1940 to fight discrimination and civil rights violations through the nation's court system. (It has been independent of the NAACP since the mid-1950s.)

Debo P. Adegbile, Acting President and Director-Counsel
99 Hudson Street

Suite 1600
New York, New York 10013
Phone: (212) 965-2200
Email: mpotter@naacpldf.org
URL: www.naacpldf.org

National Association for the Advancement of Colored People (NAACP)

Founded in 1910, the NAACP is perhaps the best-known civil rights organization in the United States. Its goals are the elimination of racial prejudice and the achievement of equal rights for all people.

Benjamin Todd Jealous, President and CEO
4805 Mt. Hope Drive
Baltimore, Maryland 21215
Phone: (410) 580-5777
URL: www.naacp.org

National Black United Fund

This group provides financial and technical support to projects that address the needs of black communities throughout the United States.

William T. Merritt, President and CEO
40 Clinton Street
5th Floor
Newark, New Jersey 07102
Phone: (973) 643-5122
Fax: (973) 648-8350
Email: nbuf@nbuf.org
URL: www.nbuf.org

National Urban League

Formed in 1911 in New York by the merger of three committees that sought to protect the rights of the city's black population, the National Urban League is best known for piloting the decades-long fight against racial discrimination in the United States. The National Urban League and its regional branches are also active in the struggle for political and economic advancement among African Americans and impoverished people of all colors.

Marc Morial, CEO & President
120 Wall Street
New York, New York 10005
Phone: (212) 558-5300
Fax: (212) 344-5332
URL: http://nul.iamempowered.com

Southern Christian Leadership Conference (SCLC)

The SCLC is an educational service agency founded in 1957 (with Martin Luther King Jr. as its first president) to aid in the integration of African Americans in all aspects of life in the United States. It continues to foster a philosophy of nonviolent resistance.

Isaac Newton Farris Jr., President
320 Auburn Avenue, N.E.
Atlanta, Georgia 30303
Phone: (800) 421-0472
URL: http://sclcnational.org

MUSEUMS AND RESEARCH CENTERS

Afro-American Historical and Genealogical Society

Founded in 1977, it encourages scholarly research in Afro-American history and genealogy.

Tamela Tenpenny-Lewis, President
P. O. Box 73067
Washington, D.C. 20056-3067
Phone: (202) 234-5350
Email: info@aahgs.org
URL: http://aahgs.org

Association for the Study of Afro-American Life and History (ASALH)

Originally named the Association for the Study of Negro Life and History, this research center was founded by Dr. Carter G. Woodson in 1915. The ASALH is committed to the collection, preservation, and promotion of black history.

Sylvia Cyrus, Executive Director
2225 Georgia Avenue N.W. Suite 331
Washington, D.C. 20059
Phone: (202) 238-5910
Fax: (202) 986-1506
Email: info@asalh.net
URL: http://asalh.net/index.html

Martin Luther King Jr. Center for Nonviolent Social Change

The center was founded in 1969 by Coretta Scott King to uphold the philosophy and work of her husband, the slain civil rights leader.

Dexter Scott King, Chairman and Chief Executive Officer
449 Auburn Avenue N.E.
Atlanta, Georgia 30312
Phone: (404) 526-8900
URL: www.thekingcenter.org

National Museum of African American History and Culture (NMAAHC)

The NMAAHC was designed to be a place where all Americans could learn about the richness and diversity of the African American experience, what it means to their lives, and how it helped us shape the United States.

1400 Constitution Ave. N.W.
Washington, D.C. 20004
Phone: (202) 633-1000
Email: info@si.edu
URL: http://nmaahc.si.edu

Schomburg Center for Research in Black Culture

An arm of the New York Public Library, the Schomburg Center was founded at the height of the Harlem Renaissance by historian Arthur A. Schomburg to preserve the historical past of people of African descent. It is widely regarded as the world's leading repository for materials and artifacts on black cultural life.

Dr. Khalil Gibran Muhammad, Director
515 Malcolm X Boulevard
New York, New York 10037-1801
Phone: (212) 491-2200
URL: www.nypl.org/locations/schomburg

SOURCES FOR ADDITIONAL STUDY

Aptheker, Herbert, ed. *A Documentary History of the Negro People in the United States.* 2 volumes. New York: Citadel Press, 1969.

Asante, Molefi Kete. *The Afrocentric Idea.* Philadelphia: Temple University Press, 1998.

Barnett, Alva, and James L. Conyers, eds. *African American Sociology: A Social Study of the Pan African Diaspora.* Chicago: Nelson-Hall Publishers, 1998.

Bennett Jr., Lerone. *Before the Mayflower: A History of Black America: The Classic Account of the Struggles and Triumphs of Black Americans.* 5th edition. New York: Penguin, 1984.

Berlin, Ira. *Many Thousands Gone: The First Two Centuries of Slavery in North America.* Cambridge, MA: Belknap Press of Harvard University Press, 1998.

———. *Generations of Captivity: A History of African-American Slaves.* Cambridge, MA: Belknap Press of Harvard University Press, 2003.

Dodson, Howard. *Becoming American: The African-American Journey.* New York: Sterling Publishing, 2009.

Franklin, John Hope, with Alfred A. Moss Jr. *From Slavery to Freedom: A History of Negro Americans.* 6th edition. New York: Knopf, 1988.

Gates, Henry Louis Jr., and Cornel West. *The Future of the Race.* New York: Vintage Books, 1997.

Gates, Henry Louis Jr. *The African-American Century: How Black Americans Have Shaped Our Country.* New York: Free Press, 2000.

Harris, Joseph E. *Africans and Their History.* New York: Penguin, 1987.

Lemann, Nicholas. *The Promised Land: The Great Black Migration and How It Changed America.* New York: Knopf, 1991.

Lynd, Staughton. *Class Conflict, Slavery, and the U.S. Constitution.* Westport, CT: Greenwood Press, 1980.

Mannix, Daniel Pratt. *Black Cargoes: A History of the Atlantic Slave Trade, 1518–1865.* New York: Viking, 1962.

Parham, Vanessa Roberts. *The African-American Child's Heritage Cookbook.* Pasadena, CA: Sandcastle Publishing, 1993.

Segal, Ronald. *The Black Diaspora: Five Centuries of the Black Experience Outside Africa.* New York: Farrar, Straus and Giroux, 1995.

Smith, Jessie Carney, and Joseph M. Palmisano, eds. *African American Almanac.* 8th edition. Farmington Hills, MI: Gale Group, 2000.

Smitherman, Geneva. *Talkin & Testifyin: The Language of Black America.* Boston: Houghton Mifflin, 1977.

Trotter, Joe William. *The African American Experience.* Boston: Houghton Mifflin, 2001.

Turner-Sadler, Joanne. *African-American History: An Introduction.* New York: Peter Lang, 2006.

Von Eschen, Penny M. *Race against Empire: Black Americans and Anticolonialism, 1937–1957.* Ithaca, NY: Cornell University Press, 1997.

Woodson, Carter G. *The Negro in Our History.* Washington, D.C.: Associated Publishers, 1962.

ALBANIAN AMERICANS

Jane Jurgens

OVERVIEW

Albanian Americans are immigrants or descendants of people from a small but ethnically distinct corner of the Balkan Peninsula in southeastern Europe. The Republic of Albania is bordered on the west by the Adriatic and Ionian seas, on the north by Montenegro and Kosovo, on the east by Macedonia, and on the south and southeast by Greece. Albania is a mountainous and hilly country located on the Strait of Otranto, which joins the Adriatic and Ionian seas. The country's total land area is 11,100 square miles (28,748 square kilometers), making it slightly larger than the state of Maryland.

According to Albania's 2011 census, the country's population was 2,831,741 (a 7 percent decrease from 2001). Regarding religious practices, 59 percent of citizens declared themselves Muslim, 10 percent Roman Catholic, 7 percent Albanian Orthodox, and 14 percent preferred not to answer. Ethnically and culturally, 83 percent declared themselves Albanian, 14 percent preferred not to answer, and the rest were Greek, Aromanian, Roma, Macedonian, Egyptian, or something other. The country has been undergoing an economic transition from a closed, centrally planned state to an open-market economy, yet it suffers from a low foreign direct investment (FDI) rate and high public debt. One of the poorest European countries, Albania relies on remittances from Albanian migrants in other countries (particularly Italy and Greece) as well as a large number of small family and subsistence farms.

Albanians first came to the United States in the late 1800s and early 1900s, settling around the Boston area and other parts of New England to work in factories, mills, and hotels. While some of these Albanians remained permanently in the United States, many moved from the United States back to southeastern Europe as Albania gained independence and underwent experiments in national sovereignty. Beginning in the 1970s significant numbers of Albanians began to migrate to the United States as Albania endured a communist government, economic transitions, and political turmoil. The Albanian American population increased as many Albanians immigrated to the United States in search of employment opportunities that were unavailable in their home country.

According to the U.S. Census Bureau's American Community Survey estimates for 2009–2011, the number of people of Albanian descent in the United States was 185,623. Originally, the majority of Albanian Americans lived in Massachusetts with smaller groups located along the Atlantic coast and in Chicago. Due to the wave of immigration resulting from the political and ethnic violence of the Kosovo War in 1999, Albanian American settlements can now also be found in Michigan, Florida, Texas, Ohio, Louisiana, and California.

HISTORY OF THE PEOPLE

Early History Albanians live in territories that were inhabited by the ancient Illyrians. Conquered by the Romans in the third century CE, they were later incorporated into the Byzantine Empire (395 CE) and were subjected to foreign invasions by Goths, Huns, Avars, Serbs, Croats, and Bulgarians. In 1468 Albania became part of the Ottoman Empire despite strong resistance by Gjergj Kastrioti Skenderbeu (the two most prevalent transliterations of this name are George Castrioti Scanderbeg and George Kastrioti Skanderbeg; 1405–1468), who is a figure of historical reverence for leading Albania's fight against foreign subjugation. At the beginning of the nineteenth century, that fight for independence intensified under the leadership of Naim Frasheri (1846–1900), Sami Frasheri (1850–1904), and Andon Zako Cajupi (1866–1930). This era was marked by an escalating sense of Albanian nationalism.

Two years before the onset of World War I, in 1912, Albania declared its independence from the Ottoman Empire. After a short period as a protectorate of the European Great Powers, Albania received full independence in 1920, first as a republic and then as a monarchy under King Zog I (1895–1961) from 1928 to 1939. In World War II, Italy invaded and occupied Albania. By 1944 a communist regime led by Enver Hoxha (1908–1985) had risen to power.

Modern Era The Albanian communist model was a particularly strict exemplar of the single-party revolutionary socialist state. Hoxha ruled with a firm grip, repressing individual rights, outlawing religious organizations, and closing the country's borders. Under Hoxha, Albania also pursued a draconian

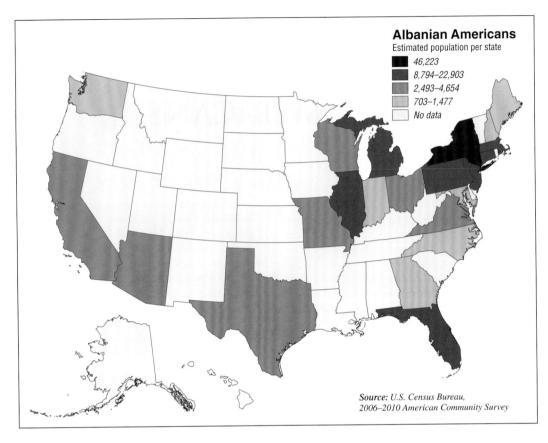

Albanian Americans
Estimated population per state

- 46,223
- 8,794–22,903
- 2,493–4,654
- 703–1,477
- No data

*Source: U.S. Census Bureau,
2006–2010 American Community Survey*

isolationist foreign policy. Travel outside the borders was extremely restricted, and its foreign allies were few. Among them was neighboring Yugoslavia, with which Hoxha broke off relations after claims of Yugoslavia's intent to annex. Albania then looked toward the Soviet Union for military support and trade, but Hoxha cut those ties in the 1960s, turning instead to China. That, too, ended over ideological differences. When Hoxha's regime abolished all religious organizations in the late 1960s, small numbers of Albanian Orthodox and Muslim clerics and adherents managed to defect and seek political asylum in the United States on grounds of religious persecution. Other dissident and anticommunist Albanians often fled to neighboring countries, including Greece and Yugoslavia. The Socialist Republic of Serbia, which was part of Yugoslavia from 1946 to 1990, included the Autonomous Province of Kosovo on the border with Albania and was inhabited largely by ethnic Albanians. Kosovo received the largest number of Albanian refugees fleeing Hoxha's regime.

In Albania industrialization and state-guided economic development remained sluggish throughout the 1960s and 1970s. Furthermore, religious and political activists faced severe suppression, especially in the 1980s. The collapse of Communist Eastern Europe in 1989 sparked rapid transformations across the Balkan Peninsula, especially in Yugoslavia, which splintered

into independent republics. One of the newly created entities was the Republic of Serbia. Inside Serbia's Kosovo region, ethnic tensions between Serbs and Kosovar Albanians escalated in the 1990s.

Hoxha died in 1985; his handpicked successor was Ramiz Alia, who became head of the country's communist party (the Albanian Labor Party, or PLA) and head of state. Albania was the last totalitarian communist nation in Europe to adopt a democratic system, spurred by University of Tirana student demonstrations in late 1990 that forced the ruling PLA to introduce some first steps of liberalization, including freedom to travel abroad and, later, to form new political parties. The Democratic Party of Albania (PD) was created as an opposition party to the PLA, which changed its name to the Socialist Party of Albania.

Albania's first multiparty elections were held in March 1991, and several reforms were enacted that same year, including the resumption of formal diplomatic ties with the United States. Alia was elected president of Albania by the newly seated Assembly of the Republic of Albania. In a symbolic act to dismantle one of the worst police states in Europe, Alia announced the dissolution of the dreaded Sigurimi, the Albanian secret police, a few months after taking office. That and other reforms failed to quell internal unrest, demonstrations, and general strikes. Alia resigned in April 1992 after new elections in which the PD won by a solid majority.

Sali Berisha of the PD became Albania's first democratically elected president in 1992. He held that office for the next five years, but the new democracy slid further into political instability. In 1997 Albania was rocked by major unrest after revelations that the investment programs the government had tacitly endorsed were little more than Ponzi-type pyramid schemes. Thus, one of Europe's poorest nations became even more impoverished, as Albanians lost what little savings they had invested in the pyramid investment funds. Unemployment figures remained high during these years, and immigration to countries in Europe and to the United States continued apace.

Albanian voters approved a new constitution in 1998 that was aimed at stabilizing the nation. The country's economic woes continued to escalate, however, with the Kosovo War and North Atlantic Treaty Organization (NATO) air strikes that began in 1999; those events prompted a half-million ethnic Albanians in Kosovo to cross the border into Albania seeking refuge. The newly implemented constitution did bring more stability to the country in the twenty-first century. Berisha's PD and the socialists jockeyed for power, and the former president became prime minister following the PD's win in the 2005 general election. The PD repeated that success in 2009, and that same year Albania became a member of NATO. Albania also submitted its formal application to become a candidate for entry into the European Union (EU) in 2009.

Nevertheless, Albania still struggles to emerge as a safe, even modestly prosperous nation guided by rule-of-law principles. Government corruption, a substandard infrastructure, organized crime, and blood feuds still trouble the country. More than a million Albanians have emigrated since 1989.

SETTLEMENT IN THE UNITED STATES

Few Albanians came to the United States before the twentieth century. The first Albanian, whose name is lost, is reported to have arrived in the United States in 1876 but soon relocated to Argentina. Kolë Kristofori (Nicholas Christopher), from the southern town of Katundi, was the first recorded Albanian to arrive in the United States, probably between 1884 and 1886. He returned to Albania and came back to the United States in 1892. In *The Albanians in America*, Constantine Demo records the names of sixteen other Albanians who either came with Kristofori or arrived soon after. They also emigrated from Katundi.

Albanians are the most recent group of Europeans to immigrate to the United States, and their numbers remained small until the 1990s. Prior to World War I, they came to the United States because of poor economic conditions, political concerns, or

A newly-arrived Albanian woman is photographed at Emigration Hall on Ellis Island, New York, 1905. AKG-IMAGES / NEWSCOM

to escape military conscription in the Turkish army. Neighboring Greece invaded southern Albania in 1913, and longstanding enmity between the two nationalities prompted another wave of migration. Many of these Albanians (between 20,000 and 30,000) who had fled Albania for political reasons returned to their homeland between 1919 and 1925. New immigration quotas enacted by the United States in the 1920s severely restricted the number of people from southern Europe who were permitted to enter the United States annually. Some Albanians were able to settle in the United States after Albania came under communist control in 1944; among this group were immigrants who had first sojourned in neighboring countries such as Yugoslavia, Greece, and Italy. After the collapse of communism in 1990, Albanians began entering the United States in increasing numbers.

During Enver Hoxha's long reign, Albania pursued a draconian, isolationist foreign policy. Travel outside the borders was extremely restricted, and its allies were few. The most strident opponents to Hoxha's regime who survived and managed to leave took up residence in Greece, the Autonomous Province of Kosovo, or the Republic of Macedonia, another border state that also belonged to the Yugoslavian federation. Kosovar Albanians also faced intense discrimination in Serbia. One factor that spurred immigration to the United States by this group was the establishment of a university in Pristina, Kosovo's main city, in the early 1970s. That created a subset of educated Kosovar Albanians who were unable to find work in Serbia due to a hiring bias for Serb nationals. Some of them began to leave Yugoslavia when that country's political chaos amplified in the 1980s, and they settled in major U.S. cities such as New York, Detroit, Michigan, and Chicago. Though college-educated, many were forced to accept entry-level jobs in the manual trades or the retail sector.

The wave of Albanians who left their impoverished country once travel restrictions were lifted in the early 1990s accounted for one of the largest population shifts in post–World War II Europe. An estimated 800,000 Albanians moved abroad between 1990 and 2000, according to Kosta Barjaba and Russell King in the book *The New Albanian Migration*. Their research indicates that by the first years of the twenty-first century, approximately one out of every five Albanians was living outside of the country's borders. A large number migrated as laborers in search of construction or agricultural work in neighboring lands such as Greece, Italy, and Serbia. The educated elite—those with college degrees and professional credentials from the main cities of Tirana, Durres, and Elbasan—chose the United States and various countries in the European Union as their destinations.

One of the most dramatic episodes in the history of Albanian immigration came in 1999 during the Kosovo War. Thousands of ethnic Albanians fled Kosovo when the conflict with Serbian military units began, and that number increased when NATO airstrikes were launched. They went to refugee camps set up by the United Nations in Macedonia, and 20,000 of them were granted permission to immediately enter the United States under a special immigration classification as refugees of war. First Lady Hillary Clinton welcomed the first planeload of Kosovar Albanians to arrive at McGuire Air Force Base at Fort Dix, New Jersey. She spoke to them under a banner that read *Mirsevini ne Amerike*, or "Welcome to America." Only some of those granted entry as war refugees had relatives in the United States; those without family ties were resettled by refugee agencies and humanitarian aid organizations that had ties to the larger Albanian American community.

Newer immigrants from Albania, who arrived after the fall of communism, are either professionals such as engineers or teachers or have found work in the construction trades or in food service. In cities such as New York, Boston, Chicago, and Detroit, the pizza monopoly once held by Italian American entrepreneurs has gradually been taken over by Albanian Americans.

Early Albanian immigrants settled around Boston and then moved to other parts of Massachusetts, where unskilled factory and textile-mill jobs were plentiful. Prior to 1920, the majority of Albanians who came to the United States originated from southern Albania.

Most were young males who either migrated for economic gain or were seeking political asylum and did not intend to remain permanently in the United States. They stayed in community barracks called *konaks*, where they could live cheaply and send money home. The *konak* gradually gave way to more permanent family dwellings as growing numbers of women and children joined Albanian men in the United States. Early Massachusetts settlements were established in Worcester, Natick, Southbridge, Cambridge, and Lowell.

As Bernd J. Fischer writes in the *Journal of Ethnic and Migration Studies*, "Determining with any certainty the number of Albanians in the US at any given time has always been an inexact science. … There are, nevertheless, educated estimates and it is assumed that by the late 1930s there were between 35,000 and 60,000 Albanians in the United States, most of them Orthodox Christians in New England. Following the Second World War there were somewhat fewer than 200,000, a number that, according to the *Albanian Catholic Bulletin*, increased to about 250,000 by the 1980s. The 1990s witnessed a rapid increase to approximately 400,000 by 1998." Fischer's article cites a rise in illegal immigration to the United States by Albanians but also the success of some who were able to enter legally through family sponsors or via the so-called green-card lottery, in which residents of nations underrepresented in the United States can apply for an entry visa. The annual event is more formally known as the Diversity Visa Lottery Program.

The Census Bureau's 2009–2011 American Community Survey 3-Year Estimates indicated that there were 185,623 people of Albanian descent living in the United States, with the highest numbers in New York state (50,253) and Michigan (25,356). Massachusetts, New Jersey, Texas, and Connecticut have noteworthy but much smaller Albanian populations, and there are also clusters of Albanians in states such as Illinois (Chicago), California (Los Angeles), Ohio (Cleveland), Pennsylvania (Philadelphia and Pittsburgh), Louisiana (New Orleans), and Florida (Miami).

LANGUAGE

Albanian is probably part of the Illyrian branch of eastern Indo-European languages. It is a descendant of Dacian, one of the ancient languages that were among the Thraco Phrygian group once spoken in Anatolia and the Balkan Peninsula. Its closest modern relative is Armenian. Today, Albanian is spoken in two major dialects (with many subdialects) in Albania and in the adjacent territories in Montenegro, Kosovo, Macedonia, and Greece—*Tosk* south of the river Shkumbini and *Gheg* in the north of the river. A third dialect (*Arberesh*) is spoken in southern Greece and southern Italy. Throughout the centuries, Albanians have been in contact with numerous civilizations, all of which have left their influence on the language. Despite outside influence, a distinct Albanian language has survived. Albanians call their language *shqip*.

Until the early twentieth century, Albanians used the Greek, Latin, and Turko-Arabic alphabets and mixtures of these alphabets. In 1908 the Congress of Manastir adopted a standard Latin alphabet of twenty-six letters, and it was made official in 1924. During the 1920s and 1930s, the government tried to establish a mixed *Tosk* and *Gheg* dialect from the Elbasan region as the official language. A standardized Albanian language, which is a mixture of *Gheg* and *Tosk* but with a prevailing *Tosk* element, was adopted in 1952. In addition to the letters of the Latin alphabet, the Albanian language adds: *ç, dh, ë, gj, ll, nj, rr, sh, th, xh,* and *zh*. Albanian is taught at such universities as the University of California–San Diego, University of Chicago, Arizona State University, and the Ohio State University. Libraries with Albanian-language collections include the Library of Congress, Chicago Public Library, Boston Public Library, New York Public Library (Donnell Library Center), and Queens Borough Public Library.

First and second generation Albanian Americans retain strong ties to their language of origin. The U.S. Census Bureau's American Community Survey reported in 2011 that an estimated 72 percent of Albanian Americans said that they spoke a language other than English at home, while 28 percent described themselves as speaking only English at home, and 34 percent reported they spoke English less than "very well."

Many ethnic Albanians who came to the United States after living in Kosovo, Macedonia, Greece, or Italy are moderately fluent in both the Albanian language and either Serbian, Greek, or Italian.

Greetings and Popular Expressions Some common expressions in the Albanian language include the following: *Po* (Yes); *Jo* (No); *Falemnderit* (Thank you); *Po, ju lutem* (Yes, please); *Mirëdita* (Hello or Good day); *Mirëmëngjes* (Good Morning); *Si jeni?* (How are you?); *Gëzohem t'ju njoh* (Pleased to meet you); *Mirëmbrëma* (Good evening); *Natën e mirë* (Good night); *Mirupafshim* (Goodbye); *Më fal / Më falni* (Excuse me); *Në rregull* (All right, or, Okay); *S'ka përse* (Don't mention it); *Shqiptarë* (Albanians).

RELIGION

Albanians in the United States are primarily Orthodox Christians, Roman Catholics, or Muslims. Currently, the Albanian Orthodox Church in the United States is divided into two ecclesiastical jurisdictions. The Albanian Orthodox Archdiocese in America (OCA) is an autocephalous church established in 1908 by Fan S. Noli, a major religious and political figure in the Albanian community. The current primate is Archbishop Nikon (born Nicholas Liolin). The headquarters of the Archdiocese, St. George Albanian

The Chying Madonna at St. Nikolas Albanian Church in Chicago, Illinois. SANTI VISALLI / GETTY IMAGES

Orthodox Cathedral, is located in South Boston. One of the oldest chapters of the St. George Cathedral was organized in Worcester, Massachusetts, in 1911. This chapter became the Church of Saint Mary's Assumption in 1915. The Albanian Orthodox Diocese of America, established in 1950 by Bishop Mark Lipa, is under the jurisdiction of the ecumenical Patriarch of Constantinople.

Most Albanian Roman Catholics came to the United States in the 1960s and 1970s mainly from territories located in today's Montenegro. Albanian Roman Catholic churches in the United States include Our Lady of Shkodra, founded in the New York City borough of the Bronx in 1969 but later relocated to Hartsdale, New York; St. Paul's Albanian Catholic Church in Rochester Hills, Michigan; and Our Lady of Albanians in Southfield, Michigan. An Italo Albanian Catholic Church, which belongs to the Eastern Byzantine rite, is also active in the United States, with a membership of more than 60,000 as of 2005.

Albanian Muslims first came to the United States around 1913. There are Albanian Islamic community centers in the New York City area, Philadelphia, Chicago, and Berkeley, California, among other places. One of the oldest Albanian mosques in the United States is the Albanian Islamic Center in Harper Woods, Michigan, which dates to the late 1940s. It hosts religious services in Albanian, Arabic, and English. A small sect of Muslims of the Bektashi Order, the First Albanian Teke Bektashiane in America, is located in Taylor, Michigan, and was founded in the United States in 1954. This sect has a small library and publishes *The Voice of Bektashism*.

In 1999 U.S. immigration officials worked with existing religious-based charities that served the Albanian immigrant community to help resettle nearly 20,000 Kosovar Albanian refugees of war who began arriving in the United States in the spring of that year. These war refugees were predominantly Muslim but were aided by groups affiliated with the Albanian Orthodox Archdiocese in America and Albanian Roman Catholic churches. Albanian Islamic Centers also provided assistance.

CULTURE AND ASSIMILATION

Fiercely proud of their unique culture and customs, Albanians have tended to resist assimilation into mainstream American life in many aspects. They have, however, thoroughly embraced what their new country has to offer. Generally, they have preserved their language and social customs while seizing opportunities for economic and educational advancement.

Traditions and Customs The Kanun (*Kanuni i Lekë Dukagjinit*) is an ancient set of civil, criminal, and family laws that still exerts influence on the lives of many Albanian Americans. The Kanun is traditionally ascribed to Leke Dukagjini (1460–1481), a compatriot and contemporary of Skanderberg. It sets forth rights and obligations regarding the church, family, and marriage. The code is based on the concepts of honor (*besa*) and blood; the individual is obligated to guard the honor of family, clan, and tribe. The rights and obligations surrounding the concept of honor have often led to the blood feud (*gjak*), which frequently lasts for generations. At the time of King Zog I's rule in the 1920s, the blood feud accounted for one out four male deaths in Albania. Enver Hoxha, Albania's communist leader after 1944, was committed to eradicating the blood feud. This code was translated into English and published in a bilingual text in 1989 in the United States.

The Kanun defines the family as a "group of human beings who live under the same roof, whose aim is to increase their number by means of marriage for their establishment and the evolution of their state and for the development of their reason and intellect." The traditional Albanian household is a patriarchy in which the head of the household is the eldest male. The principal roles of the wife are to maintain the household and raise the children. The children have a duty to honor their parents and respect their wishes.

In the late 1980s, following an influx of Albanian immigrants into the United States, *gjak* killings increased in communities such as the Pelham Parkway area of the Bronx, Boston, and Detroit. In 1990 a professor of Albanian studies at the University of Prishtina, Anton Cetta, came to the United States to implement his Commission for the Forgiveness of Blood, a reconciliation program that had achieved a notable degree of success in abolishing the practice of *gjak* killings in Kosovo.

Cuisine Albanian dishes have much in common with the foods of their neighbors. As in all Balkan countries, Albanian cuisine is influenced by what is considered today to be Turkish cuisine. Recipes have often been adapted and altered to suit American tastes. Albanians enjoy a variety of appetizers, soups, casseroles, pilaf, pies, stews, and desserts. Salads (*sallatë*) are made with tomatoes, cucumbers, lettuce, onions, peppers, olives, and feta cheese. *Sallatë me patate* is a potato salad. Soups contain a variety of ingredients, such as beans, chicken, lentils, and fish. *Paçe*, a soup made with lamb's tripe, is served at Easter. Albanian pies, *lakror* or *byrek*, are cooked with a variety of *gjellë* (filling); these fillings may be lamb, beef, leeks, onions, squash, or spinach, combined with milk, eggs, and olive oil. A *lakror* known as *brushtul lakror* is prepared with a cottage and feta cheese filling, butter, and eggs. *Domate me qepë* is a *lakror* with an onion and tomato filling.

Stews contain beef, rabbit, lamb, veal, and chicken, which are combined with cabbage, spinach, green beans, okra, or lentils. Favorites include *mish me patate* (lamb with potatoes), *çomlek* (beef with onions), and *çomlek me lepur* (rabbit stew). A popular dish among Albanian Italians living in Sicily is called *albanesi-siciliano* (olives and beef), which features brown, salted beef cubes in a sauce of tomatoes, parsley, garlic, olives, and olive oil and is served with *taccozzelli* (rectangles of pasta and goat cheese). *Dollma* is a term applied to a variety of stuffed dishes that consist of cabbage, green peppers, or vine leaves and may be filled with rice, bread, onions, and garlic. An Albanian American variation of the traditionally Greek lasagna-like dish, *moussaka*, is made with potatoes and hamburger instead of eggplant.

Albanian cuisine features a variety of candies, cookies, custards, sweet breads, and preserves, including *halva*, a confection made with sugar, flour, butter, maple syrup, water, oil, and nuts; *te matur*, a pastry filled with butter and syrup; *baklava*, a filo pastry with nuts, sugar, and cinnamon; *kadaif*, a pastry prepared with shredded dough, butter, and walnuts; and *llokume*, a Turkish paste. Popular cookies include *kurabie*, a butter cookie made without liquid; *finiqe*, a filled cookie with many variations; and *kulluraqka* or *kullure*, Albanian "tea cookies." *Të dredhura*, *bukëvale*, and *brustull* are hot sweet breads. In some local traditions, family members announce the birth of a child by cooking and distributing *petulla*, pieces of fried dough sprinkled with sugar or dipped in syrup. Albanians enjoy Turkish coffee or Albanian coffee (*kafe*), Albanian whiskey (*raki*), and wine. *Kos*, the Albanian word for yogurt, is also popular.

Albanians in the United States cook traditional dishes in their homes, as daily fare and for special occasions. Boston, and Detroit, and the Bronx in New York house many restaurants featuring Albanian cuisine. In some cases, these are humble eateries or diners centering on Mediterranean fare and offering select Albanian items.

Traditional Dress Traditional Albanian costumes share some traits with Turkish, Greek, and Slavic designs and vary depending on the region. Malësia e Madhe (a region in northern Albania and southern Montenegro), for example, is known for attire that includes close-fitting woolen trousers with black cord trim, an apron of wool with a leather belt buckled over it, and a silk jacket with long dull red sleeves with white stripes. A long sleeveless coat may be worn over the jacket along with an outer, short-sleeved jacket (*dzurdin*), and the head and neck may be covered with a white cloth. A style of male dress from southern Albania and northern Greece most often seen in the United States is the *fustanella*, a full, white pleated skirt; a black and gold jacket; a red fez with a large tassel (*puskel*); and shoes with black pompoms.

Women's clothing tends to be more colorful than that of men. Northern Albanian costumes are more ornamental and include a distinctive metal belt. Basic types of costume include a wide skirt (*xhublete*), long shirt or blouse (*krahol*), and a short woolen jacket (*xhoke*). The traditional costume of Muslim women may include a tightly pleated skirt (*kanac*) or large woolen trousers (*brekeshe*). Aprons are a pervasive feature in every type of women's costume, and there is great variety in the shape and embroidery. Albanian Americans often wear traditional costumes during independence day celebrations and other special occasions and social events.

Dances and Songs Although the musical tradition in Albania has many traits in common with neighboring countries such as Greece, much of it remains distinct. Albania has a rich heritage of musical and theatrical activities. In 1915 Albanian Americans organized the Boston Mandolin Club and the Albanian String Orchestra. They also formed amateur groups to perform plays by Albanian authors. Because a heroic sense of life has always been part of Albanian lore, ballads are often recited and sung in an epic-recitative form that celebrates fantastic heroes of the past and present. Songs may be accompanied by traditional instruments such as the *çifteli*, a two-stringed lute instrument, and the *lahuta*, a one-stringed violin.

Holidays Since Albanian Americans practice Roman Catholic, Orthodox, or Islamic faiths, they observe many religious festivals and holy days. November 28 is celebrated as Albanian Independence Day, when Albanians declared their independence from the Ottoman Empire in 1912. Since 2008 Kosovar Albanians have celebrated Kosovo Independence Day each February 17, which marks the Republic of Kosovo's declaration of independence from Serbia a decade after the Kosovo War began.

ALBANIAN PROVERBS

Besa e shqiptarit nuk shitet pazarit.

Honor cannot be sold in the bazaar.

Gjuha vete ku dhemb dhëmballa.

The tongue follows the toothache.

Dardha bije nga dardha.

The pear falls under the pear tree.

Mos i qa hallin kalorsit, se e varen këmbët.

Do not worry about how the horseman's legs come down.

Qingji i urtë pi në dy nëna.

The calm lamb drinks from two mothers.

Kush ka turp, vdes për bukë.

He who is shy dies from hunger.

FAMILY AND COMMUNITY LIFE

Albanian Americans tend to follow the nuclear-family model of their homeland, paired with strong kinship ties. The father or eldest male is considered the head of the household. Some shifts have occurred, however, with the dramatic influx of Albanians in the 1980s and 1990s.

Gender Roles The centuries-old Kanun (*Kanuni i Lekë Dukagjinit*) still exerts influence on the lives of many Albanian Americans. The strict patriarchal code enshrined in this text promotes a traditional Albanian family unit in which the head of the household is the eldest male. The wife's duties involve tending to the house and raising the children, who must strictly obey their parents. In Albanian American families, daughters generally remain at home with their parents until they marry.

Some Albanians who came of age during the communist era (1944 to 1991) felt less bound by the older traditions that required women to remain inside the home. Despite the human-rights abuses of the Hoxha regime, Albanian women enjoyed greater access to education and employment during this period. Those who left Albania in the 1980s and 1990s took with them expectations that they would fully participate in the social and economic life in their communities. Thus, Albanian American women began to organize. The *Motrat Qirijazi* (Sisters Qirjazi), the first Albanian American women's organization, was founded on March 27, 1993, in New York City, principally by Shqipe Baba. This organization serves all Albanian women in the United States, assisting and supporting them in the pursuit of unity, education, and advancement.

Some insights into the world of Albanian American women can be gleaned from estimates of the

American Community Survey, published by the U.S. Census Bureau. Of the estimated 56,326 Albanian American households in 2011, 67 percent were married-couple units and just 8 percent were female-headed households with no husband but other family members present. Over 39 percent of married couples had children under the age of eighteen, and the average family size was 3.91 persons. Among Albanians over the age of fifteen living in the United States, 62 percent were married. Fewer than 5 percent listed themselves as divorced, and 27 percent reported they had never been married. Albanian American women were slightly more likely to have attained a bachelor's degree or higher education than their male counterparts (30.6 percent of women compared to 24.9 percent of men).

Aida Orgocka, an academic specializing in economic development and immigration, published "Albanian High Skilled Migrant Women in the U.S.: The Ignored Experience" in 2005 in *The New Albanian Migration*, a volume edited by Russell King, Nicola Mai, and Stephanie Schwandner-Sievers. The women Orgocka interviewed, who had come to the United States from Albania on their own, faced discrimination in their own immigrant community. A twenty-nine-year-old woman told Orgocka that she had assisted one fellow immigrant and his family with housing and employment, but when she attained a professional position in her field, she was openly derided. "One day, I was going past a hall and there were some Albanian men chatting," she said. "As soon as they saw me, one of them said, 'Look, here comes the tramp who has lovers who find her a job.'" The woman told Orgocka this was the same person she had helped. "I do not think Albanian men have reached the point of looking at a woman as someone who can achieve something better than them," she added.

Education Most of the early Albanians who immigrated to the United States were illiterate. According to Dennis L. Nagi in *The Albanian-American Odyssey*, it was estimated that of the 5,000 Albanians in the United States in 1906, only 20 of them could read or write their own language. Due to the strong efforts of community leaders to make books, pamphlets, and other educational materials (especially the newspaper *Kombi*) available in the *konaks*, the rate of illiteracy declined significantly. By 1919, 15,000 of the 40,000 Albanian immigrants could read and write their own language. Albanians were initially suspicious of American ways of life and were often reluctant to send their children to U.S. schools. Gradually, however, they accepted that an education would provide them with the foundation for a more prosperous future in the United States.

More recent groups of Albanians—those who arrived after World War II, especially the Kosovo War refugees—have, by contrast, fully embraced new identities and have utilized access to public education. The 2011 American Community Survey 1-Year Estimate by the U.S. Census Bureau indicated that 81 percent of Albanian Americans age twenty-five and older had graduated from high school (compared with 86 percent for the U.S. population in general).

Courtship and Weddings Albanian weddings were once arranged by parents or by an intermediary matchmaker. An engagement ceremony was held between the two families, and the bride was given a gold coin as a token of the engagement. In Albania a dowry is part of the tradition, but in the United States, this has been adapted to take the form of gifts of appliances or furniture for the newlyweds. Weddings were once week-long events in Albania but have been shortened to two- or three-day parties in the United States. Whether conducted in the Orthodox Christian, Roman Catholic, or Muslim faith, an Albanian American wedding is often an elaborate affair designed to showcase the spousal couple's family standing.

EMPLOYMENT AND ECONOMIC CONDITIONS

The Albanians who came to the United States prior to 1920 were from rural backgrounds and labored as farmers, while immigrants from urban areas worked as small shopkeepers and tradesmen. The large population of Albanians that settled in Massachusetts found work mainly with the American Optical Company of Southbridge and the textile mills of New Bedford; other immigrants worked as cooks, waiters, and bellhops. Albanians soon began opening their own businesses. The most successful of these were fruit stores and restaurants. "By 1925 … most Albanians of Greater Boston could claim ownership of over three hundred grocery and fruit stores," writes Dennis Lazar Nagi in his dissertation *Ethnic Continuity as It Applies to a Less Visible National Group: The Albanian Community of Boston, Massachusetts* (1982). Today Albanians are employed in a variety of professional and enterprises. The Ghegs and Kosovars have been especially successful in the Bronx in New York City, selling and managing real estate in the Pelham Parkway and Belmont sections of the borough.

Newer immigrants from Albania, who arrived after the fall of communism, have tended to be professionals such as engineers or teachers or have found work in the construction trades or in food service. In cities such as New York, Boston, Chicago, and Detroit, the pizza monopoly once held by Italian American entrepreneurs has gradually been taken over by Albanian Americans.

POLITICS AND GOVERNMENT

Albanian Americans have always felt a strong attachment to their native country and have supported events that occur there. Both the Orthodox Church and the Albanian press have played important roles in the awakening of Albanian nationalism in the United States. The early political efforts of Albanian Americans centered on furthering the cause of Albania's independence from the Ottoman Empire by instilling a sense of pride in Albanian heritage. Early figures in the nationalist movement were Petro Nini Luarasi, who founded the first Albanian national organization

ALBANIAN BIRTHS AND BIRTHDAYS

According to some traditions in Albania, the person who tells friends and relatives that a child has been born receives a *siharik* (tip). Within three days after the birth, the family makes *petulla* (fried dough or fritters) and distributes the food to friends and other family members. A hot sweet bread (*buevale*) may also be prepared for guests who visit the mother and child. A celebration is usually held on the third day, and friends and relatives bring *petulla* and other gifts. In the Orthodox Church, this celebration may be delayed until the child is baptized. Traditionally for Albanians of the Orthodox faith, the *kumbare* and *ndrikull* (godparents) choose the name of the child to be baptized. Albanian Americans practice these traditions, too.

Many superstitions surround the birth of an Albanian child, some of which still exist among older Albanian Americans. Infants are especially vulnerable to the "evil eye" (a malevolent glance), and many Albanian mothers place a *kuleta* (amulet) on a newborn child as protection. For Christians, the *kuleta* may be a small cross; among Muslims, it may be a small triangular silver form (*hajmali*). Garlic also wards off evil. A person who touches an Albanian child or offers the child a compliment is required to say "*Mashalla*" ("As God wishes") so as not to be struck by the misfortune of the evil eye.

Among some Orthodox Christians, birthdays are not traditionally observed. Instead, the family observes a "name's day" for the saint after whom the person is named. Family and friends may gather together and wish the person a "happy nameday" and "good health and long life." The family may serve guests fruit preserves (*liko*), pastries (*të ëmbla*), Albanian whiskey (*raki*), and coffee (*kafe*). Guests are formally served in the reception room (*ode*) or the living room (*vater*) and are treated with great courtesy. Albanian Americans practice many of these traditions in the United States.

in the United States, the *Malli i Mëmëdheut* ("Longing for the Homeland"), and Sotir Petsi, who founded *Kombi*, the first-known Albanian weekly newspaper. *Kombi* actively supported an independent Albania within the Ottoman Empire, and the circulation of this early newspaper was instrumental in reducing the rate of illiteracy among Albanians in the United States. Fan S. Noli was one of the most influential figures in the Albanian nationalist movement in the United States. On January 6, 1907, he founded *Besa-Besën* ("Loyalty"), the first Albanian nationalist organization in the United States. The founding of the Albanian Orthodox Church in America in 1908 was also significant, because it gave Albanian Americans a crucial way to organize themselves, preserve their customs, and, most significantly, raise funds and awareness for the Albanian independence movement. To further Albania's freedom, Noli began publishing *Dielli* ("The Sun") in 1909. A successor of *Kombi*, *Dielli* supported liberation for Albania. Faik Konitza became the first editor of *Dielli*. To further strengthen the cause, a merger of many existing Albanian organizations into the Pan-Albanian Federation of America (*Vatra*) occurred in April 1912. *Vatra* became the principal organization to instill Albanians with a sense of national purpose.

Noli was among those who returned to Albania after World War I. These activists were hopeful that international cooperation would permit Albanians to form their own government, as vanquished parts of the Ottoman and Austro-Hungarian empires had been allowed to do in southern and eastern Europe. Noli eventually returned to the United States, and he died in Fort Lauderdale, Florida, in 1965.

The established Albanian American community played a decisive role in securing U.S. support for the Kosovo independence movement in the late 1990s. Joseph DioGuardi—a Republican from New York state and, in 1984, the first Albanian American elected to Congress—set up the Albanian American Civic League in 1989 to lobby against Serbian leader Slobodan Milosevic's discriminatory policies toward ethnic Albanians in Kosovo. Albanians in the United States and elsewhere contributed generously to fundraising efforts for both Washington lobbying and aid to the *Ushtria Çlirimtare e Kosovës*, or Kosovo Liberation Army.

In 2012 New York state's 80th Assembly District, centered in the heavily Albanian section of the Bronx around Pelham Parkway and Arthur Avenue, elected an Albanian American, Democrat Mark Gjonaj. His parents, immigrants from Montenegro, had settled in the Bronx after coming to the United States, and after graduating from St. John's University in the New York borough of Queens, Gjonaj founded a real estate company.

NOTABLE INDIVIDUALS

Academia Arshi Pipa (1920–1997), born in Scutari, Albania, taught humanities, philosophy, and Italian at various colleges and universities in Albania and in the United States.

Nicholas Pano (1934–), a professor of history, has served as the dean of arts and sciences at Western Illinois University. He made contributions to scholarly journals on the subject of Albania and authored the book *The People's Republic of Albania* (1968).

Peter R. Prifti (1924–2001), an author and translator, made significant contributions to Albanian studies and published widely on a variety of Albanian topics. His works include the books *Confrontation in Kosovo* (1999) and *Unfinished Portrait of a Country* (2005).

Stavro Skendi (1906–1989), born in Korce, Albania, was a professor of Balkan languages and culture at Columbia University from 1972 until his death.

Activism Constantine A. Chekrezi (1892–1959), an early supporter of the nationalist movement in Albania, served as editor of *Dielli* in 1914

and published *Illyria* from March to November 1916. He authored *Albania Past and Present* (1919), which is considered to be the first work in English on Albania written by an Albanian; *A History of Europe—Ancient, Medieval and Modern* (1921); an early history of Europe written in Albanian; and an English-Albanian dictionary (1923).

Christo Dako (1878–1941), an educator and a key figure in the early nationalist movement, wrote *Albania, the Master Key to the Near East* (1919).

Faik Konitza (1876–1942) was one of the more influential leaders of the Albanian community in the United States in the early twentieth century. He published the magazine *Albania* from 1897 to 1909 and was the editor of *Dielli* in 1909 and 1910 and from 1921 to 1926. He also cofounded the Pan-American Federation of America in 1912, serving as its president from 1921 to 1926, and was minister plenipotentiary of Albania from 1926 to 1939.

Fan Stylian Noli (1865–1964) is one of the best-known figures in Albanian American history. A major player in the Albanian nationalist movement, Noli founded the Albanian Orthodox Church in America in 1908.

Eftalia Tsina (1870–1953), the mother of physician Dimitra Elia, was an early promoter of Albanian social and cultural issues. In the 1920s she founded *Bashkimi*, the first Albanian women's organization in Boston.

Business Anthony Athanas (1912–2005) was a community leader and restaurateur in Boston for more than fifty years. He opened his first restaurant in Lynn, Massachusetts, in 1937 and others in 1957 and 1975. Athanas served as director of the National Restaurant Association and president of the Massachusetts Restaurant Association and won the Horatio Alger Award from the Horatio Alger Society and the Golden Door Award of the International Institute of New England.

Journalism Gjon Mili (1904–1984), a photographer for *Life* and other magazines, was known for his innovative and visionary work with color and high-speed photography. Collections of his work are housed in the Museum of Modern Art and Time-Life Library in New York, the Massachusetts Institute of Technology in Cambridge, and the Bibliotheque Nationale in Paris.

Donald Lambro (1940–) is a writer, political analyst, and investigative reporter with the *Washington Times*. His works include *Conscience of a Young Conservative* (1976), *Fat City: How Washington Wastes Your Taxes* (1980), *Washington—City of Scandals: Investigating Congress and Other Big Spenders* (1984), *Land of Opportunity: The Entrepreneurial Spirit in America* (1986), and *Future Forces: Ten Trends that Will Shape American Politics and Policies in 2000 and Beyond* (1999).

Literature Tom Perrotta (1961–) is an acclaimed author of literary fiction and screenplays. His best-known works are *Election* (1998) and *Little Children* (2004), both of which were made into Academy Award–nominated films.

Shqipe Malushi (1955–), a poet, essayist, media information specialist, and community leader, has published fiction, nonfiction, translations, essays, and newspapers articles. Her works of poetry, written in Albanian and in English, include *Memories of '72* (1972), *Exile* (1981), *Solitude* (1985), *Crossing the Bridges* (1990), and *For You* (1993). She also published a collection of short stories, *Beyond the Walls of the Forgotten Land* (1992), and a book of essays, *Transformation* (1988). In addition, she wrote and collaborated on several plays and screenplays.

Loretta Chase (1949–), born in Worcester, Massachusetts, is a popular writer of romance novels. Her books include *Don't Tempt Me* (2009), *Last Night's Scandal* (2011), and *Silk Is for Seduction* (2012).

Nexhmie Zaimi (1917–2003) wrote *Daughter of the Eagle: The Autobiography of an Albanian Girl* (1937), which describes her immigrant experience in the United States.

Music Kara DioGuardi (1970–) served as a judge on the top-rated Fox television series *American Idol* for two seasons and has written hit songs for Britney Spears, Christina Aguilera, and Kelly Clarkson.

Thomas Nassi (1892–1964), a musician and composer, graduated from the New England Conservatory of Music in 1918. He trained choirs for the Cathedral of St. George in Boston and for churches in Natick, Worcester, and Southbridge in Massachusetts between 1916 and 1918. He also arranged Byzantine liturgical responses in Albanian for mixed choirs.

Politics Stephen Peters (1907–1990) served as a research analyst in the U.S. State Department in 1945 and the Foreign Service in 1958. He wrote "Ingredients of the Communist Takeover in Albania," which was published in Thomas Hammond's 1975 volume *The Anatomy of Communist Takeovers*.

Rifat Tirana (1907–1952), an economist, was a member of the staff of the League of Nations in the 1930s. At the time of his death, he was serving as deputy chief of the U.S. Security Agency Mission to Spain. He authored *The Spoil of Europe* (1941).

Bardhyl Rifat Tirana (1937–) served as cochair of the Presidential Inaugural Committee (1976–1977) and director of the Defense Civil Preparedness Agency (1977–1979).

Joseph DioGuardi (1940–) served in the U.S. House of Representatives from 1985 to 1989 as a Republican representing the 20th Congressional District of New York. He went on to hold the post of president of the Albanian American Civic League.

Science and Medicine Andrew Elia (1906–1991) and Dimitra Tsina Elia (1906–1965), who were husband and wife, were early pioneers in the Albanian community in the field of medicine. Andrew graduated from Boston University Medical School in 1935 and was a practicing obstetrician and gynecologist in the Boston area. Dimitra was one of the first Albanian American women to practice general medicine in the United States.

Ferid Murad (1936–), a physician, won the 1998 Nobel Peace Prize in Physiology or Medicine.

Sports Lee Constantine Elia (1937–) managed Major League Baseball's Chicago Cubs (1982–1983) and Philadelphia Phillies (1987–1988). He also served as a coach for the Toronto Blue Jays, New York Yankees, and Baltimore Orioles.

Stage and Screen John Belushi (1949–1982), an actor and comedian, is best remembered for his work on the NBC network's landmark television comedy series *Saturday Night Live* (1975–1979). His movies include *National Lampoon's Animal House* (1978), *The Blues Brothers* (1980), *Continental Divide* (1981), and *Neighbors* (1981).

James Belushi (1954–) is an actor and comedian whose success followed his older brother John's. His best-known films are *K-9* (1989) and *Curly Sue* (1991), and he also starred on the ABC sitcom *According to Jim* (2001–2009).

Stan Dragoti (1932–) was a prominent director and producer in Hollywood. His film credits as a director include *Love at First Bite* (1979), *Mr. Mom* (1983), *The Man with One Red Shoe* (1985), and *Necessary Roughness* (1991).

Regis Philbin (1931–) is one of the most widely recognized names in American television. His credits include *Live! with Regis and Kelly*, *Who Wants to Be a Millionaire*, and the *Shrek* movie series.

Eliza Dushku (1980–), an Albanian American actress, has appeared on television series such as *Buffy the Vampire Slayer*, *Angel*, *Tru Calling*, and *Dollhouse*, and had parts in the movies *Bring It On* (2000) and *The New Guy* (2002).

John Cena (1977–) is an actor and a professional wrestler with the World Wrestling Federation (WWE) whose movie credits include *The Marine* (2006) and *12 Rounds* (2009).

MEDIA

PRINT

Albanian Daily News

First published in 1995, it offers coverage of Albanian news and events for an English-reading audience.

"Dervish Hima" Street
ADA Tower, No. 1
Tirana, Albania
Phone: +355 45 600 610
Fax: +355 45 600 618
Email: editoradn@albnet.net
URL: www.albaniannews.com

Dielli

An Albanian and English weekly publication. One of the oldest Albanian newspapers, it is published by the Pan Albanian Federation of America, *Vatra*. It publishes articles on social, cultural, and political events of interest to Albanians.

2437 Southern Boulevard
Bronx, New York 10458
Email: gazetadielli@gmail.com
URL: http://gazetadielli.com

Illyria

An Albanian and English bi-weekly published by the Illyrian Publishing Company, it features international news with a focus on news from the Balkans. The newspaper covers political events of interest to Albanian Americans as well as local community events.

481 8th Avenue
Suite 547
New York, New York 10001
Phone: (212) 868-2224
Fax: (212) 868-2228
Email: info@illyriapress.com
URL: www.illyriapress.com

RADIO

WCUW-91.3 FM

"Albanian Hour" is the oldest continuous Albanian radio program in the country, airing on Saturday from 8 a.m. to 10 a.m. It broadcasts local community news and events and international news from Albania.

910 Main Street
Worcester, Massachusetts 01610
Phone: (508) 753-1012
Email: wcuw@wcuw.org
URL: www.wcuw.org

ORGANIZATIONS AND ASSOCIATIONS

Albanian American Civic League

Founded in 1989, the organization is dedicated to informing the American public about the political and social problems in Albania. It operates through legislation and research to represent the interests of more than 750,000 Albanian Americans.

P.O. Box 70
Ossining, New York 10562
Phone: (718) 547-8909
Email: jjd@aacl.com
URL: www.aacl.us

Albanian-American Development Foundation (AADF)

Working with the United States Agency for International Development (USAID), the organization seeks to promote economic and political interactions between the United States and Albania. Its membership includes many Albanian Americans.

14 East 60th Street
Suite 407

New York, New York 10022
Phone: (212) 702-9102
URL: www.aadf.org

Albanian American National Organization (AANO)

Founded in 1946, it is a non-denominational cultural organization open to all Albanians and Americans of Albanian descent. With chapters throughout North America, it seeks to promote knowledge and awareness about Albanian history.

URL: www.aano.org

National Albanian American Council (NAAC)

The NAAC serves as a lobbying organization that disseminates information on economic and political affairs in the Balkans. It works to bring together Albanian Americans and work with the U.S. legislature.

1133 20th Street NW
Suite 210
Washington, D.C. 20036
Phone: (202) 466-6900
URL: www.naac.org

The Pan-Albanian Federation of America, *Vatra* (The Hearth)

Known by multiple names since its founding in 1912, *Vatra* (The Hearth) plays an active political and cultural role in the Albanian American community. It sponsors many charitable, cultural, and social events and publishes books on Albanian culture. The organization has provided scholarships for students of Albanian descent and publishes the newspaper *Dielli*.

URL: http://vatrafederation.org

MUSEUMS AND RESEARCH CENTERS

Fan S. Noli Library and Cultural Center of the Albanian Orthodox Archdiocese in America

The Fan S. Noli Library and Cultural Center contains a trove of archives, papers, and items related to the Albanian experience in America and is considered one of the leading repositories of Albanian culture outside of Europe.

St. George Albanian Orthodox Cathedral
523 East Broadway
South Boston, Massachusetts 02127-4415
Phone: (617) 268-1275
Email: albboschurch@juno.com

SOURCES FOR ADDITIONAL STUDY

Demo, Constantine. *The Albanians in America: The First Arrivals.* Boston: Society of Fatbardhesia of Katundi, 1960.

Federal Writers' Project, Works Project Administration (WPA) of Massachusetts. *The Albanian Struggle in the Old World and New.* Boston: Federal Writers' Project, 1939.

Fischer, Bernd J. "Albanian Refugees Seeking Political Asylum in the United States: Process and Problems." *Journal of Ethnic and Migration Studies* 31, no. 1 (2005): 193–208.

Nagi, Dennis L. *The Albanian-American Odyssey: A Pilot Study of the Albanian Community of Boston, Massachusetts.* New York: AMS Press, 1988.

Nahzi, Fron. "Balkan Diaspora I: The Albanian-American Community." *Kosovo: Contending Voices on Balkan Interventions.* Ed. William J. Buckley. Grand Rapids, MI: William B. Eerdmans Publishing Company, 2000.

Noli, Fan S. *Fiftieth Anniversary Book of the Albanian Orthodox Church in America, 1908–1958.* Boston: Albanian Orthodox Church, 1960.

Orgocka, Aida. "Albanian High Skilled Migrant Women in the U.S.: The Ignored Experience." *The New Albanian Migration.* Ed. Russell King, Nicola Mai, and Stephanie Schwandner-Sievers. Sussex, UK: Sussex Academic Press, 2005.

Ragaru, Nadège, and Amilda Dymi. "The Albanian-American Community in the United States: A Diaspora Coming to Visibility." *Canadian Review of Studies in Nationalism* 31, nos. 1–2 (2004): 45–63.

Trix, Frances. *The Albanians in Michigan: A Proud People from Southeast Europe.* East Lansing: Michigan State University Press, 2001.

ALEUTS

Tova Stabin

OVERVIEW

The Aleuts are an indigenous people whose ancestral home includes the Shumagin and Aleutian island groups and the western end of the mainland Alaska Peninsula, including 300-plus islands and islets. The Aleutian Islands extend from the tip of the Alaska Peninsula westward 1,200 to 1,300 miles into the Pacific Ocean, nearly to the Kamchatka Peninsula in Russia. They encompass about 6,821 square miles (17,666 square kilometers), which is comparable to the size of the state of Connecticut. These volcanic islands have a harsh climate characterized by extremely strong winds, heavy fog, and much snow (217 inches were recorded in 2000). There are differing theories about the origins of the name *Aleut*. It may come from the Aleut word *allíthuh*, meaning "community," or possibly a word from the Chukchi language (of the Chukchi people from eastern Siberia) meaning "islands." The Aleuts call themselves *Unangan*, which means "original people." Some activists within the group have rallied to stop using the name *Aleuts* and only use *Unangan*.

According to a number of sources, including the Aleutian Pribilof Island Community Development Association, at the time of the Aleuts' first contact with Europeans in the mid-1700s, their population was between 12,000 and 15,000. Aleut society was divided into a class structure in which chiefs or nobles were at the top, followed by commoners and then slaves, mostly women. Aleuts depended primarily on the sea for their subsistence, hunting sea animals, including seals, sea lions, whales, birds, and fish, and gathering clams, bird eggs, and seaweed. In addition to food, these resources were used for clothing, medicine, and rituals. Nothing went to waste—seal fat, for example, was burned for heat and light.

Today the Aleuts live on the Alaska coast, Aleutian Islands, Pribilof Islands, and Commander Islands. The Pribilof villages of St. Paul and St. George have the largest Aleut communities. For thousands of years the Aleuts lived in villages spread over various sheltered harbors across the Aleutians, but they have had to relocate many times since white people started arriving on their lands. For example, Russian fur traders forced them to move to the Pribilof Islands to hunt in the 1700s, and the U.S. government sent them to internment camps in southeast Alaska during World War II. The Aleut economy of the Pribilof Island communities took a devastating blow when the U.S. government abandoned support of commercial fur seal harvesting in the early 1980s due to the declining fur market and pressure from the animal rights movement.

According to the U.S. Census Bureau, the Aleut population in 2010 was 19,282 (as a basis for comparison, the capacity of a baseball stadium such as Chicago's Wrigley Field or San Francisco's AT&T Park is about twice that number). The Aleut Corporation estimates that about one-third of Aleuts live in the Aleutians, mainly on the Pribilof Islands, about one-third reside in the Anchorage area, and one-third are scattered throughout the lower forty-eight states, primarily in Washington and California.

HISTORY OF THE PEOPLE

Early History Early Aleut culture and language is estimated to have come into existence 9,000 years ago. Many anthropologists believe Aleuts came from coastal Asia with early Inuits. Aleuts lived in villages that had harbors where they could easily access the sea, from which they derived their subsistence economy. These ports also allowed them to see if enemies from other villages were coming. They lived in semi-subterranean houses called *barabaras*, whose roofs were covered with a layer of sod.

Russians began to arrive in the Aleutians in the mid-1700s. In 1724 Tsar Peter the Great of Russia commissioned the Danish navigator Vitus Bering (1681–1741) to find out whether North America and Siberia were connected by land. While many voyagers did not survive these harsh expeditions—including Bering, who died of scurvy during his second expedition—those who returned to Russia brought with them sea otter skins, thereby beginning a "fur rush." Russian fur-trading companies first sent Siberian *promyshlenikis*, "contract" workers who were usually serfs or townspeople, in the mid-eighteenth century. As the demand for furs increased, the Russians used brutal means against the Aleuts—such as rape, murder, and kidnapping—in order to increase the trade. The Russians wiped out villages and took children and women hostage to ensure against being attacked. Despite resistance that included destroying a fleet of five Russian ships in 1763, the Aleuts remained oppressed. Some of the original Russian hunters from 1745 were tried in Russian courts because of this brutal treatment, but the Aleuts were nevertheless forced to continue to work for the fur traders. By the latter part of the 1700s, the sea otters used for fur were virtually hunted out of existence. In 1786, however, Russian navigator Gavriil Pribilof discovered the uninhabited Aamix Islands, a breeding site of fur seals, allowing the Russian fur trade to continue for another 100 years.

By 1799 Aleut areas were under the administration of the Russian-American Company, which had a monopoly on the fur trade. The company encouraged Russian Orthodox missionaries to come to the islands, and the first Russian Orthodox Church in Unalaska was built in 1808. In 1824 a Russian Orthodox priest, Father Ioann Veniaminov, was able to convert many Aleuts to the Russian Orthodox religion in part because he fought for the rights of the Aleuts under Russian rule. Conversion furthered Russian influence on the Aleuts' traditional way of life. Additionally, the Russians caused many deaths by introducing diseases to which Aleuts had no immunity, such as smallpox. In all, the Russian colonizers had a devastating effect on the Aleut population. By 1834 the number of Aleuts had dropped to 2,500 from an estimated 12,000–15,000 before the arrival of Russians in the mid-1700s.

In 1867 Russia sold Alaska and the Aleutian Islands to the United States, though the Commander Islands remained under Russian jurisdiction. By the time of the U.S. purchase, the Russians had subjugated the Aleuts to the point where hostilities had subsided and the Aleuts had been granted full Russian citizenship. Fur hunting by U.S. companies began immediately and was very aggressive, impacting the environment and Aleut life. At first the Aleuts were treated fairly by a few private monopolies that paid wages somewhat equivalent to what other U.S. industrial workers earned. When the government took over the fur seal industry in the Pribilof Islands, however, it treated the Aleuts as if they were in servitude. The Aleuts lost their rights as Russian citizens and became virtually wards of the state under U.S. jurisdiction. During the late nineteenth century, sealskin coats had become so popular that a number of countries started high-seas hunts for them. The U.S. government was supposed to oversee the harvest, but it did not, and by 1910 the northern fur seal population had been depleted by one-third.

With fewer opportunities to support themselves by seal hunting, some Aleuts turned to fishing in the early twentieth century, creating new villages that harvested and processed cod and salmon. In 1911 Russia, Japan, Great Britain (for Canada), and the United States signed an international wildlife conservation treaty applying to fur seals. It prohibited high-seas killing, regulated commercial harvesting, and instituted killing techniques that were more humane. These new regulations helped restore the seal population and later provided Aleuts with some employment and the ability to return to one of their major food supplies.

In 1912 Alaska became a territory of the United States, and the following year the Aleutian Islands were designated as the Aleutian Islands Reservation by an executive order of President William Howard Taft, protecting the islands' wildlife. From the 1920s through the 1940s, tuberculosis struck the Aleut community, killing many within it. After the Great Depression, the fur market crashed, and many villages related to the trade were abandoned. Additionally, in the late 1930s canneries that processed codfish and salmon began to close as the fish populations diminished.

Modern Era During World War II, the Japanese attacked the Aleutian Islands. In 1942 they captured Attu and Kiska islands, and Attu villagers were taken to Japan as prisoners of war. The next year the United States regained control of the island, whereupon residents of most of the eastern Aleut villages were moved to internment camps in abandoned canneries in southeast Alaska at locations such as Funter Bay. The living conditions in these camps were miserable, with little food, heat, sanitation, or medical support. Many Aleuts died, particularly elders, who would normally teach traditions to younger generations, and children, who represented the future of the community. Thirty-two Aleuts died at the Funter Bay camp, seventeen at Killisnoo, twenty at Ward Lake, and five at Burnett Inlet.

After the war, the Aleuts returned to their villages, only to find that many of their homes and possessions had been destroyed by military personnel. Thus, many Aleuts were forced to settle elsewhere. In 1988 Congress passed the Aleut Restitution Act to begin restitution to Aleut victims of the internment camps. The environmental impact of the war continues to affect the Aleutians and the Aleut people decades later, with toxins still found in their groundwater. A 2012 report by the U.S. Fish and Wildlife Service conveyed the need for the continued cleanup of debris and toxic waste in the region from World War II.

While commercial fishing and a cash economy (as opposed to a trade or subsistence economy) grew for the Aleuts after World War II, they usually held jobs that were on the lowest end of the economic spectrum. In 1959 Alaska became a state. After a conference addressing Alaska Native aboriginal land rights in 1966, the native people founded the Alaska Federation of Natives (AFN), with more than 400 Alaska Natives representing seventeen organizations. Flore Lekanoff, an Aleut from St. George, was elected chairperson, and from 1966 to 1971, the AFN worked primarily on trying to secure a just and fair land settlement. In 1971 President Richard Nixon signed the Alaska Native Claims Settlement Act (ANCSA), which transferred land titles to Alaska Native regional corporations and local village corporations. The Aleut Corporation was thereby formed to foster economic, social, and cultural growth within the community.

Controversial nuclear testing took place in the Aleutians during the 1960s and 1970s. In 1965 an underground nuclear bomb, "Long Shot," was detonated on Amchitka Island, and in 1971 one called "Cannikin" was exploded on the same island. Greenpeace, a large independent direct-action environmental organization, was created in 1969 partly in response to nuclear testing on Amchitka Island. In 1994 the Amchitka nuclear testing facility was officially closed.

From the mid-1970s to the mid-1980s, environmental and animal-rights groups began to pressure the U.S. government to take away support from the fur seal industry on the Pribilof Islands. The Aleuts, who had depended on such hunting for thousands of years before colonization, were harassed and misrepresented, and their hunting rights were legally challenged. The price of seal pelts dropped significantly, largely as a result of this conflict. To control the negative public outcry and also save tax dollars, the U.S. government under President Ronald Reagan in 1983 withdrew a $6.2 million annual allocation to the Pribilof Islands. The U.S. government also withdrew from the international fur seal treaty, effectively ending commercial sealing in the United States. After much lobbying by and for the Aleuts, the federal government established a $20 million trust fund to help diversify the Aleut economy. Aleuts in the Pribilofs built harbors where crab and halibut fishing boats could dock and also to attract fish processors to the islands. In 1996 Congress passed the Magnuson Fishery Conservation and Management Act, giving American fishermen the first chance to harvest fish within 200 miles of the U.S. coast and ensuring "the conservation and management of the fisheries."

The Aleut International Association (AIA) was created in 1998 to deal with environmental and cultural issues to the "extended Aleut family" that shares issues across the borders of the U.S. and Russia; it is a permanent part of the Arctic Council. In 2004 the AIA was granted Special Consultive Status by the United Nations' Economic and Social Council.

Today, Aleuts continue to be involved with issues that affect the precious environment they live in. They participated in the 2009 Indigenous Peoples' Global Summit on Climate Change as well as the Arctic Marine Shipping Assessment's work to gauge the impact of increased shipping activity on the Arctic environment, economy, and society.

SETTLEMENT IN THE UNITED STATES

Many anthropologists believe Aleuts came across coastal Asia with the Inuits. As reported in *Nature* magazine in 2011, an international team studying DNA sequences found that Native descendants came from three migrations. According to coauthor David Reich, a professor of genetics at Harvard Medical School, "the Asian lineages that contributed some of the DNA to Eskimo-Aleut speakers and the Na-Dene-speaking Chipewyan from Canada are more closely related to present-day East Asian populations." Additionally, states the article, "the Naukan and coastal Chukchi from north-eastern Siberia carry 'First American' DNA. Thus, Eskimo-Aleut speakers migrated back to Asia, bringing Native American genes."

When the Russians first contacted them in the eighteenth century, the Aleuts occupied all Aleutian Islands west to Attu Island on the western tip of the Alaska Peninsula and the Shumagin Islands south of the Alaska Peninsula. Generally, they settled by protected harbors, sometimes between two bays, and built semi-subterranean houses, or houses that were partially underground. These houses sometimes held up to 40 families, which were usually related, and formed villages of up to 150 people. The Aleuts also built small, non-permanent places to live at hunting and fishing sites.

The Russian occupation during the mid-eighteenth through early nineteenth centuries brought about large forced population resettlement. Fur traders took Aleuts from their villages and forced them to live where the hunting was best. During the early years of this violent occupation, some villages were wiped out completely or abandoned. Many Aleuts moved to Morzhovoi and Belkofski near the end of the Alaska Peninsula and on the Pribilof Islands, which were important locations for the hunting needs of the Russian traders.

After the United States acquired Alaska in 1867, the near-extermination of the sea otter forced Aleuts to abandon villages for lack of a sustainable livelihood. In some villages, people began trapping foxes for the fur trade; these villages were able to survive until about the early 1940s. During the first half of the twentieth century, new villages sprung up in places where people could harvest and process cod and salmon, such as in Company Harbor, Ikatan, and False Pass. However, when codfish disappeared and the salmon industry diminished, many of these villages could not continue. In the twenty-first century, the largest Aleut villages are on the islands of St. Paul and St. George (one village on each island). Aleut communities are also found in the eastern Aleutian Islands at Akutan, Cold Bay, False Pass, King Cove, and Sand Point. Additionally, Aleuts live in the Alaskan cities of Fairbanks and Anchorage, as well as in the contiguous United States, primarily Washington and California.

LANGUAGE

The Aleut language, Unangam Tunuu (or Unangan), belongs to the Eskaleut language family and shares roots with the Inuit language. Linguists estimate that

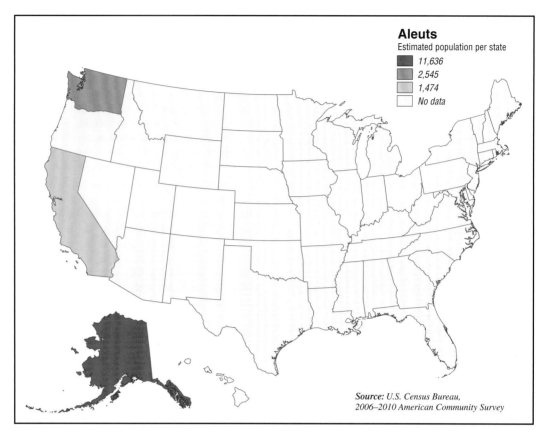

Aleuts

Estimated population per state

- 11,636
- 2,545
- 1,474
- No data

*Source: U.S. Census Bureau,
2006–2010 American Community Survey*

the Aleut language separated from the earlier Inuit (Eskimo) languages close to 4,000 years ago. Unangam Tunuu has three dialects: Eastern Aleut, Atkan Aleut, and Attu, which is now extinct except for a creolized version that is spoken on Bering Island. Estimates of the number of remaining speakers range from 100 to 300. According to Helen Corbett and Susanne Swibold in *Endangered Peoples of the Arctic: Struggles to Survive and Thrive*:

> […] linguists predict it [the Aleut language] may be extinct by the year 2055. Only the elders still speak it in the Pribilof villages. Attempts to teach it to younger generations through the school have not been successful. The Aleut language is tied to an intimate knowledge of the land and sea, rules of conduct, and a unique way of knowing. The processes of modernization and assimilation into a Western mainstream culture have displaced the language from its context, rendering it a cultural artifact.

Aleut was not a written language until Father Ioann (John) Veniaminov, a Russian Orthodox priest, started to develop a writing system in 1824 so that he could translate religious and educational tracts into the Aleut language. In the mid-twentieth century, linguist Knut Bergsland started working with Aleut speakers such as William Dirks Sr. and Moses Dirks, an Aleut linguist, to create a modern writing system and develop bilingual dictionaries. Bergsland also published an Aleut dictionary in 1994 and a grammar guide in 1997.

Speaking native languages in Alaskan public schools was forbidden from the late nineteenth through mid-twentieth centuries. Aleut was not used in schools until the 1970s, when activists forced the government to allow instruction in native languages. Some Aleut language courses were subsequently developed.

Greetings and Popular Expressions The following are some common Aleut words and expressions: *qawax* (sea lion); *qawaadax* (young sea lion); *laaqudax* (fur seal); *isux* (hair seal); *slukax* (seagull); *chulugidax* (young seagull); *iqyax* (skin boat); *udax* (bay); *chagix* (halibut); *chiknax* (limpet); *Aang, Unangax* (Hello, Aleut); *tayaǧuǧ* (man); *ayagaǧ* (woman); *aǧathaǧ* (sun); *tugithaǧ* (moon); *taangaǧ* (water); *tutalagakuq* (I don't understand); *qaǧaasakung* (thank you).

RELIGION

As a result of the integration of Russian Orthodoxy into Aleut culture, there is a lack of information about traditional Aleut religion before the group's contact with the Russians. According to traditional Aleut beliefs, the sun is a creator deity, sunlight and seawater are sacred, and the directions of east and above are associated with the sacred creator. The Aleut creation story includes an island of four mountains and four beings from the sky that land in the grasses. There are good or helpful spirits (*aglikhaiakh*) and evil or harmful spirits (*khoughkh*) that influence daily life. Animal, human, and natural spirits are to be appeased and honored through a variety of rituals. Aleut men, for instance, honored the sea mammal spirits by wearing highly decorated hunting costumes. Aleuts made offerings with animal skins and used charms and amulets. Shamans used dancing, drumming, and singing to mediate between the "material world" and the "spiritual world" and could also heal the sick, read the future, and help people succeed in hunting or war. According to their spiritual practices, souls are able to move between three worlds: earth, an upper sphere, and a lower sphere.

Many rituals revolved around death, which was seen as a rite of passage. After a death, there would be a forty-day feast during which people would honor the deceased with dancing, drumming, singing, and masks. Some Aleuts would mummify a dead body to preserve the person's spirit. High-ranking Aleuts had cave burials or were laid to rest in stone or wood structures. Sometimes people were buried near homes so that their spirits would maintain proximity to their families.

Russian fur traders first introduced Russian Orthodoxy to the Aleuts. The first missionaries arrived in late eighteenth century and baptized a number of Aleuts. One of the missionaries, Hieromonk Makary, was so appalled by how the Aleuts were being treated by the fur traders that he protested to the tsar about it upon returning to Russia. Other missionaries also intervened on behalf of the Aleuts, who, in turn, formed a strong allegiance to the church. This bond was further strengthened by the emphasis missionaries placed on involving the Aleuts in church leadership and governance. One of the original monks to come to the Aleuts, Father Herman, is revered by the Russian Orthodox Aleuts. The church canonized him in 1971 for performing miracles such as healing the sick and turning back a tsunami.

In the 1820s the Russian American Company sent priests to the Aleuts, paying them salaries to convert the natives to Russian Orthodoxy. One such missionary, Father Ioann Veniaminov, had a strong influence on the Aleuts. Not only did he convert Aleuts, but he also built churches and chapels in many villages, opened schools, taught Aleuts to speak, read, and write in Russian, and trained them to be priests. One way he connected with the Aleuts was by learning their language, Unangan, and preaching in it. Additionally, Veniaminov and an Aleut named Ivan Pan'Kov translated religious and educational works into Unangan, significantly impacting the culture. (Veniaminov was sainted by the church in 1977.) By the mid-1800s, Russian Orthodoxy had become part of Aleut culture and spirituality. Some indigenous practices were integrated into Russian Orthodoxy.

Russian Orthodoxy is an important part of the life of the Aleut community in contemporary times. The majority of Aleuts are baptized, married, and buried by the Russian Orthodox Church. It is common for songs in church to be sung in Unangan and Slavonic (the liturgical language of the Russian Orthodox Church) as well as in English. Priests bless important activities such as seal hunts and berry picking, and they also bless homes yearly. In smaller villages where priests are not available, Aleut lay readers lead services, though priests come for special services such as funerals.

CULTURE AND ASSIMILATION

The Aleuts were subject to forced assimilation first by the Russians and then by the United States, primarily in service to the fur industry. The Aleut language, spiritual practices, cultural traditions, and political structures were largely decimated. The Aleuts were forced to hunt in places away from their native villages, which hastened the demise of their way of life. War, starvation, diseases such as smallpox and scarlet fever, and enslavement reduced their population so greatly that some historians have called it a genocide. During World War II, the Aleuts were sent to internment camps, where deaths abounded. Many of those who survived found that their villages had been destroyed during the war. The Aleuts' traditional economy, from which their cultural beliefs and customs had stemmed, was changed to a wage-based system. In the later twentieth and early twenty-first centuries, a wide range of environmental issues and disasters impacted Aleut culture. These included environmentalists with non-indigenous orientations misrepresenting Aleut hunting practices, environmental disasters, and legal issues that concerned fishing rights and land rights. Additionally, a high rate of intermarriage, with Russians in particular, translated into further assimilation for the Aleut people.

Starting in the late twentieth century, the Aleuts made intensive efforts to revitalize their culture through programs such as the Pribilof Islands Stewardship Program, which connects Aleut youths to their environment by imparting both traditional knowledge and Western scientific information about the sea and sea life, including hunting and building Aleut kayaks (*bidarka*). Participants also learn Aleut songs, drumming, and dancing. The Marine Messengers Program takes students from the Stewardship Program to visit villages and towns in Alaska to speak about how they work to care for the Bering Sea and, thus, their community and culture.

Cuisine The Aleut diet once consisted of sea mammals such as sea lions and whale; fish and shellfish such as salmon, halibut, cod, shrimp, and crab;

PRESERVING TRADITION AND HEALTH

In 2012, as part of its Aleut Diet Program, the St. George Traditional Council taught children how to prepare traditional foods, which were then served to people visiting while on ecotourism cruises. The meals included fur seal hearts and livers, fur seal meatloaf, fermented flipper, reindeer stew, fish pie, and moss berry jelly. Additionally, in 2013 the Aleutian and Pribilof Islands Association published a book about local traditional foods that includes historical and present uses, preservation and preparation techniques, recipes, and harvesting, cultural, and nutritional information.

seaweed; big game such as reindeer; small game and birds such as ptarmigan, geese, and ducks; bird eggs; and herbs, plants, and berries. Many Aleut today continue hunting, fishing, and gathering but also eat non-Native foods that are imported.

Aleuts traditionally ate most of their food raw, though some was cooked over a pit. Generally, people did not stockpile food over the winter, but they did dry some fish and meats, usually by placing them on racks in the sun or over an open fire, which added a smoky flavor. Mammal fat was rendered to supplement their diets. Cow parsnip (*saqudax*) or *putchki*, which tastes like celery, was and still is commonly eaten. The roots of purple orchids (*quungdiix*) are also a staple.

Traditional Dress The traditional dress of the Aleuts was strongly connected to their subsistence economy, the strong harsh weather of their environment, and their cultural heritage. Men and women wore long parkas made of sea otter fur or bird skin; the men's parkas had hoods, while the women's had only collars. Waterproof rain parkas were usually made from seal, sea lion intestines, or esophagus and were called *kamleikas*, a Siberian Russian term. Kamleikas were tied to the hatch of a *baidarka*, a hunting kayak, to keep the hunter bound to his boat. A parka could take an entire year to make.

In the winter, sealskin boots were sometimes worn; the soles were often made from the flippers of sea lions. Shoes were not worn in the summer. Men wore *chagudax*, cone-shaped bentwood hats with visors that each hunter painted and then decorated, usually with the whiskers of sea lions. Both men and women wore ornaments on their lips called *labrets*, and girls received chin tattoos at puberty. Ceremonial clothes were sometimes made from puffin skins. These were sometimes painted, generally in geometric patterns, and feathers, whiskers, and fringes were also used for decoration.

Today the Aleut still wear some traditional dress in response to the weather (such as parkas), for

ceremonial and other occasions, and as part of their cultural identity (such as crab necklaces). They also wear more mainstream clothing.

Dances and Songs Singing, dancing, drumming, and storytelling continue to be important parts of the Aleut culture, whether for entertainment or for ceremonies such as those honoring the dead. Traditionally, each village had its own songs and stories glorifying its history and ancestors. Dancers wore masks that had a realistic look. In winter village chiefs would sometimes invite other villages for contests in dance and storytelling.

The revitalization of Aleut culture has sparked new interest in traditional dancing. Dance troupes include the *Atxam Taligisniikangis* (Atka Dancers), *Chalukam Axasniikan* (Nikolski Dancers), and *Adaagim Taligisniikangis* (Adak Dancers). These groups not only help villages learn traditional dances, but also tour Alaska, New York, California, Washington, Hawaii, and North Dakota. Additionally, dance troupes perform at "ethno-tours," packages sponsored by some Aleut organizations that enable participants to learn about Aleut cultural traditions. Unangax dance has become part of the required curriculum for students in the Aleutian Region School District.

Holidays Most Aleuts follow Russian Orthodox holidays. Easter, Christmas (also known as *Slavi* and lasting three nights starting on January 7), and Orthodox New Year are the most important occasions. A notable custom celebrated on Orthodox Christmas is called starring, or *selaviq*, commemorating the journey of the three wise kings who followed a star to the manger where Jesus was born. People carry brightly decorated stars and go door to door singing traditional songs, which usually end with the words "*Mnogaya leta*" (God grant you many years). The songs also honor those who have died in the last year. Singers are given food at each stop, including maple-frosted donuts, fish pie (*piruk*), smoked salmon, candy, and cookies. Easter is considered the most holy of the holidays, and the forty days before it are seen as a time for spiritual cleansing.

Health Care Issues and Practices Prior to European contact, Aleut society had advanced medical knowledge and strong healing traditions. The Aleuts detected the similarities between sea mammals and humans, had names for the major internal organs, could mummify bodies, and sometimes conducted autopsies to determine the cause of death. Shamans, or healers, used different types of spiritual and practical means to cure sickness, including acupuncture, bloodletting, and regional plants. By the time the Russian occupation was firmly rooted in the mid-1800s, much of Aleut traditional healing, especially the spiritual aspects, had been lost. Today, Aleuts are trying to revive the herbal medicine part of their tradition. Sharon Svarny-Livingston, an Aleut from Unalaska, has been researching and writing about Aleut herbal medicine since the 1990s.

The Aleut Elders Task Force, renamed the Unangam Ludaagingin Task Force, was created in 2005 by a collaboration of the Aleutian Pribilof Islands Association, Aleutian Housing Authority, and the Eastern Aleutian Tribes. In its own words, it helps to create a "community-based, comprehensive elder care and end-of-life services available in every regional Community." In 2012 the Aleut Diet Program was initiated to promote healthy preparation of local and traditional foods.

FAMILY AND COMMUNITY LIFE

Family and community have served as a means of survival for the Aleuts. Traditionally, semi-subterranean homes (*barabaras*), featuring a main room and separate rooms for different age groups, were often made up of large extended families. While monogamy was common, polygamy was permitted. Often everyone in a village was related by blood or marriage.

Villages had a hierarchal social structure, with chiefs as the leaders, followed by "common" people and then slaves (usually women), who often had been taken hostage in wars with other villages. Children, meanwhile, depended on close relatives to care for them. Chiefs received a share of each hunt, and in return they helped protect the hunting grounds, arbitrate disputes, and lead in wars with other villages. Chiefs were generally the wealthiest people in the village, had the largest families, and lived closest to survival resources. The Aleuts valued personal property; their kayaks (*baidarka*), for instance, were individually owned and passed down through the generations. However, the Aleuts also had a strong communal sense, sharing their food and other possessions, especially with those in need.

Patricia Petrivelli, a Niiĝuĝim/Atkan Aleut anthropologist, discusses in an article on the Smithsonian Institute's Alaska Native collections website how an early Russian Orthodox priest, Father Ioann Veniaminov, viewed the values of the Aleutians. Veniaminov noted that they respected and cared for parents and elders, helped the poor, valued the family structure, showed hospitality to strangers, were brave and fearless in war, and understood the consequence of immoral actions.

Major changes to family and community came about after the Aleuts had contact with the Russians, including the start of mixed-race marriages, usually between Russian men and Aleut women. The children of these marriages were called Creoles and sometimes received privileges from the Russians, such as more education and training than other Aleuts. Intermarriage with other European ethnic groups, such as the Swedes, occurred as these people came to the Aleutian Islands. The issue of mixed-race children and grandchildren in the Aleut community came to

Native Aleut woman in Valdey, Alaska. BILL BACHMANN / ALAMY

the forefront in 1971 when the Alaska Native Claims Settlement Act was passed. The act allotted cash settlements and land grants to Natives. This was particularly important in the Aleut community because its population was so tiny. In fact, the Aleut Corporation was one of the smallest of the Native corporations founded in the 1970s.

Most Aleuts today live in a nuclear-family setting, partly as a result of the influence of Russian Orthodoxy. Because the Aleuts have moved from a subsistence to primarily a cash economy, and because villages no longer go to war with one another, the extended family is not as essential as it once was. However, the Aleuts still have a great sense of community. Some elders, for instance, will not eat seal meat unless it has been butchered, preserved, and prepared by a family member. Family units run day-boat fisheries in the way that families came together for fur seal hunts in the past.

Gender Roles Traditionally, gender roles were assigned at a young age. Women would oversee the girls, while men would be responsible for training the boys. Girls learned household duties such as sewing and cooking, and boys were schooled in hunting and using a kayak. It was often the maternal uncle, not the father, who taught a boy to hunt. As for recreation, boys and men played wrestling games, while the girls' contests usually involved balancing feats.

Sometimes a boy who was considered particularly beautiful or feminine would be raised as a *berdaches* (two-spirit), also called a *shopan* or *achnucek*. He would dress in feminine clothes, and his grooming would include having his body hair plucked. Berdaches were greatly esteemed. Some became shamans or married wealthy men, sometimes raising the social status of the family. Much less frequently, girls were raised in the manner of boys.

Once a girl began to menstruate, she would stay with the adult women in menstrual huts for a few days and be subject to certain food and behavioral restrictions. Men believed being near a menstruating female would bring bad luck in hunting. Childbirth also took place in huts, where the new mother and baby briefly stayed before re-entering the community.

Aleut women were expert basket weavers, and today they are internationally known for this skill. Grass baskets (*qiigam aygaaxsii*), usually made from rye grasses, were dyed with berry juice; some were so tightly woven that they could hold water. Women also made containers from seal intestines.

Men followed a code of ethics for hunting, including dividing the meat amongst family members and deferring to elders. Men took great pride in their wooden hunting hats (*chagudax*). Women, meanwhile, gathered berries, seaweed, and shellfish such as crabs. Some men had secret whale-hunting societies, and their wives performed rituals for these hunts.

Gender roles among the Aleuts are less restrictive in the twenty-first century. Until the late twentieth century, almost all Russian Orthodox lay readers were male; now, though, more women are taking on that role. Furthermore, a number of women have assumed leadership positions in regional and local corporations and community organizations. For instance, in 2013 an Aleut woman, Kathy Griesbaum, was the chair of the Aleut Foundation.

Education For thousands of years Aleuts educated their children in skills such as hunting and basket weaving, arts such as dancing, and spiritual practices. When Russian Orthodox clergy first arrived in the eighteenth century, however, they began to establish formal schools. Father Ioann Veniaminov helped the Aleut to become literate in Russian and then, with Aleut Ivan Pan'Kov, to formulate an alphabet and written language of Aleut. Literacy, however, was a mixed blessing. It helped to change Aleut culture in certain positive ways, enabling the people to relate to more mainstream cultures, which was especially necessary as the economy became more cash-based. However, the loss of an oral tradition weakened relationships and customs. Family and community members who had once spoken with each other to share information and stories began to rely more on the written word. Thus, younger generations no longer looked toward their elders for knowledge.

The first U.S. public school in Unalaska opened in 1883, sixteen years after the United States purchased Alaska. By the mid-twentieth century there were substantial numbers of government-run and religious schools. In the late twentieth century, however, the Aleut community began instituting cultural heritage and traditional education as part of the school curriculum, and collaborative efforts between schools and community organizations were put in place.

The Alaska Department of Education and Early Development reported in 2006 that the Aleut dropout rate was 2.3 percent and the high school graduation rate was 89.7 percent. Despite these impressive statistics, many young adults must leave for cities because of a lack of job opportunities in rural areas. When these families depart, schools are forced to close because of declining enrollment, thereby robbing rural communities of cultural resources.

The Aleutian Region School District serves three Aleut communities in the Western Aleutian Islands: Nikolski, Atka, and Adak. It also keeps contact with Russian Aleuts from the Commander Islands. The curriculum includes Unangax dance classes; a student dance group has expanded to include the community at large, and it travels throughout Alaska and to other states to perform.

Courtship and Weddings Before the Aleuts had contact with the Russians, girls were allowed to marry at an early age, sometimes even before puberty. Boys, however, waited until their late teens, when they had become skilled at hunting and could provide for a family. Most relationships were monogamous. Polygamy was allowed for both men and women, but more often it was men, and wealthier ones at that, who had more than one spouse. Additionally, cross cousins were allowed to marry. Parents usually arranged a marriage, although there was no formal ceremony. Sometimes men would provide food or do other chores for a year or two for potential in-laws before the marriage was "sanctified."

The arrival of the Russian Orthodox Church brought with it new marriage laws. For example, even second cousins were no longer allowed to marry. This often meant that people had to go outside their villages in order to find suitable partners. In contemporary times, most Aleuts are Russian Orthodox and follow the proscribed Russian Orthodox Christian traditions of marriage.

EMPLOYMENT AND ECONOMIC CONDITIONS

For thousands of years, the Aleuts had a subsistence economy based mostly on the sea but also on herbs, berries, and other plants. This way of life continues to be intertwined with their cultural traditions, as they still depend on natural renewable resources. The exploitation of these resources by non-indigenous peoples has greatly impacted the economic outlook of the Aleuts.

With the arrival in the mid-eighteenth century of Russians who wanted to make large profits selling furs, the economy and the culture of the Aleuts began to change. The fur traders, armed with guns and other weaponry, were able to colonize the Aleuts despite resistance. After the initial years, Russian officials and businesspeople began to regulate the actions of the fur traders, establishing a formal economic system with the Aleuts through the Russian American Company in 1799. Until 1867, when the United States bought Alaska, the Aleuts were paid and had the opportunity to become full Russian citizens. Thus, the Aleuts became more involved in a cash economy, no longer relying solely on their own means to meet their needs. They also became more interested in using European goods. Some fell into debt to Russian traders.

An export economy started as soon as the United States purchased Alaska. The United States did not regulate hunting in the seas, and the sea otter population became severely diminished. This, in turn, impacted the Aleuts' ability to hunt, leading them even further away from a subsistence economy. In the 1900s the Aleuts became involved in commercial fisheries and canneries. Here, too, an important part of the Aleut economy was destroyed, this time by overfishing. By the late 1930s, the abundant codfish population was nearly exterminated, although it began to recover in around 1990. Commercial fishing for and processing of salmon became, and continue to be, mainstays of the Aleut community, with large processing plants in places such as King Cove. Villages have economic partnerships with seafood companies. In 1990 the government of St. Paul completed a modification of its harbor to accommodate large floating processors and factory trawlers. Many Aleuts in St. Paul fish for halibut and harvest crab. Thus, many Aleuts' livelihoods depend on sustainable natural resources, which are challenged by overfishing, climate change, and environmental destruction and policies. Additionally, the Aleuts must compete with other commercial entities.

The Aleut Corporation helps manage the money of the group. It was one of thirteen regional native corporations established in 1971 by the Alaska Native Claims Settlement Act; it received a settlement of $19.5 million, 66,000 acres of surface lands, and 1.572 million acres of subsurface estate. According to the Aleut Corporation website, the corporation's "primary areas of business are real estate, government operations and maintenance contracting, aggregate sales, and investments in oil and gas producing properties and marketable securities." It

Aleut man processes halibut. DAN PARRETT / GLOW IMAGES

provides dividends to Aleut members who are shareholders. The corporation's foundation, the Aleut Foundation, is described on its website as supporting "the economic and social needs of the Aleut people with scholarships for post secondary education, career development and burial assistance for shareholders of The Aleut Corporation."

Many Aleuts' livelihoods depend on sustainable natural resources, which are challenged by overfishing, climate change, and environmental destruction and policies. Additionally, the Aleuts must compete with other commercial entities.

POLITICS AND GOVERNMENT

Traditional Aleut villages served as basic political units, complete with alliances between villages that were forged for reasons that included increasing wealth and territory. However, after Russian colonization caused a severe population decline and forced migration to new islands and villages, the hostilities between villages effectively stopped. Despite the oppressive policies of the Russians, they honored the political system within tribal villages. The United States, on the other hand, did not. Even after World War II, when many Aleuts returned from internment camps and formed a tribal council, U.S. government treasury agents interfered with the council's work and governance.

After the Alaska Native Claims Settlement Act, the Aleuts had much more political power over their lives and their community. Native corporations such as the Aleut Corporation began to oversee much land and economic management and development.

Individual or affiliated villages, towns, and islands might have city councils, school district boards, tribal councils, and corporations that have a range of political responsibilities, and sometimes these various groups vie for control. Often each village has a leader who holds multiple elected or appointed positions on the school board, city council, or a corporation. These people are highly respected within the village. Both women and men hold political positions, and in the early twenty-first century, there were more women than men in official tribal capacities. Some people gain political positions because of family status, while others rely on education, work or government experience, or connections and success with communities outside the village. Additionally, being a successful fisherman can bring political power, as fishing is so essential to the economy and culture.

In 1976 the Aleutian Pribilof Islands Association was created. It is the federally recognized tribal organization of the Aleuts. According to its website, the association "contracts with federal, state and local governments as well as securing private funding to provide a broad spectrum of services throughout the region. These services include health, education, social, psychological, employment and vocational training, and public safety services."

Policy and laws set or withdrawn by the federal government over fishing and hunting have had a great impact on the Aleut community. For instance, the federal government's withdrawal from the commercial fur seal harvest in the mid-1980s created challenging political, economic, and cultural issues for the Aleuts. After years of being required to adhere to the policies of the government, Aleut leaders had to manage a variety of economic issues in ways that could prove successful in mainstream Western culture but would not diminish their values and culture.

The Aleuts have frequently been politically active in order to gain control of their lives, community, and heritage, as well as to redress past discrimination. Even while being interned during World War II, the women of the Funter Bay internment camp petitioned the federal government about the appalling conditions at the camp, stating, "We people of this place want a better place than this to live. This place is no place for a living creature." They ended the petition by saying, "We all have rights to speak for ourselves." In the 1980s the Aleuts went to court and appealed to Congress for financial restitution and a formal apology from the federal government for their forced internment. In 1987 U.S. Representative Tom Foley, along with 166 co-sponsors, introduced the Aleut Restitution Act of 1988. The bill was amended in 1993 to increase the original payment of $1.4 million to $4.7 million and was to include damage or destruction of church property. A formal apology was never made to the Aleuts.

NOTABLE INDIVIDUALS

Activism Lillie H. McGarvey (?–1987) held many positions in the Aleut community, including serving as president of the Aleut Corporation, secretary/treasurer of the Aleut League, president of the Native Women of Alaska, director of the Aleut League Alcohol Rehabilitation Project, and chairperson of the Alaska Native Health Board. After her death, the Anchorage Native Women's Commission created the Lillie McGarvey Mentoring Project in her honor. The program matches young minority women with female leaders to mentor them for careers.

Larry Merculieff, an activist from St. Paul Island, has served in various political and community positions, including as manager of St. Paul Island, commissioner of the Alaska Department of Commerce and Economic Development, president and CEO of Tanadgusix Corporation, chairman of the board of the Aleut Corporation, and general manager of Central Bering Sea Fishermen's Association. He has also been active in many groups and committees concerned with environmental, fish, and wildlife preservation in Alaska, including the National Research Council Committee on the Bering Sea Ecosystem and the Alaska Indigenous Council on Marine Mammals, for which he was chairman. He was one of four Native Americans at the White House Conference on the Oceans during President Bill Clinton's administration. In 2001 Merculieff was featured on a Discovery Channel documentary about Aleut history and spiritual traditions.

Art Thomas Stream (1941–) was born on Kodiak Island and moved to Seattle, Washington. He worked as an abstract artist, surrealist, cartoonist, and miniature artist. In 1981 he founded Streamline Studios and began working as a scrimshander (scrimshaw is the art of etching in ivory or bone) and soapstone carver. His work reflects and honors Aleut culture.

Lois Chichinoff Thadei, basket weaver, was born into a Tlingit and Haida community in southeast Alaska. She harvests perennial grasses and cures them in an ancient Aleut method for her basket material. She has won awards such as the Washington State Arts Commission Master and Apprentice Award (2010), the Washington State Historical Museum Native Art Show award (2009), and the First People's Fund Cultural Capitol Fellowship (2008).

Peter Lind Sr. (1930–) is known for creating traditional Aleut ceremonial hunting hats (*chagudax*). Of Russian Aleut descent, he was born in Chignik, Alaska.

Andrew Gronholdt (1915–1998) was an Aleut artist who made *chagudax*. He was born on Sand Point on Popof Island in the Shumagin Islands. The book *Chagudax: A Small Window into the Life of an Aleut Bentwood Hat Carver* (2012), published after his death, is a combination of his dairies and illustrations of his art.

Education Nicolai Galaktionoff (1935–2012) was born in the now-abandoned village of Makushin on Unalaska Island. He is best known for his work to keep the Unangan language alive not only by speaking the language and passing it on to his family and younger generations but also by working with linguists, anthropologists, and historians who recorded him in order to preserve pronunciations.

MEDIA

While there are no radio stations, television stations, or newspapers dedicated strictly to the Aleuts, outlets such as the radio station KUCB provide significant information on the Aleuts. In addition, the Aleut Corporation publishes a newsletter, the *Aleutian Current*, that updates shareholders on corporation news and events.

ORGANIZATIONS AND ASSOCIATIONS

Aleut Corporation

The Aleut Corporation is one of the thirteen regional Native corporations that were established in 1971 under the terms of the Alaska Native Claims Settlement Act (ANCSA). Its mission is to promote economic, cultural, and social growth for its shareholders through its subsidiaries, partnerships, and foundation.

4000 Old Seward Highway
Suite 300
Anchorage, Alaska 99503
Phone: (907) 561-4300
Fax: (907) 563-4328
Email: receptionist@aleutcorp.com
URL: www.aleutcorp.com

Aleut Foundation

The mission of the Aleut Foundation is, in its own words, to "support the economic and social needs of the Aleut people with scholarships for post secondary education, career development and burial assistance for shareholders of The Aleut Corporation."

703 West Tudor Road
Suite 102
Anchorage, Alaska 99503-6650
Phone: (907) 646-1929
Fax: (907) 646-1949
Email: taf@thealeutfoundation.org
URL: www.thealeutfoundation.org

Aleut International Association (AIA)

The AIA was formed by the Aleutian Pribilof Islands Association and the Association of the Indigenous Peoples of the North of the Aleut District of the Kamchatka Region of the Russian Federation. Its mission is to "address environmental and cultural concerns of the extended Aleut family," namely Russian and American Aleuts. The AIA is a permanent participant of the Arctic Council.

James Gamble, Interim Executive Director
333 West 4th Avenue
Suite 301
Anchorage, Alaska 99501
Phone: (907) 332-5388
Fax: (907) 332-5380
Email: aia@alaska.net
URL: www.aleut-international.org

The Aleutian Pribilof Islands Association, Inc. (APIA)

The federally recognized tribal organization of the Aleut people in Alaska. As it states, it "contracts with federal, state and local governments as well as securing private funding to provide a broad spectrum of services throughout the region. These services include health, education, social, psychological, employment and vocational training, and public safety services." The APIA operates the Aleut Heritage Library and Archive and the annual summer Urban Unangax Culture Camp, where children and adults can learn traditional skills.

Mark Snigaroff, Chair, Board of Directors
1131 East International Airport Road
Anchorage, Alaska 99518
Phone: (907) 276-2700
Fax: (907) 279-4351
Email: apiai@apiai.org
URL: www.apiai.org

Tanadgusix Corporation (TDX)

Tanadgusix Corporation (TDX) is an Alaska Native village corporation created under the ANCSA to help provide for the economic well-being of the indigenous people who reside in St. Paul.

615 E 82nd Avenue
Suite 200
Anchorage, Alaska 99518
Phone: (907) 278-2312
Fax: (907) 278-2316
Email: maryjanem@tdxcorp.com
URL: www.tanadgusix.com

MUSEUMS AND RESEARCH CENTERS

Alaska Native Knowledge Network (ANKN)

The ANKN states that it is "designed to serve as a resource for compiling and exchanging information related to Alaska Native knowledge systems and ways of knowing." Its offerings include curriculum libraries and publications.

University of Alaska Fairbanks
Burnnell Building
Room 117
P.O. Box 756730
Fairbanks, Alaska 99775-6730
Phone: (907) 474-1902
Fax: (907) 474-1957
URL: www.ankn.uaf.edu

Aleutian Pribilof Islands Association Aleut Heritage Library and Archive

A collection that includes books, articles, photographs, audio and video recordings, and other artifacts related to Unangax history and culture.

1131 East International Airport Road
Anchorage, Alaska 99518
Phone: (907) 276-2700
Fax: (907) 279-4351
Email: apiai@apiai.org
URL: www.apiai.com

The Arctic Studies Center

Established in 1988, this center is part of the Smithsonian Institution's National Museum of Natural History. Focusing specifically on studies of northern peoples, it brings together researchers with community scholars.

625 C Street
Anchorage, Alaska 99501
Phone: (907) 929-9207
Fax: (907) 929-9232
Email: crowella@si.edu
URL: www.mnh.si.edu/arctic/

The Museum of the Aleutians

Founded in 1999, this museum is dedicated to promoting public awareness of the cultural history of the Aleutian Islands. It houses some 500,000 artworks, artifacts, and manuscripts.

Zoya Johnson, Executive Director
314 Salmon Way
P.O. Box 648
Unalaska, Alaska 99685

Phone: (907) 581-5150
Fax: (907) 581-6682
Email: mota@aleutians.org
URL: www.aleutians.org

SOURCES FOR ADDITIONAL STUDY

Aleutians: Cradle of the Storms. Portland: Oregon Public Broadcasting, 2002. DVD.

Bielawski, E. *In Search of Ancient Alaska: Solving the Mysteries of the Past.* Anchorage: Alaska Northwest Books, 2007.

Corbett, Helen D., and Susanne M. Swibold. "The Aleuts of the Pribilof Islands, Alaska." In *Endangered Peoples of the Arctic: Struggles to Survive and Thrive.* Edited by Milton M. R. Freeman, 1–16. Westport, CT: Greenwood Press, 2000.

Ray, Dorothy Jean. *Aleut and Eskimo Art: Tradition and Innovation in South Alaska.* Seattle: University of Washington Press, 1981.

Reedy-Maschner, Katherine L. *Aleut Identities: Tradition and Modernity in an Indigenous Fishery.* Montreal: McGill-Queen's Native and Northern Series, 2010.

Turner, Lucien M., and Ray Hudson. *An Aleutian Ethnography.* Fairbanks: University of Alaska Press, 2008.

Veltre, Douglas W., and Allen P. McCartney. "Russian Exploitation of Aleuts and Fur Seals: The Archaeology of Eighteenth and Early-Nineteenth-Century Settlements in the Pribilof Islands, Alaska." *Historical Archaeology* 36, no. 3 (2002): 8–17.

Veltre, Douglas W., and Melvin A. Smith. "Historical Overview of Archaeological Research in the Aleut Region of Alaska." *Human Biology* 82, nos. 5–6 (2010): 487–506.

ALGERIAN AMERICANS

Olivia Miller

OVERVIEW

Algerian Americans are immigrants or descendants of people from Algeria, a country in North Africa that gained independence from France in 1962. The northern coast of Algeria is set along the Mediterranean Sea; in Arabic the country's name is the same as that of its capital, Algiers (*al-Jazai'r*, "the islands"), referring to two small islands found in the Bay of Algiers. Algeria is bordered to the east by Tunisia and Libya, to the south by Niger and Mali, and to the west by Mauritania, Western Sahara, and Morocco. The Sahara Desert covers 80 percent of the country. Mountain ranges dominate the North and Southeast. Algeria's total land area is 919,595 square miles (2,381,740 square kilometers), which is more than three times the size of Texas.

According to the *CIA World Factbook*, Algeria's population was more than 37 million in 2012. The Berbers are Algeria's indigenous ethnic group, and more than 99 percent of the population is of Berber descent. More than 80 percent of Algerians, however, identify themselves instead as Arab, forming the country's culturally and politically dominant group. Less than one percent of Algerians are of European descent. Islam is the state religion in Algeria, and 99 percent of Algerians are Sunni Muslim. The remaining one percent are Christians and Jews. Although Algeria has significant oil and natural gas reserves, per capita income in 2011 was only about $7,400 (about a fifth of per capita income in France).

Few Algerians immigrated to the United States before the twentieth century, and until the 1960s the U.S. government categorized immigrants from North Africa as "other Africans," not by their country of origin. In 1975 fewer than a hundred Algerians immigrated to the United States, but by the mid-1980s this number had grown, and 1,364 Algerian immigrants arrived in 2011.

The U.S. Census Bureau's 2006–2010 American Community Survey estimated that there were more than 14,716 Algerian Americans in the country. Large Algerian American populations are found in Texas, New York City, Miami, and Chicago. Dallas, Texas, has a large African (and North African) community and draws significant numbers of new immigrants.

HISTORY OF THE PEOPLE

Early History Around 900 BCE the region was populated by Berbers, a group from North Africa that was influenced by Carthaginians, Romans, and Byzantines. Beginning in the second century BCE the Romans built urban centers and maintained a military presence there. Much of what became Algeria was next ruled by Vandals, a Germanic tribe, who were in turn conquered in around 640 CE by Arabs, who brought Islam to the region.

In the early sixteenth century, Algeria became a province of the Ottoman Empire. The Ottomans were accepted in Algeria in part because they helped defend the area against the Spanish, who had been in conflict with Muslims since the thirteenth century and extended their campaign into North Africa. A number of Muslims and Jews from Spain settled in Algerian cities.

Modern Era In the 1830s France invaded Algeria, which then had a population of three million Muslims, and annexed it as a colony. France developed Algerian agriculture, mining, and manufacturing, centering the economy on small industry and a highly developed export trade. Algerian and European groups formed two separate subcultures with very little interaction or intermarriage. Many Algerians lost their lands to colonists, traditional leaders were eliminated if they did not cooperate with the French, and Muslims paid higher taxes than the European settlers. The colonial regime seriously hindered the overall education of Algerian Muslims who, prior to French rule, relied on religious schools to learn to read and write. It also confiscated religious endowment property (*awqaf*) that wealthy individuals had bequeathed to fund religious activities.

Although Algerians were not French citizens, France enlisted a large number of Algerians during World War I, and many lost their lives, leading to increased support for the Young Algerians, a nationalist group that had been founded just before the war. In 1926 the first group to call for Algerian independence, the Star of North Africa, was formed in Paris. In 1940, during World War II, France was defeated by Germany, and Algeria came under the rule of the Vichy government of southern France, which collaborated with Germany. Two years later, in November

1942, an Allied force of British and U.S. troops landed in the Algerian cities Algiers and Oran and were joined by Algerian Muslims fighting for their homeland, though some Algerians at the time were working with the Germans. At the end of the war, an Algerian demonstration in Sétif against the colonial system was harshly suppressed by the French. Algerians continued to demand the creation of an independent Algerian state federated with France. Instead, in 1947 they were granted an assembly, allowing them a small voice in self-government.

During the War of Independence (1954–1962) against France, nearly one million Algerians died. Upon independence, approximately one million Europeans, including 140,000 Jews, left Algeria. Most of those departing had French citizenship and did not identify with Arab culture. In the early 1980s the total foreign population was estimated at roughly 117,000. Of this number, about 75,000 were Europeans, including about 45,000 who were French. Many foreigners worked as technicians and teachers.

After independence in 1962, Algeria was led by a one-party, secular government, headed by President Ahmed Ben Bella, which organized public-sector enterprises into state corporations in an economy described as Algerian socialism. But Islamic activists who wanted to eliminate the legacy of Algeria's colonial past and to redefine Algerian identity clashed with the existing political system. In 1965 a coup d'état overthrew Ben Bella, who was replaced by Houari Boumedienne. The subsequent push to become more Arabic was seen as a means of national unity and was used by the government as a tool to ensure national sovereignty. Algerian street signs and shop signs were changed to Arabic, although 60 percent of the population at that time could not read Arabic.

Many Algerian Americans came to the United States to obtain a better education, to flee instability in Algeria, or because of fear of attack by fundamentalists who condemned their behavior. Professionals such as scientists, physicians, and academics have settled widely across the United States, often in communities without other Algerian Americans.

The pressure to Arabize was resisted by Berber population groups, such as the Kabyles, the Chaouia, the Tuareg, and the Mzabt. The Berbers, who constituted about one-fifth of the Algerian population, had resisted foreign influences since ancient times. They had fought against the Phoenicians, the Romans, the Ottoman Turks, and the French. In the fighting against France between 1954 and 1962, Berber men from Kabylie, a region in the north, participated in larger numbers than their share of the population warranted. After independence, the Berbers

maintained a strong ethnic consciousness and a determination to preserve their distinctive cultural identity and language.

A new constitution in 1989 dropped the word *socialist* from the official description of the country and guaranteed freedom of expression, association, and meeting, though it also withdrew the guarantee of women's rights that had been granted in the 1976 constitution. This same year saw the formation of the Islamic Salvation Front (FIS), an organization that sought to create a single Islamic state in which Islamic law would be strictly applied. In 1992, just before the second round of elections, the government banned the FIS and declared a state of emergency. A prolonged civil war followed, and between 1992 and 2002 more than 150,000 Algerians died in the violence. During this period there was also a sharp rise in emigration from Algeria.

In April 1999 Abdelaziz Bouteflika, backed by the military, won a presidential election in which all six other candidates had withdrawn to protest fraud. Even though there was an elected parliament, the main opposition party, the FIS, remained banned. At the time of Bouteflika's election, the Algerian government had contained the threat from Islamist rebels. Despite creating political upheaval, his election did not cause increased emigration. In fact, Bouteflika initiated a policy of reconciliation with moderate Islamists, giving them a degree of freedom of expression and persuading some to return to the country.

In 2001, in response to protests and boycotts, the government made concessions, such as legalizing the opposition, as well as naming Tamazight (Berber) as a national language and allowing it to be taught in schools. During the so-called Arab Spring in 2010, Algerians took to the streets to demand regime change and called for economic reforms. Algeria lifted its nineteen-year state of emergency on February 24, 2011.

SETTLEMENT IN THE UNITED STATES

Little is known about Algerian immigrants to the United States before the second half of the twentieth century. In the late 1700s Jacob Raphael Cohen, of Algerian origin, was the chief rabbi of Philadelphia. *The Algerine Spy in Pennsylvania*, a book by Peter Markoe published in Philadelphia in 1787, includes the fictional dispatches of a spy from Algiers reporting about the new formed United States. In immigration records until 1899 and in census records until 1920, all Arabs were recorded together in a category known as "Turkey in Asia." Until the 1960s North African Arabs were counted as "other African." Significant immigration of Muslims to the United States did not occur because Muslims feared that they would not be permitted to maintain their traditions. Census records suggest that only a few hundred Muslim men from all countries immigrated to the United States between 1900 and 1914.

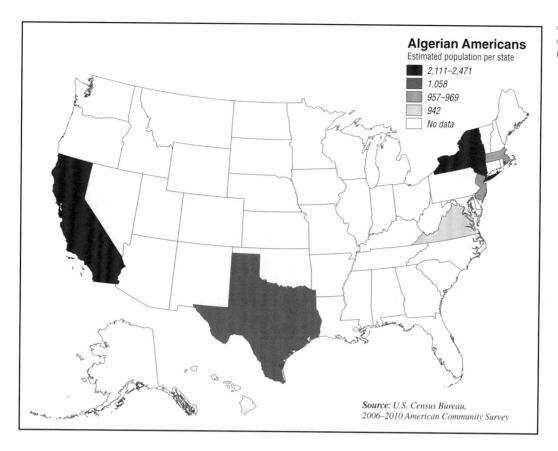

Algerian Americans
Estimated population per state

- 2,111–2,471
- 1,058
- 957–969
- 942
- No data

Source: U.S. Census Bureau, 2006–2010 American Community Survey

Algeria was introduced as an immigrant category in the United States in 1975, and 72 Algerians immigrated that year. Immigrant numbers increased gradually, and in 1984 there were 197 immigrants; 14 were relatives of U.S. citizens, and 31 were admitted on the basis of occupational preference. In 1998 the winners of the U.S. Diversity Visa (DV) program's lottery included 1,378 Algerians. The DV lottery makes available 55,000 permanent resident visas annually to persons from countries with low rates of immigration to the United States.

According to the U.S. Census Bureau's American Community Survey for 2006–2010, there were approximately 14,716 people of Algerian ancestry living in the United States. Of this group, 63 percent were foreign-born. In November 2009 Algeria and the United States entered into a new immigration agreement that eased immigration restrictions.

Algerian Americans have settled primarily in urban areas, such as New York City, Miami, Washington, D.C., Los Angeles, and Boston, as well as Dallas, Austin, and Houston, Texas. Many Algerian Americans came to the United States to obtain a better education, to flee instability in Algeria, or because of fear of attack by fundamentalists who condemned their behavior. Professionals such as scientists, physicians, and academics have settled widely across the United States, often in communities without other Algerian Americans.

Algerian Americans have formed associations, such as the Algerian-American Association of Greater Washington, which sponsors events and promotes Algerian heritage in the community. Many of these organizations aim to strengthen friendship and cooperation between the United States and Algeria.

LANGUAGE

Ethnic communities in Algeria have been distinguished primarily by language. The original language of Algeria is Tamazight (Berber). Arabic was introduced to the coastal regions by Arab conquerors in the seventh and eighth centuries CE. The language was adopted gradually across Algeria, but Berber remained the mother tongue in many rural areas. In Algeria, Berber and Arabic have mixed so that many words are swapped. In some Arabic-speaking areas, the words for various flora and fauna are still in Berber. Berber place names are numerous throughout the country.

The French language was imposed during colonization, which in Algeria began earlier and ended later than in the other nations of the Maghreb (the western part of North Africa). French remains common among Algerians, and many publications in Algeria are in French.

Arabic, the language of the majority of Algerians and the official language of the country, is a Semitic tongue related to Hebrew, Aramaic, and Amharic. The dominant language throughout North Africa and

ALGERIAN PROVERBS

- If you want the object to be solid, mold it out of your own clay.

- None but a mule denies his origin.

- The friend is known in a time of difficulty.

- An intelligent enemy is better than an ignorant friend.

- The iron is struck while it is hot.

- He who has been bitten by a snake is afraid of a palmetto cord.

- One day is in favor of you and the next is against you.

- God brings to all wheat its measure. (Meaning: it is natural to marry a person of one's own class or position.)

- Ask the experienced one, don't ask the doctor. (The answer a woman gives when she is reproved for speaking ill of another woman.)

- The forest is only burnt by its own wood. (The complaint of a parent whose child causes him trouble.)

- The son of a mouse will only turn out to be a digger. (Meaning: children become like their parents.)

- If your friend is honey, don't eat it all. (Meaning: you should not demand too much from your friend.)

- He who mixes with the grocer smells his perfume. (Meaning: you should be in the company of people from whom you may learn useful things.)

the Middle East, it is psychologically and sociologically important as the vehicle of Islam and Arab culture. Classical Arabic is the essential base of written Arabic and formal speech throughout the Arab world, including Algeria. The religious, scientific, historical, and literary heritage of Arabic people is transmitted in classical Arabic. Arabic scholars or individuals with a good classical education from any country with Arab heritage can converse with one another. The language of schools and the media in Algeria is modern standard Arabic.

Many Algerian immigrants in the United States are bilingual or multilingual. Second and third generation Algerian Americans often speak a mixture of Arabic and Berber at home with their parents or older family members. They typically learn this around the dinner table or at religion classes at the local mosque.

RELIGION

Most Algerian Americans are Muslim, though they are not always strict about their faith. Some do not belong to an Islamic center or mosque, and many find it difficult to perform the five daily prayers of their religion or to find *halal* food in the United States. However, because Algerian Americans come from a country in which rigorous adherence to Islamic practice is not stressed in all social sectors, they are adept at maintaining their religious traditions within American society.

Because more than two million Muslims live in the United States, there are mosques in many communities, and Algerian Americans worship at mosques alongside Muslims of other ancestries. As a result, these mosques tie Algerian Americans to the larger Muslim community in their locality. *Umma*, the Arabic word for "community," makes no distinction between a citizen of a particular country and the worldwide Muslim community. Most Algerian Americans observe Ramadan, a month of fasting, and they emphasize the main Muslim celebrations of the year, Eid al-Adha and Eid al-Fitr. As in other Muslim communities in the West, Algerian Americans have experienced a gradual loss of specifically Islamic values with each succeeding generation.

CULTURE AND ASSIMILATION

Many Algerian Americans are highly educated with professional occupations. Algerian women who immigrate to the United States usually avoid the *hijab* (the head scarf veil worn with a loose gown as a symbol of modest Islamic dress). They generally have fewer children and cook fewer meals, gradually adapting to American social customs. There is no segregation of sexes at social gatherings in homes and public settings except among the most traditional Muslims. Algerian Americans sometimes have as much difficulty gaining acceptance among American-born African Americans as they do among whites.

Algerian Americans who hold to Muslim beliefs purposely resist many aspects of assimilation as an expression of their religion. Their children, however, learn English and adapt to the new culture, and by the second and third generations, Algerian Americans are well assimilated and more similar to other Americans in their views on drinking, dancing, dating, and marriage. Traditionally marriages are arranged in Algeria, but most Algerian American couples select their own spouses.

Cuisine Many Algerian Americans prepare traditional Algerian cuisine. A common dish is *chorba*, a lamb, tomato, and coriander soup served with slices of lemon. A popular Algerian salad is made with sweet red peppers, tomatoes, sliced cucumber, onion, anchovy, boiled eggs, and basil or cilantro seasoned with olive oil and vinegar.

Other favorites include variations of *couscous* (a type of pasta shaped like tiny pellets), made of Baobab leaves, millet flour, and meat. One variety of Algerian couscous is made with onion, yellow zucchini squash, red potatoes, green pepper, garbanzo beans, vegetable stock, tomato paste, whole cloves, cayenne, and turmeric. As in other North African countries, meat stews are cooked in a *tagine*, an earthenware dish with a tall cover shaped like a cone or a dome. The stew, also called *tagine*, is made with chicken or lamb and flavored with olives or onions and okra or prunes. Another common meat dish is *L'Ham El HLou*, which is made with lamb, cinnamon, prunes, and raisins. Algerian desserts are light and delicate. Many dishes feature honey and dates, common ingredients in North Africa, but others, like crepes, reflect the French presence in Algeria.

Traditional Dress Traditional Algerian dress, also worn with minor variations by Berbers, has been replaced for the most part in Algeria by European clothing, except in rural areas. Traditionally a man wore a loose cotton shirt, usually covered by another reaching to the knees, and an outer garment of white cotton or wool draped so that the right arm remained free below the elbow. On the head was a red fez with a piece of cloth wound around it as a turban. Shepherds wore a muslin turban, loose baggy pants, and a leather girdle around a cloak. The turban was wound so that a loop of material hanging below the chin could be pulled up to cover the face. Women of nomadic tribes did not cover their faces, and they wore a shirt and pants (less bulky than men's trousers) under one or more belted dresses of printed cotton. The *hijab*, the head scarf worn with a loose gown that allows nothing but the hands and face to be seen, was not a traditional form of dress in Algeria.

Berber men in Kabylie, a region bordering the Mediterranean, wore a *burnous*, a full-length cloak with a hood woven out of very fine white or brown wool. The *fota*, a piece of cloth usually red, yellow, and black, was worn at the hips by Kabyle women. Kabyle women wore brightly colored loose dresses with a woolen belt and head scarves. Tuareg men, living in the south, wore a distinctive blue *litham*, a veil wound around the head to form a hood that covered the mouth and nose.

As the vast majority of Algerian immigrants to the United States come from urban environments in which modern, Western dress is common, most Algerian Americans dress much like other Americans. Algerian American women, however, often wear what is considered modern Islamic dress: a long skirt with a *hijab*.

Dances and Songs *Chaabi* is a popular type of traditional Algerian folk music characteristic of the region of Algiers. *Raï* mixes traditional Algerian

CHORBA HAMRA

Ingredients

1 tablespoon olive oil
½ pound lamb, cubed
1 large onion, chopped
2 teaspoons ground coriander
½ teaspoon cayenne
1 pinch black pepper
1 pinch cinnamon
1 teaspoon salt
1 pound tomatoes, crushed
1 large potato, sliced
1 large carrot, sliced
1 medium zucchini, sliced
1 stalk celery, chopped
1 can chickpeas
¼ pound vermicelli
6 cups vegetable broth
1 medium lemon, thinly sliced

Preparation

Heat oil until shimmering. Sauté in oil lamb, onion, coriander, cayenne, black pepper, cinnamon, and salt. When meat is well browned, add 6 cups broth. Bring to boil. Add all vegetables. Cover, reduce heat and simmer until vegetables are tender. Return to a medium boil. Add the pasta and cook until done.

Serve in bowls with a slice of lemon on top.

Serves 4

vocal styles with Western rhythms, synthesizers, and electronic magnification technology. It originated in northwestern Algeria in the 1970s. Spread through locally produced cassettes, *raï* has become popular throughout the world. The most prominent performers live in France. An Arabic word meaning "opinion," *raï* provoked the Algerian government, which banned it from being played on the radio until 1985, and militant fundamentalists were responsible for the death of *raï* singer Cheb Hasni. Another musician, Cheb Khaled, known as the king of *raï*, moved to Paris after being threatened by fundamentalists.

Holidays The most important Algerian national holiday is Revolution Day, on November 1, which celebrates the beginning of Algeria's revolution against France on that day in 1954. Independence Day, on July 5, recognizes Algeria's independence from France in 1962 and remains an important date for Algerian Americans. The Algerian-American Association of

Greater Washington, for example, held a special event in 2012 to celebrate the fiftieth anniversary of Independence Day, featuring Algerian dances and a show of traditional outfits. National Day, on June 19, commemorates the coup d'état against Algerian leader Ahmed Ben Bella in 1965.

For many Algerian Americans the Muslim religion's holidays are the most important. These include Ramadan, the Islamic month of fasting; Eid al-Fitr, the Islamic feast that signifies the end of Ramadan; and Eid al-Adha, the festival of sacrifice, celebrated on the last day of the *hajj*, the annual pilgrimage to Mecca required of all Muslims at least once in their lifetime.

FAMILY AND COMMUNITY LIFE
Before the War of Independence, the basic family unit in Algeria was the extended family, consisting of grandparents, their married sons and families, unmarried sons, unmarried daughters (or divorced or widowed daughters as well as their children), and occasionally other related adults. The patriarchal structure of the family meant the senior male member made all major decisions affecting family welfare, divided land and work assignments, and represented the family in dealings with outsiders. Within the home, each married couple usually had their own rooms opening onto the family courtyard, and they prepared meals separately. Women spent their lives under male authority, either of their father or husband, and devoted themselves entirely to the activities of the home. Children were raised by all members of the group, who passed on to them the concept and value of family solidarity.

Before Algeria achieved independence, divorce was common. As a result, marriage contracts typically stipulated the terms of divorce. Although only a man could initiate a divorce, a woman could ask the court to grant a divorce. Men who divorced their wives were obligated to pay the amount set forth in the marriage contract, while women who were allowed divorce by a court were forced to give up their right to these funds. An exception to this rule was when an Islamic judge recognized that a wife had been abused, in which case the judge could issue a decree divorce that would allow the wife to retain her right to the money agreed upon in the couple's marriage contract.

Because a woman gained status in her husband's home when she produced sons, mothers loved and favored their boys, often nursing them longer than they nursed girls. The relation between a mother and her son remained warm and intimate, whereas the father was a more distant figure. Families expressed solidarity by adhering to a code of honor that obligated members to provide aid to relatives in need and, if moving to a city to find work, to seek out and stay with family members. Among Berber groups, the honor and wealth of the lineage were so important that blood revenge was justified in their defense.

Algeria continues to have one of the most conservative legal codes concerning marriage, strictly observing Islamic marriage requirements. The legal age for marriage is twenty-one for men, eighteen for women. Upon marriage the bride traditionally went to the household, village, or neighborhood of the bridegroom's family, where she lived under the authority of her mother-in-law. In present-day Algeria a newly married couple will often take housing where they can find it. Divorce and polygamy were permitted in the classical Muslim law of marriage. In Algeria polygamy is now rare, and divorce is common. Women in Algeria have been allowed to legally file for divorce since 1959, but they face greater restrictions than men. For instance, men can file for divorce without providing justification, but women may only do so under certain conditions. Women's rights after divorce, particularly regarding financial support and child custody, remain a contentious issue in Algeria.

Compared to the average family size in Algeria, which was estimated to be 6.68 in 2008, Algerian American families tend to be small. According to the American Community Survey's estimates for 2006–2010, the average family size among Algerian Americans was 3.62 people, only slightly larger than the national average of 3.17. In the United States familial ties for Algerian Americans have loosened, and family relationships usually do not follow traditional customs of living space and decision making. Algerian American families prefer to live in separate quarters, have fewer children, and run their lives independently.

Gender Roles In Algeria women are traditionally regarded as weaker than men in mind, body, and spirit, and the honor of the family depends largely on the conduct of its women. Consequently, women are expected to be decorous, modest, and discreet. The slightest implication of impropriety, especially if publicly acknowledged, can damage the family's honor. Female virginity before marriage and fidelity afterward are considered essential to the maintenance of family honor. If they discover a transgression, men are traditionally bound to punish the offending woman. Girls are brought up to believe that they are inferior to men and must cater to them, and boys are taught to believe that they are entitled to that care.

Women's access to higher education in Algeria has improved significantly in the twenty-first century, even though rights to employment, political power, and autonomy are limited. By 2007 more than half of university students in Algeria were women, in part because some men in Algeria no longer see university education as useful for economic advancement. Although typically women return to the home after schooling, increasing numbers of women are entering the workforce, causing concern within the fundamentalist Islamic community about the role of women.

Algerian Americans Jillali Hamroune, Hocine Ameur, and Ahmin Merzouk stand in Bryant Park, New York, in 2009. They work, respectively, as a carpenter, a teacher, and a construction worker. FRANCO PAGETTI / VII / CORBIS

In the United States the majority of Algerian American women are more secular than their Algerian counterparts, though some maintain roles consistent with orthodox Islamic belief. To a large degree, this is an outcome of the fact that Algerian American women generally obtain higher levels of education than women in Algeria.

Education Algerian Americans as a group have a high level of educational attainment. According to the American Community Survey's estimates for 2006–2010, the vast majority of Algerian Americans, 91 percent, had a high school diploma or its equivalent (compared with 85 percent for the total U.S. population), and 51.6 percent had a bachelor's degree or higher (compared with 27.9 percent for the total U.S. population), and 23.5 percent had a graduate or professional degree (compared with 10.3 percent for the total U.S. population).

Compared with their peers in Algeria, Algerian American students have greater educational opportunities. Although education in Algeria became compulsory in 1976 for children between six and fifteen years old, about 20 percent of men and 40 percent of women were illiterate in 2002. Despite government support for technical training programs, Algeria has a critical shortage of workers in fields requiring technical skills.

After gaining independence from France in 1962, Algeria replaced French with Arabic in the schools and required students to study the Quran. The government has subsequently allowed French back into the classroom and tried to moderate the

influence of fundamentalist Islam in the schools, but religion remains an important focus of study. Algerians who attend university abroad tend to go to France as well as other European countries and the United States. For some Algerian students, education in the United States requires adjustment, as classes—for example, in history—are not taught from a pro-Islam perspective.

Courtship and Weddings Marriages in Algeria have traditionally been arranged, and only after a couple was engaged would they visit each other's homes and date. At a traditional wedding party, guests remain until the bride and groom retire to a room nearby and consummate the marriage. The bride's undergarments or bedclothes stained with hymeneal blood are then publicly displayed. The rate of arranged marriages has declined in Algeria along with increased education and urbanization, and many couples forego the traditional family celebration. In contemporary Algeria, the display of stained bedclothes is practiced only in very traditional, rural areas. In America, this tradition is very rarely, if ever, maintained.

Algerian Americans typically follow American dating patterns, choose their own spouses, and do not have traditional celebrations. Some Algerian Americans opt for secular weddings, especially when marrying outside the Algerian American community, as is increasingly common. In these cases, some discomfort may be caused among the bride's or groom's relatives. However, marriage outside the community has become increasingly common and accepted, especially among the well-educated and professional classes.

Funerals American Muslims, including Algerian Americans, attempt to follow traditional Islamic practices when a death occurs. According to traditional Muslim practice, burial takes place as quickly as possible, preferably within twenty-four hours of death. This is not always possible in the United States, where autopsies are sometimes required and funeral homes are more accustomed to burying bodies a few days after death. The deceased is washed, wrapped in a shroud, and carried to a cemetery. A casket is not typically used, but some states require it. Either at the deathbed or at the grave, the *shahada* (a declaration of the oneness of God) is whispered into the ear of the deceased. The body is placed in the grave with the face oriented toward Mecca. In the United States the number of Muslim cemeteries has been growing, and an increasing number of multidenominational cemeteries set aside a section to accommodate Muslims. Like other members of the American Muslim community, Algerian Americans maintain, when possible, traditional Islamic practices within local cemeteries, whether they are multidenominational or Muslim.

EMPLOYMENT AND ECONOMIC CONDITIONS

After Algeria's independence in 1962, the socialist orientation of the state discouraged the development of a class of small business owners and resulted in strong public anticapitalist sentiment. Economic liberalization under Chadli Bendjedid, president of Algeria from 1979 to 1992, transformed many state-owned enterprises into private entities and fostered the growth of an active and cohesive group of professional associations of small business owners, or *patronat*. The *patronat* has strongly supported government reforms and has persisted in its lobbying efforts. Some of its member associations include the Algerian Confederation of Employers, the General Confederation of Algerian Economic Operators, and the General Union of Algerian Merchants and Artisans. Algerian workers did not have the right to form autonomous labor unions until the Law on Trade Union Activity was passed by the National Assembly in June 1990.

In 2003 the labor force in Algeria was an estimated 11 million people. About 32 percent worked in government, 14 percent in agriculture, 10 percent in construction and public works, 13 percent in industry, and 14 percent in trade. The unemployment rate in 2011 was about 10 percent. Women officially constituted only about 20 percent of the labor force but were highly represented in certain fields requiring advanced education, including law and medicine.

Of the 197 Algerians who immigrated to the United States in 1984, 116 were professionals, and 81 had no occupation. Some were spouses of Algerian Americans already living in the United States. Since that time many Algerian immigrants have been well educated and employed as physicians, academics, and engineers. In general, Algerian American workers receive higher salaries and have more opportunities for advancement than their counterparts in Algeria, and the U.S. economy is more receptive to entrepreneurs, especially for women.

POLITICS AND GOVERNMENT

The United States and Algeria have endured a sometimes rocky relationship from the beginning of U.S. history. In the eighteenth century European maritime powers paid the tribute demanded by rulers of North Africa states (Algiers, Tunis, Tripoli, and Morocco) to prevent attacks on their ships by corsairs (pirates). After gaining independence from England, the United States government planned to construct warships to deal with the threat, but in 1797 it concluded a treaty with the ruler of Algiers guaranteeing payment of the tribute, amounting to $10 million over a twelve-year period. Payments in ransom and tribute to the privateering states amounted to 20 percent of U.S. government annual revenues in 1800.

After Algeria gained independence from France in 1962, Algeria's commitment to socialism, as well as the desire of its Islamists for a global revolution against Western capitalism and imperialism, antagonized relations with the United States. Algeria broke diplomatic relations with the United States in 1967 following the June 1967 war between Israel and its neighboring states of Egypt, Syria, and Jordan. Relations remained strained throughout the 1970s, though increased demands in the United States for energy and a growing Algerian need for capital and technical assistance resulted in renewed interaction between the two countries. In 1980 the United States imported more than $2.8 billion worth of oil from Algeria, making it Algeria's largest export market. In 1990 Algeria received $25.8 million in U.S. financial assistance and bought $1 billion in imports from the United States.

In the United States, Algerian Americans have been represented in politics and government largely through organizations supporting the interests of Arab Americans. The National Association of Arab-Americans, a foreign policy lobbying organization, was founded in 1972 to formulate and work toward a nonpartisan U.S. policy agenda in the Middle East and Arab nations. The American-Arab Anti-Discrimination Committee (ADC), formed in 1980, is committed to defending the rights of people of Arab descent and promoting their cultural heritage. The ADC, which is the largest Arab American grassroots organization in the United States, is at the forefront of combating defamation and negative stereotyping of Arab Americans in the media and wherever else it is practiced.

NOTABLE INDIVIDUALS

Literature Claire Messud, novelist and creative writing professor, was born in Greenwich, Connecticut, in 1966. Her father was Algerian, and her mother was Canadian. Messud has taught creative writing at several universities, including the University of Maryland, Amherst College, and Kenyon College, and has won awards from the American Academy of Arts and Letters. She is best known for her 2006 novel *The Emperor's Children*.

Medicine Elias Zerhouni, radiologist and medical researcher, was born in Algiers in 1951. He immigrated to the United States following his medical training in Algeria and completed his residency at Johns Hopkins University. He served as consultant to the administration of President Ronald Reagan and to the World Health Organization. In 2002 President George W. Bush appointed Zerhouni as the fifteenth director of the National Institute of Health.

Stage and Screen Yasmine Bleeth, an actress best known for her work on the American TV show *Baywatch*, was born in New York in 1968 to an Algerian mother and an American father. In 1995 *People* magazine named Bleeth as one of the "50 Most Beautiful People in the World."

MEDIA

The Amazigh Voice

A newsletter published quarterly since 1992, it informs members and other interested persons about Amazigh (Berber) language and culture and acts as a medium for the exchange of ideas and information. It is distributed worldwide and is also online.

P.O. Box 1702
Bayonne, New Jersey 07002
Phone: (201) 388-1586
Fax: (201) 650-6046
URL: www.amazigh-voice.com

Award-winning American novelist and creative writing instructor, Claire Messud is the daughter of a Canadian mother and French Algerian father. RON BULL / TORONTO STAR / GETTY IMAGES

ORGANIZATIONS AND ASSOCIATIONS

Algerian-American Association of Greater Washington

An organization founded in 1992 to provide social, cultural, and educational events for Algerian Americans in the Washington, D.C., area.

Smail Farid, President
P.O. Box 65063
Washington, D.C. 20035-5063
URL: www.aaagw.org

Algerian American Association of Northern California

An organization established in 1992 to develop and strengthen ties between Algerian Americans and others in Northern California and the nation in general.

Chakib Khemici, President
P.O. Box 2213
Cupertino, California 95015
URL: www.aaa-nc.org

Amazigh Cultural Association in America (ACAA)

An association organized and operated exclusively for cultural, educational, and scientific purposes to contribute to saving, promoting, and enriching the Amazigh (Berber) language and culture.

Akli Gana, President
442 Route 206 North
Suite 163
Bedminster, New Jersey 07921
Phone: (215) 592-7492
URL: www.tamazgha.org

Middle East & Islamic Studies Collection, Cornell University Library

A collection containing political documents, studies, maps, and other printed artifacts on Algerian culture and history.

Ali Houissa, Middle East & Islamic Studies Bibliographer
Collection Development Department
504 Olin Library

Cornell University
Ithaca, New York 14853
Phone: (607) 255-5752
URL: www.library.cornell.edu/colldev/mideast

SOURCES FOR ADDITIONAL STUDY

Arthur, John A. *Invisible Sojourners: African Immigrant Diaspora in the United States*. Santa Barbara, CA: Praeger, 2000.

Christelow, Allan. *Algerians without Borders: The Making of a Global Frontier Society*. Gainesville: University Press of Florida, 2012.

Entelis, John P., and Phillip C. Naylor. *State and Society in Algeria*. Boulder, CO: Westview Press, 1992.

Messaoudi, Khalida. *Unbowed: An Algerian Woman Confronts Islamic Fundamentalism*. Translated by Anne C. Vila. Philadelphia: University of Pennsylvania Press, 1998.

Metz, Helen Chapin. *Algeria: A Country Study*. Washington, D.C.: Federal Research Division, Library of Congress, 1984.

Ruedy, John. *Modern Algeria: The Origins and Development of a Nation*. Bloomington: Indiana University Press, 2005.

AMISH

Donald B. Kraybill

OVERVIEW

The Amish in the United States are a religious and cultural group that came to America in the eighteenth and nineteenth centuries from what is today the Alsace region of northeastern France. They are one of the more unique cultural groups in the United States. Their rejection of automobiles, use of horse-drawn farm machinery, and distinctive clothing set them apart from the high-tech culture of modern life. Extinct in their European homeland since 1937, today the Amish live in more than 400 settlements in 30 states and the Canadian province of Ontario. They function without a national organization or an annual convention. Local church districts—congregations of 25 to 35 families—are the heart of Amish life and hold the primary ecclesiastical authority.

The Amish came to the United States in two waves: 1736–1770 and 1815–1860. Their first U.S. settlements were in southeastern Pennsylvania. Eventually, they followed the frontier to other counties in Pennsylvania, then to Ohio, Indiana, and other Midwestern states. The Amish and a similar group, the Mennonites, are both descendants of early Anabaptists, but they split in the early seventeenth century. Mennonites, named for the religious leader Menno Simons, were somewhat more liberal in their acceptance of modern developments, while the Amish were followers of Jakob Ammann's more conservative practice. In the 1960s there was a reformist movement, or schism, among the Amish that resulted in a division into New Order Amish and Old Order Amish. The two groups share a great many similarities, but the smaller New Order Amish, some in Ohio and some in Pennsylvania, are a little more open to technology, allow for air travel, and are more prohibitive of alcohol and tobacco use. They are often referred to as the Amish Brotherhood.

By 2013, Amish communities had more than 280,000 adherents. Nearly two-thirds live in Ohio, Pennsylvania, and Indiana. Other sizable communities are in Iowa, Michigan, Missouri, New York, Wisconsin, Illinois, and Kentucky. Few Amish live west of the Mississippi or in the deep South. The Young Center for Anabaptist and Pietist Studies at Elizabethtown College reported that in 2013 the Amish population was doubling every 18 to 20 years because each Amish couple averages seven children, and 85 percent of Amish youth join the church formally as young adults and remain dedicated to it for the rest of their lives.

HISTORY OF THE PEOPLE

Early History The roots of the Amish stretch back to sixteenth-century Europe. Impatient with the pace of the Protestant Reformation, youthful reformers in Zurich, Switzerland, outraged religious authorities by baptizing each other in January 1525. The rebaptism of adults was then a crime punishable by death. Baptism, in the dissidents' view, was only meaningful for adults who had made a voluntary confession of faith. Because they were already baptized as infants in the Catholic Church, the radicals were dubbed "Anabaptists," or rebaptizers, by their detractors. Anabaptism, also known as the Radical Reformation, spread through the Cantons of Switzerland, Germany, and the Netherlands.

The rapid spread of Anabaptist groups threatened civil and religious authorities, who soon sent "Anabaptist hunters" to stalk the reformers. The first martyr was drowned in 1527. Over the next few decades, thousands of Anabaptists were burned at the stake, drowned in rivers, starved in prisons, or beheaded. The 1,200-page *Martyrs Mirror*, first published in Dutch in 1660 and later in German and English, records the carnage. Many Amish have a German edition of the *Martyrs Mirror* in their homes today.

The Swiss Anabaptists sought to follow the ways of Jesus in daily life, loving their enemies, forgiving insults, and turning the other cheek. Some Anabaptist groups resorted to violence, but many repudiated force and resolved to live peaceably even with adversaries. The risk of execution tested their faith in the power of suffering love. Although some recanted, many died for their faith. Harsh persecution pushed many Anabaptists underground and into rural hideaways. Swiss Anabaptism took root in rural soil. The sting of persecution, however, divided the church and the larger society in Anabaptist minds. The Anabaptists believed that the kingdoms of this world, anchored in the use of coercion, clashed with the peaceable kingdom of God.

By 1660 some Swiss Anabaptists had migrated north to the Alsace region of present-day France, which borders southwestern Germany. The Amish emerged in 1693 when Swiss and South German Anabaptists split into two streams: Amish and Mennonite. Jakob Ammann, an elder of the Alsatian church, sought to revitalize the Anabaptist movement in 1693. He proposed holding communion twice a year rather than the typical Swiss practice of once a year. He argued that Anabaptist Christians in obedience to Christ should wash each other's feet in the communion service. To promote doctrinal purity and spiritual discipline, Ammann forbade fashionable dress and the trimming of beards, and he administered a strict discipline in his congregations. Appealing to New Testament teachings, Ammann advocated the shunning of excommunicated members. Ammann's followers, eventually called Amish, soon became another sect in the Anabaptist family.

Modern Era In the century following Ammann's death, sometime between 1712 and 1730, Amish endured rounds of persecution by both local communities and changing governments. While the Swiss tried to purge their country of Anabaptists, the French sometimes sought Amish for their purported hard work and skilled farming. The French Revolution granted equal French citizenship to the Amish but also required military service, which the Amish doctrine of pacifism did not allow. Although they were granted an exception to the service by paying a tax, their way of life was precarious. When Napoleon overthrew the French government, the Amish were again threatened with conscription into the military. By this time, the United States beckoned, and the numbers of Amish in Europe declined. In addition to emigration, another contributing factor to their European decline was that the Amish in Europe were typically tenant farmers rather than landowners, making it difficult for them to form supportive communities. The congregations slowly dissolved or merged with Mennonite congregations, as happened when the last European Amish congregation in Ixheim, Germany, merged with a local Mennonite church in 1937.

SETTLEMENT IN THE UNITED STATES

Searching for political stability and religious freedom, the Amish came to North America in two waves, first in the mid-1700s and then beginning in the early 1800s. Amish immigrants to North America came at the same time as other sizable groups of German-speaking immigrants. For the Amish, who had endured severe persecution for the religious faith for nearly two centuries in Europe, the promise of openly practicing their religion without discrimination or harassment was a major enticement. Moreover, because of economic and political instability, social upheaval, and the devastation of frequent wars, Amish people also were motivated to emigrate to establish their own communities in a new country where they could enjoy more stability and control over their lives.

Between 1736 and 1770, about 500 Amish arrived in Philadelphia and settled in the southeastern Pennsylvania counties of Berks, Chester, and Lancaster. By 1767 some of these families had moved west into Somerset County, and by 1791, others had purchased farms in Pennsylvania's Kishacoquillas Valley. Descendants of these eighteenth-century arrivals eventually moved westward to establish communities from eastern Ohio (in 1809) to Iowa (in 1840).

A second wave of some 3,000 Amish immigrants arrived in North America between 1815 and 1860, seeking both economic opportunity and freedom from compulsory military service, which by then was becoming more common in Europe. Very few of these nineteenth-century newcomers set up homes in Pennsylvania, although some traveled through the state and found temporary shelter among fellow church members there. Because of high land prices in the East, most nineteenth-century Amish immigrants headed west. Some arrived in eastern ports, while others arrived on European cotton ships docking in New Orleans and then traveled up the Mississippi River and its tributaries to new homes in Illinois, Indiana, Iowa, Ohio, and Ontario. Both waves of immigrants acknowledged one another as Amish even though economic factors and kinship networks largely determined where they settled.

Amish immigrants came from rural areas in Europe where they had developed a strong tradition of agriculture. Virtually all of them arriving in North America sought to purchase land where they could establish small farms to sustain their families and small communities of 15 to 30 households. They did not establish land reservations or sequester themselves in isolated areas, but rather they lived among other German immigrants. Although Amish people carried distinct religious convictions (such as pacifism), they shared many folkways with other German immigrants as well as a German dialect that eventually became known as Pennsylvania Dutch. The challenges they faced establishing their communities were in many ways similar to those of other German immigrants who settled in rural areas.

LANGUAGE

The Amish speak English, German, and a dialect known as Pennsylvania German or Pennsylvania Dutch. The dialect is the Amish native tongue and should not be confused with the Dutch language of the Netherlands. Originally a German dialect, Pennsylvania Dutch was spoken by Germanic settlers in southeastern Pennsylvania. The pronunciation of the word *Deutsche* (the German word for "German") gradually became *Dutch* in English, and eventually the dialect became known as Pennsylvania Dutch. Even the Amish who live outside of Pennsylvania speak the Pennsylvania German dialect. In Amish culture, the dialect is used mainly as a form of oral communication: It is the language of work, family, and friendship.

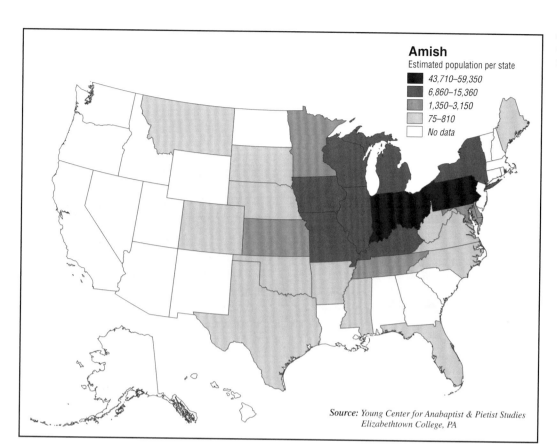

Amish
Estimated population per state

- 43,710–59,350
- 6,860–15,360
- 1,350–3,150
- 75–810
- No data

*Source: Young Center for Anabaptist & Pietist Studies
Elizabethtown College, PA*

Pennsylvania Dutch is children's first language until they learn English in the Amish school. Students learn to read, write, and speak English from their Amish teachers, who learned it from their Amish teachers. But Pennsylvania Dutch prevails in friendly banter on the playground. By the end of the eighth grade, young Amish have developed basic competence in English, although it may be spoken with what sounds like a German accent. Adults are able to communicate in fluent English with their non-Amish neighbors. When talking among themselves, the Amish sometimes mix English words with the dialect, especially when discussing technical issues. Letters are often written in English, with salutations and occasional phrases in the dialect. Competence in English varies directly with occupational roles and frequency of interaction with English speakers. Ministers are often the ones who are best able to read German. Idioms of the dialect are frequently mixed with German in Amish sacred writings. Although children study formal German in school, they do not speak it on a regular basis.

Greetings and Popular Expressions Common Pennsylvania Dutch greetings and other expressions include the following: *Gude Mariye* (Good morning); *Gut-n-Owed* (Good evening); *Wie geht's?* (How are you?); *En frehlicher Grischtdsaag* (Merry Christmas); *Frehlich Neiyaahr* (Happy

New Year); *Kumm ball widder* (Come soon again). When inviting others to gather around a table to eat, a host might say *Kumm esse*.

RELIGION

The Amish are quite religious, yet their communities reveal no church buildings or sacred symbols, and there is no formal religious education in Amish schools. However, religious meanings pervade all aspects of Amish lives. Religion is practiced, not debated. Silent prayers before and after meals embroider each day with reverence. The Amish way of living and being requires neither proselytizing nor formal theology.

The *Ordnung*, a religious blueprint for expected behavior, regulates private, public, and ceremonial conduct. Unwritten in most settlements, the Ordnung is passed on by oral tradition. The Ordnung marks expected Amish conduct, such as the male tradition of wearing a beard without a mustache, traveling via a buggy, and speaking the dialect. It also specifies taboos, including divorce, filing a lawsuit, wearing jewelry, owning a car, and attending college. The understandings evolve over the years and are updated as the church faces new issues, such as embryo transplants in cattle, using cell phones and computers, and working in factories. Core understandings, such as wearing a beard, relying on horses and buggies, and terminating formal education at the eighth grade, span all Amish settlements, but the finer points of the Ordnung vary considerably among the forty different tribes of Amish.

Although ordained leaders update the Ordnung in periodic meetings, each bishop interprets it for his local congregation. Thus, dress styles and the use of cell phones and battery-powered appliances may vary by church district. Once embedded in the Ordnung and established as tradition, the rules rarely change. As new issues face the church, leaders identify those which may be detrimental to community life. Changes deemed to be nonthreatening to their way of life, such as weed-whackers and trampolines, may be overlooked and gradually slip into Amish culture. Battery-powered video cameras, which might lead to other video entanglements with the outside world, would surely be forbidden.

Children learn the ways of the Ordnung by observing adults. The Ordnung defines the way things are in a child's mind. Teenagers, free from the supervision of the church, sometimes flirt with worldly ways and flaunt the Ordnung. At baptism, however, young adults between the ages of sixteen and twenty-two declare their Christian faith and vow to uphold the Ordnung for the rest of their lives. Those who break their promise face excommunication and shunning. Those choosing not to be baptized may gradually drift away from the community, but they are welcome to return to their families without the stigma of shunning.

Worship Services Worship services held in Amish homes reaffirm the moral order of Amish life. Church districts hold services every other Sunday. A group of 200 or more, including neighbors and relatives who have an "off Sunday," gather for worship. They meet in a farmhouse, the basement of a newer home, or in a shed or barn. A fellowship meal at noon and informal visiting follow the three-hour morning service.

Most Amish do not actively evangelize. They welcome outsiders, but few make the cultural leap. Membership in some settlements doubles every eighteen to twenty years. Their growth is fueled by a robust birth rate that averages seven children per family.

The simple but unwritten liturgy revolves around hymn singing and two sermons. Without the aid of organs, offerings, candles, crosses, robes, or flowers, members yield themselves to God in the spirit of humility. The congregation sings from the *Ausbund*, a hymnal of German songs without musical notations that date back to the sixteenth-century Anabaptists. The tunes, passed across the generations by memory, are sung in unison without any musical accompaniment. The slow, chant-like cadence means a single song may stretch over

twenty minutes. Extemporaneous or prepared sermons, preached in the Pennsylvania German dialect, recount biblical stories as well as lessons from farm life. Preachers exhort members to be obedient to Amish ways.

Communion services, held each autumn and spring, frame the religious year. These ritual high points emphasize self-examination and spiritual rejuvenation. Sins are confessed and members reaffirm their vow to uphold the Ordnung. Communion is held when the congregation is at peace, when all members are in harmony with the Ordnung. The six- to eight-hour communion service includes preaching, a light meal during the service, and the commemoration of Christ's death with bread and wine. Pairs of members wash each other's feet, in a ritual that reenacts Jesus's washing of his disciples' feet during Passover. At the end of the communion, service members give an alms offering to the deacon, the only time that offerings are collected in Amish services.

Excommunication Baptism, worship, and communion are sacred rites that revitalize and preserve the Ordnung. But the Amish, like everyone else, forget, rebel, experiment, and stray. Major transgressions are confessed publicly in a members meeting following the worship service. Violations of the Ordnung—using a tractor in the field, posing for a television camera, flying on an airplane, filing a lawsuit, joining a political organization, or opening a questionable business—are confessed publicly. Public confession of sins diminishes self-will, reminds members of the supreme value of submission, restores the wayward into the community of faith, and underscores the lines of faithfulness which encircle the community.

The headstrong who spurn the advice of elders and refuse to confess their sin face a six-week probation. The next step is the *Meidung*, or shunning, which involves rites of shaming, especially at public gatherings. For example, someone who is shunned will be seated at a separate table at a wedding meal. For the unrepentant, social avoidance becomes a lifetime quarantine. If their stubbornness does not mellow into repentance, they face excommunication. Members terminate social interaction and financial transactions with the excommunicated. However, even years after their excommunication, they can be restored to full membership if they confess their sins and agree to affirm the teachings of the church.

CULTURE AND ASSIMILATION

The Amish have been able to maintain a distinctive ethnic subculture by successfully resisting acculturation and assimilation. They do this by emphasizing their separation from the world, rejecting higher education, selectively using technology, and restricting close interaction with outsiders.

Traditions, Customs, and Beliefs At first glance all of North America's Amish groups appear pressed from the same cultural mold. A deeper look reveals many differences among the forty Amish affiliations. For instance, some of them forbid milking machines, while others depend on them. Mechanical hay balers widely used in some areas are taboo in others. Prescribed buggy tops are gray or black in many affiliations, but other groups have white or yellow tops. Buttons on clothing are banished in many groups but acceptable in others. The dead are embalmed in one settlement but not in another. Some bishops permit telephones in small shops, but others do not. Artificial insemination of livestock is acceptable in one district but not in another. In some communities virtually all the men are farmers, but in others many adults work in small shops and cottage industries. In still other settlements Amish persons work in rural factories operated by non-Amish persons. Practices vary between church districts even within the same settlement.

Several distinctive badges of ethnic identity unite the Old Order Amish across North America: horse-and-buggy transportation; the use of horses and mules for field work; plain dress in many variations; a beard and shaven upper lip for men; a prayer cap for women; the Pennsylvania German dialect; worship in homes; eighth-grade, parochial schooling; the rejection of electricity from public utility lines; and taboos on the ownership of televisions and computers.

Amish life pivots on *Gelassenheit* (pronounced "Ge-las-en-hite"), the cornerstone of Amish values. Roughly translated, this German word means submission, or yielding to a higher authority. It entails self-surrender, resignation to God's will, yielding to others, self-denial, contentment, and a quiet spirit. The religious meaning of Gelassenheit expresses itself in a quiet and reserved personality and places the needs of others above self. It nurtures a subdued self marked by modesty and reserve, gentle handshakes, lower voices, and slower strides. Children learn the essence of Gelassenheit in a favorite verse: "I must be a Christian child, / Gentle, patient, meek, and mild, / Must be honest, simple, true, / I must cheerfully obey, / Giving up my will and way."

Another favorite saying explains that *JOY* means *Jesus* first, *Yourself* last, and *Others* in between. As the cornerstone of Amish culture, Gelassenheit collides with the bold, assertive individualism of modern life that seeks and rewards personal achievement, self-fulfillment, and individual recognition at every turn.

The spirit of Gelassenheit expresses itself in obedience, humility, and simplicity. To Amish thinking, obedience to the will of God is *the* cardinal religious value. Disobedience is dangerous. Unconfessed, it leads to eternal separation. Obedience is coupled with humility in Amish life. Pride, a religious term for unbridled individualism, is discouraged. Amish teachers remind students that the middle letter of pride is *I*. Proud individuals display the spirit of arrogance, not Gelassenheit. They are pushy, bold, and forward. What non-Amish consider proper credit for one's accomplishments is what the Amish view as the hankerings of a vain spirit. The Amish contend that pride disturbs the equality and tranquility of an orderly community. The humble person freely gives of self in the service of community without seeking recognition.

Simplicity is also esteemed in Amish life. Simplicity in clothing, household decor, architecture, and worship nurtures equality and orderliness. Fancy and gaudy decorations lead to pride. Luxury and convenience cultivates vanity. The tools of self-adornment—make-up, jewelry, wristwatches, and wedding rings—are taboo and viewed as signs of pride.

Most Amish do not actively evangelize. They welcome outsiders, but few make the cultural leap. Membership in some settlements doubles every eighteen to twenty years. Their growth is fueled by a robust birth rate that averages seven children per family. The defection rate varies by settlement, but is usually less than 15 percent. Thus, six out of seven children, on average, remain Amish throughout their lives.

Beyond biological reproduction, a dual strategy of resistance and compromise has enabled the Amish to flourish in the modern world. They have resisted acculturation by constructing social fences around their community. Core values are translated into visible symbols of identity. Badges of ethnicity—horse, buggy, lantern, dialect, and dress—draw sharp contours between Amish and modern life.

The Amish resist the forces of modernization in other ways. Cultural ties to the outside world are curbed by speaking the dialect, marrying within the group, spurning television, prohibiting higher education, and limiting social interaction with outsiders. Privately operated schools insulate Amish youth from the contaminating influence of worldly peers. The temptations of the outside world, however, have always been a factor in Amish life. During *rumschpringen*, or "running around," which happens between the ages of sixteen and the early twenties, Amish youth engage in social activities with their friends and begin courtship with those of the opposite sex. In this period, some Amish teenagers and young adults may flirt with such temptations as drinking and driving cars before they accept baptism and assume their adult responsibilities within the Amish community. Though the vast bulk of rumschpringen behavior is, for the most part, relatively mild and quiet, it occasionally includes more extreme activities. In 1998, for example, two Amish men in Lancaster County were charged with selling cocaine to other young people in their community.

Amish children use scooters to get to school in Lancaster County, Pennsylvania. H. MARK WEIDMAN PHOTOGRAPHY / ALAMY

And in 1999, as many as forty Amish teenagers turned violent after a drinking binge and seriously vandalized an Amish farmstead. Community elders abhor such events, which are rare. An overwhelming majority of youth engage in recreational activities within their communities that are supervised by parents.

The survival strategy of the Amish also involves cultural compromises, which sometimes results in odd mixtures of tradition and progress. Tractors may be used at Amish barns but not in fields. Horses and mules pull modern farm machinery in some settlements. Twelve-volt electricity from batteries is acceptable, but not electricity that comes from public utility lines. Hydraulic and air pressure are used instead of electricity to operate modern machines in many Amish carpentry and mechanical shops. Members frequently ride in cars or vans, but are not permitted to drive them. Telephones, kept out of Amish homes, are installed along farm lanes and in shops. Modern gas appliances fill Amish kitchens in some states, and lanterns illuminate modern bathrooms in some Amish homes.

These riddles of Amish life reflect delicate bargains that the Amish have struck between their desire to maintain tradition while enjoying the fruits of progress. The Amish are willing to change but not at the expense of communal values and ethnic identity. They use modern technology but not when it disrupts family and community stability. Viewed within the context of Amish history, the compromises are reasonable ways of achieving community goals and preserving core values while permitting selective modernization. Such flexibility boosts the economic vitality of the community and also helps retain the allegiance of Amish youth.

Cuisine Food preferences among the Amish vary somewhat from state to state. Breakfast fare for many families includes eggs, fried potatoes, toast, and in some communities, commercially manufactured cereals such as cornflakes. Typical breakfast foods in Pennsylvania also include shoofly pie, a molasses pie that is sometimes dipped in or covered with coffee or milk; stewed crackers in warm milk; mush made from corn meal; and sausage. Puddings and scrapple (a pan fried mixture of cornmeal or flour and pork scraps) are also breakfast favorites. Puddings consist of ground liver, heart, and kidneys from pork and beef.

For farm families the mid-day dinner is usually the largest meal of the day. Noontime dinners and evening suppers often include beef or chicken dishes, and vegetables in season from the family garden, such as peas, corn, green beans, lima beans, and carrots. Mashed potatoes covered with beef gravy, noodles with brown butter, chicken potpie, and sauerkraut are regional favorites. For side dishes and desserts there are applesauce, cornstarch pudding, tapioca, and fruit pies in season, such as apple, rhubarb, pumpkin, and snitz pies made with dried apples. Potato soup and chicken-corn-noodle soup are commonplace. In summer months, cold fruit soups consisting of strawberries, raspberries, or blueberries added to milk and bread cubes appear on Amish tables. Meadow tea, homemade root beer, and instant drink mixes are used in the summer.

Food preservation and preparation for large families and sizable gatherings is an enormous undertaking. Each community has a traditional menu that is typically served at large meals following church services, weddings, and funerals. Host families often bake three dozen pies for the noontime meal following the biweekly church service. Quantities of canned food vary by family size and preference but it is not uncommon for a family to can 150 quarts of apple sauce, 100 quarts of peaches, 60 quarts of pears, 50 quarts of grape juice, and 50 quarts of pizza sauce at a time.

Amish communities are not self-sufficient. They buy food products and other household items from commercial stores, as well as from retail establishments operated by the Amish and Mennonites themselves. The growing use of instant pudding, instant drinks, snack foods, and canned soups reflects time constraints and the difficulties of cooking from scratch for large families. The use of commercial food rises as families leave the farm and especially as women take on entrepreneurial roles.

Traditional Dress The Amish church prescribes dress regulations for its members, but the unwritten standards vary considerably by settlement. Men are expected to wear a wide brim hat and a vest when they appear in public. In winter months and at church services they wear a black suit coat, which is typically fastened with hooks and eyes rather than with buttons. Men use suspenders instead of belts. As soon as they are married, men grow a beard.

Amish women are expected to wear a prayer covering and a bonnet when they appear in public settings. Most women wear a cape over their dresses as well as a white apron. The three parts of the dress are often fastened together with straight pins. Various colors, including green, brown, blue, and lavender, are permitted for men's shirts and women's dresses, but designs and figures in the fabric are taboo. Although young girls do not wear a prayer covering, Amish

SHOOFLY PIE

Ingredients

1 cup dark molasses

¾ cup boiling water

1 teaspoon baking soda, dissolved in hot water

1 egg, beaten

⅔ cup brown sugar

¼ cup butter

1 cup flour

dash of salt

1 9-inch unbaked pie crust

Preparation

Preheat oven to 400°F.

To make syrup: Dissolve baking soda in boiling water, then mix with molasses in medium bowl. Whisk in egg. Pour mixture into pie shell.

To make crumb mixture: In another bowl, mix the flour, brown sugar, shortening or butter. Spread this onto the molasses mixture.

Bake at 400°F for 10 minutes, then reduce heat to 350°F and bake until center of pie is set, about 35 minutes. Cool on a rack until the pie is firm, about 45 minutes.

children are typically dressed similarly to their parents. Most Amish make their own clothes, although shoes are also often store-bought.

Traditional Arts and Crafts The Amish are widely known for their handmade crafts such as quilts, furniture and cabinets, baskets, and toys. Because of their reputation for being well-made and sturdy, Amish crafts are desirable retail items outside of Amish communities, and many Amish have thriving small businesses to sell their crafts to tourists and even online (though the online stores are run by non-Amish). However, the heart of traditional Amish crafts is their usefulness in the home or on the farm. Each community of Amish quilters has its own style that changes slowly over time. Amish quilts are characterized by black or brown fabric off setting other solid, bright or pastel colors with generally simple piecing designs and more elaborate stitching. Amish furniture is made in many styles and is characterized by carefully chosen solid hardwood.

Holidays The Amish share some national holidays with their non-Amish neighbors and add others of their own; thus the Amish calendar underscores both their participation in and separation from the larger world. As conscientious objectors, they have little enthusiasm for patriotic days with a military flair. Memorial Day, Veterans Day, and the Fourth of July are barely noticed. Labor Day stirs little interest. The witches and goblins of Halloween run contrary to Amish conventions; pumpkins may be displayed in some settlements, but without cut faces. Martin Luther King Jr.'s birthday slips by unnoticed in many rural enclaves.

Amish holidays mark the rhythm of the seasons and religious celebrations. A day for prayer and fasting precedes the October communion service in some communities. Fall weddings provide ample holidays of another sort. Amish celebrate Thanksgiving Day with turkey dinners and family gatherings. New Year's Day is a quiet time for family gatherings. In many communities a second day is added to the celebrations of Christmas, Easter, and Pentecost. The regular holiday, a sacred time, flows with quiet family activities. The following day, or second Christmas, Easter Monday, and Pentecost Monday, provides time for recreation, visiting, and sometimes shopping. Ascension day, the day prior to Pentecost, is a holiday for visiting, fishing, and other forms of recreation.

Christmas and Easter festivities are devoid of commercial trappings. Families exchange Christmas cards and gifts. Some presents are homemade crafts and practical gifts but are increasingly store bought. Homes are decorated with greens, but not Christmas trees, stockings, lights, Santa Claus, or mistletoe. Although eggs are sometimes painted and children may receive a basket of candy, the Easter bunny does not visit Amish homes. Instead, these sacred holidays revolve around religious customs and family gatherings. Birthdays are celebrated at home and school with cakes and gifts. Parents often share a special snack of cookies or popsicles with school friends to honor a child's birthday.

Health Care Issues and Practices The Amish use modern medical services to some extent. Lacking professionals within their ranks, they rely on the services of dentists, optometrists, nurses, and physicians in local health centers, clinics, and hospitals. They cite no biblical injunctions against modern health care, but they do believe that God is the ultimate healer. Despite the absence of religious taboos on health care, Amish practices differ from prevailing patterns.

The Amish generally do not subscribe to commercial health insurance. Some communities have organized church aid plans for families with special medical costs. In other settlements special offerings are collected for members who are hit with catastrophic medical bills. The Amish are unlikely to seek medical attention for minor aches or illnesses and are more apt to follow folk remedies and drink herbal teas. Although they do not object to surgery or other forms of high-tech treatment, they rarely employ heroic life-saving interventions.

In addition to home remedies, church members often seek healing outside orthodox medical circles.

The search for natural healing leads them to vitamins, homeopathic remedies, health foods, reflexologists, chiropractors, and the services of specialized clinics. These cultural habits are shaped by many factors: conservative rural values, a preference for natural antidotes, a sense of discomfort in high-tech settings, difficulties accessing health care, a willingness to suffer, and belief in the providence of God.

Birthing practices vary in different settlements. In some communities most babies are born at home under the supervision of trained non-Amish midwives. In other settlements most children are born in hospitals or at local birthing clinics. Children can attend Amish schools without immunizations, but some parents follow the advice of family doctors or midwives and immunize their children. Lax immunization is often due to cost, distance, misinformation, or lack of interest. Occasional outbreaks of German measles, whooping cough, polio, and other contagious diseases have prompted public health campaigns to immunize Amish children. Amish elders usually encourage others to cooperate with such efforts. In recent years various health providers have made special efforts to immunize Amish children.

Marriages within small communities and the lack of new converts restricts the genetic pool of Amish society, and it is not unusual for second cousins to marry. Such intermarriage does not necessarily produce medical problems. When unique recessive traits are common in a closed community, certain diseases are more likely to occur. However, a restricted gene pool may offer protection from other hereditary diseases.

The Amish are ideal subjects for genetic research because their exceptional genealogical records, endogamy, and sizable families make it fairly easy to track hereditary traits across centuries. Some Amish resist mainstream medical treatments, but many others willingly cooperate with medical professionals gathering DNA samples for scientific studies.

In 1989 Holmes Morton and his wife, Caroline, established the Clinic for Special Children near Strasburg, Pennsylvania, to provide diagnostic and comprehensive medical care for Amish and Mennonite children with inherited genetic diseases. Morton and his staff have identified the molecular basis for common disorders in Amish communities and can now test for some 120 genetic conditions. The clinic provides diagnostic services and comprehensive outpatient care for more than two thousand patients in several states.

A similar clinic serving Amish people in Ohio and eight other states, Das Deutsch Center, was initiated by Heng Wang in 2000 in Middlefield, Ohio. Providing state-of-the-art clinical care and diagnostic testing, the center has identified and treated more than seventy rare and genetic disorders in Midwestern Amish communities. These two clinics also serve non-Amish children with rare inherited diseases. A handful of other similar clinics other Amish communities in several states are in the early stages of development.

Since 1995 Alan R. Shuldiner of the University of Maryland has conducted scientific investigations of some six thousand Amish people who have cooperated to advance scientific information about various diseases. Many of the Amish participants receive free medical evaluations and screenings for common diseases. The research staff at Shuldiner's Amish Research Clinic have investigated a variety of health issues typical in the larger society such as obesity, longevity, blood pressure, osteoporosis, mood disorders, and diabetes. The clinic's research team has produced dozens of scientific articles yielding new health information that will benefit Amish and English patients alike.

Death and Burial Rituals With the elderly living at home, the gradual loss of health prepares family members for the final passage. Accompanied by quiet grief, death comes gracefully, the final benediction to a good life and entry into the bliss of eternity. Although funeral practices vary from community to community, the preparations reflect core Amish values, as family and friends yield to eternal verities.

The community springs into action at the word of a death. Family and friends in the local church district assume barn and household chores, freeing the immediate family. Well-established funeral rituals unburden the family from worrisome choices. Three couples are appointed to extend invitations and supervise funeral arrangements: food preparation, seating arrangements, and the coordination of a large number of horses and carriages.

In most settlements a non-Amish undertaker moves the body to a funeral home for embalming. The body, without cosmetic improvements, returns to the home in a simple, hardwood coffin within a day. Family members of the same sex dress the body in white. White garments symbolize the final passage into a new and better eternal life. Tailoring the white clothes prior to death helps to prepare the family for the season of grief. Women often wear the white cape and apron worn at their wedding.

Friends and relatives visit the family and view the body in a room on the first floor of the home for two days prior to the funeral. Meanwhile community members dig the grave by hand in a nearby family cemetery as others oversee the daily chores of the bereaved. Several hundred guests attend the funeral in a barn or home, typically on the morning of the third day after death. During the service, ministers read hymns and scriptures, offer prayers, and preach a sermon.

The hearse, a large, black carriage pulled by horses, leads a long procession of other carriages to the burial ground on the edge of a farm. After a brief viewing and graveside service, pallbearers lower the coffin

An Amish auction in Montgomery County, upstate New York. PHILIP SCALIA / ALAMY

and shovel soil into the grave as the bishop reads a hymn. The spot is marked by a small headstone identical in size to all the others in the graveyard. Close friends and family members then return to the home for a meal prepared by members of the local congregation. Bereaved women, especially close relatives, may signal their mourning by wearing a black dress in public for as long as a year. Although an occasion for grief, death is nevertheless received gracefully as the ultimate surrender to God's higher ways.

Recreational Activities Various social gatherings bring members together for times of fellowship and fun beyond biweekly worship. Young people gather in homes for Sunday evening singing. Married couples sometimes gather with old friends to sing for shut-ins and the elderly in their homes. *Work frolics* blend work and play together in Amish life. Parents gather for *preschool frolics* to prepare schools for September classes. End-of-school picnics bring parents and students together for an afternoon of food and games.

Quilting bees and barn raisings mix goodwill, levity, and hard work for young and old alike. Other moments of collective work (cleaning up after a fire, plowing for an ill neighbor, canning for a sick mother, threshing wheat, and filling a silo) involve neighbors and extended families in episodes of charity, sweat, and fun. Adult sisters, sometimes numbering as many as five or six, often gather for a sisters day, which blends laughter with cleaning, quilting, canning, or gardening.

Public auctions of farm equipment are often held in February and March and attract crowds in preparation for springtime farming. Besides opportunities to bid on equipment, the day-long auctions offer ample time for farm talk and friendly fun. Games of cornerball in a nearby field or barnyard often compete with the drama of the auction. Household auctions and horse sales provide other times to socialize. Family gatherings at religious holidays and summer family reunions link members into familial networks. Single women sometimes gather at a cabin or a home for a weekend of fun. Special meetings of persons with unique interests, often called reunions, are on the rise and attract Amish from many states: harnessmakers, cabinetmakers, woodworkers, blacksmiths, businesswomen, teachers, the disabled, and the like. The disabled have gathered annually for a number of years.

Among youth, seasonal athletics are common: softball, sledding, skating, hockey, and swimming. Volleyball is a widespread favorite. Fishing and hunting for small game are preferred sports on farms and woodlands. In recent years some Amish men have purchased hunting cabins in the mountains where they hunt white-tailed deer. Deep-sea fishing trips are common summertime jaunts for men in Pennsylvania. Others prefer camping and canoeing. Pitching quoits, a game similar to a ring toss, is common at family reunions and picnics.

Idleness is viewed as the devil's workshop. But the rise of cottage industries and the availability of ready cash has brought more recreational activities to Amish culture. Amish recreation is group oriented and nature oriented. For vacations, the Amish may take trips to other settlements and stop at scenic sites along the way. Some couples travel to Florida in the winter and live in an Amish village in Sarasota that is frequented by travelers from settlements in several states. Trips to distant sites in search of special medical care sometimes include scenic tours. Although some Amish travel by train or bus, chartered vans are the most popular mode. Traveling together with family, friends, and extended kin allow these groups to further cement their bonds.

FAMILY AND COMMUNITY LIFE

The *immediate family*, the *extended family*, and the *church district* form the building blocks of Amish society. Amish parents typically raise about seven children, but ten or more children is not uncommon. About 50 percent of the population is under eighteen years of age. A person will often have more than 75 first cousins and a typical grandparent will count more than 35 grandchildren. Members of the extended family usually live nearby, across the field, down the lane, or beyond the hill. Youth grow up in this thick network of family relations where they are rarely alone, always embedded in a caring community in time of need and disaster. The elderly retire at home, usually in a small apartment built onto the main house of a homestead. Because the Amish reject government aid, virtually no families receive public assistance. The community provides a supportive social network from cradle to grave.

A church district comprises 25 to 35 families and is the basic social and religious unit beyond the family. Roads and streams mark the boundaries of districts. Members are required to participate in the district in which they live. A district's geographic size varies with the density of the Amish population. As districts expand, they divide.

A bishop, two preachers, and a deacon share leadership responsibilities in each district without formal pay or education. The bishop, as spiritual elder, officiates at baptisms, weddings, communions, funerals, ordinations, and membership meetings. The church district is church, club, family, and precinct all wrapped up in a neighborhood parish. Periodic meetings of ordained leaders link the districts of a settlement into a loose federation. Leisure, work, education, worship, and friendship revolve around the district, although families may travel to other settlements or even out of state to visit relatives and friends.

Amish society is not bureaucratic. There is no centralized national office, symbolic national figurehead, or institutional headquarters. Apart from schools, a publishing operation, and regional historical libraries, formal institutions do not exist. A loosely organized national committee handles relations with the federal government for all the settlements, and small regional committees funnel funds to the schools, mutual aid, and historical libraries.

The status symbols that mark much of modern American life (education, income, occupation, and consumer goods) are lacking in Amish society, making those families relatively homogeneous. Their agrarian heritage places everyone on more or less equal footing. However, the recent rise of Amish-owned small businesses in some settlements and factory work in others has disturbed some of this social equality by creating three social classes: day laborers who work in shops, farmers who have equity in land, and entrepreneurs who operate some 12,000 Amish businesses. Despite these newer differences, social equality is maintained by adherence to traditional styles of dress and transportation and even the custom of having equal-sized tombstones.

The practice of mutual aid also distinguishes Amish society. Mutual aid means the community bands together to help its individual families. The mutual aid technique perhaps most associated with the Amish is the barn raising. During this activity, all the able-bodied men in a community gather and build a barn in the space of a day or two. The women provide the meals, and the hard work is lessened by many hands and through an atmosphere of celebration. Mutual aid is practiced during harvest times and in times of disaster. For example, if a family's house is destroyed by fire or a storm, all will gather to help clean up debris, rehabilitate the building, or construct a new one. This, in part, illustrates why the Amish have no need for homeowners' insurance. Other forms of mutual aid include quilting bees, preparing the schoolhouse for the new year, and canning vegetables for the winter, not to mention the assistance needed with ceremonies such as weddings and funerals.

Gender Roles Amish society is based upon a soft patriarchy. Although school teachers are generally women, men assume most leadership roles. Women can nominate men to serve in ministerial roles, but they themselves are excluded from formal church roles; however, they can vote in church business meetings. Some women feel that because the men make the rules, modern equipment is permitted more readily in barns and shops than in homes. In recent years some women have become entrepreneurs who operate small quilt, craft, and food stores.

Although husband and wife preside over distinct spheres of domestic life, many tasks are shared. A wife may ask her husband to assist in the garden, and he may ask her to help in the barn or fields. The isolated housewife is rarely found in Amish society. The husband holds spiritual authority in the home, but spouses have considerable freedom within their distinctive spheres.

Education The Amish supported public education when it revolved around one-room schools in the first half of the twentieth century. Under local control, the one-room rural schools posed little threat to Amish values. The massive consolidation of public schools and growing pressure to attend high school sparked clashes between the Amish and officials in several states in the middle of the twentieth century. Confrontations in several other states led to arrests and brief stints in jail. After legal skirmishes in several states, the U.S. Supreme Court gave its blessing to the eighth-grade Amish school system in 1972, stating that "there can be no assumption that today's majority is 'right' and the Amish and others are 'wrong.'" The Court concluded that "a way of life that is odd or even erratic but interferes with no rights or interests of others is not to be condemned because it is different."

By 2013 the Amish operated more than 2,000 private schools for some 55,000 Amish children. Many of the schools have one room with 25 to 35 pupils and one teacher who is responsible for teaching all eight grades. A few Amish children attend rural public schools in some states.

A scripture reading and prayer opens each school day, but religion is not formally taught in the school. The curriculum includes reading, arithmetic, spelling, grammar, penmanship, history, and geography. Both English and German are taught. Parents want children to learn German to enhance their ability to read religious writings, many of which are written in formal German. Science and sex education are missing in the curriculum, as are sports, dances, clubs, music instruction, and computers.

A local board of three to five fathers organizes the school, hires a teacher, approves the curriculum, oversees the budget, and supervises maintenance. Teachers receive about $25 to $35 per day. The cost per child is roughly $500 per year, about 20 times lower than many public schools where per pupil costs often top $104,000. Amish parents pay public school taxes as well as taxes for their own school.

Schools play a critical role in the preservation of Amish culture. They not only reinforce Amish values, but they also shield youth from contaminating ideas. Moreover, schools limit friendships to the students' Amish peers and impede the flow of Amish youth into higher education and professional life. Amish schools promote practical skills to prepare their graduates for success in Amish society. Some selective testing indicates that Amish pupils compare favorably with rural peers in public schools on standardized tests of basic skills.

Amish teachers, trained in Amish schools, are not required to be certified in most states. Often the brightest and best of Amish students, they return to the classroom in their late teens and early twenties to teach. Amish school directors select them for their ability to teach and their commitment to Amish values. These are usually single women, who will quit teaching when they get married. Periodic meetings with other teachers, a monthly teachers' magazine, and ample common sense prepare them for the task of teaching thirty students in eight grades. With three or four pupils per grade, teachers often teach two grades at a time. Pupils in other classes ponder assignments, listen to previews of next year's lessons, or hear reviews of past work. Some textbooks are recycled from public schools while others are produced by Amish publishers. The ethos of the classroom accents cooperative activity, obedience, respect, diligence, kindness, and the natural world. Daily recess often involves softball and other traditional games.

Amish schools exhibit a social continuity rarely found in public education. With many families sending several children to a school, teachers may relate to as few as a dozen households. Teachers know parents personally and the circumstances surrounding each child. In some cases, children have the same teacher for all eight grades. Indeed, all the children from a family may have the same teacher for their entire school career.

Courtship and Weddings The wedding season is a festive time in Amish life. Coming on the heels of the harvest, weddings are typically held on Tuesdays and Thursdays from late October through early December in the Lancaster Pennsylvania settlement. In many other settlements weddings may occur throughout the year, but typically not in July and August. Larger communities may have as many as 150 weddings in one season, and 15 weddings may be scattered across the settlement on the same day. Typically staged in the home of the bride, these joyous events may involve upwards of 350 guests, two meals, singing, snacks, festivities, and a three-hour service. The specific practices vary from settlement to settlement.

The Amish typically marry in their early twenties. A couple may date for one to two years before

OLD ORDER AND LIBERAL AMISH

In the late nineteenth century some clusters of Amish formed more progressive Amish-Mennonite churches as industrialization became an influence in everyday rural life. Members of these churches eventually merged with Mennonite churches and made some concessions to twentieth-century culture. The Beachy Amish (founded in 1927 by the bishop Moses M. Beachy in 1927), for instance, support mission work and sometimes travel overseas for it. Some Beachy Amish own cars, although radio and television are still prohibited. The more conservative guardians of the heritage became known as the Old Order Amish.

In the course of the twentieth century, the Old Order Amish diversified their ranks into some 40 different Amish subgroups. Each of these groups has different regulations, accepted practices, and symbols (such as the color of their buggies). The Swartzentruber Amish, for example, were founded in 1917 in Ohio and are among the strictest of the Old Order groups. No indoor plumbing is allowed, and their homes are devoid of almost any unnecessary decoration. Their clothing is dark, and men wear only one suspender instead of two.

Thus, it is difficult to speak about "the Amish," because so many different groups adhere to that name. The most traditional of these, for example, have outdoor toilets and austere homes, whereas more liberal groups have state-of-the-art bathrooms and—apart from electricity—well-appointed homes. Members of latter group sometimes permit families to install phones in their homes, use electricity from public utilities, and use tractors in their fields.

announcing their engagement. Bishops will only marry a couple if they are both members of the church. The church does not arrange marriages, but it does place its blessing on the pair through an old ritual. Prior to the wedding, the groom takes a letter signed by church elders to the bride's deacon testifying to the groom's good standing in his home district. The bride's deacon then meets with her to verify the marriage plans.

The wedding day is an enormous undertaking for the bride's family and for the relatives and friends who assist with preparations. Efforts to clean up the property, paint rooms, fix furniture, pull weeds, and pave driveways begin weeks in advance. The logistics of preparing meals and snacks for several hundred guests are taxing. According to custom, the day before the wedding the groom slaughters several dozen chickens. The noontime wedding menu includes chicken roast—chicken mixed with bread filling, and served with gravy, mashed potatoes, creamed celery, pepper cabbage, and other items. Desserts include pears, peaches, puddings, dozens of pies, and hundreds of cookies and doughnuts.

The three-hour service—without flowers, rings, or instrumental music—is similar to an Amish worship service. The wedding includes congregational singing, prayers, wedding vows, and two sermons. Four single friends serve the bride and groom as attendants: no one is designated maid of honor or best man. Amish brides typically make their own wedding dresses from blue or purple material crafted in traditional styles. In addition to the groom's new but customary black coat and vest, he and his attendants often wear small black bow ties.

Games, snacks, and singing follow the noon meal. Young people are paired off somewhat randomly for the singing. Following the evening meal another more lively singing takes place in which couples who are dating pair off—arousing considerable interest because this may be their first public appearance. Festivities may continue until nearly midnight as guests gradually leave. Some guests, invited to several weddings on the same day, may rotate between them.

Newly married couples usually set up housekeeping in the spring after their wedding. Until then the groom may live at the bride's home or continue to live with his parents. Couples do not take a traditional honeymoon, but visit relatives on weekends during the winter months. Several newlywed couples may visit together, sometimes staying overnight at the home of close relatives. During these visits, family and friends present gifts to the newlyweds to add to the bride's dowry, which often consists of furniture. Young men begin growing a beard, the functional equivalent of a wedding ring, soon after their marriage. They are expected to have a "full stand" by the springtime communion.

Relations with Other Americans Amish culture and religion stresses separation from the world. Galvanized by European persecution and sanctioned by scripture, the Amish divide the social world into two pathways: the straight, narrow way of life, and the broad, easy road to destruction. Amish life embodies the narrow way of self-denial. The larger social world symbolizes the broad road of vanity and vice. The term *world*, in Amish thinking, refers to the outside society and its values, vices, practices, and institutions. Media reports of greed, fraud, scandal, drugs, violence, divorce, and abuse confirm that the world teems with values that run counter to theirs.

The gulf between church and world guides practical decisions. Products and practices that might undermine community life, such as high school, cars, cameras, television, and self-propelled farm machinery, are tagged "worldly." Not all new products receive this label—only those that threaten community values. Definitions of worldliness vary within and between Amish settlements, yielding a complicated maze of practices.

Despite this separation from the world, many Americans are curious about the Amish way of life and millions visit Amish communities each year as tourists. Some 10 million tourists visit Lancaster County in Eastern Pennsylvania annually. Other major sites of

Amish tourism include Holmes County Ohio (near the town of Worcester); Shipshewana, Indiana; and Arthur, Illinois. Dozens of non-Amish entrepreneurs in these areas have developed Amish-themed enterprises that include tours, films, interpretive centers, restaurants, hotels, and retail shops that cater to tourists. In addition, cyber tourism on film and video on cable channels has grown since 2000. This cyber tourism ranges from accurate documentaries such as *The Amish*, produced by the American Experience (which aired in February 2012), to fictional and exploitive portrayals of Amish life such as *Breaking Amish* and *The Amish Mafia* (both of which aired in 2012).

Philanthropy Building on their beliefs in mutual aid and spirit of sharing and caring, Amish communities also help outsiders by donating to benefits for disaster relief, hosting charity auctions, and joining with Mennonites and other Anabaptists to raise money for international aid and service projects, as well as disaster cleanup in the United States. Amish have participated in raising millions of dollars with the Mennonite Disaster Service and Christian Aid Ministries for relief in Haiti, Bosnia, and even in Louisiana after Hurricane Katrina.

Surnames As a mostly closed community, the Amish have a relatively small number of surnames—around 200—and a few names tend to predominate in particular areas. The most common surnames include Miller, Stoltzfus, Yoder, and Schwartz. Other common names include Hershberger, Hochstetler, Troyer, Schrock, Fisher, Lapp, and Zook.

EMPLOYMENT AND ECONOMIC CONDITIONS

Amish life is rooted in farming. But since the middle of the twentieth century, some of the older and larger Amish settlements in Indiana, Ohio, and Pennsylvania have shifted to nonfarm occupations because of the pressures of urbanization. As urbanization devoured prime farmland, prices soared. For example, land in the heart of Pennsylvania's Lancaster Amish settlement sold for $300 an acre in 1940. In the 1990s the same land sold for $8,000, and in 2013 an acre went for $15,000.

Scarce and expensive farmland in some of the older settlements presents a problem, as does the demographic squeeze caused by their growing population. The community has coped with the crisis in several ways. First, farms have been subdivided into smaller units with intensive cropping and higher concentrations of livestock. Second, some families have migrated to the rural areas of other states where farms can be purchased at much lower prices. Third, in some settlements a majority of families no longer farm, but instead work in small shops, rural factories, or in various trades. However, even ex-farmers insist that the farm remains the best place to raise a family.

The rise of cottage industries and small shops marks an historic turn in Amish life. These new

An Amish man in Amish Country, Pennsylvania. ALAMYBEST / ALAMY

enterprises, numbering up to 12,000 by 2013, have dramatically reshaped Amish society. By the late 1990s, such small industries employed more than half the Amish adults in Lancaster County, and by 2013, 60 percent of Amish households received their primary income from small businesses. Amish retail shops sell dry goods, furniture, shoes, hardware, and wholesale foods. Church members now work as carpenters, plumbers, painters, and self-trained accountants.

The new industries come in three forms. Home-based operations lodged on farms or by newly built homes employ a few family members and neighbors. Bakeshops, craft shops, hardware stores, health food stores, quilt shops, flower shops, and repair shops of all sorts are just a few of the hundreds of home-based operations. Work in these settings revolves around the family. A growing number of these small cottage industries cater to tourists, but many serve the needs of Amish and non-Amish neighbors alike.

Larger shops and manufacturing concerns are housed in newly constructed buildings on the edge of farms or on commercial plots. These formal shops with five to ten employees manufacture farm machinery, hydraulic equipment, storage barns, furniture, and cabinetry. Some metal fabrication shops arrange subcontracts with other manufacturers. The larger shops are efficient and profitable. Low overhead, minimal advertising, austere management, modest wages, quality workmanship, and sheer hard work grant many shops a competitive edge in the marketplace.

Mobile work crews constitute a third type of industry. Amish construction groups travel to building sites for commercial and residential construction. The construction crews travel in hired vehicles and in some settlements they are permitted to use electric tools powered by portable generators and on-site electricity.

The rise of cottage industries may, in the long run, disturb the equality of Amish life by encouraging a three-tier society of farmers, entrepreneurs, and day laborers. Parents worry that youth working a forty-hour week with loose cash in their pockets will snub traditional Amish values of simplicity and frugality. The new industries also increase contact with the outside world, which will surely prompt even more changes in Amish life. Despite the occupational changes, virtually no Amish are unemployed or receive government unemployment benefits.

Doing business in the twenty-first century also necessarily involves the challenge of technology. Amish business owners in the more progressive affiliations may use third-party providers for websites and e-mail accounts. The shift from farming to business is the most significant change in Amish communities since they immigrated to the United States in the eighteenth century.

POLITICS AND GOVERNMENT
Although the Amish support and respect civil government, they also keep a healthy distance from it. On the one hand, they follow biblical admonitions to obey and pray for rulers and encourage members to be law-abiding citizens. On the other hand, government epitomizes worldly culture and the use of force. European persecutors of the Anabaptists were often government officials. Modern governments engage in warfare, use capital punishment, and impose their will through laws. Believing that such coercion and violence is in opposition to the gentle spirit of Jesus, the Amish reject the use of force, including litigation.

When civil law and religious conscience collide, the Amish are not afraid to take a stand and will obey God rather than man, even if it brings imprisonment. They have clashed with government officials over the use of hard hats, zoning regulations, workers' compensation, and building codes for schools. However, as conscientious objectors, many have received farm deferments or served in alternative service programs during times of military draft. The Amish refuse to serve on juries.

The church forbids membership in political organizations and holding public office for several reasons. First, running for office is viewed as arrogant and out of character with esteemed Amish values of humility and modesty. Second, officeholding violates the religious principle of separation from the world. Finally, public officials must be prepared to use legal force if necessary to settle civic disputes. The exercise of legal force runs counter to the Amish stance of nonresistance. Voting, however, is viewed as a personal matter. Although the church does not prohibit it, few persons vote. Those who do vote are likely to be younger businessmen concerned about local issues. In the 2004 presidential election, for example, only 13 percent of eligible Amish adults voted.

The Amish pay federal and state income taxes, sales taxes, real estate taxes, and personal property taxes. Indeed, they pay school taxes twice, for both public and Amish schools. Following biblical injunctions, the Amish are exempt from Social Security tax. They view Social Security as a national insurance program, not a tax. Congressional legislation, passed in 1965, exempts self-employed Amish persons from Social Security. Amish persons employed in Amish businesses were also exempted by congressional legislation in 1988. Those who do not qualify for the exemption, such as Amish employees in non-Amish businesses, must pay Social Security without reaping its benefits. Likewise, the Amish do not receive Medicare and Medicaid.

The Amish object to government aid for a number of reasons. They contend that the church should assume responsibility for the social welfare of its own members. The aged, infirm, senile, and disabled are cared for, whenever possible, within extended family networks. To turn the care of these people over to the state would abdicate this fundamental tenet of faith. Furthermore, federal aid in the form of Social Security or Medicare would erode dependency on the church and undercut its programs of mutual aid, which the Amish have organized to assist their members with fire and storm damages and with medical expenses.

Government subsidies, or what the Amish call handouts, have been stridently opposed. Championing self-sufficiency and the separation of church and state, the Amish worry that the hand that feeds them will also control them. Over the years they have stubbornly refused direct subsidies even for agricultural programs designed for farmers in distress. Amish farmers do, however, receive indirect subsidies through agricultural price-support programs.

In 1967 some Amish lay leaders formed the National Amish Steering Committee in order to speak with a common voice on legal issues related to state and especially federal government. The Steering Committee has worked with government officials to resolve disputes related to conscientious objection, zoning, slow-moving vehicle emblems, Social Security, workers' compensation, photo identification, and the wearing of hard hats at construction sites. When the Amish faced voter identification problems in Pennsylvania in 2012, the steering committee worked out an exemption for them with state officials. Likewise, the Steering Committee negotiated an exemption for Amish people from the 2010 Patient Protection and Affordable Care Act, allowing the Amish to forgo purchasing commercial health insurance mandated by the federal government. Informally organized, the Steering Committee is the only Amish organization that is national in scope.

MEDIA

PRINT

Arthur Graphic Clarion

Newspaper of the Illinois Amish country.

Allen Mann, Editor
113 E. Illinois Street
Arthur, Illinois 61911
Phone: (217) 543-2151
Fax: (217) 543-2152
Email: info@thearthurgraphic.com
URL: www.thearthurgraphic.com

Die Botschaft

Weekly English newspaper with correspondents from many states that serves Old Order Mennonite and Old Order Amish communities.

Brookshire Publications, Inc.
420 Weaver Road
Millersburg, Pennsylvania 17061

The Budget

Weekly Amish/Mennonite community newspaper.

George R. Smith, National Editor
Sugarcreek Budget Publishers, Inc.
134 North Factory Street
P.O. Box 249
Sugarcreek, Ohio 44681-0249
Phone: (216) 852-4634
Fax: (216) 852-4421
URL: www.thebudgetnewspaper.com/

The Diary

Monthly publication that lists migrations, marriages, births, and deaths. It also carries news and feature articles.

Pequea Publishers
P.O. Box 98
Gordonville, Pennsylvania 17529

Keepers at Home

A journal for Amish and other women who abide by the biblical precept to be keepers of the home.

2673 Township Road 421
Sugarcreek, Ohio 44681

Mennonite Quarterly Review

Scholarly journal covering Mennonite, Amish, Hutterian Brethren, Anabaptist, Radical Reformation, and related history and religious thought.

John D. Roth, Editor
Mennonite Historical Society
1700 South Main Street
Goshen College
Goshen, Indiana 46526
Phone: (574) 535-7433
Fax: (574) 535-7438
Email: mqr@goshen.edu.
URL: www.goshen.edu/mqr/

Plain Communities Business Exchange

A monthly newspaper/magazine that targets Amish, Mennonites, and other plain communities throughout the fifty states. The publication provides a link between wholesalers, retailers, and potential customers.

Phone: (888) 692-2499
Fax: (888) 692-8108
URL: www.plaincommunities.com
Millersburg, Pennsylvania 17061

ORGANIZATIONS AND ASSOCIATIONS

Lancaster Mennonite Historical Society (LMHS)

Individuals interested in the historical background, theology, culture, and genealogy of Mennonite and Amish related groups originating in Pennsylvania. Collects and preserves archival materials. Publishes the *Mirror* bimonthly.

Rolando L. Santiago, Director
2215 Millstream Road
Lancaster, Pennsylvania 17602-1499
Phone: (717) 393-9745
Fax: (717) 393-8751
URL: www.lmhs.org

MUSEUMS AND RESEARCH CENTERS

Amish & Mennonite Heritage Center

A welcome center for tourists in the midst of the largest Amish settlement in the United States that contains many historical artifacts and documents.

5798 County Road 77
P.O. Box 324
Berlin, Ohio 44610-0324
Phone: (330) 893-3192
URL: www.behalt.com

Mennonite Historical Library

A large collection of Anabaptist historical materials that covers the Radical Reformation, the Amish, and the Hutterites in addition to the Mennonites.

Good Library
Goshen College

Goshen, Indiana 46526
Phone: (574) 535-7418
Fax: (574) 535-7438
Email: mhl@goshen.edu
URL: www.goshen.edu/mhl/

Ohio Amish Library

A library operated by and for the Amish of the community.

4292 SR39
Millersburg, Ohio 44654
Phone: (330) 893-4011

Pequea Bruderschaft Library

An Amish-operated library that is open only on Saturday mornings.

P.O. Box 25
Gordonville, Pennsylvania 17529

The Young Center for the Study of Anabaptist and Pietist Groups

Elizabethtown College
One Alpha Drive
Elizabethtown, Pennsylvania 17022
Phone: (717) 361-1470
Email: youngctr@etown.edu
URL: http://www.etown.edu/centers/young-center/

SOURCES FOR ADDITIONAL STUDY

Davies, Bess Twiston. "Meet the Modern Amish—Smart, Savvy and Up to Date." *Times* (London), May 5, 2012.

Hurst, Charles E., and David L. McConnell. *An Amish Paradox: Diversity and Change in the World's Largest Amish Community*. Baltimore: Johns Hopkins University Press, 2010.

Kraybill, Donald B., and Gertrude Enders Huntington. "The Amish Family." In *Ethnic Families in America: Patterns and Variations*, 5th ed., edited by Roosevelt H. Wright Jr., Charles H. Mindel, Thanh Van Tran, and Robert W. Habenstein, 437–60. Boston: Pearson, 2012.

Kraybill, Donald B., and Steven M. Nolt. *Amish Enterprise: From Plows to Profits*. 2nd ed. Baltimore: Johns Hopkins University Press, 2004.

Kraybill, Donald B., Steven M. Nolt, and Erik J. Wesner. "Sources of Enterprise Success in Amish Communities." *Journal of Enterprising Communities: People and Places in the Global Economy* 5, no. 2 (2011): 112–30.

Kraybill, Donald B., Karen Johnson-Weiner, and Steven M. Nolt. *The Amish*. Baltimore: Johns Hopkins University Press, 2013.

Stevick, Richard A. *Growing Up Amish: The Teenage Years*. Baltimore: Johns Hopkins University Press, 2007.

Umble, Diane Z., and David Weaver-Zercher. *The Amish and the Media*. Baltimore: Johns Hopkins University Press, 2008.

APACHE

D. L. Birchfield

OVERVIEW

The Apache are an indigenous, or native, people whose ancestors inhabited the southwestern United States. More than a dozen separate groups once ranged over an area that included northern and eastern Arizona, New Mexico, central and western Texas, southern Colorado, and western Oklahoma and Kansas, lands notable for mountains, large mesas, and deep canyons protecting fertile valleys. The name *Apache* came into English through Spanish, either as the Spanish form of the Zuni word for Navajo (a closely related tribe), *ʔápaču*; as the Spanish version of the Yavapai word for enemy, *apachu*; or from *mapache*, the Spanish word for raccoon. The Apache call themselves *Inde*, meaning simply "people."

The large number of affiliated tribes and the enormous area across which they ranged makes it difficult to estimate the pre-Columbian population of the Apache. Like the other tribes of the Great Plains, the Apache were hunters and gatherers who followed bison and other game and used small indigenous dogs to pull travois loaded with their portable possessions. Their nomadic nature and the multiple routes used by the various groups to reach the Southwest in the pre-Columbian period led to their dispersal throughout the region, from the Lipan, Jicarilla, and Mescalero Apache in western Texas and New Mexico to the Tonto and San Carlos Apache in Arizona. While nomadic, the Apache did carry on trade with the Pueblo peoples of the Four Corners region, trading bison meat and skins for maize and woven materials.

The United States currently recognizes the following Apache groups: the Apache Tribe of Oklahoma, with its headquarters in Anadarko; the Fort Sill Apache Tribe of Oklahoma, headquartered in Apache; the Jicarilla Apache Nation of the Jicarilla Apache Reservation, New Mexico; the Mescalero Apache Tribe of the Mescalero Reservation, New Mexico; the Fort McDowell Yavapai Nation of Maricopa County, Arizona; the San Carlos Apache Tribe of the San Carlos Reservation in Gila County, Arizona; the Tonto Apache Tribe of Arizona; the White Mountain Apache Tribe of the Fort Apache Reservation, Arizona; and the Yavapai-Apache Nation of the Camp Verde Indian Reservation, Arizona. The majority of these groups were forcibly removed to reservations by the federal government during the decades of the Apache Wars (1849–1886) as part of an attempt to promote Anglo colonization of lands in Arizona and New Mexico annexed by the United States after the Mexican-American War (1846–1848). While gaming and tourism have recently helped strengthen the economies of many of the Apache reservations, the Apache, in common with many native groups, suffer from a marked lack of economic opportunity, their communities plagued by unemployment, poor education, and the problems often associated with endemic poverty, including crime and drug use.

During the 2010 U.S. Census, 63,193 people (slightly more than the population of West Hartford, Connecticut) self-identified as Apache, with another 6,501 claiming membership in more than one tribe, including the Apache. This is an increase over the 2000 Census, when 56,060 claimed membership. The majority of modern Apache live either on reservations or—as in the case of the Oklahoma-based Kiowa-Apache Tribe—in Tribal Jurisdictional Areas, federally recognized areas created after the dissolution of Oklahoma's Indian Reservations in 1934. Smaller numbers live in major metropolitan centers near the reservations, such as Oklahoma City and Phoenix. An Apache community has developed in the agricultural regions of southern California, where the people moved to find work as farm laborers. The states with the highest population of Apache are Arizona, California, Texas, Colorado, New Mexico, and Oklahoma.

HISTORY OF THE PEOPLE

Early History A Southern Athapaskan people, presumably from southern Canada, the Apache began to migrate southward sometime after the year 1000. Their arrival in the southwestern United States, however, has long been a subject of debate among historians; theories and estimates are complicated by the migratory and preliterate nature of the Apache as well as by the immense range of their various settlements, which reached from Texas to Arizona. A popular theory argues that the Apache migrated south through the Rocky Mountains in the fourteenth century, slowly expanding into lands either abandoned or loosely controlled by other native groups. In any case, the Apache quickly acclimated to their new territory and settled into the regular pattern of hunter-gatherers, following bison and other large game animals and trading with other, more settled peoples.

As with almost all other native groups, the lives of the Apache were changed forever by the arrival of Europeans, in this case the Spaniards who colonized Mexico. While early contacts were mainly peaceful, the desire of Spanish authorities to extend their control into the upper valley of the Rio Grande (in modern-day northern New Mexico) brought them into conflict with the Apache. In 1598 the expedition of Juan de Oñate entered the Pueblo country of the upper Rio Grande with the intention of establishing a permanent Spanish colony in the region. Oñate succeeded, founding the town of Santa Fe in 1610. One immediate effect was the disruption of the traditional native trading economy. Prior to the arrival of the Spanish, the Apache and the Pueblo had enjoyed a mercantile relationship, with the Pueblo trading their agricultural products and pottery to the Apache in exchange for buffalo robes and dried meat. Early Spaniards in the region described the annual visits of whole Apache tribes at trade fairs, primarily at the pueblos of Taos and Picuris, with awe. Soon, however, the Spanish began confiscating the Pueblo surpluses originally used for trade.

Few native groups resisted the encroachment of Anglo-American culture as long or as fiercely as the Apache. One of the last Native American nations to abandon military resistance to the U.S. government, the Apache were equally determined to resist the policy of forced assimilation or "Americanization" that followed the end of armed conflict.

In the 1700s the Lipan Apache, a small group that had broken away from the Eastern Apache in the 1600s and migrated into Texas and northern Mexico, were enslaved by Spanish explorers and settlers from Mexico. They were forced to work on ranches and in mines. The surviving Lipan Apache were relocated to the Mescalero Apache Reservation in New Mexico in 1903.

A larger and more disruptive incursion occurred with the historic southward migration of the Comanche Nation, which began around 1700. By about 1725 the Comanche had established their authority throughout the whole of the Southern Plains region, pushing the Jicarilla north of Santa Fe and the Mescalero south of Santa Fe into the mountains of northern New Mexico. Denied access to the buffalo herds by the Comanche, the Apache turned to raiding Spanish cattle and horses, which put them in conflict with the Spanish authorities. When the Spanish settlers managed to conclude a peace treaty with the Comanche in 1786, they used their new allies, along with Navajo auxiliaries and

Spanish troops, to begin the pacification of their northern frontier. Individual Apache groups were hunted down and cornered, then offered a subsidy sufficient for their maintenance if they would settle near a Spanish mission, refrain from raiding Spanish livestock, and live peacefully. One by one, the Apache groups accepted the terms. The peace, though little studied by modern scholars, is thought to have endured until near the end of the Spanish colonial era.

The beginning of the Mexican-American War in 1846 disrupted this peace. The Americans, eager to open the new territories to Anglo settlement and mining, began to encroach on traditional Apache lands in the newly acquired territories of Arizona and New Mexico. The Apache responded by raiding Anglo settlements in an attempt to push the invaders out. Lacking both Spanish diplomatic skills and the Spanish understanding of the Apache, the Americans sought to subjugate the tribes militarily, initiating a period of bloody conflict that lasted for decades. Although the Apache fought fiercely, the various bands gradually surrendered to the U.S. authorities, ground down by the larger numbers of the Americans. One group, led by the warrior Geronimo (1829–1909), held out in Arizona until they were almost exterminated, but their resistance ended in 1886, and many of the survivors were sent to Florida as prisoners of war.

Modern Era Over the next decades the U.S. government created a number of formal reservations throughout the Southwest as territory for the various Apache groups. Faced with official malfeasance, legal conflicts over jurisdiction, and forced attempts at assimilation, along with disease and poverty, the Apache struggled to survive economically and culturally under the government-mandated reservation system. Because of the unique status of Oklahoma as the "Indian Territory" and the simultaneous need to dissolve the existing reservations there as a necessary precursor to statehood, Apache in Oklahoma were allotted lands individually rather than under common ownership, as on a reservation, under the General Allotment Act of 1887 (also known as the Dawes Act). In 1907 the Oklahoma Apache became citizens of the new state of Oklahoma and of the United States. Apache in Arizona and New Mexico were not granted U.S. citizenship until 1924. Since the 1950s the United States has attempted to terminate its governmental relationship with Indian tribes; it has adopted a policy of assisting the tribes in achieving some measure of self-determination. The U.S. Supreme Court has upheld some attributes of sovereignty for Indian nations. In recent years Apache tribal enterprises such as ski areas, resorts, casinos, and lumber mills have helped alleviate chronically high rates of unemployment on the reservations, and bilingual and bicultural educational programs have resulted from direct Apache involvement in the educational process. Federally recognized contemporary

Apache tribal governments are located in Arizona, New Mexico, and Oklahoma. Apache reservations exist in Arizona and New Mexico.

SETTLEMENT IN THE UNITED STATES

The homeland of the Apache—the Grand Apacheria—was a vast region stretching from what is now central Arizona in the west to present-day central and south Texas in the east, and from northern Mexico in the south to the high plains of what became eastern Colorado in the north. This region was originally divided between Eastern and Western Apache. Eastern Apache were Plains Apache. In the days before the horse—and before the historic southward migration of the Comanche Nation in the early 1700s—the Plains Apache were the lords of the southern Plains. Western Apache lived primarily on the western side of the Continental Divide in the mountains of present-day Arizona and western New Mexico. When the Comanche adopted the use of the horse and migrated southward out of what is now Wyoming, they displaced the Eastern Apache from the southern Great Plains to the mountainous country of what eventually became eastern New Mexico.

Following their defeat by the U.S. military, most Apache were confined to reservation areas determined by the government. They were more fortunate than many tribes in that their reservations were on or near their traditional lands. They also benefited from the isolated location of their reservations, which made it easier to maintain their distinctive culture. At the same time, there was a lack of economic opportunity, and during the twentieth century, some Apache dispersed into the general population, moving to cities in the Southwest and eventually migrating to other parts of the country. Changes in U.S. policy regarding tribal rights and Indian lands have gradually improved the economic outlook for those on the reservations, however, and some groups among the Apache have taken advantage of their scenic locations to develop recreational facilities such as ski areas and other tourist attractions.

Apache populations today may be found on reservations and areas of jurisdiction in Oklahoma, Arizona, Texas, and New Mexico. The San Carlos Reservation in eastern Arizona occupies 1,900,000 acres; and the Fort Apache Reservation, administratively divided from San Carlos in 1897, occupies 1,665,000 acres. Fort Apache is home to the Coyotero Apache, a group that includes the Cibecue and White Mountain Apache. The San Carlos Reservation lost most of its best farmland when the Coolidge Dam was completed in 1930. Mount Graham, 10,720 feet in elevation, is sacred land to the Apache. It stands at the southern end of the reservation.

The Camp Verde Reservation occupies approximately 500 acres in central Arizona. This reservation, in several small fragments, is shared by an

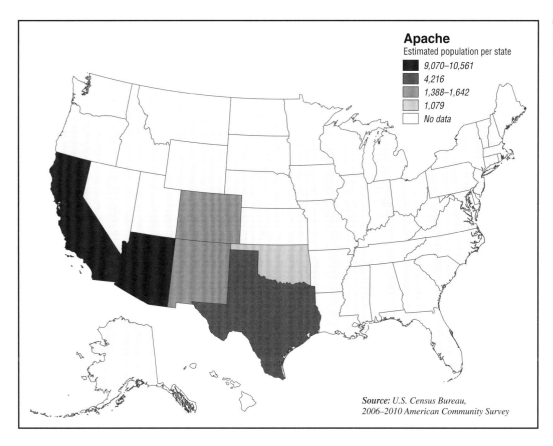

Apache
Estimated population per state

- 9,070–10,561
- 4,216
- 1,388–1,642
- 1,079
- No data

Source: U.S. Census Bureau, 2006–2010 American Community Survey

approximately equal number of Tonto Apache and Yavapai living in three communities, at Camp Verde, Middle Verde, and Clarksdale. About half of the tribal members live on the reservation. Approximately 280 acres at Middle Verde are suitable for agriculture.

The Mescalero Reservation occupies 460,000 acres in southeastern New Mexico in the Sacramento Mountains northeast of Alamogordo. The Jicarilla Reservation occupies 750,000 acres in north-central New Mexico. There are two divisions among the Jicarilla: the Olleros ("Pot-makers") and the Llaneros ("Plains People"). *Jicarilla* is a Spanish word meaning "Little Basket." In 1907 the original reservation was expanded with the addition of a large block of land to the south. In the 1920s most Jicarilla raised stock. Many lived on isolated ranches until drought began to make sheep rearing unprofitable. By the end of the 1950s, 90 percent of the Jicarilla had left the reservation and moved to the vicinity of the agency town of Dulce, in part to search for increased economic opportunity.

Apache in Oklahoma, except for the native Kiowa-Apache, are descendants of the 340 members of Geronimo's band of Chiricahua Apache. The Chiricahua were held as prisoners of war, first in 1886 at Fort Marion, Florida; then for seven years at Mount Vernon Barracks, Alabama; and finally at Fort Sill, Oklahoma. They remained prisoners of war on the Fort Sill Military Reservation until 1913, when the few remaining Chiricahua were allotted lands on the former Kiowa-Comanche Reservation, not far from Fort Sill. The Kiowa-Apache were given allotments near the communities of Fort Cobb and Apache in Caddo County, Oklahoma.

Today large numbers of Apache reside in Oklahoma, California, New Mexico, Arizona, Texas, and Colorado.

LANGUAGE

The language of the Apache is part of the larger family of languages of the Athapascan peoples. Athapascan (the name of the language itself) has four branches: Northern Athapascan, Southwestern Athapascan, Pacific Coast Athapascan, and Eyak, a southeastern Alaska isolate. The Athapascan language family is one of three families within the Na-Dene language phylum; the other two, the Tlingit family and the Haida family, are language isolates in the far north—Tlingit in southeastern Alaska and Haida in British Columbia. Na-Dene is one of the most widely distributed language phyla in North America. The Southwestern Athapascan language, sometimes called Apachean, has seven dialects: Navajo, Western Apache, Chiricahua, Mescalero, Jicarilla, Lipan, and Kiowa-Apache. These have been roughly divided by linguists into two main groups: the Western Apache languages, including the San Carlos, Chiricahua, and Mescalero dialects; and an Eastern branch, consisting of Jicarilla and Lipan.

The language of the Plains Apache, while formerly counted among the Eastern languages, is now considered to be a unique, but related, language group.

While census figures show that the vast majority of Apache speak English as their primary language, the survival of their native languages is an issue of great importance, particularly in light of aging populations and the loss of the few remaining native speakers. Their language is central to their rituals and ceremonies and is seen by many as an important part of their collective identity. Many tribes over the last decade have begun to emphasize the teaching of native languages, both in schools and to adult learners. Many schools and universities, in particular the University of Arizona, have begun programs to ensure the survival of the Apache languages through documentation and linguistic study. The recording and documentation of native languages, however, is a matter of some controversy among native speakers, who see their language as one of the few elements of their society not affected by Anglo influence.

RELIGION

Traditional Apache religion is based on the concept of *diye*, or sacred power. This power derives from and supports connection with the landscape, which plays a vital part in the stories and ceremonies that form the foundation of Apache spiritual life. The complex Apache mythology features culture heroes, such as White-Painted Woman (also called Changing Woman) and Child of the Water, who are responsible for creating various aspects of the natural and human worlds. Costumed dancers reenact key aspects of Apache mythology in various ceremonies, and rituals are used to mark important tribal events such as harvest and life passages, including puberty. Shamans (also called medicine people) are believed to have a special gift of vision that allows them to learn from spirit beings, to bring fortune to the tribe, and to heal the sick.

Spanish missionaries initiated the process of eradicating traditional Indian religious practices, and many Apache eventually became Christians. In addition, the understanding and practice of traditional Apache religion is closely tied to native language, so English-only education tended to deprive Indian children of their religion as well as their cultural identity. Interest in preserving or regaining traditional language and culture has increased, however, not only on the reservations but also among Apache living elsewhere. Some Apache have maintained a spiritual commitment to their traditional religion, while many others value the stories and rituals as part of their cultural heritage rather than as a form of religious practice.

CULTURE AND ASSIMILATION

Few native groups resisted the encroachment of Anglo-American culture as long or as fiercely as the Apache. One of the last Native American nations to abandon military resistance to the U.S. government, the Apache were equally determined to resist the policy of forced assimilation or "Americanization" that followed the end of armed conflict. Viewing with suspicion and mistrust the culture and religion of their supplanters, the Apache struggled to retain their collective identity and traditions. Their cultural independence was in part responsible for negative portrayals of Apache in American popular culture, which often depicted them as savages or villains. By the later twentieth century, however, a revised understanding of American history had greatly reduced the stereotyping of Native Americans. The question of assimilation remains complex, and, like other tribes, the Apache assert that they were deprived of their cultural heritage and economic rights by systematic oppression and injustice that is ongoing. Some Apache today have chosen to adopt a generic American lifestyle, but many others try to find a balance that incorporates the values and advantages of their traditional culture with the opportunities and conveniences of modern American life.

Cuisine Because of their migratory culture and the often austere nature of the lands they inhabited, Apache cuisine was necessarily limited. Their traditional diet relied heavily on hunted game such as bison, deer, and elk, and was light on vegetables, except for those wild plants that could be gathered locally and what corn could be acquired by trade with the Pueblo peoples. The Apache avoided many smaller animals, including those with scales and those that lived in water, considering them unclean. Meat was often boiled, sometimes with potatoes and chiles, and served with a traditional fried bread, *chigustei*, cooked on embers or heated rocks.

One staple of some Apache tribes was napolitos, or prickly pear cactus, which was dethorned, boiled, and then fried with onions. Mescal, a large desert agave plant, was another uniquely traditional Apache food and is still occasionally harvested and prepared. The proper season for harvesting is May or June, when massive red flowers begin to appear in the mescal patches. The plant is dug out of the ground and stripped, leaving a white bulb two to three feet in circumference. A large cooking pit is dug, about 15 feet long, 4 feet wide, and 4 feet deep, large enough to cook about 2,000 pounds of mescal. The bottom of the pit is lined with stones, on top of which fires are built. The mescal is layered on top of the stones, covered with a layer of straw, and then with a layer of dirt. When cooked, the mescal is a fibrous, sticky, syrupy substance with a flavor similar to molasses. Portions are also dried in thin layers, which can last indefinitely without spoiling and in the past provided the Apache with lightweight rations for extended journeys.

Dances and Songs Ritual dance and song play a large part in traditional Apache culture. During the White Mountain Apache Sunrise Dance, girls undergoing the rite of passage to womanhood present an

TRADITIONAL ARTS AND CRAFTS

San Carlos Apache women are famous for their twined burden baskets, traditional conical baskets with leather straps for collecting, carrying, and storing food that are still in use today. Another San Carlos specialty is coiled basketry, featuring complex designs in black devil's claw, a desert flower common in the Southwest with claw-shaped seedpods that can be up to 15 inches long. Although they originally constructed baskets entirely of yucca and the bear claw plant, the Apache gradually began to include strips of the tough seedpod of the devil's claw, both to increase the toughness of the final product and for the aesthetic quality of the seed pods, which contrasted with the lighter tone of the yucca and bear claw. Mescalero Apache women fashion sandals and bags from mescal fibers.

elaborate dance that lasts three to six hours and is performed twice to thirty-two songs and prayers. The Crown Dance, or Mountain Spirit Dance, is a masked dance in which the participants impersonate deities of the mountains—specifically the *Gans*, or mountain spirits. The Apache Fire Dance is also a masked dance. Musical instruments that accompany the dancers include the water drum, the handheld rattle, and the human voice. Another traditional instrument still used in ritual and ceremonial events is the bullroarer, a thin piece of wood suspended from a string and swung in a circle.

Because of their religious and ceremonial nature, not all dances are open to the public. Some dances, however, are often performed specifically for local civic and tourist events. The Yavapai-Apache at Camp Verde, Arizona, occasionally present public performances of the Mountain Spirit Dance. The San Carlos and White Mountain Apache in Arizona perform the Sunrise Dance and Mountain Spirit Dance throughout the summer, but their traditional dances are most easily observed at the San Carlos and White Mountain tribal fairs.

Oklahoma Apache sometimes perform the Fire Dance at the annual American Indian Exposition in Anadarko, Oklahoma. The Fort Sill Apache in Oklahoma and the Mescalero Apache in New Mexico hold annual visits to one another's communities, where both groups' Gan dancers participate in all-night dances. A major ritual for the Kiowa-Apache of Oklahoma, revived in around 1960, is held by the Manatidie, or Blackfeet Society, a group of male warriors. Members perform a dance—also called the Manatidie—many times during the year and hold a large annual four-day festival during which the ceremony is performed in daylight, leaving the evenings free for social dancing and performances by other groups. The largest and most frequent ceremony among the Plains Apache, the Manatidie is a core of contemporary Kiowa-Apache identity.

Holidays Perhaps the most fundamental and enduring Apache holiday is the *na'ii'ees*, a puberty ceremony for girls held in spring or summer. Often referred to as the Sunrise Ceremony, the event usually lasts for four days and marks the passage to adulthood of one or several young women, who become imbued with the spirit of White-Painted Woman. A medicine man is selected to prepare the sacred items for the event, including an eagle feather for the girl's hair, deerskin clothing, and paint made from corn and clay. During the ceremony the parents choose godparents for the girl or girls. The tradition renews the life of the tribe; everyone plays a part in various rituals and social activities, including singing, dancing, prayers, and gift-giving. An important Apache tradition often included in the Sunrise Ceremony is the appearance of masked dancers representing the mountain spirits.

Apache celebrate a number of holidays each year. The San Carlos Apache Tribal Fair is celebrated annually over Veterans Day weekend at San Carlos, Arizona. The Tonto Apache and Yavapai-Apache perform public dances each year at the Coconino Center for the Arts, Flagstaff, Arizona, on the Fourth of July. The White Mountain Apache host the Apache Tribal Fair, which usually occurs on Labor Day weekend, at Whiteriver, Arizona. The Jicarilla Apache host the Little Beaver Rodeo and Powwow, usually in late July, and the Gojiiya Feast Day on September 14 and 15 each year, at Dulce, New Mexico. The Mescalero Apache Gahan Ceremonial occurs each year on July 1 through 4 at Mescalero, New Mexico. Apache in Oklahoma participate in the huge, weeklong American Indian Exposition in Anadarko, Oklahoma, each August.

Health Care Issues and Practices Apache suffered devastating health problems from the last decades of the nineteenth century through most of the twentieth century. Many of these problems are associated with malnutrition, poverty, and despair. Contagious diseases such as tuberculosis have been particularly deadly. Once tuberculosis was introduced among the Jicarilla, it spread at an alarming rate. The establishment of schools beginning in 1903 gave the tuberculosis bacteria a means of contaminating the entire tribe. By 1914, 90 percent of the Jicarilla suffered from tuberculosis. Between 1900 and 1920 one-quarter of the people died. One of the reservation schools was converted into a tuberculosis sanitarium in an attempt to address the crisis. The sanitarium was not closed until 1940.

Traditionally, *telapi* (fermented corn sprouts), in the words of one elder, "made people feel good about each other and what they were doing together." Since European contact, however, alcohol has become an insidious, destructive force among the Apache, a byproduct of demoralization and despair, that has led to significant health problems as well as crime. A recent study found that alcohol was a factor in more than 85 percent of the major crimes on both the Fort Apache and San Carlos reservations. Tribal leaders have attempted to address alcohol abuse by trying to create tribal enterprise, by fostering and encouraging bilingual and bicultural educational opportunities, and by trying to make it possible for Apache to gain more control over their lives.

Although many contemporary Apache utilize scientific medicine, they may also incorporate age-old approaches to health care, using herbal preparations for prevention or treatment of illness, as well as rituals prescribed by a traditional healer.

FAMILY AND COMMUNITY LIFE

For the Apache the family is the primary unit of political and cultural life. Apache have never been a unified nation politically, and individual Apache tribes, until very recently, have never had a centralized government, traditional or otherwise. Extended family groups acted entirely independently of one another. At intervals during the year, a number of these family groups, related by dialect, custom, intermarriage, and geographical proximity, came together, as conditions and circumstances allowed. These groups might be identifiable as a tribal division, but they almost never acted together as a tribe or nation—not even when faced with the overwhelming threat of the Comanche migration into their southern Plains territory. The existence of these many different, independent, extended family groups of Apache made it impossible for the Spanish, the Mexicans, or the Americans to deal with the Apache Nation as a whole. Each individual group had to be treated separately, an undertaking that proved difficult for each colonizer who attempted to establish authority within the Apache homeland.

Marriage and Divorce Apache culture is matrilineal. Once married, the man joins the wife's extended family, so that she is surrounded by her relatives. Spousal abuse is practically unknown in such a system. Apache children are deeply loved and respected. Child custody quarrels are also unknown; should the marriage not endure, the children remain with the mother's family. Marital harmony is encouraged by a custom forbidding the wife's mother to speak to, or even be in the presence of, her son-in-law. No such stricture applies to the wife's grandmother, who is frequently a powerful presence in family life.

Education Beginning in the 1880s, many Apache children were sent by the white authorities to Carlisle Indian School in Pennsylvania, the first off-reservation boarding school specifically for native children. Although the school was altruistic in theory, its singular focus on assimilation into white culture

made it a difficult environment for the children sent there. They were given new European names, stripped of their native identities, and separated from their cultures and traditions. Considered at the time a "noble experiment," the Carlisle experience was a dark time for many Apache children, resulting in deep emotional conflicts.

After the end of hostilities between the Apache and the U.S. military and the establishment of permanent reservations, government and mission-sponsored schools were established among the Apache. These schools, both the secular and the religious, pursued vigorous assimilationist policies, including English-only instruction. As a result of this system of imposed acculturation, 80 percent of the Apache in Arizona spoke English by 1952. Reservation schools were often substandard and inadequately funded and were seen by many natives as merely a tool of cultural colonialism. The schools and formal education in general became a subject of some controversy among native populations.

In recent years Apache have increasingly viewed education as a way to improve the economic outlook for younger generations, and more parents actively participate in decisions involving the schooling of their children, supported by professional educators, specialists, and researchers from both government and academia. This partnership has resulted in exemplary bilingual and bicultural programs at the public schools at the San Carlos and Fort Apache reservations, especially in the elementary grades. Another example can be found

in New Mexico, where in 1959 the Jicarilla incorporated their school district with those of the surrounding Hispanic towns. In thirty years the school board came to include four Jicarilla members, including the editor of the tribal newspaper. The benefits of this partnership improved educational opportunities for both native and nonnative students, as demonstrated in 1988, when the Jicarilla school district was chosen New Mexico School District of the Year.

Some Apache communities, including the more conservative and traditional Cibecue community at White Mountain Reservation, have extended the economic opportunity paradigm to encompass the use of education as a method for the preservation of native culture and tradition and as a tool to develop human resources. Educated tribal members are finding ways for the tribe to engage in economic activity that will allow more of its people to remain on the reservation, thus preserving the collective tribal community and culture.

EMPLOYMENT AND ECONOMIC CONDITIONS

Long periods of poor opportunity and unemployment have affected all parts of the Apache Nation. Many Apache have addressed the problem by leaving the reservations to find work in larger cities, particularly in the building and construction trades. Numerous others, though, have chosen to stay on their ancestral lands. Of those, particularly in the years after the establishment of the reservation, many were agricultural

and employment for all Apache tribes. Skiing and winter sports venues, arts and crafts, and tribal festivals and ceremonies all draw large numbers of tourists to Apache lands every year, contributing considerably to the local economies. The White Mountain tribe owns and operates the Sunrise Park Ski Area and summer resort, three miles south of McNary, Arizona. The ski area has seven lifts and generates $9 million in revenue per year. Another tribally owned enterprise that benefits from tourism is the White Mountain Apache Motel and Restaurant. In addition, the White Mountain Apache Tribal Fair brings in tourists from around the country.

The Jicarilla Apache also operate a ski enterprise, offering equipment rentals and trails for a cross-country skiing program during the winter months. In addition, the gift shop at the Jicarilla museum provides an outlet for the sale of locally crafted Jicarilla traditional items, including basketry, beadwork, feather work, and finely tanned buckskin leather.

In New Mexico many members of the Mescalero Apache find employment at their ski resort, Ski Apache, near Ruidoso, New Mexico, while others work at the tribal museum and visitor center in Mescalero, Arizona. A 440-room Mescalero resort, the Inn of the Mountain Gods, also near Ruidoso, has a gift shop, several restaurants, and an eighteen-hole golf course. The resort offers casino gambling, horseback riding, skeet and trap shooting, and tennis.

The small reservation of the Yavapai-Apache has fewer than 300 acres of land suitable for agriculture. The tourist complex at the Montezuma Castle National Monument—where the tribe owns the 75 acres of land surrounding the monument—is therefore an important source of employment and revenue.

Hunting and fishing also provide jobs and bring money into the local economies at a number of Apache reservations. Deer and elk hunting are especially popular on the Jicarilla reservation. The Jicarilla also maintain five campgrounds where camping is available for a fee. Other popular campgrounds are maintained by the Mescalero Apache, the San Carlos Apache, and the White Mountain Apache.

According to the 2010 U.S. Census, among those people who self-identified as Apache, 8.2 percent were unemployed, with 44.8 percent listed as "not in the work force." Households earning less than $14,999 per year made up 22.8 percent of the population; 22.2 percent of households were under the poverty line; and 26 percent of adults over the age of eighteen lived under the poverty line.

POLITICS AND GOVERNMENT

Apache were granted U.S. citizenship under the Indian Citizenship Act of 1924. The Apache tribes are federally recognized. They have established tribal governments under the Indian Reorganization Act of 1934,

workers and stockmen. As tribes began to exert more control over their reservations and natural resources in the 1960s and beyond, Apache were able to find employment in native lumber and mining interests, as well as in native tourist industries such as resorts and casinos.

Over the last decades, many of the Apache tribes have worked to create these economic and employment opportunities within their reservations. In Arizona cattle and grazing have become a major source of both employment and revenue. This is particularly true of the San Carlos Reservation, which faced many obstacles in getting their reservation lands back. By 1925 the Bureau of Indian Affairs had leased nearly all of the San Carlos Reservation to non-Indian cattlemen, who demonstrated no concern about overgrazing. In addition, most of the best San Carlos farmland was flooded when Coolidge Dam was completed in 1930. Recreational concessions around the lake benefit mostly non-Natives. By the end of the 1930s, the tribe regained control of its rangeland, and most San Carlos Apache became stockmen. Today, the San Carlos Apache cattle operation generates more than $1 million in sales annually. Grazing, timber, and mining leases provide additional revenue.

In those areas where cattle husbandry is not practical, as in the mountain regions of Arizona and New Mexico, timber has become a comparable source of tribal revenue and employment. The Fort Apache Timber Company in Whiteriver, Arizona, is owned and operated by the White Mountain Apache. Approximately 720,000 acres of the reservation is timberland. The company employs about four hundred Apache workers, produces 100 million board feet of lumber annually, and has a gross annual income of about $30 million.

While cattle and timber have helped some reservations increase their economic opportunities, tourism has become one of the largest sources of revenue

also known as the Wheeler-Howard Act, and they successfully withstood attempts by the U.S. government to implement its policy of terminating the separate legal status of Indian tribes during the 1950s. While allowing some measure of self-determination, the Wheeler-Howard Act has caused problems for virtually every Indian nation in the United States. The act subverts traditional Native American forms of government and imposes an alien system mixing American corporate and governmental structures on native peoples. Invariably, the most traditional people in each tribe have had little to say about their own affairs, as the most heavily acculturated and educated mixed-blood factions have dominated tribal affairs in these imposed systems. Frequently, tribal governments have been little more than convenient facades to facilitate access to on-reservation mineral and timber resources in arrangements that benefit everyone but the tribal members whose resources are exploited. The struggle for tribal control of both above- and below-ground resources has shaped the development of many of the Apache tribes.

The Apache did not legally acquire the right to practice their Native religion until the passage of the American Indian Religious Freedom Act of 1978. Other important rights, and some attributes of sovereignty, have been restored to them by such legislation as the Indian Civil Rights Act of 1966, the Indian Self-Determination and Educational Assistance Act of 1975, and the Indian Child Welfare Act of 1978. Since the passage of the Indian Claims Commission Act of 1946, the Jicarilla have been awarded nearly $10 million in compensation for land unjustly taken from them, but the United States refuses to negotiate the return of any of this land. In *Merrion v. Jicarilla Apache Tribe* (1982), the U.S. Supreme Court ruled in favor of the Jicarilla in an important case concerning issues of tribal sovereignty, holding that the tribe has the right to impose tribal taxes upon minerals extracted from their lands.

NOTABLE INDIVIDUALS

Art Allan Houser (1914–1994) was a Chiricahua Apache sculptor known for his six decades of work in wood, marble, stone, and bronze. Houser's works can be seen on the front lawn of the Oklahoma State Capitol and on the campus of the University of Oklahoma in Norman. His son, Bob Haozous (1943–), is also a sculptor; he is known for his monumental, and often politically charged, public sculptures.

Vanessa Paukeigope Jennings (1952–) is a Kiowa and Kiowa-Apache artist known for her work as a regalia maker, clothing designer, cradle board maker, and bead artist. In 1989 Jennings was named a National Heritage Fellow and a Living National Treasure by the U.S. Congress.

Literature Jose L. Garza/Blue Heron, Coahuilateca and Apache, is a Native American poet and Native American educator. His poetry has appeared in such

publications as *Akwe:kon Journal*, of the American Indian Program at Cornell University, *Native Sun*, *New Rain Anthology*, *Wayne Review*, *Triage*, and *Wooster Review*. Garza has taught at Edinboro University in Pennsylvania and has served as a regional coordinator of Wordcraft Circle of Native American Mentor and Apprentice Writers.

Jimmy Santiago Baca (1952–) is a writer, poet, and educator of Apache descent. His poetry collections include *Immigrants in Our Own Land* (1979), *Martin and Meditations on the South Valley* (1987), and *Spring Poems Along the Rio Grande* (2007). Baca has won the American Book Award for poetry, a Pushcart Prize, and the Hispanic Heritage Award in Literature.

Politics Mildred Cleghorn (1910–1997), educator and cultural activist, was a Chiricahua Apache born to parents under prisoner-of-war status. She later became the first chairperson of the Fort Sill Apache tribe, serving in the position from 1976 to 1995. Apache political leader and activist Ronnie Lupe has served as tribal chairman of the White Mountain Apache since 1966 and has helped secure his people's sovereign rights over the resources of their lands.

Stage and Screen Joanelle Romero (1957–) is a Native American filmmaker and actress of Apache, Cheyenne, Jewish, and Spanish descent. She founded Red Nation Celebration, a nonprofit advocate for Native American performing arts, as well as Red Nation Media, a Native American media outlet.

An Apache-Choctaw logger holds a chainsaw as he surveys the land near Zwolle, Louisiana. PHILIP GOULD / CORBIS

MEDIA

PRINT

Arizona Silver Belt

E-newspaper serving Globe, Arizona, and the nearby San Carlos Apache Reservation.

Holly Sow, Editor
298 North Pine Street
Globe, Arizona 85501
Phone: (928) 425-7121
Fax: (928) 425-7001
Email: news@silverbelt.com
URL: www.silverbelt.com

Fort Apache Scout

Biweekly community newspaper.

Sky Nez, Editor
P.O. Box 898
Whiteriver, Arizona 85941
Phone: (520) 338-4813

Gila River Indian News

Newspaper published by the Gila River Indian Community in Arizona.

Roberto A. Jackson, Editor
P.O. Box 97
Sacaton, Arizona 85247
Phone: (520) 562-9715
Fax: (520) 562-9712
URL: www.gilariver.org/news

Jicarilla Chieftain

Biweekly paper published by the Jicarilla Apache Nation.

Mary F. Polanco, Editor
P.O. Box 507
Dulce, New Mexico 87528
Phone: (505) 759-3242
Fax: (505) 759-3005

RADIO

KCIE 90.5 FM

Jicarilla Apache radio station.

Lisa Vigil-Gomez, Station Manager
P.O. Box 603
Dulce, New Mexico 87528
Phone: (505) 759-3681
Fax: (505) 759-9140
Email: kcie@zianet.com
URL: www.nv1.org/kcie.html

KGAK 1330 AM

AM radio station serving listeners on the Jicarilla Apache Reservation and environs.

401 East Coal Road
Gallup, New Mexico 87301
Phone: (505) 863-4444
Fax: (505) 722-7381

KNNB 88.1 FM

White Mountain Apache radio station with an eclectic and ethnic format eighteen hours daily.

Udell Opaha, General Manager
Highway 73
Skill Center Road
P.O. Box 310
Whiteriver, Arizona 85941
Phone: (520) 338-5229
Fax: (520) 338-1744

ORGANIZATIONS AND ASSOCIATIONS

TRIBAL ORGANIZATIONS

Apache Tribe of Oklahoma

P.O. Box 1330
Anadarko, Oklahoma 73005
Phone: (405) 247-9493
Fax: (405) 247-2686
URL: www.apachetribe.org

Chiricahua Apache Tribe

P.O. Box 50955
Albuquerque, New Mexico 87181
Phone: (505) 299-2276
Email: info@chiricahuaapache.org
URL: www.chiricahuaapache.org

Fort Sill Apache Tribe of Oklahoma

Oklahoma Office:

43187 U.S. Highway 281
Apache, Oklahoma 73006
Phone: (405) 588-2298
Fax: (405) 588-3313

New Mexico Office:

20885 Frontage Road
Deming, New Mexico 88030
Phone: (575) 544-0073
Fax: (575) 544-0224
URL: fortsillapache-nsn.gov

Jicarilla Apache Tribe

P.O. Box 147
Dulce, New Mexico 87528
Phone: (505) 759-3242
Fax: (505) 759-3005
URL: www.jicarillaonline.com

Kiowa Tribe of Oklahoma

P.O. Box 369
Carnegie, Oklahoma 73015
Phone: (405) 654-2300
Fax: (405) 654-2188
URL: www.kiowatribe.org

Lipan Apache Tribe of Texas

P.O. Box 5218
McAllen, Texas 78502
Phone: (956) 648-9336
Email: contact@lipanapache.org
URL: www.lipanapache.org

Mescalero Apache Tribe

P.O. Box 176
Mescalero, New Mexico 88340
Phone: (505) 671-4495
Fax: (505) 671-4495

San Carlos Apache Tribe

P.O. Box 1240
San Carlos, Arizona 85550
Phone: (520) 475-2361
Fax: (520) 475-2567
URL: www.sancarlosapache.com/home.htm

Tonto Apache Tribal Council

Tonto Reservation No. 30
Payson, Arizona 85541
Phone: (520) 474-5000
Fax: (520) 474-9125

White Mountain Apache Tribe

P.O. Box 700
Whiteriver, Arizona 85941
Phone: (520) 338-4346
Fax: (520) 338-1514
URL: www.wmat.nsn.us

Yavapai-Apache Tribe

P.O. Box 1188
Camp Verde, Arizona 86322
Phone: (520) 567-3649
Fax: (520) 567-9455
URL: www.yavapai-apache.org

STATE INDIAN AFFAIRS OFFICES

Arizona Commission of Indian Affairs

Kristine FireThunder, Executive Director
State Capitol Building-Executive Tower
1700 West Washington Street
Suite 430
Phoenix, Arizona 85007
Phone: (602) 542-4421
Fax: (602) 542-3712
Email: iainfo@az.gov
URL: www.indianaffairs.state.az.us

New Mexico Indian Affairs Department

Arthur Allison, Cabinet Secretary
Wendell Chino Building, Second Floor
1220 South Saint Francis Drive
Santa Fe, New Mexico 87505
Phone: (505) 476-1600
Fax: (505) 476-1601
Email: arthur.allison@state.nm.us
URL: www.iad.state.nm.us

Oklahoma Indian Affairs Commission

Barbara Warner, Executive Director
4545 North Lincoln Boulevard
Suite 282
Oklahoma City, Oklahoma 73105
Phone: (405) 521-3828
Fax: (405) 522-4427
URL: www.oiac.ok.gov

MUSEUMS AND RESEARCH CENTERS

Center for Indian Education

Part of the Arizona State University School of Transformation, the center focuses on research and language education and trains and prepares indigenous scholars.

302 Farmer Education Building, Room 302
Tempe, Arizona 85287

Gila River Arts and Crafts Center Museum

Displays include reconstructed traditional houses of the Apache, Maricopa, Papago, and Pima and arts and crafts of more than thirty Southwestern tribes.

P.O. Box 457
Sacaton, Arizona 85247
Phone: (520) 315-3411
Fax: (520) 315-3968

SOURCES FOR ADDITIONAL STUDY

Britten, Thomas A. *The Lipan Apaches: People of Wind and Lightning*. Albuquerque: University of New Mexico Press, 2009.

Buskirk, Winfred. *The Western Apache*. Norman: University of Oklahoma Press, 1986.

Dwyer, Helen, and D. L. Birchfield. *Apache History and Culture*. New York: Gareth Stevens Publishers, 2012.

Forbes, Jack D. *Apache, Navajo, and Spaniard*. Norman: University of Oklahoma Press, 1994.

Kenner, Charles L. *A History of New Mexican-Plains Indian Relations*. Norman: University of Oklahoma Press, 1994.

Meadows, William. *Kiowa, Apache, and Comanche Military Societies*. Austin: University of Texas Press, 1999.

Mort, Terry. *Wrath of Cochise: The Bascom Affair and the Origins of the Apache Wars*. N.p.: Pegasus Books, 2013.

Perry, Richard J. *Apache Reservation: Indigenous Peoples and the American State*. Austin: University of Texas Press, 1993.

Schweinfurth, Kay Parker. *Prayer on Top of the Earth: The Spiritual Universe of the Apaches*. Boulder: University Press of Colorado, 2002.

Stockel, H. Henrietta. *Women of the Apache Nation: Voices of Truth*. Reno: University of Nevada Press, 1991.

Stockel, H. Henrietta, and Marian D. Kelley. *Drumbeats from Mescalero: Conversations with Apache Elders, Warriors, and Horseholders*. College Station: Texas A&M University Press, 2011.

Sturtevant, William C. gen. ed. *Handbook of North American Indians*. Vol. 10, *Southwest*, edited by Alfonso Ortiz and Vol. 13, *Plains*, edited by Raymond J. DeMallie. Washington, D.C.: Smithsonian Institution, 1983; 2001.

Tiller, Veronica E. V., and Mary M. Velarde. *The Jicarilla Apache of Dulce*. Charleston, SC: Arcadia Publishing, 2012.

ARAB AMERICANS
Nabeel Abraham

OVERVIEW

Arab Americans are immigrants or descendants of people from the Arabic-speaking world, an area that spans twenty-two countries in the Middle East and in West, North, and East Africa. To the west and north are the Atlantic Ocean and the Mediterranean Sea, and to the east are the Persian Gulf and the Indian Ocean. The countries include Algeria, Bahrain, Comoros, Djibouti, Egypt, Iraq, Jordan, Kuwait, Lebanon, Libya, Mauritania, Morocco, Oman, Palestine, Qatar, Saudi Arabia, Somalia, Sudan, Syria, Tunisia, the United Arab Emirates, and Yemen. In some of these countries Arabic is the only spoken language. In others Arabic is one of two or more official languages. The geography of the Arab world varies from deserts, rivers, and mountains to areas used to grow crops and raise animals. The area known as the Fertile Crescent, which lies between the Euphrates and Tigris Rivers, contains some of the richest agricultural land in the world. With an area of more than five million square miles (more than thirteen million square kilometers), the Arab world is roughly half the size of North America.

According to the *CIA World Factbook*, which used 2012 estimates when available, the population of the Arab world (not including Palestine) was 348,814,780. The Palestinian News and Information Agency estimated that the 2012 population of Palestine was 4.29 million, with 2.65 million living on the West Bank and 1.64 million living on the Gaza Strip. Islam is the major religion of the region, but there are also large populations of Christians, Jews, and Zoroastrians. In Iraq, for instance, 97 percent of the population was Muslim. In Lebanon and Syria, which are more religiously diverse, the percentage of Muslims was 59 and 74, respectively. Both countries have significant Christian populations. The standard of living varies greatly among the countries, ranging from oil-rich Qatar, which had an annual per capita income of $104,300, to war-torn Somalia, which was the fourth-poorest nation in the world, with an annual per capita income of $600. According to the United Nations Development Programme, one of the major economic problems affecting the area was that 30 percent of the region's youth was unemployed, and more than half of the total population of the area was under the age of twenty-four.

The first significant wave of Arab immigration to the United States occurred in the late nineteenth century, when Lebanese and Syrians arrived in search of improved economic opportunities. Many early Arab immigrants first supported themselves through peddling and eventually worked in factories, opened small stores, and became homesteaders. The post-World War I era was relatively hospitable to new Arab immigrants, many of whom succeeded economically and pursued educational advancement. However, legal restrictions hindered their ability to naturalize, and the passage of the National Origin Act in 1924 limited the number of Arab immigrants to 100 per year. After World War II the U.S government made it easier for educated and middle-class Arabs to immigrate to the United States. Mostly male, these Arab students often married American women, and large numbers remained permanently in the United States. A new surge of Arab immigrants began arriving in the 1990s. Unlike earlier immigrants, who were overwhelmingly Christian, these more recent immigrants were predominantly Muslim.

According to the 2011 American Community Survey, there were 1,769,251 people of Arab ancestry living in the United States. However, it is widely believed that such census figures underrepresent the true Arab American population. The Arab American Institute, for example, contended that there were 3.5 million people of Arab ancestry living in the United States. Most early Arab immigrants settled in the Northeast or Midwest. A prominent Arab American community has been established in the Detroit metropolitan area. In 2012, one-third of Arab Americans resided in California, Michigan, or New York. Other areas of significant Arab settlement include Illinois, Maryland, Massachusetts, New Jersey, Ohio, Texas, and Virginia.

HISTORY OF THE PEOPLE

Early History The history of the Arab world spans fifteen centuries and twenty-two individual countries, which have been united by a common language and by cultural ties. Ethnic Arabs inhabited the Arabian Peninsula and neighboring areas. With the rise of Islam in the seventh century CE and its phenomenal expansion over parts of Asia, Africa, and Europe, Arabic culture and language spread to the newly conquered peoples.

Over time Arab identity lost its purely ethnic roots as millions in the Middle East and North Africa adopted the Arabic language and integrated Arab culture with that of their own.

In the 1950s and 1960s, Arab countries were resonating with nationalist ideologies and the Arab world was filled with promise and hope, especially regarding the question of Palestine and Arab national unity.

Modern Era The term *Arab* is a cultural, linguistic, and political designation. It is often incorrectly applied to individuals from countries such as Pakistan and Iran who do not speak Arabic. The term embraces numerous national and regional groups as well as many non-Muslim religious minorities. Arab Christians, particularly in Egypt, Syria, Iraq, Palestine, and Jordan, constitute roughly 10 percent of the population. In Lebanon, Christians of various sects approach just under half of the population, while in Egypt, Christians compose between 10 and 15 percent of the population. Outside the Arab world, the stereotype of Arabs as nomads has persisted, but such groups have always formed only a small minority of the Arab population. The contemporary population is heavily urbanized, with large populations settling in cities such as Cairo and Istanbul. Those who remain in rural areas tend to be involved in agriculture and fishing, and much of that takes place at the subsistence level.

While sharing many common traits, the countries within the Arab world are also diverse, and their histories have been shaped by internal events and their access to economic resources. These countries range from highly developed nations such as Egypt and Syria to Somalia, which is one of the most underdeveloped

and poorest nations in the world. In 1945 seven of the Arab-speaking nations came together to form the Arab League to promote closer political, economic, and cultural links among member states. The charter members of the Arab League were Egypt, Iraq, Lebanon, Saudi Arabia, Syria, Transjordan (now Jordan), and Yemen. Today each of the Arab League's twenty-two members is bound by any unanimous decisions made by the league's council, which serves as the governing body of the organization. Despite the efforts of the Arab League, the modern history of the Arab world has been filled with strife. The Arab-Israeli conflict, for instance, claimed 200,000 lives and displaced 3 million people between 1948 and 1990. Sudan and Somalia have been involved in internal strife. Conflict within the region has historically led to large groups fleeing their homelands.

SETTLEMENT IN THE UNITED STATES

Arabic-speaking immigrants arrived in the United States in three significant waves. The first occurred between the late 1800s and World War I and consisted mainly of immigrants from Greater Syria, an Arab province of the Ottoman Empire until the Ottoman collapse in 1918. Following the breakup of the empire, the province was partitioned into the separate political entities of Syria, Lebanon, Palestine, and Transjordan. The majority of immigrants in this wave belonged to Christian minorities, though as many as 20 percent were Muslim. Although some scholars claim that these immigrants left their native countries for religious or political reasons, other evidence suggests that they were drawn to the United States and elsewhere by economic opportunity.

Of the approximately 60,000 Arabs who immigrated to the United States between 1899 and 1910, approximately half were illiterate, many were unskilled, and a majority were males, some of whom were married but were forced to leave their families behind. Like other economically motivated immigrants during this period, Arabs left with the intention of earning money and returning home to live out the remainder of their lives in relative prosperity. But the majority of these migrants stayed, bringing their families over when they were able or marrying American women and gaining citizenship.

In addition to this larger pattern of immigration, a small group of Arab writers, poets, and artists took up residence in major urban centers such as New York and Boston. The most famous of the group was Kahlil Gibran (1883–1931), author of *The Prophet* and numerous other works. Curiously, this literary circle, which came to be known as the Pen League (*al-Rabita al-Qalamiyya*), had a negligible influence on the early Arab American communities in the United States. The Pen League's greatest impact was on arts and letters in Lebanon, Egypt, and other Arab countries.

Early immigrants settled in the urban areas of the Northeast and Midwest, in states such as New York,

Massachusetts, Pennsylvania, Michigan, and Ohio. By 1940 a fifth of the estimated 350,000 Arabs resided in three cities—New York, Boston, and Detroit. In these urban areas the immigrants clustered in ethnic neighborhoods. Although many found work in the industrial factories and textile mills that propelled the U.S. economy in the first half of the twentieth century, some also chose the life of itinerant salesmen, peddling dry goods and other sundry items across the heartland. Others homesteaded on the Great Plains and in rural areas of the South.

Very few Arabic-speaking immigrants made their way across the Atlantic during the interwar period, which was marked by the Great Depression and anti-immigrant sentiment. Immigration resumed, however, after the close of World War II, especially from the 1950s to the mid-1960s. Unlike the earlier influx, this second wave included many more Muslims. It also included refugees who had been displaced by the 1948 Palestine War that culminated in the establishment of Israel. This period also witnessed the arrival of many Arabic-speaking professionals and university students who often chose to remain in the United States after completion of their training. Mid-century immigrants tended to settle where jobs were available. Those with few skills drifted to the established Arab communities in the industrial towns of the East Coast and Midwest, while those with professional skills ventured to the new suburbs around the major industrial cities or to rural towns.

In the mid-1960s, when U.S. immigration laws were liberalized, a much larger and more diverse Arab migration began, and it continued into the twenty-first century. This migration included many professionals, entrepreneurs, and unskilled and semiskilled laborers. These immigrants often fled political instability and wars engulfing their home countries. They included Lebanese Shi'a Muslims from southern Lebanon, Palestinians from the Israeli-occupied West Bank, and Iraqis of all political persuasions. But many professionals from these and other countries, such as Syria, Egypt, and Jordan, and unskilled workers from Yemen also emigrated in search of better economic opportunities. Had conditions been more hospitable in their home countries, it is doubtful that many of these immigrants would have emigrated.

LANGUAGE

The Arabic language retains a classical literary form that is employed on formal occasions, such as speeches and university lectures, and in most forms of writing. Everyday speech is the province of the many and varied regional and local dialects. It is these dialects and, in the case of highly assimilated Arab Americans, their remnants that a visitor among Arab Americans is likely to encounter.

Each national group has its own particular dialect, and there are regional and local subdialects found within each group. For the most part speakers of different dialects are able to make themselves understood when

Arab Americans in Dearborn, Michigan. JIM WEST / ALAMY

communicating with those who speak other dialects. This is especially true when closely related dialects (for example, Lebanese, Syrian, Palestinian, and Jordanian) are involved and less so among geographically distant dialects. The great exception is the Egyptian dialect, which is familiar to most speakers of Arabic because of the widespread influence of the Egyptian movie and recording industries and the dominant cultural role that Egypt has traditionally played in the Middle East.

According to the 2011 American Community Survey estimates, 43 percent of Arab Americans spoke only English in their homes, while 57 percent spoke a language other than English in their homes. The majority of the latter (79 percent) indicated, however, that they spoke English "very well." Lebanese Americans were among the Arab American subgroups most likely to speak only English in their homes (69 percent), and Iraqi Americans were among the Arab American subgroups least likely to speak only English in their homes (17 percent).

RELIGION

While a vast majority of Arab Americans were Christians during the initial significant period of migration in the early twentieth century, Muslim immigration began to outpace that of Christians later in the twentieth century. By the early twenty-first century, Muslims accounted for half of the Arab American community.

Arab Christians are generally divided between Eastern rite churches (Orthodox) and the Latin rite (Uniate) churches (Maronites, Melkite, and Chaldean). In the beginning all Middle Eastern churches followed Eastern rites. Over the centuries schisms occurred in which the seceders switched allegiance to Rome, forming the Uniate churches. Although the Uniate churches formally submit to the authority of the Roman pope and conform to Latin rites, they continue to maintain their own patriarchs and internal autonomy. Like the Eastern churches, the Uniates also allow priests to marry (though monks and bishops must remain celibate).

Arab Muslims are nominally divided between Sunni and Shi'a, the two major branches of Islam.

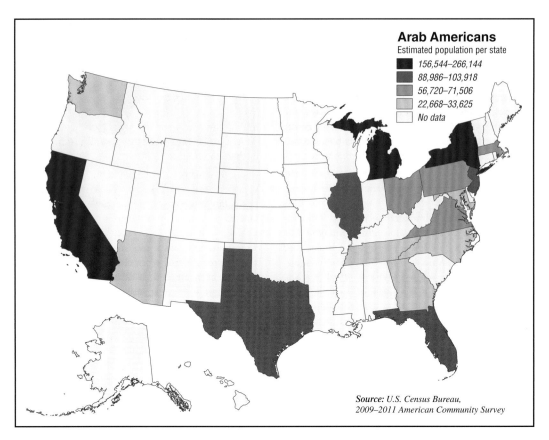

Arab Americans
Estimated population per state

- 156,544–266,144
- 88,986–103,918
- 56,720–71,506
- 22,668–33,625
- No data

*Source: U.S. Census Bureau,
2009–2011 American Community Survey*

The schism dates to an early conflict in Islam over the succession of the *Caliphate*—leader—of the religious community following the death of the Prophet Muhammad. The Sunni faction won out, eliminating leaders of the opposing faction led by the Prophet's nephew, Ali, and his sons. Ali's followers came to be known as the *Shi'a*—the partisans. Over time the Shi'a developed unique theological doctrines and practices. The majority of Arab American Muslims are Sunni. Arab Shi'a are mostly from Lebanon and Iraq as well as northern Yemen.

Arab American Muslims tend to be devout practitioners of their faith and observe the Five Pillars of Islam. *Shahadah* is the sincere declaration of the Muslim faith. *Salat* is the practice of praying five times a day, beginning with a morning prayer. If a mosque is accessible, men perform this initial prayer there, while women pray at home. Prayers follow at midday, in the afternoon, in the evening, and at night and are typically performed at home, work, or wherever else the faithful find themselves. *Hajj* is an annual pilgrimage to Mecca that Islamic men and women are required to make at least once in their lifetime. *Sawm* is fasting from dawn to sunset during the holy month of Ramadan. The fifth of these central tenets of Islamic faith is *Zakat*, which is tithing to benefit the needy. Muslims also abide by a set of Islamic dietary guidelines that make foods permissible (*halal*) to consume.

While tensions exist between mainstream American culture and the Muslim American community, American institutions have become increasingly accommodating of Muslim Americans' need to meet their various religious obligations. For example, many workplaces allow Muslim employees breaks to pray during the workday. Still, friction between American culture and Islamic religious practice persists. This can be seen in the difficulty that Muslim Americans have had in tithing as a result of increasing federal pressure on Islamic charities, which have been suspected of aiding terrorism, in the wake of terrorist attacks in the United States on September 11, 2001.

CULTURE AND ASSIMILATION

The assimilation of early Arab immigrants into American society was facilitated by the fact that the majority of those immigrants were Christian. Aside from barely discernible Arabic names beneath Anglicized surnames and a preference for some Old World dishes, they retained few traces of their ethnic roots. Many were successful, and some achieved celebrity status.

At the turn of the century, when the first emigrants left the Arab world, their homelands languished under Ottoman Turkish rule, then four centuries old. Arab and regional national consciousness was still nascent. By the time a new immigration wave began at mid-century, the Arab world was in the process of shaking off the European colonial rule, which had carved up much of the Middle East after the breakup of the Ottoman Empire at the end of World War I. In the 1950s and 1960s the Arab countries were resonating with nationalist ideologies, and the Arab world was filled with promise and hope, especially regarding Arab national unity and the independence of Palestine. These ideological currents profoundly influenced many of the postwar immigrants. This group, too, was able to assimilate into mainstream society without much resistance. The establishment of cultural clubs, political committees, houses of worship, and Arabic language schools helped maintain a cultural identity and a political awareness among many new arrivals and their children.

Arriving in the 1970s and 1980s, the third wave of Arab immigration was composed primarily of Muslims, who had greater difficulty assimilating to American culture. These new immigrants often opted to remain on the outskirts of society, even while adopting many American cultural mores. The third wave has been the driving force behind the recent upsurge in the establishment of Muslim schools, mosques, charities, and Arabic language classes.

Collectively many Arab Americans have experienced cultural marginalization. Arabs, Muslims, and Middle Easterners generally have been vilified in the news media, in Hollywood productions, in pulp novels, and in political discourse. Arab Americans cope with their marginality in three different ways: denying their ethnic identity, withdrawing into an ethnic enclave, or engaging mainstream society through information campaigns aimed at the news media, book publishers, politicians, and schools. Many Arab Americans adapt these strategies in combination or alternate between them during the course of their lives. The informational campaigns adopted by Arab Americans typically center, thematically, on the inherent unfairness of stereotyping Arabs, Muslims, and Middle Easterners in a society founded on equal opportunity. In 1999 the cable television network TNT announced that it would never again show movies such as *Shadow Warriors 2: Assault on Death Mountain* and *Thunder in Paradise* that blatantly bash Arabs and Arab Americans.

The types of Arab Americans who choose to deny their ethnic background cover the spectrum: recent arrivals, assimilated immigrants, and native born. Among the American born, denial takes the form of a complete break with one's ethnicity in favor of wholesale adoption of American culture. Others, particularly immigrants, tend to stress their distinctiveness from Arab and Islamic culture, as when Iraqi Christians stress their Chaldean identity as opposed to their Iraqi affiliation.

Arab Americans who opt to withdraw into an ethnic enclave tend to be recent immigrants. Running the gamut from unskilled workers to middle-class professionals, this group prefers to live in ethnic neighborhoods or close to other members of the same group in the suburbs. They believe that their ethnic culture and religious traditions are alien to American culture. As a result, they typically resist assimilation. They believe that cultural marginalization is the price of living in American society. That said, many who live in ethnic enclaves, especially the children of immigrants, are eager to participate in mainstream American life and escape the cultural marginalization of their community.

Those who advocate engaging society head-on seek to win societal acceptance of Arab Americans as an integral part of the cultural plurality of the United States. The integrationists adopt several strategies. Some stress the common bonds between Arab or Islamic values and American values, emphasizing strong family ties. They also focus on the commonalities between Christianity and Islam. Others seek to confront anti-Arab stereotyping and racism by emphasizing that they are Americans who happen to be of Arab ancestry. Along with well-assimilated, native-born Arab Americans, this group also consists of foreign-born professionals who wish to maintain their ethnic identity free from stigmatization by the wider culture. Other Arab Americans, however, embrace their ethnic identity and seek to benefit both from strong ethnic ties and from affirmative action-like policies in order succeed in business and politics.

According to the 2009–2011 American Community Survey estimates, 57.4 percent of Arab Americans were native-born U.S. citizens. Among the foreign-born Arab American population, 56.8 percent had become naturalized citizens.

Assimilation has been particularly difficult for all Arab American groups in the wake of the terrorist attacks of September 11, 2001. Because the attack was conducted by Arabs within the al-Qaeda terrorist organization, many Americans began equating being Arab with being a terrorist. While many Arab Americans never experienced direct discrimination, the number of hate crimes committed against Arab Americans increased significantly after the al-Qaeda attacks. The Council of American-Islamic Relations and the United States Commission on Civil Rights announced that 600 reports of hate crimes were filed in the months following September 2001. Studies conducted after the attacks have revealed a subtle prejudice that has negatively affected the lives of most Arab Americans. The most common perpetrators of prejudice, according to Arab Americans, are not individuals but the federal government and the American media. The term "flying while Arab" was coined to describe the suspicion that Arab Americans face when boarding airplanes. The result of the attacks has been that many Arab Americans feel that they are neither wholly Arab nor wholly American. One group of Arab Americans responded to the identity crisis by creating a series of forums, known as Building Respect in Diverse Groups to Enhance Sensitivity, or BRIDGES, in Detroit to work with law enforcement to apprehend terrorists while protecting the civil liberties of other Arab Americans. The prejudice that resulted from the 2001 attacks also, however, drove assimilation among the Arab American community, as some within the community sought to avoid discrimination by blending into mainstream American culture.

Traditions and Customs Customs center on hospitality associated with food, socializing with family and friends, and a preference for residing close to relatives. Educational achievement and economic advancement are viewed positively, as are the maintenance of strong family ties and the preservation of female chastity and fidelity. Arab American beliefs about the United States are extremely positive, particularly regarding the availability of economic opportunities and political freedoms. Socially, however, Arab Americans feel that American society is highly violent, rather promiscuous, too lenient toward offenders, and somewhat lax on family values.

A common American stereotype about Arabs emphasizes that they are by definition Muslims and therefore are bloodthirsty, fanatical, and anti-Western. Another misconception is that Iranians are Arabs, when most Iranians are Persians who speak Farsi, an Indo-European language, which uses Arabic script. Arabic, on the other hand, belongs to the Semitic language family. Other misconceptions and stereotypes involve the perception of Arabs as nomads and the widespread suppression of the rights of women. For the most part the American media has perpetuated the stereotype of the Arab male as a terrorist or a sheik and the stereotype of the Arab female as a downtrodden wife or as a promiscuous belly dancer. Since 2001 negative conceptions of Arab Americans have proliferated significantly as American culture has become increasingly fearful of and hostile toward the Islamic religion, which many equate with Arab culture. According to a 2004 Pew Forum on Religion and Public Life poll, four in ten Americans had an unfavorable view of Islam. The growth of Islamophobia had significant and far-reaching consequences for the Arab American community, which was subject to increased scrutiny from law enforcement and to restrictions on religious freedom. Muslims in the United States have been the targets of attacks and harassment, and mosques have been the targets of protests.

Stereotypes of Arab culture and society abound in Western literary works, scholarly research, and the news and entertainment media. Typical of the fiction genre is Leon Uris's celebrated novel *Exodus* (1958), in which the Arab country of Palestine is repeatedly depicted as a "fruitless, listless, dying land." Arabs opposed to the creation of the state of Israel are described as the "dregs of humanity, thieves, murderers, highway robbers, dope runners and white slavers." More generally, Arabs are "dirty," "crafty," and "corrupt." Uris amplified these characterizations in his 1985 work, *The Haj.* These and other examples are examined in Janice J. Terry's *Mistaken Identity: Arab Stereotypes in Popular Writing* (1985). A study of the cultural antecedents of Arab and Muslim stereotyping in Western culture is found in Edward W. Said's highly acclaimed work, *Orientalism* (1978). News media coverage is critiqued in Said's *Covering Islam* (1981); television portrayals of Arabs are examined in Jack Shaheen's *The TV Arab* (1984).

Cuisine The most pronounced dietary injunction followed by Arab Muslims is the religious prohibition of the consumption of pork. Many Arab Christians also disdain the consumption of pork, but for cultural reasons. Muslims are required to consume meat that is ritually slaughtered (*halal*). In response to the growing demand for *halal* meats, many enterprising Arab American grocers have in recent years set up *halal* meat markets.

Arab Americans have a distinctive cuisine centered on lamb, rice, bread, fresh salads, and highly seasoned dishes. The Middle Eastern diet consists of many ingredients not found in the average American kitchen, such as chickpeas, lentils, fava beans, ground sesame seed oil, feta cheese, dates, and figs. Many Arab dishes, such as stuffed zucchini or green peppers and stuffed grape or cabbage leaves, are highly labor-intensive.

For the most part Arab Americans prepare and consume traditional Arab cuisine, including hummus, a spread made primarily of mashed chickpeas; tabouli, a salad composed of bulgur, garlic, onion, tomato, and parsley; falafel, deep fried balls of chickpeas or fava beans; kibbeh, a ground meat dish; and kebabs, skewered and roasted meats. Arab foods are also increasingly popular among the American population at large. This has led to a proliferation of Arab restaurants not only in cities such as Detroit and New York but also in areas without large Arab American populations.

Traditional Dress In their day-to-day lives most Arab Americans wear common Western clothing but dress conservatively. Female Arab American Muslims also typically wear the traditional Islamic *hijab,* a scarf or cloth that is used to cover one's head. Worn in fidelity to Islamic principles and as an expression of modesty, the *hijab* is the most visible marker of Muslim identity in the United States. Some Arab American men wear the *keffiyeh,* a typically cotton scarf worn on the head. Many foreign-born Arab men of all ages are fond of carrying worry beads, which they unconsciously run through their fingers while engaging in conversation or while walking. Some Arab and other Muslim women occasionally don long, shapeless dresses, commonly called Islamic dresses, in addition to a *hijab* or other headscarf.

Greetings and Popular Expressions Some basic Arabic greetings, with pronunciation, include *marhaba* ("mar-ha-ba")—"hello," and its response *ahlen* ("ah-len")—"welcome" (colloquial greetings in Lebanese, Syrian, Palestinian, and Jordanian dialects). Egyptians would say *Azayyak* ("az-zay-yak")—"How are you?" and its response *quwayyas* ("qu-whey-yes")—"fine." A more formal greeting, readily understood throughout the Arabic-speaking world is: *asalaam 'a laykum* ("a-sa-lamb ah-laykum")—"greetings, peace be upon you." The proper response is *wa 'a laykum asalaam* ("wa-ah-laykum a-sa-lamb")—"and, peace be upon you, too." Because of the inherent hospitality of Arab households, it is proper to say *Al-hamdu lilah*— Thanks be to God—to signify the end of a meal.

Holidays The three religious holidays celebrated by Arab American Muslims are also celebrated by Muslims everywhere. They are Ramadan, Eid al-Fitr, and Eid al-Adha. Ramadan is a month-long dawn-to-dusk fast that occurs during the ninth month of the Islamic calendar. Ramadan is a month of self-discipline as well as spiritual and physical purification. The fast requires complete abstinence from food, drink (including water), tobacco, and sex from sunrise to sunset during the entire month. Eid al-Fitr marks the end of Ramadan. A cross between Thanksgiving and Christmas, the Eid is a festive and joyous occasion for Muslims everywhere. Eid al-Adha, the Feast of the Sacrifice, commemorates the Prophet Abraham's willingness to sacrifice his son Ishmael in obedience to God. According to the Quran, the Muslim holy book that is considered to be the word of God, the angel Gabriel intervened at the last moment, substituting a lamb in place of Ishmael. The holiday is held in conjunction with the *Hajj*, the pilgrimage to Mecca, in which increasing numbers of American Muslims participate.

Some Arab Muslim families celebrate the birth of Jesus at Christmas. Muslims recognize Jesus as an important prophet but do not consider him divine. They use the occasion of Christmas to exchange gifts, and some have adopted the custom of decorating a Christmas tree. Arab American Christians observe major Christian holidays. Followers of Eastern rite churches (Egyptian Copts, Syrian Orthodox, and Greek Orthodox) celebrate Christmas on the Epiphany, January 6. Easter is observed on the Sunday after Passover rather than on the date established by the Roman Catholic Church. In addition, the Eastern Churches, particularly the Coptic church, mark numerous religious occasions, saints' days, and the like throughout the year.

FAMILY AND COMMUNITY LIFE

In traditional Arab society, members of two or three generations would dwell in a single household or, in wealthier families, in a family compound. This extended household centered around a married man and some of his adult sons and their families.

ARAB PROVERBS

es-seqiye l-jerye la n-nahr-al-magTu'
> The flowing brook rather than the dry river.

okhfod sawtakwa qawwe Hijtak
> Lower your voice to strengthen your argument.

khabbe qershak el-abiyad la-yomak el aswad
> Hide your white money for your black day.

illi biyeshrub elbahar maa bighaD elsaaqia
> He who has drunk the sea does not choke on a brook.

tu3awwid 3uSfuur fii al-kaff
> A thousand cranes in the air are not worth one sparrow in the fist.

idha kaan al-qamr ma3ak laa tabaalii al-nujuum
> If the moon be with thee, thou needest not to care about the stars.

A grandparent might also have resided in the household. A variation on this structure was for several brothers and their respective families to reside in a compound with a grandparent and other elderly relatives. These traditional family structures have begun to deteriorate and change as the majority of Arabs have moved to cities.

Among Arab Americans, the large extended family constituting a single household has traditionally been found only among recent immigrants. As families acculturate and assimilate, they tend to form nuclear families with, occasionally, the addition of an elderly grandparent and an unmarried adult child. In some communities adult married children set up a household near their parents and married siblings. This arrangement allows the maintenance of extended family networks while enjoying the benefits of living in a nuclear family. The economic downturn of the early twenty-first century led to an increase in the number of multi-generational households among the Arab American community.

Gender Roles Boys and girls are reared differently, though the degree of that difference is determined by the level of assimilation. Boys are generally given greater latitude than girls. At the extreme end of the spectrum, girls are expected to marry at a relatively young age, and their schooling is not considered as important as that of boys. High school is the upper limit for girls in very traditional immigrant homes, though some postsecondary education is expected among educated households. In many Arab American families, however, women are more likely than men to attend college, as men are expected to pursue occupations that are considered inappropriate for women rather than pursue higher education. This is true of more conservative Arab Americans, such as Yemeni Americans, and more liberal Arab Americans, such as Chaldean Americans.

The daughters of professionals are usually encouraged to pursue careers. Middle Eastern families tend to favor boys over girls, and this preference extends to wide segments of the Arab American community. In a few traditional homes girls are not allowed to ride bicycles or play certain sports, while boys are otherwise indulged. The oldest son usually enjoys a measure of authority over younger siblings, especially his sisters, because he is expected to eventually carry the mantle of authority held by the father.

Within the countries of the Arab world, the status of women is dependent on a number of factors that include religion, social class, level of urbanization and education, and whether the country is dominated by civil, customary, or religious law. Many Arab men and women subsequently experience culture shock when dealing with American women and with the changing gender roles in their own families.

Within traditional Arab American families, formal authority lies with the husband or father, just as it does in Arab society. Women play important roles in socializing children, preserving kinship ties, and maintaining social and religious traditions. The degree of hospitality in the home is considered a measure of a family's standing among Arabs everywhere.

Outside the home the role of Arab American women has fluctuated with the ebb and flow of the immigration tide. While Arab American women continue to be less likely to be employed than those in the general population, large numbers have joined the workforce and have taken on changing societal and familial roles. As communities become assimilated, women tend to assume leadership roles in community organizations in the mosque or church or in community-wide endeavors such as the organization of parochial schools. With each new influx of immigrants, assimilated women tend to lose ground in institutions that attract new immigrants (e.g., the mosque). Women who at one time were among the leadership sometimes find themselves quickly taking a back seat or even being ousted from the institution. In other cases, however, women gain power and influence as their skills and experience are regarded as invaluable by new immigrants who must rely on these assimilated women for help navigating a new culture.

Education Education is highly valued among wide segments of the community. Affluent households prefer private schools. Working class and middle class members tend to send their children to public schools.

A recent trend in some Arab American Muslim communities is the growth of Islamic parochial schools. These schools are favored by recent immigrants of all classes. Between 2006 and 2011 the number of such schools increased by 25 percent. By 2011 there were about 250 in operation in the United States. In addition to learning traditional subjects, students are taught the Arabic language, religion, and history. After the fifth grade female students are required to wear headscarves.

As a group, Arab Americans tend to be better educated than the general population. Data from the 2011 American Community Survey revealed that 88 percent of Arab Americans over the age of twenty-five have received a high school diploma. Some 46 percent of Arab Americans have obtained a bachelor's degree. Egyptians tend to be the most highly educated of Arab Americans, with 96 percent completing high school and 67 percent completing college. Iraqis tend to be the least educated, with 76 percent finishing high school but only 33 percent obtaining bachelor's degrees.

Courtship and Weddings While casual American-style dating is very common among later generations of Arab Americans and among those who do not live in ethnic enclaves, newly arrived Arab immigrants often adhere to traditional Arab courtship and marriage practices. For these immigrants, American-style dating is virtually nonexistent because it conflicts with strict cultural norms about female chastity. The norm stipulates that a female should be chaste prior to marriage and remain faithful once wed. Similar standards apply to males, but expectations are reduced and the consequences of violations are not as severe. The ethics relating to female chastity cut across social class, religious denomination, and even ethnic lines, as they are found with equal vigor in virtually every Middle Eastern ethnic and national group. Real or alleged violations of the sexual mores by a female are assumed to damage her reputation and diminish her chances of finding a suitable marriage partner. According to Arab culture, such behavior also shames her family, especially her male kinsmen.

Another traditional Islamic marriage practice that some Arab American immigrants maintain is the trial period that follows the enactment of the marriage contract (*kitb al-kitab*). This period can last months or even a year or more. If successful, the marriage will be consummated after a public ceremony. During this period the family of an engaged woman will frequently permit her to go out with her fiancé. Some families insist that a chaperone be present or that the fiancé visit with the bride at her home, where the couple may be allowed to visit privately and get to know one another. It is perfectly acceptable for one or both parties to terminate the engagement at this point rather than face the prospect of an unhappy marriage. Though adhered to by some, this practice is rare among Arab Americans, especially those of later generations.

While traditional Arab culture prefers endogamous marriages between cousins, this preference is not typically maintained among modern Arab Americans, although some immigrant families do preserve the practice. Among highly assimilated and native-born Arab Americans, marriage between cousins is very rare. However, most Arab Americans do demonstrate a strong preference for religious endogamy in the selection of marriage partners. In this, Arab Americans retain a deeply rooted Middle Eastern bias. Middle Easterners do not approve of interreligious marriages. However, interdenominational marriages are not uncommon among educated Arab Americans. Arab Americans find it easier to marry a non-Arab of a different religious background than enter into an interreligious marriage with a fellow Arab American. This is especially true of Arab American men, who find it easier than Arab women to marry an outsider, as men typically spend more time working or attending school outside the Arab American community. There is a powerful familial resistance to letting Arab American women marry outside the group. An Arab Muslim woman who was unable to find a mate from within her group could marry a non-Arab Muslim (e.g., Pakistani, Indian, or Iranian). Arab Christian women facing a similar situation would opt to marry an outsider as long he was Christian.

Like cousin endogamy, arranged marriages are more common among recent immigrants than among later generations of Arab Americans. Arranged marriages run the gamut from the individual having no voice in the matter and no prior acquaintance with a prospective marriage partner to the family arranging a meeting between their son or daughter and a prospective mate they have selected. In the latter situation the son or daughter will usually make the final decision. This pattern is prevalent among assimilated immigrant and native-born families, especially if they are educated or have high aspirations for their children. Some working-class immigrant families arrange the marriage of their daughters, who are sometimes legal minors, to men in the home country. This practice is limited to a small minority. In selecting a marriage partner, attention is paid to family standing and reputation.

The traditional Arab custom of segregating the sexes before marriage is inevitably weakening because American society poses many opportunities for unrelated males and females to meet at school or on the job. Consequently, there is a detectable increase in the number of cases of romantic involvement among young Arab Americans in cities where large numbers of Arab Americans reside. But many

Portrait of a young Arab girl in Los Angeles, 1998. PHOTOGRAPH BY CATHERINE KARNOW. CORBIS. REPRODUCED BY PERMISSION.

of these relations are cut short by families because they fail to win their approval.

The 2009–2011 American Community Survey (ACS) estimated that 53.8 percent of Arab Americans age fifteen or older were married, compared with 49.0 percent of the general U.S. population. Divorce, once unheard of in Arab society, is increasingly making a presence among Arab Americans, although it is still less common for Arab Americans to be divorced (7.1 percent of those age fifteen or older) compared with the general U.S. population (10.8 percent).

Relations with Other Americans While early Arab American immigrants were largely accepted and integrated into American culture, relations began to sour for native-born Arab Americans after the June 1967 Arab-Israeli War. This situation worsened after the Arab oil embargo and the quadrupling of world oil prices that followed in the wake of the October 1973 Arab-Israeli War. Another important factor in heightening negative conceptions of Arabs was the American media's heavy coverage of the rise of militant Palestinian factions, such as the Palestinian Liberation Organization (PLO), that carried out attacks on Israelis in the late 1960s and the 1970s.

With the fall of the Shah and the rise of Ayatollah Khomeini to power in Iran (a large, non-Arab country) in 1979 came another oil shortage and price shock that further exacerbated anti-Middle Eastern sentiment in the United States. Then, on November 4, 1979, Iranian Islamic revolutionaries stormed the United States embassy in Tehran and took more than sixty Americans hostage. Over the next year media coverage of the Iranian hostage crisis, as the event became known, proliferated the notion of Islam as being a violent and irrational religion. Arabs and Muslims were vilified as bloodthirsty terrorists, greedy oil sheiks, and religious fanatics by the mass media, politicians, and political commentators. Congress began passing a series of bills that gave the federal government increased power to track down suspected terrorists.

For the better part of the 1980s Arab Americans lived in an increasing state of apprehension as the Reagan administration waged a war on international terrorism, and tensions ensued from the two U.S. attacks against Libya and the U.S. involvement in Lebanon following Israel's 1982 invasion of that country. The mid-1980s ushered in a spate of anti-Arab hate crimes.

Then, in 1990, Iraq invaded Kuwait. Fearful of a disruption to the world's oil supply and of instability in the region, the United States organized international sanctions aimed at motivating Iraq to withdraw its troops from its oil-rich neighbor. The sanctions failed to achieve their goal, however, and in early 1991 American and allied troops first bombed, then invaded, Iraq. This military offensive compelled Iraq to remove its troops from Kuwait, but Iraqi president Saddam Hussein remained in power. The Gulf War, as it was known, exacerbated the growing American antipathy for Arab culture and was felt by Arab Americans, who were increasingly the objects of prejudice and stereotyping. The feeling against Arab Americans continued to build throughout the end of the twentieth century and continued on into the early twenty-first century.

On September 11, 2001, members of al-Qaeda, an Arab terrorist organization, hijacked three jetliners and attacked the World Trade Center in New York City and the Pentagon in Washington, D.C. A fourth plane was brought down near Shanksville, Pennsylvania, by passengers before it could reach its target. Nearly 3,000 people lost their lives, and Arab Americans became the chief target of suspicion and hostility. The number of hate crimes proliferated. A

mosque in Dallas was set afire, and an Arab community center in Chicago was bombed. Schools in New Orleans were forced to close to protect Arab American students.

Within a month of the al-Qaeda attacks, Congress passed the Uniting and Strengthening America by Providing Tools Required to Intercept and Obstruct Terrorism Act, better known as the USA Patriot Act. The act gave federal officials the authority to bypass constitutional protections designed to protect the rights of those suspected of committing crimes. Some 1,200 Arab American males were detained for questioning, but only four were ever charged with any crime. All visas for Arab American males traveling to countries with known links to terrorism were suspended, and the Immigration and Naturalization Service began targeting male immigrants from Afghanistan, Libya, Saudi Arabia, Syria, and Afghanistan in addition to those from Islamic countries such as Iran and Pakistan. Interest in learning about Arab languages, religions, and culture increased significantly, and some Arab American feminists wore headscarves to indicate their support for Arab women. Nevertheless, they considered themselves Americans first and Arabs second.

EMPLOYMENT AND ECONOMIC CONDITIONS

Most Arab Americans tend to do well economically after immigrating to the United States. How well they do is dependent on a number of variables that include their own social class and educational background as well as their country of origin. According to the 2009–2011 American Community Survey estimates, 44.5 percent of employed Arab Americans were in managerial, business, science, or arts occupations, compared with 35.9 percent of the general U.S. labor force. Arab Americans were less likely to work in service occupations (13.8 percent of Arab Americans compared with 18.0 percent of the general U.S. population). The variation by country of origin can be seen in the example of Moroccan Americans, who were more likely to work in service jobs (21.4 percent) than Arab Americans in general.

According to the 2011 American Community Survey, the median annual income for Arab American families was $51,363, compared with $50,502 for the general population. Arab Americans from Lebanon, Syria, and Egypt were better off economically than immigrants from other Arab-speaking nations. Some 19 percent of Arab Americans lived in poverty in 2011, compared with 12 percent of the general population. Poverty rates were highest among households with a single mother and a child under five years of age. In general, Arab Americans tend to cluster in both the highest income and highest education brackets and in the lowest income and

A resident of Dearborn, Michigan, demonstrates in front of the Federal Courthouse in Detroit, Michigan, where suspected terrorist Umar Farouk Abdulmutallab, a 23-year old Nigerian, was arraigned on January 8, 2010. The defendent attempted to blow up Northwest Airlines Flight 253 on Christmas day in 2009. BILL PUGLIANO / GETTY IMAGES

lowest educational attainment brackets, based on when and where they came from and how long they have been in the country.

POLITICS AND GOVERNMENT

Although politically marginalized, Arab Americans have attempted to gain a voice in U.S. foreign policy throughout the twentieth century and into the twenty-first century. One of the most important national organizations dedicated to such a purpose was the Association of Arab American University Graduates, Inc. (AAUG). Founded in the aftermath of the devastating Arab defeat by Israel in the June 1967 war, the AAUG sought to educate Americans about the Arab, and especially the Palestinian, side of the conflict. The group continues to serve as an important forum for debating issues of concern to Arab Americans. The early 1970s saw the establishment of the National Association of

Arab Americans, the first Arab American organization devoted exclusively to lobbying on foreign policy issues. In 2002 the National Association of Arab Americans merged with the American-Arab Anti-Discrimination Committee (ADC), which had been founded in 1980 by former U.S. Senator James Abourezk of South Dakota. While not a lobby, ADC sensitizes the news media to issues of stereotyping. The organization has had less success with the entertainment media. More recently the Arab American Institute (AAI) was established to encourage greater participation of Arab Americans in the electoral process as voters, party delegates, or candidates for office.

Arab Americans became increasingly active politically in the late twentieth century, and that activity increased after September 11, 2001. Much of that activity was directed at teaching other Americans to respect Arab American culture and to fight discrimination, such as racial profiling and suspension of civil liberties for Arab Americans. High-profile Arab American politicians included George Mitchell, the former Senate majority leader. Former U.S. Representative Mary Rose Oakar continued to serve as a major voice for Arab Americans. Mitchell E. Daniels Jr., the governor of Indiana, and John Baldacci, a former governor of Maine, are also Arab Americans, as are former White House Cabinet officials John Sununu and Donna Shalala. The Arab American Leadership Council plays a major role in assisting Arab Americans in running for political office or seeking out appointed positions.

In 1996, despite identifying more strongly with the Republican Party, Arab Americans expressed a preference for Democrat Bill Clinton (43.4 percent) over Republican Bob Dole (29.6 percent). During the 2000 election George W. Bush made a concentrated effort to meet with Arab leaders, and 44.5 percent of Arab Americans supported his presidential bid. Within the post-September 11, 2001, environment and Bush's War on Terror, which included the War in Iraq, support for the Republican Party declined significantly, with 54 percent supporting Democrat Barack Obama in 2008. During the 2012 presidential election fifty-five Arab Americans from eighteen states served as delegates to the Democratic Convention. A poll taken in September 2012 indicated that Arab Americans continued to favor Obama (54 percent) over Republican Mitt Romney (33 percent).

NOTABLE INDIVIDUALS

Arab Americans have made important contributions in virtually every field of endeavor, from government to belles lettres. One Arab American even became the Queen of Jordan when she married King Hussein in 1978. Queen Noor was born Lisa Halaby (1951–) in Washington, D.C., to Syrian American parents.

Academia Among the many Arab American academics, Edward W. Said (1935–2003) stands out as a world-class intellectual. Born in Jerusalem, Palestine, and educated at Princeton and Harvard universities, Said achieved international renown as a scholar in the fields of literary criticism and comparative literature. As an Arab Christian, he spent a good deal of time defending Islam. Epistemologist Nassim Nicholas Taleb (1960–) is a world-renowned specialist in randomness, probability, and uncertainty. He authored *The Black Swan* (2007), which has been called one of the most influential books of the post–World War II era. Other Arab American scholars include Fouad A. Ajami (1945–), a Lebanese American who is an expert on Middle Eastern affairs, and Mostafa A. El-Sayed (1933–), an Egyptian American who specialized in chemical physics.

Activism The best-known Arab American activist is Ralph Nader (1935), who had a major influence on such issues as consumer rights and automobile safety. Nader was a candidate for president of the United States five times between 1992 and 2008. Another prominent activist was Andy Lightner (1946–), the founder of Mothers against Drunk Driving.

Broadcasting Arab Americans have also played a significant role in the broadcasting industry. Lebanese American Danny Thomas (1914–1991) was the star of the 1950s sitcom *Make Room for Daddy* and produced several popular shows of the 1960s, including *The Andy Griffith Show* and *The Dick Van Dyke Show*. Today Thomas is best remembered as the founder of the St. Jude's children's charity. His daughter Marlo Thomas (1938–), the star of *That Girl*, continued his work with St. Jude in addition to acting and supporting feminist causes. Jamie Farr (1934–) portrayed cross-dressing Corporal Klinger on the television sitcom *M*A*S*H*. Tony Shalhoub (1953–) is one of the foremost Arab American television stars in the early twenty-first century as a result of his Emmy-winning series *Monk*, in which he portrayed a detective with obsessive compulsive disorder. Actress Wendie Malick (1950–) has appeared in a number of television shows, including *Just Shoot Me* and *Hot in Cleveland*. Casey Kasem (1933–), best known for hosting the radio program *American Top 40*, which kept Americans abreast of popular music for decades, was also the voice of Shaggy in the popular cartoon series *Scooby Doo*.

Business Steve Jobs (1955–2011), the cofounder of Apple Computers, was of partial Arab descent, as his biological father was a Syrian immigrant. Over the course of his career at Apple, Jobs was widely regarded as one of the most innovative and influential entrepreneurs of the personal computer industry. The son of Lebanese immigrants, Paul Orfalea (1947–) grew up in southern California, where he founded the first Kinko's store in 1970. Over the next several decades, Kinko's grew to become a nationwide chain of outlets offering copying, printing, and binding before being sold to Federal Express in 2004. Jacques Nasser (1947–) was born in Lebanon and went on to become the president and CEO of Ford Motor Company.

Fashion Joseph Abboud (1950–) is an award-winning menswear fashion designer of Lebanese descent. He also wrote a memoir about the fashion industry and is an activist in the field of breast cancer research. He purchased JA Apparel in 2011 for $90 million. Rami Kasho, a Palestinian American fashion designer, was featured on the television show *Project Runway*.

Film Moustapha Akkad (1930–2005) produced the blockbuster *Halloween* thrillers. He was killed at the hands of an Iraqi suicide bomber while attending a wedding in Jordan. Oscar winner F. Murray Abraham (1939–) is best known for his portrayal of Antonio Salieri in *Amadeus* in 1984. Actress Kathy Najimy (1957–) is an award-winning comic actor who played a nun in the movies *Sister Act* and *Sister Act II* and a witch in *Hocus Pocus* before becoming known as the voice of Peggy Hill in *King of the Hill*. Actress and producer Salma Hayek (1966–) is of Lebanese-Mexican descent. She was known for films such as *Frieda* and for creating the television show *Ugly Betty*. Mario Kassar (1952–) is the former head of Carolco Pictures, which produced hit films such as *Rocky*, *Rambo*, and *Terminator*.

Government A number of Arab Americans have been recognized for their contributions to government at various levels, through elected and appointed positions. The first Arab American to be elected to the U.S. Senate was Democrat James Abourezk (1931–), a former U.S. Representative from South Dakota, who earned a reputation as a fighter for Native American and other minority rights while in Congress (1973–79). Former Senate Majority Leader George Mitchell (1933–), a Democrat from Maine, is the offspring of a Lebanese mother and an Irish father. Mitchell served in Congress from 1980 to 1995. Mary Rose Oakar (1940–), an Ohio Democrat, was a strong force for women and minority rights during her congressional tenure (1977–1993). Democrat Nick Joe Rahall II (1949–) represents West Virginia's Third Congressional District, Republican Charles W. Boustany Jr. (1956–), a cardiovascular surgeon, represents Louisiana's Third District, and Republican Darrell Issa (1953–) represented California's Forty-Ninth District. Republican Mitchell E. Daniels Jr. (1949–), the son of Syrian immigrants, was the governor of Indiana, and Democrat John Baldacci (1955–) served as the governor of Maine from 2003 to 2011.

Republican Ray LaHood (1945–), a former Illinois congressman, became the secretary of transportation in 2009. Other prominent Arab American members of presidential cabinets include Donna Shalala (1941–), who served as secretary of health and human services in the Clinton administration, and John E. Sununu (1941–), who served as George H. W. Bush's chief of staff.

Literature There are numerous notable Arab American poets. Khaled Mattawa (1964–), who was born in Libya and immigrated to the United States in his teens, authored of four books of poetry and translated nine books of contemporary Arabic poetry. Mattawa also coedited two anthologies of Arab American literature and was awarded the Academy of American Poets Fellowship Prize and a Guggenheim fellowship, among many other awards and honors. Other important Arab American poets include the Palestinian American Naomi Shihab Nye (1952–), the Lebanese American Lawrence Joseph (1948–), and Sam Hazo (1928–). There are also many important Arab American writers of fiction. Novelist Mona Simpson (1957–) is the author of numerous books, including *Anywhere But Here* and *My Hollywood*, is a recipient of the Whiting Prize and other awards. The Iraqi novelist Mahmoud Saeed (1939–) immigrated to the United States in 1999, fleeing persecution in his homeland for his important and controversial work. After arriving in the United States, Saeed continued to write and publish. The son of a Lebanese immigrant,

Vance Bourjaily (1922–2010) was a prolific writer of fiction and nonfiction whose published works included the critically acclaimed novel *Brill among the Ruins*. William Peter Blatty (1928–), also the son of Lebanese immigrants, is the author of the novel *The Exorcist* along with other works of fiction and screenplays.

Journalism Helen Thomas (1920–1913), a White House reporter for United Press International, covered the presidency from 1961 to 2010.

Film Screenwriter Callie Khouri (1957–) received an Oscar award for Best Original Screenplay in 1990 for *Thelma and Louise*. Writer and director Tom Shadyac (1958–) was responsible for *Ace Ventura: Pet Detective* and the 1998 remake of *The Nutty Professor*.

Music Singer Paul Anka (1941–), who was born in Canada to Lebanese parents, rose to the top of the pop charts in the 1950s. Formerly a judge on the television show *American Idol*, Paula Abdul (1962–), a singer, dancer, television personality, and choreographer, was born to a Syrian father who arrived in the United States via Brazil. Born Tiffany Renee Darwish in 1972, the singer popularly known as Tiffany was raised in California by her Lebanese/Syrian father. She is best known for hits such as "I Think We're Alone Now" and "I Saw Him Standing There." Singer Shakira (1977–), the daughter of a Lebanese father and a Colombian mother, combines the heritage of both countries in her music. Musician Frank Zappa (1940–1993) was an icon of the American rock scene. His eldest son, Dweezil (1969–), put together a tribute act, *Zappa Plays Zappa*, honoring his father in 2008. Zappa's eldest child, Moon (1967–), was also a musician and an actress; his son Ahmet (1974–) was a musician, writer, producer, and publisher; and his youngest daughter, Diva (1979–), was an artist and an actress.

Science and Medicine Dr. Farouk El-Baz (1938–), a prominent Arab American scientist, was a lunar geologist who assisted in planning the Apollo moon landings. Dr. Michael DeBakey (1908–2008), the inventor of the heart pump, was a Lebanese American. Elias Corey (1928–) of Harvard University won the 1990 Nobel Prize for Chemistry. George A. Doumani made discoveries that helped prove the theory of continental drift.

Sports Doug Flutie (1962–) won the Heisman Trophy in 1984 and quarterbacked the Toronto Argonauts to a championship in the Canadian Football League. He also played in the NFL for the Buffalo Bills, Chicago Bears, San Diego Chargers, and New England Patriots. Lebanese-born Rony Seikaly (1965–), who played for the Miami Heat, Orlando Magic, and New Jersey Nets, is considered the most famous of Arab American basketball players. Jeff George (1967–) played quarterback for teams that included the Indianapolis Colts, Atlanta Falcons, Oakland Raiders, Minnesota Vikings, Washington Redskins, and Seattle Seahawks.

Other Arab Americans who made notable contributions to the world of sports include Bill George (1929–1982), Abe Gibron (1925–), Rich Kotite (1942–), and Drew Haddad (1978–) in the NFL; Joe Lahoud (1947–) and Sam Khalifa (1963–) in Major League Baseball; George Maloof Sr. (1923–1980), former owner of the Houston Rockets, and his sons Joe (1955–) and Gavin Maloof (1966–), owners of the Sacramento Kings in the NBA. Bobby Rahal (1953–) won the Indianapolis 500 in 1986 and went on to become an all-time earnings champion and team owner. Yasser Seirawan (1960–) is a four-time national chess champion and grandmaster, and Jennifer Shahade (1980–) won the United States Women's Chess Championships in 2002 and 2004.

MEDIA

Traditionally supportive of a number of local radio and cable and broadcast television programs as well as print media, members of the Arab American community have increasingly begun to rely on nationally produced programming and on international broadcasts from their various homelands. Through the Internet, Arab Americans have instant access to newspapers, magazines, television shows, and radio in their native languages. Satellite television also offers Arab Americans access to channels such as ART (Arabic Radio and Television Network), the Lebanese Broadcasting Corporation, and MTV Arabic.

PRINT

Al Jadid Magazine

Founded in 1997, this magazine regularly publishes thought-provoking articles and translations about Arab and Arab American culture.

Elie Chalala, Editor
P. O. Box 241342
Los Angeles, California 90024-1342
Phone: (310) 227-6777
Email: aljadid@aljadid.com
URL: www.aljadid.com

American-Arab Message

Religious and political weekly printed in Arabic and English; founded in 1937.

Rev. Imam Muhammad A.H. Karoub
17514 Woodward Avenue
Detroit, Michigan 48203
Phone: (313) 868-2266
Fax: (313) 868-2267

Arab American News

Founded in 1986 and covering the Arab world and the United States, this newspaper bills itself as providing "news, views, and interviews" of interest to Arab Americans.

Osama Siblani, Publisher
5706 Chase Road
Dearborn, Michigan 48126
Phone: (313) 582-4888
URL: www.arabamericannews.com

Arab Studies Quarterly

Magazine covering Arab affairs, the Middle East, and U.S. foreign policy that is published by Pluto journals through the auspices of the Center for Islamic and Middle Eastern Studies of California State University.

Ibrahim G. Aoudé, Editor
5500 University Parkway
San Bernardino, California 92407-2318
Phone: (909) 537-3778
Email: E-mail: aoude@hawaii-edu
URL: http://arabstudiesquarterly.plutojournals.org

Jusoor: The Arab American Journal of Cultural Exchange

First published in 1992, Jusoor ("Bridges") is a quarterly that includes poetry and essays on politics and the arts.

Munir Akash, Editor
P.O. Box 34163
Bethesda, Maryland 20827-0163
Phone: (301) 263-0289
Fax: (301) 263-0255
Email: jusoor@aol.com

ORGANIZATIONS AND ASSOCIATIONS

American Arab Anti-Discrimination Committee (ADC)

Founded in 1980 by former U.S. Senator James Abourezk to combat negative and defamatory stereotyping of Arab Americans and their cultural heritage, ADC offers live streaming via ADC TV. It is the country's largest grassroots Arab American organization.

Warren David, President
1990 M Street
Suite 610
Washington, D.C. 20036
Phone: (202) 244-2990
Fax: (202) 333-3980
Email: adc@adc.org
URL: www.adc.org

Arab American Historical Foundation

Encourages the preservation of Arab American history, publications, and art. Publishes quarterly *Arab American Historian*.

Joseph R. Haiek, President/Founder
P.O. Box 291159
Los Angeles, California 90029
Phone: (818) 507-0333
Email: ArabAmericanHistory@yahoo.com
URL: www.arabamericanhistory.org

Arab American Institute (AAI)

Dedicated to involving Arab Americans in electoral politics, mobilizing votes and funds behind Arab American candidates at various levels of government. The Institute also encourages Arab Americans to become involved in the Democratic and Republican parties.

Dr. James Zogby, President/Founder
1600 K Street, NW
Suite 601

Washington, D.C. 20006
Phone: (202) 429-9210
Fax: (202) 429-9214
Email: webmaster@aaiusa.org
URL: www.aaiusa.org

Arab American Political Action Committee (AAPAC)

AAPAC was formed by a group of Arab American
professionals to organize and encourage the political
activities of Arab Americans.

Miriam Saad Bazzi, President
P. O. Box 925
Dearborn, Michigan 48121
Phone: (313) 582-4888
Email: RSVP@aapac.org
URL: www.aapac.org

ACCESS

Started by a group of volunteers in 1971, ACCESS was
created to assist the Arab immigrant population
adapt to life in the United States and is now the
largest Arab American human services nonprofit in
the country.

Hassan Jaber, Executive Director
2651 Saulino Court
Dearborn, Michigan 48120
Phone: (313) 842-7010
Fax: (313) 842-5150
Email: hjaber@accesscommunity.org
URL: www.accesscommunity.org

Association of Arab American University Graduates, Inc. (AAUG)

The oldest national Arab American organization. Founded
in the aftermath of the Arab defeat in the June 1967
Arab-Israeli War to inform Americans of the Arab
viewpoint. AAUG's membership consists mostly of
academics and other professionals. The organization
sponsors intellectual forums and conferences and
publishes books as well as the journal *Arab Studies
Quarterly*.

William J. Gedeon, President
2121 Wisconsin Avenue, NW
Suite 310
Washington, D.C. 20007
Phone: (202) 337-7717
Fax: (202) 337-3302
Email: aai@usg.org

Najda: Women Concerned About the Middle East

Promotes understanding between Americans and Arabs
by offering educational programs and audiovisual
presentations on Middle Eastern history, art, culture,
and current events.

Audrey Shabbas, President
P. O. Box 7152
Berkeley, California 94707
Phone: (510) 549-3512

National Network of Arab American Communities

Founded in 2004, the organization coordinates the efforts
of Arab American community groups and provides
them with a voice at the national level.

Nadia Tonova, Director
C/O ACCESS
2651 Saulino Court
Dearborn, Michigan 48120
Phone: (313) 843-2844
Fax: (313) 554-2801
Email: ntonova@accesscommunity.org
URL: http://nnaac.org

MUSEUMS AND RESEARCH CENTERS

Several universities have Arab American (or Middle
Eastern American) studies programs, including the
University of Southern California; the University of
Michigan, Ann Arbor; the University of Michigan,
Dearborn; the City University of New York; and the
University of South Florida.

While there is only one museum devoted solely to Arab
Americans as a group, there are various archives
devoted to collecting the papers and related
memorabilia of Arab Americans.

Arab Americans, Chaldeans, and Muslims in Michigan Collections

Bentley Historical Library

University of Michigan

Karen Jania, Reference Division Head
1150 Beal Avenue
Ann Arbor, Michigan 48109-2113
Phone: (734) 764-3482
Email: bentley.ref@umich.edu
URL: http://bentley.umich.edu/research/guides/
arab_americans

Arab American National Museum

Drawing on the contributions of a large local Arab
American community, this museum promotes Arab
American history and culture.

Anan Ameri, Director
13624 Michigan Avenue
Dearborn, Michigan 48126
Phone: (313) 582-2266
Fax: (313) 582-1086
Email: aameri@accesscommunity.org
URL: www.arabamericanmuseum.org

Faris and Yamna Naff Family Arab American Collection

Kay Peterson
Archives Center, National Museum of History,
Smithsonian Institution
12th, 14th, and Constitution Avenue
Washington, D.C. 20560-0601
Phone: (202) 633-3270
Fax: (202) 786-2453
Email: archivescenter@sci.edu

Near Eastern American Collection

Haven Hawley, Director
Immigration History Research Center, Andersen
Library, University of Minnesota
222 21st Avenue, South

Minneapolis, Minnesota 55455
Phone: (612) 625-4800.
Fax: (612) 626-0018
Email: ihrc@umn.edu
URL: www.ihrc.umn.edu

Near East Collection, Sterling Memorial Library

The oldest collection of Arab materials in the United States, Yale University's Near East Collection was established in 1840 by Professor Edward Elbridge Salisbury, an expert in Arabic language and culture.

Roberta Dougherty
P. O. Box 208240
New Haven, Connecticut 06520-8240
Phone: (203) 423-1373
Email: Roberta.dougherty@yale.edu
URL: www.library.yale.edu/neareast

SOURCES FOR ADDITIONAL STUDY

Abraham, Nabeel, et al., eds. *Arab Detroit 9/11: Life in the Terror Decade.* Detroit: Wayne State University Press, 2011.

Ameri, Anan, and Holly Arida. *Daily Life of Arab Americans in the 21st Century.* Westport, CT: Greenwood, 2012.

Alsultany, Evelyn. *Arabs and Muslims in the Media: Race and Representation after 9/11.* New York: New York University Press, 2012.

Bakalian, Anny, and Mehdi Bozorgmehr. *Backlash 9/11: Middle Eastern and Muslim Americans Respond.* Berkeley: University of California Press, 2009.

Haddad, Yvonne Yazbeck. *Becoming American?: The Forging of Arab Muslim Identity in Pluralist America.* Waco, TX: Baylor University Press, 2011.

———. *Not Quite American: The Shaping of Arab and Muslim Identity in the United States.* Waco, TX: Baylor University Press, 2004.

Howell, Sally, and Andrew Shryock. "Cracking Down on Diaspora: Arab Detroit and America's 'War on Terror'." *Anthropological Quarterly* 76.3 (2003): 443–62.

McCarus, Ernest, ed. *The Development of Arab-American Identity.* Ann Arbor: University of Michigan Press, 1994.

Naff, Alixa. *Becoming American: The Early Arab Immigrant Experience.* Carbondale: Southern Illinois University Press, 1985.

Naber, Nadine. *Arab America: Gender, Cultural Politics, and Activism.* New York: New York University Press, 2012.

ARGENTINEAN AMERICANS

Julio Rodriguez

OVERVIEW

Argentinean Americans are immigrants or descendants of people from Argentina, a country on the southeast tip of South America. Argentina is bordered by Chile to the west and south, Bolivia and Paraguay to the north, and Brazil and Uruguay to the northeast. Much of its eastern coastline is bordered by the South Atlantic Ocean. Argentina claims sovereignty over part of Antarctica, the Falkland Islands (Spanish: Islas Malvinas), and South Georgia and the South Sandwich Islands. Argentina has six main regions: The Pampas are fertile lowlands located in the center and east; Mesopotamia is a lowland enclosed by the Paraná and Uruguay rivers; the Gran Chaco is between Mesopotamia and the Andes; Cuyo is at the east side of the Andes; the Argentine Northwest is at the north of the Andes; and Patagonia is a large plateau to the south. The Republic of Argentina comprises 1,078,000 square miles (2,791,810 square kilometers), just over 15 percent of the continent's surface. Its area, including the South Atlantic islands and the Antarctic sector, covers 2.35 million square miles, which is about one-third the size of the United States.

According to the 2010 census conducted by Argentina's National Institute of Statistics and Census, Argentina had a population of 40,117,096. The World Christian Database indicates that, in 2010, Argentineans were 92.1 percent Christian, 3.1 percent agnostic, 1.9 percent Muslim, 1.3 percent Jewish, 0.9 percent atheist, and 0.9 percent Buddhist and other faiths. For the most part, Argentinean Christians are Roman Catholic; estimates show that Catholics make up between 70 percent and 90 percent of the population. Argentina's economy is the third largest in Latin America, and Argentineans enjoy an upper-middle-income economy with a high quality of life. Within Latin America, Argentina has the fifth highest nominal GDP per capita and the highest in terms of purchasing power.

Early Argentineans began to arrive in the United States in the 1960s in search of greater economic possibilities. Reflecting significant Italian as well as Spanish influence, Argentineans constitute a small immigrant population of mostly professionals, scientists, artists, and craftspeople, mainly of European descent (British, French, German, Jewish, Italian, Polish), who were

escaping political and economic trouble in Argentina. Prior to the 1970s, the Argentineans who immigrated to the United States were classified in the category of "Other Hispanics," and consequently, statistics about immigrants from Argentina do not exist for that time period. The majority of Argentinean immigrants settled in metropolitan areas, especially New York City, where 20 percent of them lived in the 1970s. New York was a popular destination because of its existing Argentinean and Italian communities (many Argentineans are of Italian origin). In the first decade of the twenty-first century, another wave of Argentineans immigrated to the United States, prompted by the poor employment opportunities that followed the 2001–2002 economic collapse in Argentina.

According to 2011 estimates by the U.S. Census Bureau's American Community Survey, the number of people of Argentinean descent living in the United States is 240,195 (a number comparable to the entire population of Madison, Wisconsin, or Saint Petersberg, Florida). Areas with significant populations of Argentinean Americans include New York City, Los Angeles, and south Florida.

HISTORY OF THE PEOPLE

Early History About 300,000 American Indians were scattered throughout the large area that is now Argentina when the Spaniards arrived in the sixteenth century. These Indians fell into at least ten distinct groups with various lifestyles. The Guaraní, for example, farmed the fertile river valleys. More typical in the south were the Onas, who lived by hunting animals such as the ostrich and seal and by gathering mollusks. Farther north, the Araucanians roamed the grasslands in bands of one to two hundred families, living off the wild animals that abounded in the area. Other tribes populating the area included the Incas in the northwest, the Charrúas in the east, and the Quechuas, Tehuelches, and Huarpes in the central and western regions. The Pampas inhabited the plains of the same name.

The arrival of explorer Juan Díaz de Solís in 1516 marked the beginning of three hundred years of rule by Spain. More than fifty years would pass before Buenos Aires (now the nation's capital) was founded in 1580, and it was to remain little more than a village for the next two centuries. There were a sufficient number of Spanish women to generate pure Spanish families, and thus began the Creole (Spanish born in the New World) elite. Unions between Spanish men and Indian women produced mestizo offspring, who grew into the artisans and laborers of colonial towns or the herdspeople and wagoners of the early countryside. Black slaves entered the country in the seventeenth and eighteenth centuries, becoming servants and artisans, caring for livestock, and planting or harvesting.

In 1776 political leadership of the large area claimed by the Spanish crown was centered at Buenos Aires. British troops tried to seize Buenos Aires in 1806, but residents fought them off and a decade later, in 1816, declared independence from Spain at the urging of the national hero José de San Martín. Buenos Aires was made the country's capital in 1862.

Modern Era In 1930 the national government experienced a military takeover, an event that would repeat itself several times in the coming years. In 1943 Argentinean soldiers seized control while Colonel Juan Domingo Perón Sosa began to gain support from the lower classes. In 1946 Perón was elected president and proceeded to become the workers' champion, backing labor unions, social security, shorter hours, higher medical benefits, and so on. His charismatic second wife, Eva (Evita) Duarte, inspired the masses as well, but in the long term Perón's policies raised expectations that remained unfulfilled. Exiled in 1955, he returned to lead the country again in 1973, then died the following year and was succeeded by his third wife and vice president, María Estela Martínez de Perón, who was deposed in 1976. Thus began a period of fierce repression that is often called the "Dirty War." Lasting until 1983, this period was characterized by imprisonment, torture, and murder of citizens who opposed the military. An alleged 15,000 to 30,000 Argentineans, many of them Jews, "disappeared" during this period, giving rise to the charge of anti-Semitism. Meanwhile the Argentinean military was defeated by Britain in a 1982 war over ownership of the Islas Malvinas (Falkland Islands).

The Argentineans demonstrated against their government in 1982 and 1983, managing to elect Raúl Alfonsín as president in 1983. Alfonsín's record as a champion of human rights and his reputation as a lawyer boded well for the people. However, although some high-ranking officials were convicted on charges of kidnapping, torture, and homicide, military uprisings led to the passage of the Ley de la Obediencia Debida (Law of Due Obedience) and the Punto Final (Stopping Point), limiting the extent of prosecution of people who participated in political violence during the "Dirty War." In part through the efforts of journalist Horacio Verbitsky, former naval officer Adolfo Scilingo's human rights violations during the "Dirty War" were brought to international attention, and he was convicted under Spain's universal

jurisdiction laws in 2005. His conviction was considered a rare glimpse of justice for the many victims of Argentina's "Dirty War."

Carlos Menem's presidency (1989–1999) was marked by radical free-market reform and widespread government corruption, leading to major economic crisis. After a series of interim presidencies, Eduardo Duhalde took over leadership of the country in 2002, announcing that Argentina would default on $140 billion (U.S. dollars) in foreign debt.

In 2003 Néstor Kirchner became president, reversing amnesty laws that had previously protected officials from being charged for atrocities committed during the "Dirty War." A popular leader, Kirchner stood against government corruption and put the Argentinean economy on the road to recovery. At the end of his term in 2007, his wife, Cristina Fernández de Kirchner, became Argentina's first elected woman president.

Despite its relative recovery from the economic crisis of 2001–2002, the expansionary policies of Nestor Kirchner and Cristina Fernández de Kirchner have led to high inflation. Fallout from the European debt crisis coupled with government-imposed currency and import restrictions has hurt confidence in the Argentinean economy both at home and abroad.

SETTLEMENT IN THE UNITED STATES

Prior to the 1970s, Argentinean immigrants were classified by the U.S. government within the broad category of "Other Hispanics," and immigration statistics from before that time do not exist. Nonetheless, Argentinean immigrants to the United States are a relatively new group. In 1970 there were 44,803 Argentinean immigrants in the United States. The 1990 U.S. Census, which counted 92,563 Argentinean-born U.S. residents, indicates that Argentinean immigration doubled between 1970 and 1990.

Early Argentinean immigrants came to the United States, primarily during the 1960s, for greater economic opportunities. The majority of these immigrants were well-educated professionals, including a substantial number of medical doctors and scientists. Later immigrants—those who began to immigrate to the United States during the mid- to late-1970s—fled their homeland to escape political persecution during the "Dirty War." The members of this group were more diverse and less educated than their predecessors, although their educational attainment tended to be higher than that of Argentina's overall population.

In the 1970s, 20 percent of the Argentineans in the United States resided in the New York metropolitan area. In the 1980s this percentage increased to just over 23 percent. This is partially due to the fact that New York City already had a large Argentinean population as well as many Italian immigrants from other countries, which made New York attractive to Italian Argentineans. New York City also has a

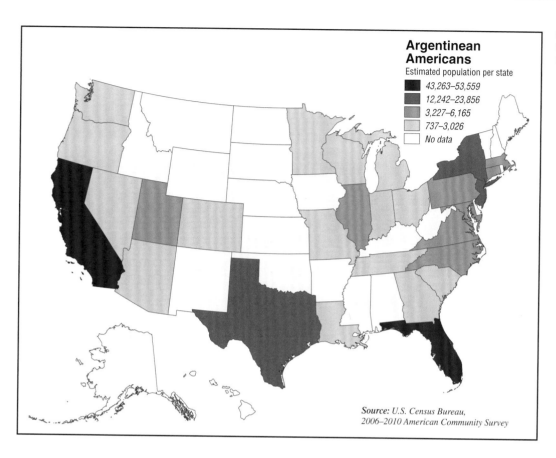

Argentinean Americans
Estimated population per state

- 43,263–53,559
- 12,242–23,856
- 3,227–6,165
- 737–3,026
- No data

Source: U.S. Census Bureau, 2006–2010 American Community Survey

number of organizations in place to assist its large Argentinean population, including the Argentine-American Chamber of Commerce, which promotes business ventures between Argentina and the United States, and the Argentine-North American Association for the Advancement of Science, Technology and Culture. Overall, Argentinean Americans seem to prefer metropolitan areas, such as New York City, where 17,363 Argentinean Americans were counted in the 1990 U.S. Census, and Los Angeles, home to 15,115 Argentinean immigrants in 1990.

In 2001 and 2002 Argentina's economy weakened, and employment opportunities became scarce. The economic collapse, in conjunction with the possibility of entry under family reunification provisions, prompted a new wave of Argentinean immigrants to the United States. Between 2000 and 2004, 17,306 Argentineans entered the United States as permanent residents. In response, the U.S. Justice Department tightened rules for temporary visas to discourage illegal residence.

Statistics show that Argentinean American immigrants, as a group, have fewer children than Argentineans; young Argentinean Americans make up between 17 and 19 percent of the Argentinean American population. There is also a higher proportion of married Argentinean American individuals at all ages, particularly between the ages of twenty and

twenty-nine. Likewise, the number of separated and divorced individuals is significantly higher in the United States.

LANGUAGE

The official language of Argentina is Castilian Spanish. Nevertheless, other languages and dialects are still in use in some communities of the country. Among the native languages, Guaraní is probably the most widespread; it is spoken mainly in the north and northeast of Argentina. Among the Spanish and Italian communities, some people speak their native tongues. In Buenos Aires, newspapers are published in English, Yiddish, German, and Italian. The variety of Spanish spoken in Argentina is referred to as "Spanish from the Río de la Plata." This variety extends throughout Argentina and Uruguay and has some particular characteristics regarding phonology, morphology, and vocabulary.

Differences in phonology (pronunciation) can usually be associated with the geographic location of the speaker. For example, in the metropolitan area of Buenos Aires, the letters *y* and *ll* in Spanish are pronounced similarly to the English *j* in "John." Elsewhere in the Americas or Spain those letters tend to be pronounced as the English *y* in "yawn."

Probably the most significant morphological characteristic of Argentinean Spanish is the verb form for the second person singular pronoun, which in standard Spanish is *tú* ("you" singular, in informal conversational style), and in Argentinean Spanish is *vos*. The verb form accompanying this personal pronoun is different from its equivalent in standard Spanish. For example: *tú juegas* (you play) in standard Spanish is *vos jugás* in Argentinean Spanish. In the present tense, this form can be derived from the conjugated verb of the second person plural used in Spain: *vosotros* (you all). The use of *vos* in Argentinean Spanish is known as *voseo*, and it is still the source of some controversy. Some Argentineans believe this form to be incorrect and sometimes disrespectful. It has even been considered a national disgrace. The argument is that the use of the *voseo* form unnecessarily separates the Argentineans and Uruguayans—who use it—from other Spanish-speaking peoples.

As in other South and Central American countries, local Spanish language has been enriched by numerous terms borrowed from native languages. For example, the words *vicuña* (vicuna) and *choclo* (corn, or *maíz* in standard Spanish) have been borrowed from the Quechua language. Immigrants have also made important linguistic contributions to the variety of Spanish spoken in Argentina, especially the Italians. In Lunfardo (Argentinean slang) there are countless words derived from Italian. Their usage is widespread in informal, everyday language. For example, the verb *laburar* (to work) in Lunfardo comes from the Italian word *laborare*, while the standard Spanish verb is *trabajar*. The common Argentinean greeting *chau*, which in Argentina is used to say "bye-bye," comes from the Italian word *ciao* (hello).

In some cases, the linguistic influence of Castilian Spanish upon a community of speakers of a different language has given rise to a new language variety. For example, in Belgrano (Buenos Aires) there is an important community of German immigrants. The variety of German spoken there is known as "Belgrano-Deutsch" and uses terms such as the verb *lechen* (to milk, from *melken* in standard German), derived from the Spanish word *leche* (milk).

Bueno, meaning "good," is a common Spanish word, but in Argentina it is essential, serving to indicate agreement as well as praise. Similarly, the expression *mira vos* is a ubiquitous phrase meaning "Is that right?," "Really," or "Wow!" *Todo bien* is used either to ask how someone is doing or to respond that one is doing well, whereas *viste* (which means "You know?") is a popular way to ask for validation at the end of a statement.

RELIGION

The rituals and ceremonies of Roman Catholicism are widespread throughout Argentina. The Declaration of Rights, which prefaces the Argentinean Constitution, states that the Roman Catholic religion shall be protected by the state since the majority of Argentineans profess this faith. Nevertheless, the Argentinean Constitution does guarantee freedom of religion, and a stipulation providing that the president of the country be a Roman Catholic was removed in 1994. During the 1990s and 2000s the Argentinean Catholic Church has undergone a significant crisis, reflected not only in absenteeism in the churches but also in the small number of seminary students and novices. It is therefore common for many Argentineans to affirm their religious beliefs and simultaneously confess their lack of involvement within the church. The *CIA World Factbook* suggests that, although 92 percent of the country is Catholic, only 20 percent actively practice their faith. There seems to be a corresponding trend among Argentinean immigrants in the United States.

CULTURE AND ASSIMILATION

Argentina's diverse population challenges any attempt to classify Argentinean Americans by ethnicity. Some common terms applied to the peoples of South America are "Hispanic" and "Latino." These terms present problems when they are used to define Argentinean Americans as well as many other peoples from the Americas. The word *Hispanic* derives from the Latin word *Hispania*, a proper name in Latin that describes the area also known as the Iberian Peninsula (Spain and Portugal). To apply this term to Argentinean Americans, as the questionnaire for the 1990 U.S. Census did, excludes almost half of their population, most of whom are Italian born or of Italian descent. The term *Latino* also presents some major difficulties in describing the cultural and ethnic diversity of South America, which extends far beyond its Latin European heritage. The term *Latin America* bluntly excludes the native peoples of Central and South America, as well as its numerous immigrant groups who have little in common with the Latin European countries.

Cuisine Argentinean cuisine is very rich and includes a variety of traditional recipes that have been passed on from generation to generation. Traditional Argentinean cuisine is based on dishes made with vegetables and meat, such as *mazamorra* (a porridge-like side dish made with corn), *locro* (a meat and vegetable soup), and *empanadas* (meat turnovers).

Argentina is perhaps best known for its beef. As John Hamill wrote: "There is this secret place, south of the border, where polite society hasn't totally surrendered to the body sculptors and cholesterol cops. Down there, people in restaurants, perfectly respectable people, still openly order huge, rare steaks" ("Where the 'Bife' Is," *Travel Holiday* 174 [March 1991]: 36–38). The excellence of Argentinean beef is known worldwide. Traditional Argentinean specialties are *asado* (grilled meat and ribs), *parrillada* (Argentinean mixed barbecue), and *empanadas*.

Immigrant groups have significantly contributed to the cuisine of Argentina. Along with the traditional dishes, Italian pasta is often the main course on the

Sunday table. There is a popular belief that on the 29th of each month eating *ñoquis* (gnocchi, an Italian pasta) brings good fortune. A ritual has evolved out of this belief that consists of placing money, usually a flattened bill that is tied up into a bow, under the plate. The Spanish settlers also contributed to the wealth of the Argentinean cuisine. Typically Spanish dishes are derived from pork, such as *chorizo* (sausage), bacon, and *jamón serrano* (pork ham cooked in salt).

Another Argentinean specialty is *dulce de leche*, a type of thick caramel made with highly condensed milk. One of the most popular sweet treats in Argentina, it is usually eaten on toast spread over butter. Argentinean cuisine has evolved a variety of desserts and pastries based on this product.

A traditional Argentinean beverage is *mate*, a type of tea grown in the north of the country. The tea is prepared in a small potlike container, called a *mate*, which is usually made from a carved, dried gourd. Curing techniques, intended to protect the gourd from cracking when water is poured into it, vary according to the region of the country and determine the taste of the beverage. Probably the two most widely known curing techniques use milk or ashes. After being cured, *mate* is prepared in the gourd by adding the tea, called *yerba mate*, and water. The tea is sipped directly from the gourd with a straw.

A traditional Argentinean custom following meals is the *sobremesa*. This word lacks a precise equivalent in English, but it describes the time spent sitting at the table after a meal in conversation, providing family members a chance to exchange ideas and discuss various issues. Argentinean meals usually consist of a light breakfast and a hearty lunch and dinner. Dinner is usually served after 9:00 p.m. In some regions of the country, people still take a *siesta* (nap) after lunch. Even in rather big cities, such as Mendoza, this custom is still observed. Business hours have been adapted to this custom. Most activities cease soon after midday and restart at about 4:00 p.m. Even the street traffic significantly wanes during these hours.

Traditional Dress The most popular Argentinean character, often presented as a symbol of Argentinean tradition, is the *gaucho*. Although the *gaucho* is almost extinct, his attire is sometimes worn for parades and national celebrations such as the Day of Tradition. The attire of the *gaucho* has evolved with time. Originally, it consisted of a simple garment known as the *chiripá*, a diaperlike cloth pulled over lacy leggings, which was usually worn with a *poncho*. The *gaucho*'s traditional pants became baggy trousers that were fastened with a leather belt adorned with coins and silver and an elaborate buckle. A neckerchief and a short-brimmed straw hat were also occasionally worn. A traditional Argentinean woman, or *china*, would typically wear a long loose dress, fastened at the waist and sleeves. Sometimes the material of the dress would have colorful patterns, typically flowery ones, which would match the flowers in her hair.

ARGENTINEAN LOCRO

Ingredients

2 cans navy beans

2 tablespoons vegetable oil

1 pound chorizo, bratwurst, or other spicy sausage

1 pound stewing beef, cut into bite-sized pieces

2 cups frozen corn

2 carrots, peeled and sliced into bite-sized pieces

1 large winter squash, peeled and chopped into 1-inch cubes

¼ pound smoked bacon, diced

32 ounces chicken broth

3 tablespoons vegetable oil

1 large onion, finely chopped

1 red pepper, finely chopped

1 teaspoon paprika

chili powder

salt and pepper to taste

½ cup chopped green onions

Preparation

For soup:

Drain the navy beans and add them to a large pot. Heat 2 tablespoons of vegetable oil in a skillet and sauté the chorizo and the stewing beef until lightly browned. Cool and slice the sausages into bite-sized pieces. Add beef and sausage to the pot with the beans. Add corn, carrots, squash, and bacon to pot. Add the chicken broth. If necessary add water to cover the beans and meat by an inch.

Simmer the meat, beans, and vegetables on low to medium heat for about an hour, then taste and check for seasoning. The soup should be thicker and the beef should be getting tender. Season with salt and pepper to taste.

Simmer for 30 minutes to an hour longer, until the beef is tender and the stew tastes very flavorful. Add a little water from time to time if necessary. While the soup is cooking, make the sauce.

For the sauce:

Heat 3 tablespoons of oil in the same skillet that was used to cook the sausage. Add the chopped onion and red pepper. Season with a teaspoon of paprika, chile powder, salt, and pepper to taste. Cook until the vegetables are soft, about 5 minutes.

Serve soup hot, with the sauce on the side, and garnish each bowl with chopped green onions.

Holidays One of the more popular Argentinean holidays is the Day of Tradition, celebrated on November 10. This festivity includes parades in the towns and cities of the country and folkloric shows known as *peñas*. In these *peñas* folkloric music is played by regional groups, and traditional food, such as *asado* and *empanadas*, is sold at small stands. In some *peñas* it is possible to attend a rodeo, where skillful horse riders, usually dressed as *gauchos*, display their equestrian abilities.

Due to the influence of immigrant groups, Christmas in Argentina is usually celebrated much like it is in Spain or Italy. A Christmas tree, usually artificial and covered by cotton snow, is set up in every home. Often, a manger is arranged under the tree to evoke the birth of Jesus Christ. The nativity is also dramatized by religious groups at churches, theaters, and public squares during the week preceding Christmas. This practice is called *Pesebre Viviente* ("Living Manger"). Like Americans, Argentineans celebrate the coming of Santa Claus (called "Papá Noel"), who is said to travel in a deer-driven sleigh with Christmas presents for the children. The two most important family reunions take place during Christmas and New Year's. Christmas is traditionally considered a religious celebration, whereas New Year's is a national celebration. Among young people it is customary to have dinner with their families, participate in the toast (which is often made at midnight), and afterward meet friends and dance until dawn. The Christmas dinner typically consists of a very rich meal, high in calories. Certain traditional European Christmas foods are commonly served, including *turrón* (a Spanish candy made with honey, sugar, and egg whites) and *panetone* (a sweet bread loaf that originated in Italy).

Another important religious celebration is Epiphany, which in Argentina is known as the Day of the Three Wise Men. It is celebrated on the sixth of January. Children are instructed by their parents to leave their shoes at the foot of the bed or under the Christmas tree. They are also supposed to leave a glass of water for the wise men and some grass for the camels they ride. The children usually write a letter with their requests for presents and leave it with the shoes, water, and grass. On the night of the fifth of January, children typically go to bed very early in the evening, expecting to get up early to receive their presents. On the following morning, the sidewalks and public squares are filled with children playing with their new toys.

Argentina's diverse population challenges any attempt to classify Argentinean Americans by ethnicity. Some common terms applied to the peoples of South America are "Hispanic" and "Latino." These terms present problems when they are used to define Argentinean Americans as well as many other peoples from the Americas.

FAMILY AND COMMUNITY LIFE

Because of their strong Spanish and Italian heritage, the Argentinean family is characterized by the close relationships traditionally maintained by these peoples. In Argentina family reunions are usually carried out on a weekly basis. Sundays and observed national holidays are often spent with relatives and friends, and typically an *asado* (Argentinean barbecue) or Italian pasta is the favorite choice for lunch.

The family, which typically extends to include cousins, aunts, uncles, in-laws, and sometimes even the families of the in-laws, is often the focus of social life in Argentina, especially after marriage. Grandparents play an important role within the family. Children usually spend a longer time living with their parents than they do in the United States. Sometimes they stay with them until they get married. Although this situation is at times imposed by economic necessity, there are also some gender biases in this respect. For example, women who live alone run the risk of being negatively labeled. In the cities this situation is better tolerated but it is considered odd. Argentinean families are usually not as geographically widespread as their American counterparts.

Gender Roles Gender roles in Argentinean society have changed in the last few decades. Although daily tasks such as cooking, laundry, care of the children, and shopping are still the domain of women, the number of women who pursue careers in addition to fulfilling their roles as mothers and wives is increasing. Little by little, women have been entering typically male-dominated fields such as politics, economics, engineering, and law. Argentina was, in fact, the first country in the Americas to have a woman president.

The situation of Argentinean immigrants in the United States tends to be somewhat different. In a 1988 study about migrant Argentinean women called "Migrant Careers and Well Being of Women," one of the interviewed subjects affirmed: "I only go out with my husband," "I live locked up," "I'm afraid to go out." This report further states: "for those married women who wanted to return to Argentina there was family conflict, since most husbands wished to remain permanently in the United States." Yet, it states, "the unmarried seemed better adjusted and reported more freedom and less family pressure than in Argentina. For instance, one respondent reported 'A woman in the United States can live alone, work, travel, and nobody thinks anything bad of her. In Argentina they would think I am crazy.' Another interviewee reported 'As a single woman, I would have a more restricted life in Argentina—there is more machismo.'"

In Argentina it is usual for couples to ask their parents or a sibling to babysit for their children. These conveniences are often unavailable to immigrant women who may find it necessary to look after the children and postpone their own work or professional career. For example, in the report cited above, an Argentinean immigrant woman stated: "I miss the family. I have to do everything at home by myself. If I lived in Argentina my mother, sister or friend would take care of the children sometimes. Here even when I don't feel well I have to continue working."

Education Education is praised by Argentineans as one of the most important assets an individual can have. Education is also valued among Argentinean Americans, 39 percent of whom have achieved a bachelor's degree or higher, according to 2011 estimates by the American Community Survey. In Argentina private and public institutions offer a wide range of possibilities for elementary, high school, and university education. The choice between a public or private institution often depends on the economic capabilities of the family. In the last few years there has been a significant surge in the number of bilingual schools. Perhaps the most common combination is Spanish and English, but there are also renowned elementary and high schools that offer bilingual instruction in Spanish and Italian, or Spanish and German. Religious schools are also widespread, and during the 1990s they started to open to coed education.

In Argentina education is mandatory from six to fourteen years of age. Elementary school ranges from the first to the seventh year, whereas high school is optional and can comprise between five to seven years of study in some vocational schools. Universities are either private or government-financed. Government-financed universities are free and often the only admission requirement is completion of a high school degree, although some universities may request an entrance examination. Careers that enjoy a certain social prestige, such as medicine, law, engineering, and economics, are popular vocations among young students. Because of such educational attainment, most Argentinean immigrants have assimilated relatively well in the United States, particularly in careers associated with science and academia.

Courtship and Weddings The wedding ceremony commonly consists of three main events. The first is the bride and bridegroom's shower party, which varies according to the social class and region of the country. In the middle class it usually consists of parties separately organized for the bride and bridegroom by their friends. The second event is the formal wedding, which is held before a state officer, usually a judge of the peace at the local civil registry. This establishes the matrimonial contract and the legal rights of the couple. Both the bridegroom and bride typically wear formal clothes for this event, which usually takes place in the morning on a business day. Two witnesses—commonly friends of the couple—are required to sign the entry in the book of civil matrimony. After the ceremony, the people present throw rice on the couple as they leave the building. Rice stands as a symbol for wishes of prosperity and fertility.

The third celebration consists of the church wedding ceremony, attended by the families and friends of the bride and bridegroom. After the ceremony, the newlywed couple greets friends and family at the entrance of the church and again rice is thrown on the couple, symbolizing economic prosperity and a fruitful marriage. Afterward there is usually a party that is often very structured. The wedding pictures of almost any couple include these ritualized customs: cutting the cake and dancing the waltz. The wedding cake often has strings coming out of it that are attached to little gifts inside. Single women each pull a string and the item they receive symbolizes their romantic fate. For instance, if a woman pulls out a little ring, it means she will marry next; if she pulls out a thimble, she will never marry; and if she pulls out a lock—like a small padlock—her parents will not allow her to get married anytime soon. Argentinian Americans maintain many of these traditions in the United States. However, strict adherence to these wedding customs has diminished, especially among later generations.

Baptisms Children have a very important role in Argentinean culture. Traditionally they are protected in the family from the world of adults. There are many celebrations that are actually intended for children, such as Epiphany, Christmas, the Day of the Children, and baptism. In a Catholic family baptism is the first ceremony in which children participate. During this ceremony the newborn is assigned godparents, who are usually relatives or friends of the family. Traditionally, the Argentinean president becomes the godfather of a family's seventh son, which is a rare occurrence. The commitment that the godparents make includes providing advice and spiritual guidance to the godchild. Sometimes they are also expected to look after the children in case of the parents' unexpected death. To be a godparent today, in the United States, is symbolic of the confirmation of the close bond or friendship between the parents and the selected godparents. In Catholic families it is also very common to have a set of godparents for the wedding ceremony. Usually the godparents are another couple whose function is to give advice on matrimonial matters to the newlyweds.

Los Quince Another traditional party celebration, representing the turning point between adolescence and womanhood, is informally known as *Los Quince*. Held on a girl's fifteenth birthday, the celebration is usually organized by the relatives and friends of the teenage girl. She wears a dress similar to the white dress worn by brides, although the color can be other than white, such as pink or light blue. Customarily, the father dances a waltz with his daughter after dinner, followed by the girl's godfather and her friends, while the rest of the guests stand in a circle. In some cases the whole family attends mass in church before the party. The tradition of celebrating *Los Quince* remains strong among Argentinean Americans.

EMPLOYMENT AND ECONOMIC CONDITIONS

Many Argentineans in the United States are characterized by their high level of education: technicians, skilled workers, and professionals in general make up

Nancy Sutley (1962–), as Chair of the Council on Environmental Quality, testifies in a hearing of the federal Oil Spill Commission investigating a spill, 2010. Sutley's parents emigrated to New York from Argentina. ZUMA PRESS, INC. / ALAMY

proposing and designing the carbon credit emissions trading market underlying the Kyoto Protocol.

Luís Angel Caffarelli (1948–) is a highly respected mathematician and professor who has taught at the University of Chicago, the Institute for Advanced Study in Princeton, New Jersey, and the University of Texas at Austin. Harvard graduate Enrique Anderson-Imbert (1910–2000) taught Hispanic literature and wrote several works on such figures as the Nicaraguan poet Rubén Darío and former Argentinean president Faustino Sarmiento. Dermatologist Irma Gigli (1931–) was a director at the University of California at San Diego and taught at Harvard, New York University, and the University of Texas at Houston.

Eduardo Daniel Sontag (1951–) is a professor of mathematics at Rutgers University, working in systems biology and control theory and engineering. His work in control theory led to the introduction of the concept of input-to-state stability (ISS), a stability theory notion for nonlinear systems, and control-Lyapunov functions. In systems biology, Sontag and David Angeli introduced the concept of input/output monotone systems. In theory of computation, he proved the first results on computational complexity in nonlinear controllability, and he introduced, together with his student Hava Siegelmann, a new approach to analog computation and super-Turing computing.

Art Architect, critic, and educator Susana Torre (1944–) has developed a career combining architectural and urban design with teaching and writing. Torre was the first woman invited to design a building in Columbus, Indiana; she organized and curated the first major exhibition of American women architects; and she edited the book *Women in American Architecture: A Historic and Contemporary Perspective*. Torre is a cofounder of *Heresies, A Feminist Journal on Art and Politics*, and she served on the editorial board of *Chrysalis* between 1976 and 1978.

Government Nancy Sutley (1962–), born in New York to a mother from Argentina, was appointed chair of the White House Council on Environmental Quality (CEQ) in 2009, serving as the principal environmental policy adviser to President Barack Obama. Prior to her appointment, Sutley was the deputy mayor for Energy and Environment for the city of Los Angeles, California. She received her bachelor's degree from Cornell University and her master's in public policy from Harvard University.

Journalism Pablo Kleinman (1971–) began working as a journalist in 1989 as the first Latin American correspondent for *Billboard Magazine*. He was editor in chief of the Spanish-language political journal *Diario de América* and is also a frequent columnist on political and social issues for several different publications in Latin America, Spain, the United States, and the Middle East. He has been a pioneer of the development of online services in Latin America,

the majority of Argentinean immigrants in the United States. However, statistics show about 50 percent of the Argentineans who entered the United States from 1965 to 1970 were manual laborers. This is likely due to the fact that periods of economic and political stability in Argentina had limited prospects not only for professionals but also for people involved in other occupations. Immigration then became more massive and included people from different social classes. The statistics showed that, by 1970, the percentage of Argentineans with ten or more years of education was four times higher in the United States than in Argentina. According to the 1990 U.S. Census, about 21 percent of the Argentinean immigrants residing in the metropolitan areas of Los Angeles and New York had a bachelor's degree or higher.

The percentage of Argentineans in the marketplace who are between twenty-five and fifty-nine years old has been increasing. In 1980, 58 percent of Argentinean women immigrants between twenty-five and fifty-nine years old could be found in the workplace, compared with 52 percent of the general female U.S. population and 24 percent in other South and Central American countries. The United States seems to offer women increased opportunities for employment. Male Argentinean Americans tend to participate in activities such as manufacturing industries, commerce, transportation, communication, and construction. They have a lower participation in activities such as agriculture, hunting, fishing, and silviculture (forestry).

NOTABLE INDIVIDUALS

Academia Graciela Chichilnisky (1944–) is a mathematical economist and an expert on climate change. Born and raised in Argentina, she moved to the United States in the 1960s to pursue graduate studies in mathematics at MIT and the University of California at Berkeley. In 1977 she became a professor of economics at Columbia University. Chichilnisky is known for authoring an early draft of WorldPol, the first democratic organization proposal in cyberspace.

Andrés Oppenheimer (1951–) is the Latin American editor and syndicated foreign affairs columnist with the *Miami Herald*. His column, "The Oppenheimer Report," appears twice a week in the *Miami Herald* along with more than sixty other U.S. and foreign newspapers. As a member of the *Miami Herald* team that uncovered the Iran-Contra scandal, he is the cowinner of the 1987 Pulitzer Prize. He was selected by the *Forbes Media Guide* as one of the "500 most important journalists" of the United States in 1993 and by *Poder Magazine* as one of the "100 most powerful people" in Latin America in 2002 and 2008.

Music Composer Lalo Schifrin (1932–) wrote the music for the television series *Mission Impossible* and is also noted for his work with Clint Eastwood in the 1960s, 1970s, and 1980s. He has won multiple Grammy Awards (with twenty-one nominations), a Cable ACE Award, and six Oscar nominations, and he has a star on the Hollywood Walk of Fame.

Juan Fernando Silvetti Adorno (1944–2003), professionally known as Bebu Silvetti, was an Argentinean pianist, composer, conductor, arranger, and record producer. Popularly known for the 1977 instrumental disco hit "Lluvia De Primavera" ("Spring Rain" in English), Silvetti was also a successful, Grammy-winning producer for a wide variety of Latin and international music performers. In 2001 he topped *Billboard Magazine*'s year-end "Hot Latin Tracks Producer Chart," and in 2002 he received the Billboard Producer of the Year Award. In 2003 Silvetti received the Latin Grammy Award for Producer of the Year.

Sports Efrain Chacurian (1924–) was a member of the U.S. National Soccer Team in 1953 and 1954, and he was inducted into the National Soccer Hall of Fame in 1992. Angelo DiBernardo (1956–) played professionally in the North American Soccer League and Major Indoor Soccer League. He also represented the United States at the 1984 Summer Olympics. Claudio Reyna (1973–) played professionally in the North American Soccer League and Major Indoor Soccer League, representing the United States at the 1984 Summer Olympics. He was the captain of the U.S. men's national team before retiring from international football following the United States' exit from the 2006 FIFA World Cup.

Diana Taurasi (1982–) is a professional basketball player who plays for the Phoenix Mercury in the Women's National Basketball Association (WNBA) and for UMMC Ekaterinburg of Russia. In 2011 she was voted one of the top fifteen players in WNBA history by fans. Luis Alberto Scola Balvoa (1980–) is a professional basketball player for the Phoenix Suns of the National Basketball Association (NBA). He was named to the NBA All-Rookie First Team in 2008.

Diver Verónica Ribot-Canales (1962–) became a U.S. citizen in September 1991, and in 1992 she

Argentinean American Diana Taurasi (1982–) plays professional basketball for the Phoenix Mercury in the WNBA and also the Russian team UMMC Ekaterinburg. DMITRY ARGUNOV / ALAMY

switched her sports nationality from Argentina to the United States. She has competed in three Olympics (1984, 1988, and 1992, all for Argentina), and she won twelve South American championship titles for Argentina.

Stage and Screen Lorenzo Lamas (1958–) is an American actor known for playing Lance Cumson on the popular 1980s soap opera *Falcon Crest*, Reno Raines on the 1990s crime drama *Renegade*, and Hector Ramirez on the daytime soap opera *The Bold and the Beautiful*.

Actress and singer Mía Maestro (1978–) is best known for her role as Nadia Santos in the television drama *Alias* (2001–2006) and as Christina Kahlo in the film *Frida* (2002). She also appeared in the *Twilight* series of films (2011 and 2012).

ORGANIZATIONS AND ASSOCIATIONS

Argentine-American Chamber of Commerce

Located in New York City, this organization promotes business ventures between Argentina and the United States.

630 Fifth Avenue
25th Floor
Rockefeller Center
New York, New York 10111
Phone: (212) 698-2238
Email: argentinechamber@argentinechamber.org
URL: www.argentinechamber.org

Argentine Association of Los Angeles

Encourages development of friendship and mutual help among Argentine nationals residing in California; gives advice and helps Argentine nationals in need; develops cultural, educational, and social activities and promotes sports; and promotes the development of the arts and cultural exchange programs.

2100 North Glenoaks Boulevard
Burbank, California 91504
Phone: (818) 567-0901
Email: info@aalaonline.com
URL: www.aalaonline.com

The Argentine Cultural Center

Promotes greater awareness and understanding of the Argentinean culture in the United States through community development, educational, and cultural programs.

20 West Park Avenue
Long Beach, New York 11561
Phone: (516) 849-1470
Email: info@theargentineculturalcenter.org
URL: www.theargentineculturalcenter.org

La Escuela Argentina

Prepares students of all nationalities in the development of strong oral and written communication in Castilian and in the acquisition, in that language, of knowledge of literature, social sciences, geography, history, and civics.

9029 Bradley Boulevard
Potomac, Maryland 20854
Phone: (301) 365-0955
Email: administracion@escuelaargentina.org
URL: www.escuelaargentina.org

MUSEUMS AND RESEARCH CENTERS

Academia Nacional de la Historia de la República Argentina (National Academy of History of the Argentine Republic)

A nonprofit learned society established to foster the study and dissemination of Argentinean history.

Balcarce 139
Buenos Aires
Argentina C1064AAC
Phone: +54 4343-4416
URL: www.an-historia.org.ar

Museo Histórico Nacional (National Historical Museum)

A museum dedicated to the history of Argentina, exhibiting objects relating to the May Revolution and the Argentine War of Independence.

Defensa 1600—Parque Lezama
Buenos Aires
Argentina C1143AAH
Phone: +54 4307-1182
Email: aamhn@aamhn.org.ar
URL: www.aamhn.org.ar

SOURCES FOR ADDITIONAL STUDY

Cattan, Peter. "The Diversity of Hispanics in the U.S. Work Force." *Monthly Labor Review*, 116, no. 8 (August 1993): 3.

Freidenberg, Judith, et al. "Migrant Careers and Well Being of Women." *International Migration Review* 22, no. 2 (1988): 208–25.

Lattes, Alfredo E., and Enrique Oteiza, eds. *The Dynamics of Argentine Migration, 1955–1984: Democracy and the Return of Expatriates*. Geneva, Switzerland: United Nations Research Institute for Social Development, 1987.

Norden, Deborah, and Roberto Russell. *The United States and Argentina: Changing Relations in a Changing World*. New York Routledge, 2002.

Romero, Luis Alberto. *A History of Argentina in the Twentieth Century*. State College: Pennsylvania State University Press, 2003.

Sheinin, David. *Argentina and the United States: An Alliance Contained*. Athens: University of Georgia Press, 2006.

Tulchin, Joseph S. *Argentina and the United States: A Conflicted Relationship*. Boston: Twayne, 1990.

ARMENIAN AMERICANS
Harold Takooshian

OVERVIEW

Armenian Americans are immigrants or descendants of people from the Republic of Armenia, a country located in the South Caucasus region of Eurasia. Armenia is bordered on the north and east by Georgia and Azerbaijan, and on the south and west by Iran and Turkey. Located on the northeastern portion of the Armenian Plateau, Armenia is a mountainous country with nearly half of its area at 6,562 feet above sea level and containing small forests, rivers, and volcanoes. Armenia's total land area is 11,484 square miles (29,743 square kilometers), which is slightly smaller than the state of Maryland.

At the time of the 2011 census conducted by the National Statistical Service of the Republic of Armenia, Armenia had a population of 2,871,509 people. The vast majority of Armenians practice Christianity, with over 90 percent of the population belonging to the Armenian Apostolic Church. The Armenian economy ranks 134th in the world, owing largely to the lingering effects of the dissolution of the Soviet Union in 1991 and its dependence on other countries for oil and gas. However, since the late 1990s Armenia's economy has gradually stabilized as the growth of the telecommunications industry and the privatization of energy-distribution industries and other enterprises throughout the country have secured outside investment in the economy. Even so, the Armenian economy still relies heavily upon remittances received from Armenians living abroad.

The first significant wave of Armenians came to the United States in the mid-1890s when Sultan Abdülhamid II began large-scale persecution of the Armenian population in the Ottoman Empire. From 1895 to 1900 approximately 2,500 Armenians came to the United States each year, many from what is present-day Armenia but significant numbers from Turkey, Russia, and Syria, as well, because Abdülhamid had displaced numerous Armenians throughout the empire and exiled many others to points in the Middle East. Most of these immigrants settled in New York City, Boston, and other industrial cities along the mid-Atlantic seaboard and took whatever factory work they could find. Between 1965 and 1991 large numbers of Armenians came to United States from the Armenian expatriate communities in

Syria, Lebanon, and Egypt in reaction to recurring Arab-Israeli violence. Others came from Romania and Bulgaria to escape ethnic prejudice. Members of the latter waves of immigrants joined established communities in the East and in California. Since the dissolution of the Soviet Union in 1991, most Armenian immigrants to the United States have come from the Republic of Armenia.

The U.S. Census Bureau's American Community Survey (ACS) estimates for 2006–2010 reported that 447,580 people of Armenian descent were living in the United States. Other organizations, such as the University of Michigan–Dearborn and the Armenian National Committee of America, offer estimates ranging between 800,000 and 1,500,000. According to the ACS, the largest number of Americans of Armenian descent were residing in California (241,323). States with smaller, but significant, populations of Armenian Americans included Massachusetts (28,471), New York (24,803), Michigan (17,345), New Jersey (15,816), and Florida (13,446).

HISTORY OF THE PEOPLE

Early History Over the course of the first millennium BCE, the Armenian people built a high civilization in Asia Minor, along trade routes connecting Greece, Turkey, and the Middle East. The Armenians were known for their business acumen and artistic achievement. However, due to their location and their relatively sparse numbers, the Armenians were vulnerable to waves of invading Assyrian, Greek, Roman, and Persian conquerors. The Romans and Persians fought over the state of Armenia and the neighboring territory throughout the first four centuries of the Common Era, and later the Byzantines took control of the area until Muslim invaders arrived in 651 CE.

Although the exact date is disputed, it is known that sometime early in the fourth century CE, the state of Armenia became the first to adopt Christianity as its national religion, some twenty years before the emperor Constantine declared it the state religion of the Roman Empire. A century later, however, Armenia came under Persian rule, and when the Persian ruler Yazdegerd II attempted to suppress Christianity, Armenia's small army defiantly stood firm to defend its faith. At the Battle of Avarair in 451, Persia's victory over the Armenian Christians proved so costly that it finally allowed Armenians to maintain their religious freedom.

The Armenians maintained their religious freedom in the following centuries as the surrounding area came under the influence of various Turkic Muslim leaders. When European Crusaders in the twelfth century entered the Near East, they found prosperous Armenian communities living among the Muslims while also maintaining the Holy Sepulchre in Jerusalem and other Christian sites. Under 400 years of Ottoman Turkish rule (1512–1908), the Christian Armenian minority were an industrious, educated elite within the sultan's empire. They were known for their exceptionally high rate of literacy, success in business, and taste in art. Nevertheless, because they were Christians, Armenians were treated as second-class citizens by the Ottoman aristocracy. In 1894 this abiding prejudice transformed into open hostility, as Sultan Abdülhamid II initiated a series of purges against the Armenians, killing over 100,000 in a two-year period and sending countless others into exile in the Middle East and Russia. Those that remained lived in hiding throughout Turkey.

Modern Era After fighting with the Russians and the Persians steadily for three centuries, the Ottoman Empire fell in 1908, giving way to the Committee of Union and Progress, a secular nationalist group commonly known as the Young Turks, a group that deeply mistrusted the Armenians. In 1909 they slaughtered between 15,000 and 20,000 Armenians living in Adana, an agricultural city in southern Turkey. In 1915 the Turkish government attempted to eradicate the Armenians, killing well over a million Armenians and exiling others throughout World War I and into the 1920s. This mass slaughter has since been called the Armenian genocide and is also known among Armenians as "the Great Crime." Although the Armenians had been suffering at the hands of the Young Turks for many years prior to 1915, it is widely acknowledged that the Great Crime began on April 24, 1915, when the Young Turks assassinated 250 Armenian intellectuals in Constantinople. The mass extermination of able-bodied men and forced migrations of women and children to Syria began shortly thereafter.

On May 28, 1918, after a failed attempt at aligning in a federation with neighboring Georgia and Azerbaijan, Armenian nationalists formed the Democratic Republic of Armenia, which lasted for two years until Turkey declared war on Armenia in 1920 and took back land that it had lost in World War I. In November 1920, the Soviet army occupied Armenia, forcing the Turkish army to withdraw and formally incorporating Armenia, along with Georgia and Azerbaijan, into the Soviet Union in 1922. The three states were known collectively as the Transcaucasian

Socialist Federative Soviet Republic (S.F.S.R.), and for almost fifteen years they benefited from Soviet protection without having to subscribe completely to the mandates of Soviet communism. That changed in 1936 when Soviet leader Joseph Stalin dissolved the Transcaucasian S.F.S.R., making the Armenian Soviet Socialist Republic (Armenian S.S.R.) the smallest of the Soviet Union's fifteen republics.

Protected from its neighbors and forced to manufacture goods for the U.S.S.R., Armenia benefited economically from Soviet rule to some extent. However, strong currents of nationalism persisted as the Soviets deprived Armenians of basic freedoms, such as speech and assembly, and as tension with Azerbaijan escalated over the mistreatment of the numerous ethnic Armenians living in that country. Nationalist sentiment became more fervent in the mid-1960s, when Armenians began to call the nations of the world to hold Turkey accountable for the Great Crime of 1915. By the late 1980s, Armenian nationalist were demanding statehood, primarily because of two events. First, in February 1988 hostility between Azerbaijanis and Armenians in Azerbaijan's Nagorno-Karabakh region erupted into armed conflict between Armenia and Azerbaijan that would displace thousands of Armenians over the course of six years. Second, in December of that year an earthquake struck northern Armenia, killing over 25,000 people, leaving another 500,000 homeless, and destroying the infrastructure of three industrial Armenian cities. In the aftermath, the international community recognized that the severity of the damage was due more to lax Soviet building and maintenance codes than to the force of the quake.

Armenia declared its independence from the Soviet Union on September 21, 1991—three months before Soviet Russia's collapse—and faced numerous challenges in its first two decades as a sovereign state. Initially the transition to a free-market economy was fraught with setbacks and corruption, but over the course of the 1990s, as more of the leading industries were privatized, Armenia secured foreign aid and benefited from the assistance of wealthy investors in the Armenian diaspora. Even so, economic progress has been tempered by internal and external political challenges. In the mid-1990s, after a tense ceasefire agreement ended the Nagorno-Karabakh War in 1994, Turkey and Azerbaijan imposed a blockade on Armenia that halted the flow of vital resources into the country. With its economy threatened by the blockade, Armenian politics turned hostile and eventually devolved into violence. On October 29, 1999, seven members of the opposition party, including the prime minister and the speaker of Parliament, were assassinated by a terrorist organization widely believed to be linked to then-president Robert Korcharyan. Korcharyan remained president until 2008, when he was succeeded by prime minister and political ally Serzh Sargsyan in what is widely recognized as a fraudulent election. In the spring of 2011, when a revolutionary wave known as the Arab Spring swept through the Middle East, Armenians followed suit. They openly protested the Sargsyan government and demanded democratic reforms, the release of political prisoners, and a public investigation into the government-sponsored violence that had occurred in 2008.

SETTLEMENT IN THE UNITED STATES

The first documented case of Armenian immigration to North America is the arrival of "Martin the Armenian," who was brought as a farmer to the Virginia Colony by governor George Yeardley in 1618, two years before the pilgrims arrived at Plymouth Rock. It is believed that a few fellow Armenians may have followed this early settler, but in total the Armenian population in the colonies was negligible. Armenians began coming to the United States in small but steady numbers in the nineteenth century, when Protestant missionaries in the Ottoman Empire encouraged them to attend American colleges and return to Armenia to work as teachers and doctors (and thereby help them win more converts). About 70 of these students stayed in the United States. They were joined by a handful of Armenian businessmen who had left the Ottoman Empire with the hope of making a fortune in the United States. In the 1870s and 1880s about 1,500 Armenian artisans came to the United States from Kharpert, an overcrowded city in present-day Turkey, in search of a better market for their goods. Most of these immigrants settled in New York and Massachusetts.

For three decades, beginning in the mid-1890s and continuing through the mid-1920s, large numbers of Armenians came to the United States from points throughout the Ottoman Empire to escape persecution from the Turks. Tension between the Armenians and Turks began to escalate in the early 1890s when Armenians in Merzifon, Tokat, and Sason (all in present-day Turkey) began asking for social reforms that had recently been implemented among the Romanians, Bulgarians, Serbians, and others living in the western region of the Ottoman Empire. Sultan Abdülhamid II responded violently to Armenian protests, killing 10,000 demonstrators in Sason in 1894 and another 100,000 throughout the empire the following year. Armenians left the empire in massive numbers, fleeing to Russia, the Middle East, Eastern Europe, northern Africa, the United States, and Canada. By 1900, when the Ottomans implemented restrictions making it difficult for Armenians to escape, well over 10,000 had immigrated to the United States, settling primarily in the East and working in steel factories, textile mills, and rubber-manufacturing plants.

Armenian immigration to the United States waned at the turn of the century, except for a small group of Armenian Protestants who came from Russia to escape religious persecution. Most of these immigrants ended up in Fresno, California, where they worked in agriculture. By 1914, when migration ceased due to the start of World War I, approximately 2,500 Armenians were living in the Fresno settlement. They sought to improve their circumstances as quickly as possible, many saving to buy a small plot of land to farm, others buying small vineyards and selling wine. Upon receiving word that prospects were good in California, some of those who had settled in the eastern United States also moved west and tried their hand at winemaking. They tended to stay in the Fresno area until the Great Depression, when falling prices forced them to move to San Francisco and Los Angeles.

Armenian immigration to the eastern United States spiked again in 1910, when more than 5,000 Armenians came to the United States to escape persecution at the hands of the Young Turks, the nationalist government that had replaced the deposed caliphate in 1908. In 1913 more than 9,000 Armenians came to the United States as the Young Turks continued their anti-Armenian policies, which at the time included squeezing tax dollars out of Armenian businesspeople. During World War I (1914–1918), Armenian migration to the eastern United States came to a halt.

Unlike most immigrants to the United States at the turn of the century, the incoming Armenians were primarily literate urban dwellers who had a background in skilled labor or who had run their own businesses while they lived in the Ottoman Empire. When they came to the United States, they accepted unskilled work but sought to move up the socioeconomic ladder as quickly as possible. Many saved their money until they could open their own shops or moved to the Midwest to earn more money as wage laborers in the auto industry. Many of those who stayed in the East and opened their own shops ran grocery stores or meat markets, which were likely to turn a profit for anyone who had the money to start the business. Others started businesses in the trades they knew. There were many Armenian tailors, shoemakers, and rug sellers in the eastern United States.

Immediately after World War I, Armenians—mostly women and children who had spent the war years in camps in Syria, Greece, and Egypt—began coming to the United States in large numbers again, with over 10,000 arriving in 1920 alone and approximately 24,000 coming between 1920 and 1924. Migration halted again in 1924 with the passage of the Immigration Act of 1924, which many historians believe discriminated against migrants from Eastern Europe and Asia.

Armenians did not begin migrating to the United States again until 1948, when the passage of the Displaced Persons Act temporarily suspended quotas for peoples displaced by World War II and allowed 4,500 Armenian refugees to enter the country.

In 1965 the Nationality Act eliminated the quota system altogether and ushered in another wave of Armenian immigrants, most of them from expatriate

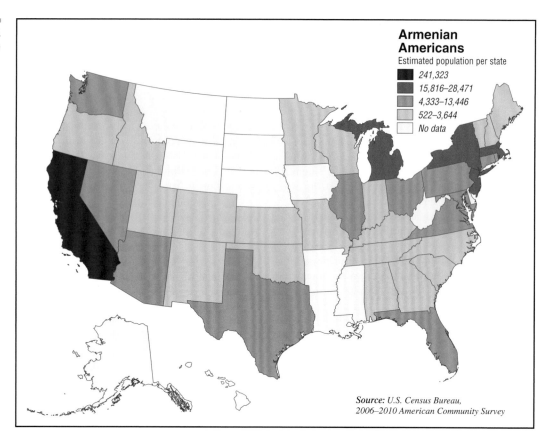

Armenian Americans
Estimated population per state

- 241,323
- 15,816–28,471
- 4,333–13,446
- 522–3,644
- No data

*Source: U.S. Census Bureau,
2006–2010 American Community Survey*

communities in the Middle East who were trying to escape the violence there. It is estimated that as many as 30,000 Armenians left the Middle East in the 1960s and early 1970s looking for new homes in the United States, Canada, and Europe.

Like the Armenians who came at the turn of the century, the members of this wave of Armenian immigrants were skilled laborers and businessmen who took what work they could find and tried immediately to improve their lot in the United States. While large numbers of these Armenians moved to New York City, they tended to avoid the other Armenian communities in New England and chose instead to move to Los Angeles and San Francisco. Since the 1975 Lebanese civil war, Los Angeles has replaced war-torn Beirut as the "first city" of the Armenian diaspora—the largest Armenian community outside of Armenia. The majority of Armenian immigrants to the United States since the 1970s has settled in greater Los Angeles, bringing the Armenian community's size there to around 200,000, according to American Community Survey estimates for 2006–2010. This includes some 30,000 Armenians who left Soviet Armenia between 1960 and 1984. In addition to New York and California, according to the American Community Survey, other states with large numbers of Armenian Americans include Massachusetts, Florida, New Jersey, and Michigan.

In the late 1980s and early 1990s, Armenian immigration to the United States increased again due to the Spitak earthquake in 1988, the Nagorno-Karabakh War (1988–1994), and the dissolution of the Soviet Union in 1991. The 1990 U.S. Census counted 308,096 Americans who cited their ancestry as "Armenian," up from 212,621 in 1980. Between 1992 and 1997, nearly 23,000 Armenians immigrated to the United States, according to the U.S. Immigration and Naturalization Service. According to the 2010 Census, 483,366 people identified as Armenian American, up from 385,488 in 2000.

Armenians possess one of the highest literacy rates of any immigrant group and have found success in nearly every field, from manufacturing and agriculture to technological and professional fields. Although many first- and second-generation Armenian Americans encountered financial hardships upon first immigrating to the United States, their children and grandchildren have experienced relative economic stability, with a poverty rate of close to 10 percent. Armenians continue to leave their country due to the unstable political and economic conditions, but as Armenia steadily adopts democratic reforms, members of the diaspora have been returning there, bringing their knowledge, skills, and money to the developing country.

LANGUAGE

The Armenian language is an independent branch of the Indo-European group of languages. Because it separated from its Indo-European origins thousands of years ago, it is not closely related to any other existing language. Its syntactical rules make it a concise language, expressing much meaning in few words. One unique aspect of Armenian is its alphabet. When Armenians converted to Christianity in the early part of the fourth century, they had their own language but, with no alphabet, they relied on Greek and Assyrian for writing. In the first decade of the fifth century, Mesrob Mashtots (353–439), a scholarly monk, invented a 36-character alphabet and transcribed the Bible into Armenian. His efforts ushered in a golden age of literature in Armenia, and the nearby Georgians soon commissioned Mesrob to invent an alphabet for their language. Armenians today continue to use Mesrob's original 36 characters (now 38), and they regard him as a national hero.

The spoken Armenian of Mesrob's era has evolved over the centuries. This classical Armenian, called *Krapar*, is used now only in religious services. Modern spoken Armenian has two dialects. The slightly more guttural "Eastern" Armenian is used by Armenians still living in Armenia as well as those in Iran and in the post-Soviet nations. "Western" Armenian is common among Armenians in every other nation throughout the diaspora—in the Middle East, Europe, and the Americas. With effort, speakers of the two dialects can understand each other's pronunciation, much the way Portuguese can comprehend Spanish.

First-generation Armenian Americans have tended to pick up English quickly, and second- and third-generation Armenian Americans have typically abandoned Armenian. In the early twentieth century, Armenian American parents spoke a hybrid of Armenian and English with their children that they called "kitchen Armenian." The children tended to speak Armenian outside the home. Third-generation Armenians spoke almost no Armenian at all. Armenians in the diaspora community have begun to worry about the survival of their language and have made efforts to encourage their children to learn Armenian. Armenian is taught at several American colleges and universities, including Stanford University, Boston College, Harvard University, the University of Michigan, and the University of Pennsylvania. Library collections in the Armenian language may be found wherever there is a large Armenian American population. Los Angeles, Chicago, Boston, New York, Detroit, and Cleveland public libraries all have good Armenian-language holdings.

Greetings and Popular Expressions Some common greetings and expressions in Armenian include the following: *Parev*—Hello; *Inch bes es?*—How are you? *Pari louys*—Good morning; *Ksher pari*—Good night; *Pari janabar!*—A good trip!; *Hachoghootiun*—Good luck; *Pari ygak*—Welcome; *Ayo*—Yes; *Voch*—No; *Shnor hagalem*—Thank you; *Paree yegak*—You're welcome; *Abris!*—Well done!; *Oorish or ge desnevink*—See you again; *Shnor nor dari*—Happy New Year;

Shnor soorp dznoort—Merry Christmas; *"Kristos haryav ee merelots"*—"Christ is risen!" (an Easter greeting); *"Ortnial eh harutiun Kristosi!"*—"Blessed is Christ risen!" (said in reply); *Asvadz ortne kezi*—God bless you; *Ge sihrem kezi*—I like you/it; *Hye es?*—Are you Armenian?

RELIGION

The Armenian Apostolic Church, an Oriental Orthodox Christian church, was founded in the first decade of the fourth century, when Gregory the Illuminator began converting large numbers of Armenians to Christianity. Despite these widespread conversions, members of the church consider Thaddeus and Bartholomew, two of Jesus's apostles believed to have proselytized in Armenia in the first century, to be the true founders of the church. Some historians, however, regard the apostles' visit to Armenia as myth or legend. Soon after his own conversion, King Tiridates III appointed Gregory as the first Catholicos, or head of the Armenian Church, and commissioned the building of a cathedral in Echmiadzin, Armenia, which remains the seat of the supreme Catholicos of the worldwide Armenian Apostolic Church.

With the exception of a small minority of Jews in Armenia, there is no other known group of non-Christian Armenians, making Christianity practically a defining feature of Armenian identity.

Practicing Christian Armenians fall into one of three church bodies—Orthodox, Protestant, or Roman Catholic. By far the largest congregation among Armenian Americans is the Armenian Apostolic Church. In the United States, Armenian Apostolic Church priests are elected by laymen and ordained by bishops, but confirmed by the Patriarch, who resides in Armenia. There are lower priests (called *kahanas*) who are allowed to marry. The Armenian Apostolic Church also has higher servants of God (called *vartabeds*) who remain celibate so that they may become bishops. The liturgy (called the *Badarak* in Armenian) is conducted in classical Armenian (*Krapar*) and lasts three hours, but the sermons can be delivered in both English and Armenian. The Apostolic Church typically does not portend to influence its members on social issues of the day—like premarital sex, birth control, homosexuality—and it does not proselytize among non-Armenians. In the United States, the church has been the locus of social and communal life. Many churches offer Armenian classes, help the new immigrants settle in their new homes, and organize activities to educate and entertain their parishioners.

In 1933 the Armenian Apostolic Church in the United States split into two factions over a disagreement on Soviet Russia that erupted into violence. While some argued that Soviet rule over Armenia was necessary, even as native Armenians were losing individual freedom under Stalin, the nationalists among the church members rejected Soviet rule. When nine known nationalists,

or Tashnags as they are called, were convicted of the December 24, 1933, assassination of Archbishop Levon Tourian in New York City, the disagreement became irreparable. Over three decades later, in 1968, with the conflict unresolved, the Tashnags formally created their own prelacy aligning themselves with the Catholicos based in Antelias, Lebanon, rather than the Catholicos based in Echmiadzin. The Armenian Apostolic Church has some 120 parishes in North America, with about 40 churches under the Prelacy.

Protestantism among Armenians dates back to American missionary activity in Anatolia, which began in the early nineteenth century. They were supposed to preach to the Muslims, but the Ottomans did not allow it, so they proselytized to the Armenians. Approximately 10 to 15 percent of Armenian Americans belong to Protestant congregations, most of them in the Armenian Evangelical Union of North America. These Armenians have a reputation as an unusually educated and financially prosperous segment within the Armenian American community. For many decades, Protestant Armenian Americans were known for their relatively quick assimilation into American culture, as they were far less likely than members of the Armenian Apostolic Church to maintain Armenian cultural traditions. However, this trend shifted in the 1970s, when Armenian Protestant churches in the United States held formal meetings with Armenian Apostolic Church leaders and began to incorporate some aspects of the Apostolic service, namely hymns and wine at the Eucharist, into their service. A small group of Armenians practice

Roman Catholicism, with parishes in New York City, Los Angeles, Philadelphia, and Detroit.

CULTURE AND ASSIMILATION

Throughout the diaspora, Armenians have developed a pattern of quick acculturation and slow assimilation. Armenians quickly acculturate to their society, learning the language, attending school, and adapting to economic and political life. Meanwhile, they are resistant to assimilation, maintaining their own schools, churches, associations, and networks of intra-marriage and friendship. For the Armenians who arrived at the turn of the twentieth century, it was especially important that their children marry an Armenian. Because a high percentage of Armenian immigrants were successful in business, Armenians tended to adapt easily to the American business climate. Many of these immigrants became successful entrepreneurs and artisans within years after arriving in the United States, even though they may have initially taken unskilled jobs.

Cuisine The Armenian diet is rich in dairy, oils, and red meats. It emphasizes subtlety of flavors and textures, with many herbs and spices. It also includes nonmeat dishes to accommodate Lent each spring. Because so much time and effort is needed—for marinating, stuffing, and stewing—Armenian restaurants in the United States lean toward expensive multicourse evening fare, not fast food or take-out. Traditional Armenian foods fall into two categories, the shared and the distinctive.

The shared part of the Armenian diet consists of the Mediterranean foods widely familiar among Arabs,

ARMENIAN PROVERBS

- We learn more from a clever rival than a stupid ally.

- It burns only where the fire falls.

- Wherever there are two Armenians there are at least three opinions.

- Mouth to mouth, the splinter becomes a log.

- The older we get, the more our parents know.

- Jealousy first hurts the jealous.

- Money brings wisdom to some, and makes others act foolish.

- In marriage, as in death, you go either to heaven or to hell.

- I'm boss, you're boss. So who grinds the flour?

- Lock your door well: don't make a thief of your neighbor.

- The evil tongue is sharper than a razor, with no remedy for what it cuts.

- The fish begins to smell from its head.

- Fear the man who doesn't fear God.

- A narrow mind has a broad tongue; a sweet tongue will bring the snake from its hole.

- See the mother, marry the girl.

Turks, and Greeks. This includes appetizers such as *humus* (chickpea dip), *baba ganoush* (eggplant dip), *tabouleh* (bulgur wheat salad), *madzoon* (yogurt); main courses like *pilaf* (rice), *imam bayildi* (eggplant casserole), *foule* (beans), *falafel* (chickpea fritters), meat cut into cubes called *kebabs* for barbecue (*shish kebab*) or boiling (*tass kebab*), or ground into *kufta* (meatballs); bakery and desserts like pita bread, *baklawa*, *bourma*, *halawi*, *halvah*, *mamoul*, and *lokhoom*; and beverages like Armenian coffee (also Turkish coffee) and *oghi* (an anise-flavored alcoholic drink, the equivalent of *ouzo* in Greece and *arak* in Lebanon).

The distinctive part of the Armenian diet is unlikely to be found outside an Armenian home or restaurant. This includes appetizers like Armenian string cheese, *manti* (dumplings), *tourshou* (pickled vegetables), *tahnabour* (yogurt soup), *jajik* (spicy yogurt), *basterma* (spicy dried beef), *lahmajun* (ground meat pizza), *midia* (mussels); main courses like *harisse* (lamb pottage), *boeregs* (flaky pastry stuffed with meat,

cheese, or vegetables), *soujuk* (sausage), *tourlu* (vegetable stew), *sarma* (grape leaves stuffed with meat or onion and spices), *dolma* (stuffed zuchini, tomato, eggplant, and other vegetables), *khash* (boiled hooves); bakery and desserts like *lavash* (thin flat bread), *katah* (butter/egg pastry), *choereg* (egg/anise pastry), *katayif* (pancakes stuffed with walnut or cheese and baked), *gatnabour* (rice pudding), *kourabia* (sugar cookies), *kaymak* (thick cream); and beverages like *tahn* (a tart yogurt drink).

Traditional recipes go back centuries. Their preparation, which is typically demanding, has become almost a symbol of survival for Armenians. A vivid example of this occurs each September for the feast of the Cross in Musa Dagh or Musa Ler (Moses's Mountain), the only Armenian village left in the Republic of Turkey today (near Antakya along the Mediterranean). Armenians gather by the thousands at the village of Musa Dagh to share *harrise* porridge for two days and participate in dancing and merriment. This celebrates the survival of a village (as described in Franz Werfel's 1933 novel *Forty Days of Musa Dagh*).

Dances and Songs First-generation Armenian Americans who came to the United States at the turn of the century attempted to preserve Armenian musical culture. Often at dinner parties and picnics Armenian children would be asked to sing traditional songs as an adult played the *oud* (lute) or the *doumbeg* (hand drum). Armenian Americans were known to play the recordings of Armenian composers and singers. The most famous of the Armenian composers was Gomidas Vartabed (1869–1935), who suffered a breakdown during the Armenian genocide and never recovered his sanity, and the most popular singer from the old country was Armen Shah Mouradian (1878–1939). In the 1920s Armenian operas were popular in the United States, and in the 1950s Armenian choir groups were popular in New York and Boston. Dance troupes from Soviet Armenia have drawn capacity crowds when they have toured the United States, and Armenian Americans are known to be especially proud of this aspect of their heritage.

Holidays Traditional holidays celebrated by Armenian Americans include January 6, Armenian Christmas (Epiphany in most other Christian churches, marking the three Magi's visit to Christ); February 10, St. Vartan's Day, commemorating martyr Vartan Mamigonian's battle for religious freedom against the Persians in 451 CE; religious springtime holidays such as Lent, Palm Sunday, Maundy Thursday, Good Friday, and Easter; April 24, Genocide Victims Memorial Day, a day of speeches and marches remembering the date in 1915 when the notables and intellectuals of the Armenian community in Constantinople were rounded up and taken away, never to be seen again; May 28, Independence Day, celebrating the short-lived freedom of the Republic of Armenia from 1918 to 1920, after 500 years of

ARMENIAN SURNAMES

Armenians often have distinctive surnames, which their familiar -*ian* endings make easily recognizable. In about the eighteenth century most Armenians in Anatolia took surnames ending with -*ian*, meaning "of," such as Tashjian (the tailor's family) or Artounian (Artoun's family). In the United States most traditional Armenian surnames today end in -*ian* (like Artounian), which is sometimes spelled -*yan* (as in Artounyan), -*ians* (Artounians), or the more ancient -*ooni* (Artooni). In other cases, Armenians can often detect surnames just by their Armenian root, despite some other suffix adjusted to fit a diaspora Armenian into a local host nation—such as Artounoff (Russia), Artounoglu (Turkey), or Artounescu (Romania). In the United States in the early twentieth century, some Armenians shed their distinctive surnames, typically for briefer ones, but today Armenian Americans take greater pride in their heritage, so name changes are uncommon.

Turkish suzerainty; September 21, the declaration of independence from the Soviet Union in 1991; and December 7, the Day of Remembrance of Victims of the 1988 Earthquake. Armenian Americans celebrate the traditional holidays of the Armenian Apostolic Church, and of the national holidays, they observe the Victims Memorial Day most closely.

FAMILY AND COMMUNITY LIFE

First-generation Armenian American families that arrived at the turn of the century remained very close-knit and conservative. Parents were known to forbid dancing, cosmetics, and unchaperoned dating. Women typically spent weekends cooking in the event that another family stopped by for dinner unannounced. These semi-spontaneous Sunday dinners were a mainstay of the first Armenian American communities on the East Coast, as were large picnics in the spring and summer. These events were known to include as many as 5,000 people and often featured speeches, athletic contests, and concerts.

In the 1960s and 1970s, when later waves of first-generation immigrants arrived in well-established Armenian communities in New York City and Los Angeles, there was some tension between the newcomers and the second- and third-generation Armenian Americans who had assimilated into American culture. New arrivals often wanted to join established groups but tended to be frustrated because they were typically denied leadership positions in these organizations. Some of the new arrivals attempted to revive the Sunday dinners and picnics in their communities, but these were not often well attended by those who had long abandoned these traditions. The wealthier Armenian families that came from the Middle East tended to be

conservative nationalists; they funded programs to revive the Armenian language and sponsored schools that taught the Armenian curriculum.

Gender Roles Armenian Americans have a history of encouraging women to work. As far back as 1910, 25 percent of Armenian American homes reported income from a woman. This remained constant among Armenian immigrants who arrived after World War I, because many of these arrivals were single women with children. Despite earning wages, however, first-generation Armenian American women still bore the burden of most domestic responsibilities. They were expected to take pride in their kitchens and pass cooking skills on to their daughters as well as to instill in their children a sense of their heritage by teaching them Armenian history. Subsequent generations of Armenian American women have been encouraged to work outside the home, and as Armenian Americans have continued to assimilate into the larger culture, women have enjoyed greater socioeconomic freedoms. Consequently, Armenian American social organizations have seen a decline in female membership. With so many women entering the labor force and raising families, they have little time to head up organizations like the Armenian Women's Guild, which experienced a 30 percent drop in membership between 1978 and 2002.

Education Education has been a high priority in Armenians' ancestral culture. A 1986 survey of 584 Armenian Americans found that 41 percent of immigrants, 43 percent of first-generation, and 69 percent of second-generation Armenians had completed a college degree. Another survey of Armenian American adolescents in 1990 found 83 percent plan to attend college. The 1990 U.S. Census similarly found that 41 percent of all Armenian American adults reported some college education—with a baccalaureate completed by 23 percent of men and 19 percent of women. Though these data vary, they all confirm a picture of a people seeking higher education. This trend continued into the early twenty-first century. The American Community Survey estimated in 2011 that 88 percent of Armenian Americans (87 percent of men and 88 percent of women) had graduated from high school, while approximately 40 percent (41 percent of men and 39 percent of women) had earned a bachelor's degree or higher.

There are more than thirty Armenian day schools in North America, educating over 5,500 pupils. Founded by Armenians migrating from the Middle East between 1960 and 1990, these institutions primarily aim to foster ethnic identity, but evidence also documents their effectiveness in preparing students for academic success, in at least two ways. These schools achieve unusually high averages on standardized national tests like the California Achievement Tests, even though the majority of their pupils are foreign-born ESL (English as a Second Language) students.

Graduates of these schools typically go on to scholarships and other successes in their higher education.

In the early twentieth century about twenty U.S. universities offered some program in Armenian studies. By 2005 endowed chairs in Armenian studies existed at University of California, Berkeley; University of California, Los Angeles; California State University, Fresno; Columbia University; Harvard University; the University of Michigan; and the University of Pennsylvania.

EMPLOYMENT AND ECONOMIC CONDITIONS

The majority of early Armenian immigrants took unskilled jobs in wire mills, garment factories, silk mills, or vineyards in California. Second-generation Armenian Americans were more professional and often obtained managerial positions. Third-generation Armenian Americans, as well as Armenian immigrants who came after World War II, were well educated and largely attracted to careers in business; they also had a penchant toward engineering, medicine, the sciences, and technology. These immigrants have tended to do well economically, with a large fraction achieving affluence within their first generation in the United States, primarily by working long hours in their own family businesses.

Americans of Armenian descent have continued to find success in many fields of employment.

According to the American Community Survey's estimates in 2011, 42 percent of the eligible population of Armenian Americans were employed in management, business, science, and arts professions, and close to 25 percent were employed in educational, health care, and social services. The ACS also estimated that Armenian American households had a median income of $55,420, slightly higher than the national average of $52,762. Individually, however, Armenian American men had a median income of approximately $53,000 a year, almost $10,000 higher than the median income for female Armenian Americans.

POLITICS AND GOVERNMENT

Armenian Americans have an influential ethnic lobby in the United States. Armenian American organizations and politicians have helped to normalize relations between the United States and Armenia, providing for economic, material, and diplomatic assistance to the country, including nearly two billion dollars annually for humanitarian aid and disaster relief. In spite of the lobbying groups' many successes, Armenian Americans have yet to realize their most important goal: formal recognition of the Armenian genocide by the United States government. Although President Reagan, President Clinton, both Bush administrations, and the Obama administration have recognized the event as a tragedy and a massacre, as of 2013 no U.S. administration had formally described it as "genocide."

A group of Armenian immigrant women weave a rug on a loom. CORBIS-BETTMANN. REPRODUCED BY PERMISSION.

With regard to American politics, Armenian Americans have been active in almost every level of government in both political parties. Notable politicians include Steven Derounian (1918–2007), a U.S. congressman who represented New York from 1952 to 1964, and Walter Karabian (1938–), who was a California state senator for several years. Republican Harry Tutunjian served as mayor of Troy, New York, between 2003 and 2012. Democrat Joe Simitian (1953–) served as a California state senator between 2004 and 2012, and in 2010 Paul Krekorian (1960–), a Democrat, was elected to the Los Angeles City Council for District 2. Anna Eshoo (1942–) represented California's 14th district in the U.S. House of Representatives between 1993 and 2013, until redistricting. In 2012 she was elected as the Representative for California's 18th district. Jacki Speier (1950–), also a Democrat, served in the California State Assembly from 1986 to 1996, the California State Senate from 1998 to 2006, and the U.S. House of Representatives beginning in 2008.

In the 1990s a few Armenian Americans returned to Armenia, securing influential political positions. Raffi Hovannisian (1959–) was appointed the foreign minister of Armenia in 1991. After resigning the following year, Hovannisian assumed a role as one of the major opposition leaders in Armenia. Sebouh "Steve" Tashjian served as the first minister of energy, and Gerard Libaridian (1945–) served as an advisor to President Levon Ter-Petrosyan.

Armenian Americans have an influential ethnic lobby in the United States. Armenian American organizations and politicians have helped to normalize relations between the United States and Armenia, providing for economic, material, and diplomatic assistance to the country, including nearly two billion dollars annually for humanitarian aid and disaster relief.

NOTABLE INDIVIDUALS

Academia James der Derian (1955–) is the director of the Centre for International Security Studies at the University of Sydney and a research professor at Watson Institute for International Studies at Brown University. His publications include *Virtuous War: Mapping the Military-Industrial-Media-Entertainment Network* (2009) and *Antidiplomacy: Spies, Terror, Speed and War* (1992).

Kamer Daron Acemoğlu (1967–), the Elizabeth and James Killian Professor of Economics at MIT, is widely recognized as one of the leading economists in the United States. In 2005 Acemoğlu was awarded the John Bates Clark Medal, given to an accomplished economist under the age of forty who has made significant contributions to the field.

Paul Boghossian is the Silver Professor of Philosophy at New York University, where he also served as Chair of Philosophy from 1994 to 2004. He is director of the New York Institute of Philosophy. His publications include *Fear of Knowledge: Against Relativism and Constructivism* (2006), which was recognized by *Choice*, a leading reviewer of academic publications, as an Outstanding Academic Book in 2006, and *Content and Justification: Philosophical Papers* (2008).

Vartan Gregorian (1934–) holds a PhD in history from Stanford University and has served as dean of the Faculty of Arts and Sciences at the University of Pennsylvania (1974–1978), president of the New York Public Library (1981–1988), and president of Brown University (1988–1997). In 1997 Gregorian became president of the Carnegie Corporation of New York, one of the most prestigious educational foundations in the United States.

Art Arshile Gorky (1904–1948) was an Armenian American painter whose work, many believe, influenced the New York City painters who would later develop abstract expressionism. Born in Khorgom, a small town near the eastern border of present-day Turkey, Gorky fled his home with his mother and three sisters in 1915 to escape the Armenian genocide.

Harry Naltchayan (1925–1994), a photographer of Armenian descent born in Beirut, came to the United States when he was twenty-three and worked for the *Washington Post* for thirty-five years. He was a veteran of numerous dangerous assignments in the Middle East and won several awards for his work, including first place in the World Press Photo Contest in 1982 for a picture of Richard Nixon, Gerald Ford, Ronald Reagan, and Jimmy Carter that is known among photojournalists as "Modern Day Rushmore."

Business Alex Manoogian (1901–1996), a Detroit-based entrepreneur, founded the Masco Corporation, which consists of over twenty companies that sell home-building and home-improvement products. As of 2013 the Masco Corporation had 32,500 employees and an estimated annual revenue of over $10 billion. In 1966 Manoogian donated his home to the city of Detroit, and it has served as the official mayor's mansion since that time.

Kirk Kerkorian (1917–), former owner of film studio Metro-Goldwyn-Mayer (MGM), participated in the building of several famous resorts in Las Vegas, including Caesar's Palace and the International Hotel.

David Shakarian (1914–1984) was the founder of General Nutrition Centers, Inc. (GNC), which sells nutritional products including vitamins, energy bars, and supplements to physical fitness enthusiasts. Shakarian opened his first store under the name Lackzoom in 1935 in Pittsburgh (he did not adopt the name General Nutrition Center until the 1960s).

Literature Eric Bogosian (1953–) is an Armenian American playwright best known for the Pulitzer-Prize finalist *Talk Radio* (1987), a brash play about a late-night radio host who takes calls from a series of troubled callers as producers observe his work to determine whether or not they will give the DJ his big break and air his show on national radio. Bogosian himself played the lead in the play's original run. It was adapted into a successful movie by Oliver Stone in 1988. Bogosian has had a number of other plays produced and staged numerous one-man shows off-Broadway. He has also acted in several other films and television shows, including *Law and Order: Criminal Intent*, on which he played a regular character from 2006 to 2010.

Michael Arlen (1895–1956), born Dikran Kouyoumdijan to Armenian parents in Bulgaria, published nine novels, including a number of the psychological thrillers. Most notable is *The Green Hat* (1924), which was adapted into a play and, after a successful run on Broadway, a movie that was banned in the United States for references to homosexuality and venereal disease. Later in his career Arlen wrote science fiction and overtly political novels. The best known of these works is *The Flying Dutchman* (1939), which criticizes German politics in the years leading up to World War II.

Nancy Kricorian (1961–) is an Armenian American writer whose publications include the novel *All the Light There Was* (2013). Kricorian's poetry has appeared in numerous American literary magazines. She has held teaching posts at several leading institutions, including Yale and Columbia universities.

William Saroyan (1908–1981), an Armenian American playwright, is perhaps best known for refusing the Pulitzer Prize for *The Time of Your Life* (1939), a play set in a shabby San Francisco bar where the main character, Joe, amuses himself by encouraging a collection of eccentrics to pursue their ambitions. A prolific writer, Saroyan published more than forty novels and plays as well as sixteen short stories.

Medicine Varaztad Kazanjian (1879–1974) was an Armenian American oral surgeon widely recognized as one of the leaders in the field of modern plastic surgery. Kazanjian was moved to pursue innovations in reconstructive surgery by his experiences volunteering for the Harvard Medical Corps in World War I.

Jack Kevorkian (1928–2011) was an Armenian American pathologist and a polarizing figure in the medical community, as well as in American popular culture, for claiming that terminally ill patients had a right to die. Kevorkian is said to have helped well over 100 terminal patients commit suicide. He was unsuccessfully tried for second-degree murder four times and was finally convicted in 1999 after *60 Minutes* aired a videotape of Kevorkian administering a lethal injection to a terminal patient named Thomas Youk. After his release from prison in 2007, Kevorkian lectured at

An Armenian baker displays his wares. AP PHOTO / REED SAXON

universities throughout the United States and made numerous television appearances. In 2008 he ran unsuccessfully for U.S. Congress from Michigan's ninth congressional district.

Raymond Damadian (1936–), an Armenian American physician, gained fame for inventing the first Magnetic Resonance (MR) Scanning Machine. After over seven years of development, Damadian and his team performed the first MRI on a human being on July 3, 1977.

Music Alan Hovhaness (1911–2000), born Alan Vaness Chakmakjian, was an Armenian American composer who wrote more than 500 original works. Hovhaness did not become a full-time composer until 1951, when he left a teaching post at the Boston Conservatory and moved to New York. In the early part of his career, Hovhaness studied Armenian culture closely and attempted to incorporate aspects of it into his work. In the late 1950s he embarked on a trip through Asia in order to draw from a wider range of influences. He spent the final twenty years of his prolific career in Seattle.

Cathy Berberian (1925–1983) was an Armenian American soprano known for interpreting works of avant-garde composers such as John Cage, Igor Stravinsky, and Sylvano Bussotti. In addition to her work in classical music, Berbian also released *Beatles Arias*, a 1967 album in which she covers twelve Beatles songs arranged as chamber music and sung in a baroque style.

Public Affairs Charles Garry (1909–1991) was an Armenian American attorney whose clients included the Black Panther Party, the Peoples Temple (a cult founded by Jim Jones and made infamous by a mass suicide in 1978 at their settlement in Guyana), and the Oakland Seven (San Francisco–based anti-Vietnam war protestors). Garry began representing the Peoples Temple in 1977 in several cases in which they asserted that the U.S. government had conspired to undermine their community in Guyana. Garry eventually came to believe that there was no such conspiracy. Although he continued to practice law after the mass suicide of 1978, his days as a high-profile civil rights attorney were over.

George Deukmejian (1928–), a Republican, was the governor of California from 1983 to 1991. Popular among California conservatives for his stance on crime, Deukmejian was nearly chosen in 1984 to be Ronald Reagan's running mate. George H. W. Bush also considered asking to Deukmejian to run with him on the Republican presidential ticket in 1988.

Raffi Hovannisian (1959–) is an Armenian American who was born in California to parents who had survived the Armenian genocide. He immigrated to Armenia in 1990 and served as the country's minister of foreign affairs from 1991 to 1992. Hovannisian founded the Armenian Center for National and International Studies in 1994. He ran for president of Armenia in 2013 but lost, earning 37 percent of the vote.

Sports Andre Agassi (1970–) is a former professional tennis player who won more than 60 titles including four Australian Open championships and the 1992 Wimbledon championship. His father was an Iranian-born ethnic Armenian. In 2010 Agassi published *Open*, a candid autobiography in which he discusses his struggles with celebrity and admits to drug use.

Ara Parseghian (1923–) is a professional football player and college head football coach. He won two national titles as head coach at the University of Notre Dame.

Stage and Screen Akim Tamiroff (1899–1972), an Armenian actor, was born in what is now the country of Georgia and moved to the United States in 1923. He appeared in more than sixty Hollywood movies between 1932 and 1972. In 1943 he won the Golden Globe for Best Supporting Actor for his role as Pablo in *For Whom the Bell Tolls*, an adaptation of Ernest Hemingway's 1940 novel.

Arlene Francis (1907–2001) was an Armenian American actress who appeared in numerous Broadway plays, hosted a New York–based radio show for twenty-five years, and appeared on numerous game shows, including *Match Game*, *Password*, and most notably *What's My Line?*, for which she served as a panelist on numerous occasions throughout its twenty-five-year run from 1950 to 1975.

Cher (1946–) is an Armenian American singer and actress who first became famous performing folk songs in the mid-1960s with Sonny Bono, her husband at the time. After their musical careers sputtered at the end of the 1960s, the duo regained their popularity with a variety show, *The Sonny & Cher Comedy Hour*, which aired for four seasons (1971–1974) on CBS. The couple divorced in 1977, at which point Cher launched a successful solo music and acting career, appearing in numerous critically acclaimed and popular films, including *Silkwood*, *The Witches of Eastwick*, and *Moonstruck*. She won an Academy Award in 1988 for her performance in *Moonstruck*. Her most famous single is "If I Could Turn Back Time," which was released in 1989 and hit number 3 on the Billboard singles chart. Cher is the only performer to have won an Emmy Award, a Grammy Award, and an Academy Award.

Kim Kardashian (1980–) is an Armenian American reality television star who has appeared on *Keeping Up with the Kardashians*, *Kourtney and Kim Take New York*, and *Kourtney and Kim Take Miami*. A fixture on the tabloid covers in the early twenty-first century, Kardashian drew considerable scorn from the public when she filed for divorce after having been married to professional basketball player Kris Humphries for just seventy-two days.

Ross Bagdasarian Sr. (1919–1972) was a singer and actor who best known for creating *Alvin and the Chipmunks*. Working under the stage name David Seville, Bagdasarian appeared in the Broadway production of William Saroyan's *The Time of Your Life* and had small parts in numerous Hollywood films. In 1958 Badasarian's song "Witch Doctor" hit number one on American music charts, and the following year he won two Grammy Awards for a *Chipmunks* Christmas song.

Rouben Mamoulian (1897–1987) was an Armenian American director born in present-day Georgia. He came to the United States in 1922, when he accepted a teaching position at the Eastman School of Music. After directing several successful talkies in the 1930s, including what is widely considered to be the best adaptation of *Dr. Jekyll and Mr. Hyde*, Mamoulian emerged as on one of Hollywood's leading directors with the success of *The Mark of Zorro* (1940). He also directed the original Broadway production of

Oklahoma!, for which he earned widespread critical and popular acclaim.

Steven Zaillian (1953–) has written screenplays for critically acclaimed films such as *Schindler's List* (1993), *Searching for Bobby Fischer* (1993), *Gangs of New York* (2002), *All the King's Men* (2006), *Moneyball* (2011), and *The Girl with the Dragon Tattoo* (2011).

MEDIA

PRINT

Armenian Mirror-Spectator

Weekly community newspaper founded in 1932 and published in Armenian and English.

Alin K. Gregorian, Editor
Baikar Association, Inc.
755 Mount Auburn Street
Watertown, Massachusetts 02472-1509
Phone: (617) 924-4420
Fax: (617) 924-2887
Email: editor@mirrorspectator.com
URL: www.mirrorspectator.com

Armenian Observer

A weekly, English-only Armenian newspaper based in Hollywood, California, that has been in circulation since 1969. The paper covers issues local, national, and international issues concerning Armenia and the diaspora.

Osheen Keshishian, Editor
6646 Hollywood Boulevard No. 210
Los Angeles, California 90028
Phone: (323) 467-6767
Email: okesh@aol.com
URL: www.thearmenianobserver.com

Armenian Reporter International

An independent, English-language Armenian news weekly that since 1967 has covered Armenian American community news; U.S. and international politics as they relate to Armenians; Armenia and Nagorno-Karabakh; and Armenians in arts, culture, and entertainment.

Vincent Lima, Managing Editor
2727 West Alameda Boulevard
Burbank, California 91505
Phone: (718) 380-3636
Fax: (718) 380-8057
URL: www.reporter.am

Armenian Review

A quarterly academic journal on Armenian issues, published since 1948 by the largest Armenian political party, the Armenian Revolutionary Federation.

Asbed Kotchikian
80 Bigelow Avenue
Watertown, Massachusetts 02172
Phone: (617) 926-4037
Email: editor@armenianreview.org
URL: www.armenianreview.org

Armenian Weekly

A periodical covering Armenian interests in English.

Vahe Habeshian, Editor
Hairenik Association, Inc.
80 Bigelow Avenue
Watertown, Massachusetts 02472
Phone: (617) 926-3974
Fax: (617) 926-1750
Email: armenianweekly@hairenik.com
URL: www.armenianweekly.com

California Courier

English-language ethnic newspaper covering news and commentary for Armenian Americans.

Harut Sassounian, Editor
P.O. Box 5390
Glendale, California 91221
Phone: (818) 409-0949

RADIO

Armenian Radio Hour of New Jersey

Broadcasts Armenian music and information of interest to Armenian Americans living in New Jersey and New York City on 89.5 FM every Sunday from 2:00 to 4:00 p.m.

15 Hart Drive South
South Orange, New Jersey 07079
URL: www.armenianradionj.net

ORGANIZATIONS AND ASSOCIATIONS

Armenian Assembly of America (AAA)

Founded in 1972, AAA is a nonprofit public affairs office that tries to communicate the Armenian voice to government, increase the involvement of Armenians in public affairs, and sponsor activities fostering unity among Armenian groups.

Bryan Ardouny, Executive Director
1334 G Street NW
Suite 200
Washington, D.C. 20005
Phone: (202) 393-3434
Fax: (202) 638-4904
Email: info@aaainc.org
URL: www.aaainc.org

Armenian General Benevolent Union (AGBU)

Founded in 1906 in Egypt by statesman Boghos Nubar, this wealthy service group operates internationally, with some sixty chapters in North America. AGBU resources are focused on specific projects chosen by its Honorary Life President and Central Committee—sponsoring its own schools, scholarships, relief efforts, cultural and youth groups, and, since 1991, a free English-language news magazine. More than any major diaspora group, AGBU has had close ties with Armenia, in both the Soviet and post-Soviet eras.

Berge Setrakian, President
55 East 59th Street
New York, New York 10022-1112
Phone: (212) 319-6383

Fax: (212) 319-6507
Email: hello@agbu.org
URL: agbu.org

Armenian National Committee (ANC)

Founded in 1958, the ANC is a political lobby group for Armenian Americans.

Aram S. Hamparian, Executive Director
1711 N Street NW
Washington, D.C. 20036
Phone: (202) 775-1918
Fax: (202) 775-5648
Email: anca@anca.org
URL: www.anca.org

Armenian Network of America (ANA)

A nonpolitical social organization founded in 1983. With chapters in several U.S. cities, ANA appeals to young professionals.

Meganoosh Avakian, President
P.O. Box 100865
Arlington, Virginia 22210-3865
Email: info@Armnet.org
URL: www.armnet.org

Society for Armenian Studies (SAS)

Promotes the study of Armenia and related geographic areas, as well as issues related to the history and culture of Armenia.

Barlow Der Mugrdechian, SAS Secretariat
Armenian Studies Program
California State University, Fresno
5245 North Backer Avenue PB4
Fresno, California 93740-8001
Phone: (559) 278-2669
Fax: (559) 278-2129
Email: barlowd@csufresno.edu
URL: www.fresnostate.edu/artshum/armenianstudies/sas/

MUSEUMS AND RESEARCH CENTERS

Armenian Library and Museum of America (ALMA)

ALMA houses a library of over 10,000 volumes and audiovisual materials as well as several permanent and visiting collections of Armenian artifacts dating as far back as 3000 BCE.

65 Main Street
Watertown, Massachusetts 02472
Phone: (617) 926-2562
Fax: (617) 926-0175
URL: www.almainc.org

National Association for Armenian Studies and Research (NAASR)

NAASR fosters the study of Armenian history, culture, and language on an active, scholarly, and continuous basis in American institutions of higher education. The association publishes a newsletter, the *Journal of Armenian Studies*. Its building houses its large mail-order bookshop and a library of more than 12,000 volumes, 100 periodicals, and diverse audio-visual materials.

Raffi P. Yeghiayan, Board Chairman
395 Concord Avenue
Belmont, Massachusetts 02478-3049
Phone: (617) 489-1610
Fax: (617) 484-1759
Email: hq@naasr.org
URL: naasr.org

SOURCES FOR ADDITIONAL STUDY

Alexander, Benjamin F. "Contested Memories, Divided Diaspora: Armenian Americans, the Thousand-Day Republic, and the Polarized Response to an Archbishop's Murder." *Journal of American Ethnic History* 27, no. 1 (2007): 32–59.

Aslanian, Sebouh David. *From the Indian Ocean to the Mediterranean: The Global Trade Networks of Armenian Merchants in New Julfa.* Berkeley: University of California Press, 2011.

Bagdikian, Ben H. *Double Vision: Reflections on My Heritage, Life, and Profession.* Boston: Beacon Press, 1995.

Bakalian, Anny P. *Armenian-Americans: From Being to Feeling Armenian.* New Brunswick, NJ: Transaction, 1993.

"A Century of Armenians in America: New Social Science Research." Special Issue, *Journal of the Society for Armenian Studies* 17–18 (2008).

Douglas, Daniel, and Anny Bakalian. "Sub-Ethnic Diversity: Armenians in the United States." *Journal of the Society for Armenian Studies* 18, no. 2 (2009): 37–51.

Hovannisian, Richard G., ed. *The Armenian Genocide: Cultural and Ethical Legacies.* New Brunswick: Transaction, 2008.

Jendian, Matthew A. *Becoming American, Remaining Ethnic: The Case of Armenian-Americans in Central California.* New York: LFB Scholarly Publishing LLC, 2008.

Mirak, Robert. *Torn between Two Lands.* Cambridge, MA: Harvard University Press, 1983.

Panossian, Razmik. *The Armenians: From Kings and Priests to Merchants and Commissars.* New York: Columbia University Press, 2006.

ASIAN INDIAN AMERICANS
Tinaz Pavri

OVERVIEW

Asian Indian Americans are immigrants or descendants of immigrants from India, the most populous country in South Asia. Bounded by Nepal and the Himalayan mountains to the north, Pakistan to the northwest, the Indian Ocean to the south, the Arabian Sea to the west, and the Bay of Bengal to the east, India occupies about 1,560,000 square miles, making it approximately half the size of the United States.

Second in population only to China, India is home to around 1.2 billion people of diverse ethnicity, religion, and language, as reported by 2011 World Bank figures. About 80.5 percent of all Indians are Hindus. Approximately 13.4 percent are Muslims, and smaller minorities include Christians, Sikhs, Buddhists, Jains, and Zoroastrians. Although official Indian languages include Hindi, which is spoken by about 40 percent of the population, and English, hundreds of dialects are also spoken in India. In recent years, India has ceased to be looked upon as a poor country and is considered one of the ten largest economies in the world.

Asian Indians began to arrive in the United States in the middle of the nineteenth century. The earliest were Sikhs, a religious subgroup, who worked in agriculture and construction on the west coast. Immigration accelerated during the 1960s, with many Indians arriving to receive higher education. This trend continued in the early twenty-first century. According to the *Chronicle of Higher Education*, in 2012 India sent the second-highest number of students for study in the United States. Asian Indians also arrived to take jobs in the information technology industry and other professional arenas as well as in the service industry.

According to the 2010 U.S. Census, 3.2 million Asian Indians live in the United States. They are spread throughout the country, although the largest communities tend to be in large metropolitan areas such as New York and Chicago.

HISTORY OF THE PEOPLE

Early History One of the world's oldest civilizations, the Indus Valley civilization (2500–1700 BCE) flourished across present-day India, Bangladesh, and Pakistan. Dravidians comprised India's earliest ethnic group. They gradually moved south as migrating Aryan tribes entered the region. These tribes established many empires, including the Nanda and Gupta kingdoms in northern India. Alexander the Great invaded northern India in the fourth century BCE.

The first Islamic presence, through Arab traders in southern India, occurred around the seventh century. In about the tenth century, Islamic raiders began their invasions of India. The earliest invaders were the Turks, followed by members of the Moghul Dynasty in the sixteenth century. The Moghul Dynasty established a thriving empire in northern India. These Muslim invasions resulted in the conversion of a section of the populace to Islam, establishing forever a significant Muslim society in India.

By 1600 the British had established a presence in India through the East India Company, a trading company that exported raw materials such as spices out of India to the West. Britain then strengthened its hold over its Indian colony by installing a parliament, courts, and bureaucracy. Several independent Hindu and Muslim kingdoms, however, continued to exist within the broader framework of British rule. The British army existed to maintain internal order and control uprisings against the colonizing government by the Indian people.

Modern Era In 1885 the British sanctioned the formation of the Indian National Congress, of which an offshoot, the Congress party, remained one of India's most important political parties. The British hoped that the party would quell growing resistance to British rule by co-opting some of India's most politically aware and educated individuals into the bounds of British rule. Instead, the Indian National Congress became the vehicle through which Indians coordinated their struggle for freedom from British rule. An indigenous independence movement spearheaded by Mahatma Gandhi and Jawaharlal Nehru—later free India's first prime minister—gained strength in the early twentieth century.

India's movement for independence was marked by nonviolence as hundreds of thousands of Indians responded to Gandhi's call for *satyagraha*, which means to be steadfast in truth. *Satyagraha* involved nonviolent protest through passive noncooperation with the British at every level. Indians simply refused

to participate in any activity over which there was British supervision, thus making it impossible for the British to continue to govern India.

Britain formally relinquished its hold over India in 1947, and two sovereign countries, India and Pakistan, were created out of British India. The partition of the two nations was a result of irreconcilable differences between Hindu and Muslim leadership. India became mostly Hindu and Pakistan was mostly Muslim. Modern India, however, was a secular nation.

Nehru and his political party, the Congress, remained in power until his death in 1964. Leaving a lasting legacy, Nehru molded independent India's economy, society, and polity. Lal Bahadur Shastri became India's second prime minister, and upon his death was succeeded by Nehru's daughter Indira Gandhi, who remained in power until 1977, when, for the first time, the Congress lost in parliamentary elections, to the opposition Janata party. Indira's loss was largely due to the increasingly authoritarian tactics she had adopted before she was voted out of power. Morarji Desai, the leader of the Janata party, became India's fourth prime minister.

Indira Gandhi and the Congress returned to power in 1980, and upon her assassination in 1984 her son Rajiv Gandhi was elected prime minister. In 1991 Rajiv Gandhi was assassinated by a Tamil suicide bomber. In 1994 the Congress, with Narasimha Rao as prime minister, instituted unprecedented and far-reaching economic reforms in the country. The Rao government succeeded in some measure in dismantling Nehru's socialist-style restrictions on the economy and private industry. By the early twenty-first century, India's exports had increased significantly, its foreign exchange reserves were at their highest levels in decades, and the economy appeared robust after weathering the global recession of 2008.

Economic liberalization, however, caused widening discrepancies between the wealthy and the poor. Moreover, a rising tide of religious fundamentalism, religious tensions, and frequent terrorist attacks threatened India's otherwise promising future. For the first time since independence, a powerful political party, the Bharatiya Janata Party (Indian People's Party), whose rise in Indian politics during the 1980s and 1990s was meteoric, challenged the prevalent belief in and acceptance of India's secularism, maintaining instead that India was a Hindu state. The party led the government from 1998 to 2004 and found widespread support in some areas of India and in some sections of the Asian Indian community in the United States and Europe. Coalition governments became the norm in Indian politics.

SETTLEMENT IN THE UNITED STATES

In many accounts, immigrants to the United States from India, Pakistan, and Bangladesh are referred to as Asian Indians. The first Asian Indians, or Indian Americans, as they are also known, arrived in the United States as early as the middle of the nineteenth century. By the end of the nineteenth century, about two thousand Indians, most of them Sikhs (a religious minority from India's Punjab region), settled on the West Coast of the United States, having come in search of economic opportunity. The majority of Sikhs worked in agriculture and construction. Other Asian Indians came as merchants and traders; many worked in lumber mills and logging camps in the western states of Oregon, Washington, and California, where they rented bunkhouses, acquired knowledge of English, and assumed Western dress. Most of the Sikhs, however, refused to cut their hair or beards or forsake the wearing of turbans their religion required. In 1907 about two thousand Indians, alongside other immigrants from China, Japan, Korea, Norway, and Italy, worked on the building of the Western Pacific Railway in California. Other Indians helped build bridges and tunnels for California's other railroad projects.

Between 1910 and 1920, as agricultural work in California began to become more abundant and better paying, many Indian immigrants turned to the fields and orchards for employment. For many of the immigrants who had come from villages in rural India, farming was both familiar and preferable. There is evidence that Indians began to bargain, often successfully, for better wages during this time. Some Indians eventually settled permanently in the California valleys where they worked. Despite the 1913 Alien Land Law, enacted by the California legislature to discourage Japanese immigrants from purchasing land, many Asian Indians bought land; by 1920 Asian Indians owned 38,000 acres in California's Imperial Valley and 85,000 acres in the Sacramento Valley. Because there was virtually no immigration by Indian women during this time, it was not unheard of for Indian males to marry Mexican women and raise families.

At the beginning of the twentieth century, about one hundred Indian students studied in universities across the United States. During the summers, Indian students in California often worked in the fields and orchards alongside their countrymen. A small group of Indian immigrants also came to the United States as political refugees from British rule. To them, the United States seemed the ideal place for their revolutionary activities. In fact, many of these revolutionaries returned to India in the early part of the twentieth century to assume important roles in the struggle for independence.

The turn of the century also saw increasing violence against Asian Indians in the western states. White workers occasionally organized expulsions of Indians from the communities in which they worked. Some Indians who had migrated for economic reasons returned to India after they had saved respectable sums of money in the United States; others stayed, putting down roots in the West. The immigration of Indians to the United States was tightly controlled by the

American government during this time, and Indians applying for visas to travel to the United States were often rejected. The Asiatic Exclusion League was organized in 1907 to encourage the expulsion of Asian workers, including Indians. In addition, several pieces of legislation were introduced in the United States, specifically the congressional exclusion laws of 1917 and 1923 that attempted either to restrict the entry of Indians and other Asians or to deny them residence and citizenship rights. Some of these were defeated, while others were adopted. For instance, a literacy clause was added to a number of bills, requiring that immigrants pass a literacy test to be considered eligible for citizenship, thus effectively barring many Indians.

In July 1946 Congress passed a bill allowing naturalization for Indians, and in 1957 the first Asian Indian congressman, Dalip Saund, was elected to Congress. Like many early Indian immigrants, Saund came to the United States from Punjab and had worked in the fields and farms of California. He also earned a doctorate at the University of California at Berkeley. While more educated and professional Indians began to enter the United States, immigration restrictions and tight quotas ensured that only small numbers of Indians entered, prior to 1965. Overall, approximately six thousand Asian Indians immigrated to the United States between 1947 and 1965.

After 1965 a second significant wave of Indian immigration began, spurred by a change in U.S. immigration law that lifted quotas and restrictions and allowed significant numbers of Asians to immigrate. Between 1965 and 1974, Indian immigration to the United States increased at a rate greater than that from almost any other country. This wave of immigrants was very different from the earliest Indian immigrants—Indians that emigrated after 1965 were overwhelmingly urban, professional, and highly educated and quickly engaged in gainful employment in many American cities. Many had prior exposure to Western society and education, and their transition to the United States was therefore relatively smooth. More than one hundred thousand such professionals and their families entered the United States in the decade after 1965.

Almost 40 percent of all Indian immigrants who entered the United States in the decades after 1965 arrived on student or exchange visitor visas, in some cases with their spouses and dependents. Most students pursued graduate degrees in a variety of disciplines. They were often able to find promising jobs and prosper economically, and many became permanent residents and then citizens. The number of Indian students in the United States increased to 104,000, as of 2011. Many will no doubt remain in the United States to swell the ranks of Asian Indian Americans.

The 2010 U.S. Census reports 3.2 million Asian Indians in the United States, and they are one of the fastest-growing ethnic groups in the United States.

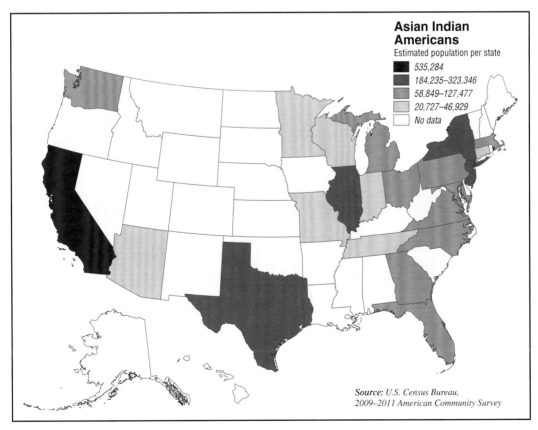

Source: U.S. Census Bureau, 2009–2011 American Community Survey

New York, California, and New Jersey are the states with the highest concentrations of Asian Indians. In California, where the first Indian immigrants arrived, the cities of San Francisco and Los Angeles are home to the oldest established Asian Indian communities in the United States.

In general, the Asian Indian community has preferred to settle in the larger American cities rather than smaller towns, especially in New York, Los Angeles, San Francisco, Chicago, and more recently, Atlanta. This appears to reflect both the availability of jobs in larger cities and the personal preference of living in urban, ethnically diverse environments, which are evocative of the Indian cities that many of the post-1965 immigrants originally came from. Still, there are sizeable Asian Indian communities in suburban areas, including Silver Springs (Maryland), San Jose and Fremont (California), and Queens (New York). Many highly educated Asian Indian immigrants have little trouble assimilating into the mainstream of American life.

LANGUAGE

India is a multilingual country with several language families and hundreds of languages and dialects. About twenty-four of these dialects are spoken by over one million people. This diversity is reflected in the Asian Indian community in America. First-generation Indians continue to speak their native language within the family—with spouses, members of the extended family, and friends within the community. Most also speak English fluently, which has eased the transition to American society for many Indian immigrants.

Regional linguistic differences are prevalent. Hindi is spoken mostly by Asian Indians from northern India and is generally not spoken by southern Indians. Immigrants from the states of southern India speak regional languages such as Tamil, Telegu, or Malayalam. A substantial number of immigrants from western India, particularly those from the state of Gujarat, continue to speak Gujarati, while those from the region of Bengal speak Bengali. Most second- and third-generation Asian Indians understand the language spoken by their parents and extended family but tend not to speak it themselves. Many Asian Indians are multilingual and speak several Indian languages. Thus, a Gujarati speaker was likely to know Hindi, as well.

Greetings and Popular Expressions Common Asian Indian greetings tend to be in Hindi or Hindustani, and include such greetings as *namaste* (pronounced "namastay"), the equivalent of "hello." This greeting is usually accompanied by the palms of one's hands pressed together against the chest. *Aapkaisehai* is the equivalent of the universal query "how are you?" *Theek* ("fine") is the response. For Muslims, the traditional Islamic greetings of *salaam aleikum* (pronounced "sullahm allaykum"), "peace be upon you," is the most common.

RELIGION

The earliest Hindu *mandir*, or temple, in the United States—the "old temple"—existed in San Francisco as early as 1920, but in general the religious needs of Hindu Asian Indians prior to the 1950s were served mainly through ethnic and community organizations such as the Hindu Society of India. Since the 1950s, Hindu and Sikh temples have been built in cities with high concentrations of Asian Indians such as New York, Los Angeles, and Chicago, while Asian Muslims worship at mosques and Christians at existing churches. Many Indian Christian denominations exist, such as the Indian Orthodox church, the Syrian-Malabar Church, or the Church of North India. By the early twenty-first century, there were thousands of places of worship for Asian Indians around the United States.

All Hindus, regardless of their regional differences and the particular gods they worship, tend to worship at available temples, although many large cities had multiple temples reflecting differences in worship according to community, region, and language. Brahmin priests typically lead the service and recite from scriptures. Services can be conducted in Sanskrit, Hindi, or the regional languages. *Poojas*, or religious ceremonies that celebrate auspicious occasions such as the birth of a child, are also performed by priests. Although some priests serve full time, others might have a second occupation in addition to performing priestly duties.

Although some Asian Indians visited temples regularly, others limited their visits to important religious occasions. Because Hinduism tends to be less formally organized than other religions, prayer meetings can also be conducted at individuals' homes. It is also quite common for Asian Indian homes to have a small room or a part of a room reserved for prayer and meditation. Such household shrines were central to a family's religious life.

Many Asian Indians practice Islam. Many Asian Indian Muslims attend mosques with Muslims who trace their origins to other parts of the world or in primarily South Asian mosques.

The Asian Indian community in the United States also included small numbers of Buddhists, as well as Jains, followers of Mahavira. The most unique feature of the Jain religion, which was founded in the sixth century BCE, is its belief in the doctrine of *ahimsa*, or nonviolence. This belief leads Jains to practice strict vegetarianism. The Jains in the United States had their own temples for worship. Buddhists, Jains, and Hindus all placed a great value on personal austerity and were concerned with the final escape from the cycle of birth and rebirth known as reincarnation.

Small but significant Zoroastrian, or Parsi, communities settled in cities such as New York and Los Angeles. The Parsis came to India as refugees from Arab-invaded Persia in the ninth and tenth centuries;

they made significant economic and social contributions to the country. Earliest reports of Parsi immigrants to the United States dated from the turn of the twentieth century, when groups of Parsis entered the country as merchants and traders.

Of all the Asian Indian religious communities, the Sikhs are the oldest and tend to be the most well organized in terms of religious activity. Sikhism is different from Hinduism, in its belief in one God. Sikhs follow the teachings of Guru Nanak, the founder of the religion, and worship in temples called *gurudwaras*. Services in *gurudwaras* are held about once a week as well as on religious occasions. Tenets of the Sikh religion include wearing a turban on the head for males and a symbolic bangle called a *kara* around their wrists. In addition, orthodox Sikh males cannot cut their hair or beards. This custom is still followed to by many in the community; others choose to give up the wearing of the turban and cut their hair.

Although some of these religious communities sometimes have tense relations in India, conflict is uncommon in the United States.

CULTURE AND ASSIMILATION

Asian Indians have quietly entered many segments of the American economy and society while still retaining their culture. Most Asian Indian families strive to preserve traditional Indian values and transmit these to their children. Offspring are often encouraged to marry within the community and maintain their Indian heritage by taking language, dance, and culture classes. Such classes are offered at many temples and community centers. As they have become one of the fastest-growing minorities in the United States, Asian Indian Americans are both visible and recognizable in American society. Even as earlier immigrants and their descendants have assimilated, newer immigrants have tended to maintain strong ties to their immediate community. Asian Indians are sometimes typecast in American society as industrious, prosperous, and professionally and educationally advanced. However, the occupational profile presented by the Asian Indian community in the early twenty-first century is one of increasing diversity. Although a large number of Asian Indians are professionals and others own small businesses, some are employed as semi- or nonskilled workers.

Traditions and Customs The Asian Indian community in the United States in the early twenty-first century is an ethnically diverse one. One can distinguish among subgroups who trace their roots to different regions or states within India, who speak different languages, eat different foods, and follow distinct customs. Some of the most populous Indian groups within the United States are Gujaratis, Bengalis, Punjabis, Marathis, and Tamils. They come from a number of the Indian states, or regions, each of which has its own language. It is more likely that

An Asian Indian woman from Rockville, Maryland, holds a tray of food, 1993. PHOTOGRAPH BY CATHERINE KARNOW. CORBIS. REPRODUCED BY PERMISSION.

these subgroups will interact socially and celebrate important occasions with members of their own subcommunity rather than the larger Indian community. However, there are occasions, such as the celebration of India's day of independence, when the Asian Indian community come together as one.

Cuisine The majority of Asian Indian Americans have retained diets rooted in Indian cuisine. Indian food is prepared with a variety of herbs and spices, including cumin, turmeric, chili powder, ginger, and garlic. All Asian Indians eat a variety of dal (lentil), bean, and *chaval* (rice) dishes. Hindus generally will not eat beef for religious reasons, whereas Muslims eschew pork. Second-generation Asian Indians are more likely to ignore these religious taboos.

Tandoori, clay-baked chicken or fish marinated in yogurt and spices, is a popular northern Indian dish. *Biryani*, or flavored rice with vegetables and meats, is served on festive occasions, often accompanied by a cooling yogurt sauce called *raita*. Southern Indian dishes such as *masala*, *dosai* (crepes filled with spiced potatoes), or *idlis*, and steamed rice cakes are also popular. Indian cuisine is largely dependent on the region of India from which a subcommunity traced its roots. Caste may also play a role.

Green chutneys made of mint or coriander accompany a variety of savory fritters such as the triangular, stuffed samosas. Pickled vegetables and fruits such as lemons or mangoes are popular accompaniments to meals. A variety of unleavened breads, such as naan, *roti*, and *paratha*, are also widely eaten. Finally, "sweetmeats" such as *halvah* or *halwa* (of which there are various types, but most often made with crushed semolina wheat, ghee, and sugar) and *burfi* (made with sweetened condensed milk and sugar and often flavored with fruit, nuts, or spices) can often round off a festive meal.

Traditional Indian cooking tends to be a time-consuming process, and Asian Indians in the United States developed shortcuts involving mechanical gadgets and canned substitutes in preparing Indian meals. However, most families continue to eat freshly prepared Indian food for the main meal of the day. Indeed, the evening meal often serve as the time when family will get together to discuss their daily activities. The average Asian Indian family tends not to eat out as often as other American families because of the importance accorded to eating together at the family table. Meal preparation still tends to be the domain of females of the house, and daughters are expected to help, although rigid gender roles are changing. Older generation Asian Indians might still eat with their hands rather than with utensils, especially in their homes.

Traditional Dress Many Asian Indian American women wear the sari—yards of colorful embroidered or printed silk, polyester, or cotton wrapped around the body—at community functions and celebrations such as weddings. At such occasions, both men and women might also wear the *kameez* or *kurta*, also made of silk or fine cotton, a long shirt worn over tight-fitting leggings. Shawls made of silk or wool and elaborately embroidered or woven with gold or silver threads or beads and draped around the shoulders are an added touch to women's costumes. On a daily basis, Western attire is the norm, except among the older generation. Women might wear on their foreheads a *bindi*, or ornamental dot, which sometimes indicates they are married but is also worn as a fashion accessory at celebrations.

Asian Indians are very fond of gold jewelry, and many women wear simple gold ornaments such as rings, earrings, bangles, and necklaces every day, and more elaborate ones at special occasions. Jewelry is often passed down through the generations from mother to daughter or daughter-in-law.

Traditional Arts and Crafts Asian Indian community centers often offer classes on traditional arts and crafts such as batik painting and puppet making, thereby allowing for these skills to be perpetuated in the United States. Traditional Indian dances such as *bharatanatyam* are taught, and plays centered on revered epics such as the Mahabharata are performed. The painting of women's hands in delicate patterns with henna is traditionally done for weddings. This ancient practice traces traditional patterns filled with ancient symbols on the backs of the hands.

Dances and Songs Asian Indian preferences in music ranges from Indian classical music, which might include instruments such as the stringed sitar, tabla (drums), and the harmonium, to popular music from Indian films and the West. Indian classical music dates back several thousand years and gained a wider audience after India's independence. Indian film music, often a fusion of Indian and Western rock, rap, or pop music, also has a widespread following both in India and within the community in the United States.

Carnatic music, the classical music of southern India, commonly employs such musical instruments as the *veena*, a stringed instrument, and a range of violins. Carnatic music usually accompanies *bharatanatyam*, a classical dance in which dancers enact mythological tales, emulating ancient temple carvings of men and women with their body, hand, and eye movements.

Indian folk dances such as the exuberant *bhangra* from the Punjab region are popular at celebratory gatherings of the community. In this dance, dancers throw their arms in the air and simulate the actions of the farmer at work with his sickle. Traditional *bhangra* music is increasingly fused with elements of hip-hop, rap, and reggae. "Bollywood" songs and music are very popular within the Asian Indian community and, increasingly, within the larger American community.

Holidays In addition to universal celebrations such as International New Year's Day, Asian Indians celebrate India's day of independence from the British on August 15 and Republic Day on January 26. Many religious celebrations are also observed, the most important including Diwali, the festival of lights celebrating the return home of the Lord Rama, and Holi, the Hindu festival of colors celebrating spring. On these days, sweets are distributed among friends and family. Oil lamps, or *diyas*, are lit on Diwali. The community often organizes a traditional dinner with entertainment to mark the holiday.

Major festivals for Muslims include Eid al-Fitr, which marks the end of Ramadan, the month of fasting. It is celebrated with prayers and visits with friends. Asian Indian Christians celebrate Christmas

In Dag Hammarskjold Plaza in New York on Sunday, March 31, 2013, the spring holiday of Holi is celebrated by throwing and wearing colored powder. FRANCES M. ROBERTS / NEWSCOM

and Easter. Navaratri ("nine nights") is one of the most famous and popular festivals in India and is a major festival for diaspora Indians. Gujaratis dance the *garbha* during this fall celebration. Increasingly, Asian Indian Americans celebrate Thanksgiving as a major holiday.

Health Care Issues and Practices Most Asian Indian Americans accept the role of modern medicine and pay careful attention to health matters. Ayurvedic medicine has many adherents within the community. Ayurveda emphasizes spiritual healing as an essential component of physical healing and bases its cures on herbs and natural ingredients such as raw garlic and ginger. Ayurveda also focuses on preventive healing. One of its most famous proponents is Deepak Chopra (1946–), an India-born doctor whose book *Ageless Body, Timeless Mind* (1993) makes a case for the practice of ayurveda and sold over a million copies in the United States. Homeopathic medicine also has adherents among the community.

Some members of the Asian Indian American community practice yoga. The ancient practice of yoga dates back several thousand years. It combined

a routine of exercise and meditation to maintain the balance between body and mind. Practiced correctly, yoga is said to enable the individual to relieve daily stresses and strains and to achieve full potential as a human being. Various asanas, or poses, are held by the individual in practicing yoga.

Asian Indian Americans are less inclined to seek out assistance for mental health problems than physical health problems. This relates to the limited discussion about and prevailing stigmas attached to mental health issues in India. The traditional Indian belief has been that mental problems will eventually take care of themselves and that the family rather than outside experts should take care of the mentally ill. This attitude might change as prevailing societal beliefs about mental health are assimilated by the community.

Death and Burial Rituals Rituals relating to death vary within each religious community. Hindus cremate their dead, with elaborate rituals for the preparation of the body and a prominent role played by the elder son in the final rites. The ceremony is referred to as *antimsanskar*, or final rites. In India the cremation traditionally takes place on a wooden pyre, and

ASIAN INDIAN PROVERBS

Common proverbs in Hindi include *"jangle me mornacha, kisnedekha?"* which translates as "who saw a peacock dancing in the woods?" Its meaning alludes to the fact that to be recognized, one must first be observed. Another proverb that underlines the importance of human life is *"jaan he to jahan he,"* meaning only if life itself is preserved can there be a world.

the body, which is often dressed in gold-ornamented clothing, burns over several hours. This is in contrast to electric cremation common in the United States. Garlands of flowers, incense sticks, and ghee (clarified butter) are placed on the stretcher along with the body. Many Hindus in the Asian Indian American community, especially among the older generation, wish to have their ashes returned to India to be scattered in the Ganges River. So many bring ashes to India that the Indian government issued guidelines—"Procedures for Carrying Ashes of a Deceased to India"—that outlined the documentation necessary to do so. Muslims bury their dead according to Sharia law and Islamic traditions. The dead body is ritually cleansed and prepared, and prayers are said. Christians bury their dead in accordance with Christian traditions.

Asian Indian families generally receive much community support upon the death of a family member. Members of the community provide both comfort and material help in times of bereavement.

Recreational Activities Within the community, the older generation tends to socialize extensively with other families within the larger Asian Indian community and specifically within their ethnoreligious group. Elaborate dinners are held in family homes where community members are invited. First-generation Asian Indians tend not be great fans of traditional American sports such as baseball or football, preferring soccer or cricket. Watching Bollywood films is very popular across the community. Younger and second-generation Asian Indians are active in recreational activities of interest to the larger American community.

FAMILY AND COMMUNITY LIFE

For the most part, Asian Indians tend to live in nuclear families in the United States, although it is common for members of the extended family, particularly grandparents, to visit for months at a time. It is also fairly common, particularly after 1965, for Asian Indian Americans to encourage their siblings to emigrate from India and provide them with financial and emotional support until they are well settled in the United States. Family ties are very strong, and it

is considered the responsibility of more prosperous members to look after their less well-to-do relatives. Relatively low percentages of Asian Indian families receive public assistance. This is due to both the relative affluence in the community and the tendency for extended family members to provide financial support in times of need.

Gender Roles By the early twenty-first century, Asian Indian women had made great progress in both India and the United States. In India, Indira Gandhi once held the highest seat in government—prime minister—and women are represented in all walks of life, although gender stereotyping persisted, especially in communities with lower levels of education. In the United States, while many women continue to perform traditional household tasks of cooking and caring for children, a large number of Asian Indian women, particularly second- and third-generation women, pursue their own professional careers and life choices and are highly successful. Asian Indian women hold many high-profile positions in American society. For the most part, the Asian Indian community in the United States does not mirror the preference for sons over daughters as continues to be prevalent in parts of India. Daughters, however, still tend to be more sheltered by families than sons.

Education Asian Indian Americans highly value education, and children are encouraged to excel at school. As a result of high parental expectations, Asian Indians are overrepresented in events such as the national spelling and geography bees. According to the 2010 U.S. Census, 70 percent of Asian Indian Americans held at least an undergraduate degree. This percentage is higher than most other ethnic groups in the United States. Many also attend graduate school and pursue such professions as medicine, business administration, engineering, and law. Many Asian Indians are professors in colleges and universities across the United States.

Courtship and Weddings In the early twenty-first century, arranged marriages were still very common in India, and dating was not a traditional Indian custom. Asian Indian parents tend to frown upon the practice, but they are yielding to their offspring's demands to be allowed to date. The preference is still for the selection of a marriage partner from within the subgroup of the larger community and with the full approval and consent of the parents. Family or community members are often involved in the selection of a suitable mate. The family and educational backgrounds of the potential partner are thoroughly examined before introductions were made. Asian Indians believe their children would be happier if they were married to someone who shares the same history, tradition, religion, and social customs and who could impart these values to their children, thus ensuring the continuity of the community. They believe that such marriages made within the community tend to be more stable and longer lasting than those that cross community boundaries. However, cross-cultural and interreligious marriages are becoming more frequent, especially with second and later generation Asian Indian Americans.

Weddings in the Asian Indian community are often elaborate affairs, sometimes stretching over several days and including several hundred guests. In traditional Hindu ceremonies the bride and groom exchange garlands of flowers and circle ceremonial fire three to seven times. The bride often wears red sari and gold ornaments. She might also have her hands and feet painted in intricate designs with henna, a tradition called *mehendi*. The groom might wear the traditional northern Indian dress of a *churidar kameez*, or tight leggings made of silk or fine cotton, and a long shirt, or opt for a Western-style suit. A Brahman priest conducts the ceremony.

Dancing and Indian and Western music is fairly common at Asian Indian American weddings, a result of the assimilation of American customs. Some weddings might include *shehnai* music, or a thin, wailing music played on an oboe-like instrument. This music is traditionally played at Hindu weddings in India. Feasts of traditional foods are prepared for guests, and traditional Hindu or Muslim rites are observed. Often, family members prepared the feast themselves, although it is increasingly common to engage professional caterers.

Relations with Other Americans Many Asian Indian Americans tend to live lives integrated with other Americans. Raising children and the school and sports activities that go with that task bring them into the mainstream of American life. Many, however, tend to celebrate special occasions within the parameters of their subgroup. The younger generations tend to be more assimilated than the older generations, and many marry outside of the community. One issue within the Asian Indian American community is the Americanization of second-generation Asian Indian immigrants. The phrase "American Born Confused Desi" ("ABCD") refers to American-born Asian Indians and is often used derogatorily to imply that they were neither American nor Asian Indian. *Desi* comes from the Urdu and Hindi word *des*, meaning "homeland."

Philanthropy As the Asian Indian American community has become more successful in the United States, they have increased their profile in the philanthropic world. Many donations are made to colleges and universities across the United States. For example, doctors Kiran and Pallavi Patel have donated up to $25 million to the University of South Florida. This includes the establishment of the Patel College of Global Sustainability. The Sheth Family Foundation helps the greater Atlanta community. Many successful Silicon Valley entrepreneurs give to charities in both India and the United States.

Founded in 2001, the America India Foundation donated tens of millions of dollars to charities in India. In addition, many temples and houses of worship engaged in charity work.

The Asian Indian community in the United States in the early twenty-first century is an ethnically diverse one. One can distinguish among subgroups who trace their roots to different regions or states within India, who speak different languages, eat different foods, and follow distinct customs.

Surnames Surnames indicated to which subcommunity an Asian Indian traced its heritage. Many common surnames were distinguishable in terms of the region and community in India that they originally came from. Hence, Patel and Mehta have their origins in Gujarat, while Gupta, Mehra, or Kumar had northern Indian origins. Singh is a last name that always indicated the Sikh community. Asian Indian Muslims might have Islamic last names such as Khan or Ahmed, but some would have names particularized by region as well, as with Kashmiri Muslims, who could have a last name such as Agha. In general, southern Indian names tend to be longer, such as Kumaraswamy or Rajagopalan. Certain last names were derived from caste and subcaste; for instance, Nair or Naidu. Others were derived from lineage or occupation. For instance, Parsis carried last names such as Captain, Dastur ("priest"), and Batliwalla (a trader of glass and bottles).

EMPLOYMENT AND ECONOMIC CONDITIONS

The economic profile of Asian Indian Americans had changed dramatically over time. Whereas the first immigrants were agricultural and manual laborers, by the early twenty-first century, significant numbers of Asian Indians were engaged in professions such as medicine, accounting, and engineering. Many Asian Indians who entered the United States as students remained and became respected professors and academics. In fact, a 2004 report by the Census Bureau based on 2000 U.S. Census figures indicated that a higher percentage of Asian Indian Americans was engaged in managerial positions than any other ethnic group in the United States.

Indian immigrants to the United States sometimes have been unable to practice the profession for which they were trained in India due to either a lack of employment opportunities or the lack of American certification. In such cases, like law, for instance, they have either chosen alternative occupations or have retrained themselves in another field. Doctors and engineers have been among the most successful in finding employment in the field within which they were trained. A U.S. Census report released in March 2012 based on 2010 Census figures lists Asian Indian Americans' median household income as $90,711.

Many Asian Indian Americans own small businesses such as travel agencies, Indian groceries, and garment stores, particularly in neighborhoods where a strong Asian Indian community exists, such as Flushing, in the New York City borough of Queens; or on Devon Avenue in Chicago. Many own fast-food franchises and gas stations across the country. Asian Indian Americans own or operate about 47 percent of the motels in the United States and almost 37 percent of all hotels and motels combined. Extended families often help relatives with the initial investment necessary, further strengthening Asian Indians' dominance of this business niche. Around 70 percent of all Indian motel owners share the same surname—Patel—indicating that they are members of the Gujarati Hindu Patel subcaste.

POLITICS AND GOVERNMENT

Indian immigrants were actively involved in the struggle for residence and citizenship rights in the early part of the twentieth century. Inspiring leaders like Dalip Saund, who later became a congressman in 1957, and rebels such as Taraknath Das mobilized the Indian community in California to strike back against anti-Indian violence and exclusion. The Ghadar Party, organized by Indians and Sikhs, was formed in San Francisco between 1913 and 1914 to realize the goal of revolution in India; it then organized in the United States around the immigration issue.

Earlier generations of Asian Indians have tended not to play particularly active roles in modern American politics. Some Asian Indians continue to identify themselves with the politics of India rather than the United States. There are signs, however, that this noninvolvement is changing. Since the 1980s the community actively raised funds for their candidates of choice. A 2009 National Asian American Survey from Rutgers University reports that 72 percent of the Asian Indians surveyed said that they were "most likely to vote." Many young Asian Indian Americans work on Capitol Hill and in state legislatures, gaining valuable experience for the future, and some politicians are beginning to realize the power of the community to raise capital. During the 2012 presidential campaign, the Asian Indian community raised millions of dollars for candidates in both parties. The Association of Indians in America launched a successful campaign to have Asian Indian Americans included within the "Asian or Pacific Islander" category rather than the "Caucasian/White" category in the census, believing that the conferring of this minority status would bring benefits to the community. Accordingly, Asian Indians are currently classified under the "Asian or Pacific Islander" category.

Asian Indians in the United States engaged in unprecedented political activity when armed conflict broke out in 1999 between India and Pakistan over the contested area of Kashmir. Asian Indian immigrants began to lobby Congress and write letters to the editors of American newspapers in support of India's position. In addition, they sent assistance to aid Asian Indian soldiers and their families. Asian Indian activists have increasingly used the Internet to garner support in the United States for Asian Indian causes.

In the early twenty-first century, the most visible successes of the Asian Indians in U.S. politics were represented by Bobby Jindal, who was elected governor of Louisiana in 2007, and Nikki Haley, who was elected governor of South Carolina in 2010.

Because Asian Indian Americans are geographically dispersed, they could not easily form powerful voting blocs. Historically, a greater percentage of Asian Indians tended to vote for Democratic rather than Republican candidates, and this trend continued in 2008 and 2012, with well over fifty percent of Asian Indians voting for President Barack Obama.

Relations with India Asian Indian Americans retain close ties to India, maintaining contact with friends and relatives and often travelling to India at regular intervals. They remain interested in Indian politics because of these ties and contributed to the election campaigns of Indian politicians. Contributions from the Asian Indian community to different political parties in India is also quite common, as is the phenomenon of Indian political party leaders travelling to the United States to make their case to the community. The government of India even created a designation for "persons of Indian origin" (PIO) or ancestry who were born or whose ancestors were born in India but was no longer an Indian citizen and lived in another country. Those with a PIO card could travel to India without acquiring a visa and invest money or purchase property in India.

India considers its Indian communities abroad very important. Even though there had been concern over the years of a "brain drain" from India, a phenomenon where India's best talent moved to the United States and Europe, the feeling in the early twenty-first century was that India could gain both economically and culturally from its emigrants. Indians who emigrated abroad are viewed as ambassadors for India, and it is hoped their achievements would make the country proud. Indeed, unique achievements by Asian Indians in the United States and Europe are often showcased by the Indian media. For example, the success of American astronaut Sunita Williams and Governor Bobby Jindal were widely covered in the Indian press.

In times of natural disaster such as floods or earthquakes in India, the Asian Indian American community sent generous contributions. Second-generation Asian Indian students demonstrated an interest in travelling to India on study projects. Asian Indians watch the liberalizing economic reforms underway in India with great interest and note potential avenues for trade and investment. Many Asian Indians maintain nonresident savings accounts in India, through which they can make investments in private businesses in different parts of the country.

NOTABLE INDIVIDUALS

Academia Asian Indians serve as distinguished faculty members at prestigious universities and colleges throughout the United States. The following includes a handful of the countless Asian Indian Americans who made names for themselves in academia. Shanti Swarup Gupta (1925–2002), a statistician, taught statistics and mathematics at Stanford and Purdue universities and was the recipient of numerous awards in the field. Jayadev Misra (1947–), a computer science educator and winner of several national awards in software and hardware design, is a professor of computer science at the University of Texas at Austin. Rustum Roy (1924–2010), a materials scientist, had been a member of the faculty at Pennsylvania State University from 1950. Gayatri Chakravorti Spivak (1942–) is a respected literary critic and professor at Columbia University. Jagdish Sheth (1938–) is Kellstadt Professor of Marketing at Emory University. The first Asian Indian American president of a university was Beheruz Sethna (1948–) of the University of West Georgia. Jamshed Bharucha (1956–) became the president of the Cooper Union in 2011. Amartya Sen (1933–) is a Harvard professor and economist who was awarded the 1998 Nobel Memorial Prize in Economic Sciences.

Art Natvar Bhavsar (1934–) is a painter. His work is part of the permanent collections of museums such as the Boston Fine Arts Museum, Metropolitan Museum of Art, and Whitney Museum of American Art in New York.

Commerce and Industry Indra Nooyi (1955–) is the influential CEO of PepsiCo. Vikram Pandit (1957–) rose in the ranks of the banking industry to become the chief executive of Citigroup from 2007 to 2012.

Culinary Arts Madhur Jaffrey (1933–) is the author of several popular books on Indian cuisine and the broader cuisine of East Asia. Her works include *Madhur Jaffrey's World-of-the-East Vegetarian Cooking*, *An Invitation to Indian Cooking*, and *Taste of India*. Her book *A Taste of the Far East* won the James Beard award for cookbook of the year in 1994. She also appeared on the television series "Indian Cookery and Far Eastern Cookery." Aarti Sequeira (1978–) hosted the show "Aarti Party" on the Food Network cable channel.

Economics Ravi Batra (1943–) is an economist whose books *The Great Depression of 1990* (published in 1987) and *Surviving the Great Depression of 1990* (published in 1988) attained best-seller status. Jagdish Bhagwati (1934–), a renowned economist specializing in the economics of underdevelopment, wrote several books on the subject. He is a professor of economics and law at Columbia University.

New York artist and Indian expatriate Natvar Bhavsar (1934–) stands in front of one of his works at the Mira Godard Gallery in Toronto, 2005. RENE JOHNSTON / ZUMA PRESS / NEWSCOM

Fashion Rachel Roy (1974–) is an important fashion designer whose clothing lines are sold at major department stores.

Film Ismail Merchant (1936–2005) was a world-renowned film producer who, with his partner James Ivory, produced and directed such award-winning films as *A Room with a View* (1986), *Howard's End* (1990), and *The Remains of the Day* (1993). Merchant also produced *The Courtesans of Bombay* (1983) and *In Custody* (1993). In addition, Merchant was a successful cookbook author, having written *Ismail Merchant's Indian Cuisine* and *Ismail Merchant's Passionate Meals*. Director Mira Nair (1957–) directed *Mississippi Masala* (1991) starring Denzel Washington, which addressed the adjustments Asian Indians must make while living in the United States. M. Night Shyamalan (1970–) directed several successful Hollywood films with supernatural themes, including *The Sixth Sense* (1999) and *The Happening* (2008).

Government Dalip Saund (1899–1973) became a U.S. congressman in 1957. Born in the Punjab region of India, he immigrated to the United States in 1920. He earned a PhD in mathematics from the University of California at Berkeley and was one of the earliest activists fighting for the citizenship and residence rights of Asian Indians in the United States.

Many Asian Indian Americans had been appointed to administrative positions. Joy Cherian (1942–) was Equal Employment Opportunities Commissioner from 1990 to 1994. In 1982 Cherian founded the Indian American Forum for Political Education, and in the early twenty-first century headed a consulting firm. Kumar Barve (1958–) was the first Asian Indian in the country to be elected to a state legislature, in 1990. Arthur Lall (1911–1998) was involved in numerous international negotiations, wrote extensively on diplomacy and negotiations (including the 1966 book *Modern International Negotiator*), and taught at Columbia University.

Asian Indian Americans also served as mayors: John Abraham (1945–) in Teaneck, New Jersey; David Dhillon in El Centro, California; and Bala K. Srinivas (1930–) in Hollywood Park, Texas. Governors included Nikki Haley (1972–) of South Carolina and Bobby Jindal (1971–) of Louisiana. Notable appointees in the administration of President Barack Obama included the actor Kal Penn (1977–), who serves in the White House Office of Public Engagement; Farah Pandith (1968–), who is U.S. Special Representative to Muslim Communities; Geeta Pasi, the ambassador to the Republic of Djibouti, appointed in 2011; and Sonny Ramaswamy (1951–), director of the National Institute of Food and Agriculture.

Journalism Fareed Zakaria (1964–) is host a weekly news and international politics show on CNN, *Fareed Zakaria GPS*. He is also an editor of *Time* magazine. Sanjay Gupta (1969–) is a neurosurgeon who was also a television personality who reported on health and science issues. He appeared on numerous news segments on CNN.

Literature Asian Indian fiction writers include Bharati Mukherjee (1940–), professor of English at Columbia University, who is awarded the National Book Critics Circle Award for *The Middleman and Other Stories* (1988). Ved Mehta (1934–) is author of his autobiography *Face to Face* (1957) and the autobiographical novel *Daddyji* (1972). Folklorist and poet A. K. Ramanujan (1929–1993) wrote the book of poems *Speaking of Siva* (1973). Kirin Narayan (1959–) is the author of *Love, Stars, and All That* (1994), a novel about Asian Indian experiences in the United States, and *My Family and Other Saints* (2008). Chitra Bannerjee Divakaruni (1957–) wrote *Oleander Girl* (2013) and *One Amazing Thing* (2010). Jhumpa Lahiri (1967–) won the Pulitzer Prize in 2000 for *The Interpreter of Maladies*; she is also the author of the acclaimed novel *The Namesake* (2003), featuring an Asian Indian American family, which was made into a film of the same name.

Dhan Gopal Mukerji (1890–1936) was one of the first Asian Indian Americans to write for children. His works included both animal fantasies such as *The Chief of the Herd* (1929) and novels, such as *Gay Neck: The Story of a Pigeon*, which won the Newbery Medal in 1927.

Music Zubin Mehta (1936–), musician and conductor, was born in Bombay into a family that practiced Zoroastrianism. He served as music director of a number of orchestras, including the Los Angeles Philharmonic, Israel Philharmonic, and New York Philharmonic. The pianist-composer Vijay Iyer (1971–) won numerous awards for his albums. Several Asian Indian musicians established schools in the United States to keep Indian culture alive among young Asian Indians. One such musician was Ali Akbar Khan (1922–2009), an Indian classical musician who came to the United States in 1955 after an invitation from violinist Yehudi Menuhin and formed a school in California's Bay Area. Norah Jones (1979–), singer-songwriter and pianist, is the daughter of famed sitar player Ravi Shankar. She won numerous Grammy Awards and was named by *Billboard* as top jazz artist for 2000–2009. Jones has released several studio albums, including *Come Away with Me* (2002), *The Fall* (2009), and *Little Broken Hearts* (2012).

Politics Dinesh D'Souza (1961–), a graduate of Dartmouth and an outspoken conservative, was appointed a domestic policy advisor in the Reagan administration. D'Souza has been a fellow at the American Enterprise Institute and is the author of numerous books, including *What's So Great about America* (2002); in 2012 he cowrote and directed the documentary *2016: Obama's America*.

Science and Medicine Asian Indian Americans have made numerous advancements in science and technology, and the following individuals represented a small sample. Hargobind Khorana (1922–2011) won the Nobel Prize in Medicine in 1968. Vijay Prabhakar practiced medicine for many years with the Indian Health Service, a branch of the U.S. Department of Health and Human Services, which provides health care to Native Americans. Subrahmanyan Chandrasekhar (1910–1995), a theoretical astrophysicist, won the Nobel Prize in Physics in 1983. Amar Bose (1929–2013) was the founder, chairman of the board, and technical director of the Bose Corporation, known for its innovative stereo speaker systems. Bose was also a professor at the Massachusetts Institute of Technology. Statistician Calyampudi Radhakrishna Rao (1920–) was awarded the National Medal of Science in 2002 by President George W. Bush.

Asian Indians have initiated numerous technology startups in Silicon Valley. Entrepreneurs such as Vivek Wadhwa and Shantanu Narayen (1963–) achieved great success in the field of information technology. Siddhartha Mukherjee (1970–) is a physician, scientist, and author whose book *The Emperor of*

All Maladies: A Biography of Cancer won the Pulitzer Prize for General Nonfiction in 2011. Sunita Williams (1965–) is a former astronaut with NASA. Deepak Chopra (1946–), an endocrinologist turned ayurvedic practitioner, published a series of highly successful books, including *Ageless Body, Timeless Mind: The Quantum Alternative to Growing Old* (1993) and *God: A Story of Revelation* (2012). Atul Gawande (1965–), a surgeon, is the author of the book *The Checklist Manifesto* (2009), and he has written extensively on medicine and public health for the *New Yorker*.

Stage and Screen Actress Mindy Kaling (1979–), the screen name of Vera Chokalingam, is best known for her work in the television comedy series *The Office*. Kal Penn (1977–) is a well-known actor who starred in the films *The Namesake* (2006) and the *Harold and Kumar* films. Aziz Ansari (1983–) is an actor and comedian who is featured on the NBC television series *Parks and Recreation*.

MEDIA

PRINT

India Abroad

This weekly newspaper was first published in 1970, making it the oldest Asian Indian newspaper in the United States. It focuses on news about the community in the United States and news from India.

Ajit Balakrishnan, Chairman and Publisher
43 West 24th Street
New York, New York 10010
Phone: (212) 929-1727
URL: www.indiaabroad.com

India Currents

This is a monthly newsmagazine focusing on issues of interest to the Asian Indian community.

Vandana Kumar, Publisher
1885 Lundy Avenue #220
San Jose, California 95131
Phone: (408) 774-6966
Fax: (408) 324-0477
Email: info@indiacurrent.com
URL: www.indiacurrents.com

News India

This weekly newspaper features articles and news on India and the Asian Indian community.

Parikh Worldwide Media
37 West 20th Street
Suite 1009
New York, New York 10011
Phone: (212) 675-7515
Fax: (212) 675-7624
URL: www.newsindia-times.com

RADIO

There are many FM and AM radio programs broadcast in Hindi across the United States. In addition, there are some programs that are broadcast in other regional Indian languages such as Gujarati, Marathi, or Tamil. Most of these originated in cities with significant Asian Indian populations. Hindi radio programs include those on KEST-AM in San Francisco; WSBC-AM in Chicago; WEEF-AM in Highland Park, Illinois; WAIF-FM in Cincinnati, Ohio; and KPFT-FM in Houston, Texas.

TV Asia

TV Asia telecasts news and feature programs of interest to the Indian community nationally.

76 National Road
Edison, New Jersey 08817
Phone: (732) 650-1100
URL: www.tvasiausa.com

ORGANIZATIONS AND ASSOCIATIONS

A distinction must be made between organizations that base membership upon an encompassing Asian Indian identity and those that are linked more closely to different regions and states within India, such as the Maharashtrian or Tamil organizations in different U.S. states. In addition, religion-based groups such as Sikh or Zoroastrian organizations also exist. The following is a list of organizations that serve all Asian Indians without distinction of religion, language, or region.

Association of Indians in America

An organization for immigrants of Asian Indian ancestry living in the United States. Seeks to continue Indian cultural activities in the United States and to encourage full Asian Indian participation as citizens and residents of America.

Anismesh Goenka, President
26 Pleasant Lane
Oyster Bay, New York 11771
Phone: (516) 624-2460
Fax: (718) 497-5320
Email: agoenka@aol.com
URL: www.aianational.com

National Federation of Indian American Associations (NFIA)

This federation represents interests of Asian Indians in the United States and promotes Indian culture and values. Attempts to influence legislation in favor of the community.

Lal K. Motwani, President
319 Summit Hall Road
Gaithersburg, Maryland 20877
Phone: (301) 926-3013
Fax: (301) 926-3378
Email: info@nfia.net
URL: www.nfia.net

Network of Indian Professionals (NetIP)

This nonprofit group seeks to help Asian Indian Americans advance personally and professionally. Also works to improve the community.

Email: info@netip.org
URL: www.netip.org

MUSEUMS AND RESEARCH CENTERS

The American Institute of India Studies (AIIS)

AIIS supports research, offers training in Indian languages, promotes knowledge of Indian culture, and supports book publications and articles about India.

1130 East 59th Street
Chicago, Illinois 60637
Phone: (773) 702-8638
Email: aiis@uchicago.edu
URL: www.indiastudies.org

Madhusudan and Kiran C. Dhar India Studies Program

The program promotes research and teaching on all aspects of the Indian subcontinent.

Mahusudan and Kiran C. Dhar India Studies Program
Indiana University
825 East 8th Street
Bloomington, Indiana 47408-3842
Phone: (812) 855-5798
Fax: (852) 856-4658
URL: www.indiana.edu/~isp

South Asia Institute at Columbia University (SAI)

SAI coordinates activities at Columbia University that relate to study of Bangladesh, Bhutan, India, the Maldives, Nepal, Pakistan and Sri Lanka.

305 International Affairs
420 West 118th Street
New York, New York 10027
Phone: (212) 854-8401
Email: ke2131@columbia.edu
URL: www.sai.columbia.edu

South Asia Studies Program at the University of Pennsylvania

The South Asia Studies Department is a close-knit community of interdisciplinary scholars that combine expertise in the languages, literatures, histories, and cultures of South Asia.

820 Williams Hall
Philadelphia, Pennsylvania 19104-6305
Phone: (215) 898-7475
Fax: (215) 573-2138
Email: daudali@sas.upenn.edu
URL: www.southasia.upenn.edu

South Asian Studies Program at Princeton University

A comprehensive undergraduate and graduate program that offers the study of sociopolitical, economic, and religious aspects of India and Pakistan.

Department of Anthropology
132 Aaron Burr Hall
Princeton University
Princeton, New Jersey 08544
Phone: (609) 258-6814
Fax: (609) 258-1032
Email: ideces@princeton.edu
URL: www.princeton.edu/sas

SOURCES FOR ADDITIONAL STUDY

Bacon, Jean. *Life Lines: Community, Family, and Assimilation among Asian Indian Immigrants.* New York: Oxford University Press, 1996.

Das Gupta, Monisha. *Unruly Immigrants: Rights, Activism, and Transnational South Asian Politics in the United States.* Durham, NC: Duke University Press, 2006.

George, Sheba Mariam. *When Women Come First: Gender and Class in Transnational Migration.* Berkeley: University of California Press, 2005.

Helwig, Arthur, and Usha Helwig, eds. *An Immigrant Success Story: East Indians in America.* Philadelphia: University of Pennsylvania Press, 1990.

Joshi, Khyati Y. *New Roots in America's Sacred Ground: Religion, Race and Ethnicity in Indian America.* New Brunswick, NJ: Rutgers University Press, 2006.

Khandelwal, Madhulika S. *Becoming American, Being Indian: An Immigrant Community in New York City.* Ithaca, NY: Cornell University Press, 2002.

Maira, Sunaina Marr. *Desis in the House: Indian American Youth Culture in NYC.* Philadelphia: Temple University Press, 2002.

Rangaswamy, Padma. *Namaste America: Indian Immigrants in an American Metropolis.* University Park: Pennsylvania State University Press, 2000.

Rudrappa, Sharmila. *Ethnic Routes to Becoming American: Indian Immigrants and the Cultures of Citizenship.* New Brunswick, NJ: Rutgers University Press, 2004.

Shukla, Sandhya. *India Abroad: Diasporic Cultures of Postwar America and England.* Princeton, NJ: Princeton University Press, 2003.

Takaki, Ronald. *India in the West: South Asians in America.* New York: Chelsea House, 1995.

AUSTRALIAN AMERICANS
Ken Cuthbertson

OVERVIEW

Australian Americans are immigrants or descendants of people from the Commonwealth of Australia, which lies between the South Pacific and Indian Oceans. The world's sixth-largest nation, Australia is the only country in the world that is also a continent. The Commonwealth includes numerous islands, some more than a hundred miles from the mainland, including Tasmania, which lies off the southeastern coast. Over 70 percent of Australia is arid or semi-arid desert. The most remote parts are commonly referred to as the Outback. Australia covers an area of 2,966,150 square miles (7,682,293 square kilometers)—almost as large as the continental United States, excluding Alaska.

Although Australia's 2011 census found the national population to be 21.5 million, the Australian Bureau of Statistics estimated the population in 2012 to be higher, around 22.8 million, due to immigration and underreporting on the census. Over 60 percent of the population identifies as Christian, while 25 percent claims no religious affiliation. Australia is one of the wealthiest countries in the world, with a median household wealth of around A$59,200 (US$62,200), compared to just US$53,000 in the United States. It has the twelfth-largest economy in the world on the strength of its mineral exports, primarily iron ore—though the global recession that began in the late 2000s has threatened to undercut decades of strong economic growth.

Australians first arrived in the United States in significant numbers during the gold rush of the 1850s, settling throughout the western United States in search of wealth and opportunity. Due to military and economic cooperation between the U.S. and Australian governments during World War II and the Vietnam War, Australian immigration to the United States remained steady throughout the mid-twentieth century. From the 1990s through the first decade of the twenty-first century, a large number of young, upwardly mobile Australians began seeking better employment opportunities in the United States, the United Kingdom, and Asia. Over one million Australians live abroad in what has been termed the Australian diaspora. Many of these immigrants have not sought permanent residence in other countries, however. A 2002 study by the Australian Department of Statistics, for example, found that half of all Australian emigrants stated that they intended to return home in the future, and upwards of 20 percent did in fact return.

In 2011 the U.S. Census Bureau estimated the total number of persons of Australian descent living in the United States to be around 90,000. Of the 33,000 born outside of the United States, 22,500 did not claim permanent residence. Areas with high concentrations of Australian Americans include New York City, San Francisco, and Houston, Texas.

HISTORY OF THE PEOPLE

Early History Mainland Australia's first inhabitants were nomadic hunters who arrived around 35,000 BCE. Anthropologists believe these Aborigines came from Southeast Asia by crossing a land bridge that existed at the time. Another group of original inhabitants, the Torres Strait Islanders, descended from ancient Melanesians and Papua New Guineans and now live primarily in the islands of the northern Torres Strait. There is some evidence that Chinese mariners visited the north coast of Australia near the present-day city of Darwin as early as the fourteenth century. However, their impact was minimal. European exploration of the region began in 1606, when Dutch explorer Willem Jansz sailed into the Gulf of Carpentaria. During the next thirty years, Dutch navigators charted much of the northern and western coastline of what they called New Holland.

In 1770, when British explorer James Cook landed at Botany Bay, near the present-day city of Sydney, he claimed the whole of the east coast of Australia for Britain, naming it New South Wales. Between 1769 and 1777, he visited Australia and neighboring New Zealand three times, making several unsuccessful attempts at colonization. The American Revolution became the impetus for large-scale British colonization of Australia as the government in London, which had been transporting petty criminals to the North American colonies, had to find a new destination for its prisoners. Botany Bay in southeastern Australia seemed the ideal site: it was 14,000 miles from England, uncolonized by other European powers, enjoyed a favorable climate, and was strategically located to help provide security for Great Britain's long-distance shipping lines to India.

In 1787 the British government dispatched a fleet of eleven ships under the command of captain Arthur Phillip to establish a penal colony at Botany Bay. Phillip landed on January 26, 1788, with about 1,000 settlers, more than half of whom were convicts. Men outnumbered the women nearly three to one. England transported more than 160,000 men, women, and children to Australia until the practice officially ended in 1868. Robert Hughes, an Australian-born art critic for *Time* magazine, in his popular 1987 book *The Fatal Shore: A History of Transportation of Convicts to Australia, 1787–1868*, calls it the "largest forced exile of citizens at the behest of a European government in pre-modern history."

In the beginning, most of the people exiled to Australia from Great Britain were conspicuously unfit for survival in their new home. To the Aborigines who encountered them, it must have seemed that the colonists lived on the edge of starvation in the midst of plenty. However, the relationship between the colonists and the estimated 300,000 indigenous people who inhabited Australia in the 1780s was marked by mutual misunderstanding at the best of times and outright hostility the rest of the time. The bloody policy of pacification by force, which was practiced by whites in the mid-nineteenth century in order to seize control of tribal lands, caused many Aborigines to seek refuge in the vast, arid Outback.

Meanwhile the white population grew slowly and steadily as more people arrived from the United Kingdom. By the late 1850s, six British colonies (some of which were founded by free settlers) had taken root on the island continent with about 400,000 white settlers. At the time, there were an estimated thirteen million sheep—or *jumbucks* as they are known in Australian slang—as it had become apparent that the country was well suited to production of wool and mutton.

In the 1920s and early 1930s, the Australian government, recognizing the need to protect what remained of the native population, established a series of Aboriginal land reserves. A large number of critics now charge that the effect of the reservations has been to segregate and ghettoize Aboriginal people rather than to preserve their traditional culture and way of life. Other government programs, such as boarding schools and child protective services, were also the subject of controversy for their attempts to alter the Aboriginal way of life. Today Australia's native population has shrunk to about 50,000 full-blooded Aborigines; about 160,000 have mixed blood.

Modern Era The Commonwealth of Australia was proclaimed in Sydney on January 1, 1901, uniting the six colonies of New South Wales, Tasmania (then Van Diemen's Land), Western Australia, South Australia, Victoria, and Queensland. The six colonies were refashioned as states united in a political federation that received its own legislature, head of government, and courts. The federal government is led by an elected prime minister, who is the leader of the party that wins the most seats in the federal legislature in any general election. Australia's federal government consists of a bicameral legislature—the 72-member Senate and the 145-member House of Representatives.

In 1901 King George V of England formally opened the new federal parliament at Melbourne (in 1927 the national capital was moved to Canberra, which was designed by American architect Walter Burley Griffin). The year 1901 also saw the passage of a restrictive immigration law intended to ensure that Australia remained predominantly white; it effectively barred most Asians and other people of color from entering the country. However, Australia proved to be progressive in at least one important regard: women were granted the vote in 1902, sixteen years before women in Great Britain were enfranchised. In addition, Australia's organized labor movement took advantage of ethnic solidarity and a shortage of workers to press for and win a range of social welfare benefits several decades before workers in England, Europe, or North America. To this day, organized labor is a powerful force in Australian society, though labor unions have been under siege in recent years by conservative politicians and business interests. As a result, the total number of union members in Australia has fallen from around 40 percent of the workforce in 1992 to just 18 percent in 2012.

In the early twentieth century, Australians mainly looked west to London for commerce, defense, political, and cultural guidance. However, with Britain's decline as a world power, Australia drew closer to the United States. Despite ongoing squabbles over tariffs and foreign policy matters, American books, magazines, movies, cars, and other consumer goods began to flood the Australian market in the 1920s. To the dismay of Australian nationalists, one spinoff of this trend was an acceleration of the Americanization of Australia, which was briefly slowed by the Great Depression. When Britain granted former colonies such as Australia and Canada full control over their external affairs in 1937, Washington and Canberra moved to establish formal diplomatic relations, and the Americanization of Australia accelerated again.

As a member of the British Commonwealth, Australia was part of the Allied forces during World War II. Most Australians felt that with Great Britain reeling, the United States offered the only hope of fending off a Japanese invasion. Australia became the main American supply base in the Pacific, and about one million American GIs were stationed there or visited the country in the years between 1942 and 1945. By 1944 almost 40 percent of Australia's imports came from the United States, while just 25 percent of its exports went to the United States. However, with the end of the war in the Pacific, old antagonisms resurfaced between the two countries, particularly surrounding discriminatory tariff policies that favored Australia's Commonwealth trading partners. Nonetheless, the war changed Australia in some fundamental and profound ways: for one, the country was no longer content to allow Britain to dictate its foreign policy. Thus, when the establishment of the United Nations was discussed at the San Francisco Conference in 1945, Australia rejected its former role as a small power and insisted on middle-power status.

In 1946 Washington and Canberra established full diplomatic relations. Meanwhile, a heated political debate erupted in Australia over the future direction of the country and the extent to which foreign corporations should be allowed to invest in the Australian economy. While a vocal segment of public opinion expressed fear of becoming too closely aligned with the United States, others wanted to partner with Americans to stem the spread of communism in Southeast Asia. As a result, in September 1951, Australia joined New Zealand and the United States in the ANZUS defense treaty. Three years later, these nations became partners with Britain, France, Pakistan, the Philippines, and Thailand in the Southeast Asia Treaty Organization.

Since the mid-1960s, both of Australia's major political parties, the Labor Party and the Coalition (a combination of the Liberal and National parties), have supported an end to discriminatory immigration policies. Changes to these policies have turned Australia into a Eurasian melting pot. One-third of immigrants now come from Asian countries. In anticipation of the 1997 reversion of the British Crown colony of Hong Kong to Chinese control, many former residents of Hong Kong relocated to Australia. In 2011, for the first time, Chinese immigrants became the country's largest immigrant group.

Demographic diversification has brought changes to Australia's economy and traditional patterns of international trade. An ever-increasing percentage of the country's commerce is with the booming Pacific-rim nations of Japan, China, and Korea. The United States ranks as Australia's third-largest trading partner—although Australia no longer ranks among the United States' top twenty-five trading partners. Even so, Australian–American relations remain friendly, and American culture exerts a profound impact on life Down Under.

Australia's population today includes about 548,000 Aborigines and Torres Strait Islanders, many of whom are of mixed ancestry. Many Aborigines live in traditional communities on reservations that have been set up in rural areas of the country, but a growing number of aboriginal young people have moved into the cities. The results have been traumatic: poverty, cultural dislocation, dispossession, and disease have taken

a deadly toll. Many of the Aboriginal people in cities live in substandard housing and lack adequate health care. The unemployment rate among Aborigines is six times the national average, while those who have jobs earn only about half the average national wage. In 2007 Australian Olympic athletes Cathy Freeman and Ian Thorpe launched the Close the Gap campaign, aimed at bringing indigenous health care and life expectancy more in line with national averages.

SETTLEMENT IN THE UNITED STATES

Although Australians have a recorded presence of almost two hundred years on American soil, they have contributed minimally to the total U.S. immigration figures. Data compiled by the U.S. Immigration and Naturalization Service indicate that about 16,200 Australians came to the United States in the seventy years from 1820 to 1890—an average of slightly more than 230 per year. The average increased to around 1,000 per year in the first half of the twentieth century and has increased to about 2,000 per year since then.

Evidence indicates that beginning in the mid-nineteenth century, most Australians who immigrated to America settled in and around San Francisco, and to a lesser extent in Los Angeles. (California was not part of the United States until 1848.) Apart from their peculiar clipped accents, which sounded vaguely British to undiscerning American ears, Australians easily blended into American society—much more easily than in British society, where class divisions were rigid. Often the British regarded anyone from the colonies as a provincial philistine.

The California gold rush in January 1848 sparked the first major wave of emigration from Australia to the United States. Groups of would-be prospectors chartered ships to take them on the monthlong 8,000-mile voyage to the United States. Among them were many of the ex-convicts who had been deported from Great Britain to the colony of Australia. Called Sydney Ducks, these fearsome immigrants introduced organized crime into the area and caused the California legislature to attempt to prohibit the entry of convicted criminals. However, gold was but the initial attraction; many were seduced upon their arrival in California by what they saw as liberal land ownership laws and the limitless economic prospects of life in the United States. From August 1850 through May 1851, more than eight hundred Aussies sailed out of Sydney harbor bound for California. Most made new lives in the United States and never returned home. On March 1, 1851, a writer for the *Sydney Morning Herald* decried this exodus of "persons of a better class, who have been industrious and thrifty, and who carry with them the means of settling down in a new world as respectable and substantial settlers."

As the U.S. Civil War raged from 1861 to 1865, immigration of Australians to the United States virtually disappeared. Statistics show that from January

1861 to June 1870 only around thirty Australians made the move across the Pacific. This situation changed in the late 1870s, following the end of the Civil War, as the U.S. economy expanded and trade increased. Regular steamship service was inaugurated between Melbourne and Sydney and ports on the U.S. west coast. Interestingly, the better the economic conditions were in Australia, the more likely Australians were to pack up and go; but when times were tough, they tended to stay home. Thus, in the years between 1871 and 1880, when conditions were favorable, 8,930 Australians immigrated to the United States. During the next two decades, as the world economy faltered, those numbers fell by half, a pattern that continued into the next century.

Before World War I, the vast majority of Australians who came to the United States did so as visitors en route to England. The standard itinerary for travelers was to sail to San Francisco and see the United States while journeying by rail to New York. From there, the tourists sailed to London. The trip was tremendously expensive, and although it was several weeks shorter than the mind-numbing 14,000-mile ocean voyage to London, it was still difficult and time-consuming. Thus, only well-to-do travelers could afford it.

With the 1941 outbreak of war with Japan, the nature of relations between Australia and the United States changed dramatically. In the boom years after the war, immigration to the United States, which had dwindled to about 2,300 persons during the lean years of the 1930s, increased. This was largely due to two important factors: a rapidly expanding U.S. economy and the exodus of 15,000 Australian war brides who married American servicemen stationed in Australia during the war.

With few exceptions, the number of Australians receiving permanent resident status in the United States grew steadily after 1960. During the 1960s, nearly 15,000 immigrants from Australia were granted residence in the United States, a figure that jumped to more than 18,500 during the 1970s. In the late 1980s a deep worldwide recession hit the resource-based economy of Australia, resulting in high unemployment and hardship. The number of Australian immigrants fell to around 17,000. In the 1990s, as the Australian economy began to strengthen, that number jumped to over 24,200, remaining steady throughout the 2000s. From 1980 (when the U.S. Census Bureau began recording ancestry data) to 2010, the number of U.S. residents claiming Australian ancestry increased from around 53,700 to over 90,000. Around 75 percent of all employed Australian immigrants since 2000 have found work in management, sales, or education, seemingly confirming the notion that highly skilled Australians have looked to the United States and elsewhere for economic and employment opportunities.

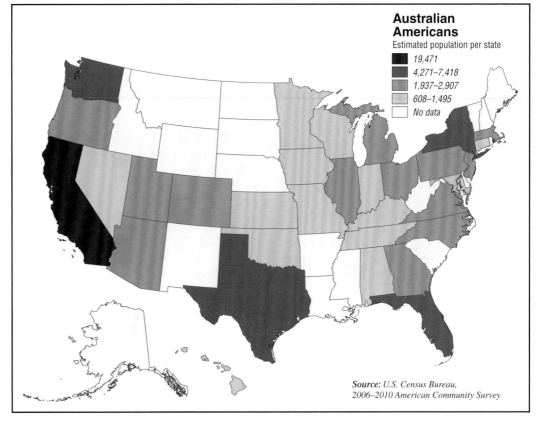

Source: U.S. Census Bureau, 2006–2010 American Community Survey

LANGUAGE

English is spoken in Australia, though with some marked differences from American or even British English, from which it is derived. In 1966 an Australian named Afferbeck Lauder published a tongue-in-cheek book titled *Let Stalk Strine*, which means "Let's Talk Australian" (*Strine* is the telescoped form of the word *Australian*). Lauder was later revealed to be Alistair Morrison, an artist-turned-linguist who was poking good-natured fun at his fellow Australians and their accents—accents that make *lady* sound like "lydy" and *mate* like "mite." In the 1970 book *The Australian Language*, linguist Sidney Baker does what H. L. Mencken did for American English, identifying more than five thousand words or phrases that are distinctly Australian.

Greetings and Popular Expressions A few distinctively Australian words and expressions are *abo*—an Aborigine; *billabong*—a watering hole, usually for livestock; *billy*—a container for boiling water for tea; *bloke*—a man; *bonzer*—great, terrific; *boomer*—a kangaroo; *chook*—a chicken; *Digger*—an Aussie soldier; *dingo*—a wild dog; *dinki-di*—the real thing; *dinkum, fair dinkum*—honest, genuine; *grazier*—a rancher; *joey*—a baby kangaroo; *jumbuck*—a sheep; *ocker*—a good, ordinary Aussie; *Oz*—short for Australia; *pom*—an English person; *shout*—a round of drinks in a pub; *swagman*—a hobo or bushman; *tinny*—a can of beer; *tucker*—food; and *ute*—a pickup or utility truck.

RELIGION

Australian Americans are predominantly Christian. Statistics suggest that Australian society has been becoming increasingly secular, with nearly a third of all people having no religion (or failing to respond to the question when polled by census takers). However, 25.3 percent are Roman Catholic and 17.1 percent are Anglican or Episcopalian. Only about 7 percent adhere to non-Christian religions, with Muslims, Hindus, Buddhists, and Jews constituting the bulk of that segment. Given these numbers, it is reasonable to assume that most church-going Australian Americans are adherents to the Episcopalian or Roman Catholic Churches, both of which are active in the United States.

CULTURE AND ASSIMILATION

Australians in the United States assimilate easily because they come from a Westernized industrial state with many similarities to the United States in language, culture, and social structure. According to Harvard professor Ross Terrill, Australians have a great deal in common with Americans when it comes to outlook and temperament; both are easygoing and casual in their relationships with others. Like Americans, Terrill writes, Australians "have an anti-authoritarian streak that seems to echo the contempt of the convict for his keepers and betters." Apart from their accents, Australians are almost indistinguishable from Americans, particularly because the vast majority of Australians who immigrate to the United States are white. Thus, they tend to blend in and adapt easily to the American lifestyle, which in urban areas is very similar that of their homeland.

Data about Australian Americans must be extrapolated from demographic information compiled by the Australian government. Indications are that they live a lifestyle strikingly similar to that of many Americans. Data show that the average age of the population—like that of the United States and most other industrialized nations—is growing older. In 2011 the median age of Australians was about thirty-four years. There has been a dramatic increase in recent years in the number of single-person and two-person households in Australia. In 2011, 24 percent of Australian households had just one person, and 34 percent had but two. These numbers are generally maintained in the Australian American population and reflect the fact that Australians are more mobile than ever. Young people leave home at an earlier age, and one out of three marriages ends in divorce, a rate that lags behind the U.S. divorce rate, which is over 50 percent. Australians tend to be socially conservative. As a result, their society still tends to be male dominated; a working father, stay-at-home mother, and one or two children remains a powerful cultural image.

Traditions and Customs In *The Australian Legend* (1958), Australian historian Russell Ward sketches an image of the archetypal Aussie. He notes that while Aussies have a reputation as a hard-living, rebellious, and gregarious people, the reality is quite the opposite: "Far from being the weather-beaten bushmen of popular imagination, today's Australian belongs to the most urbanized big country on earth." Even so, in the collective American mind, the old image persists, bolstered by the 1986 movie *Crocodile Dundee* and its numerous sequels, which star Australian actor Paul Hogan as a wily bushman who visits New York City. Apart from Hogan's likeable persona, much of the fun in the film stems from the juxtaposition of American and Aussie cultures. Discussing the popularity of *Crocodile Dundee* in the *Journal of Popular Culture* in 1990, authors Ruth Abbey and Jo

Australians in the United States assimilate easily because they come from a Westernized industrial state with many similarities to the United States in language, culture, and social structure.

Crawford note that to American eyes, Paul Hogan was Australian "through and through." What is more, the character he plays echoes Davy Crockett, the fabled American woodsman. This meshes comfortably with the prevailing view that Australia is a latter-day

Australian Americans' love of Vegemite has made this spreadable brewers' yeast by-product widely available in the U.S. FINNBARR WEBSTER / ALAMY

version of what the United States once was: a simpler, more honest and open society.

The Australian tourism industry actively promoted *Crocodile Dundee* in the United States, causing a dramatic jump in American tourism in Australia in the late 1980s. Ever since, Australian culture has enjoyed unprecedented popularity in North America. In 2004 a number of Australian tourism and trade groups launched a promotional campaign called "G'Day USA: Australia Week" to encourage American investment and tourism in Australia. The campaign, which has become the largest promotional event sponsored by a foreign country in the United States, includes food and wine conventions, fashion shows, concerts, and other showcases for Australian art, business, and culture. The campaign has been enormously successful, causing Australian airline Qantas to double the amount of transnational flights it offers.

Cuisine The emergence of a distinctive Australian culinary style in recent years may be the byproduct of a growing sense of nationalism as Australia moved away from Britain and forged its own identity—largely spurred by the vast number of immigrants since immigration restrictions were eased in 1973. Australians continue to be big meat eaters: beef, lamb, and seafood are standard fare, often smothered in heavy sauces or served in the form of meat pies called pasties. A quintessential Australian meal might

be a barbecue-grilled steak or lamb chop. Two dietary staples from earlier times are an unleavened bread called damper that is cooked over a fire, and billy tea, a strong, robust hot drink that is brewed in an open pot. For dessert, favorites include peach melba, fruit-flavored ice creams, and pavlova, a rich meringue dish that was named after a famous Russian ballerina who toured the country in the early twentieth century.

In colonial times, rum was the preferred form of alcohol. However, tastes have changed; wine and beer are popular nowadays. Australia began developing its own domestic wine industry in the early nineteenth century, and wines from Down Under are today recognized as among the world's best. As such, they are readily available at liquor stores throughout the United States and are a tasty reminder of life back home for transplanted Aussies. On a per-capita basis, Aussies drink about twice as much wine each year as Americans. They also enjoy ice-cold beer, which tends to be stronger and darker than most American brews. In recent years, Australian beer has earned a small share of the American market, no doubt in part because of demand from Aussies living in the United States.

Australian Americans often find foods from home, or "tucker," in American grocery stores and specialty shops. Ingredients like vegemite, a salty vegetable spread used on toast and sandwiches, are available in most areas with high concentrations of Australian immigrants, such as California and New York. Import companies such as Simply Australian (www.simplyoz.com) cater to Australian Americans by offering familiar products like meat pies, pavlova, Weet-Bix breakfast cereal, teas, and such sweets as Tim Tam and Violet Crumble bars.

Traditional Costumes Australians do not have any unusual or distinctive national costumes. One of the few distinctive pieces of clothing worn by Australians is the wide-brimmed khaki bush hat with the brim turned up on one side. The hat, which has sometimes been worn by Australian soldiers, has become something of a national symbol and is occasionally worn by Australian Americans.

Dances and Songs When most Americans think of Australian music, the first tune that springs to mind is often "Waltzing Matilda." But Australia's musical heritage is long, rich, and varied. The country's distance from Western cultural centers such as London and New York has resulted in a vibrant and highly original commercial style, particularly with respect to music and film. The traditional music of nonindigenous Australia, which has its roots in Irish folk music, and bush dancing, which is similar to square dancing without a caller, are popular. Homegrown pop vocalists such as Helen Reddy and Olivia Newton-John (born in England but raised in Australia), and opera diva Joan Sutherland have found receptive audiences in the United States and around the world, as have Australian rock-and-roll bands such as INXS, AC/DC, Jet, the Vines, Silverchair, Little River Band, Hunters and Collectors, Midnight Oil, and Men Without Hats. Other Australian bands such as Yothu Yindi and Warumpi, which are not well known outside the country, have revitalized Australian music with a unique fusion of mainstream rock and roll and elements of the music of Australia's Aboriginal peoples.

Holidays Predominantly Christian, Australian Americans celebrate most of the religious holidays on the Christian calendar. However, because the seasons are reversed in the Southern Hemisphere, Australia's Christmas occurs in midsummer. For that reason, Aussies do not share in many of the same yuletide traditions that Americans keep. For example, after attending church, Australians typically spend December 25 at the beach or gathered around a swimming pool, sipping cold drinks—making Australian Americans' first holiday season in the United States something of an adjustment.

Secular holidays that Australians everywhere celebrate include January 26, Australia Day—the country's national holiday. The date, which commemorates the 1788 arrival at Botany Bay of the first convict settlers under the command of captain Arthur Phillip, is akin to the U.S. Fourth of July holiday. Another important holiday is Anzac Day, April 25. On this day, Aussies everywhere pause to honor the memory of the nation's soldiers who died in the World War I battle at Gallipoli in Turkey. Many attend dawn memorial services, and it is quite common to play two-up, a gambling game long associated with Australian soldiers (commonly known as Diggers), throughout the day. Australian Americans observe this holiday at ceremonies typically organized by the Australian consulate or by expatriate groups. Another military-related holiday, Armistice Day, is commonly celebrated by Australians around the world on November 11 to commemorate the end of World War I.

The most common method of celebration for Australians is a casual barbeque, or "barbie," in which a group of friends eat grilled meats, seafood, and vegetables; drink cold beverages; and perhaps play popular games like cricket or Aussie-rules football. Since Americans also tend to gather around the grill on holidays, Australian Americans are largely able to maintain this informal tradition in the United States.

FAMILY AND COMMUNITY LIFE

Like Australians, Australian Americans are an informal, avid outdoor people with a hearty appetite for life and sports. Because Australia has a temperate climate all year round, outdoor sports such as tennis, cricket, rugby, Australian-rules football, golf, swimming, and sailing are popular both with spectators and participants. The national pastimes of barbecuing and sun worshipping are somewhat less strenuous. In fact, Australians spend so much time in the sun in their

PAVLOVA

Ingredients

    4 egg whites at room temperature

    ⅔ cup white sugar

    4 teaspoons cornstarch

    ½ teaspoons white vinegar

    1 teaspoon vanilla extract

    1 cup heavy whipping cream

    1 cup fresh fruit (kiwis and strawberries are traditional)

    parchment paper

Preparation

Preheat oven to 250°F.

Put the egg whites in a large glass bowl. Add vinegar and whisk until it becomes foamy. Slowly add in sugar and continue to whisk until a stiff meringue is formed. Add the cornstarch and vanilla, whisking a few more times. (Do not over-whisk)

Wet the parchment paper and line the baking sheet with it. Use a spoon to mound the meringue onto the paper, making a well in the middle so that it is somewhat bowl shaped. Continue to layer the meringue up on the sides to create a deeper bowl.

Place the meringue in the oven for 45 minutes. Turn the heat off and leave the meringue in for another hour, or until it is completely cool.

While the meringue is cooling, cut up your fruit into appetizing, bite-sized pieces and whip the cream until stiff.

Remove the meringue bowl from the oven. Fill the meringue bowl with whipped cream and put the fruit on top.

Serve immediately.

Serves 8–10

backyards and at the beach that the country has one of the world's highest rates of skin cancer, with nearly two-thirds of the population being diagnosed with some form of the disease by age seventy.

Gender Roles Although Australian families have traditionally been headed by a male breadwinner with women in the domestic role, changes are occurring. Australia was one of the first countries to grant women the right to vote, though high levels of inequality between genders still exist: women are significantly underrepresented in positions of power, are paid far less than men for performing the same jobs, and are at increased risk for physical and sexual abuse, particularly in indigenous communities. Although such problems are also present in the United States, there is some evidence that Australian women see the United States as a place where they are more likely to succeed on their own. According to the 2010 U.S. Census, there were over 36,000 women of Australian descent over age eighteen residing in the United States, compared to just over 34,000 Australian American men. Of these women, 4,500 were foreign-born, naturalized U.S. citizens (the figure is 3,200 for men). This suggests that Australian women are more likely than Australian men to make their residence in the United States permanent. These numbers agree with a study conducted by the Australian Bureau of Statistics, which found that between the years 2004 and 2010, women were more likely than men to depart permanently.

Although Australian American women aged thirty-five to fifty are four times as likely to be married than unmarried, those aged twenty to thirty-four are more likely to be unmarried. These statistics fall in line with general trends in the United States, suggesting that young Australian American women are similarly independent. Australian American women are also more likely than men to live on their own and to raise children as a single parent. In fact, the U.S. Census Bureau reported in 2011 that approximately 30 percent of all Australian American women were enrolled in college or graduate school, placing them on par with their male counterparts and the general female population of the United States in that age range—though women are far less likely to obtain high-wage jobs after college. Nevertheless, Australian American women are clearly redefining their social roles in the twenty-first century; they are more educated and less dependent on husbands or partners for financial support than in past years. Many have reached out to other Australian American women to form support networks. For example, Australian Women in New York has published a monthly newsletter and hosted regular gatherings for students, professionals, and mothers of Australian descent since 1999.

Education Australian Americans tend to be highly educated, as they often come to the United States to pursue college degrees or to put their advanced skills to greater use. In 2011 the U.S. Census Bureau reported that 93 percent of all Australian Americans age twenty-five or over held a high school diploma as opposed to 86 percent of the general population, and 45 percent held a bachelor's degree or higher as opposed to 28 percent of the general population. The Australian government actively encourages college students to study overseas, and a recent report by the Institute of International Education found that there were 3,848 Australian college students studying in the United States in 2012, an increase of nearly 45 percent since 2001. Australian Americans attend public schools over private schools by a three-to-one margin.

EMPLOYMENT AND ECONOMIC CONDITIONS

According to the American Community Survey's estimates in 2010, the most common types of employment for Australian Americans are education and health care (22 percent) or professional, scientific, or management positions (16 percent). However, it is largely impossible to describe a type of work or location of work that characterizes most Australian Americans. Because they have been and remain so widely scattered throughout the United States, and because they have so easily assimilated into American society, they have not established an identifiable ethnic presence in the United States. Their similarity in most respects to other Americans has made them unidentifiable and virtually invisible in most areas of American life. The place Australian Americans tend to congregate is on the Internet. There are Australian groups on online forums such as Yahoo! and on independently operated forums like Mates Up-Over (www.matesupover.com). They also come together over sporting events, such as the Australian-rules football grand final, the rugby league grand final, or the Melbourne Cup horse race, which are broadcast live on cable television or via satellite.

POLITICS AND GOVERNMENT

Acknowledgement of the Australian diaspora in the early 2000s has led the Australian government to make greater efforts at maintaining ties to expatriates. Various cultural organizations and commercial associations sponsored directly or indirectly by the government are now working to encourage Australian Americans and American business representatives to lobby state and federal politicians to be more favorably disposed toward Australia. One such program, Expatriate Connect, attempts to match skilled Aussies living overseas with Australian small businesses so that those businesses might expand their reach in the international market. Another organization, Advance Australian Professionals in America, is partially funded by the Australian government and seeks to turn Australian American professionals into political and cultural ambassadors.

NOTABLE INDIVIDUALS

Journalism Rupert Murdoch (1931–), one of the United States' most powerful media magnates, was born in Australia. He owned a host of important media properties, including the *Chicago Sun Times*, *New York Post*, and *Boston Herald* newspapers, and 20th Century Fox movie studios. CNN television journalist Soledad O'Brien (1966–) is a second-generation Australian American.

Literature Jill Ker Conway (1934–), an award-winning memoirist and historian who was the first female president of Smith College in Massachusetts, was born in New South Wales and came to the United States in 1960. Her 1989 memoir *The Road from Coorain* was adapted as a television movie in 2002.

Music Singer Helen Reddy (1941–), who had a Grammy-winning single—"I Am Woman"—in 1972, became an American citizen in 1968. Singer Rick

Springfield (1949–), who had a number one hit in 1968 with his song "Jessie's Girl," became a U.S. citizen in 2006. Renowned bassist Michael "Flea" Balzary (1962–), best known for his work with the rock group Red Hot Chili Peppers, was born near Melbourne and immigrated to the United States with his family at the age of five.

Sports Greg Norman (1955–), a highly successful professional golfer holds dual citizenship in the United States and his native Australia. Matthew Brabham (1994–), grandson of Australian Formula 1 racing legend Sir Jack Brabham and winner of the 2012 Cooper Tires USF2000 Championship, also has dual citizenship in the United States and Australia. Tennis legend John Newcombe (1944–) maintains a home and a tennis academy in New Braunfels, Texas. Kyrie Irving (1992–), 2012 NBA Rookie of the Year, was born in Melbourne and moved to the United States at the age of two. Patrick "Patty" Mills (1988–), the first indigenous Australian NBA basketball player, plays for the San Antonio Spurs.

Stage and Screen Screen actor Rod Taylor (1930–), known for his leading role in Alfred Hitchcock's *The Birds* (1963), was born in Sydney and moved to the United States in the mid-1950s. Actress Mia Farrow (1945–), known for her roles in films such as *Rosemary's Baby* (1968), *The Purple Rose of Cairo* (1985), and *Crimes and Misdemeanors* (1989), is the daughter of Australian director John Farrow. Actress Nicole Kidman (1967–) has dual citizenship because she was born in Hawaii to Australian parents. Kidman won an Oscar for her performance in the 2002 film *The Hours*.

MEDIA

TELEVISION

Australian Broadcasting Corporation

Australia's national public broadcasting station, available for streaming online and via satellite in the United States.

2000 M Street NW
Suite 660
Washington, D.C. 20036
Phone: (202) 466-8575
Fax: (202) 626-5188
URL: www.abc.net.au

Channel 9 Australia

One of the oldest and most popular television stations in Australia.

6255 Sunset Boulevard
Suite 1500
Los Angeles, California 90028
Phone: (323) 461-3853
Fax: (323) 461-3018
URL: www.channelnine.ninemsn.com.au

Australian American Mia Farrow is well known for her activism and acting career. DAN CALLISTER / ALAMY

Network 10 Australia

A prominent Australian free-to-air television station with offices in Los Angeles.

3440 Motor Avenue
Los Angeles, California 90034
Phone: (310) 287-2501
Fax: (310) 287-2505
URL: www.ten.com.au

ORGANIZATIONS AND ASSOCIATIONS

Advance

This global organization of Australian professionals seeks to partner skilled expatriate Australians with Australian businesses and to provide opportunity for Australian professionals around the world.

Serafina Maiorano, Chief Executive Officer
150 E 42nd Street
34th Floor
New York, New York 10017
Phone: (212) 682-2885
Fax: (212) 682-2066
Email: serafina@advance.org
URL: www.advance.org

American Australian Association

Encourages closer ties between the United States and Australia, and organizes events across the United States to encourage networking among Australian Americans.

Frances M. Cassidy, President
1251 Avenue of the Americas

New York, New York 10020
Phone: (212) 338-6860
Fax: (212) 338-6864
Email: information@aaanyc.org
URL: www.americanaustralian.org

Australian American Chamber of Commerce, San Francisco Chapter

This organization promotes business, cultural, and social relations between the United States and Australia in California.

Dawn Lillington, Executive Director
P.O. Box 471285
San Francisco, California 94147
Phone: (415) 485-6718
Email: chamber@sfaussies.com
URL: www.sfaussies.com

Australian New Zealand American Chamber of Commerce, Midwest Chapter

This organization promotes business, cultural, and social relations between the United States and Australia in the Midwest region.

Cameron McLeod, President
P.O. Box 64308
Chicago, Illinois 60664-4308
Phone: (312) 458-9846
Fax: (312) 896-5032
Email: infoanzacc@anzacc-midwest.org
URL: www.anzaccmidwest.org

Australia New Zealand America Society

This organization seeks to expand educational and cultural opportunities in the Pacific Northwest.

Greg Pearce, President
18525 NW Village Park Drive
Issaquah, Washington 98027
Phone: (425) 865-0375
Email: anzas@comcast.net
URL: www.anzas.org

MUSEUMS AND RESEARCH CENTERS

Australian and New Zealand Studies Association of North America

This academic association promotes teaching about Australia and the scholarly investigation of Australian topics and issues throughout institutions of higher education in North America.

Patty O'Brien, President
Email: pao4@georgetown.edu
URL: www.anzsana.net

Edward A. Clark Center for Australian & New Zealand Studies

Established in 1988, this center was named after a former U.S. ambassador to Australia from 1967 to 1968. It conducts teaching programs, research

projects, and international outreach activities that focus on Australian matters and on U.S.–Australia relations.

Dr. Rhonda Evans Case, Interim Director
Harry Ransom Center
Suite 3.362
University of Texas
Austin, Texas 78713-7219
Phone: (512) 471-9607
Fax: (512) 471-8869
Email: evanscaser@ecu.edu
URL: www.utexas.edu/cola/centers/cas

Georgetown University Center for Australian and New Zealand Studies

Established in 1995 by the School of Foreign Service at Georgetown University in Washington, D.C., this center is partially funded by the government of Australia; offers courses on Australian history, government, and culture; and often arranges lectures by visiting professors from Australia and New Zealand.

Dr. Alan Tidwell, Director
ICC 232
Georgetown University
Washington, D.C. 20057
Phone: (202) 687-7464
Fax: (202) 687-5528
Email: act35@georgetown.edu
URL: http://canz.georgetown.edu

SOURCES FOR ADDITIONAL STUDY

Arnold, Caroline. *Australia Today*. New York: Franklin Watts, 1987.

Bateson, Charles. *Gold Fleet for California: Forty-Niners from Australia and New Zealand*. Auckland: Minerva, 1963.

Clancy, Laurie. *Culture and Customs of Australia*. Westport, CT: Greenwood, 2004.

Constable, George, et al., eds. *Australia*. New York: Time-Life Books, 1985.

Hughes, Robert. *The Fatal Shore: A History of The Transportation of Convicts to Australia, 1787–1868*. New York: Knopf, 1987.

Kelton, Maryanne. *"More Than an Ally?": Contemporary Australia–US Relations*. Aldershot, UK: Ashgate, 2008.

Moore, John Hammond, ed. *Australians in America: 1876–1976*. Brisbane: University of Queensland Press, 1977.

Renwick, George W. *Interact: Guidelines for Australians and North Americans*. Chicago: Intercultural Press, 1980.

Siracusa, Joseph M., and David G. Coleman. *Australia Looks to America: Australian–American Relations, since Pearl Harbor*. Claremont, CA: Regina Books, 2006.

Smith, Robin E., ed. *Australia*. Canberra: Australian Government Printing Service, 1992.

Austrian Americans

J. Sydney Jones

OVERVIEW

Austrian Americans are immigrants or descendants of people from Austria, a landlocked country in central Europe. Austria is bordered by Germany, Switzerland, and Liechtenstein to the west; the Czech Republic to the north; Slovakia and Hungary to the east; and Slovenia and Italy to the south. The Danube River, Europe's second-longest river and the only major European river that flows eastward, flows through Austria. The total land area of the country is 31,832 square miles (82,445 square kilometers), about twice the size of Switzerland and slightly smaller than the state of Maine.

According to the *CIA World Factbook*, Austria's population was 8,219,743 in July 2012. Most Austrians (73.6 percent) are Roman Catholics. The rest of the population is divided among Protestants (4.7 percent), Muslims (4.2 percent), and other faiths (3.5 percent). More than 10 percent of Austrians identify with no religious group. In 2011 Austria's GDP per capita was $42,400, making it the eighteenth-wealthiest country in the world. The Austrian economy is heavily dependent upon a large service sector, which in 2011 contributed nearly 70 percent of the nation's GDP.

Although Austrians began immigrating to the British colonies in the New World before the United States existed as a nation, it was not until the mid-nineteenth century that they began arriving in significant numbers. Between 1860 and 1900 the number of German-speaking Austrians in the United States increased dramatically, reaching 275,000 by 1900. They settled primarily in urban centers of the United States where they were able to find jobs in the stockyards of Chicago and the coal mines of Pennsylvania. In the first two decades after World War II, a new wave of Austrians from many different backgrounds immigrated to the United States to escape the chaos and desolation of their homeland in the immediate postwar era. As Austria developed into a democratic nation with a stable economy, immigration to the United States declined and by 2012 had become negligible.

The U.S. Census Bureau estimates that in 2010 there were 684,214 people of Austrian descent living in the United States, a number comparable to the population of El Paso, Texas. Less than 0.2 percent of the population identify themselves as Austrian, as compared to 13 percent of the population who identify themselves as being of German ancestry. The states with the highest number of Austrian Americans among their inhabitants include New York, California, and Pennsylvania.

HISTORY OF THE PEOPLE

Early History Austria's very name denotes its history. *Ostmark* or *Ostarichi* ("eastern provinces" or "borderland"), as it was known during the reign of Charlemagne (768–814), eventually became the German *Österreich*, or "Austria" in Latin. As an eastern kingdom—more bulwark than principality, more fortress than palace—Austria bordered the civilized world. The first human inhabitants of this rugged environment were Stone Age hunters who lived 80,000 to 150,000 years ago. Permanent settlements were established in early Paleolithic times. Though little remains of that distant period, an early Iron Age settlement was unearthed at Hallstatt in the western lake district of present-day Austria. The Celts arrived around 400 BCE, and the Romans, in search of iron-ore deposits, invaded 200 years later. The Romans established three provinces in the area by 15 BCE. They introduced the grape to the hills surrounding the eastern reaches of the Danube near a settlement they called *Vindobona*, later known as *Wien*, or "Vienna" in English.

For the next four centuries the Romans fought Germanic invasions, eventually losing but establishing a fortification line along the Danube River, upon which many modern Austrian cities were built. With the fall of Rome, barbarian tribes such as the Bavarians from the west and Mongolian Avars from the east settled the region, bringing new cultural influences. One Germanic tribe, the Franks, was particularly interested in the area, and by the end of the eighth century Charlemagne succeeded in subduing the other claimants, Christianizing the region and creating a largely Germanic province for his Holy Roman Empire. This Ostmark did not hold long. Incursions from the east by the Magyars around 900 CE unsettled the region once again, until the Magyars too were subdued.

The political and territorial concept of Austria came about in 976 when the eastern province was granted to the House of Babenberg. For the next three centuries this powerful family would rule the eastern borderland, eventually choosing Vienna as their seat. By the twelfth century Austria had become a dukedom and a flourishing trade center. With the death of the line of Babenberg in 1246, the dukedom was voted first to Ottokar II, king of Bohemia, who was defeated in battle by a member of a Swiss noble house, Rudolf IV of Habsburg. The Habsburgs would rule not only Austria but also large parts of Europe and the New World until 1918. They created a central European empire around the region of Austria that extended into Bohemia, Hungary, Yugoslavia, Poland, Spain, and the Netherlands. Throughout the Habsburgs' reign, the empire acted as a bulwark against eastern invasion by Turks and Magyars, and through both diplomacy and strategic marriages, the family established a civilization that would be the envy of the world. Under such emperors as Rudolf and Charles V and the empress Maria Theresa, universities were established, and Vienna became synonymous with music, fostering such composers as Joseph Haydn, Wolfgang Amadeus Mozart, Ludwig van Beethoven, Franz Schubert, and Johannes Brahms.

When the Napoleonic Wars ended the power of the Holy Roman Empire, the Austrian, or Habsburg, Empire took its place in central Europe, and its foreign minister, Clemens Metternich-Winneburg, consolidated power to make a unified German state. The democratic revolutions of 1848 temporarily destabilized the country, but under the rule of Franz Joseph a strong government again rose to power. The Austrian Empire faced increasing nationalistic pressure, however. First the Magyars in Hungary won a compromise with Vienna, creating the Austro-Hungarian Empire in 1867. Other ethnic minorities in the polyglot empire pressed for independence, and eventually, with the assassination of Archduke Ferdinand by a Serbian extremist in Sarajevo in 1914, the world was plunged into a war that destroyed the Austrian Empire.

Modern Era In 1918, with the abdication of Karl I, the last Habsburg, the modern Republic of Austria was founded. Now a smaller country, it comprised only the original Germanic provinces with 7 million inhabitants. The postwar years were characterized by a struggle for economic survival and the question of union with Germany. Clashes between left- and right-wing factions increased throughout the 1920s, culminating on February 12, 1934, in what became known as the February Uprising. Members of *Heimwehr*, a militia of the dominant right-wing Christian Socialist Party, operating as a police force, tried to search the left-wing Social Democrats' party headquarters in Linz and sparked an open conflict that spread quickly to Vienna. Within four days the rebellion was crushed, several hundred were dead, the Social Democratic Party and its affiliated labor unions were banned, its leaders executed or in exile, and the Austrofascists in control. The multiparty system in Austria had been

destroyed. In 1938 Adolf Hitler invaded Austria and one day later proclaimed his native country a province of Germany. A month later, a controlled, retroactive referendum that Jews and Roma were not allowed to take part in yielded a 99 percent vote in favor of union with Germany.

During the early years of World War II, German military victories and Austria's geographical isolation spared the country the full effect of the conflict. Almost a million Austrians fought with German troops. By 1943, however, Austrian support for the war and for the German union had begun to erode. In 1945 Allied forces advanced into Austria, and soon afterward Germany surrendered unconditionally.

At the end of the war, the four Allied powers divided Austria into four occupation zones. The Western Allies initially were reluctant to recognize Austria's provisional government but did so in October 1945 after it became clear that the separatist feelings that had surfaced among the provinces after World War I were not a concern. Indeed, the provisional government and provincial sentiments supported a common Austrian identity. In November of 1945 the first national election since 1930 was held. The Western Allies, pleased with Austria's democratic direction, pushed for the country to have greater control over its own affairs in 1946, allowing the Austrian government to nationalize German assets, despite objections from the Soviet Union. Perhaps the most significant victory was Austria's participation in the European Recovery Program, better known as the Marshall Plan. Membership in the Organization for European Economic Co-operation, which emerged from the Marshall Plan and served to determine how aid was to be used, expedited Austria's alliance with the West and provided the economic basis for a stable parliamentary democracy.

On May 15, 1955, the Austrian State Treaty was signed, forbidding unification with Germany and the restoration of the Hapsburgs and protecting Austria's Croat and Slovene minorities. Later that year the last of the Soviet and Western troops that had occupied Austria were withdrawn. The next decades saw Austria's Western sympathies clarified, particularly when the country offered sanctuary to those fleeing the Soviet invasion of Hungary in 1956 and of Czechoslovakia in 1968.

During the immediate postwar period, Austria provided some restitution and compensation for Nazi victims, but the Amnesty Act of 1948 restored full citizenship to most of the more than half a million Austrians who had registered as ex-Nazis in 1946. Only about 42,000 people who were categorized as more implicated in the atrocities remained excluded from full citizenship. One of the reinstated was Kurt Waldheim, a diplomat who served two terms (1972–1982) as secretary general of the United Nations. Despite the revelation of evidence of his Nazi activities,

Waldheim was elected president of Austria in 1986. The resulting international furor tarnished Austria's reputation, ultimately compelling it to reexamine its history. Original restitution measures for Nazi victims ultimately were deemed inadequate, and since 1994 Austria has committed to providing victims and heirs of victims some $1 billion in restitution.

Bruno Kreisky (1911–1990) was the most significant chancellor of Austria's postwar years. From 1970 to 1983 he led the nation during a period of domestic prosperity and growing international stature. Kreisky enjoyed a longevity that no leader since the Hapsburgs had known, earning him the informal title of "Kaiser Bruno." Austria joined the European Union in 1995 and entered the EU Economic and Monetary Union in 1999, adopting the euro currency.

SETTLEMENT IN THE UNITED STATES

Austrian emigration patterns have been difficult to determine. There was no state known as Austria until 1918; prior to that, the then-sprawling Habsburg Empire, an amalgam of a dozen nationalities, encompassed the idea of Austria. Therefore, Austrian immigration can rightly be seen as the immigration of Czech, Polish, Hungarian, Slovenian, Serbian, and Croatian peoples as well as a plethora of other national and ethnic groups. Additionally, immigrants themselves were often unclear about their countries of origin. A German-speaking person born in Prague in 1855, for example, was Czech but was also part of the larger Austrian Empire—Austrian, in fact—and may have considered himself German. Immigrants thus may have listed the Czech Republic, Austria, and/or Germany as their country of origin. This study will confine itself to German Austrian emigration patterns.

The earliest documented German Austrian settlers in America were some fifty families of Protestants from Salzburg who arrived in the colony of Georgia in 1734 after fleeing religious persecution. Granted free passage and land, they established the settlement of Ebenezer near Savannah. Despite initial difficulties with poor land, sickness, and a relocation of their community, they grew and prospered as new families of immigrants arrived. Although the Revolutionary War destroyed their settlements, one of these Austrian settlers, Johann Adam Treutlen, became the first elected governor of the new state of Georgia.

Few Austrians immigrated to the United States during the first half of the nineteenth century; fewer than 1,000 Austrians were listed in official surveys by 1850. Those who did come settled in Illinois and Iowa and were supported by 100 to 200 Catholic priests sent from both Germany and Austria to oversee the settlers' religious training and education. The Leopoldine Stiftung, an Austrian foundation that supported such missionaries, funded priests not only for the newly emigrated but also for Native Americans. Priests such as Francis Xavier Weninger (1805–1888)

spread the Gospel to Austrian immigrants in the Midwest and black slaves in New Orleans. Bishop Frederic Baraga (1797–1868) was one of the most active priests among the Native Americans, working and preaching in northern Michigan. John Nepomuk Neumann (1811–1860) established numerous schools in the Philadelphia area and was a proponent of the retention of German culture and language.

Tyroleans provided a further segment of early nineteenth-century immigration to the United States. Mostly peasants, these Tyroleans came to the New World in search of land, yet few had the money they needed to turn their dreams into reality. Other early immigrants fled the oppressive Metternich regime, such as Samuel Ludvigh (1801–1869), a

During the years 1901 to 1910 alone, more than 2.1 million Austrian citizens arrived on American shores to become one of the ten most populous immigrant groups in the United States. The Austrians—cosmopolitan and either Catholic or Jewish—avoided the rural, Protestant, conservative areas of the country.

democratic intellectual who eventually founded *Die Fackel*, a well-known German-language periodical in Baltimore. The 1848 revolutions in Austria saw a small but influential tide of political refugees. These so-called Forty-eighters were mostly anticlerical and held strong antislavery views as well. Though they were few in number, they had a lasting influence on not only politics and journalism but also on medicine and music. They were mostly free-thinking, well-educated liberals who found assimilation a wearisome process in their newly adopted country. Their presence also upset the conservative Americans. Among these Forty-eighters were many Austrian Jews. Most of the Forty-eighters became abolitionists in the United States, joining the new Republican Party despite the fact that the Democratic Party traditionally showed more openness to immigrants. It has been conjectured that their votes helped Abraham Lincoln win the 1860 presidential election.

Immigration statistics are difficult to interpret for the years between 1861 and 1910, as the U.S. Bureau of Immigration categorized all the inhabitants of the Austro-Hungarian Empire together. During these decades immigration swelled, with estimates of German-speaking Austrians in the United States reaching 275,000 by 1900. Immigrants were encouraged by relaxed emigration laws at home; by the construction of more railways, which allowed easy access to the ports of Europe from their mountainous homeland; by general overpopulation in Europe; and by migration from the farm to the city as Western society became increasingly industrialized. The United States thus became a destination for displaced Austrian agrarian workers. Many

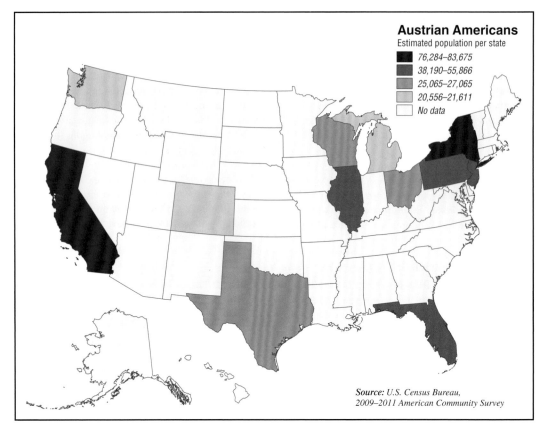

Austrian Americans
Estimated population per state

- 76,284–83,675
- 38,190–55,866
- 25,065–27,065
- 20,556–21,611
- No data

Source: U.S. Census Bureau, 2009–2011 American Community Survey

Austrians found employment in the United States as miners, servants, and common laborers. Others flocked to the cities of the Northeast and Midwest—New York, Pittsburgh, and Chicago—where many first- and second-generation Austrians still live. The 1880s witnessed massive immigration to the United States from all parts of Europe, Austria included, with more than 5 million arriving during that ten-year period. But if peasants were being displaced from the land in Austria, much the same situation was at play in the American Midwest, where mechanization was revolutionizing agriculture. Therefore, newly arrived immigrants, dreaming of a plot of farmland, were largely disappointed. Many of these new arrivals came from Burgenland, an agricultural province to the southeast of Vienna.

During the years 1901 to 1910 alone, more than 2.1 million Austrian citizens arrived on American shores to become one of the ten most populous immigrant groups in the United States. The Austrians—cosmopolitan and either Catholic or Jewish—avoided the rural, Protestant, conservative areas of the country. Fathers left families behind in Austria, hoping to save money working in Chicago stockyards and Pennsylvania cement and steel factories. More than 35 percent of them returned to their native home with their savings.

With the onset of the First World War, Austrian immigration stopped for a time. Even during the postwar period of 1919 to 1924, fewer than 20,000

Austrians came to the United States, most of them from Burgenland. The passage of a restrictive immigration law in 1924 further curtailed Austrian immigration, first to a limit of 785 and then to 1,413 persons per year. Austrian immigration slowed to a trickle during the years of the Great Depression.

A new wave of immigrants from Austria began arriving in the late 1930s. Unlike earlier immigrants who were largely unskilled laborers from the provinces, these new arrivals were mostly well-educated urban Jews fleeing Hitler's new regime. In 1938 Austria had become incorporated into the Third Reich, and anti-Semitism had become a daily fact of life. In the three-year period between the *Anschluss*, or annexation by Germany, and the outbreak of all-out war in 1941, some 29,000 Jewish Austrians immigrated to the United States. These were generally highly skilled professionals in medicine, architecture, law, and the arts and included men of international renown: composers Arnold Schoenberg (1874–1951) and Erich Wolfgang Korngold (1897–1957); author Franz Werfel (1890–1945); and stage and film directors Max Reinhardt (1873–1943) and Otto Preminger (1906–1986). The Jewish Austrian intellectual elite was, in fact, scattered around the globe in the diaspora caused by the Second World War.

Some 40,000 Austrians entered the United States from 1945 to 1960. U.S. immigration quotas again limited and diverted immigration to other countries such as Canada and Australia. By the 1960s, as Austria became an established democratic state with a prospering economy and effective social services, immigration declined, and return migration increased. Between 1992 and 2011, fewer than 500 immigrants arrived annually to the United States. The U.S. Census Bureau's American Community Survey reported 684,214 people of Austrian descent living in the United States in 2011; 45 percent of those born in Austria were sixty-five years of age or older. By the end of the first decade of the twenty-first century, Austrian immigration to the United States had become negligible.

LANGUAGE

Austria and Germany are, to paraphrase Winston Churchill's famous quip about England and the United States, two countries separated by a common language. That Austria is a German-speaking country seems to come as a surprise to many Americans. Germans also have great fun scratching their heads over Austrianisms (for instance, the German *kartoffel* becomes *erdapfel*, or apple of the earth, in Austria). However, Austrian German, apart from having a lighter, more singsong accent and some regional words, is no different from standard German than Canadian English is from American English. The umlaut (ä, ö, ü) is the primary diacritical mark over vowels and is sometimes expressed by an *e* after the vowel instead of employing the diacritic.

As English is an offshoot of Old German, there are enough similarities between the two languages to make language assimilation a reasonably easy task for Austrian Americans. The *v* for *w* confusion is an especially difficult phonetic problem, as German has no unaspirated pronunciation of *w*. Another pronunciation difficulty is the English diphthong *th* for which German has no equivalent, resulting in the thick *s* so caricatured by stage and screen actors.

Given that few Austrian Americans today are first-generation immigrants—the group most likely to speak their native language in the home—English is commonly spoken in the community. In 1990 there were 1.5 million people over the age of five speaking German in the home, a small number of whom were Austrian. By 2000 German was no longer among the ten foreign languages most frequently spoken at home. In 2011 the U.S. Census Bureau estimated that 92.1 percent of Austrian Americans spoke English at home, and that only 1.3 percent reported speaking English "less than well" (American Community Survey estimate for 2009-2011). However, many Austrian Americans are bilingual. By some estimates, as many as one-third speak both German and English.

Greetings and Popular Expressions Typical Austrian greetings and farewells include the more formal Germanisms (with pronunciation) such as *guten Tag* (gooten tahg)—"good day"; *guten Abend* (gooten ahbend)—"good evening"; and *auf Wiedersehen* (ouf veedersayen)—"good-bye." Less formal Austrian expressions are *Grüss Gott* (groos gote)—literally "greetings from God," but used as "hello" or "hi"; and *servus* (sairvoos)—both "hello" and "good-bye," used by younger people and between good friends. Other polite expressions—for which Austrian German seems to have an overabundance—include *bitte* (bietuh)— both "please" and "you're welcome"; *Danke vielmals* (dahnka feelmahls)—"thanks very much"; and *Es tut mir sehr leid* (es toot meer sair lied)—"I'm very sorry." Seasonal expressions include *Frohe Weihnachten* (frohuh vienahkten)—"Merry Christmas"—and *Prosit Neujahr* (proezit noy yahr)—"Happy New Year." *Zum wohl* (tzoom vole)—"To your health"—is a typical toast.

RELIGION

The first Austrian Americans came in search of religious freedom. Approximately 500 people arrived in Savannah, Georgia, on March 12, 1734. The Jerusalem Evangelical Lutheran Church built in 1769 still stands in what is now Rincon, Georgia, the oldest continuing Lutheran congregation in the same building in the United States, and descendants of the original Salzbugers still live in Effingham and Chatham counties.

Despite the Protestantism of that early group, most Austrian immigrants were Roman Catholics who brought their religion with them to America. Austrian missionaries, mainly Jesuits, baptized Native Americans and helped chart the New World from the seventeenth century on. But by the nineteenth century that mission had changed, for newly arrived Austrian immigrants, disdained by Irish Catholic priests who spoke no German, were clamoring for Austrian priests. Partly to meet this need and partly to convert new souls to Catholicism, the Leopoldine Stiftung, or Leopoldine Society, was established in 1829. Collecting weekly donations throughout the Habsburg Empire, the foundation sent money and priests into North America to bring faith to the frontier. Through such contributions, more than 400 churches were built on the East Coast, in the Midwest, and in what was then known as Indian country further west. The Jesuits were especially active during this period in cities such as Cincinnati and St. Louis. The Benedictines and Franciscans were also represented by both priests and nuns. These priests founded bishoprics and built congregations in the thousands. One unfortunate reaction to this was an intensification of nativist tendencies, or anti-immigrant sentiments. This influx of priests was looked upon as a conspiracy to upset the balance of the population in the United States with Roman Catholics imported from Europe. For many years such nativist sentiments made it difficult for Austrian immigrants to fully assimilate into U.S. society.

On the whole, the formal traditions and rights of the Catholic Church in the United States and in Austria were the same, but external pressures differed. New waves of Austrian immigrants, especially those fleeing Nazism, also changed the religious makeup of the groups as a whole. For the most part, arrivals between 1933 and 1945 were Jewish. Therefore, as with the U.S. population in general, Austrian Americans in the late twentieth and early twenty-first century have become more secular and less faith-bound.

CULTURE AND ASSIMILATION

During the late nineteenth century, some Americans feared the radical element among German and Austrian immigrants. The Chicago Haymarket Riot of 1886—the violent aftermath of a demonstration by German-born laborers—particularly intensified such feelings and pushed other Germans and Austrians to assert their loyalty to American values. Austrian Americans also suffered from the anti-German sentiments that were prevalent in the years prior to and during World War I. Before the United States was engaged in war against the German and Austro-Hungarian empires, many German-language newspapers expressed pro-German views and defended Germany against what they saw as the threat of British imperialism. When Congress declared war in April 1917, nearly all these newspapers immediately declared their loyalty to the United States, but their earlier statements were public record and provoked discrimination and—in some cases—actual attacks on anything associated with Germany. Austrian Americans were included in the backlash. German-sounding names for schools, streets, and towns were changed. German and Austrian music were eliminated from public performances, and businesses and homes were vandalized. German-language newspapers closed their doors voluntarily or forcibly. German-language books were burned, and classes in the German language were eliminated from schools. President Woodrow Wilson questioned the patriotism of "hyphenated Americans." Many German and Austrian Americans responded by changing their names and assimilating more fully into the dominant U.S. culture.

Although similar feelings arose during World War II, they never reached the intensity or pervasiveness displayed during World War I. By the end of the twentieth century, there was little evidence of a distinct Austrian American culture. Even the cultural roots emphasis of the 1970s had little discernible effect on the community. As emigration from Austria declined and as Austrian Americans established in the United States moved into second and third generations and beyond, assimilation increased substantially.

Traditions and Customs Austrian traditions, maintained most faithfully by those living in the mountainous region of western Austria, center mainly on the seasons. *Fasching* is an old winter custom that traditionally takes place in February. In its pagan form, it was an attempt to drive out the evil spirits of winter and prepare for spring. Processions of villagers dressed in varieties of masked costumes and ringing cowbells symbolized the fight of spring against winter. Some of these processions still take place in parts of Tyrol and Styria, but the Fasching has generally evolved into a procession of carnival balls linked with Lent and the passion of Easter.

Similarly, the old spring festivals wherein village children would parade with boughs decorated with ivy and pretzels to celebrate the reawakening of the sun have been replaced by Palm Sunday and Corpus Christi celebrations. May Day, with the dance around the maypole, is still a much celebrated event in villages all over Austria. The festival of the summer solstice, announced by bonfires on the hills, still takes place in parts of Salzburg, under the name of St. John's Night.

Harvest festivals of autumn, linked with apple and wine gathering, have a long tradition throughout Austria. Harvest fairs are still a vital part of the autumn season, and the wine harvest, from grape picking and pressing through the various stages of wine fermentation, is an affair closely monitored by many Austrians. The pine bough outside a winery signals to customers that new wine is available. The thanksgiving festival of Saint Leonard, patron saint of livestock, is a reminder of a pagan harvest celebration.

Perhaps best known and most retained by Austrian immigrants in the United States are traditions of the Christmas season, the beginning of which is marked by St. Nicholas Day on December 6. Good children are rewarded with apples and nuts in their stockings, whereas bad ones receive only lumps of coal. Caroling and the Christmas tree are but two of the Austrian and German contributions to the American celebrations of yuletide. The Christmas carol "Silent Night," one of the most beloved songs of Christmas services in the United States, was written by two Austrians and was first sung on Christmas Eve in 1818 at the midnight mass of St. Nicholas Church in Oberndorf, Austria.

As customs and beliefs from Austria have been incorporated by the Catholic Church, many Austrian Americans have retained the feast days of their native country, though without the pageantry or connection to their original purpose. The Austrian custom of placing a pine tree atop newly constructed houses has become a traditional ceremony for U.S. ironworkers as well, many of whom are of Central European origin. The fir tree, as mentioned, has become a staple of American Christmas. Yet overall, Austrian customs have become barely recognizable in the United States.

Austrian American councils around the country preserve their cultural traditions in a limited fashion through such activities as Viennese Balls, St. Nicholas events for children, and observance of Austrian American Day, first proclaimed by former President Bill Clinton on September 25, 1997. Most societies also hold a monthly or quarterly *stammtisch*, an informal group meeting where food and conversation are shared. Originally the word also referred to the large, often round, table that was reserved for the regulars who gathered in a particular place to drink beer, play cards, socialize, and hold lively discussions, frequently of a political nature.

Cuisine Austrian cuisine relies heavily on meat, especially pork. The famous dish *wiener schnitzel*, pork or veal fried in bread crumbs, is among the many recipes that were imported along with the immigrants. *Goulash*, a spicy Hungarian stew, is another item that has found its way onto the American table, as has *sauerkraut*, both a German and an Austrian specialty. Sausages, called *wurst* in German, have become so popular in the United States that names such as *wiener* (from *wienerwurst*) and *frankfurter* (from Frankfurt in Germany) are synonymous with a whole class of food. Pastries and desserts are also Austrian specialties; Austrian favorites include *Sachertorte*, a heavy chocolate concoction closely connected with Vienna's Hotel Sacher; *linzertorte*, more of a tart than cake and stuffed with apricot jam; and the famous pastry *apfelstrudel*, a flaky sort of pie stuffed with apples. The list of such sweets is lengthy, and many of them have found places, under different names, as staples of American cuisine. Breads are another Austrian contribution to the world's foods: the rye breads of both Germany and Austria are dense and long-lasting with a hearty flavor.

Austrian beer, such as the light lagers and heavier *Bock*—brewed for Christmas and Easter—is on par with the better-known German varieties. Early immigrants of both nationalities brought the fondness for barley and hops with them, and many Austrians founded breweries in the United States. Wines, especially the tart white wines of the Wachau region of the Danube and the refined, complex varietals of Gumpoldskirchen to the south of Vienna, have become world famous as well. The Austrian love for the new wine, or *heuriger*, is witnessed by dozens of drinking songs. The simple wine tavern, owned and operated by the vintner and his family, combines the best of a picnic with dining out.

Traditional Dress In Austria the traditional costumes, or *trachten*, are still fashionable, not only for the rural population but for city dwellers as well. Most typical and best known by those outside Austria is the *dirndl*. Both village girls and Viennese matrons can be seen wearing this pleated skirt covered by a brightly colored apron and surmounted by a tight-fitting bodice. White blouses are worn under the bodice, sometimes embroidered, sometimes with lace. For men the typical *trachten* is the *steirer anzug*, a collarless variation of a hunting costume, usually gray with green piping and trim, which can be worn for both formal and informal occasions. The *wetterfleck*, a long loden cape, is also still worn, as are knickers of elk hide or wool. *Lederhosen*, or leather shorts, associated with both Germany and Austria, are still typical summer wear in much of Austria. Austrian Americans reserve traditional dress for special occasions such as parties to celebrate their shared culture.

Dances and Songs From simple *lieder*, or songs, to symphonies and operas, Austrian music has enriched the cultural life of the Western world. Vienna in particular was the home of native Austrian and German composers alike who created the classical idiom. Men such as Haydn, Mozart, Beethoven, Schubert, and Brahms developed symphony and chamber music. More modern composers such as Anton Bruckner, Gustav Mahler, and Arnold Schoenberg—the latter immigrated to the United States—expanded the boundaries of tonality and structure in musical composition.

Austria is also synonymous with the waltz, developed from an earlier peasant dance and made famous through the music of Johann Strauss and Joseph Lanner. The Viennese operetta has also influenced the musical taste of the world, helping to develop the form of the modern musical. Johann Strauss Jr. is one of many who pioneered the form, and a Viennese, Frederick Loewe, helped to transform it on Broadway by writing the lyrics to such famous musicals as *My Fair Lady* and *Camelot*. Austrian Americans take pride in their rich musical heritage, and local Austrian American councils frequently host formal Strauss balls and sponsor concerts of Austrian music.

Holidays Beyond such traditional holidays as Christmas, New Year's, and Easter, Austrian Americans cannot be said to celebrate various feast and seasonal days as a group. The more cosmopolitan immigrants from Vienna, for example, were and are much more internationalist in outlook than fellow Austrian immigrants from Burgenland, who hold to more traditional customs even in the United States. This latter group, former residents of a rural, agricultural area and generally Catholic, are more likely to observe such traditional feasts as St. Leonard's Day in November, St. Nicholas Day on December 6, and Corpus Christi in June, as well as such seasonal festivities as harvest festivals for wine in October.

Health Care Issues and Practices The medical tradition in Austria is long and noteworthy. The Viennese have contributed medical innovations such as antisepsis and therapies such as psychoanalysis to the world. Austrian Americans place a high value on health care. They also bring with them the idea of medical care as a birthright, for in Austria such care has been part of a broad government-run social program during much of the twentieth century. There are no documented congenital diseases specific to Austrian Americans.

rapidly into their new country, adapting to the ways of the United States and being influenced by the same cultural trends that affected native-born Americans: the increasing importance of the role of women in the twentieth century; the decline of the nuclear family, including a rising divorce rate; and the mobility of citizens—both geographically and economically. The variety of Austrian immigrants also changed during this century. Once mainly agrarian workers who congregated in urban areas despite their desire to settle on the land, immigrants from Austria—especially after the First World War—tended to be better educated with a larger world view. The flight of the Jewish Austrian intelligentsia during the Nazi period especially affected the assimilation patterns. These professional classes placed a high premium on education for both male and female children. Thus, Austrian immigrants became skilled workers and professionals.

Gender Roles Austrians who have immigrated to the United States in the twenty-first century arrive from a culture that has seen significant changes in the roles of women. Austrian legislation has attempted to address gender inequities in labor by providing compensation for the unpaid labor of women in many households and for the dual responsibilities of single parents. The United States makes no such provisions, and the change may require some adjustment. Attitudes toward homosexuality in the two countries also are reflected in some legal differences. Although open hostility within most traditional religious communities is the norm in both countries, Austria legalized civil unions for same-sex couples on January 1, 2010, excluding adoption and artificial insemination from the rights granted. A majority of Americans support same-sex unions, but most states deny recognition to gay marriages and make no provision for civil unions.

EMPLOYMENT AND ECONOMIC CONDITIONS

As with all examinations of Austrian immigration, occupational statistics suffer from the inconsistent distinction between ethnic groups among the Austro-Hungarian immigrants. German-speaking Austrians did settle in the center of the country to become farmers, but exact numbers are unclear. Prior to 1900 Austro-Hungarian immigrants were also laborers, saloon keepers, waiters, and steel workers. Statistics that are available from 1900, however, indicate that a high proportion of later arrivals found work as tailors, miners, and peddlers. By the mid-twentieth century, these same occupational trends still prevailed, with tailoring and the clothing industry in general employing large numbers of Austrian Americans. The food industry was also heavily weighted with Austrians, who worked as bakers, restaurateurs, and meatpackers. Mining was a predominant occupation among Austrians as well.

In the half century since then, Austrian Americans have branched out into all fields: medicine, law,

FAMILY AND COMMUNITY LIFE

Initially, many of the immigrants from Austria were males who came to the United States to earn and save money and then returned home. Most often, these early immigrants would live together in crowded rooming houses or in primitive hostels in urban centers of the industrial northeast. As permanent immigration patterns replaced this more nomadic style, the structure of the Austrian family became transplanted to the United States. Typically a tight nuclear family, the Austrian family has few of the characteristics of the extended Mediterranean family. The father ruled the economic life of the family, but the strong matriarch was boss at home. As in Austria, male children were favored. Sundays were a sacrosanct family time together. In general, few outsiders were allowed the informal "Du" greeting or even invited into the home.

This tight structure soon broke down, however, in the more egalitarian American environment. Overall, Austrian immigrants tended to assimilate

entertainment, management, and technology, as well as the traditional service industries where many of them started as new immigrants. Given the high rate of assimilation among Austrian Americans and the small number of Austrian immigrants entering the United States in the twenty-first century, no new patterns of employment can be determined.

POLITICS AND GOVERNMENT

The earliest notable political influence wielded by Austrian Americans came through the pens and the votes of the Forty-eighters. These liberal refugees from the failed revolts of 1848 were strongly abolitionist and pro-Lincoln. Later arrivals during the half century of mass immigration from Austro-Hungary (1860–1910) packed the ranks of unskilled labor and of the fledgling labor movement in the United States. Indeed, the deaths of ten Austro-Hungarian laborers during an 1897 mining strike in Lattimer, Pennsylvania, prompted a demand for indemnity by the embassy of Austro-Hungary.

Immigrants in the 1930s and 1940s tended to have strong socialist beliefs and formed organizations such as the American Friends of Austrian Labor to help promote labor issues. During World War II an Austrian government in exile was attempted in the United States, but fighting between factions of the refugees, specifically between Social Democrats and Christian Socialists, prevented any concerted action on that front. The creation of the Austrian battalion—the 101st Infantry Battalion—became the center of a debate that raged among Austrian Americans. Groups such as Austria Action and the Austrian Labor Committee opposed such a formation, fearing it would become the vanguard of the restoration of the Habsburg monarchy under Otto von Habsburg after the war. On the other side, the Free Austrian Movement advocated such a battalion, even if it meant aligning the right with the left among the recruits. A scant six months after its formation, the Austrian battalion was disbanded. Despite this failure, the debate occasioned by the creation of the battalion helped to bring to the forefront of American discussion the role of Austrian Americans and of Austria itself in the Second World War. Austrian Americans were not interned, and Austria itself was declared one of the first victims of Nazism in the Moscow Declaration of November 1, 1943. The restoration of its independence was made an Allied war aim.

Little information on Austrian American voting patterns exists, though early Jewish Austrian immigrants and Austrian socialists tended to vote Democrat rather than Republican. Interesting in this context is the career of Victor Berger (1860–1929), an Austrian who not only influenced labor organizer Eugene V. Debs in becoming a socialist but also became the first socialist to sit in the House of Representatives in Washington.

On the whole, Austrians of the first generation maintain close links with Austria, returning periodically to their place of birth. Even Jewish Austrians who had to flee the Holocaust return to visit and sometimes to retire in their homeland.

NOTABLE INDIVIDUALS

Austrian Americans have made lasting contributions in all fields of American life, though seldom are their Austrian roots emphasized. From the arts to the world of science, this immigrant population has made its mark.

Academia Joseph Alois Schumpeter (1883–1950) was a well-known critic of Marxism and an authority on business cycles. Another notable Austrian American economist was Ludwig von Mises (1881–1973), a critic of the planned economies of socialist countries.

Other Austrian Americans in the fields of literature and history have done much to generate interest in Austria and Central Europe: Harry Zohn (1924–2001) was a much-published professor of German literature at Brandeis University, and the Viennese Robert A. Kann's (1906–1981) *A History of the Habsburg Empire* has become a standard reference. R. John Rath (1910–2001) helped to centralize Austrian studies with his work at Rice University and then at the University of Minnesota. These are only a few of the many notable Austrian American historians at work in this country.

Vienna-born sociologist Paul Lazarsfeld (1901–1976) was one of the most influential social scientists of his era. Professor of sociology at Columbia University for three decades, he served as the fifty-second president of the American Sociological Association. Peter Drucker (1909–2005), author, professor, and management consultant, has been described as "the man who invented management." Drucker received the Presidential Medal of Freedom, the nation's highest civilian honor, in 2002. Heinz Politzer (1910–1978), writer, literary critic, literary historian, and professor of German at Berkeley, was a major figure in Kafka scholarship. He devoted three decades to the writing of *Franz Kafka: Parable and Paradox* (1962). Gerda Kronstein Lerner (1920–), who immigrated to the United States in 1939, is an author, a historian, and a professor emerita of history at the University of Wisconsin, Madison. A pioneer in the field of women's history, she taught what is believed to be the first women's history course at the New School for Social Research, New York City, in 1963. Egon Schwarz (1922–), professor emeritus at Washington University in St. Louis, has been a visiting scholar at more than a dozen universities in Austria and the United States. He is an influential voice in the scholarship of Austrian/German literature of the nineteenth and twentieth centuries. Robert von Dassanowsky (1960–), professor of film studies and director of the Film Studies Program at the University of Colorado at Colorado Springs, was elected to the European Academy of Sciences and Arts in 2001 and as of late 2012 serves as a U.S. delegate to the organization. He has written several books and in 2012 served as editor of *Quentin Tarantino's "Inglourious Basterds": A Manipulation of Metacinema* and *World Film Locations: Vienna*.

Art and Architecture Austrian artists who came to the United States include the artist and architect Joseph Urban (1872–1933); the sculptor and architectural designer Karl Bitter (1867–1915); Joseph Margulies (1896–1984), who painted and etched scenes of the New York ghetto; and Greta Kempton (1901–1991), who is best known for the official portrait of President Harry S. Truman. Curator René d'Harnoncourt (1901–1968), born in Vienna, eventually became director of contemporary art at the Museum of Modern Art in New York. Max Fleischer (1885–1972) was one of the pioneers of the animated cartoon; his creations include Betty Boop and Popeye.

The exodus from Austria caused by the rise of Hitler brought to the United States such distinguished artists as the expressionist painters Franz Lerch (1895–1977) and Max Oppenheimer (1885–1956), and the graphic artist John W. Winkler (1890–1979).

The best known of all Austrian American architects is Richard Neutra (1892–1970), whose name is synonymous with the steel and concrete structures he pioneered in California. Other modern architects include R. M. Schindler (1887–1953) and Victor Gruen (1903–1980), who immigrated in 1938 and whose environmental architecture helped transform such cities as Los Angeles, Detroit, and Fort Worth. Frederick John Kiesler (1896–1965) was known as an innovative architect whose set designs, interiors, and bold floating architectural designs earned him a reputation as a maverick and visionary.

Business Franz Martin Drexel (1792–1863), a native of Voralberg, founded the banking house of Drexel and Company in Philadelphia, which later gave rise to the House of Morgan. Another immigrant from Voralberg, John Michael Kohler (1844–1900), built one of the largest plumbing outfitters in the United States, which later became the Kohler Company, and introduced the enamel-coated bathtub. August Brentano (1831–1886) was an impoverished Austrian immigrant who turned a newspaper stand into a large bookshop chain. The development of department stores in the United States also owes a debt to Austrian American Nathan M. Ohrbach (1885–1990), founder of the Ohrbach stores. John Daniel Hertz Sr. (1879–1961), an Austrian Czech, made his name synonymous with rental cars.

Tourism in the United States has also been enhanced by the Austrian-style ski resorts and schools in Sun Valley developed by Felix Schaffgotsch (1904–1942). The Arlberg technique in skiing was promoted by Hannes Schneider (1890–1955) in Jackson, New Hampshire, and later resorts such as Aspen and Heavenly Valley were made famous by their Austrian instructors.

In technology, the 1978 invention of a text scanner by Austrian American Ray Kurzweil (1948–) has opened a new world for blind readers. Austrian American Wolfgang Puck (1949–) is a chef, restaurateur, and television personality. His companies include Wolfgang Puck Fine Dining Group, which operates a growing number of fine dining establishments in cities throughout North America; and Wolfgang Puck Worldwide, which operates and franchises Wolfgang Puck–branded restaurants as well as licenses Puck's name for a variety of consumer goods, including kitchenware, cookbooks, and food products.

Fashion Austrian American fashion designers have included Nettie Rosenstein (1890–1980), a winner of the prestigious Coty Award for clothing design, and the Vienna-born Rudi Gernreich (1922–1985), who created the topless bathing suits of the 1960s.

Journalism Among journalists, the foremost name is Joseph Pulitzer (1847–1911). Though claimed by both Hungarians and Austrians, Pulitzer spoke German and had a Hungarian father and an Austrian mother. The founder of the *St. Louis Post-Dispatch* and owner of the *New York World*, Pulitzer is remembered for the prize in journalism that he endowed. He was one of many Austro-Hungarians involved in journalism in nineteenth-century America. Others include Gustav Pollak (1848–1919), a contributor to the *Nation* and the *Evening Post*, and Joseph Keppler (1838–1894), an innovator in color cartoons and owner of the humorous magazine *Puck*. A more recent publishing venture involving an Austrian American is the *New Yorker*, whose founding president, Raoul H. Fleischmann (1885–1969), was born in Bad Ischl, Austria.

Law and Society One of the best-known Austrian Americans in the legal field was Felix Frankfurter (1882–1965), a native of Vienna, who was a justice on the Supreme Court for twenty-three years. The Spingarn Medal, awarded yearly to an outstanding African American leader, was created by Joel Elias Spingarn (1875–1939), one of the founders of the National Association for the Advancement of Colored People (NAACP) and the son of an Austrian immigrant.

Literature Franz Werfel (1890–1945), though born in Prague, was a thoroughly Austrian writer. He and his wife fled the Nazis and came to the United States in 1940. His *Song of Bernadette* (1943) became a best seller in the United States, and the Werfels settled in Beverly Hills. The children's writer and illustrator Ludwig Bemelmans (1898–1962) was born in South Tyrol and settled in New York as a youth. His famous Madeline stories continue to charm young readers. Hermann Broch (1886–1951), one of the most influential of modern Austrian writers, known for such novels as *The Sleepwalkers* (1931–1932) and *The Death of Virgil* (1945) was another refugee from Hitler's Europe and taught at both Princeton and Yale.

Medicine Among Austrian American Nobel laureates in medicine were Karl Landsteiner (1868–1943), who discovered blood types, and the German Austrian Otto Loewi (1873–1961), a cowinner of the Nobel for his work in the chemical transmission of nerve impulses.

Loewi came to New York University after he was driven out of Graz by the Nazis. Many other Austrian Americans have also left their mark in the United States both as practitioners and educators, but perhaps none so methodically as the psychoanalysts who spread Sigmund Freud's work to the United States. These include A. A. Brill (1874–1947), the Columbia professor and Freud translator; Heinz Werner (1890–1964); Paul Federn (1871–1950); Otto Rank (1884–1939), a Freud disciple; and Theodor Reik (1888–1969), the New York psychoanalyst. This group of immigrants was not limited to Freudians, however. Alexandra Adler (1901–2001), daughter of Alfred Adler, who is generally known as the second great Viennese psychoanalyst, came to the United States to work at both Harvard and Duke. Bruno Bettelheim (1903–1990) was also a native of Vienna; he became known for his treatment of autistic children and for his popular writings. The list of those both in medicine and mental health who were driven out of Austria during the reign of Hitler is long and impressive. Viennese-born Eric Kandel (1929–), professor and director of the Kavli Institute for Brain Science at Columbia University's College of Physicians and Surgeons, received the Nobel Prize in Physiology or Medicine in 2000, along with colleagues Arvid Carlsson and Paul Greengard, for research on the neurological mechanisms of memory.

Music Arnold Schoenberg (1874–1951), creator of the twelve-tone system and a pioneer of modern music, fled the rise of Nazism in 1933 and continued composing and teaching at both the University of Southern California and the University of California, Los Angeles. Frederick Loewe (1904–1988), a native Viennese, was the lyricist in the team of Lerner and Loewe who helped transform the American musical. The folk singer and actor Theodore Bikel (1924–) was born in Vienna and came to the United States via Israel and London. Paul Wittgenstein (1887–1961), brother of the philosopher and a pianist of note, settled in New York after 1938. Having lost his right arm in the First World War, Wittgenstein became famous for playing with one hand, and major composers such as Maurice Ravel wrote music for the left hand for him. Austrian immigrants Maria and Georg von Trapp and their children arrived in the United States in 1938 and settled in Pennsylvania, where they earned their living by singing baroque and folk music and running a music camp. The fictionalized account of their lives, *The Sound of Music*, opened on Broadway in 1959 and was soon followed by a major motion picture in 1965.

Science Three of Austria's four Nobel Prize winners in physics immigrated to the United States. They include Victor Franz Hess (1883–1964), the discoverer of cosmic rays; Isidor Isaac Rabi (1898–1988), a physicist at Columbia; and Wolfgang Pauli (1900–1958). Otto Halpern (1899–1982) also contributed to the defense effort of his new homeland by his invention of a counter-radar device. Distinguished

Action hero and former Governor of California Arnold Schwarzenegger (1947–) is an Austrian American. JOHN BARR / LIAISON / GETTY IMAGES

chemists include Ernst Berl (1877–1946), who came to the United States to work on explosives and chemical warfare, and Herman Francis Mark (1895–1992), whose work in synthetic plastics led to the development of such materials as nylon and orlon. Edwin Salpeter (1924–2008), who was the J. G. White Distinguished Professor of Physical Sciences Emeritus at Cornell University at the time of his death, was an eminent astrophysicist whose research encompassed black holes and missile defense systems.

Stage and Screen The earliest contribution of Austrian Americans is found in the theater. Many of the earliest theater houses in this country were built by Austrian immigrants who brought their love for theater with them. Prominent arrivals from Austria include the impresario Max Reinhardt (1873–1943). Famous for his *Everyman* production at the Salzburg Festival and for a school of dramatics in Vienna,

Hedy Lamarr (1914–2000), originally from Austria, was a U.S. film actress and engineer. PICTORIAL PRESS LTD / ALAMY

actors as Rudolph Schildkraut (1895–1964), Paul Muni (1895–1967), Hedy Lamarr (1915–2000), Oskar Homolka (1898–1978), and Bibi Besch (1940–1996). An impressive group of film directors also hail from Austria: Erich von Stroheim (1885–1957), whose film *Greed* (1924) is considered a modern masterpiece; Josef von Sternberg (1894–1969), the father of gangster films and even better known as Marlene Dietrich's director; Fred Zinnemann (1907–1997), the director of *High Noon* (1952); Billy Wilder (1906–2002), whose many accomplishments include *The Apartment* (1960) and *Sunset Blvd.* (1950); and Otto Preminger (1906–1986), a boyhood friend of Wilder's in Vienna and director of such film classics as *Anatomy of a Murder* (1959) and *Exodus* (1960). Friedrich Christian Anton "Fritz" Lang (1890–1976), known primarily as a filmmaker and screenwriter, made twenty-three movies in Hollywood, where he continued to work in the film noir genre for which his most famous film, *M* (made before he immigrated to the United States), served as precursor.

Vicki Baum (1888–1960), Gina Kaus (1883–1985), and Salka Viertel (1889–1978) were all successful screenwriters in Hollywood.

MEDIA

PRINT

transforum

This online publication is published three times annually by the Austrian Cultural Forum New York, an agency funded by the Austrian government to represent Austrian culture in the United States. It concentrates on cultural affairs such as exhibitions and exchanges.

Andreas Stadler, Editor in Chief
11 East 52nd Street
New York, New York 10022
Phone: (212) 319-5300
Fax: (212) 644-8660
Email: editor@acfny.org
URL: www.acfny.org/transforum/transforum-14/

Austrian Information

Newsletter/magazine on Austrian news, events, and personalities published quarterly by the Austrian Press and Information Service.

Alice Irwin, Editor in Chief
3524 International Court NW
Washington, D.C. 20008-3027
Phone: (202) 895-6775
Fax: (202) 895-6722
Email: austroinfo@austria.org
URL: www.austria.org

Ariadne Press

Publishes studies on Austrian culture, literature, and film; works of Austrian American writers; and translations of Austrian authors.

Reinhardt worked in Hollywood and New York after immigrating to escape the Nazis. Actor Paul Henreid (1908–1992) is best known for a classic scene in *Now Voyager* (1942), in which his debonair character lights two cigarettes simultaneously and passes one to Bette Davis, and for his role as the idealistic Victor Laszlo in *Casablanca* (1942).

Arnold Schwarzenegger (1947–), born near Graz, Austria, immigrated to the United States in 1968. By the 1980s he had become a major star of action movies, including *Conan the Barbarian* (1982) and *The Terminator* (1984), as well as its two sequels—*Terminator 2: Judgment Day* (1991) and *Terminator 3: Rise of the Machines* (2003). On October 8, 2003, with 48.6 percent of the vote, he became the thirty-eighth governor of California. After a second term as governor, he returned to his acting career, appearing in *The Expendables 2* in 2012.

Other Austrian Americans involved in theater and film include such well-known stage and screen

270 Goins Court
Riverside, California 92507
Phone: (909) 684-9202
Fax: (909) 779-0449
Email: ariadnepress@aol.com
URL: www.ariadnebooks.com

Other regional German-language newspapers and magazines, such as California's *Neue Presse* and the *Staats Zeitung*, operate throughout the United States, though none are specifically oriented to or targeted at an Austrian readership.

RADIO AND TELEVISION

Though the short-wave broadcasts of the Austrian Broadcasting Company, ORF, can be picked up in the United States, and various cable networks air German-language programming on their international channels, there is no domestically produced programming that targets the Austrian American audience.

ORGANIZATIONS AND ASSOCIATIONS

In general, Austrian Americans, because of diverse interests and ethnic backgrounds, have tended to favor small regional organizations and clubs over national ones. Most of these societies are organized by province of origin, and those of the Burgenland contingent are the most pervasive. In addition, urban areas such as Chicago, New York, Los Angeles, and Miami Beach tend to have associations for the promulgation of Austrian culture. The Austrian-American Councils of the United States is an umbrella organization that provides a networking base for twenty-seven regional and local councils scattered across the United States, Mexico, and Canada. The members hold annual meetings, usually in the fall around the time of Austrian-American Day, with the support of the World Federation of Austrians Abroad. Other Austrian societies and organizations are united by such common themes as music or literature or by shared history as with those who fled Austrian Nazism or Hitler. The following are a sampling of regional fraternal and cultural associations.

American-Austrian Cultural Society

Founded in 1954, the organization fosters friendship between the United States and Austria; promotes Austrian culture; and supports educational programs about Austrian arts, science, and trade in the metropolitan area of Washington, D.C.

Ms. Ulrike Wiesner, President
5618 Dover Court
Alexandria, Virginia 22312
Phone: (703) 941-0227
Email: American_Austrian_Society@yahoo.com
URL: www.american-austrian-cultural-society.com

Austrian American Council Midwest

The council works with local Austrian clubs throughout the Midwest to promote Austrian history and culture. It also fosters goodwill and better understanding between the people of the United States and Austria.

Gerhard Kaes, President
5319 West Sunnyside
Chicago, Illinois 60630
Phone: (773) 685-1481
Email: gkaes@sbcglobal.net
URL: www.aacmidwest.com/index.html

Austrian American Council West

The council sponsors Austrian cultural events, encourages Austrian artists and arts, and supports a variety of humanitarian causes. It also fosters increased understanding between people of the United States and Austria.

Veronika Reinelt, President
2701 Forrester Drive
Los Angeles, California 90064
Phone: (818) 507-5904
Fax: (818) 507-1907
Email: aacw@att.net
URL: www.aacwest.com/index.html

Austrian-American Society of Pennsylvania

Incorporated as a nonprofit organization in 1981, the purpose of the organization is to promote appreciation and understanding of Austrian culture, history, tradition, and language through social and cultural events, educational programs, and other activities.

Renate M. Donnelly, President
10 Village Circle
Newtown Square, Pennsylvania 19073-2927
Phone: (610) 356-3271
Fax: (610) 356-4710
Email: info@aasop.org
URL: www.aasop.org

Austro-American Association of Boston

Founded in 1944, the organization was established to further interest in Austria and Austrian culture and to promote friendship between Austria and the United States. Members are drawn from Boston and throughout New England.

Traude Acker, President
67 Bridle Path
Sudbury, Massachusetts 01776
Phone: (978) 579-2191
Email: traudeaustria@hotmail.com
URL: www.austria-boston.org/index.asp

Austrian Studies Association

Formerly known as the Modern Austrian Literature and Culture Association, it is the only North American association devoted to scholarship on all aspects of Austrian, Austro-Hungarian, and Hapsburg territory cultural life from the eighteenth century to the present. The association holds an annual conference and publishes the quarterly *Journal of Austrian Studies*.

Robert Dassanowsky
Email: austrianstudiesassociation@gmail.com
URL: www.austrian-studies.org

Office of Science and Technology

This office provides an interface between Austria and North America in the areas of science, research, and research policy. It publishes the free online magazine *bridges*.

Philipp Marxgut, Director
3524 International Court NW
Washington, D.C. 20008
Phone: (202) 895-6700
Fax: (202) 895-6750
Email: austroinfo@austria.org
URL: www.ostina.org

MUSEUMS AND RESEARCH CENTERS

Austrian Cultural Institute Forum New York

Part of the cultural affairs section of the Austrian Consulate General, the institute is responsible for cultural and scientific relations between Austria and the United States. It maintains a reference library specializing in Austrian history, art, and folklore and organizes lectures and panel discussions as well as educational exchanges.

11 East 52nd Street
New York, New York 10022
Phone: (212) 319-5300
Fax: (212) 644-8660
Email: desk@acfny.org
URL: www.acfny.org

Dietrich W. Botstiber Institute for Austrian American Studies (BIAAS)

The institute promotes an understanding of the relationship between the United States and Austria through two Fulbright-Botstiber visiting professorships, one in Austria and the other in the United States, jointly sponsored with the Austrian-American Educational Commission. BIAAS also offers an annual fellowship in Austrian American studies; provides grants for work; and sponsors programs in the fields of history, politics, economics, law, literature, poetry, music, and translations.

Carlie Numi, Deputy Administrator
200 E. State Street, Suite 306-A
Media, Pennsylvania 19063
Phone: (610) 566-3375
Fax: (610) 566-3376
Email: cnumi@botstiber.org
URL: www.botstiber.org/austrian/index.html

Center for Austrian Studies

Located at the University of Minnesota, the center conducts research on Austrian history and publishes a newsletter, three times annually, as well as the *Austrian History Yearbook*.

Klaas van der Sanden, Interim Director
University of Minnesota
314 Social Sciences Building

267 19th Avenue S
Minneapolis, Minnesota 55455
Phone: (612) 624-9811
Fax: (612) 626-9004
Email: casahy@.umn.edu
URL: www.cas.umn.edu

German-American Heritage Museum of the USA

The museum tells the story of all Americans of German-speaking ancestry and their role in shaping the United States. The museum collects, records, preserves, and exhibits artifacts related to the history and legacy of German, Swiss, Austrian, and Slovakian Americans.

Bern E. Deichmann, President
719 Sixth Street NW
Washington, D.C. 20001
Phone: (202) 467-5000
Fax: (202) 467-5440
Email: info@gahmusa.org
URL: http://gahmusa.org/gahm/gahm.html

Neue Galerie New York, Museum for German and Austrian Art

The museum is devoted to early twentieth-century German and Austrian art and design, displayed on two exhibition floors. The second-floor galleries are dedicated to fine and decorative arts from Vienna circa 1900.

Renée Price, Director
1048 Fifth Avenue
New York, New York 10028
Phone: (212) 628-6200
Fax: (212) 628-8824
Email: museum@neuegalerie.org
URL: www.neuegalerie.org

SOURCES FOR ADDITIONAL STUDY

Boernstein, Henry. *Memoirs of a Nobody*. Edited and translated by Steven Rowan. Detroit: Wayne University Press, 1997.

Goldner, Franz. *Austrian Emigration 1938 to 1945*. New York: Frederick Ungar, 1979.

Good, David F., and Ruth Wodak, eds. *From World War to Waldheim: Culture and Politics in Austria and the United States*. New York: Berghahn Books, 1999.

Perloff, Marjorie. *The Vienna Paradox*. New York: New Directions, 2004.

Spalek, John, Adrienne Ash, and Sandra Hawrylchak. *Guide to Archival Materials of German-Speaking Emigrants to the U.S. after 1933*. Charlottesville: University of Virginia Press, 1978.

Spaulding, E. Wilder. *The Quiet Invaders: The Story of the Austrian Impact upon America*. Vienna: Österreichische Bundesverlag, 1968.

Stadler, Friedrich, and Peter Weibel, eds. *Vertreibung der Vernunft: The Cultural Exodus from Austria*. New York: Springer-Verlag, 1995.

AZERBAIJANI AMERICANS
Grace Waitman

OVERVIEW

Azerbaijani Americans are immigrants or descendants of immigrants from Azerbaijan, a constitutional republic on the western coast of the Caspian Sea. Azerbaijan is located in a region known as the Caucasus, a large tract of land between the Caspian Sea and the Black Sea that is at the border of Europe and Asia. Azerbaijan shares borders with Iran to the south, Armenia to the west, Georgia to the northwest, and Russia to the north. The Nakhchivan Autonomous Republic, a landlocked semi-sovereign area spanning 2,124 square miles (5,500 square kilometers) and situated between Armenia and Iran, is also considered part of Azerbaijan. In total, Azerbaijan covers approximately 33,436 square miles (86,600 square kilometers), an area slightly larger than the state of South Carolina.

Azerbaijan's population was an estimated 9.59 million in 2013, according to the *CIA World Factbook*. However, scholars agree that there are likely somewhere between 20 and 30 million ethnic Azerbaijanis living in northern Iran, though the Iranian government does not release population counts of the various ethnic groups living there. Most citizens of Azerbaijan are Muslim (approximately 96 percent), with small segments of the population identifying themselves as Russian Orthodox, Armenian Orthodox, Christian, and Jewish. Ethnic groups in Azerbaijan include the Azeri (90.6 percent), Dagestani (2.2 percent), Russians (1.8 percent), and Armenians (1.5 percent). The economy of Azerbaijan is based on oil production that grew steadily in the first decade of the twenty-first century due to the completion of the Baku-Tbilisi-Ceyhan pipeline, which runs through Azerbaijan, Armenia, and Turkey and connects the vast oil and gas fields in the Caspian Sea to trade routes in the Mediterranean Sea. Azerbaijan is among the top ten oil suppliers to the European Union.

Azerbaijanis, or Azeri Turks as they often call themselves, began immigrating to the United States in the middle of the twentieth century after World War II and settled primarily in New York and New Jersey. Large numbers have also established residence in California, Texas, Minnesota, and Florida. After arriving in the United States, many Azerbaijanis found blue-collar jobs and formed communal organizations such as the Azerbaijani Society of America

that fostered a sense of solidarity and helped members of the immigrant group maintain a connection to Azerbaijan. Another wave of Azeris immigrated to the United States between 1988 and 1994, when the country was at war with Armenia. Over 75 percent of Azeris who have immigrated to the United States come from countries other than Azerbaijan, with the most significant population of Azeris coming from Iran and sizable numbers from Russia and Turkey.

Precise data for Azerbaijani Americans is difficult to obtain because the U.S. Census Bureau does not include Azerbaijani as an ancestry group when compiling population data. Moreover, some Azerbaijani immigrants who have come to the United States from Iran self-identify as Iranian; other Azerbaijani immigrants may self-identify as Turkish because Azerbaijanis are a Turkic people. Nevertheless, the Network of Azerbaijani Americans from Iran (NAAI) and the Azerbaijani-American Council both estimate that there are approximately 400,000 people of Azerbaijani origin living in the United States, with up to 300,000, and perhaps as many as 350,000, coming from Iran.

HISTORY OF THE PEOPLE

Early History In the 1960s archeologists found evidence of a proto-human settlement dating back more than 300,000 years at the Azykh Cave in the Nagorno-Karabakh region of Azerbaijan. From 900 to 700 BCE the area was populated by an Iranian tribe called the Medes as well as the Scythians, a nomadic people that migrated from north of the Black Sea and eventually settled in the South Caucasus, an area that includes present-day Georgia, Turkey, Azerbaijan, and northern Iran. The kingdoms established by the Medes and the Scythians in the South Caucasus were absorbed into the Persian empire in approximately 550 BCE. While under Persian control, the people of the Azerbaijan region practiced the Zoroastrian religion.

Just over two centuries later, Alexander the Great displaced the Persians, and subsequently the area was subject to numerous cultural influences, including the Greeks, the Romans, and the Caucasian Albanians, until various local Caucasian tribes regained control in approximately 200 BCE. Christian influences began to enter the region in the first century CE, and

Christianity spread rapidly in the early 300s due to the charisma of Gregory the Illuminator, an Armenian prophet who converted nobles and tribal leaders throughout the area. Christianity and Zoroastrianism remained the principal religions in the southern Caucasus until the Muslim conquest in the seventh century brought Sunni Islam to the region and initiated the decline of rival faiths.

Turkic tribes from Central Asia, all of which practiced Sunni Muslim, began to invade the southern Caucasus early in the eleventh century, and by 1030 the Ghaznavids had seized control of the northern portion of present-day Azerbaijan. The Ghaznavids were followed quickly in 1055 by another Turkic people, the Seljuqs, who revived Persian culture and brought more than a century of prosperity to the region. The flowering of the arts and sciences, the development of schools, and the renaissance in architecture ended abruptly in the 1230s when Mongol invaders sacked the Seljuq empire, destroying several major cities in present-day Azerbaijan. The Mongols remained in control of much of the South Caucasus until they were expelled in 1380 by Tamerlane, a Turkic emperor originally based in Samarkand, or present-day Uzbekistan. Tamerlane's vassals ruled briefly in Azerbaijan before giving way in the mid-1400s to the Shirvanshahs, a Sunni dynasty that had intermittently controlled areas of present-day Azerbaijan since approximately 850 CE. In 1462 the Shirvanshahs entered into a series of skirmishes with the Safavids, a Sufi religious order that practiced Shia Islam and was based in Ardabil in northern Iran. In 1501 the Safavids invaded Baku, the capital of present-day Azerbaijan, and massacred the Shirvanshahs. Fighting persisted over the course of the sixteenth century until the Safavids, under the rule of Shah Abbas, were finally able to regain control of Azerbaijan in 1601 and establish Shia Islam in the region.

In the 1700s Azerbaijan was occupied by the Ottomans and by the Russians, as the Safavid dynasty, based in present-day Iran, began to crumble due to a series of attacks from numerous enemies along all its borders. The Russians gained control of the Azerbaijani region with the signing of the Treaty of Gulistan in 1813 at the end of the first Russo-Persian War and the Treaty of Turkmenchay in 1828, which concluded the second Russo-Persian War and established the current border between Iran and Azerbaijan. In an attempt to maintain dominion over the region and to mitigate the influence of Persian culture in Azerbaijan, the Russians encouraged the migration of non-Orthodox Russian Christians, in addition to Germans and Armenians to the region. In 1870 oil was discovered near the Caspian Sea in the city of Baku, and over the next thirty years the population of Baku increased by 250 percent as migrating Russian and Armenian businessmen assumed control of the oil enterprise and ruled over both the local Azeri population and transplanted workers from throughout the Russian Empire.

Modern Era In the years of the oil boom and through the turn of the twentieth century, a left-wing intelligentsia, influenced by socialist ideas that had been circulating in Europe, had been growing steadily in Azerbaijan, especially in Baku. Forced to meet underground for decades, the group's ideas began to spread rapidly with the start of World War I in 1914 and later with the abdication of Tsar Nicholas II and the subsequent institution of Bolshevik rule in Russia. In 1918 a democratic republic was established in Azerbaijan, the first in the Islamic world, but these swift changes brought violence as the Azeris tried to expel the Armenians and groups of Bolsheviks in Baku persecuted Muslims. Azerbaijan sustained its independence for two years before succumbing to the Soviet Red Army in 1920. During the 1930s, Soviet leader Joseph Stalin purged the Azerbaijani intelligentsia, killing all suspected dissidents and eliminating any hope that the country would soon free itself of Soviet rule. Azerbaijan was a primary supplier of oil to the Soviet Union throughout World War II and after, through the 1950s, until the oil field of Baku were depleted and the Soviet Union looked elsewhere for oil and gas.

No longer able to depend on oil revenues, Azerbaijan became one of the poorest of the Soviet Republics in the 1960s, and ethnic violence between Azeris and Armenians returned to the region and continued through the 1990s. The focal points of the tension was the Nargorno-Karabakh region in Azerbaijan, where the highest concentration of Armenians lived, and the city of Baku, where anti-Armenian sentiment was most virulent. The Soviet Army was repeatedly called to the area to suppress anti-Armenian violence, and by the late 1980s the fighting between Azerbaijan and Armenia was recognized in international circles as a full-scale war. With an anti-Soviet movement gathering force in Baku, the Red Army interceded and killed over 100 dissidents in the Azerbaijani capital on January 19 and 20, 1990. Known as Black January, this period of time is considered by Azeri nationalists to be the first days of a reestablishment of the Azerbaijan Republic, which had been dormant since the 1920 invasion of the Red Army. However, Azerbaijan did not formally declare its independence until August 30, 1991, four months prior to the dissolution of the Soviet Union.

The war with Armenia continued to escalate in the early 1990s and reached its zenith with the Khojaly Massacre on February 26, 1992, when Armenian nationals, with the help of the Russian army, killed more than 500 Azeris in Khojaly, a city in the Nagorno-Karabakh area of Azerbaijan. Azeris throughout the world recognize the event as ethnic cleansing, and each year gather to commemorate the tragedy. In the years leading up to the Khojaly

Massacre, over 250,000 Azeris had been expelled from Armenia. An uneasy ceasefire between Armenia and Azerbaijan was proclaimed in 1994, and shortly thereafter a plundered Azerbaijan took the first steps toward economic recovery. On December 12, 1994, the Contract of the Century, which secured $60 billion of international investment in the Azerbaijan oil industry went into effect, and in 1998 the Azerbaijani parliament ratified plans to build the Baku-Tbilisi-Ceyhan pipeline. Construction began in 2002. Throughout the early 2000s large deposits of natural gas have been discovered in Baku, continuing the resurrection of the Azerbaijani economy and transforming the country into one of the world's largest suppliers of natural gas.

SETTLEMENT IN THE UNITED STATES

The first Azerbaijani immigrant on record entered the United States in the early twentieth century through Ellis Island. After World War II a larger wave of Azeri immigrants arrived, many of whom had been detained in German prison camps during the war. It is impossible to know how many of these immigrants had lived in Azerbaijan before they were displaced by the war and how many had lived elsewhere in the Caucasus, in places such as northern Iran, southern Russia, and eastern Turkey. Immigrants from this period settled primarily in New York City, especially Brooklyn, and New Jersey, where they created the Azerbaijan Society of America in 1957. By the 1970s the Azerbaijani American population also occupied other areas of the United States, including California, Texas, Minnesota, and Florida.

In the late 1980s through the mid-1990s, the United States government conferred refugee status on 14,205 Azeris who had fled the country during the war with Armenia. Nonprofit agencies helped Azerbaijani refugees find homes in every state in the union, with the majority of these immigrants taking up residence in the established Azerbaijani American communities in Los Angeles and the Brooklyn borough of New York City. These Azerbaijanis had sustained strong ties with their home country, to the extent that several major U.S. cities formed a "sister city" relationship with cities in Azerbaijan, especially Baku. For example, Baku has a "sister city" relationship with Houston, Texas, and Honolulu, Hawaii. Similar connections exist between Newark, New Jersey, and Ganja in Azerbaijan; and between Monterey, California, and Lankaran in Azerbaijan. Other states with large numbers of Azerbaijani Americans include New Jersey, Texas, Minnesota, and Florida.

LANGUAGE

The official language of Azerbaijan is Azeri, a language in the Turkic family of languages. While over 90 percent of the population of Azerbaijan speaks Azeri, the language is also prevalent in Iran, where approximately 30 million people speak Azeri, and in the region of Borchali in southern Georgia, which is home to almost 40,000 people of Azerbaijani origin. Other languages used by Azerbaijanis include Dagestani, Russian, and Armenian. Azerbaijani immigrants have tended to learn English quickly. However, in the United States there are a considerable number of language programs

The next wave of Azeri immigrants, who arrived in the 1990s, likewise depended on family members as well as other members of established Azeri communities in the United States to ease the trauma of displacement and relocation. In California, relocation programs arranged for a relative to meet arriving Azerbaijanis at the airport.

available for persons interested in learning Azeri. The most notable of these is the Summer Language Workshop at the Indiana University–Bloomington, which has offered Azeri classes since 1990. In addition, many Azeri organizations in the United States offer language classes to promote the usage of Azeri among second- and third-generation Azerbaijani Americans. For example, the Azerbaijani American Cultural Association, founded in Miami, Florida, offers these classes as a way to promote knowledge about Azerbaijan and its culture.

Greetings and Popular Expressions Common greetings and expressions in Azeri include the following:

Xoş gəlmişsiniz!—Welcome!; *Salam əleyküm*—Hello; *Əleyküm salam*—Hello (in reply); *Siz necəsiniz?*—How are you? (formal); *Necəsiz? / Sən necəsən?*—How are you? (informal); *Sağ olun, yaxşıyam*—Thanks, I'm fine; *Nə var?*—What's up?; *Tanış olmağıma çox şadam*—Pleased to meet you; *Çox şadam*—Pleased to meet you (in reply); *Sabahınız xeyir*—Good morning; *Axşamınız xeyir*—Good evening; *Sağ olun / Salamat qalın / Görüşənədək*—Goodbye (formal); *Sağol / Xudahafiz*—Goodbye (informal); *Yaxşı günlər!*—Have a nice day!; *Nuş olsun!*—Bon appetit!; *Üzr istəyirəm / Bağışlayın*—Excuse me.

RELIGION

Almost 95 percent of the population in Azerbaijan practices Islam. Of that Muslim majority, 85 percent is Shia and 15 percent is Sunni. In Nargorno-Karabakh, where the population is overwhelmingly Armenian, most people belong to the Armenian Apostolic Church. There are small but significant Jewish, Christian, and Hindu populations in Azerbaijan as well. Zoroastrianism was the primary religion in Azerbaijan from the first millennium BCE through the Arab invasions of the seventh century. While few Azeris have practiced Zoroastrianism since that time, aspects of Zoroastrian culture remain prevalent in contemporary Azerbaijani society. For example, Nowruz, the Persian New Year celebrated each year at the beginning of spring on the Western calendar, is among the most popular holidays in Azerbaijan.

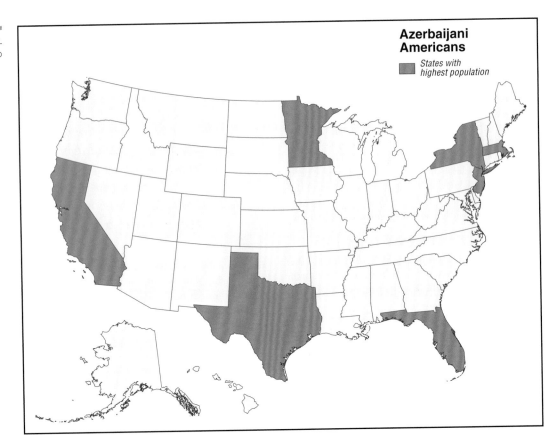

Azerbaijani Americans

☐ States with
highest population

Azerbaijan is officially a secular state, and in the early twenty-first century it was widely recognized as one of the most irreligious countries among the predominately Islam nations of the world. Several government agencies, most notably the State Committee for Work with Religious Associations, actively promote freedom of religion in Azerbaijan. Nevertheless, with the increase of tension between Muslim nations and the West in the early twenty-first century, the International Relations Security Network (ISN) has noted increasing numbers of Azerbaijani youth joining radical sects. In the United States, Azerbaijani Americans tend to practice Islam more ardently than their forebears in Azerbaijan, but Azeri immigrants have a sense of ethnic solidarity and pay less attention than native Azerbaijanis to sectarian differences within their faith.

CULTURE AND ASSIMILATION

Azerbaijani Americans have sustained close ties with Azerbaijan, whether they came to the United States to escape the Nagorno-Karabakh War or arrived in the first wave in the 1950s. They have formed numerous organizations seeking to keep members of the immigrant group informed about current events in Azerbaijan, and they promote strong relations between the United States and Azerbaijan. The first wave of Azeri immigrants from Azerbaijan was insular, with almost 80 percent

choosing to marry within the immigrant group. Azeri immigrants from other countries, such as Iran and Turkey, were likely to live within communities with other Azeris who had migrated from the same country. The immigrants who came in the second wave, during the Nagorno-Karabakh War, tended to join existing Azeri communities but assimilated much more quickly than their predecessors in the United States, most likely because members of this second group arrived as refugees and were seeking a brand new life.

Cuisine The staple dish in Azerbaijan is *plov*, saffron rice cooked in a mix of spices and sometimes served with meat and vegetables. Other traditional dishes include *dolmas* (vegetables such as grape leaves, tomatoes, or peppers stuffed with meat and rice) and kebabs, or *shashlyks*, as skewered meats are called in Azerbaijan. Kebabs that feature chicken roasted in a clay oven called a *təndir* (the same type of oven that is called a *tandoor* in India and Pakistan) are a national favorite. Another favorite is *kourma* with *alycha* (a type of plum) and lemon, which consists of pieces of mutton served on the bone and prepared using onions, saffron, and tomatoes. Azerbaijani cuisine also includes sweets such as *badam-buri*, a pastry that contains almonds and sugar; *pakhlava* (baklava), a pastry covered with syrup and served with chopped nuts sprinkled on top, and *halva*, a sweet popular throughout the Middle East that is made with either malted wheat or ground nuts or sesame seeds. Azeris also enjoy fruit pastries seasoned with saffron. The preferred beverage in Azerbaijan is black tea. Many Azerbaijani American organizations offer festivals that feature foods native to Azerbaijan. Some groups, such as the Azerbaijani American Cultural Association based in Miami, offer Azerbaijani cooking classes as a means of preserving Azeri culture. Many Azerbaijani Americans share food during holidays, such as during the month of Ramadan.

Dances and Songs Azerbaijani music often combines storytelling and poetry with mournful instrumentation. *Mugham* is a form of classical Azerbaijani music that combines poetry with improvised musical interludes. The nature of the improvisation varies from region to region in Azerbaijan. *Meykhana* is a form of rap or spoken word poetry rendered in rhymed verse by one or more performers. When performed solo, artists are known to improvise their verse. The *ashiq* form consists of stories and poems sung with the accompaniment of string instruments. Azeri American organizations often host concerts featuring professional musicians trained in the one of the Azeri musical styles. One of the most popular of Azeri musicians is Emin Agalarov (1979–), who performs under the name Emin and sings in English. Emin was trained by Muslim Magomayev (1942–2008), an Azerbaijani opera singer who also had a Sinatra-like lounge act and covered pop songs. Emin, too, is famous for his Frank Sinatra and Elvis Presley covers but also writes and performs original pop songs. Many college campuses, notably Indiana University, regularly host cultural events featuring classical Azerbaijani music.

Holidays Many Azerbaijani Americans celebrate the traditional Muslim holidays, such as Eid al-Fitr, which is the breaking of the fast at the end of Ramadan. Azerbaijani Americans also observe Nowruz, the Persian New Year, at the beginning of spring, although this is not a weeklong holiday in the United States as it is in Azerbaijan.

However, public holidays that commemorate key moments in Azerbaijani history have a larger place in the national consciousness than religious and traditional holidays. The most significant of these national holidays is Republic Day, celebrated each year on May 28 to observe Azerbaijani freedom from Russian rule. This day has a significant place in the national memory because Azerbaijan was the first democratic republic in the Islamic world and because it was able to maintain its freedom for only two years before Soviet Russia took control of the country. The day is marked with a military parade through the streets of Baku. In the United States, large segments of the Azerbaijani American community—those

AZERBAIJANI PROVERBS

Ağıl başda olar, yaşda olmaz.

Intelligence is in the head, not in the age. (Meaning: You do not have to be old to be intelligent.)

Bir buğda əkməsən, min buğda biçməzsən.

Without sowing a single wheat you would not harvest thousand ones. (Meaning: One small action can help change what happens in the future.)

Əvvəl düşün, sonra danış.

First think, then speak.

Kiminin əvvəli, kiminin axırı.

Someone's end is someone's beginning.

Köpəyin qarnı tox gərək.

Dog has to have its stomach full. (Meaning: Treat those in your service well and they, in turn, will treat you well.)

Bilməmək eyib deyil, soruşmamaq eyibdir.

Shameful is not the one who doesn't know, but the one who doesn't ask.

Ağac bar verəndə baş ın aşağı dikər.

Tree would bend when it bears fruit. (Meaning: One should be modest even if he or becomes rich and influential.)

who emigrated from Iran—are likely to let Republic Day and other national holidays pass without much notice. However, some members of the Azeri community in the United States commemorate the holiday by attending speeches hosted by the Azerbaijani Consulate. In Los Angeles, the Consulate General addresses a large audience of up to a few hundred people that includes members of the immigrant community as well as university professors, politicians from neighboring states, and dignitaries in the Los Angeles area.

Azeris throughout the world observe the anniversary of the massacre of "Black January" to mourn the death of Azeri citizens killed by the Red Army in Baku in 1990. Likewise, each year Azeris commemorate the Khojaly Massacre of February 26, 1992. In 1993, two years after the fall of the Soviet Union, Azerbaijani president Heydar Aliyev declared December 31 Solidarity Day, and it has since been observed both within the country and by Azeri expatriates abroad. In addition, many Azerbaijani Americans celebrate traditional U.S. holidays like Thanksgiving and New Year's Day.

In Cleveland, Ohio, Azeri President Heydar Aliyev (1923–2003) is embraced by an Azerbaijani American woman during his visit to the memorial cemetery of the fighters who had died for the independence of Azerbaijan, in Baku, 1998. YURI KOCHETKOV / AFP / GETTY IMAGES

FAMILY AND COMMUNITY LIFE

In Azerbaijan the extended family is the primary unit in society, a tradition born of the fact that for centuries rural Azerbaijani families worked collaboratively on a shared piece of land to ensure sustenance and survival. Modern families no longer exercise this type of shared occupational structure, but families still rely strongly on one another and may receive both financial and emotional assistance from relatives. Azeri immigrants who came in the aftermath of World War II established close-knit communities in the United States, and like many people starting with very little in a new country, these immigrants relied on each other to build new lives in their adopted country. The next wave of Azeri immigrants, who arrived in the 1990s, likewise depended on family members as well as other members of established Azeri communities in the United States to ease the trauma of displacement and relocation. In California, relocation programs arranged for a relative to meet arriving Azerbaijanis at the airport. This was part of the process of establishing the identity of the refugees and was often necessary before further services, such as finding the new arrival an apartment and procuring an identity card, could be rendered.

Gender Roles In Azerbaijan traditional gender roles are typically observed. Men are expected to provide for their families, while women look after the domestic responsibilities of cooking, cleaning, and raising children. While women do work outside the home, they frequently pursue stereotypically feminine occupations like teaching or nursing. Outside the major cities, especially Baku, women do not visit restaurants or tea houses alone. Traditional gender roles remain largely intact throughout much of the Azerbaijani American community, though these roles are not as rigidly prescribed in the United States.

Azeri women have also taken an active role in helping female refugees adapt to life in the United States. For example, the Azerbaijani American Women's Association, established in 2006 and headquartered in California, offers support and promotes awareness of the experiences of Azeri women who immigrated in the 1990s. This organization not only serves the needs of Azerbaijani American women but has also established connections with other women's organizations in the United States.

Education Because Azerbaijanis are not included as an ancestry group by the U.S. Census Bureau, academic statistics for Azeris are difficult to obtain. Many of the refugees arriving in the 1990s sought the help of religious organizations to educate their children and help them learn English and make the transition to the U.S. school curriculum. Cooperative arrangements between Azerbaijan and the United States have created learning opportunities for the young people of both countries. For example, the Azerbaijani-American Youth Social Association has sponsored educational projects that engage youth from both nations in volunteer-based activities that allow participants to learn more about the culture of the other country.

Courtship and Weddings While love marriages are on the rise in Azerbaijan, arranged marriages are the norm in many communities and most women live with their parents prior to marriage. Even in the case of love marriages, most Azerbaijanis seek the approval of the parents. After approval is granted, the bride's parents typically host a party, either in their home or, more commonly, in a banquet hall. As part of this celebration, the couple receive an ornamental box that contains their engagement rings. The rings are initially secured together by a red ribbon; this is cut in a ceremony, after which time the couple each dons their respective rings. Chocolates are often included in the box, signifying adding sweetness to the union. The bride spends the day before the wedding with female friends and family members, celebrating with more sweets and having her hands decorated with henna. After the wedding the newlyweds do not typically go on a honeymoon but rather move into the groom's parents' home. During the first few months of marriage, the bride learns from her mother-in-law how to cook and care for her husband. Azerbaijani Americans are less likely to enter into arranged marriages and typically abide by American wedding traditions such as rehearsal dinners and honeymoons.

EMPLOYMENT AND ECONOMIC CONDITIONS

The Azeris who came to the United States in the 1950s typically found blue-collar employment in the East Coast region. However, there was a small contingent among this group that had escaped

Azerbaijan in 1920, at the dawn of Soviet rule, and spent over thirty years living as merchants in Eastern Europe before coming to the United States. Many of these people opened small businesses in the United States. Many of the refugees who arrived in the 1990s were highly educated people who had left professional jobs in Azerbaijan. In the United States, these people typically accepted lower-level jobs and large pay cuts.

POLITICS AND GOVERNMENT

Azeris throughout the world are a politically conscious people who keep track of politics in Azerbaijan and continue to celebrate the most important holidays on the national calendar. In the United States, several Azerbaijani Americans organizations have established "sister city" relationships between major metropolitan areas in the United States and Azerbaijan. In 2010 these organizations partnered with the U.S. Census Bureau to gather data on the Azeri communities in the United States. In addition, Azerbaijani Americans have participated in U.S. politics, most notably by petitioning Congress to admit Azeri refugees from the Nagorno-Karabakh War. Some grassroots organizations have publicly supported President Barack Obama.

NOTABLE INDIVIDUALS

Academia Max Black (1909–1988) was a philosopher, physicist, and mathematician who studied under Bertrand Russell and Ludwig Wittgenstein at Cambridge University and later made important contributions in the field of analytic philosophy. Black was born in Baku (which at the time was part of the Russian Empire), raised in London, and moved to the United States in the latter part of his academic career. He lectured in the philosophy departments at the University of Illinois at Urbana-Champagne and at Cornell University.

Ali Javan (1926–) is an Azeri physicist born in Tehran who immigrated to the United States in 1948. Javan joined the faculty at the Massachusetts Institute of Technology (MIT) in 1961 and has served as professor emeritus there since 1964. Javan's accomplishments include inventing the gas laser, which made fiber optic communication possible, and developing the first instrument that could accurately measure the speed of light.

Lotfali A. Zadeh (1921–) is a mathematician, electrical engineer, and computer scientist who received his PhD from Columbia University in 1949 and became a professor at the University of California at Berkeley in 1959. Zadeh was born in Baku, but his father was an Azeri Iranian who had been raised in Tehran. When he was ten, Zadeh moved with his family to Tehran and spent thirteen years there before moving to the United States and enrolling at MIT.

Art Semyon Bilmes (1955–) is an Azerbaijani American commercial artist whose clients include

AZERBAIJANI ADVOCACY GROUPS

Azerbaijani Americans are very active in politics, especially concerning their advocacy for the need to establish and maintain a strong relationship between Azerbaijan and the United States. The majority of the Azerbaijani organizations in the United States are designed to promote greater awareness of and knowledge concerning Azerbaijani customs and traditions. While this might not seem like an overtly political objective, Azerbaijani Americans who have membership in these organizations frequently view these goals as a means of advocating for understanding of their heritage and culture.

Many of these groups were established in the aftermath of the massive wave of Azerbaijani refugees who arrived on U.S. soil during the early and mid-1990s. Because of the struggles that Azerbaijan underwent after its independence from Soviet control, especially in its war with Armenia, the national pride of Azerbaijanis prompts them to engage in efforts to make their nation and its distinctive identity more visible to mainstream America. To this end, other organizations have taken as their explicit purpose the goal of elevating grassroots initiatives designed to cultivate cultural, scholarly, and academic exchanges between Azerbaijan and the United States.

CBS, Western Union, Citibank, and Smirnoff Vodka. In 1990 Bilmes opened the Ashland Academy of Art, in Ashland, Oregon, an independent art school with a curriculum modeled on the classical European academies. The school remained open for thirteen years until 2003, when Bilmes closed it and subsequently moved with his family to Maui, Hawaii, where he opened an art school called Atelier Maui.

Music Sona Aslanova (1924–2011) was an Azerbaijani soprano who moved to the United States in 1994. Aslanova sang opera and folk music and became famous during tours of the Soviet Union when she performed in operas composed by renowned Azerbaijani composer Uzeyir Hajibeyov. In the prime of her career, Aslanova was frequently cast in movies and live radio broadcasts.

Bella Davidovich (1928–) is an Azerbaijani pianist classically trained in Moscow. A prodigy, Davidovich showed signs of musical genius at age six and was performing classical pieces at leading venues by age eleven. Her professional career began in 1944 and spanned twenty-eight seasons, during which time she was considered among the finest pianists in the Soviet Union and Eastern Europe. Davidovich retired in 1977 and the following year immigrated to the United States, where she accepted a teaching position at the Juilliard School.

Mstislav Rostropovich (1927–2007) was a cellist born in Baku to aristocrats of Russian and Polish descent. He moved to Moscow in 1943 and by his mid-twenties was considered to be among the best cellists in the world. However, Rostropovich was also a human rights activist, and his political beliefs derailed his career in the Soviet Union. He was exiled in 1974 and settled with his wife in Washington, D.C., where he accepted a position as conductor of the U.S. National Symphony Orchestra in 1977. He continued in that post until 1994 and made frequent visits to Russia after the fall of the Soviet Union in 1991. At the end of his life, in addition to his home in the United States, Rostropovich maintained homes in three other countries, including two residences in Russia.

Sports Kristin Fraser (1980–) is a figure skater born in Palo Alto, California, who competed for Azerbaijan in the 2002 and 2006 Winter Olympic Games with Igor Lukanin, a Soviet-born skater who has also competed for Germany in international events. Lukanin and Fraser have won four Azerbaijani national champions together. They married in December 2010.

MEDIA

Azerbaijan International

Launched in 1996, this online magazine boasts on its masthead that it is the "World's Largest Web Site about Azerbaijan." As of 2013 the site had compiled more than 2,250 articles and 6,350 photos relating to Azerbaijan.

P.O. Box 5217
Sherman Oaks, California 91413
Phone: (310) 440-8000
Email: ai@artnet.net
URL: http://azer.com/

Azerbaijan Review

Monthly newspaper published in New York since 2007; languages included are Azeri, Russian, and English.

Email: info@AzeriAmerica.com
URL: www.azeriamerica.com/index_files/Azerbaijan-ReviewSource.htm

ORGANIZATIONS AND ASSOCIATIONS

Azerbaijan Cultural Society of Northern California

Hosts educational and social events that bring together the Azerbaijani American community in Northern California.

16400 Lark Avenue
Suite 260
Los Gatos, California 95032
Email: secretary@acsnc.org
URL: www.acsnc.org

Azerbaijani American Cultural Association

Founded in 2006 to promote Azerbaijani culture in South Florida. Hosts the "Days of Azerbaijan" festival and numerous conferences to educate local residents.

137 Golden Isles Drive #1414
Hallandale Beach, Florida 33009
URL: http://azerbaijaniamerican.com/

Azerbaijani American Women's Association

Identifies and addresses issues that Azerbaijani women face in the United States and in Azerbaijan, hosts educational and social events that promote Azerbaijani culture, and conducts philanthropic activities.

1573 San Ponte Road
Corona, California 92882
Phone: (951) 372-9193
Email: aawa.info@gmail.com
URL: http://aawausa.org/

U.S. Azeris Network

Builds alliances among the various Azerbaijani American organizations throughout the United States as well as with Turkic and other diasporic communities; promotes voter awareness and encourages Azerbaijani Americans to participate in American political debate.

P.O. Box 76044
Washington, D.C. 20013-6044
Email: info@usazeris.org
URL: www.usazeris.org

MUSEUMS AND RESEARCH CENTERS

American Research Institute of the South Caucasus

Hosts reading groups and lectures on countries in the South Caucasus and supports research on Azerbaijan, Armenia, and Georgia.

Leyla Rustamli, Resident Director for Azerbaijan
Department of Anthropology, Purdue University
700 West State Street
Suite 219
West Lafayette, Indiana 47907
Email: azerbaijan@arisc.org
URL: www.arisc.org

SOURCES FOR ADDITIONAL STUDY

Alstadt, Audrey L. *Azerbaijani Turks*. Palo Alto, CA: Hoover Institution Press, 1992.

De Waal, Thomas. *The Caucasus: An Introduction*. Oxford, UK: Oxford University Press, 2010.

Goodrich, Lauren, Peter Zeihan, and George Friedman. *A Crucible of Nations: The Geopolitics of the Caucasus*. Austin, TX: Stratfor Global Intelligence, 2011.

Goltz, Thomas. *Azerbaijan Diary: A Rogue Reporter's Adventures in an Oil-Rich, War-Torn, Post-Soviet Republic*. Armonk, NY: M.E. Sharpe, 1998.

Hasanli, Jamil. *At the Dawn of the Cold War: The Soviet-American Crisis over Iranian Azerbaijan*. New York: Rowman and Littlefield Publishers, 2006.

Lerman, Zvi, and David Sedik. *Rural Transition in Azerbaijan*. Lexington, VA: Lexington Books, 2010.

Ordubadi, Mămmăd Săid. *Years of Blood: A History of the Armenian-Muslim Clashes in the Caucasus, 1905–1906*. Reading, UK: Ithaca Press, 2011.

Roudik, Peter L. *Culture and Customs of the Caucasus*. Westport, CT: Greenwood Press, 2008.

Said, Kurban. *Ali and Nino: A Love Story*. Trans. Jenia Graman. New York: Overlook Press, 1996.

Swietochowski, Tadeusz. *Russia and Azerbaijan: A Borderland in Transition*. New York: Columbia University Press, 1995.

BAHAMIAN AMERICANS

Carol Brennan

OVERVIEW

Bahamian Americans are immigrants or descendants of people from the Commonwealth of the Bahamas, an archipelago in the western Atlantic Ocean. Serving as a gateway to the Gulf of Mexico, the Bahamas sit at a strategic juncture between the United States, Cuba, Haiti, and the Dominican Republic. Nassau, the capital, is approximately 280 miles (450 kilometers) from Florida. The archipelago, consisting of more than seven hundred islands, belongs to a vast oceanic mass known as the Bahama Banks; the majority of the Bahamian isles are small, uninhabited atolls or outcroppings of reefs. The islands' total combined land mass is 5,359 square miles (13,880 square kilometers), roughly equivalent to the size of Connecticut or Puerto Rico.

The *CIA World Factbook* lists the 2012 population of the Bahamas as 316,182. Black Bahamians, descendants of slaves taken from Africa to various parts of the Western Hemisphere between 1500 and the early 1800s, made up 85 percent of the population in 2012; another 12 percent of Bahamians were of European heritage, followed by a combined total of 3 percent who claimed Hispanic or Asian ethnicities. Religious affiliation hews to the Protestant denominations, with about 67 percent of Bahamians describing themselves as belonging to the Baptist, Anglican, Methodist, or other churches. The remainder are Roman Catholics, who make up 14 percent of the population, followed by other Christian denominations. One of the most elite tropical vacation destinations in the Americas, the Bahamas is also a financial services hub, and the nation's standard of living is among the highest in the Caribbean.

The first Bahamians in America landed in Florida as far back as the late 1700s. More came to the Florida Keys as marine salvagers or commercial fishermen in the early nineteenth century. Beginning in the 1880s and 1890s, black Bahamians began arriving in larger numbers to work as citrus pickers in South Florida groves and then as construction laborers and workers at other menial jobs. In the 1950s many black Bahamians sent their children to the thriving historically black colleges and universities in the American South. More recent Bahamian immigrants have tended to come to the United States

temporarily for educational opportunities or to earn professional credentials.

The U.S. Census Bureau's American Community Survey reported that in 2009–2011, an estimated 48,739 U.S. residents claimed Bahamian ancestry. The figure corresponds to the population of a medium-sized U.S. municipality like Danville, Virginia, or Cleveland Heights, Ohio. South Florida remains home to the largest numbers of Bahamian Americans, and significant numbers also live in the New York City area. Others have settled in Georgia, Texas, North Carolina, and New Jersey.

HISTORY OF THE PEOPLE

Early History The original inhabitants of the Bahamas were the Lucayans, an Amerindian people belonging to the larger Taíno group. The Lucayan population was estimated at about 40,000 before the arrival of the first European explorers of record in the Caribbean in the 1490s. The explorer Christopher Columbus first set foot in the Western Hemisphere in the Bahamas when the crew of the *Pinta* disembarked on October 12, 1492. The exact location is unknown, though conjecture points to the island of San Salvador. Columbus wrote that the indigenous Lucayans seemed peaceful and without weapons that posed any threat to the outsiders. Over the next three decades, the Lucayans were removed entirely; Spanish conquistadors seized them as slaves to work in the gold mines on the island of Hispaniola (present-day Haiti and the Dominican Republic), where they died of maltreatment and disease.

The Bahamas are believed to have been uninhabited for more than 130 years, between roughly 1520 (the date the Spanish last recorded seizing a small number of Lucayans) and 1647 (when colonists and slaves arrived from Bermuda). Bermuda, a group of islands lying some 600 miles off the coast of North Carolina, was home to a permanent English colony established in the early 1600s that had prospered but had quickly become overcrowded. Domestic tensions grew in the colony as a result of the English Civil War of the 1640s, and a group of anti-Royalist Puritans left Bermuda to set up their own colony in the Bahamas in 1647, registering as the Company of Eleutheran Adventurers. About seventy people were in the party, including slaves of African origin. They struggled in their early years on the island of Eleuthera; and their cause was taken up by New England Puritans, who raised funds and sent a supply ship to help them. In gratitude the Eleutherans sent back a quantity of brazilwood timber, some of which was used to construct buildings on the Harvard College campus in Massachusetts.

English settlement in the Bahamas increased over the next half-century, with new ports established on other islands in the chain, among them the future capital city of Nassau on New Providence Island. The Bahamas' position as a gateway from the Atlantic Ocean into the Gulf of Mexico made the islands an ideal hideout for pirates, and English colonial authorities spent several years attempting to eradicate the archipelago's reputation as a lawless pirate haven. An economic compromise was worked out after the Bahamas became a crown colony of Britain in 1718. The deal permitted Bahamians—whose economy relied heavily on the ubiquitous piracy in the Caribbean—a newly created concession for marine salvage work in Caribbean waters. These specialists were called wreckers, and their license to salvage already damaged ships marked a quasi-legitimate step up from the illegal enterprise of outright piracy. Salvaged cargo, rather than pillaged loot, could now be sold at auction in Nassau and other ports, and the British crown received a cut of the proceeds by way of a tax.

After Britain was defeated in the American Revolutionary War, about 7,000 Loyalists from the American colonies fled to the Bahamas, lured by land grants from Britain to bring their large-scale agricultural enterprises—and slaves—to the still-underpopulated islands of the chain. Exuma Island was one of those settled by Loyalists, but cotton and other crops failed in the climate there.

When the slave trade was abolished in the British Empire in 1807, the Bahamas became a designated settlement destination for slaves seized en route to North and South America, and the Afro-Bahamian population grew. From 1808 to 1838 colonial authorities offered the arriving West Africans either repatriation to the African nation of Sierra Leone or a fourteen-year apprenticeship program in which they could work as agricultural laborers or learn a trade. About 5,000 Africans came to the Bahamas under this unusual set of circumstances and stayed. The camps set up to house them became havens for runaway slaves, and although these rescued captives retained a strong West African identity, they also demonstrated deep allegiance to the Bahamas and the British crown for generations to come.

Slavery itself was formally abolished in the British Empire by Parliament in 1833. Former slaves became indentured servants or tenant farmers to their former masters and remained poor. They worked as domestic servants, conch fishermen, or sisal fiber harvesters. Others moved away from the main islands and took up ocean salt mining or sponge diving, both labor-intensive endeavors that were barely remunerative. In the late nineteenth century, some black Bahamians were able to own land and in this way gain the right to vote in local elections, but the group remained largely disenfranchised. A *New York Times* correspondent visited the colony during the first weeks of the American Civil War to report on what happens when a large population of emancipated blacks remains in place after slavery is abolished. The correspondent found that black Bahamians live "in the most barren localities that it is possible to find on the Island. The huts are crowded together—they look dilapidated and filthy—and the inhabitants make no efforts whatever to raise food for domestic use. The people are as smart and intelligent as any negroes in the world, but they are disposed to be insolent to whites, and are strongly imbued with the prejudices of caste."

Modern Era Economic and racial disparities in the Bahamas continued well into the twentieth century. In fact, the colony was considered so unimportant that Edward, Duke of Windsor (who had abdicated as Edward VIII, the disgraced king of England), was assigned to serve as its governor-general during World War II. For generations the country's wealth and power been concentrated among the white elite, the still adamantly pro-British descendants of the Loyalist settlers; however, in the postwar years, as Britain shed its colonial holdings, the majority black Bahamians began agitating for a greater public role in the economic, political, and social spheres.

In 1964 the Bahamas became a self-governing colony. Black and liberal Bahamians rallied under the banner of the Progressive Liberal Party (PLP). The old guard, representing the island's conservative white elite, organized themselves as the United Bahamian Party. A major turning point in the history of the Bahamas came in 1967, when a young black attorney and member of parliament, Lynden O. Pindling (1930–2000), was able to form a majority government. As the country's first black prime minister, Pindling led the Bahamas to independence on July 10, 1973. Since then the Bahamas have been an independent Commonwealth country and parliamentary constitutional monarchy, with a governor-general representing the British monarch. Pindling remained in office until the early 1990s as the nation continued to prosper from favorable tax legislation and bank secrecy laws. Its pristine beaches and unpolluted waters turned it into a major tourist destination in the 1950s and 1960s, especially after nearby Cuba fell to the communist insurgents led by Fidel Castro (1926–). Pindling was the first of a long line of black leaders of the Bahamas, and the country has remained largely peaceful and prosperous—in contrast to Haiti, the Dominican Republic, Jamaica, and other Caribbean

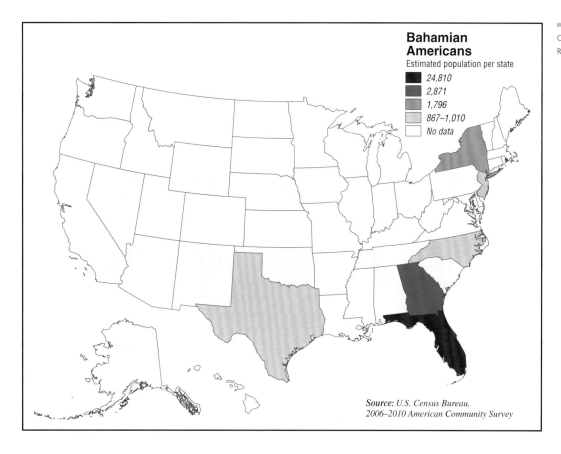

Bahamian Americans
Estimated population per state

- 24,810
- 2,871
- 1,796
- 867–1,010
- No data

*Source: U.S. Census Bureau,
2006–2010 American Community Survey*

nations. As a result, in the post–World War II era, immigration to the United States from the Bahamas has been low in comparison to those nations.

SETTLEMENT IN THE UNITED STATES

The first Bahamians to settle in what later became the United States were sailors and land squatters of various races and ethnicities who came to Florida, many of them to the Keys, in the late eighteenth century. An archipelago with its own complex topography, the Florida Keys offered the riches of shipwrecks on its shoals. The land was apparently fertile, there were pristine beaches, and communities of Seminoles and other indigenous groups were sparse. Largely inaccessible by land routes until well into the twentieth century, the Keys had belonged to the Spanish since the sixteenth century. The Spaniards were briefly driven out by the English in the late eighteenth century and never permanently resettled the area. In 1820 they ceded the land to the United States. Especially during these decades of transition, a particular attraction of the Keys was the absence of any formal governmental authority. Key West (the island village at the far tip of the Keys) had been known to fishermen and marine salvage hunters from both the Bahamas and Cuba for generations. In the 1820s, after the United States instituted new laws governing marine salvaging of ships found off U.S. coastal waters, another wave of predominantly white settlers arrived from the Bahamas. Key West became a center of a new marine salvage industry in the 1850s, attracting other settlers, too, including Afro-Caribbean peoples and Spanish-heritage immigrants descended from Spanish settlers in Hispaniola, Cuba, and parts of Central and South America.

Bahamians in Florida were known as "Conch" (pronounced "conk"), after the shellfish that is a staple of the Bahamian diet; conchs are found in abundance in the Florida Keys where the majority of the settlers from the Bahamas lived. In the mid-nineteenth century, Conch Bahamian families dominated the economy of Key West. White Bahamians eventually adopted the term "Conch Nation" as their own informal collective name, trumpeting their heritage as the first permanent settlers of European origin in the Keys. By the 1890s Key West was home to about 8,000 former Bahamians. Afro-Bahamians came in small numbers and built homes on Petronia Street, off the city's main thoroughfare, Duval Street. This district became known as Bahamian Village, though Afro-Cubans also lived there.

Black Bahamians immigrated to South Florida in much larger numbers in the first years of the twentieth century as part of what was known in the Bahamas as the Miami Craze. The first wave was largely made up of temporary residents and was tied to Florida's emergence as a major citrus producer and then as a tourist destination. From 1905 to 1912, both black and white Bahamians in Florida worked on the Flagler Florida East Coast Railway, lured by wages of $1.50 a day; comparable day rates on the Bahamian island of New Providence were between 25 and 50 cents a day. Black Bahamians also cleared land and dug drainage canals for the newly developing farms of South Florida, while others worked in the construction trades as the region began attracting tourists. Many Bahamian men moved back and forth between Florida and the Bahamas, sending money home and retaining close kinship ties. Most traveled on the regular mail boat that ran between Nassau and other ports in the Bahamas to Florida, paying the $5 passage fee per trip. They lived in rooming houses in humble villages around Biscayne Bay, the future site of Miami. Some of these quarters had been built as houses by Seminole, Creek, and other Native Americans who sparsely populated the area before Miami became a boom town almost overnight in the late 1890s.

South Floridians' demand for cheap labor peaked in the years before World War I, just as conditions for black Bahamians were at a low point at home. In the postslavery period, whites in the Bahamas had imposed what was called the "truck" system on the poorest black Bahamians: the tenant farmers, sponge divers, and salt rakers. Taking its name from the French word *troquer* (to barter), the truck system offered compensation for work in the form of commodity credits instead of actual wages. The system was destructive not only for black Bahamians but also for the Bahamian economy as a whole, which suffered as black Bahamians left in droves for better-paying jobs in Florida. By 1914 an estimated 5,000 black Bahamians lived in South Florida, mostly on the outskirts of the recently incorporated city of Miami.

Afro-Bahamians in Miami soon eclipsed the Keys' Conch population as the largest group of Bahamians in the United States. They built Bahamian-style cottages in places called Kebo and Lemon City, which evolved into Miami's Coconut Grove and Little Haiti neighborhoods. As in Bahamian Village in Key West, the frame cottages were single- or two-story homes, and the immigrants were known to disdain apartment-style dwellings as unsafe. These black Bahamian Americans retained a strong group identity. Emancipated decades before their American brethren, they were better educated in a British colonial system that, while unfair, was not as punitive as elsewhere; many were skilled tradesmen who had benefited from the apprentice training system in the Bahamas. Moreover, Afro-Bahamians were generally already accustomed to mixing with whites. Business and farm owners in Florida considered them excellent employees, well-trained as workers yet suitably deferential.

As Miami expanded rapidly in the first decades of the twentieth century, blacks of Bahamian origin worked as day laborers, on the city's busy cargo docks, and in more permanent jobs as domestic workers and hotel employees. Technically, they remained British crown subjects, and their numbers swelled to the point that the British Foreign Office had to appoint a vice-consul for Miami. As they prospered, black Bahamians also chafed at the racial segregation of the American South. They were appalled by police brutality and the white mob violence that erupted in Miami and other Florida cities, and as a result some opted for a further and more permanent journey to New York City, which had a significant black Caribbean-born population by the eve of World War I. Settling in the Harlem neighborhood, black Bahamians joined a flourishing segment of equally industrious black West Indians who worked as domestics, in the hotel and food-service industries, and even as small business owners.

The Johnson-Reed Act, passed by the U.S. Congress in 1924, sharply curtailed the number of persons of color permitted entry visas into the United States, causing a steep drop in immigration from the Bahamas. During World War II, however, a new wave of Bahamians was allowed to immigrate to alleviate wartime labor shortages. About 5,000 came as temporary migrants as part of a 1943 deal struck by the governor-general, the Duke of Windsor. Known as "the Contract" or "the Program" in the Bahamas, the migrant-labor system was similar to the Bracero (manual laborer) Program involving Mexicans in Texas and other parts of the southwestern United States. Some Bahamians became migrant laborers in Florida citrus groves, and others agreed to work on farms in Georgia and Alabama and even on Midwestern dairy farms. The U.S. Farm Security Administration work-visa program remained in place for two decades before it was ended in 1963.

Four years later the Bahamas became one of the newest black-majority-governed nations in the Caribbean and Latin American world. Immigration to the United States slowed considerably, especially in comparison to the flight of those seeking refuge from terrible economic and social conditions in such places as Haiti and Jamaica. Those Bahamians who did immigrate tended to seek higher education or work experience in professions such as medicine or engineering. They came as single adults, remained unmarried or married Bahamians, and generally kept their Bahamian citizenship rather than becoming Americans (Bahamian law forbids dual citizenship).

According to the 2010 U.S. Census, Florida was still the state with the largest population of Americans of Bahamian descent (24,810). Other states with small, but significant, numbers of Bahamian Americans include Georgia, New York, Texas, North Carolina, and New Jersey.

LANGUAGE

English has been the predominant language in the Bahamas since the British Eleutheran Adventurers arrived in the 1640s. Bahamian Standard English

In Coconut Grove, Florida, a traditional Bahamian enclave, people enjoy the Junkanoo parade at the Goombay Festival in 2009. The festival celebrates the legacy of the Bahamian-rooted community. JOE RAEDLE / GETTY IMAGES

(BSE) is taught in the schools and retains British spelling and forms of punctuation. However, a spoken patois is one of the features of authentic Afro-Bahamian culture and has traveled with immigrant populations. Black Bahamian Americans still speak it amongst themselves in social settings, even in relatively assimilated American families. The patois features a lilting colonial British accent, a more simplified grammar, and the use of such terms as "dem" and "dose" for "them" and "those," for example. Another notable feature is the repetition of words: a Bahamian will concur with another speaker by saying "true-true," for example. "Sip-sip" is a similar word for "gossip."

RELIGION

The first Europeans in the Bahamas came in search of religious freedom. The men and women of the Eleutheran Company were Puritans, and the Anglican religion of the Church of England became predominant as the island nation grew. Afro-Bahamians adopted Anglicanism or, later, were swayed by the Methodist or Baptist churches, both of which had a large missionary presences on the island in the nineteenth century. Christian leaders played a key role in the suppression of *obeah* among Afro-Bahamians. A practice that includes both traditional healing arts and sorcery, obeah migrated with slaves from West Africa and helped them retain their connection to traditional culture. The obeah-man or obeah-woman, a figure of respect in the community, used both rituals and herbal remedies to treat the sick. Obeah practices also became a way for slaves and ex-slaves to exact revenge on their enemies, either bodily or upon property—for example, by cursing crops. Obeah practices came with Bahamian immigrants to Florida.

One of the first Bahamian American churches in the United States was St. Peter's Episcopal Church on Duval Street in Key West, erected in 1838 to serve the Conch Bahamians of the Anglican faith. Afro-Bahamians in Key West founded the parish of St. Peter's in 1872. In Miami in 1897 the first permanent black Bahamian settlers founded St. Agnes Episcopal

HOLDING ON TO HERITAGE THROUGH COOKING

Rachel L. Swarns, a *New York Times* journalist, wrote of her Bahamian heritage and the erosion of its foodways in a 2012 article titled "Holding On to Heritage before It Slips Away": "Our ties to the islands dwindled over the years as relatives migrated or died, but we maintained our connections in other ways, sharing meals of conch fritters and coconut candy, boiled grouper and johnnycakes with friends and family." Swarns added that she yearned to cook old family recipes but had no nearby kin left with whom she could share the dishes. "My children have never known what it is like to squeeze into a kitchen full of Bahamian women serving up fried fish and family stories," Swarns remarked. "Suddenly, I've found myself grappling to hold on to something I never imagined I might lose."

Church, which played a decisive role in the community for decades, as would Christ Episcopal Church in Coconut Grove, founded in 1901. Bahamian Baptists in Coconut Grove were led by the Reverend Samuel A. Sampson, who organized the 56th Baptist Church congregation. In 1896 they built a house of worship on Charles Avenue called St. Agnes Missionary Baptist Church, which became Macedonia Missionary Baptist Church in the early 1920s. All of the aforementioned parishes still have active congregations.

A spoken patois is one of the features of authentic Afro-Bahamian culture and has traveled with immigrant populations. Black Bahamian Americans still speak it amongst themselves in social settings, even in relatively assimilated American families.

CULTURE AND ASSIMILATION

Bahamian Americans are well integrated into mainstream American life but retain ties to their homeland through kinship, travel, and a few cultural distinctions.

Traditions and Customs The most notable Bahamian cultural event in the United States is the annual Junkanoo Parade, which celebrates a venerable Afro-Bahamian tradition. Slaveholders in the British Caribbean customarily gave their workers a day of rest on December 26, known as Boxing Day throughout the British Commonwealth, along with New Year's Day. This respite permitted Afro-Bahamians to rest, socialize with family, and honor their West African traditions. The celebrations evolved into the music-and-costume extravaganza known as Junkanoo, which is a major event in Nassau even in the twenty-first century, when it takes place on New Year's Day.

The word *Junkanoo* may be a corruption of "John Canoe," a mythical African prince and possible slave trader who was said to have pushed back against English and Dutch encroachment and seized one slave operation for himself. It may also be derived from the Yoruba word *gensinconnu*, or masked person. The Yoruba of West Africa traditionally held a festival to honor their ancestors as part of a belief system called Egungun. Celebrants paraded behind large, elaborate masks and headdresses constructed from wood, animal skins, and other natural resources at their disposal; in the Junkanoo variant, these are made from humbler materials such as crepe paper and cloth. In Nassau only parade marchers dress up; revelers turn out en masse to pay their respects. The musicians beat a drum called a *goombay*, which is made from a hammered metal chamber with a goatskin stretched over it to make a playing surface. They also ring cowbells and blow empty conch shells, which sound like foghorns. Key West holds its Junkanoo in October to coincide with its Halloween tourist season, and Miami holds its Junkanoo during an annual June Bahamian culture week.

Cuisine Bahamians on the islands and in Florida still favor the humble but delicious conch, an edible mollusk. Conch can be eaten in a variety of ways, from raw to fried, and is a dining-out staple in most southern Florida restaurants, especially in the Keys. In Key West "conch" is a term appended to practically everything, linking the freewheeling spirit of the outpost to the first white Bahamian settlers.

Bahamian dishes are heavily spiced and have some West African touches. The traditional Bahamian breakfast is boiled fish and grits. Pigeon peas and rice is another culinary staple. Pigeon peas are not peas but rather a legume brought from West Africa that Europeans first called the "Congo pea." Also known as a gandule, tropical green bean, or no-eyed pea, the crop flourishes in subtropical climates around the world, even in Asia. For Afro-Bahamians in the United States, pigeon peas and rice, made with onion and salted pork, is a comfort food and a link to their heritage. Souse is another black Bahamian dish still served at holiday gatherings, often with a side of grits or johnnycake (a large, dense, slightly sweet baking powder biscuit). Souse is a simple soup made from water, onions, lime juice, celery, bell peppers, and, usually, chicken, though oxtail, pigs' feet, or sheep's tongue may also be used.

Dances and Songs Besides referring to the goatskin drum originating in West Africa, goombay is a form of calypso music that Afro-Bahamians brought with them to Florida. The African American literary icon Zora Neale Hurston, also a trained anthropologist, wrote extensively of Afro-Caribbean traditions in Florida during her lifetime. In an essay she authored for the Works Progress Administration (reprinted in Michael Craton and Gail Saunders's 1989 work *Islanders in the Stream:*

A History of the Bahamian People), Hurston reported that *Goombay* performances were loosely organized social occasions and compared them to other American Afro-Caribbean events. "The dance movements are more arresting; perhaps because the Bahamian offerings are more savage," she observed. "Nightly in Palm Beach, Fort Pierce, Miami, Key West and other cities of the Florida east coast, the hot drum heads throb and the African-Bahamian folk arts seep into the soil of America."

Goombay music is a feature of annual festivals celebrating Afro-Bahamian heritage in several Florida cities. The largest of these is held in Miami during the first weekend in June and attracts as many as a half-million spectators. Miami's Goombay Festival includes a Junkanoo parade, performances by the Royal Bahamas Police Band, and a street market where traditional Bahamian crafts and foods are sold. Ensembles such as the Sunshine Junkanoo Band and the Miami Junkanoo Band regularly play at cultural events in the Bahamas, too, including Nassau's Junkanoo event every January 1.

Holidays Bahamian Americans celebrate Junkanoo on December 26 and January 1, but unlike the parade that is a major event in Nassau, immigrants observe the event in more low-key private family gatherings. For many years the original Afro-Bahamian settlers in Florida continued to celebrate August 1, the day of their emancipation from slavery in the British Empire. In some communities black Bahamian settlers even carried on the venerable English tradition of Guy Fawkes Night on November 5. This date commemorates the foiling of the Gunpowder Plot in 1605,

when rebels planned to blow up the House of Lords in London along with King James I. Guy Fawkes Night celebrations migrated to the British colonies, where Royalists celebrated the survival of the monarchy as they did back home in England by burning effigies of the treasonous Fawkes. In the 1930s, when Florida law enforcement authorities understood that black Bahamian immigrants were burning an effigy of a white person every November 5, the Fawkes Night revelries were outlawed.

Twenty-first century Bahamian Americans observe Bahamian Independence Day on July 10, the date in 1973 when the Bahamas became an independent, black-majority-rule nation. The Bahamian Consulate-General in Miami stages a series of weekend-long events commemorating Afro-Bahamian life, including a Junkanoo parade, goombay music, and a visit from the Royal Bahamas Police Force Band.

Health Care Issues and Practices The first Afro-Bahamians in America brought with them their reliance on traditional herbal medicines and remedies, many of which had roots in West African practices.

FAMILY AND COMMUNITY LIFE

As islanders Bahamians tended to forge and keep close-knit kinship ties, even during the most active period of immigration to the United States between 1880 and 1930.

Gender Roles In the postslavery era women were accustomed to being left to fend for themselves for extended periods, especially those on the poorer Out Islands (which were isolated from the earlier-settled islands of New Providence and Grand Bahama). Their husbands were often absent for weeks at a time, working as spongers, salt collectors, or fishermen. Mothers and wives enjoyed an unusual degree of economic decision-making power and moral authority in their households and extended families. This pattern continued when young Bahamian men began leaving home to seek work in the booming South Florida economy. Eventually, entire families began immigrating to the Miami area on a more permanent basis. As in the islands Afro-Bahamian women maintained some independence even in this more traditional, settled family life. They usually worked outside the home, often as domestics or laundresses in private homes. They were active in their church communities and formed their own service clubs and social organizations or lodges.

Education Bahamians place a premium on education, and in the United States the majority of new immigrants sent their children to the segregated public schools in the Miami area. The temporary Afro-Bahamian college student immigrants in the 1950s and 1960s sought an education at historically black schools in the American South and at public universities in the New York City area.

Courtship and Weddings In British-regulated Bahamian society, interracial unions were strongly discouraged, a practice that continued among Afro-Bahamians in the United States. Dating and engagement were followed by a church wedding.

Relations with Other Americans Bahamian Americans tended to separate themselves from other Afro-Caribbean immigrants in South Florida, particularly from Haitians. Black Haitians spoke Haitian Creole or French, practiced Roman Catholicism, and were viewed as a negative influence on the more socially conservative Afro-Bahamians.

Death and Burial Rituals In the early 1900s the Afro-Bahamian community in Miami raised funds and secured municipal permission to erect the Coconut Grove Colored Cemetery. Founded in 1904, it replaced an earlier burial site and features the distinctive limestone above-ground tombs that are common to Bahamian burial practices. The Coconut Grove graveyard is sometimes erroneously reported to have been the filming location used for some scenes in pop star Michael Jackson's pioneering long-form 1983 video "Thriller."

EMPLOYMENT AND ECONOMIC CONDITIONS

The first Bahamian Americans used their tropical climate construction trade skills to help settlers in South Florida and the Keys build well-ventilated, insect-proof, hurricane-ready homes and resorts. They also built roads and were vital to Henry Flagler's Florida East Coast Railway. The family members who joined them in Miami worked as domestics, cooks, and citrus pickers. Many became small business owners and prospered in the segregation-era South. Their offspring attained college educations and were among the first solidly African American middle class.

POLITICS AND GOVERNMENT

The Afro-Bahamian immigrants who came during the Miami Craze were elated about the economic opportunities the building boom afforded them, but they were also appalled by the brutal racism of the segregated Southern United States. In the Bahamas they had certainly experienced discrimination, but a history of island revolts in the Caribbean had forced white colonists—confined as they were by the sea, and with limited militia on hand—to treat slaves with more tolerance. This carried over to the post-emancipation era, and newly arrived Afro-Bahamian blacks were shocked at the restrictions placed on them in Florida. Some took up the cause of the United Negro Improvement Association (UNIA), an early civil rights group formed by Marcus Garvey. Born in Jamaica in 1887, Garvey was educated at the University of London and settled in Harlem in 1916, founding the newspaper *Negro World*. Afro-Bahamians in Miami and New York City were a strong support base for Garvey's organization; at the height of UNIA's popularity just after World War I, there were twelve chapters of the group in Florida alone. UNIA added multiple for-profit sidelines that eventually ran afoul of U.S. law. Garvey was deported to Jamaica in 1927, and one of his successors as UNIA president was Nassau-born Frederick A. Toote.

During the most tumultuous years of the civil rights movement in America, the pastor of Coconut Grove's Christ Episcopal Church, Father Theodore R. Gibson (1915–1982), played an active role in improving conditions for blacks of all origins in the Miami area. Gibson's Bahamian parents had come to South Florida during the Miami Craze and then separated. Gibson spent large portions of his childhood with his grandparents in George Town, on the Bahamian island of Exuma, which he said shaped both pride in his heritage and his religious convictions. He became head of Miami's chapter of the National Association for the Advancement of Colored People (NAACP) and eventually won a seat on the county board of commissioners. It was Gibson who forced local authorities to extend the sewer system to Coconut Grove's streets in the 1960s, and he also worked to end school segregation.

NOTABLE INDIVIDUALS

Broadcasting Al Roker (1954–) is a longtime national meteorologist for NBC's *The Today Show*. He was born in Queens, New York, to parents of Jamaican and Bahamian heritage and began visiting his father's relatives in the Bahamas as a teenager. One of several books he has published is *Al Roker's*

Hassle-Free Holiday Cookbook (2007), which features a few traditional Bahamian recipes for the Boxing Day/Junkanoo celebrations.

Government In 2010, after a long career in public education and public service, Frederica Wilson (1942–) became the first Bahamian American elected to Congress. A Miami native whose Bahamian-born grandmother was a strong influence in her life, Wilson successfully petitioned the Speaker of the House to allow her to bypass a rule prohibiting the wearing of hats when Congress is in session. Wilson wears hats in honor of her late grandmother, who worked as a laundress.

Literature James Weldon Johnson (1871–1938) was one of the first major African American literary figures. Johnson was a writer, an activist, a founding member of the National Association for the Advancement of Colored People (NAACP), and a guiding light of the literary movement known as the Harlem Renaissance. His mother, Helen Louise Dillet, was born into a free black family in Nassau in the 1840s and later became the first black woman to teach school in Florida. Johnson's maternal grandfather was a prosperous Haitian immigrant who became a landowner in the Bahamas and even served in the colonial House of Assembly. The long tradition of activism in Johnson's maternal line—dating all the way back to the Haitian slave revolt of 1804, which his grandfather had witnessed and which had created the world's first black-ruled republic—was an instrumental force in Johnson's writings that helped him define the African American experience.

Music Julian "Cannonball" Adderley (1928–1975) was a renowned jazz musician born to Bahamian immigrants in Florida. He played saxophone in bands that backed Ray Charles and Miles Davis and later formed the Cannonball Adderley Quintet with his brother Nathaniel.

Stage and Screen Actor Sidney Poitier (1927–) is one of the Bahamian American community's most respected achievers. Born in Miami to parents from Cat Island in the Bahamas, Poitier has had a long career on the New York stage and in film. In 1964 he became the first African American performer to win the Academy Award for Best Actor or Actress, which he won for the 1963 film *Lilies of the Field*.

Esther Rolle (1920–1998) had a long career on the New York stage, in film, and on television. A native of Pompano Beach, Florida, she came from a large Bahamian immigrant family and gained fame in black theater in the 1950s. Pioneering television producer Norman Lear cast her as the housekeeper to the titular brassy feminist in *Maude*, a 1970s sitcom spin-off of the top-rated *All in the Family* series. Rolle's character, Florida Evans, proved so appealing that she was given her own series, *Good Times*, which ran for six seasons on CBS from 1974 to 1979.

Harlem Renaissance author, poet, and historian James Weldon Johnson was also Bahamian. CHARLES H. PHILLIPS / TIME LIFE PICTURES / GETTY IMAGES

Another *All in the Family* spin-off that was one of the top-rated sitcoms of the era, *The Jeffersons*, featured Roxie Roker (1929–1995) as Helen Willis, a neighbor of upwardly mobile George and Louise Jefferson. Roker's Willis and her on-screen husband were one of prime-time television's first interracial couples. Roker was born in Miami to Bahamian immigrant Albert Roker. Her cousin Al Roker (1954–) is a meteorologist for *The Today Show*. Roxie Roker's son Lenny Kravitz (1964–) is a multiple Grammy Award–winning rock musician and songwriter.

MEDIA

The Bahamas Weekly

The Afro-Bahamian diaspora's main news source.

Phone: (242) 352-2988
Email: info@thebahamasweekly.com
URL: www.thebahamasweekly.com

Nassau Guardian

Bahamian Americans keep up with news of the islands through Internet versions of the *Nassau Guardian*, the Bahamas' oldest newspaper.

Anthony Ferguson, President
4 Carter Street
P.O. Box N-3011
Oakes Field
Nassau, Paradise Island
Bahamas
Phone: (242) 302-2300
Fax: (242) 328-6883
URL: www.thenassauguardian.com

ORGANIZATIONS AND ASSOCIATIONS

Bahamian American Association, Inc. (BAAI)

Founded in 1912 as the Nassau Bahamas Association of New York, this group began as mutual-aid society and social organization for Bahamians living in New York City. Under the motto "Perseverance, Tenacity, and Courage," the BAAI boasts a long history of promoting Bahamian American educational achievements, business aspirations, and the economic and political development of Afro-Bahamians in the Bahamas. In the 1940s the organization bought a property in Harlem that became its cultural center. The Bahamian Student's Association was created as an offshoot in 1959. In 2002 the Nassau Bahamas Association of New York was reorganized and renamed the Bahamian American Association, Inc. (BAAI).

William R. Dames, President
211 West 137th Street
New York, New York 10030-2406
Email: thebaai@hotmail.com
URL: www.thebaai.org

Bahamian American Cultural Society

Founded in 1991 as a book-drive effort to aid schools in the Bahamas, this group works to promote Bahamian heritage in the United States, especially in the New York City area. It offers genealogical research tools; sponsors exhibitions of Bahamian artists and music events, including a late-summer cultural day held at one of the Hudson River piers; and promotes heritage tourism in the Bahamas.

Beryl Edgecombe, President
400 Second Avenue
Suite 8D
New York, New York 10010-9998
Phone: (212) 213 0562
Fax: (212) 725 8979
Email: bacsorg@earthlink.net
URL: www.bahamianamericanculturalsociety.org

National Association of the Bahamas

This Miami-based service organization promotes cross-cultural ties to the Bahamas and aids Bahamian students studying in the United States. It holds an annual picnic and scholarship fundraising gala featuring Junkanoo music.

Rosamon L. Gomez, President
St. Bernard de Clairvaux Episcopal Church
16711 West Dixie Highway
North Miami Beach, Florida 33160
Phone: (954) 673-0980
Email: rosamongomez@gmail.com
URL: www.nabmiami.org

MUSEUMS AND RESEARCH CENTERS

The Black Archives, History and Research Foundation of South Florida, Inc.

Founded in 1977 by Dorothy Jenkins Fields, a Bahamian American, the organization preserves the Afro-Caribbean contributions to the history and development of South Florida and the city of Miami.

Timothy A. Barber
5400 NW 22nd Avenue
Miami, Florida 33142
Phone: (305) 636-2390
Fax: (305) 636-2391
Email: baf@theblackarchives.org
URL: www.theblackarchives.org

Schomburg Center for Research in Black Culture of the New York Public Library

The leading archival source for the history of the African diaspora in New York City, the Schomburg Center is a trove of archival materials honoring the contributions of black New Yorkers to American culture, music, art, literature, and political activism.

Khalil Gibran Muhammad, Director
515 Malcolm X Boulevard
New York, New York 10037-1801
Phone: (212) 491-2200
URL: http://www.nypl.org/locations/schomburg

W. E. B. Du Bois Institute for African and African American Research-Harvard University

The preeminent research authority on African American history and contemporary life.

Dr. Henry Louis Gates, Jr., Director
104 Mount Auburn Street
Room 3R
Cambridge, Massachusetts 02138
Phone: (617) 495-8508
Fax: (617) 495-8511
URL: http://dubois.fas.harvard.edu

SOURCES FOR ADDITIONAL STUDY

Craton, Michael, and Gail Saunders. *Islanders in the Stream: A History of the Bahamian People*. Vol. 2, *From the Ending of Slavery to the Twenty-first Century*. Athens: University of Georgia Press, 1998.

Reimers, David M. *Other Immigrants: The Global Origins of the American People*. New York: New York University Press, 2005.

"Resources of the Bahamas." *New York Times*, June 30, 1861.

Swarns, Rachel L. "Holding On to Heritage before It Slips Away." *New York Times*, Sept. 18, 2012.

West-Dur´n, Alan, ed. *African Caribbeans: A Reference Guide*. Westport, CT: Greenwood Publishing Group, 2003.

BANGLADESHI AMERICANS

J. Sydney Jones

OVERVIEW

Bangladeshi Americans are immigrants or descendants of immigrants from Bangladesh, a country located in Southeast Asia. Bangladesh (formally known as the People's Republic of Bangladesh) is bounded to the east, north, and west by the much larger country of India, with which it shares a 2,500-mile border. To the southeast, Bangladesh shares a 119-mile border with Myanmar (Burma). To the south of Bangladesh lies the Bay of Bengal. Fully two-thirds of Bangladesh is made up of low-lying delta land, through which the many branches of the Ganges, Brahmaputra, and Meghna rivers flow to the sea. Flooding via the Bay of Bengal is both a gift and a curse, providing the nutrients and water supply for Bangladesh's three-crop rice production, but also displacing thousands of Bangladeshis annually. Bangladesh covers an area of 55,598 square miles (143,998 square kilometers) and is roughly the size of Wisconsin.

According to the Bangladesh Bureau of Statistics' Population and Housing Census, the population of Bangladesh was more than 14 million in 2011. Some 90 percent of Bangladesh is Muslim, and the remaining population is divided among Hindu, Christian, Buddhist, and Animist. The majority of the population considers itself Bengali. The non-Bengali minority encompasses the Adivasi (Indigenous) peoples and the Urdu-speaking population. The Adivasis (also known by the more political term "Jumma") are divided into many groups, which include the Chakma, Marma, Tripura, Tanchangya, Chak, Pankho, Mru, Murung, Bawm, Lushai, Khyang, Gurkha, Assamese, Santal, and Khumi. The majority of indigenous people live in the Chittagong Hill Tracts area of southeastern Bangladesh, which has a unique Adivasi culture that is distinct from that of the rest of Bangladesh. There are also Adivasis in some flatland areas. Bangladesh is one of the most densely populated countries in the world, and this population pressure contributes to economic stress and disparity. While economic indicators in Bangladesh have been weak since independence, the country has made substantial improvements in the prosperity of its poorest strata. Annual income per person, for example, has risen from $540 in 1990 to $1,909 as of 2011. The national poverty rate is high—31.5 percent

as of 2010—but has declined significantly since 1992, when it was 56.6 percent. Some 45 percent of the workforce is engaged in agriculture. Bangladesh is the world's second largest garments exporter, exceeded only by China. The country earned approximately $19 billion from garments in 2012, servicing brands such as Walmart, Nike, and Disney.

Early immigrants who came to the United States in the late nineteenth century from what is now Bangladesh were identified as Indian. They initially settled in California and other western states, as well as in cities such as New York, Detroit, New Orleans, and Baltimore. They built railroads, worked in factories, cut lumber, settled homesteads, and worked as traders. After Bangladesh won its independence from Pakistan in 1971, a second wave of immigrants began to arrive in the United States. Some of these people came because, no longer being part of Pakistan, migration was easier. In the late 1970s, others came as the political situation in the then independent Bangladesh continued to deteriorate. These new immigrants were mostly young male professionals seeking employment opportunities. The most substantial wave of Bangladeshi American immigration occurred after 2000 and was a result of the Diversity Immigrant Visa Program, which provided diversity visas (DVs) to immigrants from countries such as Bangladesh with low rates of immigration to the United States. Following the September 11, 2001, terrorist attacks, however, immigration officials began to place more hurdles, such as longer wait times and in-depth security checks, in the way of those seeking to migrate from Muslim-majority countries. This resulted in a drop in the number of Bangladeshis allowed in the United States.

According to U.S. Census data, the population of Bangladeshi Americans doubled between 2000 and 2010, rising to 147,300 in 2010. Unofficial estimates, which take undocumented immigrants into consideration, place that number as high as 250,000. Bangladeshi Americans are a very young migrant population, with seven in ten born outside the United States. Only about half have become American citizens. In New York during this period, Bangladeshis were the fastest growing new migrant group. Other areas of with significant Bangladeshi American populations include California, Florida, and Michigan.

HISTORY OF THE PEOPLE

Early History While Bangladesh gained independence in 1971, the area it occupies has a long cultural history. Originally known as Bengal, the region of the eastern Indian subcontinent around the Bay of Bengal has been settled since the first centuries of the Common Era and has a recorded history of over two millennia. The earliest inhabitants of the region were of mixed Mongoloid, Austric, and Dravidian heritage. This early civilization had highly developed arts, trade, and agriculture. Between 2000 and 1500 BCE, much of this was swept aside after invasions by Aryans, which brought the Sanskrit language and Vedic Hinduism to India. Bangladeshis are primarily descendants of the non-Aryan inhabitants of the region, with a very small portion also claiming descent from merchants and travelers from the Persian, Turkic, and Arab regions.

Bengal has a rich literary heritage, as written records in Bengali date back to the ninth or tenth century. Under the Buddhist Pala kings, Bengal was first unified politically between the eighth and twelfth centuries. At the height of its power in the early ninth century, this Pala empire included all of Bengal and most of Assam and Bihar.

The Hindu Sena Empire took the place of the Pala Empire in the late eleventh century but by about 1200 was already suffering from repeated incursions by invading Muslim armies led by Muhammad Bhaktyar. Muslim domination lasted until the Battle of Plassey in 1757, in which the British, under Robert Clive, defeated the Muslim ruler of the region and established British rule. However, more than 500 years of Muslim rule in the area left a lasting and rich legacy. Bengali Muslim rulers generally sponsored the arts and sciences at their courts and became patrons of poets, both Hindu and Muslim. A high point of Bengali literature was reached between the fifteenth and seventeenth centuries. During this time period, large numbers of Bengali, especially in the eastern region (today's Bangladesh), converted from Hinduism and Buddhism to Islam. This had a lasting effect in the region, in effect creating two Bengals—one in the west that was majority Hindu, and one in the east that was majority Muslim.

Modern Era With the defeat of the Muslim ruler Siraj-ud-Daula at the Battle of Plassey, Bengal fell under British rule. In 1905 the British partitioned Bengal into Muslim and Hindu areas, but the partition was revoked in 1912 due to protest from the Hindu political class. Thereafter, Bengal remained a unified part of the British Raj until 1947. Two legacies of British rule were the English language and a European-style educational system.

During the nearly two centuries of British rule, the rift between Muslims and Hindus widened. The 1857 Sepoy Mutiny was a crucial factor in this, since the British analysis concluded that, in many cities, Muslim soldiers had been the leaders of the rebellion, even though Hindu soldiers had also participated. Thereafter, British imperial policy strategically exacerbated various divisions between the two main religious groups so as to head off any possibility of another united Hindu-Muslim rebellion against the British. In cities like Delhi, intellectual and economic control shifted from the Muslim to the Hindu population, due to the British policy of gradually disempowering the Muslim population. At the end of the Raj, the stage was thus set for a partition of the Indian Empire based on the two main religious groupings. India remained primarily Hindu, while the state of Pakistan was formed for Muslims. East Bengal became East Pakistan and was separated from West Pakistan by more than a thousand miles, with India in between the two wings of Pakistan.

Relations between the two wings of Pakistan were poor from the outset, as the Bengalis in East Pakistan distrusted their fellow Pakistanis in West Pakistan. East and West Pakistan were culturally and linguistically distinct from one another with only a shared religion in common. The beginning of mistrust came in 1952, when East Pakistan resisted an attempt by the Urdu-speaking elite section of West Pakistan to make Urdu the official language of the entire country.

Later in the 1950s, the Pakistani military took control of the political system and suspended the democratic process. Due to the military's overwhelming base in West Pakistan, this further exacerbated tensions between the two Pakistans. Though East Pakistan had the majority of the population of the new country, and though it accounted for much of the foreign exchange through its rice and jute production and the activities of the port of Chittagong, it held far less political power than West Pakistan. Less than 13 percent of Pakistani government employees were Bengali, and less than 10 percent of high-ranking army officials were from the eastern wing of the newly constituted Pakistan. Only 36 percent of the national budget was spent in East Pakistan.

By the early 1960s, a movement for regional autonomy in East Pakistan began to form under the leadership of Sheikh Mujibur Rahman, who was popularly known as Sheikh Mujib. In 1966 Sheikh Mujib was imprisoned on conspiracy charges. When the charges were finally dismissed, he emerged from prison a national hero. Three years later, after sustained anti-army protests in both wings of Pakistan, General Ayub Khan stepped down and was replaced by General Yahya Khan. In an attempt to alleviate an increasingly tense political situation, Yahya allowed the first free elections under universal franchise since the army took control of Pakistan in the 1950s. This election, held in 1970, was the first one where the Bengali numerical majority's votes were counted on the basis of one person, one vote. Sheikh Mujib and his Awami League party won an absolute majority of all Pakistan assembly seats, but West Pakistani politician Zulfiqar

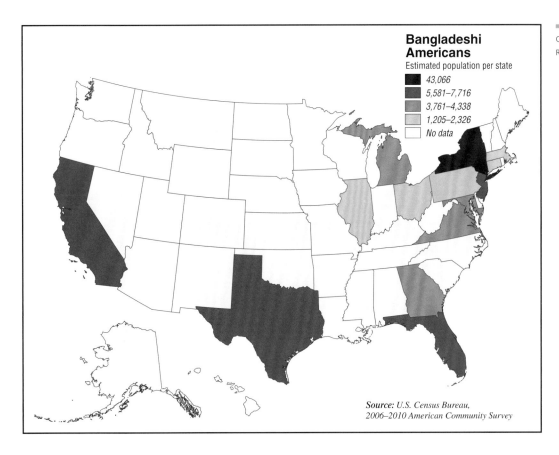

Bangladeshi Americans

Estimated population per state

- 43,066
- 5,581–7,716
- 3,761–4,338
- 1,205–2,326
- No data

Source: U.S. Census Bureau, 2006–2010 American Community Survey

Ali Bhutto refused to accept the result. The subsequent negotiations broke down and the army postponed the assembly, inflaming the situation.

In March 1971, the Pakistani military launched a secret military crackdown, arresting all Awami League leaders and killing thousands of people in the universities and other political nerve centers. East Pakistan subsequently proclaimed its independence as a free nation. West Pakistan jailed Sheikh Mujib and declared East Pakistan a rebel province. Some ten million people fled to India and Bengali rebels set up training camps inside India and fought a guerrilla war against the well-armed Pakistani military. During a nine-month war, Pakistani soldiers were accused of carrying out genocidal attacks, targeting Hindu Bengalis, and also using lists of teachers, students, and other professionals to decide who would be picked up.

India allied itself with Bangladesh (East Pakistan) to defeat Pakistani forces in what became known as Bangladesh's War of Independence. By the time the war ended on December 16, the conflict had claimed between half a million and three million lives, according to differing estimates, and had displaced ten million people. Thousands of Bangladeshi women had also been raped by Pakistani forces. At war's end, the exiled government returned from Calcutta, India, to Dhaka, and Mujib was released from Pakistani prison to become the first leader of the newly independent

Bangladesh. The war left much of the nation, including its economy, in ruins. Economic recovery was slow since tea plantations in northern Sylhet and the jute mills that fueled industry had been destroyed. Many of the millions who had fled the country returned after independence only to find their homes and villages in ruins. However, a new nation, Bangladesh, had been formed, made up of the former East Bengal as well as the former Sylhet district of Assam.

In 1975 Sheikh Mujib attempted to strengthen his hold on power by banning all political parties but his own Awami League. A coup led by army officers followed, and Mujib was killed. After a series of coups and military regimes during the late 1970s and 1980s, a massive pro-democracy movement gripped the country in 1990 and mobilized reform. Many analysts consider 1990 the last noble moment of all-party, mass political mobilization, comparing it with the 1968 movement that led to the ouster of General Ayub Khan and the 1971 movement that led to the Independence War.

Begum Zia of the Bangladesh Nationalist Party (BNP) became the first female prime minister of the country in 1991. She was succeeded in 1996 by Sheikh Hasina Wajed of the Awami League, daughter of the country's first leader, Mujib. Over the last two decades Zia and Hasina have alternated control of power, with the exception of the two-year, military-backed "Caretaker Government" of 2006 to 2008.

Bangladesh has weathered attempts at military dictatorship and has made room within its borders for diverse religious groups. It can be characterized as having a fragile democracy, where the military always has the potential to intervene. While the country's intellectual class often discusses the need for a "third force" to challenge the Awami League-BNP duopoly, so far no such force has succeeded at the polls. The brief and failed election campaign of Nobel laureate Muhammad Yunus of the Grameen Bank further weakened the "third force" scenario. However, in spite of unstable governance, the country has made impressive improvements, and Nobel laureate Amartya Sen recently cited Bangladesh as having better results on certain human health indicators than India. However, overpopulation does continue to motivate large numbers of Bangladeshi to seek better opportunities in countries such as the United States.

SETTLEMENT IN THE UNITED STATES

As the nation-state of Bangladesh did not come into existence until 1971, there were no "Bangladeshi" immigrants per se to the United States until after that time. However, immigrants from the Bengali region to the United States have been arriving since 1887. Their numbers were small, in part because of discriminatory immigration laws that allowed citizenship only to Caucasians. These immigrants included dissident student activists, both Hindu and Muslim, who fled to the United States after the partition of Bengal in 1905. Small groups of these male students settled on the west coast, primarily in San Francisco, Oregon, and Washington. Such student immigrants were from both West and East Bengal and numbered only in the hundreds.

Merchant marines also immigrated in small numbers in the early years of the twentieth century. Escaping poverty, they simply jumped ship after docking in New York or San Francisco. As anti-miscegenation laws forbade their marrying white women, this first wave of male immigrants from Bengal married mostly Mexican, African American, or Creole women and also formed communities with these ethnic groups.

Though some of the early Bengali immigrants, such as the student activist Taraknath Das, tested the discriminatory immigration and naturalization laws, little changed in the first half of the twentieth century. Das was able to gain citizenship by proving to a clerk that anthropologists officially labeled his race Caucasian. A handful of Bengali and Indian immigrants won citizenship on these grounds, until the 1924 Immigration Act further restricted citizenship rights. Court battles ensued, and finally, in 1946, naturalization was granted to all Indians, including both Muslim and Hindu Bengalis. A quota of 100 immigrants per year was set, and in 1965, Indian and Pakistani immigrants were given the same status as other nationalities.

In the 1960s, just prior to independence, many East Bengalis had fled to the United States to avoid political persecution, or, in the case of religious minorities, to avoid religious discrimination. These immigrant groups were generally composed of well-educated and affluent professionals. With the creation of Bangladesh in 1971, official immigration records became separate from those of Indians and Pakistanis.

Since 1971, the number of immigrants from this region has increased annually. In 1973, 154 Bangladeshi immigrants arrived in the United States; 147 in 1974; 404 in 1975, and 590 in 1976. These immigrants were mostly younger men who were leaving behind the hard economic and political times of the still-developing Bangladesh. The overpopulation of the region and subsequent poverty continue to be the main reasons for emigration from Bangladesh.

By 1980 there were an estimated 3,500 Bangladeshis in the United States, 200 of whom had already become U.S. citizens. However, these numbers severely underestimate the undocumented portion of this population. They settled in every state of the union but were concentrated in the urban areas of New York, New Jersey, and California. Fully a third of these early immigrants were professionals, and many of the remaining two-thirds were white-collar workers. Immigrants within this wave tended to be men (60 percent) under the age of thirty-nine. About half of these immigrants were already married when they arrived, with families awaiting immigration once the spouse was settled. They formed civic organizations and clubs in the locales where they settled, and they tended to keep to their ethnic and religious communities. Bangladeshi immigrants typically supported Democratic candidates, in part as a result of Republican support for Pakistan during the independence movement.

In the 1980s both documented and undocumented immigrants continued to arrive from Bangladesh in large numbers. Between 1982 and 1992, the U.S. Immigration and Naturalization Service legally admitted 28,850 Bangladeshis. Another 6,000 Bangladeshis also won diversity visas through a lottery between 1988 and 1993. By the 1990s, estimates of undocumented Bangladeshi immigrants had reached as high as 150,000. In 1998 it was estimated that there were more than 100,000 Bangladeshi Americans living in New York City alone, and the area of 36th Avenue in Astoria began to be identified as "Mini Bangladesh" because of the large number of Bangladeshi restaurants in the area. Other large enclaves of Bangladeshis were found in Los Angeles, Miami, Washington, D.C., and Atlanta. In Los Angeles, the Bangladeshi community is centered in and around the downtown area, where shop and restaurant signs are often in Bengali. As immigrants began to settle in the United States, the networks of kinship brought in smaller groups of migrants, composed of family and friends.

A third and most significant wave came in the 1990s and 2000s as a result of the Diversity Immigrant Visa Program. Because this program did not give preference to immigrants based on their professional skills or educational achievements, the number of non-professionals was much higher (some argue the majority) in this new group. As a result, a majority of them went into blue-collar jobs, such as taxi driving, restaurant work, and operating newspaper stands and fruit stands.

While New York remained home to the largest number of Bangladeshi Americans, the economic downturn of the early twenty-first century forced large numbers of Bangladeshi Americans to leave the area to seek out job opportunities in Michigan, where they found opportunity in the small businesses that support the automobile industry. Often, Bangladeshis were drawn to economically blighted areas where they could live inexpensively and start new businesses at low cost. In Hamtramck, Michigan, for example, an influx of new Bangladeshi migrants has started to turn parts of the city's devastated economy around toward some measure of solvency. Others sought out new lives in Florida and in large cities such as Los Angeles, Dallas, Atlanta, and Chicago.

Recent immigrants from Bangladesh also included groups of the indigenous Adivasi peoples of the Chittagong Hill Tracts, with their distinct culture. They had left Bangladesh to escape repression by the military, which continues to control the Chittagong Hill Tracts, in spite of a 1997 peace accord that was supposed to end the military's presence. Other Bangladeshis had arrived in the United States indirectly via the Middle East, Australia, or Africa. Though these immigrants tended to be more geographically mobile than earlier immigrants from Bengal and Bangladesh, most still preserved strong ties to Bangladesh and become involved in local organizations that reflected their religious, ethnic, or geographical affiliations in their home country.

According to 2000 U.S. Census figures, there were 41,280 Bangladeshis of single ancestry living in the United States. By 2010 the official count had reached 147,300. Data from 2007 to 2009 indicates that 73 percent of recent Bangladeshi immigrants are foreign born, and 41 percent arrived in the United States after 2000. Between 2001 and 2010, there were 86,158 immigrant visas issued by the U.S. Immigration and Naturalization Service to Bangladeshis. Some 41 percent of those were sponsored by family members already living in the United States, and 33 percent had an immediate family member who had already immigrated to America. Only 6 percent were sponsored by employers. Some 64 percent of those immigrants were

between the ages of eighteen and sixty-four. Most were Muslim, but some were Hindu, Buddhist, and Christian. Almost all Bangladeshi Americans continue to maintain strong cultural ties with others from their homeland.

LANGUAGE

Bengali, or Bangla, is the language spoken by most of the people of Bangladesh as well as those in the Indian state of Bengal and parts of Assam. More than 200 million people worldwide speak Bengali, making it one of the world's most widely spoken language groups. Part of the Indo-Aryan subfamily of the Indo-European family of languages, Bengali is derived from Sanskrit.

For the Bangladeshi, Bengali is more than a language; it is a cultural identity. One of the first measures that West Pakistan employed in 1952 in its attempt to incorporate East Pakistan was to proclaim Urdu the national language of the country. That measure failed, and after the 1971 independence war, Bengali replaced English in government documents and in most levels of public administration, as well as on street and commercial signs. Schools, too, began to switch from teaching in English to teaching in Bengali after independence. For example, St. Joseph, one of the top schools in Dhaka, switched from the Cambridge system to Bengali-medium in 1973. In the 2000s, however, this trend reversed and the prevalence of English-medium schools, especially in the capital of Dhaka, increased. Bilingual phrasing in both English and Bengali is now widespread on street signs, in shop names, and on billboards. This has led to great anxiety among the cultural class and to several attempts to reduce the increasing presence of English. Among many factors, this was due largely to a growing economic sector, including telecommunications, banking, and advertising, that required English-educated young professionals. Though English continues to be a strong and growing second language in Bangladesh, Bengali is still the official language of government and education. On a street and vernacular level, many Bengalis have some listening comprehension of Hindi due to the popularity of Indian Bollywood films. Rural areas primarily continue to use Bengali speech, often using a local dialect.

Until the 1930s, formal Bengali, *sadhu bhasha*, was used for literary, printed matter, while the colloquial language, *cholito bhasha*, was the medium of more informal discourse. Now, however, the colloquial is used for all forms. Most Bangladeshis speak *cholito bhasha* as well as their own local dialects. Some of those, such as that spoken in Sylhet (*Sylheti*), Chittagong (*Chatgayya*), and Noakhali (*Noakhaillya*), have been somewhat affected by Arab-Persian influences. Loan words from English, Arabic, Portuguese, Persian, and Hindi are common in Bengali in general, reflecting the history of the nation as a trading and convergence point. Famous writers in Bengali include the 1913 Nobel laureate Rabindranath

BANGLADESHI PROVERBS

Bengali is a language rich in proverbs, many of them reflecting the moral values and ethics of a rural, agrarian society. Homey virtues are represented in the saying "All are kings in their own houses," while meeting one's own consequences are reflected in "Like sin, like atonement." Food becomes a metaphor in many proverbs: "Have I drawn a harrow over your ripe corn?" is said to someone who, without reason, wants to harm the speaker; and "He has spoiled my already served rice!" is used to described a situation when something, after much effort, begins to take effect and then is set back or ruined by some outside force or person.

Ignorant actions are mocked in proverbs such as "Cutting the root below and watering the bush above," and "Standing below the tree while felling it." Things that last briefly are caught in the phrase "'Tis a palm tree's shade," while "An ocean of wisdom" can be applied to wise men and fools alike, the latter with a sarcastic voice. Doing one's best in spite of all is reflected in "One puts on a rag rather than go naked," while the effects of inattention are summed up in "It comes in through one ear, but it goes out at the other." Along the same lines, giddy oversight is summed up in "Blind with both his eyes open!" and the futility of striving for the unreachable is represented in "'Tis sand mixed up with molasses." Peasant irony and understanding of material realities are represented in "He who has money may ask for judgment."

Shomoy bohia jaey nodir sroter praye

Time flows away with the river stream. (Time is precious; do not waste it.)

Chokh moner ayna

The eyes are the mirror of the soul.

Karo poush mash, karo shorbonash

For some it is the month of *Paush*, for others a great disaster. (*Paush* is when crops come in.)

GREETINGS AND POPULAR EXPRESSIONS

Assalam-u-alaykum (*Muslim*) *or* nomoshkaar (*Hindu*)

Hello

Shuprobhat

Good morning

Khoda hafiz (*Muslim*) *or* biday (*general, though less common*)

Good-bye

Shubhoratri

Good night

Ji (*more polite, to an elder*) *or* hya (*more informal*)

Yes

Na

No

Dhonnobad

Thank you

Kemon achen?

How are you?

Bhaalo achi

I am fine.

Apnaar (*or* tomaar *for less formal*) nam ki?

What is your name?

Ami bujhlam na?

I did not understand.

Apni Ingreji bolte paren?

Do you speak English?

Tagore, a Hindu, whose poems, songs, and stories lovingly document Bengali life, and Kazi Nazrul Islam, a Muslim poet who is widely known as the poetic voice of a more rebellious, assertive Bengali identity. The fact that the two most prominent poets of modern Bengal are a Hindu and a Muslim is cited as an example of Bengal's religious pluralism.

Among Bangladeshi Americans, 92 percent continue to speak their own language within their homes, and it is estimated that 188,452 individuals speak Bengali within the United States. Nearly half of all Bangladeshi Americans are considered to have Limited English Proficiency, and a fourth of them have been labeled linguistically isolated because of that language barrier. This is particularly true of older immigrants. When interacting with other Bangladeshi Americans, many speak a combination of Bengali and English.

RELIGION

Some 90 percent of Bangladeshis follow the tenets of Islam, which was the state religion of Bangladesh from 1988, when the military regime changed the constitution, until 2011, when the Fifteenth Amendment to the Bangladeshi Constitution officially made Bangladesh a secular state and made secularism an essential feature of the state.

Three Bangladeshi
American friends in
Brooklyn, NYC. DAVID
GROSSMAN / ALAMY

Most Bangladeshi Muslims are of the Sunni sect, with a small number of Shi'ite Muslims. There are also smaller numbers of other sects, such as Ahmadiya Muslims, Baha'i, and Aga Khani. About 10 percent of the population is Hindu; the remaining population consists of Buddhists, Christians, and followers of various other sects. Among Bangladeshi Americans, the majority of those entering the United States after 2000 have been Muslim, though there are also small but significant Bengali Hindu, Bengali Christian, and Adivasi (which is primarily Buddhist) communities in the United States. Muslim Bangladeshi Americans have been involved in building mosques and in fighting for their right to work and live peacefully in a society that is largely Christian and where Muslim Americans have been under severe scrutiny since the terrorist attacks in the United States on September 11, 2001.

In American cities with large Muslim populations, such as New York and Detroit, Bangladeshi Muslims are able to practice their religious faith within a diverse community of Muslims. This increases connections outside the Bangladeshi American community. Bangladeshi Americans living in areas without substantial Muslim communities often face difficulties in practicing their faith, such as having to drive great distances to reach the nearest mosque. The same is generally true of Bangladeshi Hindus, who have access to Hindu temples in cities such as New York, Los Angeles, Phoenix, and Boston but have difficulty finding a religious community in smaller American cities and in rural areas.

CULTURE AND ASSIMILATION

Overall, Bangladeshis are fairly recent arrivals to the United States and tend to maintain ethnic enclaves in the areas where they settle. Having won a war of independence and the right to self-identity in the subcontinent, the immigrants who come to America have attempted to preserve their new identities as Bangladeshi Americans.

For these newer immigrants, preserving religious and cultural identities as Bangladeshi has remained important. Among second- and third-generation Bangladeshi Americans, teaching members of younger generations to respect that identity and learn that history has become a major priority. In central Florida, for instance, a group of Bangladeshi Americans holds monthly social gatherings, where they speak their own language, eat their own food, listen to their own music, and wear the traditional clothing of Bangladesh. However, these meetings also tend to reflect the mixed cultures of the group, with communication often being conducted in a combination of English and Bengali; American food shares the table with traditional Bangladeshi dishes, and jeans and T-shirts appear frequently, particularly among the young. This same pattern is repeated in other cities, especially where entire families are living together (it is more difficult when it is only male migrants alone in America). New York is home to the largest group of Bangladeshi Americans in the country, and members of the community within the New York/New Jersey area have made a sincere effort to promote the Bangladeshi culture through events

BHAPA CHINGRI

Ingredients

10–12 Pieces of prawns

3½ ounces mustard oil

½ fresh coconut, cut into small chunks

5 tablespoons chile paste and white mustard

2 teaspoons turmeric powder

sugar and salt to taste

10–12 pieces green chile, chopped Banana leaves

Preparation

Wash prawn pieces and then immerse in salt water for about 5 minutes.

Pulse coconut in food processor until a paste forms; do not over process. Combine oil, coconut paste, chile/mustard paste, salt, turmeric and sugar, mix well.

Remove the prawns from the water and dry with a paper towel. Place prawns in the coconut mixture and marinate for 5 hours in the refrigerator.

After prawns have marinated, place 1 each on a banana leaf. Sprinkle chopped green chile on each prawn and cover it with another leaf.

Place banana leaf packages in a pressure cooker and cook for about ten minutes.

Serve immediately.

such as the annual Bangladeshi Festival. They also established the Bangladesh Theatre of America, an off-Broadway folk and music theater. While still a university student, attorney Nuren Haider wrote the children's musical *Amra Harainee (We Are Not Lost)* to teach the children of Bangladeshi Americans about their heritage.

Traditions and Customs Bangladeshi culture, as reflected in its traditions and customs, has a rich mixture of Islamic, Hindu, Buddhist, and Christian influences, along with more ancient traditions and practices. Most Bangladeshi Americans are aware of, and take great pride in, the long history of their people. Though separated from their homeland, they continue to celebrate and honor the beauty of Bangladeshi culture's great achievements in art, drama, literature, and dance. The culinary traditions of Bangladesh also endure in the United States. In New York, for example, there are renowned Bangladeshi restaurant "blocks" in Queens, Brooklyn, and the Bronx that draw Bangladeshi visitors from near and far. That said, the cultural richness of Bangladesh continues to evolve within the Bangladeshi American community, which

blends traditional customs and attitudes with those of America's diverse multicultural milieu.

Cuisine Rice is the mainstay of the Bangladeshi diet. In Bangladesh the cultivation of this crop occupies 80 percent of the cultivated land and is grown in three crops. A summer rice, *aus*, is harvested in July or August, after which the autumn rice, or *amon*, is planted, still using the water from monsoon season. A third crop, the winter rice, *boro*, is grown from December through April.

In addition to this staple, Bangladeshis eat all sorts of fish, another mainstay in the Bangladeshi diet. Meat is also consumed, except pork, which is forbidden by Islamic tradition. (However, other communities, especially Adivasi and Christian communities, do eat pork.) Like much of the food on the subcontinent, Bangladeshi cuisine is highly spiced, and common spices include mustard, fenugreek seed, and cumin. Curries are popular, as is rice pilaf, and Bangladeshi cuisine is also noted for a variety of milk-based sweets such as *roso golla*. A typical meal for a Bangladeshi American might include fish, vegetables, rice, and a dessert. Fish and vegetables are also combined in dishes such as *bhapa* and *ghanho*.

Among the Bangladeshi American population, it is very common to prepare and consume traditional Bangladeshi cuisine. In addition, as the Bangladeshi American population has grown, restaurants that serve this cuisine have opened in American cities such as New York and Atlanta. These restaurants, which sometimes serve Indian as well as Bangladeshi food, cater to a broader population and serve this cultural cuisine to Americans who are not of Bangladeshi descent. In fact, due to the need to attract non-Bengali customers, many restaurants located outside immigrant enclaves brand themselves as "Indian," even though the majority of them are owned and managed by Bangladeshis.

Traditional Dress Traditionally, one of the few overt differences between Muslims and Hindus in Bangladesh was in their form of dress. Muslim men tended to wear a sarong-like garment, the *lungi*, which was tied around the waist. This garment was worn with a short vest. Muslim men also wore beards, as is traditional in many Muslim cultures. Hindu men, however, traditionally wore the *dhoti*, a pleated white garment that was brought between the legs and tied in front. The educated classes of men often wore loose-fitting, lightweight cotton trousers called *pajamas* (from which the English word is derived) with a collarless, knee-length shirt, known as the *panjabi*. For traditional ceremonies, such as weddings, the *sherwani* and *churidar*, a calf-length tunic and tight-fitting trousers, were often seen, accompanied by a turban.

While such traditional dress is still sometimes worn, the distinctions between what Hindus and Muslims wear in Bengal have broken down. The *lungi*, for example, is very common but is no longer worn only by Muslims. *Pajamas*, too, are now worn by a wide swath of the population, while *dhotis* are decreasingly common.

Most Bangladeshi Americans wear western clothing in their daily lives, but they might don traditional clothing for special occasions or when gathering with other Bangladeshi Americans. Some Bangladeshi American Muslim women wear headscarves in public for religious reasons. A number of Bangladeshi American Muslim women have joined with other Muslim women in filing lawsuits to protect their right to wear headscarves on the job. However, some ceased wearing head coverings in the years following the September 11, 2001, terrorist attacks, fearing discrimination against Muslims.

Traditional Music and Dance Bengali tradition is rich in music and dance, and much of it is story-based. This strong folk tradition has remained alive in many Bangladeshi American communities, where holidays and festival times are celebrated with Bangladeshi dance and song as well as with drama and poetry. Many of the string and percussion instruments employed are common to the subcontinent as a whole.

There are four main categories of music in the culture: classical, light classical, devotional, and popular. In its popular music, however, Bangladesh proves to be most original, developing forms for which there are no real equivalents outside the borders of Bangladesh. Characterized by spontaneity and high energy, these include *bhatiali*, *bhawaiya*, *jari*, *sari*, *marfati*, and *baul*.

Bangladeshi culture also has highly developed forms of dance, including such classical dances as *kathakali* and *bharata-natya*, both of which are typical throughout the subcontinent. However, specific to Bangladesh are indigenous dances such as *dhali*, *baul*, *maipuri*, and snake dances. These hearken back to Adivasi and communal life and describe various aspects of that lifestyle. These dances are performed on certain festival days. In both music and dance, improvisation is considered the primary goal.

The technology of the World Wide Web allows Bangladeshi Americans to listen to the music of their homeland 24/7, and websites keep them abreast of current musical trends. A group of Bangladeshi Americans has also formed the nonprofit organization Bangladesh American Band Alliance (BABA) to present Bangladeshi music to American audiences, and Bangladeshi American events are regularly held in cities with large Bangladeshi American populations to honor this music and culture.

Holidays While the Bangladeshi American community joins in such universal celebrations as New Year's, and in such American festivities as July Fourth and Thanksgiving, the real festivals and holiday occasions for them are religious and cultural in nature. For Bangladeshi Muslims, the two most important holidays are Eid-al-Fitr, which marks the end of Ramadan, the month of fasting, and Eid-al-Adha, the festival of sacrifice, which observes the pilgrimage to Mecca. For

Bangladeshi Hindus, important holidays are Durga Puja, which celebrates the Hindu goddess Durga, and Saraswati Puja, which celebrates the Hindu goddess Saraswati. These holidays are often celebrated with an exchange of visits between friends and relatives, and increasingly with festivals of song and dance. Additionally, Hindus celebrate other *pujas*, or festivals, honoring various gods and goddesses.

Some Bangladeshi American Muslim women wear headscarves in public for religious reasons. A number of Bangladeshi American Muslim women have joined with other Muslim women in filing lawsuits to protect their right to wear headscarves on the job. However, some ceased wearing head coverings in the years following the September 11, 2001, terrorist attacks, fearing discrimination against Muslims.

Most Bangladeshi Americans also celebrate secular and cultural Bangladeshi holidays. *Pohela Boishakh* is celebrated on April 14 in honor of the beginning of the Bengali calendar year. National Mourning Day is celebrated on February 21 to honor those who gave their lives in 1952 during the language riots to have Bangla declared the official language of Bangladesh. Bangladeshis celebrate two anniversaries of the nation's independence from Pakistan: on March 26, Independence Day, they memorialize the day that Bangladesh began the war for independence; on December 16, Victory Day, they memorialize the surrender of the Pakistan army and the formation of the People's Republic of Bangladesh. They also commemorate December 14 as Martyred Intellectual Day, in honor of the people killed by the Pakistan army and by local collaborators in the last days of the 1971 war.

Health Care Issues and Practices No specific disease or illness has been identified as being unusually prevalent among Bangladeshi Americans except for diabetes, which is common due to the high starch content of their diet. The community as a whole accepts the practices of Western medicine, though many still work within the framework of the alternative medical practices of the subcontinent, including, among some Hindus, adherence to the Ayurvedic beliefs in spiritual healing and the use of herbs for preventive treatment. *Kabiraji*, which is another form of herbal treatment, is practiced by both Muslims and Hindus.

Health problems have been a particular issue among older Bangladeshi Americans for whom the language barrier presents a major problem because 83 percent of this group is not proficient in English. There is also a tendency among this group to demonstrate distrust of western healthcare practices, which often leads senior Bangladeshi Americans to ignore health warnings. Diabetics may neglect monitoring their blood glucose levels, and many fail to take medications as prescribed. The problem is exacerbated among those who do not have health insurance and who, therefore, delay seeing a health professional.

FAMILY AND COMMUNITY LIFE

A majority Muslim nation, Bangladesh largely escaped the defining caste system of its Hindu neighbor, India. Social organization in the rural districts is based on the village or family (*paribar* or *gushti*), generally consisting of a complete or incomplete patrilineal extended household and residing in a homestead. This is combined into the larger unit of extended family house, sometimes called the *ghar*. The extended household works lands jointly, and food is served in a communal kitchen. The idea of nuclear family is somewhat alien in villages, although it is becoming more common in cities.

From this basic (*bari*) level, extended kinship ties are also patrilineal, based on real or assumed relationships. Such a kinship system becomes incredibly complex, and there are a variety of words to describe relatives of varying degrees. Thus "uncle," for example, can have several names. The father's brother is called *chacha*, while the mother's brother is *mama*; the father's sister's husband is *phupha*, and the mother's sister's husband is *khalu*.

Bangladeshi society is woven together by this intricate kinship system, and even those not related by blood but who are simply older and thus worthy of respect become an aunt (*chachi*) or uncle (*chacha*), grandfather (*dada*) or grandmother (*dadi*). The use of such kinship names even extends to people of the same generation, who become *bhai* (brother, used for men older than you) or *apa* (sister, used for women older than you). Thus, in the United States, Bangladeshis may find some initial difficulty in using people's names instead of kinship titles.

The *bari*, or household, consists of an extended family, typically married sons on the paternal side. Great respect is shown the father, or *abba*, and mother, *amma*. Older brothers are also shown such respect. This model, however, tends to break down in the United States, where the necessities of earning a living often send both parents out into the workforce. Immigration regulations also lead to fracturing with the family structure. For example, restrictions on certain visas preclude immigrants from bringing their families with them to the United States. These visa restrictions disproportionately affect working-class immigrants. Among professionals, family migrations are more common.

Bangladeshi Americans of the first generation see themselves primarily as members of a complex family relationship rather than as individuals making their own way in the world. In addition to forming close ties to other Bangladeshi Americans, they have forged relationships with other American Muslims and with other South Asian immigrants. The typical *bari* relationship of Bangladesh has already been altered to more of the nuclear family model of the United States wherein unmarried children reside with their parents until they are married and then move away to form their own new family.

Gender Roles As with the rest of the subcontinent, women in Bangladeshi society were traditionally in the home in the role of nurturers while the men were the breadwinners. This has changed in recent decades, however, as result of various factors. First, the increased availability of contraceptives has allowed women greater autonomy. Second, the garments industry, which employs millions of women, has become a multi-billion-dollar industry. Third, microcredit programs, which are small loans and which primarily target women, have proliferated. As result, Bangladeshi women have been empowered economically and, thus, socially and politically.

Though traditional gender roles have begun to break down in Bangladesh, women in the first generation of Bangladeshi Americans tend to adhere more closely to the gender expectations of their native culture than to those of mainstream America. This is exacerbated by the fact that, although they may have worked in Bangladesh, in America they often have a difficult time finding employment and cannot easily do the late-night, hazardous jobs such as driving a taxi or working in a deli, which the male immigrants are able to do. Thus, there may sometimes be a reversal of their position as a result of migration. Younger women, on the other hand, have entered into the educational and professional worlds of the United States while attempting to honor the culture of their homeland and respect their parents.

Education In general, people in Bangladesh attend school for an average of eight years. While 61 percent of men and boys are considered literate, only 52 percent of women and girls meet this requirement. More recent immigrants often arrive in the United States lacking English-language educational skills. Other Bangladeshi immigrants, however, have often arrived with a strong desire for education, particularly those who came to America as college students. The offspring of second- and third-generation Bangladeshi Americans tend to be well educated. Overall, 81 percent of Bangladeshi Americans living in the United States between 2007 and 2009 had obtained high school diplomas, and 47 percent had graduated college with a bachelor's degree or higher.

Courtship and Weddings Arranged marriages are still somewhat common within the Bangladeshi American community, but the practice is beginning to fade away. Arranged marriages were previously the dominant custom in Bangladesh. Young couples, after they have been selected for each other, may exchange photos and even talk with each other long distance before the marriage. Arranged marriages are still common in Bangladesh, but the custom is fading away quickly among the educated middle class and elites.

Factors that are causing this change in Bangladeshi cities include the huge growth of coeducational schools and cities and an increase in women entering the workforce who desire to choose their own partners. In the United States, where dating and individual choice are customary, arranged marriages are sometimes less common. At the same time, for a Bangladeshi American wishing to marry someone from the same background, some level of "arranging" may become necessary due to the difficulty of finding a partner in America, which is in part a result of the larger male population within recent migrants.

The fact that a prospective son-in-law lives in the United States is often seen as a plus for a Bangladeshi bride's family, promising enhanced opportunities for the couple. Young Bangladeshi men living in the United States often marry other Bangladeshis, flying back to Bangladesh for the ceremony with brides chosen by their families. Many Muslim females within the Bangladeshi American community opt to eschew dating in the American sense for cultural reasons, but this is also changing rapidly in the next generation.

The wedding ceremony itself can be an extended celebration lasting several days. Muslim and Hindu rites are generally observed for such ceremonies, which are accompanied by feasting and the signing of the marital agreement by bride and groom. Often the wedding is held at community centers and accompanied by traditional Bangladeshi or Bengali music. Traditional clothing is common among both brides and grooms, and religious customs often dictate whether traditional or westernized clothing is worn. Even when weddings are westernized to some extent, they generally include Bangladeshi music and food.

Relations with Other Americans Bangladeshi Americans are predominantly Muslim, but these religious ties stretch thinly across cultural lines. Bangladeshi Americans are thus a tightly knit group. Bengali by heritage, Bangladeshi Americans often affiliate with that ethnic minority in the United States, including Bangladeshis of other religions and Bengalis from West Bengal, India (who are statistically more likely to be Hindu). Bengalis of both religious persuasions may associate with each other because of their shared cultural bonds. However, at the larger, organized level, the Bangladeshi community generally separates itself from Indian Bengalis, reflecting the national boundaries of their homeland. This may also reflect the fact that the Bangladeshi American can associate only with an idea of "Bangladesh," while the Bengali from India can choose to associate with "Bengali" (which can be both Indian and Bangladeshi) and "Indian." Some of this is overcome especially among young, progressive groups of Bengalis from both countries, who may make a conscious decision to unite based on culture and language, across national borders.

Bangladeshi Americans also seek out other groups with which they share commonalities such as other American Muslims, including African Americans, and other immigrants from South Asian countries. All of this is made more complex by the fact that although a majority of Bangladeshi Americans are Muslim, not all of them are.

Following the events of 9/11, some Bangladeshi Americans became targets of hate crimes. This is particularly ironic given that a large number of Bangladeshis, including those who worked as waiters in the Windows of the World restaurant, were killed in the attack on the Twin Towers. In Texas, for instance, Rais Bhuiyan was shot while filling in for a friend at a gas station. While Bhuiyan survived the attack, his assailant, Mark Anthony Stroman, managed to kill both a Pakistani American and an Indian American during his crime spree. Rais Bhuiyan made national headlines when he appealed to stop the execution of Stroman, saying that his understanding of Islam required him to save every human life. He later formed an organization called *World Without Hate*. In New York, a number of Bangladeshi Americans have been physically or verbally harassed. In another case that made national headlines, Bangladeshi American taxi driver Ahmed H. Sharif had his neck slashed but survived the attack. He was later received as a "hero" by New York mayor Michael Bloomberg. As a result of such incidents, Bangladeshi Americans have banded together to fight hate crimes, and some of the younger generation have started to enter the legal, social work, and organizing professions. These include the prominent lawyer Aziz Huq, who clerked for Justice Ruth Bader Ginsburg at the U.S. Supreme Court, worked on several prominent cases involving post-9/11 issues, and is currently a professor at the University of Chicago law school.

EMPLOYMENT AND ECONOMIC CONDITIONS

Traditionally, only the more educated and skilled classes of Bangladeshi society were able to immigrate to the United States. Early statistics gathered with the first decade of Bangladeshi immigrations showed that a third of these immigrants had professional training and the vast majority of the rest had marketable skills. They typically worked in professions such as engineering, economics, architecture, and medicine.

However, in the 1990s, the new wave of immigration, partly swelled with diversity visa lottery winners, included immigrants with fewer skills and less education. While the new wave brought a large number of computer technicians who found work in Silicon Valley in California, it also brought many who were unskilled. Those immigrants found work clerking in convenience stores, driving cabs, or working in various service industries. Many street vendors in New York are also of Bangladeshi origin.

According to data gathered by the Census Bureau in 2007–2009, the per capita income of Bangladeshi Americans is $16,784. Roughly one in five live in poverty, and the poverty rate of children and seniors within that group is the highest found among any Asian American group. However, only 3 percent of that group receives cash forms of public assistance. Some 7 percent of those over the age of sixteen are unemployed. One-third of Bangladeshi Americans are employed in sales and office work, and nearly a third are engaged in managerial and professional work. Those who came to the United States as college students are generally the most successful, working as engineers, doctors, scientists, and college professors. Some 17 percent work in production, transportation, and material moving, and another 17 percent are employed in service occupations. Many women sell food and crafts to supplement family income. Less than half (44 percent) of Bangladeshi Americans own their own homes, a trend that worsened during the housing meltdown of 2008 and 2009, and the group is the least likely of all Asian Americans to do so. Almost a fourth live in overcrowded households, and one in four have no health insurance.

POLITICS AND GOVERNMENT

Many Bangladeshi immigrants arrive in the United States with a strong political identity because of their conflicted history, and they tend to continue to exercise their political tendencies as Bangladeshi Americans.

Jawed Karim (1979–), whose father is a Bangladeshi American, co-founded YouTube. com. MARTIN KLIMEK / ZUMAPRESS / NEWSCOM

Closely aligned with the Democratic Party for both political and cultural reasons, Bangladeshi Americans, like other Asian Americans, express strong support for Democratic tenets. The group feels a particular affinity for President Barack Obama. In order to promote the particular political interests of Bangladeshi Americans, the Bangladeshi American Democratic Party was established in south Florida in 2002. In the 2012 U.S. elections, New York exit polls showed Bangladeshi Americans as the third largest ethnic group in terms of turnout. Ninety-six percent of Bangladeshi Americans voted for President Barack Obama. This represented the largest percentage of any group to vote for Obama.

The Bangladeshi American Community Council works with Bangladeshi Americans to promote political involvement. The group also pays homage to politicians who represent the group at state and local levels. With strong support from both the African American and Latino populations, in 2010, Hansen Clarke, an attorney whose father is Bangladeshi and whose mother is African American, became the first Bangladeshi American to be elected to Congress, representing Michigan's 13th District. In 2012 Mohammed Akhtaruzzaman won a seat on the city council in Paterson, New Jersey. Inventor, writer, and activist Nuran Nabi had already broken ground for Bangladeshi Americans in that area by becoming the first Bangladeshi American to win elected office in New Jersey in 2006.

NOTABLE INDIVIDUALS

Academia Aziz Huq is a professor of law at the University of Chicago and was a clerk for Justice Ruth Bader Ginsburg in the U.S. Supreme Court. Huq specialized in national security cases and was director of the Liberty and National Security project at the Brennan Center in New York. He is the author of *Unchecked and Unbalanced: Presidential Power in a Time of Terror* (2007), which deals with the expansion of federal powers after the terrorist attacks of September 11, 2001. Maqsudal Alam is a microbiologist at the University of Hawaii who specializes in the study of genomics. Asif Azam Siddiqui (1966–) is a history professor at Fordham University who specializes in the history of science and technology. He has authored a number of books on the subject of space exploration. Elora Shehabuddin is an associate professor of humanities and political science at Rice University and the author of two books, *Reshaping the Holy: Democracy, Development, and Muslim Women in Bangladesh* (2008) and *Empowering Rural Women: The Impact of Grameen Bank in Bangladesh* (1992). Naveeda Khan is an assistant professor in anthropology at Johns Hopkins University, and the author of *Muslim Becoming: Aspiration and Skepticism in Pakistan* (2012). Ali Riaz is professor and the chair of the department of politics and government at Illinois State University. He is the author of several books, including *Religion and Politics in South Asia* (2010). Dr. Dina Siddiqi is an independent scholar who divides her time between the

United States and Bangladesh. She works on academic projects as well as conducting research with feminist organizations in Bangladesh such as *Ain o Salish Kendra*. Lamia Karim is an associate professor of anthropology at the University of Oregon in Eugene and the author of *Microfinance and Its Discontents: Women in Debt in Bangladesh* (2011).

Architecture Both an architect and an engineer, Fazlur Rhaman Khan (1929–1982) was one of the most prominent Bangladeshi Americans to have migrated to the United States before 1971. His legacy of designs has kept his name alive as an innovative thinker. His work can be seen in buildings such as the John Hancock Center and the Willis Tower (formerly known as the Sears Tower), which is the tallest building in the United States.

Art Hassan Elahi (1972–), a professor at the University of Maryland, is an interdisciplinary artist whose experience being tracked and interrogated by the FBI for being an alleged terrorist has informed his work, which explores questions of identity, privacy, and surveillance in the contemporary world. Elahi's work has been exhibited at the Venice Biennale and around the world. Fariba S. Alam is a visual artist, born in Massachusetts, of Bangladeshi descent. Her work integrates tile work, archival photography, and self-portraiture in order to create large-scale photographs and installations. Throughout her work, she reimagines cultural artifacts, geometric patterns in nature, and Islamic architecture. Naeem Mohaiemen (1969–) is a writer and visual artist whose museum projects look at the contradictions of borders, wars, and belonging in South Asia. His work has been included in various shows, including as part of Visible Collective at the Whitney Biennial of American Art. Anoka Faruqee (1972–) is a painter who has exhibited her work in group and solo exhibitions in the United States and in Asia. She is an associate professor at the Yale School of Art, where she is also acting director of graduate studies of the painting and printmaking department.

Business Jawed Karim (1979–) is a cofounder of YouTube and is responsible for much of the technology behind PayPal. Born in Germany to a German mother and a Bangladeshi father, he moved to the United States in 1980. Frequently listed by *Forbes* as one of the richest men in the world, entrepreneur and engineer Sal Khan (1976–), who received his MBA from Harvard University, made a fortune as the manager of a hedge fund before quitting to run the Khan Academy, a web-based tutorial system that aims to provide free education to students around the world.

Music Operatic soprano Monica Yunus (1979–) was born in Chittagong to a Bangladeshi father, Nobel Peace Prize winner Muhammad Yunus, and a Russian American mother. A folk rock singer/songwriter, Hamza Jahangir released his first album, *Kothai Jabo*,

in 2012. Born Mohammed Kabir, urban hip-hop artist MOBONIX is a former Marine whose musical talents were shaped in part by his mother, who played with a Bengali band. A Bengali American, jazz musician Badal Roy, who was discovered by jazz legend Miles Davis, is considered the world's most noted tabla (Indian drum) player. Born in Bangladesh, singer Palbasha Siddique (1991–) grew up in Minnesota. Performing with her band Melange, she sings in both Bengali and English.

Politics Democrat Hansen Clarke (1957–) served in the Michigan House of Representatives from 1991 to 1992 and again from 1999 to 2002. He won election to the state senate in 2003 and remained in that position until 2011 when he became the first Bangladeshi American to serve in the U.S. Congress, where he represents Michigan's 13th District. His father is a Bangladeshi American, and his mother is an African American. A politician, inventor, activist, and a writer, Nuran Nabi has chronicled the history of Bangladesh's War of Independence in *Bullets of '71: A Freedom Fighter's Story* (2010). In 2006 he became the first Bangladeshi American to win an elected position in the state of New Jersey.

MEDIA

Bangladeshi Americans have 24/7 access to radio and television stations as well as newspapers and magazines in both their own language and English via the Internet. In areas with large Bangladeshi American communities, a number of weekly print newspapers that cover Bangladesh as well as the Bangladeshi diaspora in the United States and the American Muslim community are available. In New York City, more newspapers are printed in Bengali than in any other South Asian language. The City Planning Department estimates that there are almost as many Urdu speakers as Bengali speakers in the city, but Bengali newspapers outnumber Urdu newspapers two to one.

PRINT

Thikana

Started in 1990, *Thikana* is the oldest of New York's Bangladeshi newspapers and continues to offer Bengali-language coverage of news affecting the Bangladeshi American community.

11-35-45th Avenue
Long Island City, New York 11101
Phone: (718) 472-0700
Fax: (718) 361-5356
Email: wthikana@aol.com; thikana@mindspring.com
URL: www.thikana.net

Weekly Bangalee

Since 1991, this weekly newspaper has chronicled both national and international news in the Bengali language for South Asian Americans.

86-16 Queens Boulevard
Suite 202

Elmhurst, New York 11373
Phone: (718) 639-1177
Fax: (718) 565-8101
Email: weeklybangalee@gmail.com
URL: http://weeklybangalee.com/home

Weekly Parichoy

Published in both Bengali and English, this newspaper is updated each Wednesday, covering both national and international news.

72-32 Broadway
Suite 404
Jackson Heights, New York 11372
Phone: (347) 686-8329 or (917) 749-1179
Fax: (718) 559-4835
Email: parichoy@gmail.com
URL: www.parichoy.com

TELEVISION

WNVC-TV (56)

Operating under the MHz umbrella, this public broadcasting station offers international programming in the Washington, D.C., area and offers Asian programming on Saturday mornings.

8101-A Lee Highway
Falls Church, Virginia 22042
Phone: (703) 698-9682
URL: www.mhznetworks.org

ORGANIZATIONS AND ASSOCIATIONS

Bangladesh American Band Alliance (BABA)

BABA was formed in 2005 to forge alliances among all Bangla bands and other cultural organizations in the United States, in order to promote Bangladeshi culture among young people.

Phone: (703) 629-3150 or (410) 320-4961
Email: jangi1@hotmail.com or ssuhas@comcast.net
URL: www.babamusic.net

Bangladesh Association of America (BAAI)

Established in 1972 to serve the needs of the Washington, D.C., Bangladeshi American community.

Sajda Solaiman, President
6850 Fernholly Court
Springfield, Virginia 22150
Phone: (301) 258-0088
URL: www.baaidc.com

Bangladeshi Medical Association of North America (BMANA)

Seeks to bring together physicians who are from or were trained in Bangladesh to network for further training or placement in North America.

Dilip Sarkar, MD, President
87-46 68th Street
Jamaica, New York 11432
Phone: (757) 621-6755
Fax: (718) 621-7655
URL: www.bmana.org/index.php

DRUM

DRUM was founded in 2000 to build the power of South Asian low-wage immigrant workers, youth, and families in New York City to win economic and educational justice, and civil and immigrant rights.

72-18 Roosevelt Avenue
Jackson Heights, New York 11372
Phone: (718) 205-3036
Fax: (718) 205-3037
Email: info@drumnyc.org
URL: www.drumnyc.org

Federation of Bangladeshi Associations in North America (FOBANA)

FOBANA is organization of Bangladeshi associations that aims to encourage Bangladeshi Americans to gather to celebrate their success and introduce their vibrant culture in the United States.

Duke Khan, Convener
1090 Vermont Avenue NW
Suite 910
Washington, D.C. 20005
Phone: (770) 317-8229, or (770) 882-1293
Email: dukekhan@gmail.com or fobanaec@gmail.com
URL: www.fobanaonline.com

Sakhi for South Asian Women

Sakhi aims to end violence against women, particularly in the South Asian community in the United States.

P.O. Box 2020
Greeley Square Station
New York, New York 10001
Phone: (212) 714-9153
Email: contactus@sakhi.org
URL: www.sakhi.org

MUSEUMS AND RESEARCH CENTERS

American Institute of Bangladesh Studies

A consortium of member colleges and universities organized to encourage and support research on the history and culture of Bangladesh. Headquartered at Pennsylvania State University, It was founded in 1989 by Professor Craig Baxter.

Laura Hammond, Administrative Program Manager
203 Ingram Hall,
1155 Conservatory Drive
Madison, Wisconsin 53706
Phone: (608) 261-1194
Email: aibsinfo@aibs.net
URL: www.aibs.net

Bangladesh American Center

The groundbreaking for this center, which promotes the history and culture of Bangladesh and of Bangladeshi Americans, took place on March 18, 2011.

Hasan Rahman, Center Director
1314 Renn Road
Houston, Texas 77083
URL: www.bachouston.org

SOURCES FOR ADDITIONAL STUDY

Bald, Vivak. *Bengali Harlem and the Lost Histories of South Asian America*. Cambridge: Harvard University Press, 2013.

Baluja, Kagri Glagstad. *Gender Roles at Home and Abroad: The Adaptation of Bangladeshi Immigrants*. New York: LFB Scholarly Publications, 2003.

Foner, Nancy. *Across Generations: Immigrant Families in America*. New York: New York University Press, 2009.

Harris, Michael S. "Bangladeshis," in *American Immigrant Cultures: Builders of a Nation*, edited by David Levinson and Melvin Ember. New York: Macmillan Reference, 1997.

Karim, Elora. *Microfinance and Its Discontents*. Minneapolis: University of Minnesota Press, 2011.

Kibria, Nazli. *Muslims in Motion: Islam and National Identity in the Bangladeshi Diaspora*. New Brunswick: Rutgers University Press, 2011.

Lewis, David. *Bangladesh: Politics, Economics, and Civil Society*. New York: Cambridge University Press, 2011.

Novak, James J. *Bangladeshi: Reflections on the Water*. Indianapolis: Indiana University Press, 1993.

Shehabuddin, Elora. *Reshaping the Holy: Democracy, Development, and Muslim Women in Bangladesh*. New York: Columbia University Press, 2008.

BARBADIAN AMERICANS

Lloyd E. Mulraine

OVERVIEW

Barbadian Americans are immigrants from or descendants of people from the island of Barbados. A small Caribbean nation in the Lesser Antilles, Barbados is the easternmost island in the West Indies island chain, which stretches south from southeast Florida to the northern coast of South America. Barbados's nearest neighbor, the island of St. Vincent, is 109 miles (176 kilometers) due west. Though nominally north of the equator, Barbados is considerably closer to Caracas, Venezuela (524 miles or 844 kilometers), than to Miami, Florida, in the United States (1,586 miles or 2,553 kilometers). The island is one-sixth the size of Rhode Island (the smallest state in the United States), measuring 21 miles (30 kilometers) long and 14 miles (22 kilometers) across at its widest point, with a surface area of 166 square miles (431 square kilometers). Although relatively flat, Barbados is made up mostly of coral that rises gently from the west coast in a series of terraces to a ridge in the center, where the island's highest point, Mt. Hillaby, reaches 1,115 feet.

A 2009 estimate by the *CIA World Factbook* listed the population of Barbados at 284,589. While this placed Barbados as only the 180th most populous nation, its small geographic size meant that it was ranked as the fourth most densely populated nation in the Americas and the eighteenth globally. Close to 90 percent of the island's population is of African ethnic origin, 4 percent is white (mainly English and Scottish), 1 percent is East Indian, and 3 percent is of mixed race (including Lebanese and Syrian Christians, Ashkenazi Jews, and Indo Guyanese). Approximately 70 percent of the population nominally belongs to the Anglican/Episcopal church, an important aspect of the island's long, unbroken connection with England, while the rest is Methodist, Moravian, Roman Catholic, Church of God, Seventh-day Adventist, Pentecostal, and a host of other religions. Barbados has a traditionally strong economy based on manufacturing and tourism. In 2011 the International Monetary Fund listed Barbados as the fifty-first richest country in the world by per capita gross domestic product (GDP) and as one of the sixty-six "High Income Countries" in the world, with a per capita GDP of $23,416.

While white Barbadian planters often invested in lands in the American colonies during the seventeenth and eighteenth centuries, widespread emigration from Barbados to the United States began early in the twentieth century. Between 1900 and 1920, as many as 100,000 West Indians, including a significant number from Barbados, came to the United States. A number of the initial Barbadian immigrants were professionals, but the majority were semi-skilled workers who settled in the northeastern United States, particularly New York City and Philadelphia, Pennsylvania. These numbers declined drastically in the decades immediately preceding and following World War II, largely because of restrictive immigration laws passed in the United States, such as the McCarran-Walter Immigration and Nationality Act of 1952, which placed a quota on the number of West Indians who could move to the country each year. After this quota was abolished in 1965 and Barbados gained its independence in 1966, the immigration of both skilled and unskilled Barbadians began to increase. As with previous generations, these new arrivals tended to settle in the northeastern United States, particularly in New York City and its borough of Brooklyn.

The 2010 U.S. Census estimated that there were more than 100,000 Barbadian Americans living in the United States (comparable to the population of West Palm Beach, Florida, or Flint, Michigan). Most Barbadian Americans continue to live in the northeastern United States, with up to 70 percent located in New York City and Philadelphia and a smaller percentage in Massachusetts and New Jersey.

HISTORY OF THE PEOPLE

Early History According to historical accounts, various Amerindian civilizations flourished in Barbados from around 350 CE to the early sixteenth century. The first wave of settlers were the Arawak-speaking Saladoid-Barrancoid people from the mouth of the Orinoco River in what is now Venezuela; they occupied the island from about 350 to 650 CE. Archeological findings reveal that they were skilled in farming, fishing, and ceramics. In about 800, a second wave of Amerindian migrants, the Igneri, occupied the island. They were expert fishermen, and they also grew crops of cassava, potato, and maize. These settlers also produced cotton textile goods and were noted for their ceramics. A third wave of migrants, the Kalinago, whom the Spaniards called Caribs, settled on the island during the mid-thirteenth century. More materially developed and politically organized, they quickly subdued and dominated their predecessors.

After centuries of settlement on the island, frequent Spanish raids for slaves in the sixteenth century drastically reduced the local population, to such an extent that by the 1540s Spanish officials considered the area uninhabited. Many natives were transported to Hispaniola (the island that today consists of Haiti and the Dominican Republic) and other Spanish-ruled islands to work on the sugar plantations and in mines. Many other natives simply left by choice for the safety of other neighboring islands.

The imperial forces of Spain, France, England, and the Netherlands all competed to find potentially profitable islands in the Caribbean during this period, but it was the English who finally settled Barbados. In 1625, when the first English ship, the *Olive Blossom*, accidentally arrived in Barbados while returning to England from Brazil, the captain, John Powell, and his crew claimed the island on behalf of King James I.

The English mariners who arrived in Barbados in 1625 were the first Europeans to begin its colonization. On February 17, 1627, Powell's brother Henry Powell landed the *William and John* at the present site of Holetown village and founded the second British colony in the Caribbean (the first being St. Kitts in 1623). The ship arrived bearing eighty English settlers and ten African slaves. These early colonists survived on farming while exporting tobacco and cotton. Later that year Powell brought thirty-two Indians from Guiana who were to live as free people while teaching the English settlers the art of tropical agriculture and regional political geography.

In 1629 Henry Hawley arrived on the island and assumed the governorship. He was a strong, ruthless ruler whose leadership helped to establish political and economic conditions for the development of a society dominated by a small landed elite. In 1636, Hawley issued a proclamation that all blacks and Indians, along with their offspring, brought to the island were to be received as lifelong slaves. Barbados thus developed into the first successful English slave plantation society in the New World. At the same time, there developed a white underclass of indentured servants consisting of voluntary workers, political refugees, transported convicts, and others. By 1640 the social structure of the island consisted of masters, servants, and slaves. The slaves and their posterity were subject to their masters forever, while servants were indentured for five years. After serving their terms, released servants were often supplied with money and land to start their own farms. As a result, the population of the colony grew rapidly; there were 40,000 people living in Barbados in 1640, mostly English yeomen farmers and indentured servants drawn there by the opportunity to acquire cheap land and compete in an open economic system.

Sugarcane cultivation began in 1637 and led to substantial changes in the colony's economic and social development. Production of tobacco, the island's main crop, was in decline and was quickly displaced by sugarcane. The sugar industry prospered, attracting white planters and merchants from a number of European countries. Soon Barbados became the richest colony in the New World.

This was to have a profound effect on the social development of the island, as the white planters perceived that African slaves could work much harder in the tropical climate than white indentured servants. In the 1630s, the island's African population was less than 800. By 1643, this number had increased to slightly less than 6,000, and by 1660 Barbados had developed into a plantation-dominated society in which slaves outnumbered whites by a two-to-one margin. It is estimated that between 1640 and 1807, the year the British Parliament abolished the slave trade in British territories, including Barbados, some 387,000 African slaves were brought to Barbados.

An unexpected result of this was the introduction of a new racial group to the island. During the seventeenth century, mulattos—born of white masters and black slave women—began to populate the colony. They were called "coloreds," and many were freed by their masters/fathers. By the eighteenth century, a small community of free persons of mixed racial identity existed in the colony. However, these free-coloreds were quickly perceived as a potential threat to the island's political and social systems, both by white Barbadians (who were determined to exclude them from white society) and by slaves (who were despised by the free-coloreds). As a result, whites made every effort to attach the stigma of racial and genetic inferiority to free-coloreds, resulting in the passage of discriminatory legislation in 1721. The new law stated that only white male Christian citizens of Great Britain who owned at least ten acres of land or a house having an annual taxable value of ten pounds could vote, be elected to public office, or serve on juries.

Despite being excluded by whites, free-coloreds sought to distance themselves from their slave ancestry and took a strong pro-slavery stand when imperial legislative action at the beginning of the nineteenth century tended toward improvement of the slaves' condition. By 1831 the franchise was extended to free-colored men; however, the property-owning requirements continued to apply to all voters. Thus, only a small minority gained voting rights. With the advent of a general emancipation, the free-colored people lost their status as a separate caste.

In 1833 the British Parliament passed a law that would free the slaves in the West Indies the following year. The slaves in Barbados, like the rest of the West Indies, became free on August 1, 1834. However, the emancipated people were not entirely free; they were subjected to a four-year apprenticeship period. In

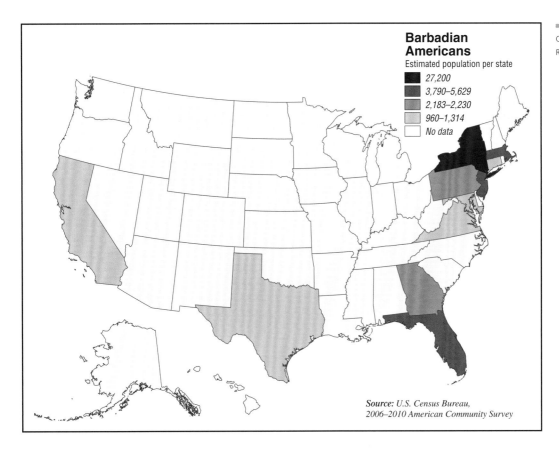

Barbadian Americans

Estimated population per state

- 27,200
- 3,790–5,629
- 2,183–2,230
- 960–1,314
- No data

Source: U.S. Census Bureau, 2006–2010 American Community Survey

addition, the Contract Act was passed in 1840, which essentially gave the planters a continued hold on the emancipated slaves, a condition that lasted well into the next century.

Modern Era Much of the twentieth century was marked by the struggle for political rights among all classes and by efforts for the island to achieve political independence within the British Empire. Although Barbados had originally been a proprietary colony of the crown, it was, by the 1830s, the political center of the British Windward Islands, a colony that also included Grenada, the Grenadines, St. Lucia, and St. Vincent. Until 1885, when the capital shifted to the island of Grenada, Bridgeport (the capital of Barbados) was the Windward Islands' administrative center. This distinction brought the island a certain regional political prominence, though it did little to establish Barbados as an autonomous part of the larger British Empire since the Windward Islands had no legislative authority and no power to raise revenue or levy taxes.

This arrangement proved highly unpopular, particularly among Barbadians, who wished to gain not only their political independence but also their own cultural and ethnic identity. British attempts in the 1870s to strengthen the system into a formal federation of colonies sparked considerable opposition in Barbados, from both the white planter and colored merchant classes. The poorer laboring classes went so far as to riot in support of the federation scheme, which they hoped would allow them to leave Barbados in search of greater economic opportunities on other islands. However, the vocal opposition of the merchant and landed classes eventually led the British to withdraw their federation idea. Barbados left the British Windward Islands system in 1885.

The conflict over federation demonstrated the inherent imbalance of political power within the island. Because of the high-income requirement for voting rights, local politics was dominated by the white planter class, leaving the vast majority of the islanders, including all women, barred from participation. Years of dissatisfaction with these conditions, along with continuing economic distress and a burgeoning nationalism, eventually led to widespread riots throughout much of the British West Indies, including Barbados in the 1930s.

In the new era of political and economic progress created by the unrest of the 1930s, Barbados again turned its attention to gaining independence from the British Empire. In 1958 Barbados and nine other British Caribbean territories joined together to form the West Indian Federation, a separate nation within the British Commonwealth. Grantley Adams, the first premier of Barbados, became the prime minister of the federation. This new nation hoped to achieve self-government, economic viability, and independence, but the federation collapsed in 1962, fatally crippled by the nationalistic tendencies of its member states. Barbados reverted to its former status as a colony and began to negotiate with the British government for independence within the new British Commonwealth of Nations. Under the Westminster System, which guaranteed former British colonies autonomy, sovereignty, and equality of status with both the United Kingdom and all other Commonwealth nations, Barbados finally gained its independence on November 30, 1966, becoming a sovereign state within the Commonwealth.

This period of external change was mirrored in the domestic politics of the island. Since the late 1930s domestic politics had been dominated by Adams and his Barbados Labour Party (BLP). Though active and vocal supporters of the monarchy, Adams and the BLP spearheaded a program to increase democracy and social and economic equality, which culminated in the end of the income qualifications that had dominated the island's political life for decades. This was soon followed by the granting of voting rights to women. By 1958 Adams and his BLP had managed to wrest political power from the entrenched planter class, a struggle that culminated in Adams becoming the nation's premier.

Once secure in its power, the Adams government was soon challenged by new groups that desired to continue the economic and social reforms of the 1940s. The most successful of these splinter groups was the Democratic Labour Party (DLP) of Errol Walton Barrow, which quickly became a popular liberal alternative to Adams's government, itself seen as increasingly conservative, in part due to Adam's continued support of the monarchy. Ousting Adams's chosen successor as premier in 1961, Barrow and the DLP began another round of progressive reforms on the island, including the creation of a free educational system, which was particularly important since access to educational opportunities had previously been closely controlled by the planter aristocracy. It was under Barrow's stewardship that Barbados became an independent nation within the larger British Commonwealth in 1966 and a member of both the United Nations and the Organization of American States.

Since gaining its independence, Barbados has maintained a stable democratic government, with power passing back and forth between the BLP and the DLP. During the 1970s, several smaller political groups, such as the National Democratic Party, the People's Democratic Congress, and the People's Pressure Movement, formed to compete with the two larger parties, but power has remained in the hands of the established parties.

SETTLEMENT IN THE UNITED STATES

Despite the position of Barbados within the British Empire in North America and its economic ties with colonial America, widespread immigration of Barbadians to the United States did not begin until the twentieth century. This was largely due to the status of the African Barbadians, which kept them tied to the island both legally and economically. Only when slavery was abolished and the African Barbadians, both black and of mixed race, gained their legal freedom could they begin to leave the island for new shores.

The Barbadian connection to America dates back to the 1660s, when close links were established between Barbados and the Carolinas. Sir John Colleton, a prominent Barbadian planter, was among the first to suggest the establishment of a colony there, and a permanent colony was formed in 1670 in what is known today as Charleston, South Carolina. Many prominent Barbadian merchants and planters subsequently migrated to Carolina. These Barbadians contributed agricultural knowledge to the fledgling colony through their introduction of the sugar trade, and they were major influences in both the development of the southern economy and "planter" culture. A modern remnant of their contributions to southern culture is Gullah, the dialect of the Carolina coast and islands, which closely resembles the Barbadian language.

It is difficult to establish exact information regarding Barbadian Americans because the United States Census classifies all Barbadians within a larger "British West Indian" category. However, it is estimated that between 1900 and 1920, nearly 100,000 Barbadians immigrated to North America, with the majority settling in New York, Philadelphia, and Chicago. Available evidence suggests that as many as 50 percent of these immigrants were skilled or white-collar workers, including large numbers of doctors, lawyers, and clergymen, as well as many students. This constituted a high percentage when compared to those of many other immigrant groups. Experts attribute it to the strong British educational system on the island, which allowed some Barbadian immigrants to arrive in the United States with a higher level of literacy and education than other groups.

By the 1920s Barbadian immigration to the United States had diminished significantly, the result of discriminatory immigration laws passed during that decade. The most notable of these was the Immigration Act of 1924, also known as the Johnson-Reed Act, which utilized a complex "National Origins Formula" to limit the number of people who could enter the country annually to 2 percent of the number of their countrymen who were residents in the United States according to the 1890 Census. Reflecting the isolationism and nativism within the United States at the time, these laws clearly favored the immigration of northern Europeans over other ethnic groups. While West Indians fared better than Asian immigrants, many of whom were completely barred from entry in the United States, the Johnson-Reed Act dramatically curtailed immigration until the 1960s.

Despite these limitations, in the early 1940s, small numbers of Barbadians were brought to the United States as laborers to support the war effort. A sizable number of these workers came to Chicago, which was an important manufacturing and logistics hub. The Chicago Historical Society notes in its *Encyclopedia of Chicago* that, while Barbadian immigrants worked to create a separate identity from that of Chicago's African Americans, they nevertheless encountered prejudice, not only because of their race but also because of their British cultural heritage. As a result, most Barbadians chose to work and socialize with other West Indian immigrant groups, forming political and charitable organizations such as the American West Indian Association, which sponsored festivals, charitable activities, and visits to Chicago by prominent Caribbean political figures. Bonds among the West Indian groups were also strengthened through sports, particularly cricket, the popularity of which had spawned more than a half-dozen West Indian teams by the 1950s. These teams still play in summer leagues throughout Chicago. In general, cricket has provided Barbadians and other West Indians with an important opportunity for social interaction.

Following the immigration increase during World War II, the numbers dropped again. The McCarran-Walter Immigration and Naturalization Act of 1952 continued the spirit of the Immigration Act of 1924 by establishing an annual quota of only 800 immigrants for all British territories in the West Indies, including Barbados.

With the establishment of Barbadian independence and the loosening of U.S. immigration policy in the 1960s, however, large-scale emigration from the island became possible. This process began with the passage of the Immigration and Nationality Act of 1965, also known as the Hart-Celler Act, which abolished the quotas that had been in place since the 1920s and replaced them with a system that focused on the skills of potential immigrants and on their family connections to U.S. citizens or residents. This approach was partly an attempt to increase the number of skilled and white-collar immigrants entering the country, and it included legal provisions for family reunification, formalizing the process now often referred to as "chain immigration."

After 1965, Barbadian immigration increased to an average of approximately 2,000 people per year. The majority were unskilled workers or laborers. The rate of Barbadian immigration slowed by the 1990s, with U.S. Census figures showing approximately 800 immigrants per year entering the United States from 1992 to 2002. This decrease was partially the result of a shift of Barbadian immigration to Canada. The Migration Policy Institute notes that these numbers continued to drop in the 2000s. In 2011, for example, 455 Barbadians immigrated to the United States.

BARBADIAN PROVERBS

Barbadians decorate their speech with proverbs. While modern Barbadian Americans have little use for such sayings in daily life, these phrases remain an important part of their culture and heritage. Here are some noteworthy examples, as collected by G. Addison Forde in his book *De Mortar-Pestle: A Collection of Barbadian Proverbs* (1987):

- Duh is more in de mortar dan de pestle.
- If crab don' walk 'bout, crab don' get fat.
- Cockroach en' had no right at hen party.
- De higher de monkey climb, de more 'e show 'e tail.
- Donkey en' have no right in horse race.
- Don' wait till de horse get out to shut de stable door.
- Play wid puppy an' 'e lick yuh mout.

According to the 1990 *Census of Population Report*, 82 percent of Barbadian immigrants lived in the Northeast, mostly in New York. More than 11 percent resided in the South, approximately 4 percent in the West, and almost 2 percent in the Midwest. The five states with the highest Barbadian populations were New York (22,298), Massachusetts (3,393), Florida (1,770), New Jersey (1,678), and California (1,160). Unlike Chinese Americans or Italian Americans, Barbadian Americans—and West Indians in general—do not form small enclaves in the American cities where they live. Instead, they tend to settle wherever they can find jobs, most often in the administrative service and health care sectors, or affordable housing, and they strive for upward mobility and opportunities to improve their lives.

LANGUAGE

Barbadians are often referred to as "Bajans," which is also the term for their unique dialect. It is said that no matter how many years Bajans spend away from Barbados, they never lose this distinctive way of speaking. Use of standard English by Barbadians depends to a great extent on the level of education of the speaker, but even many highly educated Bajans employ certain colloquialisms that are unique among Caribbean natives. In ordinary social settings, Bajans prefer to speak Bajan, but when the occasion warrants, they slip into a language that is more nearly standard English. There are also regional differences in speech on the island, particularly among people who live in the parishes of St. Lucy and St. Philip.

The USA national cricket team is mainly comprised of expatriates from former British protectorates such as India and Barbados who remain enthusiastic about the sport.
AP IMAGES / ADAM BUTLER

Bajan is a language much like the creole dialects spoken in other areas of the Caribbean or in West Africa. Some creoles have an English base, while others are rooted in French, but each is distinctive. Although educators often discourage the use of Bajan, this language is a vital part of Barbadians' cultural heritage. Bajan has a distinctive accent, whether spoken by white or black or by educated or uneducated Barbadians. Among certain peculiarities of the language, pointed out by linguists, is the use of compounds that in standard English are redundant. Examples are "boar-hog," meaning "boar"; "sparrow-bird," meaning "sparrow"; and "big-big," meaning "very large." Although there are fewer words of African origin in the language than in some of the other creole dialects, such words as *coucou, conkie, wunnah* and *backra* definitely have an African base.

While Barbados developed a traditional language and dialect that has had a wide influence throughout the Caribbean and select parts of the Southern United States, Barbados, as a result of its colonial history, is an Anglophone country, meaning that English has been

the predominant language on the island since the seventeenth century. Thus, Barbadian immigrants to the United States are fluent in English, an important factor in their assimilation and their ability to capitalize on economic and educational opportunities.

RELIGION

Because there is no record of the religion of the first settlers on Barbados, the Amerindians, the first documented religion on the island is the Anglican Church. It is almost certain that the early slaves brought their religions from Africa to the island. At the time of settlement of Barbados by the English, Anglicanism was the state religion in England. Thus, Anglicanism became the dominant religion in Barbados for many years. The island was divided into eleven parishes in the seventeenth century, and these parishes still exist today. There is a church in each parish, along with other meeting places. Until 1969, the church was fully endowed by the government, and it enjoyed the privileges of a state church, with its bishops and clergy paid from general tax receipts.

In the seventeenth century, Irish indentured servants brought Roman Catholicism to Barbados, and Jews and Quakers were among other religious groups that also arrived, followed by Moravians and Methodists in the late eighteenth century. In the late nineteenth century, the Christian Mission and other revivalist religions appeared, and today there are more than 100 Christian religions, as well as Judaism, Islam, and Hinduism. Anglicanism has lost much of its religious influence, although it still claims 70 percent of the population.

Traditionally, Barbadians who have immigrated to the United States have not left their religions behind. Predominantly Anglican, the early Barbadian immigrants were often denied access to white Episcopal churches in the United States on account of their race. In response, immigrant communities, particularly in New York, began to establish their own Anglican churches, such as Saint Augustine and Christ Church in Brooklyn. Established as parts of existing Anglican and Episcopal Diocese in the United States, these churches were never part of the larger Barbadian Anglican Communion. While these domestic parishes have retained much of the native faith's historically liberal policy toward the ordination of women and education, they have developed a separate administrative identity within the United States. In recent times, the increasing diversity found in many of the neighborhoods served by these churches has led to many of these parishes becoming more multi-ethnic and less traditionally Barbadian, further blurring any connections with the native church in Barbados.

While the majority of Barbadian immigrants have retained their Anglican faith in the United States, West Indian Methodist and American Episcopal parishes were also built in Harlem and the Bronx in New York. Many churches still exists in all five New York boroughs that serve as social, political, and community centers for Barbadian immigrants.

CULTURE AND ASSIMILATION

Subject to much of the same racial prejudice and injustice as American blacks, early Barbadian immigrants to the United States struggled to establish their own identity. Settling mainly in the more ethnically diverse northeastern United States, the new arrivals quickly established churches and social groups, particularly sports clubs, as means of both developing a unique identity and maintaining their connections to their homeland. While many Barbadians quickly assimilated into American society, they have, as a group, remained important contributors to the economy and culture back on Barbados.

Traditions and Customs Barbadians have a variety of traditions that are handed down from generation to generation, typically by word of mouth. Many traditions can be traced to Africa or Europe. For example, a Barbadian custom that was influenced

PICKLED BREADFRUIT

Ingredients

1 breadfruit (can substitute with 3 green bananas or 1 yam)

1 lime, juiced

1 onion, finely chopped

½ sweet pepper, finely chopped

salt and pepper

Preparation

Peel, core and cube an under-ripe breadfruit into 1-inch slices. Heat a pot of water to boiling. Put in 2 tablespoons of salt and boil breadfruit until tender. Strain and place cooked breadfruit into a serving dish.

Mix lime juice, onion, sweet pepper, and salt and pepper. Pour this over the breadfruit. Keep warm and when ready to serve, spread with butter. Salted fish or meat is a good accompaniment for this dish.

Recipe courtesy of Cedric King

by English settlers is the belief that saying "rabbit rabbit" on the first day of every month will ensure good luck for that month. Many Barbadian beliefs, however, are rooted in the country's own distinct culture. For example, a baby is allowed to cry at times because crying is believed to help develop the voice. Children should not cry during the night, though, because a *duppy* (ghost) might steal the infant's voice, making it hoarse the next day.

Like many longtime British colonies, Barbados has adapted many social traditions from its colonial heritage, including a deep connection to the Anglican Church, a fierce love of politics and social justice, a passionate belief in education, and a fanatical love of cricket. Among Barbadian immigrants to the United States, these ideals—rather than traditional festivals, cuisine, and art—have continued to flourish. Cricket, in particular, has long been a centerpiece of the Barbadian American experience in the United States, and dozens of Barbadian and West Indian cricket teams provide both an important source of social identity and a meaningful connection to the people's island roots.

Cuisine The national dish of Barbados is *coucou* and flying fish. *Coucou* is a corn-flour paste prepared exactly as it was in some parts of Africa, where it was called *foo-foo*. Sometimes it is made with okra, which is allowed to boil into the sauce. The corn flour is then added and stirred in, shaped into balls, and served with flying fish steamed in a rich gravy. Flying fish may also be fried in a batter or roasted.

Another traditional Barbadian meal is *conkie*, which is a delicacy in Ghana, where it is known as *kenkey*. *Conkie* is a form of bread made with Indian corn flour with sweet potato, pumpkin, and other ingredients. The dough is wrapped in the broad leaf of the banana plant, which is placed in some boiling water and allowed to steam until cooked. Although *conkie* can be eaten at any time of the year, it is now eaten mainly at Independence time. Pepper-pot is another Barbadian specialty. It is a concoction of hot peppers, spices, sugar, cassareep (a flavoring syrup made from cassava root), and salted meat such as beef and/or pork and is eaten with rice or another starch. This dish also originated in Ghana.

In addition, Barbadians enjoy pudding and souse, traditionally a special Saturday meal. The intestines of the pig are meticulously cleaned and stuffed with such ingredients as sweet potatoes, peppers, and much seasoning and are allowed to boil until cooked. Sometimes the blood of the pig is included in the ingredients. When this occurs, the dish is called black pudding. Souse, made from the head and feet of the pig, is pickled with breadfruit or sweet potatoes and cooked into a stew. It is usually served with the pudding.

Many of these dishes continue to be part of the daily diet of Barbadian Americans, and several restaurants, particularly in New York City, specialize in traditional Bajan cuisine. Among the offerings are *coucou* and flying fish, souse, and dumplings. These foods are enjoyed not only by Barbadian Americans but also by people from different cultures. Brooklyn, New York, is home to some of the best-known Bajan restaurants, including Culpeppers and Cocks Restaurant in the Crown Heights section.

Dances and Songs Barbados is an island rich in entertainment, notably songs and dance. Some of Barbados' traditional dances, such as the Jean and Johnny, no longer exist on the island, but the Maypole dance can still be found there. Many modern dance groups, influenced to some extent by African culture, have sprung up across the island. Nightly entertainment at hotels and clubs consists of a floor show of limbo and folk dancing and live bands. Many talented performers dressed in colorful costumes provide professional-quality productions at local theaters. The Crop Over Festival, a harvest celebration, features costume bands, folk music, and calypso competitions. Crop Over has become a major element in the island's tourism industry. In fact, Barbadian Americans often return home for the festival. While few of these entertainment forms remain important to Barbadian American culture, calypso music and dance form important parts of religious and secular festivals and events in the United States, not only as a representation of traditional Barbadian culture but also as a larger symbol of the West Indian identity.

Holidays Barbadians refer to all of their holidays as "Bank Holidays." These include New Year's Day,

January 1; Errol Barrow Day, January 21; Good Friday, late March or early April; Easter Monday; May Day, May 2; Whit Monday, usually in May; Kadooment Day, August 1; United Nations Day, October 3; Independence Day, November 30; Christmas Day, December 25; and Boxing Day, December 26. Many of these holidays are clearly religious holidays, influenced by the presence of the Anglican Church. Good Friday is an especially important holiday in Barbados.

Perhaps one of the most festive celebrations in Barbados is Crop Over, which was most likely influenced by the Harvest Festival of the Anglican Church and the Yam Festivals of West Africa. Historical evidence indicates that as early as 1798, a manager of Newton Plantation in Barbados held a dinner and dance for the slaves, in celebration of the completion of the sugarcane harvest. It was revived in 1973 as a civic festival.

Crop Over takes place during the last three weeks of June and the first week of July. The early portion of the festival is dominated by events in the rural areas: fairs, cane-cutting competitions, open-air concerts, "stick licking," native dancing, and handicraft and art displays. On the first Saturday in July, the celebration moves to Bridgetown. Sunday is known as Cohobblepot and is marked by various cultural events and the naming of the Crop Over Queen. The finale occurs on Monday, or Kadooment, during which there are band competitions and a march from the National Stadium to the Garrison Savannah.

It is not practical for Barbadians living in the United States to observe many of these holidays, as they are the English equivalents of U.S. federal holidays and, thus, have no American analogues. However, other holidays, such as Good Friday, Easter, Christmas, and New Year's, are celebrated in much the same way among Barbadian Americans as they are back in Barbados, with eating, drinking, dancing, and the exchange of gifts. Moreover, Barbadian Americans have developed their own set of holidays and festivals, particularly Barbadian Independence Day celebrations and Chicago's famous Carifete Caribbean Festival on the Midway Plaisance, both of which include parades, calypso music and dance, and traditional foods and drink. Barbadians also participate in celebrations within the larger culture of West Indian immigrants, including Miami's Carnival and the Brooklyn Labor Day Carnival.

Funerals There are also many customs regarding funerals. It is traditional to bury the dead without shoes so that they will not be heard when they are walking around as ghosts. It is also considered unwise to enter a graveyard if one has a sore, as this will make it very difficult for the sore to heal. After returning home from a funeral, one should enter the house backward to stop ghosts from entering the house as well; this is supposed to be effective because once the ghost walks in the footsteps, it will be facing away from the door and will be fooled into leaving. In addition, opening an umbrella indoors invites ghosts into the house; therefore, an umbrella should be placed unopened in a corner to dry.

FAMILY AND COMMUNITY LIFE

Proudly referring to itself as "Little England," Barbados has always retained a very English view of family and gender roles, a result of its long colonial experience and traditional relationship with the Anglican Church. This focus on family, faith, and education stood early Barbadian immigrants to the United States well, gaining them economic opportunity and allowing them, for the most part, to avoid the same legal and social inequities that were forced on American blacks. However, while their traditional views on religion and education have remained important facets of their cultural identity, the pressure among Barbadian Americans to assimilate and the economic imperatives of chain migration have steadily changed the traditional notions of family and gender roles to conform more to modern American norms.

Gender Roles Like most West Indians, Barbadians are family-oriented. Any disruption to the family affects all concerned. The roles of family members are clearly defined, and Barbadians follow them rigorously. There is man's work, woman's work, and children's work. Even though both parents might work outside the home, the woman is responsible for all domestic chores, such as cooking, grocery shopping, and laundering. Children's chores include washing dishes, sweeping the house and yard, getting rid of garbage, and taking care of domestic animals. Typically, the father is the head of the household. He is the wage earner and he is often revered by the rest of the family.

The act of immigration has often severely challenged these traditional roles and has often forced Barbadian Americans to at least temporarily alter their usual roles and expectations. Barbadians who immigrate to the United States often do so for social, political, educational, or economic reasons. All come "to better themselves." Like other immigrant groups that follow the pattern of "chain" or "serial" migration, many Barbadians leave behind spouses and/or children on the assumption that they will send for them when it is economically viable. The resulting separation often puts a tremendous emotional strain on the family members, especially children, who are often left behind with grandparents, other family members, or friends. The effects can be compounded by a number of economic and logistical concerns, which can postpone, sometimes indefinitely, the reunion of the family in the United States.

While it once was the male head of the family who initially immigrated, that trend has reversed in recent decades, with increasing numbers of women arriving first. The demand for domestic workers in the 1950s and the increasing numbers of women seeking education and employment in nursing and health care in recent years has greatly increased the number of female immigrants to the United States. This has, in turn, helped to fundamentally change the traditional social and economic roles of Barbadian women in the United States. The cultural experience and economic stability provided by their time in the United States often allow women to assume more of a leadership position once they are reunited with the rest of their family. In recent years, modern Barbadian American women have used this change in status to become important leaders in their churches and in the many national and regional Barbadian American advocacy groups.

Weddings Most weddings in Barbados are performed in a church. Weddings are always held on Saturday because it is considered bad luck to be married on Friday. Traditionally, the bride wears a white gown and a veil. The groom, who arrives before the bride, sits in the front of the church with his best man. He is not supposed to look back until the bride arrives inside the church, at which time he stands and waits until she arrives at his side. A minister then performs the ceremony, which varies according to the wishes of the couple or the status of the family. At the end of the ceremony, the wedding party leaves the church and drives in a procession to the reception hall or house, honking horns as it moves along. The uninvited guests usually leave their businesses and hang around the church or on the side of the road to see the bride. Several superstitions are associated with marriage. The bride must never make her own wedding dress, and it should remain unfinished until the day of the wedding; the gown's finishing touches should be done while the bride is dressing for the wedding. It is bad luck if the bridegroom sees the wedding dress before the day of the wedding, if it rains on the day of the wedding (especially if the bride gets wet), or if a cat or a dog eats any of the wedding cake.

Marketing Barbados as a destination for weddings has become an important part of the Barbadian tourist industry and has reinforced traditional native wedding traditions and rituals. Barbadian Americans wishing to have a traditional native wedding often return to the island to formalize their union, while others remain in the United States and conform to the traditional requirements of their individual church or faith.

EMPLOYMENT AND ECONOMIC CONDITIONS

Like most immigrant groups, modern Barbadians come to the United States in search of economic opportunities than cannot be found in their homeland. At home, economic opportunities do not keep pace with population growth, and salaries and wages often lag behind the cost of living. While earlier immigrants were often educated, skilled workers, the majority of modern immigrants initially find jobs as clerical workers, operators, craftsmen, foremen, sales workers, private household workers, service workers, managers, officials, foremen, and laborers. To enter the job market, many accept low-paying jobs they would consider beneath them at home, using these jobs to gather enough resources to attend technical and professional schools and colleges and, thus, move up the economic ladder. Their success at achieving upward mobility can be seen in the large number of second- and third-generation Barbadian Americans who have gained recognition in politics, the arts, and entertainment.

I left Barbados because the jobs were scarce. I decided to take a chance and come to this new country. There were a lot of us from the West Indies. We heard this was a good, new country where you had the opportunity to better your circumstances.

Lyle Small in 1921, cited in *Ellis Island: An Illustrated History of the Immigrant Experience*, edited by Ivan Chermayeff et al. (New York: Macmillan, 1991).

According to the 2010 Census, 69.5 percent of Barbadian Americans over the age of sixteen were part of the work force, with 69.3 percent in the civilian sector and 0.2 percent in the military. Of those in the civilian labor force, 34 percent were in management, business, science, and arts occupations, while 25.6 percent were in the sales and office jobs and 24.8 percent were in the service sector. The estimated median family income for those employed was $52,165. The percentage of unemployed was estimated to be 7.1 percent.

While the economic downturn of the 2000s affected Barbadian Americans as much as other groups in the United States, the low wages and high cost of living in Barbados still made immigration a viable alternative. This gap has become a major focus of Barbadian economic planning, as many governmental and advocacy groups have begun targeting the immigrant community to boost revenue on the island. Barbadian Americans are seen by Barbados as both a source of tourism and a means of capital and support for businesses and public projects.

POLITICS AND GOVERNMENT

Unlike most of the other Caribbean islands settled by Britain, Barbados experienced unbroken British colonial rule for almost 350 years. The country's government is structured after the British Parliament. The Barbadian Parliament consists of a Senate and a House of Assembly. The main political parties in Barbados are the Democratic Labor Party, Barbados Labor Party, and the National Democratic Party.

Barbadians have a passion for politics. Their love for their country is no doubt a major factor in their high level of political involvement. Because of their pride in and attachment to their homeland, Barbadian Americans remain actively involved in the politics of Barbados. Many zealously continue to monitor changes and developments in government, as well as financially contribute to their favorite political parties.

Many Barbadian Americans, though traditionally supporters of the Democratic Party and part of the "New Deal coalition" of minorities that has long been the basis of postwar Democratic politics, demonstrate only a passive interest in American politics. There is, however, much support among Barbadian Americans for immigrant education in the United States through scholarships and grants. Nevertheless, many of the largest Barbadian American organizations are either American adjuncts of Barbadian groups, such as the U.S.-based branches of the Barbadian Labour Party and the Barbados Cancer Society, or are focused on politics and causes at home.

NOTABLE INDIVIDUALS

Law and Law Enforcement Charles Gittens (1928–2011) was a second-generation Barbadian American who became the first black United States Secret Service agent. After serving in the U.S. Army and graduating from North Carolina Central University, Gittens joined the Secret Service in 1953. During his distinguished career, he rose to become the head of the Washington, D.C., office of the Secret Service before retiring in 1979. Following his retirement, Gittens joined the Department of Justice's elite Office of Special Investigations.

Lloyd Sealy (1917–1985) was the first black New York City Police Department officer to command a police precinct and to achieve the rank of assistant chief inspector. In 1966 he became the first black officer to become a borough commander, heading the Brooklyn North Patrol Command. After his retirement, Sealy became an associate professor of law and police science at John Jay College of Criminal Justice, where the library is named in his honor.

Journalism Gwen Ifill (1955–), journalist, television newscaster, and moderator, is the executive producer and moderator of the long-running PBS public-affairs program *Washington Week in Review*.

Literature Paule Marshall (1929–), a MacArthur Fellow and Dos Passos Prize–winning author and poet, is best known for her novel *Brown Girl, Brownstones* (1959). A protégé of the great Harlem poet Langston Hughes, Marshall taught at the University of California at Berkeley and Yale, and he served as the Helen Gould Sheppard Chair of Literature and Culture at New York University.

Music Grandmaster Flash (1958–) is a Barbadian-born hip-hop pioneer, musician, and disc jockey. He is credited with many of the technical and musical innovations that were central to the development of rap and hip-hop, including the creation of the cross-fader, a switch that allows the disc jockey to seamlessly move from one turntable to another without a break in the music, and the popularization of basic disc jockey touches such as backspin and scratching.

L. L. Cool J (1968–), a rap musician and actor, starred in the CBS drama *NCIS Los Angeles*.

Singer Robyn Rihanna Fenty (1988–), known simply as Rihanna, was born in Barbados and came to the United States when she was sixteen. She went on to become one of the most successful performers in pop music.

Politics and Government Shirley Chisolm (1924–2005) was born in New York City and raised by her grandparents in Barbados. Chisolm was the first black congresswomen in the United States, serving seven terms from 1969 to 1983. She was also the first black female Democratic candidate for president, garnering 152 first-ballot votes at the 1972 convention.

Eric Holder (1952–) was the eighty-second attorney general of the United States and first to be black, and he also served as a federal judge. Holder was the deputy attorney general under President Bill Clinton before becoming President Barack Obama's attorney general in 2008.

Sports Christian Taylor (1990–) was a gold medalist in the triple jump at the 2012 London Olympics who also competed in the 200- and 400-meter dashes and long jump. While at the University of Florida, Taylor won numerous National Collegiate Athletic Association indoor and outdoor titles in the triple jump. He also captured the title in the triple jump at the 2011 World Championships.

Stage and Screen Cuba Gooding Jr. (1968–), actor, gained recognition for roles in films such as *Boyz in the Hood*, *As Good as it Gets*, and *Men of Honor*. In 1996 his portrayal of football star Rod Tidwell in the hit film *Jerry Maguire* earned him the Academy Award for Best Supporting Actor. Gooding's father, Cuba Gooding Sr., was the lead singer for the popular 1970s soul group the Main Ingredient.

MEDIA

PRINT

Carib News

Carib News is an in-depth weekly newspaper published for English-speaking Caribbean readers living in the United States.

Carl Rodney, Editor
15 West 39th Street
13th Floor
New York, New York 10018
Phone: (212) 944-1991
Fax: (212) 944-2089
Email: info@nycaribnews.com
URL: www.nycaribnews.com

RADIO

WLIB-AM (1250)

This New York City station broadcasts music, sports, and news from the Caribbean on Fridays and Saturdays from 7 a.m. to 7 p.m.

Skip Dillard, Operations Manager/
Program Director
Phone: (212) 447-1000
Fax: (212) 447-5211
Email: info@wlib.com
URL: www.wlib.com

WVIP-FM (93.5)

Located in New Rochelle, New York, this world-ethnic station broadcasts Caribbean news and music every day.

William O'Shaughnessy, General Manager
1 Broadcast Forum
New Rochelle, New York 10801
Phone: (914) 636-1460
Fax: (914) 636-2900
URL: www.wviphd.com

Barbadian American Christian Taylor won the gold medal for the U.S. in the triple jump during the 2012 Summer Olympics. IAN MACNICOL / GETTY IMAGES

One Caribbean Radio (105.1)

Broadcasting from Brooklyn, New York, this station provides news and music to the Caribbean Diaspora community of New York.

Phone: (718) 622-1081
Email: info@onecaribbeanradio.com
URL: www.onecaribbeanradio.com

WAVS 1170 AM Radio

Based in Davie, Florida, WAVS is the longest-running Caribbean station in the United States, servicing Broward and Dade Counties.

Dean Hooper, Station Manager
6360 SW 41st Place, Davie
Florida 33314
Phone: (954) 584-1170
Fax: (954) 581-6441
Email: info@wavs1170.com
URL: www.wavs1170.com

ORGANIZATIONS AND ASSOCIATIONS

Barbados American Charitable Organization of New Jersey

Founded in 1979, the Barbados American Charitable Organization of New Jersey is a 5013C nonprofit group that supports charitable and educational projects in Barbados, the Caribbean, and the United States.

Miguel Edghill, President
2560 U.S. Highway 22 East #157
Scotch Plains, New Jersey 07076
Phone: (908) 753-2546
Email: baconjinc@gmail.com
URL: www.baconj.org

Barbados Association of Greater Houston

Promotes education at the highest levels. It provides financial and tutorial assistance and advocating for social appreciation and understanding by performing public service in the community.

Shontelle Hunte, President
6610 Harwin Drive #156
Houston, Texas 77036
Phone: (713) 977-0787
Email: info@barbadoshouston.com
URL: www.barbadoshouston.com

Barbados Cancer Association U.S.

This U.S.-based branch of the Barbados Cancer Association is dedicated to minimizing the impact of cancer on the Barbadian community in the United States by promoting prevention, early detection, and prompt treatment of cancer.

P.O. Box 3094
Grand Central Station
New York, New York 10163-3094
URL: www.barbadoscancerusa.org

Barbados Diaspora Collective

The Barbados Diaspora Collective is a group of Barbadian American organizations that has partnered with the government of Barbados to establish a facility on the island to provide hospice services for Barbadians dying of cancer and other chronic diseases.

410 Lakeview Road
Suite 202
New Hyde Park, New York 11042
Phone: (806) 519-2226
Email: info@bdcusa.org
URL: www.bdcusa.org

Council of Barbadian Organizations

Established in 1993, the Council of Barbadian Organizations is an umbrella group that manages and supports the efforts of member groups with educational and professional programs.

Linda Watson-Lorde
P.O. Box 2222
Church Street Station
New York, New York 10008-2222
Phone: (718) 909-8763
Email: info@cbony.org
URL: www.cbony.org

MUSEUMS AND RESEARCH CENTERS

Institute for Caribbean Studies

This is a nonpartisan, not-for-profit advocacy organization that brings together public and private sectors, nongovernmental organizations, and scholars to advance the interests of Caribbean Americans.

Claire Alicia Nelson, President
1629 K Street NW
Suite 300
Washington, D.C. 20001
Phone: (202) 638-0460
Email: icsdcorg@gmail.com
URL: www.icsdc.org/home

Center for Latin American and Caribbean Studies at New York University

Founded in 1966, New York University's Center for Latin American and Caribbean Studies is a respected leader in teaching and research, recognized for its K-12 curriculum planning, graduate studies program, and public events.

Sisa Bárbara Holguín, Program Administrator
King Juan Carlos I of Spain Center (KJCC)
53 Washington Square South
Floor 4W
New York, New York 10012
Phone: (212) 998-8686
Fax: (212) 995-4163
Email: clacs.info@nyu.edu
URL: www.clacs.as.nyu.edu

SOURCES FOR ADDITIONAL STUDY

Beckles, Hilary McD. *A History of Barbados: From Amerindian Settlement to Nation-State*. Cambridge: Cambridge University Press, 1990.

Chamberlain, Mary. *Empire and Nation-Building in the Caribbean: Barbados, 1937–66*. Manchester; New York: Manchester University Press, 2010.

Fenigsen, Janina. "'A Broke-Up Mirror': Representing Bajan in Print." *Cultural Anthropology: Journal of the Society for Cultural Anthropology* 14, no.1 (1999): 61–87.

———. "'Flying at Half-Mast'? Voices, Genres, and Orthographies in Barbadian Creole." In *Variations in the Caribbean: From Creole Continua to Individual Agency*. Edited by Lars Hinrichs and Joseph T. Farquharson, 107–32. Philadelphia: John Benjamins Pub. Company, 2011.

Frazer, Henry, et al. *A–Z of Barbadian Heritage*. Kingston: Heinemann Publishers (Caribbean) Limited, 1990.

Hoyos, F. A. *Barbados: Our Island Home*. London: Macmillan Publishers, 1984.

LaBrucherie, Roger A. *A Barbados Journey*. Pine Valley: Imagenes Press, 1985.

Marshall, Paule. *Brown Girl, Brownstones*. Old Westbury: Feminist Press, 1981.

Murray, David A. B. *Flaming Souls: Homosexuality, Homophobia, and Social Change in Barbados*. Toronto: University of Toronto Press, 2012.

Puckrein, Gary A. *Little England: Plantation Society and Anglo-Barbadian Politics, 1627–1700*. New York: New York University Press, 1984.

BASQUE AMERICANS

Elizabeth Shostak

OVERVIEW

The Basque Country is not an independent state but a region in the western Pyrenees that straddles the border between France and Spain. It is bordered by the Bay of Biscay to the north, France to the northeast, and Spain to the south and west. In Spain, where six-sevenths of its territory lies, the Basque Country was established as an "autonomous community" in 1979. The Basque Country in Spain consists of the provinces of Alava, Guipuzcoa, Navarre, and Vizcaya (Bizkaia). Its capital is Vitoria (Gasteiz), and other principal cities include Donostia-San Sebastián and Bilbao. In France the Basque Country comprises the regions of Labourd, Basse Navarre, and Soule. Much of the Basque Country is composed of rugged mountains, and the terrain is suitable for intensive cultivation on small farms. Measuring only about one hundred miles from end to end, the Basque Country is about the size of Maryland.

The Basque Country had just over 2.1 million inhabitants in 2012, with 92 percent living in the Spanish portion, according to Basque government estimates. The region is overwhelmingly Roman Catholic in its religious orientation. Traditionally, Basques were sailors, fishermen, and agricultural workers. Life in the contemporary Basque Country is similar in quality to that in its sovereign nations of Spain and France. While violence from separatist groups has harmed the Basque Country's ability to create a tourist industry, the region still draws tourists, especially to the picturesque and historical city of Donostia-San Sebastián. Rich in natural resources, the Basque Country in Spain embraced manufacturing in the post-fascist 1970s, resulting in four-fifths of the population living in or near the largest city, Bilbao. The Basque Country subsequently weathered the debt crisis that pummeled the Spanish economy in the late 2000s, brought on by a drop in tourism and real estate sales combined with fiscal mismanagement.

Basques first began significant migration to the United States in the late nineteenth century. Many in this first wave of Basque immigrants to the United States came via Argentina. Basques then began to come directly from the Basque Country to the United States, and this pattern of immigration peaked between 1910 and 1920. While many of these early Basque immigrants initially came seeking easy riches in the gold rush, they discovered various economic opportunities in the western United States, particularly in California, Idaho, Oregon, and Nevada. Basque immigrants most frequently became sheepherders, due to the enormous demand for sheep in the American West as well Basques' difficulty acquiring cattle as a result of their low social standing. Over time, Basque immigrants established a strong cultural presence in the western United States. Immigration regulations after 1920 made immigration to the United States less feasible, and an improved Basque economy from the 1970s made it less attractive. Nevertheless, some recent immigrants have come to join relatives, to study English, and to earn college degrees.

According to the Census Bureau's American Community Survey estimates for 2009–2011, the number of U.S. residents claiming Basque ancestry is relatively small, 54,432 (about half the size of the population of Springfield, Illinois). However, this number is probably inaccurate due to Basque Americans sometimes falling under the status of Spanish or French rather than their own ethnic grouping. Basques have generally done well integrating into American communities while also leaving their imprint on the communities where they settled. A strong sense of ethnic pride, particularly since World War II, has led to strong cultural expressions throughout the western United States, including a dedicated academic research center—the Center for Basque Studies at the University of Nevada, Reno—established in 1967.

HISTORY OF THE PEOPLE

Early History Although the Basques have perhaps the oldest civilization on the European continent, their precise origin remains unknown. The Basques lived in the Pyrenees before the arrival of Indo-European tribes during the second millennium BCE. When Christianity was introduced by the Romans, the Basque tribes resisted conversion, and they avoided occupation during the Muslim conquest of the Iberian Peninsula during the eighth century. The success of this resistance to outside influence was largely an outcome of the remoteness of the mountainous terrain that the Basques occupied. While other groups on the Iberian Peninsula were conquered by the Moors, the Banu Qasi dynasty formed an autonomous principality in Basque territory in the 700s. In the ninth century, the Banu Qasi dynasty coexisted harmoniously with the kingdom of Navarre, which formed in 824 CE. Evidence shows that the Basques also successfully defended themselves against invasions by earlier groups, including the Visigoths, Franks, and Normans. Navarre was the first and only Basque political state, and during the reign of King Santxo the Great (999–1035), many Basque-speaking regions, including that of the Banu Qasi dynasty, were unified under its jurisdiction. The kingdom withstood many challenges and was able to maintain independence for some 700 years. In 1512, however, Castilian (Spanish) forces conquered and occupied the kingdom. The northern section of the region was ceded to France, and the rest incorporated into Spanish territory.

Because Arab invaders did not vanquish the Basques, the Spanish crown considered them hidalgos, or noblemen. This status allowed individuals of relatively modest backgrounds to find powerful positions within civic and church administrations. During the years when Spain concentrated on building colonies in the New World, several of the Basque elite were given important government posts in Latin America. In this way, a tradition of emigration was established among the Basques. In both France and Spain, the Basques enjoyed a large degree of political autonomy as well as economic and military privileges, which had been codified in *fueros* (bodies of traditional law) since the eleventh century.

Modern Era By the late eighteenth century, political turmoil in both France and Spain had taken its toll among the Basques. The French revolution and the Napoleonic campaigns brought invading armies to the Basque territory in France; soon thereafter, during the 1830s, many Basques in Spain supported the conservative pretender to the Spanish throne, Don Carlos, whose cause was brutally defeated. His supporters were forced to flee the country, and many Basques made their way to Spanish colonies in the Americas and joined Basque communities that had already been established. When the Basques supported the Carlist rebellion of the 1870s, the Spanish government retaliated by abolishing the *fueros*.

The creation of the Spanish Republic in 1931 split loyalties in the Basque Country. The regions of Guipuzcoa, Vizcaya (Bizkaia), and Alava supported the republic, hoping that the government would grant them autonomous status. Navarre however, vigorously opposed the republic. The ensuing civil war attracted international attention. The Nazi bombing of the Vizcayan city of Guernica, memorialized in a painting of that name by Pablo Picasso, was seen as a brutal suppression of Basque nationalist hopes. At the war's end in 1937, many Basques went into exile. When right-wing dictator Francisco Franco assumed power in 1939, his government instituted harsh anti-Basque policies, most notoriously the suppression of the Basque language.

After Franco's rule ended with his death in 1975 and the liberal Spanish monarchy was established, Basques pushed for self-government. In 1979 the statute of autonomy recognized the Basque Country as an autonomous community, but radical Basque factions were not satisfied. The military wing of the *Euzkadi Ta Azkatasuna* ("Basque Homeland and Liberty," known as ETA) was responsible for many bombings and other terrorist activities intended to press Basque demands for complete political independence. Since the late 1970s, calls for Basque unity and an independent Basque state have been hampered by the division of the Basque Country between France and Spain. Proindependence politicians controlled the Basque political scene until 2009, when legislation went into effect banning far-left political parties, a response to the violent tactics and political power of ETA. For the first time since the Franco era, Spanish nationalist parties controlled over half the seats in the Basque parliament. In October 2011, following an international peace conference in Spain, ETA announced a permanent ceasefire and heralded what many hoped would be a new era of diplomacy between the independence movement and the nations of Spain and France.

SETTLEMENT IN THE UNITED STATES

Renowned as seafarers, Basque fishermen and sailors had probably reached American waters well before the voyage of Columbus in 1492. They were among the first Europeans to hunt whales off the northeastern coast of North America. When Columbus recruited his sailing crew, Basques made up the largest ethnic group on board, and they continued to participate in voyages across the Atlantic during the earliest years of European exploration of the continent. A few educated Basques held administrative posts in Spanish California, and several of the priests who founded missions there in the late 1500s were Basques. Large-scale immigration to the United States did not begin until the late 1800s, however.

The California gold rush brought the first waves of Basque immigrants to the United States, but most of these adventurers did not come directly from Europe. Instead, they generally were Basques who had immigrated earlier to Spanish colonies in South America. During the period of Spanish colonization, Basques from Spain had often taken administrative posts overseas. Political exiles also found their way to South America. In the 1820s Basque immigrants were welcomed in Argentina, where they were able to procure unused rangeland on which to raise sheep. There, they learned about transhumance, a specific ranching and herding method, which some eventually brought with them to North America.

When gold was discovered in California in 1848, Basques in South America were well positioned to take advantage of the opportunity. They could sail quickly to California, arriving well in advance of

Europeans or even residents of the United States' eastern regions. Many European-born Basques living in South America came to California by this route. Large numbers of French Basques also came directly from Europe, sailing around the South American continent to San Francisco. Although it is difficult to determine the precise number of Basques who came to the United States during the gold rush because many were counted as South Americans, it is evident that at least several hundred entered the country in 1848.

Basque immigrants were not successful with mining and soon migrated from the gold fields to the ranchlands of southern California. Familiar with the South American style of ranching, the Basques quickly established themselves in the area as cattle herders. Because herding was an isolating activity, the job attracted single men, primarily between the ages of sixteen and thirty; Basque women were almost nonexistent in the United States until these men became financially established and sent for wives from Europe. Later, after a Basque American population had been established, Basque women came to the United States independently, to work in boardinghouses.

As Basques entered the ranching business, they began to raise sheep, due to discrimination they encountered among American cattlemen. Though not their first choice of livestock, sheep proved more resilient than cattle to drought and flooding. The type of ranching Basques had learned in South America, transhumance, also proved successful. It required sheep to be moved across a large open area according to seasonal needs. The animals wintered in lowland areas that the Basques either leased or purchased, and they summered in the high grazing lands of the Sierra Nevada mountains. Conditions in the West proved quite suitable for transhumance, and during the 1860s the number of sheep in California more than doubled.

Los Angeles had become the center of the Basque community in California in the 1840s and remained its largest settlement through the late 1800s. By 1886, about two thousand Basques lived in Los Angeles, and the city's downtown area had a distinct Basque district, complete with Basque boardinghouses and handball courts. As Basques increased their herds, however, the California ranges became crowded. By 1870, Basques had begun to spread into northern California and also Nevada, where gold and silver strikes had created a booming economy and an increased demand for sheep to feed the new miners. During the 1890s, Basques moved into Oregon and southern Idaho. By 1910, Basques had spread into all the open-range areas of the West.

The success Basque immigrants found in sheepherding caused significant conflict, however, with the area's settled ranchers, especially cattle ranchers. At the time, grazing was permitted on public lands on a first-come basis, but ranchers who owned private holdings wanted to use adjacent public ranges as their own exclusive property. These settled ranchers resented the presence of itinerant Basque sheepherders and began harassing them and spreading anti-Basque sentiment. As the national forest system developed in the late nineteenth and early twentieth centuries, most of the mountain rangeland in the West became part of that system. Although some grazing was still permitted, rights were denied to aliens and to herders who did not own ranch property—a practice that, in effect, targeted Basques. In 1934 the Taylor Grazing Act placed almost all remaining public rangeland under federal control, with the same grazing restrictions. This law effectively ended itinerant herding, and, coming at the height of the Great Depression, caused severe economic hardship to the Basque community. As a result, many Basque shepherds returned to Europe. Those who had been able to buy land, however, remained in the United States and sometimes prospered.

As their operations expanded, Basques in the United States began to send back to Europe for additional helpers. The pattern of recruitment continued until strict immigration laws in 1924 limited the annual quota of Spanish nationals to a mere 131; these regulations effectively stopped additional immigration from the Basque Country. After World War II, however, the situation changed. Sheepherders had become so scarce that Senator Patrick McCarran of Nevada sponsored legislation to exempt European herders from immigration quotas. Over the next decade more than five thousand European Basques applied for jobs on U.S. ranches. By the late twentieth century, however, the American sheep industry was in serious decline, decreasing the need for new immigrants to take herding jobs. Basques often remained in the business, however, as ranch owners and managers, or sought out other careers. Basque immigration also slowed significantly after 1970 in the wake of improved economic conditions in the Basque Country.

> We were in the foothills of the Basque country, but night had fallen and everything about us was lost in obscurity. Yet, as fleeting as glimpses out of memory, scenes that told us where we were, caught and hung momentarily in the passing headlights of our car, and then were gone in the darkness. There was a little boy in a beret and short trousers, and under his arm a loaf of bread that seemed as long as he was. There was a crude, wooden cart pulled by two oxen, whose nodding heads kept rhythm with the gay fringes on their horns. There was a girl in a scarf and bright peasant dress, visiting with her young man at the juncture of a country lane, whose eyes our lights brushed in passing, and whose laughter tinkled after us in the night like tiny bells.
>
> Robert Laxalt, *Sweet Promised Land* (Harper & Brothers Publishing, New York, 1957).

For a variety of reasons, it is difficult to determine the number of people of Basque ancestry living in the United States. One reason is that many of the first Basque immigrants were counted as "Chileans"

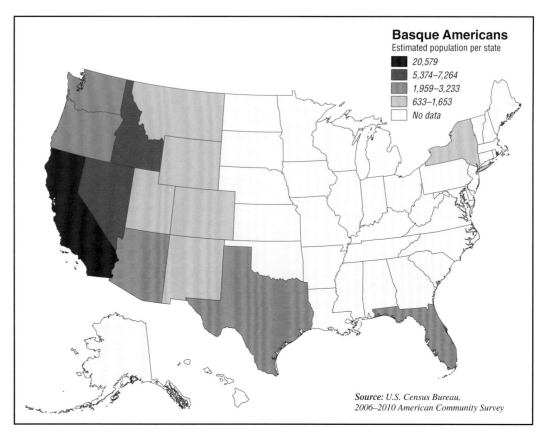

Basque Americans
Estimated population per state

- 20,579
- 5,374–7,264
- 1,959–3,233
- 633–1,653
- No data

Source: U.S. Census Bureau, 2006–2010 American Community Survey

(an umbrella term for all South Americans). Further, before the recognition of the Basque Country, Basque immigrants were often categorized as either "French" or "Spanish," and anti-Basque sentiment frequently led people to sustain these inaccurate national affiliations. The Census Bureau's American Community Survey (2009–2011) estimated the number of U.S. residents claiming Basque ancestry to be 54,432, though this number is likely lower than the actual population.

Although most Basque Americans are found in the western parts of the country, some communities were established on the East Coast. After the transcontinental railroad was completed in 1869, Basques from Europe did not have to sail all the way around South America to reach California; they could make the much shorter ocean journey to New York City and then take the train from there to the western states. Many did in fact follow this plan, but some remained in the city and established a small but close-knit Basque community there. Small Basque communities also sprang up in Connecticut, Rhode Island, Washington, D.C., and Florida, in part as a result of a gambling industry that emerged on the East Coast around the Basque game of Jai-Alai.

Immigration patterns among the Basques reflected their regional distinctions in Europe. Those who settled in California, central Nevada, Arizona, New Mexico, Colorado, Wyoming, and Montana were generally from France or Navarre, while those

who moved to northern Nevada, Idaho, and Oregon came from the Spanish province of Vizcaya. These groups traditionally tended to remain relatively separate in the United States. In 1973, however, the North American Basque Organization (NABO) was founded to encourage cohesion among Basque Americans and to promote the "perpetuation of 'Basqueness.'"

LANGUAGE

The Basque language, Euskara (also spelled Euskera), has ancient origins that remain obscure. Linguists have been unable to establish a relationship between the Basque language and any other known language groups. Although some faint similarities with Finnish, Georgian, and Quechua have been found, these connections remain inconclusive and researchers have been unable to agree on a relationship between Basque and any other known language. The fact that several Basque words for tools derive from the Basque word for "stone" (*haitz*) has led specialists to suggest that the language is among the most ancient in Europe and may link Basque culture to the prehistoric people who created the Lascaux cave paintings.

Basque is considered a particularly difficult language to learn. Basques joke that the devil himself spent years trying to learn the language in order to tempt the Basque people, but after seven years had mastered only two words, *ez* and *bai* ("no" and "yes"). The basic structure of Euskara uses agglutination, or the practice of adding prefixes or suffixes to words to create different meanings. Although Euskara shows influences from Celtic and Iberian languages as well as from Latin, it has remained largely unchanged for centuries. It has not, however, enjoyed a strong literary tradition. Works in Euskara were not transcribed in writing; instead, the language was passed down orally. The first printed book in Euskara did not appear until 1545. Some scholars consider this a central reason that the Basques did not produce a particularly rich literature.

Several regional dialects of Basque include Guipuzcoan, Alto Navarro Septentrional, Alto Navarro Meridional, Biscayan, and Anvala. Souletin (Zuberera), spoken by Basques in France, is the dialect most distinct from the others. Because this proliferation of dialects was a hindrance to greater Basque unity in Europe, in the late 1960s a unified Basque language known as Batua was developed. Verb forms in Batua were modeled on the Guipuzcoan dialect. Batua also standardized spelling. It has not, however, been introduced to the United States, where Basque speakers continue to use the dialects they inherited from their immigrant ancestors.

One estimate from the late 1990s suggests that Euskara is spoken by close to a million people in the Basque Country, but other accounts place the number around 700,000. About 8,100 people in the United States count themselves as *Euskaldunak*, or Basque-language speakers. The language was suppressed in Spain during Franco's dictatorship, but interest in preserving Euskara increased as the Basque separatist movement grew stronger in the latter half of the twentieth century. Basques' pride in their heritage had led to the creation of several organizations in the United States dedicated to preserving Basque culture and sustaining the language, both through academic research and language courses open to Basques and the larger community.

RELIGION

As a result of their geographic isolation and the spread of Islam during the Banu Qasi dynasty, the Basques were fairly late to convert to Christianity. However, they became primarily Roman Catholic beginning in approximately the eleventh century, and they brought this faith with them to the United States. Although the Basques who worked as sheepherders in the remote American west often found it difficult to attend mass, the Roman Catholic Church has played an important role in the lives of Basque Americans. According to Father Jean Eliçagaray, isolated sheepherders often kept their faith by repeating the prayers and hymns they had learned by heart in Euskara. Having the Catholic liturgy available in their native language was very important; Father Eliçagaray himself was part of a twentieth-century lineage of Basque priests requested and sent to oversee Basque American dioceses. For a period beginning in the 1960s, the U.S.

Catholic Conference sponsored a Basque priest from France to minister to Basque Americans in the western states and to celebrate masses in Euskara; these were broadcast by various radio stations in the west. Catholic rituals such as baptisms and first communions are important social as well as religious events for the Basque community.

CULTURE AND ASSIMILATION

Basques who worked as sheepherders experienced a lonely life. They spent long months alone on the range, moving from place to place. When they returned to the towns at the end of the season, they rented rooms at Basque boardinghouses, known as *ostatuak* or *hotelak*, where they could socialize with their countrymen, speak their native language, and enjoy Basque food and drink. These boardinghouses served an essential role in maintaining Basque culture among a group who were scattered over a wide geographic area. They also became places where Basque men could meet potential wives among the young women recruited from the Basque Country to work as boardinghouse maids. Other men, once they were financially established, sent back to Europe for wives, who joined them in the United States. In this way, Basque American families maintained a strong ethnic identity through the first generation. Often, other young male relatives from the Basque Country came to help with the herds, further cementing family bonds.

The conflict between established ranchers and itinerant Basque sheepherders in the late nineteenth and early twentieth centuries created some prejudice toward Basque immigrants and caused economic and political discrimination against them. Some families recall hearing epithets such as "dirty black Basco" or "tramp." Even worse was the physical intimidation some suffered at the instigation of landed interests during the height of the western range wars, during which their camps were sometimes vandalized and herds killed. Yet Basques were also respected as hard workers who were frugal with their money and conservative in their politics. After federal legislation from 1934 ended competition for grazing rights, anti-Basque sentiment began to disappear. By the later decades of the twentieth century, the Basque sheepherder had acquired a highly romantic image—the opposite of the negative stereotype from earlier years.

Basque immigrants tended to remain clannish at first, socializing with other Basques—often from the same villages in Europe—and patronizing Basque businesses. However, by the second and third generations, this pattern began to change. Intermarriage with other ethnic groups became more common, and many parents urged their children to learn English—to the extent that, by 1970, only about eight thousand Basque Americans knew their ancestral language. In addition, Basques assimilated well because, unlike some immigrant groups, Basque Americans were scattered over a vast land area and never established an ethnic majority in any town or even county. It was imperative, therefore, that Basque immigrants did business with and lived among an ethnically different majority. At the same time, it is possible that their relatively small numbers motivated Basque Americans to emphasize their ethnic traditions more consciously than larger immigrant groups have done. The Basques recognize a person's right to claim Basque ethnicity if he or she has only one Basque ancestor and encourage Basques scattered throughout the country to participate actively in the many associations and festivals that have sprung up since the 1960s.

Basque culture largely relies on an oral tradition to propagate itself. This may have started with the dominance of Latin as a written language during the Middle Ages, helping establish the Basque oral tradition. The oral tradition also helped sustain Basque language and culture during the oppression of Franco's regime. The Spanish dictator occupied the Basque Country in 1937 and banned Basque cultural expressions, including the teaching or speaking of Euskera. By the time of Franco's death in 1975, the Basque language was almost nonexistent. Fortunately,

a concerted effort revived the language in the Basque Country and elsewhere.

Basque Americans have also embraced the oral foundation of their cultural heritage. Not only have they sustained the tradition through stories, song, and dance, but also, contemporary Basques support Basque language schools, where many Basque Americans and their children study the language. As a testament to the Basque American cultural heritage and the importance of oral tradition to it, the Idaho Oral History Center recorded the stories of many Basque Americans, providing a record of their experiences and an important resource for researchers.

Traditions and Customs The Basque identity is based on a deeply held sense of the Basques' distinctness from other cultures. Their language, for example, includes some negative terms for non-Basques. Although Basques accepted Christianity, they maintained myths and legends of supernatural creatures, including Tartaro, a one-eyed giant who is usually outwitted by humans. Basques also have legends of the Basa-Jaun and his wife, Basa-Andre, wild forest creatures who are sometimes depicted as

At the Trailing of the Sheep Parade on Main Street in Ketchum, Idaho, sheep are moved to their winter pastures. David R. Frazier Photolibrary, Inc. / Alamy

mischievous beings but other times described as an ogre and a witch. Basque fairies are called *laminak*, and, like fairies in Celtic legend, they supposedly live underground. Basques folktales often mention *astiya* (witches), sorcerers, magicians, and the Black Sabbath.

Elaborate masquerades or folk plays, part dance and part theater, are an ancient part of Basque culture. Scholars have found links between these events and Greek drama, as well as medieval miracle and mystery plays. Many derive from the romances of Charlemagne, and others are taken from biblical or classical subjects. Characters often include such villains as devils, infidels, demons, and sometimes Englishmen, and the action emphasizes the struggle between good and evil. The forces of good always prevail. Actors dress in colorful costumes and incorporate song, dance, and exaggerated gestures into their performances. Often, a chorus plays an important part. Masquerades have served as the basis for some of the more intricate dances performed by Basque American dance troupes.

Art Although Basque American individuals have not established themselves as notable visual artists, immigrant sheepherders developed an art form unique to the American West. The herders carved the trunks of aspen trees, often cutting their initials and dates into the bark, but sometimes adding short thoughts, poems, or drawings—often about women or sex, but also about politics, sports, hometowns, and other topics. As time passed, the aspen would produce scar tissue around the cuts in a manner that outlined them. As many as five hundred thousand such carved trees may exist in the western states. One carver who signed his name "Borel" appeared to have had some formal art training, and the trees he carved are near Kyburz Flat in California's Tahoe National Forest. Dr. Joxe Mallea of the University of Nevada, Reno, who specialized in the study of Basque tree carvings and has been instrumental in their preservation on public land, called Borel "an amazing carver."

The single most significant piece of art for Basque Americans is the National Basque Monument in Nevada. Unveiled in Reno on August 27, 1989, the five-ton bronze piece was created by renowned Basque sculptor Nestor Basterretxea (1924–), who named it *Bakardade* ("Solitude"). The sculpture depicts a sheepherder carrying a lamb on his back under a full moon. Not all Basque Americans appreciated the memorial's abstract design, and some complained that it did not adequately memorialize their history. Yet the committee that approved the design felt that the memorial would stimulate discussion about Basque cultural heritage.

Cuisine Basque cuisine, based on simple peasant dishes made with fresh ingredients, is admired as one of the most delicious in Europe. Food is a serious

and pleasurable thing for the Basques, who emphasize fresh, homegrown ingredients and simple preparation. The Basque Country's rich culinary tradition has grown increasingly sophisticated in recent years. According to the celebrity chef Anthony Bourdain, the region has "more Michelin stars per capita than anywhere else in the world," a reference to the venerable restaurant rating system.

Salt-cod (*bacalao*) and beans are staple ingredients of the Basque Country table, and olive oil, garlic, tomatoes, and peppers are often used. Farmers traditionally make their own cheese from sheep's milk and also mill their own cider (*sagardo*). Snacks or appetizers (tapas) are popular, as are sausages known as chorizo (*txorixos* or *txistorras*). Tuna, anchovies, and sardines are also popular. When meat is served at the Basque table, it is usually lamb, beef, or pork. Main dishes are customarily accompanied by a simple salad, sometimes made with vegetables picked minutes before from the household garden, and they are almost always served with the region's Rioja wines. Festive dishes include *pastel vasco* or *gateau basque*, a custard-filled cake essential for any celebration. Another special dessert is *intzaursala*, a creamy dish made with ground walnuts boiled with water and sugar and then cooked with milk.

According to María José Sevilla in *Life and Food in the Basque Country*, the cuisine of Basques in France differs from that of Basques in Spain. French Basques live a bit farther inland, and their food is based more on meat than fish. Similarly, Basques in the United States have had to adapt their cooking to ingredients readily available in the western areas of the country. Lamb replaced fish as a food staple for Basque herders and ranchers in the United States, and beans and potatoes were also regularly cooked. Even during his lonely months out on the range, the Basque herder would always cook himself a hearty meal—often a lamb stew with potatoes and beans—and consume it with sourdough bread and plenty of robust red wine. Herders continued this practice even during the Prohibition years, when the sale of alcohol was outlawed in the United States. Somehow, Basques made sure that red wine was always available.

Large, group barbecues have been very popular among Basque Americans; homemade chorizo and red wines are plentiful at these events. Because early Basque boardinghouses served dinners to large numbers of residents, this "family style" dining around a large table came to be considered a Basque tradition—although it is one that evolved in response to American conditions and is not customary in Europe. Although Basque Americans make up a very small percentage of the U.S. population, Basque restaurants are plentiful in several areas of the country. Throughout the western states and especially in California, Nevada, and Idaho, both large and small cities boast Basque restaurants.

LAMB STEW

Ingredients

4 pounds of lamb shoulder cut into pieces oil or lard

3 onions, diced

3 cloves garlic, crushed

3 carrots, cut into pieces

½ small dried red pepper, seeds removed and minced

1 cup red wine

1½ cups chicken broth

salt to taste

6 medium potatoes, cut into pieces

1 cup chopped cilantro

Preparation

Brown lamb in oil or lard with onion, garlic, carrot, and pepper. When vegetables are soft and meat is getting tinges of brown add salt to taste, cilantro, wine and broth to cover. Cook for an hour or until meat is getting tender. While meat is simmering, heat oil or lard in a skillet and brown potatoes. When meat has simmered for an hour, add potatoes. Cook until done.

Traditional Dress Perhaps the most recognizable piece of traditional Basque attire is the *txapella*, or beret, worn by many Basque men as they go about their daily business or socialize. This beret is still worn in the Basque Country today, when all other daily dress is contemporary. Basque men also wear the beret with traditional costumes, including the red and white worn during the annual festival of San Fermin. Today, Basques and Basque Americans alike only wear folk costumes during festivals, usually in presentations of traditional dance. Male dancers typically wear white pants and shirts, with a red *geriko* (sash) around their waists, along with white shoes with red laces. Sometimes they wear long white stockings with elaborate red lacings up to the knee and a pair of bells just below the knee to ward off evil spirits. Some dance costumes include a black vest, and the men always wear the *txapella*. Women dancers also wear white stockings with elaborate lacings. Their blouses are white, and their full skirts are sometimes green (more common among Basques of French origin) and sometimes red (among Basques of Spanish origin). The women wear black vests and white head scarves. On their feet they wear *abarkak*, or leather shoes.

Dances and Songs Dance is a central and very colorful part of Basque life. According to the Southern California Basque dance troupe Gauden Bat, there are more than four hundred different Basque folk dances, many of which are associated with particular regions.

Only men perform traditional or ritual dances, while both men and women perform recreational dances. Many of the most celebrated Basque folk dances involve arm movements with sticks, swords, or hoops and demand great agility. John Ysursa, an American expert in Basque culture, has emphasized the influence of Basque dances on other traditions, pointing out that some steps in modern ballet may have derived from Basque folk dances.

As early as the 1930s, Basque Americans began organizing festivals that included dancing, along with music and other activities. These festivals have expanded since the 1960s. The Oinkari Basque Dancers of Idaho, incorporated in 1964, have toured extensively at Basque American cultural events as well as at national venues and World's Fair exhibitions. The troupe lists an extensive repertoire that includes both secular and religious dances. Since their inception, the Oinkari Basque Dancers have learned and perform dances from all the Basque regions. One of their most colorful dances is from the *Zuberoa'ko Maskarada*, or Zuberoan masquerades. Scholars believe that it originated as part of an ancient fertility rite. Dancers come forward one by one and perform individual steps around a wine glass, finally stepping onto it and then leaping away. Another thrilling dance is the *Amaia'ko Ezpata Dantza*, the sword dance of *Amaia*, based on the history of the Basques in the seventh century. Eighteen men, formed to represent two armies, perform the piece, which involves high kicks and spinning twists.

In the *Xemein'go Dantza*, a dance symbolizing the struggle between good and evil, a dozen sword-bearing men dance in a circle around their leader, who is believed to represent the archangel Michael. They then hoist him onto their swords and lift him above their heads, as two men dance in front. The *Kaxarranka*, a dance from the fishing town of Lekeitio, is performed to honor Saint Peter, patron saint of fishermen. In this dance, six to eight men carry a large arch on which a man dances high above their heads. The procession winds through the town, stopping at designated areas. The *donibane* is usually performed at night around an open fire and is associated with the feast of Saint John.

Songs are also integral to Basque cultural functions. Among the best known are "*Gernika'ko Arbolo*," which honors the Tree of Gernika, a symbol of Basque democracy, and "*Boga, Boga*," which describes the difficult life of fishermen. "*Aitoren Ixkuntz Zarra*" tells of the beauties of the Basque language and urges the Basque people to speak their native tongue. Indeed, Basque choirs have been organized in the United States as a means of preserving the Basque language and culture. The choir Anaiak Danok ("We Are All Brothers") performed in Boise during the 1970s. It became the Bihotzetik Basque Choir in 1986 and recorded its first album, *Biotzetik, From the Heart*, in 2000.

Music is extremely important in Basque culture. Old songs are sung at festivals, and summer music camps in the United States enable children to learn traditional instruments such as the *txistu* (flute) and the tambourine. Basque musicians also play the violin and accordion, though use of the violin is less common among in the United States than in the Basque Country. Central to Basque musical culture are the *bertsolariak*, poets who compete in festivals by improvising songs on any subject. Although *bertsolari* competitions are common at Basque American gatherings, Nancy Zubiri points out in *A Travel Guide to Basque America* that all the *bertsolariak* in the United States by the 1990s were from the Basque Country, and not American born. The linguistic fluency required by the art form, specialists believe, has been almost impossible to acquire in the United States.

Holidays Basques celebrate the main Christian holidays but also enjoy their own unique holidays and festivals. The biggest holiday among Basques is the feast of their patron saint, Ignatius of Loyola, founder of the Jesuit order. It is celebrated on the last weekend in July and includes a mass and picnic, music, dancing, and sports contests. The famous running of the bulls to celebrate the festival of Saint Fermin takes place in the Basque city of Pamplona, also in July of each year. Basque Americans in different states organize specific festivities throughout the year. In Boise they have held an annual Sheepherders' Ball since 1929. Basque Americans have also held several *jaialdi*, or international festivals, at which athletes, musicians, and dancers from the Basque Country and the United States have performed.

Health Care Issues and Practices Although there have been no health or psychological issues identified as specific to Basque Americans, Basques do have distinct physiological traits. Of all European peoples, Basques have the highest rate of blood type O and the lowest incidence of blood type B. They also have the highest rate in the world of Rh negative blood factor.

FAMILY AND COMMUNITY LIFE

Early Basques Americans' traditionally solitary lifestyle caused Basque immigrants to develop a high degree of independence and self-sufficiency. For herders on the high ranges or ranchers at remote settlements, opportunities for socializing were few. Eager and diligent workers, Basques preferred to work for themselves or for a family business when possible. Basque Americans did not begin organizing cultural groups until about the 1930s, but even then Basques of French origin and those of Spanish origin had little contact with one another. In 1973, however, a group of Basque Americans formed the North American Basque Organizations, Inc., to unite the various local groups and promote more interaction among Basque Americans of different backgrounds. In *A Travel Guide to Basque America*, Zubiri observes that although Basque Americans continue to harbor some regional differences, they consider it important to work together to preserve their unique cultural heritage.

Gender Roles Women and men in Basque American households traditionally worked hard to make their ranches or small businesses work. Women packed food and supplies to send out to the herders,

The Oinkari Basque Dancers perform at the Trailing of the Sheep Festival in Hailey, Idaho. DAVID R. FRAZIER PHOTOLIBRARY, INC. / ALAMY

BASQUE PROVERBS

Azeria solas ematen zaukanean ari, gogo emak heure oiloari.

> When the fox is engaging you in conversation, keep an eye on your chicken.

Dakien guztia ez derrala, ahala oro jan ez dezala.

> Don't say as much as you know and don't eat as much as you can.

Danbolin ordainduak soinu txarra jotzen du.

> A drummer paid in advance doesn't play good music.

Dezagun gutxi, dezagun beti.

> Let us have little, but let us always have enough.

Dirua, mutilik hoberena eta nagusirik txarrena.

> Money is the best of servants, but the worst of bosses.

Diruak malkarrak zelaitzen.

> Money can turn rough, hilly terrain into flat fields.

Ez naiz joaten elizara, maingu naizelako; joaten naiz tabernara, ardoa on zaidalako.

> I don't go to church, because I'm lame, but I do go to the bar, because I like the wine.

and they also cooked, sewed, and performed countless physical chores around the ranch. Although in many ways this kind of work resembled the responsibilities held by Basque women in Europe, in the American west families often lived at far greater distances from one another than they had in the Basque Country and were much more isolated. Louis Irigaray, a California Basque shepherd and singer, wrote in his memoir that his mother found ranch life boring and profoundly lonely. In towns, Basque American women also played significant roles. Paquita Garatea, a professor of history, researched women's work in Basque American communities, and she found that many boardinghouses and hotels were run by men and their wives but that the women played a central, if not dominant, role.

As later generations of Basque Americans grew further from their ancestral roots, they assimilated with the values of mainstream American culture, including intermarrying and attending college or joining the mainstream workforce—regardless of gender in any particularly "Basque" way. With the interest in revivifying Basque culture that began in the 1960s and

continues today, both men and women launched programs and organizations, and both boys and girls participate in Basque language learning, dance and choral troupes, and festivals.

Courtship and Weddings During the first decades of Basque immigration, many men sent for their wives in Europe to join them in the United States. If the man had accumulated enough money to afford the trip, he might return to the Basque Country to choose a wife from his own village. Other men asked a matchmaker to arrange marriages for them. Many Basque boardinghouses employed maids from the Basque Country, who were frequently courted and wed by patrons. In later generations, however, Basque men more often courted local women of various ethnic backgrounds.

Basque American weddings are often gala affairs, with the entire Basque community in attendance. After the church ceremony, a large feast is held, complete with good wine, music, song, and dance. Weddings provide a welcome opportunity to socialize and strengthen community ties.

Funerals Funerals are taken very seriously by Basques and serve as an occasion for Basque Americans to affirm their ethnic bonds. They consider it important to attend funerals of other Basques even when they scarcely know the family involved and sometimes travel hundreds of miles to be present. This funerary obligation was of particular importance during the early 1900s, when many Basques in the United States lived isolated lives on the range and had few social contacts. Their families back in the Basque Country worried that these men might die alone, deprived of a proper burial ceremony. Consequently, the Basque American community took great care to bury each of their dead with due ceremony.

In the United States, Basques have formed associations to help provide flowers and memorial services for their deceased. In Mexico, Cuba, Argentina, and Venezuela, they established their own burial crypts and cemeteries. Basque associations in New York City and Boise offered their members burial insurance. Basque funerals follow the rituals of the Catholic Church, and if a Basque priest is available, he offers the funeral mass in Euskara. Until about the mid-1940s, it was customary to hold a *gauela*, or wake, at the home of the deceased or at a Basque hotel. It was also traditional to make a financial donation for a mass for the deceased, a practice that the mourners reciprocated when the occasion arose. After the ceremony, a funeral feast was always held.

Recreational Activities Basques have brought several unique sports to the United States, and they enjoy participating in athletic contests at festivals. Many of these events can be traced to the physical work Basques performed in the Pyrenees. Wood chopping is a very popular event at Basque American festivals, as are weight carrying and stone lifting, all of which allow athletes to demonstrate their skill as well as their strength and endurance.

Handball games are also an essential part of Basque American life. Pelota, or handball, was developed from the medieval game of *jeu de paume*. According to Zubiri, Basques invented the basic modern handball game as well as several variations. Jai alai, played with basketlike extensions (*txistera*) that are fastened to the wrist, is probably the best-known of these variations. Basque immigrants began building pelota courts (called "frontons") soon after they arrived in the United States, and their love of the sport is considered an important factor in unifying the American Basque community. From the earliest days of Basque immigration, weekly pelota matches were held throughout the western states, enabling people scattered over a large geographic area to come together for competitions. Until World War II, every significant Basque community in the United States had at least one pelota court. Jai alai, on the other hand, has been most popular in Florida, the first state to boast a professional team, as well as in Connecticut. *Mus*, a card game, is another common pastime when Basque Americans get together.

Interactions with Other Americans Basques have lived successfully among different ethnic groups in the United States. Because of their small numbers, they have had to work and associate with many non-Basques, but they have also supported each other through clubs, sports, and other activities. Although Basque Americans express a deep appreciation of their distinct culture, intermarriage is not discouraged.

EMPLOYMENT AND ECONOMIC CONDITIONS

Basque Americans are unusual in that they are, as an ethnic group, associated almost exclusively with one business: sheepherding. Yet, significant as their presence has been in that industry, they have also succeeded in several other enterprises. They have traditionally worked in agricultural jobs or at manual labor. In addition to ranching and herding, Basque Americans have opened small businesses such as dairy farms or turned their boardinghouses into restaurants. Less often, they have taken urban jobs in meat-packing plants, bakeries, or construction. Relatively few Basque immigrants have entered professional fields—a trend that some have linked to the group's traditional indifference toward higher education. However, this is less true of later generations of Basque Americans, who are more likely to attend college and work as bankers, lawyers, politicians, and in other professions.

POLITICS AND GOVERNMENT

Most Basques who settled in the American west expected their stay to be temporary. They planned to work for a few years, save money, and then return to the Basque homeland. Though in the end many remained in the United States, their ambivalence about where they should finally settle caused many to delay the process of obtaining U.S. citizenship. Thus the political involvement of the first few generations of Basque immigrants was relatively low. More recently, Basque Americans have participated in American politics and, as with the majority of the population in western states, have generally supported conservative causes and the Republican Party. Although Basques have served as mayors or other local officials, few have sought higher office.

Basque Americans have remained generally indifferent to political events in either France or Spain. Further, the Basque separatist cause has elicited little enthusiasm from Basque Americans. Although some groups and individuals in Idaho have denounced Spanish government crackdowns on Basque separatist activities, other Basque Americans throughout the west have expressed no interest in the matter, which they consider an urban and middle-class movement unrelated to their rural concerns. This attitude differs markedly from the views of Basques throughout Mexico and South America, who have generally showed strong support for Basque nationalism. However, the Basque Country and the Basque government of the autonomous region have been known to help finance Basque cultural activities in the United States.

Military Service During World War I, many Basque immigrants were harshly criticized for refusing to serve in the U.S. army. Some who were drafted chose to renounce their new citizenship to avoid service. Often, these men were denied the chance to reapply for citizenship—a condition that deprived them of grazing rights in the western states. In their study *Amerikanuak: Basques in the New World*, William A. Douglass and Jon Bilbao state that this apathy toward military service was consistent with the Basque pattern of indifference to political causes in either Spain or France. Douglass and Bilbao report that throughout the late 1800s and early 1900s, the rates of military evasion in the Basque provinces was consistently high. Military service was not a significant issue among Basque Americans, however, during World War II. Former Idaho secretary of state Pete Cenarrusa, for example, proudly cited his record as a Marine fighter pilot during that war. He retired with the rank of major.

NOTABLE INDIVIDUALS

Academia The University of Nevada, Reno, has an acclaimed Basque Studies program. It offers course work in Basque language, history, and culture and publishes the Basque Book Series, which numbers more than thirty titles. As of 2005, Boise State University has also formed a Basque Studies program. It boasts the highest number of Basque students in a program outside of the Basque Country. The University of California, Santa Barbara, and California State University, Bakersfield, have also for formed initiatives in Basque Studies. Together, these programs have begun to form a Basque Studies consortium that publishes an academic journal.

John Etchemendy (1952–) was appointed the provost of Stanford University in 2000. He received his doctorate in philosophy from Stanford in 1982 and joined the faculty there in 1983.

Journalism Robert F. Erburu (1930–) was the publisher of the *Los Angeles Times* and was president, CEO (1981), and chairman of the board (1986) of its parent company, the Times Mirror Co. After his retirement, he became a notable philanthropist, serving on several boards and committees, including the chairman of the board for the National Gallery of Art and honorary trustee of the Brookings Institution.

Literature Basque Americans have been relatively slow to establish a literary tradition, in part because so much of their background was based on an oral culture and in part because they came to the United States with little education. In addition, most of the Basque intelligentsia who emigrated chose to go to South America rather than the United States, leaving the American West with virtually no foundation to support Basque literature. One writer, however, received extensive recognition. Robert Laxalt (1923–2001), brother of politician Paul Laxalt, earned critical acclaim for his books exploring the Basque American experience. *Sweet Promised Land* (1988), Laxalt's first book, is a memoir of his immigrant father. In *The Basque Hotel* (1993), he chronicles the coming of age of a young boy whose parents run a boardinghouse in Nevada. *Child of the Holy Ghost* (1992) tells of his journey to the Basque Country to discover his parents' roots, and *The Governor's Mansion* (1994) recounts how an oldest son enters politics in Nevada. *The Land of My Fathers: A Son's Return to the Basque Country* (1999) explores Laxalt's experience moving his family to the Basque Country in the 1960s and his attempt to understand his cultural heritage. *Time of the Rabies* (2000), a novella, tells of ranchers fighting a rabies epidemic in the 1920s.

Music Among the more celebrated Basque American musicians was accordion player Jim Jausoro (1920–2004). Jausoro and his partner, Domingo Ansotegui (1913–1981), began playing dance music at Basque festivals and gatherings in the 1940s and eventually became quite well known. From 1960 Jausoro played regularly for Boise's Oinkari Basque Dancers. In 1985 he was chosen as one of twelve master traditional artists in the United States to receive the National Heritage Award from the National Endowment for the Arts. Jausoro also received a lifetime achievement award from the North American Basque Organization. In 2004, a few months before he died, Jausoro accompanied the Oinkari Basque Dancers to Washington, D.C., where they performed at the Library of Congress and the Kennedy Center.

The singer and actor David Archuleta (1990–) is of Basque descent on his father's side. He was the youngest contestant on the popular TV show *American Idol* and finished as the runner-up in 2008.

Politics Pete T. Cenarrusa was a fighter pilot during World War II and served nine terms as an Idaho state representative beginning in 1950—three times as speaker of the house. He became Idaho's secretary of state in 1967 by appointment and was elected seven times, until his retirement in 2002—making him the longest-serving secretary of state in U.S. history and the longest-serving elected official in Idaho state history. Cenarrusa served as the national dean of the secretaries of state in 1999.

Other Basques have served as politicians. Paul Laxalt (1922–) is one of the few who sought national office. He became governor of Nevada in 1966 and was elected to the U.S. Senate in 1974, becoming the first Basque American to be elected to a federal post. Anthony Yturri (1914–1999) served several terms in the Oregon senate. In Nevada, Peter Echeverria (1918–2000) served as a state legislator and as chairman of the Nevada Gaming Commission. Democrat John Garamendi (1945–), a graduate of the University of California, Berkeley, spent several years in California state politics after a Peace Corps stint in Ethiopia. Despite several failed campaigns, including a bid for governor in 1994, he was elected lieutenant governor of California in January 2008 and elected as U.S. representative for California's tenth district in November 2009.

Science and Medicine Florence Bascom (1862–1945) was the first woman hired by the U.S. Geological Survey, in 1896. She was also an associate editor of the journal *American Geologist* from 1896 to 1908 and was featured prominently in, ironically, the first edition of *American Men of Science* in 1906. During her graduate school courses, she was forced to sit behind a screen in order to not "distract" the male students. In addition to conducting geological research, Bascom taught at several colleges, including the Hampton Institute for Negroes and American Indians (now Hampton University) in Virginia and Bryn Mawr College.

Sports Benny "the Jet" Urquidez (1952–) is a world-renowned boxer and martial artist. He became particularly well known for his flamboyant fighting style. Further, he competed across various fighting styles, from karate to *muay thai*. After retiring from professional competition, Urquidez developed his free-form martial arts system, which combines several different fighting styles and that Urquidez calls Ukidokan karate.

Stage and Screen José Iturbi (1895–1980) was a renowned pianist, composer, and movie star. He trained as a classical musician, and fostering the appreciation of classical music in the modern era became one of his biggest causes. In his Hollywood films, including *Anchors Aweigh* (1945) and *Three Daring Daughters* (1948), he generally played himself. Iturbi's recording of Chopin's "Polonaise in A-flat" (recorded in 1944) was a massive hit that stayed on the charts for 219 weeks.

MEDIA

Two Basque-language newspapers were published in the Los Angeles area during the late 1800s. Lawyer Martin Biscailuz (1861–1899) published *Escualdun Gazeta*, the first newspaper in the world printed exclusively in the Basque language, during the 1880s. When Biscailuz's reputation suffered after his alleged mismanagement of a wealthy client's estate, the paper folded and was succeeded by *California'ko Eskual Herria*, published by journalist José Goytino. During the 1890s the large population of Basques in central California prompted the *Bakersfield Daily Californian* to print occasional articles in Basque, and during the 1930s the *Boise Capital News* also included stories in Basque. From 1973 to 1977, Brian Wardle, a non-Basque from Boise, published a newspaper called *The Voice of the Basques*.

PRINT

Newsletter of the Center for Basque Studies

Semiannual publication covering the Basque Studies Program and Basque-related news. Carries articles about Basques and news of research in Basque studies. In 2011 the newsletter went entirely digital, and editions could be downloaded from the website or e-mailed directly to readers.

Sandra Ott, Editor
Center for Basque Studies University of Nevada
MS/2322, Reno
Nevada 89557-2322
Phone: (775) 784-4854
Fax: (775) 784-1355
Email: basque@unr.edu
URL: http://basque.unr.edu/index.html

EuskalKultura.com

Clearinghouse for news and information about the Basque diaspora and Basque culture outside the geographical limits of *Euskal Herria* (the Basque Country). Features news, information of other Basque-related resources, and genealogy aids. Content in English, Spanish, and Euskara.

Paseo de Bera Bera 79, Donostia-San Sebastián
20009
Spain
Phone: +34 943-50447
URL: www.euskalkultura.com

ORGANIZATIONS AND ASSOCIATIONS

The Basque Center

Provides meeting space and social activities as well as rehearsal space for the Oinkari Basque Dancers and the Boise'ko Gasteak Dancers (a children's group).

Patty Gabica
601 Grove Street
Boise, Idaho 83702
Phone: (208) 342-9983
Email: info@basquecenter.com
URL: http://basquecenter.com

Basque Educational Organization (BEO)

Founded in 1983; offers Basque language, dance, music, and sports classes; sponsors theater and educational programs; and maintains a museum and reference library.

P.O. Box 31861
San Francisco, California 94131-0861
Email: info@BasqueEd.org
URL: www.basqueed.org

North American Basque Organizations, Inc. (NABO)

Umbrella organization that includes local clubs; maintains cultural relations with the Basque government, the French Basque Cultural Institute, and other international centers; sponsors music festivals, summer camps, and sporting events; maintains website; and publishes the weekly newsletter *Astero*.

15850 Old Hickory Lane
Chino Hills, California 91709
Phone: (909) 597-4526
Email: info@nabasque.org
URL: www.nabasque.org

MUSEUMS AND RESEARCH CENTERS

Basque Museum and Cultural Center

Maintains museum displays, classrooms, archives, and a research library. Exhibits include a preserved Basque home and boardinghouse.

611 Grove Street
Boise, Idaho 83702
Phone: (208) 343-2671
Email: info@basquemuseum.com
URL: www.basquemuseum.com

Basque Studies Program at Boise State University

A multidisciplinary program in which students study language, culture, history, and political challenges of the Basque Country and Basques in America.

David Lachiondo, Director
1103 Grant Avenue
Boise, Idaho 83725
Phone: (208) 425-5331
Email: basquestudies@boisestate.edu
URL: http://sspa.boisestate.edu/basquestudies

The Center for Basque Studies

Based at the University of Nevada, Reno, the center is an international research organization that also publishes widely in Basque-related studies. It offers language and Basque-focused courses for undergraduate and graduate students and hosts scholars and conferences related to Basque culture and history.

Center for Basque Studies University of Nevada, Reno
Reno, Nevada 89557-2322
Phone: (775) 784-4854
Email: basque@unr.edu
URL: http://basque.unr.edu/index.html

SOURCES FOR ADDITIONAL STUDY

Douglass, William A., and Jon Bilbao. *Amerikanuak: Basques in the New World*. Reno: University of Nevada Press, 1975.

Echeverria, Jeronima. *Home Away from Home: A History of Basque Boardinghouses*. Reno: University of Nevada Press, 1999.

Etulain, Richard W., and Jeronima Echeverria, eds. *Portraits of Basques in the New World*. Reno: University of Nevada Press, 1999.

Irigaray, Louis, and Theodore Taylor. *A Shepherd Watches, a Shepherd Sings: Growing Up a Basque Shepherd in California's San Joaquin Valley*. Garden City, NY: Doubleday & Company, 1977.

Laxalt, Robert. *Sweet Promised Land*. Harper & Row, 1957. Reprint, Reno: University of Nevada Press, 1988.

Mallea-Olaetxe, J. *Speaking through the Aspens: Basque Tree Carvings in California and Nevada*. Reno: University of Nevada Press, 2000.

Río, David. *Robert Laxalt: The Voice of the Basques in American Literature*. Reno: Center for Basque Studies, University of Nevada, Reno, 2007.

Sevilla, María José. *Life and Food in the Basque Country*. New York: New Amsterdam Books, 1990.

Urza, Carmelo. *Solitude: Art and Symbolism in the National Basque Monument*. Reno: University of Nevada Press, 1993.

White, Linda, and Cameron Watson, eds. *Amatxi, Amuma, Amona: Writings in Honor of Basque Women*. Reno: Center for Basque Studies, University of Nevada, 2003.

Zubiri, Nancy. *A Travel Guide to Basque America: Families, Feasts, and Festivals*. 2nd ed. Reno: University of Nevada Press, 2006.

BELARUSAN AMERICANS

Vitaut Kipel

OVERVIEW

Belarusan Americans are immigrants or descendants of people from Belarus, a landlocked country located in Eastern Europe. Belarus is bordered by Poland to the west, Russia to the east, Ukraine to the south, and Lithuania/Latvia to the north and northwest. Glacial scouring accounts for the flatness of the terrain, much of which is forested and marshy. The total land area, which includes more than 11,000 lakes and 20,000 rivers, is 80,154 square miles (207,600 square kilometers)—an area slightly smaller than the state of Kansas.

According to a census conducted by the Belarus government and funded by the UN Population Commission, the country had a population of about 9.7 million in October 2009. Belarus has shown an annual population decrease of 0.36 percent since 2007, and the *CIA World Factbook* estimated the population to be about 9.6 million as of July 2012. The country's population is 83 percent Belarusan, 9 percent Russian, 3.1 percent Polish, 1.7 percent Ukrainian, and 3.2 percent other. According to the commissioner on Religions and Nationalities of the Republic of Belarus, 48.3 percent adhered to Eastern Orthodoxy, 41.1 percent irreligion, 7.1 percent Catholicism, and 3.5 percent other religions. Belarus, once part of the former Soviet Union, has a relatively well-developed industry base, of which nearly 80 percent is state controlled. According to the World Bank Classification, Belarus's economy falls in the lower-middle income category and is ranked sixty-one in total GDP. In the twenty-first century, Belarus has maintained a steady growth rate in industry, but in 2011 the economy began experiencing hyperinflation, which caused the government to implement a series of currency controls.

The first significant wave of immigrants to the United States from Belarus occurred from about 1880 through the 1930s. The majority immigrated for economic and political reasons and settled in New York, Boston, Baltimore, and Philadelphia. The post-World War II era (1948 through the early 1950s) also saw a notable increase in immigration, with more than 50,000 Belarusans coming to the United States. They moved throughout the fifty states, the greatest number settling in industrial cities and mining regions between Illinois and New York. Most shared fervent anticommunist sentiments. Since the collapse of the Soviet Union in the 1990s, the United States has seen another influx of Belarusans, many of Jewish heritage.

It is difficult to determine the number of Americans with Belarusan ancestry, because census and immigration statistics have recorded Belarusan immigrants as Polish or Russian. In 2011 the U.S. Census Bureau's American Community Survey estimated that 57,818 people living in the United States were born in Belarus (2009–2011 estimate). This number is comparable to, for example, the population of Cheyenne, the state capital of Wyoming. The largest concentrations of recent Belarusan immigrants have settled in the metropolitan New York area, New Jersey, Cleveland, Chicago, Detroit, and Los Angeles. They have emigrated for political, economic, and familial reasons.

HISTORY OF THE PEOPLE

Early History Early civilizations populated the territory that is now Belarus in the middle Paleolithic Period (100,000–40,000 BCE); the first significant settlements emerged about 25,000 years ago. The Dryhavichy, Kryvichy, and Radzimichy peoples settled the area between the seventh and ninth centuries CE, followed by the first state formations in the principalities of Polotsk, Smalensk, and Turov in the ninth and tenth centuries. These principalities formed a unified structure, thus establishing by the thirteenth century the Grand Duchy of Lithuania—a commonwealth that became an important political power in Eastern Europe over the next several centuries. The Grand Duchy of Lithuania recognized Belarusan as the official language. The cities of Navahradak (thirteenth century) and Vilnius (sixteenth century) served as the capitals of this large, multinational, influential state.

The Grand Duchy of Lithuania was formed as a defense against the Teutonic knights, the Turks, and the Golden Horde of Mongol Tartars, and it gradually reached its peak of influence in the fourteenth century under Vytautas the Great. In 1386 Grand Duke Jogaila was crowned king of Poland. The joint forces of Poland and Lithuania won the famous Battle of Grundwald in 1410. In 1569 the Polish-Lithuanian Commonwealth was created; this, in turn, led to the federative state of Rzeczpospolita. In 1583 the new state fought and won the Livonian War against Muscovy.

The beginnings of Russian influence and domination over the Belarusan territories can be traced back to the seventeenth century, when the easternmost parts of Belarus were incorporated into the Russian Empire. After the three Partitions of Poland in 1772, 1793, and 1795 by Russia, Prussia, and Austria, Belarus was absorbed entirely into Russia and underwent severe Russification—that is, Russian acculturation. This process of cultural assimilation was systematically justified and encouraged by Tsars Alexander I and Nicholas I and remained vigorous through the reigns of successive tsars—particularly that of Tsar Alexander II (reigned 1855–1881)—and the subsequent decades of the Soviet regime. The word *Belarus* was abolished and replaced by the deliberately vague geographical concept "Northwest Territory." The use of the Belarusan language was also outlawed, and Tsar Nicholas I mandated that all communication would henceforth take place in Russian. Beginning in the 1830s the government adopted a policy of forced deportation of Belarusans to the northern regions of the Empire. In addition, an enormous surplus of the local labor force led to a large wave of emigration. Thus, beginning with the last two decades of the nineteenth century and into the early years of World War I, hundreds of thousands of Belarusan peasants migrated out of their homeland to Siberia and the United States.

Despite the efforts of Russian administrators to eliminate any characteristics of Belarusan separateness—political or cultural—an ethnic awareness emerged among Belarusans toward the last quarter of the nineteenth century. In 1902 the first Belarusan political party, the Belarusian Revolutionary Hramada, was established. This was soon followed by numerous cultural and religious organizations, publishing groups, and a teachers' union. However, the real impetus for a widespread revival of Belarusan consciousness and the development of a mass movement was the appearance of Belarusan-language newspapers: first the short-lived *Nasa Dola* (1906) and then its successor, *Nasa Niva* (1906–1915), both published in Vilna.

Modern Era The high point of Belarusan political activity during the prewar period and the World War I years was the convening of the all-Belarusan Congress in December 1917 in the capital city of Minsk. The Council, elected at this Congress in 1918, adopted a resolution declaring the independence of Belarus in the form of the Belarusan Democratic Republic. This new democratic state was short-lived, however. Bolshevik armed forces interrupted the Congress and overran the Republic.

The Bolsheviks moved quickly to catch up with the national aspirations of the people. On January 1, 1919, they proclaimed the Belarusan Soviet Socialist Republic (abbreviated as BSSR). This event had a positive influence on the general populace as the leadership of the newly established Belarusan Soviet Republic improved the economy, political administration,

educational system, and cultural life. Many Belarusans who had migrated to Western Europe and the United States returned to their homeland. Unfortunately, according to the terms of the Treaty of Riga, signed in 1921, a significant part of Belarusan ethnic territory was given over to the new Polish state.

In the early and mid-1920s, Belarusan national life flourished in both the eastern (under the Soviets) and the western (under the Poles) territories. There were hundreds of Belarusan schools, publishing houses, and other expressions of cultural life. The Belarusan national movement reached its peak in eastern and western Belarus during the 1920s.

Uncomfortable with the growth of the Belarus national movement, Polish administrators began to curb Belarusan political activities in the mid-1920s, closing Belarusan schools, outlawing Belarusan-language newspapers, and harassing Belarusan religious communities. By the early 1930s the Belarusan movement in Poland had been totally crushed, with its leaders either imprisoned or emigrated—primarily to Soviet Belarus. The systematic persecution of nationally conscious Belarusans in Soviet Belarus began several years later. Soviet Belarus experienced numerous purges, with the peak years being 1930, 1933, and 1937 to 1938.

The Belarusan Soviet Socialist Republic and Western Belarus were reunited into a single state in September 1939 when Soviet troops occupied the eastern part of the Polish state. The occupation of Western Belarus by Soviet armed forces proved costly to the Belarusans: thousands of Belarusans were deported to Siberia, numerous leaders were shot, and all Belarusan activity was suppressed.

The German *Wehrmacht* occupied Belarusan territory just a few weeks after the beginning of the German-Soviet War, on June 22, 1941. A number of Belarusan political leaders cooperated with the German occupiers, but any hope of new political freedom under German rule was dashed by the spring of 1944 when the Soviet army advanced westward and occupied Belarusan territory.

World War II devastated Belarus. More than 9,000 villages and 200 towns were destroyed, and approximately six million Belarusans lost their lives. The territory of Belarus was once again Balkanized. Parts of Belarusan ethnic territory were divided up and handed over to Poland, Lithuania, and Latvia, with the largest portion going to the Russian Federation. Hundreds of thousands of Belarusans were resettled in Siberia, and thousands of others emigrated as a result of the war. Almost two decades would pass before Belarus recovered from the devastation of World War II.

Despite the denigration of Belarusan culture, a sizable segment of the population resisted Russification. By 1985 a powerful revival process had become evident. Belarusan schools began to open, Belarusan

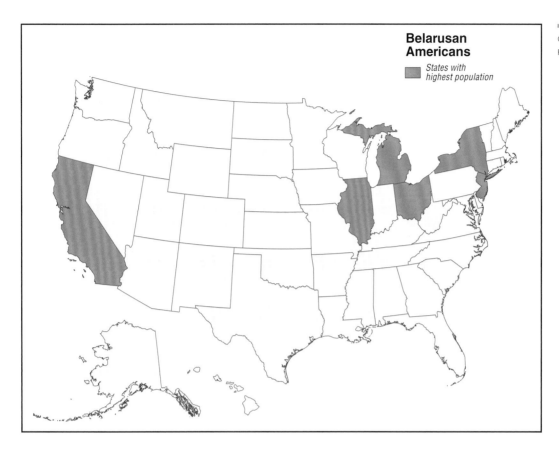

Belarusan Americans

▨ States with highest population

became the official language of the Republic, and numerous societies fostered a new esteem for the language and culture. The national revival also led to the emergence of the Belarusan Popular Front, a national political movement functioning as a democratic opposition party in the parliament of the Republic. Belarus became an independent state in 1991, seceding from the former Soviet Union. However, the election of Alexander Lukashenko as president in 1994 marked a turn toward international isolation.

Lukashenko was elected president of Belarus for a second term (2001–2006), a third term (2006–2011), and a fourth, with early elections held in 2010. Lukashenko has been labeled "Europe's last dictator," and the European Union has condemned him for human rights violations. The political situation further isolated Belarus from the European Union and the United States. This, in turn, strengthened Lukashenko's belief that Belarusan interests were in close alignment with the systems and structures of the Russian Federation. In 2011 Belarus's economy suffered hyperinflation. In 2012 Lukashenko blamed journalists for the economic crisis, threatening to close off the country's borders.

With attention focused on Lukashenko's leadership, many have forgotten that more than two million people inhabit areas that are still subject to radioactive contamination from the 1986 accident at the Chernobyl (in the Ukraine, just south of the Belarus border) nuclear power plant. This was an economic, ecological, and social catastrophe for Belarus. The long-term effects are still subject to speculation and have been addressed by environmental organizations such as Greenpeace.

SETTLEMENT IN THE UNITED STATES

Some people believe that the earliest Belarusan immigrants in America settled in the Colony of Virginia in the early 1600s. They cite the fact that Captain John Smith, who became the first governor of Virginia in 1608, visited Belarus in 1603. Thus, it is possible that Smith brought Belarusans with him to Virginia, together with Polish or Ukrainian manufacturing specialists. Many scholars, however, maintain that the historical connection between John Smith and Belarus is tenuous.

Mass emigration from Belarus began during the final decades of the nineteenth century and lasted until World War I. At the outset, emigration from Belarus was directed toward the industrial cities in Poland, to Riga in Latvia, to St. Petersburg in Russia, to the mines in Ukraine and Siberia, and later, to the United States. Libava and northern Germany were the main points of departure, whereas New York, Philadelphia, Boston, and Baltimore were the main gates of entry to the United States. Unfortunately, the ethnicity of the Belarusan immigrants was not properly registered upon arrival. Instead, they were routinely registered as Russians (having Russian Imperial passports and being of the Eastern Orthodox religion) or as Poles, if they were Roman Catholics.

Belarusans who arrived in the United States after World War I were predominantly political immigrants, mainly from Western Europe and Poland. They numbered only a few thousand persons because of U.S. opposition to immigration during the Great Depression as well as anti-Semitic sentiments, but the relatively small number of immigrants was still able to found several Belarusan organizations.

Belarusans arrived in sizable numbers in the period following World War II, from 1948 to the early 1950s. During this period about 50,000 Belarusans immigrated to the United States; for the most part, they were individuals with "displaced person" status who had left Europe for political reasons. These immigrants represented a very broad spectrum of the Belarusan nation, but they had one trait in common: fervent anticommunism. The great majority of them were nationally conscious Belarusans filled with the political resolve to reestablish an independent democratic Belarusan state, the Belarusan Democratic Republic. They came from a variety of countries, the majority of them from West Germany and Austria, but many from Great Britain, France, Italy, Belgium, Denmark, and other countries in South America and northern Africa. These lands had been their first stopovers after the events of World War II prompted them to leave Belarus. These immigrants represented several distinct categories: former prisoners of war of the Polish and Soviet armies; former émigrés who had left Belarus shortly after World War I or in 1939, when the Soviets invaded Poland; persons who had worked in Germany during the war as *Ostarbeiters*; refugees who had fled Belarus in 1943 or 1944; and post–World War II defectors and dissidents.

Emigration waves from Belarus during the 1980s were relatively small as compared with previous waves. People emigrated for various reasons: political, economic, and filial (to reunite with families). Most of these immigrants were of Jewish Belarusan background. Since the fall of the Soviet Union in the 1990s, immigration from Belarus to the United States has increased, especially by individuals who are rejoining family members in the United States.

Because official databases in the United States are unable to provide accurate numbers for Belarusans entering the country, widely varying figures have appeared in print. Belarusan researchers have attempted to calculate the number of Belarusans immigrating to the United States. On the high end, researchers count between 1 and 1.5 million, while the Belarusan Institute of Arts and Sciences (U.S.) suggests the number is between 600,000 and 650,000. The 1980 U.S. Census counted 7,328, but the 1990 Census tallied only 4,277. The 2000 U.S. Census counted 38,505 U.S. residents who were born in Belarus, and in 2011 the total was an estimated 57,818, according to the American Community Survey, conducted by the U.S. Census Bureau.

LANGUAGE

The Belarusan language is a part of the East Slavic group of languages, which includes Ukrainian and Russian. The language of Belarusan Americans has specific features. Many Americanisms have entered the everyday Belarusan language, but these are often so assimilated to the lexical and phonological patterns of Belarusan that they do not seem foreign to the language; for example, compare the word *radio*—which was popularized in the 1920s in the United States— with the Belarusan equivalent, *radyjo*. Meanwhile, a peculiar phenomenon is evident in the language of thousands of Belarusan immigrants who came prior to World War I. These people claimed to speak Russian but were in fact speaking a Russified Belarusan, often with the admixture of Yiddish words. Unfortunately, because of the lack of language professionals working for the U.S. Census, this mélange of languages, which actually has a Belarusan base, was recorded as Russian.

Numerous associations, including the Belarusan American Community Center in Cleveland, Ohio, seek to preserve the native Belarusan language for members of the next generation. Common Belarusan greetings include "Preevyet," or "Hi," and "Dobri Dyehn," or "Good Day."

RELIGION

After World War II Belarusans began to establish their own distinct churches in the United States. The majority of Belarusan immigrants were of the Eastern Orthodox faith. The formal organization of Belarusan Orthodox activities dates from 1949 to 1950, when parishes were founded as part of the Belarusan Autocephalous Orthodox Church (BAOC). Organizational work for the BAOC began in North America under the guidance of Archbishop Vasil, who established his residence in New York City. Liturgical services were conducted in Belarusan. The BAOC conducted an extensive school program that was involved in providing aid to Chernobyl victims. The Chernobyl nuclear accident in 1986 devastated Belarus. Nearly 20 percent of the agricultural land was contaminated, affecting not only the health of thousands of Belarusans but also their livelihoods.

Belarusan Catholics of the Latin Rite have not formed parishes of their own in the United States. Consequently, some Belarusan American Roman Catholics have devoted themselves to civic activities within Belarusan Orthodox communities. Belarusan Catholics of the Byzantine-Slavic Rite (Uniates) organized their own parish in Chicago, primarily through the efforts of two Belarusan activists, Reverend John Tarasevich and his nephew Reverend Uladzimir Tarasevich.

BELARUSAN PROVERBS

- A devil will spot a peer and take him for a beer.

- Wolf is not a shepherd, goat is not a gardener.

- Magpie tells the news to a post, the post spreads it coast to coast.

- Like an angel he ascended, and like a devil descended.

- While one tree stump burned, another's back was warmed.

- God knew why he did not give horns to a pig.

CULTURE AND ASSIMILATION

Belarusans assimilated into the mainstream of American society with relative ease. Because of this, many Belarusans recognized the urgency of cultural preservation. The Belarusan American Association, together with a number of other groups, developed a system of supplementary secondary schools in Belarusan communities where the American-born generations receive education in the language, culture, and religious traditions of Belarus. The task of representing Belarusan culture at various venues throughout the United States has been assumed by choirs, theatrical groups, and musical and dance ensembles.

Perhaps because of their willingness to assimilate, Belarusan Americans faced neither extreme nativism nor racist resistance from other ethnic groups. However, they were sorely misunderstood because on entry into the United States, many were registered as Russians and Poles. Part of the misperception also stems from terminology. As political concepts, the terms "Byelorussia," "Byelorussian," and—since 1991—"Belarus" and "Belarusans" are all relatively new. For most Americans, the term "Byelorussia" was not known until the end of World War II, when the Byelorussian Soviet Socialist Republic became a charter member of the newly forming United Nations. Prior to World War II, the terms more familiar to Americans were "White Russia" and "White Russians" or "White Ruthenia" and "White Ruthenians." The term "White" in these various formulations is simply the literal translation of *byelo-* or *byela-*.

Traditions and Customs Belarusan customs (some of which are shared with neighboring Slavic nations) typically interweave elements of nature, especially agriculture, with pagan and Christian components. Most customs are related to the calendar, ceremonial events, and games. Many customs with roots in Belarus are observed by Belarusan Americans. In the

United States groups such as the Belarusan American Community Centers in Strongsville, Ohio, and South River, New Jersey, sponsor festivals celebrating Belarusan culture at which Belarusan folk music is performed, frequently accompanied by traditional Belarusan dance and costumes. Although the lifestyles of our modern, technological age are not conducive to maintaining folk traditions, it is remarkable how many of them have survived through both time and the Belarusan diaspora. This is especially evident when one examines the thirty-six volumes on Belarusan ethnography published as *Bielaruskaja Narodnaja Tvorcasc* by the Academy of Sciences in Minsk, Belarus, between 1977 and 1993.

Cuisine Cuisine plays an important role in manifesting the hospitality, cordiality, and friendliness implicit in the traditional Belarusan greeting "A guest in the house is God in the house." Belarus is located in the forest, grain, and potato belts of Eastern Europe, and many traditional Belarusan recipes incorporated the riches of the land. Favorite dishes include a wide variety of grains, various mushrooms, meats, and many kinds of fish dishes. These same ingredients were both cheap and easily obtainable for Belarusan immigrants in the United States, and therefore many recipes remained popular for practical reasons. There are, of course, a number of items that Belarusans have in common with their Slavic neighbors, including *halubcy* (stuffed cabbage), borscht, and *kaubasa* (kielbasy). One popular comestible well known to many Americans is the bagel. The traditional bagel comes from the town of Smarhon in the northwestern part of Belarus. However, the potato is, without question, the most famous food of Belarus. The Belarusan housewife has close to 100 ways of preparing potato dishes for every occasion. Likewise, potato dishes are common in Belarusan American cooking due to both tradition and practicality.

Traditional dishes include *draniki* (fried potato pancakes) and *babka* (oven-baked mashed potatoes and lard); various sauces such as *mochanka* (made from mushrooms) and *poliuka*, which accompanies *bliny* (another variety of potato pancake) or meat dishes; soups such as *zatirki* combined with meatballs or dough balls; and desserts such as *kisel* (fruit jellies).

Traditional Costumes The traditional clothing of Belarus was sometimes worn in the United States on holidays (particularly during the Christmas and Easter seasons) by both men and women. Now it can be seen mostly at folk festivals, though it is also worn by dance ensembles at performing art centers and universities and is on exhibit in museums.

The most visible and expressive Belarusan folk art is found in national apparel, where the predominant colors are red, white, black, and occasionally green. Symmetric and geometric designs are the most common features of Belarusan decorative patterns. There are distinct patterns, designs, and materials for men and women. A woman's holiday dress of homespun material consists of a white linen blouse, always ornamented with embroidery or a woven design; an apron, usually of white linen with embroidery; a long pleated skirt of colorful woolen material; a vest, laced or buttoned in the front, often with slits from the waist down; and a headdress. The man's costume is composed of linen trousers and a shirt. The shirt is long, always embroidered, and worn with a handwoven belt or sash.

Traditional Arts and Crafts Among the Belarusan crafts that are widespread in the United States are woven rugs and embroidered table covers and bedspreads. Handwoven belts and embroidered towels are perhaps most prized. Towels have particular significance because they are used for a number of solemn occasions, including weddings and christenings, and for adorning religious orthodox icons, such as portraits of saints. Belarusan American families have dozens of towels for all types of events. Pottery, straw incrustations, and woodcarving are also popular age-old Belarusan crafts practiced throughout the United States. These items are typically adorned with simple geometric designs and are put to more practical uses, rather than kept as art objects.

Dances and Songs Scholars trace the origins of Belarusan music to pagan times. A national characteristic is the tendency to form instrumental groups. Every village in the home country has its own musicians, and that pattern has been replicated in the United States, with virtually every Belarusan community having its own orchestra. The most commonly used instruments are the violin (*skrypka*), accordion (*bajan*), cymbals, pipe (*dudka*), and tambourine.

An important part of the Belarusan musical heritage is the huge repertoire of songs, suitable for every occasion, including birth, marriage, death, entering military service, the change of seasons, work, and leisure. Belarusans sing solos and duets and harmonize in ensembles and choirs. The rich and elaborately lyrical songs that form the basis of Belarusan folk music have a special appeal for Belarusans. Singing is often accompanied by one or more instruments, very often the *husli* (psaltery). The lullaby is especially popular in Belarusan families. Generations of children have grown up learning the lyrics to these songs, which are sung to them by their mothers and grandmothers.

Dancing has similarly enjoyed a millennium-long life span in Belarus, and this tradition has continued in the United States. Belarusan folk dancing is characterized by the richness of its composition, uncomplicated movements, and a small number of rapid steps. Folk dances are often accompanied by songs expressing the feelings, work habits, and lifestyle of the people. Ethnographers have identified more than 100 Belarusan folk dances, many of which are performed in the United States. The legacy of song and dance is an aspect of the native culture that is shared by both old and new immigrants, transcending generational barriers.

Holidays Among Belarusan Americans, traditional Belarusan practices and customs are seen most frequently during the holiday seasons. The Christmas season, for example, includes many unique customs. One of the most cherished and carefully preserved traditions is the celebration of *kuccia*, a very solemn and elaborate supper on Christmas Eve. Twelve or more dishes are prepared and served. Each dish is served in a specific order, with a portion set aside for the ancestors. The pot holding the *kuccia* (a special barley confection) is placed in the corner of the room under the religious icons. After the family says grace, the *kuccia* is the first course served. Another widely observed custom is the decoration of the Christmas tree with handmade Belarusan ornaments. As a rule, the entire family takes part in the ceremony, with the oldest family members contributing most of the craftsmanship. Caroling, more widespread than any other Christmas tradition, is solidly maintained by Belarusan Americans both of the older and younger generations, with the latter employing this custom as a means of fundraising for cultural organizations.

The Easter season is another occasion for the observance of traditional customs among Belarusan Americans. The season begins with a period of fasting, followed by *Vierbnica* (Palm Sunday) and flower-arranging competitions to see who can create the finest bouquet. Following the Easter Liturgy, the priest blesses colored eggs, sausage, *babka* (special Easter bread), and cheese. An Easter breakfast, *Razhavieny*, is held in the parish hall where traditional foods are served. Easter Sunday is given over to visiting friends and relatives and to playing various games, such as cracking the Easter eggs.

The most widely observed sanctified feast day is that of Saint Euphrosynia of Polacak, the patron saint of Belarus. Her feast day, May 23, is traditionally celebrated by all Belarusans. Belarusan Americans also have a special devotion to Saint Cyril of Turov, whose feast day falls on April 28. The Mother of God of Zyrovicy is the patroness of many Belarusan churches. Her patronal feast is May 20. Other church-related customs and anniversaries observed by Belarusan Americans are *Adzihitrya* (Guide), observed on August 10; the Feast of Pentecost/Whitsunday; and the Feast of All the Saints of Belarus (the third Sunday after Pentecost). Belarusan Roman Catholics observe the feast of Our Lady of Vostraja Brama in Vilna on November 16 and Saint Mary of Budslau on July 2, among others.

Nonreligious holidays include March 25, which celebrates Belarus's independence from Russia in 1918, and August 25, which celebrates its independence from the former Soviet Union (1991). Both are important to Belarusan Americans, many of whom emigrated in order to be free of Communist rule.

FAMILY AND COMMUNITY LIFE

During the nineteenth and early twentieth centuries, the typical Belarusan family was a large communal group. Incorporating distant relatives or even strangers, the family was held together by the work each contributed to the farm rather than by blood relationships. Most often the father or grandfather acted as family head. He assigned the men jobs and acted as trustee for the family property, which was collectively owned. Although modern Belarusan and Belarusan American families no longer interact in the same way, some of the family leader's authority remains. For instance, at family gatherings, the head sits in the place of honor, with the other men grouped by rank around him.

Gender Roles Although gender roles in Belarus remain traditional in the sense that men are typically the breadwinners and women take care of the children and household, Belarusan American women have assimilated with ease into American culture. They have joined many women's organizations and typically have careers. Belarusan American women have also shown support for women's organizations that have recently sprung up in Belarus, such as the Women's Liberal Association and the League of Women Electors. However, despite Belarusan American women's efforts, Belarusan culture still strongly adheres to sex-role stereotypes.

Education Many organizations and associations have been created for the purpose of educating Belarusan American youth, primarily by promoting and preserving Belarusan traditions. The Belarusan-American Association (BAZA), for example, has worked with numerous organizations and communities to create secondary schools in order to preserve the Belarusan language and culture in the United States. BAZA helps publish books and periodicals on Belarusan topics. Other groups, such as the Belarusan Youth Movement of America, focus not only on educational and cultural projects in the United States but also on promoting democracy and human rights in Belarus.

Surnames Widespread and recognizable, traditional Belarusan surnames include Barsuk, Kalosha, Kresla, Savionak, and Sienka. Belarusan surnames are often based on geographical origin (e.g., Babruiski, Minskii, Mogilevskii, Slutski, and Vilenski). Many others derive from baptismal names (e.g., Jakubau, Haponau, Kazimirau, or such diminutives as Jakubionak and Hapanionak). The most typical Belarusan surnames are those with the suffixes "-ovich" or "-ievich," such as Dashkievich, Mickievich, Zmitrovich. Others derive from occupations (e.g., Dziak, Hrabar, Mular).

EMPLOYMENT AND ECONOMIC CONDITIONS

Upon entering the United States in the nineteenth and early twentieth centuries, most Belarusan Americans moved to mining towns and industrial cities. They worked in mines and in industrial jobs ranging from textiles and shoes to steel and machinery. Today many immigrants, particularly those of Jewish origin, move for filial reasons (to reunite with families) rather than for political and economic reasons. They receive support from family if necessary and assimilate with ease, taking on jobs involving both skilled and unskilled labor, depending on the individual's work experience. Hyperinflation in Belarus has spurred increased immigration to the United States; many Belarusans of the Jewish faith have joined family in Israel.

POLITICS AND GOVERNMENT

Relations with Belarus The idea of Belarusan statehood and separateness began to surface in non-Belarusan publications such as the newspapers *Novyi Mir*, *Russkii Golos*, and *Novoye Russkoye Slovo*. These Russian American newspapers not only published materials of interest to Belarusan immigrants but also wholeheartedly supported Belarusan independence and the establishment of Belarusan ethnic organizations. Through contacts with the homeland and the printed word, the concepts of national separateness, national self-awareness, and Belarusan independence were communicated to the Belarusan American immigrant communities, inspiring them to come together and form specifically Belarusan ethnic organizations.

The political activities of Belarusan groups consist mainly of lobbying various political groups and individual political leaders to support the idea of a democratic and independent Belarusan state. The Belarusan American Association has been a champion in this undertaking in the recent past, having written thousands of memoranda and visited hundreds of legislators at all levels to solicit political support for Belarus's independence movement. The Belarusian Youth Movement of America is also active in the political life of American Belarusans. They continue to bring letters of attention concerning the political situation in Belarus to the U.S. government.

NOTABLE INDIVIDUALS

Belarusan Americans are immigrants or descendants of people from Belarus. Because Belarus was recently part of the former Soviet Union, some of the individuals listed below were previously and inaccurately labeled Russian American.

Academia Noam Chomsky (1928–) is a linguist, philosopher, logician, historian, and activist who has taught at the Massachusetts Institute of Technology (MIT) for more than fifty years. He has written more than 100 books, including *Manufacturing Consent: The Political Economy of the Mass Media* (1988), and is considered one of the most important scholars of the twentieth century.

Art Yelena Tylkina (1965–) is a fine artist born in Belarus and living in New York. Her works have won numerous awards and have appeared in many museums, including the Belarus Museum in Brooklyn, New York, and the Museum of Contemporary Art in Baltimore, Maryland.

Belarusan American author
Gary Vaynerchuck (1975–).
EUGENE GOLOGURSKY /
GETTY IMAGES

Business David Sarnoff (1891–1971) was a businessman and executive at the electronics company RCA. Sarnoff was inducted into the National Association of Broadcasters Hall of Fame in 1977 and was posthumously inducted into the Radio Hall of Fame in 1989. The David Sarnoff Library, located in Princeton Junction, New Jersey, contains many historical items from his life.

Fashion Ralph Lauren (1939–) is a fashion designer most famous for his Ralph Lauren Polo label. His company reported revenues of 5 billion dollars for the 2009 fiscal year. Lauren has won many awards and was decorated Chevalier de la Legion d'honneur by French president Nicolas Sarkozy.

Film Film actor Kirk Douglas (1916–) is considered to be one of the finest male actors in Hollywood history and received an Academy Honorary Award in 1996. He has starred in many well-known movies, including Disney's *20,000 Leagues Under the Sea* (1954), *Gunfight at the O.K. Corral* (1957), and *Spartacus* (1960).

Michael Douglas (1944–), son of Kirk Douglas, is an actor and producer. He has won three Golden Globe Awards and two Academy Awards, including an award for best actor for his role in *Wall Street* (1987).

Harrison Ford (1942–) is a film actor best known for his role as Han Solo in the original *Star Wars* trilogy. He also starred in the *Indiana Jones* franchise.

Literature Isaac Asimov (1920–1992) was a prolific science fiction writer best known for his *Foundation Trilogy* and *I, Robot*, a collection of short stories first published in 1950. Asimov won multiple Hugo and Nebula Awards, and was posthumously inducted into the Science Fiction and Fantasy Hall of Fame in 1997.

Media Larry King (1933–) is a television and radio host known for his program *Larry King Live*, which aired on CNN for twenty-five years. King is recognized as a philanthropist, airing programs to help those in need after the natural disasters of Hurricane Katrina (2005) and the Haiti earthquake of 2010.

Jazep Varonka (1891–1952) served as the prime minister of the Belarusan National Republic before coming to the United States in 1923. He started the first Belarusan newspaper in the United States, *The White Ruthenian Tribune* (1926), and pioneered radio broadcasts in the Belarusan language (1929).

Music Irving Berlin (1888–1989), a prolific songwriter, composer, and lyricist, wrote scores for nineteen Broadway shows, including *Annie Get Your Gun* (1946), and eighteen Hollywood films, including *Easter Parade* (1948) and *White Christmas* (1954). He is considered by many to be one of the world's greatest songwriters.

MEDIA

Belarus Digest

Bimonthly online newsletter providing nonpartisan analysis of Belarus-related events from around the world. It was launched in Washington, D.C., in 2008 by Yarik Kryvoi.

Yarik Kryvoi, Editor in Chief
URL: www.belarusdigest.com

Belarus Today

Weekly English-language paper that includes politics, economy, culture, science and technology, entertainment, and sports.

URL: http://belarustoday.info/?new_lang_id=2

Belarus TV

A satellite television station owned by Belteleradio Company, which also operates the radio station Radio Belarus. Founded in 2005, the company broadcasts children's programs, sporting and music events, and news to Belarusan/Russian-speaking people living abroad.

9 Makayonka Street
Minsk, Belarus 220807
Phone: +375 17 389-61-46
Fax: +375 17 267-84-32
Email: belarus-tv@tvr.by
URL: www.tvr.by/eng

Belarusian Telegraph Agency

Provides Belarusan news in English, including politics, economy, culture, and sports.

URL: www.belta.by/en

ORGANIZATIONS AND ASSOCIATIONS

Belarusan American Association, Inc. (BAZA)

Promotes the preservation and celebration of Belarusan history and culture in the United States.

166-34 Gothic Drive
Jamaica, New York 11432
Phone: (908) 247-1822
Email: baza.hq@hotmail.com
URL: www.bazahq.org

Belarusan American Community Center

Preserves and furthers Belarusan heritage, language, and culture.

11022 Webster Road
Strongsville, Ohio 44136
Phone: (440) 572-3008
Fax: (440) 572-3008
Email: bacc@polacak.org
URL: www.polacak.org

Belarusan Youth Movement of America

Focuses on educational, social, and cultural projects and aims to develop democracy and human rights in Belarus.

URL: www.belmov.org

North American Association for Belarusian Studies

Seeks to promote research and teaching in Belarusian studies, including the fields of linguistics, history, art, anthropology, political science, and economics.

Email: maria.survilla@wartburg.edu
URL: www.belarusianstudies.org
Contact: Maria Paula Survilla, President

MUSEUMS AND RESEARCH CENTERS

Center for Slavic, Eurasian, and East European Studies at Duke University

303 Languages Building
105 Campus Drive
Durham, North Carolina 27708
Phone: (919) 660-3157
Fax: (919) 660-3188
URL: www.duke.edu/web/CSEEES

Department of Russian and Slavic Studies at New York University

19 University Place
New York, NY 10003
Phone: (212) 998-8050
Fax: (212) 995-4557
Email: eliot.borenstein@nyu.edu

World-renowned designer, Ralph Lauren, was born in the Bronx to Jewish parents who had emigrated from Belarus. THEO WARGO / WIREIMAGE / GETTY IMAGES

SOURCES FOR ADDITIONAL STUDY

Belarus: Then and Now (series). Minneapolis, MN: Lerner Publications, 1993.

Byelorussian Cultural Tradition in America. New Brunswick, NJ: Rutgers University, 1983.

Dowswell, Paul. *The Chernobyl Disaster*. London: Hodder Wayland, 2003.

Kipel, Vitaut. *Belarusans in the United States*. Lanham, MD: University Press of America, 1999.

Mort, Valzhyna. *Factory of Tears*. Trans. Elizabeth and Franz Wright. Port Townsend, WA: Copper Canyon Press, 2008.

Odrach, Theodore. *Wave of Terror*. Trans. Erma Odrach. Chicago: Academy Chicago Publishers, 2008.

Roberts, Nigel. *Belarus: The Bradt Travel Guide*. New York: The Globe Pequot Press, 2011.

Zaprudnik, Jan. *Historical Dictionary of Belarus*. Lanham, MD: Scarecrow Press, 1998.

BELGIAN AMERICANS

Jane Stewart Cook

OVERVIEW

Belgian Americans are immigrants from Belgium or the American descendants of immigrants from Belgium. Belgium, whose official name is the Kingdom of Belgium, is a densely populated country not much larger than the state of Maryland. It covers an area of 11,781 square miles (30,519 square kilometers), bounded on the north by the Netherlands, on the west by France, and on the east by Germany and the tiny nation of Luxembourg. The country is divided into three regions: Northern Lowlands, Central Lowlands, and Southern Hilly Region. Belgium's strategic location has earned the country the sobriquet "the crossroads of Europe." Brussels, its capital city, is just a three-hour drive from The Hague, the capital of the Netherlands, and from Paris, the capital of France.

According to the U.S. State Department, the population of Belgium was about 10.5 million in 2012. The Flemish, who reside in Flanders, the northern half of the country, speak Dutch. They make up the majority of Belgium's population. Wallonia, roughly the southern of the country, is occupied by the French-speaking Walloons. One percent of the population speaks German, principally those who reside near the German border. About 75 percent of Belgians are Roman Catholic, with Protestants, Jews, and Muslims making up the remainder of the population. Belgium has a relatively high GDP, ranked thirty-second in the world in 2012. However, the nation's economy is especially vulnerable to volatility in world markets, and several Belgian banks experienced severe negative effects from the international financial crisis that began in 2008.

The first Belgians arrived in the United States in the seventeenth century. The period of greatest Belgian immigration began was in the nineteenth century. Belgian immigrants first settled primarily in New York and New Jersey, but by the 1840s many Belgians were settling in the Midwest. The majority of nineteenth-century Belgian immigrants were farmers, miners, and other manual laborers. Following World War II, many middle-class professionals from Belgium immigrated to the United States seeking employment in the areas of science, technology, or education. Owing to stable political and economic conditions in Belgium during the second half of the

twentieth century and the early twenty-first century, Belgian immigration decreased dramatically. In the early twenty-first century most Belgian immigrants were highly trained professionals who were seeking career advancement and middle- to upper-class youth who were pursuing higher education.

According to the U.S. Census, the number of people of Belgian descent residing in the United States in 2010 was about 345,000—approximately twice the population of Providence, Rhode Island. Small numbers of Belgian Americans can be found in many parts of the country, with the biggest concentrations in the rural areas of Wisconsin, Michigan, and Illinois. In 2012 Wisconsin had the largest population of Belgian Americans, the majority of them residing in three counties: Door, Brown, and Kewaunee. Belgian Americans who live in cities have largely assimilated into American society and no longer live in immigrant communities.

HISTORY OF THE PEOPLE

Early History From approximately 57 BCE to 431 CE, Rome ruled over Gaul, an area of what is now France, Belgium, Luxembourg, and Germany. The land was inhabited at the time by independent tribes of Celtic origin. Julius Caesar's account of his efforts to subdue the area provides the first written record of what came to be called Belgium. The Romans considered Belgium a defensive barrier against the Franks, Germanic tribes that settled in what is now Flanders. The difference in languages spoken in the region continued to the preset day, with the Germanic speech in the north eventually evolving into Dutch and the Latin of Rome spoken to its south eventually developing into French.

With the collapse of the Roman Empire in the fifth century, the Franks held sway for more than 550 years. After the death of the Frankish king Louis the Pious in 840, the Frankish empire was divided roughly into France, the Holy Roman Empire (Germany), and the "Middle Kingdom," which extended from the area of the Low Countries, including Belgium, to northern Italy. In 1516 Belgium became a possession of Spain and remained so until 1713, when the country was given to Austria as settlement in the War of the Spanish Succession. Belgium was annexed by France in 1795, and after Napoleon's defeat in the Battle of Waterloo in 1815, it was placed under the rule of the Netherlands. In 1830 Belgium declared its independence, adopted a constitution, and chose its first king, Leopold I. He was succeeded in 1865 by his son Leopold II.

Modern Era During World War I, Belgium was overrun by Germany. More than 80,000 Belgians died in the conflict. However, under the personal command of their "soldier king," Albert I, Belgium managed to hold on to some territory until the defeat of the Germans by Allied forces in 1918. In World War II, Adolf Hitler bombed Belgium into submission and took its new king, Leopold III, prisoner until the end of the war. The arrival of Allied forces in 1944 was followed by the Battle of the Bulge, a major German offensive that took place in part on Belgian soil. It turned into a decisive Allied victory that hastened the end of the war. Belgium rebuilt its war-torn country, became a founding member of the United Nations and the North Atlantic Treaty Organization, and by the 1960s was enjoying a prosperous economy. Belgium has been a leader in the movement toward European economic integration, and in 1958 it became a founding member of the European Economic Community.

Belgian society has become increasingly divided in the late twentieth and early twenty-first centuries owing to linguistic, political, and economic differences between French-speaking Wallonia and Dutch-speaking Flanders. These divisions led to the enforcement of an official linguistic border beginning in the 1960s and the formation of Flemish and Francophone cultural councils in 1970. Belgium's three main economic regions—Wallonia, Flanders, and Brussels—continue to maintain a certain level of political, cultural, and linguistic autonomy to this day.

Belgium is a founding member of the European Union (EU). Officially established in 1993, the EU had roots in the European Economic Community and the European Coal and Steel Community dating to the 1950s. The EU introduced the euro as its currency in 1999 and, after the Belgian franc was phased out, circulation of the euro in Belgium officially began in 2002. Belgium is the location of the EU's headquarters. Several other pivotal international organizations, including the North Atlantic Treaty Organization (NATO), are also centered in Belgium. In 2003 Belgium legally recognized same-sex marriage, becoming only the second country in the world to do so. Adoption by same-sex partners was not included in the law, however, and it was not until 2006 that the parliament legalized adoption by same-sex couples. By that year, 3,500 same-sex couples had married in Belgium.

Over the past several decades Flanders has experienced rapid economic development while Wallonia's steel and coal industries have suffered. Consequently, Flanders and its Flemish inhabitants have gained greater economic and political power. Belgium underwent a political crisis beginning in 2007 caused by growing tensions between the Flemish and the Walloons. Powerful Flanders accused the Walloons of being dependent on Flemish economic assistance, while the Walloon community accused Flanders of having a segregationist language policy. The crisis resulted in the dissolution of both houses of parliament in May 2010 after the parliament adopted a declaration that called for constitutional review. Although the crisis subsided after prolonged formal negotiations in 2011, political divisiveness within the country remained high, and there was soon renewed talk of Belgian partition.

SETTLEMENT IN THE UNITED STATES

In the seventeenth century Belgians participated in the early European settlement of what is now Manhattan. Many historians believe that Peter Minuit, who acted as purchasing agent for the West Indian Company when Manhattan Island was bought from the resident Native Americans, was a Walloon, or at least of Belgian heritage.

Henry C. Bayer, in his book *The Belgians, First Settlers in New York and in the Middle States*, discusses Belgian settlements at Wallabout (Long Island), Staten Island, and several places in New Jersey, including Hoboken, Jersey City, Pavonia, Communipaw, and Wallkill. These place names are derived names used by the Walloons who settled there or from the Dutch version of Walloon words used to describe a locale. For example, Hoboken is named after a town in Belgium. Pavonia got its name when a Fleming, Michael Pauw, purchased land on the Jersey shore. Translating his own name, Pauw (which in Flemish and Dutch means "peacock"), into Latin, he got "Pavonia." Wallkill is the Dutch word for "Walloon's Stream."

A notable name connected with American early history is Lord Baltimore, whose relatives were prominent aristocrats in Flemish Belgium. Some Belgian officers fought during the Revolutionary War, including Charles De Pauw—the aide-de-camp to Lafayette, the French general who fought for the United States—Ensign Thomas Van Gaasbeck, Captain Jacques Rapalje, and Captain Anthony Van Etten.

Belgians came to the United States in greatest numbers during the nineteenth century. The reasons they immigrated were the same for many other western Europeans—financial opportunity and a better life for their families. Belgian immigration records do not appear until 1820. From 1820 to 1910, the number of Belgian immigrants was 104,000, and from 1910 to 1950, some 62,000 Belgians came to the United States. During the period from 1847 to 1849, when disease and economic deprivation were the lot for many in Belgium, the number of Belgian immigrants to the United States reached 6,000 to 7,000 a year. Most of those coming to the United States at that time

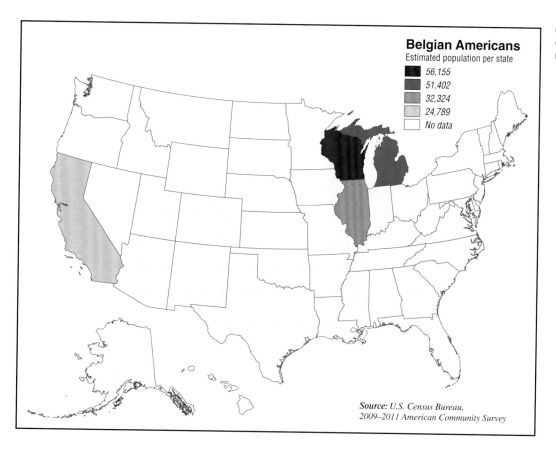

Belgian Americans
Estimated population per state

- 56,155
- 51,402
- 32,324
- 24,789
- No data

*Source: U.S. Census Bureau,
2009–2011 American Community Survey*

were small landowners (farmers), agricultural laborers, and miners; craftspeople such as carpenters, masons, and cabinetmakers; and other skilled tradespeople, such as glassblowers and lace makers.

In the nineteenth century Belgian American settlement patterns reflected work opportunities. The glass industry attracted many Belgian Americans to West Virginia and Pennsylvania. Detroit, Michigan, attracted building tradespeople. Door, Brown, and Kewaunee counties in Wisconsin attracted those seeking farmland. This rural region of Wisconsin became one of the most unique cultural regions in the United States and is often referred to as the "Belgian Ethnic Island." Considerable numbers settled in Indiana. Substantial pockets of Belgian Americans can also be found in Illinois, Minnesota, North Dakota, Ohio, Kentucky, Florida, Washington, and Oregon. Many towns and cities across the United States bear the names of their counterparts in Belgium, including Liege, Charleroi, Ghent, Antwerp, Namur, Rosiere, and Brussels.

The Belgian American settlement in Detroit took place mainly between 1880 and 1910. Most of the new arrivals were skilled Flemish craftspeople. Detroit's early industrial and manufacturing growth was fueled in great part by their skills in the building trades and in transportation. According to Jozef Kadijk, whose 1963 lecture at Loyola University

in Chicago appears in *Belgians in the United States*, approximately 10,000 residents of Detroit at that time were born in Belgium. Taking their descendants into account is said to increase that figure to 50,000. Most of the Wisconsin Belgians were Walloons from the areas of Brabant and Liege, Belgium. They had begun arriving in substantial numbers by 1853, following the lure of farmland that could be purchased from $0.50 to $1.25 an acre. Here they cleared fields, felled trees, and built rude log shelters to house their families. Writing to their countrymen back home about their satisfaction with their new lives, they soon were joined by thousands of fellow Belgian immigrants. The 1860 census shows about 4,300 foreign-born Belgians living in Brown and Kewaunee counties.

Following World War II, many middle-class and urban professionals left Belgium for the United States, seeking work in universities, laboratories, and industrial corporations. Altogether, it is estimated that from 1820 to 1970 approximately 200,000 Belgian immigrants settled in the United States. Each year since 1950, a fixed quota of 1,350 has remained unfilled, and by 2010 Belgians represented less than 0.1 percent of the foreign-born population, according to the U.S. Census. The few Belgians who immigrated to the United States in the late twentieth and early twenty-first centuries did so for career or educational opportunities.

FLEMISH PROVERBS

Stel niet uit tot morgen wat je heden kunt doen.

Delay not until tomorrow what you can do now.

Wie hierbinnen komt zijn onze vrienden.

Those who enter here are our friends.

Avondrood brengt water in de sloot.

Red sky at night brings water in the stream.

Beter een half ei dan een lege dop.

Better half an egg than an empty shell.

Zwijgen en denken kan niemand krenken.

Silence and thinking hurts no one.

LANGUAGE

The official languages of Belgium are Dutch, French, and German. Because of geographic and cultural circumstances, a natural language boundary runs west to east, roughly through the center of the country. Dutch, commonly referred to as Flemish, is spoken in the northern part of the country, and Walloon, a local dialect of French, is spoken in the southern part. (German is spoken by a small minority—about one percent of Belgium's population—along Belgium's border with Germany.) Because of their proximity to France, Walloons hold the French language in high regard, using it as the standard for their own. The Flemings, in contrast, share many customs and beliefs, as well as the Dutch language, with the people of the Netherlands.

In the past, attempts to force an official adoption of either French or Dutch by towns along the language boundary caused great dissension. To settle these disputes, laws were passed in the early 1960s making the language boundary permanent. As a result, both Dutch and French are the official languages, and two distinct cultures flourish side by side. Many Belgians switch back and forth between the two languages, using their native dialect with family and friends and either Dutch or French in public or formal situations. Even though both Dutch and French are the official languages of the country, they are still not regarded by all Belgians as equal in value. The following proverbs illustrate how the two languages are viewed: French in the parlor, Flemish in the kitchen; You speak the language of the man whose bread you eat; It is necessary to cease being Flemish in order to become Belgian.

Belgian immigrants in the United States used the primary language they spoke in their homeland in Belgium. Before World War I, the Flemish and Walloon languages were commonly used by first-generation Belgians. Gradually, most Belgian Americans lost the ability to speak either Dutch or French. Immigrant parents were eager to have their children learn English, and today few retain more than a word or two in the old language. Individuals who were at least fifty years old in the mid-1970s spoke French in a family environment but had to speak English in school. By 2010, with the majority of the Belgian American population consisting of at least third- or fourth-generation immigrants, more than 90 percent of Belgian-origin individuals reported speaking only English at home.

RELIGION

The majority of Belgian Americans are of the Roman Catholic faith, although some are Presbyterians and Episcopalians. By 1900, Belgian religious orders were thriving in sixteen states. The Sisters of Notre Dame, from Namur, Belgium, were successful in establishing bilingual schools in fourteen of those states; the Benedictines built missions in the western part of the country, and the Jesuits, who founded St. Louis University in 1818, were able to expand the reach of the university through the use of Belgian teachers and benefactors. Nevertheless, Belgian immigrants often had no churches of their own, mainly because they assimilated at a faster rate in the more populous areas, attending Catholic churches founded by other ethnic Catholics, such as German or French Americans. Two of the more homogeneous groups—in Door County, Wisconsin, and Detroit, Michigan—were successful in establishing churches of their own.

In 1853 the Belgian missionary Father Edward Daems helped a group of immigrants establish a community in northeastern Wisconsin in an area called Bay Settlement. They called it *Aux premiers Belges*— The First Belgians. By 1860 St. Hubert's Church in Bay Settlement and St. Mary's in Namur were built. Other Belgian churches established during the nineteenth century in Door County were St. Michael's, St. John the Baptist, and St. Joseph's. In 1861 the French Presbyterian Church was established in Green Bay. Small roadside chapels were also built to serve those who lived too far away to attend parish churches regularly. The chapels were named by worshipers in honor of patron saints.

In 1834 Father Bonduel of Commnes, Belgium, became the first priest to be ordained in Detroit. The first Catholic College (1836) in Detroit was operated by Flemish Belgian priests, and the first school for girls was founded by an order of Belgian nuns in 1834. By 1857, Catholics in Detroit were a sizable group. However, they had no church of their own and were, at that time, worshipping with other Catholics at St. Anne's Church. This was remedied in 1884, when the first Belgian parish was established.

With the consolidation of many Catholic parishes throughout the United States, even Belgian Americans in small, stable communities may no longer attend an ethnically affiliated church. As with, for example, the German Catholic and the French Catholic parish churches in the United States, many U.S. Belgian Catholic parishes have died out or have merged with other parishes. Remnants of Belgian Catholicism still remain, however, in parts of rural United States—particularly Wisconsin—where small votive chapels built by Belgian families dating back to the nineteenth and early twentieth centuries are still used. Today Belgian Americans use the chapels as places of prayer and for small religious gatherings. In the early 1990s there were twenty-four chapels still being used actively by Belgian Americans in Door County, Wisconsin

CULTURE AND ASSIMILATION

Belgians are western Europeans, and as such, generally presented a familiar religious and cultural background in their new homeland. Stereotypical notions as to traits of character often depict the Dutch-influenced Fleming as reserved, stubborn, practical, and vigorous, while the passion of France is observed in the Walloon's wit, extroversion, and quickness of mind and temper. It is true that whether Flemish or Walloon, the influences of the Netherlands, Germany, and France upon their language, religion, and social customs are evident. This helped to make their assimilation easier—although they sometimes met with a strong anti-Catholic sentiment, which equated allegiance to the Roman Catholic Church with disloyalty to the United States, in many parts of the United States. In early days rural populations tended to remain homogeneous, separated mainly by distance from other communities. They relied on others of their own group to help them survive. Strong identification with one's own group gave comfort and protection to those sharing a common language and heritage. However, the Walloons who settled in northeast Wisconsin found their way made easier because of the established French Catholic communities. In general, the Flemings, with higher education levels and sought-after job skills, suffered less prejudice than the Walloons, the majority of whom were poor, unskilled, and illiterate. Through their industry and thrift, however, these poor farmers soon won the respect of their neighbors.

In time, Belgian Americans became admired not only for their industry and down-to-earth outlook but also for their sociable character and friendly manner. With growing access to transportation, employment, and education, and the settlement of other nationalities nearby, Belgians began to seek interaction with others outside their group. Belgian hospitality and the retention of many old-world customs and traditions gave color and vitality to the communities in which they resided. Another factor that both hastened assimilation and fostered ethnic pride was the tragic experience of Belgium during World War I and World War II. The sympathy extended to Belgian Americans by others led them to emphasize their origins and culture.

Traditions and Customs It is said that a Belgian, whether Fleming or Walloon, is an inveterate hand shaker. On meeting, greeting, and parting, prolonged handshakes are the rule. This custom is thought to stem from ancient times, when a man's handshake proved he held no weapon. Belgians' belief in the value of the community and their sturdy outlook on life have helped them recover from plague, famine, World War I, World War II, and economic depression. Those characteristics have also contributed to the progress and well-being of Belgian Americans. For example, in 1871 a devastating Wisconsin forest fire (known as the "Peshtigo Fire") destroyed land, farms, and residences in an area 6 miles wide and 60 miles long. The Belgian communities of northeast Wisconsin were destroyed, leaving 5,000 homeless to face the coming winter, but by 1874 the resilient inhabitants of the area had managed to completely rebuild their communities. Up to the time of the fire, most homes had been built of wood, because it was plentiful and cheap. After the fire, however, many new homes and other structures were built of red brick. Trimmed in white and sturdy and square in design, they were reminiscent of buildings in the Belgian homeland. Even today, many fine examples of this form of architecture can be found throughout the Belgian farming communities in Wisconsin.

Many Belgian Americans lived long distances from hospitals or doctors, and many others could not afford medical services. Therefore, folk remedies and home cures were common. A poultice made of flax seed and applied to the chest was thought to help with fever and colds. Other remedies used include "King of Pain" liniment for aches and sprains, "Sunrise Herb Tea" for constipation, and cobwebs placed on wounds to stop bleeding.

Every ethnic group that came to the United States in the nineteenth century could not help but be influenced by other cultures. As ties with the old country weakened, these groups became more and more Americanized, and for the most part they were eager to do so. All groups, however, kept land-of-origin customs and beliefs alive through religious and social practices. Belgian Americans have been very successful in preserving their secular and religious traditions.

Cuisine Belgians have a love affair with food and revere the act of eating. To rush through a meal is thought to be uncivilized behavior. Belgian food is hearty and rich, and it is often accompanied by beer. Indeed, there are more than three hundred varieties of beer brewed in Belgium, and the amount of beer consumed nationally, per capita, is second only to Germany. Although many dishes in Belgian cooking are the same for the Flemish and the Walloons, there are differences. For example, Flemish cooking features sweet-salt and sweet-sour mixtures (such as sauerkraut and pickles). Nutmeg is a favored spice in Flemish cooking. Walloon cuisine is based on French techniques and ingredients, and its favored seasoning is garlic.

As in Belgium, a typical Belgian American family meal begins with a thick vegetable soup, followed by meat and vegetables. Pork sausages made with cabbage and seasonings are called *tripes à l'djote* (or Belgian tripe); *boulettes* are meatballs. *Djote*, or "jut," is cooked cabbage and potatoes seasoned with browned butter, pepper, salt, and nutmeg, while *potasse* is a dish of potatoes, red cabbage, and side pork (which is the same cut as bacon, but uncured). A homemade cottage cheese called *kaset* is often included with the meal. This spreadable cheese is cured in crocks and used like butter. For dessert there is Belgian pie, which is an open-faced tart filled with custard or cottage cheese, then topped with layers of prunes or apples.

Some traditional Flemish foods include: *geperste kop*, or head cheese, which is not cheese but the renderings from a pig's head, ears, and stomach made into a jellylike product; *olie bollen*, a raised doughnut made with apples; and *advocaat*, a liqueur made of grain alcohol, vanilla, eggs, milk, and sugar. Both Flemish and Walloon cultures share the traditional use of Belgian endive (chicory) in their cooking. Mussels are also a food that is commonly prepared in both Flemish and Walloon communities. Traditionally eaten during the summer, mussels are steamed in their shells in large pots and are served in many different sauces, although vegetable broth is the most traditional flavoring.

A pastry called *cougnou*, which is shaped like the baby Jesus, is a special Christmas treat for Walloons. Another Walloon Christmas tradition is a wafflelike cookie called *bona*, or *guilette*, which is made with a special baking iron. The Belgian waffle, called *gället*, although a traditional food eaten on New Year's Day, has been Americanized and is commonly found on restaurant menus.

Belgians have been known for their expertise in bread baking. Traditionally, a huge outdoor oven was used for baking. The oven, made of masonry and stone, protruded from a structure called the bakehouse, which was also made of masonry and stone and had walls two feet thick. The bakehouse chimney and interior of the oven were red brick. The oven could bake as many as fifty loaves of bread at one time. After the bread finished baking, the oven would be just hot enough for baking pies. Some of these picturesque ovens still exist in rural Belgian American communities, although few of them are still in use.

Clothing The early Belgian immigrants were usually clothed in homespun cloth and caps. Wooden shoes called *sabots* (by Walloons) or *klompen* (by the Flemish) were traditional footwear for men, women, and children. They wore these shoes outdoors and left them by the door when entering the house. Some immigrants brought from Belgium the knowledge and the tools for making wooden shoes. Belgian Americans who could afford them wore wooden shoes decorated with carvings of leaves and flowers. Children sometimes used their wooden shoes as skates or sleds.

Belgian lace, the fine handwork that originated in sixteenth-century Flanders, is often used to trim religious vestments, altar cloths, handkerchiefs, tablecloths, napkins, and bed linens. This fine art used to be practiced by Belgian immigrants wherever they settled in the United States.

The organizers of the kermis (also spelled kermess or kermesse)—a Belgian harvest festival—wear red, white, and blue sashes while leading the people of the community in a procession to a church where they give thanks. Belgian Americans who are assimilated into American culture rarely wear this traditional clothing.

Dances and Songs At the kermis festivities, people sing revolutionary songs of the old country, such as the Brabanconne and the Marseillaise. During the procession to church, people perform the "Dance of the Dust" on the dirt road. This dance honors the soil from which the harvest is reaped. At social gatherings, Belgians may sing drinking songs such as "Society of the Long Clay Pipe" (a Walloon song) and songs from particular Belgian towns and cities. "Li Bia Bouquet," for example, honors the province of Namur. Local bands that play at weddings, festivals, and other social occasions typically consist of cornet, slide trombone, violin, clarinet, and bass drum, and they offer waltzes, quadrilles, and two-steps.

Holidays The festival of kermis (also spelled kermess or kermesse) celebrates the harvest and generally lasts six consecutive weeks. The festival has long been observed in the United States. Masses are held to give thanks, and there is much feasting, dancing, and singing. Games that are played include the card game called "conion" and a greased-pole climb. The celebration of kermis has persisted to the present day in rural Belgian American communities.

In the past many Belgian Americans would celebrate Assumption Day (August 15), which honors the Virgin Mary and her ascension into heaven. In rural areas a field mass was part of the celebration. This holiday celebration began in the morning, with clergy clad in white vestments and a choir singing Gregorian chant. Although Assumption Day is still honored by some devout Catholics of Belgian origin, the tradition is no longer as common among today's Belgian American communities.

Another Catholic holiday celebrated by Belgian Americans is Rogation Day. On the last Monday in May, people would traditionally gather to petition the Virgin Mary for her blessings on their new plantings. A procession would be made to the church or shrine honoring the Virgin. Young girls dressed in white with long veils would strew flowers along the way. Although this tradition is still alive among devout Catholics, as with Assumption Day it is not as widely practiced by Belgian Americans today.

Belgian Americans celebrate traditional religious holidays such as Christmas and Easter. They also celebrate St. Nicholas Day, on December 6. In the early days, men of the community would dress up like St. Nicholas (the Dutch version of Santa Claus) and go from house to house, leaving candy and small presents for the children. Today, for many Belgian Americans, this holiday marks the beginning of the Christmas season.

Health Care Issues and Practices There are no documented physical or mental afflictions that affect Belgian Americans any more than affect the general population. Belgian Americans have access to health and life insurance through their employers or at their own expense. However, in the past, beneficial societies would be formed to provide this coverage, usually for a nominal monthly fee. These benefits often exist in some form today to the extent that membership is held in various Belgian fraternal and religious organizations.

FAMILY AND COMMUNITY LIFE

The most immediate concern of Belgian immigrants who arrived in the United States during the nineteenth century was survival. Those who settled in the Midwest often came with only a few meager possessions. Often, they settled in what was then only wilderness, and they needed all their mental and physical resources to make it through their first winter. Their awareness of their inability to return to their homes in Belgium, combined with the comfort and assistance

of the Catholic clergy, pulled them through this difficult transition period. These early families set to work clearing the land, building shelters, and planting crops. Men, women, and children all worked in the fields and tended the animals. Belgian Americans who settled in cities took work where they could find it to support their families. The most fortunate were those who came with craft skills, since the country was growing and such workers were in demand. As Belgian Americans became established in their new country, they began to form organizations to help the sick and poor among them. They also maintained ties with those they left behind in Belgium. As a result, many more Belgian immigrants came to the United States to join their friends and relatives. As years went by, the initially crude homesteads and rocky fields in rural Belgian American settlements became productive family farms, and job opportunities in the cities led many Belgian Americans to become business owners or to enter professions.

Belgian American populations are heavily concentrated in the Midwest, where the second and third generations have tended to carry on the work traditions of their forebears. Detroit, for example, has many Belgian descendants employed in the construction and transportation industries. Well-kept Belgian farms dot small Wisconsin communities, even though many farmers may work second jobs at paper mills or in other industries for their main source of income.

At Belgian restaurant, Petite Abeille, in New York City, 2007. MANTEL / SIPA PRESS/0701081501 / NEWSCOM

Today, the grandchildren and great-grandchildren of nineteenth-century Belgian immigrants have assimilated fully into the educational and occupational roles of twentieth-century society.

During the second half of the twentieth century, the Belgian Ethnic Island in Door County and surrounding counties in Wisconsin began to erode as a close-knit Belgian American community. Many older Belgian American farmers seeking retirement found that no one in the family was interested in carrying on the family business, intimidated by the great demands of the dairy industry. As a result, many Belgian American farmers began to sell their property in five-acre parcels to buyers who were primarily investing in vacation or retirement homes. Due to high appreciation in property value in northern Door, there was a growing demand for the more affordable property in the southern area of the peninsula, much of which was owned by Belgian American farmers. This influx of outsiders caused growing erosion of the formerly tight-knit Belgian Ethnic Island. The expansion of State Highway 57 into an interstate made the lower area of the Door County region easily accessible, bringing more vacationers and tourists as part of a process of ex-urbanization. These factors have caused the further dispersal of Belgian Americans to different areas of Wisconsin and elsewhere in the United States. Nevertheless, strong Belgian American cultural traditions do persist, especially in architecture, folk culture, and diet. These traditions continue to bring members of the community together to celebrate their common origins.

Gender Roles Belgian American families tended to be large. There were strong social and religious taboos against divorce. In the early days of Belgian immigrants' arrival to the United States, rural women were expected to work in the fields as well as in the home. Traditional roles for men and women were observed, and any deviation was often censured. Women cared for children, ran the household, and cooked the meals, while men worked outside the home, assumed active roles in the Belgian American community, and often socialized with other men at local saloons or bowling alleys. Men's social and sporting clubs provided them with a social outlet outside the family sphere. Some of these still exist in rural areas, including the Cadieux Café Feather Bowling Club in Fraser, Michigan, and the Belgian American Men's Century Club in Detroit, Michigan. Even though it was not uncommon for widows to carry on their deceased husband's occupation, especially that of farming, it was frowned upon if women assumed community leadership roles, except on a social basis. Children also had chores to do at an early age, and gender-based chores were commonly assigned. On farms, they also helped with planting and harvest, and as a result, were often absent from school during those times of the year. However, these early immigrants respected teachers and education.

Although most second generation young women attended elementary school, very few went on to high school. Teaching was one of the few approved professions for women during the nineteenth century.

To this day, Belgian American women continue to work on farms with men in rural areas in Wisconsin and Michigan. However, Belgian American women in rural areas are less likely to participate actively in the public sector, since traditional Belgian gender divisions have been maintained to some extent in these regions. The majority of their socializing is among women within the Belgian American community, and several organizations still exist that facilitate such interaction, including the Queen Elizabeth Circle in Warren, Michigan, and the Women's Century Club in Detroit. Urbanized Belgian Americans, however, are much more likely to adhere to liberal American notions of gender equality, and women today thus have access to many of the same career and educational opportunities as men.

Courtship and Weddings During the nineteenth century, the young bride (sixteen to twenty was a common marrying age) prepared for her wedding by filling her hope chest with handmade quilts, tablecloths, and linens. Her friends often gave her a bridal shower. It was taken for granted that she would marry within the Catholic religion. Rural communities often held twilight wedding masses so that men would have time to be away from their fields.

A wedding celebration commonly lasted all day and all night. Typically 300 to 600 people would be invited. In the early days of Belgian American settlement, the wedding couple went from house to house, extending a personal invitation. Once held in the bride's family home, the celebration now often takes place at a local hall or country club. It was customary for neighbor women to help prepare the food, and preparation took many days. A very festive atmosphere surrounded the entire event. The guests ate and drank all day, and in the evening there was a wedding dance. The gift opening took place after the wedding dinner, and gifts were displayed for all the guests to see. Money was rarely given as a gift. Many of these same customs apply today, especially in the more homogeneous Belgian communities. Nevertheless, with the erosion of the Belgian American ethnic enclaves, more and more young women of Belgian descent married outside of the Belgian American community, into mixed cultural marriages. This further dispersed the community as many brides moved away with their husbands.

Funerals After the announcement of a death in the Belgian American community, a wake is held for friends and family. It is customary to have an open casket for viewing of the deceased. The body is taken to the church for a Catholic mass the following day. Funeral masses in memory of the dead person are held throughout the year, having been paid for by relatives and friends. A funeral dinner is held for all mourners. The dinner is usually put on by a group of church women, whose

special task is providing this service to members of the church. It is customary for friends and neighbors to send food to the home of the deceased. Other funeral customs from the past still persist in some form today. The rosary is still said at the wake. A procession of vehicles from the church to the cemetery is a usual occurrence. The wearing of dark, or black, clothing is observed today by only the most traditional mourners but once was an expected ritual for the family. This usually went on for at least one year. During this time family members did not attend festive or social events. Tying a purple or black ribbon on the door of the dead person's home and the wearing of a black arm band by men in the family were other mourning customs of an earlier time.

EMPLOYMENT AND ECONOMIC CONDITIONS

Beginning in the nineteenth century, many Belgian Americans worked as farmers or manual laborers in industries such as mining and construction. As the manufacturing industry took off in midwestern cities such as Detroit, Michigan, many Belgian Americans found work in automobile factories. As educational opportunities expanded for second and third generation Belgian immigrants, they began to enter the professional sector and pursue jobs in education, technology, business, and other areas. The arrival of more highly educated Belgian immigrants following World War II also increased the professionalization of the Belgian American community in the United States. Today Belgian Americans are employed in many different industries, working as manual laborers, skilled laborers, and professionals.

Belgian Americans in rural areas continue to dedicate themselves to farming, although many families have been forced to seek secondary employment outside of the farm to stay afloat financially. There are a number of small businesses owned by Belgian Americans, especially within rural areas that cater to the population of Belgian origin. Many of these businesses suffered as a result of the economic crisis that began in the United States in 2007. Belgian Americans working in the manufacturing and construction industries were also laid off as a result of this crisis, and families faced the same financial difficulties as the rest of the American working and middle classes. Fortunately, there are many Belgian American organizations in the United States that work to support the Belgian American community, and they served as a resource during this difficult period. Among these organizations are the Belgian American Association, the United Belgian American Societies of Detroit, and the St. Charles Beneficial Society.

POLITICS AND GOVERNMENT

At first, Belgian Americans paid little attention to the American system of government. Exercising the right to vote and to have an influence in local affairs came gradually, as Belgian Americans learned the English language and began to establish leadership among themselves. Soon they began to draw upon their community leaders for various offices—town assessor, justice of the peace, superintendent of schools. As a group, Belgian Americans realized the power of their vote and began to exert greater influence in the communities where they resided. Owing to their independent spirit, the community preferred to band together politically to solve their problems, rather than passively waiting for outsiders to order their affairs.

Several Belgian Americans have been actively involved in U.S. politics since the early twentieth century, including Raymond Goldsmith, who worked for the Securities and Exchange Commission in the mid-1900s; Louis C. Rabaut, who was a Michigan congressman in the 1930s and 1940s; and Anne-Marie Slaughter, who served as Director of Policy Planning for the U.S. State Department from 2009 to 2011. Because of the small size of the Belgian American population and their assimilation into American culture, however, Belgian American politicians today have not found it necessary to act as advocates for their community.

On a national scale, Belgian Americans responded as a distinct group to Belgium's tragic experience during World War I and World War II. The Flemish, especially, made a strong effort to avoid being associated in people's minds with the Germans. In general, assimilation was hastened by wartime experiences. Belgian American veterans' and fraternal organizations came into being during this time.

Military Belgian Americans fought in the U.S. War of Independence. The American Civil War came shortly after the greatest influx of Belgian immigrants, and as American citizens, many were called to serve. In rural communities this caused great hardship, as women and children struggled to support themselves by working the farms alone. Belgian Americans also fought in both World War I and World War II. Their efforts were made more poignant by Belgium's devastation by

the German army in both wars. It has been noted that during World War I, Belgian Americans gave so generously to the children who were victims of that war, that an official delegation from Belgium was sent to the United States in 1917 to honor their efforts. Belgian Americans also served in subsequent military engagements in Korea and Vietnam. It is likely that members of the Belgian American community have also served in military conflicts in the early twenty-first century, including Iraq and Afghanistan, although there are not specific statistics available owing to the small size of the Belgian American population.

Relations with Belgium Very few Belgian immigrants returned to Belgium, but the tie between the old country and the new has never been severed. From the beginning, letters went back and forth, telling of conditions in the United States and urging those left behind to join the new arrivals. As years went by, Belgians gradually became Americanized. Even so, however, the connection with Belgium remained. The outpouring of aid from Belgians in the United States during World War I and World War II is certainly proof of their continued bond to the homeland. Organizations such as the World War Veterans sent groups to Belgium and also received official delegations from there—often at the highest political and governmental levels. The Belgian American Educational Foundation grew out of the World War I Commission for the Relief of Belgium. This organization promotes and facilitates exchanges among the academic, artistic, and scientific communities of Belgium and the United States. The religious connection between the two countries remains strong, largely because of the ongoing work of Catholic missions in the United States by such Belgian Catholic orders as the Norbertines and the Crosiers (Holy Cross Fathers). Even more so, the modern-day interest in researching one's forebears has led many Belgian Americans to reconnect with their mother country. Whether Walloon or Flemish, it reflects Belgian Americans' pride in their ancestry and customs. Since the 1970s librarians across the country, and especially in the Midwest, note the rise in requests for genealogical information in this search for Belgian roots.

NOTABLE INDIVIDUALS

Academia George Sarton (1884-1956) was a brilliant science historian who traced the cultural and technical evolution of science from its beginnings to the modern day. Other Belgian Americans who have made significant contributions to their academic specialty include economist Robert Triffin (1911-1993) and economic historian Raymond de Roover (1904-1972).

Emile L. Boulpaep (1938–) is a professor of cellular and molecular physiology and the director of Medical and Graduate Studies at Yale University. He served as the president of the Belgian American Educational Foundation beginning in 1977 and was a board member of the Francqui Foundation.

Boulpaep discovered physicochemical characteristics of cell membranes that provided insight into a number of kidney and heart disorders. In 1992 he was awarded the prestigious Christoffel Plantin Prize, which honors the achievements of Belgians living in other countries.

Commerce and Industry Washington Charles De Pauw (1822–1887) was an industrialist whose method of manufacturing plate glass secured his fortune; much of his wealth was used to benefit the city of New Albany, Indiana, where his plant was located. Peter Corteville (1881-1966) founded the Belgian Press, a Detroit printing company that published a prominent Belgian American weekly newspaper, the *Gazette van Detroit*, which at one point attained a circulation of almost 10,000.

Sophie Vandebroek is a successful businesswoman who became Xerox's chief technology officer and the president of the Xerox Innovation Group in 2006. Vandebroek was born in Leuven, Belgium, and is a Fulbright Fellow and a Fellow of the Belgian-American Educational Foundation. In 2012 Belgium named her the Information and Communications Technology (ICT) Personality of the Year.

Fashion Anne Elisabeth Jane "Liz" Claiborne (1929-2007) was a Belgian American fashion designer and entrepreneur who was born in Brussels, Belgium. Claiborne cofounded Liz Claiborne Inc., which in 1986 became the first company founded by a woman to make the Fortune 500 list of the largest U.S. corporations. Claiborne started her fashion line with the goal of designing practical clothes for working women. By 1989, when Claiborne retired from active management, the company had experienced tremendous growth and had expanded into several new divisions to become a well-known fashion house.

Film Audrey Hepburn (1929-1993) was an actress and humanitarian who was revered as both a film and fashion icon. Born in Ixelles, Belgium, Hepburn spent her childhood traveling between Belgium, the Netherlands, and England. Hepburn was one of the leading actresses during Hollywood's Golden Age, and she is ranked third on the list of female screen legends in the history of American cinema.

Jean-Claude Camille François Van Varenberg (1960–), professionally known as Jean-Claude Van Damme, is a Belgian actor, director and martial artist. Born in Brussels, Belgium, he moved to the United States in the 1980s to pursue a film career. Van Damme is best known for his martial arts action films, including *Bloodsport* (1988) and *Timecop* (1994).

Literature Georges Simenon (1903-1989) is famous for his psychological detective stories and is the creator of the popular character Inspector Maigret. He is the author of more than two hundred works. He came to the United States during World War II, and he later lived in Switzerland.

Eleanore Marie Sarton (1912–1995), whose pen name was May Sarton, was a Belgian American poet and novelist. Sarton was born in Wondelgem, Belgium, but her family moved to the United States in her early childhood. Many of her works, such as the novel *Mrs. Stevens Hears the Mermaids Singing* (1965), reflect on lesbian identity.

Music One traditional form of music in Belgium involves playing the carillon, a bell tower comprised of fixed, chromatically tuned bells that are sounded by hammers controlled from a keyboard. Belgian American practitioners of the carillon art have flourished in the United States. Jos D'hollander (1934–) was one of the foremost carillonneurs in the country and is the former carillonneur of the Park Avenue Baptist Church in New York City. Other famous carillonneurs were Antoon Brees of Riverside Church of New York and Cranbrook Church in Detroit, and Camiel Lefevre of Bok Tower in Florida. Lefevre was the first graduate of the world's first carillon school in Mechelen, Belgium, which was founded in 1922 and funded by the Belgian American Education Foundation.

Vivica Genaux (1969–) is a coloratura mezzo-soprano born to an American father of Belgian-Welsh descent. Genaux has sung in major operas, including *The Barber of Seville* at the Metropolitan Opera and *L'italiana in Algeri* at Opéra National de Paris.

Religion Catholic missionary-explorers were active across the United States beginning in the seventeenth century. Two of the most notable are Father Louis Hennepin, a Franciscan, and Father Pierre-Jean de Smet, a Jesuit. Father Hennepin (1614-1705) joined the 1678 La Salle expedition to explore the Mississippi River; he was the first European to sketch and describe Niagara Falls. In 1683 he wrote a comprehensive treatment of the Upper Mississippi Valley; sixty editions of this book were published in most of the major European languages. Father de Smet (1801-1873) was a notable pioneer in the exploration of the nineteenth-century frontier. From 1845 to 1873 he traveled thousands of miles in undeveloped western territory. As a missionary, perhaps his most important work was with the Native Americans, and he played a prominent role in the final peace treaty with the Sioux leader Sitting Bull. Father Joseph Damien De Veuster (1840-1889) devoted his life to the care of lepers in Hawaii. Better known as Father Damien, he contracted leprosy himself in 1885. He was beatified by the Catholic Church in 1993, 104 years after his death.

Science and Medicine Karel J. Van de Poele (1846-1895) is known as "the father of the electric trolley." By 1869, his electrical streetcars were operating in Detroit. He founded the Van de Poele Electric Light Company and invented the dynamo, which served to power American industry in its early days. Jean-Charles Houzeau de Lehaie (1820-1888) has been called the "Belgian von Humboldt" for his work in the fields of astronomy, mathematics, physics, botany, politics, journalism, and literature. He was born in Belgium and arrived in New Orleans in 1857. He was actively involved in politics at the time of the Civil War and campaigned against slavery. Karel Bossart (1904-1975) was called the father of the Atlas missile. His engineering work in the missile field culminated in 1958, when he received the U. S. Air Force's Exceptional Civilian Award for developing the first intercontinental ballistic missile. He was a graduate of Massachusetts Institute of Technology. George Washington Goethals (1858-1928) is known as the builder of the Panama Canal. An engineer, administrator, and soldier, he spent seven years overseeing its construction, and was the Canal Zone's first civil governor. Georges Van Biesbroeck (1880-1974) was an astronomer at Yerkes Observatory in Wisconsin. He is noted for lending support to Einstein's Theory of Relativity by verifying its prediction that light is slightly distorted as it passes close by the sun.

Albert Claude (1898-1983) was a joint recipient in 1974 of the Nobel Prize in Medicine for his work on the structure of the cell; he was also a pioneer in the development of biological electron microscopy. Kevin M. De Cock is a Belgian-born American scientist and infectious-disease specialist. He served as the Director of the U.S. Centers for Disease Control and Prevention's (CDC) Center for Global Health beginning in 2010. Dr. De Cock previously served as the director of the World Health Organization (WHO) Department of HIV/AIDS from 2006 to 2009. He has won numerous awards, including the Chalmers Medal, presented by the Royal Society of Tropical Medicine and Hygiene.

MEDIA

PRINT

Two Flemish newspapers, the *Gazette van Moline* and *Gazette van Detroit*, were the largest Belgian publications in the early twentieth century. The *Gazette van Moline*, founded in 1907, was the first Flemish newspaper in the United States. It ceased publication in 1921. The *Gazette van Detroit* was founded in 1914 and was still being published in 2012 after having been rescued from the brink of collapse in 2006 by several Belgian investors.

Belgian Laces

Official quarterly bulletin of the Belgian Researchers, Inc., and the Belgian American Heritage Society. It is described as "the link between people of like ancestry and like interest on both sides of the ocean."

Regine Brindle, President and Editor
495 East 5th Street
Peru, Indiana 46970
Phone: (765) 473-5667
Email: tbr2008@live.com
URL: www.rootsweb.ancestry.com/-inbr/belgian_laces.htm

Flemish American Heritage

Triannual magazine printed by the Genealogical Society of Flemish Americans.

Judith Elskens, Editor
18740 Thirteen Mile Road
Roseville, Michigan 48066
Phone: (586) 777-2720
Email: FlemishLibrary@gmail.com
URL: www.flemishlibrary.org/

Gazette Di Waloniye Wisconsin

French-language quarterly periodical that serves to connect the Belgian Americans of Northeastern Wisconsin with Belgians in Belgium.

Willy Monfils, Editor
770 Chemin de la Boscaille
B-7457
Walhain, Belgium

ORGANIZATIONS AND ASSOCIATIONS

Belgian-American Association

Focuses on fostering awareness and appreciation between the United States and Belgium. Promotes social and cultural activities within its membership and works to preserve Belgian heritage in the United States.

Arsene Van Vooren, President
P.O. Box 140,
St. Clair Shores, Michigan 48080-0140
Phone: (586) 771-7926
URL: www.thebaa.us

Belgian American Chamber of Commerce

Founded in 1925 for a membership that includes Belgian exporters and American importers of Belgian products. Publishes the *Belgian American Trade Review*, a quarterly journal that contains company profiles, information on Belgian products, and Port of Antwerp news.

Tamara Zouboff, Executive Director
C/o KBC Bank
1177 Avenue of the Americas, 8th Floor
New York, New York 10036
Phone: (212) 541-0779
Email: info@belcham.org
URL: www.belcham.org

Belgian American Educational Foundation

Founded in 1920 to promote closer relations and exchange of intellectual ideas between Belgium and the United States through fellowships granted to graduate students of one country for study and research in the other. Assists higher education and scientific research. Commemorates the work of the Commission for Relief in Belgium and associated organizations during World War I.

Emile Boulpaep, President
195 Church Street, 10th Floor
New Haven, Connecticut 06510-2009
Phone: (203) 777-5765

Email: emile.boulpaep@yale.edu
URL: www.baef.be/documents/home.xml?
lang=en

Belgian American Heritage Society of West Virginia

Founded in 1992 to promote the social and intellectual advancement of West Virginia Belgians. Serves as a resource for those interested in Belgian genealogy, history, and culture.

Marlene Reed, President
340 Buckhannon Avenue
Clarksburg, West Virginia 26301
Phone: (304) 623-4484
Email: bahsofwv@aol.com

The Peninsula Belgian American Club

Nonprofit organization located in Namur, Wisconsin. Founded in 1964 with the purpose of keeping Belgian heritage alive.

Jim Lampereur, President
1255 North 12th Place,
Sturgeon Bay, Wisconsin 54235-1159
Phone: (920) 866-2189
Email: joyce.lampereur@greenbaynet.com
URL: www.belgianamerican.org

MUSEUMS AND RESEARCH CENTERS

The Belgian Researchers

Provides books, periodicals, and other materials for genealogical research. Principal objective: "Keep our Belgian heritage alive in our hearts and in the hearts of our posterity." Publishes *Belgian Laces*, the official quarterly newsletter.

Regine Brindle, President and Editor
495 East 5th Street
Peru, Indiana 46970
Phone: (765) 473-5667
Email: tbr2008@live.com
URL: www.rootsweb.ancestry.com/-inbr/index.html

Center for Belgian Culture of Western Illinois

Promotes Flemish history and culture and provides leadership in perpetuating Belgian heritage and teaching the values of Belgian culture.

Kevin DeRoo, President
712 Eighteenth Avenue
Moline, Illinois 61265-3837

Phone: (309) 762-0167
Email: info@belgianmuseumquadcities.org
URL: www.belgianmuseumquadcities.org

Genealogical Society of Flemish Americans

Provides information and library materials pertaining to Flemish genealogical research. Publishes *Flemish American Heritage*.

Judith Elskens, Editor
18740 Thirteen Mile Road
Roseville, Michigan 48066
Phone: (586) 777-2720
Email: FlemishLibrary@gmail.com
URL: www.flemishlibrary.org

University of Wisconsin–Green Bay Special Collections Library/Belgian American Ethnic Resource Center

Cooperative project of the State Historical Society of Wisconsin and the University of Wisconsin–Green Bay. Holdings include materials on persons of Belgian descent whose families originally settled in Brown, Kewaunee, and Door counties. Materials include family papers, church records, photographs, oral-history interviews, and records of school districts and towns.

Debra L. Anderson, Special Collections Librarian
2420 Nicolet Drive
Green Bay, Wisconsin 54311-7001
Phone: (920) 465-2539
Email: libraryweb@uwgb.edu
URL: www.wisconsinhistory.org/libraryarchives/arcnet/greenbay.asp

SOURCES FOR ADDITIONAL STUDY

Amato, Joseph. *Servants of the Land: God, Family and Farm, the Trinity of Belgian Economic Folkways in Southwestern Minnesota*. Marshall, Minnesota: Crossings Press, 1990.

Belgians in the United States. Brussels, Belgium: Ministry of Foreign Affairs, 1976.

Bernardo, Stephanie. *The Ethnic Almanac*. Garden City, New York: Dolphin Books, Doubleday & Company, 1981.

Cook, Bernard. *Belgians in Michigan*. East Lansing: Michigan State University Press, 2007.

Laatsch, William, and Charles Calkins. "Belgians in Wisconsin." *To Build in a New Land: Ethnic Landscapes in North America*, ed. Allen Noble. Baltimore: John Hopkins, 1992.

Sabbe, Philemon D., and Leon Buyse. *Belgians in America*. Belgium: Lannoo, Tielt, 1960.

BELIZEAN AMERICANS
Tova Stabin

OVERVIEW

Belizean Americans are immigrants or descendants of people from Belize, formerly known as British Honduras, a country located in Central America. Belize is bordered by the Mexico to the north, Guatemala to the west and south, and by the Caribbean Sea to the east. Belize has the second-largest barrier reef in the world, with hundreds of small islands called *cayes*. It has two seasons: the dry season (February to July) and the wet season (August to January). It is 8,867 square miles (22,966 square kilometers) in size, or slightly smaller than Massachusetts.

According to the 2010 Population and Housing Census of Belize, the population of Belize was 312,698, with the median age being 21.3 years old. The vast majority of Belizeans are Christian. The 2010 census estimated that approximately 40 percent of Belizeans were Roman Catholic, 8 percent were Pentecostal, and smaller percentages were other Christian denominations, such as Seventh Day Adventists, Anglicans, Mennonites, Baptist, Methodists, Nazarenes, and Jehovah's Witnesses. Approximately 10 percent of the population practices other religions, including the Baha'i Faith, Buddhism, Hinduism, Islam and Mormonism. Indigenous, Caribbean, and African spiritual practices or folk religions can also be found, such as *Obeah*, a mystical and healing tradition originating in West Africa that slaves brought with them. A little over 15 percent of Belizeans say they are not affiliated with any religion (twice as many as in the 2000 census). Belize is made up of many ethnic groups. The 2010 Belizean government census reported that approximately 49 to 50 percent of the population were mestizos (people with mixed European and indigenous ancestry), 21 percent Creoles (people with some African ancestry), 10 percent full-blooded Mayans, and 4.6 percent Garifunas or Garinagus, also called Black Caribs. Garifunas originally came from St. Vincent, settled in Honduras, and then immigrated to Belize; they are a mix of African, Arawak, and Caribbean ancestry. About 6 percent are classified in the census as "mixed ethnic origin," and 10 percent are "other," including German Mennonites, Asians, and Europeans. In the 1980s and 1990s the Belizean government encouraged immigration from Chinese areas such as Hong Kong and Taiwan. There is a great gap between the rich and the poor. The 2010 *CIA Factbook* indicated that more than four out of ten people lived in poverty. The average per-capita income in 2012 was $8,412.08 (ranked ninety-third in the world). Tourism is the number one industry.

Belizeans began migrating to the United States in the early 1900s and settled mostly in New York and other large cities, such as Chicago. These early immigrants were primarily middle-class Protestants who were ethnically Creole. Due to labor shortages in the United States caused by so many men fighting in World War II, several hundred Belizean men were recruited to work in the United States during and after the war. These workers first came to states in the South and then went to northern states such as Massachusetts. Belizean immigration continued during the 1950s and 1960s due to the poor economy in Belize and the growing economy in the United States. Between 2000 and 2009, Belizean immigrants had the second-highest naturalization rate (61.2 percent) among all Central American immigrant groups.

According to U.S. State Department estimates, the number of Belizean Americans in 2012 was more than 100,000, which roughly equates to the population of Flint, Michigan. Except for Belize itself, the United States is home to the largest population of Belizeans in the world. Los Angeles has the most Belizean immigrants, with between 50,000 and 55,000. Belizean American communities can also be found in the large cities, Chicago, New York, Houston, New Orleans, and Miami.

HISTORY OF THE PEOPLE

Early History Belize was one of the Mayan city-states during the "classic" Mayan period between the third and ninth centuries CE. Mayan culture flourished in Belize, Honduras, Guatemala, southern Mexico (Yucatan region), and El Salvador. After about the year 1000, however, Mayan culture and population began to decline.

In 1494 the Treaty of Tordesillas was signed between Portugal and Spain to "apportion" land explored by Christopher Columbus and other late-fifteenth-century explorers. Belize came under Spanish rule, and in the sixteenth century Spaniards journeyed to Belize to find gold, though they found none.

Despite "ruling" Belize, Spain did not have settlements there, opening the land up to British buccaneers and then woodcutters (later known as Baymen), who harvested and sold logwood and mahogany found in Belizean forests. Unable to control the Mayans and force them to be laborers, Baymen brought many slaves from Africa to help log the forests. By 1800 there were about 4,000 people living in the British settlement (3,000 black slaves, 900 mixed-race coloreds and free blacks, and 100 white colonists). Efforts were made to keep the slaves divided so that the white colonists could stay in power, but throughout the late 1700s and early 1800s, there were many slave revolts, as well as resistance from the Mayans over land and labor. Slavery was abolished in 1838 in the British Caribbean, although discrimination continued toward the freed slaves, who were not allowed to own land. By the late 1800s, with the use of troops, weapons, laws, and foreign help, the Mayans were forced from their land in Belize. In the mid-1800s, a war in the Yucatan Peninsula between mestizos and privileged Spanish-descended landlords prompted many mestizos to flee to Belize; by the 1860s, the population of Belize had nearly doubled because of this migration. In 1859 Spain and Britain signed a treaty over control of Belize, resulting in Belize becoming a colony of British Honduras in 1861 and a crown colony (a colony of Britain represented by a governor) in 1871.

Modern Era Belizean nationalism emerged in the early twentieth century. Belizean citizens, mainly Creole, were recruited to fight with the British during World War I. However, they were severely discriminated against, and when they returned to Belize, they started protests against British rule. The idea of nationalism continued to grow in the 1930s with a group called the Unemployed Brigade, which organized poor people of color to stage strikes, boycotts, and protests against rich white business owners. An economic crisis occurred during and directly after World War II, due mainly to export markets being closed. This precipitated many large and sometime violent protests against British rule. By the 1950s, a national independence party, the People's United Party (PUP) was formed. They organized a general strike that forced Britain to make some political concessions, such as universal suffrage and limited rule by the British. By 1964 the region was self-governing, and the capital was relocated to Belmopan seven years later. In 1973 its name was changed from British Honduras to Belize.

Belize did not become an independent state, however, until 1981, largely because of disputed borders with Guatemala. In the 1859 treaty between Spain and Britain, it was stated that Guatemala would recognize Belize if a road was built between Belize City and Guatemala City. Britain never built the road, and Guatemala contended that the treaty was, therefore, void. Guatemala finally recognized Belize in 1992 but continued its territorial claim to about

half of Belize (the southern portion and its islands). The Organization of American States was unsuccessful in negotiating an agreement between Belize and Guatemala, but in 2008, it was able to persuade Guatemala and Belize to sign an agreement to have a referendum in both countries that would bring the dispute to arbitration in the International Court of Justice in The Hague, Netherlands. The referendum was to be held in October 2013 with a settlement expected a few years later.

SETTLEMENT IN THE UNITED STATES

Belizean men were recruited to work in the southern and then northern United States, such as in Massachusetts, during World War II because of labor shortages created by U.S. involvement in the conflict. In the 1950s, with the U.S. economy booming and that in Belize faltering, a small but steady stream of Belizeans continued to immigrate to the United States.

Immigration increased after 1961 when Hurricane Hattie devastated much of Belize; part of the U.S. assistance involved granting refugee status to Belizean immigrants. While the economy did improve marginally in Belize in the 1970s, most jobs were in the government sector. There was little training available for technical or professional positions, and as the lack of upward job mobility persisted, Belizeans continued to come to the United States in order to gain educations and learn new job skills. Notably during the 1960s and 1970s, the immigration of Belizean women to the United States increased, as more traditionally female job openings, such as for nurses and domestics, became available. Until the late 1970s, New York and Chicago had the largest numbers of Belizean Americans. Most Belizeans in New York were from middle-class urban centers in Belize, while those in Chicago came from rural areas.

By the 1980s, there were enough Belizean Americans that other Belizeans immigrated to join family members, especially those like Creoles and Garifunas from the middle class, who had enough economic privilege to travel. These immigrants sought jobs in professions such as teaching and nursing.

Before independence was declared in Belize, many Belizeans came to the United States with British visas and then stayed illegally after the visas had expired. Generally, these immigrants migrated through New Orleans, Miami, or border towns in Mexico, often then traveling to northern locales like New York. Some Belizeans married non-Belizeans or were sponsored by relatives, which enabled them to change their status to legal. Others achieved a legal status by working in jobs that were part of occupational preference quotas for immigrants. Many of these were in traditionally female occupations such as nursing or the domestic sector. Some male immigrants worked toward a legal status by signing up for the armed services, especially during the Vietnam War. Overall, however, the path to legalization was difficult because

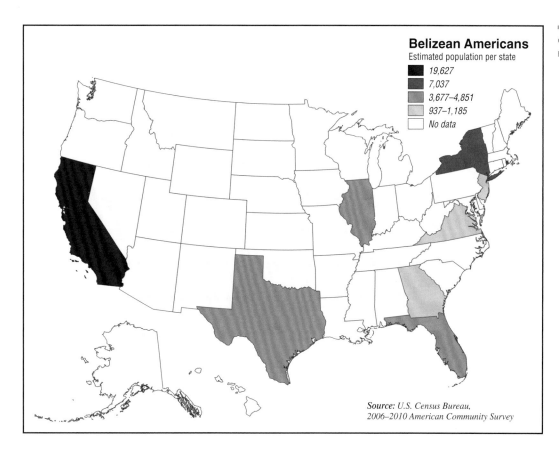

Belizean Americans
Estimated population per state

- 19,627
- 7,037
- 3,677–4,851
- 937–1,185
- No data

Source: U.S. Census Bureau,
2006–2010 American Community Survey

Belizeans were classified as part of the British Empire, and the U.S. immigration quotas were small for Brits.

The last large wave of Belizean immigration to the United States occurred around the time Belize declared independence, from the late 1970s to the mid-1980s. In addition to their general economic concerns, many of these immigrants opposed the new Belizean government. They had no faith in the government's stability, especially economically, and opposed what they perceived to be the "Latinization" of the country. Most immigrants during this time were sponsored by family or friends already in the United States. Unlike many previous immigrants, they came from all points in Belize, not only from the major cities. Furthermore, their ranks included mestizos in addition to Creoles and Garifunas.

At the time of Belizean independence, an economic crisis gripped Belize. The 20,000 to 30,000 Belizeans who immigrated to the United States during the 1980s were motivated, in part, to send money back home to family members, who were often struggling economically. The United States Embassy in Belize estimated that by 1984, about one-fourth of Belizeans (roughly 55,000) were living in the United States, mostly in New York City, Los Angeles, Chicago, Miami, and New Orleans. Two out of three, according to the estimate, were in the United States illegally. Many were also fairly young, in the range of twenty to thirty-four years old. The 1986 Immigration Reform

and Control Act allowed many undocumented Belizeans to become legal through an amnesty provision for immigrants who entered the United States before 1982 and established "roots" in the country.

By the mid-1990s, immigration from Belize had slowed down dramatically, from about 18,000 in the 1980s to about 9,000 in the 1990s to less than 1,000 per year from 2000 to 2004, according to the 2004 *Yearbook of Immigration Statistics* from the Department of Homeland Security. Many Belizean Americans had been in the United States for some time, and family members who wanted to join them had generally already done so. United States immigration laws also became stricter. Furthermore, with the economic picture improving in Belize, many Belizeans were less motivated to leave their country. Nevertheless, some Belizeans have immigrated anyway because of the better educational opportunities in the United States. Tourism also has sparked immigration. A rise in U.S. citizens vacationing in Belize has brought more interaction between people of the two countries. This has translated into more marriages between Americans and Belizeans, especially between Belizean women and non-Belizean men. Many of these couples have settled in the United States.

By the 2000s, over 45 percent of all Belizeans lived in the United States. A 2011 report by the Migration Policy Institute report on Central American immigrants in the United States notes that in 2009, Belizeans made up 1.9 percent of all Central American immigrants in the United States and had the highest U.S. naturalization rate (61.2 percent) of all Central American immigrant groups. The study also reported that 69.6 percent of Belizean immigrants were working-age adults, 43.6 percent were men, and 16.5 percent lived in poverty. The largest ethnic group of Belizean Americans continues to be Creoles, but mestizos now make up a sizable portion, too.

The heaviest concentration Belizean Americans is in the Los Angeles area, with 50,000 to 55,000. Other large Belizean American communities are in southern Florida, New Orleans, Houston, New York, and Chicago. Like other immigrant groups, Belizean Americans were impacted by the U.S. recession in the 2000s and became somewhat more dispersed as they searched for jobs all over the United States.

LANGUAGE

English is the official language of Belize. While most Belizeans speak English, much of the population also uses what is often known as Belize *Kriol* (Creole) English or BC. Belize *Kriol* is mainly an oral language, though there is a developing written form. The language originally developed as a mix of the West African languages of the slaves who were brought to Belize and the English spoken by slave owners; it enabled slave owners to communicate with their slaves. It was later combined with the Jamaican language due to the many Jamaicans who were brought to the Belizean colony. Although considered an English dialect, *Kriol* English is difficult to understand for those who speak only American or British English.

Spanish is widely used by mestizos, who are growing in population. A number of Mayan languages are also spoken, including *Kekchi*, *Mopán*, and *Yucatán*. Another relatively common language is *Garifuna*, also known as Black Carib and *Moreno*. While English is the language used in schools, Spanish and/or *Kriol* are sometimes spoken in early grades if those are the main dialects in the children's homes.

The majority of Belizean Americans speak English, particularly as many immigrants came from middle-class and educated backgrounds in Belize. Thus, they do not confront as many linguistic barriers in school or at work as some other Latin American immigrant groups. Some schools exist that preserve the languages spoken in Belize, such as the Garifuna Culture and Language Academy in Los Angeles. Garifuna is spoken not only in Belize, but also in Honduras, Guatemala, and Nicaragua.

Here are some common Kriol expressions/greetings: *Weh di go aan* ("Hello"); *Da how yu di du?* ("How are you?"); *Aarait* ("Fine, thank you"); *Fu chroo?* ("Is that so?"); *Si yoo lata* ("See you later"); *Evryting gud/aarite* ("Everything's fine"); *Gud maanin* ("Good morning").

RELIGION

Although there are not specific Belizean American churches, many Belizean immigrants attend churches or church schools that have large numbers of people

BELIZEAN PROVERBS

Here are some Belize *Kriol* proverbs:

Plantain no eat like rice.

When you are hungry or it's hard times, eat (or do) what's necessary even if you are not used to it or you don't like it.

A lia is fugetful.

A dishonest person isn't consistent.

Wahnti wahnti kyah geti an geti geti nuh wahnti.

You want what you can't have.

If yo no chek di wata, no teck off yo shoe.

Look before you leap.

Dah no so, dah naily so.

Where there's smoke, there's fire.

Punkin neva bear waatamelen.

The pumpkin vine never bears watermelon.

Wait bruk down bridge.

Don't make me wait too long.

Fishaman neva say e fish 'tink.

A fisherman never thinks his fish stink.

One day belly full neva fatten maaga dawg.

One meal along won't change someone's life.

Sleep wit' yo' own eye.

Don't depend on what others say, trust yourself.

One one craboo fill barrel.

Every little bit counts.

from their ethnic group, such as St. Michael's of Los Angeles, a Catholic church. Christians from Belize and other Central American countries, such as the Garifunas, often join together religious organizations like the Evangelical Garifuna Council of Churches in the Bronx in New York City. The interdenominational Garifuna Seminary was founded in 2009 with pastors from Belize, Honduras, Guatemala, and the United States. It is located in Corozal, Belize.

Belizean mestizos might attend one of the many Spanish Catholic or Christian congregations in the United States. The majority of Latinos are Catholic, and 41 percent of the Latino Protestant congregations are Pentecostal. These statistics loosely mirror the religious affiliations in Belize, where the majority of the population is Catholic and the largest Protestant denomination is Pentecostal. Mystical and spiritual tradition from indigenous and African cultures is also followed by certain Belizean American groups.

CULTURE AND ASSIMILATION

Though Belize is the most sparsely populated country in Central America, it has many distinct ethnicities. Additionally, since Belize only recently became an independent country (1981), its national identity is not as strong as those of many other nations. Thus, there are relatively few cultural groups and organizations that encompass the country as a whole. Those that do exist are generally in the larger immigrant communities, and they include the Belize Cultural Foundation and the Belize Culture and Heritage Association in Illinois. The Consortium for Belizean Development, which assists Belizeans all over the world, was started in Washington, D.C., but is now comprised of central, eastern, and western regional groups. It undertakes a number of initiatives, including holding fundraisers to assist with educational needs in Belize and among Belizean Americans and cultural events such as the Elegant Flair Dance Company Cultural Dance Tour.

It is not uncommon for different Belizean ethnic groups, such as the Garifunas or mestizos, to join together with people from other countries in Latin America or the Caribbean. While their countries of origin may be different, these people may have more in common with each other than with Belizean Americans as a whole. Additionally, while English is the official language of Belize, some of these ethnic groups may share some other common language, such as Spanish for those who are mestizos. Some Belizean Americans, especially the Creoles and Garifunas, who still make up the majority of Belizean American immigrants, relate most closely to Caribbean immigrant communities, while those who are mestizo or Mayan feel stronger connections to Latin American immigrant groups.

For Belizean Americans, assimilation into mainstream can be more dependent on ethnic or racial heritage than their country of origin. Those with darker skin and who are not proficient in English, for instance, experience more discrimination and can feel more isolated. They are more likely to live in neighborhoods or communities where the people share their experiences, culture, and language.

Belize is the only Central American country with a British/English cultural and linguistic tradition, although there are other English-speaking communities in Central America, such as in Panama and Nicaragua with the Bluefields. Additionally, British Guyana in South America is similar in that it is an English-speaking territory surrounded by Spanish-speaking neighbors. Belizean Americans and people from those other English-speaking communities are sometimes separated from Spanish-speaking Central or South American immigrants because of language and cultural issues. However, the ability to speak English can also facilitate a smoother transition to the United States. While other languages are widely spoken in Belize, notably Belize *Kriol* and Spanish, most people are at least relatively fluent in English. Research indicates that English proficiency helps immigrants to economically integrate into American society by allowing them to mesh better with the educational system and also attain skilled jobs that pay higher wages. Belizean Americans, along with Panamanian Americans and Costa Rican Americans, have the highest high school graduation rates among Central American immigrants, according to the Migration Immigration Resource in 2006.

Since English is the official language of Belize, it has also been been relatively easy to "send" American culture to Belize. Dating to the 1960s, there has been much U.S. mass media in Belize, including radio, music, newspapers, magazines, and television. Additionally, Belizean Americans send packages with American products, such as clothing, to relatives who still are living in Belize, America tourism has been on the rise, and middle- and upper-class Americans sometimes retire in Belize. Later waves of Belizean immigrants have had an easier time assimilating to the United States because of this exposure.

Since Belizean Americans come from a country with a wide range of ethnicities, they embrace many traditions and cultures. A Belizean American may, for instance, tell Anancy stories that come from an African tradition, listen to the punta rock that originated from Belizean Garifunas, play the British game cricket, and eat mestizo or Mayan foods such as tamales or corn dishes.

Traditions and Customs Since Belizean Americans come from a country with a wide range of ethnicities, they embrace many traditions and cultures. A Belizean American may, for instance, tell Anancy stories that come from an African tradition, listen to the *punta* rock that originated from Belizean Garifunas, play the British game cricket, and eat mestizo or Mayan foods such as tamales or corn dishes. Additionally, Belizean Americans have been strongly impacted by Caribbean culture and are viewed as being "laid back" in their approach to life.

In larger Belizean American communities, Belizean Americans maintain their Belizean identity by coming together for large celebrations on important occasions such as Belize Independence Day each September. These celebrations usually involve Belizean dancing, food, storytelling, and music, and guests from Belize are sometimes invited. These occasions embrace the multiple ethnic and cultural traditions of Belize, as well as mainstream American culture (such as American rock and roll bands and fair food). Often

HUDUT

Ingredients

4 large green plantains, peeled

2 large ripe plantains, peeled

2 cups coconut milk

1 cup white onion, sliced thin

4 garlic cloves, minced

2 whole habanero peppers, deseeded

1 bunch wild basil

salt and freshly ground black pepper, to taste

4 medium yellowtail snapper fish, scaled & cleaned

water for coconut milk and softening of the plantain in the Mata bowl, as needed

Preparation

Peel and boil the green and ripe plantain in a pot of salted water until soft. In a saucepot, add the coconut milk, onion, garlic, habanero and basil and cook over medium heat. Bring to a gentle simmer stirring occasionally. To the rich coconut broth, add the whole fish and continue to simmer until the fish is cooked. Remove the cooked plantain from water and place them in a food processor while still warm. Process until smooth. Add water and salt as necessary. Remove the smooth plantain (Hudut) from the food processor and reserve.

Serve soup while hot with spoonfuls of the Hudut dropped on top.

they help raise money for, say, scholarships for Belizean Americans or for causes that are deemed important to the community

Cuisine Belizean cuisine is a reflection of the various ethnic groups that make up the country, with influences including Caribbean, Creole, Mexican, and Mayan foods. Garifunas, for instance, commonly eat *hudut*, a dish made with green plantains that are mashed into a fish stew made with coconut milk. There are regional differences in the cuisine. For example, Belizeans who live near the sea depend more on seafood, while Mayans grow corn and use it for soft tortillas in their daily diet. Notable corn dishes include *garnaches*, which are flat fried corn circles with beans, cheese and onions.

Rice and beans (either red or black), often cooked with meat or meat fat, are staples of Belizean food. Since Belize borders the Caribbean, seafood is plentiful, including conch, red snapper, and squid. Chicken and oxtail dishes are also common, as are wild game such as iguana and deer.

Fish and meat stews are popular, and meats and fish are also used in meat pies and tamales, also called *dukunu*. Soups are also commonplace, such as *escabeche*

(made with chicken and an onion broth), *chirmole* or *relleno* (made with black beans), and varieties featuring seafood such as conch. Coconut is a common ingredient used for cooking rice and desserts such as coconut tarts. Bread made from wheat, corn, or cassava (such as *bammie*) is eaten with most meals, and pancake-type dishes like Johnny Cakes (a sweet pancake) are popular. Fry Jacks, a deep-fried puff pastry akin to *beignets* or *sopapillas*, are often eaten for breakfast (which is referred to as "tea") with beans and eggs.

There is no shortage of desserts, from lemon pie, milk cake (caramel cake), and cassava cake to bread pudding, sweet potato pone (or pound, a type of pudding), and coconut tarts. Fresh fruit juices made with watermelons, limes, or oranges are common, as are seaweed drinks made with seaweed and mixed usually with milk, cinnamon, nutmeg, and vanilla. Belikin is a popular Belizean brand of beer, and rum is often mixed with coconut milk.

Belizeans use a wide variety of spices and herbs, some common in the United States (oregano, thyme, ginger, garlic) and others more rare (annatto or achiote). Garifunas sometimes use seaweed to season their food. Mixed seasonings such as red or black *recardo* pastes come from Mayan and Mexican traditions. Red *recardo* is made from annato, garlic, black pepper, onion, and vinegar and is used in tamales and meat dishes; black *recardo* is made from burned corn tortillas, onion, garlic, cloves, and vinegar and is generally used for bean dishes. Hot peppers are also common. Maria Sharp's hot sauce is famous internationally, including among Belizean Americans. It contains habernero peppers (used in many Belizean dishes), carrots, onions, limejuice, vinegar, and spices.

Belizean Americans embrace general Belizean culinary traditions. Belizean restaurants are generally found in communities with larger populations of Belizean Americans, such as Los Angeles, Chicago, and New York City. They are often family-run and frequented by Belizean Americans wanting "home cooking" in addition to the general population. Little Belize in southern California, owned by Belizean Americans, is a well-known example.

Traditional Dress Since Western clothes are common in Belize, most Belizean Americans have no problem adapting to fashion styles in the United States. Due to the heat, Belizeans tend to dress casually, and that sometimes carries over to the attire worn by Belizean Americans. Men sometimes wear *guayaberas*, a loose-fitting white shirt that is generally pleated and is worn in many Latin American and Caribbean countries. Belizean Americans from particular ethnic groups may wear more traditional dress, especially for special occasions, celebrations, or dance performances. Mayan women, for example, might wear embroidered blouses and colored skirts, while Garifunas sometimes dress in colorful blouses and head scarves.

Dances and Songs The music of Belize includes influences from both Central America and the Caribbean. *Punta* rock, which is popular in both Belize and the United States, draws on Garifuna rhythms, though the styles of reggae, calypso, merengue, salsa, and hip-hop are also incorporated. *Punta* rock blends percussion instruments such as drums, turtle shells, and *shakes* (rattles) with electric guitars and keyboards, and the accompanying dance style features shuffling steps that call for heavy use of the hips. *Brukdown*, another traditional music of Belize that originated in logging camps, is created by turning objects such as bottles and tables into percussion instruments. It is not as popular as *punta* rock in either Belize or the United States.

Music and dance are major parts of Belizean American celebrations. Music is often a central aspect of Belizean Independence Day festivities, which are often highlighted by performances from native Belizeans, such as well-known singer Tony Wright. Dance groups from different Belizean traditions also perform at Belizean American celebrations; for example, the Elegant Flair Dance Group was featured at a Belizean Independence Day celebration in southern California in 2011.

Specific Belizean ethnic groups come together to form dance groups to keep their traditions alive in the United States. The *Lidereibuga* (powerful) Garifuna Ensemble, for example, is a dancing, singing, and drumming group that emerged from the Garifuna Language & Culture Academy in Los Angeles. It states that its objective is "to preserve our traditional and contemporary Garifuna songs, dances, and drumming. As Garifuna women and men connected to the lands of Belize, Guatemala, Honduras, Nicaragua, and Yurumein (St. Vincent), we are the lifeline of the Garifuna culture and it is our legacy to maintain and share it with the world."

Holidays The main holidays celebrated by Belizean Americans are Belizean Independence Day (September 21) and Belizean National Day (September 10), also called Saint George's Caye Day. In places with many Belizean Americans, these holidays are generally celebrated with large community-wide events that sometimes last for two days. They are usually held outdoors, and the dance and musical entertainment, such as *punta* rock, reflects the multiple ethnic groups of Belize. Belizean Americans sometimes travel from distant locations in the United States for the celebrations in major cities like Los Angeles. These events are not, however, all fun and games. Churches with large Belizean American memberships sometimes hold services for Belizean Independence Day.

Garifuna Settlement Day is November 19 and celebrates when the first large group of Garifuna people came to Belize, Guatemala, and Nicaragua in the early 1830s. U.S. celebrations of Garifuna Settlement Day began in the 1960s in Los Angeles, where there is now a Garifuna Settlement Day organization. In 2011

Illinois governor Pat Quinn proclaimed the month of November to be Garifuna-American Heritage Month in his state in a response to a petition by the Garinagu Lun Awanseruni members. Dancing, food, drumming, and parties are part of the festivities.

Since many Belizeans are Christian, they also celebrate Christmas and Easter. In Skokie, Illinois, an annual Christmas Bram is staged by the Belize Culture and Heritage Association. A Christmas Bram is when people dance and play music in the streets in a parade-like manner; the rhythm of the percussion-based music is described as *bram! bram! bram!* In Belize, *Carnaval*, similar to Mardi Gras, is celebrated just prior to Lent by the Spanish-speaking population; Spanish-speaking Belizean Americans sometimes join with other Central American immigrants in celebrating *Carnaval* in the United States.

Health Care Issues and Practices Belizean Americans generally adhere to Western medical practices. Some specific ethnic groups also utilize more traditional or indigenous types of folk medicine and healing. For instance, a Belize *Kriol* cure for a cut is to peel a banana or a plaintain, rub salt on it, and then place it on the wound. Among Mayans, a traditional healer employs herbs and other remedies for everyday ailments. With the rise of "alternative" medicine in the United States, the demand for herbal medicines has increased. In cities with large numbers of Belizean Americans, healthcare outreach programs have been initiated for Belizean immigrants, especially those who are economically disadvantaged. Los Angeles, for example, has the Belize Cancer Center.

FAMILY AND COMMUNITY LIFE

The family, both nuclear and extended, is important in Belizean American culture for both social and economic reasons. The later waves of Belizean immigrants were able to come to the United States because of social networks with family members who were already established there. Belizean Americans maintain ties to relatives in Belize; some, in fact, immigrated to the United States simply so that they could get better jobs and send money to their family members back home. Sometimes Belizeans have shuttled between the two countries depending on economic opportunities. Cultural celebrations such as Belize Independence Day help to strengthen relationships among Belizean Americans. By Belizean standards, the majority of Belizean American immigrants come from middle-class or higher backgrounds where Western ideas of family life are embraced.

In Belize single-mother families are typical, partially because large numbers of men have immigrated to the United States and elsewhere to find work. Grandparents sometimes care for children. Family sizes differ depending on the ethnic group; mestizos, for example, tend to have more children. Various Belizean ethnic groups have particular family traditions or rituals. The *dügü*, for instance, is a religious ceremony involving the extended family in Garifuna communities. Ancestors are called upon to help with healing and/or other serious family problems; a mass is held, followed by two days of continuous singing, dancing, and drumming. Mestizos have *quinciñeras* that celebrates a girl's transition to womanhood on her fifteenth birthday. The most recent waves of Belizean immigrants tend to be younger and have fewer family and other ties to Belize.

Gender Roles While males generally dominate economically and socially, Creole families are traditionally considered matriarchal. The matriarchal structure developed partially from the history of male slaves working far away in logging camps while the women labored close to home and presided over the family. The concept of *machismo* is evident in Belizean culture, but it is less strongly ingrained than in some other Latin American countries.

The occupations of Belizean Americans generally follow traditional gender lines: women often are domestics, teachers, and nurses, while men are skilled manual workers and business managers. These roles have a historical relationship to the immigration patterns of Belizean Americans, such as men being recruited to come work in the United States during World War II, occupational preference laws that allowed women to immigrate if they were nurses or teachers, and, beginning the 1990s, women being brought to the United States to be domestic workers by Americans who were tourists in Belize. Since the 1990s, American television shows, other media like the Internet, and the rise of tourism have influenced the gender roles of Belizeans, making them more akin to those in the United States.

Education In Belize, though a high percentage of the population is literate and school is compulsory until age twelve, only about half of the people continue to high school, and fewer go on to higher education. The University of Belize, which opened in 2000, is the only comprehensive university in Belize. Most schools in Belize are subsidized by the government and are parochial, and some Belizean immigrants continue to send their children to parochial schools in the United States, such as St. Michael's Catholic School in Los Angeles.

From the 1960s through the 1980s, some Belizeans felt that the government of the United Democratic Party was so focused on gaining independence that it was not enacting educational policies that would lead to better jobs. This prompted Belizeans to immigrate to the United States, where they felt the educational opportunities were better. In O. Nigel Bolland's *Belize: A New Nation in Central America*, he writes of the poor training available in professional and technical sectors in Belize in the 1980s. In addition, 2006 report from Migration Information Source pinpoints differences in the educational levels of later

waves of immigrants: "Though the emigration rate [from Belize] has fallen, its effects may have become more pronounced since more educated Belizeans are leaving. As noted in the country's official census report, half of emigrants held high school degrees while the percentage with post-high school education rose 64 percent above the rate recorded in 1991."

Belizean American organizations such as the Belize Cultural Foundation focus on providing educational (and economic) advancement for Belizeans in the United States and Belize. Meanwhile, the Concerned Belizeans of Chicago organizes benefits to provide school supplies and scholarships for students in Belize.

Relations with Other Americans For Belizeans, social, familial, and economic ties to their home country remain as strong, or become even stronger, once they immigrate to the United States. For this reason, Belizeans are often called a transnational people. While the English proficiency of Belizean immigrants allows them to assimilate more easily into mainstream U.S. culture than some other immigrant groups, they maintain strong ethnic identities. It is not uncommon for Belizeans to immigrate to the United States with the idea of eventually returning to Belize. Many continue to send funds to family or even to Belizean entrepreneurs who might "field test" ideas in Belize. Businesses such as the American Belizean Investment Company identify and fund small-scale business opportunities in Belize. The Belize Post Office reported that in 1996, $2 million in postal orders were cashed, and this does not include other ways of sending money to Belize, such as by Western Union.

Belizean Americans tend to identify with groups that have similar ethnic origins. For example, mestizos have a connection to the Latino community, while Belize Creoles relate to Caribbean Americans. Dark-skinned Belizean Americans and those whose main language is not English suffer the same types of discrimination and prejudice as other people of color and non-English-speaking immigrants in the United States.

EMPLOYMENT AND ECONOMIC CONDITIONS

Traditionally, most Belizeans have immigrated to the United States to improve their economic circumstances. In the 1940s and early 1950s, Belizean men were recruited for agricultural work such as citrus farming in Florida and for industrial jobs in the north due to manpower shortages caused by World War II. In the 1960s occupational preference quotas included domestics and nurses, jobs that attracted female Belizeans; in the 1970s a demand for low-wage service workers in large urban centers was met by more Belizean immigrants. When tourism in Belize grew in the 1990s and 2000s, some families from the United States would bring Belizean women back with them to be their live-in domestic help. In fact, the majority of Belizean American women were employed as domestics in the 1990s. In the Chicago Belizean American community, many Belizean American men worked in construction or as carpenters.

Many Belizean Americans have come to the United States for a higher education, but upon obtaining their degrees, they have often been unable to find jobs in their fields back in Belize. Thus, Belizeans who receive degrees in, say, computer science or engineering choose to settle more permanently in the United States. Some Belizean Americans are doctors and nurses or are in the banking world. As is the case with many immigrant groups, Belizean Americans have opened Belizean restaurants or small businesses that cater to their culture. Other Belizean Americans work in "transnational enterprises," small- to medium-sized businesses that might have "outlets" in both Belize and the United States.

Organizations such as the Belize Cultural Foundation of California focus on the economic situation of Belizean Americans. The foundation defines itself as a "philanthropic organization of concerned Belizean Americans united to promote the economic advancement of the Belizean community, with a focus on economic and educational empowerment, and public advocacy to improve the quality of life in Belize and the United States."

POLITICS AND GOVERNMENT

The specific voting patterns of Belizean Americans have not been documented. However, people from ethnic groups with which Belizean Americans are connected, such as blacks and Latinos, tend to vote Democratic.

Belizean Americans maintain close ties with the political process in their home country. In fact, major Belizean political parties send members to the United States to garner support from Belizean Americans for elections and policies. There has been, however, some conflict surrounding Belizean Americans' dual citizenship in terms of voting rights and participation in other Belizean affairs. After the United Democratic Party came to power in Belize in 1984, it granted dual citizenship to Belizean Americans who had lost their citizenship when Belize became independent in 1981 under the People's United Party. However, this legislation did not specify the right to vote (among other rights, such as land ownership). There has been movement toward changing some of these laws. Proponents feel that because Belizean Americans contribute so much economically to Belize, they should be allowed to continue to vote and have other Belizean rights, even if they are U.S. citizens.

NOTABLE INDIVIDUALS

Activists Cheryl L. Noralez is a Belizean American activist and promoter of Garifuna culture, was the founder and president of the Garifuna Heritage Foundation United and also established the Garifuna

Belizean American Milt Palacio (1978–) is depicted playing basketball in Turin, Italy in 2009. FRANCESCO RICHIERI/EB / GETTY IMAGES

Language & Culture Academy in 2005. Born in Belize, she moved to Los Angeles when she was four years old.

Literature Zee Edgell (1940–) was born Zelma Inez Tucker in Belize City and eventually became a resident of the United States. She is a journalist, novelist, women's right advocate, and college professor. Edgell held numerous prestigious positions, such as director of the Department of Women's Affairs of Belize, head of the Women's Bureau of Belize, secretary to the governing board for Concerned Women For Family Planning in Dacca, Bangladesh, and UNICEF consultant to the Somali Women's Democratic Organization in Mogadishu, Somali. She taught at the University College of Belize, Old Dominion University, Kent State University, and the University of Wisconsin. Her first novel, *Berka Lamb*, was published in 1982, followed by *In Times Like These* (1991) and *The Festival of San Joaquin* (1997). All of her novels involve the

Former track and field world champion, and professional basketball player, Marion Jones (1975–) is a citizen of both the United States and Belize. EVERETT COLLECTION INC / ALAMY

history of Belize and its diverse ethnic and cultural traditions. In 2009 she was awarded an honorary doctorate of letters from the University of the West Indies.

Music Shyne (1978–) is a Belizean American rapper who was born Jamal Michael Barrow in Belize City. In 2006 he legally changed his name to Moses Michael Levi to reflect his grandmother's Jewish heritage. His father, Dean Barrow, became prime minister of Belize in 2008. Shyne moved to Brooklyn, New York, at age thirteen with his mother. His albums include *Shyne* (2000), *Godfather Buried Alive* (2004) and *Shyne's Third Studio Album* (2013). In 1999 he was involved in a shooting in a New York club and was sentenced to ten years in prison in 2001. *Godfather Buried Alive* came out while he was in jail, and most of the tracks were previously recorded. After being released from prison in 2009, he was deported because, while he had a green card, he had not naturalized as an American citizen. He lived in Jerusalem as an Orthodox Jew in 2010. In early 2013, he garnered publicity for a series of Twitter rants against President Barack Obama in which he insisted the president do something to address violence on the streets of Chicago and help him be able to return to the United States.

Lisa Tucker (1989–), singer and actress, was born in California to parents of Belizean and African American descent. Her music includes pop, R&B, and rock. She was among the top ten finalists on *American Idol* in 2002 when she was sixteen years old. Her acting credits include TV shows such as *Zoey 101*

(2007–2008), *90210* (2009), *The Game* (2009), *The Vampire Dairies* (2011), and *The Following* (2013).

Frankie "Pa-G" Garcia is a Garifuna American musician who was born in Brooklyn, New York, and raised in Dangriga,. He played the *primero* drums (providing cross rhythms) and *segundo* drums (providing tempo and bass) as well as the turtle shells, maracas, congas, guitar, and bass. In the 1990s, Garcia began playing *punta* rock with bands such as Pen Cayetano, Turtle Shell Band, and Ugurau Band and also drummed for dance groups. In the studio, he performed on albums such as *Trival Vibes* (2000) by Bredda David and *Hot Party Vibes* (2007) by the Caribbean Dynamics Band. He has toured in the United States, Europe, and Latin America. Garcia received the Isabel Flores Award for Garifuna drumming in 2010.

Science and Medicine Avery August (1966–) is a Belizean American born in Belize City who immigrated to Los Angeles with his family after a year of study at Belize Technical College. He then received a Bachelor of Science degree from California Statue University and a Ph.D. from Cornell University. Starting in 2010, he was the chair of the Department of Microbiology and Immunology at Cornell University. His areas of research were the regulation of T cell activation and the development of lung immune responses.

Sports Marion Jones (1975–), a Belizean American born in Los Angeles to a Belizean mother and an African American father, was a track and field star and a basketball player. She was part of the 1994 North Carolina Tar Heels women's basketball team that won the National Collegiate Athletic Association championship. In 2000 she became the first woman to win five medals during an Olympics. However, she was stripped of her medals in 2007 after admitting to using performance-enhancing drugs and served six months in federal prison. After her release from prison, Jones became a motivational speaker whose goal was to help others cope with life-challenging events. In 2010 she published a book, *On the Right Track: From Olympic Downfall to Finding Forgiveness and the Strength to Overcome and Succeed*, and played for the Tulsa Shock in the Women's National Basketball Association.

Chito Martinez (1965–), born Reyenaldo Ignacio Martinez in Belize, was a Belizean American baseball player. He was drafted by the Kansas City Royals in 1984 and played for the Baltimore Orioles from 1991 to 1993.

Milt Palacio (1978–), basketball player, was born in Los Angeles to Belizean parents. He played point guard in the National Basketball Association for the Vancouver Grizzlies, Boston Celtics, Phoenix Suns, Cleveland Cavaliers, Toronto Raptors, and Utah Jazz. He also played professionally in Europe for teams in Serbia, Russia, Greece, Spain, and Lithuania.

Verno Jeremias Phillips (1969–), a Belizean American born in Belize City, is a boxer whose nickname was the "Cool Ruler." He held titles in the

National Boxing Association's light middleweight division (2002), the International Boxing Federation's light middleweight division (2004, 2008), and the Trans America middleweight division (2006).

Stage and Screen Arlen Escarpeta (1981–), Belizean American actor, has appeared in films such as *We Are Marshall* (2006), *Friday the 13th* (2009), and *Final Destination Five* (2011) and television series such as *American Dreams*, *The Client List*, *House*, *Law & Order: Special Victims Unit*, *Without A Trace*, *Cold Case*, *Judging Amy*, and *ER*.

Kareem Ferguson was a Belizean American actor and director who was born in Belize. He was a member of the Actors Gang Theater and Ensemble Studio Theater in California. In 2011 his performance in the play *Free Man of Color* garnered a nomination from the National Association for the Advancement of Colored People for an award for best lead actor.

MEDIA

While there are no specific Belizean American newspapers or radio and TV programming, the Belizean American community stays abreast of news from Belize via online sources. Most Belizean newspapers can be read online, and many Belizean radio stations can be streamed from the Internet. Links to these can be found on *www.belizenews.com*.

ORGANIZATIONS AND ASSOCIATIONS

Belize Cultural Foundation

Established in 2000, the Belize Cultural Foundation is, as it describes itself, a "philanthropic organization of concerned Belizean Americans united to promote the economic advancement of the Belizean community, with a focus on economic and educational empowerment, and public advocacy to improve the quality of life in Belize and the United States."

George Greenwood, Founding Member
34197 Lake Breeze Drive
Yucaipa, California 92399
Phone: (323) 251-4220
Fax: (909) 746-8728
Email: belizeculturalfoundation@gmail.com
URL: http://belizeculturalfoundation.org/

Belize Culture and Heritage Association (BCHA)

BCHA was established in 2005 and has the following motto: "One Country, Many Cultures," It aims to represent and educate the Belizean community.

P.O. Box 345
Evanston, Illinois 60204
Email: info@haceb.org
URL: http://www.haceb.org

Belize in America

Belize in America bills itself as an "online hub that displays, promotes and broadcasts all of Belize's rich and diverse culture in America." In addition to news

and discussion forums, it provides information on business, entertainment, education, culture, and various events.

Cyril Garcia, Publisher and Senior Editor
211 South State College Boulevard
Suite 417
Anaheim, California 92806
Email: info@BelizeinAmerica.net
URL: http://belizeinamerica.net

Concerned Belizean Association of Los Angeles

This organization provides information on matters concerning Belizeans and sponsors various events for Belizeans in the Los Angeles area.

Phyllis Palacio, President
3940 Roxton Avenue
Los Angeles, California 90008
Phone: (323) 295-3612
Email: rox3940@aol.com

Garifuna American Heritage Foundation United (GAHFU)

The GAHFU states that its mission "is to serve the Garifuna-American community in the greater Los Angeles area, the Untied States and abroad through cultural programs, outreach, advocacy and social services programs."

Cheryl Noralez, Chief Executive Officer and Founder
2127 Atlantic Avenue
Long Beach, California 90806
Phone: (323) 898-6841
Email: gahfuinc@garifunaheritagefoundation.org
URL: www.garifunaheritagefoundation.org

MUSEUMS AND RESEARCH CENTERS

There are no research centers or museums in the United States specifically dedicated to Belizean Americans. However, institutions such as Belize's National Institute of Culture and History in Belize do outreach and collaborations with other countries, as well as publish information in print and on online.

SOURCES FOR ADDITIONAL STUDY

Babcock, Elizabeth C., and Dennis Conway. "Why International Migration Has Important Consequences for the Development of Belize." *Conference of Latin Americanist Geographers Yearbook 2000* 26, no. 1: 71–89.

"Belizeans." *Encyclopedia of Chicago History*. Encyclopedia of Chicago History, 2005. Web. 21 Jan 2013.

Straughan, Jerome F. *Belizean Immigrants in Los Angeles*. Los Angeles: University of Southern California, 2004.

———. "Emigration from Belize since 1981." In *Taking Stock: Belize at 25 Years of Independence*. Ed. Barbara Balbone and Joseph Palacio. Benque Viejo del Carmen, Belize: Cubola, 2007.

Wilk, Richard R. "Real Belizean Food: Building Local Identity in the Transnational Caribbean." *American Anthropologist*, June 1999: 244–55.

BLACKFOOT

Richard C. Hanes and Matthew T. Pifer

OVERVIEW

The Blackfoot Nation, a confederacy of Native American tribes, originally lived in what are now northern Montana and the Canadian provinces of Alberta and Saskatchewan. Their traditional territory stretched from the North Saskatchewan River in Canada in the north to the Yellowstone River in Montana to the south, and from the Rocky Mountains in the west to the Great Sand Hills in Saskatchewan to the east. High rolling plains, steep cliffs, and long harsh winters distinguish the Blackfoot territory. The name *Blackfoot* is the English translation of *Siksika*, a Blackfoot/Siksika-language word that refers to the dark-colored moccasins worn by some Blackfoot; some say their moccasins were blackened by prairie fire ash or dyes. The term *Blackfoot* is more commonly used in Canada, while *Blackfeet* is more commonly used in the United States.

Population estimates of the Blackfoot before contact with the Europeans vary. In 1790 Donald McKenzie, an early European explorer and fur trader, estimated that there were about 9,000 Blackfoot. In 1832 George Catlin, a European artist of Native Americans, estimated that the Blackfoot confederation population was 16,500. The early Blackfoot were nomads and lived in bands of about 10 to 30 lodges (about 80 to 240 people); people were able to move from one band to another, and sometimes entire bands split and individuals joined new bands. The Blackfoot Nation is a confederation of several distinct tribes or nations, including the South Piegan (or Pikuni) that live in Montana and the Akainawa (or the Blood or Kainai), the North Peigan (the spelling used in Canada), and the Siksika (or North Blackfoot) that are in the Canadian area. Before Europeans arrived, nomadic Blackfoot followed animal herds, especially buffalo, and also migrated in seasonal rounds to areas where roots, berries, and other plants were ready to be used for food or medicine. They hunted buffalo to use for food, shelter, and clothing. Their nomadic way of life following animals and vegetation allowed them to be self-sufficient, even through harsh winters.

The Blackfeet Indian Reservation in the United States is in northwestern Montana and is about the size of Delaware. The Blackfoot are one of six tribes in the United States still living on ancestral land. Beginning in the 1830s Blackfoot land was appropriated and tribal members were forced to move onto reservations to make room for white settlers through a series of manipulative treaties, massacres, presidential orders, and Congressional acts. Additionally, European colonization created an environment in which the buffalo came close to extinction, making it impossible for the Blackfoot to maintain their subsistence-based way of life. Oil drilling on Blackfoot land was an important part of the economy from the 1920s to the 1980s, when economic factors in the oil industry and elsewhere made energy companies less interested in drilling and production on the reservation. In 2009, however, new fracking technologies (hydraulic fracturing of rocks that allows gas and oil to be extracted) and rising oil prices made oil drillers again interested in the oil on Blackfoot land. The environmental and spiritual consequences of fracking, however, make its use controversial when posited against high unemployment and the poor economy found on the reservation.

According to the 2010 U.S. Census, 10,405 people lived on the Blackfeet Reservation. According to the Blackfeet Enrollment Department, as of late 2011 the Blackfoot Nation consisted of 16,924 enrolled tribal members and an estimated 4,500 tribal descendants, making it the largest tribe in Montana and one of the largest tribes in the United States. About 8,500 enrolled Blackfoot live on the reservation, as do Blackfoot descendants, Indians from other tribes, and non-Indians. About 7,500 Blackfoot members live elsewhere in the United States and worldwide. Two other U.S. states with significant numbers of Blackfoot are California and Washington. In 2000, members of the traditional Blackfoot Confederacy issued a declaration rejecting the United States' and Canada's jurisdiction over them and began to call themselves the Blackfoot Nation rather than the Blackfoot Confederacy; the U.S. federal government ignored the declaration.

HISTORY OF THE PEOPLE

Early History Archeological evidence shows that the Blackfoot have lived for thousands of years in and around their current location. The bones of the Blackfoot and the bones of buffalo more than 6,000

years old were found at a buffalo jump (a cliff where hunters killed the animals by driving them over the edge) near the reservation. The archeological site of this buffalo jump was declared a World Heritage Site by UNESCO in 1981.

In early times the Blackfoot roamed the plains to follow herds of buffalo. They used dogs to pull *travois*, frame structures consisting of two long poles attached to the dogs' sides used to drag loads over land. This period was called the Dog Days. Scouts would report the location of herds, and then the camp would pack up to go hunt the buffalo. During the Dog Days the Blackfoot used arrows and lances in wars with their enemies, including the Shoshone, the Plains Cree, the Sioux, the Flathead, and the Assiniboin. Often they allied in battle with their neighbors the Gros Ventre and the Sarcee. By the mid-nineteenth century they had pushed their enemies, particularly the Shoshone, Flathead, and Kootenai, west across the Rocky Mountains.

The Dog Days came before the horse and gun era that began around 1750. The Blackfoot called horses *ponokamita* (elk dogs). Horses changed the way of life of the Blackfoot. Horses could carry more and run faster than dogs. Horses were also used for barter—healers and dreamers who designed shields could be paid with horses, for instance. Warriors would raid other tribes in order to get the best horses. While individuals did not keep many horses, wealth could be measured by how many horses a person gave away.

In the mid-eighteenth century fur trappers exploring the West hoped to establish trading relationships with the Native populations; they were the first non-Indians to visit the region. The first trapper to provide an extensive written record of the Blackfoot was David Thompson, an agent for the Hudson's Bay Company who traveled into Blackfoot territory in 1787. From then until the near extermination of buffalo in 1883, trading companies impacted the life of the Blackfoot, economically and socially. The companies, for instance, introduced the Blackfoot to new technologies, such as guns, and introduced new diseases, most notably smallpox. Smallpox epidemics devastated the Blackfoot population in 1781, 1837, and 1869. In 1837 approximately 6,000 people, or half the tribe, died.

The first whiskey traders moved into Blackfoot territory around 1830. They were followed by settlers, missionaries, soldiers, and government representatives. Many tried to "civilize" the Blackfoot and force them onto reservations in order to make room for white settlers. Alcohol was introduced into the tribe. Blackfoot culture and social structures began to deteriorate, chiefs were not as influential, and buffalo and wildlife populations started to decrease.

In the mid-nineteenth century the Blackfoot began to cede much of their territory through various treaties and agreements, the first of which was the 1855 agreement known as Lame Bull's Treaty after the Piegan chief who signed it. The Blackfoot people believed their homeland was guaranteed if they shared hunting rights with other tribes (in agreements that were to be for ninety-nine years) and if they allowed safe passage for others through Blackfoot territory in order to construct roads, railways, telegraph lines, military posts, and settlements. In exchange, the U.S. government was to provide the Blackfoot with needed goods and funds. This treaty ceded much traditional Blackfoot territory within U.S. borders and left a reserve for the tribe's use. However, in 1862 and 1863 gold was found in the common hunting ground and within Blackfoot lands. Mining camps were set up and miners trespassed into Blackfoot country looking for gold. More than 15,000 miners worked and explored in and around Blackfoot country. By 1865, ten years after the treaty was signed, there were virtually no more bison in the shared hunting ground. These settlers and miners also introduced new diseases that the Blackfoot had not been previously exposed to and, thus, had no resistance to. Scarlet fever killed more than 1,000 Blackfoot in 1864.

New treaties in 1865 and 1868 significantly decreased the size of Blackfoot territory along the southern boundary. Continued pressures from expanding white settlements led to resistance by some Blackfoot. In retaliation, the U.S. Cavalry, commanded by Major Eugene M. Baker, indiscriminately massacred 173 Blackfoot in 1870 at Chief Heavy Runner's Piegan camp on the Marias River. Baker believed the camp was hostile, but in fact it consisted primarily of women, children, and elders recovering from smallpox.

In 1871 the U.S. Congress resolved that Native American nations were not separate nations and, thus, instead of negotiating treaties presidential orders and Congressional acts would be used to appropriate land. Three years later an executive order further reduced the Blackfoot territory in Montana and formally established a reservation on the eastern flanks of the Rocky Mountains next to the Canadian border. The U.S. government moved the southern boundary of the reservation 200 miles northward and opened the land to settlements but did not give any compensation to the tribe. In the north, the Canadian government established reservations (called reserves) in Alberta for the Blackfoot in 1877 through Treaty No. 7, which ceded much of the traditional Native territory. The Bloods reserved almost 350,000 acres, the North Blackfoot more than 178,000 acres, and the North Peigan more than 113,000 acres. Additional land in the United States was relinquished through agreements in 1887 and 1896.

With industrialization on the rise in the late nineteenth century, buffalo herds that were already stressed began to be hunted even more. New factories with steam engines had driving belts that needed durable material. Buffalo hide was some of the strongest material available for these belts. As the population grew in the eastern United States, demand increased

for buffalo robes for winter coats and for blankets used in sleds and open carriages. Some men who were dislocated by the Civil War moved to Montana territory and started to trade in buffalo hides.

The last buffalo hunt by the Blackfoot took place in 1882. Buffalo were on the verge of extinction, radically affecting the Blackfoot diet, which had consisted primarily of buffalo. The buffalo population on the plains dropped from nearly five million in 1870 to almost zero in 1875, leaving the Blackfoot dependent on government goods for survival. Many moved to the Badger Creek Agency for supplies, but rations were often not available. In what came to be known as "Starvation Winter," the tribe was nearly wiped out; about one out of every four Blackfoot was killed, leaving fewer than 3,000 tribe members remaining. The ridge behind Badger Creek Agency is still known as Ghost Ridge because of the number of people who were buried there. Since the time of the first treaty, 80 percent of the people had died, and the buffalo were virtually gone. The deaths from Starvation Winter combined with the mass invasion of white people also resulted in a high rate of intermarriage between white men and Blackfoot women.

In 1887 white ranchers near the reservation pressured the U.S. government to hold land cession hearings. These hearings were held during the severe wintertime when it was difficult for the Blackfoot to attend, and thus a bare majority of leaders agreed to split the reservation into three separate agencies and relinquished more land for $125,000 per year for ten years.

In 1896 the Northern Rockies were taken from the tribe for $1.5 million. Speculators were unable to find the rich minerals they hoped would be there, so they proceeded to use the land to create Glacier National Park. As late as 1925 there was pressure on the Blackfoot to give away more land to expand the park.

Lands within the Blackfeet Reservation were allotted to individual tribal members between 1907 and 1911 under the General Allotment Act of 1887. Each enrolled member of the Blackfoot tribe was granted an allotment of land within the reservation. In many cases these allotments were split, making management of the lands difficult. This process also led to "excess" lands falling into non-Indian ownership. Any land that was not accounted for could be sold to the public, which left nearly 800,000 acres open for settlement.

During the late nineteenth century, the U.S. and Canadian governments, viewing the Blackfoot as a financial burden, sent the children to boarding schools in an attempt at a forced assimilation of the next generation. Some were first sent to the Carlisle Indian Industrial School in Pennsylvania and later to boarding schools in Montana for ten or eleven months of the year. Families were broken up, and children were dressed in non-native uniforms and forbidden to speak their native language or practice important traditional customs, such as smudging. Additionally, children were abused by staff, and the atmosphere encouraged hostility and mistreatment between children. Many of these children began to lose their cultural pride and their connection with family and community, developing low self-esteem and other negative patterns, all of which affected the Blackfoot community for generations.

Modern Era American Indians became U.S. citizens in 1924. Ten years later, according to the terms of the 1934 Indian Reorganization Act, the Blackfoot became an "IRA Tribe," receiving several guarantees from the U.S. federal government. For example, the act stopped reservation land from being sold to non-Indians by giving trust land status to the tribe while the federal government holds the legal title; beneficial interest is with the tribe. This also gave the tribe a legal basis for sovereignty and self-governance. After this act, the Blackfoot adopted their own constitution. The Blackfeet Tribal Business Council was created in 1935 to manage reservation business and administrative affairs. The U.S. government provided credit to help the Blackfoot expand cattle ranches, which improved some tribe members' economic situation. During World War II, many Blackfoot served in the military, and others worked off the reservation.

In 1964 thirty Blackfoot were killed and hundreds were left homeless by a flood that destroyed Two Medicine River Dam. From this catastrophe came the impetus to create housing and industrial development programs that helped build schools, improve hospitals, and provide adequate housing. The Community Action Program, Neighborhood Youth Corps, Volunteers in Service to America (VISTA), senior citizen programs, and a series of Economic Development Administration projects provided assistance. In the 1970s the Blackfeet Indian Housing Authority sponsored, for instance, Mutual Help Housing, a project that required people to contribute their own labor to building a house they would live in. This program not only provided shelter but also helped unemployed Blackfoot acquire employment skills. During these years oil and gas revenues and natural minerals found on the reservation also helped the Blackfoot's economic situation.

Blackfeet Community College in Browning, Montana, opened in 1974. In 1978 Glacier National Park considered fencing its border with the Blackfeet Reservation, but Blackfoot complaints and at least one Congressional intervention stopped the fencing from being completed. Also that year Congress passed the Indian Child Welfare Act, which granted tribal governments the power to rule in child custody cases. In 1979 the state of Montana passed a law stipulating that in order to hold a position on or near reservation land, public school teachers must take classes in Native

American studies. During the 1960s and 1970s there was a strong movement toward re-embracing Blackfoot culture and language. Elders were encouraged to teach the "old ways" and language to the younger generation. By the 1980s and 1990s dictionaries, grammar books, and language courses were created, while local Head Start programs taught about Blackfoot language and culture.

In 1998 all four Blackfoot tribes began a movement to re-establish the Blackfoot Confederacy, made up of the United States Blackfeet and the Canadian Blackfoot, Peigan, and Blood tribes. The Blackfoot Confederacy represents all Blackfoot people, working with museums to repatriate "tribal treasures," dealing with border issues between Canada and the United States, and helping to bring jobs and government funding to the tribes.

In 2000, members of the traditional Blackfoot Confederacy issued a three-page declaration "rejecting Canada's and the United States' jurisdiction over their traditional territory and reverting to the state of affairs that existed before European contact." They began to call themselves the Blackfoot Nation, rather than the Blackfoot Confederacy. Each of the tribal members present at the meeting where the declaration was issued spoke of being marginalized by the Indian Act or by the federally recognized government on their home territory; they were not supportive of the elected governments. The federal government ignored the declaration.

In 2008 the Blackfoot Digital Library was created to be an educational resource and share the true stories of Blackfoot families, as well as to respond to misrepresentations of the tribal past and present.

Although the Jay Treaty of 1794 granted North American tribes freedom to travel between the United States and Canada, in 2009 a new requirement made it necessary for people to show passports when crossing the border. Many Blackfoot were stopped and questioned at the border, and some were denied entry. This is particularly difficult for tribes from nations such as the Blackfoot, who have reservations on both sides of the border.

Contemporary challenges for the Blackfoot are high unemployment, issues regarding treaty and water rights, and high rates of alcoholism and suicide. The Blackfoot Nation has established its own alcohol-prevention programs for youth that provides practical, psychological, and spiritual guidance that aligns with Blackfoot cultural traditions and beliefs.

SETTLEMENT IN THE UNITED STATES

Four reservations compose the Blackfoot Nation. The sole United States reservation is the Blackfeet Reservation in Montana, which is more than 1.5 million acres in size, containing a diverse landscape of mountains and hills and lakes and rivers. The other three reservations are located in Alberta, Canada: the Blackfoot Reserve on the Bow River, the Blood

Reserve situated between the Belly and St. Mary rivers, and the smaller Peigan (Piikani) Reserve located a short distance west of the Blood Reserve.

Archeological digs show that Blackfoot were hunting buffalo on Blackfoot territory 6,000 years ago. The Blackfoot were nomadic hunters and gatherers traversing the plains in small bands, each with a chief; there was no central chief. They had alliances with the Gros Ventre and Sari tribes but were often at war with other tribes, including the Shoshone, Plains Cree, Flathead, and Assiniboine. A nomadic lifestyle allowed the Blackfoot to be self-sufficient in harsh conditions. They were considered one of the most powerful tribes of the northern Great Plains. They continued to be able to support their families and communities by following the buffalo and plant life of the plains until white settlers took over much of their territory and created an environment in which the buffalo, the Blackfoot's main economic source, were virtually extinct.

While more than half of the enrolled tribal members lived on the reservation in 2011, there have been various dispersals of the tribe in modern history. Beginning in the late nineteenth century, the U.S. government sent many children to boarding schools in Montana (on and off the reservation) and elsewhere in the United States. During World War II many Blackfoot men were soldiers or moved off the reservation. By the end of World War II, nearly one-third of

U.S. Blackfoot had moved off the reservation. After World War II was over, Blackfoot who served in the military or who went elsewhere for work returned to the reservation, creating a labor surplus and making it hard to find work. Many Blackfoot moved to other states and found only low-paying jobs and experienced discrimination; some later returned to the reservation. These dispersals also meant that the Blackfoot language was lost, as were some cultural traditions. After World War II and through the beginning of the twenty-first century, high unemployment was a main reason for Blackfoot to leave the reservation. Some also left to pursue higher educational opportunities not available on the reservation; some returned after graduating, while others needed to seek employment elsewhere with their new skills. While Montana still remains the state with the highest population of Blackfoot, California, and Washington are also home to significant numbers.

LANGUAGE

Blackfoot, or Siksika, is an Algonquian language spoken by more than 8,000 people in southern Alberta and northern Montana. The Blackfoot Algonquian dialect is related to the languages of several Plains, Eastern Woodlands, and Great Lakes tribes. When migrating west, the Blackfoot encountered Athapascan-, Shoshonean-, and Siouan-speaking tribes. The Blackfoot recorded their traditional stories and important events,

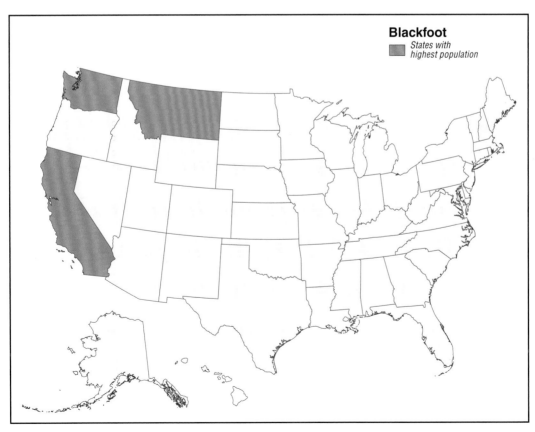

Blackfoot
States with highest population

such as wars, in pictographs on the inside and outside surfaces of tipis and on their buffalo robes. People recorded the most significant events of a particular year by painting the event on hides called "winter counts." In the 1800s British clergyman John William Tims developed a written language using symbols to represent sounds and used this to translate the Bible into the Blackfoot language. While the Siksika (Blackfoot), Kainai (Blood), Ammskaapipiikani (Southern Piegan in the United States), and Apatohsihpiikani (Northern Peigan in Canada) all speak the Blackfoot language, over time each has developed slight linguistic variations—different words for the same thing or different pronunciations.

Forcing Blackfoot children to go to boarding schools where speaking their native language was forbidden almost made the Blackfoot language extinct. A movement in the 1960s and 1970s encouraged elders to pass down the language. By 1989 a Blackfoot dictionary had been published, and in 1991 a Blackfoot grammar book was published. The Blackfoot language is taught in schools on or near the reservation as well as at the Blackfeet Language Studies Department at Blackfeet Community College. In 1987 the Piegan Institute was created as a language-survival school to counteract the loss of the Blackfoot language. The institute runs the Cuts Wood School immersion program in kindergarten through eighth grade with the objectives to "increase the number of Blackfoot-language speakers, to increase the cultural knowledge base of community members, and to actively influence positive community-based change. Our national objectives are to promote support for Native language issues through advocacy and education and to provide a voice to the national and international dialogue on Native Language restoration." In 1995 the Nizipuhwahsin Center opened as a Blackfoot-language immersion school that has full-day programming for children ages five through twelve. By the first decade of the twenty-first century, Blackfoot-language immersion schools had been established in Browning, Montana, including Cuts Wood, Lost Children, and Moccasin Flat School. At Moccasin Flat School a sign on the door reads "Please do not speak English here." Blackfoot language-resource sites have been established on the Internet.

Greetings and Popular Expressions Examples of Blackfoot greetings, expressions, and commonly used terms include the following:

Tsá kaanistáópííhpa?

How are you?

Amo(i)stsi míiinistsi iikááhsiiyaawa

These berries are good.

Póóhsapoot!

Come here!

Nitsíksstaa nááhksoyssi

I want to eat.

Kikáta'yáakohkottsspommóóhpa?

Can I help you?

Tsimá kítsitokoyihpa?

Where do you live?

Isstónnatsstoyiiwa

It's extremely cold.

Ookáán

sun dance

Ássa!

Hey!

Inihkatsimat!

Help!

Wa'piski-wiya's

white man

RELIGION

The Blackfoot are a profoundly religious people who believe that the physical and supernatural worlds are interconnected and that spiritual powers can be transferred through dreams. According to Malcolm McFee in *Modern Blackfeet: Montanans on a Reservation* (1972), "All of the Blackfeet universe was invested with a pervasive supernatural power that could be met with in the natural environment." The Blackfoot sought these powers, believing the life of the land and their own lives were irrevocably bound.

In the supernatural world the most important figure is the Creator or the Sun (*Nah-too-si*), who is thought to be everywhere and part of everyone. *Nah-too-si* is often personified as the *Na'pi*, the Old Man, which loosely translates into "man and the light of early morning sunrise." Na'pi encompasses the full range of human attributes. Na'pi's wife is *Ksah-koom-aukie*, Earth Woman.

Blackfeet believe in good and evil spirits. If someone lives and acts like a wicked person, he or she will be separated from the good spirits and will have to remain close to death. Sometimes evil spirits can harm or haunt people out of revenge or jealousy. *Sta-au* is the ghost of cruel people. Spirits also live in animals; owls are thought to be the spirits of medicine people, for instance.

Spiritual powers can be transferred to people in the form of songs that contact spirit powers. Spirit powers can come through animals, birds, or supernatural beings. A person can fast to show a need for help in order to earn a spirit's pity. The spirit might then bestow the power to heal others or help people succeed in war. An animal's power or the power of a natural element can be bestowed in a dream. The animal, often appearing in human form, provides the dreamer with a list of the objects, songs, and rituals necessary to use this power. The dreamer gathers the items and places them in a medicine bundle (pouch).

Medicine bundles are a central part of Blackfoot spiritual life. Historically, bundles were wrapped in rawhide, but in modern times they are wrapped in cloth or hides. There are more than fifty medicine bundles, including beaver bundles, medicine pipe bundles, and sun dance bundles. Bundles contain items needed for particular rituals or ceremonies, such as tobacco, sweet grass, paint, or a knife; songs are associated with the bundles. The most powerful medicine bundle is the beaver medicine bundle. According to John C. Ewers, author of *The Blackfeet: Raiders on the Northwestern Plains*, this bundle was used by the Beaver Men to charm the buffalo and to assist in the planting of the sacred tobacco used in the medicine pipe ritual performed after the first thunder was heard. Medicine bundles were continually traded among members of the tribe in elaborate ceremonies in which the physical pouch and its constituent power were transferred from one owner to another.

The *Okan* (sun dance or medicine lodge ceremony) is the most important religious ceremony of the year and is held every summer when the serviceberries are ripe. It is a ceremony of prayer, sacrifice, and renewal that requires a special circular lodge. Traditionally all tribal members come into the lodge to pray, sing, dance, and confess war deeds. As a result of performing the sun dance, Blackfoot prayers are carried up to the Creator, who blesses the participants with well-being and an abundance of buffalo.

Traditionally the *Okan* was initiated by a woman in one of the Blackfoot bands. A woman who vowed to take on the responsibilities of sponsoring the sun dance was called the "vow woman." Typically a woman would do this as a display of gratitude to the sun for the survival of someone in her family. If, for example, a brother or sister had somehow narrowly escaped death, a woman in that person's family would seek to become the vow woman. The vow woman was required to fast prior to the sun dance, prepare food for the sun dance, have a sacred headdress, and learn complex prayers.

As word spread about the vow woman and the location of the sun dance, bands of Blackfoot would move toward the site of the dance and would begin to prepare the sun dance lodge at the center of a circle camp. Once the lodge was erected around the central cottonwood pole, the dance began, and it lasted four days. During this time the dancers, who had taken their own sacred vows, fasted from food and water. They called to the sun, through sacred songs and chants, to grant them power, luck, or success. Some pierced their breasts for ritualistic purposes or made other physical sacrifices to suffer and prove the sincerity of their prayers, as was common in many other ancient cultures. The sun dance was considered barbaric by Catholic missionaries, who tried to suppress it in the late nineteenth and early twentieth centuries. From the 1890s to 1934 the sun dance was illegal, but the Blackfoot practiced it in secret. Since 1934 the sun dance has been held for eight days every summer.

A Blackfoot burial platform. A Native American man stands over the remains of his son's body outside a structure that has the young warrior's possessions attached to it, 1912. THE LIBRARY OF CONGRESS

Other important religious rituals include the sweat lodge and vision quests. Sweat lodges are used to cleanse the spirit. Usually built along a riverbank, the sweat lodge uses rocks for fire, sage for the floor, and willows for the frame; all these items are gathered ceremoniously. Traditionally women were not allowed to participate in sweat lodges, but many lodges are now open to all. Vision quests are generally performed by youths wanting to enter the adult world. The quests are usually prompted by a dream and involve purifying oneself for four consecutive days in a sweat lodge before going high in the mountains to seek a guardian spirit, often in the form of an animal, who acts as a guide in daily activities and important events.

During the nineteenth century Catholicism became a major religion among the Blackfoot. Catholic Jesuits, or "black robes," were the first Christian missionaries to reach the Blackfoot bands. In 1859 Catholic Jesuits erected the St. Peter's Mission near Choteau on the Teton River. Methodists arrived shortly after the Jesuits, and they made their own attempts to convert Blackfoot spiritual life. Agent John Young, a Methodist minister, managed to get the Jesuits banned from the Blackfoot reservation during the Starvation Winter of 1883–1884, but the Jesuits, led by Peter Prando, established themselves just across the reservation boundary on the south side of Birch Creek. Catholics became well established on the reservation and for many years operated the Holy Family Mission boarding school. Evangelical Christianity also has a strong following on the Blackfeet Reservation today.

While most Blackfoot today consider themselves Christian, traditional religious practices involving medicine bundles, the sun dance, and sweat lodges are still prominently practiced. The Blackfoot avoid eating fish or using canoes, because they believe that rivers and lakes hold special power attributed to underwater people called the *Suyitapis*. The Suyitapis are the power source for medicine bundles, painted lodge covers, and other sacred items. A traditional disdain for fishing persists for many, despite the rich on-reservation fisheries.

CULTURE AND ASSIMILATION

The Blackfoot have a rich heritage of traditions, customs, beliefs, art, and stories. Despite attempts at forced assimilation by white European Americans, the Blackfoot have struggled and have been able to maintain much of their culture, language, way of life, and way of thinking. As stated on the Blackfeet Nation website, attacks on the Blackfoot way of life "culminated in the late 1800s with the official government policy of assimilation. The assumption behind this misguided, paternal policy was that the white way of life was best, and therefore Indians should stop being Indians and start living, acting, and thinking like whites. In other words: 'Become civilized like us, and you will be happier and better off.' … [but] Indians like being Indians. Indians want to be Indians. Indians will always fight to remain Indians."

European Americans tried to eradicate Blackfoot culture by sending the children to boarding schools, but today Blackfoot communities run their own schools that teach traditional Blackfoot culture and language alongside general curriculum.

Blackfoot people were originally nomads, following seasonal rounds in groups. Only in the summer would the entire tribe come together for the sun dance, which also strengthened social and tribal bonds. Blackfoot people maintained this traditional nomadic lifestyle until the late 1800s, when the buffalo were near extinction due to European colonization. They were forced to adapt their way of life and struggled a great deal economically while also suffering from exposure to diseases such as smallpox, which killed many. Eventually they were able to establish a new way of life and an economy based on farming, ranching, and resource extraction. Elders continue to pass on traditions and language.

Some of the stereotypes of the Blackfoot are typical of stereotypes of many Native Americans in the United States. They are often portrayed as lazy, stupid, or promiscuous. These stereotypes derive from a lack of understanding of tribal traditions and views regarding work, education, social relationships, and culture. Additionally, like many tribes today, Blackfoot are often portrayed solely in traditional garb and as historical figures rather than as people living contemporary lives in which they honor their traditions. Blackfoot in particular have been described as savage and hostile. This stereotype and associated prejudices arose from the Blackfoot resistance to white settlers who were trying to take their land and force them to assimilate.

Some of these white settlers, believing that Blackfoot were hostile, indiscriminately massacred Blackfoot members, such as at the massacre at Heavy Runner's Piegan camp in 1870. The U.S. Cavalry believed the tribe was hostile and so attacked a camp that was primarily populated by women, children, and elders recovering from smallpox, a disease introduced to the Blackfoot by white settlers.

While Blackfoot people maintain and embrace their culture, language, and identity, they work alongside and relate to mainstream society. Like many other cultures, they struggle to pass on their traditions to youth who can be lured by high-tech entertainment and mainstream culture and values.

Traditions and Customs The Blackfoot traditionally relied on the buffalo for food, clothing, shelter, and much of their domestic and military equipment. The pervasive use of the buffalo in Blackfoot culture provides the basis for Alfred Vaughan's claim, recorded by John C. Ewers, that the buffalo was the Blackfoot's "Staff of Life." Until the near extermination of the buffalo in the early 1880s, they roamed the plains in extraordinarily large herds. Several hunting methods were used throughout Blackfoot history, such as the "buffalo surround" and cliff drives. However, once the Blackfoot acquired the horse and mastered its use, they preferred charging the buffalo on these fast and well-trained "buffalo runners." This method of hunting brought together courage and skill, traits the Blackfoot valued highly.

The traditional shelter of the Blackfoot was a tipi that normally housed one family of about eight individuals. According to Ewers, the typical household was composed of two men, three women, and three children. About nineteen pine poles, each averaging 18 feet in length, made up the tipi's frame. Between six and twenty buffalo skins, often decorated with pictures of animals and geometric designs, covered the poles. The tipi is sacred, and each one has a story and unique identity. It is forbidden for a tipi to be copied or replicated. It may be transferred to another group only by elaborate rituals.

Furnishings for a tipi included buffalo robe beds and willow backrests. The tipi's design allowed for easy movement, a necessity given the traditionally nomadic nature of the Blackfoot hunting lifestyle. After the buffalo's disappearance and the creation of reservations during the latter half of the nineteenth century, canvas tents and the log cabin replaced the tipi. The log cabin was a symbol of the new sedentary lifestyle. Ranching, agriculture, and seasonal labor then became the primary means of survival, although subsistence hunting remained an important source of food in many families. While Blackfoot generally now live in houses, many families still have tipis built in the traditional ways, except that heavy cloth is used rather than buffalo hides.

Seasonal events are very important, including the four-day summer celebration called North American

Indian Days and the quintessential sun dance, which not only involves sacred ceremonies but also provides an opportunity for Blackfoot to get together, share views and ideas, and socialize.

The 1982 film *The Drum Is the Heart*, produced by Randy Croce, traces how long-standing Blackfoot traditions are still a part of modern celebrations. The film shows ceremonial costumes, tipi decoration, social interactions, and the ongoing role of powwows.

Cuisine Buffalo meat, the traditional staple of the Blackfoot diet, was boiled, roasted, or dried. Dried meat was stored in rawhide pouches. It was also made into *pemmican*, a mixture of ground buffalo meat, serviceberries, and marrow grease. Pemmican was an important food source during the winter and other times when buffalo were scarce. *Depuyer* was a substitute for bread and eaten with lean or dried meats. Depuyer is the fatty substance taken from the backbone of bison. It is dipped quickly into hot grease and then hung up in a smokehouse. In addition to buffalo, men hunted larger game, such as deer, moose, mountain sheep, antelope, and elk. The Blackfoot supplemented their diet with berries and other foods gathered from the plains. Women gathered roots, prairie turnips, bitterroot, and camas bulbs in the early summer. They picked wild serviceberries, choke cherries, and buffalo or bull berries in the fall and gathered the bark of the cottonwood tree, enjoying its sweet interior. Blackfoot also ate the eggs of ducks and other waterfowl. Fish, reptiles, and grizzly bears were generally considered unfit for consumption.

Red meat is still a staple in Blackfoot homes, and dried meat is still prepared in the "old ways." The loss of land and resources of the late nineteenth and twentieth centuries led to a change in diet based on the availability of American foodstuffs, such as flour. Fry bread or bannock (an unleavened flat bread) is also eaten. Most Blackfoot primarily have a typical modern American diet.

Traditional Dress Traditionally, the Blackfoot made their clothing from the hides of buffalo, deer, elk, and antelope. The women tailored dresses for themselves from the durable and pliable skins of antelope or mountain sheep. These dresses were ankle length and sleeveless, with straps to hold them up. They were decorated with porcupine quills, cut fringes, and simple geometric designs that were often colored with earth pigments. In the winter separate skin sleeves were added to these dresses along with a buffalo robe. The women also wore necklaces of sweet grass and bracelets of elk or deer teeth. Clothing changed as contact with white traders increased. Many women began to use wool and other types of cloth to make many of their garments. They often decorated their clothing with glass beads. The buffalo robe, however, for reasons of warmth and comfort, remained important through the nineteenth century.

The men wore antelope or mountain sheep skin leggings, shirts, breechcloths, and moccasins. In the winter they wore a long buffalo robe, often decorated with earth pigments or plant dyes and elaborate porcupine quill embroidery. They also wore necklaces made from the claws and teeth of bears and from braided sweet grass. In general this dress was common among Blackfoot men until the last decade of the nineteenth century. At this time what was called "citizen's dress," according to Ewers, became popular, due to pressure from missionaries and the disappearance of the buffalo. Citizen's dress consisted of a coat, trousers, and moccasins, which were preferred over the inflexible shoes of the white man.

Traditional dress is worn at traditional or social gatherings on the reservation, such as at the North American Indian Days or when on the powwow circuit. Sometimes multitribal designs are used for powwows. Everyday modern clothing is not infrequently blended with traditional dress and ornaments.

Dances and Songs Traditionally the Blackfoot had numerous dance societies, each having a social and religious function. Dances, usually performed at summer gatherings, reflected the Blackfoot emphasis on hunting and war. Men were honored in the dances for bravery in battle or for generosity in sharing meat from a hunt. The Blackfoot sun dance was a major annual dance ceremony involving the construction of a special circular lodge. Men fasted, prayed, and danced from the wall of the lodge to a central pole and back to the wall. Voluntary piercing of the chest for ritual purposes was sometimes a concluding feature of the dance.

Today the Blackfoot hold the North American Indian Days Celebration in Browning, Montana, every July. The large powwow draws Native and non-Native peoples from throughout the region for singing, dancing, socializing, and a rodeo. It is one of the largest gatherings of Native people on the continent. On the powwow circuit the Blackfoot share their dance styles and songs with other Native people from around the country. The powwows feature dance and drumming competitions with prize money. The Blackfoot have also revitalized the Black Lodge Society, which aims to revive Blackfoot songs and dances.

Dancing in general is an important part of Blackfoot socializing. Individuals also host informal round dances, owl dances, and snake dances in their homes. More formal dances are held during Christmas or other mainstream holidays.

Traditionally Blackfoot music is mainly for religious and ceremonial purposes. Music is to be treated with respect, as it can have supernatural powers. Music is seen as a way to receive communications from supernatural forces and can be serious or humorous. The term for "music" and "song" is the same. There is virtually no music that is not without song. However, there is a separate word for "drumming" that is sometimes used for singing songs that accompany drumming. Songs are identified by which event they are used for rather than who composed the song.

The Blackfoot used two types of drums. For the sun dance a section of tree trunk with skin stretched over both ends was traditionally used, similar to what is seen at contemporary powwows. The other type of percussion instrument was like a tambourine, with hide stretched over a broad wooden hoop. Rattles were traditionally used for various ceremonies, with the type varying depending on the particular ceremony. Some were made of hide, others of buffalo hooves. Whistles with single holes were used in the sun dance.

Health Care Issues and Practices The Blackfoot believe spirits to be an active and vital to everyday life. Therefore they viewed illness as the visible presence of an evil spirit in a person's body. Consequently, such illness required the expertise of a professional medicine man or woman, who had acquired, through a vision, the ability to heal the sick by removing evil spirits. In their visions a supernatural power instructed the medicine people,

who then called upon this power to assist them during healing ceremonies. Ewers, in *Indian Life on the Upper Missouri*, observes that upon the conclusion of the traditional healing ceremony a medicine person might physically remove some object from the sick person, presenting it as proof that the ceremony had been successful. Lesser injuries, such as cuts, were treated with medicinal herbs. The medicine person commonly acquired such knowledge through an apprenticeship. Traditionally horses were offered as payment for a medicine person's services. As old people die without passing on the information and skills of traditional healing, these ways are being lost.

The health of the tribe declined when the Blackfoot were forced to move to the reservations, children were sent to boarding schools, and the buffalo and many of the traditionally used plants were wiped out as a food source. The European diet and the introduction of alcohol contributed to the rise of heart disease, stroke, high blood pressure, cancer, diabetes, dental disease, and more. Studies have shown that heart disease and associated premature deaths are higher among Native Americans than among any other racial or ethnic group in the United States.

Traditional Chicken Dance costume for the Blackfoot Nation. MICHAEL WHEATLEY / ALL CANADA PHOTOS / GETTY IMAGES

The Blackfeet Indian Hospital, operated under the Indian Health Service, is located in Browning and provides local health services to the Blackfeet Reservation. In addition to hospital services, it includes a Women's Health Center, a diabetic clinic, and a pharmacy.

FAMILY AND COMMUNITY LIFE

The family unit was, and continues to be, an important part of Blackfoot society. It usually consisted of a husband, a wife (or sometimes wives), children, and sometimes an elder unable to live alone or a young male who is "raised" by the husband and acts as his helper. Grandparents, and sometimes all elders, are called *naas*. Polygamy increased in the late 1800s when disease and war killed many males. "Good families" were those who were well provided for, including ownership of horses. The oldest members of the family had the most respected positions.

The other social structure of importance was the clan, sometimes called a camp or a band, which consisted of about ten to thirty lodges (about 80 to 240 people). The makeup of a clan was generally related to the members' maternal or paternal lineage. A clan needed to be large enough to defend itself yet small enough to be organized for daily life. Each group had leaders who were sometimes members of the same family. Different leaders held different responsibilities: one leader could be responsible for hunting and another for leading battles during war. Major decisions were generally made by consensus, and a good leader was seen as being able to bring about consensus. Individuals in bands did not have to stay together. If there was a dispute about leadership, for instance, a member could leave one band and join another. If the entire band was struggling, the entire band could break up and members could join other bands.

Many of the same values of the importance of and reverence for family and social structure still exist today in the Blackfoot tribe. This can be somewhat attributed to the remoteness and often inaccessibility of the reservation in the winter, making people dependent on one another for survival as well as being somewhat less influenced by "big city life."

Gender Roles While gender roles definitively existed, they were not as strict as in some other tribes and cultures. For instance, both genders did storytelling, artwork, music, and traditional medicine/healing, and both played roles in religious ceremonies, although men played more prominent and leadership roles. Girls and boys learned to ride horses at an early age. While men were the vast majority of hunters and warriors, sometimes young women without children would help in battle or herd stolen horses to the tribe. Men would sometimes sew their own clothing. Proscribed gender roles continue to change in contemporary times. For instance, while traditionally men did sweat lodges, today many lodges are open to men and women.

Some commonly held gender roles did exist in Blackfoot society, such as women being in charge of the home and men "going out in the world." Women's work included tasks such as cooking (including butchering, curing, and preparing meat), cleaning, childrearing, and gathering wild plants and berries. As a result women owned nearly all of the household property. Men were primarily hunters and warriors who brought back needed family supplies from the hunt. Men also made tools for hunting and war and sometimes eating utensils made from buffalo bones, horns, or hides. Women's domain over the home, however, also included tasks that might traditionally be considered part of Western male gender roles because they encompassed certain types of physical strength. Women were in charge of building the family home, the tipi, and dragging the posts for the home when the tribe moved. Blackfoot women were also in charge of the long and hard work of hide tanning. Hides were staked on the ground and scraped to remove fat, meat, and hair and then rubbed with mixtures of animal brains, liver, and fat to produce softer skins. After drying in the sun, the hide was soaked in water, rolled in a bundle, cured, and stretched and scraped again. Each hide required many hours of labor. Blackfoot women were judged by the number and quality of hides they produced.

Gender roles began in childhood with children imitating their future adult roles. Boys might play with bows and arrows, snare gophers, or have spear-throwing contests, while girls might make tiny travois and play with dolls. Boys and girls played a hockey game called "batting ours."

Blackfoot had men's and women's societies. Men's societies were generally war societies with names such as "the Bulls" or "Crazy-Dogs." To become a member of a society, young men had to prove their bravery, generosity, honesty, and other traits. Women had to prove their "high character" to join the *Motoki* societies of women. Some men's and women's societies continue today. Generally they are composed of people of similar ages, and every four years an entire membership enters the next older society. Older society members give the rights of membership to newer members and present them with gifts.

Education Western educational facilities were introduced to the Montana reservation in the late nineteenth century. Holy Family Mission, a Catholic boarding school that operated until 1936, was the earliest non-Indian educational institution on the Blackfeet Reservation. U.S. government programs sent Blackfoot children to the residential Carlisle Indian Industrial School in Pennsylvania in 1889 and to other boarding schools across the United States and in Montana. After that residential/boarding schools began to appear on the reservation. Willow Creek Boarding School, west of present-day Browning, was opened in 1892. The Cut Bank Boarding school was built in 1904 on Cut Bank Creek. Residential boarding schools, which children were forced to attend for ten or eleven months of the year, tried to eradicate Blackfoot culture by forced assimilation, forbidding the practice of traditional customs, dress, and language. Children caught practicing traditional ways were severely punished. Physical and sexual abuse was also present. Children were separated from their families and community, depriving them of family love, support, and values. Their self-esteem eroded from the treatment they received in the schools. Additionally, the schools were underfunded, so many children had to grow their own food and stuff their own mattresses with straw. The severe impact of these schools on Blackfoot youth and the community has lasted for five to six generations. Some have called these schools an act of war. The Cut Bank Boarding school operated until the 1960s, when children were bused into Browning public schools. The tribe currently operates a boarding school on the reservation, and some tribal members now choose to send their children to off-reservation boarding schools.

Public schools began to open on the Blackfeet Reservation in about 1910, with about twenty operating until roughly 1960. In the 1950s, when more people moved out of rural areas, school attendance there dropped. Schools became more centralized and rural children were bused to schools near Browning. In public schools Blackfoot children were expected to suppress their culture and were taught to strive to go to college and move off the reservation. Remaining on the reservation, even with a job, was looked down upon. However, unlike in the boarding schools, children in public schools remained with their families and communities, where their culture, language, values, and traditional ways were affirmed.

In the 1930s federal programs provided funds for college and vocational education for the Blackfoot. More than 120 Blackfoot held college degrees by 1950.

As with many tribes, a renewal of Blackfoot tribal traditions and customs occurred in the late twentieth century, highlighted by education initiatives. In 1978 Congress passed the Tribally Controlled Community College Assistance Act promising federal funds to encourage reservations to develop local postsecondary schools, primarily two-year colleges with associate-degree programs whose graduates could go into clerical or skilled-trades jobs. Blackfeet Community College, established in 1976, was one of these projects. In 1979 all Montana public school teachers on or near the reservation were required to be familiar with Native American studies. Based on the 1972 state constitution and a twenty-first-century state law known as "Indian Education for All," all children attending public schools in Montana are required to learn about the history and culture of Native Americans.

Blackfoot communities now have their own primary, middle, and secondary schools and Head Start programs that blend general curriculum with lessons in the Blackfoot language and culture. Elders sharing their wisdom and teaching traditional knowledge is an essential part of the school curriculum. The cultural presence is intended to help raise students' self-esteem and scholastic achievement.

In 1980 Blackfeet Community College ended its ties with Flathead Valley Community College and became a separate institution, allowing it to more effectively respond to the needs and interests of local students. In 1985 Blackfeet Community College received accreditation. The college is a member of the American Indian Higher Education Consortium and the American Indian Science and Engineering Society. Accreditation was reaffirmed in 2000 after an extensive self-study review process. The Blackfeet Tribal Business Council appoints the board of trustees of the college.

Courtship and Weddings Marriage traditionally played an important role in the social and economic lives of the Blackfoot. Marriages were arranged by close friends or relatives or were prearranged by the bride's parents when she was still a child. Before any wedding could take place, the man needed to convince the bride's father, relatives, or friends that he was worthy. This condition of marriage meant he had to prove that he was a powerful warrior, a competent hunter, and an economically stable husband. Due to these requirements, very few men married before the age of twenty-one. The wedding ritual centered on the couple's families offering horses, household goods, and robes A new couple lived either in their own hut or in that of the husband's family. Because there were often more women than men in the tribe as a result of war casualties, a man was permitted more than one wife and would commonly marry the sister (or sisters) of his first wife. Men and women were allowed to leave their spouses for reasons such as unfaithfulness, neglect, or cruelty.

EMPLOYMENT AND ECONOMIC CONDITIONS

Throughout the eighteenth and early nineteenth centuries, Blackfoot followed seasonal rounds in bands. The territory ranged from the edge of the Saskatchewan forests in the north to the Missouri River country to the south. The buffalo helped the Blackfoot to be self-sufficient, providing them with food, clothing, blankets, hides, shoes, containers, shields for battle, and even thread (from sinew from the backbone) and rattles (from hoofs). With the near extinction of buffalo in 1883, the traditional economy was destroyed, and many Blackfoot died from starvation.

With the buffalo gone and the Blackfoot pushed onto reservations, raising cattle seemed the most logical economic system to the Blackfoot and non-Indian observers alike. However, Indian government agents, claiming that the dry plains could flourish with irrigation, insisted that the Blackfoot become farmers. In 1907 the U.S. government gave the Blackfoot authority to allot "surplus" land to individual families on the reservation; a year later a large irrigation project was built. As predicted, farming was not economically sustainable, and by 1915 the emphasis had shifted from farming to ranching. Some Blackfoot were able to prosper by grazing their own herds, while others leased their lands to stockraisers. Some started selling land to non-Indians just to survive. Approximately 30 percent of the reservation fell into non-Indian hands. The tribe lost more than 200,000 acres during this period. Tribal members contested the allotment process, and in 1919 President Woodrow Wilson signed legislation repealing the 1907 Blackfeet Allotment Act and returned all surplus lands to the tribe.

In the 1920s a Five Year Industrial Program helped relieve economic stress. During the Great Depression, the Indian Division of the Civilian Conservation Corps and the Works Progress Administration brought employment to the reservation. In the 1940s and early 1950s, vocational training programs were available to the Blackfoot.

In 1964 Two Medicine River Dam flooded, killing thirty Blackfoot and leaving hundreds homeless. This proved to be catalyst for starting a huge new housing program along with a major industrial development program. The effects of President Lyndon Johnson's "Great Society" programs to eliminate poverty and racial injustice were felt on the reservation. They provided temporary relief in certain areas of tribal life as schools were built, hospital facilities improved, and adequate housing was made available to more tribal members. The Community Action Program, Neighborhood Youth Corps, VISTA (Volunteers in Service to America), and Senior Citizen Programs provided assistance to the tribe, as did a series of Economic Development Administration projects.

In the second half of the twentieth century, the Blackfoot won two substantial monetary judgments from the United States. Money was awarded in compensation for irregularities associated with the 1888 relinquishment of vast areas in eastern Montana. In 1982 a $29 million settlement for unfair federal accounting practices with tribal funds was awarded.

Other economic growth was seen in the Blackfoot tribe in the mid- and late twentieth century. Under the guidance of tribal leader Earl Old Person, a major recreational complex, an industrial park, a museum and research center, housing developments, and a community center were constructed on the reservation. The Blackfeet Writing Company, which made pens and pencils, was established in Browning in 1971; it closed in the late 1990s. Other ventures were unsuccessful, such as lumber mills and the purchase of the American Calendar Company in 1988.

In 1990 the Blackfoot, along with other tribes, including the Sioux, Cheyenne, and Crow, formed the Montana Indian Manufacturer's Network to promote jobs for Indians in economically depressed areas. The foundation was the subject of a 1992 film, *Tribal Business in the Global Marketplace*, produced and written by Carol Rand and directed by Thomas Hudson.

European Americans tried to eradicate Blackfoot culture by sending the children to boarding schools, but today Blackfoot communities run their own schools that teach traditional Blackfoot culture and language alongside general curriculum.

Oil has been and remains a significant part of the Blackfoot economy as well as a controversial subject in the tribe. In 1902 the oil was discovered by a copper miner on Swift Creek. Commercial oil drilling began in the 1920s and continued to its height in the 1980s, with 643 oil wells (50 million barrels produced annually) and 47 producing gas wells in 1982. Oil provided 90 percent of the Blackfoot annual income.

The demand and price for oil and gas has affected, and continues to affect, the tribe's economic situation. Some of the largest energy companies in the world had oil leases on the reservation, but many of these leases did not favor the tribe. A leasing contract in 1975 with Damson Oil was more equitable and gave the tribe the right to participate in management decisions and profit sharing in return for assuming some of the risk. This contract helped to ensure that subsequent contracts were more equitable. However, oil and gas companies kept all the production logs, and in 1981 there were accounting discrepancies in the figures for the amount of oil and gas that was being taken from the reservation. After this case the tribe began to more closely monitor exploration and production of oil and gas. In addition to accessing all the logs, a tribal elders' committee monitors all lease sales and seismic activity, both for financial oversight and to ensure that sacred and religious sites are respected.

By the end of the 1980s, economic factors in the oil industry and elsewhere had made energy companies less interested in drilling and production on the reservation. In 2009, however, new fracking technologies (hydraulic fracturing of rocks that allows gas and oil to be extracted) and rising oil prices made oil drillers again interested in the oil-rich Blackfeet Reservation land. Within the tribe there is division over the issue of using fracking. With unemployment in the tribe at about 70 percent, according to a 2012 *New York Times* article, some tribal members have welcomed the oil drillers as a source of jobs. Money from oil companies has allowed the Blackfoot to pay off debt and build new businesses, such as a tribe-owned grocery store. Other tribal members have serious concerns about

BLACKFOOT MILITARY SOCIETIES

Military societies, called *aiinikiks*, were a basic element of Blackfoot society. The Blackfoot had strong and friendly relations with the Athapascan-speaking Sarcee to the north and were generally friendly with the Gros Ventre. However, long-term enemies existed among the Nez Perce, the Flathead, the Northern Shoshoni, the Crow, the Cree, the Assiniboine, and others. War leaders were believed to possess supernatural powers acquired through visions guaranteeing success. Hostile interaction with other tribes was a means of acquiring honor, usually accomplished through the capture of property. Successful exploits were exhibited on tipi covers or buffalo robes. Honor was earned by being exposed to danger more than by actually killing an enemy. These interactions with other groups were an important means of gaining better social standing. However, trade relationships were generally maintained even with enemy tribes. The military societies also served domestic services, such as policing camps, overseeing camp moves, and organizing defense from external threats.

fracking's impact on the environment. The damage it causes can affect the tribe's way of life, including the ability to have vision quests in the mountains.

In the late 1990s and early 2000s, the Blackfeet Tribal Business Council, the governing council of the tribe, established and created numbers of new projects, programs, and enterprises. For instance, in 1999 the council approved the establishment of Siyeh Corporation in Browning to "generate business development, create jobs, produce revenue, and advance the economic self-sufficiency of the Tribe by managing its tribal enterprises." In addition to running casinos, Siyeh also manages several enterprises, including the Blackfeet Heritage Center and Art Gallery. In 2009 the council created Chief Mountain Technologies to provide information technology and professional business services for government agencies.

POLITICS AND GOVERNMENT

For the Blackfoot of Montana, the 1934 Indian Recognition Act began their modern economic and political development. Under the authority of the act, the Blackfoot chose to write a constitution establishing a tribal council. The governmental changes placed remaining tribally owned lands into a more stable federal trust status and provided loans for economic pursuits, such as raising livestock and for education.

The Montana Blackfeet Reservation is led by the Tribal Business Council, which is composed of nine members elected to four-year terms to promote political stability. Terms are staggered, with elections held every two years. Any member of the tribe eighteen years or older can vote in any election, but all voting takes place on the reservation. The council is headquartered in Browning, the largest of five reservation communities.

The tribe is much larger than it was in 1934 and is organizationally more complex, so council members now work full-time and often meet several times a week. The tribal constitution empowers the council to negotiate with all federal, state, and local government agencies on behalf of the tribe; provide legal counsel for tribe members; prevent the "sale, disposition, lease or encumbrance of tribal lands, interests in lands or other tribal assets, without consent of the tribe"; manage economic tribal affairs and enterprises, including oil leases and oil royalties; regulate and license tribal business or professional activities; establish minor courts for intertribal disputes; and encourage and foster Indian arts, crafts, culture, and traditions.

The Blackfoot also participate in U.S. government politics and have been elected to local, state, and federal government positions as Democrats and Republicans.

NOTABLE INDIVIDUALS

Activism Earl Old Person (1929–) is a highly esteemed and honored Indian leader and activist. He was born in Browning, Montana, to Juniper and Molly (Bear Medicine) Old Person, who were from prominent families on the Blackfeet Reservation. By the time he was seven, Old Person had begun presenting Blackfoot culture via songs and dances at statewide events. At the age of twenty-five, he became the youngest member of the Blackfeet Tribal Business Council, the governing council of the tribe. He was elected as its chairman in 1964 and, except for two years, held that position into the 1990s. Old Person also served as president of the National Congress of American Indians from 1969 to 1971 and president of the Affiliated Tribes of the Northwest from 1967 to 1972. He was chosen in 1971 as a member of the board of the National Indian Banking Committee. In 1977 he was appointed task force chairman of the Bureau of Indian Affairs (BIA) reorganization. He was to recommend to the secretary of the interior changes in BIA policy that Indian leaders throughout the United States were interested in making. He won the prestigious Indian Council Fire Award in 1977 and traveled extensively to meet with dignitaries and celebrities. In 1978 Old Person was given the honorary lifetime appointment as chief of the Blackfoot Nation. In 1990 he was elected vice-president of the National Congress of American Indians (NCAI), a national political interest group that lobbies on behalf of U.S. tribes. In 1998 he was awarded the Jeanette Rankin Civil Liberties Award by the American Civil Liberties Union of Montana. In 2007 he was inducted into the Montana Indian Hall of Fame.

Elouise Pepion (1945–2011) was a great-granddaughter of Mountain Chief, one of the legendary leaders of the Blackfoot Nation. She was a founder of the first land trust in Indian country and was a trustee for the Nature Conservancy of Montana. During a tenure as the tribe's treasurer that lasted for more than a decade, she found irregularities in the management of the funds held in trust by the United

States for the tribe and for individual Indians. The funds were from government fees for lands leased for lumber, oil production, grazing, gas, and minerals, which the government was supposed to pay as royalties to Indian owners. Along with the Intertribal Monitoring Association, which Pepion served as president, she sought reform in the 1980s and 1990s. When this did not work, she asked renowned lawyers and the Native American Rights Fund to begin a class action suit in 1996 to force reform and account for trust funds belonging to individuals. The suit, *Cobell v. Salazar*, went on until 2009, when a settlement was reached with the government. In 2010 Congress passed a bill to appropriate money for President Obama's settlement of $3.4 billion dollars. Most individuals were to receive a settlement of about $1,800. The case was appealed and upheld in 2012 by a three-judge panel of the U.S. Court of Appeals for the District of Columbia Circuit. Pepion won many awards and honors during her life, including a Genius Grant from the MacArthur Foundation's Fellowship Program (1997). In 2011 Senate majority leader Harry Reid cosponsored legislation to award her the Congressional Gold Medal.

Art King Kuka (1946–2004) was born in Browning, Montana. He earned a BFA at the University of Montana, Missoula, and attended the Institute of American Indian Arts in Santa Fe, New Mexico, in the mid-1960s. He worked in watercolors, oils, bronze, steel, silver, and gold. His art reflected his commitment to his culture and spirituality. His embossed lithographs are called Kukagraphs and are made from a printing process he developed and perfected. Kuka was also a poet whose work was published in several anthologies, including *The Whispering Wind* (1991) and *Voices of the Rainbow* (1992).

Education Richard Sanderville (ca. 1873–1957), part Piegan, grew up on the Montana Blackfeet Reservation and became a student in the use of traditional sign language. He inherited this interest from his father and grandfather, who also served as interpreters between the Blackfoot and European Americans from the fur-trade era onward. He was among the first group of Blackfoot enrolled at the Carlisle Indian School in Pennsylvania. Sanderville later served on the Blackfoot tribal council. Seeking to relieve the poverty of the area in the 1920s, he helped organize the Piegan Farming and Livestock Association. Sanderville helped develop the dictionary of the Indian sign language with the Smithsonian Institution in Washington, D.C., in the 1930s. He was also instrumental in establishing the Museum of the Plains Indian on the Blackfeet Reservation in 1941 in an effort to preserve tribal history.

Film George Burdeau (1944–) received a degree in communications from the University of Washington and did graduate work at the Anthropology Film Center and Institute of American Indian Arts in Santa Fe, New Mexico. Burdeau has produced, directed, and written more than thirty films and television productions. He received a Peabody Award for *Surviving Columbus* (1992) and an Emmy Award for *The Native Americans/ The Plains* (1996). His film *Backbone to the World: The Blackfeet* (1997) is about the Blackfoot tribe's struggle to find a new identity. In 2000 he directed the documentary *Who Owns the Past?* Burdeau was the founding dean of the Communications Department of the Institute of American Indian Arts and director of the National Center for the Production of Native Images, both in Santa Fe, New Mexico. He was the first Native American director in the Directors Guild of America. He has served as chairman of the Indian Arts and Crafts Board, board member of the Institute for the Preservation of the Original Languages of Americas, board chair of the Institute of Native Culture and Communication, and founding board member of the Native American Public Broadcasting Consortium.

Government Melinda Gopher (1965–) is a civil, treaty, and political rights activist as well as a paralegal, feature writer, and screenwriter. She ran as a Democrat for the U.S. House of Representatives in 2010 and 2012.

Denise Juneau (1967–) was the first American Indian woman to be elected to statewide executive office in Montana. A Democrat, Juneau served as Montana's state superintendent of public instruction and spoke at the 2012 Democratic National Convention.

Donna Jean Hutchinson (1949–), a Republican, was elected to the Arkansas House of Representatives in 2007. Her son Jeremy Hutchinson (1974–), also a Republican, was elected to the Arkansas State Senate in 2011.

Literature James Welch (1940–2003) is considered the founding author of the Native American Renaissance. He employed his Native background in writing about the human relationship to the natural landscape, Indian mythology, cultural traditions, tribal history, and the plight of Native life in the nineteenth and twentieth centuries. His novel *Fools Crow* (1986; republished in 2007) received several literary awards, and he received a Lifetime Achievement Award from the Native Writers' Circle of the Americas in 1997. Welch cowrote (with Paul Stekler) the Emmy Award–winning documentary *Last Stand at Little Bighorn* for the PBS *American Experience* series. Welch and Stekler also wrote the nonfiction book *Killing Custer: The Battle of Little Bighorn and the Fate of the Plains Indians* (1994). Welch's other novels include *Winter in the Blood* (1974), *The Death of Jim Loney* (1979), *The Indian Lawyer* (1990), and *The Heartsong of Charging Elk* (2000). His books of poetry include *Riding the Earthboy 40* (1971). He taught at Cornell University and the University of Washington.

Music The Grammy-nominated Black Lodge Singers is one of the most renowned northern-style drum groups on the powwow circuit. Members of the group include Kenny Scabby Robe, a Blackfoot, his wife, Louise, from the Yakama nation, and their twelve sons. The group recorded more than twenty albums and was nominated for a Grammy in 1994 for Best Traditional Folk Album for its collaboration with R. Carlos Nakai and William Eaton on the album *Ancestral Voices*. The Black Lodge Singers also received Grammy nominations for *Tribute to the Elders* (2001), *Weasel Tail's Dream* (2002), and *More Kids' Pow-Wow Songs* (2006).

Sports Joe "The Boss" Hipp (1962–), a professional heavyweight boxer, was the first Native American to challenge for the World Boxing Association (WBA) Heavyweight Championship. Hipp won the World Boxing Federation Intercontinental Heavyweight Championship in 1991, and in 1994 he won the North American Boxing Federation title. In 1995 he fought Bruce Seldon in Las Vegas for the WBA heavyweight title, losing in ten rounds. In 2009 he was inducted into the American Indian Athletic Hall of Fame. In 2005 he founded the All Nations Foundation to encourage Native American youth to strive for achievement and excellence in sports, academics, and health and fitness.

Stage and Screen Steve Reevis (1962–) is an actor best known for his role as Shep Proudfoot in the Academy Award–winning film *Fargo* (1996), for which he won an award from First Americans in the Arts. He also acted in *Last of the Dogmen* (1995), *The Missing* (2003), and *The Longest Yard* (2005). He has had guest roles on many television series, including *Line of Fire*, *Bones*, and the miniseries *Into the West*.

MEDIA

Blackfeet TV

Blackfeet TV is an on-demand streaming media service providing locally produced tribal news, community and special interest programs, and videos.

URL: http://blackfeet.tv

Glacier Reporter

Includes news, sports, a business directory, obituaries, blogs, and a calendar for the Browning area.

Brian Kavanagh, Publisher
John McGill, Editor
P.O. Box 349
Browning, Montana 59417
Phone: (406) 338-2090
Fax: (406) 338-2410
Email: glacrptr@3rivers.net
URL: http://cutbankpioneerpress.com/glacier_reporter/

KBWG 107.5 FM–*Ksistsikam ayikinaan* (Voice from nowhere), Thunder Radio

A community radio station begun in 2010 that broadcasts in English and the Blackfoot language. It features music, news, talk, language lessons, and stories from elders.

Phone: (406) 338-5298
Email: KBWG107.5@gmail.com
URL: www.browningmontana.com/kbwglp.html

Piikani Sun

Indian-owned quarterly publication featuring articles on various topics, including spirituality, tribal governance, music and books, and stories from elders.

Spirit Talk Culture Institute
P.O. Box 477
East Glacier, In the Blackfoot Nation 59434-0477
Canada
Phone: (406) 338-2882
URL: www.blackfoot.org/piikanisun.php

ORGANIZATIONS AND ASSOCIATIONS

Blackfeet Community College

Tribally controlled two-year college chartered by the Blackfeet Tribal Business Council in 1974.

Dr. Billie Jo Kipp, President
P.O. Box 819
Browning, Montana 59417-0819
1 Agency Square
Browning, Montana 59417
Phone: (406) 338-5411
Fax: (406) 338-3272
Email: rkipp@bfcc.edu
URL: http://bfcc.edu/

Blackfeet Nation

Phone: (406) 338-7521
Fax: (406) 338-7530
URL: www.blackfeetnation.com

MUSEUMS AND RESEARCH CENTERS

Blackfeet Heritage Center & Art Gallery

Opened in 2002, the center exhibits and sells items ranging from a large selection of historical and traditional books as well as beadwork, jewelry, drums, paintings, and more by more than 500 artists from sixteen North American tribes.

333 Central Avenue West
Browning, Montana 59417
Phone: (406) 338-5661
Fax: 406-338-5665
Email: sales@blackfeetnationstore.com
URL: http://blackfeetnationstore.com/store/

Blackfoot Digital Library

An educational resource hosted by Red Crow Community College.

URL: http://blackfootdigitallibrary.org

Montana Historical Society Museum

Founded in 1865, the museum provides information on the cultural history of Montana, including newspapers, photograph archives, unpublished diaries and manuscripts, and an extensive library.

The museum also publishes the quarterly periodical *Montana: The Magazine of Western History*.

Jennifer Bottomly-O'Looney, Senior Curator
225 North Roberts
P.O. Box 201201
Helena, Montana 59620
Phone: (406) 444-4753
Email: jbottomly-o'looney@mt.gov
URL: http://mhs.mt.gov/museum/

Museum of the Plains Indian and Crafts Center

Founded in 1941, the museum is operated by the Indian Arts and Crafts Board of the United States Department of Interior, promoting the historic and contemporary Native American arts of Northern Plains Native cultures.

Loretta Pepion
P.O. Box 410
Junction of Highway 2 & 89
Browning, Montana 59417
Phone: (406) 338-2230
Fax: (406) 338-7404
Email: mpi@3rivers.net
URL: www.blackfeetcountry.com/museum.html

SOURCES FOR ADDITIONAL STUDY

Bastien, Betty. *Blackfoot Ways of Knowing: The Worldview of the Siksikaitsitapi*. Calgary, Alberta: University of Calgary Press, 2004.

Blackfoot Gallery Committee and Glenbow Museum. *The Story of the Blackfoot People: Nitsitapiisinni*. Buffalo, NY: Firefly, 2001.

Crowshoe, Reg, and Sybille Manneschnidt. *Akak'stiman: A Blackfoot Framework for Decision-Making and Mediation Processes*. Calgary, Alberta: University of Calgary Press, 2002.

Dempsey, Hugh A. *Firewater: The Impact of the Whisky Trade on the Blackfoot Nation*. Calgary, Alberta: Fifth House, Ltd., 2002.

Ewers, John C. *The Blackfeet: Raiders on the Northwestern Plains*. Norman: University of Oklahoma Press, 1958.

Lokensgard, Kenneth Hayes. *Blackfoot Religion and the Consequences of Cultural Commoditization*. Burlington, VT: Ashgate Publishing, 2010.

McClintock, Walter. *The Old North Trail: Life, Legends and Religion of the Blackfeet Indians*. Lincoln: University of Nebraska Press, 1992.

BOLIVIAN AMERICANS

Tim Eigo

OVERVIEW

Bolivian Americans are immigrants or descendants of people from the central South American country of Bolivia. The only landlocked country in the Western Hemisphere, Bolivia is bordered to the west by Chile and Peru, to the south by Argentina, to the southeast by Paraguay, and to the east and north by Brazil. One of the most striking features of Bolivia is its high plateau, or *Altiplano*, which is also home to most of its multiethnic population. The Altiplano sits between two chains of the Andes Mountains and is one of the highest inhabited regions in the world, reaching an average height of 12,000 feet (3,658 meters). The valleys and ridges of the Andes's eastern slopes are called the *Yungas*, where 30 percent of the country's population lives. Three-fifths of Bolivia is sparsely populated, particularly in the lowlands. Altogether, Bolivia covers an expanse of land twice as large as Texas.

According to the World Bank, the 2011 population of Bolivia was approximately 10 million people. Of all the South American countries, Bolivia has the largest percentage (60 percent) of indigenous peoples, including the Aymara, Quechua, Kallawayas, Chipayas, and Guarani. The next largest ethnic group in the Bolivian population is the mestizos, those of mixed-race heritage, who make up 30 percent of the population. Finally, nearly 10 percent of the Bolivian population is of Spanish origin. There is also a small population of Japanese Bolivians living primarily in the lowland areas. The majority of Bolivians are Roman Catholic, although in many areas indigenous beliefs are practiced alongside Catholicism. Bolivia is considered a developing nation; between one-half and two-thirds of the population, many of them subsistence farmers, live in poverty. Exports of natural gas and oil, textiles, and minerals—including silver, tin, and lithium—make up the bulk of the Bolivian economy.

Bolivians first immigrated to the United States in significant numbers following the 1952 Bolivian National Revolution. Many of these immigrants were political dissidents or middle-income professionals. A second wave of immigration occurred in the 1980s during a period of hyperinflation in Bolivia. These immigrants were primarily lower-income workers laboring in manual labor or the service industry. This pattern continued into the late 1990s, but rising political tensions between the U.S. and Bolivian governments, along with the looming financial crisis, led most Bolivian immigrants to settle in countries like Argentina, Brazil, and Spain in the 2000s and early 2010s.

According to the 2010 U.S. Census, there are 99,210 people of Bolivian descent living in the United States, making them the third smallest Hispanic group in the country, less than one half of 1 percent of the size of the Mexican American population. However, some Bolivian and Latin American organizations, such as the Economic Commission for Latin America (ECLA), believe the number may be as high as 366,000, people when undocumented immigrants are accounted for. The highest concentration of Bolivian Americans resides in the Washington, D.C., metropolitan area. Compared with other immigrant populations, a relatively small number of Bolivians become naturalized American citizens, with many seeking only temporary employment or education as a means of supporting family members still living in Bolivia.

HISTORY OF THE PEOPLE

Early History To those in the relatively recently settled Western Hemisphere—and, in fact, to most people anywhere in the world—the length of Bolivian history is staggering. When the Spanish arrived to conquer South America in the 1500s, they found a land that had been populated and civilized for thousands of years. From around 400 CE until around 1000 CE, the Tiahuanaco culture thrived, though it had inhabited western Bolivian since as far back as 1500 BCE. Its center for ritual and ceremonies was on the shores of Lake Titicaca, the largest navigable lake in the world and a dominant part of Bolivia's geography. The Tiahuanaco culture was highly developed and prosperous. It had superb transportation systems, a road network, irrigation, and striking building techniques.

The Aymara Indians subsequently invaded, probably from Chile. At the end of the fifteenth century, the Peruvian Incas swept over the area. Their rule continued until the arrival of the Spaniards in the 1530s. Spanish rule was known as the colonial period and was marked by the development of cities, the oppression of the Indians, and the missionary work of the Catholic Church.

The struggle for independence from Spain began in the seventeenth century, and the most significant rebellion occurred when the Aymara and Quechua united at the end of the eighteenth century. Their leader, Tupac Katari, was eventually captured and executed, but the rebels continued to resist, and for more than a hundred days, about eighty thousand Indians besieged the capital city of La Paz. General Antonio José de Sucre, who fought alongside Simón Bolívar, finally gained independence from Spain in 1825. The new nation was a republic, with a senate and a house of representatives, an executive branch, and a judiciary. A few decades after Bolivia obtained its independence, it lost two disastrous wars to Chile, and in the process, lost its only coastal access. It lost a third war in 1932, this time with Paraguay, which further reduced its land holdings. Even at the end of the twentieth century, such setbacks continued to weigh heavily on the Bolivian psyche and affected political actions in La Paz.

Modern Era In addition to being a silver exporter, the republic of Bolivia also became a leading supplier of tin for the world's markets. Ironically, the poor working conditions in the mines led to the evolution of Bolivia's modern political state; conditions in the mines were so abhorrent that a middle-class and workers' party, the National Revolutionary Movement, or MNR, formed. Under the leadership of President Paz Estenssoro in the 1950s, the MNR nationalized the mines, taking them from private companies and transferring ownership to the government. The MNR also began land and industrial reforms. For the first time, Indian and mestizo farmers and the working poor had an opportunity to own the land that they and their ancestors had toiled on for generations. However, political tumult continued and ultimately resulted in the 1964 overthrow of President Estenssoro, leading to almost twenty years of military rule.

Gladys Gomez, a Bolivian American beauty queen, holds U.S. and Bolivian flags in New York City, 1962. PHOTOGRAPH BY MARTY HANLEY. CORBIS / BETTMANN. REPRODUCED BY PERMISSION.

From the 1970s onward, Bolivia suffered setbacks due to rampant inflation, other deteriorating economic conditions, and a series of military dictators. A dramatic crash in the world market for tin also severely impacted the economy. However, since 1985 efforts have been made to stabilize and diversify the economy, and in 2010, major credit agencies upgraded their rating of Bolivia's economy. Bolivia's economy has always been dominated by mining and cattle and sheep herding, but the illegal growing of coca had become a major problem by the 1980s. From coca leaves, a paste can be made, which then is used to make cocaine. In the 1990s, the Bolivian government sought to reduce the drug trade in cooperation with the United States Drug Enforcement Administration (DEA). This process was made difficult by the fact that coca has always been a part of the daily lives of millions of Bolivians. As many as 350,000 Bolivians make their living as coca growers, and with the 2006 election of Indian Aymara leader Evo Morales—a prominent supporter of the coca growers' trade union—as president of Bolivia, coca production is once again on the rise. The illegal manufacture and sale of cocaine has been a major point of contention between the United States and Bolivia, especially during the administration of George W. Bush, when the U.S. ambassador and several American DEA agents were expelled from Bolivia for purportedly conspiring to overthrow the government. While relations improved somewhat under the Barack Obama administration, the relationship between the two countries continued to be shaky.

Bolivian immigrants tend to travel to the United States primarily seeking greater economic and educational opportunities. As such, they fare better than do those who do so seeking political asylum, such as Salvadorans and Nicaraguans. Also, Bolivians who immigrate to North America often come from large cities and therefore adapt more easily to American urban areas. They are well educated and have high professional aspirations. Their families are usually intact, and their children do well in school because the parents come from a higher educational background. In the 1990s Stephanie Griffith, an activist in immigrant communities, stated that, of all recent immigrants, the Bolivians come closest to achieving the American dream.

SETTLEMENT IN THE UNITED STATES

Since 1820 more than a million immigrants from Central and South America have settled in the United States, but who they were or where they came from remains a mystery. It was not until 1960 that the U.S. Census Bureau categorized these immigrants by their nation of origin. Because of this, and because the total number of Bolivian immigrants to this country has been relatively small, estimates of Bolivian immigration to the United States may be impossible to determine.

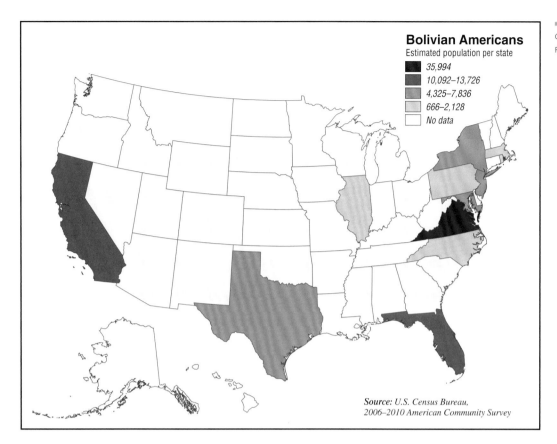

Bolivian Americans
Estimated population per state

- 35,994
- 10,092–13,726
- 4,325–7,836
- 666–2,128
- No data

Source: U.S. Census Bureau,
2006–2010 American Community Survey

Between 2001 and 2010, Bolivians who sought permanent-resident status in the United States numbered 22,695. However, the average number of Bolivians naturalized every year is 457. This suggests that Bolivian Americans have a continued interest in remaining Bolivians and may hold open the possibility of returning to South America. Additionally, many Bolivians enter the country on tourist or other short-term visas, which further complicates immigration data.

Although relatively few Bolivians immigrate to the United States, those who do are often clerical workers who can afford to travel such a long distance from home. This exodus, or "brain drain," of educated workers has harmed Bolivia and South America as a whole. It is a middle-class migration from one of the poorest nations in the world. While these workers enjoy relatively high standards of living in Bolivia, they hope for better opportunities for themselves and their children. These educated workers largely settle in urban centers on the West Coast, in the Northeast, and in the Gulf states, where there are Bolivian or other South American immigrant communities that offer support and cultural ties to home. Oftentimes, and especially during the financial crisis of the late 2000s, educated Bolivian immigrants find themselves having to take jobs for which they are overqualified, such as in construction or the service industry.

The largest communities of Bolivian Americans are in Washington, D.C., Maryland, and Virginia.

There are also significant Bolivian populations in Miami, New York City, Los Angeles, and Chicago. The 2010 U.S. Census indicated that about 37,600 Bolivian Americans lived in and around Washington, D.C.

LANGUAGE

Bolivian languages include at least thirty indigenous languages, as well as Spanish and other languages spoken by descendants of immigrants to Bolivia. According to the Bolivian Constitution, rewritten in 2009, all thirty-seven indigenous languages as well as Spanish are considered official languages of the state. The most prominent indigenous languages are Quechua, Aymara, and Guaraní. Spanish and Quechua are spoken primarily in the Andes region, while Aymara is mainly spoken in the Altiplano around Lake Titicaca, and Guaraní in the southeast along the border with Paraguay. Formerly dismissed as simply the languages of poor Indians, Quechua and Aymara have gained favor since the late twentieth century due to increasing attempts to preserve Bolivia's customs, particularly under the presidency of Evo Morales, himself an Aymara Indian. Quechua is primarily an oral language, but it is one with international importance. Originally spoken during the Incan Empire, Quechua is still spoken by about 10 million people in Peru, Bolivia, Ecuador, Argentina, and Chile. About 3 million people in Bolivia and Peru speak Aymara. It has survived for centuries despite efforts to eliminate its use. Spanish remains the predominant language in Bolivia and is used in all modern forms of communication, including art, business, and broadcasting. However, all civil servants are required to speak and conduct business in at least one indigenous language, and efforts have been made to include indigenous languages in educational institutions.

Bolivian Americans, when they do not speak English, usually speak Spanish in addition to any indigenous language they may speak. Bolivian American schoolchildren new to the United States, for whom English is a second or third language, have experienced increased difficulties becoming adept at English, as support and funding for bilingual education shrinks in the United States. Some private organizations, such as Escuela Bolivia in Virginia, attempt to meet this need by offering English-as-a-second-language classes and academic tutoring as well as cultural programs for Bolivian and other Hispanic immigrants.

Greetings Nonverbal communication is important to Bolivians when they meet and converse. Bolivians who are descended from Europeans often use their hands when they speak, whereas indigenous people from the highlands normally do not gesture. Similarly, urban dwellers often greet each other with a single kiss on the cheek, especially if they are friends or acquaintances. Men usually shake hands and perhaps embrace. Indigenous people shake hands very lightly and pat each other's shoulders as if to embrace. They do not embrace or kiss. Bolivian Americans tend to utilize expansive gestures when they communicate. This is due to the fact that most Bolivian Americans are of European ancestry.

RELIGION

The majority of Bolivians, about 80 percent, identify as Roman Catholic, but various Protestant sects are gaining in popularity, as well as a renewed interest in or adherence to traditional indigenous beliefs. Although the state is officially secular, the strong Catholic influence can be seen in certain policies, such as the lack of access to birth control or abortion. Many indigenous communities interweave pre-Columbian and Christian symbols in their religious practices. In 2009 the Bolivian government decided to recognize the celebration of the Aymaran New Year, or Wilka Kuti (return of the Sun), an event that celebrates the beginning of a new solar cycle with the arrival of the winter solstice. In particular, worship and ritual related to Pachamama, a traditional Andean fertility goddess, are significant. Pachamama, which translates to "Mother World" in Quechua, is often thanked or toasted by a ritual spilling of chicha, a fermented maize drink. This may be done daily, with more elaborate ceremonies occurring on special events, such as the beginning of a trip. The traditions of Pachamama have also influenced environmental legislation, such as the Law of the Rights of Mother Earth, passed in 2010. Another

ancient god who plays a role in everyday life is Ekeko, "dwarf" in Aymara. Especially favored among mestizos, he is believed to oversee the finding of a spouse, providing shelter, and luck in business.

One famous Bolivian folktale is about Mount Illimani, which towers over the city of La Paz. According to the legend, there once were two mountains where one now stands, but the god who created them could not decide which he liked more. Finally, he decided it was Illimani, and threw a boulder at the other, sending the mountaintop rolling far away. "*Sajama*," he said, meaning, "Go away." Today, the distant mountain is still called Sajama. The shortened peak that sits next to Illimani is today called Mururata, meaning "beheaded."

Bolivian Americans generally continue to practice their Catholic faith but may adhere less to indigenous beliefs, particularly if they do not live in an area with a Bolivian community. However, many of the festivals celebrated by Bolivian Americans incorporate both Catholic and indigenous elements, such as the Festival of the Virgin of Urkupina, which is celebrated by the Rhode Island Bolivian-American Association every August. Many Bolivian Americans celebrate El Día de Todos Santos, or All Saints' Day, a major Catholic feast day that honors the numerous saints recognized by the church on the first of each November, and also venerate Our Lady of Copacabana, the patron saint of Bolivia, on August 5.

CULTURE AND ASSIMILATION

Bolivian Americans generally find that their skills and experience prepare them well for life in the United States, although the initial period of adjustment may be challenging. However, in the 1990s and 2000s, anti-immigrant sentiments increased in many areas of the country, particularly toward the rapidly growing Mexican American population, and these feelings often failed to distinguish between Mexican and other Latin American immigrants and between legal and illegal immigrants. Thus, the move to the United States can be challenging for Bolivians, especially those who primarily speak an indigenous language rather than Spanish, as well as for those who lack family or community support networks.

Traditions, Customs, and Beliefs Bolivian Americans seek to instill in their children a strong sense of the culture of the country from which they emigrated. As such, children's education includes Bolivian history, traditional dances, and music. In regions with larger Bolivian American populations, there are often cultural organizations to support this education. For example, Virginia's Liga Incopea, a soccer league featuring teams of Bolivian immigrants organized loosely around the participants' city or village of origin, raises money to support various projects in Bolivia and fosters a sense of community among Bolivian Americans, encouraging other Bolivian Americans to attend the games and socialize with one another. In addition, social media such as Facebook have made it easier for Bolivian Americans to connect with each other and their relatives in Bolivia.

Cuisine As in most countries, the Bolivian diet is influenced by region and by income. Most meals in Bolivia, however, include meat, usually served with potatoes, rice, or both. Bolivian cuisine is similar to traditional Spanish cuisine and infused with traditional native Bolivian foods such as *quinua* (or quinoa, a seed that is typically boiled and eaten like rice) and *chuño* (freeze-dried high-altitude potatoes). Bolivian cuisine is also influenced by other major immigrants to the region, including German, Italian, Russian, and Basque. Near Santa Cruz are large wheat fields, and Bolivia imports large quantities of wheat from the United States. In the highlands, potatoes are the staple food. In the lowlands, the staples are rice, plantain, and yucca. Fewer fresh vegetables are available to those in the highlands. While most of the Bolivian diet is rich in carbohydrates, in rural areas other kinds of food may be more scarce, leading to nutritional deficiencies.

Some popular Bolivian recipes include *silpancho*, pounded beef with an egg cooked on top; *thimpu*, a spicy stew cooked with vegetables; and *fricase*, pork soup seasoned with yellow hot peppers. Also central to the urban Bolivian diet is street food such as *salteñas*, oval pies stuffed with various fillings and eaten as a quick meal. They are similar to empanadas, which are usually filled with beef, chicken, or cheese. Diets in the lowlands include wild animals such as the armadillo. The most common Bolivian drink is black tea, which is usually served strong with lots of sugar. Maté, made by steeping the dried leaves and stems of the yerba maté plant in hot water, is also a popular drink.

Due to the availability of South American produce and other foods in the United States, Bolivian Americans have been successful in incorporating much of their native cuisine into their everyday diets. In areas with a high concentration of Bolivian immigrants, Bolivian restaurants and bakeries have become increasingly popular, not just among Bolivian Americans but with other Americans as well, who often appreciate the familiar dependence upon meat and carbohydrates in Bolivian cuisine. As Americans have taken an interest in street food in recent years, a number of Bolivian food trucks have appeared in the Washington metropolitan area, serving hearty dishes like peanut soup, empanadas, salteñas, and *chicharrón*, a dish made with fried pork rinds.

Traditional Costumes Bolivian clothing varies greatly between regions, indigenous cultures, and income levels. In addition, traditional clothing often reflects a combination of indigenous traditions and colonial Spanish influences. Traditionally, Bolivian men living on the Altiplano would wear homemade trousers and a woven poncho. Today, they are more likely to wear factory-made clothes imported from other countries. For headgear, however, the *chulla*, a woolen cap with earflaps, remains a staple of the wardrobe.

Traditional native clothing for women includes an apron over a long skirt and many underskirts. An embroidered blouse and cardigan-style sweater is also worn. A shawl, which is usually in the form of a colorful rectangle, serves many purposes, from carrying a child on the back to creating a shopping pouch. While the wool of the alpaca, a llama-like animal, is a traditional fiber, it is now often too expensive for native Bolivians, although alpaca sweaters and shawls are frequently sold to tourists. Bolivians are also known for their jewelry, particularly that made with silver, an abundant resource in Bolivia. Many Bolivian women wear silver necklaces, earrings, or bracelets.

One of the more striking types of Bolivian clothing is the bowler hat worn by Aymara women. Known as a *bombin*, it was introduced to Bolivia by British railway workers. It is uncertain why more women than men tend to wear the bombin. For many years, a factory in Italy manufactured bombins for the Bolivian market, but they are now made locally by Bolivians.

On most days, Bolivian Americans tend to wear typical American-style clothing, including jeans and t-shirts or more formal business attire, with the occasional addition of traditional Bolivian accessories such as a woven poncho, alpaca sweater, chulla, or handmade jewelry. During celebrations such as National Hispanic American Heritage Month, celebrated each year in the United States from September 15 to October 15, it is not uncommon to find Bolivian American women wearing the bombin or a flowing skirt known as a *pollera*, and people of both genders wearing colorful woven clothing representative of the type of clothes traditionally worn on the Altiplano. In the United Sates as well as in Bolivia, however, there is something of a generation gap when it comes to clothing, with younger generations largely turning away from traditional Bolivian clothing and embracing a more modern style.

Music Bolivian music reflects the continuing pride and interest in indigenous traditions. The use of pre-Columbian musical instruments remains an important part of Bolivian music. One of those instruments is the *siku*, a series of vertical flutes bound together. Bolivian music also uses the *charango*, which is a cross between the mandolin, guitar, and banjo. Originally, the soundbox of the charango was made from the shell of an armadillo, which gave it a unique sound and appearance. During the 1990s Bolivian music began to incorporate lyrics into traditionally mournful Andean music, creating a new genre. Bolivian musicians continue to fuse traditional music, instruments, and lyrics with pop, jazz, and rock sounds. Greater distribution through the Internet has made it easier for Bolivian Americans to listen to music from their native land and has allowed Bolivian and other Andean musicians to gain international fans. The popular Bolivian rock band Octavia, for example, toured the United States in the late 1990s, focusing

Children in traditional Bolivian costumes brighten the Annual Dance Parade along Broadway in New York City. DAVID GROSSMAN / ALAMY

on areas with significant Bolivian populations, such as Florida, Virginia, and New York.

Dances and Songs More than five hundred ceremonial dances can be traced to Bolivia. These dances often represent important events in Bolivian culture, including hunting, harvesting, and weaving. One dance performed at festivals is the *diablada*, or devil dance, which is believed to have originated in Oruro, Bolivia, as a fusion of indigenous and Catholic traditions. Another famous festival dance is the *morenada*, the dance of the black slaves, which may have been inspired both by the suffering of African slaves brought to Bolivia, as well as traditional Aymara dances. Other popular dances include the *tarqueada*; a llama-herding dance known as the *llamerada*; the *kullawada*, which is known as the dance of the weavers; and the *wayno*, a dance of the Quechua and the Aymara.

In the United States, traditional Bolivian dances are popular among Bolivian Americans, and dance groups are considered an important way of maintaining cultural ties to Bolivia. During the late twentieth century, Bolivian dances began to appeal to a broader audience as well and became one of the most visible examples of Bolivian culture in the United States. Performances by

groups of Bolivian American folk dancers from around the country have increased in recent years, with younger generations viewing the dances as a source of pride. The Comite Pro-Bolivia, an umbrella organization of arts and dance groups, organizes many school parades and other appearances year-round. Held every year on the first Sunday of August, the Bolivian National Day Festival is sponsored by the Arlington (Virginia) Department of Parks and Recreation and attracts about 10,000 visitors. Examples of Bolivian dancing can be viewed online via a number of blogs devoted to the art form and on sites like YouTube.

Holidays Bolivian Americans maintain strong ties with Bolivia. This is emphasized by the fervor with which they celebrate Bolivian holidays in the United States. Because Bolivian Americans are primarily Roman Catholic, they celebrate the major Catholic holidays, such as Christmas, Easter, and All Saints' Day, as well as feast days of particular or local significance to Bolivians. They also celebrate Bolivia's Labor Day and Independence Day on August 6.

Festivals in Bolivia are common and often fuse elements from the Catholic faith and from pre-Columbian customs. The Festival of the Cross, which originated with the Aymara Indians, is celebrated on May 3. Another Aymara festival is *Alacitas*, the Festival of Abundance, which takes place in La Paz and the Lake Titicaca region on January 25. During Alacitas honor is given to Ekeko, who brings good luck. One of the most famous of Bolivia's festivals is Carnival in Oruro, which takes place before the Catholic season of Lent. In this mining town, workers seek the protection of the Virgin of the Mines. During the Oruro Carnival, the *diablada* is performed.

Health Care Issues and Practices In terms of key health indicators, Bolivia ranks very low among Western Hemisphere countries. Malnutrition and sanitation problems are responsible for many of the health problems in the Bolivian population. Bolivia also has an extremely high child and maternal mortality rate. In addition, cocaine addiction has increased since the 1980s, when the illegal drug trade expanded. However, in the 2000s reforms began with international support, particularly targeting women and children and expanding vaccination programs. A 2011 United Nations report indicated small but steady progress in the areas of maternal and infant mortality.

Bolivian Americans, particularly urban professionals with broad access to medical care, tend to have much better health statistics. Undocumented immigrants or those who come from poor or rural areas, however, often find it difficult to obtain health care in the United States, as the cost of insurance or medical bills for uninsured laborers can be prohibitive. In the late 2000s it was reported that a blood disease known as Chagas, which can remain dormant for years before suddenly becoming fatal, was affecting hundreds of thousands of immigrants from Latin America, with Bolivian Americans having the highest rate of infection.

FAMILY AND COMMUNITY LIFE

Gender Roles Bolivian culture tends to emphasize traditional gender roles and division of labor. Men hold positions of public authority, while women are primarily responsible for the domestic sphere. In rural areas, however, the division of labor in agricultural tasks may be more flexible. Women also tend to be primarily responsible for the transmission of cultural skills and traditions such as weaving, songs, and dances. Since the 1990s, legal efforts have been made to address violence against women. The 2010 constitution contains provisions that strengthen women's rights, including prohibition of gender discrimination and requiring equal pay for equal work. President Evo Morales also nominated several women to his cabinet. However, women are still disproportionately affected by violence, illiteracy, and poverty. Bolivian women also suffer from high rates of maternal mortality and often lack access to health care.

Bolivian American women, particularly second- and third-generation Americans, have largely embraced the ideal of gender equality. They are often highly educated and are serving as heads of their households with greater frequency. Women now make up the majority of immigrants arriving from Bolivia, and studies have shown that they are contributing to a greater share of remittances—money earned in the United States but sent back to relatives in Bolivia—over the last decade. While many Bolivian American men often feel undervalued due to the lack of high-paying jobs available to them, Bolivian American women have embraced the educational and employment opportunities available to them in the United States and are achieving greater social status as a result.

Education In colonial times, only upper-class men were educated, either privately or in schools run by the Catholic Church. In 1828, President Antonio José de Sucre ordered public schools to be established in all states (known as "departments"); however, on the eve of the 1952 revolution, less than one-third of the adult population was literate. Efforts have been made to increase literacy, and as of 2008, according to United Nations standards, Bolivia was declared free of illiteracy. Nonetheless, in rural areas levels of functional literacy still remain low.

Education in Bolivia is free and compulsory for children between seven and fourteen years of age. In rural areas of Bolivia, however, schools are underfunded, people are spread far and wide across the countryside, and children are needed to work on the farms. Children in rural areas often receive less than five years of schooling, compared with nine years for urban children. In 2008, the first indigenous universities were established with the goal of increasing opportunities for those populations.

Bolivian females tend to be less educated than their male counterparts. Only 65 percent of girls in rural areas receive any schooling and may attend school only until the third grade before they are expected to stay at home and help with housekeeping and child care. Bolivian women have an illiteracy rate of 38 percent compared with a 14.5 percent rate among men.

Education levels among Bolivian Americans vary. Many Bolivian immigrants are high school or college graduates, and they often obtain jobs in corporations, in health care, or in government. In the 2010 U.S. Census, it was found that 34 percent of Bolivian Americans over the age of twenty-five have a bachelor's degree or higher, making them one of the more highly educated Hispanic populations in the United States. Bolivian Americans from rural or indigenous regions have less schooling and often work as manual laborers or in the service industry. As with other immigrant and minority populations in the United States, programs have been created that are specifically designed to serve the needs of Bolivian American students and preserve cultural traditions and values. For example, at the Bolivian School in Arlington, Virginia, roughly 250 students practice their math and other lessons in Spanish, sing "Que Bonita Bandera" ("What a Pretty

Flag") and other patriotic Bolivian songs, and listen to folktales in native dialects.

Courtship and Weddings Traditionally, marriage is seen by both indigenous and Hispanic cultures in Bolivia as an important commitment to a broad family network. In rural Bolivia, it is common for a man and a woman to live together before marrying. The couple usually lives in the house of the man's family. They may live together for years, and even have children, before they save enough money to formally celebrate their union. There might also be a series of different ceremonies, including a formal betrothal, a traditional indigenous ritual, a Roman Catholic ceremony, a planting ritual, and a housewarming.

Urban weddings among Bolivians of European descent are similar to those performed in the United States. Among mestizos and other indigenous peoples, weddings are lavish affairs. After the ceremony, the bride and groom enter a specially decorated taxi, along with the best man and parents of the bride and groom. All of the other guests ride in a chartered bus, which takes them to a large party.

Bolivian American weddings are often performed in Catholic churches, and the bride and groom wear typical wedding clothing such as a tuxedo for the groom and a white dress for the bride. In some instances, the groom will present the bride with gold coins that are then blessed by the priest as a symbol of the groom's commitment to support his bride. The reception usually features Bolivian folk music, with the bride and groom dancing a *cueca*, a courtship dance traditional to several Latin American countries. The parents of the bride and groom then give speeches in support of the new couple, and the celebration commences. Dances among attendants are usually performed in lines separated by gender, with a line of men facing a line of their female partners. Bolivian food and drink, such as *signani*, a grape-based liquor that is Bolivia's national drink, or *chicha*, a corn-based beer, are generously served.

Funerals Funeral services in Bolivia often include a mixture of Catholic theology and indigenous beliefs. Mestizos participate in an expensive service known as *velorio.*, which is similar to a wake. The wake, or viewing of the deceased's body, occurs in a room in which all of the relatives and friends sit against the four walls. There, they pass limitless servings of cocktails, hot punches, and beer, as well as coca leaves and cigarettes. The next morning, the casket is carried to the cemetery. The guests extend their condolences to the family and may then return to the funeral celebration. The next day, the immediate family completes the funeral rite.

For mestizos who live near La Paz, completing the funeral rite includes a hike to the Choqueapu River, where the family washes the clothing of the deceased person. While the clothes dry, the family eats a picnic lunch and then builds a bonfire to burn the clothes. This ritual brings peace to the mourners and releases the soul of the deceased into the next world.

While Bolivian Americans mostly adhere to typical American funeral customs, they often retain a greater sense of connection to the deceased after they are buried. Bolivian Americans, along with many other Latin Americans, celebrate *El Día de los Muertos*, the Day of the Dead, on November 2, the day after All Saints' Day. On this day it is thought that the souls of the dead return to the world, and Bolivian Americans visit the graves of their loved ones to hold conversations with and offer food to nourish the departed on their journey back to the afterlife. Decidedly joyous affairs, Day of the Dead celebrations have become annual community events featuring Latino music, art, dancing, and food in areas with large Hispanic populations.

EMPLOYMENT AND ECONOMIC CONDITIONS

Like immigrants from other Central and South American countries, Bolivian Americans have relatively high levels of income and education. Their median income is higher than that of other Hispanic groups, such as Puerto Ricans, Cubans, and Mexicans. Also, a higher percentage of Central and South Americans work in managerial, professional, and other white-collar occupations than members of other Hispanic groups.

Many Bolivian Americans highly value education, which has allowed them to do well economically. Upon arrival in the United States, they are often employed as clerical and administrative workers. By pursuing further education, Bolivian Americans often advance into managerial positions. A large percentage of Bolivian Americans have held government jobs or positions in American corporations. Multinational companies often benefit from their skills and facility with foreign languages. Bolivian Americans have made inroads in academia, as well, and many teach about issues related to their former homeland.

Immigration into the United States is often tied to the economy of an immigrant's home country, and Bolivia is no exception. One measure of Bolivia's economic health is its fluctuating trade balance with the United States. In the early 1990s Bolivia had a positive trade balance with the United States. In other words, Bolivia exported more to the United States than it imported from it. By 1992 and 1993, however, that balance had shifted, causing Bolivia to have trade deficits with the United States during those years of $60 million and $25 million, respectively. These amounts are relatively small, but they added to a national debt that was staggering for such a poor nation. In fact, the International Monetary Fund and the United States forgave some of Bolivia's debt in the 1990s and again in the mid-2000s, releasing it from its obligation to repay them. While Bolivia once again enjoyed a positive trade balance with the United States totaling nearly $238 million in 2011, American aid to the country dropped to just $42 million—a decline of $80 million since 2007—as political tensions continued to strain U.S.-Bolivian relations.

Bolivian Americans are employed in a variety of careers in the United States. Among those immigrants who provided occupation information to the U.S. immigration authorities, the largest single occupation category in 1993 was professional specialty and technical workers. The next largest group of Bolivian Americans identified themselves as operators, fabricators, and laborers. About two-thirds of Bolivian immigrants in 1993 chose not to identify their occupation, a percentage that is consistent with immigrants from most countries. In the twenty-first century, a contracting U.S. economy has forced most educated Bolivian immigrants to take low-paying jobs as laborers, field workers, and hospitality staff. As a result, many Bolivians have stopped viewing the United States as a desirable destination, with many temporary residents choosing not to renew their visas and to seek greater opportunity elsewhere.

POLITICS AND GOVERNMENT

For Bolivian Americans, the political system of the United States is quite familiar. Both countries have a constitution that guarantees basic freedoms, a government with three separate branches, and a Congress that is divided into two houses. However, Bolivia's government has experienced upheaval and several military coups since its nineteenth-century struggle for independence from the Spanish.

Bolivian American participation in American politics has been focused on improving the living conditions in Bolivia and other areas of South America, as well as on issues relating to immigration, including amnesty and bilingual education. During the 1990s Bolivian Americans developed a strong desire to influence politics within their homeland. In 1990 the Bolivian Committee, a coalition of eight groups that promote Bolivian culture in Washington, D.C., petitioned Bolivia's president to allow expatriates to vote in Bolivian elections. In 2009 Bolivian expatriates were eligible for the first time to vote in the Bolivian general election for the president, vice president, and legislative assembly. During the 2000s American and Bolivian political and diplomatic relations became significantly strained, in part due to disagreements about narcotics policy and heavy tension between newly elected President Morales and the Bush administration. In 2011 both countries made gradual steps towards reestablishing relationships, although tension remained, particularly due to Morales's support for Venezuelan president Hugo Chavez.

NOTABLE INDIVIDUALS

Academia Eduardo A. Gamarra (1957–) is an assistant professor at Florida International University in Miami, Florida. He is the coauthor of *Revolution*

and Reaction: Bolivia, 1964–1985 (1988) and *Latin America and Caribbean Contemporary Record* (1990). In the 1990s he researched the stabilization of democracy in Latin America. Gamarra is a cofounder of Newlink Research, a consulting firm dedicated to electoral and public policy campaigns throughout Latin America.

Leo Spitzer (1939–) is a professor of history at Dartmouth College in Hanover, New Hampshire. He was born in La Paz, the child of refugees from Nazi persecution in Austria. His written work includes *Hotel Bolivia: The Culture of Memory in a Refuge from Nazism* (1974). His research concerns have centered on colonialism and racism in Latin America, Africa, and Central Europe as well as issues of historical memory, refugees, and depictions of trauma in photography and film.

Jaime Escalante (1930–2010) was a renowned teacher of mathematics whose story was told in the award-winning film *Stand and Deliver* (1987). This movie documented his life as a calculus teacher in East Los Angeles, where he encouraged his students, primarily low-income Latinos, to view studying advanced math as an opportunity for future success. He was born in La Paz.

Art Juan Fernando Bastos (1958–) is an American portrait artist of Bolivian descent. He has painted portraits of celebrities (including actress Charlize Theron and author Gore Vidal) and high-society figures and was featured in a 1999 *New York Times* article about the reemergence of portraiture. He has also created works that fuse his Catholic upbringing with Andean myths and traditional themes, such as the Lake Titicaca mermaids. He lives and works in Los Angeles.

Antonio Sotomayor (1904–1982) was a renowned painter and illustrator of books. His work also includes a number of historical murals that are painted on the walls of California buildings, churches, and hotels. His illustrations can be seen in *Best Birthday* (by Quail Hawkins, 1954); *Relatos Chilenos* (by Arturo Torres Rioscco, 1956); and *Stan Delaplane's Mexico* (by Stanton Delaplane, 1976). Sotomayor also wrote two children's books: *Khasa Goes to the Fiesta* (1967), and *Balloons: The First Two Hundred Years* (1972).

Government Cecilia Muñoz (1962–) is a civil rights activist who serves as director of the White House Domestic Policy Council under President Barack Obama and previously worked as director of intergovernmental affairs. She also served as senior vice president for the Office of Research, Advocacy and Legislation at the National Council of La Raza, a nonprofit organization dedicated to improving opportunities for Hispanic Americans and overseeing advocacy activities that cover issues of importance to immigrants. In 2000 she received a prestigious MacArthur Fellowship for her work on civil rights and immigration policy reform. She was also featured in

Episode 12, "Last Best Chance," of the HBO documentary How Democracy Works Now: Twelve Stories (2010). Her parents emigrated from La Paz.

Journalism Hugo Estenssoro (1946–) is accomplished in many fields. He is prominent as a magazine and newspaper photographer (for which work he has won awards), and he has edited a book of poetry (*Antología de Poesía Brasileña* [*An Anthology of Brazilian Poetry*], 1967). He has also written as a correspondent for numerous magazines both abroad and in the United States. In his correspondence, Estenssoro has interviewed Latin American heads of state and political and literary figures in the United States. In the 1990s, he was a resident of New York City.

Literature Ben Mikaelsen was born in La Paz in 1952. He is the author of several children's and young-adult books, including *Rescue Josh McGuire* (1991), *Sparrow Hawk Red* (1993), *Countdown* (1997), *Petey* (1998), and *Tree Girl* (2005). Mikaelsen's stories often focus on his characters developing a harmonious relationship with nature. Mikaelsen lives in Bozeman, Montana.

Music Jaime Laredo (1941–) is an award-winning violinist who, early on, was noted for his virtuoso performances. He first performed when he was eight years old. His likeness has appeared on a Bolivian airmail stamp. He also plays viola and has recorded piano quartets with violinist Isaac Stern, cellist Yo-Yo Ma, and pianist Emanuel Ax, as well as collaborating with renowned pianist Glenn Gould. In 2012 Laredo was appointed to the strings faculty at the Cleveland Institute of Music.

Jaime Mendoza-Nava (1925–2005) was a Bolivian American composer and conductor born in La Paz. He studied at the Juilliard School, the Madrid Royal Conservatory, and the Sorbonne. Later he was on the staff of Walt Disney Studios, and his works were recorded by MGM Records. Much of his music is inspired by the pentatonic music of the Andes. In Hollywood, he also had several credits as a sound editor and provided scores for many films, including *The Boys in Company C*, *A Boy and His Dog*, and *Equinox*.

Sports Marco Etcheverry (1970–) is an accomplished athlete well known to fans of professional soccer. Before his stellar career with the D.C. United team, he was already one of Bolivia's most famous athletes. He played for soccer clubs from Chile to Spain and traveled the world with various Bolivian national teams. He is the captain of his team and a hero to thousands of Bolivian immigrants in the Washington area. Etcheverry led D.C. United to championship wins in both 1996 and 1997. In 1998 Etcheverry had a career high ten goals and matched a personal best with nineteen assists for a total of thirty-nine points. Nicknamed "El Diablo," Etcheverry and his countryman Jaime Moreno are the only two players in league history to reach double figures in goals and assists.

Jaime Moreno (1974–) is a former Bolivian soccer player now serving as Youth Academy Technical Training Coach for D.C. United in Major League Soccer and as the head coach of D.C. United's U-23 side. He was the all-time leading scorer in Major League Soccer at the time of his retirement.

Jennifer "The Bolivian Queen" Salinas (1982–) is a professional boxer with a record of thirteen wins and three losses. The daughter of Bolivian immigrants, she was born in Virginia but spent most of her childhood in Bolivia before returning to the United States at fifteen. Salinas frequently makes charitable donations of sporting goods and other athletic materials to organizations in Bolivia and has been the guest of president Evo Morales at the presidential palace in La Paz.

Stage and Screen Raquel Welch (1940–) is an accomplished actress who has appeared in a number of films and on stage. Her film work includes *Fantastic Voyage* (1966), *One Million Years BC* (1967), *The Oldest Profession* (1967), *The Biggest Bundle of Them All* (1968), *100 Rifles* (1969), *Myra Breckinridge* (1969), *Mother, Jugs, and Speed* (1976), *Tortilla Soup* (2001), *Legally Blonde* (2001), and *Forget About It* (2006). Welch won a Golden Globe Award for Best Actress for her work in *The Three Musketeers* (1974). She acted on Broadway in *Woman of the Year* (1982). She has also appeared as a guest star on numerous television programs, including *Seinfeld*, *Sabrina the Teenage Witch*, and the PBS series *American Family: Journey of Dreams* (2002–2004), the first original American primetime TV drama to feature a primarily Latino cast.

MEDIA

Los Tiempos

The largest newspaper in Cochamba, Bolivia, *Los Tiempos*, began publishing a weekly version of the newspaper in the Washington metropolitan area in 2004.

URL: www.lostiempos.com

Bolivia Web

Collates news articles regarding Bolivia from around the web, as well as linking to numerous Bolivian newspapers, relevant blogs, and streaming Bolivian radio.

URL: www.boliviaweb.com

Bolivia Weekly

Offers English-language Bolivian news and a weekly podcast discussing current events in Bolivia.

URL: www.boliviaweekly.com

Upside Down World

An online magazine dedicated to activism and politics in Latin America. Includes a section on Bolivia.

URL: http://upsidedownworld.org/main/bolivia-archives-31

ORGANIZATIONS AND ASSOCIATIONS

Asociación de Damas Bolivianas

> P.O. Box 77653
> San Francisco, California 94107
> Email: damasbolivianas@gmail.com
> URL: www.damasbolivianas.com

Bolivian-American Chamber of Commerce, Inc.

Promotes trade, commerce, and investment between the United States and Bolivia.

> 909 Third Avenue #6721
> New York, New York 10150
> Email: bacc@bolivia-us.org
> URL: www.bolivia-us.org

Bolivian Medical Society and Professional Associates, Inc.

Serves Bolivian Americans in health-related fields.

> Dr. Jaime F. Marquez
> 9105 Redwood Avenue
> Bethesda, Maryland 20817
> Phone: (301) 891-6040

Comite Pro-Bolivia (Pro-Bolivia Committee)

Umbrella organization made up of ten arts groups, located in the United States and in Bolivia, with the purpose of preserving and performing Bolivian folk dances in the United States.

> P.O. Box 10117
> Arlington, Virginia 22210
> Phone: (703) 461-4197
> Fax: (703) 751-2251
> Email: probolivia@yahoo.com
> URL: http://jaguar.pg.cc.md.us/ProBolivia/

Embassy of the Plurinational State of Bolivia

Provides news, cultural, and travel information regarding Bolivia.

> 3014 Massachusetts Avenue NW
> Washington, D.C. 20008

> Phone: (202) 483-4410
> URL: www.bolivia-usa.org

Rhode Island Bolivian-American Association

Organization devoted to promoting Bolivian culture throughout Rhode Island.

> P.O. Box 114329
> North Providence, Rhode Island 02911
> Email: info@ribaa.org
> URL: www.ribaa.org/index.html

SOURCES FOR ADDITIONAL STUDY

Blair, David Nelson. *The Land and People of Bolivia*. New York: J. B. Lippincott, 1990.

Griffith, Stephanie. "Bolivians Reach for the American Dream: Well Educated Immigrants with High Aspirations Work Hard, Prosper in D.C. Area," *Washington Post*, May 8, 1990.

Klein, Herbert S. *Bolivia: The Evolution of a Multi-Ethnic Society*. 2nd ed. New York: Oxford University Press, 1992.

Kohl, Benjamin, Linda C. Farthing, and Felix Muruchi. *From the Mines to the Streets: A Bolivian Activist's Life*. Austin: University of Texas Press, 2012.

Morales, Waltraud Queiser. *Bolivia: Land of Struggle*. Boulder, CO: Westview Press, 1992.

Pateman, Robert. *Bolivia*. New York: Marshall Cavendish, 1995.

Paz-Soldan, Edmundo. "Obsessive Signs of Identity: Bolivians in the United States." In *The Other Latinos*, ed. José Luis Falconi and José Antonio Mazzoti. Cambridge, MA: David Rockefeller Center for Latin American Studies at Harvard, 2008.

Sánchez-H., José. *My Mother's Bolivian Kitchen: Recipes and Recollections*. New York: Hippocrene Books, 2005.

Schuster, Angela M. "Sacred Bolivian Textiles Returned," *Archaeology*, January/February 1993, 20–22.

Skiemeier, James F. *The Bolivian Revolution and the United States: 1952 to the Present*. University Park: Pennsylvania State University Press, 2011.

BOSNIAN AMERICANS

Olivia Miller

OVERVIEW

Bosnian Americans are immigrants from or descendants of people from Bosnia-Herzegovina, a republic of the former Yugoslavia, which is located on the Balkan Peninsula in Eastern Europe. Bosnia-Herzegovina is bordered to the north and west by Croatia, to the east by Serbia, and to the south by Montenegro and the Adriatic Sea. The northern portion of the country, Bosnia, is mountainous and wooded, whereas Herzegovina, to the south, is primarily flatland. The republic has a land area of 19,741 square miles (51,129 square kilometers), slightly less than that of West Virginia.

In 2012 the *CIA World Factbook* estimated the population of Bosnia-Herzegovina to be nearly 3.9 million people. This figure was significantly lower than that of the 1991 census—the last census performed—which listed 4.3 million. During the Bosnian War (1992–1995), the country was devastated by ethnic cleansing and brutal warfare between Bosnian Serbs and non-Serbs. The population includes Catholic Bosnian Croats (15 percent), Eastern Orthodox Bosnian Serbs (31 percent), and Bosnian Muslims, also known as Bosniaks (48 percent), whose ancestors converted from Christianity under the Ottoman Empire centuries ago. Some historians have pointed out that the residents of Bosnia are ethnically similar but have chosen to identify as Croats or Serbs primarily for religious or political reasons. Since the war, Bosnia-Herzegovina has achieved a tenuous peace. The twenty-first century has been marked by modest economic gains due to relatively lax trade restrictions and growing exports of metals and wood products. Nevertheless, political infighting and religious tensions continue to pose major challenges to the future of the country.

Serb immigrants began to arrive in the United States in the first half of the nineteenth century and helped settle the American west, working in fishing or shipping in cities such as San Francisco, New Orleans, and Galveston, Texas. Bosnian Muslims also settled in the Midwest in the early 1900s, helping to establish some of the first Muslim communities in cities such as Chicago, Milwaukee, and St. Louis. For most of the twentieth century, accurate immigration figures for Bosnians were impossible to obtain. Until 1918 the U.S. Immigration Service counted Croatians from Dalmatia, Bosnia, and Herzegovina separately from other Croatians, who were classified as Slovenians. From 1918 through 1992, when Congress voted to recognize Bosnia and Herzegovina as an independent nation and began admitting Bosnian refugees, Croatians were listed as Yugoslavs. Since 1993 the United States has admitted more than 300,000 refugees and immigrants from Bosnia and Herzegovina, though many have returned to Bosnia and Herzegovina as conditions in the region have improved.

According to 2009–2011 estimates by the U.S. Census Bureau's American Community Survey, the number of U.S. residents who were born in Bosnia is 119,187, roughly equivalent to the population of Charleston, South Carolina. The U.S. Census Bureau has not tracked statistics for Americans with Bosnian heritage; the Embassy of Bosnia and Herzegovina suggests that the number may be around 350,000. Cities with the greatest concentration of Bosnian Americans include New York, Atlanta, Chicago, St. Louis, and San Francisco.

HISTORY OF THE PEOPLE

Early History In the first few centuries CE, the Roman Empire controlled Bosnia. After the empire disintegrated, various powers sought control of the land. Slavs were living in Bosnia by the seventh century, and by the tenth century they had an independent state. In the ninth century the two kingdoms of Serbia and Croatia were established.

Bosnia briefly lost its independence to Hungary in the twelfth century but regained it around 1180. It prospered and expanded under three especially powerful rulers: Ban Kulin, who reigned from 1180 to 1204; Ban Stephen Kotromanic, who ruled from 1322 to 1353; and King Stephen Tvrtko, who reigned from 1353 to 1391. After Tvrtko's death, internal struggles weakened the nation. The neighboring Ottoman Turks were becoming increasingly aggressive, and they conquered Bosnia in 1463. For more than four hundred years, Bosnia was an important province of the Ottoman Empire. Islam was the official religion, though non-Muslim faiths were tolerated. Indeed, in the Ottoman era, many Jews came from Spain, where they faced persecution or death at the hands of the Catholic Inquisition, and found a tolerant home in Bosnia.

By the nineteenth century, however, many Bosnians had become dissatisfied with Ottoman rule. Clashes between peasants and landowners were frequent, and there was tension between Christians and Muslims. Foreign powers became interested in the region. At the Congress of Berlin in 1878, following the end of the Russo-Turkish War (1877–1878), Austria-Hungary took over the administration of Bosnia-Herzegovina. Many Bosnian Muslims, who thought the new rulers favored Serbian interests, emigrated to Turkey and other parts of the Ottoman Empire.

The Austro-Hungarian government formally annexed Bosnia-Herzegovina in 1908. Nationalists in Serbia, who had hoped to make Bosnia-Herzegovina part of a great Serb nation, were outraged. In 1914 in Sarajevo a Serb nationalist assassinated Archduke Franz Ferdinand, the heir to the Austro-Hungarian throne, and precipitated World War I (1914–1918). At the end of the war came the creation of the South Slav state, which together with Serbia became the Kingdom of Yugoslavia. Bosnia's Muslim Slavs were urged to register themselves as Serbs or Croats. In 1941 Nazi Germany, under the leadership of Adolf Hitler, invaded Yugoslavia. The Nazis set up a puppet Croatian state, incorporating all of Bosnia and Herzegovina, but persecuted and killed Serbs, Gypsies, and Jews, as well as Croats who opposed the regime. Yugoslav communist Josip Broz Tito led a multiethnic force against Germany, and at the end of World War II, he became premier of Yugoslavia. Under Tito's rule, Yugoslavia was a one-party dictatorship that restricted religious practice for thirty-five years.

Modern Era After Tito's death in 1980, the presidents of the six republics and two autonomous regions ruled Yugoslavia by committee, which led to political instability and fragmentation, as well as a weakened economy that persisted throughout the 1980s. This institutional and economic weakness helped create a rise in nationalism during the 1980s among Yugoslavia's component republics. The Muslim-led government of Bosnia and Herzegovina declared its independence from Yugoslavia in March 1992. The following month, the United States and the European community recognized the sovereignty of Bosnia and Herzegovina. Interethnic fighting began when the Yugoslav National Army, under the leadership of Slobodan Milosevic, attacked Sarajevo. Milosevic, the leader of Serbia, sought to unite all Serbian lands and to purge the regions of non-Serb populations. Serbs, Croats, and Muslims fought to expand or keep their territories within Bosnia. By mid-1995 most of the country was in the hands of Bosnian Serbs who were accused of conducting "ethnic cleansing"—the systematic killing or expulsion of other ethnic groups—which resulted in the deaths of around 200,000 people and the displacement of more than 2 million more. In December 1995 the war was officially ended with the signing of the Dayton Agreement, which stipulated

that Yugoslavia recognize and respect the newly independent countries of Croatia and Bosnia-Herzegovina as sovereign nations. At that time, more than one million Bosnians remained displaced within the borders of the republic. At least one million more were living as refugees in twenty-five other countries, primarily in the neighboring Yugoslavia and its former republics but also throughout western Europe.

Throughout the late 1990s and early 2000s, the United Nations maintained a peacekeeping force of 60,000 troops and arbitrated disputes in Bosnia. The European Union assumed these duties in 2004 with a contingent of 7,000 troops, which was reduced to 2,500 in 2007. The international community also sought to bring the Serbian leaders responsible for the atrocities in Bosnia to trial for war crimes. Milosevic was arrested in October 2000 and eventually underwent a four-year trial at The Hague in the Netherlands before dying in his cell in 2006. A total of 160 other political and military leaders, including Bosnian Serb president Radovan Karadžić and top general Ratko Mladić, were indicted and subsequently arrested under the auspices of the United Nations' International Criminal Tribunal for the former Yugoslavia. As of 2012 many of these trials were still ongoing, but the sight of such reviled figures in shackles helped many Bosnian refugees achieve a small sense of closure to a devastating period of destruction and upheaval.

SETTLEMENT IN THE UNITED STATES

There were six waves of Serbian/Croatian immigration to the United States. The earliest occurred from 1820 to 1880. The largest wave of Yugoslav immigrants took place from 1880 to 1914, when approximately 100,000 Serbs arrived in the United States. Most were unskilled laborers who fled the Austro-Hungarian policies of forced assimilation. Croatian and Serbian immigrants were largely young, impoverished peasant men. In the United States they settled in the major industrial cities of the East and Midwest, working long hours at low-paying jobs, like other industrial laborers of the era.

The third wave happened between World War I and World War II. From 1921 to 1930, 49,064 immigrants arrived in the United States from Yugoslavia. These interwar years were times of Serbian nationalist fervor. The Yugoslav regime became increasingly dictatorial, ruling provinces through military governors. Immigrants sought freedom from ethnic oppression by coming to the United States. The number of immigrants dropped to 5,835 in the decade from 1931 to 1941, and then decreased to 1,576 in 1941, when Germany took control of Yugoslavia. Immigration was further reduced during the postwar years when the Communist Party under Tito took over the country and restricted emigration. The fourth wave was made up of displaced persons and war refugees from 1945 until 1965.

The fifth major surge began in the 1960s, when 20,381 Yugoslavians immigrated, a surge that

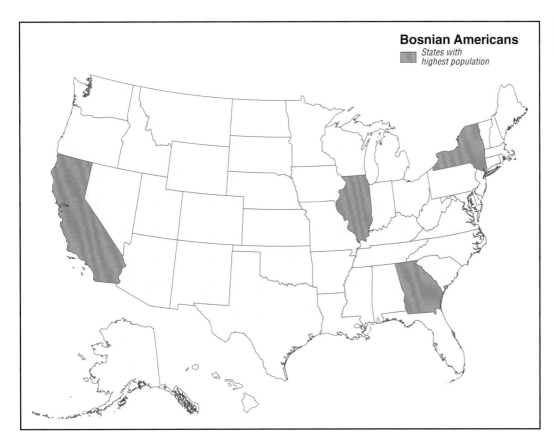

Bosnian Americans
States with highest population

continued into the next decade with 30,540 more immigrants. During the years of Tito's rule, Yugoslavia received economic and diplomatic support from the United States, which aimed to use the anti-Soviet Tito to stem the spread of Soviet-style communism. In the 1970s U.S. secretary of state Henry Kissinger stated that the United States would risk nuclear war on Yugoslavia's behalf. From 1981 to 1990, 19,200 Yugoslavians immigrated to the United States. These Croatian and Serbian immigrants were intellectuals, artists, and professionals who adapted easily to life in the United States.

The sixth wave came as a response to disintegrating political stability after Bosnia declared its independence from Yugoslavia in 1992. These immigrants were primarily Muslims who had been pushed out by Serbs fighting to create a Serb-only region. From 1991 to 1994, 11,500 immigrated. The number fell to 8,300 in 1995, then rose to 11,900 in 1996. In 1994, with the U.S. Census records listing Bosnians as a separate category, 337 refugees were granted permanent residence. An additional 3,818 refugees were granted permanent residency in 1995 and 6,246 more in 1996. From 2001 to 2009, another 88,000 Bosnians received permanent resident status. Bosnian refugees settled into communities all over the United States, with the highest concentration in the Midwest. Most received help from charitable organizations as well as aid from the immigrants who preceded them.

Most Bosnian immigrants have settled quickly into long-established ethnic enclaves. Bosnian Serbs tend to settle with other Serbs and Bosnian Croats in local Croatian communities. Until the war in the 1990s, Bosnian Muslim immigrants had been so few in number that there was no Bosnian Muslim community into which they could integrate. They concentrated in urban areas, some of which now have significant Bosnian Muslim populations. In the Astoria section of New York City, for instance, Bosnian Muslims built a mosque that was dedicated in 1997.

Of the 258,000 Americans of Yugoslavian ancestry living in the United States in 1990, 37 percent lived in the West, 23 percent lived in the Northeast, 28 percent lived in the Midwest, and 12 percent lived in the South. Cities with large Yugoslavian American populations included Chicago, New York, Newark, Detroit, St. Louis, Des Moines, Atlanta, Houston, Miami, and Jacksonville. According to the 1990 Census, the highest concentration of Serbs, Croats, and Bosnian Muslims lived in a neighborhood near 185th Street in eastern Cleveland. After 1992, Bosnian Americans who came as refugees began to settle increasingly in fast-growing enclaves in cities such as New York, St. Louis, St. Petersburg, Chicago, Salt Lake City, and Waynesboro, Pennsylvania. In St. Louis, for example, the Bosnian population had been smaller than 1,000 in the early 1990s, but by 2011 it had reached 70,000; of these a great majority are Bosniaks (Muslims).

About 15,000 Bosnian refugees settled in the Queens borough of New York City in the mid-1990s, though that number has since been cut in half, with a number of refugees moving elsewhere or returning to Bosnia. As is true of other immigrant populations, Bosnian refugees in the United States are especially attracted to established ethnic communities because many refugees are separated from immediate family members. It often takes several years to reunite families, so the Bosnian community provides needed social support.

LANGUAGE

The official language of Bosnia-Herzegovina is Bosnian, also called Serbo-Croatian. The language goes by different names because of the country's ethnic differences and rivalries. People in the Muslim-controlled sector call it Bosnian, whereas those in Croat areas call it Croatian, and those in Serb areas refer to it as Serbian.

Bosnian belongs to the Slavic branch of the Indo-European language family and more specifically to the group of South Slavic languages, which includes Bulgarian, Macedonian, and Slovenian. A few Bosnian words are recognizably related to English. The Bosnian word *sin* means "son," and Bosnian *sestra* means "sister." Bosnian has many borrowed words from other European languages, including English, Turkish, Arabic, and Persian.

Bosnian is written in either the Cyrillic or the Latin alphabet. Its letters are generally pronounced as they are in English, with certain exceptions. The letter *c* is pronounced "ts"; the letter *ć* is pronounced similarly to "tch" but with a thinner sound, more like the thickened "t" in "future"; *č* is pronounced "tch" as in "match"; *dj* is pronounced roughly like "j" in "jam"; *j* is pronounced "y," as in "Yugoslavia"; *s* is pronounced "sh"; and *z* is pronounced "zh" as in "Zhivago."

Bosnian Americans generally have little difficulty pronouncing English, although the "th" and "w" sounds may give some trouble. They may also find some English verbs hard to understand. Bosnian uses fewer auxiliary verbs, such as "be" and "do," than English, and Bosnian speakers may be puzzled by questions in English, in which the auxiliary verb comes before the subject, as in "Did you eat?"

Greetings and Popular Expressions During the war, one of the most frequently asked questions was "*Sta je tvoje ime?*" (pronounced stah-yeah-tVOya), which means "what is your name?" in Bosnian; name was a major clue to ethnicity.

RELIGION

Many Bosnians treat their religion the same way as many Americans do, as something restricted to weekly church attendance and major religious holidays. The Yugoslav government discouraged religious fundamentalism, as did the religious community itself, reflecting

BOSNIAN PROVERBS

Iver ne pada daleko od klade.
> A splinter doesn't land far from the trunk.

Tko drugome jamu kopa sam u nju pada.
> Whoever digs a trap for others ends up in it himself.

Uzdaj se u se i u svoje kljuse!
> Trust yourself and your horse!

years of accommodation between religion and the communist state. Religious affiliation in Yugoslavia, however, was closely linked with the politics of nationality. Centuries-old animosities among the Eastern Orthodox Serbs, the Roman Catholic Croats, and the Bosnian Muslims remained a divisive factor in the 1990s and 2000s, though the basis was more economic power than religious fervor. There also was lingering resentment over forced conversions of Orthodox Serbs to Roman Catholicism by ultranationalist Croatian priests during World War II.

According to the 2010 U.S. Census, there were 122 Serbian Orthodox churches in the United States and Canada with a total membership of around 69,000. Serbian Orthodox churches serve as a social center as well as a place of worship. Serbian Bosnian Americans celebrate a family's religious anniversary, the *krsna slava* ("christening celebration"), each year. *Slava*, as it is commonly called, commemorates the conversion of the family's ancestors to Christianity in the ninth century, and on this day families feast and receive the visit of a priest. Bosnian Serbs also celebrate Easter with feasting and special ceremonies.

CULTURE AND ASSIMILATION

Bosnia-Herzegovina's population comprises three main groups: Serbs, who are Eastern Orthodox; Croats, who are Catholic; and Muslims (or Bosniaks). Each group has its distinct beliefs, traditions, and customs. Bosnian American communities have informal networks of communication such as places of worship, which provide a gathering spot for religious activities as well as weddings, baptisms (for Croats and Serbs), and funerals.

Like many immigrant groups, especially refugees, Bosnian refugees face many challenges in the United States. They must start over, learning a new language, new customs, and new skills. One Bosnian American refugee described this adjustment to the *St. Petersburg Times* as "in some ways like being a blind man who wants to take care of himself but is powerless to do so." Because their immigration was not necessarily by choice, they often find the experience more overwhelming in comparison to immigrants who were eager to come to the United States. Learning English is the first step that Bosnians take once they reach the United States, though many Bosnians speak several European languages, especially German, as many Bosnians took refuge in Germany during the war and learned the language. Established Bosnian communities offer services such as English-language classes; computer training classes; no-cost legal aid; and instruction on understanding health insurance, buying a home, and managing other complicated aspects of American life. Established communities also usually provide a place for worship.

In the 2000s more than one million Bosnian refugees remained in the United States even though the war ended in 1995. Many cannot return to Bosnia because the boundaries of territories have changed and their homes are in a divided country. Although they are usually forced to take lower status jobs to make ends meet, Bosnian Americans often seek higher education and better employment opportunities, as most Americans do. Many also Americanize their names, which are difficult for Americans to pronounce. Earlier immigrants often discovered with surprise that immigration officials had Americanized their names on the documents that admitted them to the country.

A number of Bosnian American organizations have encouraged cultural crossover through public festivals and gatherings celebrating Bosnian and Herzegovinian heritage. In Salt Lake City, home to more than 5,000 Bosnian immigrants, an annual Living Traditions Festival includes Bosnian dance and music performances by the American Bosnian and Herzegovinian Association of Utah. Likewise, since 2003 the United Bosnian Association and the Bosnian Chamber of Commerce in St. Louis have held an annual Bosnian Day/Bosanski Festival featuring Bosnian cuisine, music, and folk dancing.

Cuisine The cuisine of Bosnia reflects influences from central Europe, the Balkans, and the Middle East. One popular traditional dish is *cevapcici* (kabobs), which are made from ground beef and spices that are shaped into little cylinders, cooked on an open fire, and served on *somun*, a thick pita bread, along with grilled onions. Another meat dish is *pljeskavica*, a patty made with a mixture of ground meat (lamb, beef, or pork). *Bosanski lonac* is a slow-roasted mixture of layers of meat and vegetables eaten with chunks of brown bread. It is usually served in a vaselike ceramic pot. Serbian meat and fish dishes are typically cooked first and then braised with vegetables such as tomatoes and green peppers. A condiment called *ajvar*, made from red bell peppers and garlic, often accompanies meat and bread dishes.

Mediterranean and Middle Eastern influences are evident in *aschinicas* (pronounced ash-chee-nee-tsa-as), restaurants offering various kinds of cooked meat, filled vegetables called *dolmas*, kabobs, and salads, with Greek baklava for dessert. The filling for dolmas most often consists of ground meat, rice, spices, and various kinds of chopped vegetables. Containers can be hollowed-out peppers, potatoes, or onions. Some dolmas

In Clearwater, Florida, Mija Kazazic, who lost part of her leg in the Yugoslavian War, and Winter the dolphin, who lost his tail in a fishing accident, swim together. Both Kazazic and Winter have prosthetic limbs. BARRY BLAND / BARCROFT MEDIA / GETTY IMAGES

A young Bosnian immigrant makes Bosnian pita, which is a phyllo pastry filled with either ground beef, cheese, potatoes, or spinach and cheese. BARRY CHIN / THE BOSTON GLOBE / GETTY IMAGES

are made from cabbage leaves, grape leaves, kale, or some other leaf large enough and softened enough by cooking that it can be wrapped around the little ball made of the filling. When enough pieces are made, they are stacked in a tureen that is then covered with its own lid or with a piece of parchment tightly tied around its neck. The dish is then cooked slowly on a low, covered fire.

Pita, pastry filled with meat or vegetables, is another distinctive Bosnian dish. In other parts of the former Yugoslavia, pitas that are meat-filled are called *burek*. Pita meat pie is often the final course of a meal or is served as a light supper on its own.

Orthodox Bosnians and Bosnian Americans include special dishes in their Easter celebrations. In Orthodox tradition, after the midnight service, the congregation walks around the church seven times carrying candles, then goes home to a supper that includes hard-boiled eggs that have been dyed and decorated, and *pasca*, a round, sweet yeast cake filled with either sour cream or cottage cheese.

Homemade brandy, known as *rakija* in the former Yugoslavia but exported to the United States as *slivovitz* (plum brandy) or *loza* (grape brandy or *grapa*), is the liquor of choice for men on most occasions. Women may opt instead for fruit juice. Other popular nonalcoholic beverages include Turkish-style coffee (*kahva*, *kafa*, or *kava*), a thin yogurt drink called *kefir*, and a tea known as *salep*.

Bosnian Americans have successfully incorporated much of their native cuisine into their diet and have introduced a number of traditional foods to the rest of the population in areas with high concentrations of Bosnian immigrants. Although Bosnian Americans, particularly younger generations, are typically eager to assimilate and often give foods more familiar-sounding names in restaurants—calling *lepinja*, a puffy flatbread, "white bread," for example—entrées such as dolmas; lamb, beef, or veal kabobs; cevapcici with ajvar; pljeskavica; and smoked sausages known as *suho meso* have become popular throughout the Midwest, along with Bosnian coffees and desserts such as baklava.

Traditional Dress For centuries Bosnia was well known for having the widest variety of folk costumes of any region of the former Yugoslavia. Today these outfits serve as stage costumes rather than street wear. Traditionally, older men wore breeches, a cummerbund, a striped shirt, a vest, and even a fez, a felt hat that was usually red. These garments were often colorful and richly embroidered. The typical women's costume was a fine linen blouse embroidered with floral or folk motifs worn under a vest called a *jelek* that was cut low under the breast and made of velvet, embroidered with silver or gold thread. A colorful skirt was covered by an apron and worn on top of a white linen petticoat that showed beneath the skirt. The baggy trousers worn by women, called *dimije*, spread to all three ethnic groups as a folk costume, though each group wore different colors as specified by the Ottoman Empire. *Dimije* were rare on the streets of cities before World War II, but they were common in rural districts and among the older women within the cities. Traditional fashion lore dictated that you could tell how high in the mountains a woman's village was by how high on the ankles she tied her *dimije* to keep the hems out of the snow.

The devout Muslim women of Bosnia have not traditionally worn the chador familiar in fundamentalist Muslim countries. The chador is a garment that covers women from head to toe. Bosnian Muslim women instead wear hijabs (head scarves) and raincoats as symbolic substitutes for the chador, particularly on religious holidays.

Most Bosnian Americans have adopted the typical American style of dress. Because Bosnians typically view their religion more as a cultural or political identifier, many Bosnian American Muslim women no longer wear a hijab in public.

Music and Dance Music and dance reflect Bosnia's great diversity. During the years of Tito's rule, Bosnian amateur folklore groups, called cultural art societies, flourished throughout the region. They were required to perform the folk music and dances of all three major ethnic groups. Some such troupes also performed contemporary plays, modern dance, choral works, and ballet.

Bosnian music can be divided into rural and urban traditions. The rural tradition is characterized by such musical styles as *ravne pjesme* (flat song) of limited scale; *ganga*, an almost shouted polyphonic style, and other types of songs that may be accompanied on the *shargija* (a simple long-necked lute), the wooden flute, or the *diple* (a droneless bagpipe). The urban is more in the Turkish style, with its melismatic singing—more than one note per syllable—and accompaniment on the *saz*, a larger and more elaborate version of the *shargija*. Epic poems, an ancient tradition, are still sung to the sound of the *gusle*, a single-string bowed fiddle. Although Bosnia's Jewish population was decimated by World War II, its influence remains apparent in folk songs sung in Ladino, a dialect descended from fifteenth-century Spanish.

In the 1990s and 2000s, the influence of Western pop music and of new native pop music in a folkish style, played on the accordion, became apparent. For instance, pop singer Dino Merlin (Edin Derviśhalidović) incorporates elements of Western dance and pop music into his songs and has become extremely popular among Bosnians around the globe, touring the United States in 2009 to the delight of

many Bosnian immigrants. But modern influences have not displaced *sevdalinka*. With a name derived from the Turkish word *sevda* (love), *sevdalinka* songs have been the dominant form of music in Bosnia and Herzegovina, and have served as a source of comfort for displaced Bosnians everywhere. Incorporating both Western and Eastern elements, these deeply emotional songs speak metaphorically and symbolically of love won and lost, much like American country western music. Sevdah North America, located in Seattle, Washington, encourages Bosnian Americans to maintain an emotional connection to their home country through the lyrics and melodies of *sevdalinka* and hosts an annual "Evening of Sevdah" concert to provide all members of the local community with an opportunity to experience one of the most popular forms of Bosnian music.

In the 2000s more than one million Bosnian refugees remained in the United States even though the war ended in 1995. Many cannot return to Bosnia because the boundaries of territories have changed and their homes are in a divided country.

Bosnia has one of the richest yet least known of all the regional folk dance traditions of the former Yugoslavia. Dances range from the *nijemo kolo*, accompanied only by the sound of stamping feet and the clash of silver ornaments on the women's aprons, to line dances in which the sexes are segregated as they are in the Middle East, to Croatian and Serbian dances similar to those performed across the borders in their native regions. A number of dance groups in America, such as Iowa's K.U.D. Kolo dance troupe, perform traditional Bosnian and Herzegovinian dances at festivals, concerts, and other cultural events. Many such groups are open to enrollment from elementary and high school students, thereby fostering new generations of Bosnian Americans with knowledge of and appreciation for their cultural heritage.

In the United States, Bosnian Serbs' culture is centered on music. Choirs and *tamburica* orchestras have been a part of local communities since 1901, when the Gorski Vijenac (Mountain Wreath) choir of Pittsburgh was founded. The tamburica is a South Slavic stringed instrument similar to a mandolin. It exists in five different sizes and musical ranges. The Bosnian community in St. Louis holds an annual Tamburitza Extravaganza Festival where as many as twenty bands from all over the country perform. In Pittsburgh, the Duquesne University Tamburitzans, a dance troupe whose members are all Duquesne students, was founded in the 1930s. The group not only trains new performers but also maintains a cultural center at the university.

Sviraj (pronounced svee-rye, with a rolled *r*) is a popular group of ethnic Balkan musicians who preserve their heritage through performances that celebrate the music of eastern Europe. *Sviraj* means "Play on!" in Serbian and Croatian. The music has its roots in Serbia, Croatia, Macedonia, Bosnia, Dalmatia, and Romania.

Holidays Bosnian Americans observe the holidays of their individual religions. The Serbian Orthodox Church uses the Julian calendar, which is thirteen days behind the Gregorian one commonly used in the West. Serb Bosnian Americans follow this calendar for holidays. For example, Orthodox Christmas falls on January 7 rather than December 25. Eastern Orthodox Christian families also celebrate the *Slava*, or saint's name day, of each member of the family. Muslim Bosnian Americans follow Islam's holidays and calendar, including Ramadan, the month of ritual fasting. At the end of Ramadan, a period called Bajram, they exchange visits and small gifts during the three days. Croat Bosnian Americans observe Catholic holidays.

FAMILY AND COMMUNITY LIFE

In most Bosnian American families, both husband and wife work outside the home, but the wife still has the primary responsibility for housework and cooking. In Bosnia the effects of the wars of the twentieth century and migration away from rural areas after World War II have resulted in fewer extended families living together. However, Bosnian Americans tend to live with extended family members, though this is likely to end as Bosnians acclimate to American culture and become more financially successful. Bosniaks tend to have fewer relative connections already living in the United States because prior to 1992 there were few Muslim immigrants. Polygamy as a Muslim custom last existed in Bosnia in the early 1950s, and then only in one isolated region of the country, Cazinska Krajina. Most Bosnian marriages follow the modern custom of love matches, and arranged marriage between families has largely disappeared. In recent decades, about a third of all urban marriages in Bosnia have been between partners from different religious and ethnic backgrounds. Family size has been decreasing as education and prosperity have increased.

Gender Roles Traditionally, women played subservient roles in Yugoslavia's patriarchal families, especially in the country's remote mountainous regions. In the interwar period, laws codified women's subservient status. Industrialization and urbanization in the communist era changed traditional family patterns. This trend was most pronounced in the more developed northern and western urban areas. The number of women employed outside the home rose from 396,463 in 1948 to 2.4 million in 1985. As women began working away

from home, they became more independent. In the 1980s the percentage of women in low-level political and management positions was equal to that of men, but this was not the case for upper management positions.

Many Bosnian American women refugees have lost everything and have become the heads of households for the first time. They face the challenge of rebuilding their lives in a new country and adapting to a new culture and language while providing food, shelter, and education for themselves and their surviving relatives. Many were financially dependent on their spouses before the war and consequently have no marketable skills or entrepreneurial experience. By 2011, however, the U.S. Census Bureau's American Community Survey estimate for 2009–2011 indicated that among Bosnian-born U.S. residents, a greater percentage of women (19.6 percent) than men (15.8 percent) were working in management, business, science, or arts occupations, a gender balance similar to that of the total U.S. population (33 percent of males and 39 percent of females work in these professions).

Education The literacy rate in Bosnia was 92 percent prior to the civil war that began in 1992. Education through the eighth grade was compulsory for both boys and girls, after which a student could opt for either a vocational trade school or a more academically oriented route. There were university faculties in the larger cities, along with a community college-type option called "workers' universities."

The first wave of Bosnian immigrants and refugees to arrive in the 1990s found it difficult to succeed in American schools due to the language barrier, poor economic situations in the cities in which they settled, and a lack of supportive organizations that could address some of the problems they faced. Many of these young immigrants left school to pursue jobs that would support their families, which often lacked a primary breadwinner due to the devastation caused by the war. However, younger Bosnian Americans have fared increasingly well as students, garnering undergraduate and advanced degrees often with the help of various cultural organizations. Still, there remains some concern that educated Bosnian Americans are leaving their communities for wealthier communities elsewhere, leaving less educated Bosnian Americans without strong role models to encourage them to remain in school.

Courtship and Weddings In 1992, when the war started in Bosnia, approximately 40 percent of the registered marriages in urban centers were between ethnically mixed Bosnians. Bosnian American wedding ceremonies often reflect this mix, including traditions from both ethnic groups involved and often eschewing the traditional customs of their religions for a more secular approach. The bride usually wears white and is attended by bridesmaids. Men wear suits, sometimes accompanied by capes. There are many flowers, and there is much drinking and dancing. The food includes Bosnian biscuits, a coffee-cake-like bread with walnuts, raisins, and chocolate.

An Islamic tradition of giving handwoven carpets (*kilims*) and knotted rugs as wedding gifts lasted for centuries. The custom of giving a personally woven dowry rug, with the couple's initials and date of marriage, disappeared only in the 1990s. Bosnian Americans do, however, typically adhere to the tradition of the groom and his family providing gifts for the bride as a kind of symbolic dowry.

A traditional dance called *kolo*, in which participants join hands and form a line that winds its way around the dance floor, is commonly performed at Bosnian American weddings. *Sevdah* music is usually played, and traditional foods such as pita are typically served, but in many other aspects Bosnian American wedding ceremonies resemble the typical American-style wedding.

Relations with Other Americans It is important to understand that the contributing basis of hostility among twentieth-century Bosnians has largely been due to economic reasons, not religious ones. As all three groups became more secular, religious-based conflict actually diminished. But economically and politically, Bosnian Muslim landowners were resented by Catholic Croats and Orthodox Christian Serbs. American Bosnians do not face the same political pressures, so the different ethnic communities coexist relatively peacefully in American cities. Bosnian Americans often marry across ethnic lines, which gives them a powerful reason to stay in the United States. If people in a mixed marriage return to Bosnia, they are not usually accepted by either person's ethnic group.

After the attacks of September 11, 2001, many Bosniaks were faced with increased suspicion from other Americans, who associated all followers of Islam with Muslim extremism and terrorism. In 2007 an eighteen-year-old Bosnian Muslim refugee, Sulejman Talović, went on a shooting spree at Trolley Square Mall in Salt Lake City, Utah, killing five people and reigniting fears concerning Bosniaks and terrorism. Subsequently, many Bosnian Americans were forced to either hide their religious affiliation or to speak out against violence despite the fact that Talović was not motivated by religious or political beliefs.

Surnames Almost all Bosnian family names end with the suffix *ic*, which essentially means "child of," much like the use of the suffix "son" in English names such as Johnson. Women's first names tend to end in the letter *a* or *ica*, pronounced EET-sa. Family names are often an indication of ethnicity. *Sulejmanagic*, for example, is a Muslim name, as are others containing such Islamic or Turkish roots as *hadj* or *bey*, pronounced "beg." Children receive their father's last name. Hence, someone with an Islamic-sounding root in his or her last name may be presumed to be, at least by heritage, a Muslim.

POLITICS AND GOVERNMENT

Croatian and Serbian Americans organized labor unions and strikes for better working conditions as early as 1913. The oldest Croatian fraternal associations, Slavonian Illyrian Mutual Benevolent Society, founded in 1857 in San Francisco, and the United Slavonian Benevolent Association of New Orleans, founded in 1874, provided financial help to families of injured immigrants. Croatian and Serbian Americans formed many groups dedicated to influencing policies of their homeland. In the United States, Croatian Americans have traditionally been strong supporters of the Democratic Party.

Bosnian Americans speak out about conditions in their former homeland. For example, in an interview on CNN's *Larry King Live*, professional basketball player Vlade Divac of the Sacramento Kings said Americans have been misled about the situation in Yugoslavia. Divac reported that his relations with some NBA players had been affected by his Serbian heritage.

Relations with Former Country The United States supported Yugoslavia under Tito's rule because Tito had broken with Soviet leader Joseph Stalin. The United States provided economic and military assistance to prevent Soviet aggression in the area. But with the fall of communism and the dissolution of the Soviet Union, Yugoslavia lost its strategic importance to the United States. When the war broke out in 1992, James Baker, secretary of state under President George Bush, was quoted as saying, "We don't have a dog in that fight." Eventually, however, the United States became involved in finding a peaceful solution to the civil strife in Bosnia. On November 21, 1995, the General Framework Agreement for Peace in Bosnia and Herzegovina (the Dayton-Paris Agreement) was concluded as a result of a U.S.-led peace initiative after three years of peacemaking efforts by the international community. When the Dayton Peace Accord was signed the following month, UN Secretary-General Boutros Boutros Ghali thanked U.S. president Bill Clinton for his role. The last U.S. troops left Bosnia and Herzegovina in 2004 but, although many Bosnian refugees desire to return to their homeland, most are skeptical of the continued political gridlock in the country and have put off returning until the prospects for peace and prosperity improve.

NOTABLE INDIVIDUALS

Film Karl Malden (Mladen Sekulovich; 1912–2009) was born in Chicago to a Serbian father from the Herzegovina region and a Czech mother. Following a lengthy stage and screen career spanning from the 1950s to the

1980s, in which he won both an Oscar and a Prime-time Emmy Award, Malden was named the head of the Academy of Motion Picture Arts and Sciences in 1988. He was given a star on the Hollywood Walk of Fame in 1960 and received a Life Achievement Award from the Screen Actors Guild in 2004.

Literature Aleksandar Hemon was born in Sarajevo and began living in the United States in 1992; he had been on a visit to Chicago when the Bosnian War broke out, and he was unable to return home. Hemon was awarded a Guggenheim Fellowship in 2003 and a MacArthur Foundation "genius grant" in 2004. His acclaimed novel *The Lazarus Project* (2008) was a National Book Award finalist, and his short fiction has been published in the *New Yorker*, *Ploughshares*, and the prestigious anthology *Best American Short Stories*.

Music Tomo Milicević is a guitar player for the band 30 Seconds to Mars. Born in Sarajevo in 1979, Milicević and his family immigrated to Troy, Michigan, in the late 1980s. He joined 30 Seconds to Mars, which is fronted by actor Jared Leto, in 2003, and has recorded two albums with the group, *A Beautiful Lie* (2005) and *This Is War* (2009).

MEDIA

Bosnako-Americka Televizija (Bosnian-American Television)

The first Bosnian American TV station, founded in New York in 1999. Has been available in the United States and Canada since 2000.

Email: info@batv.tv
URL: www.batv.tv

RTV BosTel

A Bosnian American television station founded in Chicago in 2001. Broadcasts twenty-four hours a day throughout North America.

URL: www.rtvbostel.com

Sabah

A major weekly newspaper founded in 1997 that serves the Bosnian immigrant community in the United States, with a circulation of more than 20,000 readers, primarily in the Midwest.

Sukrija Dzidzovic, Founder and Publisher
5003 Gravois Avenue
St. Louis, Missouri 63116
Phone: (314) 351-0201
Fax: (314) 351-0297
Email: sabahbos@aol.com
URL: www.sabahusa.com

ORGANIZATIONS AND ASSOCIATIONS

Bosnian-American Cultural Association

Works to preserve Bosnian culture and teach Americans about Bosnia.

Dr. Hasim Kosovic
1810 North Pfingsten Road
Northbrook, Illinois 60062
Phone: (312) 334-2323

Congress of North American Bosniaks

An umbrella organization for a number of Bosnian American Muslim (Bosniak) cultural groups that presents a yearly convention of Bosniaks in different cities throughout North America.

P.O. Box 651
Skokie, Illinois 60076
Phone: (847) 677-9136
URL: www.bosniak.org

Jerrahi Order of America

Bosnian cultural, educational, and social relief organization affiliated with a traditional Muslim Sufi order and made up of Muslims from diverse backgrounds. The Jerrahi Order has branches in New York, California, Indiana, Seattle, and Bosnia.

884 Chestnut Ridge Road
Chestnut Ridge, New York 10977
Phone: (845) 352-5518
Email: info@jerrahi.org
URL: www.jerrahi.org

New England Friends of Bosnia and Herzegovina

Grassroots organization that aims to support Bosnian Americans through cultural and other activities as well as to promote a long-term and just peace in Bosnia and Herzegovina. Organizes speaker series, interviews, conferences, rallies, and humanitarian aid drives. Originally focused on serving western Massachusetts; now provides resources to organizations and individuals all across the United States.

2400 Massachusetts Avenue
Cambridge, Massachusetts 02140
Phone: (617) 714-4641
URL: www.nefbih.org

MUSEUMS AND RESEARCH CENTERS

Bosnian American Genocide Institute and Education Center

Sanja Seferovic Drnovsek
6219 North Sheridan Road
Chicago, Illinois 60660
Phone: (773) 941-2824
Email: sanja.bagi@gmail.com
URL: www.baginst.org

Bosnian American Library of Chicago

Selena Seferovic
Bosnian American Library of Chicago at Conrad Sulzer Public Library
4455 North Lincoln Avenue
Chicago, Illinois 60614
Phone: (773) 831-1942
Email: selena@bosnianlibrarychicago.com
URL: www.bosnianlibrarychicago.com

SOURCES FOR ADDITIONAL STUDY

Clark, Arthur L. *Bosnia: What Every American Should Know.* New York: Berkley Books, 1996.

Kisslinger, Jerome. *The Serbian Americans.* New York: Chelsea House Publishers, 1990.

Malcolm, Noel. *Bosnia: A Short History.* New York: New York University Press, 1996.

Puskar, Samira. *Bosnian Americans of Chicagoland.* Charleston, SC: Arcadia, 2007.

Shapiro, E. *The Croatian Americans.* New York: Chelsea House Publishers, 1989.

Silber, Laura, and Allan Little. *Yugoslavia: Death of a Nation.* New York: Penguin, 1995 and 1996.

Tekavec, Valerie. *Teenage Refugees from Bosnia-Herzegovina Speak Out.* New York: Rosen Publishing Group, 1995.

BRAZILIAN AMERICANS

Alphine W. Jefferson

OVERVIEW

Brazilian Americans are immigrants or descendants of people from the República Federativa do Brasil, or the Federative Republic of Brazil, the largest country in South America, encompassing nearly 45 percent of the continent's land mass. Brazil is located in east-central South America and is bounded to the north by French Guiana, Guyana, Venezuela, and Suriname, to the northwest by Colombia, to the west by Peru, Bolivia, Paraguay, and Argentina, to the south by Uruguay, and to the east by the Atlantic Ocean. The Amazon River runs through northern Brazil. The rain forest of the Amazon Basin, which makes up 60 percent of the world's rain forest, covers about half of Brazil.

According to *CIA World Factbook* estimates for 2012, Brazil has a population of approximately 199 million people of various ethnicities, making it the world's fifth most populous country. Europeans (primarily Portuguese explorers) came to Brazil at the end of the fifteenth century; by the twenty-first century, people of Portuguese descent made up a slight majority of the population. Among the other ethnic groups in the country are Africans, Italians, Germans, Japanese, and indigenous peoples (primarily of the Tupí-Guaraní linguistic families). In the 2010 Brazilian census, 47.7 percent identified themselves as *brancas* (white), 43 percent as *pardo* (multiracial), 7.6 percent as *preto* (black), 1.1 percent as Asian, and 0.4 percent as Native American. Racial identification, and terminology, in Brazil is different from that in the United States, and may shift depending on various considerations. For instance, in a 2000 survey in Rio de Janeiro, 38 percent of people who identified as white also reported having some African ancestry. The 2010 Brazilian census reported that 65 percent of Brazilians were Roman Catholic and 22 percent were Protestant. According to the Jewish Virtual Library, in 2010 there were approximately 150,000 Jews in Brazil. There were also 35,000 Muslims in Brazil according to the 2010 census. Many Brazilians who subscribe to one of the mainline religions also practice other religious traditions, including Spiritism, Candomblé, Macumba, Umbanda, or Santería. These religious practices are informed by Roman Catholicism and traditional African and Amerindian religious ceremonies. In 2012 Brazil had the world's seventh-largest economy. With

20 percent of the population working in agriculture and 14 percent in industry, it exported equipment, iron ore, soybeans, footwear, coffee, and automobiles. Although income inequality has been notoriously high in Brazil, the beginning of the twenty-first century saw a marked and steady improvement in this area.

Although the United States Census did not specifically count Brazilians before 1960, the census that year included 27,855 Brazilians. The 2005 *Yearbook of Immigration Statistics* reports that in the decade 1960–1969, 29,238 Brazilians obtained permanent resident status in the United States. The decade 1990–1999 saw legal immigration peak at 50,744. Until 1980, California and New York had the highest concentrations of Brazilians. The first significant immigration occurred after 1986, when 1.4 million Brazilians left their home country. It is not known how many came to the United States, however. In 2001 the Brazilian Ministry of Foreign Affairs estimated the number of Brazilians in the United States to be somewhere between 800,000 and 1.1 million. Almost half of those who came to the United States settled in the Northeast (primarily New York, Massachusetts, and New Jersey), and the majority of the rest settled in the southern United States. After 2005, however, the number of legal Brazilian immigrants living in the United States began to increase more slowly. As a result of stricter immigration enforcement and the weakened U.S. economy, some Brazilians decided their best opportunities lay at home. A notable exception to this was in New Orleans after Hurricane Katrina destroyed much of it in 2005; several thousand Brazilians came for construction jobs rebuilding the city. In addition, in 2005 Brazilian television aired 203 episodes of a tremendously popular *telenovela* (soap opera) titled *América*, which focused on the life of an illegal Brazilian immigrant in the United States. In a widely reprinted article in the *Latin American Herald Tribune*, "Soap Opera Lures Brazilians to U.S," authorities cited *América* in their search for answers to the fourfold increase in undocumented Brazilians detained in the United States in 2005.

The U.S. Census Bureau estimated in 2010 that there were 347,346 Brazilian Americans; of these about two-thirds were born in Brazil. In 2007, however, the Brazilian government had estimated that there were

1.1 million Brazilians in the United States, many more than the official count. By 2007 the two states with the largest contingent of Brazilians (40 percent of the total) were Florida (22 percent) and Massachusetts (18 percent), whereas California (with 9.5 percent) and New York (with 7.5 percent) were home to only 17 percent of all Brazilians residing in the United States, having been surpassed by New Jersey, with 10.4 percent. In 2010, 44 percent of Brazilian Americans still lived in the Northeast.

HISTORY OF THE PEOPLE

Early History Archaeological evidence suggests that Brazil may have been inhabited as early as forty thousand years ago. Various native peoples are known to have lived in Brazil for thousands of years. The first European to lay claim to the region was Pedro Cabral, who discovered and claimed the land for Portugal in 1500. The next year, Italian explorer Amerigo Vespucci sailed along the South American coast. Brazil's first settlement was established at Salvador da Bahia, named after the Portuguese city of Salvador. For the next three centuries, Brazil would be ruled by Portugal as a colony.

In 1533 the first Africans were forcibly brought to Brazil to work as slaves, primarily on coffee and sugar plantations. Native peoples living along the coast of Brazil were pushed to the interior of the country by the Portuguese as early as 1616. The coastal areas of the country were then settled by the Portuguese colonists. The Treaty of Madrid, signed in 1750, defined Brazil's borders, which were remarkably similar to the nation's modern boundaries.

Brazil was ruled by Portugal as a colony until 1808. That year the French emperor Napoleón Bonaparte invaded Portugal, touching off the bloody Peninsular War. The Portuguese royal family, led by King Dom João VI, fled from Napoleón's army and reestablished its kingdom in Brazil, first in Salvador and later in Rio de Janeiro. Dom João returned to Portugal in 1821, leaving his son Dom Pedro I as regent. Pedro I declared Brazil's independence on September 7, 1822. His son Dom Pedro II succeeded him in 1831 and ruled until 1889.

From the sixteenth century through 1888, when slavery was abolished in Brazil, the country obtained 37 percent of all African slaves traded worldwide, and more than 3 million slaves were sent there (compared with the approximately 650,000 that went to the United States).

Modern Era A federal republic was established following an 1889 coup, and for the next forty-one years the Brazilian government was a constitutional democracy. Getúlio Vargas, a member of the revolutionary Liberal Alliance, staged a military coup in 1930, establishing a dictatorship and ruling as governor for the next fifteen years. During World War II, Brazil sustained considerable economic growth. A series of

elected presidents followed Vargas, but in 1964, as a result of popular frustration with steadily rising inflation, economic stagnation, and various other social problems, the military staged yet another coup. Then-president João Goulart was deposed, and army marshall Humberto Castelo Branco officially became president on April 11, 1964.

The military continued to choose government officials until 1982, when a period of liberalization began in Brazil. In 1989 Fernando Collor de Mello became president in the nation's first direct presidential election in decades; however, Collor de Mello, famed for his wide-reaching economic reforms, was accused of accepting bribes in 1992, and on September 29 of that year, he was impeached by the Brazilian government for political corruption. He was succeeded by his vice president, Franco Itmar, who officially took office on October 2, 1992. Two years later, former foreign and finance minister Fernando Henrique Cardoso won a hotly contested presidential election against the favored candidate, populist Luis Inacio "Lula" da Silva, a trade union leader. Cardoso remained president until 2002 when Lula, finally, after his fourth attempt, won the presidency. Lula was reelected in 2006. In 2010 his chief of staff and hoped-for successor, Dilma Rousseff, was elected president. Rousseff, a leftist who had been tortured by the military government in the 1970s, was the first woman and first economist to become the Brazilian head of state.

SETTLEMENT IN THE UNITED STATES

Some sources claim that the earliest immigrants from Brazil to the United States were probably eight Jewish Brazilians who entered the country in 1654. But Brazilian American immigration information is not very reliable; the U.S. Immigration and Naturalization Service did not tabulate Brazilians as a separate group entering the United States until 1960. Before that, Brazilians were counted in a group that included all South Americans. It is known that between 1820 and 1960, 234,761 people of South American origin entered the United States, with peak waves of South American immigrants entering from 1841 to 1850 and from 1911 to 1930. It is impossible to tell how many of these South Americans were from Brazil. According to the 1960 U.S. Census, however, 27,885 people of reported Brazilian ancestry were living in the United States.

From 1960 until the mid-1980s, there was a relatively even pattern of Brazilian immigration to the United States; estimates suggest that between 1,500 and 2,300 Brazilians immigrated each year, mainly from southern and south-central Brazil, including the states of Espírito Santo, Minas Gerais, Rio de Janeiro, São Paulo, Paraná, Santa Catarina, and Rio Grande do Sul. The majority of these immigrants were of European heritage and came from the middle and upper-middle classes of Brazilian society.

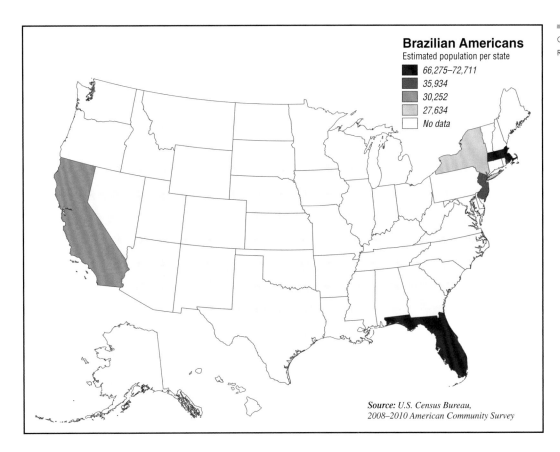

Brazilian Americans
Estimated population per state
- 66,275–72,711
- 35,934
- 30,252
- 27,634
- No data

Source: U.S. Census Bureau,
2008–2010 American Community Survey

During the mid-1980s, Brazil's economy began to deteriorate rapidly; in 1990 the annual inflation rate reached 1,795 percent. Despite the economic reforms of President Collor de Mello, incomes continued to drop by nearly 30 percent, and many Brazilians lost faith in their government. The Brazilian government estimates that between 1986 and 1990, 1.4 million Brazilians left the country permanently—many of them immigrating to the United States, while others headed for Japan and various countries in South America and Europe.

According to Maxine Margolis in *Little Brazil: An Ethnography of Brazilian Immigrants in New York City*, Brazilian immigration to the United States did not begin on a significant scale until the mid-1980s. Between 1987 and 1991, 20,800 Brazilians immigrated to the United States, with 8,133 entering the country in 1991 alone. Again, the majority of these immigrants were middle- or upper-middle-class members of Brazilian society, and most of them came from southern or south-central Brazil. The 1990 U.S. Census indicated that there were about 60,000 Brazilians living and working in the United States, but because Brazilian Americans were only counted in the census if they wrote "Brazilian" in the "Other Hispanic" category—a misnomer because Brazilians are not Hispanic—this number was most likely too small. Other sources suggested that there were approximately 100,000 Brazilians, documented and

undocumented, living in the New York area alone. In addition, there were sizable Brazilian communities in Boston, Los Angeles, Miami, Phoenix, and Washington, D.C.

As Brazil's economic conditions worsened in the 1980s and 1990s, the American consulate found that many more Brazilians wanted to immigrate to the United States than quotas legally allowed. Consequently, beginning in the mid-1980s, a significant percentage of all Brazilian immigration to the United States was undocumented. The most common way for Brazilians to illegally enter the United States was to overstay a tourist visa, fade into established Brazilian communities, and obtain low-skill, low-wage work. A riskier method of gaining entry was with false passports and/or green cards. A number of professional immigration services—legitimate and otherwise—operated in both the United States and Brazil to assist those wishing to come to the United States. Some Brazilians entered the United States on their own, via the Mexican border, but this was extremely time-consuming, dangerous, and expensive. Undocumented persons make up a large percentage of the Brazilian population in the United States, thereby skewing census and immigration data.

Nearly half of all Brazilian Americans live in the northeastern United States, primarily in the states of New York, New Jersey, and Massachusetts. However, Florida is the state with the largest total number of

Brazilian Americans, and a sizable population also resides in California. First-generation Brazilians tend to congregate in areas where other Brazilian Americans are living—such as Astoria, a neighborhood in the New York City borough of Queens—especially if they speak little or no English. However, second- and third-generation Brazilian Americans are more likely to have gained financial independence and therefore may relocate to areas with fewer or no other Brazilian Americans. These neighborhoods do not preserve Brazilian cultural heritage as closely as do many first-generation neighborhoods. It is estimated that the majority of illegal Brazilian immigrants live in New York City; however, because they are largely undocumented, their exact places of residence are difficult to ascertain. In her 2009 doctoral dissertation, *Tropical Brazucas: Brazilians in South Florida and the Imaginary of National Identity*, Brazilian American Rosana Resende notes that in addition to Miami-Dade County, large concentrations of Brazilians were found north of Miami, in Broward County. "I had heard that Broward was … *the* place to go to for 'real' Brazilian food, meant for Brazilians."

LANGUAGE

Although Portuguese is not the only language spoken in Brazil, it is the official language of the nation and the native language of most Brazilian immigrants. Portuguese is a Romance language, similar in some ways to Spanish, French, and Italian, and is spoken by about 250 million people worldwide. There are two major differences between Brazilian Portuguese and the Portuguese spoken in Portugal: first, the Brazilian vocabulary is larger by several thousand words; second, the pronunciation is softer. Brazilian Portuguese has adopted words and phrases from the Tupí-Guaraní languages of Brazil's native peoples, as well as from the various languages spoken by the West Africans who were brought to Brazil as slaves. It was these African languages that influenced the softening of the Brazilian Portuguese pronunciation. In 1992 Brazilian Portuguese became the international standard for textbook production and writing because Brazilians make up 75 percent of the world's Portuguese speakers.

Of the 347,346 people of Brazilian ancestry recorded in the 2010 U.S. Census, 18 percent spoke only English, 82 percent spoke English and another language, and 38 percent said they did not speak English very well. Because Brazilian Americans often retain close ties with their home culture and language, several urban areas with high concentrations of Brazilian immigrants feature radio broadcasts in Portuguese and publish Portuguese-language newspapers and periodicals.

Greetings and Popular Expressions Common greetings and expressions in Brazilian Portuguese include: *Bom dia*—Good morning; *Boa tarde*—Good afternoon; *Boa noite*—Good night; *Como vai?*—How are you? (literally, how is it going?) *Obrigado*—Thank you (masculine); *Obrigada*—Thank you (feminine); *De nada*—You're welcome; *Pois não*—Certainly; or, Don't mention it; *Passe bem*—Goodbye; *Até amanhã*—See you tomorrow; *Que horas são?*—What time is it?; *Como se chama a senhora (a senhorita)?*—What's your name?

RELIGION

Although the majority of Brazilian Americans are Roman Catholic, a growing number belong to Protestant denominations, particularly Assembleias churches such as the Assemblies of God (Assembléia de Deus). In addition, small percentages of Brazilian Americans practice Spiritism, a faith based on communication with the spirits of the dead. Others follow Umbanda, a combination of Spiritism, folk Catholicism, and African-Brazilian beliefs and rituals. Candomblé, an African-Brazilian religion that originates from the Brazilian state of Bahia, is very popular not only there but also in other parts of the Portuguese diaspora. Little is known about the existence of these religions in the United States because their practitioners fear censure from both Brazilians and Americans. There are also Brazilian Jews in the United States, including at least one rabbi, in Kansas City, who is an authority on the history of the hidden Jews in Latin America, including Brazil. Among historians of the Portuguese Inquisition and the settling of Brazil, estimates of Brazilian descendants of Jews who were forced to convert to Catholicism range from thousands to millions. Beginning in the 1990s, there was a movement among many of these people to reclaim their Jewish heritage.

With 123 million self-declared Catholics, Brazil has the largest number of Catholics in the world. At the same time, only 20 percent of Brazilian Catholics attend mass or participate in church activities regularly. In areas of the United States with large Brazilian immigrant communities, Catholic churches such as St. Paul's Catholic Church in Tampa, Florida; Five Wounds Portuguese National Church in San Jose, California; Madonna Queen of the Universe Shrine in East Boston, Massachusetts; and Our Lady of Fatima in Riverdale, Maryland, offer mass in Portuguese. In New York City, the largest and best-known Roman Catholic church with services in Portuguese is Our Lady of Perpetual Help in Manhattan. This church features a prominently displayed statue of Nossa Senhora Aparecida (Our Lady of Aparecida)—considered by many Brazilians to be the patron saint of Brazil—and serves as a center for many Brazilian Americans to congregate, worship together, and reinforce their cultural identity.

At least 10 percent of Brazilian Americans belong to one of several Protestant churches. In the United States, particularly in the Northeast, most Brazilian American Protestants are either Pentecostals or Baptists. Pentecostal Brazilian Americans tend to socialize primarily with members of their church, and therefore Pentecostal churches—several of which have services in Portuguese—often become the center of the social lives of most members. Baptist Brazilian Americans tend to socialize more outside of the church. Some Baptist churches in the United States, such as the Baptist Church of the Portuguese Language in Queens, New York City, offer services in Portuguese. In addition to the Pentecostal and Baptist denominations, the Universal Church (a Protestant sect which is Brazilian in origin) and Seventh-day Adventist Church also attract Brazilian American believers.

Spiritism is a Brazilian practice that combines science, philosophy, and Christian morality and follows the teachings of Allan Kardec, a nineteenth-century French philosopher who set forth his principles in two books: *The Book of the Spirits* and *The Book of the Mediums*. Spiritists, who tend to be white and middle-class, believe in communication with the dead via spirit mediums. Small groups of Brazilian American Spiritists meet in communities with large Brazilian American populations as a way of maintaining social cohesion.

Alan Patrick Marcus, who studied the small immigrant Brazilian community in Marietta, Georgia, found that "posters in Portuguese on store-walls advertise time-schedules for services for churches including the Georgia Brazilian Assembly of God Church, Ministerio de Madureira Campo de Atlanta, Ministerio International Ebenezer, Church of God, Assembleia de Deus em Marietta, and the Congresso de Jovens (Conference for Youth)." Marcus also found that among Brazilians who have traveled back and forth between the United States and Brazil, Pentecostal churches provided important connections such as help finding employment, housing, and schooling and filling other social service needs.

CULTURE AND ASSIMILATION

Significant Brazilian immigration to the United States did not begin until near the end of the twentieth century, and for several reasons Brazilian Americans remained unfamiliar to other Americans. Sometimes they were incorrectly grouped with Spanish-speaking people from other Latin American countries, obscuring the particulars of Brazil's Portuguese, African, and native origins. Their often undocumented status also contributed to the community's insularity. Brazilians were best known as phenomenal soccer players, and for dancing the *lambada* and the *samba* and participating in their globally famous street parties—especially during Carnaval. Despite the limited perceptions these stereotypes created, Brazilian Americans maintained pride in their cultural traditions and continued to celebrate their Brazilian heritage both in private and in public.

Traditions and Customs Brazilians have many traditions, customs, and beliefs that have existed for

A Brazilian immigrant at her naturalization ceremony for new American citizens. 2007 JOE RAEDLE / GETTY IMAGES

hundreds of years and are integral to Brazilian culture. Though common throughout much of the country and observed by all racial groups, many of these practices can be traced to the traditional beliefs and practices of African, native, and European folk culture. Indeed, some scholars observe that the fusion of different cultural beliefs, religious practice, music, and cuisine finds its greatest expression in Brazil. Religious rituals, military and political rallies, festivals, and family celebrations are important parts of Brazilian society regardless of class or race. Brazilians also give parties to celebrate such events as *futebol* (soccer) matches, practices, and victories. Soccer is such an important part of Brazilian and Brazilian American life that it is not uncommon to see hundreds of people gathered around a single small television set watching a game outdoors. In many ways, this is more than just watching sports; it is an affirmation of community.

Brazilian Americans have preserved their cultural heritage by maintaining some of Brazil's customs, traditions, and beliefs, including the value and importance of the extended family and the observance of Brazilian festivals and holidays, which celebrate Brazilian culture. These cultural traditions have changed over time as more and more Brazilian Americans are assimilated into mainstream American life and culture. In a 2005 interview at a Pinellas Park, Florida, emporium that features Brazilian, Portuguese, and Hispanic foods, a Brazilian American mother named Joyce Alves described coming to the store for special ingredients

BRAZILIAN AMERICAN GATHERING PLACES

According to Alan Patrick Marcus's 2009 study of Brazilian immigrants, supermarkets and stores that feature Brazilian foods were important gathering places. He also found that different communities in the United States were magnets for Brazilians from different states in Brazil, each with their own particular cuisine. Goianos (from the state of Goias) in Marietta, Georgia, looked for products such as pequi, an important fruit from Goias. In Framingham, Massachusetts, he found immigrants from the state of Minas Gerais looking for a particular vegetable. As one female Brazilian American interviewee in her twenties told him in Marietta: "To come to the padaria [Brazilian bakery] … and to speak Portuguese really hit home. … We speak the same language, think and eat similar. … This is my home, but Brazil is home in my heart." Hence, for Brazilian Americans (as for many immigrants), there is a strong connection with one's native culture through the eating of certain foods.

and getting ready for the Christmas holiday. "It is traditional, said Alves, to serve hors d'oeuvres such as coxinha de galinha, made with mashed potato and chicken, pastels, a deep-fried stuffed pastry, and codfish cakes. 'People usually start coming to your house about 9 p.m.,' Alves said. A bigger meal is customarily served after midnight, but Alves said her Americanized family now serves everything together." (Waveney Ann Moore, "Happy Heritage," *St. Petersburg [FL] Times*, December 7, 2005.)

Cuisine Brazil is a country filled with people of many different backgrounds and origins; its cooking reflects its multicultural roots. Brazilian cooking has been influenced by African, Native American, Spanish, Portuguese, Italian, German, and even Japanese cuisines. In particular, Brazilian cooking reflects the cooking styles of the African slaves who were brought to Brazil beginning in the sixteenth century. *Dendê* (palm oil), coconut milk, spicy peppers, *feijão* (black beans), and *farinha* (manioc flour) are principal ingredients in Brazilian dishes that have African origins. The national dish of Brazil, *feijoada*, consists of a variety of smoked or sun-dried meats and sausages, black beans, and a sauce made from the juices of the beans and the meats. It is usually served with sliced oranges, shredded kale or collard greens, *farofa* (toasted manioc flour), and various hot sauces and condiments. Popular beverages include Brahma, a brand of Brazilian beer; *caipirinhas* and *batidas*, tropical drinks made with rum and *cachaça* (a sugarcane liquor); and *guaraná*, a popular Brazilian soft drink made from the berries of the *guaraní* tree. Brazilian Americans also introduced another popular drink and dietary supplement to the American market: The

açai berry has created a sensation in the United States through the multiple health and wellness claims of its many suppliers.

Other Brazilian foods that are popular among Brazilian Americans and can be found in many Brazilian restaurants in the United States include *churrasco à rodizio*, a meal of barbecued chicken, pork, and beef served with rice, black beans, French fries, and potato salad; *frango à passarinho* (literally, "chicken in the style of a little bird"), small pieces of chicken wrapped in garlic leaves; *moqueca*, a fish stew native to the Brazilian state of Bahia; and *bacalhau*, or codfish casserole. Brazilian-style steakhouses, or churrascarias, are popular among non-Brazilian Americans as well as Brazilians and can be found in all areas of the United States where Brazilians have settled. During Brazilian parties or street festivals, a variety of Brazilian snack foods are served. Among them are *kibe*, fried snacks of Lebanese origin; *acarajé*, a deep-fried black bean fritter filled with spicy sauces, shrimp, green peppers, and chiles; and *pasteis*, a pastry filled with meat, shrimp, or olives.

Traditional Dress There are different traditional costumes for different states and regions of Brazil. In the United States, particular dress and flamboyant costumes continue to be worn during annual parades, festivals, and Carnaval. One such costume, worn by women from the state of Bahia (referred to as "Baianas"), consists of a huge, hooped white skirt; a white bodice with elaborate sleeves; strings of colorful looped beads worn around the neck; and an elaborately wrapped white turban. The costume is worn to perform an annual ceremony in Salvador, Brazil, known as *Lavagem* (meaning "cleansing"), in which the Baianas carry vases full of flowers and perfumed water in a procession to the Bonfim Church, where they then wash the steps. In the United States, a version of the ceremony, the "Lavagem da Rue 46" (cleansing of 46th Street), is performed every September at the annual Brazilian Day Festival (Brazilian Independence Day) in Manhattan's Little Brazil.

Tiny string bikinis, called *fio dental*, or "dental floss," are worn by many Brazilian women on the beach. For everyday wear, most Brazilians and Brazilian Americans dress in American-style clothing.

Holidays For the many states, cities, and communities in Brazil with patron saints, it is customary to hold festivals each year on the saints' feast days. During Holy Week—the week before Easter Sunday, which is seen as one of the most important weeks of the year—Brazilians re-create the passion and the resurrection of Jesus Christ. Some Brazilian communities also re-create the events of the birth of Jesus during the Christmas season. Military parades are common in Brazil as a way of celebrating state holidays, such as Brazilian Independence Day, which occurs during Fatherland Week, the first week in September.

Another major Brazilian festival is Carnaval, a nationwide celebration that takes place during the four days before the beginning of Lent. Many prefestival events, however, start up to two months earlier. In many ways, Carnaval is considered to be the quintessential expression of Brazilian culture, and Brazilian Americans are proud to celebrate the event. Carnaval festivities are also becoming increasingly popular among non-Brazilians in the United States.

Festa do Iemanjá is a solemn ceremony held on New Year's Eve that honors the West African *orisha* (deity) Iemanjá (also spelled Yemanjá), the Queen of the Sea. It is a major rite in Rio de Janeiro and Bahia. Flowers, perfumes, fruits, and even jewelry are tossed into the sea to please the mother of the waters and gain her protection for a new year. Also this time, many Brazilians place on their wrists a cloth bracelet bearing the phrase "Lembra do Senhor do Bonfim do Bahia," which translates as "Remember the lord of Bonfim of Bahia." (This is a reference to a famous church in Bahia, Igreja do Nossa Senhor do Bonfim (Church of Our Lord of the Good End [i.e., good death]), built in 1745 and famous for its healing powers.)

Brazilian Americans celebrate secular American holidays, such as the Fourth of July, Thanksgiving Day, and New Year's Day, and Christian Brazilian Americans also celebrate such holidays as Christmas and Easter by attending church services and having special meals and ceremonies at home. Many of these services are held in Portuguese with Brazilian music. Few Brazilian Americans feel any conflict about maintaining bicultural religious and secular holiday practices.

On Brazil's Independence Day, there are feasts in many Brazilian American communities, particularly in large cities in the northeastern region of the country, such as Boston, New York City, and Newark, New Jersey. Independence Day, celebrated each September 7, marks Brazil's liberation from Portugal. The largest celebration by far is the Brazilian Independence Day Parade and Street Fair, which has been held annually since 1985 on New York's West 46th Street ("Little Brazil"). The all-day street festival attracts thousands of people, predominantly Brazilian Americans, from throughout the Northeast; participants wear green and gold, Brazil's colors, dance to Brazilian music, and enjoy Brazilian food and drink.

Health Care Issues and Practices There are no documented health or mental health problems specific to Brazilian Americans. Brazilian Americans generally obtain health insurance at their own expense or through their employers. Most Brazilian Americans who live illegally in the United States have no health insurance and enter the health bureaucracy at risk. Many also rely on "faith healing," a practice commonly associated with one or more of their religious traditions.

Brazilian American Spiritists practice alternative or homeopathic approaches to health and medicine. Instead of traditional medical techniques, Spiritists use such practices as past-life therapy, dispossession and exorcism therapies, acupuncture, color therapy, yoga therapy, and homeopathy. A well-known Brazilian faith healer whose influence has spread to the United States is João Teixeira da Faria (1942–), popularly known as João de Deus (John of God). One of his ambassadors in the United States is Rio de Janeiro–born Susie Verde, who has conducted healing circles in Boulder, Fort Collins, and Denver, Colorado, as well as around the world. Most Brazilian Americans do not consider these practices to contradict their Catholic faith or beliefs.

Funerals The death of beloved Brazilian race car driver Aytron Senna (1960–1994) allowed the entire world to see how Brazilians deal with death. Within minutes of his demise in the Grand Prix in Italy, thousands of Brazilians flocked to his home in São Paulo, stood outside on the walls, and cried for days. Senna's funeral service went on for hours; every major Brazilian political and religious leader eulogized him. Coverage of the event saturated every aspect of the media for more than a week. Brazilians in the United States also noted his death in a series of services and rituals. In this instance, the entire globe saw how a nation mourned a national hero.

In Brazil, the color of mourning is black. Usually, a large picture of the deceased is on display at the funeral service. Generally speaking, bodies in Brazil

A Brazilian American father and daughter enjoy the festivities at the 23rd annual Brazil Day Festival in Midtown Manhattan, NY. RICHARD B. LEVINE / NEWSCOM

are not embalmed, so most burials occur within twenty-four hours. In addition to mourning, funerals function as vehicles for public displays of emotion, belonging, and connection. Women are expected to wear heavy veils and to actively mourn the dead. Sociological sources indicate that unrestrained displays of raw emotion are such a basic part of Brazilian culture that they are expected and encouraged. Thus, it is customary to give fainting mourners sugar water to calm them.

Funeral customs vary from place to place and are informed by the religious traditions of the deceased. In the northeastern part of Brazil, the dead are paraded through the streets in their coffins, with family and friends walking behind as they leave the *necrotério* (morgue and funeral home) and proceed to the cemetery. Among the middle and upper classes in urban areas, cars and hearses are used. For many Catholics, a special mass is held fifteen days after the burial; this signifies the final act of public mourning.

Many Brazilian Americans travel to Brazil as often as they can in order to maintain contact with extended family members who remain in the homeland. Even for Brazilian Americans who have lived in the United States for many years, the social and cultural value placed on the family usually remains intact. These visits back home affirm the unity of the extended family unit.

FAMILY AND COMMUNITY LIFE

Brazilian social life centers on the family. It is not uncommon for Brazilians to see members of their extended families—married siblings, grandparents, aunts, cousins, and other relations—on a daily basis. Family is also very important to Brazilian Americans. Many Brazilians are encouraged to immigrate to the United States by family members who have already made the journey. New immigrants often live with other family members or close friends until they find homes of their own, especially in larger Brazilian American communities where family members almost always live near one another. Many Brazilian Americans travel to Brazil as often as they can in order to maintain contact with extended family members who remain in the homeland. Even for Brazilian Americans who have lived in the United States for many years, the social and cultural value placed on the family usually remains intact. These visits back home affirm the unity of the extended family unit.

In Brazil, social status is very important. Educated Brazilians are socialized from an early age to show respect in speech and conduct to those of higher social status. Individualism in many forms is generally dismissed by Brazilians as egotistical behavior, since Brazilians tend to focus on the family and the community rather than on the individual. Each step in the life cycle—christening, going to school, confirmation, entering the workforce—is viewed as a rite of passage. In making these significant steps, Brazilians often have many mediators—usually older family members and friends—who counsel them in understanding their rights and responsibilities as one person in a larger group.

Economic and social necessity have eroded the bonds of the traditional extended family structure in immigrant communities throughout the United States. In the 1990s many Brazilian immigrants to the United States were single. Others were married men and women who sometimes left their spouses and children at home until they could afford to send for them. Until they found their own houses or apartments, Brazilians usually stayed with friends or at cheap boarding houses (often Brazilian-run) in cities with large Brazilian communities, such as New York or Newark. After single people establish themselves in the United States, they facilitate the immigration of other family members. Brazilian Americans often help each other find jobs and adequate housing as well as share cultural information and news from Brazil. Some Brazilians move to the United States with their immediate families—particularly those who have jobs before they arrive or enough money to last until they can find employment.

As the standard of living for Brazilian immigrants begin to rise, many invest in such modern conveniences as television sets, microwave ovens, and stereo equipment. (These items are seen as luxuries because they are so expensive in Brazil.) A common concern for many Brazilian Americans is the welfare of their family members living in Brazil. Many Brazilian Americans send money to friends and family back home. Charitable organizations sponsor drives to collect money and clothing for the poor in Brazil on a regular basis. In addition, those who travel back to Brazil for the holidays often carry large numbers of items purchased in the United States. There is little organized charitable work by Brazilian Americans to help other Brazilian Americans in need when they arrive. Their fear of detection and deportation partially explains this fact.

Gender Roles Brazilian women, at home and in the United States, were long portrayed as exotic and desirable, pictured as tanned and scantily dressed (or feathered and high-heeled during Carnaval). In her 2008 essay "Looking for New Worlds: Brazilian Women as International Migrants," Adriana Piscitelli argues that "racialized and sexualized notions about Brazilian styles of femininity that attract 'sex tourists' to the country also mark female international migrants." Rosana Resende also addresses this issue, recalling in her dissertation, "Even my prudish sexagenarian mother has been misread as 'hot-to-trot'—no deep necklines, no red lips, no tight pants—on the mere fact that she is Brazilian." In her interviews with Brazilian American women, Resende found that they identified with a high level of sensuality, but not with promiscuity. They have a positive relationship to sexuality and the human body in general. The stereotype of Brazilian women has ramifications for both women and men in dating and courtship. Brazilian women can neither ignore nor negate this mythologized image. Indeed Brazilian men feel the need to compete with non-Brazilian men for the most desirable Brazilian women. Nonetheless, among the twenty-nine South Florida women Resende interviewed, only four were in relationships with non-Brazilians; of the seventeen men interviewed, only one was married to a non-Brazilian. Therefore, attitudes about the reality of this competition are unfounded.

Many married, middle-class women in Brazil do not work outside the home, even if they have advanced university degrees. It is common in Brazil—even among the lower-middle class—for households to employ servants and maids. Many Brazilian women must adapt to new roles and obtain outside employment when they immigrate to the United States because it is usually a financial necessity. According to Margolis, these adjustments in roles can cause many problems for immigrants, particularly for married couples in which the woman is making more money than the man. Moreover, middle-class women who had cooks and housekeepers in Brazil are somewhat disheartened by the reality of having to assume those same roles in the United States in order to find employment. The women Resende interviewed expressed mixed feelings related to their job opportunities in the United States. They were pleased about their ability to work and be respected for their labor despite their age or sex; however, unless their English was very good, many were forced to take jobs quite below their professional training and social position.

Weddings In Brazil, wedding customs conform to the major practices of each religious denomination. The road to matrimony starts with a large engagement reception, where the families of the intended come together; the man gives the woman a simple gold wedding band, which is worn on the right hand prior to the marriage. During the wedding ceremony, the ring is placed on the left hand. Western traditions have influenced weddings in Brazil, making services similar to those in North America.

In general, the bride wears white and the groom dons formal wear. Instead of bridesmaids and groomsmen, the *padrinho* (godfather) and *madrinho* (godmother) of both the bride and groom form the wedding party. The service follows the traditional liturgical rites of the church to which they belong.

These traditions are so strong that even heavily Americanized young Brazilian American couples are forced to follow the dictates of their parents in these sacred ceremonies.

The reception is a gala, cross-generational affair, with plenty of food, liquor, music, and dancing. Usually, an older male relative will discreetly gather small monetary donations and present them to the couple before they leave for the honeymoon. Depending on the status of the family, honeymoons can range from a simple night in a room of a crowded house to a week on the beach—a favorite honeymoon spot. Couples who return to Brazil for their nuptials usually have bigger and more elaborate ceremonies than they can afford in the States.

Baptisms Baptismal traditions are determined by the religious denomination of the family. For Catholics, the child is baptized in infancy and later, after reaching the "age of understanding" (usually between eight and twelve), he or she is formally confirmed. The child's godparents play an important role, taking vows to love, protect, and, if necessary, provide for the child. White baptismal clothing is absolutely essential; poor parents reportedly will even spend their food money to acquire the appropriate dress. After the actual baptismal service, the child is showered with presents at a lavish reception. This tradition is very important to Brazilian Americans because being so far from home can create many commitments as well as obligations to ensure the child's proper religious education.

Education Many Brazilian immigrants to the United States have university degrees and held skilled jobs in Brazil. By 2007 nearly 32 percent of all Brazilian Americans twenty-five years of age and older had at least graduated college—30 percent of males and 33 percent of females, according to a report by the Center for Latin American, Caribbean and Latino Studies at the City University of New York. However, these immigrants often have difficulty finding desirable jobs in the United States because the requirements for degrees are different in Brazil—and because many Brazilian Americans, even those with advanced education, are not fluent in English. Illegal immigrants are largely excluded from the American labor market, since they pose a legal risk to prospective employers. Overall, second- and third-generation immigrants are more likely to have skilled, high-paying jobs, as they have been educated in the United States, are more likely to be fluent in English, and have legal permanent resident status. In 2003, with the help of the Brazil-USA Cultural Center of Florida, South Florida opened a bilingual Portuguese/English public school program at Ada B. Merritt K-8 Center in Miami. Public schools in a growing number of districts, including Cambridge and Framingham, Massachusetts; Newark, New Jersey; Danbury, Connecticut; and Providence, Rhode Island, also offered bilingual Portuguese/English instruction.

EMPLOYMENT AND ECONOMIC CONDITIONS

Because Brazilian immigrants who entered the United States prior to 1960 were not documented separately, little information exists on their employment history. According to the 2010 U.S. Census, of the 274,926 Brazilian Americans who were over the age of sixteen, 75.4 percent were a part of the labor force and had higher employment rates than any other racial/ethnic group in the United States. Almost half of Brazilian American women work in service occupations, whereas Brazilian men are more evenly spread across all occupational categories.

Margolis conducted research on Brazilian immigrant workers in New York City (the majority being illegal immigrants). She found that restaurant work was the most common form of labor for male Brazilians who had recently immigrated to the United States. Many other undocumented Brazilian males took jobs in construction or with small companies that pay wages in cash; others work as street vendors or as shoe shiners in the informal economy. The vast majority of female Brazilian immigrants to the United States, both legal and illegal, took jobs in domestic service and in child care, usually for private households. Margolis notes that some Brazilian women take jobs as restaurant workers, street vendors, or in some aspect of the entertainment industry. Her findings also indicate that illegal immigrants tend to take positions where they can be paid "under the table," avoiding possible detection or deportation by immigration authorities.

Many male Brazilians found work in the construction industry as laborers and sometimes saving to start their own small businesses. These Brazilians were vulnerable to changes in the construction industry. For instance, many thousands came to New Orleans to work on the rebuilding of much of the city after Hurricane Katrina in 2005. In the following years, however, the severe downturn in the American housing industry had significant effect on Brazilian American communities as previously employed households had to rely on charity or their families and friends for support. This reality was noted in the December 4, 2007, *New York Times* in an article titled "Brazilians Giving Up on Their American Dream."

POLITICS AND GOVERNMENT

Hardly any information exists about Brazilian American participation in the electoral process in the United States; however, Brazilian Americans are usually actively involved with politics in Brazil. First-generation immigrants, Brazilian Americans who remain close to family members still living in Brazil, and businesspeople with ties to Brazil are especially interested in the political situation in the homeland. Only in cities with large Brazilian American populations are there any Brazilian American elected officials. Most of these serve in local and regional offices.

Relations with Brazil During the 1989 Brazilian presidential election—the first direct presidential election since 1964—many Brazilian Americans became involved in the election process. Brazilian Americans who were still eligible to vote through the Brazilian consulate organized themselves in support of each of the candidates. Fernando Collor de Mello, who won the election and was later impeached, was supported most heavily by businesspeople and wealthier Brazilian Americans. Collor de Mello ran against Luis Inacio "Lula" da Silva, a trade union leader and Labor Party candidate who received support from many middle-class Brazilian American merchants and newer immigrants.

Despite the fact that many Brazilian Americans were very interested and involved in the presidential campaign, relatively few of the eligible immigrants voted through the Brazilian consulate; the consulate apparently did not advertise the necessity of registering in June for the November election. Undocumented Brazilian immigrants to the United States, who were eligible to vote in their elections at home, generally did not do so because they feared being reported to immigration authorities. Of the Brazilian Americans who did cast ballots, most voted for da Silva.

Two years after Collor de Mello's impeachment, former government minister Fernando Henrique Cardoso won the 1994 presidential election against da Silva, the favored candidate. Finally, in 2002 da Silva won election and served until 2010. During these years,

Brazil's economy grew, and despite widely publicized violence and income inequality, Brazil took a leadership role in the world. Brazilian Americans feel a deep pride in their home country, which, in addition to soccer, sun, and samba, became known for economic growth and political stability as well. In addition, Brazil is a noted leader in the production of alternative fuels, hybrid cars, and exported goods.

NOTABLE INDIVIDUALS

Several Brazilian Americans have made significant contributions to American culture, particularly in music, literature, journalism, and sports.

Academia Numerous Brazilian American professors and students have contributed to American colleges and universities. Roberto DaMatta is professor emeritus of anthropology at the University of Notre Dame. He has written many books about Brazilian culture and society.

João José Reis, who earned a PhD in history from the University of Minnesota has taught at the University of London and Stanford University and has been awarded many prestigious awards and fellowships. He spends time and teaches in both Brazil and the United States.

Business David Neeleman, born in Sao Paulo in 1959 is the founder of JetBlue and Azul Brazilian airlines. He lived in Brazil until he was five and then moved to Utah. Neeleman is an unconventional CEO, donating his salary to the company's employees and flying coach on the planes his company owned.

Eduardo Luiz Saverin was a Brazilian American until he immigrated to Singapore in 2009 and renounced his American citizenship. He and Mark Zuckerberg, a fellow Harvard undergraduate student, created Facebook in 2004.

Journalism Brazilian American journalist Jota Alves founded the New York monthly newspaper the *Brazilians* and also started the tradition of the New York City Brazilian Independence Day Parade and Street Fair in 1985.

Music The pop singer, songwriter, and musician Monica da Silva was born in Michigan to a Brazilian mother from Belém in northeast Brazil and an American father. She was raised in Miami and in Brazil. Her 2012 album *Brazilian Beat* was put out by Putumaya, a popular world music label.

Vinicius Cantuária was born in Manaus, Amazonas, Brazil, living there until he was seven, when his family moved to Rio. As singer, songwriter, guitarist, and percussionist, his career includes several genres of Brazilian music. He works from his studio in New York and has put out over a dozen albums.

Religion Rabbi Jacques Cukierkorn, an expert on descendants of Jews who were forced to convert to Catholicism during the Spanish Inquisition, was born in São Paulo. He is the spiritual leader of Reform Jewish congregations in Kansas City, Missouri, and is the author of a Portuguese language guide to Judaism.

Sports A U.S. National Soccer Hall of Famer, Carlos Alberto Torres played for the New York Cosmos from 1977 through 1982. Before joining the Cosmos, he had played for more than a decade for major Brazilian clubs and was captain of the Brazilian team that won the 1970 World Cup.

Stage and Screen Popular television and film actress Morena Baccarin was born in 1979 in Rio de Janeiro. Her mother was the stage and screen actress Vera Setta, and her father was a journalist. Her first film was *Perfume*, in 2001. In 2013 she was nominated for a Screen Actors Guild Award for her work in the Showtime series *Homeland*.

The actress Sônia Braga was born in 1950 in Maringa, Parana State, Brazil. She began her career acting on Brazilian television and has acted in many films, including *Kiss of the Spider Woman* (1985), for which she was nominated for a Golden Globe, and *The Milagro Beanfield War* (1988). She has appeared in many television series, including *The Cosby Show, Law and Order, Alias, Sex and the City*, and *Brothers and Sisters*.

Brazilian American singer singer Bebel Gilberto (1966–), daughter of Brazilian singers João Gilberto (1931–) and Miúcha (1937–), performs at the Brasil Summerfest in New York City, 2012. ROB KIM / GETTY IMAGES

MEDIA

In her research on the South Florida Brazilian community, Rosana Resende noted that there were ten to fifteen print publications making up the Brazilian ethnic press in South Florida alone, available free of charge in most of the three hundred business establishments serving the community. About these papers she wrote that they "are not likely to be the main source of news for anyone. In this day of instant worldwide news, weekly, biweekly, and monthly publications are hardly the best way to keep oneself informed. Rather, it seems as if they serve as a touchpoint for the community. They provide the opportunity to read, in Portuguese, about local events, to indulge in stories about Brazilian celebrities, who may or may not be coming through South Florida, and to have both U.S. and Brazilian national events and policies discussed by journalists who, like their readers, have a foot in both nations."

PRINT

Brasil/Brazil Revista de Literatura Brasileira/A Journal of Brazilian Literature

A scholarly journal of Brazilian literature with text in English and Portuguese.

Nelson H. Vieira, Editor

or

Regina Zilberman, Editor
Brown University
Department of Portuguese and Brazilian Studies
Box O
Providence, Rhode Island 02912
Phone: (401) 863-3042
Fax: (401) 863-7261
Email: Brasil_Brazil@Brown.edu
URL: www.brown.edu/Departments/Portuguese_Brazilian_Studies/publications/brasil.html

Brazilian Times

Founded in 1988, the *Brazilian Times* publishes newspapers in New York and Massachusetts and the *Brazil Times Magazine*.

Edirson Paiva, Publisher
P.O. Box 447
Somerville, Massachusetts 02143
Email: bt@braziliantimes.com
URL: www.braziliantimes.com

The Brazilians

Monthly magazine published in both Portuguese and English, it seeks to promote Brazilian culture and includes business information, news, and articles on Brazilian music, art, and traditions.

16 West Forty-Sixth Street
New York, New York
Phone: (212) 398-6464
URL: http://thebrasilians.com

The Florida Review

Biweekly newspaper published in Portuguese (with a small section in Spanish). Designed to meet the needs of both Brazilian Americans and Brazilians visiting the United States, it provides world and community news, cultural information from Brazil, and other services and is distributed throughout the United States and in major Brazilian cities.

Marcos Ommati, Editor
801 Bayshore Drive
Box 19
Miami, Florida 33131
Phone: (305) 374-5235

Gazeta Brazilian News

News service serving the Brazilian Community.

Zigomar Vuelma, Publisher
Fernanda Cirino, Editor in Chief
4390 North Federal Highway
Suite 207
Fort Lauderdale, Florida 33308
Phone: (954) 938-9292

Email: vuelma@gazetanews.com
Email: news@gazetanews.com
URL: http://gazetanews.com

Luso-Brazilian Review

Severino J. Albuquerque (Brazilian Literature and Culture), University of Wisconsin–Madison; Peter M. Beattie (History and Social Sciences), Michigan State University; Ellen W. Sapega (Portuguese and Luso-African Literature and Culture), University of Wisconsin—Madison, Coeditors

University of Wisconsin–Madison
1018 Van Hise Hall
1220 Linden Drive
Madison, Wisconsin 53706

Soul Brasil

Brazilian Printing Media in the United States; "Go Green" concept pioneer, based in Los Angeles; focuses on promoting Brazilian culture in the United States as well as conscious living on mother earth. Provides up-to-date Brazilian events in Los Angeles and the rest of California, more than two hundred free articles for research, and exclusive web features about Brazilian people & their culture. Distributed free in 276 locations throughout Southern California.

Phone: (818) 508-8753
URL: www.soulbrasil.com

RADIO

KLBS (AM 1330)

Portuguese Radio Network

Ethnic Radio of Los Banos

A Portuguese-language station with daily broadcasts from 6:30 a.m. to 8:00 p.m. Programming includes news, community information, Brazilian music, and interviews.

401 Pacheco Boulevard
Los Banos, California 93635
Phone: (209) 826-0578 (office)
Phone: (209) 826-4996 (requests)
Fax: (209) 826-1906

WRYM (AM 840)

Broadcasts in Portuguese on Sunday morning, 5:00 a.m.–6:30 a.m.

Albino Baptista
1056 Willard Avenue
Newington, Connecticut 06111-3540
Phone: (860) 666-5646
Fax: (860) 666-5647

ORGANIZATIONS AND ASSOCIATIONS

Brazilian American Chamber of Commerce

This organization, which was founded in 1968, has more than three hundred members, many of which are corporate. The Chamber of Commerce promotes the interests of business in Brazil and in the United States. It publishes a newsletter and the *Brazilian American Business Review Directory*.

Tony Sayegh, President
509 Madison Avenue
Suite 304
New York, New York 10022
Phone: (212) 751-4691
Fax: (212) 751-7692
Email: info@brazilcham.com
URL: http://brazilcham.com

Brazilian American Cultural Center (BCC)

The mission of the Cultural Center is to promote the culture and art of Brazil and Brazilian America. It also sponsors programs and exhibits about Brazilian history, art, and music and publishes the *Brazilians*.

20 West 46th Street
New York, New York 10036
Phone: (212) 730-0515

Brazilian Immigrant Center, Inc.

Primarily supports the Brazilian and Latino/a immigrant communities. In 2011 it served more than three thousand members of the Brazilian American community who were seeking information about their labor, immigration, tenant, consumer, civil, or human rights.

Natalicia Tracy, Executive Director
14 Harvard Avenue
2nd Floor
Allston, Massachusetts 02134
Phone: (617) 783-8001, extension 101
Fax: 617-562-1404
Email: ntracy@braziliancenter.org

Brazilian Women's Group

Founded by a group of women interested in discussing the issues of being an immigrant woman from Brazil in this country, the goals of the group are to provide support to the Brazilian families living in the Greater Boston area; to be an information vehicle to the community; to help community members in their search for solutions to their problems; to promote Brazilian cultural activities for the community.

Heloisa Maria Galvao, Executive Director
569 Cambridge Street
Allston, Massachusetts 02134
Phone: (617) 787-0557, extension 14 or 15
Fax: (617) 779-9586
Email: mulherbrasileira@verdeamarelo.org
URL: www.verdeamarelo.org

Centro Cultural Brasil-USA (Brazil-USA Cultural Center)

Adriana Riquet Sabino, President
80 Southwest Eighth Street
Suite 2600
Miami, Florida 33130
Phone: (305) 376-8864
Fax: (305) 376-8865
Email: ccbu@centroculturalbrasilusa.org
URL: www.centroculturalbrasilusa.org

MUSEUMS AND RESEARCH CENTERS

Brazilian-American Cultural Institute Archives

Claire T. Carney Library Archives and Special Collections

Ferreira-Mendes Portuguese-American Archives

The Claire T. Carney Library houses the archives of the Brazilian-American Cultural Institute, which closed in 2008, when the government of Brazil discontinued funding it. The institute was a nonprofit organization established to promote awareness in the United States about the music, art, and culture of Brazil. Its 8,000-volume bilingual library has been integrated into the Claire T. Carney Library's general collections.

University of Massachusetts–Dartmouth
285 Old Westport Road
North Dartmouth, Massachusetts 02747-2300
Phone: (508) 999-8750
URL: http://libblog.lib.umassd.edu/category/ferreira-mendes-portuguese-american-archives

SOURCES FOR ADDITIONAL STUDY

Bernstein, Nina, and Elizabeth Dwoskin. "Brazilians Giving Up Their American Dream." *New York Times*, December 4, 2007.

Beserra, Bernadete. *Brazilian Immigrants in the United States: Cultural Imperialism and Social Class.* New York: LFB Scholarly Publications, 2003.

Gibson, Annie M. N. *Post-Katrina Brazucas: Brazilian Immigrants in New Orleans.* New Orleans: Uno Press, 2012.

Guimaraes, Duval B. "The Brazilians in the United States." *Soul Brasil Magazine*, n.d. www.soulbrasil.com/index.php?page=br-usa/21.php&lang=en&ms_lang=en.

Jouët-Pastré, Clémence, and Leticia J. Braga. *Becoming Brazuca: Brazilian Immigration to the United States.* Cambridge, MA: Harvard University David Rockefeller Center for Latin American Studies, 2008.

Llana, Sara Miller. "Reverse Brain Drain Pulls Brazilians Home, and Europeans with Them." *Christian Science Monitor*, October 21, 2012.

Marcus, Alan Patrick. "(Re)creating Places and Spaces in Two Countries: Brazilian Transnational Migration Processes." *Journal of Cultural Geography* 26, no. 2 (2009): 173+.

Margolis, Maxine L. *Good-bye, Brazil: Émigrés from the Land of Soccer and Samba.* Madison: University of Wisconsin Press, 2013.

———. *Little Brazil: An Ethnography of Brazilian Immigrants in New York City.* Princeton, NJ: Princeton University Press, 1994.

Piscitelli, Adriana. "Looking for New Worlds: Brazilian Women as International Migrants." *Signs: Journal of Women in Culture and Society* 33, no. 4 (2008): 784–93.

Resende, Rosana D. *Tropical Brazucas: Brazilians in South Florida and the Imaginary of National Identity.* Doctoral Dissertation. Gainesville: University of Florida, 2009.

Santos, Fernanda. "Sounds of Little Brazil, Bursting with Pride." *New York Times*, August 31, 2008.

Bulgarian Americans

Eleanor Yu

OVERVIEW

Bulgarian Americans come from or are American descendants of people from Bulgaria, a small country on the east coast of the Balkan Peninsula in southeastern Europe. Bulgaria boasts a varied topography, with flatlands in the north (the Danubian Plateau) and center (the Thracian Plain) and two large mountain ranges spanning the country from west to east—the Balkans across the center and the Rhodopes across the south. The Danube River separates Bulgaria from Romania and forms the country's northern border. Bulgaria shares its western border with Serbia and Macedonia and its southern border with Greece and Turkey. The Black Sea coastline bounds the country to the east. Its land area is approximately 42,823 square miles, or 110,550 square kilometers, making it slightly larger than the state of Tennessee.

Bulgaria's population was about 7.4 million in 2011, according to the U.S. State Department. Approximately two-thirds of the population is urban, with over one million people living in the capital city of Sofia. About 76 percent of Bulgarians belong to the Bulgarian Orthodox Church. Smaller numbers of citizens are Muslim (10 percent), Protestant (0.9 percent), Roman Catholic (0.7 percent), and other religious faiths. In 2011, ethnic Bulgarians accounted for 84.8 percent of the population, ethnic Turks 8.8 percent, ethnic Romanians 4.6 percent, and others (including ethnic Macedonians, Armenians, Russians, and Greeks) less than 1 percent. Since the country cast off Soviet-sponsored communism in 1989, Bulgarians have increasingly turned to public worship, and religious observance has been on the upswing. Bulgaria suffered sharp economic ramifications as its communist government collapsed. However, a series of reforms in the 1990s and 2000s improved conditions greatly, and Bulgaria joined the European Union in 2007. Bulgaria has a diverse economy—with strengths in agriculture and industry, as well as business-friendly policies such as a flat corporate tax rate—but its growth has been slowed by a sluggish global economy, lingering government corruption, and organized crime.

Bulgarians first began coming to the United States in great numbers in the first decade of the twentieth century, generally settling in the Midwest or northeast, where those who were uneducated could find labor in factories and mills or on farms. A second wave of Bulgarians immigrated to the United States to escape the rise of communism following World War II. These educated, highly skilled Bulgarians sought freedom and economic opportunities. Since the fall of communism in Bulgaria in 1989, the number of Bulgarians who have arrived in the United States has increased due to their new eligibility for the U.S. State Department's green card lottery, which has made immigration easier. These more recent immigrants are a diverse group, with varying levels of education and employment backgrounds. Since the mid-1990s the Bulgarian American population has begun to concentrate in Chicago, which now boasts the largest Bulgarian immigrant population in the world.

According to the 2011 American Community Survey, an estimated 101,379 Bulgarian Americans live in the United States. Although Bulgarian immigrants historically have tended not to settle in established Bulgarian communities in the United States, that trend has begun to change in the past twenty years, as Chicago has emerged as a hub for Bulgarian American people, cultural institutions, churches, and businesses. Chicago, though, is by no means the only destination for Bulgarian immigrants. Bulgarians have generally settled anywhere they have thought they can thrive economically, such as agricultural and manufacturing areas in the Midwest; northeastern metropolises such as New York, Boston, and Washington, D.C.; and west coast cities such as Los Angeles.

HISTORY OF THE PEOPLE

Early History The First Bulgarian Kingdom arose in the early ninth century. In 865 Bulgarian Tsar Boris I, perhaps seeking to stabilize relations with Byzantium, made Eastern Orthodox Christianity the official state religion. Shortly after, Bulgaria established its own patriarchate, independent of the Eastern Orthodox Church in Constantinople. Not only did this mean the Bulgarian Orthodox Church could conduct its services in the Slavic language, but it also kept ecclesiastical authority within the country's borders. The close identification of the Bulgarian Orthodox religion with the nation was a thread that wove through much of the country's history, as the church repeatedly found itself shouldering the burden of nation building and acting as sanctuary to Bulgarian culture.

Under the reign of Boris I's son, Tsar Simeon (893-927), the First Bulgarian Empire reached its maximum size and its golden age of art, literature, and commerce. After Simeon's reign, the empire began to decline. It was plagued by constant warfare against the Byzantines, the Magyars, and the Kievan Russians and by internal disarray. By 1018 the whole of Bulgaria had fallen once more under the sway of Byzantine rule.

The Second Bulgarian Empire began in 1185, when the brothers Asen and Peter forced the weakening Byzantine Empire to recognize an independent Bulgarian state. With the ascension of Asen II (1218-1241), medieval Bulgaria reached its zenith in cultural development and in territorial growth. The kingdom extended from the Adriatic Sea to the Black Sea, touching the Aegean Sea at its southern frontier and enveloping the city of Belgrade (today the capital of Serbia) in the north. Trade flourished, as did education, religion, and the arts. Bulgaria entered a second and more brilliant "golden age."

This period of relative tranquility ended around 1240, when Tartar invaders were cutting a swath through Europe. Bulgaria, torn by internal dissension and unable to repel the Tartars' frequent raiding parties, was forced to pay tribute to the invaders. The Tartars were driven out in 1300, followed by another period of expansion and prosperity.

As the fourteenth century neared an end, a new threat emerged at the southern frontier of the Bulgarian kingdom: the armies of the Ottoman Empire, which had already gained a foothold on the European shores of the Aegean Sea. In 1385 Sofia became the first major Bulgarian city to fall to the Ottoman Empire. The Turks wasted no time in crushing what remained of Bulgarian resistance and imposed a five-century-long rule over Bulgaria.

Turkish colonization had profound short- and long-term effects on the development of the Bulgarian nation. While looting Orthodox monasteries, Turkish troops destroyed masterpieces of Bulgarian culture, including scores of paintings, frescoes, and manuscripts from the golden ages. Stripped of its independence as well as its riches, the Bulgarian Orthodox Church was made a sub-patriarchate of the Greek Orthodox Church for four centuries. Many Bulgarians were enslaved, forced to convert to Islam, or exiled to other parts of the Ottoman Empire. The Turks replaced the existing social structure with a more oppressive form of feudalism, rewarding Turkish landlords and converts to Islam with the most fertile land while burdening Bulgarian peasants with heavy local and state taxes.

Bulgarians were, however, permitted a limited form of local self-government. They spoke their native tongue among themselves without restriction. The Bulgarian artisan and merchant classes prospered as they sold food and cloth to the rest of the Ottoman Empire. The empire's centralized government left remote mountain villages and monasteries untouched.

As a result, the villages were able to preserve Bulgarian culture, while the monasteries served as a refuge for literature and religious learning.

From the monasteries, a wave of nationalist feeling fanned out to the rest of the country in the 1760s. At the same time, the Ottoman Empire, increasingly plagued by corruption and misrule, was sliding ever closer to its eventual disintegration. One monk in particular, Father Paisii of Hilendar, is credited with stoking the flames of the Bulgarian National Revival. His history of the Bulgarian people encouraged his compatriots to agitate for Bulgarian-language schools and ecclesiastical independence from the Greek Orthodox Church.

In 1870, worn down by revolts and European enemies, the Ottoman sultan conceded the autonomy of the Bulgarian church and mandated the creation of the Bulgarian Exarchate. Meanwhile, Bulgarian expatriates in Serbia and Romania, dissatisfied by the slow pace of Turkish reform, were forming armed, revolutionary groups that sought the violent overthrow of the Turks. In 1876 the Bucharest-based Bulgarian Revolutionary Central Committee organized the April Uprising against the Turks. Although that revolt failed, the brutal Ottoman reprisals, which resulted in the death of 30,000 Bulgarians, drew Europe's attention to what had previously been considered an Ottoman backwater.

Modern Era Outraged on behalf of its little "Slavic brother" and backed by international public opinion, Russia led the clamor for Bulgarian autonomy. The major European powers tried to secure reforms from the sultan through diplomacy. Negotiations foundered, however, on the question of autonomous Bulgarian provinces, and Tsar Alexander II of Russia declared war on Turkey in April 1877.

The eight-month War of Liberation ended in Turkish defeat. In March 1878 Russia imposed upon the Turks the Treaty of San Stefano, which created a Russian-protected "Big Bulgaria" that encompassed Bulgaria proper and most of Macedonia and Thrace. Fearing Russia's growing influence in the Balkans, the western European powers dismantled the treaty within months. In July 1878 the Congress of Berlin reduced the size of Bulgaria by two-thirds and confined the new nation to the area between the Danube River and the Balkan Mountains.

Pro-Bulgarian sentiment simmered in the Turkish provinces of Macedonia, Thrace, and Eastern Rumelia. In particular, uprisings persisted in Macedonia, where a large portion of the populace spoke a Bulgarian dialect and adhered to the Bulgarian Orthodox faith. Formed in 1893, the Internal Macedonian Revolutionary Organization (IMRO) dedicated itself to armed rebellion. The IMRO's most memorable revolt, the Ilinden, or St. Ilya's Day uprising, on August 2, 1903, ended in the deaths of thousands of Macedonians and the destruction of entire villages at the hands of the Turkish army.

Bulgaria's territorial ambitions led it into the successive Balkan Wars of 1912 and 1913. Covetous of its lost territories, Bulgaria joined Serbia and Greece in 1912 in a successful offensive against Turkey. Then, when Greece and Serbia each claimed large portions of Macedonia, Bulgaria turned on its erstwhile allies, only to lose to them in 1913. Although forced to yield some land, Bulgaria finished the wars with a net gain in territory.

In World War I, the promise of gaining Serbian Macedonia enticed Bulgaria into an alliance with the Central Powers (Germany, Austria-Hungary, and Ottoman Turkey). In the 1930s the authoritarian King Boris III cemented Bulgaria's relationship with fascist Germany and Italy. Hoping to recover Thrace and Macedonia, Bulgaria again allied itself to the losing side, this time in World War II. It declared war on the Allies on December 13, 1941. However, Boris successfully resisted sending Bulgarian troops to bolster Germany's eastern front. Nor did the Bulgarian people support Nazi Germany's anti-Jewish policies; although Boris acquiesced to a number of repressive measures against Jews, he staved off the Nazi-ordered deportation of 50,000 Bulgarian Jews.

The Soviet army invaded Bulgaria in September 1944, only hours after the Soviet Union declared war on the Balkan country. Shortly afterward, a coalition of Bulgarian resistance groups, dominated by the communists, seized control of the government. Under the eye of the occupying Soviet army, the Bulgarian communists abolished the monarchy and established the People's Republic in September 1946. A new constitution, modeled on the Soviet constitution, was drafted in 1947. Soviet troops withdrew from Bulgaria that same year.

The communists consolidated their power over the next four decades, giving Bulgaria a reputation as Moscow's most loyal Warsaw Pact ally. Under the leadership of Vulko Chervenkov (1949-1956) and Todor Zhivkov (1956-1989), Bulgarian foreign and domestic policy rarely strayed from the Soviet Union's. Evidence indicates that the Bulgarian state security police, the Durzhavna Sigurnost, often acted in lieu of the KGB, accepting assignments from which Moscow wanted to distance itself.

As the 1980s drew to a close, the shock waves of Soviet *perestroika* reverberated across eastern Europe. Bulgarians articulated their unhappiness with the regime through public protests and increasingly visible dissident activity. On November 10, 1989, one day after the fall of the Berlin Wall, reformers within the Communist Party forced the resignation of Zhivkov.

Post-communist Bulgaria made an uneasy transition to capitalism, as the privatization of state-run enterprises proceeded slowly. A soaring crime rate and an economic crisis even led some to call for the restoration of the monarchy and others to rally for a return to communism. However, a series of reforms

in the late 1990s and early 2000s improved Bulgaria's economy. In 2001 the country also elected its first prime minister to come from the deposed monarchy: Simeon Saxe-Coburg-Gotha. Stabilization from the economic reforms and a political push for democracy and European integration allowed Bulgaria to join the European Union (EU) on January 1, 2001, and the North Atlantic Treaty Organization (NATO) on March 29, 2004. Despite these advancements, Bulgaria fell victim to the global recession of the late 2000s and suffered an economic downturn. However, fiscal responsibility and a relatively small amount of debt have buffered Bulgaria from the catastrophes experienced by other European nations, such as Greece and Spain.

Aside from the rare adventurer, few Bulgarians settled in the United States before the great immigration wave of the early twentieth century, when thousands of southern and eastern Europeans altered America's ethnic makeup.

SETTLEMENT IN THE UNITED STATES
Bulgarians have a long tradition, dating to the Byzantine period, of fleeing political turmoil in their country. Every unsuccessful revolt against the Turks in the eighteenth and nineteenth centuries was accompanied by mass migrations of Bulgarians to Russia, the Ukraine, Moldavia, Hungary, Romania, Serbia, and other Balkan nations. Expatriate Bulgarian communities formed and thrived in some of those countries. Today an estimated two million ethnic Bulgarians live beyond the country's borders, with the vast majority residing in Russia and Romania.

Aside from the rare adventurer, few Bulgarians settled in the United States before the great immigration wave of the early twentieth century, when thousands of southern and eastern Europeans altered America's ethnic makeup. The earliest documented Bulgarian immigrants were converts to Protestantism who arrived around the middle of the nineteenth century to pursue higher education in the United States, as Nikolay G. Altankov notes in *The Bulgarian-Americans* (1979). Their passages were funded by American Protestant groups intent on grooming talented natives for missionary work back in Bulgaria. Although some Bulgarian students did return home to spread the gospel, others chose to remain in the United States, settling in their adopted country with their families. Noteworthy early Bulgarian Americans include Ilya S. Iovchev, who arrived in 1870 and became a journalist, and Hristo Balabanov, who came to the United States in 1876, earned a medical degree, and then established a practice in Tacoma, Washington, in 1890.

Bulgarians first started immigrating to the United States in large numbers between 1903 and 1910. During this period, approximately 50,000 Bulgarians from Turkish-occupied Macedonia and from Bulgaria proper, or "the kingdom," arrived in the United States. Economic opportunity was the primary attraction for Bulgarians from "the kingdom," as they wanted to escape overpopulation and unemployment in their native regions. Macedonian-Bulgarians had an additional impetus to emigrate: the unsuccessful St. Ilya's Day revolt of 1903 drew brutal reprisals from the Turkish army, which laid waste to three Macedonian provinces and killed 5,000 revolutionaries and villagers. Some 330,000 homeless Macedonians fled to Bulgaria. Within months, the largest wave of Bulgarian and Macedonian Bulgarian emigration had begun.

After 1910, political developments continued to influence the ebb and flow of emigration from Bulgaria. Territorial loss following the Balkan Wars and the First World War drove between 400,000 and 700,000 ethnic Bulgarians from Aegean Thrace, Macedonia, and Dobrudzha into Bulgaria proper. Their arrival strained the already limited economic resources of the country and led many Bulgarians to seek work abroad.

For typical Bulgarian immigrants of the early twentieth century, passage to the United States was not obstacle-free. With little of value to their names, peasants would sell their land and livestock, mortgage their farms, or take high-interest loans from steamship agents in order to fund their transatlantic trips. Such costly outlays meant there was no turning back. Some immigrants began their journeys at Danube River ports, traveling to Vienna and continuing overland by train to any number of European port cities (such as Hamburg, Le Havre, and Trieste), where they spent up to a week or more in detention camps before boarding ships to New York. Others embarked from the Greek ports of Piraeus or Salonika. Although their points of departure varied, most immigrants spent the month-long ocean voyage in steerage, in the hold of the ship, where crowded, unsanitary conditions and poor food encouraged the spread of disease. Many Bulgarians sought to avoid stringent entrance exams at Ellis Island, the immigration station in New York City, by entering the country illegally through Canada or Mexico.

Emigration from Bulgaria never boomed the way it did from some other southern or eastern European countries, and in 1924 the National Origins Immigration Act limited the number of Bulgarians who could enter the United States to a mere 100 per year. From 1924 until the lifting of the national origins quota restrictions in 1965, only 7,660 Bulgarians were officially admitted to the United States. Historians believe thousands more made the United States their home during this period, entering illegally via Canada or Mexico or with non-Bulgarian passports issued by the country of their last residence rather than the country of their birth. Consequently, many Bulgarians have likely been recorded as Turks, Greeks, Serbs, Romanians, Russians, or Yugoslavs. At one point, U.S. immigration statistics did not distinguish Bulgarians from Serbs and Montenegrins. The 1924 quota restrictions affected not only the dimension of Bulgarian immigration but also its character. Most of the immigrants of the interwar years (1919-1939) were women and children joining husbands and fathers who had already established themselves in the United States. Otherwise, emigration from Bulgaria during these years had dwindled to a trickle.

The early immigrants tended to settle in Slavic or Balkan enclaves in the Midwest and the Northeast, where unskilled laborers could find work in factories, mills, and mines. The earliest recorded Bulgarian communities arose shortly after the turn of the century in the cities of Steelton and Philadelphia in Pennsylvania; Cleveland and Dayton in Ohio; Chicago; St. Louis, Missouri; and New York City. Smaller numbers of Bulgarians settled in the West or Northwest as farmers or railroad workers. Between 1910 and 1914, a group of ethnic Bulgarians from Bessarabia established a farming community in North Dakota. Another group established itself in Yakima, Washington, as fruit growers. Nevertheless, the most popular destination for new arrivals was the Midwest, where, for instance, the Illinois cities of Granite City and Madison counted more than 6,000 Bulgarian inhabitants in 1907. As the automobile industry grew, Detroit became home to the largest concentration of Bulgarians in the United States—there were 7,000 in the city in 1910, with an additional 1,500 scattered in nearby areas of Michigan.

The rise of the communist state in 1945 precipitated a new wave of immigration. Thousands fled in the wake of the Soviet invasion of Bulgaria in 1944. Following retreating German troops to Germany or Austria, some Bulgarians settled in western European countries; others entered the United States under the Displaced Persons Act of 1947. A handful became Americans under the auspices of a 1944 congressional act that granted citizenship to refugees who were accepted into U.S. military service overseas. Until the Bulgarian borders were sealed in 1949, refugees continued to leave by the thousands. The route to America was often circuitous, with refugees typically spending several years in non-communist European countries such as Greece, Turkey, Italy, Austria, and Germany or in South America before finally coming to the United States. In contrast to the earlier immigrants, those from after the war were primarily political refugees and professionals who left Bulgaria with no expectation of returning. After 1956 the flow of postwar refugees slowed to a mere 100 to 300 a year, but periodic relaxations on travel or border regulations continued to give the determined occasion to flee.

In 1989 the demise of single-party rule in Bulgaria brought an end to communist restraints on travel and opened the country's borders. Bulgaria's economic instability under the new government led many

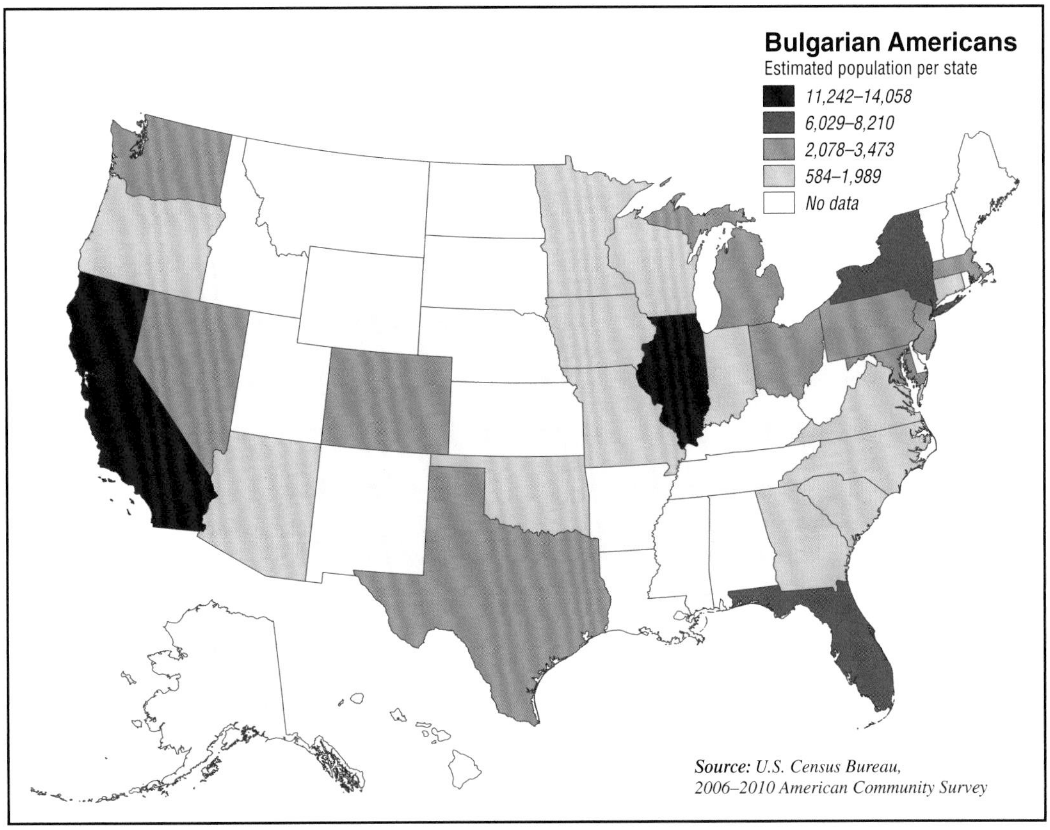

Bulgarians to leave for western European countries or the United States. Bulgarians no longer needed to seek political asylum in order to immigrate to the United States; they were allowed access to the green card lottery, which awards a fixed number of visas (50,000) annually to citizens of countries with low immigration rates. When Bulgaria qualified for the lottery in the mid-1990s, immigration of Bulgarians to the United States increased to a rate of about 1,000 per year. Unlike those who left Bulgaria during the Cold War, these immigrants were not predominantly skilled workers and professionals in fields such a medicine, law, and business. Rather, they were a diverse group of professionals and laborers, rich and poor, young and old. As immigration has increased and diversified, it has also focused on Chicago, in particular the city's northwest suburbs. There, churches, businesses, and schools have emerged to meet the demands of a Bulgarian population that has grown dramatically.

The 1990 U.S. Census placed the official number of people of Bulgarian ancestry living in the United States at 20,894. Some twenty years later, in 2011, that number had topped 100,000, according to the Census Bureau's American Community Survey. While Chicago is the heart of this community, there are Bulgarian Americans around the United States. Michigan continues to be home to a large number of Bulgarian Americans, with an estimated 10,000 living there today. Other cities with large Bulgarian American populations include Gary, Fort Wayne, and Indianapolis in Indiana; Lorain, Toledo, Cleveland, Youngstown, and Akron in Ohio; and Los Angeles. Pittsburgh, Pennsylvania, once a hub for Bulgarians, has declined as a destination in recent years, while the greater New York and Los Angeles areas have attracted growing numbers of immigrants.

LANGUAGE

Bulgarian is a South Slavic language, closely related to Serbo-Croatian and Slovenian and more distantly to Russian. It is one of the oldest written languages in Europe. Like Russian, Bulgarian uses the twenty-nine-character Cyrillic alphabet, which was adapted from the Greek alphabet in the ninth century to accommodate the sounds of the Old Slavonic tongue. The Orthodox missionaries Cyril and Methodius created this alphabet for the spoken Slavic language, and their disciples Kliment and Naum translated religious texts into Old Church Slavonic using the script, which they named Cyrillic after its creator. The alphabet spread from early medieval Bulgaria to other Slavic civilizations. With substantial justification, Bulgarians consider their native tongue the *ur*-Slavic language that influenced all other Slavic languages.

As a language, Bulgarian has been influenced by its contact with other civilizations. It retains more than 2,000 words from the pre-Cyrillic Old Slavonic tongue. Four centuries of Greek Orthodox supervision over the Bulgarian church has added Greek religious terms, as well as some Greek words used in daily life, to the Bulgarian language. The Turks, then the Russians, donated vocabulary relating to political, economic, and day-to-day life. Although the official state language is Bulgarian, Turkish survived several waves of repression during the communist reign and is the primary language of about 8 percent of citizens. The postwar era introduced a number of western European words to Bulgarian, especially in the fields of technology and science.

Typically, Bulgarian immigrants to the United States are linguistically divided. While they use English in their interactions outside the Bulgarian American community, they often speak Bulgarian at home as well as in Bulgarian stores, churches, and schools. Bulgarian Americans place a high value on retaining their native language, and it is common for Bulgarian immigrants to encourage their children to learn and to practice using the Bulgarian language. To do so, Bulgarian Americans often exclusively speak Bulgarian at home. Some Bulgarian Americans also send their children to Bulgarian American schools, which typically meet once a week and teach Bulgarian language and culture. The Bulgarian-American Cultural Center in Sarasota, Florida, teaches Bulgarian-language courses and also hosts cultural events in order to educate American-born Bulgarian American children about their ancestral culture. Similarly, the Bulgarian Community Center in Washington, D.C., and the Bulgarian-American Center Madara in Boston and New York preserve and promote Bulgarian culture for both Bulgarian Americans and the broader community. In Chicago, there are some seven Bulgarian schools, many of which are affiliated with Bulgarian churches.

In order to encourage language development and cultural connection, some Bulgarian Americans also send their children to stay with relatives in Bulgaria over summer vacation. In addition to offering a more affordable form of childcare during the long break from school, these visits are seen by Bulgarian Americans as a way to keep their children connected to their foreign relatives.

Greetings and other popular expressions in Bulgarian include:

Zdravei—Hello;

Kak ste?—How are you?;

Blagodarya—Thank you;

Nyama zashto—You're welcome;

Molya—Please;

Izvinete—Excuse me;

Dobro utro—Good morning;

Dobar den—Good day;

Dobar vecher—Good evening;

Leka nosht—Good night;

Dovizhdane—Goodbye;

Chestito—Congratulations;

BULGARIAN PROVERBS

Bulgarian proverbs usually rhyme in the original language. Even in translation, however, they still convey common Bulgarian values such as hard work and respect for friends.

Бързата кучка слепи ги ражда.

(A hasty bitch gives birth to blind puppies.)

На ВЪлка вратЪт му е дебел, защото си вЪрши работата сам.

(The wolf has a thick neck, because he does his job on his own.)

Насила хубост не става.

(You can't make something beautiful with force.)

Много баби, хилаво бебе.

(Too many midwives deliver a sickly baby.)

Капка по капка - вир става.

(Drop by drop, a whole lake becomes.)

Chestit rozhden den—Happy birthday;

Chestita nova godina—Happy new year;

Nazdrava—To your health.

RELIGION

Most Bulgarian Americans belong, at least nominally, to the Bulgarian Orthodox Church, an independent national branch of Eastern Orthodoxy. The first Bulgarian church in America was established in 1909 in Granite City, Illinois. Shortly thereafter, the Holy Synod, the church's Sofia-based ruling body, authorized the dedication of a second church, Holy Annunciation, in Steelton, Pennsylvania. In the succeeding decades, thirty additional Bulgarian churches were founded, all under the jurisdiction of the Holy Synod. Many of these no longer exist. Administratively, the churches belonged to the Bulgarian Eastern Orthodox Mission for the United States and Canada. In 1938 the mother church elevated the mission to the level of a diocese and installed Bishop Andrei Velichki (d. 1972) as its titular head. However, the rise of communism in Bulgaria contributed to a growing friction between the American churches and the authorities in Sofia until nine churches finally broke relations with the Holy Synod in 1963. They established an independent diocese headed by Bishop Kyril Yoncheff.

In subsequent years the Bulgarian American churchgoing community became increasingly polarized, as some people continued to attend churches that recognized the authority of the Holy Synod in Bulgaria and others refused to go to churches that they believed were compromised by ties to the communist regime. Even after the collapse of communism, a bitter divide still separates churches of the independent diocese from those of the loyalist diocese.

The church has nonetheless remained at the heart of community life. For many Bulgarian Americans, it serves as a haven for Bulgarian culture. Orthodox Bulgarians can attend services conducted entirely in Bulgarian and then go to social events organized by church groups or simply exchange gossip and argue politics. New immigrants may take advantage of support services offered at the church, such as English lessons or job counseling services.

CULTURE AND ASSIMILATION

As an ethnic group, Bulgarian Americans do not have a conspicuous or clearly defined image in the United States. Scholars have attributed the group's low profile to a number of factors. Bulgarian immigration, even at its height (1907-1910), was never comparable to that of southern or eastern European nationalities. Bulgarian immigration was also practically nonexistent before 1900. Those who did come led largely nomadic lives or were dispersed around the country and tended not to form distinct ethnic communities. There were no "little Bulgarias" from which the American public could draw its stereotypes.

According to Nikolay Altankov, the first scholar to make an extensive study of Bulgarian Americans, the group's own attitudes may have encouraged the indifference of the general public. Far from being vocal or visible, Bulgarians tend to shy away from involvement in public life. With some exceptions, they prefer to devote their energies to friends and families rather than to politics or ethnic activities.

When the early immigrants did attract notice, their "Bulgarian-ness" was often obscured by their identification with other Slavs. During the heyday of Bulgarian immigration, outsiders might have recognized Granite City's "Hungary Hollow" as an eastern European enclave, but few bothered to distinguish Bulgarians from their Magyar or Slavic neighbors. Insofar as Bulgarians were confused with larger Slavic groups—or "Slavs," a collection of only loosely connected cultures—they encountered the same prejudices as those immigrants. Their opportunities for employment were limited, and they took the low-paying, unskilled, and often dangerous work that the native-born refused. They also faced the inevitable derogatory epithets. Established Americans looked down on the newcomers, whose unfamiliar customs and lack of English skills alienated them from the mainstream and whose poverty forced them to live in crowded, unsanitary conditions. Indeed, several misconceptions surrounded "Slavs" and, in turn, Bulgarians. One such stereotype emphasized a predilection for violence, largely based on a perception that the men drank excessively and were brutal toward their wives. Another stereotype centered on a lack of personal grooming and domestic care, though this misconception applied to almost all immigrants who lived in relative poverty.

By contrast, immigrants who arrived during the Cold War as political refugees received a more welcome reception. For one, their strong anticommunist stance inspired sympathy. For another, they were better educated, more cosmopolitan, and more highly skilled than their predecessors. As academics, doctors, engineers, and small business owners, they had stronger financial prospects in their adopted country. However, because their numbers were small and they were even less likely to settle in specifically Bulgarian neighborhoods, they failed to raise the profile of Bulgarian Americans.

> While I am not a whole American, neither am I what I was when I first landed here; that is, a Bulgarian. … I have outwardly and inwardly deviated so much from a Bulgarian that when recently visiting in that country I felt like a foreigner. … In Bulgaria I am not wholly a Bulgarian; in the United States not wholly an American.
>
> Stoyan Christowe in 1919, cited in *Ellis Island: An Illustrated History of the Immigrant Experience*, edited by Ivan Chermayeff et al. (New York: Macmillan, 1991).

The descendants of the early immigrants, the second generation, often chose to live in non-Bulgarian neighborhoods and marry out of their ethnicity. Educated in American schools and steeped in American culture, they were eager to cast aside the "differentness" that marked their parents. Increasingly, they spoke only English. Observance of Bulgarian customs went the way of regular attendance at a Bulgarian church. In short, second generation Bulgarian Americans assimilated into American life, frequently at the expense of ethnic heritage. Yet their children, from a relatively comfortable vantage point as third generation Americans, are feeling the draw of their past. Many Americans of Bulgarian descent are rediscovering their ethnic roots. Bulgarian folk dance and music, in particular, are enjoying a new popularity among Bulgarians and non-Bulgarians alike. For example, in Chicago the group Horo, which was founded in 2003, presents a diverse repertoire of Bulgarian dances set to folk music and has grown in popularity both within and without the local Bulgarian American community. Classes on Bulgarian dance and festivals celebrating Bulgarian dance and music also attract people with no Bulgarian roots.

Traditions and Customs In Bulgaria, practice of traditions varies from region to region. A city dweller, for instance, might not adhere as strictly to tradition as a villager does. And the customs the urbanite follows differ from those practiced by the farmer, whose life is shaped by close ties to the land and a greater dependency on the vagaries of nature. Historical circumstance has exacted a toll, somewhat estranging the postwar generations of Bulgarians, educated under communism, from the beliefs of their ancestors.

Although Bulgarian immigrants bring their traditions to their adopted country, their American-born children, in their haste to assimilate, may be eager to shed long-held customs. Nonetheless, Bulgarian Americans, in general, make a point to retain their ties to the customs of their homeland. For example, it is common for Bulgarians to practice certain traditions marking rites of passage, such as the *Proshtupulnik*, which celebrates a child's first steps, or the practice of breaking bread at a wedding reception, which supposedly reveals details about the future marriage. In order to combat the deterioration of cultural tradition, Bulgarian Americans have also successfully established schools to teach Bulgarian history and language, festivals to celebrate traditional music and dance, and churches that serve as centers for Bulgarian cultural activities.

Cuisine Like the cuisines of its Balkan neighbors, Bulgarian cooking has assimilated many elements of Turkish cuisine. There is an emphasis on dairy products, mainly yogurt and cheese; on nuts, especially the walnuts and sunflower seeds of the Tundzha Valley; and on fresh, seasonal fruits and vegetables. Traditional meat dishes—stews, sausages, kebabs (grilled meats)—are most often made of lamb, veal, or pork. Also popular are chicken, beef, brains, kidney, and liver. Bulgarian dishes are generally spicier than those of neighboring countries, and cooks are liberal in their use of herbs and strongly flavored condiments such as garlic and chili peppers.

Because many of the ingredients in Bulgarian cuisine are available in the United States, many Bulgarian Americans have continued cooking and consuming the dishes that are enjoyed in Bulgaria. For example, Bulgarian Americans can make their own versions of roasted red pepper and eggplant puree or buy variations at well-stocked grocery stores and online. They can also recreate Bulgarian versions of dishes such as *mousaka*, or stuffed bell peppers. If the traditional brined cheese *sirene* is difficult to find, they can easily substitute feta, which is widely available in American grocery stores. Family meals among Bulgarian Americans often are elaborate and frequently feature meat. Conversely, the diets of poor,

early immigrant laborers tended to reflect their humble living conditions.

Traditional breakfasts are simple, eaten at home before the workday begins. The breakfast usually consists of bread, fruit, and cheese—the most familiar being *sirene*, a salty, feta-like cheese, and *kashkaval*, a hard cheese similar to cheddar—which are washed down with a glass of yogurt (*kiselo mlyako*) or *boza*, a millet drink. Midday meals tend to be soups or fried dishes, cooked in butter or oil, while grilled meat and spicy stews, preceded by a salad tossed in yogurt or in oil, are the mainstays of evening meals. Bulgarians have traditionally relied on numerous light snacks (fruit, cheese, bread, and other baked goods), eaten throughout the day, to sustain them as they labored in the fields or pastures or, later, in factories and mines.

The classic Bulgarian dishes are simple and hearty. The "national soup," *tarator*, is a cold cucumber and yogurt soup seasoned with dill and garlic and topped with chopped walnuts. Another popular starter, the *salata shopska*, is a mixed salad of tomatoes, cucumbers, cabbage, peppers, and onions tossed in vinegar and sunflower oil and sprinkled with a light layer of crumbled cheese. Bulgarian meals are invariably accompanied by the oven-baked bread known as *pitka*, which is served with *ciubritsa*, an aromatic condiment with a native herb resembling tarragon at its base.

Of the traditional Bulgarian main dishes, *gyuvech* is the best known. Baked in an earthenware dish, it is a rich, spicy stew of various vegetables—usually some combination of peppers, chilies, onions, tomatoes, eggplant, and beans—cooked with meaty chunks of veal, pork, lamb, or beef and slathered with a yogurt-egg sauce that bakes into a crust. *Sarmi*, also popular, is made by stuffing cabbage leaves with minced meat and rice. Other common meat dishes are *kebabche*, a grilled patty of minced pork, lamb, and veal flavored with garlic, and *kyufte*, a meatball of the same ingredients, as well as the more universal chops and filets of veal and pork.

Desserts also reflect Bulgaria's history and its unique geopolitical position: the Middle Eastern pastry baklava, a layered pastry of chopped nuts drenched in honey, is as common as *garash*, a chocolate layer cake with central European antecedents. Local fruits make another post-dinner favorite, such as strawberries, raspberries, plums, cherries, peaches, apples, and grapes. Coffee, or *kafe*, is consumed Turkish-style or as European espresso.

Dances and Songs Music and dance are central to Bulgarian culture, binding together the community in times of both oppression and in celebration. Significantly, there are few strictly solo performances of folk dance or music, which speaks to the communal aspect of these expressions. Songs are used to commemorate religious occasions, traditional holidays, past wars and other historical events, births, marriages, deaths, departures, and harvests. Even religious services are chanted in song-like fashion rather than read. Songs and dances are very much a part of the fabric of daily life, as well. Shepherds can still be heard in the Rhodope Mountains playing plaintive songs to their flocks, using the traditional goatskin bagpipe. In villages and cities alike, a Bulgarian youth will announce romantic intentions by challenging the object of his or her interests to a dance contest. And any given performance of the popular line dance, the *horo*, will include participants of all ages in its circle.

Because Bulgarian music and dance are so community-oriented, they are preserved among immigrants only to the extent that there is a close-knit community. Early Bulgarian immigrants often held evening parties, or *vecherinka*, at Bulgarian-owned saloons or coffee houses, where workers sought release from their long, difficult days in song, dance, and drink. Saints' days and holidays were greeted with the greatest festivity, as men performed variations on the basic *horo*, or circular line dance. The immigrants could briefly forget their hardships in lively dances like the *ruchenitsa*, which allowed them to showcase their agility in leaps and squats, or the *kopenitsa*, with its tricky, rhythmically complex steps. Increasingly isolated from Bulgarian American daily life, however, traditional music and dance are relegated today to weddings and other special events or to the occasional performance at ethnic festivals.

Although its role in Bulgarian American life has perhaps declined, Bulgarian folk music has inspired a recent generation of Western artists, from American pop singers David Byrne and Paul Simon to English singer-songwriter Kate Bush to the ranks of non-Bulgarian Americans who have formed traditional Bulgarian folk dance and music groups in the United States. New York City alone boasts the women's singing group Zhenska Pesen and the Bosilek Bulgarian Dance Troupe. Contemporary music from Bulgaria is also enjoying unprecedented popularity in the West, and many recordings are available on Western labels. The best known of these offerings is *Le Mystere des Voix Bulgares* (The Mystery of Bulgarian Voices), a female vocal choir that has put out several albums throughout the 1990s and 2000s.

Bulgarian music is distinguished by its rhythmic complexity, heavy ornamentation, and the stirring and slightly nasal sound of the "open-throated" singing style. Most traditional folk songs are ornately decorated solos performed by a woman against the steady drone of a bagpipe or another voice. (Songs for dancing, categorized as "useful" and, therefore, less artistic, are simpler.) In some villages, a polyphonic style arose in which the women sing in two- or three-part harmony and enhance their songs with whoops,

TARATOR (COLD YOGURT CUCUMBER SOUP)

Ingredients

2 cucumbers, peeled and chopped (or grated)

1 garlic clove, minced

4 cups plain yogurt

½ cup water

¼ teaspoon salt

2 tablespoons fresh dill, minced

2 teaspoons olive or sunflower oil

finely chopped walnuts

Preparation

Mash the garlic with salt and then add it to cucumber. Place in a large bowl and pour in the yogurt. Gradually add water until the yogurt mixture is the desired consistency. Add additional salt to taste. Add finely chopped walnuts, oil, and fresh dill.

Refrigerate at least two hours before serving to allow flavors to mix.

Serve chilled.

vibrati, and slides. The female singers are sometimes accompanied by men playing traditional Bulgarian instruments. These include, most commonly, the *ghaida*, or goatskin bagpipe; the *kaval*, a shepherd's flute made of three wooden tubes; the *gadulka*, a stringed instrument with no frets or fingerboard on its neck; the *tambura*, a lute-like stringed instrument with a long, fretted neck; and the *tapan*, a large, two-sided drum.

Holidays Bulgarian Americans celebrate Christmas (Koleda), New Year's Day (Surva), and Easter (Velikden). To a greater or lesser degree, they also observe a smattering of prominent saints' days, including St. Cyril and St. Methodius Day on May 11, St. Constantine and St. Elena Day on May 21, St. Elijah's Day (Ilinden) on July 20, the Birth of the Virgin on September 8, St. John of Rila's Day (Ivan Rilski) on October 19, St. Demetrius's Day (Dimitrovden) on October 26, the Day of the Archangels Michael and Gabriel (Arhangelovden) on November 8, and St. Nicholas's Day (Nikulden) on December 6. In addition to these primarily religious holidays, Bulgarian Americans celebrate the most important secular holiday on March 3, which marks the liberation of Bulgaria from the Turks. Immigrant families also partake in the standard American holidays, such as Thanksgiving and the Fourth of July.

Most saints' days are recognized simply by feasting or attendance at special church services, in which

candles are lit before the appropriate icon. Other saints' days coincide with seasonal celebrations of pagan origins and incorporate pre-Christian customs into a Christian framework. On New Year's Day or Saint Basil's Day, for instance, groups of young children carrying *survaknitsa*, bundles of twigs draped with colored thread and dried fruit, supposedly bring luck and prosperity to their neighbors by visiting their homes and lightly slapping them with the fruit-laden twigs. *Kukerov den* welcomes the start of the agricultural year. On the first Sunday before Lent, young men ensure fertility by parading and dancing in huge masks, or *kuker*, made of animal skins and fur. On March 1, or *Baba Marta*, people celebrate the first day of spring by wearing or giving away *martenitsa*, a good-luck charm made of two woolen balls, one red (symbolizing red cheeks) and the other white (for white skin). A second springtime fertility rite, in which unmarried women perform dances and songs, coincides with St. Lazar's Day, eight days before Easter. Summer begins on the day of St. Constantine and St. Elena, while St. Demetrius's Day, October 26, is a harvest holiday marking the end of the agricultural year.

As part of the St. Nicholas's Day celebration on December 6, Bulgarians traditionally eat carp, due to the fish having a cruciform backbone. Bulgarian Americans often have difficulty acquiring carp in American supermarkets, and thus substitute other kinds of fish that do not have the carp's symbolically significant spine.

The extent to which Bulgarian American families observe these holidays is often determined by the presence or absence of ties to a larger Bulgarian American community. That said, Bulgarian Americans do tend to celebrate many of the traditional holidays and to observe ethnic traditions. For example, it is common among Bulgarian children in the United States to color eggs on either the Thursday or Saturday before Easter, as is traditional. The first egg, according to custom, is painted red, as are the children's cheeks. Then, on Easter Sunday, kids throw their colored eggs at each other; the child with the last remaining unbroken egg is declared the winner.

FAMILY AND COMMUNITY LIFE

Bulgarian American communities took root slowly in the decades preceding the First World War. The unmarried men who first came to the United States believed their stays would be temporary. That perception, coupled with the mobile nature of their work, initially inhibited the creation of permanent communities. Nevertheless, immigrant social life came to organize itself around two types of institutions during the early part of the twentieth century: the *boort*, or boardinghouse, and the *kafene*, or cafe.

The *boort* was a Bulgarian-owned boardinghouse that allowed groups of immigrant men to save money by living together and pooling their household duties and expenses. It was usually run by a Bulgarian who had met with enough success in the United States to buy a house. Confining his private quarters to a single room or two, he would rent out the remaining room or rooms. The boardinghouse owner often held a factory job as well. If he was married, his wife and family might provide meals or other housekeeping services to the boarders for an additional fee. More often, the boarders chose to do their own chores. The typical *boort* was overcrowded and sparsely furnished. Boarders slept and ate in shifts, six or more to a single room. They often worked different rotations at the same factory or mine. Although conditions ran to the squalid, many immigrants preferred saving their earnings to living in comfort.

The *kafene* (cafe or coffeehouse) offered an escape from the rigors of work and crowded households. In addition to serving familiar food and drinks, it functioned as a center for recreation and socializing. The proprietor of a *kafene* was usually more educated and better established in his new country than was the boardinghouse owner. He had a better command of the English language than his customers and was often called upon to act in a number of different capacities, such as a translator, attorney, or travel agent. As a natural outgrowth of his multiple roles, he sometimes ran another business—i.e., a newsstand, a grocery store, a rooming house, an employment agency, or a bank—on the side.

Gender Roles Among the first generation of immigrants, family relations adhered rather closely to the traditional Bulgarian model. The close-knit family was headed by a patriarch who made all the pivotal decisions. The father's parents often lived in the household, caring for the children while the father and mother worked. Social life revolved around the extended family to a far greater degree than in western European societies. Marriages were commonly arranged by family members or professional marriage brokers.

With assimilation, however, came the disintegration of this model. Because women were relatively scarce, they were more highly valued in the immigrant community than they were in Bulgaria. Bulgarian wives, realizing how essential their labor was to their families' survival in the new country, became more independent-minded. Immigrant women were forming their own organizations and clubs as early as 1913. Bulgarian men, lacking both fluency in English and status in American society, found their patriarchal roles somewhat diminished. Their children assumed an ambassadorial role, explaining and interpreting the society and language of America to their parents. Increasingly, second-generation children left home to attend college or go to work. In contrast, grown-up children in Bulgaria left their parents' homes only to marry, settling nearby even then. As families assimilated in the United States, the traditional hierarchies flattened, giving women and children greater voices in their households.

Despite this trend toward gender equality, Bulgarian Americans tend to preserve the basic framework of male and female roles within the family structure. Women, for example, are more engaged with housekeeping duties than are men. While women typically enter the workforce along with their husbands, they also tend to perform housework after their work day has ended. Due to the nature of Bulgarian cuisine, women are often expected to make meals from scratch as well as pickle and preserve food. While immigrants in the contemporary era, being more educated, have been more likely to fit within the relatively strong gender equality in the United States, Bulgarian Americans also retain gender roles traditional to Bulgarian culture.

Traditions of Early Life According to Orthodox tradition, a child born on the day of an important saint must take that saint's name or face an unhappy life unprotected by the saint. This naming is extremely important in both Bulgarian and Bulgarian American culture, and it is celebrated annually on one's name day. On this day, friends and family come to celebrate. Guests are not invited, but are welcomed to drop in, unannounced, and they often bring presents.

Baptism is considered an important rite that establishes individual identity before the eyes of God. The godparents bring the child, dressed in new clothes for the occasion, to church. Relatives and friends are invited to attend. If either godparent has not been baptized, he or she must be baptized at that time. The priest blesses the child and then bathes the child in a tub of warm water. Then he sprinkles with holy water a fragrant plant symbolic of good health, called the *zdravets*. After the baptism, there may be a celebratory dinner at the parents' home, to which guests typically bring gifts of money. Each year thereafter, the godmother goes to church and lights a candle on the child's baptism day.

Proshtapulnik is a nonreligious tradition widely observed by Bulgarian Americans that celebrates a child's first step. Family and friends are invited to bring objects symbolic of various professions. These objects—a paint brush to symbolize art, scissors for the tailor, a pen for the writer, money for the banker, a globe for the world traveler, and so on—are arranged on a small table. The parents then roll a rounded loaf of bread toward the table and urge the newly ambulatory child to chase it. Once the bread falls at the foot of the table, the child is instructed to choose one of the objects on top. According to tradition, the child will choose the tool of his or her future profession.

Weddings Typically a month in duration, the Bulgarian engagement period seems short to most Americans. Thus, this practice has been modified in the United States, where it may be difficult to arrange wedding festivities in one month's time and where Bulgarians marry non-Bulgarians.

Traditionally, on the day of a Bulgarian wedding, the bride's family will hide their daughter in their home from the groom. The groom will then arrive and try to find his bride and take her to the wedding. Children, however, block the door and demand bribes from the groom in exchange for access. This lighthearted custom ends with the groom giving the children money and being allowed to take his bride to the wedding. Many Bulgarian Americans still practice this tradition.

The wedding ceremony, which usually takes place early in the day, is similar to other Eastern Orthodox wedding services. The priest leads the bride and groom through the service, and after they are married, guests line up to offer the bride fresh flowers. The newlyweds might then engage in a folk custom that supposedly foretells which spouse will rule over the other in married life: each tries to be the first to step on the other's foot. However, many modern couples, preferring to regard each other as equal partners, choose to forego this custom. It is also traditional among Bulgarian Americans for only a small number of witnesses to attend the ceremony. These witnesses, who are friends of the bride and groom, go on to serve as the godparents for the married couple's children and to otherwise remain involved in the new family's life.

At the reception, a feast of lavish dishes and wine is punctuated by live folk music. Guests of all ages join in the *horo*, a circular line dance, whose leader leaps and performs difficult steps while waving a long flagpole. Traditionally, the wedding band was made up of folk instruments; today it may be a union of Bulgarian folk and modern Western instruments. The band's playlist may also be divided between modern pop songs and folk music.

Funerals In Bulgaria today, a family announces a relative's death by issuing cards or fliers to acquaintances and posting notices in offices or on building walls. In the United States, these traditions have been modified. Deaths are often announced in Bulgarian American newspapers, rather than in cards, and obituaries and pictures are often posted in Bulgarian churches, which sometimes designate certain areas or rooms for remembrances of parishioners' deceased relatives.

Funeral services are usually held inside a sermon hall at the cemetery rather than at the graveside. There, a priest or employee of the cemetery leads prayers for the dead and reads a short sermon. A band plays solemn music as the coffin is led to the grave. Guests bring flowers, making sure that each bouquet includes an even number of flowers, since odd-numbered bouquets are reserved for festive occasions. Close family members dress in black for the first forty days following the funeral, and sometimes longer. Mirrors in the home of the deceased are covered with black cloth.

Forty days after the funeral, the family of the deceased holds another service to celebrate the soul's flight from the body. Followers of the Bulgarian Orthodox faith believe that the spirit leaves the body forty days after death; some say there is scientific proof the body becomes perceptibly lighter on that day. More fliers, bearing a photo of the deceased, are posted announcing the occasion. Guests congregate at the grave or at church, where they light candles for the deceased and are fed ceremonial foods. The most common dish eaten on this day is *zhito*, or boiled whole wheat topped with sugar and nuts.

EMPLOYMENT AND ECONOMIC CONDITIONS

In the nineteenth century, it had become commonplace for Bulgarian peasants from poor, mountainous regions to leave their homes and seek temporary work abroad, usually in neighboring countries. These migrant workers, called *burchevii*, wandered to such countries as Turkey and Egypt but always with the intention of returning home with their earnings. Most of the early immigrants in America were *burchevii*. They tended to be single men, usually uneducated peasants and laborers who found jobs in industrial centers, working in railroad construction or in the steel mills, mines, and automobile factories of the Midwest and Northeast.

Between 1910 and 1929, the number of Bulgarians who returned to their native country outstripped the number who immigrated to the United States. Some of the people who went back to Bulgaria did so to marry and buy plots of land with their savings. Others returned to serve in the Bulgarian army during the Balkan Wars and the First World War. Those who stayed continued working in factories and mines in order to save enough to money to enable second- and third-generation Bulgarian Americans to receive an education and enter the professional ranks of American society.

Since the fall of communism in Bulgaria in 1989 and the incumbent increase in immigration in the 1990s, the Bulgarian American population has grown and diversified. While their prospects for employment are tied significantly to their level of education and their grasp of English, most Bulgarian immigrants must settle for low-skill positions upon arrival in the United States. Many women, especially older women without special employment qualifications, work as caregivers for the elderly. Many men have worked initially as truck drivers and later established their own trucking companies. Others have worked in construction and other labor jobs. Although there are many well-educated Bulgarian immigrants with professional employment, many first-generation Bulgarian Americans pin their hopes for improved employment on their children.

POLITICS AND GOVERNMENT

The earliest Bulgarian American political organizations grew out of social need. Groups of immigrants who hailed from the same village formed mutual benefit societies in which members pledged to support each other in times of financial hardship. Patterned after similar organizations in the home country, the first-known Bulgarian organizations, founded by Macedonian

Bulgarians, arose in the United States around 1902. They reflected the predominance of Macedonian Bulgarians among the early immigrant pool. In 1906, Iliia Iovchev, a Bulgarian-born employee of the Immigration Bureau at Ellis Island, started the Bulgarian and Macedonian Immigrant Society *Prishlets* (newcomer). Its purpose was to help immigrants through the admission procedures at Ellis Island and settle in the New World. A women's charitable organization called *Bulgarkata v Amerika* devoted itself to performing charity work on behalf of both the local community and the women's native villages in 1913. That same year, the Bulgarian People's Union, the first group with a national profile, emerged. By that time, nearly thirty mutual benefit societies had been organized around the country. Their numbers continued to mount, and by 1933 there were over 200 such organizations with a total of 10,000 members.

One of the longest-lived national organizations was the Macedonian Political Organization (MPO), founded in Fort Wayne, Indiana, in 1922. With branches in many cities, it supported the claim that Macedonians are ethnically Bulgarian and promoted the creation of an independent Macedonia. From 1926 onward, the MPO published a Bulgarian-language weekly called the *Makedonska Tribuna*. The group changed its name to the Macedonian Patriotic Organization in 1952.

Some immigrants were also involved in the national political scene. Before World War II, many Bulgarian American workers were active in leftist or labor causes; some belonged to the Bulgarian Socialist Labor Federation, a group founded in 1910 that later merged with the American Socialist Labor Party. Postwar immigrants, on the other hand, tended to belong to strongly anticommunist organizations, such as the Bulgarian National Committee, set up in 1949 by former Bulgarian politician Georgi M. Dimitrov. Competing right-wing groups organized the royalist Bulgarian National Front in New York in 1958. In an attempt to unite a number of splinter groups, an anticommunist umbrella organization calling itself the American Bulgarian League arose in 1944. Its goal was to promote understanding between communist Bulgaria and America.

The fall of communism in Bulgaria has led to a revival in organizational activity in America. As new groups arise to support specific political agendas in Bulgaria, existing groups have refocused their activities to help newly arrived immigrants or to bridge cultural gaps between the United States and Bulgaria.

NOTABLE INDIVIDUALS

Art The artist Christo Javacheff (1935–), or "Christo," fled Bulgaria in 1956 and settled in New York several years later with his French-born wife and son. Before gaining admission to the United States, he studied and created art in Vienna, Geneva, and Paris. It was in Paris that Christo's signature style began to emerge, as he experimented with wrapping objects in lengths of cloth or string. Later, Christo focused on the design of monumental, nonpermanent installations for public spaces. His art interacts with existing buildings, structures, or geographical features. For example, a 1962 project titled *Rideau de Fer* (Iron Curtain) marked the first anniversary of the construction of the Berlin Wall by blocking off a busy Parisian street for three hours with an "iron curtain" constructed of 204 oil drums. Later projects continued to provide oblique, but highly visible, social commentary.

Other accomplished Bulgarian American artists include Atanas Kachamakov, a sculptor best known for illustrating the popular children's book *Dobry* (1935); Constantine Vichey, an architect and the designer of the Varig and Aeroflot offices in New York City; and Nevdon Koumrouyan, a jewelry designer whose work has been exhibited at the Smithsonian Institution.

Business Arguably the most influential Bulgarian American businessman today, Frank Popoff is chairman of the Chemical Financial Corporation. He previously served as an advisor of American Express Company. He also helmed the chemical giant Dow Chemical Company as its chief executive officer starting in 1987 and as its chairman from 1992 to 2000. Born in Bulgaria, Popoff immigrated to the United States as a small child. He joined Dow Chemical in 1959, immediately after earning his MBA from Indiana University, and rose quickly through the ranks. Popoff serves on the boards of several corporate and philanthropic organizations.

The banker Henry Karandjeff came from an earlier generation of immigrants and had a more local profile. Born in a Macedonian village in 1893, he arrived in the United States at the age of thirteen. He graduated from St. Louis University in 1919 and later founded two savings and loans banks in Granite City, Illinois. When he retired, he left a successful business to his son.

Literature and Journalism Peter Dimitrov Yankoff (1885–?) drew upon his immigrant experience to pen the 1928 novel *Peter Menikoff: The Story of a Bulgarian Boy in the Great American Melting Pot* (1928). Another Bulgarian immigrant, Boris George Petroff, wrote *Son of Danube* (1940).

The journalist Christ Anastasoff authored scores of articles, many of them about Bulgarian and Macedonian immigrants. His book *A Visit to Yugoslavia and Macedonia* was published in 1957. Boyan Choukanov catered to a primarily Bulgarian American audience as editor of the *American Bulgarian Review* and as host of the weekly cable television show *Balkan Echo* in New York City. Stephane Groueff (1922–2006), a reporter based in New York, published *Manhattan Project*, a book about the history of the development of the atomic bomb. On CNN International, the face and voice of Ralitsa Vassileva (1964–) is beamed around the world by satellite as she anchors the news network's *World Report* program.

Angela Nikodinov (1980–) is a Bulgarian American figure skater and olympic-level coach. MATTHEW STOCKMAN / GETTY IMAGES

Music Leah LaBelle (1986–) is a pop singer best known as the twelfth runner-up on the popular singing competition TV series *American Idol* in 2004. She was born Leah LaBelle Vladowski to immigrant Bulgarian parents. Her parents, who are also musicians, fled communist Bulgaria during a western European tour with their pop music groups Sreburnite Grivni and Tonika. In 2012 LaBelle recorded an album, *Sexify*.

Politics A colorful and energetic writer and politician, Stoyan Christowe (1898–1995) emigrated from his native Macedonia as a teenager in 1911. He first settled in St. Louis, Missouri, with a group of older men from his village. Christowe taught himself English and was admitted to Valparaiso University in Indiana. He became a reporter after graduating and, in 1928, was sent to the Balkans as a foreign correspondent for the *Chicago Daily News*. During the Second World War, Christowe served in Military Intelligence in the Pentagon. In 1961, he was elected a Vermont state representative, an office he held until his election to the state senate in 1965. Running as a Republican, Christowe was re-elected to four more terms before retiring in 1972. Christowe's eventful life provided excellent material for his books, which include memoirs, novels, and a volume about Macedonia.

Science and Medicine The psychiatrist George Kamen (1942–2006) was still living in Bulgaria when he pioneered the idea of group therapy in the late 1960s. The revolutionary new treatment brought him both professional acclaim and political troubles.

Because Kamen worked with groups of patients who discussed with each other their deepest thoughts and emotions, he inevitably attracted official scrutiny. Kamen soon became the target of a campaign of harassment and decided to flee Bulgaria. After several unsuccessful attempts, he escaped to Vienna and then to political asylum in West Germany. Kamen and his wife Katia, also Bulgarian, arrived in the United States in 1980, and he later established a private practice in New York City.

Sports Angela Nikodinov (1980–) is a first-generation Bulgarian American figure skater. She took the bronze medal at the U.S.Nationals in 1999 and 2001 and competed in the World Championships in 1999, 2000, and 2001. In 2000 she won the Four Continents competition. Nikodinov retired from competition in 2005 after recurring injuries and the tragic death of her mother in a car accident. She married Bulgarian figure skater Ivan Dinev in 2008, and four years later, they had their first child, a daughter. The couple coaches in the Los Angeles area, and Nikodinov sometimes skates in exhibitions.

MEDIA

Bulgaria Weekly

The biggest Bulgarian-language weekly newspaper outside of Bulgaria, based in Chicago.

Phone: (773) 237-3900
Fax: (773) 237-7739
Email: editor@bulgaria-weekly.com
URL: http://bulgaria-weekly.com

ORGANIZATIONS AND ASSOCIATIONS

Bulgarian American Business Center

Established in 1992 and based in both Fairfax, Virginia, and Sofia, Bulgaria, the Bulgarian American Business Center facilitates mutually beneficial business interactions between U.S. and Bulgarian companies.

Vladmir Ossenov, President
3754 Center Way
Fairfax, Virginia 22033-2601
Phone: (703) 385-9889 or (703) 475-3821
Email: BABCenter@gmail.com
URL: www.babcenter.org/en/about/news/default.htm

Bulgarian American Chamber of Commerce

Founded in 1993, the Bulgarian American Chamber of Commerce is a nonprofit organization that promotes cooperation among Bulgarian-owned businesses in the English-speaking world. Its annual directory contains listings of businesses, services, churches, and social organizations located in the United States, Canada, and Australia. The chamber also sponsors cultural events and visits from famous Bulgarians. Its guests have included opera soprano Ghena Dimtrova, Bulgarian president Zhelyu Zhelev, and exiled Bulgarian king Simeon.

Dr. Ogden C. Page, President
1427 North Wilcox Avenue
Hollywood, California 90028-8123
Phone: (323) 962-2414
URL: http://bulgarianamericanchamber.org

Bulgarian American Enterprise Fund

Created in 1991 under the aegis of the George H. W. Bush administration, this private investment fund is interested in developing the Bulgarian economy. The fund's activities are twofold: it invests in Bulgarian businesses in Bulgaria and encourages American companies to do business in Bulgaria.

Frank Bauer, President
333 West Wacker Drive, Suite 2080
Chicago, Illinois 60606
Phone: (312) 629-2500
Email: chicago@baefinvest.com
URL: www.baefinvest.com

Bulgarian American Society

A nonprofit organization, the Bulgarian American Society uses donations to fund humanitarian, social, and education projects in Bulgaria.

Sol Polansky, President
Meryl Steigman, Executive Director
Phone: 301-229-7509
Email: sol110@verizon.net or steigmax@verizon.net
URL: www.bulgarianamericansociety.org

SOURCES FOR ADDITIONAL STUDY

Altankov, Nikolay. *The Bulgarian-Americans*. Palo Alto, CA: Ragusan Press, 1979.

Carlson, Claudia, and David Allen. *The Bulgarian Americans*. New York: Chelsea House Publishers, 1990.

Christowe, Stoyan. *The Eagle and the Stork, an American Memoir*. New York: Harper's Magazine Press, 1976.

Pundeff, Marin V. *Bulgaria in American Perspective: Political and Cultural Issues*. New York: Columbia University Press, 1994.

Raĭchevski, Stóiàn. *America and the Bulgarians: Till the Constituent Assembly of 1879*. Sofia: National Museum of Bulgarian Books and Polygraphy, 2003.

Rice, Timothy. *Music in Bulgaria: Experiencing Music, Expressing Culture*. Cambridge: Oxford University Press, 2003.

BURMESE AMERICANS

Amy Cooper

OVERVIEW

Burmese Americans are immigrants or American descendants of people from Burma (also called Myanmar), a country in Southeast Asia. Officially renamed Myanmar by the country's military government in 1989, Burma is bordered on the north by China; on the west by India, Bangladesh, and the Bay of Bengal; on the east by Thailand, Laos, and China; and on the south by the Indian Ocean and Thailand. Mountain ranges largely encircle the nation and enclose an expanse of hills, valleys, and forests. With an area of approximately 261,220 square miles (676,550 square kilometers), Burma is about the size of the state of Texas.

Estimates by the Myanmar military government and the U.S. Central Intelligence Agency placed the country's population at about 55 million in 2012. The majority of the people, almost 90 percent, are Buddhist, and no more than 4 percent are Christians or Muslims. There are more than 130 ethnic groups in Burma, but the largest—the Burman ethnic group—accounts for more than two-thirds of the population. Other notable ethnic groups are the Kachin, Karen, Karenni, Chin, Mon, Arakanese, Rohingya, and Shan, as well as Chinese and Indians. Despite abundant national resources, Burma is the poorest country in Southeast Asia.

Since the early 1960s, there have been three waves of migration of Burmese to the United States. The first wave occurred following the military's takeover of the Burmese government in 1962. Predominantly composed of ethnic Chinese and non-Burman ethnic minorities, this group included educated professionals and skilled workers. Many of them emphasized their Chinese heritage. In the late 1980s a second wave of Burmese arrived. This group was more diverse and included Burman, Chin, Kachin, Karen, and other ethnic groups as well as Chinese. Beginning in 2006, the third wave of migration has consisted primarily of refugees escaping harsh governmental repression in Burma. This third wave, which has included many people from the Karen and Chin ethnic groups, numbered more than 70,000 by the time of the 2010 U.S. Census, which counted 100,200 Burmese in the United States.

The areas of the United States with the largest populations of Burmese Americans are the Los Angeles metropolitan area and the San Francisco Bay area. New York City, Chicago, and the state of Florida contain smaller communities. Burmese refugees have settled in significant numbers in Fort Wayne and Indianapolis, Indiana; Utica, New York; Baltimore and Rockville, Maryland; and Phoenix, Arizona, with smaller numbers also settling in Fort Worth, Texas, and Elizabeth, New Jersey.

HISTORY OF THE PEOPLE

Early History Since prehistoric times, people have inhabited Burma's coastal areas and river valleys, and as early as the ninth century CE, the Pyu people established various city-states and kingdoms. Northern Myanmar became popular as part of a trade route between China and India. The Mon people established large cities in the south and gained power, and in 1044 the leader Anawrahta took up residence in Pagan and began the first unification of Burma. In the process, Anawrahta made Theravada Buddhism the official religion and established the nucleus of modern Burma. This was Burma's classical age, as government, art, and religion flourished. Temples were built and scholars and monks dedicated themselves to the study of Theravada Buddhism. This age ended in 1364 CE with the Court of Ava, when increased interkingdom warfare divided the country. Nevertheless, by 1613 the Ava kingdom had returned and reunited Burma. For the next 200 years, Burma gained power and territory, and between 1766 and 1769 it successfully repelled four attacks by the Chinese.

In the nineteenth century the British sought to expand their colonial empire and targeted Burma. After defending itself but losing territory to the British in two wars (1824–1826 and 1852–1853), Burma fell in the Third Anglo-Burmese War (1885). Britain made Burma a colony, eliminating the monarchy, reducing the power of the Buddhist church and the *Sangha* (the religious community), and weakening the education system. The British expanded transportation systems and colonial industries for rice, rubies, oil, and timber; however, these colonial policies did not help the predominantly poor Burmese people.

The Burmese began to develop a nationalist outlook in the early 1900s. Anticolonial politics flourished among Burmese student and urban groups who built the We Burmans Association. Student unions and many Buddhist monks spread anticolonial sentiments among the Burmese peasantry. In the late 1930s, Burmese peasants fought British and Indian colonial troops for two years, and Aung San and Nu became leading figures in the struggle against colonialism. When World War II began in 1939, Burmese leaders did not support the British colonial government, which issued an arrest warrant for Aung San. Escaping to Japan, Aung San accepted Japanese aid to secure Burmese independence from the British and he helped form the Burma Independence Army (BIA). Once the Japanese army occupied Burma, however, Japan refused to grant the country independence and leave. In 1945, near the end of the war, Aung San led the BIA in a campaign with the British to expel the Japanese. After the conclusion of World War II, Britain withdrew its military administration but maintained political control. Burmese anticolonialist and nationalist organizations, which demanded full independence from Britain, formed the Anti-Fascist People's Freedom League (AFPFL) and pressured the British government. Under Aung San, the AFPFL negotiated a transfer of power from British to Burmese officials. The British agreed to Burma's independence in January 1947, and a constitution was approved on January 4, 1948. As internal political rivalries escalated, however, one faction assassinated Aung San.

Modern Era With independence, Burma adopted a parliamentary system of government. It formed the Union of Burma, with Nu as the first prime minister, but internal strife and ethnic conflicts riddled the country. The Karen National Union argued for a separation from Burma, which resulted in a civil war between disaffected ethnic groups and the official government. In 1958 General Ne Win assumed the premiership in an effort to stabilize the country's security and military. Nu won the election in February 1960, but Ne Win led a coup d'etat in 1962 and arrested several government officials including Nu, who later fled in exile to India in 1969. Suspending the constitution and placing Burma under a Revolutionary Council, Ne Win instituted a military dictatorship and a socialist state. He nationalized much of the country's industry and commerce and further isolated Burma from the outside world and international aid and investment. Facing oppression and economic challenges, many Burmese left the country. With a committee composed of representatives from several ethnic groups, Ne Win drafted a new constitution, which was ratified in December 1973. Elected president in early 1974, Ne Win and his military dictatorship then offered amnesty to political insurgents in May 1980.

During the 1980s Burma's isolation increased, its economy stagnated, and the military increased its repression of non-Burman ethnic groups. Demonstrations broke out in Rangoon and major cities on August 8, 1988. Popularly known as "8-8-88," the peaceful demonstrations included students, dissident military officials, and prodemocracy politicians who protested against the military government. In response, soldiers opened fire on unarmed protestors. General Saw Maung, who then took control of the government, imposed martial law, and established a new military regime called the State Law and Order Restoration Council (SLORC). These events also led many Burmese to leave Burma.

To appease public and international disapproval of their repression, the SLORC offered to hold elections. The daughter of Aung San, Aung San Suu Kyi, emerged as the figurehead of the prodemocracy movement. She joined democratic activists in forming the National League for Democracy (NLD). Even though the military placed Aung San Suu Kyi under house arrest before the 1990 elections, the NLD won a landslide victory, but the military government chose to ignore the results. In 1991 Aung San Suu Kyi won the Nobel Peace Prize for her democratic, nonviolent activism. The military regime renamed itself the State Peace and Development Council (SPDC) and officially changed the country's name to "Myanmar." Many Burmese opposition groups and a number of other countries (including the United States) continue to use "Burma," however, because they refuse to recognize the legitimacy of the military government. The SPDC continued its campaign of political, ethnic, and religious repression, and many more refugees fled Burma. The government received the condemnation of the United Nations, human rights organizations such as Amnesty International, and foreign governments such as the United States. Meanwhile, Burmese activists remained active in national and international opposition groups.

SETTLEMENT IN THE UNITED STATES

In 1965 the U.S. Immigration Act allowed for an increase in the number of Asian immigrants to the United States. Around the same time, political oppression, economic hardships, and the closing of universities in Burma pushed professionals, skilled workers, and entrepreneurs to seek better opportunities in the United States. This first wave of Burmese immigrants settled in large cities such as Chicago, New York, Los Angeles, Fort Worth, and Washington, D.C.

The increased repression of non-Burman ethnic groups and political dissidents by Burma's military regime in the 1980s gave rise to a second wave of Burmese migration to the United States. Some were members of the Chin, Kachin, Karen, and other ethnic groups that were fleeing persecution, and others were escaping the military government's oppression of prodemocracy activists following the "8-8-88" demonstrations. The U.S. government, however, did not usually grant them refugee status, which would have included permission to work in the United States. Many persons in the second wave of migration

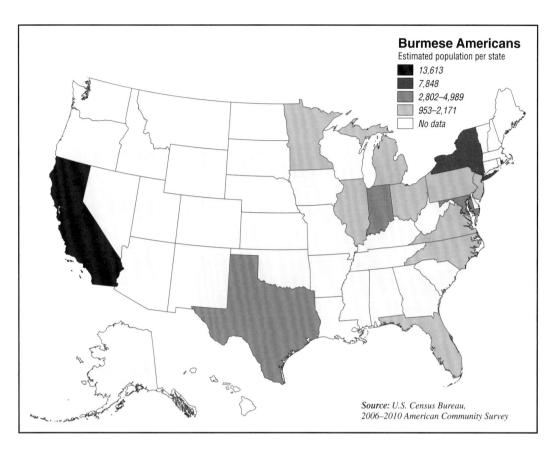

Burmese Americans
Estimated population per state

- 13,613
- 7,848
- 2,802–4,989
- 953–2,171
- No data

Source: U.S. Census Bureau,
2006–2010 American Community Survey

therefore did not have the same professional opportunities as the first wave of Burmese immigrants, and they were largely unable to obtain suitable occupations. Still, many remained in the United States illegally out of fear of returning to life under Burma's government. Some of these refugees settled near previous communities of Burmese immigrants; others settled in different locations, including Indianapolis, Indiana, which became home to the largest group, numbering an estimated nine thousand in 2012.

The third wave of migration has consisted overwhelmingly of Karen refugees, who beginning in 2005 became the target of the military regime's escalated repression of non-Burman ethnic groups. In the hill-and-valley regions of Burma, the military has harassed farmers, abused and raped women, and suppressed separatist or ethnic movements. For the most part, Karen, Mon, and other ethnic Burmese refugees did not have the professional expertise or educational background of previous Burmese immigrants. Indianapolis and Fort Wayne, Indiana, have continued to welcome large numbers of Burmese refugees, and significant numbers have also settled in Elizabeth, Fort Worth, Phoenix, and Utica.

LANGUAGE

Burmese is the primary language of Myanmar, but more than one hundred languages are spoken in the country. Burmese belongs to the Tibeto-Burmese group of languages. Speakers of Burmese first arrived from China around the ninth century CE. The language was later influenced by the Mon language, which was a source for the writing system of Burmese, and by Buddhist scriptures.

The professional, entrepreneurial, and well-educated immigrants in the first and second wave of Burmese migration are generally bilingual, speaking fluent Burmese and English. British rule before World War II had demanded instruction in both English and Burmese, and many of these immigrants spoke English as their first language. Nevertheless, Burmese is the primary language used at gatherings of immigrants and American-born Burmese Americans. Their proficiency in English has allowed many of these Burmese Americans to develop business contacts and build professional societies in the United States.

Burmese from the second and third waves of migration generally experience anxiety regarding English. Following Burma's independence, English was no longer the primary language taught in Burma, although many people continued to use it. The military regime that took power closed universities and schools and banned books and literature. Most Burmese refugees to the United States, especially those from villages and more isolated communities, had little exposure to English. This lack of familiarity with the language has severely limited their educational and professional opportunities in the United

A Burmese woman and her son, both refugees from Myanmar, tend to their crop of Burmese variety hot peppers in their plot at the Global Growers Network's Bamboo Creek Farm in Stone Mountain, Georgia USA. The incubator farm is designed for farmers who have fled their native countries. Most of the farmers grow crops native to their homeland for their own consumption and to sell to other resettled refugees nearby. EPA EUROPEAN PRESS PHOTO AGENCY B.V. / ALAMY

States, not only hindering their acculturation into American society but also reinforcing the differences between them and earlier Burmese immigrants to the United States.

There is relatively little opportunity for American-born Burmese Americans to receive formal instruction in Burmese in the United States. Four places where Burmese is taught are Northern Illinois University in DeKalb; Cornell University in Ithaca, New York; the Foreign Service Institute of the U.S. Department of State; and the Southeast Asian Studies Summer Institute (SEASSI) summer language program, which takes place at a different university every two summers.

RELIGION

Almost 90 percent of the population in Burma is Buddhist. Buddhism is a nontheistic religion that claims that suffering is unavoidable and that the root of suffering is attachment, greed, and desire. Freedom from suffering can be obtained by following what is known as the Noble Eightfold Path: Right Understanding, Right Thought, Right Speech, Right Action, Right Livelihood, Right Effort, Right Mindfulness, and

Right Concentration. Buddha's teachings are known as the *Dharma*, and they are given to a collective body of followers or a religious community called the *Sangha*.

Burmese Americans have established churches and other worship centers almost everywhere they have settled. For instance, there are numerous Buddhist temples and worship centers serving communities of Burmese Americans in the San Francisco Bay Area, Fort Worth, and Fort Wayne. The Chin people, who constitute the second-largest Burmese ethnic group in the United States, are mostly Christian. They have founded more than twenty local churches in Indianapolis alone.

The veneration of ancestors is important among Burmese Americans who retain Burmese culture. Buddhist Burmese American families display pictures of ancestors. Burmese American families of other faiths may engage in similar practices but with less intensity. Second generation Burmese Americans generally take on the religious practices of their parents. Because there are fewer religious sites for Buddhists in the United States than in Burma, the role of officials at such sites differ in the United States. In some places, religious officials such as monks serve as both religious and community leaders.

CULTURE AND ASSIMILATION

Burmese American culture and assimilation varies depending on ethnicity, religion, and time of arrival. Burmese of Chinese and Indian ethnicity classify themselves based upon their ethnicity rather than their country of origin. Because of their relatively small numbers, non-Buddhist Burmese Americans, such as Christians, commonly join groups that are more broadly based on southeast Asian identity and religion.

Burmese Americans from the first and second waves of migration tend to classify themselves in a variety of ways. Most interestingly, they often identify themselves as "Asian American" in order to belong to an acculturated group that has more options than a smaller ethnic group. Burmese refugees in the third wave of migration have taken a longer time to assimilate to American culture, partly because they have had fewer educational and professional opportunities than those in the first and second waves of migration.

Cuisine Traditional Burmese food consists primarily of rice, vegetables, and fish, and it has been influenced by Indian and Chinese culinary traditions. Burmese use *ngapi*, a preserved fish paste, to accent meals, and they commonly add garlic, ginger, fish sauce, or dried shrimp for flavoring. Popular dishes include *mohinga*, a fish soup with rice noodles, and *khaukswe*, noodles typically served with chicken stewed in coconut milk. The Burmese enjoy spicy foods and they favor fruits over processed sweets. Green tea and regular black tea are the most popular drinks.

Burmese American cuisine is primarily available in local, communal, or religious settings. Burmese Americans typically dine at home or at religious sites, a custom that is more common among Buddhists. Although few Burmese restaurants emerged with the first wave of migration, more Burmese restaurants have appeared more recently. Because of the association between Indian, Chinese, and Burmese food, the visibility of Burmese food has benefitted from the growing popularity of Chinese and Indian dining in the United States. Burmese cuisine features prominently at Burmese American professional and political gatherings.

Holidays Burmese Americans commonly observe Burma Independence Day, which commemorates the official end of British colonial rule in Burma on January 4, 1948. To celebrate, Burmese wear their traditional costume, the *lorgyi*, a tube of cloth worn by both sexes and tucked in at the waist. Buddhist, Christian, and Hindu Burmese Americans also observe the traditional holidays of their respective religions.

Of note are several holidays celebrated by Buddhist Burmese Americans. The Kason Festival, or the Watering of the Banyan Tree, is celebrated on

MOHINGA (FISH SOUP)

Ingredients

For soup base:

1 large onion, chopped

1 whole garlic head, chopped

2 inches ginger root, peeled and finely chopped

2 tablespoons paprika powder

2 pounds small rice vermicelli

¼ teaspoon turmeric

3 pounds catfish fillet or nugget, finely chopped

1 tablespoon ground black pepper

2 tablespoons fish sauce

5 tablespoons vegetable oil

4 quarts water

3 sticks of lemongrass, cut in half

1 can of banana stem, sliced (optional)

½ pound fish cake, diced

5 onions, quartered

½ cup semolina flour, dissolved in 1 cup water

2 teaspoons salt

Garnish:

6 boiled eggs, halved

6 branches cilantro, coarsely chopped

roasted, dried chili flakes

10 fried, split chickpeas

fried garlic flake in oil

Preparation

Place garlic, onion, ginger, and paprika in a small food processor and chop until a paste. Heat oil in large stock pot and sautéchili paste with turmeric until fragrant, for 5 minutes. Stir in catfish, then add black pepper, fish sauce, and continue to stir for 10 minutes. Add water, banana stem, and lemongrass. Bring to boil; reduce heat and simmer for at least three hours, adding more water as needed. For best results, allow the soup to simmer up to 5 hours.

Add quartered onions, fish cake, and semolina flour and bring liquid to a boil, at the same time stirring and scraping the bottom of the pot to prevent lumping and sticking to the bottom of the stock pot. taste the stock and add additional salt as needed.

Cook the rice vermicelli with water according to package directions. Do not overcook the vermicelli as it will impact the taste of the finished soup. Once cooked, drain and divide into 6 to 8 bowls, add fish stock, garnish with chopped cilantro, fried chickpea, boiled egg, fried garlic, oil and chili flakes for some heat.

Serves 6

Children cool off during the Burmese New Year Water Festival. New York City, 2010. FRANCES M. ROBERTS / NEWSCOM

the day of the full moon during the month of Kason (April–May) and marks the enlightenment of the Buddha at the foot of the Banyan tree. On this day, people make pilgrimages to monasteries to offer food and gifts to monks. On Thingyan, or the Water Festival of the Burmese New Year, people throw water on each other, symbolizing the washing away of bad luck and the sins of the old year. Vesak, the holiest of Buddhist holidays, celebrates the birth, enlightenment, and death of the Buddha. These three celebrations, centered on Buddhist temples, generally take place on April 8, December 8, and February 15.

FAMILY AND COMMUNITY LIFE

Immigrants who have assimilated as Burmese Americans consider the family to be very important and show great respect for their elders as well as for educators, community leaders, and religious leaders. Because Burmese immigrants were fewer in number than many other immigrant groups, they did not settle in large groups. However, they maintained contact and built community associations with other Burmese Americans in their respective regions. The Burmese Association of Texas serves the Fort Worth area, the Burmese American Professional Society links those in the San Francisco Bay Area, and other groups emerged elsewhere.

Others who have arrived in the United States from Burma share the communal and family goals of these immigrants, but they differ in other respects. Refugees fearing deportation from the United States and a return to life under Burma's military regime

were less able to organize themselves. However, outside organizations formed to assist the refugees with acculturation, assimilation, and educational information. For example, in Indiana, which is home to the largest influx of Burmese refugees, organizations such as the Burmese American Community Institute and local educational and religious institutions were set up to provide language classes and information on essential services.

EMPLOYMENT AND ECONOMIC CONDITIONS

A majority of those in the first and second waves of Burmese migration benefited from their former experience as academics, professionals, and skilled workers. After their arrival, many found employment and built professional organizations for social and cultural support. However, refugees in the second and third waves of migration lacked the educational and professional opportunities of the earlier immigrant groups. Some refugees found themselves taking employment in jobs beneath their actual educational and professional qualifications. Refugees also lacked the language skills of the first- and second-wave immigrants, hindering their employment opportunities. Nevertheless, these refugees have sought to improve their economic conditions, participating in language classes and pursuing available opportunities. The Burmese American Association of Texas provides classes to immigrants and refugees to improve their language skills in the job market, and the Burmese American Community Institute operates programs and resources to develop educational and professional opportunities. The programs assist not only Burmese high school students but also parents by providing essential information on post-high school careers and employment.

POLITICS AND GOVERNMENT

There is little information on how Burmese Americans vote in the United States. However, Burmese Americans are very active in international politics. Both Burmese immigrants and refugees overwhelmingly oppose Burma's military regime, and they have built numerous organizations in the United States to lobby for change in Burma. The Burmese American Democratic Alliance, the Burmese American Women's Alliance, and other organizations rally for support, engage in fund raising, and disseminate information about Burmese politics. In 2008 some of these activists publicized how the military government had refused international aid offered to help victims of Cyclone Nargis in Burma. In 2012 political and professional organizations of Burmese Americans promoted the visit of the prodemocracy heroine Aung San Suu Kyi to the United States when she awarded the U.S. Congressional Gold Medal.

NOTABLE INDIVIDUALS

Academia Born in New York in 1966 and the grandson of the UN Secretary-General U Thant from Burma, Thant Myint-U is a Burmese American historian who has served at Cambridge University and in the United Nations. His writings on Burma include *The Making of Modern Burma* (2001), *The River of Lost Footsteps* (2007), and *Where China Meets India* (2011).

Journalism Julie Chen (1970–) has served as a reporter and news anchor on CBS. She also has hosted *The Talk*, a daytime talk show that features a panel of women who discuss various topics.

Daughter of a Burmese immigrant, Alex Wagner (1977–) is a prominent reporter for the network MSNBC. Her work with the nonprofit organization Not on Our Watch took her to Burma to monitor and report on the country's military regime.

Literature Wendy Law-Yone (1947–) is a Burmese American fiction writer whose experiences in fleeing the Burmese military government shape much of her writing. *The Coffin Tree* (1983) concerns two Burmese refugees from a political coup, and *Irrawaddy Tango* (1993) relates the story of a young woman who

In New York City, Buddhist monks pray for Myanmar victims of Cyclone Nargis outside United Nations headquarters, 2008. MARIO TAMA / GETTY IMAGES

rises up against a dictator. Her latest book, *The Road to Wanting* (2010), focuses on a woman who lives in a boom town at the Chinese-Burmese border.

MEDIA

There is very little information published about the Burmese American community. In addition, there are no American newspapers or periodicals published in Burmese. Some material about the political situation in Burma concerning human rights is available from the National League for Democracy and on various social media sites such as Facebook and YouTube.

From Burma to New York: The Stories of Burmese Refugees

Website built by graduate students in journalism at Columbia University, provides information on refugees from Burma who make the transition to the United States. Resources include information on select refugees, the resettlement process, and Burma's history.

URL: www.fromburmatonewyork.com

Irrawaddy

Founded in Thailand by exiled Burmese journalists, this news website and magazine is perhaps the most widely read source of Burma-related news worldwide. It is published in Burmese and English.

URL: www.irrawaddy.org

National League for Democracy (NLD)

Website that provides links and information regarding the democratic movement in Burma, including discussion of human rights and political activities and developments within Burma.

URL: www.nldburma.org

Voice of America (VOA), Burmese Service

A segment of the International Broadcasting Bureau, provides information about programming broadcast to Myanmar and the United States. VOA's International Broadcasting Bureau broadcasts several programs with a Burmese focus.

URL: www.voa.gov/burmese

ORGANIZATIONS AND ASSOCIATIONS

American Burma Buddhist Association

Serves as a religious, educational, and cultural resource center to promote Buddhist thought, beliefs, and practices. Has centers in New York and New Jersey.

619 Bergen Street
Brooklyn, New York 11238
Phone: (718) 622-8019
URL: www.mahasiusa.org

Burma Project/Southeast Asia Initiative

Linked through the Open Society Foundations network, provides information on human rights in Burma.

400 West 59th Street
New York, New York 10019
Phone: (212) 548-0632
URL: www.opensocietyfoundations.org/about/programs/burma-project-southeast-asia-initiative

Burmese American Community Institute (BACI)

Works with Burmese refugees in Indiana. Provides information on educational and professional opportunities.

1503 Quinlan Court
Indianapolis, Indiana 46217
Phone: (317) 215-4979
Email: info@baci-indy.org
URL: www.baci-indy.org

Burmese American Democratic Alliance (BADA)

Promotes discussion on human rights and political activism, particularly in regard to the government of Burma.

1952 McNair Street
Palo Alto, California 94303
Phone: (415) 895-2232
Email: badaonline@gmail.com
URL: www.badasf.org

MUSEUMS AND RESEARCH CENTERS

Center for Burma Studies at Northern Illinois University

Catherine Raymond, Director
101 Pottenger House
520 College View Court
Northern Illinois University
DeKalb, Illinois 60115
Phone: (815) 753-0512
Email: craymond@niu.edu
URL: www.niu.edu/burma/index.shtml

SOURCES FOR ADDITIONAL STUDY

Aung San Suu Kyi. *Freedom from Fear and Other Writings*, ed. Michael Aris. New York: Viking, 1991.

———*Letters from Burma*. London: Penguin, 1996.

Bajoria, Jayshree. "Understanding Myanmar," Council on Foreign Relations. Council on Foreign Relations, July 10, 2012.

Fink, Christina. *Living Silence: Burma under Military Rule*. London: Zed, 2001.

Steinberg, David I. *Burma/Myanmar: What Everyone Needs to Know*. New York: Oxford University Press, 2010.

Thant Myint-U. *The Making of Modern Burma*. Cambridge: Cambridge University Press, 2001.

Thomas, William. *Aung San Suu Kyi*. Milwaukee: World Almanac Library, 2005.

CAMBODIAN AMERICANS

Carl L. Bankston III

OVERVIEW

Cambodian Americans are immigrants or descendants of people from Cambodia, a nation in mainland Southeast Asia bordered on the west and northwest by Thailand, on the north by Laos, on the east by Vietnam, and on the south by the Gulf of Thailand. The climate is tropical, with monsoon rains from May to October and a dry season from December to March. There is little variation in temperature, which is hot most of the year. There are mountains in the southwest and north, but most of the country consists of low, flat plains. Three-quarters of the land is covered with forests and woodland, and much of the land is cultivated with rice paddies. Cambodia has a total land area of 181,035 square miles, which is approximately the size of the state of Missouri.

The Kingdom of Cambodia had a population of about fifteen million people in July 2012, according to the *CIA World Factbook*. Cambodia is an overwhelmingly Buddhist country; 95 percent of the population practices Theravada Buddhism, the branch of Buddhism found in many countries in southern Asia. Other faiths include Roman Catholicism, Islam, animism, and Mahayana Buddhism—the branch found most often in northern Asia. An estimated 2.1 percent of the people in Cambodia are Muslim, mostly members of the Cham ethnic minority. Although the Cambodian economy grew rapidly from 2004 to 2008 and continued to improve even during the global economic troubles after 2008, it is still a poor country. Nearly one-third of its people live below the poverty level, and subsistence farming is still the most common occupation. Cambodia has a wealth of natural resources, including timber and minerals, and oil deposits have been found in its territorial waters. Most of its economic growth during the 2000s, though, came from the expansion of the garment industry and tourism.

Before 1975 there were almost no people of Cambodian origin in the United States. Small numbers of Cambodians, also known as Khmer, began to arrive as refugees in the late 1970s. After the U.S. Congress passed the Refugee Act of 1980, many more Cambodians began to resettle in the United States, along with rapidly growing numbers of refugees from Laos and Vietnam. In 1981 more than 38,000

Cambodian refugees reached the United States. By the time of the 1990 U.S. Census, the Cambodian American population had reached an official estimate of 150,000 people. The flow of refugees decreased in the late 1980s, but an established Cambodian American population became a basis for regular migration from Cambodia to the United States. Although Cambodians Americans were initially a greatly disadvantaged population, suffering from the traumas of

Adapting to the American economy was difficult for many people of Cambodian ancestry who arrived in the United States during the 1980s. Most had been farmers in their previous country, and in the United States they were generally settled in cities.

war and dislocation and often with little formal education, they showed a notable trend toward socioeconomic adaptation and upward mobility.

U.S. Census figures placed the Cambodian American population at 225,497 in 2010, or equal to the total population of a mid-sized American city such as Reno, Nevada. Although Cambodian Americans live in almost all parts of the United States, the largest concentrations are in California and Massachusetts. Long Beach, in southern California, and the area around Lowell, Massachusetts, are home to the nation's largest Cambodian communities.

HISTORY OF THE PEOPLE

Early History Cambodia is an ancient country with a long history that has been a source of pride and pain to the Cambodian people. The Cambodians probably lived originally in western China, but they migrated down the Mekong River valley into Indochina sometime before the common era. In Indochina, they came into contact with the highly developed civilization and culture of ancient India. From India, they took the religions of Hinduism and Buddhism and the idea of state organization as well as the concept of kingship.

The greatest period in Cambodian history was the Angkor period (ninth through fifteenth centuries), named after a huge complex of religious and public monuments. During much of this time, Cambodia, or "Kambuja-Desa," as it is called in old inscriptions, was the most powerful kingdom in Southeast Asia, governing great expanses of territory that are now part of Thailand and southern Vietnam, as well as the land that constitutes Cambodia today.

By the end of the Angkor era, the kingdom of Kambuja-Desa had come under increased pressure from the Siamese (Thai) on the west and the Vietnamese on the east. From the 1400s on, the Cambodians lost territory to both the Siamese and Vietnamese. By the 1800s Cambodia had fallen almost entirely under the control of Vietnam and Siam, and Cambodia was sealed off from the outside influences that were beginning to affect other Southeast Asian countries. In 1864 Cambodia became a French protectorate.

Modern Era Although there was a steady growth of Cambodian nationalism, the country remained at peace through the early part of the twentieth century. After World War II broke out and France was occupied by Germany, the French remained in control in Indochina, with the agreement of Germany's allies in Asia, the Japanese. In 1941 the Cambodian king, Monivong, died, and the French made Monivong's grandson, Norodom Sihanouk, king.

Sihanouk was to dominate Cambodian history for most of the half-century following his coronation. He also developed from a protégé of the French into a determined, if cautious, adherent to the cause of Cambodian independence. The occupation of Japanese troops in Southeast Asia provided many Asian colonies with evidence that the European colonists could be defeated. In 1945 Japanese troops disarmed the French colonial forces in Cambodia. At their instigation, Sihanouk declared Cambodian independence from France on March 12, 1945.

The French reestablished themselves in Cambodia after the defeat of Japan soon thereafter, but their power had been seriously weakened. Nationalist feelings continued to grow stronger in Cambodia. In France, some young Cambodian students, influenced by the French Communist Party, began to formulate ideas that combined extreme nationalism with Communist ideology. Three of these students were to become the most important leaders of the Khmer Rouge: Saloth Sar, later known as Pol Pot, Khieu Samphan, and Ieng Sary. All nationalists looked back to the time of Angkor Wat as a symbol and ideal of Cambodian greatness.

By 1953 the war in neighboring Vietnam was becoming a problem for the French, exacerbated by its momentous unpopularity in France. Cambodian resistance and the prospect of fighting another full-scale war in Cambodia led France to grant Cambodia independence on November 9, 1953, while retaining much control over its economy. In 1954, after the French had failed to reimpose their rule on Vietnam, delegates to the Geneva Conference agreed that

elections would be held in all three of the countries of Indochina. Sihanouk abdicated his throne in 1955 in favor of his father and assumed the highest office in the country as its prime minister.

Sihanouk managed to keep his country neutral during many of the long years of war that raged in Vietnam and Laos. He was, at the same time, intolerant of Cambodian leftists, whom he labeled the "Khmer Rouge," or "Red Khmer." Many of these leftists fled into the countryside.

The United States became involved in Southeast Asia to preserve a non-Communist regime in South Vietnam. The policies of Prince Sihanouk were primarily aimed at keeping Cambodia out of the war, and until about 1970, he was largely successful. His constant attempts to play the different sides in the Vietnam conflict against each other, though, resulted in hostility toward him by the pro-American governments of Thailand and South Vietnam and in suspicion of him on by the American government.

In 1970, apparently with American support, General Lon Nol staged a coup while Prince Sihanouk was on his way to France for health reasons. As the United States welcomed a more cooperative Cambodian regime, the Vietnam War had finally overtaken Cambodia. In May 1970 American and South Vietnamese forces invaded eastern Cambodia, driving the Vietnamese communist forces farther into the country.

Out of power, Sihanouk joined forces with the Khmer leftists whom he had formerly persecuted. Having the prince on their side gave the Khmer Rouge an enormous advantage in drawing support from the peasants, many of whom still regarded Sihanouk as an almost divine figure. At the same time, American aerial bombing in the Cambodian countryside, directed against both the North Vietnamese and the Khmer Rouge, caused enormous disruption of the traditional society. In the first half of 1973, before the U.S. Congress prohibited further bombing in Cambodia, American planes dropped over one hundred thousand tons of bombs on the country. In April 1975, with the United States having pulled its troops out of Vietnam and Saigon about to fall to the Vietnamese Communists, the Khmer Rouge marched into Phnom Penh.

Cambodia became an experiment in revolutionary social change known as Democratic Kampuchea. In order to create a completely new society in which everyone would be equal, the Khmer Rouge, under the leadership of Pol Pot, ordered everyone, including the elderly and sick, out of the cities and towns of Cambodia and into the countryside. Family life, all traces of individualism, and all attachments to old institutions, including religion, were abolished. A new calendar for a new era was invented, with 1975 renamed "Year Zero." All Cambodians were put to work at agricultural labor in order to build up the

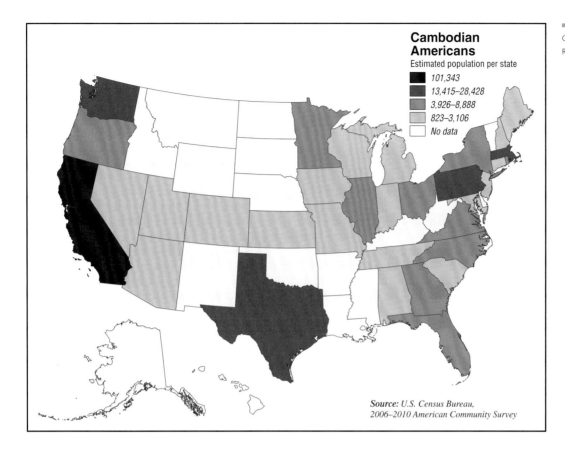

Cambodian Americans

Estimated population per state

- 101,343
- 13,415–28,428
- 3,926–8,888
- 823–3,106
- No data

*Source: U.S. Census Bureau,
2006–2010 American Community Survey*

agricultural surplus of the nation to finance rapid industrialization. In effect, these uncompromising ideals turned the entire country into a collection of forced labor camps; soldiers whose young lives had consisted mainly of bitter warfare acted as armed guards.

Estimates of the number of people who died under Pol Pot's Democratic Kampuchea regime vary from one million to two million. The number of people actually executed by the Khmer Rouge is unknowable.

Democratic Kampuchea, in addition to espousing an extreme form of socialism, was also committed to extreme nationalism. The Khmer Rouge wanted to recreate the greatness of the Angkor period, which meant retaking the areas that had become parts of Vietnam and Thailand. Border skirmishes between Cambodian and Vietnamese forces led Vietnam to invade Cambodia on Christmas Day in 1978, and by early January the Vietnamese held Phnom Penh. In the chaos of war, the rice crop went untended and thousands of Cambodians, starving and freed from the Khmer Rouge labor camps, began crossing the border into Thailand. Television cameras brought the images of these refugees into the homes of Americans and other westerners, and immigration from Cambodia to the United States began as a response to the "Cambodian refugee crisis."

Under pressure from the United States and other anticommunist and anti-Vietnamese nations, Vietnamese troops pulled out of Cambodia in 1989, leaving behind the Cambodian government they had created—the People's Republic of Kampuchea. In the meantime, with the help of anti-Vietnamese governments, the Coalition Government of Democratic Kampuchea was formed with the participation of forces loyal to the then-infamous Khmer Rouge and to the Khmer People's National Liberation Front. In 1991 all Cambodian parties signed a peace agreement in Paris that called for United Nations Transitional Authorities in Cambodia to prepare the country for a general election. In 1993 the elected representatives voted to form a coalition government composed of the two political parties that had garnered the most votes. They also decided to reestablish the monarchy with Sihanouk as king and head of state. The Khmer Rouge refused to take part in this election and continued to oppose the new government.

In 1993 Norodom Sihanok again became king, although the monarchy had relatively little real power. In 1993 Sihanouk's son, Norodom Ranariddh, was elected prime minister, but he was forced to share power with Hun Sen, a former Khmer Rouge leader who had allied himself with the invading Vietnamese. Ranariddh became first prime minister, while Hun Sen became second prime minister. In 1997 Hun Sen staged a coup and Ranariddh fled to France.

Ranariddh was able to return and participate in elections in 1998, becoming chairman of the Cambodian National Assembly. Hun Sen became sole prime minister. In 2004 Sihanouk abdicated, and his son Norodom Sihamoni, a half-brother of Ranariddh, became king. Sihanouk died on October 15, 2012. In November 2012 President Barack Obama became the first American president to visit Cambodia.

SETTLEMENT IN THE UNITED STATES

Large numbers of refugees from Cambodia started arriving in the United States only after 1979, when the U.S. refugee program began accepting Cambodians from refugee camps in Thailand. Most of these arrived in the early 1980s. Of the 118,823 foreign-born Cambodians identified by the 1990 U.S. Census, only 16,880 (or about 14 percent) had arrived before 1980.

As thousands of refugees from Vietnam, Laos, and Cambodia began to come into the United States each year, the United States developed organizational procedures for resettlement. Voluntary agencies, many of which were affiliated with American churches, had been set up by 1975 to assist the first wave of Vietnamese refugees. These agencies had the task of finding sponsors, individuals, or groups who would assume financial and personal responsibility for refugee families for up to two years. By the early 1980s refugee camps had been set up in various countries throughout Southeast Asia. Most Cambodians stayed in refugee camps in Thailand, but many who were being prepared for resettlement in the United States were sent to camps in the Philippines or elsewhere. Agencies under contract to the U.S. Department of State organized classes to teach English to familiarize refugees with American language and culture.

In 1980 and 1981, 34,107 Cambodians entered the United States. From 1982 to 1984, the influx continued, with 36,082 Cambodians entering the United States. After that time, the numbers began to diminish. In 1985 and 1986, 19,921 Cambodians reached American soil, and from 1987 to 1990, only 11,843 Cambodians were admitted. By the early 1990s prospects of a political settlement in Cambodia removed much of the perceived urgency of accepting Cambodian refugees, and immigration from Cambodia to the United States decreased to very small numbers.

By the 2000s the flow of refugees from Cambodia to the United States had essentially stopped. Between 2002 and 2011, only 84 individuals of Cambodian nationality were admitted to the United States, according to the 2011 *Yearbook of Immigration Statistics*, published by the U.S. Homeland Security Office. The number of people born in Cambodia admitted to the United States under the standard immigration category of "legal permanent residents" reached an average of roughly 3600 people per year during that same ten-year period. This modest but stable immigration

flow was largely due to the fact that U.S. immigration policy favors family members of citizens and legal residents, and a fairly large Cambodian American population had by then been established.

By 1990 the Cambodian American population had reached almost 150,000, according to the U.S. Census count, although those active in working with Cambodian immigrants warned then that the census may have undercounted this group, as the Cambodians were so new to American society and many may not have responded to the census. Ten years later, the Cambodian American population had grown to 183,769. By 2010 the numbers had grown to 255,497.

The largest concentration of Cambodian Americans is in California, where about 85,000 Cambodians, or roughly one-third of the national population, resided by 2011, according to estimates from the American Community Survey of the U.S. Census Bureau. This national population of Cambodians had grown less concentrated over time, though, since about nearly half of the people of Cambodian ethnicity had lived in California in 1990. The largest Cambodian community was in the Los Angeles–Long Beach area, where over 33,000 Cambodians lived by the beginning of the second decade of the twenty-first century, according to the U.S. Census. The area of Long Beach along the Anaheim and Atlantic corridors is known as "Cambodia Town." Outside of California, the greatest number of Cambodian Americans were found in Massachusetts, where nearly 29,000 lived. About half of the Massachusetts Cambodians (14,000) lived in and around the city of Lowell. Other states with large Cambodian populations included Washington (26,600), Texas (at least 15,200), Pennsylvania (at least 12,200, mostly in Philadelphia), Rhode Island (8,200), Connecticut (5,500), Minnesota (5,500), Georgia (4,900), Oregon (4,600), Virginia (4,100), North Carolina (4,000), New York (4,000), and Florida (3,900). Cambodian population growth in the southern states, such as Georgia, North Carolina, and Florida had been especially notable since the 1990s.

In the early 1990s only about 20 percent of foreign-born Cambodians in the United States had become naturalized U.S. citizens, but by 2011 that figure had grown to 65 percent (according to the American Community Survey estimates for 2009–2011). As of 2011 about 46 percent of Cambodian Americans had been born in the United States.

LANGUAGE

Cambodian, or Khmer, is classified by linguists as an Austro-Asiatic language, related to Mon—a language spoken in Burma (Myanmar) and western Thailand—and various tribal languages of Southeast Asia. Although many major Asian languages are tonal languages, Cambodian is not tonal; as in the European languages, tones of voice may indicate emotion, but they do not change the meanings of words. The Cambodian alphabet, which has forty-seven letters, is derived from the alphabet of ancient India, and it is similar to the Thai and Laotian alphabets, as the Thai and Lao people borrowed their systems of writing from the Cambodians.

Census estimates from 2011 showed that over three-quarters of Cambodian Americans aged five or older spoke Khmer, or Cambodian, at home. Only 60 percent of those under eighteen reported speaking their ancestral language at home, though, reflecting the beginning of a shift toward English among younger people. Although an estimated nine percent of adult Cambodian Americans could speak no English and 29 percent of adults could not speak English well, only a tiny proportion of children could not speak English, and over one-third of Cambodian American children spoke only English.

Greetings and Popular Expressions Cambodian has many sounds that are quite different from those of English, and these are represented by the letters of the Cambodian alphabet. Linguists usually use a phonetic alphabet to write these sounds in the characters used by English and other European languages, but the phrases below are written in a fashion that should provide nonspecialist speakers of American English with a fairly close approximation to their actual pronunciation: *Som chumreap sur*—Good day; *Loak sohk suh-bye jeeuh tay?*—Are you well, sir?; *Loak-srey sohk suh-bye jeeuh tay?*—Are you well, madame?; *Baht, knyom sohk suh-bye jeeuh tay*—I'm fine (from a man); *Jah, knyom sohk suh-bye jeeuh tay*—I'm fine (from a woman); *Som aw kun*—Thank you; *Sohm toh*—Excuse me, or I'm sorry; *Meun uh-wye tay*—Don't mention it, or You're welcome; *Teuh nah?*—Where are you going?; *Niyeh piesah anglay bahn tay?*—Can you speak English?; *Sdap bahn tay*—Do you understand?; *Sdap bahn*—I understand; *Sdap meun bahn*—I don't understand; *Som chumreap lea*—Good-bye.

RELIGION

Buddhism is the traditional religion of Cambodia. Before 1975 the ruler of the country was the official protector of the religion, and the monks were organized into a hierarchy overseen by the government. Monasteries and temples were found in all villages, and monks played an important role in the education of children and passing on Cambodian culture. The people also supported their local monasteries, through gifts and by giving food to monks. Monks were forbidden to handle money and had to show humility by begging for their food. Every morning, the monks would go from house to house, with their eyes downcast, holding out their begging bowls, into which the lay people would spoon rice. Although the religion was attacked by the radical Khmer Rouge during their regime and many monks were killed, the vast majority of Cambodians remain Buddhists, and the faith continues to be an important part of the national culture.

Some Cambodian Americans have converted to Christianity, either in the refugee camps or after arriving in the United States. Often these conversions have been the result of spiritual crises brought about by the tragedies of recent Cambodian history. In many cases,

The Cambodian Buddhist Temple in Hampton, Minnesota. 2007 ZUMA / ZUMA PRESS, INC / ALAMY

people felt that Buddhism had somehow failed because of the death and destruction that had occurred in their country. In other cases, Christianity has seemed attractive because it is the religion of the majority of Americans, and conversion has seemed a good way to conform to American society and express gratitude to the religious organizations that played an important part in resettling refugees in the United States.

The majority of Cambodian Americans, however, continue the practice of their traditional religion. As more Cambodians settled in this country and established their own communities, observing their religious rituals became easier. In mid-1979, the Washington, D.C.–area Cambodian Buddhist Society founded Wat Buddhikarama, reportedly the first Cambodian Buddhist temple in the United States. Three years later, in 1982, the expanding Cambodian population of Long Beach, California, led Cambodian refugees to establish Wat Kemara Buddhikaram. In mid-1985, the Khmer Buddhist Society opened the first Cambodian Buddhist temple in New York City in the Bedford Park section of the Bronx. During the following decades, Cambodian American Buddhist temples proliferated. By 2009 there were at least 109 Cambodian temples in the United States. Monasteries, or places where Buddhist monks live, are usually attached to the temples, or places of worship, and the monks are in charge of the temples and the religious rituals held in them. Cambodian Americans often see their temples as cultural centers as well as places for religious activities. Buddhist monks in the United States do not beg; rather, laypeople bring food donations to the temples.

CULTURE AND ASSIMILATION

Traditional Cambodian cultural practices were disrupted during the Khmer Rouge years. Since then, there have been efforts to reconstruct traditions and culture by people in Cambodia and by Cambodian Americans. This has been a special challenge for the latter, as they live in a new country surrounded by members of other ethnic groups. Young people, in particular, assimilate into wider American practices and often have relatively few links to ancestral practices. Nevertheless, Buddhist temples have been especially important in maintaining some aspects of traditional culture.

Traditions and Customs Traditional Cambodian culture emphasizes courtesy and respect, especially respect for elders. The hierarchical character of the culture is expressed in concepts of the body. As in neighboring Thailand and Laos, the head is conceived of as the highest part of the body spiritually as well as physically. Because the head is thought to contain the human soul, touching someone on the head is an expression of disrespect. The feet, on the other hand, are the body's lowest parts, and pointing the soles of the feet at another is extremely discourteous.

Although Cambodian Americans do shake hands when meeting other Americans, their tradition for greeting is to place both hands together at the chest or in front of the face and give a slight bow of the head. Known as the *sampeah*, this gesture is the same as the *wai* in Thailand. The greater the respect one owes to the person greeted, the higher one holds one's hands. In traditional Cambodian culture, it is considered impolite to make eye contact with an older person or with someone of superior status.

Cuisine As in other parts of Southeast Asia, rice is the basic dish in Cambodian cooking. Meats and vegetables are generally meant to accompany rice. Noodle dishes are also common. A fermented fish sauce or paste, known as *prahok*, is commonly used as a flavoring. *Prahok* is added to foods in cooking and used as a dip. The cuisine is often spicy, employing chili peppers, lemongrass, ginger, and mint. Because bananas, papayas, mangoes, and other fruits are abundant in Cambodia, these are traditionally common in the Cambodian diet. Cambodian Americans families often prepare traditional dishes in their homes. The ingredients are generally available in stores specializing in Asian foods. Some Cambodian Americans grow spices and vegetables in their own gardens.

Cambodian restaurants have not become as fashionable as Thai restaurants in the United States, but many cities with Cambodian American communities do have excellent Cambodian eating establishments, and the Los Angeles region has several Cambodian restaurants. Cambodian restaurants often serve Thai dishes as well as Cambodian dishes.

Traditional Dress The basis of traditional Cambodian dress is a tube-shaped piece of cloth that resembles a skirt. Known as the *sampot* or the *sarong* (a Malay/Indonesian term), this article of clothing derives from the historic Indian influence on Cambodia. Made of cotton or silk, it is fastened around the waist and comes in a variety of patterns and styles. A variety of shirts or tops accompany the *sampot*.

The *krama* is one of the most characteristic articles of Cambodian dress. It is a checkered scarf worn around the neck, about the shoulders, or turban-style on the head.

Among Cambodian Americans, the *sampot* and *krama* are usually only seen on older people or on relatively recent immigrants living in ethnic neighborhoods. Elaborate versions of traditional dress, however, are used in dances and on holidays and ceremonial occasions.

Traditional Arts and Crafts Cambodian crafts suffered during the Khmer Rouge period, but these began to make a comeback in the following decades. The production of traditional arts and crafts by Cambodian Americans is often limited by their participation in a modern economy of mass consumption. Nevertheless, Cambodian Americans remain proud of their traditional arts, which are often displayed on ceremonial occasions.

Cambodian American Nhep Prok is a master of the Cambodian "khimm," or stringed dulcimer. He and 100 other community members participated in an event at Peralta Hacienda Historic house, titled "Rhythm of the Refugee, a Cambodian Journey of Healing" in California, 2011. MATT VAN SAUN / DEMOTIX / CORBIS

Textile weaving has a long history in Cambodia. *Sampot*s are woven from both silk and cotton. Cambodian weavers also make pictorial tapestries, known as *pidan*, usually of silk. The *krama* is traditionally woven from cotton. In addition to these cloths, Cambodians also weave baskets and floor mats from strips of bamboo. These traditional crafts have become rare in the everyday life of Cambodian Americans, but they are still practiced in temples and cultural centers. Cambodia Town, in Long Beach, California, holds an annual Cambodian Arts and Culture Exhibition in November, in which the arts and crafts from the previous homeland are displayed.

Dances and Songs Music is important to traditional Cambodian culture, and Cambodian Americans put a great deal of effort into maintaining this link with their heritage. Traditional music ensembles perform in almost all large Cambodian communities in the United States. There are six types of music ensembles, but the type known as *areak ka* is considered the most traditional and is used for popular religious ceremonies and wedding ceremonies. The instruments used in the *areak ka* ensemble are a three-stringed fiddle, a type of monochord, a long-necked lute, and goblet-drums. Other instruments that may be found in Cambodian ensembles include a quadruple-reed oboe, several types of gongs, a large barrel drum, a flute, a two-stringed fiddle, a three-stringed zither, hammered dulcimers, cymbals, and the xylophone. Cambodian music may sound somewhat strange at first to those who are unfamiliar with Asian music.

The best-known Cambodian dance is called the "masked dance," because the dancers wear the masks of the characters they portray. The masked dance always tells the story of the *Ramayana*, an epic that the Cambodians took from ancient India. All parts in the masked dance, even those of women, are played by men. Cambodian classical ballet, or "court dance," on the other hand, has traditionally been danced by women, although men have been entering classical ballet since the 1950s. There are a number of Cambodian dancers in the United States, and the art of dance is also beginning to revive in Cambodia. Bringing this part of the culture back to life, however, has been difficult, since an estimated 90 percent of all trained dancers died during the Khmer Rouge regime. Today, traditional Cambodian dances are taught and practiced at Cambodian American temples. The classical dance troupe Cambodian-American Heritage, based in Washington D.C., has achieved wide recognition in the contemporary American art world.

Literature Much of the early literature of Cambodia is written in Sanskrit and known by modern scholars primarily from inscriptions on temples and other public buildings. Classical Cambodian literature is based on Indian models, and the *Reamker*, a Cambodian version of the Indian poem the *Ramayana*, is probably the most important piece of classical Cambodian literature. The *Reamker* is still known by Cambodians today. In the years before 1975, episodes from this poem were often acted out by dancers in the royal court or by villagers in village festivals. A collection of aphorisms, known as the *Chbab*

Cambodian American Muslim woman and children at Khmer New Year celebrations in South California. NIK WHEELER / ALAMY

(or "laws"), exists in both written and oral literature. Until recently, children were required to memorize the *Chbab* in school. Similar to the *Chbab* are the *Kotilok* (or "Art of Good Conduct"), which are fables designed to teach moral lessons.

European literary forms, such as novels, had taken root in Cambodia by the 1970s, but almost no literature was produced under the Khmer Rouge, and many intellectuals were killed during the Khmer Rouge regime. Since 1979, suffering under the Khmer Rouge has been a major theme in Cambodian literature, both in Cambodia and abroad. Among Cambodian Americans, also, the urge to bear witness to the horrors of the years from 1975 to 1979 has inspired many to write, and as a result, the autobiography is the most commonly employed literary form.

Holidays For three days in mid-April, Cambodians observe *Chaul Chnam*, the solar New Year, which is the most important and most common Cambodian holiday, and it is widely celebrated by Cambodian Americans. Many parties and dances are held during these three days, and traditional Cambodian music is usually heard. The game of *bos chhoung* remains a popular New Year's tradition among Cambodians in the United States. In this game, young men and women stand facing each other, about five feet apart. A young man takes a scarf rolled into a ball and throws it at a young woman in whom he is interested. She must catch the scarf, and if she misses it, she must sing and dance for him. If she catches the scarf, she will throw it back to him. If he misses it, he must sing and dance. For Buddhist Cambodians, the New Year festival is an important time to visit the temple to pray, meditate, and plan for the coming year.

The water festival, held in November when the flooding in Cambodia has stopped and the water starts to flow out of the Great Lake (Tonlé Sap) into the river again, is celebrated in both Cambodia and the United States. It usually involves boat races and colorful, lighted floats sailing down the river.

Health Care Issues and Practices Many older Cambodian Americans faced special mental and physical health problems resulting from their tragic recent history. Almost all lived under the extreme brutality of the Khmer Rouge regime that ruled the country from 1975 to 1979, and their native country was in a state of war both before and after. Most Cambodian refugees also spent time living in refugee camps in Thailand or other Southeast Asian countries. Health professionals and others who worked with Cambodian Americans often note that these experiences have left Cambodian refugees with a sense of powerlessness that affected many, even in the United States. Physical ailments often resulted from the emotional anguish they suffered and continued to suffer. Among those who resettled in Western countries, a strange malady appeared, often referred to as the "Pol Pot syndrome," after the leader of the Khmer Rouge. The Pol Pot syndrome included insomnia, difficulty in breathing, loss of appetite, and pains in various parts of the body.

The stress that led to such illnesses often tended to create a low general level of health for the Cambodian Americans who arrived in the refugee waves of the late twentieth century. In the "Khmer" entry in *Refugees in the United States: A Reference Handbook* (1985), May M. Ebihara notes that 84 percent of Cambodian households in California reported that at least one household member was under the care of a medical doctor, compared to 45 percent of Vietnamese households and 24 percent of Hmong and Lao households. The syndrome known as post-traumatic stress disorder, a type of delayed reaction to extreme emotional stress that affected many Vietnam veterans, is also common among older Cambodian refugees in the United States.

Traditional Cambodian healers, known as *krou Khmer*, may be found in many Cambodian American communities. Some of the techniques used by these healers are massages, "coining," and treatment with herbal medicines. Coining, or *koh khchal*, is a method of using a copper coin dipped in balm to apply pressure to acupuncture points of the body. Some Western doctors believe that this actually can be an effective means of pain relief. Coining does leave bruise marks, however, and these can alarm medical personnel and others not familiar with this practice.

Death and Burial Rituals Cambodians and other Theravada Buddhists normally cremate the dead. In a traditional Cambodian funeral, the body of the deceased is washed, dressed, and then displayed in a coffin, usually surrounded by flowers. A photograph of the deceased accompanies the body. White, not black, is the color of mourning, and family members dress in white for funeral ceremonies, and white flags are placed outside the house.

Buddhist monks are essential to performing the rituals for moving the dead from the present life to the next. The monks form part of a procession to bring the body to the place of cremation. In the United States the rituals are somewhat modified. Some Cambodian Americans have adopted the practice of wearing black as the color of mourning. Because laws in the United States do not permit bodies to be kept at home, the bodies are displayed at funeral homes, which take charge of cremations. Buddhist monks will often recite prayers by bodies at the funeral homes in the evenings or immediately before the body is taken to the crematorium or burial place.

Recreational Activities Cambodian Americans enjoy the same sports and games other Americans do. Traditional recreations, such as the game of *bos chhoung* mentioned above, are usually enjoyed during ceremonial occasions around temples or other cultural sites. Khmer kickboxing, known as *pradal serey*, is very similar to Thai kickboxing. This sport can be found in many Cambodian American communities, and there are Cambodian kickboxing schools in several locations in the United States.

Soccer is very popular with Cambodian American men. The Cambodian American Soccer Association is based in the Washington, D.C., area.; it is not ethnically exclusive and is open to members of other racial and ethnic groups.

FAMILY AND COMMUNITY LIFE

The family is extremely important to Cambodian Americans, in part because so many of them lost family members in their previous country. They tend to have very large families. Children—especially young children—are treasured, and parents treat them with a great deal of affection. However, Cambodian American families often experience stress because of conflicting expectations on the part of parents, many of whom are immigrants or grew up in immigrant families, and children, most of whom were born in the United States and have no memories of Southeast

CAMBODIAN PROVERBS

- The new rice stalk stands erect; the old stalk, full of grain, leans over.
- Travel on a river by following its bends, live in a country by following its customs.
- The small boat should not try to be a big boat.
- Don't let an angry man wash your dishes; don't let a hungry man guard your rice.
- Drop by drop, the vessel will fill; pour it, and everything will spill.
- Men have words—elephants have tusks.
- If you don't take your wife's advice, you'll have no rice seed next year.
- Don't rush to dump your rainwater when you hear the sound of thunder.
- Losing money is better than wasting words.
- If you are an egg, don't bang against a rock.
- Gain knowledge by study, wealth by work.

Asia. As younger Cambodian Americans grow up and establish their own families, Cambodian American families are becoming more similar to those of other Americans in cultural orientations and practices.

Gender Roles In Cambodia, men are responsible for providing for their families. Only men can occupy the prestigious status of the Buddhist monk. They also receive formal education, whereas Cambodian women are trained for certain tasks in the home. Contrary to other Asian cultures, Cambodian women occupy a key position in the household. Generally, the wife budgets the family assets and cares for the children. She is highly regarded by the men in her own family and by Cambodian society at large. However, many Cambodian women had their first taste of formal education in the refugee camps. In the United States, young Cambodian American women pursued their educations in large numbers, and they have often become important as breadwinners for their families.

The active roles of Cambodian American women are reflected in contemporary statistics. The 2011 American Community Survey of the Census Bureau showed that 70 percent of Cambodian American women between the ages of twenty-five and sixty-five were in the labor force, compared to 83 percent of Cambodian American men. Cambodian American women had even higher levels of college attendance

ornate brocade wrap-skirt. She also wears many bracelets, anklets, and necklaces. Grooms sometimes wear the traditional *kben* (baggy pantaloons) and jacket, but Western-style suits are becoming common.

A procession bring gifts of food and drink to the bride's home. At the beginning of the wedding, the couple sits at a table covered with flowers, fruit, candles, and sometimes a sword to chase evil spirits away. Friends and relatives take turns standing in front of the crowd to talk about the new couple. A Buddhist monk cuts a lock of hair from the bride and groom and mixes the two locks together in a bowl to symbolize the sharing of their lives. Gifts, frequently envelopes with money, are offered to the couple by guests. At the end of the wedding, the couple goes through the ritual known as *ptem*, in which knots are tied in a white string bracelet to represent the elders' blessing.

Relations with Other Americans Because Cambodian Americans have often settled in urban areas, they have frequent contact with members of other minority groups. Sometimes these encounters are troubled by cultural misunderstandings and the social problems frequently found in urban communities. In some areas with large Cambodian communities, Cambodian youth gangs have developed, in part as a matter of self-protection. Older Cambodians often see that they have much in common with their poor Asian, black, and Hispanic neighbors and will frequently distinguish these areas of "poor people" from the comfortable middle-class neighborhoods of "Americans." Most Cambodian Americans are fairly dark skinned, and they are acutely aware of prejudice in America. They sometimes internalize this prejudice and express feelings of inadequacy because of it.

It has been noted that Cambodian Americans in Texas have frequent contacts with Mexicans or Mexican Americans, and that members of the two ethnic groups accommodate one another easily. Cambodians may frequently be found as participants in Mexican American weekend markets. Many Cambodians in Texas have learned Spanish and follow Mexican customs when interacting with their Spanish-speaking peers. The area known as "Cambodia Town" in Southern California also has a substantial Mexican American population.

Cambodian Americans have high rates of intermarriage with members of other groups. By 2010 over 25 percent of married Cambodian American women and an estimated 13 percent of married Cambodian American men had spouses from another group, most often white Americans. Almost 40 percent of children with a Cambodian American mother and about 18 percent of children with a Cambodian American father had a parent who was non-Cambodian, and thus the number of people who were partly of Cambodian ancestry was growing rapidly.

Cambodian Americans tend to welcome non-Cambodians to activities in Buddhist temples and to

than men, as 57 percent of women in this ethnic group aged nineteen through twenty-one attended college in 2011, compared to 50 percent of men.

Education Lack of formal education was a serious handicap for most Cambodian Americans arriving in the United States as refugees. This continued to be a problem, especially for older group members. In 2011 over one-fourth of Cambodian American aged at least twenty-five had less than a high school education, and about 17 percent had no formal schooling. Among those aged forty or over, 40 percent had not finished high school and over one-fourth had not been to school at all.

Although Cambodian American young people did not show the high educational achievement and attainment levels of some other ethnic groups, they had made progress since group members began arriving in the United States. The majority of young people aged nineteen through twenty-one were in college by 2011, and over one-fifth of those aged twenty-five through thirty had finished four years of college.

Courtship and Weddings Traditional Cambodian wedding ceremonies are still held by Cambodian Americans, and even members of other ethnic groups who have married Cambodians have celebrated these ceremonies. Although in Cambodia marriages are often arranged by the parents, it is now common for Cambodian American young people to choose their own partners through the wider American practice of dating. The bride in a Cambodian wedding wears a *sampot*, an

holiday celebrations. Several Cambodian temples in North America offer meditation classes in English for the benefit of non-Cambodians.

Philanthropy Cambodian mutual assistance associations were established in many locations with substantial Cambodian populations during the 1980s. These generally provided help with family problems, homeless prevention, care for the elderly, translation, preparation for citizenship, and general issues of adaptation. Cambodian Buddhist temples regularly engage in philanthropic and charitable activities.

The Devata Giving Circle, an organization of Cambodian American women dedicated to raising funds to help Cambodian American girls and women, was founded in 2010. The group provided grants to community organizations dedicated to advancing the rights and opportunities of Cambodian American women.

Surnames In the United States and Europe, surnames (or family names) follow given names. Traditionally, the order is the opposite for Cambodians, with the surname first and the family name second. Cambodian Americans frequently conform to the Western practice, though. Most Cambodian family names have a single syllable. These names are numerous, but some of the most common are Chea, Lim, and Sy.

EMPLOYMENT AND ECONOMIC CONDITIONS

Adapting to the American economy was difficult for many people of Cambodian ancestry who arrived in the United States during the 1980s. Most had been farmers in their previous country, and in the United States they were generally settled in cities. Cambodian refugees had high rates of unemployment, and the jobs found by first-generation Cambodian Americans were most often low-paying jobs in service and manual labor occupations. As Cambodian Americans became a more established part of the American economy, though, they achieved substantial upward mobility, although they still tended to be concentrated in blue-collar types of employment.

By 2011, according to the American Community Survey, Cambodian Americans who were in the labor force had an unemployment rate of only about 6 percent among those aged between twenty-five and sixty-five who were not in some form of schooling. This was lower than the general American unemployment rate of 8.6 percent in that year. Cambodian American workers tended to be concentrated in semiskilled and skilled blue collar occupations. Their most common jobs, according to 2011 estimates, were assemblers of electrical equipment, machine operators, cashiers, supervisors and proprietors of sales jobs, nursing aides and orderlies, hairdressers and cosmetologists, truck drivers, and janitors. These jobs were held by about one-third of Cambodian American workers.

Cambodian Americans in the early twenty-first century were not members of a wealthy group, but they were substantially better off than the first arrivals from Cambodia. In 1990 an estimated 42 percent of families of Cambodian ethnicity were living below the poverty level; according to 2011 U.S. Census estimates, about 20 percent of all Cambodian Americans lived below the poverty level. This was somewhat higher than the poverty rate for all Americans (16 percent), but significantly lower than the poverty rate for African Americans.

The median household income of Cambodian Americans in 1990 was only $18,837, compared to $30,056 for Americans in general. By 2011, though, the median household income of Cambodian Americans was $60,000, compared to just over $50,000 for Americans in general (according to the American Community Survey). This comparatively high income level was probably due to the low unemployment rate of Cambodian Americans, to their having multiple workers per family, and to their concentration on the West Coast, a geographic region that generally had higher incomes and higher costs of living than the rest of the country.

POLITICS AND GOVERNMENT

Over the first decades after their arrival, most Cambodian Americans were concerned with questions of survival in the new country. They were not actively involved in U.S. politics but remained keenly interested in the reconstruction of their native country. Some Cambodian American organizations, such as the Cambodian Network Council, contributed to the rebuilding of Cambodia by sending trained Cambodian Americans and others to Cambodia as volunteers.

By 2013 most Cambodian Americans were U.S. citizens, by birth or naturalization, and involvement in American politics and government had become more common. In 2010 Massachusetts businessman Sam Meas, a Republican, became the first Cambodian American to run for U.S. Congress.

NOTABLE INDIVIDUALS

Journalism Dith Pran, the subject of the film *The Killing Fields*, worked as an assistant and interpreter for *New York Times* correspondent Sydney Schanberg in Cambodia. After Pran's family escaped from Cambodia on the eve of the Khmer Rouge takeover in 1975, Pran stayed behind to help save Schanberg and other journalists from execution. Although Western journalists were able to leave, Pran was trapped in Cambodia. In 1979 he escaped to Thailand, where he reunited with Schanberg. In the United States he continued to work as a photographer and journalist. His book of interviews with Khmer Rouge survivors, entitled *Children of Cambodia's Killing Fields: Memoirs by Survivors*, was published in 1997. Dith Pran died of cancer in New Jersey in 2008.

Music Sam-Ang Sam is a scholar, musician, and activist born in Pursat Province in Cambodia in 1950. He studied music at the University of Fine Arts in

Phnom Penh and afterward continued his studies in the United States, where he received a PhD in ethnomusicology from Wesleyan University. He served on the faculty at the University of Washington in Seattle until becoming director of the Cambodian Network Council (later the Cambodian American National Council) in Washington, D.C. He traveled around the world performing and teaching about Cambodian music. Chinary Ung (1942–) is a composer and professor of music at the University of California, San Diego. As a musician, Ung specializes in playing the *roneat ek* (Cambodian xylophone). He was principal curator for the 2013 Season of Cambodia Festival.

Politics Sam Meas, Massachusetts businessman and politician, was born in Kandal Province of Cambodia between 1970 and 1972. In 2010 he became the first Cambodian American to run for the U.S. House of Representatives, in an unsuccessful campaign. Two years later he ran unsuccessfully for the Massachusetts state senate. Sichan Siv, American diplomat and author, escaped from Cambodia in 1976. He served as U.S. deputy assistant secretary of state from 1989 to 1993. Siv was appointed ambassador to the United Nations by President George W. Bush in 2001 and served until 2006. In 2009 he published *Golden Bones*, his memoir of life under the Khmer Rouge and his new beginning in the United States.

Stage and Screen Haing Ngor (1940–1996), actor, physician, and author, is among the most famous Cambodian Americans, best known for his Oscar-winning portrayal of the Cambodian interpreter and journalist Dith Pran in the film *The Killing Fields* (1984). Born in rural Cambodia, he worked his way through medical school and became an obstetrician and surgeon in Phnom Penh. After the Khmer Rouge takeover in 1975, his family was killed by execution squads. He escaped to Thailand in 1979 and came to the United States in 1980. Besides having a successful acting career, he headed six organizations devoted to caring for Southeast Asian refugees and resettling them in the West. In 1996 he was murdered outside his home in Los Angeles.

Soben Huon, from Los Angeles, is part of a new generation of Cambodian Americans. Born in 1983, she attended Brigham Young University in Utah. A Cambodian classical dancer, Ms. Huon became the first non-white contestant to win the title of Miss Utah in the Miss USA contest of 2006.

MEDIA

Cambodian Radio Broadcast (106.3 KALI FM)

Radio broadcast in Khmer language on Sundays, in the Long Beach area.

The Khmer Post Media Center

Online source for Cambodian language radio, video, and other media.

P.O. Box 4073
Long Beach, California 92896
Phone: (562) 728-8972
Email: Sovannara@TheKhmerPost.com
URL: www.thekhmerpost.com

ORGANIZATIONS AND ASSOCIATIONS

Cambodian American Resource Agency (CARA)

An umbrella group that brings together volunteer organizations to provide support for community-based events involving Cambodian Americans.

Philip Lim, President
Email: info@caraweb.org
URL: www.caraweb.org

Cambodian Association of America (CAA)

Established in 1975 to help new arrivals, the CAA today provides education outreach and social programs to both Cambodians and non-Cambodians.

2390 Pacific Avenue
Long Beach, California 90806
Phone: (562) 988-1863
Fax: (562) 988-1475
URL: www.cambodianusa.com

Cambodian Family

Serves Cambodian Americans in the Santa Ana, California, area. Offers English-language training to Cambodian refugees and immigrants, provides help in finding employment, gives classes in health education and parenting skills. Also offers programs for Cambodian American youth, including a gang-prevention program, after-school classes, and Cambodian-language classes.

Sundaram Rama, Executive Director
1626 E. Fourth Street
Santa Ana, California 92701
Phone: (714) 571-1966
Fax: (714) 571-1974
URL: http://cambodianfamily.org

The Cambodian American Heritage, Inc.

An organization founded in 1980 to preserve Cambodian arts and culture in the United States. The centerpiece of the organization's work is its classical dance troupe and music ensemble.

129 Canoe Court
Fort Washington, Maryland 20744
Phone: (301) 292-6862
URL: www.cambodianheritage.org

MUSEUMS AND RESEARCH CENTERS

Cambodian American Heritage Museum and Killing Fields Memorial

Museum devoted to raising awareness of the Cambodian genocide and to celebrating the heritage and renewal of the Cambodian American community.

2831 W. Lawrence Avenue
Chicago, Illinois 60625
Phone: (773) 878-7090

Khmer Art Gallery

A Philadelphia gallery specializing in Cambodian art that displays both traditional and contemporary works in a variety of media.

319 North 11th Street
Philadelphia, Pennsylvania 19107
Phone: (215) 922-5600
Email: info@khmerartgallery.com
URL: www.khmerartgallery.com/index2.html

Southeast Asian Resource Action Center (SEARAC)

A national organization that advances the interests of Cambodian, Laotian, and Vietnamese Americans. The organization's resource center is one of the best sources of information on these groups.

1626 16th Street NW
Washington, D.C. 20009
Phone: (202) 667-4690
Email: searac@searac.org
URL: www.searac.org/content/
publications-and-materials

SOURCES FOR ADDITIONAL STUDY

Bankston, Carl L. III, and Danielle Antoinette Hidalgo. "Southeast Asia: Laos, Cambodia, and Thailand." In *The New Americans: A Guide to Immigration Since 1965*, edited by Mary Waters and Reed Ueda, 624–640. Cambridge: Harvard University Press, 2007.

———. "Temple and Society in the New World: Theravada Buddhism in North America." In *North American Buddhism: Social Scientific Perspectives*, edited by Paul D. Numrich, 51–86. New York: Brill Publishers, 2008.

———. "The Waves of War: Immigrants, Refugees, and New Americans from Southeast Asia." In *Contemporary Asian America*, 2nd edition, edited by Min Zhou and James V. Gatewood, 139–157. New York: NYU Press, 2000.

Chan, Sucheng. *Survivors: Cambodian Refugees in the United States*. Urbana, IL: University of Illinois Press, 2004.

Criddle, Joan D., and Teeda Butt Mam. *To Destroy You Is No Loss: The Odyssey of a Cambodian Family*. New York: Atlantic Monthly Press, 1987.

Das, Mitra. *Between Two Cultures: The Case of Cambodian Women in the United States*. New York: Peter Lang, 2007.

Hein, Jeremy. *Ethnic Origins: The Adaptation of Cambodian and Hmong Refugees in Four American Cities*. New York: Russell Sage Foundation, 2006.

May, Someth. *Cambodian Witness: The Autobiography of Someth May*. Edited by James Fenton. New York: Random House, 1987.

Tal, Kali, ed. *Southeast Asian-American Communities*. Woodbridge, CT: Viet Nam Generation, 1992.

Yimsut, Ronnie. *Facing the Khmer Rouge: A Cambodian Journey*. New Brunswick, NJ: Rutgers University Press, 2011.

CANADIAN AMERICANS

Marianne P. Fedunkiw

OVERVIEW

Canadian Americans are immigrants or descendants of people from Canada, a country in North America that lies to the north of the United States. Canada is surrounded on three sides by oceans: the Pacific to the west, the Arctic to the north, and the Atlantic to the east. It is the largest country in the Western Hemisphere, covering 3,849,674 square miles (9,970,610 square kilometers), including both land and freshwater areas. This is about the size of the United States plus another Montana. Its southern border with the United States, which stretches 5,525 miles (8,892 kilometers), is the longest undefended border in the world.

According to an estimate in the *CIA World Factbook*, the population of Canada was 34,300,083 in 2012. Despite Canada's large area, most of the country is frigid, uninhabited wilderness, and much of the population lives within 100 miles (160 kilometers) of the U.S. border. Approximately 60 percent of Canadians lived in urban centers, particularly in the southeastern region between Windsor, Ontario, and Quebec City, Quebec. The largest cities are Toronto, with a population of 5.7 million (about 2.5 million less than New York City), followed by Montreal, with 3.75 million (about the same as Los Angeles), and Vancouver, with 2.1 million (about the same as Chicago). More than 42 percent of Canadians are Roman Catholic, just over 27 percent are Protestant or other Christian faith, and the remainder are Muslim, unspecified, or claim no religious affiliation. Since World War II, Canada has transformed itself from a rural economy to an urban one. The economy of Canada is similar to that of the United States; it is based on high-tech jobs, manufacturing, mining, and service-sector jobs.

Although there has always been a flow of people between Canada and the United States, reliable migration data has only been kept since the 1910 U.S. Census. Migration is also somewhat seasonal: the Canadian population in the United States swells in the winter months, when many so-called snowbirds retreat from the harsh Canadian winter to the warmer climate of the Southern United States.

According to the 2010 U.S. Census, there were 704,562 people of Canadian descent living full-time in the United States—fewer people than the total population of the state of Alaska. Canadians spending the winter months in the United States tend to settle in Florida, Arizona, Texas, and Southern California.

HISTORY OF THE PEOPLE

Early History The first European explorers to visit North America are thought to be the Vikings in around 1000 CE. Some believe that there were earlier visitors to Canada, including Celtic monks fleeing the Viking invasions of the British Isles and perhaps even voyagers from Africa. Such visitors would have found a harsh, cold land occupied by often hostile native peoples. As a result, few early explorers survived or stayed long in Canada.

By the early 1500s, parts of North America were being claimed for various European thrones. Many French explorers traveled to Canada seeking a northern route to the Far East. By the 1670s the burgeoning fur trade led to the founding of the Hudson Bay Company, which is still in operation today. Settlement was not easy in the seventeenth century. By 1663 there were only twenty-five hundred French settlers, most of whom were clustered around Montreal, Quebec City, and Trois Rivières (Three Rivers), the latter being about halfway between the former two. Vicious battles took place between the French settlers and the native Iroquois, and many of the European colonies were all but destroyed. In fact, relationships with indigenous peoples often determined the pace of settlement. Jesuit missionaries, who were sent to the new land to help colonize and convert the natives to Christianity, met with considerable opposition, for example, and in many cases missions were destroyed and missionaries killed.

By 1713 the population of New France, as the Canadian colony was called, numbered fewer than twenty thousand, compared with some four hundred thousand English, Scots, and Irish settlers in the Atlantic coastal areas. The French and English began fighting over the Canadian lands, particularly the valuable beaver country around Hudson and James Bays, as well as over regions of what is today the Northeastern United States.

The French lost the Seven Years' War (also known as the French and Indian War) to the British. On February 10, 1763, France signed the Treaty of

Paris, giving Britain control over all of North America except for the Louisiana Territory, which France ceded to Spain. All that was left for France were the small islands of St. Pierre and Miquelon, off the southern coast of Newfoundland, which are still French possessions today.

Many early ties linked the areas that would become Canadian territory with those that, after 1776, would become American states. At its zenith, British Canada included not only present-day Canadian territory but also the American states of Illinois, Indiana, Michigan, Ohio, and Wisconsin. In fact, after the British conquest of New France, the "Canadian" colonies had to decide whether they wished to join the Thirteen Colonies in the latters' bid for independence or remain within the British Empire. Newfoundland, Prince Edward Island, and Quebec opted relatively quickly to remain with Britain, while Nova Scotia deliberated longer—probably because in 1776, almost two-thirds of Nova Scotia's population consisted of New England immigrants with strong ties to the American colonies. In the end, however, Nova Scotia decided to stay with Great Britain, too, rather than become the fourteenth state of the Union. American invaders did try to take part of Canada from the British in December 1775, when forces led by Benedict Arnold and Richard Montgomery unsuccessfully attacked Quebec. Furthermore, those Americans who supported British rule—the United Empire Loyalists—found refuge in Ontario and the Atlantic provinces in the later eighteenth century.

The new British rule and pressure from the revolutionaries in the Thirteen Colonies did not make for a harmonious meld of lands and peoples in Canada. Concessions were made, however, to keep Quebec in the British Empire. The Quebec Act of 1774 returned to the French Canadians their civil law based on the Napoleonic Code (still applicable today) and the freedom to practice the Roman Catholic religion. To further accommodate both French and British interests, the Constitutional Act of 1791 allowed for two separate elective legislative assemblies within the distinct provinces of Upper Canada (the largely British area to the west of the Ottawa River) and Lower Canada (present-day Quebec).

Tension between the French and English was not confined to the east, however. When the Canadian government acquired western lands from the Hudson Bay Company in 1869, Louis Riel led a group of Métis settlers in protest. The Métis, who were part European and part Native American (called *mestizos* in Spanish America), feared that the encroachment of other settlers would mean the loss of their freedom and identity.

In addition to the Loyalists fleeing the American Revolution, American farmers began entering Canada in search of cheaper land. By 1812 about 60 percent of the population of Upper Canada comprised non-Loyalist colonists from the United States. Loyalists and British made up the remaining 40 percent in about even proportions.

The most significant relationship with Americans in the early nineteenth century, however, was one of war. Many Americans believed that the British were supporting Indian attacks on the United States, while other Americans, such as the expansionist "war hawks," favored going to war to seize Upper Canada for the United States. Americans also resented Britain's imposition of a naval blockade on France, which hampered American trade with France, and Britain's seizure of thousands of British sailors on American ships, whom the British deemed deserters. As a result of these mounting tensions, American president James Madison declared war on Britain on June 1, 1812.

The War of 1812 went poorly for the Americans because they mistakenly concentrated their initial efforts on taking the eastern part of Upper Canada, including the Detroit and Niagara Rivers. The Americans believed they would be welcomed by their compatriots who had moved to Canada, but they were wrong. The Americans lost not only Detroit, but all of the American territory west of Lake Erie to General Isaac Brock's troops and his ally, the famed Shawnee chief Tecumseh. The battles of the War of 1812 continued well into 1814, with both sides making advances, but victory was on the side of the British more often. In fact, in August 1814, the British advanced as far south as Washington, D.C., burning down the Capitol and President's House in the process.

In the end, the war changed little in terms of boundaries or national possessions. But ideologically, the war fostered anti-American sentiments and corresponding loyalty to the colony itself—making the settlers view themselves as neither Loyalists nor British but Upper Canadians.

The 1830s was a decade of discontent in both Lower and Upper Canada, which culminated in the rebellions of 1837. Although relatively few people participated in the actual uprisings, the conflicts set the stage for changes in government that led to confederation in 1867. On July 1, 1867, Nova Scotia, New Brunswick, and Lower and Upper Canada joined together to form the Dominion of Canada.

Another major development in the relationship between Canada and the United States that helped propel Canada to independence centered around the American Civil War. Canada quickly opposed the war, particularly the thought of the South's winning (although many Americans believed that the British supported the South, which supplied Britain's cotton and tobacco), and hostilities between the two countries grew. The situation grew worse when many American slaves fled to freedom in Canada via the Underground Railroad and when the so-called Fenian Brotherhood—anti-British Irish Americans—attacked the Canadian village of Fort Erie in southern Ontario in the summer of 1866. The fear of annexation by the United States eventually led Canadians to forge the British North America Act in 1867, which established the Dominion of Canada. The first prime minister of Canada was Sir John A. Macdonald.

Although the western prairies and outlying parts of Ontario and Quebec—then a huge area called Rupert's Land—were not part of the confederation, the same fear of an American takeover of these lands led to an expansion of the railroad to the west, followed by an influx of settlers westward. Manitoba joined Canada as a province in 1870, followed by British Columbia in 1871, the Yukon Territory in 1898, and Alberta, Saskatchewan, and the Northwest Territories in 1905.

As for the remaining provinces, Prince Edward Island joined in 1873, and Newfoundland, the last, joined in 1949 as the province of Newfoundland and Labrador. This reluctance to officially become part of Canada perhaps explains why many Newfoundlanders who have moved to the United States identify themselves not as Canadian Americans but as "Americans of Newfoundland descent." Finally, in 1999, the eastern half of the Northwest Territories became the new Territory of Nunavut.

Modern Era The twentieth century saw continued tension between French speakers and English speakers in Canada. English-speaking Canada felt strong ties to Britain—it fought on the side of Britain in the South African Boer War (1899–1902), World War I, and World War II. The French-speaking Canadians, however, resented fighting in what they considered to be English wars, and the issue of compulsory military service drove the two groups further apart.

Meanwhile, European and Asian immigrants flowed into Canada. Much of the still-open Canadian West was built up by these new Canadians. The period between the two world wars brought a greater sense of national autonomy. By 1939 English Canadians made up only half of the population of twelve million. Another 30 percent were French, and the rest consisted of Ukrainian, Polish, German, and Scandinavian immigrants. When the Second World War began, Canada made its own decision to take part, going to battle on September 10, 1939.

The years following World War II were ones of prosperity in Canada, particularly compared with those preceding the war, which saw hardship throughout the country. The 1950s and 1960s saw decreasing trade with Britain and increasing trade with the United States. Canada also achieved greater respect internationally. Lester B. Pearson, Canadian prime minister from 1963 to 1968, won the Nobel Peace Prize in 1957 for his work in the Middle East. Pearson also served as chairman of the North Atlantic Treaty Organization (NATO) in 1951–1952 and as president of the United Nations General Assembly in 1952–1953.

SETTLEMENT IN THE UNITED STATES

Following the British victory in the French and Indian War, the British obtained the province of Canada under the terms of the Treaty of Paris in 1763, thus controlling Canada and the American Colonies. From 1763 until the American Revolution, people moved freely between the two British possessions. Following the American Revolution, some British Loyalists chose to leave the new United States and take up residence in Canada to remain under British rule, and many were granted land in Canada to replace property lost in the revolution. Relatively few Canadians immigrated to the United States in the early years of the new American republic. The eastern end of the border between Canada and the United States was set by the treaty ending the Revolutionary War in 1783 (also called the Treaty of Paris). The western portion of the boundary was settled by the Webster-Ashburton Treaty, negotiated between the two nations in 1842. The number of Canadians moving to the United States has climbed steadily since the 1850s. According to the 1990 report *Migration between the United States and Canada*, migration between the two countries was relatively unrestricted until immigration laws were

Can't you see the freedom in America? That it's not just political? Can't you see American liberty? Can't you see self-reliance and self-expression? That is the American atmosphere. … In America you can do anything you want, live anywhere you want, and, finally, do what it is that you most want to do very easily—perhaps not without what you might consider to be sacrifices, but they're not really sacrifices.

Agnes Martin in 1931, cited in *American Mosaic: The Immigrant Experience in the Words of Those Who Lived It*, edited by Joan Morrison and Charlotte Fox Zabusky (New York: Dutton, 1980).

changed in the United States in 1965 and in Canada in 1976. In the early part of the twentieth century, for example, more than 1.2 million Canadians crossed the border to live in the United States. Interestingly, this was four times the number that moved from the United States to Canada. The decade of the 1920s saw the largest exodus yet, with nearly a million Canadians heading south, primarily to take advantage of the industrial boom in the northeastern and north central states. The number of Canadians in the United States peaked at 1.3 million in 1930, after which the Great Depression and World War II slowed emigration. The flow picked up markedly in the 1950s and early 1960s, however, because of greater job opportunities and higher wages in the United States. From the 1930s to the 1980s, more than 2.3 million Canadians immigrated to the United States, but after changed U.S. immigration laws in the 1960s restricted the flow, the number of Canadian immigrants per year dropped by almost 60 percent.

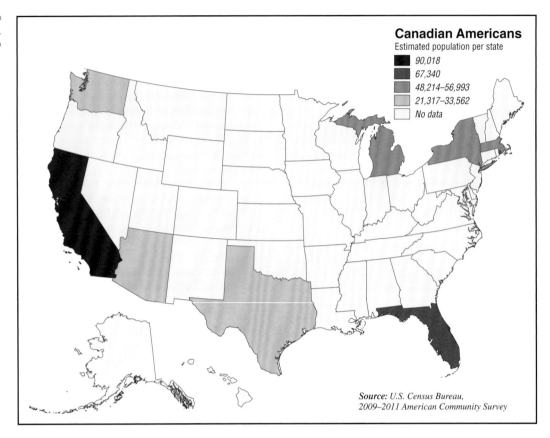

Canadian Americans
Estimated population per state

- 90,018
- 67,340
- 48,214–56,993
- 21,317–33,562
- No data

*Source: U.S. Census Bureau,
2009–2011 American Community Survey*

This decline continued through the 1980s and had a marked effect on U.S. immigration statistics. While in the early 1960s Canadians made up almost 12 percent of total immigrants in the United States, by the early 1980s that number had fallen to just 2 percent. In fact, almost 65 percent of the immigrants listed in the 1980 U.S. census had immigrated before 1960.

During periods when immigration laws were less restrictive, crossing the border from Canada was less an international migration than a movement based on economic influences—just like internal migration. When the laws tightened, the patterns became more controlled and more typical of long-distance international migration, according to *Migration between the United States and Canada*. Demographically, most Canadians who immigrated to the United States before 1960 lived in the northern states, while those who came later tended to live in states farther south. According to the 2010 U.S. Census, Canadian immigrants tend to live in warmer locations such as Florida, California, and Arizona.

LANGUAGE

Canada has two official languages, English and French. These two languages are the mother tongue for nearly 84 percent of Canadians, with 60 percent speaking primarily English and almost 24 percent French. Among other languages used by the rest of the

population are Italian, Chinese, German, Portuguese, Polish, and Ukrainian.

For the majority of Canadians who either speak English solely or another language as well as English, moving to the United States is made easier by the common language. Immigration is often more difficult for Francophones, or French-speaking Canadians, who are classified in Canada as a separate group. Other Canadians who are considered separate groups include Acadians and a number of native groups, among them the Iroquois, Tlingit, and Inuit.

Some Canadians who speak French or another non-English language might continue speaking it after immigrating to the United States, and for some Canadians ancestry is as important as nationality in forming their identity. For example, Canadian immigrants with German ancestry might identify themselves as German Americans rather than the more accurate designation German Canadian Americans.

RELIGION

Religion has been a fundamental of Canadian society since the French and British explorers arrived in the sixteenth century. The first Roman Catholic Mass in Canada was held in 1534, and the first Anglican service took place forty-four years later. The most active churches in Canada, according to recent figures, are the Roman Catholic and Anglican, although there is also strong representation by the United Church of

Canada, Judaism, Islam, Evangelical Lutheranism, and various Pentecostal faiths. Protestant Canadians who immigrate to the United States encounter certain differences in the names of their denominations; for example, Canadian Anglicans would most closely resemble American Episcopalians. Due to the similarities in religion in the United States and Canada, there are few issues for immigrants concerning religion. Most immigrants simply carry on their religious traditions in what could be referred to as sister churches in the United States.

CULTURE AND ASSIMILATION

Unlike most other immigrant groups, there is almost no language barrier separating English-speaking Canadians and Americans. This is one reason why assimilation is relatively easy. Another factor is that the two countries are close neighbors, so many traditions and customs have crossed boundaries and become familiar to both. Migration between the United States and Canada states that "the ease with which Canadian and United States immigrants are assimilated is evident from the large population of naturalized U.S. citizens among Canadian-born immigrants. … In both countries, more than 80 percent of the immigrants prior to 1980 have become naturalized citizens of the destination country."

English-speaking Canadians who moved to the United States also enjoyed the benefit of settling relatively close to their home country. Unlike immigrants from European, Asian, or African countries, Canadians could visit relatives and readily receive news from Canada via newspapers, radio, or television. Unless they had recent ethnic ties to a country that was their home before Canada, assimilation was largely a smooth procedure. Aside from an abiding interest in all things British that is held by some Canadians, traditions tended to be more generally North American than distinctively different. The media play a large role in this cultural mixing: most of Canada's population is concentrated in a thin band close to the American border, well within the range of American radio and television broadcasts, so many Canadian immigrants can still hear and see familiar programs and events.

Because of the many similarities between Canadians and Americans, common stereotypes either portray Canada as just another state or exaggerate the differences that do exist. An example of the former is an American referring to the provinces as "states," the prime minister as "the president of Canada," or Parliament or the House of Commons as "Congress" or "the Senate." Another misconception is that, because Canadian nationalism historically was built upon a wariness of American control, Canadians moving to the United States would be concerned about this issue. Therefore, the type of individual most likely to make the move would prefer American culture and want to assimilate into it. The stereotype that exaggerates differences often centers on weather, culture, and common

pastimes. Some people envision all of Canada as a land of igloos and ice, where everyone is French Canadian (or at least fully bilingual) and plays ice hockey.

The main sources of these stereotypes are television and cinema. For example, Second City Television (SCTV) in the United States in the 1970s and early 1980s produced comedy sketches and even a movie featuring beer-swilling, flannel-attired Canadian brothers Bob and Doug Mackenzie, who spoke in an exaggerated Canadian accent and ended most sentences with "eh?" Another more passive source of stereotypes is simply an incomplete knowledge of the vast and diverse country that is the northern neighbor of the United States. It would be difficult to describe the Maritimes, the Prairies, northern Ontario or Quebec, and British Columbia (not to mention mostly Inuit Nunavut) using the same words.

Differences between Canadians and Americans, though not easy to explain, do exist. In the *New York Times*, for example, Canadian nationalist and novelist Robertson Davies discusses basic differences in the underlying myths upon which each country was built:

> The myth of America is a very powerful one and one that we in Canada look toward with envy. You have your heroes. You have your great men of the past, you have your myth of tradition, of the conquering of the West, and the pioneer life and the gold rush life and all that sort of thing, which is enormously romantic, and nations feed on the romantic tradition. … [Canadians] don't go for heroes. As soon as a man begins to achieve some sort of high stature, we want to cut him down and get rid of him, embarrass him. (December 15, 1994).

Cuisine The cuisine of immigrants from Canada is influenced by the region where they grew up and the area of the United States where they moved. For example, Canadians from the Atlantic provinces (Newfoundland and Labrador, New Brunswick, Nova Scotia, and Prince Edward Island) and coastal British Columbia include a hearty amount of seafood in their diets, and this preference would not change if they immigrated to a seaboard state. A common, inexpensive dish from Quebec is poutine, a mixture of fries, cheese curds, and gravy.

Other dietary practices by immigrants from Canada are rooted in ethnic origins. Ethnocultural groups such as the Mennonites and Jews, for instance, maintain an ethnic cuisine as part of their identity.

Holidays Canadians and Americans share many of the same national holidays, although they are not always celebrated on the same days. For example, while Americans celebrate the birth of their nation on July 4, Canadians celebrate Canada Day on July 1. Both countries observe a Thanksgiving holiday, although in Canada it falls on the first Monday of October rather than on the third Thursday in November. In addition, there are Canadian provincial holidays that differ from province to province, as well as other ethnocultural holidays that citizens of either country may observe.

Health Care Issues and Practices There are no documented health problems or medical conditions specific to Canadian Americans. Recent Canadian immigrants to the United States must make a transition, however, from government-controlled health care to a private system. Canada's public health system has been in place since the 1960s, and by comparison the cost of staying healthy in the United States seems steep to Canadian Americans. In Canada, workers or employers pay a special tax to the provincial government, which in turn pays for most medical services, up to an agreed-upon limit. Most health care practitioners are self-employed and bill the provincial government directly for their services.

Canadians in Canada or in the United States have access to sophisticated medical treatment using leading-edge technology. Some Canadian physicians, however, have become disenchanted with increasing levels of government control over medicine in Canada and have moved to the United States to practice.

FAMILY AND COMMUNITY LIFE

Canada prides itself upon its multiculturalism, and its diversity supplies a context for any discussion of family and community dynamics. An Italian Canadian who moves to the United States, for example, might maintain the customs, language, and community dynamics of his or her Italian origins. Defining such a person as just Canadian would obscure those traditions. Other factors, such as cuisine, traditional clothing, and special events, can differ significantly on the basis of not only ethnic background but also the region of Canada from which an individual came.

Gender Roles Gender roles in Canada have undergone, and continue to undergo, significant changes. Traditionally Canadian women were primarily homemakers and bore the bulk of the child-rearing responsibilities. These roles were very similar to those found in the United States at the same time. According to a 2008 article on the website Canada.com titled "Gender Roles around the House Are Changing," Canadian men were beginning to be more involved in household chores such as cleaning and childcare, and 56 percent of men took at least partial responsibility for grocery shopping. There has also been a significant rise in the number of Canadian women who obtain advanced degrees, find high-paying jobs, and become the primary breadwinners. These trends are mirrored in the United States among immigrants from Canada and among Americans in general.

Education Compared with Canadians in general, Canadians who move to the United States, both men and women, have higher educational levels. According to the 2010 U.S. Census, 20.03 percent of Canadian Americans held a university degree.

In Canada there are few appreciable differences in the education of boys and girls, although some differences do exist at higher educational levels. For example, the number of female graduates of undergraduate university programs in Canada was greater than that of males from 1990 to 2010, although slightly more men than women went on to complete master's and doctoral degrees.

EMPLOYMENT AND ECONOMIC CONDITIONS

In the early twentieth century, hundreds of thousands of Canadians sought manufacturing jobs in booming American industries. In the early twenty-first century 60 percent of Canadian Americans worked in highly skilled, white collar jobs, ranging from clerical to executive administrative, a figure higher than average in the United States.

POLITICS AND GOVERNMENT

Over the years Canadian Americans have initiated little conflict within the United States, and few Canadian Americans have become involved in American politics. One exception is Jerry Simpson (1842–1905), a Populist Party representative who served three terms in Congress. Born in Westmoreland County, New Brunswick, Simpson was a self-educated man who began his career as a cook on a Great Lakes boat at age fourteen and rose to become captain. He established a farm and ranch in Kansas before entering politics.

Canadians have a strong presence in both national labor organizations (such as the Canadian Labour Congress and Canadian National Federation of Independent Unions) and international trade unions with local chapters in both Canada and the United States. Some of the international trade unions with the largest Canadian participation are the United Steelworkers of America, with 875 locals in Canada; the United Food and Commercial Workers International Union, with 175 locals in Canada; the International Association of Machinists and Aerospace Workers, with 152 lodges in Canada; and the International Brotherhood of Electrical Workers, with 121 locals in Canada.

Because Canadians tend to assimilate thoroughly into American life, it is difficult to identify group patterns in activities such as voting and participation in the armed forces. One major difference that Canadian immigrants would encounter in U.S. politics is the dominance of just two political parties. In Canada there are three national political parties, the Progressive Conservatives, the Liberals, and the New Democratic Party. In different provinces there are also other strong parties, such as the Social Democrats or Parti Québecois.

Canadian Americans' quick rate of assimilation also affects their level of participation in the political issues of their home country. Although the English-language media in border states and the

English-language, Canadian-targeted seasonal newspapers in states such as Florida and Arizona do well in presenting current Canadian events, geographical distance often leads to a sense of isolation or non-involvement. Coupled with the many similarities between Americans and Canadians, achieving a distinct sense of identity becomes a challenge for immigrant Canadians—if such is even desired. Groups such as French Canadians, who are already individualized by their separate language, culture, and long history in the United States, are better able to maintain their identity and ties to Canada. For example, this group would be very aware of the latest struggles for French independence in Canada and the rise of the separatist Parti Québecois and Bloc Québecois.

NOTABLE INDIVIDUALS

Academia Perhaps the most notable Canadian American academic is economist John Kenneth Galbraith (1908–2006), born in Iona Station, Ontario. After completing his bachelor's degree in Ontario, he went to California to pursue graduate studies. He was a professional economist from 1949 to 1975 and held a number of teaching positions in North America and Europe. His many books include *American Capitalism* (1952), *The Great Crash* (1955), and *A Short History of Financial Euphoria* (1993). He received the Medal of Freedom in 1946 for his contributions to American economics.

English professor Margaret Anne Doody (1939–), born in St. John, New Brunswick, came to the United States in 1976 as an associate professor at the University of California–Berkeley and went on to teach at Vanderbilt University in Nashville and the University of Notre Dame. She is the author of a number of books on eighteenth-century British novelist Samuel Richardson and his writings.

Film, Television, and Theater Mary Pickford (1893–1979), "America's Sweetheart," was Canadian by birth. Born Gladys Mary Smith in Toronto, she starred in silent-screen versions of *Rebecca of Sunnybrook Farm, Tess of the Storm Country*, and *Coquette*, for which she won an Oscar. She became an early pioneer of film in the United States, organizing the Mary Pickford Corporation in 1916 to produce her work and in 1919 joining Charlie Chaplin, D. W. Griffith, and husband-to-be Douglas Fairbanks to establish United Artists Company.

Another Canadian-born actor was Glenn Ford (1916–2006), originally Gwyllyn Samuel Newton Ford. Born in Quebec City, he attended high school in Santa Monica, California, and served with the United States Marines Corps during World War II. His many films include *Destroyer* (1943), *Cimarron* (1961), and *Superman* (1978). In 1958 he was named "Number One Box Office Star in America" in a poll by the *Motion Picture Herald*.

Film star Donald Sutherland (1935–) was born in St. John, New Brunswick. His films include *M*A*S*H* (1970), *Ordinary People* (1980), and *The Hunger Games* (2012).

Canadian American comedian Phil Hartman (1948–1998) was beloved by many fans and mourned after his untimely death. LYNN GOLDSMITH / CORBIS

One of the best-known Canadian names in television was that of Lorne Greene (1915–1987). Born in Ottawa, Ontario, he made his American debut on the New York stage in 1953. Among his many credits of stage, screen, and television are the movies *Peyton Place* (1957) and *Earthquake* (1974) and the television Western series *Bonanza* (1959–1973), in which he played the patriarch of the Ponderosa Ranch, Ben Cartwright.

Born in New Westminster, British Columbia, Raymond Burr (1917–1993) is perhaps best known for his title role on the television series *Perry Mason* (1957–1966). He also had the title role in the series *Ironside* from 1967 to 1975.

Another recognizable Canadian face on television and in film is William Shatner (1931–). The Montreal native has appeared on Broadway but is famous for his role as Captain James T. Kirk of the Starship *Enterprise* in the television series *Star Trek* (1966–1969) and subsequent *Star Trek* movies. Shatner followed this success with a leading role in the police series *T. J. Hooker* in the 1980s and again in the dramedy series *Boston Legal* from 2004 to 2008. He also wrote a series of science fiction novels beginning in 1989 that were adapted for television as *TekWar*.

Two younger Canadian-born actors well known for their television work are Michael J. Fox and Jason Priestley. Fox (1961–) was born in Vancouver, British Columbia. He received two Emmy Awards for his starring role in the television sitcom *Family Ties* (1982–1989) and in the late nineties starred in the sitcom *Spin City*. He has also appeared in films such as *Back to the Future* (1985) and *The Secret of My*

Success (1987). Fox works much of the time for his foundation that seeks to find a cure for Parkinson's disease, a neurological disease with which he was diagnosed in 1991. Priestley, also born in Vancouver, is best known as a leading actor in the television series *Beverly Hills 90210.*

Another Canadian American film and TV star is Jim Carrey. Carrey, an actor, comedian, and producer, has won four Golden Globe Awards and is known for his roles, for example, in the Ace Ventura movies, *Dumb and Dumber*, and *How the Grinch Stole Christmas.*

A Hollywood's hearthrob, Ryan Reynolds was born in Canada in 1976. He is best known for his role as the DC Comics superhero the Green Lantern in the 2011 movie of that name and in romantic comedies such as *The Proposal.*

A group of Canadian-born comedians have found success in the United States on the television comedy series *Saturday Night Live.* Mike Myers (1963–), born in Toronto, went on to star in the movie *Wayne's World* and as secret agent Austin Powers, as well as providing the voice for the animated ogre Shrek. Dan Aykroyd (1952–), born in Ottawa, was a star and screenwriter for the *Blues Brothers* films (1980 and 1998) and also appeared in the first two *Ghostbusters* movies (1984 and 1986), as well as in *Driving Miss Daisy* (1989).

Among those Canadian Americans who often appeared on the Broadway stage (as well as in movies and TV) are Hume Cronyn, Colleen Dewhurst, and Christopher Plummer. Actor, writer, and director Hume Cronyn (1911–2003) was born in London, Ontario, and came to the United States in 1932. He starred in countless plays—many of them with his wife, actress Jessica Tandy—including the 1978 Pulitzer Prize–winning *The Gin Game.* Cronyn was named to the Theatre Hall of Fame (1979) and Kennedy Center Honors (1986) in addition to receiving a Tony Award in 1964 and an Emmy Award in 1992. His films include *Lifeboat* (1944), *The Postman Always Rings Twice* (1946), and *Cocoon* (1985). Colleen Dewhurst (1926–1991) was born in Montreal, Quebec. Her Broadway appearances included *Desire under the Elms* (1952), *Camille* (1956), *All the Way Home* (1960), and *Moon for the Misbegotten* (1974)—the latter two earning her Tony Awards. She also directed plays and appeared in a number of films and television movies, including the 1986 miniseries *Anne of Green Gables.* She played a guest role as Murphy Brown's mother in the television series *Murphy Brown.* Her second husband was actor George C. Scott. Christopher Plummer (1929–) was born in Toronto and made his Broadway debut in 1954 in *Starcross Story.* Although he has done considerable stage work, particularly in the Shakespearean classics, he is best known for his role as Captain von Trapp in the 1965 Academy Award–winning movie *The Sound of Music.* He has

appeared in many television dramas, including the miniseries *The Thorn Birds* (1983), and has received many awards, among them a Theatre World Award (1955), two Drama Desk Awards (1973 and 1982), a Tony Award (1974), and an Emmy Award (1977). In 2012 he became the oldest actor to receive an Oscar, which he won for his lead role in the movie *Beginners.*

Journalism Television anchorman Peter Jennings (1938–2005) was born in Toronto, Ontario, and began his career in Canada, later moving to ABC News in New York City in 1964. From 1983 to 2005 he was senior editor and anchorman of ABC's *World News Tonight.* He was named Best Anchor in the United States by the *Washington Journalism Review* in 1988 and 1989.

Another Canadian American broadcast journalist, Robert (Robin) MacNeil (1931–) was born in Montreal. After studying in Canada, he became a Washington correspondent in 1963. In 1975 he served as executive editor and coanchor of the *MacNeil/Lehrer Report* on WNET-TV in New York City, and from 1983 to his retirement in 1995, he hosted the *MacNeil/Lehrer News Hour* on PBS.

Music Many Canadians continue to live in Canada while working in the United States, but singer/songwriter Paul Anka (1941–) moved to the United States soon after achieving success. Born in Ottawa, Ontario, Anka first made a hit with the song "Diana," composed in 1957. He followed it in 1959—the same year he moved to the United States—with the popular songs "Put Your Head on My Shoulder," "Crazy Love," "Lonely Boy," and "Time to Cry;" Anka also composed the theme music for *The Tonight Show Starring Johnny Carson* and penned the English-language lyrics to "My Way" (originally a French song), made famous by Frank Sinatra. He has received twenty-two songwriting awards—eighteen for most-performed songs and four for songs performed more than one million times—and fifteen gold records.

Born in Fort Macleod, Alberta, singer/songwriter Joni Mitchell (1943–) first captured attention in the United States with "Chelsea Morning" (1962). She won a Grammy Award for her album *Clouds* (1969) and a lifetime Grammy in 2002.

Science and Technology Physicist Richard Edward Taylor (1929–) was born in Medicine Hat, Alberta, and was one of three recipients of the Nobel Prize for Physics in 1990 for his work in demonstrating that protons and neutrons are made up of quarks. Taylor moved to the United States in 1952.

Orthopedic surgeon and educator John Emmett Hall (1925–) was born in Wadena, Saskatchewan, and became professor of orthopedic surgery at Harvard University Medical School in 1971.

Psychiatrist and educator Charles Shagass (1920–1993) was born in Montreal and came to the United States in 1958. He was a professor at Temple University in Philadelphia, Pennsylvania, for nearly twenty-five years and was considered an expert on brain function.

Sports Canada has given birth to some of the world's greatest athletes—particularly in professional ice hockey. Wayne Gretzky (1961–) was born in Brantford, Ontario, and holds the National Hockey League scoring title in addition to twelve league trophies. After nine years with the Edmonton Oilers, Gretzky moved to Los Angeles in 1988 to play with the Los Angeles Kings. He retired in 1999 as a member of the New York Rangers.

Gretzky's Edmonton teammate Mark Messier (1961–) was born in Edmonton. Beginning in 1991 he starred for the New York Rangers.

Brett Hull (1964–), son of hockey great Bobby Hull, was born in Belleville, Ontario. He began his professional hockey career with the Calgary Flames. From 1987 until 1998 he was a member of the St. Louis Blues, after which he played with the Dallas Stars and the Detroit RedWings. He retired in 2005 while on the roster of the Phoenix Coyotes. He was the recipient of two league trophies (Lady Byng and Hart Memorial) and held the league scoring record for goals scored from 1989 to 1992. He later become an executive for the Dallas Stars and St. Louis Blues.

Swimmer Missy Franklin (1995–), born in California to Canadian parents, debuted at the 2012 Summer Olympics at the age of seventeen and won four gold medals. She became the world record holder for the 200 meter backstroke.

Visual Arts Many Canadian artists, particularly women, have chosen to live in the United States. Henrietta Shore (1880–1963), born in Toronto, began spending half of each year in New York taking classes with the Art Students' League at the age of twenty. She immigrated to California in 1913 and became an American citizen eight years later. Her paintings of landscapes, figures, and abstract works led to a number of major solo exhibitions and a medal in the Panama-Pacific Exposition of 1915.

Agnes Martin (1912–2004) was born in Macklin, Saskatchewan, but grew up in Vancouver, British Columbia. She left for the United States at age twenty and became an American citizen at twenty-eight. She earned a master's degree in fine arts from Columbia University, spent several years painting and teaching children in New York and New Mexico, and lived in a desert hut for six years (1967–1973) in New Mexico, meditating and writing. Primarily an abstract artist, Martin often used grids of pencil or paint on paper or canvas with various textures.

Toronto-born Sylvia Stone (1928–) immigrated to New York in 1945. Stone is known for her sculpture and painted aluminum reliefs. After she married abstract painter Al Held, her paintings became less figurative and more abstract, and she also began to broaden her materials to include aluminum and other metals, plexiglass, and mirrors. Stone has taught at Brooklyn College.

During a naturalization ceremony at Faneuil Hall in Boston, Boston Red Sox left fielder Jason Bay, a native of Canada, takes an oath of citizenship with more than 350 other people in 2009. AP PHOTO / ERIC J. SHELTON

Jacqueline Winsor (1941–) was raised in St. John's, Newfoundland, and became an artist after discovering that a career as a secretary was not for her. She graduated from the Massachusetts College of Art in 1965 and went on to get her master' of fine arts degree from Rutgers University in 1967. After settling in New York, Winsor, an abstract sculptor, experimented with hemp and rope as sculpture media and went on to create boxlike structures of various materials in which the interiors are lit.

Other notable Canadian American artists include Hartwell Wyse Priest (1901–2004), born in Brantford, Ontario; sculptor Mary Abastenia Eberle (1878–1942), who was the daughter of Canadian parents living in Webster City, Iowa; and Canadian-born abstract artist Dorothea Rockburne (1932–).

MEDIA

PRINT

Coverage of Canadian issues is found in American newspapers, especially those in border states.

The American-Canadian Genealogist

Formerly the *Genealogist*, this publication of the American-Canadian Genealogical Society reports on the work of the society, which is devoted to the study of the genealogies of French Canadians and French Americans.

Gerard Savard, President
PO Box 6478
Manchester, New Hampshire 03108-6478
Phone: (603) 622-1554

RADIO

Canadian stations serve as news outlets for Canadian Americans in border states looking for information about their home country. American stations in border states also devote significant coverage to Canadian developments. Some Canadian radio programs are syndicated in the United States.

Canada Calling and *Canada This Week*

These radio programs cover Canadian news events, specifically packaged for Canadian Americans and "snowbirds" in Florida and Arizona. *Canada Calling*, first broadcast in 1952, is a five-and-a-half-minute daily radio news show broadcast on thirty stations in Florida and one station in Phoenix. *Canada This Week* is a fifteen-minute weekly summary of Canadian news events broadcast on Sundays. Both shows are broadcast from Lakefield, Ontario, just northeast of Toronto.

Prior Smith
PO Box 986
Lakefield, Ontario K0L 2H0
Phone: (705) 654-3901

Canadian Broadcasting Corporation (CBC)

As It Happens, Sunday Morning, and *Quirks and Quarks* radio programs are distributed by Public Radio International (PRI). *As It Happens,* a news commentary/documentary program, is fed to twenty-two of the fifty states. Ten cities in Minnesota alone carry the program, including KNOW-FM in St. Paul. *Sunday Morning* is heard in seventeen states, again most frequently in Minnesota but also on stations ranging from West Virginia (WVWV-FM in Huntington) to Alaska (KSKA-AM in Anchorage). The science program *Quirks and Quarks* is distributed by PRI to sixteen states.

Ann Phi, Communication Assistant
Public Radio International
100 North Sixth Street
Suite 900A
Minneapolis, Minnesota 55403
Phone: (612) 338-5000

TELEVISION

CFCF-TV

Canada Pulse News, a half-hour weekly summary of Canadian news, is shown in Florida on WFLX Fox 29 in West Palm Beach and on WTMV 32 in Tampa/St. Petersburg. Produced by CFCF-TV in Montreal, Quebec, its first season was in 1993, and it runs thirteen weeks each year.

George Goulakos, Sales Manager
CFCF-TV
405 Ogilvy Avenue
Montreal, Quebec H3N 1M4
Phone: (514) 495-6100

This Week in Canada

This half-hour program airs weekly in the winter season in select states, including Florida, Maine, Michigan, Nebraska, New York, and Virginia, on the Public Broadcasting System (PBS). It offers a selection of Canadian news events and is produced by World Affairs Television of Montreal, Quebec.

Colin Niven, Producer
World Affairs Television
600 Maisonneuve West
Suite 3230
Montreal, Quebec H3A 3J2
Phone: (514) 847-2970

ORGANIZATIONS AND ASSOCIATIONS

Association for Canadian Studies in the United States (ACSUS)

Founded in 1971, ACSUS has a membership of thirteen hundred individuals and institutions, which include business and government officials as well as librarians, professors, publishers, and students with an interest in Canada. The organization was brought together to promote scholarly activities about Canada at all educational levels. ACSUS publishes the *ACSUS Occasional Papers, American Review of Canadian Studies,* and the *Canadian Studies Update,* a quarterly newsletter. It also sponsors a biennial conference.

Johns Hopkins SAIS
1740 Massachusetts Avenue NW
Nitze 516
Washington, D.C. 20036
Phone: (202) 663-5664
Fax: (202) 663-5717
Email: info@acsus.org
URL: www.acsus.org

MUSEUMS AND RESEARCH CENTERS

Canadian-American Center (National Northeast Resource Center on Canada)

This is a joint research facility made up of Canadian studies programs at the University of Maine, the University of Vermont, and the State University of New York at Plattsburgh. Research is carried out in the fields of economics, humanities, international relations, law, and social sciences as they relate to Canada and the United States. In addition to publishing the Canadian-American Public Policy Series and Borderlands Monograph Series, the center sponsors professional meetings.

Dr. Stephen J. Hornsby, Director
University of Maine
Canadian-American Center
154 College Avenue
Orono, Maine 04473
Phone: (207) 581-4220
Fax: (207) 581-4223
Email: hornsby@maine.edu
URL: www.umain.edu/canam

Center for Canadian-American Studies

An integral unit of Western Washington University, the center focuses on Canada, including interdisciplinary studies in Canadian business, economics, politics, geography, social structure, and culture, as well as Canadian-U.S. environmental issues and problems.

Dr. Donald K. Alper
516 High Street

Canada House
Room 201
Bellingham, Washington 98225-9110
Phone: (360) 650-3728
Fax: (360) 650-3995
Email: canam@cc.wwu.edu
URL: www.wwu.edu/canam

Florida-Canada Linkage Institute

Founded in 1987, the institute promotes cultural, business, and educational exchanges between Florida and Canada. It is supported by the Florida International Affairs Commission.

Dr. Vsenia Vyrschikova, Director
University of Central Florida
Office of International Studies
PO Box 163105
Orlando, Florida 32816-1356
Phone: (407) 823-3647
Fax: (407) 882-0240
Email: feli@ucf.edu
URL: www.international.ucf.edu/fcli

Johns Hopkins University Center for Canadian Studies

Founded in 1969, the center is part of the JHU School of Advanced International Studies. Its research areas include Canadian/U.S. relations, the impact of foreign trade on Canadian culture and politics, and Canadian politics and government. Courses at the master's and doctoral degree levels are taught by resident faculty as well as visiting professors from Carleton University in Ottawa, Ontario, and Laval University in Quebec City, Quebec.

Dr. Charles F. Doran, Director
1740 Massachusetts Avenue NW
Washington, D.C. 20036

Phone: (202) 663-5714
Fax: (202) 663-5717
Email: slee255@jhu.edu
URL: http://legacy2.sais-jhu.edu/centers/canadian-studies.htm

SOURCES FOR ADDITIONAL STUDY

Bickerton, James, and Alain G. Gagnon. *Canadian Politics*. Toronto: University of Toronto Press, 2009.

Cheal, David. *Aging and Demographic Change in Canadian Context*. Toronto: University of Toronto Press, 2003.

Chiswick, Barry R., ed. *Immigration, Language, and Ethnicity: Canada and the United States*. Washington, D.C.: AEI Press. Distributed by University Press of America, 1992.

Francis, R. Douglas, Richard Jones, and Donald B. Smith. *Origins: Canadian History to Confederation*. Toronto: Holt, Rinehart and Winston, 1988.

Immigration and Naturalization Service. *Immigration Profiles: Canada*. Washington, D.C.: U.S. Department of Justice, 1991.

James, Patrick, and Mark Kasoff, eds. *Canadian Studies in the New Milennium*. 2nd ed. Toronto: University of Toronto Press, 2013.

Long, John F., M.V. George, and Edward T. Pryor. *Migration between the United States and Canada*. Washington, D.C.: Current Population Reports/Statistics Canada, February 1990.

Simpson, Jeffrey. *Star-Spangled Canadians: Canadians Living the American Dream*. Toronto: HarperCollins Canada, 2000.

Walton, Richard J. *Canada and the U.S.A.: A Background Book about Internal Conflict and the New Nationalism*. New York: Parents' Magazine Press, 1972.

CAPE VERDEAN AMERICANS

Jane E. Spear

OVERVIEW

Cape Verdean Americans are immigrants or descendants of people from the Republic of Cape Verde, an archipelago in the Atlantic Ocean located approximately 320 miles (515 kilometers) off the coast of Senegal, the westernmost country on the African continent. Cape Verde consists of ten islands, nine of which are inhabited, and multiple islets. Slightly larger than Rhode Island, the islands and islets cover an area of 1,557 square miles (4,033 square kilometers), forming two clusters, the windward islands and the leeward islands, relating to their position to the northeast wind. The windward islands are Santo Antão, São Vincente, Santa Luzia, São Nicolau, Sal, and Boa Vista, along with the islets of Branco and Raso. The leeward islands include Maio, São Tiago (or Santiago), Fogo, and Brava, plus the islets of Grande, Luís Carneiro, and Cima (also called the Rombos). The country's largest active volcano, Pico do Fogo, rises 9,281 feet above sea level.

According to a 2012 report by the World Bank, Cape Verde has a population of 500,585. More than two-thirds of Cape Verdeans report Creole ancestry, meaning they're descendants of Portuguese settlers and black Africans. Most of the population (93 percent) identifies as Roman Catholic, with approximately 5 percent of the population practicing Protestantism. The republic is also home to small Muslim and Baháʼí communities. The islands possess few natural resources, and their arid climate forces the country to import much of its food. However, by focusing on developing its tourism industry, Cape Verde has significantly increased its gross national product above the average for sub-Saharan and regional small island economies.

Cape Verdean immigrants began arriving in the United States in the mid-nineteenth century. The first wave of immigrants came aboard New England whaling ships. Throughout the nineteenth century, Cape Verdeans continued to trickle into the northeastern United States, working as seamen or finding employment in the cranberry bogs of Massachusetts. Initially the immigrants were primarily males from the lower island classes, but a severe drought and economic hardships in Cape Verde brought on by postcolonial neglect led to a surge of immigration in the twentieth

century, with those immigrants representing a broader subset of the islands' population. In the 1920s the United States enacted a series of regulations that prevented Cape Verdeans, among others, from immigrating to the country. The passage of the Immigration and Nationality Act of 1965, however, helped ease those restrictions and facilitated further immigration to the United States from Cape Verde and elsewhere. In 1975 Cape Verde achieved independence from Portugal, which had for years enforced severe restrictions on emigration from the islands. The newly independent nation authorized the establishment of a U.S. embassy in Praia, the national capital, which helped facilitate immigration to the United States. Together, the easing of U.S. immigration policy and Cape Verdean emigration policy led to a significant wave of new arrivals from the islands. Of the close to 400,000 Cape Verdeans who have immigrated to the United States, approximately 60,000 have arrived since 1966, with close to 10,000 arriving between 1992 and 2002.

According to the 2010 United States Census, 91,000 people report having Cape Verdean ancestry. However, the actual number is thought to be much higher. The Cape Verdean Embassy, for example, estimates that close to 200,000 people of Cape Verdean descent live in the United States, and a 2007 article in the *New York Times* put the estimate at closer to 265,000. As they have during most of their history in the United States, Cape Verdeans continue to settle predominantly in the Northeast, particularly in Massachusetts, Rhode Island, Connecticut, and New Jersey.

HISTORY OF THE PEOPLE

Early History The name Cape Verde means "green cape," although these dry and mountainous islands are not particularly green. In the middle of the fifteenth century, before Queen Isabella of Spain sent Christopher Columbus to discover a new route to the East, Portugal was engaged in colonial expansion. The exact date that Portuguese explorer Diogo Gomes and Genoese navigator António da Noli (working for the Portuguese king) discovered the Cape Verdean islands varies. One source suggests that they landed on the unpopulated islands as early as 1455. Other Portuguese historians maintain that the islands were discovered over the course of two voyages between 1460 and 1462. Whenever the discovery, the navigators are believed to have completed their exploration of the islands within two years. Oral traditions passed down through the centuries among the Portuguese and Cape Verdeans indicate that the islands were not always uninhabited. According to these stories, São Tiago was inhabited by the Wolofs, natives of the coastal nations of Senegal and Gambia in western Africa, and Sal was inhabited by the Lebu, Serer, and Felup people, also native to the African continent.

In 1466 King Afonso V of Portugal developed a proposal to make settling in the Cape Verdean islands more attractive. He granted a charter of privileges and placed his brother as owner of the islands, giving him jurisdiction over all inhabitants in civil and criminal matters. The inhabitants of the islands at that time may have included blacks from the African continent, white settlers from Europe, and Moors (people of mixed Arab and Berber descent). The charter allowed European settlers to organize a slave trade off the African coast, providing for the development of the islands and the expansion of slave markets in Brazil and the West Indies. The scarcity of European women inhabiting the Cape Verdean islands ultimately led to the coupling of Portuguese male settlers with native Africans, resulting in a mostly mixed-blood population.

The poor growing conditions on the islands created difficulties for the Portuguese, who were accustomed to harvesting and eating grains that could not be grown on the Cape Verdean landscape. The Portuguese brought maize (corn) from Brazil and established it as the islands' main crop. They also imported *urzela*, a natural substance used in dyes. Many of the African slaves brought to Cape Verde were expert weavers, and they wove cotton into intricately patterned materials for use in clothing and household goods. To the detriment of the natives and slaves inhabiting the islands, produce grown in Cape Verde during Portuguese occupation was returned to Portugal, rather than being used to feed the region's population.

Naturally, Europeans settled in the most fertile areas of Cape Verde. São Tiago, the largest island, was divided into feudal estates, the system of land division used in Europe. Feudal estates were passed down from one generation to the next, father to son, and were worked by tenant farmers. Working the land, especially in the difficult soil of the Cape Verdean islands, was tedious at best, and these tenant farmers generally lived grim and difficult lives. Although they were not considered slaves, tenant farmers never gained the right to own the land they farmed, subsisting on only what was left after they paid taxes to the landlord.

Similar to Britain, which sent criminals to Australia, Portugal sent many *degredados*, or convicts, to settle the Cape Verdean islands. This practice continued regularly until 1882. Many Jewish people,

especially men, also settled on the islands, usually to escape persecution in Portugal, where they faced racial and religious discrimination and were frequently robbed of their money and possessions. White settlers in Cape Verde learned to make a profit on their slaves by teaching them to speak Portuguese, allowing the slaves to be sold for a higher price.

Cape Verde experienced two major droughts in the sixteenth century, the first in 1549 and the second from 1580 to 1583. By the middle of the seventeenth century, a significant number of white settlers had decided to abandon the islands, causing a decline in the export economy. Eventually the Portuguese governing monarchy permitted slave ships in transit from Africa to the Americas to pay their customs fees before they left the coast of mainland Africa, rather than requiring them to pay the fees at the Cape Verdean islands. Consequently, the capital city of Ribeira Grande, located on the island of Santo Antão, became easy prey for pirates. Neglect pushed the city into ruins, and Praia became the new capital of the colony. The city afforded a natural fortress to protect it from roving marauders and pirates in search of valuable goods. Illegal trade brought the only consistent source of revenue to the islands, as Portuguese laws restricted trade with foreigners.

Due largely to mismanagement of the charter companies employed by the monarchy, famines increased in Cape Verde from 1696 to 1785, even when droughts were not as severe. Managers of the land did not store food during more fertile periods, and during the famine of 1773 to 1775, some inhabitants became so desperate to leave the islands that they sold themselves into slavery on foreign ships. Other slaves took advantage of the chaos that occurred during pirate attacks, escaping to the distant countryside and settling down to farm the land for themselves.

Another brutal famine during the 1830s killed an estimated one-third of the islands' population. In 1835 soldiers at Praia—most of them recruited from the Azores, a group of Portugal-owned islands in the North Atlantic—began an uprising that resulted in the slaughter of many officials. The government eventually thwarted the takeover attempt, executing the insurrectionist leaders. Subsequent uprisings in Cape Verde were similarly unsuccessful. Through news reports, Americans became aware of the famine of the early 1830s and another in 1856. While the Portuguese government offered no assistance, the people of Boston and New York sent money and provisions—eleven ships containing food set out from New York alone in 1856—to alleviate the suffering of the Cape Verdean people.

Modern Era Portugal did not outlaw the trading of slaves until 1836, long after most European countries denounced the practice. The slave trade nevertheless continued in Cape Verde, due largely to loopholes in the laws and the unscrupulous dealings of officials and businesspeople on the island. The Anglo-Portuguese Treaty of 1842 brought the first serious admonitions, preventing slaves from coming onto the Cape Verdean islands. Throughout the 1850s, Portugal continued to pass laws prohibiting slavery, yet the slave trade remained active until 1878.

Tenant farmers who remained on the Cape Verdean islands continued to be subjected to the cruel vagaries of landowners and of the land itself. Outrageous practices, such as arbitrary rent raises, often resulted in the sudden eviction of tenants, and there was little mercy for struggling residents. When a famine lasting from 1863 to 1866 killed one-third of the islands' population for the second time in thirty years, the Portuguese government began a program of forced emigration. Some Cape Verdean residents, willing to endure contract labor rather than face another threat of starvation, were sent to the equatorial islands of São Tomé and Príncipe, where cocoa production was emerging as a major operation. Other islanders settled in Senegal, while some went to the country of Guinea-Bissau in western Africa, where they established independent businesses, often trading distilled spirits made from sugar cane and other imported goods. In 1870 Guinea-Bissau fell under the control of the Portuguese, who resented these distilled-spirit operations because they competed with their own brandy-making businesses. The Portuguese eventually forced the resettled Cape Verdeans out of business, forcing them to take on low-paying government jobs.

Droughts and famines in the Cape Verdean islands continued throughout the nineteenth century and into the twentieth century. A law enacted by the Portuguese government in 1899 allowed authorities in Cape Verde to force any kind of work, no matter how low the wage or undesirable the situation, upon unemployed males. This enabled the government to maintain the workforce on the islands' cocoa plantations during another grave famine in 1902 and 1903. The harsh law remained intact when Portugal became a republic in 1910. World War I created havoc in Cape Verde, particularly for its shipping industry, and yet another famine, this one lasting from 1920 to 1922, resulted in the deaths of an estimated 30,000 people.

In 1917 the United States began prohibiting the immigration of illiterate people. This law was the precedent for harsher immigration laws enacted in the 1920s designed to stem the flow of immigrants into the country. Hundreds of Cape Verdeans had left the islands for the United States during the nineteenth and early twentieth centuries, but following the new U.S. immigration restrictions, those numbers fell drastically. Meanwhile, Portugal's transition into a republic had resulted in the establishment of a free press and school reforms on the islands, but a military coup in 1926 led to the establishment

of a one-party state in Portugal, hampering freedoms once again and making it even more difficult for the small minority of educated Cape Verdeans to be heard. In 1936 a group of intellectuals and social reformers founded a literary review known as *Claridade*, which would revolutionize Cape Verdean literature. Publication of *Claridade* continued until 1960. Although Portugal remained neutral during World War II, the Cape Verdean islands suffered the effects of travel and shipping restrictions. Famines during and immediately after the war, first from 1941 to 1943 and again from 1947 to 1949, killed an estimated 45,000 people.

In the 1950s many Cape Verdeans began immigrating to western Europe, which had been devastated by the war and was in need of workers for the booming war-recovery efforts. The largest number of Cape Verdeans settled in the Netherlands, although some settled in Portugal, where they eagerly took on the most menial of jobs to escape the hardships of famine back on the islands. Thus, Cape Verdeans in the United States were no longer the only displaced islanders sending money back to their homeland. In fact, Cape Verdeans settling in Europe sent so much money back home that those remittances became the major source of income and exchange on the islands.

Protests began mounting throughout Portuguese Africa in the 1950s. Those who resisted colonial rule in Cape Verde were subject to the terrors of the Portuguese secret police and were sometimes even incarcerated in the prison camp at Tarrafal, located on the island of São Tiago. The Portuguese government provided famine relief in 1959 in an attempt to win the people's support. Other public projects, such as roads, a desalination plant, and irrigation systems, were constructed, only to fail in a few short years. In 1956 Amílcar Cabral organized a group of Cape Verdeans and people from the mainland colony of Guinea-Bissau to form the *Partido Africano de Independência de Guiné e Cabo Verde* (African Party for the Independence of Guinea and Cape Verde), also known as the PAIGC. Although originally a peaceful movement, the PAIGC engaged in a full-scale guerrilla war against the Portuguese regime from 1963 until Cabral's assassination in 1973. Although Guinea-Bissau was granted independence in 1974, Portugal attempted to install a puppet government in Cape Verde. Residents resisted these efforts by calling for general strikes, which halted all production and services on the islands. The PAIGC and Portugal ultimately agreed to a transitional government comprised of Portuguese and Cape Verdeans. On July 5, 1975, following elections, the islands were formally established as the Republic of Cape Verde, an independent nation.

When Amílcar Cabral's widow, Ana Maria Cabral, spoke at the 1995 Festival of American Folklife at the Smithsonian Institution in Washington, D.C., she focused on her husband's and her country's struggles for independence. Before his death, Amílcar Cabral had written into Cape Verde's new constitution provisions for dual citizenship and voting, consequently formalizing the close ties that Cape Verdeans who emigrate maintain to their homeland and legally recognizing the interdependence between the diaspora (members of a culture who spread out and settle away from their homeland) and those who remain on the islands. Ana Maria Cabral noted that

> Cape Verde [had] undergone a very interesting historical process. Originally a group of uninhabited islands, the archipelago's population resulted mostly from Portuguese exiles' intermarrying with black African slaves and their descendants. Cultural colonization progressively diluted itself in a biological and social mixing that, joined with factors less than favorable to the establishment of a strong metropolitan ruling class, soon imposed on Cape Verdean society a characteristic personality. These are evident everywhere: in linguistic recreation, musical reharmonization, ancestral traces in culinary customs, and the more common manifestations of everyday life.

Two former prime ministers competed for the presidency of Cape Verde in 2001. The first was Pedro Pires, a member of the African Party for the Independence of Cape Verde (PAICV), the Cape Verdean successor to the PAIGC. The second candidate was Carlos Veiga, a member of the Movement for Democracy (MPD). Pires narrowly defeated Veiga, turning to the islands' diasporic community in hopes of stabilizing the struggling economy. Pires's strategy worked, and his partnerships with groups like the Cape Verdean American Business Organization paved the way for foreign investors to add to the yearly remittances from the islands' emigrants, which accounted for 20 percent of Cape Verde's gross national product. These investments allowed Cape Verde to address its neglected infrastructure, leading

When the children and grandchildren of the first Cape Verdean immigrants in the United States became involved in the civil rights movement of the 1960s, a new sense of solidarity with other Americans of African descent emerged.

to increased tourism and a better-funded education system. Between 2000 and 2005, Cape Verde's income rose by 5.7 percent. In 2008 Cape Verde became one of only two countries to graduate from the status of "least-developed country" to "developing country," as defined by the World Trade Organization (WTO). Pires was reelected in 2006 and served until 2011, when he stepped down and was succeeded by MPD candidate

Jorge Carlos Fonseca. Although Cape Verde's economy continues to make strides, unemployment and poverty remain high, forcing many residents to emigrate in search of better opportunities.

SETTLEMENT IN THE UNITED STATES

Massachusetts colonist John Winthrop was the first American to record contact with Cape Verdeans. In 1643 Winthrop recorded in his journal that a shipment of boat slaves had been sent from Boston to England in order to finance the purchase of African slaves from the Cape Verdean island of Maio. The first Cape Verdeans to settle in the United States did so in the middle of the nineteenth century. Most of these early settlers had boarded the New England whaling ships that stopped along Cape Verde's coast. Into the early twentieth century, before the decline of the whaling industry, Cape Verdeans were prominent on whaling ships, serving in every capacity, including as captains, harpooners, and deckhands.

Cranberries were (and still are) a chief commercial crop in Massachusetts, with numerous cranberry bogs located throughout the southeastern portion of the state, including on the Cape Cod peninsula. These bogs required a large amount of workers during harvest time and thus employed many early Cape Verdean settlers. At the end of the twentieth century, the New England area, particularly Massachusetts and Rhode Island, remained home to the largest concentrations of Cape Verdean Americans. Population estimates for Cape Verdeans living in that region vary, with figures ranging from 13,000 to 21,000. Although immigration restrictions became more stringent following the terrorist attacks of September 11, 2001, Cape Verdeans have continued to immigrate to the United States at a steady rate, with an average of 1,470 arriving yearly from 2001 to 2011.

Following World War I, a small number of Cape Verdean Americans left New England for Ohio and Michigan to fill the many positions opening in the auto, steel, and manufacturing industries. It was not unusual for Cape Verdeans to travel back and forth from their Midwestern homes to Massachusetts and Rhode Island, where their families remained. A more significant number of Cape Verdeans settled in California, especially in Sacramento and in the southern part of the state, where pockets of Portuguese immigrants had already established communities. During the lengthy factory strikes of the late 1950s and 1960s, some Cape Verdeans returned to New England to reunite with family members and find work in the cranberry bogs or on other migrant farms.

Although Cape Verde has made significant strides in improving its economy in the twenty-first century, its population continues to migrate to Europe and to the United States in search of better employment, wages, health care, and food. Many Cape Verdean Americans still find employment in the farming and fishing industries of the Northeast. However, many others are settling in urban areas, where they find

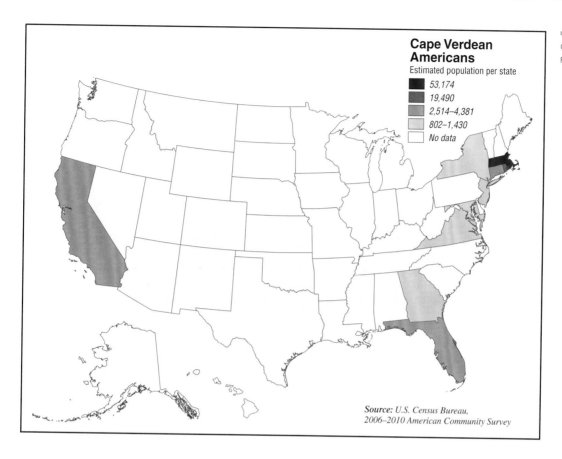

Cape Verdean Americans
Estimated population per state

■	53,174
■	19,490
■	2,514–4,381
■	802–1,430
□	No data

Source: U.S. Census Bureau, 2006–2010 American Community Survey

employment in the service and construction industries. Driven by increased access to education, some Cape Verdean Americans have branched into professional fields, becoming doctors, lawyers, and engineers.

LANGUAGE

Cape Verdean Americans speak English, Portuguese, and *Kriolu* (or *Crioulo*), a Creole language that is a mixture of the European languages of early explorers and the native tongues spoken by African slaves. Much of the Kriolu vocabulary stems from Portuguese, although many of the language's words are no longer used in twenty-first-century Portugal. The African tongues, mostly *Mande*, influenced Kriolu chiefly in the way grammar is used. Since the independent Republic of Cape Verde was established in 1975, Kriolu has become the dominant language among the islands' residents.

When Cape Verdeans came to the United States to find work in the early twentieth century, they were forced to learn English, as were other foreign-born immigrants. Many Cape Verdean American children had a difficult time in school, as they had not been given sufficient time to develop their English-speaking skills. In 1971 Massachusetts passed the Transitional Bilingual Education Act, which required school districts with twenty or more students from the same primary language background to provide transitional bilingual education programs. Other states soon adopted similar laws. In 1996 the Cape Verdean Creole Institute was founded in Boston with the goal of promoting the Cape Verdean language.

Greetings and Popular Expressions Common Kriolu expressions and greetings include: *Sin*—Yes; *Nau*—No; *Kon Lisensa*—Excuse me; *N ka ta konprende*—I do not understand; *Spera un momentu*—Wait a minute; *Pur favor, papia dibagar*—Please speak slowly; *Dja Txiga, Dimas*—Enough, too much; *Gosi li* (or g*osin li* or g*urinha sin*)—Right now; *Kumo ki bu ta txomal na Kriolu?*—What is that called in Kriolu?; *Bu ta papia Ingles?*—Do you speak English?

RELIGION

A large percentage (close to 70 percent) of Cape Verdean Americans regularly attend religious ceremonies. The majority are Roman Catholic, although some, particularly those living on the Cape Cod peninsula, belong to Protestant denominations, such as the United Methodists and the Church of the Nazarene. The religious practices of Cape Verdeans who identify as Roman Catholic often incorporate elements from African traditions, including spiritual dances, music, and shouts. Due to their African heritage, many Cape Verdeans in the United States have faced discrimination in local Roman Catholic parishes, which are more likely to tailor their services to Europeans. For most of their history, Cape Verdeans have incorporated resistance to colonialism into their spiritual practices, although some of this meaning is lost on second- and third-generation Cape Verdean Americans.

CULTURE AND ASSIMILATION

Cape Verdeans who immigrate to the United States carry with them a history of hardship and devastation. The strength they have developed by facing those challenges helps to fortify them as they tackle the obstacles of living in a foreign country. Even as they forge new lives in the United States, most Cape Verdean Americans continue to work for the betterment and survival of those who remain in their home country.

Many Cape Verdeans have faced racial prejudice in the United States. Cape Verdeans living in the United States in the nineteenth and early twentieth centuries created a distinct identity for themselves, separate from that of their African ancestors. They did not think of themselves as African Americans in the way that descendants of African slaves did. For these Cape Verdeans, their European blood was as much a part of their ancestry as their African blood. This was especially true for immigrants who settled outside the concentrated Cape Verdean communities of New England. Because a majority were Roman Catholics in a country where few African Americans shared that faith, Cape Verdean Americans more often found themselves in the company of white Catholics, particularly eastern European immigrants also struggling to blend into their new country. As a result, many Cape Verdean Americans considered themselves Portuguese and usually expressed that distinction when their identity was questioned.

Although often forced into black neighborhoods because of their skin color, early generations of Cape Verdean Americans attempted to maintain a society separate from the African Americans surrounding them. Despite these attempts, many Cape Verdean Americans married outside their community, especially with West Indians, Azoreans (people from the Azores islands), and African Americans. Nevertheless, their shared customs, language, and religion helped keep Cape Verdean Americans together in closely knit extended families. Until the middle of the twentieth century, most Cape Verdeans had large immediate families, often with five or more children.

When the children and grandchildren of the first Cape Verdean immigrants in the United States became involved in the civil rights movement of the 1960s, a new sense of solidarity with other Americans of African descent emerged. Cape Verdean Americans of the post–World War II generation in particular saw the similarities between their own struggles and the struggles of other African Americans.

By the end of the twentieth century, the Cape Verdean community in the United States had become far more self-aware and eager to celebrate its shared identity. Cape Verdean Americans scattered throughout the United States, from well-established communities in New England and Southern California to newer clusters in metropolitan areas such as Atlanta, began to renew their heritage with the younger generations. Meanwhile, financial success allowed second- and third-generation Cape Verdean Americans to pursue higher degrees and migrate to new parts of the country, including San Francisco and central Florida.

While the initial waves of Cape Verdean immigrants were made up primarily of those from the islands of Brava, Fogo, and São Nicolau, the diasporic community in the United States now includes people from every Cape Verdean island. Emigration from Cape Verde declined slightly during the first decade of the twenty-first century, but ongoing unemployment in the country continues to motivate its residents to seek better opportunities elsewhere. The Cape Verdean immigrant population in the United States has also reached a relative gender balance. Earlier immigrants were primarily young and middle-aged men, but higher demand for domestic workers has enticed more women to immigrate to the United States. According to the Cape Verdean Immigration Bureau, the percentage of women leaving the country to work elsewhere increased 15 to 20 percent during the first decade of the twenty-first century.

Traditions and Customs Roman Catholicism provides much of Cape Verde's religious heritage, but animist customs and beliefs linger in the spiritual practices of Cape Verdeans living on the islands and in the United States. A number of non-Christian customs are woven into the celebration of Roman Catholic holidays, while many Cape Verdeans who identify as Roman Catholic also believe in the power of healers and nontraditional medicine. Nuno Miranda, a healer and spiritualist revered by many Cape Verdeans in the twentieth century, was responsible for passing down many of these customs.

Cuisine Whenever food is served among Cape Verdean Americans, the most important factor is the coming together of family and friends to celebrate the gift of food and to share it with love. Perhaps the most common traditional dish among Cape Verdean Americans is *cachupa*, also known as *katxupa*. Cape Verdeans offer many slight variations of this dish, but the main ingredients are beaten corn, ground beef, bacon, sausage, pigs' feet, potatoes, dry beans, cabbage, garlic, onions, and bay leaves. These ingredients are cooked together for several hours. The two most common versions are *cachupa rica*, indicating the inclusion of meat for the *rica*, or rich, and *cachupa povera*, for the poor who cannot afford meat. Cachupa sometimes contains fish when made in the islands or in New England communities, where fish is plentiful.

Another favorite dish is *canja de galinha*, which includes chicken, rice, and tomatoes cooked with onions, garlic, sage, and bay leaves. This dish is always served at funerals or at big family celebrations. *Jagacida* is a rice dish cooked with lima or kidney beans, salt, pepper, and fresh parsley, and is served with meat or poultry. *Caldo de peixe* is a fish soup and a favorite among islanders, who rely on fish as a major food source. *Lagaropa*, a red grouper fish native to the seas surrounding the islands, is used when available. Custom dictates that when a person is suffering from too much alcohol consumption, a spicy version of the soup is necessary for recovery. For something sweet, *pudim de leite*, a simple milk pudding, is served.

Music The hardships Cape Verdeans have faced in their homeland and in the lands to which they have immigrated have resulted in a music full of melancholy, or *morna*, as the traditional ballads are known. Much of Cape Verdean music features a mixture of guitar, violin, and vocals. Song lyrics often reflect the pain of separations endured throughout the waves of emigration from the islands. In his article "The Sands of Cape Verde," John Cho, world music columnist for the *San Juan Star*, wrote, "Given such a history filled with loss and departures, plus having the Portuguese (themselves known for their pensive nature) as their European component, it is no surprise that the popular musics of Cape Verde are steeped in melancholy." Cho goes on to note that because most of Cape Verde's population is made up of the descendants of African slaves who had been cut off from their histories and were forced to live under brutal colonial rule, the themes of alienation and involuntary abandonment of roots also play a significant role in the islands' traditional music. "An obvious analogy," Cho wrote, "is the development of another great music of melancholia, the blues, also by slaves and their progeny in the United States." Many Cape Verdean Americans remain devoted to their traditional music, and some have also developed an interest in jazz.

Holidays The major holidays celebrated by Cape Verdean Americans are rooted primarily in their Christian beliefs. These holidays include Christmas (December 25), the Nativity of Saint John the Baptist (June 24), and Carnival (typically in February or March), the period of celebration preceding Ash Wednesday and beginning the season of Lent. Many other Cape Verdean holidays revolve around the celebration of saints, with most of these occurring during the months of May, June, and July, with some, such as All Saints' Day and All Souls' Day, occurring in late October and early November. In addition to celebrating Independence Day on July 4 in honor of their adopted country, Cape Verdean Americans commemorate Cape Verde's Independence Day on July 5. Many Cape Verdean Americans in the New England area celebrate the Nativity of Saint John the Baptist with traditional parades, folk dances like the *coladeira*, and special meals.

Health Care Issues and Practices Americans of Cape Verdean ancestry are not known to suffer any disease or illness specific to their ethnic group. However, like other African Americans, Cape Verdean Americans have an increased risk for high blood pressure and diabetes.

CACHUPA RICA

Ingredients

4 cups crushed dry hominy

¼ pound dried kidney beans

2 onions, chopped

2 bay leaves

2 garlic cloves, chopped

olive oil, as needed

salt

¼ pound beef, cubed

¼ pound bacon, diced

1 pig foot

4 sausages (linguiça or chouriço), thickly sliced

Paprika, to taste

2 potatoes, peeled and cut into 1-inch cubes

¼ pound savoy cabbage, coarsely chopped

2 cassavas, peeled, 1-inch dice

Chopped cilantro, for garnish

Preparation

Add the hominy, beans, half the onions, 1 of the bay leaves, 1 garlic clove, 1 tablespoon of the olive oil, and a pinch of salt to a stock pot. Cover with water and boil for 30 minutes. Turn off the heat and set aside.

In large pot or Dutch oven, heat 3 tablespoons of oil over low heat and add the beef, bacon, pig trotter, sausage, the rest of the onions, the remaining garlic clove, and bay leaf, paprika and salt to taste. Cover and simmer for 3 hours. Add water if the pan threatens to dry out.

Return the beans and hominy to a boil. Then add the meat mixture. When the beans and hominy are nearly tender, add the potatoes, cabbage, and cassavas. When the potatoes are fork-tender, remove the pot from heat.

Allow the dish to rest 30 minutes before serving. Garnish with the chopped cilantro.

As an isolated cultural group in the United States, earlier Cape Verdean immigrants often did not receive social services that addressed problems such as domestic abuse and youth violence and delinquency. This situation began to change in the 1990s, when organizations designed to provide services to immigrant populations, including Cape Verdeans, began to appear. Two such organizations serving Cape Verdean Americans in the Boston area are the Dudley Street Neighborhood Initiative, a community-based planning and organizing nonprofit located in the ethnically diverse and historically poor Roxbury neighborhood,

CAPE VERDEAN PROVERBS

Si tchuba tchobe, morre fogadu. Si ka tem tchuba, morre di sedi.

If the rains come, we die of drowning. If the rains don't come, we die of thirst.

N ka ten di agraba di mar pamodi tudu ki ten e mar ki dau.

I cannot hold a grudge against the sea, because all that I have the sea has given me.

Sacu basiu ca ta sakedu.

An empty bag can't stand up.

Cover just as your cloth permit it.

Do not bite off more than you can chew.

Many Cape Verdean proverbs continue to be passed down from the older generations born in the islands to the younger generations born in the United States. These proverbs reflect the often-troubled lives of the Cape Verdean people.

- Who stays will not go away. Who never went away will not come back anymore.

- Without leaving, there is no coming back.

- If we die in the departure, God will give us life in the return.

- A pretty girl is like a ship with all its flags windward.

- Who does not want to be a wolf should not its pelt wear.

- Who mix himself up with pigs will eat bran.

- A poor foreigner eats the raw and the undercooked.

- There is no better mirror than an old friend.

- Good calf sucks milk from all the cows.

- What is good ends soon. What is bad never ends.

and the Log School Family Education Center, located in the nearby Dorchester neighborhood, which develops programs for the betterment of immigrants, some of them not yet American citizens, who struggle with identity, poverty, and poor education.

FAMILY AND COMMUNITY LIFE

Family life is central to Cape Verdean Americans. It is the social structure around which everything else in their lives revolves. Until the latter half of the twentieth century, Cape Verdean American families were often large, with at least four or more children. As they assimilated into American culture and education levels rose, families became smaller. Cape Verdean Americans in the baby-boomer generation often had only two or three children, as compared to their parents' average of seven or eight. Family ties remain just as important in smaller families, however, and despite new affluence, better education, and greater social mobility, newer generations of Cape Verdean Americans continue to express an interest in their heritage. Groups such as the Cape Verdean American Community Development Agency, based in Rhode Island, have developed a series of programs that seek to establish greater educational and professional opportunities for Cape Verdeans while allowing them to maintain a link to their culture.

Gender Roles Gender roles among the Cape Verdean American population have shifted over time. Before Cape Verde achieved independence in 1975, emigration was limited. Of those who did immigrate to the United States, most were men. These early immigrants brought with them the patriarchal system that prevailed in Cape Verde and elsewhere under colonialism. Thus, women who were part of earlier waves of Cape Verdean immigrants were subject to pronounced discrimination that limited their ability to pursue economic, educational, and social opportunities.

After Cape Verdean independence, however, the situation began to change, as more women began immigrating to the United States. A vast majority of these women, whether or not they were married, pursued occupations outside the home. Although they found it difficult to find work in mills due to racial and gender discrimination, many of these women worked alongside men in cranberry bogs and strawberry patches. Others found work in the homes of wealthy families as maids or nannies or in other domestic capacities. Their increased economic power within the community, as well as within the family structure, helped decrease their vulnerability to patriarchal bias and discrimination. While Cape Verdean American women, like other women in the early twenty-first century, continue to struggle against the strictures of traditional gender roles, they are as likely as Cape Verdean men to receive a higher education and to work in professional capacities.

Education Education has gained increasing importance among Cape Verdean Americans. According to the 1990 United States Census, approximately 23.6 percent of the Cape Verdean American population had at least some level of college education. By 2010 that number had increased slightly, climbing to between 25 and 28 percent. This trend toward more education for both genders seems to have extended to Cape Verdeans living on the islands as well as those in the United States, with secondary and higher education becoming more the norm in both countries. Additionally, newer Cape Verdean immigrants are more likely to speak English than were earlier generations and are attending college in increasing numbers.

With more Cape Verdean Americans attending university, the immigrant community is seeing financial and social gains. Groups such as the Cape Verdean American Business Organization provide scholarships and internships for young Cape Verdean entrepreneurs. Cape Verdean Americans have also harnessed their passion for education by supporting schools in their home country. In 1975 Cape Verde had two high schools, but with support from the diasporic community, it now has approximately thirty schools and a public university with more than 3,000 students.

Courtship and Weddings Weddings are an important festivity in the islands and are influenced by Cape Verdeans' African roots. The custom of *batuque*, composed of solo dancing and responsorials from a women's chorus, is a common wedding tradition. The most traditional practitioners of this custom are on the island of São Tiago. Among some islanders, the performance involves a ritual mockery of advice to the newly married couple, sometimes composed by the male elder of the family. Variations include the lead singer taking command of the group, slowly dancing the rhythmic beat of the *batukadieras*, or drums. In the first part, the *txabeta*, the dancer in the middle of the circle, keeps time to the accelerating music with her hips. The *finacon* involves improvisational singing about events of importance to Cape Verdeans, such as the devastating famines. In his article "Traditional Festivities in Cape Verde," writer Gabriel Moacyr Rodrigues placed this custom in the context of the community. "The elder leader can be understood as a matron, the most experienced woman, who executes the hip movements that suggest the sexual act and provoke the libido." Rodrigues further noted,

> Young girls—the Batxudas—dance afterward, and their agile, sensual bodies awaken feelings in the old men around that remind them of their own love and marriage. For the young who watch, the dancer represents the desire for love. As she dances, the young girl closes her eyes and holds her hands in front of her face in a gesture of wanting to be seen and appreciated while still intending to preserve her chastity and bashfulness.

These traditional performances are not, however, generally practiced among Cape Verdean Americans, who largely observe common American wedding customs.

Death and Burial Rituals Funerals among Cape Verdean Americans of Catholic and Protestant denominations typically follow their churches' standard rituals. Most Cape Verdean Americans follow the custom of showing the body in a funeral home in the day or two before the mass, or service, and burial. Following the funeral is a celebration featuring special foods, particularly *canja*, a dish of chicken, rice, and tomatoes.

Relations with Other Americans As Cape Verdean Americans began intermarrying with African

In Rhode Island, a Cape Verdean American grandmother is reunited with her granddaughter. O. LOUIS MAZZATENTA / NATIONAL GEOGRAPHIC / GETTY IMAGES

Americans, many of them descendants of African slaves and American slaveholders, the two cultures began to share traditions and find common sympathies. Cape Verdean Americans' attempts to resuscitate their cultural identity, however, have been occasionally met with backlash. Some African American community leaders have sought to dissuade Cape Verdean Americans from separating themselves from other African American communities, believing that a split between the groups would lead them to compete for similar resources. Meanwhile, a recent influx of Brazilians to the northeastern United States has increased the amount of immigrants with Portuguese ancestry in the region, affording the Cape Verdean population a larger voice in the community.

EMPLOYMENT AND ECONOMIC CONDITIONS
The first Cape Verdean immigrants in the United States were primarily men, most of them employed in the whaling and shipbuilding industries. By the early

twentieth century, Cape Verdeans were also frequently employed in the cranberry bogs of New England. As education levels climbed, Cape Verdean Americans began taking jobs in professional fields, such as medicine, law, education, and business. Many Cape Verdeans arrived in the United States during the rise of the auto and steel industries and took jobs in those factories. By the end of the twentieth century, Cape Verdean Americans were also visible as sports figures, musicians, and politicians. The twenty-first century saw an increase in entrepreneurs and business professionals, as well as steady employment figures in the manufacturing industries.

POLITICS AND GOVERNMENT

Cape Verdean Americans have been prominent as judges and state representatives in Massachusetts and Rhode Island since the latter half of the twentieth century. They have served in both world wars, as well as in Korea, Vietnam, Iraq, and Afghanistan.

According to the constitution of the Republic of Cape Verde, all people of Cape Verdean ancestry, whether in the islands or abroad, can hold dual citizenship and actively participate in elections in their home nation. The 2011 parliament in Cape Verde included two members from New England who represented the interests of the diasporic community. Due largely to the active political participation of the islands' emigrant population, even Cape Verdeans born in United States feel a strong tie to their ancestral country.

NOTABLE INDIVIDUALS

Art Anthony Barboza (1944–) is a celebrated photographer whose work has appeared in *National Geographic*, the *New Yorker*, *Life*, and many other esteemed publications. Lindsay Grace is a prominent

new-media artist, professor, and game designer who has developed a number of games, including Polyglot Cubed, an educational tool for learning foreign languages. Joao da Lomba was a Cape Verdean whaler in the early twentieth century who was recognized for his expertly crafted scrimshaw pieces. Other early Cape Verdean American artists were known only to those who frequented the local museums of New England, such as the Kendall Whaling Museum in New Bedford, Massachusetts, where some of those items can still be found.

Government Alfred J. Gomes (1897–1974) was a prominent attorney and activist in the Boston area. Born in Cape Verde and raised in Massachusetts, Gomes graduated from Boston University Law School in 1923, a time when few Cape Verdeans completed elementary school. A prolific historian and researcher of Cape Verdean history and culture, Gomes helped to establish various scholarships, awards, and relief funds to benefit Cape Verdeans on the islands and in the United States.

Viriato "Vinny" deMacedo (1965–) was born in Cape Verde and immigrated with his family to the Boston area when he was six months old. In 1998 he was elected to the Massachusetts state legislature as the Massachusetts State Representative for the First Plymouth District. As of 2012, he was serving his seventh term in the state legislature.

Music Tavares was an R&B, funk, and soul music group that rose to fame in the late 1970s with a cover of the Bee Gees song "More Than a Woman," which was featured in the 1977 hit movie *Saturday Night Fever*. Horace Silva (1928–), more commonly known as Horace Silver, is a prominent Cape Verdean American jazz pianist and composer and a pioneer of the jazz style known as hard bop. Paul Gonsalves (1920–1974) was a prominent jazz tenor saxophonist. In his appearance at the 1956 Newport Jazz Festival as part of Duke Ellington's orchestra, Gonsalves made history with a twenty-seven chorus solo in the song "Diminuendo and Crescendo in Blue," now considered one of the all-time classic jazz performances. Ethel Ramos Harris, a Cape Verdean American violinist, established a scholarship to foster continued music education for Cape Verdean American youth. Jose Gomes Da Graca, a violinist known to most Cape Verdeans as Djedjinho, became even more popular after his death in 1994, when family members released recordings of his music. Lisa Lopes (1971–2002), also known by her stage name, Left Eye, was part of the popular American hip-hop group TLC before she died in a car accident in 2002.

Sports Dana Barros (1967–) is a retired professional basketball player who is best known for his time with the National Basketball Association (NBA) team the Boston Celtics. Wayne Fontes (1940–) is a former professional football player who coached the Detroit Lions National Football League (NFL) team from 1988 to 1996. Henry Andrade (1962–), a Cape Verdean American hurdler and dual citizen of both countries, represented Cape Verde in the 1996 Summer Olympics. Tony Gonzalez (1976–) is an NFL tight end who has played for the Kansas City Chiefs and the Atlanta Falcons. Gonzalez is considered one of the best tight ends of all time.

Stage and Screen Well known as a producer of television commercials, Ricardo Lopes headed Kelly, Denham Productions. Michael Beach (1963–) is an actor who has starred in the television series *Third Watch*, *ER*, and *Stargate Atlantis*. Stacey Dash (1967–) is an actress best known for her role in the popular movie *Clueless*. She has also appeared in the television drama *CSI: Crime Scene Investigation*.

MEDIA

Nobidade TV

Nobidade TV is a Cape Verdean program started in Rhode Island in 1988. Its mission is to educate the public about the Cape Verdean people and its culture.

213 Rhodes Street
Providence, Rhode Island 02905
Phone: (401) 603-0277
Email: cvvisions@gmail.com
URL: http://nobidadetv.com

ORGANIZATIONS AND ASSOCIATIONS

Cape Verdean American Community Development Agency

The Cape Verdean American Community Development Agency is a nonprofit organization established

to provide educational services to immigrant populations.

120 High Street
Pawtucket, Rhode Island 02860
Phone: (401) 475-9834
URL: http://cacdonline.com

Cape Verdean Association of Brockton

Established in 1977, the Cape Verdean Association of Brockton is a community-based nonprofit organization whose mission is to provide education, health, civic, social, and human services to Cape Verdeans and other people residing in the areas in and surrounding Brockton, Massachusetts.

575 North Montello Street
Brockton, Massachusetts 02301
Phone: (508) 559-0056
Fax: (508) 559-9337
URL: www.cvassociation.webs.com

Cape Verdean Association in New Bedford

The mission of the Cape Verdean Association in New Bedford is to preserve and promote Cape Verdean culture.

Raquel Dias, President
P.O. Box 5532
New Bedford, Massachusetts 02742
Phone: (508) 991-5796
Email: cvainfo@cvanb.org
URL: www.cvanb.org

Cape Verdean American and Olympic high hurdler Henry Andrade (1962–) at Cerritos College in Cerritos, California, 1996. AP PHOTO / MARK J. TERRILL

Cape Verdeans of Atlanta

Organized in 1993, Cape Verdeans of Atlanta is a nonprofit organization established to address the enhancement, preservation, and promotion of Cape Verdean culture.

Glynis Ramos-Mitchell, President
Phone: (770) 924-8331
Email: info@capeverdeansofatlanta.com
URL: http://capeverdeansofatlanta.com

MUSEUMS AND RESEARCH CENTERS

Cape Verdean Museum

The Cape Verdean Museum aims to preserve and celebrate Cape Verdean American culture and history.

Denise Oliveira, President
1003 Waterman Avenue
East Providence, Rhode Island 02914
Phone: (401) 228-7292
Email: info@capeverdeanmuseum.org
URL: www.capeverdeanmuseum.org

New Bedford Whaling Museum

The New Bedford Whaling Museum contains exhibits explaining the history of the Cape Verdeans who served on the New Bedford whaling ships, among other historical exhibits.

James Russell, President
Phone: (508) 997-0046
Fax: (508) 997-0018

Library Fax:

18 Johnny Cake Hill
New Bedford, Massachusetts 02740
Fax: (508) 207-1064
Email: frontdesk@whalingmuseum.org
URL: www.whalingmuseum.org

SOURCES FOR ADDITIONAL STUDY

Aisling, Irwin, and Colum Wilson. *Cape Verde Islands: The Bradt Travel Guide.* Chalfont St. Peter, UK: Bradt Publications, 1998.

Batalha, Luis, and Jørgen Carling, eds. *Transnational Archipelago: Cape Verdean Migration and Diaspora.* Amsterdam: Amsterdam University Press, 2008.

Beck, Sam. *Manny Almeida's Ringside Lounge: The Cape Verdeans' Struggle for Their Neighborhood.* Providence: Gávea-Brown Publications, 1992.

Carter, Katherine, and Judy Aulette. "Creole in Cape Verde: Language, Identity and Power." *Ethnography* 10, no. 2 (2009): 213–37.

Fisher, Gene A., and Suzanne Model. "Cape Verdean Identity in a Land of Black and White." *Ethnicities* 12 (2012): 354–79.

Gibau, Gina Sánchez. "Contested Identities: Narratives of Race and Ethnicity in the Cape Verdean Diaspora." *Identities: Global Studies in Culture and Power* 12, no. 3 (2005): 405–38.

Halter, Marilyn. *Between Race and Ethnicity: Cape Verdean American Immigrants, 1860–1965.* Chicago: University of Illinois Press, 1993.

———. "Diasporic Generations: Distinctions of Race, Nationality and Identity in the Cape Verdean Community, Past and Present." In *Community, Culture and the Makings of Identity: Portuguese-Americans along the Eastern Seaboard*, edited by Kimberly DaCosta Holton and Andrea Klimt. North Dartmouth: University of Massachusetts Dartmouth, 2009.

Hayden, Robert C. *African-Americans and Cape-Verdean Americans in New Bedford: A History of Community and Achievement.* Boston: Select Publications, 1993.

Lobban, Richard Andrew. *Cape Verde: Crioulo Colony to Independent Nation.* Boulder, CO: Westview Press, 1995.

Meintel, Deirdre. "Cape Verdean Transnationalism, Old and New." *Anthropologica* 44, no. 1 (2002): 25–42.

Nunes, Maria Luisa. *A Portuguese Colonial in America, Belmira Nunes Lopes: The Autobiography of a Cape Verdean American.* Pittsburgh: Latin American Literary Review Press, 1982.

CARPATHO-RUSYN AMERICANS

Paul Robert Magocsi

OVERVIEW

Carpatho-Rusyn Americans are immigrants or descendants of immigrants from a region of Europe known as Carpathian Rus' (or Ruthenia). The region is located in the geographical center of the European continent, on the northern and southern slopes of the Carpathian Mountains where Poland, Slovakia, Ukraine, and Romania meet; smaller numbers of Carpatho-Rusyns reside in neighboring northeastern Hungary and, farther south, in the province of Vojvodina in Serbia and immediately adjacent Croatia. At the outset of the twentieth century, the majority of the population of Carpathian Rus' was composed of Carpatho-Rusyns. Defined as a territory, it is primarily a land of mountains and foothills and covers just over 7,000 square miles, making it about the size of New Jersey.

Carpathian Rus' has never been an independent country, and Carpatho-Rusyns (also known in English as Carpatho-Ruthenians, or simply Ruthenians) have always lived as a national minority in one or more European states. At times, some of those states have refused even to recognize the existence of Carpatho-Rusyns. For these reasons it is difficult to determine their exact number. Informed estimates suggest that there may be just over one million Carpatho-Rusyns living in Carpathian Rus' today, although official census data from Poland, Slovakia, Ukraine, and Romania record only 56,000. Other groups in Carpathian Rus' include Poles, Slovaks, Ukrainians, Romanians, Hungarians, and Roma/Gypsies. Carpathian Rus' has traditionally been the least economically developed region of whatever country it has been a part. Its main resources are forests, mineral water springs, and salt deposits; a significant number of Carpatho-Rusyns continue to be engaged primarily in small-scale agriculture, in animal husbandry (mainly sheep), or as employees in light industrial plants, including lumber mills.

Carpatho-Rusyns began to immigrate to the United States in the 1880s. They were part of the "new immigration" of people from eastern and southern Europe that continued to increase in number until the outbreak of World War I in 1914. Most settled in the industrialized regions of the northeastern United States—in particular Pennsylvania, New York, New Jersey, Connecticut, and Ohio. By the second half of the twentieth century Carpatho-Rusyns had followed the path of other residents in the Northeast, who today are no longer employed in factories, mills, and mines, but rather—for the most part—in service industries and white-collar professions.

The Carpatho-Rusyn Research Center estimates that in 2010 there were about 620,000 people in the United States who have one or more ancestors of Carpatho-Rusyn origin. Most still live in the former industrial and steel-belt areas of the Northeastern United States, although there are an increasing number who live farther south, in Virginia and Florida, or farther west, in Arizona and California. There are no longer any towns or cities where Carpatho-Rusyns live in concentrated immigrant communities. Rather, they are scattered throughout regions surrounding cities such as New York (including northern New Jersey); Binghamton-Elmira-Johnson City in upstate New York; Scranton-Hazleton in eastern Pennsylvania; Washington, D.C., and its surrounding suburbs in Maryland and northern Virginia; and especially western Pennsylvania, where the largest number still live in small towns surrounding Pittsburgh.

HISTORY OF THE PEOPLE

As a people who never had their own independent state, Carpatho-Rusyns have been subject to the whims of the rulers and policies of the countries in which they have lived. According to present-day boundaries, historic Carpathian Rus' is located within the borders of four countries, each of which includes territory where the majority or a significant portion of the population is Carpatho-Rusyn: the Lemko Region in southeastern Poland; the Prešov Region in northeastern Slovakia; Subcarpathian Rus', or Transcarpathia, in far western Ukraine; and the Maramureş Region in north-central Romania.

Early History The ancestors of Carpatho-Rusyns—various Slavic tribes from the north and Slavicized Vlachs from the south—settled over several centuries in the foothills and valleys of the north-central Carpathian Mountains. Beginning in the sixth and seventh centuries, a tribe known as White Croats appeared, followed by other Slavs known as Rusyns, who came from what is today northwestern Ukraine.

In-migration from the north continued at least until the fifteenth or sixteenth century, at which time Vlach shepherds from the Balkans penetrated the Carpathians from the south and in the process became assimilated into the Slavic-speaking Rusyn people.

In the course of the eleventh and twelfth centuries, Carpathian Rus' came under the rule of two states: the Hungarian Kingdom on the southern slopes of the mountains (the Prešov Region, Subcarpathian Rus', and the Maramureş Region); and the Polish Kingdom on the northern slopes (the Lemko Region). During the medieval and early modern eras, three developments unfolded that were to have a lasting impact on Carpatho-Rusyn society.

The first was the late ninth-century mission undertaken by two brothers from the Byzantine (or Eastern Roman) Empire, Cyril and Methodius, who either directly or more likely through their disciples brought Christianity in its Eastern-rite form to Carpatho-Rusyns. The importance of these figures is remembered to this day in many Carpatho-Rusyn religious institutions in the United States, which are named after Saints Cyril and Methodius.

The second development concerned the enserfment of the peasantry, a practice that was legally implemented in Hungary in 1514 and in Poland in 1573. Since the vast majority of Carpatho-Rusyns were small-scale peasant agriculturalists, this meant that virtually the entire group became proprietary serfs, unable to leave their homesteads and required to perform labor duties for the landlord who "owned" them. Their subordinate social status remained in force until as late as 1848 and was a factor contributing to their impoverished status even after "emancipation." It was that ongoing rural poverty that prompted emigration abroad in the 1870s and 1880s.

The third development was the church union implemented in Poland (the Union of Brest, 1596) and in Hungary (the Union of Uzhhorod, 1646), at which time some Orthodox clergy and parishes entered into union with the Catholic Church of Rome, while others refused. The result was religious division among Carpatho-Rusyns in Europe, which has continued among immigrants and their descendants in the United States.

The political status of Carpathian Rus' changed at the end of the eighteenth century. By that time, the Hungarian Kingdom had already become part of the Austrian Empire, and in 1795 Poland disappeared from the map of Europe. The former Polish-ruled province of Galicia (which included the Lemko Region) had already been annexed to the Austrian Empire in 1772, with the result that all of Carpathian Rus' on the northern as well as southern slopes of the Carpathian Mountains was now within one state. That state, known after 1868 as the Austro-Hungarian Empire, was ruled by the Habsburg dynasty, whose long-reigning emperor, Franz Joseph (reigned 1848–1916),

was especially popular among Carpatho-Rusyns both in the homeland and among his emigrant "subjects" living temporary or permanently in the United States.

During the period of Habsburg rule under Emperor Franz Joseph, Carpatho-Rusyns were emancipated from serfdom (in 1848) and experienced what was called a national awakening. This was a process whereby an ethnic group speaking a particular language (or series of dialects) was encouraged by its leaders (the so-called intelligentsia) to become aware of their existence as a distinct people or nationality. The most influential of the post-1848 Carpatho-Rusyn "national awakeners" was priest and writer Alexander Dukhnovych (1803–1865), who is still remembered today by Carpatho-Rusyns in the United States, with commemorative events, organizations, and prizes named after him, and the singing of the Carpatho-Rusyn national hymn ("I Was, Am, and Will Remain a Rusyn") and national anthem ("Subcarpathian Rusyns, Arise from Your Deep Slumber"), whose lyrics were either written by or attributed to him.

From the outset of the national revival, Carpatho-Rusyn leaders faced several challenges. The first was to define what the term *Rusyn* meant and, in particular, the relationship of Carpatho-Rusyns to other East Slavs, or Rus' peoples—the Russians, Belarusans, and Ukrainians. They were also faced with the question of defining their identity and adopting an appropriate literary language. Were the East Slavs living in Carpathian Rus' part of the Russian nationality or the Ukrainian nationality, or did they represent a distinct Carpatho-Rusyn nationality? Analogously, should their literary language be Russian, Ukrainian, or a distinct Carpatho-Rusyn language based on local dialects? Aside from debates among leaders about which East Slavic identity to choose, the inhabitants of many villages, in particular in the lowland areas of what is today southeastern Slovakia and northeastern Hungary, were gradually losing their Carpatho-Rusyn identity though assimilation with Slovaks and Hungarians. Such controversies regarding national orientation were brought to the United States by the early immigrants and still exist among some of their descendants to the present day.

Modern Era The twentieth century brought profound changes to Central Europe, resulting in the political division of Carpathian Rus'. Following the end of World War I in late 1918, Austria-Hungary ceased to exist and Carpatho-Rusyn territory was divided among several countries. The Prešov Region and Subcarpathian Rus' south of the mountains became part of Czechoslovakia, with the exception of a few villages in the Maramureş Region that were incorporated into Romania. The Lemko Region along the northern slopes was joined to Poland. The few Rusyn settlements in the Vojvodina Region in the far south of the former Hungarian Kingdom became part of Yugoslavia. Rusyn American immigrants played an active role in the postwar political developments and were especially influential in the decision to unite most of Carpathian Rus' south of the mountains into Czechoslovakia.

Within Czechoslovakia (both Subcarpathian Rus' and the Prešov Region in Slovakia), Carpatho-Rusyns experienced a new national revival and a marked improvement in their educational and cultural standards. However, Czechoslovakia's refusal to fulfill postwar international agreements and to grant autonomy (self-rule) to Subcarpathian Rus' alienated many local leaders as well as former Rusyn American activists. Only on the eve of World War II, following the Munich Pact imposed upon Czechoslovakia by Nazi Germany, did Subcarpathian Rus' (renamed Carpatho-Ukraine on October 11, 1938) finally obtain its autonomous status. Autonomy lasted less than six months (October 1938–March 1939), however, after which Hitler destroyed what remained of Czechoslovakia and allowed Hungary to reannex Subcarpathian Rus'/Carpatho-Ukraine. Consequently, during World War II Carpathian Rus' was divided among three states: Subcarpathian Rus', the Maramureş Region, and the Vojvodina were in Hungary; the Prešov Region was in independent Slovakia; and the Lemko Region (after the destruction of Poland) was in Nazi Germany.

At the close of World War II, borders changed once again, but this time the very existence of Carpatho-Rusyns as a distinct people was also threatened. In 1945 the largest Carpatho-Rusyn territory (Subcarpathian Rus') was annexed to the Soviet Union, specifically Soviet Ukraine. The Prešov Region remained within restored Czechoslovakia; the Lemko Region was assigned to a restored Poland; and the Maramureş Region was returned to Romania. Between 1945 and 1948 all these countries came under Communist rule and were politically subordinate to the Soviet Union.

The Soviets and their Communist satellite neighboring countries "resolved" the Carpatho-Rusyn nationality question by administrative decree. Regardless of what Carpatho-Rusyns may have called themselves or believed their national identity to be, they were henceforth considered Ukrainians. The Lemko Region "Ukrainians" faced an even worse fate: between 1945 and 1947 they were either resettled to Soviet Ukraine or forcibly deported to the western regions of Poland. In neighboring Slovakia and Romania, Carpatho-Rusyns were also administratively transformed into Ukrainians during the early 1950s. In short, a Rusyn identity was banned in all countries where Carpatho-Rusyns lived, with the exception of the small group of Vojvodinian Rusyns (about 25,000 of them) in Yugoslavia. Although Yugoslavia was under Communist rule, it was not a Soviet satellite; it not only recognized its Rusyns as a distinct nationality but also actively encouraged Rusyn-language education and cultural development.

Another result of post-1945 Communist rule was the Soviet-imposed Iron Curtain, which brought the virtual end to all contact, including travel and even postal communications, between Carpatho-Rusyn immigrants in the United States and their relatives in the European homeland. This ban, which remained in force until the end of 1980s, contributed to the alienation of most Carpatho-Rusyn Americans from their ancestral homeland.

The Revolutions of 1989, which brought an end to Communist rule in Central Europe and led to the collapse of the Soviet Union two years later, had a profound impact on Carpathian Rus' and, indirectly, on Americans of Carpatho-Rusyn descent. In effect, the events of 1989 allowed for the "reestablishment" of Carpatho-Rusyns as a distinct people in their European homeland and a further revival of Carpatho-Rusyn identity in the United States.

After being cut off from the European homeland for nearly half a century, Rusyn American contact with the homeland was renewed following the Revolutions of 1989, the fall of Communism, and the collapse of the Soviet Union.

In the wake of the Communist collapse in Central and Eastern Europe, four new states came into being: Carpatho-Rusyns in the Prešov Region found themselves in independent Slovakia; those in Subcarpathian Rus'/Transcarpathia in independent Ukraine; and those in the former Yugoslavia in independent Serbia (Vojvodina) and Croatia. These states rejected their Communist totalitarian past; professed liberal democratic principles; and permitted the establishment of grassroots civic organizations, all of which professed the view that Carpatho-Rusyns represented a distinct nationality that deserved to have a newly codified Rusyn literary language taught in schools and used in the media for other cultural activity. These organizations were assisted by Carpatho-Rusyns in the United States, who, after nearly half a century of enforced separation from their relatives and friends were finally able to reconnect with the homeland.

Since 1989 the status of Carpatho-Rusyns has steadily improved, especially after several of the countries where they live (Poland, Slovakia, the Czech Republic, Hungary, and Romania) became part of the European Union during the first decade of the twenty-first century. The governments of each of those countries, as well as Serbia and Croatia, provide varying degrees of support for Rusyn-language publications, radio and television programs, theaters and cultural ensembles, and especially schools, from the elementary to university level. Only Ukraine has been reluctant to provide such support, since certain circles in the highest levels of the Ukrainian government and civic society continue to argue that Carpatho-Rusyns are not a distinct nationality, but rather a branch (sub-ethnos) of the Ukrainian nationality. Such negative views have encouraged Carpatho-Rusyns in the United States to undertake various efforts to protest against the official position of Ukraine toward Carpatho-Rusyns.

SETTLEMENT IN THE UNITED STATES

Carpatho-Rusyns began immigrating to the United States in the late 1870s and 1880s. By the outbreak of World War I, approximately 225,000 had arrived. This was to be the largest number of Carpatho-Rusyns ever to reach the United States. When emigration resumed after World War I, only about 20,000 came in the second wave. From World War II through the first decade of the twenty-first century, the numbers were smaller still—at most, 12,000. Upon arrival in the United States, the vast majority of Carpatho-Rusyns identified with the state they had left. Therefore, it is impossible to know their exact number. Based on immigration statistics and membership records in religious and secular organizations, it is reasonable to assume that there are about 620,000 Americans who have at least one ancestor of Carpatho-Rusyn background.

At the time of the first and largest wave of immigration (1880s to 1914), the Carpatho-Rusyn homeland was located entirely within the Austro-Hungarian Empire. That empire was itself divided into two parts: about three-quarters of Carpatho-Rusyns lived in the

northeastern corner of the Hungarian Kingdom, with the remainder in the Austrian province of Galicia. The economic situation for Carpatho-Rusyns was the same in both parts of Austria-Hungary. Their approximately 1,000 villages were all located in hilly or mountainous terrain from which the inhabitants eked out a subsistence-level living based on small-scale agriculture, livestock grazing (especially sheep), and seasonal labor on the richer plains of lowland Hungary. Their livelihood was always precarious, however, and following a growth in the population and shortage of land, many felt they had no choice but to immigrate to the United States.

Most of the earliest immigrants in the 1870s and 1880s were young men who hoped to work a year or so, save up their money, and then return home. Some engaged in seasonal labor and may have migrated back and forth several times between Europe and the United States in the decades before 1914. Others eventually brought their families and stayed permanently. Before World War I, movement between Europe and the United States was relatively easy for enthusiastic young laborers, but U.S. immigration restrictions (enacted in 1921 and 1924) and the imposition after 1945 of direct or indirect Soviet rule in the European homeland put an effective end to almost all cross-border emigration and seasonal migration.

Because earning money was the main goal of the immigrants, they settled primarily in the Northeast

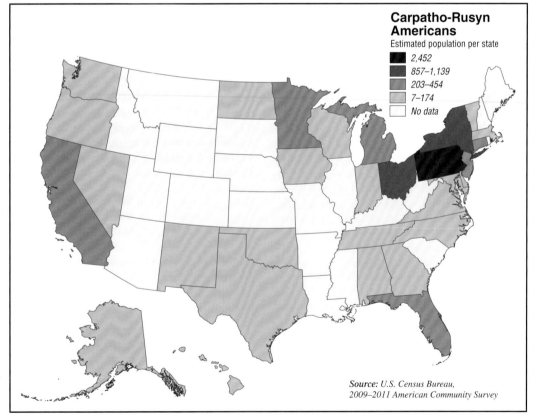

Source: U.S. Census Bureau, 2009–2011 American Community Survey

and north-central states, in particular the coal-mining region around Scranton and Wilkes-Barre in eastern Pennsylvania, and in Pittsburgh and its suburbs in the western part of that state. Other cities and metropolitan areas that attracted Carpatho-Rusyns were New York City and northeastern New Jersey; southern Connecticut; the Binghamton-Endicott-Johnson City triangle in south-central New York; Cleveland and Youngstown, Ohio; Gary and Whiting, Indiana; Detroit and Flint, Michigan; and Minneapolis, Minnesota.

LANGUAGE

Carpatho-Rusyns are Slavs by origin. They speak a series of dialects that are classified as East Slavic and that are most closely related to Ukrainian. However, because their homeland is located within a political and linguistic borderland, Carpatho-Rusyns' speech has been heavily influenced by neighboring West Slavic languages such as Slovak and Polish, as well as by Hungarian. Several attempts have been undertaken in the European homeland and in the United States to codify this unique speech pattern into a distinct Carpatho-Rusyn literary language. The most successful results have been in the Vojvodina region of Yugoslavia, where a local Rusyn literary language has existed since the early 1920s, as well as in present-day Slovakia and Poland, where a Rusyn literary language was formally codified in 1995 and 2000.

The early immigrants to the United States used Rusyn for both spoken and written communication. As early as 1892, the *Amerikansky russky viestnik* (American Rusyn Messenger) began to appear in Mahanoy City and eventually Homestead, Pennsylvania, as the weekly and, at times, three-times-weekly newspaper of the Greek Catholic Union. It was published completely in Rusyn until 1952, after which it switched gradually and then entirely to English. That newspaper was one of fifty weekly and monthly Rusyn-language publications that have appeared in the United States, including the daily newspaper *Den'* (*The Day*; New York, 1922–1926). Traditionally, the Rusyn language uses the Cyrillic alphabet. Cyrillic was initially also used in the United States, although by the 1920s a Roman-based alphabet became more widespread. Today there are no newspapers or journals published in the United States that use any form of the Rusyn language.

First generation immigrants, in particular, wanted to pass on the native language to their American-born offspring. Hence, church-sponsored parochial and weekend schools were set up, especially from 1900 to 1930. To preserve the native language, several Rusyn American grammars, readers, catechisms, and other texts were published. The language was also taught in both Byzantine Catholic and Carpatho-Russian Orthodox seminaries and used on a few radio programs during the 1940s and 1950s in New York City, Pittsburgh, Cleveland, and other cities with large Carpatho-Rusyn concentrations. At present there are no longer Rusyn-language radio programs or seminary courses. On the other hand, several adult-education classes, usually associated with a church parish or branch of the Carpatho-Rusyn Society, are being held in an effort to teach Rusyn to those who have never used it before.

Greetings and Popular Expressions Common greetings in Rusyn include the following: *Sláva Ysúsu Chrýstu* (literally Praise be to Jesus Christ, commonly Hello); *Dóbryj dyn'* (Good day); *Što sja róbyt?* (What's up?); *Jakóje vášoje imnjá* (What is your name?). Other common expressions include: *Dúže krásnȳj dyn'* (It's a beautiful day); *Ščastlývoje naródynja* (Happy birthday); and *Na zdoróvlja!* (To your health!; Cheers!)

RELIGION

Carpatho-Rusyns are Christians and, for the most part, belong to various Eastern Christian churches. They trace their Christian origins back to the second half of the ninth century, when the disciples of the Byzantine Greek monks Cyril and Methodius brought Christianity from the Eastern Roman (Byzantine) Empire to Carpathian Rus'. After 1054, when the Christian world was divided into Roman Catholic and Orthodox spheres, the Carpatho-Rusyns remained part of the Eastern tradition. Among the features that characterized the Eastern Christian tradition were churches with golden domes on the outside and an icon screen (iconostasis) on the inside separating the altar from the congregation; the use of Church Slavonic (written in the Cyrillic alphabet) instead of Latin as the liturgical language; the possibility for married men to serve as priests; and use of the Julian, or "old," calendar, according to which nonmovable feasts like Christmas were celebrated about two weeks after the Gregorian, or Western, calendar. Eastern Orthodox Christians also recognized as the nominal head of their church the ecumenical patriarch, who resided in Constantinople, the capital of the former Byzantine Empire.

The matter of church jurisdiction changed in the mid-seventeenth century, when some Carpatho-Rusyn Orthodox bishops and priests entered into union with the Roman Catholic Church. These Uniates, as they were initially called, were at first allowed to keep their Eastern rite and traditions, but they were required to accept the authority of the Pope in Rome instead of the Orthodox ecumenical patriarch. Because the Uniates continued to follow the Eastern rite and church practices derived from Byzantium, they were eventually called Greek Catholics and today are known as Byzantine Rite Catholics.

Regardless of whether Carpatho-Rusyns were Orthodox or Byzantine Rite Catholics, the church remained a central feature of their lives in the European homeland. Until well into the twentieth

The Reverend Paul J. Hicha stands before his Carpathian Russian Orthodox Catholic church in Colorado's Little Carpathia, which includes parts of El Pasco and Elbert counties. IRA GAY SEALY / THE DENVER POST VIA GETTY IMAGES

priests from the European homeland, and created mutual-benefit societies to provide insurance and worker's compensation in times of sickness or accident as well as to help support the new churches. The oldest and still the largest of these fraternal societies was the Greek Catholic Union, founded in 1892 in Wilkes-Barre, Pennsylvania, and then transferred to the suburbs of Pittsburgh in 1906. The churches and fraternals each had their services and publications in the Carpatho-Rusyn language, as well as schools in which children were taught the language of their parents. In short, during this first period, the immigrants felt that they could not be accepted fully into American society, and so they created various religious and secular organizations that would preserve their old world culture and language.

Aside from losing members to Orthodoxy, the Greek/Byzantine Rite Catholic Church was also having difficulty maintaining traditional practices. After 1929 Greek/Byzantine Rite Catholics were required by Rome to accept the practice of celibacy for their priests and to turn over all church property to their bishop—property that until then was generally held by laypersons who had built and paid for the buildings. This resulted in the "celibacy controversy," which caused great dissatisfaction and led to the defection of thousands more Greek/Byzantine Rite Catholics, who subsequently created a new American Carpatho-Russian Orthodox Church. The Greek/Byzantine Rite Catholics also gave up other traditional practices, and by the 1950s and 1960s they had changed to the Western calendar and used primarily English in their services.

The division between Orthodoxy and Byzantine Rite Catholicism in the European homeland has continued among Carpatho-Rusyn immigrants and their descendants in the United States, who today are served by three Eastern-rite churches. The Byzantine Rite Catholic Church has four eparchies (dioceses), with seats in Pittsburgh, Pennsylvania; Passaic, New Jersey; Parma, Ohio; and Phoenix, Arizona. The American Carpatho-Russian Orthodox Church has one diocese, based in Johnstown, Pennsylvania. The Orthodox Church in America (formerly the Russian Orthodox Church in North America), with its seat in Syosset (Long Island), New York, has twelve dioceses across the country. The approximate Carpatho-Rusyn membership in these churches is as follows: Byzantine Rite Catholics—195,000; Carpatho-Russian Orthodox—18,000; and Orthodox Church in America—250,000.

century, all rites of passage (births/baptisms, weddings, funerals) and civic events in Rusyn villages and towns were governed by the church calendar. In many ways, Carpatho-Rusyn culture and identity were synonymous with either the Greek/Byzantine Rite Catholics or the Orthodox Church. Virtually all of the early Carpatho-Rusyn cultural leaders, including the nineteenth-century "national awakener" Aleksander Dukhnovych, were priests.

Because religion was so important, it is not surprising that Carpatho-Rusyns tried to re-create aspects of their church-directed life after immigrating to the United States. From the very outset, however, the Byzantine Rite Catholics met with resistance from American Catholic bishops, who before World War I were intolerant of all traditions that were not in accord with American Roman Catholic norms (especially those that used "foreign" languages and followed practices that allowed married men to become priests). As a result, thousands of Greek/Byzantine Rite Catholics left their church and joined the Russian Orthodox Church of North America. This "return to the ancient faith" began as early as 1892 and was led by a priest who at the time was based in Minneapolis, Father Alexis Toth.

Unable to practice their Eastern rite within the framework of the Roman Catholic Church, Carpatho-Rusyns built their own churches, invited

In the early years of the immigration, when Carpatho-Rusyns did not yet have their own churches, many Greek/Byzantine Rite Catholics attended, and eventually joined, Roman Catholic churches. Subsequently, intermarriage increased the number of Carpatho-Rusyn Roman Catholics, who today may number as high as 80,000 to 100,000. The community's internal religious controversies and the proselytizing efforts of American Protestant churches, especially in the early decades of the twentieth century, have also resulted in the growth of several evangelical sects among Carpatho-Rusyns and conversions, especially to various Baptist churches.

CULTURE AND ASSIMILATION

From the 1880s to about 1925, Carpatho-Rusyns in the United States felt estranged both linguistically and culturally from the American world surrounding them. Not only did they speak a foreign language, but they were also members of a "strange" Eastern Christian church that initially did not exist in the United States. Like other eastern and southern Europeans, Carpatho-Rusyn immigrants were effectively segregated from the rest of American society because of their low economic status and lack of knowledge of English. They were never singled out as a group, but rather lumped together with other Slavic and Hungarian laborers and called by the opprobrious epithet *Hunkies*. However, this was a relatively short phase; by the late 1930s and 1940s the American-born sons and daughters of the original immigrants had adapted to the host society and become absorbed into the American middle class. Effectively, Americans of Carpatho-Rusyn descent are now an invisible minority within the white middle-class majority.

For nearly a half-century, the children of immigrants born in the United States increasingly rejected the old-world heritage of their parents and tried to assimilate fully into American life. New youth organizations were founded that used only English, while the most popular sports clubs, even within the pre–World War I organizations, were devoted to American sports such as baseball, basketball, bowling, and golf. In essence, Carpatho-Rusyns seemed to want to do everything possible—even at the expense of forgetting their ethnic and religious heritage—to be like other Americans. Even the international situation was helpful in this regard, as throughout virtually this entire period Carpatho-Rusyn Americans were cut off from the European homeland by the economic hardships of the 1930s, World War II, and finally the imposition of Communist rule and the creation of the Iron Curtain after 1945.

Like many other "assimilated" Americans, some third generation descendants of Carpatho-Rusyn immigrants have wanted to learn what their grandparents knew so well but what their parents tried desperately to forget. This quest for ethnic rediscovery was inspired by the nationwide telecast of the African American saga *Roots* in 1977 on top of the celebrations surrounding the bicentennial of the United States in 1976. In contrast to earlier times, American society as a whole no longer stigmatized such interest in the old world but actually encouraged the search for one's roots. Since then, an increasing number of Americans of Carpatho-Rusyn background have begun to learn

about and maintain nostalgic ties with an ancestral culture that they otherwise never really knew.

All this was made possible because of a marked revival of individual and community-based organizational activity. New organizations and community groups were founded in the late 1970s, and several new publications began to appear that dealt with all aspects of Carpatho-Rusyn culture. A scholarly organization, the Carpatho-Rusyn Research Center, was founded in 1978; since then it has distributed tens of thousands of books and maps about Rusyn culture and history and for two decades published a popular quarterly, the *Carpatho-Rusyn American* (1978–1999). The research center's existence encouraged university-based historians, linguists, and literary specialists to develop for the first time a scholarly discipline of Carpatho-Rusyn studies, and a new generation of English-language writers (Sonya Jason and Mark Wansa, among others) began to publish prose works based on Carpatho-Rusyn themes.

In order to popularize Carpatho-Rusyn culture at the grassroots level, other organizations were established or renewed in places where the group has traditionally lived, including the Rusin Association of Minnesota, the Carpatho-Rusyn Cultural Society of Michigan, and the Rusin Cultural Garden in Cleveland. This trend toward cultural renewal and the rediscovery of one's heritage was especially enhanced by the political changes that took place in Central and Eastern Europe after 1989. With the decline of Communism, visits to families and friends that effectively had been cut off by the Iron Curtain became a common occurrence.

Interaction with the homeland has also had a direct impact on activists in the United States. In 1994 several Rusyn American enthusiasts, led by John Senich Righetti, formed the Carpatho-Rusyn Society, which within a few years evolved into the largest and most effective grassroots organization dedicated to promoting Carpatho-Rusyn culture and identity in the United States. Originally based in western Pennsylvania, where its headquarters are housed in a monumental Cultural and Educational Center (the former Greek Catholic Cathedral), the Carpatho-Rusyn Society is today a national organization with vibrantly active branches in Phoenix, Arizona; Cleveland, Ohio; eastern Pennsylvania; the Lake Erie region; Washington, D.C., and its surrounding suburbs; New England; New Jersey; New York City; the Greater Pittsburgh area; Youngstown, Ohio; and the Lake Michigan region.

Traditions and Customs Although Carpatho-Rusyn immigrants and their descendants have largely adopted American cultural traditions, one tradition that has been continued in the United States is the *Vatra*, or bonfire. This event is typically a multiday festival featuring traditional foods, dances, and folk songs. Often, as the night progresses, the bravest attendees will attempt to leap over the bonfire. Since 2005, the Carpatho-Rusyn society has organized an annual *Vatra* in regions with large Rusyn populations, such as Ohio and Pennsylvania.

Cuisine Traditional Carpatho-Rusyn foods include *studenina* (jellied pigs feet), *halupki* (cabbage stuffed with meat, rice, and spices and often covered in tomato sauce), *haluski* (fried noodles or dumplings served with cabbage), *palachinke* (crepes filled with cheese or fruit), *pascha* (a bread typically baked around Easter), kielbasa sausages, and sauerkraut (a pickled cabbage condiment). *Perohy*, dough stuffed with potato and cheese, has become particularly popular in Ohio and Pennsylvania.

Traditional Dress Although most Rusyn Americans tend to wear typical American clothing, Carpatho-Rusyn folk attire can commonly be found at cultural events. Almost all traditional Carpatho-Rusyn clothing features colorful, detailed embroidery and patterns, typically on linen or wool materials. In the lowlands, men and women typically wore wider, loose-fitting shirts, trousers, dresses, or skirts, while those living in the Carpathian Mountains wore tighter-fitting attire. Men often wore collared white linen shirts and broad, colorful belts over linen or wool *gati* (trousers), while women wore long skirts, dresses, or *zapasky* (aprons), sometime accompanied by a shawl or scarf.

Dances and Songs A popular song in the Carpatho-Rusyn nationalist movement, one that has come to be recognized as a de facto national anthem for many Carpatho-Rusyns, is "*Podkarpatskije Rusiny— ostavte hlubokij son*," which means "Subcarpathian Rusyns, Arise from Your Deep Slumber." Based on the poem "I Am Rusyn," by nineteenth-century nationalist leader Aleksander Dukhnovych, the song is sung at most Carpatho-Rusyn cultural events. Another popular folk song is "*Červena ruža trojaka*," or "Red Rose," which is a slow-paced love song often sung as a lullaby.

Carpatho-Rusyns also have a long tradition of performing folk dances. Perhaps the most common dance is the *Rus'ka Pol'ka*, or Rusyn polka, a variation on the polka common to many Eastern European countries. Other traditional dances include the *Fljashkovyj Tanec*, or bottle dance, the *Sokyra Tanec*, an axe dance that can be traced to nineteenth-century forest workers, and the *Karichka*, a circle dance performed at gatherings and events.

In the latter part of the twentieth century and the beginning of the twenty-first, several new song-and-dance ensembles, the largest of which is the folk group Slavjane in Pittsburgh, were founded by third, fourth, and fifth generation descendants of the pre–World War I immigrants. Since 1961 Slavjane has performed traditional Rusyn folk dances and songs throughout the United States. Other Rusyn American dance and music ensembles include the Karpato-Rus' Ensemble and the Living Traditions Folk Ensemble.

Holidays Carpatho-Rusyn holidays are mostly religious in nature. Perhaps the most sacred of these holidays is Christmas Eve. On this day, Rusyns celebrate *Svjatyj Vecer*, or Holy Supper, which is typically a twelve-course meatless meal, with each course symbolizing one of the apostles. The table is often adorned with hay, to symbolize Christ's birth in a manger, and family members from miles around remain seated there until the last course, typically *kolaci* (strudels), has been eaten. The meal concludes with a round of Christmas carols, and the family then attends Midnight Mass. Many Carpatho-Rusyn families have given up the more explicit religious traditions involved with the "Big Supper," as it is often called, but the annual feast remains a popular custom in the United States.

Velykden (Easter) is also an important holiday among Carpatho-Rusyns and Carpatho-Rusyn Americans. Traditionally celebrated as the end of a forty-day fast for Lent, this holiday typically features an abundance of foods, including *pascha* (a bread meant to symbolize Christ), veal, pork, ham, eggs, and cheeses, especially *hrudka*, which is made from eggs and milk. Often these foods are placed in a basket that is brought to church to be blessed and then shared among other churchgoers or returned home to be consumed during a large feast. Another Easter tradition familiar to other American ethnic groups is the decoration of eggs. Known as *pysanki*, these eggs are not eaten, but are displayed in the home or given as gifts.

A secular holiday with special meaning for Carpatho-Rusyn Americans has been held annually on October 26 since 2010. Known as Carpatho-Rusyn Day, this day commemorates a gathering that took place in 1918 at Philadelphia's Independence Hall in which Carpatho-Rusyn Americans, along with representatives of other stateless ethnic groups, asserted their cultural identities with a Declaration of Common Aims. It is typically marked by cultural celebrations hosted by various Rusyn groups throughout North America.

Death and Burial Rituals Carpatho-Rusyn immigrants to the United States initially followed funeral traditions from the old world. The deceased was laid out in the family's living room, where visitations by friends and family took place. An exhibition of a typical Rusyn American wake is on permanent display at the Senator Heinz Historical Center in Pittsburgh.

Three days later a funeral service was held in a Byzantine Catholic or Orthodox church, followed by a shorter prayer service at the gravesite in cemeteries where tombstones in the Rusyn variant of the Cyrillic alphabet are still visible. Since World War II, and almost without exception, wakes have been held in funeral homes, and very rarely are there any tombstones in a language other than English. Although the practice is generally frowned upon, some of the dead are cremated and not buried within the traditional three-day time frame.

FAMILY AND COMMUNITY LIFE

In the Carpatho-Rusyn homeland, where there was a need for agricultural laborers, families were often large, with an average of six to ten children. Family homesteads might also house grandparents as well as a newly wedded son or daughter and spouse waiting to earn enough to establish their own home. Many villages were made up of three or four extended families interrelated through blood or connected by other relationships, such as godparents.

The earliest Carpatho-Rusyn immigrants were young men who moved into boarding houses. Those who remained in the United States eventually married or brought their families from Europe. The extended family structure typical of the European village was replaced by nuclear families living in individual houses or apartments that included parents and on average, three to four children.

Courtship and Weddings The traditional old-world pattern of marriages arranged by parents, sometimes with the help of a *starosta* (matchmaker), was, with rare exceptions, not followed among Carpatho-Rusyn immigrants. Instead, individuals courted and found their own partners. In the decades before World War II, parents encouraged their children to find a marriage partner of the same faith (Catholic or Orthodox) and, whenever possible, of Carpatho-Rusyn or at least Slavic background. This was relatively easier at a time when these groups lived in geographic proximity in the mining and mill towns of the Northeast United States. However, as Carpatho-Rusyns dispersed to various parts of the country and as parental pressure lessened (or was simply ignored), young people of Carpatho-Rusyn background have increasingly intermarried with Americans of non-Slavic heritage and with a religious background different than their own.

Education Carpatho-Rusyns derived from a society in which education was viewed in different ways. The children of priests and urban-based professionals made sure their children (both boys and girls) had an elementary education. The children of the vast majority of Carpatho-Rusyns, who were village-based farmers, typically attended at most a few years of elementary school. In the United States, all were required to complete elementary school and a few years of high school. Until at least the 1950s, parents did not urge their daughters to continue their education after high school but instead to get married and serve as the homemaker for a family. Boys were often encouraged to go to technical schools or to begin work as an apprentice in a trade. Since the 1960s, however, an increasing number of both young men and women have been encouraged by parents to attend colleges and universities.

Gender Roles Before the 1950s women were encouraged to become homemakers, but they were always welcome to take an active part in community activity. At least since the 1930s, women have served on the governing boards of Rusyn American fraternals, have had their own sports clubs, and have been particularly effective in establishing ladies' guilds that, through social events, have been able to raise extensive funds to help local church parishes. To this day, many ladies' guilds operate catering and small food services from the basements of churches, cooking traditional Rusyn dishes like *holubky* (stuffed cabbage) and *pirohy* (three-cornered cheese- or potato-filled dumplings) and selling them to the community at large. The profits go to the church.

EMPLOYMENT AND ECONOMIC CONDITIONS

Although the vast majority of Carpatho-Rusyns who came to the United States during the major wave of immigration before World War I left small villages where they worked as small-scale subsistence farmers or as livestock herders, only a handful found jobs in agriculture in the United States. As one priest and community activist quipped earlier in the century, "Our people do not live in America, they live *under* America!" This remark reflects the fact that many of the earliest Carpatho-Rusyn immigrants found employment in the coal-mining belt in eastern Pennsylvania. Because they lacked industrial and mining skills upon arrival, they were given the most menial tasks, such as coal splitting and carting. Carpatho-Rusyns were also attracted to the iron mines in upstate Minnesota; the lead mines of south-central Missouri; the coal mines of southern Oklahoma and Washington state; the gold, silver, and lead mines of Colorado; and the marble quarries of Vermont. But even more important than mining was the growing steel industry of Pittsburgh and its neighboring towns. The steel mills and associated industries employed most Carpatho-Rusyns who lived in western Pennsylvania and neighboring Ohio.

Even before World War I, women had to work outside the home in order to supplement the family income. With limited English-language and work skills, at first they were only able to find work as cleaning women in offices or as servants and nannies in well-to-do households. Second-generation Carpatho-Rusyn Americans were more likely to find work as retail salespersons, waitresses, and workers in light industries such as shoe, soap, and cigar factories.

Like women, the second generation of American-born men had moved slightly up the employment ladder to work as skilled and semiskilled workers, foremen, or clerical workers. By the third and fourth generation, there was a marked increase in managerial and semiprofessional occupations. Ever since the pre–World War I years, a few enterprising individuals have operated their own retail shops and businesses, although most Carpatho-Rusyns and their descendants have typically worked in factories, mills, mines, and other industries.

A 1954 image of a cemetery in Little Carpathia, a Carpatho-Rusyn enclave in Colorado. IRA GAY SEALY / THE DENVER POST VIA GETTY IMAGES

A dependence on the existing American industrial and corporate structure has, since the 1980s, had a negative effect on thousands of Carpatho-Rusyn Americans who thought the jobs or industries that they and their fathers and grandfathers worked in would always be there for themselves and their children. The widespread closing of coal mines in eastern Pennsylvania and the collapse of the United States steel industry put thousands out of work. As a result, Carpatho-Rusyns, like other middle-class working Americans in the past two decades, have had to lower their expectations about economic advancement and to retrain themselves for—and especially to encourage their children to prepare for—jobs that are no longer in coal and steel, but in electronics, computers, and service-related industries.

POLITICS AND GOVERNMENT

At least until World War I, Carpatho-Rusyns in the European homeland did not have any experience in politics. They were used to being ruled and not participating in the governing process. The result was skepticism and a deep-seated mistrust toward politics, which was to continue after immigration to the United States. Not surprisingly, first-generation Carpatho-Rusyns, and even their American-born descendants, rarely ran for public office. It was not until the 1970s that the first individuals of Carpatho-Rusyn background were to be found in elected offices beyond the local level, and by 2012 all had been from Pennsylvania, whether serving at the state governor level (Tom Ridge) or in the U.S. Congress (Joseph M. Gajdos). As for the majority of Carpatho-Rusyn Americans, their relation to political life was limited to participation in strikes, especially in the coal fields and in steel and related industries during the decades of the 1890s to 1930s. While there were some Carpatho-Rusyn political clubs established during the 1930s and 1940s to support Democratic Party candidates, these were generally few in number and short-lived.

On the other hand, Carpatho-Rusyn Americans have in the past played an active and, at times, decisive role in homeland politics. This was particularly so during the closing months of World War I, when, in anticipation of the imminent collapse of the Austro-Hungarian Empire, Carpatho-Rusyn Americans proposed various options for the future of their homeland.

In the spring and summer of 1918, both Greek/Byzantine Rite Catholic and Orthodox religious and lay leaders formed political action committees, the most important of which was the American Council of Uhro-Rusyns in Homestead, Pennsylvania. The Homestead-based council chose a young, U.S.-trained Carpatho-Rusyn lawyer, Gregory Zatkovich, to represent them. Under his leadership, the Rusyn Americans joined with other groups in the Mid-European Union in Philadelphia, lobbied the American government, and followed President Woodrow Wilson's suggestion that, since it was not feasible for Carpatho-Rusyns to have their own independent state, they might consider joining—with guarantees for full autonomy (self-rule)—the new state of Czechoslovakia. An agreement to join Czechoslovakia was reached in Philadelphia in November 1918, after which Zatkovich led a Rusyn American delegation to convince leaders in the homeland of the desirability of joining Czechoslovakia.

The "American solution" was indeed accepted in 1919 at the Paris Peace Conference. Only the Lemko Rusyns north of the mountains were left out; eventually they were incorporated into the new state of Poland. In recognition of his role, Zatkovich, although still an American citizen, was appointed by the president of Czechoslovakia to be the first governor of its eastern province, Subcarpathian Rus'.

During the 1920s and 1930s, the U.S. Carpatho-Rusyn community closely followed political events in the homeland and frequently sent protests to the League of Nations, calling on the Czechoslovak government to implement the political autonomy that had been promised but was not fully implemented in the province of Subcarpathian Rus'. The United States government, however, was by then less interested in faraway Central and Eastern Europe, and Rusyn American political influence on the homeland declined and eventually ended entirely after Subcarpathian Rus' was annexed to the Soviet Union in 1945 and the rest of Central Europe came under Soviet-inspired communist rule.

Throughout Carpatho-Rusyns' entire history in the United States, politics for most Carpatho-Rusyns has meant trying to decide and reach a consensus on the question "Who are we?" At least until about 1920, most Carpatho-Rusyns in the United States considered themselves a distinct Slavic nationality called Rusyn or Uhro-Rusyn (that is, Hungarian Rusyn). By the 1920s there was a strong tendency among many secular and religious leaders to consider Carpatho-Rusyns as just a branch of the Russian nationality. Hence, the term *Carpatho-Russian* became a popular term to describe the group. By the 1950s and 1960s, two more possible identities were added: Slovak and Ukrainian.

Since the 1970s, however, there has been a return to the group's original identity; that is, the idea that Carpatho-Rusyns are neither Russian, nor Slovak, nor Ukrainian, but rather a distinct nationality. Several of the older religious and lay organizations have reasserted the Rusyn orientation, and it has been fully embraced from the outset by all the new cultural and scholarly institutions established in the United States since the 1970s. The Rusyn orientation in the United States has been encouraged further by the Carpatho-Rusyn national revival that has been occurring in all the European homeland countries (Slovakia, Ukraine, Poland, Hungary, Romania, Serbia, and Croatia) since the Revolutions of 1989.

After being cut off from the European homeland for nearly half a century, Rusyn American contact with the homeland was renewed following the Revolutions of 1989, the end of communist rule, and the collapse of the Soviet Union in 1991. Since then, both secular and church bodies have again provided moral and financial assistance to civic organizations in Carpathian Rus'. Carpatho-Rusyns from the United States have played a particularly active role in the World Congress of Rusyns since its establishment in 1991. Subsequently, Carpatho-Rusyn American organizations and individuals have lobbied the United States and European governments on behalf of their brethren in the homeland, urging continued support for cultural and educational institutions, encouragement for Carpatho-Rusyn identification on decennial censuses, and recognition by the government of Ukraine of a distinct Carpatho-Rusyn nationality and language.

NOTABLE INDIVIDUALS

Art Undoubtedly the most famous American of Carpatho-Rusyn descent was Andy Warhol (born Andrew Warhola in 1928), the pop artist, photographer, and experimental filmmaker. At the height of his career in the 1960s and 1970s, he had become as famous as the celebrities he was immortalizing. Recalling the idealized saintly images (icons) that surrounded him

when he was growing up and attending the Byzantine Rite Catholic Church in Pittsburgh's Rusyn Valley (Ruska dolina) district, Warhol created on canvas and in photographs new iconic that epitomized American pop culture in second half of the twentieth century. After his untimely death in 1987, his older brothers, John and Paul Warhola, helped perpetuate the Carpatho-Rusyn heritage of Andy and his family. That heritage figures prominently in the Andy Warhol Museum in Pittsburgh, and with the help of the New York-based Warhol Foundation, the Warhola Family Museum of Modern Art was founded in 1992 in Medzilaborce, Slovakia, just a few miles from the Carpatho-Rusyn village of Mikova, where both of his parents were born.

Other artists of Carpatho-Rusyn descent are renowned for their work as illustrators, including Andy Warhol's nephew James Warhola (1955–), known for his work in *MAD* magazine and children's books; Steve Ditko (1927–), the comic book artist and cocreator of Spider-Man; and John Kricfalusi (1955–), animator and creator of *The Ren and Stimpy Show*.

Government Pennsylvanians have elected several Americans of Carpatho-Rusyn descent to some of the state's highest offices, including Democratic congressman Joseph M. Gaydos (1926–); Mark Singel (1953–), lieutenant governor of Pennsylvania; and Tom Ridge (1945–), Pennsylvania governor from 1995 to 2001, at which time he was appointed by the president to be the first U.S. Secretary of Homeland Security, a cabinet post created in the wake of the terrorist attacks of September 11, 2001. Another high-ranking U.S. government official was George J. Demko, a specialist on the Soviet Union who served in the 1980s as the official geographer of the United States, a post that was responsible for determining land and offshore boundaries between the United States and its neighbors.

Literature Among the several American authors of Carpatho-Rusyn heritage who have written works in either Rusyn or English, the best known is Thomas Bell (born Thomas Belejcak; 1902–1961), whose realist dramatic and prose works describe the difficult life of immigrants from central and eastern Europe during the Great Depression. His best-known work is the novel *Out of This Furnace* (1941).

Music Among the best-known musicians of Carpatho-Rusyn background are Bret Michaels (born Bret Sychak; 1963–), lead singer of the rock band Poison; the noted jazz pianist and composer of Lemko-Rusyn background Bill Evans (1929–1980); and, in a more traditional mode, the Orthodox choir director Peter J. Wilhousky (1902–1978), remembered for his classic arrangements of the Yuletide "Carol of the Bells" and the stirring "Battle Hymn of the Republic," immortalized in recordings by the Mormon Tabernacle Choir.

Andy Warhol, of Carpatho-Rusyn descent, paints the Statue of Liberty in Paris, 1986. FRANCOIS LOCHON / GAMMA-RAPHO / GETTY IMAGES

Religion It is in the area of religion that Carpatho-Rusyns have made a particularly significant contribution to American life. Four individuals stand out for their work on behalf of not only Eastern Christianity, the traditional faith of Carpatho-Rusyns, but also Roman Catholicism and American evangelical Protestantism.

The expansion of Russian Orthodoxy in the late nineteenth century is attributable largely to Father Alexis Toth (1853–1909), who has been called the "father of Orthodoxy in America." After joining the Orthodox Church in 1891, Toth set out on missionary activity and helped convert nearly 25,000 Carpatho-Rusyn Americans and other East Slavic immigrants to Orthodoxy. The church grew so rapidly that it moved its headquarters from San Francisco to New York City. In 1994 Toth was made a saint of the Orthodox Church of America.

Another Carpatho-Rusyn immigrant of great significance to the Orthodox Church was Vasyl Shkurla (1928–2008), who like Toth was originally from the area known today as Slovakia. As Metropolitan-Archbishop Laurus, primate of the Russian Orthodox Church Abroad (the Synod) based in New York City, he was the person chiefly responsible for healing the ninety-year rift (*raskol*) in Russian Orthodoxy through negotiations that led to the historic act of communion with the Orthodox Church in Russia, signed in 2007.

Miriam Teresa Demjanovich (1901–1927) was born in the United States of Carpatho-Rusyn parents. She converted to Roman Catholicism as a child and later became a nun of the Sisters of Charity. Her posthumously published collection of "spiritual conferences," *Greater Perfection* (1928), became so popular that it was translated into several languages, including Chinese. Her followers established the Sister Miriam Teresa League in New Jersey in an effort to have her proclaimed a saint in the Roman Catholic Church.

Joseph W. Tkach (1927–1995) was born to Carpatho-Rusyn parents in the United States. He became pastor general of the Worldwide Church of God in 1986, editor of the popular religious magazine *Plain Truth*, and the guiding force behind the church's syndicated news-oriented television series, "The World Tomorrow," which for many years was one of the most widely viewed religious programs in the United States.

Science and Medicine Several research scientists of Carpatho-Rusyn background have made notable discoveries or inventions. Nick Holonyak (1928–), professor of electrical and computer engineering at the University of Illinois, developed the first practical LED—a light-emitting diode (the glowing numbers on computers and other devices)—as well as the first semiconductor laser to operate in a visible spectrum. Andrew Skumanich (1929–), an astrophysicist at the National Center for Atmospheric Research in Colorado, is best known for formulating the scientific principle identified as the Skumanich law of stellar rotation. John Pazur (1922–2005), professor of biochemistry at Pennsylvania State University, spent years investigating the properties of starch and glucose, which led to the now widely used commercial production of fructose syrup from corn starch.

The scientist whose work had perhaps the most immediate impact on contemporary society is Mikulas (Mika) Popovic (1941–) of the University of Maryland's Institute of Human Virology, who was considered a key figure at the laboratory of the National Institutes of Health when it succeeded in identifying HIV as the virus that caused AIDS. His work has been the subject of investigative novels, international court cases, and a Hollywood film, *And the Band Played On* (1993), in which Popovic is depicted as one of the important scientists working on what was still an incurable medical problem.

Stage and Screen In the 1940s and 1950s, Lizabeth Scott (born Emma Matzo, 1922–) was the sultry leading lady in several Hollywood films. Sandra Dee (born Alexandra Zuck, 1942–2005) was cast in roles that depicted the typical American teenage girl of the 1950s and 1960s. Her very name was later used as a nostalgic symbol of that era in the film *Grease* (1978). In more recent years, other famous American actors of Carpatho-Rusyn descent include Meg Ryan (born Margaret Mary Hyra, 1961), known primarily for her roles in Hollywood romantic comedies; Robert Urich (1946–2002) of the television drama *Spencer for Hire*; and John Spencer (1946–2005) of TV's *The West Wing*.

MEDIA

Carpatho-Rusyn Society Heritage Radio Program

WPIT AM 730, Pittsburgh, Pennsylvania.

Dean Poloka, Host
2201 Forest Grove Road
Coraopolis, Pennsylvania 15108-3355
Phone: (412) 877-9351
Email: RusynRadio@c-rs.org
URL: www.carpathorusynsociety.org/RadioPgm

Karpatska Rus'/Carpathian Rus'

Quarterly magazine of the Lemko Association and the Carpathian Institute.

Paul Best, Editor
184 Old County Road
Higganum, Connecticut 06441-4446
Phone: (860) 345-7997
Email: lemkoassociation.org@gmail.com
URL: www.lemkoassociation.org/publications

The New Rusyn Times

A cultural-organizational publication of the Carpatho-Rusyn Society.

Richard Custer, Editor
915 Dickson Street
Munhall, Pennsylvania 15120
Phone: (412) 567-3077
Email: editor@c-rs.org
URL: www.c-rs/Publications/nrt.html

TREMBITA

The newsletter of the Rusin Association.

Karen Varian, Editor
1817 121st Avenue N.E.
Blaine, Minnesota 55449
Phone: (763) 754-7463
Email: Rusinmn@aol.com
URL: mnrusinassociation.homestead.com/Trembita.html

ORGANIZATIONS AND ASSOCIATIONS

Carpatho-Rusyn Consortium of North America

Coalition of six cultural organizations in the United States and Canada, formed in 2009, to advocate on behalf of Carpatho-Rusyns in North America and in their European countries of origin.

Karen Varian, Co-Chair
1817 121st Avenue N.E.
Blaine, Minnesota 55449
Phone: (763) 754-7463
Email: crconsortium@gmail.com
URL: www.rusynmedia.org/consortium/index.html

Carpatho-Rusyn Society, Inc.

Organization founded in 1994 to promote Carpatho-Rusyn culture and identity in the United States.

James Kaminski, President
915 Dickson Street
Munhall, Pennsylvania 15120
Phone: (416) 567-3077
Email: cfa@c-rs.org
URL: www.c-rs.org/munhall.html

Greek-Catholic Union of the USA

The oldest mutual benefit society in the United States (founded 1892), it continues to support cultural and religious activities connected to Carpatho-Rusyns.

George N. Juba, President
5400 Tuscarawas Road
Beaver, Pennsylvania 15009
Phone: (724) 495-3400; (800) 722-4428
Fax: (724) 495-3421
Email: info@gcuusa.com
URL: www.gcuusa.com

The Lemko Association

Founded in 1929, this is the oldest Rusyn American cultural/social organization. It is concerned primarily with immigrants and their descendants from the Lemko Region in present-day Poland.

Paul Best, Chairman
184 Old County Road
Higganum, Connecticut 06441-4446
Phone: (860) 345-7997
Email: lemkoassociation.org@gmail.com
URL: lemkoassociation.org

Rusin Association

Community organization to promote Carpatho-Rusyn culture and identity among residents of Minnesota and nearby states.

Karen Varian, President
2215 3rd St NE
Minneapolis, Minnesota 55418
Phone: (763) 754-7463
Email: Rusinmn@aol.com
URL: mnrusinassociation.homestead.com

MUSEUMS AND RESEARCH CENTERS

Byzantine Catholic Cultural Center

Permanent display of Carpatho-Rusyn traditional dress, art, handicrafts, religious items, and other artifacts from Europe and the United States.

Rev. Richard Plishka
2420 West 14th Street
Cleveland, Ohio 44113-4406
Phone: (216) 357-2933
Email: info@byzcathculturalcenter.org
URL: www.byzcathculturalcenter.org

Carpathian Institute

Archive and library with materials about Lemko Rusyns, and a consortium of scholars whose research is devoted to people of all national orientations in the Carpathian region.

Paul Best, Chairman
184 Old County Road
Higganum, Connecticut 06441-4446
Phone: (860) 345-7997
Email: lemkoassociation.org@gmail.com
URL: lemkoassociation.org

Carpatho-Rusyn Cultural and Educational Center

Museum, genealogical center, and meeting hall to promote cultural and social activities related to Carpatho-Rusyns.

James Kaminski, President
915 Dickson Street
Munhall, Pennsylvania 15120
Phone: (412) 567-3077
URL: www.c-rs.org

Carpatho-Rusyn Research Center, Inc.

Research and publishing house that distributes scholarly and popular reading materials on all aspects of the history and culture of Carpatho-Rusyns in Europe and North America.

Paul Robert Magocsi, President
1026 Vermont Avenue
Glassport, Pennsylvania 15045
URL: www.rusynmedia.org/Links/C-RRC

St. Nicholas Chapel Museum

A museum of unique artifacts related to the history of the Greek Catholic Union fraternal society, Byzantine/Greek Catholics, and Carpatho-Rusyns in the United States.

Christine Petty, Communications Director
5400 Tuscarawas Road
Beaver, Pennsylvania 15009
Phone: (800) 722-4428
Fax: (724) 495-3421
Email: info@gcuusa.com
URL: www.gcuusa.com

SOURCES FOR ADDITIONAL STUDY

Barriger, Lawrence. *Glory to Jesus Christ: A History of the American Carpatho-Russian Orthodox Greek Catholic Diocese.* Brookline, MA: Holy Cross Orthodox Press, 2000.

Custer, Richard. "The Influence of Clergy and Fraternal Organizations on the Development of Ethnonational Identity among Rusyn Immigrants to Pennsylvania." In *Carpatho-Rusyns and Their Neighbors,* edited by Bogdan Horbal, Patricia A. Krafcik, and Elaine Rusinko, 43–106. Fairfax, VA: Eastern Christian, 2006.

Dyrud, Keith. *The Quest for the Rusyn Soul: The Politics of Religion and Culture in Eastern Europe and America, 1890—World War I.* Philadelphia, London, and Toronto: Associated University Presses for the Balch Institute Press, 1992.

Magocsi, Paul Robert. *The Carpatho-Rusyn Americans.* New York and Philadelphia: Chelsea House, 1989.

———. *Opportunity Realized: The Greek Catholic Union's First One Hundred Years.* Beaver, PA: Greek-Catholic Union of the USA, 1994.

———. *Our People: Carpatho-Rusyns and Their Descendants in North America,* 4th ed. Wauconda, IL: Bolchazy-Carducci, 2005.

Warzeski, Walter C. "The Rusin Community in Pennsylvania." In *The Ethnic Experience in Pennsylvania,* edited by John E. Bodnar, 175–215. Lewisburg, PA: Bucknell University Press, 1973.

CATAWBA INDIAN NATION

Lisa Kroger

OVERVIEW

The Catawba are Native American people who first occupied the land along the Catawba River in what are now parts of South Carolina, North Carolina, and Virginia. They made their home in the Piedmont, a fertile plateau region between the Atlantic coastal plain and the Appalachian Mountains. Interpreters accompanying Spanish explorers in the sixteenth century described the original tribe as *Issa* or *Iswa* (yeh is-WAH), which translates as "people of the river." European settlers later began calling them and associated tribes the *Catawba*, a word used by the Yuchi tribe of the Tennessee River valley to identify the tribal groups in the Catawba River valley.

James Mooney, author of *Siouan Tribes of the East* (1894), estimated that there were as many as 6,000 Catawba people at the time of their first contact with the English in the seventeenth century. Although they were known as the fiercest warriors in the area, the Catawba were also a family-oriented culture, with extended families living together in one dwelling and performing life-sustaining tasks communally. The term *Catawba* referred to a group of twenty-two tribes, with the Issa being one of the most prominent; other distinct tribes absorbed into the Catawba Nation after European encroachment included the Cheraw, the Pee Dees, and the Sugarees. The groups subsisted mainly through hunting and small-scale farming, though the more established tribes often farmed larger plantations.

The modern Catawba Indian Nation are inhabitants of South Carolina. Under the Treaty of Pine Tree Hill (1760), the Treaty of Augusta (1763), and the Treaty of Nation Ford (1840), the tribe relinquished most of their ancestral land in exchange for a 15-square-mile reservation lying in the current counties of York and Lancaster. Pressured by the South Carolina government, the Catawba leased much of their new land to white settlers in the early nineteenth century (though few lease payments were ever collected). In 1944, under the direction of the Franklin Roosevelt administration's Indian Reorganization Act, the tribe drafted and approved their first constitution. Because of a new 1950s federal policy of terminating tribal recognition and assimilating tribal members into the dominant culture, however, the Catawba government was disbanded in 1962 and its assets were

divided among tribal members, who spent the next three decades working to regain their status as a federally recognized tribe.

In 2012 the government of the Catawba Indian Nation estimated that the tribe had more than 2,800 members. The Catawba people are unique compared to other Native American tribes in that they have traveled very little from their ancestral tribal lands. Most Catawba Indians remain in and around the city of Rock Hill, South Carolina.

HISTORY OF THE PEOPLE

Early History The Catawba are likely the descendants of the Siouan-speaking people who traveled east from the Siouan lands of the Great Plains across the Appalachian Mountains nearly a thousand years ago and settled in the Catawba River valley. By the mid-sixteenth century, in an effort to make peace and form a unified defense, they had formed the tribal groups that now make up the Catawba Indian Nation. The first recorded contact between the Catawba and European explorers was in 1540, when Spanish explorer Hernando de Soto led his men through the Piedmont on an expedition for gold. As the European settlers advanced, the Catawba families moved into the less populated mountains, forsaking all but a small remnant of their former 55,000 square miles of territory.

In 1698 the first of four major epidemics hit the Catawba people when European settlers and their African slaves brought new diseases into the area. By 1760 the native population had been decimated; according to James H. Merrell, in his *Encyclopedia of North American Indians* (1996), the tribe had been reduced "from perhaps five thousand in 1690 to less than five hundred in 1760."

Because of their diminished numbers, the Catawba needed to befriend their new neighbors if they hoped to survive. The tribes set up trade with the English, relying on them for weapons and other necessities. The Catawba even sided with the English against the French in the Seven Years' War (1754–1763; also known as the French and Indian War). Most other Indian tribes who participated in the war sided with the French, if only to oppose the British who were taking over their native lands. The Catawba's reputation for fierceness rested partly on the leadership of

King Hagler (or Nopkehee), the Catawba chief from around 1750 to 1763. He commanded the respect of the English and at the same time defended the rights of his people. Under Hagler's leadership the Catawba people resisted anglicization, managing to preserve much of their native culture.

As the British colonies grew in the late eighteenth century, the homeland of the Catawba nation was taken over by the new inhabitants. The Catawba fought back, forcing the Treaties of Pine Tree Hill (1760) and Augusta (1763), which secured them a temporary homeland consisting of 144,000 acres (225 square miles). Realizing that their nation would not thrive or even survive without peace, however, they determined to make allies of the colonists, who were growing increasingly unhappy under British rule because of what they saw as excessive taxation. To bolster relations the Catawba served as scouts for the patriots of South Carolina during the American Revolutionary War (1775–1783). By 1800 the land that made up the Catawba reservation was considered valuable farmland, though, and the state induced the Catawba to sell it. According to the 1840 Treaty of Nation Ford, the Catawba would relinquish their reservation lands to South Carolina for $5,000 worth of land elsewhere on the river banks; $2,500 in cash; and nine annual payments of $1,500. The state agreed to relocate the Catawba to North Carolina near the Cherokee Nation. The state of North Carolina was not party to this scheme, however, and the Cherokee were not welcoming. While some Catawba did relocate to Haywood County, North Carolina, most of the Catawba people returned within a decade to their ancestral homeland in South Carolina, which no longer legally belonged to them. Despite many subsequent removal efforts, the Catawba held their ground.

Modern Era In 1883, in an attempt to convert the tribe, Mormon missionaries offered assistance by building schools for Catawba children. The schools were fervently welcomed, because the Catawba could not attend the white schools of South Carolina and did not feel accepted in the black schools. While some of the tribe's difficulties were resolved in 1942, when the state of South Carolina purchased a 630-acre reservation for their use, the problem of racial categorization plagued the Catawba Indian Nation until 1943. At that point the federal government recognized them as a tribe, affording them government benefits. In 1944 South Carolina began the nearly two-decade process of granting the Catawba state citizenship (all Native Americans had been made citizens in 1924 by the federal government, but South Carolina had not cooperated).

Passed in 1944, Roosevelt's Indian Reorganization Act attempted to improve conditions for Native Americans. The U.S. government gave the Catawba 3,400 acres (5.3 square miles) of land to farm; however, the small farms were not particularly successful.

By the 1950s Washington's policy had changed to one of termination and assimilation: the federal government terminated its recognition of tribes and its trusteeship of their lands in an attempt to assimilate them into the dominant white culture. Federal recognition of the Catawba ended in 1962, and their farmlands were divided among tribal members, undermining their traditional unity.

At this time many Catawba considered themselves white and wished to assimilate into white culture, some moving to Mormon communities, where they felt more welcomed than they did in other predominately white, non-Native American populations. According to Charles M. Hudson in *The Catawba Nation* (1970), the final tribal roll, dated July 2, 1960, counted 631 members. Showing their resilience and strength as a people, the Catawba stayed united despite their diminishing population and lack of an official tribal organization; although the Catawba no longer had a constitution or official government, what was left of the tribe continued under the rule of a chief. The remaining Catawba people stayed on or near the ancestral lands, continuing to keep the culture alive through the preservation of tribal traditions, particularly the making of pottery, which they sold.

Community cohesion eventually led the tribe to petition Congress for recognition in 1973. The Catawba people argued that the 1840 Treaty of Nation Ford with South Carolina, in which they had sold their ancestral lands, was illegal and that the U.S. government had an obligation to protect their rights. To show their commitment, they updated their constitution in 1975. After two decades of persistent effort, their petition was granted. On November 20, 1993, the Catawba Indian Nation was again recognized as at tribe. The federal government also gave them $50 million in exchange for giving up their land claims against the state of South Carolina. In the decades since they reorganized as an official tribe, the Catawba Indian Nation has nearly quadrupled the enrollment recorded in 1960, largely as the result of a well-organized government and a focus on building heritage and customs within the community.

In the twenty-first century, the Catawba Indian Nation has used the federal money to rebuild their community through land purchases for the reservation and the establishment of several tribal programs, such as a housing program, a health clinic, and senior and child care facilities.

SETTLEMENT IN THE UNITED STATES

The Catawba tribe originated in the Catawba River Valley of North and South Carolina, where the tribal lands are located today; however, there has been some migration over the centuries. Under the 1844 treaty, South Carolina took possession of Catawba ancestral lands and displaced the tribe. As a result, many of the Catawba tribal members went to North Carolina,

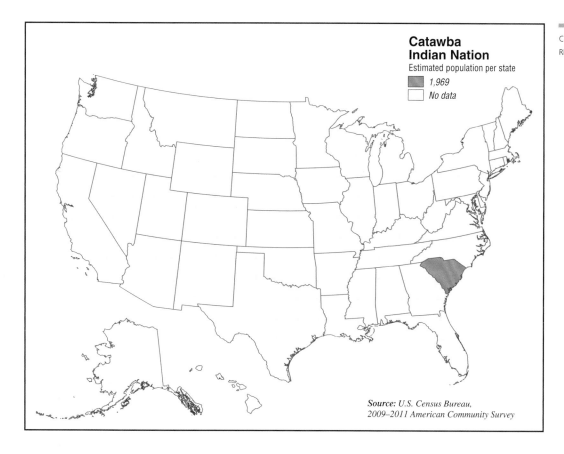

Catawba
Indian Nation
Estimated population per state
1,969
No data

*Source: U.S. Census Bureau,
2009–2011 American Community Survey*

hoping to find a life with the Cherokee, but most subsequently returned to their original homeland. According to the U.S. Census Bureau's American Community Survey estimates for 2006-2010, most Catawba still reside in South Carolina.

After the Mormon missionary schools converted tribal members to their faith near the end of the nineteenth century, the Catawba faced religious intolerance and continued poverty. A number of tribal Mormons moved west to Colorado and Utah to be closer to their church and to seek a better life; some formed new Mormon townships. A few of these missionaries made their way as far west as New Mexico while keeping strong ties to the Catawba still in South Carolina. It is characteristic of the Catawba that many who leave home in search of a better life eventually return. Some marry white spouses but never feel fully accepted into white society; others simply find life easier on the reservation, where their customs and heritage are a part of daily life. The tribe has thus managed to keep a strong presence in and near Catawba ancestral lands.

In 2000 the U.S. Bureau of Indian Affairs turned down a request by the Western Catawba (the descendants of those who followed the Mormon Church west at the end of the nineteenth century) for official recognition as part of the Catawba Indian Nation. According to the Western Catawba, the Eastern tribe has repeatedly refused them membership.

LANGUAGE

The tribe's native language is Catawba, an Eastern Siouan language that is generally considered to have been lost in 1952 with the death of Catawba elder Sallie Brown Gordon—although a few others, such as Chief Samuel Taylor Blue (1871–1959), have also been given the title of last native speaker of the language. Families of the Catawba Indian Nation speak English at home and in their community. Efforts are being made to revive the tribe's native language. As of 2009 the Catawba Cultural Center and linguist Claudia Heinemann Priest were working on compiling a Catawba-language dictionary to preserve the language and pass it on to the next generations.

RELIGION

Prior to English influence the Catawba were polytheistic. Their religion was centered on a creator and a number of lesser deities, many represented by animal spirits. In the 1880s missionaries from the Mormon Church arrived in South Carolina. The Catawba people had resisted converting to Christianity for many years, preferring their native ways to English ones. The Mormons tempted the tribe, however, partly by recognizing the small Catawba community's need for schools. The Catawba people were also more open to the Mormon faith because of the large role that Native Americans played in their religious beliefs. A large percentage of Catawba are Mormon today; however, many are members of Baptist and other Protestant churches.

CULTURE AND ASSIMILATION

The Catawba people have struggled successfully to maintain their culture and identity in the face of dwindling numbers and formidable pressure to assimilate. Regaining their status as a tribe helped them preserve their rich heritage. Although they have always interacted with the outside world, they have resisted conforming to European and American worldviews.

The Catawba Cultural Preservation Project, in conjunction with the Catawba Cultural Center, works to preserve the culture and heritage of the Catawba Indian Nation. One of the most prominent examples of their efforts is the Yap Ye Iswa Festival, which translates as the "Day of the Catawba." The festival is celebrated every year on the Saturday after Thanksgiving. Its goal is to educate both the Catawba and outsiders about the art, history, and food of the tribe. Traditional drummers and dancers perform, and pottery is on display. Catawba children can also attend after-school and summer camp programs that teach the Catawba culture to the next generation.

Traditions and Customs In an effort to preserve and celebrate their heritage and that of other native tribes, the Catawba Indian Nation holds an annual intertribal powwow. The gathering of peoples who share a common heritage is considered a sacred event. The festivities feature dance competitions in traditional and contemporary regalia, native arts and crafts, storytelling, and Catawba cuisine.

Cuisine Traditional Catawba foods include roasted corn, mutton, venison stew, collard greens, and, in contemporary times, the pan-Indian festival foods fry bread (deep-fried dough) and Indian tacos (fry bread topped with ground beef and other ingredients used in tacos, such as shredded lettuce and tomatoes). The Catawba take immense pride in their culture, including their cuisine, and use every opportunity to share their culinary heritage with the outside community. Traditional food can be found at such cultural gatherings as the tribal powwow and the Yap Ye Iswa Festival. Guests to the reservation can also request a traditional dinner of Indian tacos at the Catawba Cultural Center.

Traditional Dress Traditional Catawba clothing was usually made of deerskin; men wore loincloths and women wore knee-length skirts. In the colder months both genders wore pants. Men and women adorned themselves with beaded or copper jewelry. Ceremonial dress for men consisted of a long-sleeved leather coat, decorated with fringe, and a headdress with large feathers. Women wore a decorative long coat over a floor-length skirt. Sometimes they painted their skin.

In the twenty-first century, the Catawba only wear traditional dress to promote their culture at special events such as the yearly powwow.

Traditional Arts and Crafts Pottery is one of the Catawba tribe's most cherished traditions. Its roots can be traced back thousands of years; it predates the more famous Pueblo pottery of the Southwest Indian tribes. It is the oldest continuous ceramics tradition in North America. Catawba pottery is not glazed or painted; instead, its unique mottled surface, usually in varying colors of black, tan, and a coppery brown, comes from the clay used to make the pots and from the firing process, which begins with sun-drying the shaped clay.

Catawba pottery is much more than just a traditional art; it is a great source of pride for the Catawba Indian Nation and has been credited with helping to hold the community together during times when the tribe's future was uncertain. Anthropologist Edward Palmer traveled to the Catawba reservation in 1884 to study the pottery; his collection is in the Smithsonian today. Palmer's mission sparked the state's interest, and they promoted Catawba arts as part of their tourist industry.

In the twentieth century, Catawba potters began selling their wares to tourists in their area and at sometimes distant craft fairs, turning the products into a major source of income. The popularity of the pottery is growing, and the younger Catawba generation is interested in learning the skill.

One of the most popular styles of Catawba pottery is the Rebecca pitcher, a tall, thin pitcher with a single long, looping handle. The design is named for the Old Testament figure Rebecca, who dipped her jug into a well. Although the design is most likely not original to the Catawba tribe—some scholars believe they adapted it from the early settlers in the Piedmont area—it has become one of their best sellers.

The largest collection of Catawba Indian pottery can be found on the campus of University of South Carolina Lancaster, about 15 miles from the current reservation.

To a lesser extent the Catawba art community also produces traditional Native American beaded jewelry, dream catchers, and leather accessories. The Catawba Cultural Center offers classes on these crafts to the community.

Dances and Songs Catawba cultural events usually include traditional and contemporary drumming and dancing. Wearing full regalia, including feathered headdresses and leather fringed jackets or ribbon shirts and embroidered and beaded dresses, tribal drum groups of Catawba elders make the grand entry at powwows and other cultural events. Singing and dancing accompany the drum rhythms.

Health Care Issues and Practices The Catawba Service Unit is an ambulatory outpatient care facility serving the tribe; the unit is a combination of a medical and dental clinic, a pharmacy, a laboratory, and a nutritional department. Its goal is not only to offer health services to the Catawba people but also to educate the tribe about health-related issues. Along with modern-day health care options, the tribe recognizes long-held cultural traditions by offering herbal remedies such as gentian root and horsemint leaves for pain relief.

The Wellness Steering Committee, put together by the Catawba government, has a "Get Moving Catawba" initiative that is aimed at educating the Catawba community about healthy food and exercise options. The committee also coordinates sporting events for the benefit of a healthy community.

FAMILY AND COMMUNITY LIFE

Gender Roles Traditionally, the Catawba men were responsible for the majority of the hunting and for warfare. The tribe was known to be fierce, and men were expected to be warriors. Women were often at home, taking care of the household, the children, and the farming. Catawba society was a not a typical patriarchy, however. Women were viewed as equal to men, and they held important leadership roles in the community. In addition, both genders produced artwork and music and practiced medicine. The Catawba Indian Nation's history has been built by both male chiefs and female leaders, a tradition that continues today. As in American society more generally, societal roles have changed somewhat among the Catawba, with both men and women working outside the home.

Education Most Catawba children attend local public schools. The Catawba Indian Nation is working to make education available to all members. The tribe runs the Iswa Head Start, offering preschool education to Catawba children, as well as the Little People Academy, a licensed childcare center. The tribe also encourages college attendance by offering scholarship resources and a College Day, an informational meeting for students and their parents.

In 2008 the tribe opened the Catawba Achievement Center, which offers courses on computers, including typing, PowerPoint presentations, and cyber security. These courses are geared specifically toward teaching the older generation to use computer technology.

Courtship and Weddings Courtship and marriage among the Catawba people is determined by the couple; there are no arranged marriages. However, some Catawba members feel it is important to marry within the tribe. Marriage ceremonies are usually religious in nature, depending on the denomination of the couple.

The Catawba have promoted and marketed the more general Native American tradition of the wedding vase (a jug with two spouts), thought to have originated with the Navajo and Pueblo tribes of the American Southwest. The Catawba likely adopted the custom of incorporating the vase into their own ceremonies in the twentieth century, when their potters began to make the vases for sale. During the wedding the bride and groom drink from the jug, one from each spout. The couple then throws the pot to the

RED THUNDER CLOUD: THE FALSE CATAWBA

A late picture of Cromwell Ashbie Hawkins West, a.k.a. Red Thunder Cloud. AP PHOTO

While Sally Gordon Brown (d. 1952) was the last native speaker of Catawba, the language survived until the January 8, 1996, passing of Red Thunder Cloud, an imposter who conned a leading anthropologist and thereby learned Catawba. It was only after Red Thunder Cloud's death that scholars discovered his true identity: he was an African American, born Cromwell Ashbie Hawkins West in Newport, Rhode Island, to parents Cromwell Payne West, a drugstore proprietor, and Roberta (Hawkins) West, the daughter of one of the first black lawyers in Baltimore. Records indicate that Roberta West did not live in Newport from 1929 to 1933, and some scholars believe she may have spent this time with her children in North Carolina, near the Catawba reservation.

When he was nineteen, West presented himself to Frank G. Speck, an anthropologist from the University of Pennsylvania, as a Catawba who had studied native groups in Virginia and Rhode Island. Impressed by West's knowledge of Native American history and his gift for languages, Speck employed West as a research assistant for a project on the Shinnecocks of Long Island. During this time Speck gave West a Catawba dictionary he had compiled. West then used a letter that Speck had written on his behalf to take up residence in 1945 on the Catawba reservation, where he stayed for six months and studied the language under Chief Blue Sky and his sister, Sally Gordon Brown. Ten years later West collaborated with G. Herbert Matthews, a linguist at the Massachusetts Institute of Technology, to record the Catawba language and publish five texts, one of which falsely documented West's Catawba heritage. In this manuscript, West listed his name as Carlos Ashbie Hawk Westez and manufactured three generations of Catawba forebears on his mother's side. Eventually West settled in Worcester, Massachusetts, where he made a living selling a line of herbal tea that he called "Red Thunder Cloud's Accabonac Princess American Indian Teas."

A portrait of Anna Speakswell, a Catawba in Rock Hill, South Carolina. CATHERINE BAUKNIGHT / ZUMAPRESS / NEWSCOM

in local textile mills, jobs that had previously been unavailable to nonwhites. Many Catawba men have served in the military, and Catawba women found work in the educational and health care fields. When the Catawba Indian Nation was federally recognized once again in the 1990s, the tribe began operating a bingo parlor in Rock Hill. The bingo operation was shut down in 2002 when it lost revenue, partly because of the weakening economy and the South Carolina Education Lottery, which took a portion of the profits. In 2006 the tribe sought to operate electronic gambling machines on reservation land, but their petition was denied.

In 2012 the Catawba Indian Nation sued the state of South Carolina for the right to open a casino on reservation land, arguing that the state and federal government had granted gambling rights to the tribe in 1993. Because South Carolina only allows offshore gambling, the tribe's request was refused by a circuit judge. The casino, which could have brought an estimated 4,000 jobs, would have provided a major economic boost for the tribe. In an interview with the *Charlotte Business Journal* (February 3, 2012), Chief Bill Harris said, "The tribe's ability to engage in gambling activities is vital to its economic self-sufficiency." The Catawba continue to fight to build the $340 million casino in York County, South Carolina.

POLITICS AND GOVERNMENT

The Catawba Indian Nation has their own government, led by a general council composed of all voters eighteen and older who are enrolled members of the nation. The council meets at least twice a year to vote on all issues affecting tribal business. One responsibility of the general council is to elect an executive committee composed of a chief, an assistant chief, a secretary treasurer, and two additional committee members to oversee daily tribal business. As set forth in the Catawba Indian Nation's 1975 constitution, the general council's duties include negotiating with local, state, and federal governments; regulating the use of Catawba property and funds; and passing and enforcing ordinances within the Catawba reservation.

NOTABLE INDIVIDUALS

Art Georgia Harris (1905–1997) was an acclaimed Catawba potter. In 1997 she received a National Heritage Fellowship from the National Endowment for the Arts. Unfortunately, Harris passed away between the time of the award notification and the White House ceremony.

Sara Ayers (1919–2002) was a prominent Catawba Indian potter. Born on the South Carolina Catawba reservation, she later moved to West Columbia, South Carolina. There, along with her husband, she produced Catawba pottery that is sought by art collectors. Her work has been featured in museums and has garnered awards, including the South Carolina Folk Heritage

ground, breaking it, and counts the number of shards. According to tradition, this determines the number of children the couple will have. The vases are particularly popular among non-Catawba collectors and tourists.

EMPLOYMENT AND ECONOMIC CONDITIONS

The Catawba were traditionally farmers and hunters. In the twentieth century, after the tribe lost their official status, their lands decreased and the people scattered to some degree, so that farming efforts were less successful. The members sought a variety of jobs in their attempts assimilate into American culture and survive. Many Catawba turned to the traditional arts, particularly pottery making, and began selling their work. In the middle of the twentieth century, when they received status as official citizens, the Catawba were allowed employment

Award. A pottery piece by Ayers is on display in the White House Library.

Government King Hagler (ca. 1700–1763), also known as King Haigler or Nopkehee, was the most famous of the Catawba chiefs, ruling from the early 1750s to 1763. Hagler was instrumental in creating peaceful relationships between the Catawba nation and the people of South and North Carolina. He was killed on August 13, 1763, by Shawnee Indians.

Peter Harris (1756–1823) was a Catawba soldier in the Revolutionary War, joining the Third South Carolina Regiment under Colonel William Thompson. He was wounded at the Battle of Stono and reportedly carried a gun from that conflict every day until his death. With other Catawba tribesmen, he created a unit for Thomas Sumter in order to fight with Captain Thomas Drennan's company. Around 1783 Harris and two other Catawba traveled to England with some white men who showed them around, defrauded them, and left them. A musical based on his travels, *The Catawba Travellers*, was first performed in London in around 1795. Once back on American soil, Harris wrote the state of South Carolina requesting a pension for his services during the war. He was granted $60 a year.

Another Catawba named Peter Harris fought on the Confederate side during the Civil War (1861–1865). Held as a prisoner of war at Hart's Island in New York Harbor, he was widely recognized for his bravery. According to one account of Harris in battle, he continued to fight while crawling to safety with a wounded leg.

Sports Evans "Buck" George was an assistant chief of the Catawba Indian Nation. He played football at Clemson University in the early 1950s and in 1955 was drafted by the Washington Redskins, the first Native American to play for them. As assistant chief George was instrumental in preserving the history of his tribe. He also supported the video poker and bingo businesses that would bring the Catawba welcome revenue.

ORGANIZATIONS AND ASSOCIATIONS

Catawba Indian Nation

The Catawba Indian Nation organizes public services for the Catawba people, including scholarship opportunities and help with job placement and training. It works closely with the Catawba Cultural Center to help maintain the Catawba Indian Nation's history and cultural heritage.

Evie Stewart, Tribal Administrator
966 Avenue of the Nations
Rock Hill, South Carolina 29730
Phone: (803) 366-4792
Fax: (803) 327-4853
Email: info@catawbaindian.net
URL: www.catawbaindian.net

MUSEUMS AND RESEARCH CENTERS

Catawba Cultural Center

The Catawba Cultural Center preserves Catawba heritage while promoting the culture of the Catawba people. It offers historical exhibits and also teaches traditional arts and crafts. The center holds the yearly Catawba Pow-Wow and a Yap Ye Iswa (Day of the Catawba) Festival.

Leslie Campbell
1536 Tom Stevens Road
Rock Hill, South Carolina 29730
Phone: (803) 328-2427, ext. 238
Email: kcgw@ccppcrafts.com
URL: www.sites.google.com/site/catawbaculturalpreservation/home

The Catawba Project

The Catawba Project is conducted by the Research Laboratories of Archaeology at the University of North Carolina at Chapel Hill. The project was first formed in 2001 to document and understand how the modern Catawba Indian Nation was formed and what changes it underwent throughout the years. It is also interested in comparing the Catawba people with other Native American groups in the area, such as the Cherokee and Chickasaw.

Steve Davis, Associate Director
Research Laboratories of Archaeology
Campus Box 3120
108 Alumni Building
UNC–Chapel Hill
Chapel Hill, North Carolina 27599-3120
Phone: (919) 962-6574
Fax: (919) 962-1613
Email: rpsdavis@unc.edu
URL: http://rla.unc.edu/CatawbaProject/CatawbaProject.html

Hilton Pond Center for Piedmont Natural History

Focuses on research and education regarding the Piedmont area. It houses a collection of Catawba Indian pottery and works to educate the public about the Native Americans of the area.

Bill Hilton, Jr., Director
1432 Devinney Road
York, South Carolina 29745
Phone: (803) 684-5852
Email: education@hiltonpond.org
URL: www.hiltonpond.org

Schiele Museum of Natural History

The museum maintains on its grounds a replica of a Catawba Indian village for visitors to explore.

Ann Tippitt, Director
1500 East Garrison Boulevard
Gastonia, North Carolina 28054
Phone: (704) 866-6900
Fax: (704) 866-6041
Email: annt@cityofgastonia.com
URL: www.schielemuseum.org

University of South Carolina Lancaster Native American Studies Center

The 15,000-square-foot Native American Studies Center, established in 2012, holds the largest collection of Catawba Indian pottery in existence. It is also home to the only university research archive devoted to the Catawba people's culture and history—the Thomas J. Blumer Catawba Research Collection. With four exhibition galleries, an archaeology lab, the archives, pottery collection holdings, a Catawba language lab, classrooms, and a folklife lab, the center attracts students, scholars, and tourists from around the world.

Chris Judge, Center Director
119 South Main Street
Lancaster, South Carolina 29720
Phone: (803) 313-7172
Fax: (803) 313-7106
Email: judgec@mailbox.sc.edu
URL: http://usclancaster.sc.edu/nas/index.html

SOURCES FOR ADDITIONAL STUDY

Blumer, Thomas John. *The Catawba Indian Nation of the Carolinas.* Charleston, SC: Arcadia, 2004.

———. *Catawba Indian Nation: Treasures in History.* Charleston, SC: History Press, 2007.

———. *Catawba Indian Pottery: The Survival of a Folk Tradition.* Tuscaloosa: University of Alabama Press, 2004.

Brown, Douglas Summers. *The Catawba Indians: The People of the River.* Columbia: University of South Carolina Press, 1966.

Hudson, Charles M. *The Catawba Nation.* Athens: University of Georgia Press, 2007.

Merrell, James H. *The Indians' New World: Catawbas and Their Neighbors from European Contact through the Era of Removal.* New York: W. W. Norton and Company, 1991.

Moore, David G. *Catawba Valley Mississippian: Ceramics, Chronology, and Catawba Indians.* Tuscaloosa: University of Alabama Press, 2002.

CHALDEAN AMERICANS

Mary C. Sengstock and Sanaa Taha Al Harahsheh

OVERVIEW

Chaldean Americans are immigrants or descendants of people from the northern Tigris-Euphrates valley, presently located in the Middle Eastern nation of Iraq. Iraq is bordered by Turkey to the north, Iran to the east, Kuwait and Saudi Arabia to the south, and Jordan and Syria to the west. Iraq is approximately 432,160 square kilometers in size, making it slightly larger than the state of California.

According to the *CIA World Factbook*, the Iraqi population in 2012 was 31.1 million. The majority of Iraqis are Muslim, with about 60 percent belonging to the Shi'a sect and around 35 percent belonging to the Sunni sect. Christians and adherents of other religions represent under 5 percent of the Iraqi population. The nation's economy is largely dependent on the oil industry, though textiles and agriculture are also prominent industries. The standard of living is low, largely due to the recent wars in the area; in 2008 about 25 percent of the population was estimated by the *CIA World Factbook* to be living below the poverty level.

Chaldeans are among the minority of Iraqis who are Christian, and they began arriving in the United States around 1910. They settled in Detroit, Michigan, which was a major target of immigration in general at the time due to the growing automobile industry. A number of early Chaldean immigrants worked in the retail grocery sector, becoming major players in the Detroit grocery economy by the middle of the twentieth century. Emigration of Chaldeans from Iraq increased dramatically following World War II, as many took advantage of the student visas available at that time. These numbers increased even more after the U.S. government's immigration quota system was revised by Congress in 1965. The Iraq wars in the late twentieth and early twenty-first centuries prompted even more Chaldeans to come to the United States.

According to the 2010 U.S. Census, 105,981 immigrants from Iraq were living in the United States, up from 89,892 in 2000. Most of the Iraqi immigrants are Chaldeans, although the conditions from years of war in Iraq have led Muslims to flee the country as well. It is difficult to determine exactly how many Iraqi immigrants are Chaldeans, however,

as the U.S. Census generally uses the more generic terms *Arab* and *Iraqi*. In addition, some Chaldeans may be reluctant to respond to such questions because they prefer to identify as being of Chaldean rather than Arab or Iraqi descent. Following the earliest patterns of their immigration, most Chaldeans settle in Detroit and the surrounding area, particularly in suburbs such as Southfield and Farmington Hills. Recent Chaldean immigrants have also made homes in Arizona and California.

HISTORY OF THE PEOPLE

Early History Iraq is located on the site of ancient Mesopotamia, surrounding the Tigris and Euphrates river valleys, where some of the oldest settlements in recorded history occurred. The names, *Mesopotamia* and *Iraq* are said to refer to the location near the two rivers. In the two thousand years before the Common Era, the area was occupied by numerous tribes, including Akkadians, Assyrians, Babylonians, Jews, and Sumerians. The region is mentioned in the Bible as the location of "Ur of the Chaldees," from which the prophet Abraham is said to have originated. Many residents of the area converted to Christianity during the first century CE; Chaldeans trace their ancestors to this group. In the seventh century CE, many dwellers in the region followed Mohammed and converted to Islam, which became the dominant religion.

Modern Era The modern history of Iraq began in the sixteenth and seventeenth centuries, when the Ottoman Empire occupied the area. In the nineteenth century, the territory became a protectorate of the British government. During this era, there was some increase in the Christian population, due to missionary activities of British Protestants. By 1918 the area, still under English rule, had a population of approximately three million. Most of these people were Muslims; other groups included the Kurds, who lived to the north, near the Turkish border. Christians and Jews made up a minor portion of the population. However, their religious preferences provided them with ties to the West, so they often became involved with the British government, making them suspect among other Iraqis.

The League of Nations established Iraq as an independent nation in 1932. This was followed by World War II (1939–1945), which led to the 1948 establishment of Israel as an independent nation. The emergence of Israel enraged the Arab world, generating resentment against the Western nations as well as groups within Arab world that were believed to be aligned with the West, such as Christians and Jews. Subsequently, the Ba'th Party rose to power in Syria and began to increase its influence throughout the Middle East, including in Iraq. By 1968 a new leader, Ba'thist Saddam Hussein, had assumed control of Iraq. In 1973 further unrest occurred in Iraq with an uprising of the Kurdish population in the north. Tensions came to a head in 1980, when Iraq went to war with Iran, sparking further ethnic hostility in the area. Iraq's subsequent invasion of Kuwait in 1990 prompted Western nations including the United States to come to Kuwait's defense. Iraq was forced to withdraw from Kuwait, and the aftermath of the war featured difficulties with Iraq's postwar reconstruction, including increased tensions among minorities that were tied to power struggles and a scarcity of resources such as clean drinking water, utilities, and health care. The second Iraq War began in 2003, resulting in the fall of Saddam's government and the occupation of Iraq by U.S. forces. This further exacerbated the problems within Iraq and had particularly severe impact on minorities. In 2010 the U.S. military withdrew from Iraq.

SETTLEMENT IN THE UNITED STATES

Settlement in a new land is influenced by factors occurring in both the country of origin and the destination country. Thus, the difficult conditions in Iraq at various times in its history—from bleak economic conditions to discrimination against minorities—have compelled Iraqis to seek better opportunities in the United States. In particular, religious minorities such as Jews and Christians experienced difficulties in their homeland. Since Christians were not favored in Iraq, the impetus for Chaldeans to leave was strong. However, given the often hostile conditions in Iraq, departure was not always easy. In the first few decades of the twentieth century, migrants often lacked the economic resources to travel. Sometimes it was difficult for individuals to move from their homes to the ports that would give them access to other countries. However, since the Chaldeans, Christian in faith, often had contact with the British government, they were sometimes able to muster the resources necessary to leave.

Chaldeans found the prospect of living in a Christian-dominated nation appealing, and this was a major reason for their initial immigration to the United States in the earliest decades of the twentieth century. Many of these early Chaldean immigrants wound in the Detroit area, based on two probable factors: (1) Detroit was a major destination for immigrants of many countries at the time due to its burgeoning automobile industry, and (2) another group of Middle Eastern Christian immigrants, the Maronites from Lebanon, were also settling there. Only a handful

of Chaldeans were a part of this original migration; by 1923 there were mere dozens of Chaldeans in Detroit. Nearly all of these immigrants were men, and once they had established themselves in their new country, they brought their wives and children over from Iraq. Unlike other new arrivals to Detroit during this period, few Chaldeans sought employment in the auto industry, opting instead to service the growing Detroit population through food service, first as peddlers and later as operators of grocery stores.

The establishment of a quota system in the 1920s with measures such as the Immigration Act of 1924 curtailed all immigration to the United States. Iraq was allotted only one hundred immigrants persons per year, complicating the entry of additional Chaldeans. During World War II, immigration to the United States was limited again for most groups.

After World War II, however, the influx of immigrants increased. The impetus to come to the United States was strong for Iraqis, given mounting tensions in the Middle East such as the founding of Israel in 1948. Subsequent Chaldean immigrants were greatly assisted by their predecessors, who helped them with travel arrangements and then with becoming established in Detroit, especially in the grocery business. Chaldeans, as well as other immigrant groups, also benefited from a student visa system that was introduced after World War II. It allowed foreigners to study in the United States with the understanding that they would return to their homelands upon completing their educations. However, many students, including Chaldeans, wound up marrying American citizens and remained in the United States. This increased the number of young Chaldeans in the Detroit area. By the early 1960s, the Chaldean Catholic Church had enumerated approximately three hundred members in the community, according to M. C. Sengstock in *Chaldean-Americans: Changing Conceptions of Ethnic Identity*.

In 1965 an additional opportunity arose to assist Chaldean migration, as U.S. quota limitations were eliminated. Chaldean immigration increased dramatically throughout the remainder of the twentieth century. By 2000 the Chaldean community in Detroit was estimated to be more than 100,000 people (based on data from the Chaldean church). Additional Christians identified as either Chaldeans or related Christian groups had established communities in other areas, notably Chicago, Turlock, California; San Diego, California; Phoenix, Arizona; and the state of New York.

In the early twenty-first century, following the two Iraqi wars, the U.S. government policy admitted additional Iraqis as refugees. Unlike their predecessors who had come to the United States as students and had benefited from their ties to the American families into which they married, these refugees were often at an extreme disadvantage. Many literally came to the United States with nothing but the

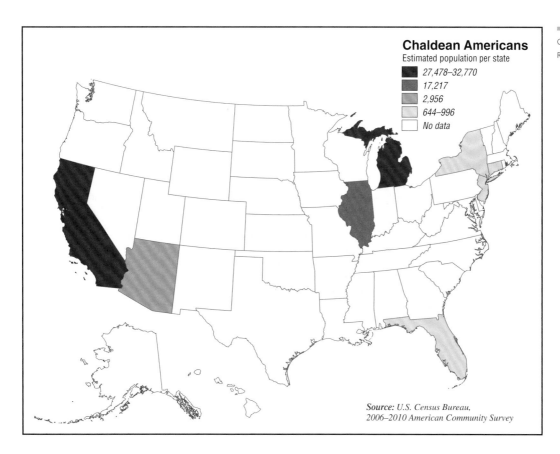

Chaldean Americans
Estimated population per state

- 27,478–32,770
- 17,217
- 2,956
- 644–996
- No data

Source: U.S. Census Bureau,
2006–2010 American Community Survey

shirts on their backs; some had lived in bare-bones refugee settlements in Syria, Lebanon, or other Middle Eastern nations for several months, or even years, prior to being able to leave the Middle East. These refugees often needed considerable assistance with health and readjustment issues upon their arrival in the United States, and social agencies in the Chaldean and Arabic communities established programs to provide this help.

The 1990 U.S. Census listed 44,916 immigrants from Iraq residing in the United States. That number had more than doubled by the time of the 2010 U.S. Census, which counted 105,981. According to U.S. Census data from earlier in the decade, the three states with the largest numbers of Iraqi immigrants were Michigan, California, and Illinois, and Detroit was the U.S. city with the greatest number of Iraqi Americans. However, statistics relating specifically to the Chaldean population are difficult to obtain. Prior to 2000, the U.S. Census had no category under which Chaldeans could feel comfortable indicating their ethnic origins. The major census category was "national origin"; thus, Chaldeans were expected to identify themselves as "Arabic" or "Iraqi." Many Chaldeans, however, prefer to identify as such, relating to their religious, cultural, and linguistic heritage within Iraq. Some might identify as "Assyrian" or "Aramaic," terms that some use to refer to their language. Either way, Chaldeans are largely

unrecognizable in census data, forcing researchers to make use of Chaldean church data to provide a more accurate record of Chaldeans in the United States. With such data, Detroit's Chaldean American community was estimated to be approximately 150,000 in 2009; Iraqi Christians (including Chaldeans and those identifying as Assyrians) in other states numbered around 30,000 to 50,000. Thus, the Chaldean American population totaled approximately 180,000 to 200,000 people.

LANGUAGE

Language among Chaldean immigrants is a complicated matter, since their traditional dialect differs from the national language of Iraq, Arabic. People of Chaldean heritage are intensely proud of their historic language, which they call Chaldean and which is a variant of ancient Aramaic, the language supposedly spoken by Jesus during his lifetime. (The language is also called Assyrian by others who speak it.) The earliest Chaldean immigrants spoke Chaldean and taught it to their American-born children. Later immigrants, specifically those who came as students after World War II, were more likely to speak Arabic and know no Chaldean at all. Consequently, there are really two ethnic languages in the Chaldean community: Chaldean and Arabic. Some Chaldean churches have begun to offer language classes, usually at the elementary level, so that children may learn their linguistic heritage. These classes tend to focus on the Chaldean language rather than Arabic.

Learning English has usually not been a problem for Chaldean immigrants, especially for the men, who pick up English rather quickly in order to work effectively in stores. Chaldeans often tell stories about having learned English from reading the labels on cans on the shelves of these stores. In some families, including both earlier immigrants and later ones, English may be the only common language.

Greetings and Popular Expressions *Shlama ilookhoon*—Hello; *Meleh shumukh?*—What is your name?; *Dakh iwet/dikh-e-wait?*—How are you?; *Ewwan randi!*—I'm fine! (response to "How are you?"); *Baseema raba*—Thank you; *Bsheina.*—Welcome; *Busho bishlama*—Good-bye; *Randa*—Good; *Taawa*—Very good; *Yoom breekha*—Good day; *Rgaan*—Please; Allaha omokh—God be with you; *Kedamtookh brikhta*—Good morning; *Raamshokh breekha*—Good night.

RELIGION

Chaldeans are Roman Catholic, practicing one of the specific rites that originated primarily in the Eastern regions of the early Christian church, such as Greece, Egypt, and, in the case of the Chaldeans, Mesopotamia. Chaldeans claim that the people of Mesopotamia were converted by the Apostle Thomas and his follower, St. Addai, on their missionary journeys in the area. The beliefs of the Chaldean rite are identical to those of the Roman Catholic Church as a whole.

The rituals followed in the Mass and other services may be quite different from those used in a Western Catholic church. The language spoken Chaldean, which is a version of old Aramaic. That their services are conducted in the language spoken by Jesus is a matter of great pride to Chaldeans. In order to accommodate the needs of new immigrants (who usually speak only Arabic) and American-born Chaldeans (who may know only English), however, some parishes offer services in Arabic and/or English in addition to Chaldean. Furthermore, changes in to the Chaldean vernacular over the centuries have meant that the ritual language is incomprehensible to most Chaldeans. Other aspects of the Chaldean rite, such as traditions of fasting and the observance of Lenten practices, also differ from those of the Western, or Latin, rite. In general, Eastern rites tend to be stricter—for example, the Lenten penitential practice is extended for a somewhat longer period. Services for special events such as weddings, funerals, and Baptisms are also different. For centuries, for example, the Western church poured water on the head, whereas Chaldeans immersed the candidate in water.

The Chaldean community has maintained the traditional Chaldean ritual rather effectively in the United States. More than a half-dozen Chaldean churches have been established in the Detroit area to serve the community. In 1982 a diocese was established to serve the entire United States, as well as Canada. However, the number of Chaldeans in the United States has grown to such an extent that in 2002 a diocese in San Diego took over the western area of the country.

Like other Catholics, Chaldeans are free to fulfill worship at any Catholic church. Many Chaldeans simply choose to attend services at the nearest Catholic church. Most Chaldeans do, however, make a special effort to attend a Chaldean church for special events such as weddings, funerals, and baptisms, particularly since Catholic rules dictate that such special services be performed by a priest of the person's own rite. In practice, though, many Catholic priests will perform these services even if they cross the boundaries of a specific rite. Some American-born Chaldeans actually prefer Western rite services because they are offered in English.

Generally, Chaldeans have a reputation for being highly committed Catholics. They are proud of their association with the Catholic Church, even though many other Christians from the East have followed the Orthodox faith. Certainly there are some who do not practice their religion devoutly and others who have ceased their participation entirely, but the maintenance of the Chaldean rite is surprisingly strong, given that Chaldeans have been in the United States for over a century and, as a result, the community has blended into American culture. It should also be noted family ties are extremely important in the Chaldean community; thus, even immigrants who are not religious often remain active in the Chaldean church through various activities.

CULTURE AND ASSIMILATION

Until the mid-twentieth century, Chaldean Americans tended to remain rather isolated from other Americans. They seemed more focused on developing their own community than fostering relationships with other groups. This began to change in the last quarter of the twentieth century, as more American-born Chaldeans grew to adulthood and became comfortable with moving outside their ethnic community. Today's Chaldean Americans are engaged in social, educational, civic, and political activities to a much greater extent than their parents and grandparents were.

Traditions and Customs An important custom for Chaldean males in Iraq was gathering at a coffee house, where the men would socialize over coffee or by smoking tobacco from a hookah, or water pipe. In the United States today, the men's tradition of gathering together continues, sometimes still over coffee or a hookah. Malls have also become centers where Chaldeans (and other Middle Easterners) meet for conversation and socializing.

Since Chaldean Americans are highly committed to marriage, their families, and the church, traditions and customs that relate to these institutions tend to be strongly supported and maintained in the community. Social events normally center on either the family or church or both. Chaldeans go to considerable lengths to ensure that the traditional Catholic religious ceremonies, such as baptisms, first communions, marriages, and funerals, are held in a Chaldean church. These events also usually involve a large social gatherings, often including several hundred family and community members.

For a baptism, the infant is elaborately dressed and the center of attention for the subsequent party. When a child nears the age for first communion (usually around seven years old), the family will frequently plan for several siblings and/or cousins to receive the sacrament together and share the joint social celebration.

Weddings are of particular importance and tend to be large affairs, with numerous bridesmaids and groomsmen and hundreds of guests. The major focus of the event, however, is the religious ceremony. Chaldean religious tradition strongly frowns on divorce, and although the breakup of marriages is more common today among Chaldean Americans, it occurs less frequently than among Americans as a whole. In the past in Iraq, marriages were traditionally arranged and couples often did not even meet each other prior to the wedding. Today, however, dating is more common both in Iraq and the United States. Nevertheless, whether a life choice involves a marriage partner or a job, the opinions of members of the extended family remain important.

A significant wedding custom, carried over to the United States from the old country, involves the groom's family giving gold to the bride. In Iraq this provided the bride with security; if she became widowed, she could sell her gold to care for herself and her children. The economic necessity of this tradition has receded into history, but both the mother and mother-in-law generally still give gold jewelry to the bride—the mother to share the family's wealth and the mother-in-law as a welcoming gesture.

Cuisine Chaldean cuisine is similar to that of other Middle Eastern nations. Among other qualities, it is rich in grains, meat, tomatoes, and potatoes. Chaldean Americans have maintained many of their traditional eating patterns, using recipes that have been passed down for generations. Popular Chaldean dishes include meat and vegetable stew, which is served with rice. A variety of different vegetables are included, such as okra, peas, and green beans. Another notable dish is *dolma*: rice mixed with meat and spices and wrapped in grape leaves or stuffed in other vegetables, such as onions or peppers. Other common Chaldean dishes include *shish kebab* (cubes of meat and vegetables grilled on skewers), *falafel* (deep fried balls of chickpeas served with tahini, a sesame sauce),

The Daughters of Mary Sisters Choir sings during a service at St. Peter's Chaldean Church in El Cajon, California, 2003. SANDY HUFFAKER / GETTY IMAGES

ASSYRIAN LENTILS

Ingredients

2 cups orange lentils, washed and picked

½ cup basmati rice, washed

6 cups water

2 tablespoons olive oil

1 medium onion, chopped

½ teaspoon curry powder

1 teaspoon salt

Preparation

Add lentils and water to 6-quart pan and bring to slow boil over medium, stirring occasionally, for 20 minutes. In a small pan, fry onion in olive oil until tender, then add curry powder and cook for 1 minute. Add onion curry mix to lentil pot and simmer for another 10-15 minutes, until rice and lentils are soft and tender to taste.

Recipe courtesy of Ator Foster

and *kibbeh* (a pie made with ground meat and wheat and baked or fried).

Baklava, also eaten by Arabs and popular in the United States, is a dessert pastry made with layers of phyllo dough covered with nuts and honey. Sesame seed candy is also very popular in Chaldean culture. Tea is typically consumed at all times of the day, with or without meals and as a social drink. Unlike their Muslim or Jewish neighbors in the Middle East, Chaldeans may consume pork and alcohol. American Chaldeans have adapted many of their food patterns to American customs. For example, Thanksgiving is much as it is in a typical American household, with a traditional turkey dinner. Side dishes, however, are likely to include Chaldean foods in addition to American offerings.

Christmas and Easter dinners are particularly important, since these are viewed as the most significant religious feasts. *Pacha*—made with lamb stomachs and intestines that are stuffed with rice and meat and are sewn shut and cooked in a broth that sometimes has the tongue or head of a lamb—is usually reserved for Christmas. It is considered a great delicacy. These feasts also involve making a cookie called *caleche*, which is stuffed with dates or walnuts and shaped into a diamond or crescent.

The extended family adds an important dimension to Chaldean dining. Dinners featuring the extended family occur often, sometimes even weekly. A large amount of food is typically cooked so that each family can take some home and eat it in the coming week. Food preparation, then, is viewed as a family activity.

Traditional Dress For both males and females, Chaldean traditional dress was based on tunics and layering. The earliest type was a rather elaborate shawl drapery worn without a tunic underneath. Later, the tunic came with various fringed shawl draperies; some of the latest types are worn without the shawl draperies. Male tunics were wrapped so that they covered the entire body and were relatively close to the figure. Women's attire featured a plain ungirded tunic and a simply draped shawl, partially covering the figure. Some women would wear a gown of velvet in blue, green, yellow, purple, brown, and other colors, with a huge silver belt and decorative necklaces of silver and gold coins or other ornaments.

Headwear is an important feature of both ancient and modern Chaldean dress. Chaldean women typically wear scarf-like wraps, and some don round, ornamental hats that resemble crowns and bear silver ornamentation that encircles the headpiece in rings. Men's headwear in contemporary Chaldean villages includes small, gently conical hats with ornamental feathers. Other men's accessories include watches, jewelry and scarves. Linen has been used from an early period for better-quality garments, but the most common material has always been wool. Cotton, leather, and papyrus were also used. Traditional Chaldean clothes bear a number of colors, such as black, yellow, gold, maroon, white, and various shades of blue and green, purple and vermilion. Today, Western clothes have largely been adopted by Chaldeans, both in the United States and Iraq. Most Chaldean Americans do not wear traditional clothes.

Arts and Crafts Some Chaldean American women have developed skills in sewing or embroidery, but their work appears resembles American patterns rather than traditional Chaldean or Middle Eastern fare. Many Chaldean craft projects carry out the community's religious traditions, such as making rosaries or religious pictures. Dolls adorned with the classic Chaldean clothing, usually that of a bride in Telkaif prior to the mid-twentieth century, come closest to constituting a traditional Chaldean craft. Several elder Chaldean American women have produced such dolls. However, making these dolls is a family tradition—there does not seem to be a widespread commercial market for them.

Dances and Songs Performed at weddings, parties, and other significant events, dances and songs have helped to define Chaldeans. Songs are performed either in Aramaic or Arabic. A *khiga*, a type of line dance, is the most popular Chaldean dance, dating to before recorded history. The accompanying song is traditionally played to welcome the bride and groom to the reception hall. The fast-paced *seskanee* is another famous dance, found mainly in the Nineveh plains among Chaldean Catholics of Alqosh and surrounding villages. Chaldean music differs by region, though many songs are about either love or war (focusing on the history of Iraq and its people). The *dowlah* (drum) and *zornah* (wind-pipe, or flute) are traditional Chaldean musical instruments that are played together at weddings and other events, either with or without singing. Today, Western dances, songs, and instruments are part of many Chaldean American parties, weddings, and other functions. However, traditional fare may also be part of the festivities.

Holidays The main holidays celebrated by Chaldean Americans are Christmas and Easter. These holidays revolve around the church, and most Chaldean Americans make a point of attending services. Religious ceremonies are traditionally conducted in Aramaic, and some traditions, such as the Lenten fast, tend to be more rigorous than those in the American Catholic Church. Families and relatives also gather together on these holidays and prepare large amounts of Chaldean food. This includes *pacha* (usually served on Christmas), meat and vegetable stew, rice, *dolma*, and *kibbeh*. Thanksgiving is also celebrated in Chaldean American households.

Health Care Issues and Practices Health care is socialized in Iraq, and the country's system was extremely advanced in the 1970s and 1980s. However, there has been a dramatic rise in disease since 1990, due to chemicals used in the Persian Gulf War and from malnutrition and bacterial diseases exacerbated by conditions resulting from the economic embargo imposed on Iraq by Western nations. Indeed, the health care system in Iraq is rapidly declining, as once-controlled maladies such as typhoid fever, measles, chicken pox, and cholera are reappearing in considerable numbers. In addition, there has been a steep increase in afflictions such as leukemia and other cancers, high blood pressure, and birth defects, related exposure to radiation from leaking uranium shells. Recent Iraqi immigrants to the United States have suffered from some of these ailments.

Furthermore, Chaldean immigrants are vulnerable to mental health problems such as depression, anxiety, and post-traumatic stress disorder for reasons that can be traced to the Iraqi wars, the overall brutal conditions in their native country, difficult experiences in refugee camps, cultural conflict, and problems adjusting to American culture. Such mental issues are stigmatized, meaning many Chaldean immigrants do not seek professional help.

Iraqi immigrants, including Chaldeans, generally trust in the U.S. health care system. Some, however, harbor negative views toward it, the result of protracted waiting times in health care facilities, the difficulty of obtaining antibiotics (which requires a doctor's prescription), the cost of medical care and insurance, or the relative absence of follow-up treatment. Thus, some Chaldean Americans shun the health care system. In fact, despite the advanced medical treatments in the United States, some Chaldean Americans still use traditional therapies such as herbal remedies.

Death and Burial Rituals In Chaldean culture, funerals are simple and somber events, and the rituals surrounding them are also generally practiced by Chaldean Americans. When a Chaldean dies, the news is passed to relatives and friends by the deceased person's immediate relatives. It is customary to first notify the priest in order to make arrangements for the funeral service and burial. Relatives gather for a last farewell before the deceased is taken to the church.

According to Chaldean liturgy, the body is immediately washed and prepared for burial. While the body is being readied, the priest and deacons conduct a funeral service that lasts more than an hour. The assembly observes the service in respectful silence, and when the washing ritual is completed and the body is dressed, it is enclosed in a casket and brought before the mourners. The priest and deacons then sing special chants about the dead. The service concludes with a reading from the scriptures, followed by several more chants.

A funeral procession is formed that heads for the cemetery. The theme of the graveside ceremony centers on hope of a glorious resurrection, and the deacon begins by exhorting the assembly to pray for the deceased. A second priestly prayer precedes the lowering of the body into the grave. To end the prayer, the priest throws a handful of earth into the grave, and those around him do the same.

After the burial, relatives, neighbors, and friends gather to console the family of the deceased. The mourning period usually lasts for three days, and friends and relatives often help to provide meals for everyone. Most female family members wear black and no makeup for one year. On the fortieth day after the burial, the family usually has a smaller church service, which is attended by close relatives and friends. The first anniversary includes another church service, at which point the long period of mourning ends.

Recreational Activities Today's Chaldean Americans engage in typical American recreational activities. The *Chaldean News*, a monthly newspaper published in suburban Detroit, often highlights the activities of Chaldean youth in a wide variety of sports, such as basketball and baseball. Chaldeans have excelled in several sports at both the high school and college levels. A handful of pastimes have been retained from the old country, though they are generally practiced by immigrants rather than the American-born Chaldeans. An example of this is *tawlee*, a board game similar to backgammon that reportedly has its origins in ancient Mesopotamia. Most Chaldeans, however, have adopted American games and recreational activities.

FAMILY AND COMMUNITY LIFE

Preserving the traditional family—with its close ties between parents, children, siblings, cousins, grandchildren, and other relatives—is always viewed by Chaldean Americans as a high priority. These relationships are the foundation of Chaldean American life.

CHALDEAN PROVERBS

Some proverbs are unique to the Chaldean community; others appear also in Arabic. Most of those listed below appear to be exclusive to Chaldeans.

Yumma me zabna chilkallah lak marisha yalleh.

A mother would rather sell her gold ankle bracelet than wake up sleeping babies.

Beyoma klosha shirattha eh bilaleh kimayakha birkatha.

By day she wears bracelets but at night she beats her thighs.

Mukhi in gouda to shami garrah.

Talk to the walls so that the roof hears.

Bera d'shatit mina maya latalqit kepa bgawa.

Don't throw stones into the well you drink water from.

Aqerwa zilla l'rishlem wla nshala adata.

The scorpion went to Jerusalem and didn't give up its habits.

Melpo, melpo, tine' dgomle lbathra.

Like camels when they urinate, their urine goes backwards.

Itha dlebokh dna'sito, nshoqla.

Kiss the hand you can't bite.

Zuza khwara, tayoma khoma.

A white penny for black tomorrows.

Zalat al'aqil kabira.

A reasonable man's mistake is very big.

Itho mbathro, itho meqamo.

One hand behind and the other in front.

Gender Roles Traditional Chaldean families, like many in the Arab world, have been largely segregated by gender. Men are typically the head of the family and are not involved in household activities or the care of children. They work outside the home. Women, meanwhile, are valued for the number of children they bear and are expected to remain in the home rather than be employed. These gender constructions begin in early childhood, though they are changing somewhat.

In the earliest years of the Chaldean immigration, men concentrated their attention on the grocery business, which required a great deal of practical skills but generally did not involve much formal education. Consequently, Chaldeans did not prize academics highly. Most immigrants went into business with little more than the minimal education they had attained prior to coming to the United States. They did, however, encourage their sons to at least graduate from high school before focusing their efforts on learning business skills. Both Chaldean boys and girls spent many hours assisting in the stores owned by their fathers and uncles. However, the boys were more likely to be groomed to run the business; their sisters were simply expected to marry, set up a household, and have children.

Chaldean American gender roles are now adapted more to U.S. society. For example, Chaldean women often obtain college educations and have profession positions. This pattern was initiated in the 1950s and 1960s, when Chaldean children began to attend college. Today both males and females generally have the same levels of education as most Americans do and can be found in fields such as business, law, medicine, dentistry, and engineering. Many Chaldean American women balance their careers with being wives and mothers.

Despite these advancements, some Chaldean American women still complain that Chaldean families prefer male children over females and that girls often have more household responsibilities than their brothers. This has led women to seek more equality with their husbands in the home, something that has not been completely accepted across the Chaldean American community. Some males have been dismayed by the greater equality experienced by their sisters and wives, especially compared to their mothers and grandmothers, and they have expressed a desire to return to the more traditional gender roles.

The pattern of spouse selection has also changed, as arranged marriages are now obsolete. Nevertheless, the extended family still has considerable input in the choice of a marriage partner. This transformation is also evident in Iraq, where Chaldeans have more freedom to choose their own spouses and are more inclined to date prior to marriage.

Education Chaldean Americans have followed an interesting path regarding education, stemming largely from their early involvement in the grocery business and their immigration patterns. Early immigrants had considerable success in business without much formal education. Thus, they downplayed the value of school and discouraged their children from pursuing higher education. This is no longer the case. Many new arrivals from Iraq come with college degrees, and American-born Chaldeans express interest in fields other than the grocery business and use education as a means to move into other professions. Detroit's Chaldean community has embraced this trend, providing college scholarships and honoring students at all levels of education who have attained diplomas in the previous year.

Courtship and Weddings Traditional Chaldean weddings in the village culture were arranged through the family of the groom. Older family members selected a young woman whom they considered an appropriate marriage partner for their son. Sometimes marriages between cousins occurred, too. In the early twentieth century, men usually married in their early twenties, when they were old enough to support a family. The bride was generally much younger than the groom, sometimes as young as eleven years old. Female relatives of the male typically visited the female relatives of the prospective bride, and a conversation was held to explore whether there might be some value in a relationship between the two families. The discussion would be discreet so that neither family would suffer embarrassment if an arrangement could not be completed. Once an agreement was reached, the couple's engagement was announced. Weddings were typically held in the home of the groom, after which there was a party that lasted as many as four days. Brides wore colorful clothing, with as much gold jewelry as their families could afford. The virginity of the bride was critical, and the groom's family often sought proof in the form of a bloody cloth following the couple's wedding night. However, once Chaldeans began to migrate from villages to Iraqi urban centers, the tradition of arranged marriage gradually declined.

In the early years of Chaldean immigration, some marriages were arranged between men who had moved to the United States and the daughters of relatives or friends in Iraq. Marriage between men who had already become U.S. citizens and women in Iraq became a mechanism of immigration. Arranged marriages among Chaldeans had disappeared in the United States by the middle to late twentieth century.

Today, Chaldean American weddings have an American feel. Brides wear long, elaborate, white gowns and veils, and grooms and their attendants don tuxedos. There are usually five or six bridesmaids and groomsmen. The weddings take place at church, usually in a major Sunday Mass, with many attendees looking on. An elaborate reception follows that might number several hundred people. The festivities last well into the night.

Relations with Other Americans Until the mid-twentieth century, Chaldean Americans tended to remain rather isolated from other Americans. They seemed more focused on developing their own community than fostering relationships with other groups. This began to change in the last quarter of the twentieth century, as more American-born Chaldeans grew to adulthood and became comfortable with moving outside their ethnic community. Today's Chaldeans are engaged in social, educational, civic, and political activities to a much greater extent than their parents and grandparents were.

Philanthropy Chaldean Americans engage in a considerable amount of philanthropy. One of their oldest philanthropic groups is the Michigan-based Chaldean Ladies of Charity, made up of women who have carried out charitable services for Chaldean families and individuals for decades. Among its achievements has been its establishment of resources for care of Chaldean elderly.

The Chaldean Federation is an umbrella for several Chaldean associations, including the Chaldean-American Bar Association, Chaldean Cultural Center, Chaldean-Middle Eastern Social Services, Chaldean American Ladies of Charity, Chaldean Community Foundation, Shenandoah Country Club, and Chaldean Outreach and Community Hope (COACH). Some of these organizations have philanthropic missions. The Chaldean Federation offers scholarships to Chaldean students and also runs numerous programs to assist recent refugees from Iraq with matters such as resettlement and deportation problems. It also engages with U.S. government officials to provide help to Chaldeans displaced by the Iraq wars.

Surnames Typical Chaldean surnames include Abbo, Abro, Acho, Binno, Bidiwid, Garmo, George, Hakim, Khami, Kherkher, Konja, Lossia, Mansour, Matti, Kashat, Najor, Namo, Sarafa, Sesi, Shamoun, Shammamy, Roumayah, Sitto, Yaldo, Yasso, Yono, Yousif, and Zeabari.

EMPLOYMENT AND ECONOMIC CONDITIONS

Many Chaldean Americans continue to work in the grocery business. In addition to independently owned grocery stores, this includes wholesale grocery supply operations, which some Chaldeans own and/or operate. At various times, Chaldeans have owned businesses that produce and/or distribute canned foods, baked goods, dairy products, and other foodstuffs to stores that are both within and outside the Chaldean network. Chaldean Americans have also been involved in businesses that provide supplies such as butcher equipment or alarms to grocery stores, as well as real estate firms that help to locate potentially profitable sites for stores.

In the latter half of the twentieth century, many Chaldean Americans began to branch out into other professions. Today there are Chaldean Americans in virtually every type of occupation, including medicine, dentistry, engineering, pharmacy, law, and education. In prior decades, Chaldean American males were primarily the ones who worked, but now many women do, too. As with other groups, Chaldean Americans were affected by the economic downturn in the 2000s. However, their business connections cushioned them to some degree, as loans were available through the Chaldean American community. Recent immigrants and refugees were more critically impacted by the recession because their jobs were less stable.

POLITICS AND GOVERNMENT

Until recently, few Chaldean Americans were involved in politics and government. Their attention was focused mainly on their internal community: family, the grocery business, and the church. In the past few decades, however, Chaldeans have moved into the political sphere in greater numbers. A Chaldean American, Waddie P. Deddeh, served for an extended period in the California state legislature from 1966 to 1992. In 2012 a member of the Chaldean community, Klint Kesto, was elected to the Michigan state legislature for the first time, and a Chaldean woman, Diane Dickow D'Agostini, served as a district judge in the Detroit area in the 2000s and 2010s. Their motivations for running for office included representing the Chaldean community and Middle Easterners in general.

NOTABLE INDIVIDUALS

Academia Amer Hanna Fatuhi, a scholar of Mesopotamian history and religious groups in Iraq, wrote *The Untold Story of Native Iraqis* (2012).

Majid Khadduri (1909–2007) founded the graduate Middle East Studies Program at Johns Hopkins University in Baltimore, Maryland.

Activism Joseph Kassab (1952–) is executive director of the Chaldean Federation of America, where he is responsible for refugee assistance programs.

Business Michael George (1933?–) is a Chaldean businessman and philanthropist in the Detroit area who served as chief executive officer of Melody Farms Dairy.

Sam Attisha (1968?–) is vice president of business development and external affairs for Cox Communications in San Diego. He was named "One of San Diego's Top Influentials" by the *Daily Transcript* newspaper.

Politics Wadie P. Deddeh (1920–) served as a senator in the California State Assembly.

Attorney Klint Kesto who was elected Michigan's legislature in November 2012 to represent the state's 39th District, which includes Commerce and West Bloomfield. In what the *Chaldean News* referred to as "an historic win," he became the first Chaldean American to be elected to the Michigan legislature.

Diane Dickow D'Agostini served as a judge in the 48th District of Oakland County in Michigan. Prior to that, she was assistant prosecutor. She is renowned for her work in preventing domestic violence.

Religion Mar Sarhad Jammo (1941–) is bishop of the Chaldean Catholic Church in the western United States, based at St. Peter's Chaldean Catholic Cathedral in El Cajon, California.

Mar Ibrahim Ibrahim (1937–) is bishop of the Chaldean Catholic Church in eastern North America, based at Mother of God Church in Southfield, Michigan.

Science and Medicine Nathima Atchoo, an obstetrician/gynecologist associated with the Gary Burnstein Community Health Clinic in Pontiac, Michigan, is known for traveling to the Middle East to treat refugees. In 2009 she received the Chaldean Humanitarian of the Year award from the Chaldean Federation of Michigan.

Hind Rassam Culhane was co-chair of the Social and Behavioral Sciences Division at Mercy College in Dobbs Ferry, New York.

Stage and Screen Heather Raffo (1970–) is a playwright and actress whose works have been presented Off-Broadway and on tour. She has exposed American audiences to Iraqi culture, notably from a female perspective.

Alia Martine Shawkat (1989–) is an actress who has appeared in a number of films and TV programs, including *Amreeka, State of Grace*, and *Arrested Development*.

A Chaldean immigrant from northern Iraq watches President George W. Bush speak about plans for Iraq at a White House press conference on Thursday March 6, 2003. JOHN GASTALDO / ZUMA PRESS / NEWSCOM

MEDIA

Chaldean Americans operate several media sources directed mainly to their ethnic community. Some media outlets, however, are aimed at other Arabic, Iraqi, or Middle Eastern groups as well.

NEWSPAPERS

Assyrian International News Agency

This agency was established in 1995 to serve the Chaldean community in El Cajon, California.

Peter BetBasoo, Editor
Email: Peter.BetBasoo@aina.org
URL: www.aina.org

Betha Kaldaya

A community newspaper published by the Chaldean American Institute.

269 East Lexington Avenue
Suite B
El Cajon, California 92020
Phone: (619) 500-3224
URL: www.bethakaldaya.com

Chaldean News

Based in Michigan, this monthly newspaper provides coverage on all aspects of Chaldean activities.

30095 Northwestern Highway
Farmington Hills, Michigan 48334
Phone: (248) 996-8360
URL: www.chaldeannews.com

Michigan Arab Times Alhadath Newspaper

This newspaper offers articles for the Arabic-speaking community in Michigan, including some materials on the Chaldeans.

URL: www.michiganarabtimes.com

Nineveh

A quarterly magazine published by the Assyrian Foundation of America, *Nineveh* contains articles in English as well as in Assyrian (Aramaic/Chaldean).

P.O. Box 2600
Berkeley, California 94702
URL: www.assyrianfoundation.org

RADIO

The Chaldean Voice

This independent radio station, accessible online, features programming of interest to Chaldeans.

25775 Berg Road
Southfield, Michigan 48034
Phone: (248) 353-1083
URL: www.chaldeanvoice.com

ORGANIZATIONS AND ASSOCIATIONS

Arab American and Chaldean Social Services Council

A nonprofit founded in 1979 that offers a number of services to Middle Eastern immigrants in southeastern Michigan. Among the organization's areas of service are health, education, and employment training.

26400 Lahser Road
Suite 330
Southfield, Michigan 48033
Phone: (248) 354-8460
URL: www.myacc.org

Chaldean American Chamber of Commerce

Helps to foster a thriving business climate for Chaldeans living in the Detroit area.

29850 Northwestern Highway
Suite 250
Southfield, Michigan 48034
URL: www.chaldeanchamber.com

Chaldean American Ladies of Charity

Founded in 1961, this organization offers assistance to needy Chaldean families in the Detroit area.

32000 Northwestern Highway
Suite 150
Southfield, Michigan 48334
Phone: (248) 538-8300
URL: www.calonline.org

Chaldean Cultural Center

Highlights the artistic achievements of Chaldeans throughout history.

5600 Walnut Lake Road
West Bloomfield, Michigan 48323
Phone: (248) 681-5050
URL: www.chaldeanculturalcenter.org

Chaldean Federation of America

Among its other missions, this organization advocates for Chaldean refugees. In addition to Michigan, it has offices in El Cajon, California, and Scottsdale, Arizona.

29850 Northwestern Highway
Suite 250
Southfield, Michigan 38034
Phone: (248) 996-8384
URL: www.chaldeanfederation.org

MUSEUMS AND RESEARCH CENTERS

As of 2012 the Chaldean Cultural Center was being built in West Bloomfield Michigan, a facility owned by leaders of the local Chaldean American community. The center will feature historical data and artifacts relating to Chaldeans.

The Arab-American National Museum, located in Dearborn, Michigan, has devoted a section of its space to the Iraqi-Chaldean community.

SOURCES FOR ADDITIONAL STUDY

Fatuhi, Amer Hanna. *The Untold Story of Native Iraqis.* Bloomington, IN: Xlibris, 2012.

Gallagher, Barbara George. *Chaldean Immigrant Women, Gender and Family.* Ann Arbor, MI: ProQuest Dissertations and Theses, 1999.

Lobe, J. "Iraq Exodus Fuels Rise in Refugees, Displaced." *Inter Press Service.* Global Policy Forum, 2007. Web. 31 Dec. 2012.

Najor, Julia. *Babylonian Cuisine: Chaldean Cookbook from the Middle East.* Detroit: National Books, International, 1981.

Schopmeyer, K. "A Demographic Portrait of Arab Detroit." In *Arab Detroit: From Margin to Mainstream*, edited by N. Abraham and A. Shryock, 61–92. Detroit, MI: Wayne State University Press, 2000.

Sengstock, Mary C. *Chaldean-Americans: Changing Conceptions of Ethnic Identity.* Staten Island, NY: Center for Migration Studies, 1999.

———. *Chaldeans in Michigan.* Lansing: Michigan State University Press, 2005.

Shikwana, Therese Hermiz. *The Relationship of Socioeconomic Status of Chaldean Parents and Their Children's Education.* Ann Arbor, MI: ProQuest Dissertations and Theses, 1997.

Spurlock, Charles Johnson. *From the Tigris to the Rouge: An Exploratory Study of Chaldean Gendered Ethnicity and Gender Transition.* ProQuest Dissertations and Theses, 2010.

CHEROKEES

Robert J. Conley

OVERVIEW

Cherokees are a Native American people whose ancestral lands were a vast area of what is now the southeastern United States. The earliest historical data indicates they lived in about 200 villages scattered throughout the present states of Alabama, Georgia, Kentucky, North Carolina, South Carolina, Virginia, and West Virginia. The original Cherokee territories consisted primarily of three main regions: the Lower Towns near the river valleys of Georgia and the Carolinas, the Middle Towns in the high country of the Blue Ridge Mountains, and the Overhill Towns on the western side of the Blue Ridge. The word *Cherokee* is believed to have evolved from a Choctaw word meaning Cave People and was adopted by Cherokees in the form of *Tsalagi* or *Jalagi*.

The Cherokee population in 1674—prior to any major contact with Europeans—was around 50,000. The Cherokee people had a settled, agricultural society, and their kinship and clan membership was matrilineal, or determined by the mother. According to traditional Cherokee religion, the world is divided into the Upper World, where protective spirits dwell; the Middle World, inhabited by humans; and the Under World, a place of bad spirits that can bring disaster and disorder. The Cherokee relied on the benevolent spirits of the Upper World to help maintain harmony and balance on Earth. As part of their religion, they performed daily rituals, prayers, and annual ceremonies. Their economy was based primarily on the cultivation of three agricultural crops—corn, beans, and squash—and also incorporated the gathering of certain native plants and hunting. Before European contact, they were a large, powerful tribe and appear to have had a relatively high standard of living compared to smaller Native American tribes.

Today there are three federally recognized Cherokee governments in the United States. The first, the Cherokee Nation, occupies all or part of fourteen counties in the northeastern portion of the state of Oklahoma. Not considered a reservation, the land is subject to what has been called "a checkerboard jurisdiction": one farm or acreage falls under tribal jurisdiction, while its neighbor is under that of the state. A second and separate federally recognized tribal government, the United Keetoowah Band of Cherokees in

Oklahoma, exists in the same area. The third government, the Eastern Band of the Cherokee Nation, is located on a Cherokee land grant in western North Carolina known as the Qualla Boundary. Current Cherokee territory is a result of the tribe's forced relocation, primarily from Georgia, by the federal government in 1838, a journey known as the Trail of Tears due to the high number of individuals who died. One of the Cherokee Nation's key sources of revenue since the late twentieth century has been tourism.

Though divided geographically, culturally, and politically, the Cherokee Nation in 2011 was made up of about 300,000 registered citizens—roughly the population of Riverside, California—according to Cherokee Nation documentation. This population is distributed across the United States, with many Cherokees living and working outside of their designated lands. The largest concentration of the group in the United States is in eastern Oklahoma, where the population of Cherokees in combination with any other race was approximately 180,000 in 2006, according to the U.S. Census Bureau's American Community Survey estimates for 2006–2008. While Oklahoma is the state with the largest Cherokee population, other states with smaller yet significant numbers of Cherokee include California, Texas, Arkansas, Florida, and North Carolina.

HISTORY OF THE PEOPLE

Early History Early Cherokee Indians lived in the Appalachian Mountains along the Tennessee River. Different clans dwelled in small villages separated by a distance that took approximately a day to travel by foot. Cherokee society depended on the cultivation of certain crops, combined with the gathering of berries and nuts and the hunting of local game. Village chieftains were the leaders of local clans and served as representatives for their villages to the larger tribe. Cherokees would trade among different villages, and occasional rivalries existed between clans.

Traditional Cherokee life began to change with the arrival of Spanish explorer Hernando de Soto in 1540. While their encounter was brief, and North America was never colonized by Spain, Native American tribes, including the Cherokee, were directly impacted by Spanish technology, culture, and disease. The Spanish conquerors introduced horses and dogs to the region, as well as violence from guns and other weaponry. The majority of Cherokee villagers fled their settlements prior to the arrival of the Spanish because of the negative reputation of Europeans among Native Americans in the region. The few Cherokee villages that did encounter Spaniards were reportedly hospitable to them, providing the explorers with food and shelter. Although de Soto died in the Cherokee country region in 1542 and Spain saw his expedition as largely a failure, the Spanish did establish several forts and settlements in the area and were involved in the mining and smelting of gold and other precious metals throughout the seventeenth century. This meant more regular contact between the Cherokee and Spanish settlers in the region during this period.

Reportedly, the Cherokee had their first contact with the English in 1654, when English colonists from the Jamestown settlement attacked a new Cherokee settlement at the falls of the James River, the site of present-day Richmond, Virginia. The English were defeated and forced to surrender. Contact between the Cherokee and explorers and traders was common in the late seventeenth century, and a treaty was reportedly signed between the tribe and the colony of South Carolina in 1684 that facilitated peaceful relations between the two societies. However, violations of this treaty by British colonists led the Cherokee to renew warfare against the foreigners in order to defend their highly coveted territory. English colonial traders began to appear among the Cherokees around 1673. Such interactions produced some mixed marriages, usually between a white trader and a Cherokee woman.

Among the most pervasive challenges the Cherokee faced during this period was their lack of immunity to European diseases. A smallpox epidemic in 1738 devastated their population; reportedly, almost half of the tribe died from the disease within a year. Although this thinned the once large and powerful tribe, Cherokee leaders continued to fight against white encroachment on their lands. In March 1775 a leader of the Dragging Canoe tribe called for the Cherokee to continue their resistance of usurpation by U.S. settlers. He spoke at Sycamore Shoals in what now is Tennessee, asking, "Should we not therefore run all risks, and incur all consequences, rather than submit to further laceration of our country? … I have my young warriors about me. We will have our lands."

The Cherokees were forced to sign one treaty after another with the U.S. government, each one giving away more land to the new nation. As early as 1803, President Thomas Jefferson planned to move all eastern Native Americans to a location west of the Mississippi River, and he signed an agreement with the state of Georgia promising to accomplish that deed as soon as possible. President Andrew Jackson actually set the so-called removal process in motion. In the meantime, the government had been doing everything in its

power to convince Cherokees to move west voluntarily, and the first to do so was the faction known as Chickamaugans. Other migrations followed in the late eighteenth and early nineteenth centuries.

The vast majority of the Cherokees, however, remained in their ancestral homelands. In 1835 the United States Congress passed the Removal Act. The Cherokee Nation, which by this time was under the administration of Principal Chief John Ross, refused to recognize the validity or the legality of the Removal Act and challenged it in court. The U.S. Supreme Court ruled in favor of the Cherokee Nation. According to Anthony Wallace in *The Long, Bitter Trail: Andrew Jackson and the Indians* (1993), President Jackson said, "Justice [John] Marshall has made his decision. Now let him enforce it." Jackson then sent negotiators into the Cherokee Nation to secure a treaty whereby it would give up all of its land in the East for land out West. The government of the Cherokee Nation refused to negotiate, but other Cherokees signed the treaty without authorization. The United States called the treaty a legal document and proceeded to force the Cherokees to live up to its terms.

Jackson ordered the U.S. Army to forcibly remove the Cherokees from their homelands in 1838. People were taken out of their homes and herded like cattle into stockades to await removal. Conditions were crowded and unsanitary, and many died in these prisons. The forced march began later that same year. While there are no statistics regarding the exact number of Cherokees who were removed, scholars have estimated that between 16,000 and 20,000 marched west over what would soon be known as the Trail of Tears. Along the way, approximately 4,000 people died, according to Russell Thornton in his 1984 *Ethnohistory* essay, "Cherokee Population Losses during the Trail of Tears: A New Perspective and a New Estimate." A few managed to escape by hiding out in the mountains.

In the West, the Cherokee split into two major factions. Those who had signed the removal treaty and all of their friends, allies, and associates had become known as the Treaty Party. They had moved west voluntarily in 1835 after having signed the treaty. The followers of Chief John Ross, who had suffered the forced removal, were known as the Ross Party. These two factions fought each other in a civil war that lasted until 1843. At the end of this domestic strife, the Cherokees rebuilt their nation, with Tahlequah, Oklahoma, becoming the capital city. They constructed new homes, schools, and churches. Despite having a treaty with the United States that guaranteed they would be left alone, this was not to be.

The Cherokee Nation was dragged into the American Civil War. Ross begged the United States to send troops to protect its neutrality as promised in the treaty, but soldiers never came. Under pressure from former Treaty Party members who had become

Confederate Cherokees, Ross was forced to sign a treaty with the Confederacy. Following the Civil War, the United States used that treaty as an excuse to punish the Cherokee Nation, making it sign yet another treaty and give up more land. Certain governmental powers were also taken away from the Cherokee Nation. The Cherokee Nation, Choctaw Nation, Chickasaw Nation, Creek Nation, and Seminole Nation were organized into what was known as Indian Territory.

Over the next half-century, the powers of the so-called Five Civilized Tribes that made up the Indian Territory were further eroded by the United States. In 1907, against the wishes of nearly all of the traditional full-blood people of all five tribes, Indian Territory was combined with Oklahoma Territory to its west to form the new state of Oklahoma.

From the beginning, the United States had no intention of dealing with Indians in the new state. If not for complications transferring land titles, all tribal governments would have been abolished; indeed, most were. The U.S. president began appointing chiefs for the five tribes when the government had need of a signature to make the transfers legal. Several appointments were made only long enough to obtain the desired signature, and these appointees became known as "Chiefs for a day."

Modern Era In 1970 President Richard Nixon affirmed Native Americans' right to self-determination, prompting a revitalization of the government of the original Cherokee Nation; the following year the Cherokees elected their own principal chief for the first time since 1902. However, this also created the uncomfortable situation of having two Cherokee governments in the same location, with the same jurisdiction and basically the same constituency. (The other, the United Keetoowah Band of Cherokee Indians in Oklahoma, was founded in the 1950s.) A conflict over political issues developed, as both sides claimed to be the only legal government for Cherokees in Oklahoma. Since then, the Cherokee Nation has grown and prospered, making its most impressive strides under the leadership of Wilma P. Mankiller (1945–2010), who served as principal chief from 1985 to 1995. Joe Byrd succeeded Mankiller, but allegations of corruption and abuse of power plagued his four-year term. In 1999 Chad Smith was elected principal chief, followed by Bill John Baker, a fourth-generation Cherokee, in 2011.

SETTLEMENT IN THE UNITED STATES

Cherokees had lived in the southeastern region of what is now the United States for centuries before their first contact with Europeans in the late sixteenth and early seventeenth centuries. During ancient times, the central city of the Cherokee Nation was Kituhwa, located near present-day Bryson City, North Carolina. Today almost half the total Cherokee population resides in Oklahoma. Other states with significant numbers of Cherokee are North Carolina, Florida, California, Arkansas, and Texas.

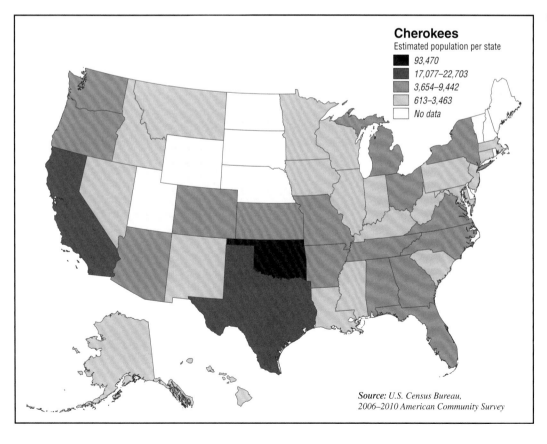

Source: U.S. Census Bureau, 2006–2010 American Community Survey

CHEROKEES

LANGUAGE

The Cherokee language belongs to the Iroquoian family of languages and is therefore related to Mohawk, Seneca, Onondaga, Oneida, Cayuga, and Tuscarora, among others. It is a complex and difficult language; for example, in his *Cherokee—English Dictionary*, Durbin Feeling lists 126 forms of a single verb. Cherokee has been a written language at least since 1821, when Sequoyah (ca. 1770–1843), a Cherokee, produced a syllabary for that purpose. (A syllabary is a writing system in which each symbol stands for an entire syllable. In the Cherokee syllabary, the symbol *A*, for example, stands for the sound "go.") Although Sequoyah is credited with inventing the syllabary, some Cherokees have taken exception to this designation, maintaining that the syllabary is an ancient Cherokee writing system that was kept secret until Sequoyah decided to make it public. Soon afterward, almost the entire Cherokee population became literate, and in 1828 the Nation began publishing a bilingual newspaper, the *Cherokee Phoenix*.

Today, the Cherokee language is still in wide use. In fact, many children grow up with it as their first language, learning English when they go to school. Bilingual education programs in the public schools also encourage continued use of the language. However, according to the U.S. Census Bureau's American Community Survey, English was the only language spoken in approximately 93 percent of Cherokee households in 2010. As of 2013 in Oklahoma specifically, there were approximately 12,000 native speakers of Cherokee, down from 15,000 in the 1970s. In other words, attempts to preserve the Cherokee language among new generations have not been particularly successful.

Greetings and Popular Expressions *Osiyo* or *'Siyo* is usually translated as "hello" and may be followed by *Tohiju?*, meaning "How are you?" or "Are you well?" One response is *tohigwu* (I am well). Other common expressions are *Wado* (Thank you); *Howa* (All right" or Okay); *Asgaya* (Man); *Achuja* (Boy); *Agehyuh* (Women); *Agehyuja* (Girl); and *Chalagihi Ayehli* or *Jalagihi Ayehli* (Cherokee Nation).

The Cherokee language is still in wide use. In fact, many children grow up with it as their first language, learning English when they go to school. Bilingual education programs in the public schools also encourage continued use of the language.

RELIGION

The ancient Cherokee belief system describes a world that is flat and floating on water. This is the world that we live on. Above it is a sky vault made of stone, which might resemble a bowl turned upside down over a saucer. The original life forms, all spirit beings, and the souls of the departed live on top of the sky vault. Life there is similar to that on Earth. The Cherokee believe that there is a world beneath the Earth that is the opposite of this one: when it is winter on Earth, it is summer down there; when it is night here, it is daytime there. Many powerful and potentially destructive spirit forces live in the world below.

It would be a mistake, however, to view the two Cherokee spirit worlds as heaven and hell. They are not defined as good and evil—although the one below is seen as tremendously chaotic—but rather as contrasts. Tribal members live in a precarious balance between them. Consequently, maintaining that balance—and thus achieving a sort of harmony—was the most important aspect of life for the traditional Cherokee. Almost all habits, rituals, and ceremonies were designed and practiced to that end. For example, Cherokee hunters would pray to the spirits of animals for forgiveness and guidance prior to killing them. Similarly, those who gathered medicinal plants, as well as roots and vegetables for sustenance, would harvest only every fourth plant that they encountered in order to allow the rest to grow and serve their purpose in the natural world. The Cherokee existence was defined by opposites: light and dark, day and night, summer and winter, male and female, earth and sky, fire and water. A balance had to be maintained to avoid a mixture of these opposites and therefore avert a disaster that would necessitate a cleansing ceremony. One such ceremony, called "going to the water," would be performed at sunrise for reasons such as illness or a bad dream. Cherokee individuals would step into a river or creek while facing east and submerge themselves in the water seven times. The ritual was thought to rid people of negative feelings and enable them to begin anew.

These religious beliefs were altered, however, upon the Cherokee's contact with English colonists, who established several different Christian denomination missions in tribal territory beginning in the early eighteenth century. Many tribal members were eager to learn English and other aspects of the "white man's" culture, which were taught by the missionaries. Over time, the New Testament was translated into Cherokee and published in the Cherokee syllabary. Christian congregations, particularly Baptists, also began to perform hymns and scriptures in the Cherokee language. Tribal communities mixed traditional Cherokee values, including the ideals of sharing and respect, into their new Christian faith. Many historians have credited the Cherokee Baptist Association, to which most Cherokees in Oklahoma belong today, with saving the Cherokee language from extinction. Although this is a subject of debate, the association has, at the very least, played a significant role in preserving the language. The association's membership is entirely native, and services in its churches are generally conducted entirely in Cherokee. A number of church members still consult traditional Cherokee healers, many of

456 GALE ENCYCLOPEDIA OF MULTICULTURAL AMERICA 3ʳᵈ EDITION, VOLUME 1

whom have actually joined Cherokee Baptist churches themselves, becoming ministers or elders within these congregations.

CULTURE AND ASSIMILATION

The process of acculturation began for the Cherokees with the introduction of European trade goods in 1673. Steel pots and knives, tomahawks, glass beads, manufactured cloth, guns, and gunpowder gradually replaced traditional products of native manufacture. Trade with Europeans also changed hunting practices, calling for large numbers of pelts and quickly endangering the population of many game animals. Clothing styles changed, too. As the centuries passed, Cherokees adopted more Western/American norms, with many tribal members living and interacting with non-Cherokees on a daily basis.

The founding of the United States as a nation and the continual growth of U.S. settlements that encroached on Cherokee territory led to intense pressure for removal of the tribe by the 1820s and 1830s. In response, a significant portion of the Cherokee, believing that their white neighbors wanted them removed because they were "savage," began a conscious effort to make themselves over and become "civilized." Part of this involved eliminating illiteracy. The Cherokee Sequoyah developed a written language, or syllabary, in 1821, and the Cherokee also hired teachers from universities in the Northeast and invited missionaries to come to their lands to teach and preach. These Cherokee became known as "progressives," and their efforts, combined with the

acculturation and assimilation process that had begun in 1673, were relatively successful in changing the lifestyles of the Cherokee. Specifically, the Cherokee community in Arkansas became quite prosperous during the nineteenth century, and many of its white neighbors regarded it favorably.

While the assimilation and prosperity of certain groups, such as those residing in Arkansas, cannot be denied, most Cherokees in the seventeenth through nineteenth centuries maintained a relatively traditional lifestyle, continuing to farm small plots (10 acres or fewer), adhering to the religious beliefs of balance and harmony with the Earth, and dwelling in tribal villages.

Traditions and Customs Some Cherokees today are almost indistinguishable from white people, and their customs, habits, and beliefs reflect those of mainstream America. However, traditional Cherokees still gather at various "stomp grounds," which are consecrated, ceremonial grounds. Each ground has its own set of religious leaders, and the ceremonies performed there are series of dances, which are done in a counter-clockwise direction around a sacred fire all night long. Attendance at the stomp grounds declined for many years, but since the 1970s there has been an increase. Although stomp dancers were very secretive for years, some groups now perform publicly to educate the general population, as well as Cherokees themselves, about the group's traditional ways and beliefs.

Cuisine The Cherokees were traditionally an agrarian people, maintaining a town garden and

Prior to the Native Nations Procession, four elders from the Cherokee nation gather to beat drums. WILLIAM S. KUTA / ALAMY

A Cherokee boy and girl in costume on the reservation. NATIONAL ARCHIVES AND RECORDS ADMINISTRATION

Traditional Dress Cherokee men once wore only a breechcloth and moccasins in warm weather. When it was colder, they added leggings and a fringed hunting jacket. Chiefs and priests wore long, full cloaks made of feathers and feather caps (not the traditional and popular Plains Indian headdress). Men shaved their heads, leaving a topknot (sometimes called a scalplock) that they allowed to grow long, and their bodies and faces were often tattooed. Women wore only a short skirt in warm weather and added a poncho-like top during the winter. Styles changed in the early nineteenth century as a result of trade with Europeans. Women began to make and wear long dresses and blouses of manufactured trade cloth, and men dressed in shirts and jackets of cloth. They also added colorful turbans. By the 1880s, Cherokees had abandoned most of their distinctive clothing in favor of dressing mostly like frontier whites.

Today, for special occasions some Cherokee men will don ribbon shirts, a contemporary pan-Indian item. A few may even dress up in hunting jackets and turbans. Women may wear traditional "tear dresses," so named because the pattern calls for tearing the fabric along straight lines rather than cutting with scissors.

Dances and Songs As previously mentioned, the stomp dance is a religious activity. It is possible today to hear stomp dance songs without actually attending a ceremony, as many are recorded on albums of Cherokee music. No traditional social dances have survived, but some Cherokees have joined in the pan-Indian practice of powwow dancing. When Cherokee singing takes place, it is almost always gospel music sung in the Cherokee language. At least one old Cherokee lullaby, titled "Oostie," has survived. Barbara McAlister, a Cherokee opera singer, sometimes performs it during her concerts. She combines the lullaby with the words of "Amazing Grace," which was sung by Cherokees during the Trail of Tears in both the Cherokee and English languages.

Holidays Traditionally, certain ceremonies were performed at specific times of the year, and they included songs and dances. The largest of these was the Green Corn Dance, celebrating the beginning of spring. Today the Cherokee Nation observes one annual holiday on September 6, which marks the anniversary of the adoption of the new constitution following the Trail of Tears. It reunited those Cherokees who had moved west on their own before the Trail of Tears with the main body of the Cherokees under the administration of Chief John Ross. For convenience, this holiday is celebrated over the Labor Day weekend in Tahlequah, Oklahoma, and is attended each year by thousands of people from all over the world. Activities include a parade through downtown Tahlequah, a state of the nation address by the principal chief, traditional games, concerts, and arts and crafts shows.

Health Issues and Practices A traditional Cherokee would say that there was a time long ago when there was no disease in the world. Then humans

individual garden plots. Women mostly tended to the crops, as they owned the gardens and the homes. They planted a wide variety of beans, pumpkins, squash, and corn. In addition to the growing of crops, women gathered many wild plants for food, including wild onions and greens, mushrooms, berries, grapes, and nuts. Deer was the main game hunted for meat, but bear, buffalo, elk, squirrel, rabbit, opossum, and other animals were also killed for food. Eventually, the Cherokees began raising cattle, hogs, chickens, and other domesticated animals acquired from Europeans.

The contemporary Cherokee diet is not much different from that of the general population of the United States, although special gatherings feature wild onions and eggs, bean bread, fry bread, grape dumplings, and sometimes fried crawdads (crayfish). A special treat is *kanuche*, made by pounding whole hickory nuts, boiling them in water, and straining the hulls out to produce a rich broth. *Kanuche* may be mixed with hominy, corn, or rice.

developed weapons. When the Cherokee acquired these new weapons, in particular bows and arrows, they were able to kill many more animals than previously. One day the animals called a council to discuss this problem, and they all agreed that people had to kill animals in order to obtain food for survival but that this killing was taking place too casually. They decided that hunters should take killing more seriously by praying, fasting, and going through a prescribed ritual. Furthermore, it was determined that hunters should kill only what was needed and then apologize to the spirits of the slain animals. If hunters failed in these regards, the animal spirits would strike him with dreadful diseases. Some of these diseases were so horrible that the plants, having overheard the council, decided to provide cures.

Traditional Cherokee healers, like those of other American Indian tribes, have always been expert at the medicinal use of plants. However, a traditional Cherokee cure almost always involves more than just the plant medicine. It also incorporates the ritualistic use of words and sometimes specific actions. Many traditional Cherokees still go to these healers to cure their ills.

Europeans brought diseases to North America that Cherokee healers did not know how to cure. As a result, a belief developed that it would take a white doctor to cure a white person's disease. Missionaries, school systems, government programs, and intermarriage also undermined Indian beliefs. Many Cherokees began to depend on white doctors for health care, either exclusively or in part.

For many years, the health of American Indians was in the hands of the United States government through its Indian Health Service (IHS). In recent years, however, tribes have begun contracting with the IHS to administer these services themselves. There are still two IHS hospitals in the Cherokee Nation, in Claremore and Tahlequah in Oklahoma. In addition, the Cherokee Nation has its own health division, which operates several rural health clinics and a number of other health programs.

Cherokees, like other Native Americans, generally face the same health problems as anyone else. Cherokees have a high occurrence of diabetes, perhaps as a result of dietary habits fostered by outside influences such as government boarding schools and the government's food distribution program for Indians. Other major health problems for the Cherokee are high rates of alcoholism, suicide, obesity, and childhood injuries. Many Cherokee leaders believe alcoholism is the primary problem facing the tribe and that it directly impacts other issues, including health, unemployment, poverty, and crime.

FAMILY AND COMMUNITY LIFE

Over time, marriage with people from other cultures and ethnic groups became more common among Cherokees. Marriage with whites and blacks, in particular, caused a drastic change in the Cherokee family structure. Cherokees have a matrilineal clan structure, or a family in which descent is traced through the female line. This framework was undermined by the insistence of white males to be considered heads of households and to pass along their own surnames to their offspring. In addition, missionaries supported this male-oriented structure.

Over the past two centuries, marked progress has been made within the Cherokee Nation regarding gender roles and education. The Cherokee have modernized substantially, incorporating certain North American values of gender equality into their culture and instilling the importance of higher education into their youth.

Gender Roles Traditional Cherokee society divided the tribal power evenly between men and women. Men were generally in charge of war, hunting, and diplomacy, and women were responsible for property, farming, and family. The role of the woman was crucial to the clan since its membership was traced through a matrilineal line. While only men could be tribal chiefs during earlier times, it was women who were the landowners. An exception to this rule was the role of Beloved Woman, which was bestowed upon highly respected women dating back at least to the eighteenth century. For example, Nanyehi (1738–1822/1824), otherwise known as Nancy Ward, was a Beloved Woman who was allowed to sit in councils and make decisions alongside tribal chiefs and other Beloved Women. Nanyehi believed in coexisting peacefully with European American settlers and served as an ambassador and peace negotiator for the Cherokee people.

A young Cherokee woman carries her child, c. 1940s. EVERETT COLLECTION / NEWSCOM

Gender roles within Cherokee culture are significantly different today, more closely resembling those of mainstream U.S. society. Many Cherokee women are chiefs, or they hold other leadership or political positions within the Cherokee Nation and the U.S. political system in general. Wilma Mankiller became chief of the Cherokee Nation in 1985, marking the first time a woman had been elevated to that position in any major American Indian tribe. Cherokee men today are able to be landowners, and many have taken over the role of farming that was previously assigned to women. However, clan relationships continue to be traced through a matrilineal line.

Education Before Oklahoma became a state and took over or closed down almost all of the Cherokee Nation's educational institutions, the tribe had its own school system. In fact, the Cherokee Nation had established the first free, compulsory public school system and the first institution of higher learning west of the Mississippi River. The tribe had produced more college graduates than the neighboring states of Arkansas and Texas combined, but that changed with Oklahoma's statehood. According to the 1970 U.S. Census, the average adult Cherokee had only five and a half years of schooling. Indeed, fewer than seventy years of being subject to the Oklahoma public schools had been devastating for the Cherokees. In the past, upon being enrolled in the first grade, Cherokee students in Oklahoma public schools had been automatically placed in slow-learner classrooms. Cherokee high school students in Oklahoma were not encouraged to apply for college and were not taken on trips with the white students to visit college campuses. Some Cherokee students attended government boarding schools for Indians, but the majority were in public schools.

Since the revitalization of the Cherokee Nation that began in the mid-1980s under the leadership of Chief Wilma Mankiller, there has been gradual improvement in the area of education. Programs for Cherokee students have been instituted in the public schools, thanks to pressure from the Cherokee Nation and the availability of federal funds for such programs. The Cherokee Nation has taken over Sequoyah High School in Tahlequah, a former federally run boarding school, and is operating it for Indian students. It has also established a complete preschool program for Cherokee children starting at age three. As for higher education, a program has been put in place to assist Cherokees in attending college. Many of the public schools that formerly discouraged Cherokee students now have Cherokee teachers, counselors, administrators, and other personnel on their staffs. Most Cherokees still attend public schools (several of which have up to 90 percent Cherokee enrollment), but over the past two decades, these institutions have become much more attuned to the needs of the tribe. In 2010, according to the U.S. Census Bureau, approximately 16.5 percent of the Cherokee population over the age of twenty-five had a bachelor's degree or higher, and nearly 80 percent of Cherokee adults were high school graduates.

Relations with Other Americans Because of their long history of intermarriage, as well as the nature of land division in eastern Oklahoma, Cherokees have long been accustomed to interacting with non-Cherokees. In fact, Cherokees have always seemed willing to accept outsiders into their ranks. Tahlequah in Cherokee County in Oklahoma, for example, has a large population of mixed-blood families, many of which are tribal members. Indians from other tribes have also moved to Tahlequah, including Creeks, Kiowas, Osages, and Navajos. Some of that is the result of intermarriage, some is not. Additionally, Tahlequah has a significant number of Hispanics and a small African American population. Those two groups have had more difficulty fitting in, although there is seldom any overt racism displayed toward them.

Cherokee interaction with blacks dates to the late 1700s and early 1800s. In an attempt to adapt to white lifestyles, some Cherokees became plantation slave owners in the South. According to historian Jim Stebinger, Cherokees held an estimated 1,600 black slaves. In contrast to white plantation owners, however, Cherokees worked alongside their slaves and also permitted interracial marriage.

EMPLOYMENT AND ECONOMIC CONDITIONS

Employment opportunities for traditional Cherokees, or those who live in Cherokee communities, are limited because they tend to stay at home. They would rather be around their families and friends and remain a part of their community than seek better opportunities elsewhere. For these Cherokees, unemployment figures are high. Major employers in the area are large nurseries in Cherokee County, Oklahoma, and large chicken-processing plants in Arkansas. The Cherokee Nation also has become a major employer in the area, though there still are not enough jobs to go around. Low-income people living in rural areas often lack dependable transportation, so even if they can secure jobs, commuting is an issue. According to 2010 U.S. Census figures, approximately 34 percent of Cherokee households had an income of $24,999 or less, with the majority of households falling well below the federal poverty level. While only 6.3 percent of working-age Cherokees were listed as unemployed in the 2010 Census, that number is somewhat deceiving. According to the Census, over 40 percent of the total population was not part of the labor force.

The Cherokee Nation offers employment-training programs, but these do no good if the individual does not want to move and there is no job opening in the area. Some Cherokees have gone through several job-training programs, becoming qualified carpenters, plumbers, and electricians, yet they remain unemployed. Many mow lawns, cut firewood, and accept various odd jobs in order to support their families. For food, they still hunt and gather plants.

POLITICS AND GOVERNMENT

Cherokee oral tradition tells of a time when the tribe was ruled by a powerful priesthood called the *ani-Kutani*. When the priests took away a young man's wife, he organized a revolt and all the priests were killed. Since then, according to the tale, the Cherokees have had a democratic government.

The Cherokee Nation today operates under a constitution ratified by Cherokee voters in 1976. The three-branch government is made up of a chief executive called the principal chief, a legislature called the tribal council, and a judicial branch called a tribunal that has three tribal justices. From its humble condition in the 1970s, the governmental system of the Cherokee Nation has become large in scale, employing 1,300 people, 85 percent of whom are Cherokees, with a $1.6 million monthly payroll.

Membership in the Cherokee Nation has no blood-percentage requirement but is based strictly on lineal descent from any person listed as Cherokee on the so-called Dawes Roll (the roll prepared by the United States government's Dawes Commission for purposes of land allotment in preparation for Oklahoma statehood). Therefore, many Cherokees complain that too many white people (usually those with less than one-fourth Cherokee blood) take advantage of tribal programs.

The Indian Self-Determination Act, known as PL 93-638, allows Indian tribes to contract with the federal government either through the Bureau of Indian Affairs or Indian Health Service to operate programs for themselves that had been previously run by those two entities. The Cherokee Nation has been taking advantage of this law since the 1970s and has contracted nearly all of the available government programs.

State governments seem to make frequent attempts to encroach into the area of tribal jurisdiction. They want to impose state hunting and fishing regulations on tribal members and collect various taxes from them. (Indians who live on a reservation do not pay federal or state income tax on money they earn on that reservation.) Issues of state infringement on tribal sovereignty, in which the Cherokee Nation has been involved in recent years, includes the state's attempt to tax tobacco sales at smoke shops and to regulate gaming. The Cherokee Nation operates high-stakes bingo parlors.

In terms of U.S. politics, there are Cherokee Democrats and Republicans, as well as independents. Cherokees are seldom, if ever, of one mind on any given issue. Generally, they only come close to reaching a consensus when the issue is tribal sovereignty. Every so often, for example, a congressman will introduce a bill to abrogate all Indian treaties and terminate all tribal governments, and the Cherokees will unite against such a measure.

CHEROKEE JUSTICE

The traditional Cherokee legal system was based on the notion of responsibility for wrongful actions rather than a Western concept of justice. The Cherokee Nation aimed to maintain harmony and balance in both the social and spiritual worlds. Thus, its religion enforced a strict moral system that required the acceptance of responsibility and paying the cost for various transgressions, such as the murder of a tribal member. As Michael J. Rutledge explains in his article "Forgiveness in the Age of Forgetfulness" for *History-sites.com* (1995), "It was believed that the murdered 'soul' or ghost would be forced to wander the earth, unable to go to the next world. This created the imbalance. The acceptance of responsibility and the death of the killer or one of his clansmen restored balance by freeing the innocent ghost, allowing him to go to the next world."

NOTABLE INDIVIDUALS

Although the Cherokee Nation is just one of more than 300 American Indian tribes in the United States, it has produced a significant number of prominent people in various areas. In addition, a number of other accomplished Americans have claimed to be of Cherokee descent, including Tom Mix, Monte Blue, John Nance Garner, Iron Eyes Cody, Walter Brennan, Johnny Cash, Burt Reynolds, James Garner, Willie Nelson, Oral Roberts, Cher, Anita Bryant, Loretta Lynn, Kevin Costner, and President Bill Clinton.

Academia Carolyn Attneave (1920–1992) was a psychologist and educator. She wrote several books, including *Family Networks* (1973) and *Beyond Clinic Walls* (1974).

Art The Cherokee Nation has a rich artistic tradition. Accomplished artists of Cherokee descent include Cecil Dick (1915–1992), known for his flat-style painting; George Cochran (1911–1992), a painter; Willard Stone (1916–1990), a sculptor and wood carver; Anna Mitchell (1926–2012), a potter; Bill Glass Jr. (1950–), a sculptor and mixed-media artist; Virginia Stroud (1949–), a painter and illustrator; Jeanne Walker Rorex (1951–), a painter; Bill Rabbit (1946–2012), a painter and jewelry maker; Traci Rabbit; a graphic artist and sculptor; Robert Annesley (1943–), a poet, graphic artist, painter, and sculptor; Jane Osti, a sculptor; Bert Seabourne (1931–), a painter; Joan Hill, a.k.a. Chese-quah (1930–), a painter and illustrator; Murv Jacob (1945–), an illustrator; Jimmie Durham (1940–), a sculptor, performance artist, and poet; and P. J. Gillam Steward, a sculptor.

Film Gary Robinson (1950–) is a writer, producer, and director of Cherokee and Choctaw ancestry. His 2011 documentary *Language of Victory* explores how American Indian soldiers from more than twenty tribes used their native languages to send secret military messages during the two world wars. Robinson also wrote the books *The Language of Victory: American Indian Code Talkers of World War I and World War II* (2011) and *From Warriors to Soldiers: A History of American Indian Service in the United States Military* (2008).

Literature Sequoyah (ca. 1770–1843), the inventor of the Cherokee syllabary, was born in what is now Tennessee and moved west before the Trail of Tears. He is thought to have died somewhere in Mexico.

Notable Cherokee writers include the following: John Rollin Ridge (1827–1867), editor of the *Sacramento Bee* newspaper and the author of *The Life and Adventures of Joaquin Murieta, the Celebrated California Bandit* (1854); John Milton Oskison (1874–1947), editor of the *New York Evening Post* and *Collier's Weekly* and author of *Brothers Three* (1935); Norman H. Russell (1921–2011), poet, educator, and author of *Indian Thoughts* (1975); Robert J. Conley (1940–), author of The Real People series of novels and recipient of the 2007 the Native Writers' Circle of the Americas' Lifetime Achievement Award; Marilou Awiakta (1936–), a poet, a storyteller, and the author of *Abiding Appalachia* (1978), *Rising Fawn and the Fire Mystery* (1983), and *Selu: Seeking the Corn Mother's Wisdom* (1993); Diane Glancy (1941–), a poet and novelist whose works include *Firesticks* (1993), *Flutie* (1998), and *The Only Piece of Furniture in the House* (1996).

Cherokee poets include Carroll Arnett (Gogisgi) (1927–1997), poet, teacher, and the author of *Rounds* (1982), *Tsalagi* (1976), *South Line* (1979), *Engine* (1988), and other books; Robin Coffee (1955–2010), a poet whose works include *Voices of the Heart* (1990) and *Sacred Seasons* (1993); Ralph Salisbury (1924–), a poet, a teacher, and the author of *A White Rainbow* (1985), *Spirit Beast Chant* (1982), *One Indian and Two Chiefs* (1993), *Pointing at the Rainbow* (1980), and other works; Gladys Cardiff (1942–), an Eastern Cherokee poet whose works include *To Frighten a Storm* (1976).

Other Cherokee writers include Thomas King (1943–), a screenwriter, a novelist, and the author of *Green Grass, Running Water* (1994) and *Medicine River* (1989); Rayna Diane Green (1942–), a writer, a folklorist, and the editor of *That's What She Said: Contemporary Poetry and Fiction by Native American Women* (1984); Geary Hobson (1941–), an educator, writer, and critic who wrote *Deer Hunting and Other Poems* (1990) and edited *The Remembered Earth: An Anthology of Contemporary American Indian Literature* (1981); Lynn Riggs (1899–1954), a playwright who wrote *Green Grow the Lilacs* (1931), which later became the Rogers and Hammerstein musical *Oklahoma!* (1943); Betty Louise Bell (1949–), the author of *Faces in the Moon* (1994); and Robert Franklin Gish (1940–), the author of *Dreams of Quivira* (1997) and *When Coyote Howls: A Lavaland Fable* (1994).

Military Nimrod Jarrett Smith (1837–1893), also known as Tsaladihi, fought in the Civil War and became the principal chief of the Eastern Band of Cherokees.

Stand Watie (1806–1871), or Degataga, served in the Civil War as commanding officer of the First Indian Brigade of the Confederate Trans-Mississippi Army.

Admiral Joseph James (Jocko) Clark (1893–1971), a World War II naval hero, was commander of the seventh fleet during the Korean War.

Music Jack F. Kilpatrick (1915–1967) was a noted composer and longtime professor of musicology at Southern Methodist University. In addition, he wrote several books with his wife, Anna Kilpatrick, that deal with Cherokee tales and language texts. Barbara McAlister (1941–), a mezzo-soprano opera singer, was born in Muskogee, Oklahoma, and performed around the world. Rita Coolidge (1945–) won multiple Grammy Awards for her country, pop, adult contemporary, and jazz songs. Lana Chapel (1956–) is a singer and songwriter of country music who, at the age of eleven, became the youngest songwriter to be signed by Broadcast Music Incorporated (BMI). Famed rock guitarist Jimi Hendrix (1942–1970) was of mixed Cherokee ancestry; his paternal great-grandmother was a full-blooded Cherokee. Gary Paul Davis (1969–), also known as Litefoot, is a Native American rapper and actor of mixed Cherokee and Chichimeca ancestry who founded the Red Vinyl record label.

Stage and Screen Frank Boudinot (1836–1864) moved to New York City in the first half of the nineteenth century to become a professional actor, using the stage name of Frank Starr. He was an officer for the Union Army during the Civil War, during which he was killed.

Victor Daniels (1899–1955), using the professional name Chief Thundercloud, was a successful film actor for more than twenty years. Among his roles, he played Tonto in the 1938 and 1939 *Lone Ranger* films and Chiricahua Apache tribal leader Geronimo in the 1939 movie *Geronimo*.

Clu Gulager (1928–), whose first name is a version of *tlu-tlu*, the Cherokee word for a "purple martin," was a film and television actor who is perhaps best remembered for his role of Deputy (later Sheriff) Ryker, on the television series *The Virginian* (1962–1971). His first series was *The Tall Man* (1960–1962), in which he played Billy the Kid. His film credits include *The Last Picture Show* (1971).

Wes Studi (1947–), a full-blooded Cherokee, received critical acclaim for his film portrayals of Magua in *The Last of the Mohicans* (1992) and Geronimo in *Geronimo: An American Legend* (1994). In addition, Studi had a role in the Academy Award–nominated film *The New World* (2005).

Dennis Weaver (1924–2006), a film and television actor, is remembered for his Emmy-winning portrayal of Chester on the television series *Gunsmoke* (1955–1975) and for starring in the series *McCloud* (1970–1977).

William Penn Adair "Will" Rogers (1879–1935) was a performer in Wild West shows and on stage before becoming a film actor, radio personality, and nationally syndicated newspaper columnist. During his lifetime, he was known as "Oklahoma's favorite son."

MEDIA

Cherokee Observer

An independent monthly newspaper.

P.O. Box 487
Blackwell, Oklahoma 74631-0487
Phone: (580) 363-5438
Email: editors@cherokeeobserver.org
URL: www.cherokeeobserver.org

The Cherokee One-Feather

The official publication of the Eastern Band of Cherokee Indians, it features news of interest to the local Cherokee tribe and to American Indians in general.

Jean Jones, Editor
P.O. Box 501
Cherokee, North Carolina 28719
Phone: (828) 554-6264
Email: rochjone@nc-cherokee.com
URL: http://theonefeather.com

The Cherokee Phoenix

The *Phoenix* is the official newspaper of the Cherokee Nation and the first to be published by Native Americans in the United States, beginning in 1829. Its publication was intermittent until the twentieth century, and it is now a monthly with a weekly digital newsletter.

Bryan Pollard, Executive Editor
P.O. Box 948
Tahlequah, Oklahoma 74465
Phone: (918) 453-5269
Fax: (918) 207-0049
Email: nicole-hill@cherokee.org
URL: www.cherokeephoenix.org

Cherokee Tribune

A community weekly newspaper that was founded in 1934.

Otis Brumby, Jr., Publisher
521 East Main Street
Canton, Georgia 30114
Phone: (770) 479-1441
Email: otis3@mdjonline.com
URL: http://cherokeetribune.com

Journal of Cherokee Studies

This publication covers historical and cultural research of Cherokees.

William Anderson, Editor
Museum of the Cherokee Indian
P.O. Box 1599
Cherokee, North Carolina 28719
Phone: (828) 497-3481
Email: infocwy@cherokeemuseum.org
URL: www.cherokeemuseum.org

ORGANIZATIONS AND ASSOCIATIONS

Cherokee Cultural Society

The purpose of this organization is to build community, preserve Cherokee heritage, and perpetrate the culture. It also publishes a monthly e-mail newsletter, the *Cherokee Messenger*.

4407 Rose Street
Houston, Texas 77007
Phone: (713) 866-4085
Email: jwilliams@sageways.com
URL: www.powersource.com/cherokee

Cherokee Nation

The federally recognized government of the Cherokee people, the Cherokee Nation has inherent sovereign status recognized by treaty and law. The seat of Cherokee Nation government is the W. W. Keeler Complex near Tahlequah, Oklahoma, the capital of the Cherokee Nation. With more than 300,000 citizens, it is the largest tribal nation in the United States.

Bill John Baker, Principal Chief
P.O. Box 948
Tahlequah, Oklahoma 74465
Phone: (918) 453-5000
Email: communications@cherokee.org
URL: www.cherokee.org

Cherokee Nation of New Jersey

Founded in 1997, it seeks to educate people about American Indians who are also of African, Hispanic, Asian, and European descent and to foster goodwill.

C. W. Longbow, Chief
182 Ellery Avenue
Newark, New Jersey 07106
Phone: (973) 489-1368

Eastern Band of Cherokee Indians

A federally recognized Native American tribe made up of 14,000 members who are descended from Cherokees who remained in the Eastern United States while others were forcefully relocated to the west in the nineteenth century. The band generally regards the Cherokees in Oklahoma as more traditional. It is located in western North Carolina in the traditional Cherokee homelands of the Qualla Boundary.

Michell Hicks, Principal Chief
P.O. Box 455
Cherokee, North Carolina 28719
Phone: (828) 497-7000
Fax: (828) 497-7007
URL: http://nc-cherokee.com

United Keetoowah Band of Cherokees in Oklahoma

A federally recognized Cherokee tribe located in Tahlequah, Oklahoma, the Keetowah identify as descendants of "Old Settlers," who were Cherokee that migrated to Oklahoma and Arkansas around 1817, before the forced relocation of Cherokees under the Indian Removal Act in the 1830s. The band has approximately 14,000 members.

Jim Ross, Chief
P.O. Box 746
Tahlequah, Oklahoma 74465
Phone: (918) 431-1818
URL: www.ukb-nsn.gov

MUSEUMS AND RESEARCH CENTERS

Cherokee Heritage Center

The Cherokee Heritage Center preserves the historical and cultural artifacts, language, and traditional crafts of the Cherokees.

21192 South Keeler Drive
Park Hill, Oklahoma 74451
Phone: (918) 456-6007
URL: www.cherokeeheritage.org

Cherokee National Historical Society (CNHS)

The CNHS operates Cherokee Heritage Center. It also publishes quarterly newsletter, *Columns*.

Karen Cooper, Executive Director
P.O. Box 515
Tahlequah, Oklahoma 74465
Phone: (888) 999-6007
Fax: (918) 456-6165
Email: tsalagi@netsites.net

The Five Civilized Tribes Museum

This institution preserves and encourages the continuation of the cultures and traditions of "The Five Civilized Tribes." In addition to housing artifacts and artwork, it has a research library.

1101 Honor Heights Drive
Muskogee, Oklahoma 74401
Phone: (918) 683-1701

Fax: (918) 683-3070
Email: 5tribesdirector@sbcglobal.net
URL: www.fivetribes.org

Museum of the Cherokee Indian

Located on the Cherokee reservation in Cherokee, North Carolina, this museum offers dramatic presentations of Cherokee history and language. It received a $3 million renovation in 1998 to include a walk along the Trail of Tears.

P.O. Box 1599
Cherokee, North Carolina 28719
Phone: (828) 497-3481
Fax: (828) 497-4985
Email: kenblank@cherokeemuseum.org
URL: www.cherokeemuseum.org

SOURCES FOR ADDITIONAL STUDY

Beard-Moose, Christina Taylor. *Public Indians, Private Cherokees: Tourism and Tradition on Tribal Ground.* Tuscaloosa: University of Alabama Press, 2009.

Bird, Traveller. *Tell Them They Lie: The Sequoyah Myth.* Los Angeles: Westernlore Press, 1971.

Collier, Peter. *When Shall They Rest? The Cherokees' Long Struggle with America.* New York: Holt, Rinehart, and Winston, 1973.

Conley, Robert J. *The Witch of Goingsnake and Other Stories.* Norman: University of Oklahoma Press, 1988.

Feeling, Durbin. *Cherokee-English Dictionary.* Tahlequah, OK: The Cherokee Nation, 1975.

Fogelson, Raymond D. *The Cherokees: A Critical Bibliography.* Bloomington: Indiana University Press, 1978.

Mankiller, Wilma P., and Michael Wallis. *Mankiller: A Chief and Her People.* New York: St. Martin's Press, 1993.

Mooney, James. *Myths of the Cherokee.* Washington, D.C.: Seventh Annual Report of the Bureau of American Ethnology, 1891.

Sturm, Circe. *Becoming Indian: The Struggle over Cherokee Identity in the Twenty-first Century.* Santa Fe, TX: School for Advanced Research Press, 2010.

Wallace, Andrew. *The Long, Bitter Trail: Andrew Jackson and the Indians.* New York: Hill and Wang, 1993.

CHEYENNE

Kristin King-Ries

OVERVIEW

The Cheyenne are a Native American people whose ancestors, before 1700, lived for several centuries in what is now the state of Minnesota. Their land was bounded by the Mississippi, Minnesota, and Upper Red Rivers. After a series of events that included incursions by neighboring tribes and white settlers, dwindling food sources, and disease, the tribe spread westward across the northern Great Plains and the Cheyenne branch of the Red River in North Dakota and southward to eastern Colorado. Tribal territory included high plains, river valleys, and mountains. The word *Cheyenne* is an English adaptation of the Dakotan word *Sahi'yena*, a diminutive form of the word *Sahi'yai* (literally, "red talkers"). The word referred to nations who spoke a non-Dakotan language but whom the Dakota did not consider to be enemies, including the Cree and Chippewa. Early European travelers heard the name from the Dakota and thought it applied exclusively to the ancestors of the present-day Cheyenne. In the Cheyenne language the tribe's name is *Tsitsistas*, which means "the people."

The population of the Cheyenne tribe before Europeans arrived was large enough that it was divided into ten separate bands. Scholar George Bird Grinnell estimated in a 1918 *American Anthropologist* article that the population in 1820 was 3,500 or more. Traditionally, the tribe was run by a Peace Council composed of forty-four chiefs, with four chiefs chosen from each of the ten bands and four senior chiefs—elder chiefs who had acquitted themselves well during their time as a band chief. According to Cheyenne oral history, the council form of government originated with the prophet Sweet Medicine, who received directives during a vision quest. By the mid-eighteenth century, the Cheyenne were living in villages on the banks of lakes and rivers, with permanent earthen lodges housing individual families. They farmed, hunted, gathered wild rice, and made pottery, regularly engaging in trade with neighboring tribes.

At the beginning of the twenty-first century, the Cheyenne tribe had two main population centers: the Northern Cheyenne Reservation in southeastern Montana (bordered on the west by the Crow Reservation and on the east by the Tongue River) and the Cheyenne and Arapaho Tribal Jurisdictional Area in central Oklahoma. In the mid-1800s, the bands of Cheyenne had become increasingly widespread and difficult to govern as a single unit, and in 1842 they split into northern and southern branches. Both were forced by the U.S. Army onto the reservation in present-day Oklahoma, then called the Darlington Agency—the Southern Cheyenne (along with their longtime allies the Arapaho tribe) in 1869 and the Northern Cheyenne in 1877. In 1884 the federal government established the reservation in Montana for the northern branch of the tribe. In 1909 the government dismantled Oklahoma reservations into allotments and stopped calling them reservations, though the tribes still refer to them as reservations outside of legal contexts. The two branches have diverged in their economic fortune in the modern era. During the twentieth and early twenty-first centuries, the Northern Cheyenne tribal government operated various agricultural, ranching, and forestry enterprises, with mixed results. The federally created joint Southern Cheyenne and Arapaho Tribes, which historically had been very poor, became quite wealthy in the first decade of the twenty-first century as a result of profits from its casinos.

According to the official website for the Northern Cheyenne Tribe, the number of enrolled members in 2013 was 10,050 people, with 4,371 living on the reservation. More than half of the tribal members have been absorbed into the broader U.S. population. The Oklahoma Indian Affairs Commission reported that the Cheyenne and Arapaho Tribes counted 12,183 enrolled members in 2011. The majority of Southern Cheyenne live in Clinton and other smaller towns and rural counties in the central western part of Oklahoma, which were part of the reservation until 1888 but are mostly now off-reservation.

HISTORY OF THE PEOPLE

Early History Historians and archeologists have pieced together the prehistory of the Cheyenne from various linguistic, archeological, and biological clues. Drawing on the fact that the Cheyenne language belongs to the Algonquian family of languages, and that the Algonquian homeland between 1200 and 900 BCE was located northeast of the Great Lakes, scholars have speculated that the early Cheyenne people (the

Chief Wolf Robe, a Southern Cheyenne chief, is depicted with a Benjamin Harrison peace medal. Silver peace medals were presented by American presidents at treaty signings and other formal ceremonies. These medals were given out beginning with the Jefferson administration through the Benjamin Harrison administration. GL ARCHIVE / ALAMY

Proto-Cheyenne) came from that area as well. Information on the tribe's whereabouts between 900 BCE and the seventeenth century is inconclusive. What is known is that at some point the Cheyenne tribe migrated west. The tribe's first recorded villages were built around Lake Superior during the seventeenth century. In this region the Cheyenne had a Northeast Woodlands lifestyle with an economy based on hunting, fishing, and gathering. They later migrated further west to what is now Minnesota and farmed along the shores of the Mississippi, Minnesota, and Upper Red rivers. At some point they also lived in earth-lodge villages farther west yet, along the Middle Missouri River, interacting with the Arikara and Mandan tribes and adopting some of their cultural practices.

Between the 1600s and early 1800s, the tribe developed a complex, well-run political structure that included three sources of authority: the Peace Chiefs of the tribal council, the priests in charge of sacred ceremonies, and the warrior chiefs of the military societies. Military societies have existed in various tribes since prehistoric times, playing the role of tribal police, warriors, and leaders for certain ceremonies. A rich oral tradition of myths, legends, and rituals grew. Cheyenne values, beliefs, and style of government originated with the wisdom of the ancient cultural hero Sweet Medicine (Mutsoyef), a prophet who said that harmonious relationships between humans, the natural world, and the spirit worlds embodied the most important aspects of existence. He taught that the highest tribal authority should be held by men of peace.

During the Minnesota era, Cheyenne villages ranged in size from sixty or seventy to more than two hundred permanent dwellings. In response to invading Chippewa and Sioux and encroachment by white settlers, the tribe moved gradually westward. Once on the Northern Plains, the Cheyenne adopted a nomadic lifestyle, living in tipis and acquiring horses in order to hunt buffalo. They grew fewer crops and supplemented their diet with wild edible plants. Every fall, members of the Cheyenne tribe joined thousands of Native Americans belonging to other Plains tribes to trade with each other at a spot on the Mississippi River. The Cheyenne were known for their excellent quillwork clothing, which they traded, along with horses, for corn. Eventually they ranged across a broad stretch of country that included parts of Kansas, Colorado, Nebraska, Oklahoma, Wyoming, the Dakotas, and Montana. Lewis and Clark encountered the tribe in 1804 and described them as socially organized and rich in horses and dogs.

In the 1830s the northern and southern bands of Cheyenne gradually parted ways. The final gathering of the whole tribe took place in Wyoming in 1842. During this time span they began trading with U.S. troops. Exposure to the germs of people of European ancestry led to outbreaks of smallpox among the Plains tribes between 1837 and 1839, and in 1849 one of the Cheyenne bands lost 50 percent of its population to a cholera epidemic. In the 1850s white settlers moved west in increasingly large numbers, and in 1851 the Plains tribes signed the Fort Laramie Treaty, giving the government permission to build railroads, roads, and settlements on their land in exchange for annuities and federal recognition of tribal sovereignty. The Cheyenne chief Lean Bear traveled to Washington, D.C., in 1862, receiving a peace medal and promises of protection for his people from President Abraham Lincoln. The U.S. government honored neither its treaties nor its promises. When gold was discovered in Montana in 1862, white settlers flooded Cheyenne lands. In 1864 Colonel John Milton Chivington and a group of militia volunteers attacked a settlement at Sand Creek in southeastern Colorado Territory, massacring nearly two hundred Cheyenne and Arapaho. During this period U.S. troops systematically slaughtered the buffalo herds, the main food source of the Cheyenne. By 1883 the buffalo population had plummeted to two hundred animals.

Late in 1868 Lieutenant Colonel George Custer and his troops attacked a Southern Cheyenne camp on the Washita River while its inhabitants slept. Many historians consider the Battle of Washita River (also known as the Washita Massacre) to be the bloodiest in Oklahoma history. The federal government's campaign

against the Cheyenne intensified, with more attacks and killings and further destruction of tribal resources. After suffering great losses at Summit Springs, Colorado, the Southern Cheyenne (and their allies the Arapaho) agreed to confinement on the Darlington Agency in exchange for peace. Until around 1880 they were able to retain their traditional band structure and way of life, even on agency lands. They were still armed and were permitted to make hunting trips off the reservation. They lived in tipis along the river and owned large herds of horses, and their religious and political institutions remained intact. As of 1880, however, the tribal members on the reservation were no longer permitted to hunt or live in tipis.

To the north, in what was to be the final full-scale fight against the U.S. Army, a coalition of Sioux, Northern Cheyenne, and Arapaho defeated Custer and his troops at Little Bighorn, Montana, in 1876. The government's retaliation was severe. The Northern Cheyenne were rounded up and forced to join the southern branch of the tribe on the Darlington Agency. Throughout their ordeals, the Northern Cheyenne remained unified in their goal to return to their homeland.

Modern Era Confined to reservations, the tribe became dependent on the federal government's Bureau of Indian Affairs (BIA) for food. The BIA was also in charge of tribal governance. The agency exercised almost unchecked power over the reservations for decades. Children were forced to go to boarding schools and learn English. The arrival of Christian missionaries on the reservations resulted in a weakening of traditional religious practices. Tribal members were moved out of tipis and into permanent housing.

During the first half of the twentieth century, life for the Northern and Southern Cheyenne remained bleak. By then, Congress had approved measures to divide both of the Cheyenne reservations into individual allotments and sell or lease the rest (which amounted to the vast majority of the tribal land) to nontribal members. Geographically separating and isolating members of the tribal community resulted in a loss of cohesion and culture.

The Southern Cheyenne tribal members were especially dispersed in small towns where they were subject to economic exploitation and discrimination. Against formidable odds, members of the southern branch of the Cheyenne managed to keep their religion alive. The religion of the Arapaho, however, did not survive the years of hardship, which caused contention within the leadership of the Cheyenne and Arapaho Tribes. The Southern Cheyenne had difficulty persuading their counterparts to vote in favor of funding traditional religious activities.

During World War II tribal members left the reservations in significant numbers for the first time since relocation, with men and women enlisting in the U.S. Army, the men as soldiers and the women as nurses. Federal programs such as the Civilian Conservation Corps and the Works Progress Administration had also offered incentives to Native Americans to migrate to big cities to work in the war effort.

In the 1960s and 1970s the Cheyenne experienced a period of growth that benefitted from greater tribal activism on a national level and increased federal funding provided by laws such as the Economic Opportunity Act of 1965 and the Indian Education Act of 1972. The civil rights movements of the 1960s and 1970s also lent strength to the nationwide Native American struggle for independence and cultural renewal and gave birth to a pan-Indian culture. The support helped the Northern and Southern Cheyenne develop programs that built on earlier efforts to preserve their religion, revive the Cheyenne language, and reaffirm the rituals and culture of their ancestors. Powwows became triannual events, providing a time and place for tribes to gather and dance, sing, honor the ways of their ancestors, and pass on their traditions to their children.

Beginning in the 1960s and continuing through the present, the Northern Cheyenne and the Cheyenne and Arapaho Tribes have demanded greater control over the use of their water rights, mineral and gas leases, timber harvests, and other natural resources. The Northern Cheyenne Tribal Council drew on the religion of Sweet Medicine to create tribal consensus; this helped them fend off major multinational energy corporations who were pressuring the government for permission to mine coal on reservation lands. The tribe has since allowed some oil exploration on the reservation, however. Meanwhile, the Cheyenne and Arapaho business committee has secured lucrative leases from energy companies for the use of tribal resources.

Pan-Indian culture, while positive in many ways, gave rise to new challenges in the late twentieth century. The particular cultures and languages of individual tribes were in danger of disappearing into a generic, unified Indian Country ethos. Increased tribal political and cultural sovereignty helped stem the tide of assimilation, but in the early twenty-first century, many Cheyenne elders still expressed concern: while efforts to preserve the language had resulted in a rich archive, they affirmed, too few of the younger generation were fluent or even proficient Cheyenne speakers. Increasingly, traditional ceremonies such as the Sun Dance were performed in English or neglected entirely. Traditional stories and storytellers no longer had a place in daily life.

In the first decade of the twenty-first century, various Cheyenne and Arapaho tribal enterprises became casino owners. The income, combined with the money from oil and gas leases, earned the tribe hundreds of millions of dollars in less than ten years. The money has allowed tribal leaders to provide a number of services to members. Each enrolled member receives annual disbursements as part of a profit-sharing plan. The newfound wealth has also resulted in political turmoil. Disputes over who controls the profits from the tribe's casinos have caused dissension among tribal members and wreaked havoc on the tribal government. In 2009 Governor Darrel Flyingman was removed from office after being accused of financial mismanagement. His successor, Governor Janice Prairie Chief-Boswell, took office in 2010 but parted ways with her lieutenant governor, Leslie Harjo, in 2011. Each accused the other of violating the tribal constitution. Both claiming to be the rightful governor, they operated two separate governments for more than two years. Some tribal members favored having the Bureau of Indian Affairs settle the matter, while others objected to that method.

SETTLEMENT IN THE UNITED STATES

In 1776, when the United States came into being, the Cheyenne tribe had been in existence for hundreds of years. They had already split into two branches, with the northern branch living in present-day Montana and Wyoming and the southern branch spread from Colorado to Oklahoma. The total population was approximately 3,500.

Under the first Treaty of Fort Laramie, signed in 1851, the U.S. government ordered the Cheyenne tribe to relocate to the Northern Plains east of the Rocky Mountains between the North Platte and Arkansas rivers. This land included a large section of present-day Colorado, the southeast corner of Wyoming, and parts of southwestern Nebraska and northwestern Kansas. Later in the 1850s a series of unfavorable treaties secured by the Commissioner of Indian Affairs lost tribes millions of acres that had been promised to them in earlier treaties. Tribes being forced further west displaced tribes already in residence, and the Plains became crowded. At the same time the vast herds of buffalo were disappearing, depriving the people of a major food source. White settlement and foreign epidemics added to the pressure on the tribes. All of these factors contributed to intertribal hostilities and conflicts between tribes and the U.S. government. In his 1988 book *The Cheyenne Nation: A Social and Demographic History*, anthropologist and historian John Moore characterizes the 1860s as "a long decade of wars that suddenly turned the Plains Indians from nomadic bison hunters to settled residents on government-run reservations."

After the 1864 Sand Creek Massacre, a particularly devastating attack on the Southern Cheyenne by federal troops, the Cheyenne and Lakota cosigned the 1867 Treaty of Medicine Lodge with the federal government. The treaty created the Great Sioux Reservation, an area that encompassed parts present-day Kansas and Oklahoma. In 1868 the U.S. government signed a second Treaty of Fort Laramie with an alliance of tribes that included the Northern Cheyenne and Northern Arapaho, promising them the western half of present-day South Dakota. The following year, however, the government broke its treaties with the Cheyenne. U.S. troops invaded the Great Sioux Reservation and defeated the Southern Cheyenne. President Ulysses S. Grant then signed an executive

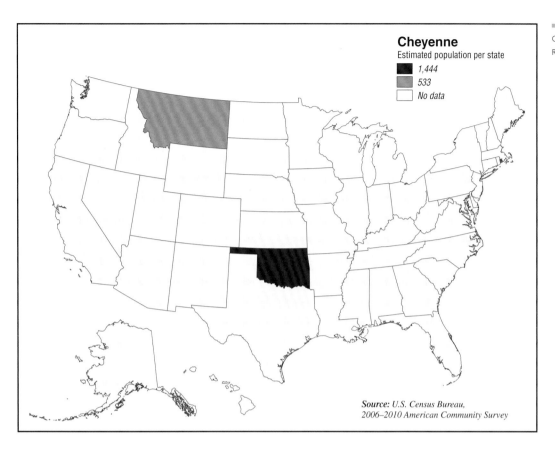

Cheyenne
Estimated population per state
■ 1,444
▨ 533
☐ No data

*Source: U.S. Census Bureau,
2006–2010 American Community Survey*

order creating the Cheyenne and Arapaho Reservation on more than four million contiguous acres of rich grazing land in Oklahoma, forcing the people to relocate once again. At this time the Southern Cheyenne and Arapaho Tribes became one tribe on paper.

For another ten years, the Northern Cheyenne tribe continued to resist the federal government from its base north of the Platte River. A war party of Northern Cheyenne and Lakota defeated General George Custer and his troops at the Battle of the Little Bighorn in 1876, and the federal government redoubled its military campaign against them. The government's efforts, combined with a severe winter in 1877, forced the surrender and relocation of many Northern Cheyenne to the same reservation as the Southern Cheyenne. Unlike the members of the southern branch, however, the Northern Cheyenne were imprisoned in crowded rooms for months on end. This situation contributed to the spread of diseases, including malaria, measles, and dysentery. Unable to hunt or gather and fed on paltry rations of unfamiliar food, the people were malnourished. These hardships, along with the mental and emotional strain of enforced inactivity and alienation from their native lands, caused many deaths.

In 1878 a band of nearly three hundred Northern Cheyenne fled Darlington Agency to make the long, perilous trek home through white settlements. U.S. soldiers pursued them, capturing 150 and detaining them at Fort Robinson, Nebraska, in January 1879. Of these, 130 escaped on January 9, but most of them died in the attempt, either killed by the U.S. Army or frozen to death. A fraction succeeded in reaching present-day Montana. After the Northern Cheyenne reservation was established there by executive order in 1884, the federal government expected the tribal members to become farmers, but soil conditions on the Montana reservation were poor, and life there became a struggle to survive.

The Southern Cheyenne held onto their Oklahoma lands for less than twenty years; in 1887 Congress passed the Dawes Act, allowing Indian land to be surveyed and divided among individual members of Indian tribes. The Oklahoma reservation was apportioned into 160-acre allotments, to be held in trust by the federal government, and the remaining acreage (six-sevenths of the reservation) was sold off to white settlers as "surplus." The sudden change resulted in the tribal members being in almost constant contact with whites. Life on the allotments was a great strain for the tribes. An estimated 20 percent of the population died during the influenza epidemic of 1918 to 1919. The federal government encouraged the Cheyenne and Arapaho allotment owners to farm their land. The shift from their former nomadic hunting life was in itself difficult, and recurrent drought hindered farming efforts. Within a few years many tribal members ended up working as hired labor for white farmers who had leased the allotments from the government.

The 1928 Northern Cheyenne Allotment Act divided portions of the northern tribe's lands into individual allotments, dissolving the tradition of communally owned land there as well. Between 1966 and 1973 the BIA leased the rest of the reservation to multinational energy companies without the knowledge or consent of tribal members. By 1974 only 260,000 of the original 447,000 reservation acres were still tribally owned. Anthropologist Gregory Campbell wrote in an 1987 article ("Northern Cheyenne Ethnicity, Religion and Coal Energy Development"), "This period is described by elders as a period of alcohol abuse and breakdown of family life." Tribal members nevertheless managed to form the Northern Cheyenne Landowner's Association, and in 1974, after a lengthy legal battle, they succeeded in terminating all coal leases on tribal land.

The passage of the federal Indian Reorganization Act (IRA) in 1934 ended the sale of Indian trust land and provided some money to recover some of the trust land that had passed out of tribal ownership. The IRA also guaranteed religious freedom for Native Americans and made it legal for American Indian tribes to create reservation governments. Such governments included a tribal constitution and a tribal council.

The governments of the two branches of the Cheyenne people differ slightly in terms of organization. In 1936 the Northern Cheyenne Tribe passed its first constitution, which established a tribal council consisting of members elected from the each of the five districts on the reservation. The Cheyenne and Arapaho Tribes ratified their constitution the following year, which created a business committee of fourteen members, consisting of seven Cheyenne members and seven Arapaho members. All tribal constitutions had to be approved by the secretary of the interior, however, who ensured that the BIA retained supervisory control over most aspects of tribal life.

After the end of World War II, tribal servicemen and women who returned to the reservations brought with them the money they had earned working for the army as well as a new knowledge of the outside world. Lifestyles on the reservations began to change in response to the influence of the dominant culture. Televisions and cars became common.

Alongside these changes the federal government pushed to end federal support and recognition for tribes by getting rid of tribal enrollment, selling off tribal lands, liquidating tribal assets, and using the proceeds to make a one-time per-capita payment to each current tribal member. The Cheyenne and Arapaho succeeded in keeping their federal tribal recognition, however, and the Northern Cheyenne also managed to avoid termination. The northern branch of the tribe began reacquiring their land, and by 2013 nearly 99 percent of the reservation was once again tribally owned.

LANGUAGE

The Cheyenne language belongs to the Algonquian family of languages. It first appeared in written form in 1896, when a Mennonite missionary wrote and published a Cheyenne dictionary. The alphabet contains fourteen letters. Various Cheyenne bands, including the Sutai Tribe, spoke dialects of the language. The Cheyenne spoken today by the two branches of the tribe is very similar. Until around 1880 almost all tribal members spoke in variations of Cheyenne exclusively. A handful were bilingual, having learned English from a white parent or family member or from living in close quarters with white people. The various Plains Indians tribes communicated through sign language, and many Cheyenne who had lived on the Plains before the reservation era knew how to sign. A tribal member named Tichkematse (Squint Eyes), imprisoned by the U.S. Army from 1875 to 1878, learned English and later taught Indian Sign Language to an anthropologist and fellow employee at the Smithsonian. Tichkematse worked at the museum as a naturalist from 1878 to 1891.

At the St. Labre Indian Mission School in Montana (established in 1884) and the BIA boarding school in Busby, Oklahoma, speaking or writing in Cheyenne was forbidden. The same was true for those children who attended public schools. They were taught that in order to succeed, they needed a white education, and many who went to the boarding schools determined that their children's first language would be English. Those sent away at a young age had little choice, since many forgot their own language. It therefore became rare for tribal members born on the reservation to grow up speaking Cheyenne at home.

Since the 1970s there has been renewed interest in preserving and passing on the language. Tribal elders and the tribal governments are working to record fluent speakers and to teach young children to speak Cheyenne. Courses in the language are offered in Montana at Chief Dull Knife College, St. Labre School, and the tribal public school; and in Oklahoma at the Cheyenne and Arapaho Tribal College and at Watonga High School. Few of the teachers were fluent in Cheyenne, making the project more challenging.

Greetings and Popular Expressions Examples of Cheyenne words and phrases include: *Hoonobb wonooyoo'cec* (haw-no-ba-won-aw-yaw-chek)—"Happy New Year"; *neaese*—"thank you"; *ma'heo'o nehnese-vatamemeno*—"Great One, take pity on us"; and *Epeva'e* (eh-peh-va)—"It is good."

RELIGION

The traditional Cheyenne religion is based on the prophecies of Sweet Medicine, a Cheyenne spiritual leader who shared his visions of the future with the tribe. According to tribal history, Sweet Medicine went on a vision quest to Bear Butte, a dome-shaped mountain in South Dakota near Sturgis. For four years he lived in a tipi on the butte and received sacred teachings from Maheo (the Wise One Above) and his servants. When Sweet Medicine returned to his people, he reorganized the tribal society into religious, political, and military institutions. In Sweet Medicine's prophecies the universe was divided into Heamahestamor (the World Above) and Atonoom (the World Below), which were in turn divided into different regions. The universe was filled with spiritual beings that manifested as birds, animals, and spirits of the dead; the environment was alive, sacred, and imbued with meaning, both cultural and religious. Sweet Medicine's visions have been passed down from generation to generation. According to scholars, he created a social contract between tribal members and their government and between tribal society and the universe.

One of the Cheyenne's rituals was the Arrow Renewal Ceremony, in which priests used *mahuts* (sacred arrows that symbolize masculinity and prosperity) and *issuwin* (a sacred buffalo hat that symbolizes femininity) before a hunt or battle to enlist the aid of spirits and ensure a successful outcome. The Sun Dance was performed annually in the spring to bring about regeneration. In general, ceremonies underscored the authority of the council chiefs and the priests. Dancing, drumming, singing, storytelling, and body painting played an integral role. Other rituals included war dances and celebrations honoring individuals, some making use of sweat lodges.

In 1872 the Bureau of Indian Affairs enacted policies that banned the tribe's annual ceremonies and sent Christian missionaries to the reservations to convert the people. Quaker missionaries were the first to arrive on the Cheyenne and Arapaho Reservation in Oklahoma in the 1870s, followed by Mennonites in 1882. Both groups founded schools and engaged in missionary activity. Catholic missionaries reached the Northern Cheyenne reservation in 1883, where they opened a church and founded the St. Labre Mission School in Lame Deer. The Mennonites followed, sending their first missionary in 1899. They also opened a church and founded a school on the Northern Cheyenne reservation. Tribal members resisted conversion and held onto their ceremonies by disguising them as other events, calling them Homecoming Celebration and Fourth of July Celebration. Typically, the first day involved a show developed to convince the Indian agent and missionaries of compliance. Once the white people went home, two or three days of traditional ceremonies began.

Today, some tribal members are Catholic, others are Protestant, and some still observe the traditional religion taught by Sweet Medicine. Some practice a combination of Christianity and traditional religion. The Cheyenne tend to view faith and religious practice as nonexclusive. Charles Little Old Man, a tribal member who participated in the Western Heritage Center's 2012 Northern Cheyenne oral history project, explained that he was raised to respect all religions. Little Old Man said his grandmother had told him, "All forms of prayer are good."

CULTURE AND ASSIMILATION

In addition to U.S. government programs aimed at erasing all aspects of the Cheyenne culture, another serious challenge for the early generations living on reservations was prejudice. Cheyenne children attending boarding schools were told by their white teachers that they were dirty and spread vermin. This stigma affected subsequent generations. Those who lived on the reservation experienced discrimination from non-Indians who lived or worked nearby, and those who moved off experienced isolation in the larger culture. Until the middle of the twentieth century, cities and towns near the reservations had signs that read "No Indians Allowed." In an interview for the Western Heritage Center's oral history project, one Northern Cheyenne woman who moved off the reservation in the 1960s described being mistaken for Mexican and not correcting the mistake because she felt ashamed of her true identity. Since that time, however, a growing number of Cheyenne tribal members have attended college and graduate school, working at high-paying and high-profile jobs, and, in certain instances, becoming successful members of both cultures.

According to interviewees for the Western Heritage Center's 2012 project, some Cheyenne who had lived or spent time off the reservation reported feeling out of place in the dominant culture, in which non-Indians still have misconceptions or are uneducated about what it means to be Cheyenne.

Traditions and Customs One very important tradition that dates back to at least 1700 and was still practiced in the early twenty-first century is the Give-Away. This ceremonial distribution of goods takes place at funerals, naming ceremonies, powwows, the Sun Dance, and other ceremonies. The tradition of gift giving is not unique to the Cheyenne Tribe. Many Northern Plains tribes practice a similar custom, though the rituals vary from tribe to tribe. In the 1800s the Cheyenne people gave horses as gifts. As circumstances changed, so did the nature of what was given away. Horses are far less common as gifts now, having been replaced with blankets, quilts, shawls, dishes, food, and money. The stated purpose of the Give-Away is to display love for a kinsman, often the givers' children. The ritual also confers prestige on the givers. In an essay in *Plains Anthropologist* (1973), scholar Katherine Weist notes that the practice results in a continual flow of goods from person to person, family to family, and tribe to tribe.

Cuisine During the farming phase of Cheyenne history, the tribe's diet included crops such as corn, squash, and beans, as well as buffalo, deer meat, and fish. The women dried meat and gathered herbs for

In Gallup, New Mexico, Cheyenne women perform a traditional dance at an InterTribal Ceremonial event. CHUCK PLACE / ALAMY

tea. Chokecherries were dried and pulped into cakes. When the tribe moved west and became a hunting culture, more meat was added to their diet, along with fruits and berries, wild mushrooms, turnips, and wild onions. The Cheyenne continued to eat corn that they bought from other tribes, and they smoked tobacco for ceremonial purposes.

Contemporary Cheyenne cuisine still uses game meat but incorporates dishes from the dominant culture as well. Sandwiches, salads, pasta, and chicken wings are some of the items offered on the menu at the Rez Restaurant at the Lucky Star Casino in Concho, Oklahoma.

Traditional Dress Women traditionally wore long, fringed deerskin dresses and high fringed boots. Men wore breechcloths with deerskin leggings and moccasins. Later, men adopted the fringed leather warrior shirts worn by other Plains tribes. These traditional

clothes were often decorated with porcupine quills, elk teeth, and shells. During ceremonies the men wore tall, feathered headdresses, which they exchanged for long war bonnets after moving to the Plains. In the late 1800s the Cheyenne people began to wear European-style cloth dresses and pants, which they decorated with quill work or beads. Today, Cheyenne dress in accordance with mainstream American style, wearing traditional clothing at powwows and other special occasions.

Traditional Arts and Crafts Traditional arts and crafts included quill embroidery: long white porcupine quills with black tips were strung together to decorate clothing and make breastplates. Quills were also used to make jewelry such as chokers. The Cheyenne decorated deerskin dresses, shirts, moccasins, leggings, and buffalo skin shields with beadwork and used beads to make jewelry. Other crafts included pottery.

Dances and Songs Dances and songs were an important part of religious ceremonies, in the sweat lodge, and at powwows. One of the more famous dance-song combinations is the Sun Dance song cycle, performed in the spring by Cheyenne tribal members to renew themselves as a people and to integrate all of the bands. The cycle consists of twelve sacred song-prayers accompanied by dancing. The Cheyenne tribe had other spiritual and war dances and songs that have been preserved and are performed at powwows, such as the Gourd Dance, the Fancy Dance, and the Straight Dance.

Holidays Traditionally, the most important holiday observed the Sun Dance, which took place over several days. The two other major holidays were the Arrow Renewal and the Hat Ceremony. Today, the Cheyenne celebrate all federal holidays along with Cheyenne holidays. Fort Robinson Outbreak Spiritual Run is a four-day, 400-mile run held from January 9 to 14. It begins at Fort Robinson, Nebraska, and ends at the tribal burial grounds in Busby, Montana. In 1996 Northern Cheyenne tribal member Philip Whiteman Jr. organized the run, in which 130 tribal members have participated each year to commemorate their ancestors who escaped from Fort Robinson on January 9, 1879. Cheyenne Victory Day, celebrated on June 25, marks the tribe's 1876 victory over Custer and his U.S. troops in the Battle of the Little Bighorn. The Sand Creek/Washita Massacre Commemoration, on November 29, honors the memory of the sleeping Cheyenne slaughtered by the Colorado Militia in 1864.

Health Care Issues and Practices Diabetes, alcoholism, and drug abuse have caused persistent health problems among Cheyenne tribal members. Both reservations have treatment programs that address these issues. All tribal members are eligible to receive health care from the federal Indian Health Services, which has a clinic that serves the Northern Cheyenne in Lame Deer, Montana, and three facilities in Oklahoma for the Cheyenne and Arapaho: one each in Concho, Watonga, and Clinton.

Death and Burial Rituals Historically, the Cheyenne tribe believed that every person had a spirit. When a person died, the spirit must be treated with respect and encouraged to move onward to the spirit world. Members of the warrior society placed the remains in a grave. According to an essay by William Tall Bull (a Northern Cheyenne historian and a nationally renowned preservationist) in the anthology *We, the Northern Cheyenne*, if a spirit looks back, it may take a child with it. Tribal members gathered at the gravesite, where a priest, such as the Keeper of the Sacred Hat, prayed, and elders offered a pipe ceremony as a sign of respect. Those gathered commemorated the life of the deceased and sang a death song. Then the dead was sent on his way with the following words: "Now that you have left, go. You do not turn around and look back." Cheyenne children were taught not to visit the graves of their people in the evening, the time of day when the spirits walk. If children visited at that hour, a spirit might follow them home and make it hard for them to sleep.

In pre-reservation-era burial ceremonies, the Cheyenne selected a high point, such as a ridge, to build a burial platform that typically had one side attached to a tree. The dead person, wrapped in layers of shawls and blankets and finally shrouded in white, was laid to rest on the platform. Family members hung household goods from the branches of the tree for the dead to take with them into the next world. A medicine pole, placed nearby with a medicine chest at its foot, and a horse (or horses), shot on the spot, were also intended for use in the next world. Mourners arrived after these rituals ended to sing death songs. Once the body had been blown to the ground or scattered, the remains were buried underground.

In the twenty-first century, burial methods have changed, but Cheyenne beliefs about death and spirits remain largely the same. The dead person is placed in a casket instead of on a burial platform, and the burial takes place right away. If the bones of Cheyenne people are uncovered during construction or archeological digs or are recovered from a museum, members of the tribe must rebury the bones on tribal land. The tribe must conduct a traditional ceremony at the gravesite similar to the one described above in order for the spirits of the dead to be at peace. Since the passage of the federal Native American Grave Protection and Repatriation Act in 1990, the skulls of dozens of Cheyenne have been returned to the tribe and reburied.

Recreational Activities Traditional Cheyenne games include lacrosse and a hoop game that involves two players throwing thin poles at a hoop covered with a net. The person who lands the most poles in the net wins the game. In some instances a third person sets the hoop in motion and the game is played while the hoop is rolling on the ground. Popular sports on the two reservations include basketball and bowling, and many participate in the annual Fort Robinson Outbreak Spiritual Run.

FAMILY AND COMMUNITY LIFE

From approximately 1680 through the first half of the 1800s, when the Cheyenne tribe was primarily an agricultural society, families tended to live in multigenerational and matrilocal (females stayed with their family of origin and males moved in with their wives' families) groups. Family units were organized into bands, and the bands were unified under the tribal council. Once the tribe moved further west and became nomadic, family structure became more fluid as suited the conditions of the Great Plains.

From the 1870s to the 1950s, families were often forced to live apart, with the young people being sent away to school. The multigenerational family remained the model, however, and when the children were home on vacation, they spent time with their grandparents and extended families.

Today, family life on the reservation varies between traditional multigenerational cohabitation and the nuclear family units typical of the dominant culture. Technology has had a tremendous impact on Cheyenne family life, bringing the outside world much closer than ever before and replacing the influence of the tribe with external influences.

In Cheyenne culture people were traditionally given two types of names: nicknames such as Crooked Foot or Howling All Night that referred to body particularities or other personal characteristics; and personal names, which are more serious, taken from spirits, birds, animals, or plants that are considered a source of power. These are the names used in major ceremonies, and though they are not kept secret, they are considered private and are only used by those close to the person.

Gender Roles In the past Cheyenne men held the leadership roles, serving as chiefs, priests, or warriors. They were responsible for hunting and providing protection. Women were traditionally in charge of the home, including the cooking, cleaning, and child rearing. The early earthen lodges were constructed by both men and women, but during the Plains era, women were in charge of erecting and disassembling the tipis. Women and girls usually trained pack horses, while the men trained hunting and war horses. There were exceptions to the customary division of labor; women who had lost husbands or sons in battle were allowed to ride and shoot, sometimes participating in the hunt. Both men and women created art and music, told stories, and practiced traditional medicine. Whereas the priests had always been primary in Cheyenne society, as wars with the United States government intensified during the second half of the nineteenth century, the more aggressive warriors of the military societies began to dominate.

Today, women play a larger role in public life. In 2013 the top three officials in the executive branch of the Cheyenne and Arapaho tribal government were women, including Governor Janice Prairie Chief-Boswell. One of the four members of the executive committee of the Northern Cheyenne Tribe is a woman—Melissa Lonebear.

Education Before the tribe encountered Europeans, learning was passed down orally. It took the form of on-the-job training, in which elders, aunts, and uncles served as teachers. Subjects ranged from language, ceremonies, and culture to botany, astronomy, and biology and covered every aspect of Cheyenne life. Later, children were forcibly removed from their homes, sometimes by armed police, and transported to white-run boarding schools, where upon arrival they were bathed in kerosene and their heads were shaved. The intent of these schools was to discipline and punish, and the focus was on teaching trades rather than on general education.

The educational opportunities for Cheyenne tribal members improved greatly after the mid-1900s. Both Cheyenne reservations have public schools for students in kindergarten through twelfth grade. By 2012 St. Labre Indian School, still a Catholic institution, had grown to 750 students spread across three campuses. Half of the staff is Native American, and the school offers courses in Cheyenne language and culture. Boarding is voluntary, and boarders are generally those who live farther than 40 miles from the school. Chief Dull Knife College, a two-year college, is in Lame Deer, Montana, on the Northern Cheyenne Reservation. Approximately half of the students go on to attend four-year programs elsewhere. In 2006 the Cheyenne and Arapaho Tribes established a two-year tribal college on the Southwestern Oklahoma State University campus in Weatherford, Oklahoma.

Courtship and Weddings Although Cheyenne men and women had some say in who they wed, until the twentieth century their choice had to be approved by both families. Cheyenne women generally married between the ages of sixteen and twenty, while men married later, between the ages of twenty and twenty-five. A man went courting by talking to his potential bride in public or by visiting her tipi and talking with her through the buffalo skin wall. Once two people became interested in one another, a matchmaker, usually an older woman from the man's family, approached the woman's family, and if the match was agreeable, a date was set. During the engagement the families prepared an elaborate set of ceremonial gifts for each other. The groom-to-be gave his betrothed's family buffalo meat or horses. The females in the bride's family made the couple a new tipi with all the furnishings, and on the day of the ceremony, the tipi was set up near the groom's family.

The ceremony began with the bride, dressed in her finest, riding a horse led by the matchmaker to the groom's tipi. The bride's entire family followed her on foot, leading horses, which they gave the groom's family as gifts. The two families ate a meal together in the

groom's family's tipi and then exchanged gifts. Finally, the families escorted the couple to their new tipi.

Surnames In Cheyenne culture people were traditionally given two types of names: nicknames such as Crooked Foot or Howling All Night that referred to body particularities or other personal characteristics; and personal names, which are more serious, taken from spirits, birds, animals, or plants that are considered a source of power. These are the names used in major ceremonies, and though they are not kept secret, they are considered private and are only used by those close to the person. Some examples are Lonelodge, Tallbear, Little Thunder, and Killsback. People can change their name if they believe the current name is unlucky, if they want to indicate a change in status, or if they feel a new name would help heal an illness.

Boys traditionally received their serious name when they reached puberty and after they had joined a war party for the first time. The boy's eldest aunt on his father's side bestowed the name. Current practice is to give the new name when a boy joins in one of the annual ceremonies for the first time or when he finishes high school. Girls, also named by their paternal aunt, have traditionally received a grownup name at birth and carried it throughout life.

When dealing with the outside world, contemporary tribal members use "office" names, which are English names handed down from the father's family and kept on file by the BIA—for example, Edward Red Hat, Katie Bull Coming, and Roy Nightwalker. In the early twenty-first century, as a result of marriages with partners outside the tribe, some members have names of European origin.

EMPLOYMENT AND ECONOMIC CONDITIONS

The main sources of employment on the Northern Cheyenne Reservation are the schools, the federal government, the tribal government, power companies, and construction companies. Tribal members also farm, ranch, and own small businesses. According to the tribal website, as of 2012 the unemployment rate was 46 percent, significantly higher than the national average of approximately 8 percent. During the 2012 tribal elections, candidates cited poverty and unemployment as the most critical issues facing the tribe at that time.

Moore wrote that in 1970 the unemployment rate among the Cheyenne and Arapaho Tribes was as high as 82 percent; the median income of these families was 15 percent of what their white neighbors earned. By 2013 the Oklahoma tribe had a much larger economy than the Northern Cheyenne. In the 1990s the tribe opened the Lucky Star Casino, a 40,000-square-foot complex in Concho, Oklahoma, that offers gaming, a restaurant, and an event center for concerts. Cheyenne and Arapaho businesses have earned the tribe profits in the hundreds of millions. Tribal energy leases to Chesapeake Energy Incorporated have garnered millions of dollars in revenue as well. In 2011 the tribe joined with West Wind Energy LLC to create a wind turbine operation in Concho that provides power for the casino, hospital, and other tribal operations.

POLITICS AND GOVERNMENT

The political division the government created between the Northern and Southern Cheyenne disregarded their strong ties. Although they wished to live in different geographic locations, the two branches of the tribe have always considered themselves to belong to one Cheyenne nation. Both the Northern Cheyenne and the Cheyenne and Arapaho Tribes have a constitutional form of government. The northern tribe amended its 1936 constitution and bylaws in 1996. The Cheyenne and Arapaho Tribes ratified amendments and bylaws to their 1937 Wheeler-Howard Act constitution in 1975 and again in 2006.

The Northern Cheyenne Reservation's government has three branches. The executive branch is made up of a president, vice president, secretary, and treasurer. Elections are held every two years, and elected officials serve staggered four-year terms. The judicial branch consists of two trial judges, a clerk of court, and a bailiff. The third branch, the legislature, comprises ten elected representatives, two from each of five legislative districts. The body passes laws, guards tribal land and sovereignty, and serves the people. The tribe still appoints a Council of Chiefs but the chiefs serve in honorary positions and are not involved in the day-to-day operations of the reservation. Ben Nighthorse Campbell, a Northern Cheyenne Peace Chief, was elected to represent Colorado in the U.S. House of Representatives in 1987 and served the state in the U.S. Senate from 1992 to 2005.

The Cheyenne and Arapaho Reservation also has three branches of government, but its structure is slightly different. Their executive branch is composed of four members who are elected every four years, and the positions are governor, lieutenant governor, chief of staff, and chief executive policy analyst. The executive branch also includes five administrative departments: administration; housing; education; social services; and treasury. The tribal council is composed of all tribal members over the age of eighteen and meets annually. The judicial branch, in addition to having a trial court with four judges, comprises a judicial commission and a supreme court with a chief justice and three associate justices. The legislative branches are similarly endowed with the power to pass laws, guard tribal land and sovereignty, and serve the people. The Southern Cheyenne still have Peace Chiefs, but like the Northern Cheyenne's Council of Chiefs, these positions are honorary.

In recent years there have been struggles within the Cheyenne and Arapaho Tribal Government with tribal members concerned about management and control of revenues. In 2009 then-governor Darrell

Flyingman was removed from office. Janice Prairie Chief-Boswell became tribal governor in 2010, with Leslie Wandrie-Harjo as her lieutenant governor. Shortly after assuming office, Wandrie-Harjo accused Prairie Chief-Boswell of misconduct concerning tribal finances. For two years the two officers were embroiled in a dispute. The instability resulted in the First Bank of Trust Company freezing millions of dollars in tribal assets. The BIA intervened, and a special election was held in 2012 in which Janice Prairie Chief-Boswell was reelected as governor of the tribes.

With regard to national politics, voter turnout is reportedly low among those living on the Cheyenne and Arapaho Reservation. The tribal government in Concho informed its constituents that Native Americans made up 11.1 percent of the eligible voter population in Oklahoma during the 2012 elections. They provided information and encouraged tribal members to register and vote.

NOTABLE INDIVIDUALS

Art Bentley Spang (1960–) is a Northern Cheyenne tribal member and an artist, writer, and curator. His family moved off the reservation when he was four years old, and he has lived in Seattle, in Alaska, and on the northwestern coast of the United States. Spang graduated from Montana State University Billings with a degree in art and earned an MFA from the University of Wisconsin-Madison. He began his career creating sculpture and metal works and has become a multimedia artist, videographer, performance artist, and photographer. He has exhibited at the Denver Art Museum, the Heard Museum in Phoenix, the Brooklyn Museum, and many other art institutions around the world. In 1992 he spent a year as a community scholar at the Smithsonian Institute, and in 2004 he received a Paul Allen Foundation Grant.

Civic Leadership W. Richard West Jr. (1943–) founded the Smithsonian's National Museum of the American Indian Southern Cheyenne in 1990. His father, a Cheyenne tribal member, was sent to boarding school at the age of six and subsequently obtained a BA and an MA in art. He spent his working life as an artist and university professor. West graduated from Harvard with an MA in American history and from Stanford Law School with a JD. He has been awarded honorary degrees by Dartmouth and Amherst colleges. He served at the Museum of the American Indian until 2007. A Peace Chief of the Southern Cheyenne, he has served the tribe in many capacities. In 2012 he was named president and CEO of UCLA's Autry National Center of the American West.

Film Chris Eyre (1968–), a member of the Cheyenne and Arapaho Tribes, is a film director and producer. He directed such films as Smoke Signals, which won an award for best film at the Sundance Film Festival. Others directorial credits include two movies produced by Robert Redford and based on

Tony Hillerman mystery novels. He has also worked on documentary films and in television. In 2012 he was appointed the chair of the film department at the Santa Fe University of Art and Design.

Government Ben Nighthorse Campbell (1933–), a former U.S. member of Congress, was born in Auburn, California. His father, a Northern Cheyenne tribal member, spent much of his childhood at the Crow Agency boarding school in Montana. In 1951 Nighthorse Campbell dropped out of high school to join the U.S. Air Force and was awarded medals for conduct in the Korean War. He received a B from San Jose State University in California and also studied in Japan at Meiji University. At the 1964 Summer Olympics, he competed as a member of the U.S. sumo wrestling team. He served the state of Colorado in the House of Representatives (1987–1993) and later in the Senate (1993–2005). As of 2012 he ran his own consulting firm and served on the policy, budget, and development committees for the Smithsonian's National Museum of the American Indian. He is one of the forty-four Northern Cheyenne who serve on the Council of Chiefs.

Literature Suzan Shown Harjo (1945–) is a poet, a writer, and a Native American policy advocate who has helped to recover millions of acres of native lands. In the mid-1960s she produced the first Native American news show in the United States. As of 2013 she was serving as the president of Morning Star Institute, a Native American rights group based in Washington, D.C.

MEDIA

Cheyenne and Arapaho TV, K47MU-D

Launched in 2012, this public broadcast station is designed to serve Cheyenne and Arapaho tribal members with educational and instructional programs dedicated to preserving the Cheyenne and Arapaho languages. The program was developed by the tribes' Department of Education to provide state-of-the-art media training for students interested in a career in broadcasting. The station reaches an estimated 40,000 viewers.

Lisa Liebl, Public Relations/Executive Office
Concho, Oklahoma
Phone: (405) 623-0023
Email: lliebl@c-a-tribes.org
URL: www.catv47.wordpress.com

Cheyenne and Arapaho Tribal Tribune

A bimonthly newspaper in print and online that covers news, obituaries, and community announcements for people living on the reservation and in surrounding areas. In 2011 the news staff won four Native American Journalist Association awards for excellence.

Rosemary Stephens, Editor in Chief
700 North Black Kettle Boulevard
P.O. Box 167

Concho, Oklahoma 73022
Phone: (405) 422-7446
URL: www.c-a-tribes.org/tribal-news

Northern Cheyenne Tribal News

This is a feature of the larger tribal website.

P.O. Box 128
Lame Deer, Montana 59043
Phone: (406) 477-6284
Fax: (406) 477-6210
URL: www.cheyennenation.com/news.html

ORGANIZATIONS AND ASSOCIATIONS

Cheyenne and Arapaho Tribes

Ida Hoffman, Chief of Staff
Phone: (800) 247-4612
Fax: (405) 422-8225
URL: www.c-a-tribes.org

Montana-Wyoming Tribal Leaders Council

A nonprofit organization dedicated to preserving and maintaining tribal lands, advocating for tribal rights, and advancing the lives of Native American tribes in Montana and Wyoming. The council's work includes fostering intertribal cooperation, promoting tribal welfare and wellness, and engaging in policy work and lobbying on the state and national levels.

Gordon Belcourt, Executive Director
175 North 27th Street
Suite 1003
Billings, Montana 59101
Phone: (406) 252-2550
Fax: (406) 252-6355
URL: www.mtwytlc.org

Northern Cheyenne Tribe

Melissa Lonebear, Tribal Secretary
P.O. Box 128
Lame Deer, Montana 59043
Phone: (406) 477-6284
Fax: (406) 477-6210
URL: www.cheyennenation.com

MUSEUMS AND RESEARCH CENTERS

Cheyenne Indian Museum

This museum in Ashland, Montana, has a collection of Plains Indian artifacts and features a documentary about the St. Labre School.

1000 Tongue River Road
Ashland, Montana 59003
Phone: (406) 784-4500

Chief Dull Knife College Cultural Center

The center is located on the Chief Dull Knife College campus in Lame Deer. Exhibits include a recently commissioned portrait of Chief Dull Knife.

P.O. Box 128
Lame Deer, Montana 59043

Colorado Historical Society

A regional museum with historical resources on the Cheyenne people.

Cheryl Graham, Education Programs
1200 Broadway
Denver, Colorado 80203
Phone: (303) 447-8679
URL: www.historycolorado.org

The Denver Art Museum

This museum has an exhibit and website called Cheyenne Visions II that includes historical objects, art (both historic pieces and contemporary work), and a historical timeline of the Cheyenne people.

100 West 14th Avenue Parkway
Denver, Colorado 80204
Email: nativeart@denverartmuseum.org
URL: www.denverartmuseum.org

Jessie Mullin Picture Museum

A private museum exhibiting a collection of Northern Cheyenne photographs, paintings, maps, and old census rolls, in addition to photos of all past tribal presidents.

Janet Mullin
509 Cheyenne Avenue
P.O. Box 922
Lame Deer, Montana 59043
Phone: (406) 477-6460

SOURCES FOR ADDITIONAL STUDY

Berthrong, Donald J. *The Cheyenne and Arapaho Ordeal: Reservation and Agency Life in the Indian Territory, 1875–1907*. Norman: University of Oklahoma Press, 1992.

Campbell, Gregory. "Northern Cheyenne Ethnicity, Religion and Coal Development." *Plains Anthropologist* 32, no. 118 (1987): 378–88. *JSTOR*.

Fowler, Loretta. *Tribal Sovereignty and the Historical Imagination: Cheyenne-Arapaho Politics*. Lincoln: University of Nebraska Press, 2002.

Grinnell, George Bird. "Early Cheyenne Villages." *American Anthropologist* 20, no. 4 (1918): 359–80.

Little Bear, Richard E. *We, the Northern Cheyenne People: Our Land, Our History, Our Culture*. Lame Deer, MT: Chief Dull Knife College, 2008.

Moore, John H. *The Cheyenne Nation: A Social and Demographic History*. Lincoln: University of Nebraska Press, 1988.

Schlesier, Karl H. "Action Anthropology and the Southern Cheyenne." *Current Anthropology* 15, no. 3 (1974): 277–83. *JSTOR*.

Stewart, Donald D. "Cheyenne Arapaho Assimilation." *Phylon* 13, no. 2 (1952): 120–26.

Weist, Katherine. "Giving Away: Ceremonial Distribution of Goods among the Northern Cheyenne of Southeast Montana." *Plains Anthropologist* 18, no. 60 (1973): 97–103. *JSTOR*.

Weist, Tom. *A History of the Cheyenne People*. Billings: Montana Council for Indian Education, 1977.

CHILEAN AMERICANS

Phyllis J. Burson

OVERVIEW

Chilean Americans are immigrants or descendants of people from Chile, a country located on the west coast of South America. Chile is bounded by Peru on the north, Bolivia and Argentina on the east, and the South Pacific Ocean on the west. Chile is a long, narrow country, about 100 miles wide and 2,600 miles long. Its land mass measures 292,258 square miles (756,945 square kilometers), making it slightly larger than Texas.

According to a July 2012 estimate by the U.S. Central Intelligence Agency, Chile's population was approximately seventeen million. Almost 70 percent of the population was Roman Catholic and about 15 percent was Protestant. A small percentage was Jewish. The vast majority, 95 percent, was of European-Indian (*mestizo*) and European origin; 4 percent was Mapuche, an indigenous group. An estimated 89 percent of the people lived in urban areas. Mining, agriculture, light manufacturing, and fish products are important to the economy, and international trade helps make Chile's economy one of the strongest in South America.

Chileans began migrating to the United States, particularly California, in the 1790s on merchant ships; a significant wave came during the Gold Rush of the 1850s. In the latter half of the twentieth century, Chilean immigrants came to the United States seeking either political asylum or better economic opportunities. Since 1990 most Chileans have come to the United States searching for better education that would lead to better job prospects.

The 2010 U.S. Census estimated that there are over 126,000 people of Chilean descent living in the United States today, only 0.3 percent of the total Hispanic population. California, Florida, and New York have the highest population of Chilean Americans; New York City and Miami, followed by Los Angeles, are the urban areas with the largest Chilean communities.

HISTORY OF THE PEOPLE

Early History The name *Chile* comes from a Mapuche word meaning "land's end," a reference to the fact that Chile stretches to the tip of South America. Indigenous groups migrated into the area of modern Chile at least 10,000 years ago. In the early fifteenth century A.D. the Incan empire began to expand from its center in Peru into present-day Chile. At the height of the empire, it stretched 3,000 miles along the Andes, extending into what is now southern Chile. The Incan advance was halted by the Mapuche, who still live in southern Chile, and by the Spanish, who invaded the Incan capital in present-day Peru in 1532. The first Europeans began to explore Chile in 1535, claiming it for the Spanish crown in 1536 and founding Santiago in 1541. Over the next several years, the overwhelming majority of the indigenous population died because they lacked immunity for diseases, such as measles, brought by the Europeans. As a result, most of the indigenous groups were easily defeated by the Spaniards. The Mapuche, however, successfully resisted the invaders.

Extensive intermarriage occurred between Europeans and Mapuche, and *mestizos* (persons of European-Indian ancestry) make up two-thirds of the current Chilean population. The Spanish introduced Roman Catholicism and a land-tenure system that created a small, wealthy landowning class and a large, landless peasant class. Over time, those born in South America grew to resent foreign domination by Spain.

Modern Era On September 18, 1810, Chileans set up a rebel government. After several battles, Bernardo O'Higgins (1778–1842) and José de San Martín (1778–1850) led the Chileans to victory. On February 12, 1818, they proclaimed Chile's independence from Spain. Bernardo O'Higgins became the first head of government and is honored as the father of Chilean independence.

In the War of the Pacific (1879–1883) against Peru and Bolivia, Chile increased its area by one-third and gained valuable mineral resources, including deposits of nitrate, a natural fertilizer.

During the first half of the twentieth century, several governmental reforms took place. Church and state became separate, ensuring freedom of worship. Women gained the vote, and the government set up free, compulsory primary education. The Chileans were proud of their democratic tradition, with regular elections and freedom of the press. Many considered Chile to be the most stable

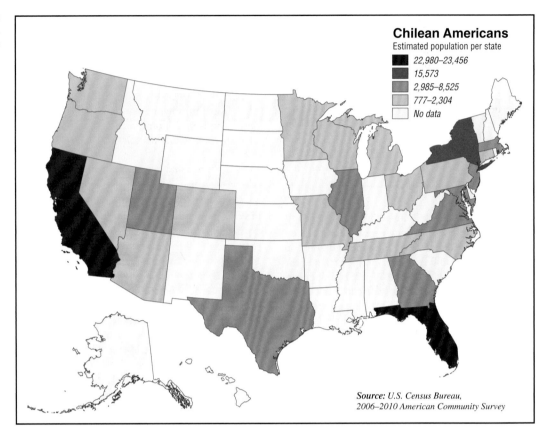

Chilean Americans
Estimated population per state

- 22,980–23,456
- 15,573
- 2,985–8,525
- 777–2,304
- No data

*Source: U.S. Census Bureau,
2006–2010 American Community Survey*

democracy in South America and, thus, were unprepared for the violence of the 1970s.

In 1970 Salvador Allende (1908–1973), a Marxist and an organizer of the Socialist Party in Chile, became president. He instituted far-reaching social reforms, but these contributed to an economic crisis and widespread dissatisfaction. The U.S. Central Intelligence Agency, fearful of Allende's socialist policies, secretly supported groups hostile to the government. On September 11, 1973, Augusto Pinochet (1915–2006) led a military coup and established an authoritarian government. During the coup, Allende lost his life.

Pinochet took strict control over the press, radio, television, and school system. The government repeatedly violated civil and human rights. Many journalists and other intellectuals were killed, imprisoned, or forced into exile. About one million people, almost one-tenth of the population, left Chile during the Pinochet dictatorship. However, the government succeeded in building a strong economy. In October 1988, Pinochet lost a national plebiscite designed to keep him in power for another eight years. As a result, he was constitutionally obligated to step down. Evidence indicates that Pinochet contemplated defying the plebiscite results, but that his top military officers refused to support such a move. Thus, in 1990, after sixteen years of military rule in Chile, the moderate Patricio Aylwin (1918–) took office. Aylwin

and his successor, Eduardo Frei, who took office in 1994, moved Chile toward more freedom and openness while maintaining economic growth.

In 2000 Ricardo Lagos, Socialist Party candidate of the Center-Left Concertación coalition, took office; the Socialists continued to control the presidency when Chile's first female president, Michelle Bachelet Jeria, was elected. Bachelet was succeeded by Sebastián Piñera in 2010. The twenty-first century saw several events that put Chile in the forefront of the news around the world. In February 2010, the sixth largest earthquake in the world since 1900 hit Chile, causing massive and widespread damage. In August of the same year, a mine in northern Chile collapsed, trapping the miners beneath the ground. The Chilean government carried out a successful rescue of thirty-three men who had been trapped underground for seventeen days.

SETTLEMENT IN THE UNITED STATES

Because of its strategic position on world trade routes and long coastline, a lively trade developed between Chile and other parts of the world. Until the Panama Canal was completed in the early twentieth century, many ships traveling between the east and west coasts of the United States made the long journey around Cape Horn at the southern tip of South America. They stopped in Valparaíso and other ports to sell goods and replenish their stores. Significant immigration to Chile did not end with the coming of the Spaniards. A significant number of Germans, Italians, Irish, English, Greeks, Yugoslavs, Lebanese, and others came to Chile during the nineteenth and twentieth centuries because of economic hardship or political difficulties in their countries of origin. Chile's many diverse groups earned the country the nickname "the United States of South America." The diversity is also reflected in the variety of surnames found in the country. Typical last names are Spanish, such as López; German, such as Hahn; Irish, such as O'Connell; or English, such as Lee. More than two-thirds of the population is mixed European and Indian, with brown eyes and dark brown, almost black, hair. However, some Chileans are blue-eyed blonds and others have red hair.

As early as the 1790s, merchant ships from Chile began to arrive at the California coast. The first large wave of immigrants from Chile to the United States occurred during the California Gold Rush of 1848–1849. Carlos López tells the story in his book *Chilenos in California: A Study of the 1850, 1852, and 1860 Censuses*. Ships arriving at the port of Valparaíso first brought the news of the discovery of the precious metal, along with samples of gold dust. The Chilean economy was in crisis and ship owners, hoping to create business, spread wild rumors about the abundance of gold in California. Thousands of Chileans crammed the ships to make their fortunes. Some of the first Chileans to arrive were experienced miners. They taught the "anglos" better techniques of panning for and extracting gold. In order to crush ore, these miners improved an existing device, expertly fashioning huge stone wheels to be used in what came to be called "Chili mills." Adventurers came, too, including the prominent Vicente Pérez Rosales (1807–1886), who kept a record of his trip in his diary. In San Francisco, the Chileans settled in an area called "Chilecito" (Little Chile). When a new shipload of Chileans arrived, they were welcomed and instructed in the ways of California by the Chilecito community. On July 15, 1849, residents of Chilecito were attacked and robbed. Chileans suffered other discrimination; the government passed a foreign miners tax. Further, in the summer of 1850 there was a move to expel foreigners, especially Chileans and Mexicans, from the mines. Thousands of Chileans returned to San Francisco, though many remained in the mining towns. Perhaps half of the Chilean prospectorsers eventually returned to Chile, disappointed with the difference between the romantic stories they had heard and the realities of nineteenth-century California.

The Chileans who remained in California retained an active ethnic identity for some time. They often lived in areas called Chilitowns, speaking Spanish and cooking their traditional foods. To keep in contact, they established newspapers and local clubs. In 1867 a Chilean American newspaper appeared in San Francisco. In translation, its name was "the voice of Chile and of the American republics."

Later, it merged with a Mexican American paper, providing news of interest to Chileans and Mexicans in San Francisco until 1883. Local organizations all over California provided a way for Chilean Americans to continue their traditions and support each other socially and financially.

Though many of the prospectorsers who settled permanently in California retained their interest in the mother country, the majority of them married non-Chileans. Over time, Chilean Americans spread out all over California and into neighboring states. As their children learned English in school and mixed with the wider society, the high rate of intermarriage with non-Chileans continued. The ethnic neighborhoods, newspapers, and clubs disappeared as the interests of Chilean Americans changed.

From the time of the Gold Rush until the 1960s, a small number of immigrants trickled into the United States from Chile. Young people from upper-class Chilean families came to the United States to attend college or graduate school, and frequently remained. Single men whose companies sent them to Chile often returned with South American brides. Exporters, sailors, and professionals immigrated to the United States to increase their economic or career opportunities.

However, significant immigration into the United States did not begin to occur until the latter half of the 1960s. At that time, a larger number of Chileans began to emigrate in hopes of increasing their economic opportunities. They knew they could find better jobs and a higher standard of living in the United States. Young Chileans pursuing their educations were also spurred to immigrate by growth in academic exchange programs and the emergence of Chilean area studies programs at American universities. Another important factor in the increased Chilean immigration to the United States was the Alliance for Progress, an economic development program launched in 1961 by the United States in partnership with twenty-two Latin American nations, including Chile. Aimed to boost economic growth and counter the appeal of communism, the program also had the effect of bolstering the connection between—and increasing immigration between—America and Latin American neighbors such as Chile.

The overthrow of Allende in 1973 and the establishment of a military dictatorship led to a large exodus of Chileans. Pinochet was determined to rid the country of divisive elements. Chief among his targets were leftist political leaders, labor leaders, and working-class community leaders, as well as journalists, radical students, intellectuals, and other professionals. Many fled for their lives to Europe, other parts of Latin America, the United States, and Canada. The size of the group that came to the United States was small in comparison to those who emigrated to other countries. Some countries persuaded Pinochet to exile Chilean dissidents rather than imprison or kill them. The United States offered to take Chilean refugees under a program for so-called political parolees.

Many of the refugees were ill prepared for the transition to life in North America. They lacked employment, housing, or contacts with Chileans already here to ease their entry into the United States. Some were sent in the middle of winter to areas of heavy snow, for which their California-like climate had not prepared them. A number of churches responded to these needs. In one well-known case, an Irish priest, Father Chouchulain Moriarty, heard of the plight of the immigrants. He dedicated himself to assisting the newly arriving Chileans to adjust to American life. Father Moriarty established a program in the Roman Catholic Church of the Sacred Heart in San Jose, California. New arrivals were housed in the church convent building, and helped to find jobs, secure permanent housing, and learn English. Because of the reputation of Father Moriarty's work, political parolees from all over California and as far away as the Midwest traveled to San Jose to become part of the program.

Throughout the Pinochet regime, Chileans continued to immigrate to the United States, for both political and economic reasons. Those who have come since 1990, when the military regime ended, are immigrating primarily for economic reasons. Though the Chilean economy is growing, there is still a large class of poor people in the country.

Beginning in 1988, Chilean exiles were allowed, and later encouraged, to return home. In that year President Pinochet decreed that all those in exile could return to Chile. After he came into office in 1990, President Aylwin established a generous program for Chileans who returned, including financial assistance and other benefits. A substantial number of those in exile did return, including some living in the United States, eager to reunite with their families and to be part of a more democratic Chile.

Most of the Chilean American population has arrived during the past 25 years. As of 2010, the U.S. census indicated that there were about 126,810 persons of Chilean ancestry in the United States. About 97,337 of these had been born in Chile. Thus, less than one-tenth of all Chilean Americans were born here. The overwhelming majority are first-generation immigrants who retain close emotional ties to their country of origin. Many visit their families in Chile periodically or send their children there for vacations. A small percentage, especially academics and business people, spend some of their time in the United States and some in Chile, pursuing their careers on two continents.

Most Chileans who come to the United States settle in or around cities. They come from a highly urbanized country and find it compatible to settle in a metropolitan area. Cities provide the jobs they need and the opportunity to interact with other Chileans.

They especially gravitate toward California, New York City, and Florida because of the large Spanish-speaking populations in these areas. They know they will be able to find jobs where they can use their Spanish language and communicate with bosses. Furthermore, Chileans feel an emotional tie to states such as Florida, where there is a substantial Latin influence. By far, the largest number of Chilean Americans live in California. States with the next largest numbers of Chileans are, in order from greatest to fewest: New York, Florida, New Jersey, and Texas. Many settled in Canada, especially Toronto and Montreal, during the Pinochet regime. At that time, the Canadian government allowed them special entry visas for humanitarian reasons.

LANGUAGE

Virtually all Chilean Americans speak Spanish, though some have come from parts of Chile where German, Italian, or another language was spoken in their homes. Their accent depends on social class and region of the country from which they came. Frequently, Chileans omit the "s" sound in words, and sometimes drop out the last syllable of a longer word. (In the greetings listed below, the "s" sound is retained, because it is used in conversation where there is reason to be formal.)

Chileans make great use of the suffixes "-ito" and "-ita," word endings that literally mean "little" but translates more accurately in this context as an indicator of familiarity. A friend named Norma may be referred to affectionately as Normita (nor-*mee*-tah), literally meaning "little Norma."

Greetings and Popular Expressions Friends and family commonly greet each other with the *abrazo* (ah-bra-zoh). This is a handshake and hug, sometimes with a kiss on the right cheek. The *abrazo* is repeated upon parting. Other greetings (with pronunciation) include: *¡Hola! ¿Qué hubo?* (oh-lah kay oo-boh)—How are you?; *¿Cómo está?* (koh-moh ess-tah)—How are you?; *¡Gusto de verte!* (goo-stoh day vehr-tay)—Nice to see you!; *¡Buenos días!* (bway-nohs dee-ahs)—Good day!; *¡Chao!* (chow)—Good-bye! To express appreciation for their host's food, Chileans say: *¡Es rico!* (ess ree-koh)—It's delicious!

RELIGION

Because such a high proportion of Chileans are Roman Catholic, most of those who immigrate to the United States are of this faith. The global nature of the church, with its shared beliefs and practices, eases the transition for a Catholic from Santiago to San Francisco or New York. Chileans find that, although the churches may look different and the congregation and priest may speak English, the order of the mass is the same, and there are still familiar traditions, such as lighting prayer candles. Chileans often attend churches in which there are services in Spanish. Sometimes they organize local events especially attractive to other Chilean Catholics, such as those connected with patron saints.

Victor Toro stands near a mural depicting the history of Latin American immigration. After entering the U.S. illegally, Toro spent 30 years in New York City as a community activist and volunteer for humanitarian causes. AP PHOTO / BEBETO MATTHEWS

In Chile, baptisms are often performed when the child is about two months old. Godparents are chosen who agree to raise the child in the faith if the parents should die. At age eight, children take their first communion. Another set of godparents may be added at this time; sometimes the child is allowed to choose them. Some Chilean Americans Catholics keep this tradition alive today.

Protestant immigrants often join the denominations in North America in which they had been active at home. Santiago has one of the world's largest Pentecostal churches, so many Chileans look for Pentecostal congregations in the United States. Many German Chileans join Baptist or Lutheran churches. Other Chileans join the Seventh Day Adventist church. Like the Roman Catholics, the Protestants often search for congregations where Spanish is used. A small group of Jewish Chileans have also come to the United States. Like the Roman Catholics, they have a worldwide sense of community with others who share the Jewish faith and traditions.

CULTURE AND ASSIMILATION

There are three major reasons Chileans have come to the United States during the past 25 years. The first group, small in number, left Chile because of the political repression of the Pinochet regime. Many of these immigrants are of middle- or upper-class origin. A significant proportion of them arrived with advanced educations and well-developed skills. They had contacts with other Chilean exiles and a sense of identity from their shared commitment to a democratic Chile. After a period of adjustment, many of them were able to pursue skilled jobs or professions. Unfortunately, others, who lacked skills or whose professional certifications were not recognized in the United States, were forced to take low-level jobs in which they were unable to use their skills. Some had been politically active students or union leaders in Chile who did not enter the United States with easily transferable skills.

The second important contingent immigrated to the United States as students, teachers, and scholars. Of this group, most are middle- and upper-class

Chileans who come to the United States to pursue university degrees. A number of Chilean academics and professionals have also come to the United States in order to accept positions within the American university system.

Most immigrants, however, fall into the third group. They have come to the United States searching for economic opportunities. Many of these are poorer, with less education and fewer skills than the group of political exiles. They often find it necessary to take jobs at the lower end of the pay scale. A typical pattern is to find a job as a babysitter or in the construction industry, where fluency in English is of limited importance. As time permits, they attend English classes or get secretarial or technical training, eventually acquiring more desirable jobs. Chilean Americans work hard to secure education and training so as to better themselves.

Because Chile is far away and does not share borders with the United States, immigrants cannot simply cross a border to enter the country. They must save money and work hard to get here. Such enterprising immigrants often have high motivation and additional skills, as well as American relatives or other contacts. These facts ease their transition into the American economy.

Because they share the Spanish language, Chileans often interact with other Latinos in church, at work, and around the neighborhood. This frequently leads to friendships and sometimes to marriage. Chileans also have a high rate of intermarriage with other U.S. citizens, which is contributing to their assimilation into mainstream society. Although most Chilean Americans are eager to learn or improve their English, some find it more comfortable to live and work in Spanish-speaking neighborhoods.

Chilean Americans find themselves in the position of being a minority within a minority. That is, Chileans make up a tiny part of the Latino population in the country, itself a minority group. Many Chileans feel quite separate from Central American or Caribbean people; they have never tasted Mexican food and their accents are quite different from Puerto Ricans. Yet the dominant white majority considers them all to be Latinos, making few distinctions. Indeed, most books about Latinos, such as Milton Meltzer's *Hispanic Americans* (1982), fail to discuss Chileans at all, focusing only on the larger Latino groups in the United States. Because Chilean Americans are such a small group numerically, most mainstream Americans do not know enough about Chileans to have well-defined ideas of how they differ from other Latinos.

Traditions and Customs Chileans have a reputation for being a friendly people, and this tradition is maintained by Chilean Americans. According to a well-known folk song, "If you go to Chile, the country folk will come to greet you and you will see that Chileans love a friend from far away." Unlike certain other Latin countries, guests wait to be invited into the home. They usually greet the head of the family first to show respect. Visitors often spend time asking about the family, including the children.

When Chilean Americans come to the United States, they find the pattern of the regular work day not too different from that of their native country. Business people are accustomed to working from nine to five, perhaps staying a few hours extra to finish work. Although this has changed in the larger Chilean cities, many more Chileans are used to coming home for lunch hour than is true in the United States. Although some Chileans take a nap after lunch, the *siesta* is not as entrenched a tradition as it is in some other Latin American countries.

Chileans commonly eat four times a day. They have breakfast, a late lunch, tea at about five, and a late dinner. In Chile, lunch is typically the largest meal of the day. Afternoon tea is served in late afternoon around five or six o'clock. People eat sandwiches or, sometimes, cakes, and drink tea. Chile is one Latin country where tea is a more popular drink than coffee. Dinner is often eaten between eight-thirty and ten-thirty, but some Chilean Americans report they have, on occasion, left the table at two o'clock in the morning. Chilean Americans are often forced to change their eating patterns by the necessity of leaving for work early in the morning and taking coffee breaks at the times designated by their employers rather than by their traditions. Some Chileans are so poor that they can only afford one substantial meal a day. Chilean Americans from poor backgrounds often eat better in the United States, even when working at low-paying jobs, than they were able to do in Chile.

Cuisine The fishing industry is larger in Chile than in any other Latin American country except Peru. Seafood has long been an important part of the diet, with approximately 200 types of fish available. Fish is inexpensive, so it is eaten by almost all Chileans. The types of seafood they eat include mussels, scallops, clams, crabs, lobsters, abalone, and sea urchins. The conger eel is a national specialty; there are many ways to prepare it in both simple and elegant dishes. Chilean Americans adapt their seafood cooking to the varieties of fish and shellfish that are available in North America. They enjoy soups, stews, and seafood combinations.

Many traditional dishes contain beans and corn, reflecting the Indian heritage of the country. Most Chilean bean recipes call for *porotos*, or cranberry beans. The climate of the country allows beans to grow during most of the year, so they are a natural for inclusion in many dishes. Chilean corn is somewhat different from that grown in the United States. In some Chilean varieties, the ears are much larger than their North American cousins. One very popular dish, *porotos granados*, contains beans, corn, squash, garlic, and onion.

Many recipes, such as *pastel de choclo* (corn and meat pie), call for unripe corn. In this dish, ground corn, sprinkled with sugar before baking, replaces the upper crust found in meat pies made in the United States.

Empanadas—pockets of dough filled with meat or cheese, onions, olives, raisins, hardboiled eggs, and spices that are baked or fried—are one of the favorite traditional foods of Chilean Americans. They are eaten as snacks or one course of a meal and are a favorite treat for holidays. *Humitas* are made from grated corn, onions, and spices. Traditionally, these are wrapped in corn husks and cooked in boiling water.

Wine is a popular drink among Chileans. South of Santiago lies a stretch of Chile's central valley that is superb wine-growing country. The early Spaniards introduced vineyards to Chile so that they could grow wine for use in the Catholic mass. From the time when a French winegrower was imported to improve the wine, Chileans have used European methods to make wine and have won prizes for their specialties. Another alcoholic drink, also made from grapes, is called *pisco*. A favorite drink is the pisco sour, in which *pisco* is served with lemon juice, sugar, beaten egg whites, and ice. Chileans also use fermented grapes to make another popular drink that they call *chicha*.

Traditional Dress Chileans are generally not attracted to the casualness and what some consider to be sloppiness of dress in the United States. Even those who are poor make an effort to avoid wearing tattered clothing. Styles generally follow fashion trends set in Europe. Chilean Americans tend to get more dressed up for the same event than people in the United States. For example, men usually go to restaurants in suits. Over time, Chilean Americans tend to become more relaxed in their dress while still enjoying more formal dress. Sometimes conflicts arise between immigrants and their children, who wish to adopt the sloppier appearance of other teenagers.

Traditional Arts and Crafts As in the other Andean countries of Peru and Bolivia, basketry, carvings of stone and wood, copperware, and lapis lazuli jewelry are common in Chile. These crafts have remained popular among Chilean Americans. One type of Chilean craft, the *arpillera*, is a wall hanging made with bits of cloth sewn together to create a picture. These arpillera were typically created by Chilean women as a kind of political resistance, particularly important during the Pinochet regime. Chilean Americans still look at these woven tapestries as an important part of their history and culture. In 2007 Chilean-American poet Marjorie Agosín published a book titled *Tapestries of Hope, Threads of Love: The Arpillera Movement in Chile*, which details the art's role in political and social change.

Dances and Songs Chilean Americans enjoy watching and performing dances. In some cities there are dance groups where people get together periodically to enjoy traditional dances.

CHILEAN FOLKLORE

Chile's rich store of folklore, sayings, and supernatural beliefs is derived from its European and Indian past, as well as its relation to the mountains and the ocean. One saying, related to the water, is that the shrimp who falls asleep is carried away by the current. Tuesday (not Friday) the thirteenth is considered to be an unlucky day. Another saying is that faraway loves are loves of idiots. Some traditional Chilean folk beliefs are identical to those in the United States. For example, Chileans also say that breaking a mirror will bring seven years of bad luck.

Some believe that the spirits of the dead are responsible for strange noises. It is said that spirits of the dead will visit those who work late at night. Also, neighbors may say that someone who is suddenly lucky has entered into an agreement with the devil. Some of these ideas are more common in the Chilean countryside than in the cities. Though many Chileans and Chilean Americans repeat them, they do not always believe them.

The so-called national dance of Chile is the *cueca*, which depicts the courting behavior of the rooster and the hen. Characteristic of this dance are stamping and the use of scarves. The man may use the scarf to pull the woman toward him, and she may use it to cover her face in a flirtatious manner. The *cueca* may be performed in formal attire or a more rural outfit.

The formal ballroom attire for men is based on the traditional dress of the Chilean cowboy. This consists of black pants, a colorful sash, a white shirt, and a black bolero jacket. A waist-length, brightly colored, handwoven woolen poncho is worn over the bolero, or sometimes thrown over the shoulder. The man wears fringed leggings and high, pointed leather boots with large decorative spurs. He wears a flat, wide-brimmed straw or, sometimes, a fancy leather hat. Women wear a straight black skirt with a slit from which can be seen layers and layers of white lace. She wears a white blouse, a black bolero jacket, and a hat like her partner's.

In the folk version of the *cueca*, the man wears rural work pants with a shirt open at the neck with the sleeves rolled up. He wears the traditional woven straw hat and boots or sandals, depending on what part of the country is being represented. As in the more formal costume, the man will wear a short, colorful poncho. The woman wears a dress gathered at the waist with a round collar and lace at the cuffs. The dress may be plaid or flowered, with white lace underneath.

Another popular dance is the *refalosa*. In this dance, scarves are also used, but the typical movements are sliding, rather than stamping, as in the *cueca*. Other dance traditions in Chile are those originating on Easter Island that feature pelvic thrusting, and the skimming dances characteristic of the fishing villages of the area of Chiloe.

Traditional Music Chileans in the United States continue a social tradition called *peña*, which consists getting together to play and listen to music and commonly includes telling long jokes and enjoying food. For many years during the military regime of Pinochet, Violeta Parra, a well-known Chilean composer and singer, lived in a tent in Santiago and held a famous *peña* every weekend. She wanted Chileans to return to their traditional folk music and instruments, rather than merely to copy songs from the United States or other countries. Under her influence, many young musicians, some of whom later immigrated to the United States, began to play traditional Chilean folk music. They used instruments such as the *quena*, a small Indian flute, and a stringed instrument from the Andes Mountains. In the United States, a *peña* is sometimes held in a local restaurant on a certain evening of the week. Chileans bring their guitars and other instruments; everyone enjoys the singing and the fellowship.

One type of folk music that Chile shares with Bolivia and Peru is Andean music. Chilean-born René Iribarren plays Andean music in the United States with a group called Alborada, or "dawn." Iribarren, who plays ten different instruments, is the composer for the group.

Holidays Chileans celebrate Independence Day on September 18th. On that day in 1810, *criollos* (settlers born in Chile rather than Spain) began their struggle for independence from Spain and set up a government. In Chile fairs are held in cities and towns during the week before and the week after September 18. People build booths with thatched roofs in which to sell food, exhibit crafts, and put on entertainment. In some parts of the United States, Chileans hold similar fairs on Independence Day. There is an annual Independence Day festival in northern Virginia, called *ramada*, referring to the branches that are used to make the booths constructed for the celebration. Visitors to the fair enjoy traditional crafts, sing the national anthem, dance the *cueca*, listen to folk music from the Andes and other parts of the country, and eat plenty of *empanadas*.

Christmas is celebrated in Chile on December 25, just as it is in the United States. Children and adults stay up late on Christmas Eve to eat a big family meal. Some people go to mass. At midnight everyone opens presents, including small children who have stayed up for the event. Chilean Americans have, in general, kept the tradition of opening presents at midnight and allowing children to stay up. Most Chilean Americans also continue the tradition of a relaxed Christmas Day, with perhaps an outing.

Health Care Issues and Practices Public health in Chile has improved in the past twenty years, with falling infant mortality and longer life expectancy. There do not appear to be any special diseases specific to Chileans. Many Chilean Americans believe in the effectiveness of herbal teas for a variety of illnesses. They call such teas *aguita*, which translates to mean "little waters."

FAMILY AND COMMUNITY LIFE

Chileans have strong family ties. Traditionally, the father is the head of the family, but the mother makes many decisions within the home. Chilean women often speak out and take stands on both private and public issues. They have a tradition of being politically, as well as socially, active in their communities. In the United States they are an important part of the self-help and cultural groups that are active in many cities.

Children are taught to give respect to their parents and the elderly. Young boys are typically given more freedom than girls. Teenagers are usually allowed to date by about age 16, with the emphasis on group activities. It is common for children to live at home until they marry. Even after they have families of their own, children often return home to spend Sundays and holidays with their parents. Chilean Americans have kept this strong emphasis on family, though they have assimilated to American culture, particularly regarding how long a single child may remain at home once he or she reaches adulthood.

Gender Roles Machismo, the cult of male superiority and dominance, is still a fact of life in Chile. However, women have more opportunities in comparison to some other Latin countries and recent changes in Chilean social customs reflect an increasingly egalitarian treatment of the sexes. An increasing number of women work outside the home. The majority of these are domestics, but there are also teachers, secretaries, social workers, and other professionals. Women make up 30 percent of the work force. There is some opportunity for women to gain career advancement.

Children frequently have a party for their birthday and another on the day of the saint for whom they were named. Since many children in Chile are named Juan or Juana, St. John's Day is a big day for parties. Chilean American birthdays more closely resemble those of the typical American child, usually celebrated with a small gathering or family dinner on the day of the child's birth. Chilean American children usually have fewer toys than the typical child raised in the United States. Children are more likely to receive gifts of candy than toys from their friends at birthday parties.

Education Chile has one of the best-educated populations in Latin America, with a literacy rate of 94 percent for men and 93 percent for women. Eight years of education are free and compulsory. Chileans value learning and are proud of their educational system; they consider education to be a way to a better life. Parents often urge their children to complete their education before marrying. If their means are limited and they must choose between educating sons or daughters, sons are often chosen. Many Roman

Members of the Chilean community in Hollywood, California, watched the rescue of the Chilean miners with the rest of the world in 2010. Here they celebrate after the miners were released. ZUMA PRESS, INC. / ALAMY

Catholic parents prefer to send their children to religious schools. Several thousand Chilean American students are pursuing degrees in higher education. Although they are enrolled in a wide variety of programs, two particularly popular fields are natural science and engineering. These fields are seen as leading to promising careers. In addition, students are attracted by the well-equipped laboratories and other technical apparatus available at universities in the United States.

Courtship and Weddings Chileans often have two marriage ceremonies, one civil and the other religious. These are frequently performed on different days, with the civil ceremony perhaps several days before the church service. At weddings, the bride traditionally keeps the groom waiting, and she will typically not appear until thirty to sixty minutes after everyone else has arrived at the church. The bride wears white, but the groom seldom wears a tuxedo unless it is a high-society wedding. There is not usually a wedding party; the bride and groom go through the ceremony without attendants. The reception is often a sit-down meal.

EMPLOYMENT AND ECONOMIC CONDITIONS

Many Chileans immigrated to the United States as political exiles during the 1970s and 1980s; these immigrants, as a group, were well educated and highly skilled. After a short period of adjustment, many of them became highly successful professionals in a variety of fields. More recent immigrants, who did not benefit from the same educational background as their predecessors, have had to take low-paying jobs—such as babysitting, construction, and maintenance—in which a lack of fluency in English does not create communication problems. Over time, however, many of these individuals have obtained training in English as well as technical training, helping them improve their economic status.

POLITICS AND GOVERNMENT

The political orientation of Chilean Americans tends to vary with their socioeconomic status and background. Most Chileans of upper-class or business backgrounds favor the Republican Party. Chileans of lower-class backgrounds and those who fled Chile because of Pinochet generally favor the Democratic Party. Since the majority of Chileans have arrived during the past twenty-five years, when membership in labor unions in the United States was declining, and they are not entrenched in manufacturing jobs, Chileans have not been especially active in union politics. Those who have lost their jobs often do not feel comfortable using unemployment benefits; they have a strong desire to support themselves. Second-generation Chilean Americans, born and raised in this country, are becoming more involved in the issues of domestic Latino politics. Few Chilean Americans have been active in the military, but this will change as more native-born children grow up.

Chilean-born Isabel Allende (1942–) is the author of the novel *House of Spirits*, as well as a number of other well-received works of fiction and memoirs. J. COUNTESS / GETTY IMAGES

The Chilean Americans who came to the United States during the California gold rush and their descendants took a strong interest in events in Chile. During the War of the Pacific in the nineteenth century, local organizations in California raised considerable money to support the Chilean war effort and help the needy back home. A century later, after the military coup by Pinochet, Chilean Americans took an active part in protesting the repressive actions of his government. A number of writers in exile in the United States centered their work on themes related to political and social conditions in Chile. In addition, local groups raised money to help families of the "disappeared" Chilean citizens who had simply vanished because Pinochet had decreed their death. Beginning in 1974, women in Chile created *arpilleras*, a type of tapestry, to show the cruelty of the Pinochet regime. These could not be sold openly in Chile, but some Americans helped to sell them in the United States as a way of publicizing the human rights violations. Many local groups in the United States continue to raise funds for social programs in Chile.

NOTABLE INDIVIDUALS

Chilean Americans have contributed to American life in many realms, including literature, the arts, science, social science, music, and business.

Academia Arturo Valenzuela is a political scientist and an expert on the political system in Chile. Having worked at both Georgetown University and Duke University, Valenzuela moved from the academic realm to the political when he served as U.S. Deputy Assistant Secretary for Inter-American Affairs under the supervision of President Bill Clinton. In 2009 he was named Assistant Secretary of State for Western Hemisphere Affairs by President Barack Obama.

Art Artistic expression is another strong tradition in Chilean culture. Many Chilean Americans contribute to art, sculpture, and photography in the United States.

Montserrat Castedo (1941–) is an artist and tapestry maker. She places bits of colored fabric, some of which she dyes herself, on a percale background stretched across an easel. Castedo focuses on the theme of peace and harmony in nature. After many years of residence in the United States, she returned to live in Chile but retained her ties with the United States, where her work was exhibited.

Raimundo Rubio (1956–) is a contemporary, avant-garde painter. He uses surrealistic techniques, placing unrelated objects together in the same picture. He comes from a family of Chilean intellectuals; his father and brother are poets. Trained in Chile as a painter, Rubio came to the United States in 1979. Exhibits of his work have appeared in Miami, Washington, D.C., and Spain. In October 1994 he opened a one-person show in New York. Since then, he has continued to show his art regularly, including a 2004 show at the Corcoran Gallery of Art in Washington, D.C., and a 2009 exhibit at New York's Chelsea Hotel.

The sculptor and painter who signs her works with the name Pía (1953–) works mostly with a variety of types of wood but also in stone. She views her work as closely connected to Easter Island, a small land mass with ancient traditions in the Pacific Ocean west of Chile. Photographer Luis Salvatierra (1948–), born in Valparaíso, came to the United States in 1974 because of the military coup. He spent considerable time documenting the Latino community in Washington, D.C. More recently, he has worked at translating Pablo Neruda's poetry into photography.

Business Chileans are also involved in business, some at the national and international level. Andrés Bande (1944–) is a business executive who was born in Santiago who has served as president of Ameritech International, a worldwide telecommunications company based in Chicago. He has also served as executive vice president of US West International, a regional Bell company, which he reorganized and expanded. Bande has been active in organizations for Latinos, including a group that promotes excellence in education.

Literature Much of the work of Chilean American writers is concerned with the plight of those who suffered under the military rule of

Pinochet. Indeed, many of the writers are themselves exiles, voluntarily or involuntarily, from the military regime. Isabel Allende (1942–), whose diplomat father was a cousin of the ousted president, Salvador Allende, is a novelist. After the coup, she participated in getting information out of Chile about those whom Pinochet was torturing. Afterward, fearing for her life, she fled the country, eventually moving to the United States in 1988. Her first novel, *The House of the Spirits*, has been translated into twenty-seven languages and was released as a film in 1994. The novel is loosely autobiographical, drawing on her experiences of being raised by her grandfather and clairvoyant grandmother. Other novels include *Of Love and Shadows, Eva Luna, City of the Beasts*, and *The Island Beneath the Sea*.

Ariel Dorfman (1942–) is a well-known author, journalist, and educator who has lived in exile from Chile for many years. His works include *Last Song of Manuel Sendero, My House Is on Fire, Mascara, Hard Rain*, and a play called *Death and the Maiden*. One of Dorfman's themes is the state of being in exile. Dorfman was the subject of the 2007 documentary *A Promise to the Dead*.

Fernando Alegría (1918–2005) is a poet and novelist and has been a university professor of Spanish American literature. His work reflects his commitment to his Chilean ancestry and to improving the lot of the poor and oppressed. One of his favorite themes is the hero; he published a book about the Mapuchan leader Lautaro (1943). His *Allende: A Novel* is a fictionalized biography of Salvador Allende. His other works include *Chilean Spring* and *The Funhouse*.

Writer and poet Marjorie Agosín (1955–) grew up in Chile and has taught literature at Wellesley College. Her writings express her concern about the social conditions of women and the political repression in Chile. In 2002 the Chilean government gave her the Gabriela Mistral Medal of Honor for Life Achievement. Cecilia Vicuna (1947–), a poet, artist, and political activist, has published sixteen books in the United States. Elena Castedo is an author whose book *Paradise* was one of five finalists for the National Book Award in 1993.

Music Many Chileans also excel in classical music. Pianist Claudio Arrao (1903–1991) was known throughout the world. A child prodigy, Arrao played for the president of Chile when he was only six years old. Later, Arrao went to Germany to study, where he remained for a number of years. In 1941 he moved to New York City and lived there until his death. Arrao traveled throughout the world giving concerts. He is considered to have been one of the most outstanding interpreters of Beethoven's piano music.

A number of other Chilean Americans are classical musicians, including conductors Juan Pablo Tzyuierdo and Maximiliano Valdés. Juan Orrego Salas is a composer and has taught at the Indiana University school of music in Bloomington, Indiana. Roberto Díaz, who comes from a Chilean musical family, has served as first violist for the National Symphony Orchestra at the Kennedy Center in Washington, D.C.

ORGANIZATIONS AND ASSOCIATIONS

Perhaps because large-scale immigration has occurred only since the 1970s and 1980s, relatively late compared to other immigrant groups, Chilean American organizations are local rather than national. Many such groups are oriented toward helping other Chileans with their adjustment to the United States. Some groups raise money to send to Chile to support social or political causes there. Another focus is the sponsorship of dance groups or other cultural activities to educate children and teenagers about Chilean traditions.

La Peña Cultural Center

A community center located in the San Francisco Bay area devoted to promoting peace and cultivating social and cultural awareness. The center was formed in response to the political unrest of Chile's dictatorial government in the late 1970s, and today La Peña is a "safe-haven" for Chilean immigrants.

Paul Chin, Executive Director
3105 Shattuck Avenue
Berkeley, California 94705
Phone: (510) 849-2568
Email: info@lapena.org
URL: www.lapena.org

North American-Chilean Chamber of Commerce

Active since it was founded in 1918, promotes understanding of the political, economic, and regulatory issues for business and trade between Chile and the United States.

Mario J. Paredes, President
866 United Nations Plaza
Suite 4019
New York, New York 10017
Phone: (212) 317-1959
Fax: (212) 758-8598
Email: info@nacchamber.com
URL: www.nacchamber.com

MUSEUMS AND RESEARCH CENTERS

Archives and Special Collections at the Thomas J. Dodd Research Center

It has about 2,500 volumes, including many rare books, about the history, literature, and politics of Chile from the sixteenth to the twentieth century. Located at the University of Connecticut.

Marisol Ramos, Curator of Latin America and Caribbean Collections, Special Collections Department

405 Babbidge Road
Unit 1205
Storrs, Connecticut 06269
Phone: (860) 486-2734
Fax: (860) 486-6100
Email: Marisol.ramos@lib.uconn.edu
URL: doddcenter.uconn.edu/asc/collections/cd/cd_lac
.htm

Organization of American States, Art Museum of the Americas

Includes exhibits of Chilean American artists and sculptors in its Art Museum of the Americas.

Andrés Navia
Art Museum of the Americas
201 18th Street NW
Washington, D.C. 20005
Phone: (202) 458-6016
Fax: (202) 458-6021
Email: artmus@oas.org
URL: www.museum.oas.org

SOURCES FOR ADDITIONAL STUDY

Chilean Writers in Exile: Eight Short Novels, edited by Fernando Alegria. Trumansburg, New York: Crossing Press, 1982.

Eastmond, Marita. *The Dilemmas of Exile: Chilean Refugees in the U.S.A.* Göteborg, Sweden: Acta Universitatis Gothoburgensis, 1997.

Faugsted, George Edward. *The Chilenos in the California Gold Rush.* San Francisco: R and E Research Associates, 1973.

Lopez, Carlos. *Chilenos in California: A Study of the 1850 and 1860 Censuses.* San Francisco: R and E Research Associates, 1973.

Military Rule in Chile: Dictatorship and Oppositions, edited by J. S. Valenzuela and A. Valenzuela. Baltimore: Johns Hopkins University Press, 1986.

Pike, F. B. *Chile and the United States: 1880–1962.* Notre Dame, Indiana: University of Notre Dame Press, 1963.

Romero, Simon. "Mine Saga in Chile Captivates Bolivians." *New York Times*, October 11, 2010.

CHINESE AMERICANS

Ling-chi Wang

OVERVIEW

Chinese Americans are immigrants or descendants of immigrants from China, the third-largest country in the world, which occupies a significant portion of Southeast Asia. The land mass, 3,657,765 square miles (9,700,000 square kilometers), or as big as all of Europe, is bounded to the north by Russia and Mongolia, to the west by Russia and India, to the southwest by the Himalayas, to the south by Indochina and the South China Sea, and to the east by the Yellow Sea and the Pacific Ocean. Three major rivers flow through China: the Huanghe (Yellow) River in the north; the Yangzi in the heartland; and the Zhujiang (Pearl River) in the south. Most (85 percent) of China's land is nonarable, and the rest is regularly plagued by flood and drought.

Today China has a population of 1,343,239,923 people (2011), one-fifth of humanity. Han Chinese make up 91 percent of the population; the remaining 6 percent are made up of the 55 non-Han minorities, the most prominent of whom are the Zhuang, Hui, Uighur, Yi, Tibetan, Miao, Mongol, Korean, and Yao. Each of these minorities has its own history, religion, language, and culture. While China remains a communist nation it has become a major world economic powerhouse and is one of the United States' largest trading partners.

According to the U.S. government, the first Chinese immigrants arrived in 1820, and 325 men arrived in 1849, during the California Gold Rush. By 1852 there were 25,000 immigrants and that number had grown to over 100,000 by 1880. Chinese immigrants provided much of the labor for the Transcontinental Railroad. Most Chinese immigrants came looking for better opportunities and to escape crushing poverty at home. Economic growth in modern-day China has not slowed immigration; actually it has allowed more people to immigrate for education and business opportunities. Throughout the twentieth century, and particularly after a series of economic reforms designed to increase productivity and allow greater participation in the global economy were initiated in the late 1970s, Chinese migrants began leaving the country in large numbers. Today there are an estimated 50 million Chinese living outside of the country, making them the largest immigrant group in the

world. The majority of these "Overseas Chinese" have settled in Southeast Asia, but many live in Europe, Africa, and North America. In 2010, Asians overtook Latinos as the largest group of immigrant arrivals in the United States, and Chinese immigrants made up the largest percentage of all immigrants from Asia at 22.6 percent. These numbers, however, are complicated by the fact that the Census Bureau includes people from Hong Kong and Taiwan, as well as Chinese citizens who were living in other countries in Southeast Asia in their totals.

The 2010 U.S. Census identified 3,794,673 Chinese Americans. Chinese Americans make up 1.2 percent of the total U.S. population. Areas of significant Chinese American population include New York City, San Francisco, Los Angeles, Boston, Washington, D.C., Chicago, Honolulu, and Seattle. Chinese Americans no longer exclusively live in Chinatowns; they are integrated into the larger population.

HISTORY OF THE PEOPLE

Early History Historians have estimated that Chinese civilization began about five thousand years ago in the Huanghe (Yellow River) basin and the middle Yangzi region. Legends have it that Huangdi (the Yellow Emperor) defeated his rival tribes, established the first Chinese kingdom, made himself *tienzi*, or the "Son of Heaven," and invented many things for the benefit of his people, including clothing, boats, carts, medicine, the compass, and writing. Following Huangdi, historians believe that the Xia Dynasty (2100–1600 BCE) was the first dynasty of China and marked the beginning of Chinese history. Xia, weakened by corruption in its final decades, was eventually conquered by a Shang king to the east, who established the Shang Dynasty (1600–1100 BCE). The Shang achievements can be readily seen from the remnants of its spectacular palaces, well-crafted giant bronze cauldrons, refined jade carvings, and massive written records. During the Zhou Dynasty (1100–771 BCE), the Chinese idea of the emperor as the "Son of Heaven" who derived his mandate from heaven, was firmly established. In the highly organized feudal society, the Zhou royal family ruled over hundreds of feudal states.

Beginning in 770 BCE, Chinese history entered two periods of turmoil and war: the Spring/Autumn

(770–476 BCE) and the Warring States (475–221 BCE). During these 550 years, the former feudal states engaged in perpetual wars and brutal conquests. During the same time, China witnessed unprecedented progress in agriculture, science, and technology and reached the golden age of Chinese philosophy and literature. Confucius (551–479 BCE), founder of Confucianism; Laozi (sixth century), the founder of Daoism; the egalitarian Mozi (480–420 BCE); and Han-fei (280–233 BCE), founder of legalism, defined the character of Chinese civilization and made profound and enduring contributions to the intellectual history of the world.

Qin Shi Huangdi of the Qin state finally crushed all the rival states and emerged as the sole ruler of the Chinese empire in 221 BCE. Qin extended the borders of China; imposed harsh laws; completed the Great Wall; built a transportation network; and standardized weights, measures, currency, and, most important, the Chinese writing system. The brutality of his rule soon led to widespread rebellion, and the Qin rule was eventually replaced by the Han Dynasty (206 BCE–220 CE). The Han emperor firmly established the Chinese state under Confucianism and created an educational and civil service system that remained in use until 1911. During this period, China came into contact with the Roman Empire and with India.

During the Sui-Tang era, China traded extensively by land and by sea with the known world, and Islam, Judaism, Zoroastrianism, and Christianity were brought into China. But Tang began to decline toward the end of the eighth century, causing rebellions of warlords from within and invasions from without. After Tang, China was again divided. In 1211 Genghis Khan, a Mongolian leader, began the invasion into China from the north, but the conquest was not completed until 1279 under Kublai Khan, his grandson, who established the Yuan Dynasty (1271–1368) in China. During Mongolian rule, China traded extensively with Europe, and Marco Polo brought China's achievements to European attention.

The decline of the Ming Dynasty (1368–1644) led to the conquest of China for the second time by a foreign power, the Manchu, from the northeast. The Manchu established the Qing Dynasty (1644–1911) and again expanded China's borders. Like the Mongols, however, the Manchu conquerors were also conquered and absorbed by the Chinese. Failed reform within the Qing administration, internal pressure through various organized rebellions, external pressure from the major Western powers, and military defeat by Japan in 1895 all led China to become increasingly isolated and weak. Many Chinese left the country as refugees during this period, settling primarily in countries in Southeast Asia though some also travelled westward in search of economic opportunity.

Modern Era China's isolation was finally broken when the British defeated China in the Opium War (1839–1842), forcing China to open its ports to international trade and exposing China over the next hundred years to Western domination. Under the yoke of imperialism and mounting political corruption and internal unrest, especially the Taiping Uprising, the Qing Dynasty collapsed in a revolution led by Dr. Sun Yat-sen in 1911. During this time significant immigration to the United States began.

The new Republic of China, under the leadership of Sun, his dictatorial successor Chiang Kai-shek, and the Nationalist Party (Guomindang or Kuomintang), proved both weak and corrupt. From the invasion by Japan, which began in 1931, to a strong insurgent movement led by Communist Mao Tse-tung, the Chiang regime was severely undermined and eventually ousted from China in 1949, retreating to Taiwan under U.S. military protection. Mao established the People's Republic of China, free from foreign domination for the first time since the Opium War. His alliance with the Soviet Union in the 1950s, however, led to China's isolation throughout the Cold War. His engagement with U.S. forces in Korea and support of the North Vietnamese in Vietnam made China the enemy of the United States. The United States–China detente was initiated in the historic meeting between President Richard Nixon and Mao Tse-tung and Chou Enlai in 1972. In 1978, under the leadership of Deng Xiaoping, China also undertook a series of bold economic and social reforms. These reforms were aimed at modernizing the country: the government began to actively encourage Chinese students to attend universities in industrialized nations and opened up the nation's economy to trade with the West. In 1979 the United States broke ties with Taiwan and normalized its relations with China, making the United States a major destination for Chinese students and job seekers. Since the end of the Cold War, China has become a major political and economic power in an increasingly economically integrated yet disorderly world.

SETTLEMENT IN THE UNITED STATES

In many respects, the motivations for Chinese to go to the United States are similar to those of most immigrants; some came to the "Gold Mountain" (*Jinshan* in Mandarin or *Gumsaan* in Cantonese), the United States, to seek better economic opportunity, while others were compelled to leave China either as contract laborers or refugees. They brought with them their language, culture, social institutions, and customs, and over time, they made lasting contributions to their adopted country and tried to become an integral part of the U.S. population.

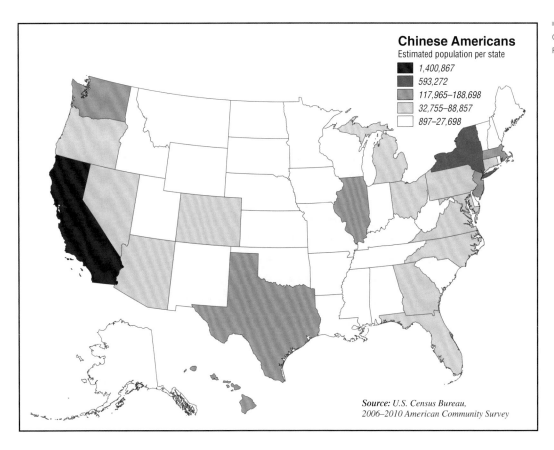

Chinese Americans
Estimated population per state

- 1,400,867
- 593,272
- 117,965–188,698
- 32,755–88,857
- 897–27,698

Source: U.S. Census Bureau,
2006–2010 American Community Survey

However, their collective experience as a racial minority, since they first arrived in the mid-nineteenth century, differs significantly from the European immigrant groups and other racial minorities. Chinese were singled out for discrimination through laws enacted by states in which they had settled; they were the first immigrant group to be targeted for exclusion and denial of citizenship by the U.S. government in 1882. Their encounter with Euro-Americans has been shaped not just by their cultural roots and self-perceptions but also by the changing bilateral relations between the United States and China. The steady infusion of immigrants from China and Taiwan and easy access to traditional and popular cultures from China, Taiwan, and Hong Kong, through telecommunication and trans-Pacific travel, have helped create a new Chinese America that is as diverse as it is fast-changing. Chinese American influence in politics, culture, and science is felt as much in the United States as it is in China, Taiwan, and Hong Kong.

The movement of the Chinese population within China (called the *han*, or *tang*, people in pre-twentieth century China and *huaqiao*, or *huaren*, in the twentieth century), has continued throughout the five-thousand-year history of China. *Huaqiao* (literally, sojourning Chinese), or more accurately *huaren* (persons of Chinese descent), is a term commonly used for Chinese residing outside of China proper or overseas.

Ancient Chinese legends and writings, most notably the fifth-century account by Weishen of a land called Fusang, suggest the presence of Chinese in North America centuries before Christopher Columbus, and a few Chinese were reported to be among the settlers in the colonies on the east coast in the eighteenth century. Significant Chinese immigration to the West Coast of the United States (*Jinshan*) did not begin until the California Gold Rush.

Chinese immigration can be roughly divided into three periods: 1849–1882, 1882–1965, and 1965 to the present. The first period, also known as the first wave, began shortly after the Gold Rush in California and ended abruptly with the passage of the Chinese Exclusion Act of 1882, the first race-based immigration law. During this period, the Chinese could act like other pioneers of the West and were allowed to immigrate or travel freely between China and San Francisco. Thousands of Chinese, mostly young male peasants, left their villages in the rural counties around the Zhujiang, or Pearl River, delta in Guangdong Province in southern China to search for better economic opportunities in in the American West. They found jobs extracting metals and minerals, constructing a vast railroad network, reclaiming swamplands, building irrigation systems, working as migrant agricultural laborers, developing the fishing industry, and operating highly competitive, labor-intensive manufacturing industries in the western states. The temporary nature of some of these jobs, together with the strong anti-Chinese sentiment that greeted them upon their arrival, prevented most of them from becoming permanent settlers. Under these circumstances, most of the laborers had only limited objectives: to advance their own and their families' economic well-being during their sojourn and to return to their ancestral villages to enjoy the fruits of their labor during retirement. At the end of the first period, the Chinese population in the United States was about 110,000, or one-fifth of one percent of the U.S. total.

When Chinese labor was no longer needed and political agitation against the Chinese intensified, the U.S. Congress enacted a series of very harsh anti-Chinese laws, beginning in 1882 with the Chinese Exclusion Act, designed to exclude Chinese immigrants and deny naturalization and democratic rights to those already in the United States. Throughout most of the second period (the period of exclusion; 1882–1943), only diplomats, merchants, and students and their dependents were allowed to travel between the United States and China. Cooperation between China and the United States during World War II brought increased scrutiny to the exclusion of Chinese immigrants and the poor treatment of Chinese Americans by the United States, and led to a loosening or outright repeal of many laws that had affected them. The Chinese exclusion laws were repealed by Congress and Chinese residents were granted the right to naturalization, and 105 Chinese immigrants per year were granted access in 1943. After the war, Chinese American war brides were allowed to enter the country beginning in 1946. Otherwise, throughout this period, Chinese Americans were confined largely to segregated ghettos, called Chinatowns, in major cities and isolated pockets in rural areas across the country. Deprived of their democratic rights, they made extensive use of the courts and diplomatic channels to defend themselves, but with limited success.

The civil rights movement in the 1960s, particularly the enactment of the Civil Rights Act of 1964 and the Immigration and Nationality Act of 1965, finally ushered in a new era, the third period in Chinese American immigration history. Chinese Americans were liberated from a structure of racial oppression. The former legislation restored many of the basic rights denied Chinese Americans, while the latter abolished the racist law that severely restricted Chinese immigration and prevented Chinese Americans from being reunited with their loved ones. Under these new laws, thousands of Chinese came to the United States each year to reunite with their families and young Chinese Americans mobilized to demand racial equality and social justice.

Equally significant are two other types of Chinese immigrants who have been entering the United States since the early 1970s. The first type consists of highly select and well-educated Chinese. No less than 250,000 Chinese intellectuals, scientists, and engineers have come to the United States for advanced degrees. Most of them have stayed to contribute to U.S. preeminence in science and technology. The second type is made up of tens of thousands of Chinese immigrants who have entered the United States to escape either political instability or repression throughout East and Southeast Asia, the result of a dramatic reversal of the U.S. Cold War policies toward China in 1972 and toward Vietnam in 1975. Some of these are Chinese from the upper and middle classes of Taiwan, Hong Kong, and throughout Southeast Asia who want long-term security for themselves, their businesses, and their children. Others are ethnic Chinese from Vietnam and Cambodia who became impoverished refugees and "boat people" when Vietnam implemented its anti-Chinese "ethnic cleansing" policies in 1978. It was this steady infusion of Chinese immigrants that accounted for the substantial increase of the Chinese American population, amounting to 3.7 million in the (2010) census, making them the largest Asian American group in the United States.

Economic development and racial exclusion defined the patterns of Chinese American settlement. Before the Chinese Exclusion Act of 1882, the patterns of Chinese settlement followed the patterns of economic development of the western states. Since mining and railway construction dominated the western economy, Chinese immigrants settled mostly in California and states west of the Rocky Mountains. As these industries declined and anti-Chinese agitation intensified, the Chinese retreated—and sometimes were forced by mainstream society—into small import-export businesses and labor-intensive manufacturing (garments, wool, cigars, and shoes) and service industries (laundry, domestic work, and restaurants) in such rising cities as San Francisco, New York, Boston, Philadelphia, Chicago, Los Angeles, and Seattle; into agriculture in rural communities in California; and into small retail business in black rural communities in the deep South. Some Chinese found themselves systematically evicted from jobs, land, and businesses and their rights, privileges, and sanctuaries in mainstream society permanently suspended. By the early twentieth century, over 80 percent of the Chinese population were found in Chinatowns in major cities in the United States. The concentration of Chinese Americans in Chinatowns further restricted their employment options.

Chinatowns remained isolated and ignored by the American mainstream until after World War II. After the war, as the United States became a racially more open and tolerant society, emigration from the Chinatowns began. With new employment opportunities, a steady stream of Chinese Americans moved into new neighborhoods in cities and into sprawling suburbs, built around the rising military-industrial complex during the Cold War. As the new waves of postwar immigrants arrived, the poor moved into historic Chinatowns and the more affluent settled into new neighborhoods and suburbs, creating the so-called new Chinatowns in cities including San Francisco, Los Angeles, New York, and Houston, and a string of suburbs with strong Chinese American presence, such as the ones along Interstate 10 west of Los Angeles and Highway 101 between San Francisco and San Jose. The new immigrants brought new cultural and economic vitality into both the new and the old communities even as they actively interacted with their Euro-American counterparts.

From interactions under ghetto confinement, to the rise of a suburban Chinese American middle class, to the revitalization of historic Chinatowns, Chinese American communities across the United States have become more diverse, dynamic, and divided, with the arrival of new waves of immigrants creating new conflicts as well as opportunities that are uniquely Chinese American.

The growth and proliferation of the Chinese American population in the last three decades also aroused resentment and hostility in cities and suburbs and in the spheres of education and employment. For example, some neighborhoods and suburbs, most notably San Francisco and Monterey Park, California, tried to curb Chinese American population growth and business expansion by restrictive zoning. Chinese American achievements in education, seen with increasing apprehension in some cases, have led to the use of discriminatory means to slow down or reverse their enrollment in select schools and colleges. Since the early 1980s, there has been a steady increase in incidents of racial violence reported. These trends have been viewed with increasing alarm by Chinese Americans across the United States.

LANGUAGE

Most prewar Chinese arrived in the United States knowing only the various dialects of Cantonese (*Yue*), one of the major branches of Chinese spoken in the Zhujiang delta. The maintenance of Chinese has been carried out by a strong network of community language schools and Chinese-language newspapers. However, with the arrival of new immigrants from other parts of China and the world after World War II, virtually all major Chinese dialects were brought to America. Most prominent among these are Cantonese, Mandarin (Putonghua), Minnan, Chaozhou, Shanghai, and Kejia. Fortunately, one common written Chinese helps communication across dialects.

Today, Chinese is maintained through homes, community language schools, newspapers, radio, and television, and increasingly through foreign language classes at mainstream schools and universities. The rapid increase of immigrants after 1965 also gave rise to growing demand for equality of educational opportunity in the form of bilingual education, a demand that resulted in a 1974 U.S. Supreme Court decision in *Lau vs. Nichols*, a case brought by Chinese American parents in San Francisco. Hand in hand with this trend is the teaching of Mandarin or *Putonghua*, China's national spoken language, in public and community schools.

Greetings and Popular Expressions Cantonese greetings and other popular expressions include: *Nei hou ma?* (How are you?); *Hou loi mou gin* (Long time no see); *Seg zo fan mei?* (Have you eaten?); *Zoi gin* (Good-bye); *Zou tao* (Good night); *Deg han loi co* (Let's get together again); *Do ze* (Thank you); *M'sai hag hei* (Don't mention it); *Gung hei* (Congratulations); and *Gung hei Fad coi* (Have a prosperous New Year).

Mandarin greetings and other popular expressions include: *Ni hao* (How do you do?); *Xiexie* (Thank you); *Bu yong xie* or *Bu yong keqi* (Don't mention it); *Dui bu qi* (Excuse me); *Mei guanxi* (It's okay); and *Zaijian* (Good-bye).

RELIGION

Because the Chinese American community today is very diverse, it is impossible to associate it with a single religion. There are Christians as well as Buddhists, Daoists, Confucianists, Muslims, and atheists. Chinese churches and temples (*miao*) are found wherever there are Chinese Americans. Most of the old temples are found in historic Chinatowns. For example, in San Francisco's Chinatown in 1892, no fewer than fifteen temples were present. Some of the temples were dedicated to the Goddess of Heaven (*Tienhou*)—also the god of seamen, fishermen, travelers, and wanderers—while others were dedicated to Emperor Guangong (*Guandi*), a warrior god. Modern temples, such as the one in Hacienda Heights, California, were built by more recent Chinese immigrants from Taiwan. Likewise, Christian churches catering to specific Chinese dialects are found in old Chinatowns as well as in the suburbs.

The majority of contemporary Chinese Americans could be characterized as irreligious by Western standards of religion. This does not mean, however, that most of them are devoid of any religious feeling or that they do not practice any religion at all. The majority, in fact, practice some form of Buddhism or Daoism, folk religions, and ancestral worship.

Generally speaking, Chinese are pragmatic in their approach to life and religion. Many are somewhat superstitious: they believe in the doctrines of *fengsui*, which are intended to help in the organization of home or business, and they do not want to do anything they personally think is likely to offend the gods or the ways of nature. Toward this end, they choose which deities they want to worship and they worship them through certain objects or locations in nature. They also worship their ancestors, folk heroes,

MAPO TOFU

Ingredients

½ cup low sodium chicken broth

1 teaspoon cornstarch

2 teaspoons soy sauce

1 teaspoon sugar

1 tablespoon sesame oil

2 medium cloves garlic, minced

2 teaspoons ginger, peeled and minced

4 green onions, white part only, minced

1 tablespoon fermented black beans, roughly chopped (black bean paste will also work)

½ teaspoon Sichuan peppercorns, black seeds removed then ground (optional)

6 ounces ground pork

2 teaspoons doubanjiang (chili bean paste)

14 ounce block of silken tofu, drained and cut into ¾-inch cubes

green part of green onions minced for garnish

Preparation

Add the chicken stock, cornstarch, soy sauce and sugar to a small bowl and stir to combine.

Heat a wok or large skillet until hot. Add the sesame oil, garlic, ginger and green onions and stir-fry with a spatula until fragrant. Add the black beans and Sichuan pepper and continue stir-frying.

Add the ground pork and use the spatula to break up all clumps. When the pork is cooked, add the doubanjiang and stir to distribute. Add the tofu, and toss gently to mix.

Stir the stock mixture to incorporate anything that may have settled to the bottom and then pour it over the pork and tofu. Toss to coat, then simmer until the sauce thickens.

Garnish with the green parts of the green onions and then serve with hot rice.

animals, or their representations in idols or images, as if they are gods. To these representations, they offer respect and ritual offerings, burning incense, ritual papers, and paper objects to help maintain order and to bring good luck. This is perhaps why Chinese rarely become religious fanatics, evangelical, or driven to convert others. Above all, Chinese respect other people's religions as much as they respect their own.

Like most ethnic groups in America, Chinese Americans have many unique rituals and moral teachings. Rituals are observed, learned, and practiced at home and in community temples or village ancestral halls. In the absence of ancestral halls in the United States, they perform rituals at miniature altars at home, in their places of business, and in sanctuaries found in district and family associations in Chinatowns. Festivals and important dates in one's family are observed through rituals and banquets. Beliefs or teachings, to most Chinese, are simply ethical wisdom or precepts for living right or in harmony with nature or gods. They are taught through deeds, moral tales, and ethical principles, at home and in temples. Over the centuries, these teachings have combined major ideas and wisdom from Confucianism, Buddhism, and Daoism with local folk religions and village lore.

CULTURE AND ASSIMILATION

Throughout the second half of the nineteenth century and the early decades of the twentieth, Chinatown was a permanent home for the Chinese who were cut off from China and yet disenfranchised from the Euro-American mainstream. Assimilation was never a viable choice for Chinese Americans, who were excluded and denied citizenship because they were deemed nonassimilable by the white mainstream.

In 1852 Governor John Bigler of California demanded Chinese exclusion on the grounds they were nonassimilable. In 1854 the California Supreme Court, in *Hall v. People*, ruled that Chinese testimony against whites was inadmissible in a court of law because "the same rule which would admit them to testify, would admit them to all the equal rights of citizenship; and we might soon see them at the polls, in the jury box, upon the bench, and in our legislative halls." By congressional statutes and judicial decisions, Chinese immigrants were made ineligible for naturalization, rendering them politically disenfranchised in a so-called democracy and exposing them to frequent and flagrant violations of their constitutional rights.

Chinese Americans could not understand how the United States could use gunboat diplomacy to open the door of China and at the same time use democracy to close the door to Chinese Americans. The bitter encounter with American democracy and hypocrisy planted a seed of modern Chinese nationalism, which led the Chinese Americans to fight for equal rights at home and to orient their collective will toward freeing China from imperialist domination. They linked the racial oppression of the Chinese in the United States to the impotence of China.

Life within the Chinatown ghetto, therefore, was hard but not stagnant. Legally discriminated against and politically disenfranchised, Chinese Americans established their roots in Chinatowns, fought racism through aggressive litigation and diplomatic channels, and participated actively in various economic development projects and political movements to modernize China and create avenues for integrating into American society. Despite such efforts, for many members of the American-born generation who made a concerted effort to assimilate, mainstream society remained inhospitable.

In the nineteenth century, most Chinese immigrants saw no future in the United States and oriented their lives toward eventual return to China, called *luoye-guigen* ("fallen leaves return to their roots"). With this sojourner mentality, they developed a high degree of tolerance for hardship and racial discrimination and maintained a frugal Chinese lifestyle, which included living modestly; observing Chinese customs and festivals through family and district associations; sending regular remittance to parents, wives, and children; and maintaining village ancestral halls and charities. Parents tried to instill Chinese language and culture in their children, send them to Chinese schools in the community or in China, motivate them to excel in American education, and, above all, arrange marriages. The parents in Louis Chu's *Eat a Bowl of Tea* (1961) tried to find their son a bride in villages in the Zhujiang delta. For the most part, their sole aspiration was to work hard and save enough to retire in comfort back in the villages from which they came.

They also joined social organizations. District associations (*huiguan*) and family associations (*gongsuo*), respectively, represented the collective interest and well-being of persons from the same villages or counties and persons with the same family names. These ascriptive organizations provided aid and comfort to their members, arbitrated disputes, helped find jobs and housing, established schools and temples, and sponsored social and cultural events. Most of these organizations had branches in different Chinatowns, enabling members to travel from one city to another. Together, these organizations formed the Chinese Consolidated Benevolent Association, a de facto ghetto government, to settle disputes among individuals and organizations and to represent the community's interests with both U.S. and Chinese governments, at times through civil disobedience, passive resistance, and litigation—such as when it urged all resident Chinese citizens to resist registering themselves with the U.S. government under the Geary Act of 1893 and challenged the Act before the Supreme Court—and at other times through diplomatic channels and grassroots protests instigated in China. Their activities brought mixed blessings to the community. At times, these organizations became too powerful and oppressive, and they also obstructed social and political progress. Without question, they left an enduring legacy in Chinese America.

Outside groups also engaged with the early Chinese American community, often in the hopes of furthering their own agendas. Into these uniquely American ghettos came a string of Protestant and Catholic missionaries, establishing churches and schools and trying to convert and assimilate the Chinese, as well as a steady stream of political factions and reformers from China, advancing their agendas for modernizing China and recruiting Chinese Americans to support and work for their causes. Both were agents of change, but they worked on different constituencies and at cross purposes: one tried to assimilate them, while the other tried to instill in them a cultural and political loyalty to China.

Virtually all major Christian churches established missions and schools in San Francisco's Chinatown, the largest in the United States and the center of cultural, economic, and political life of Chinese in North America. Among the most enduring institutions were the YMCA and YWCA, the St. Mary's Chinese Mission School, and the Cameron House, a Presbyterian home for "rescued" Chinese prostitutes. The churches, in general, were more successful in winning converts among the American-born generation.

Proportionally smaller in number, those Chinese Americans who were exposed to a segregated but American education very quickly became aware of their inferior status. Many became ashamed of their appearance, status, and culture. Self-hatred and the need to be accepted by white society became their primary obsession. In practice this meant the rejection of their cultural and linguistic heritage and the pursuit of thoroughgoing Americanization: adoption of American values, personality traits, and social behaviors and conversion to Christianity.

Denying their racial and cultural identity failed to gain them social acceptance in the period before World War II. Most found themselves still shut out of the mainstream and were prevented from competing for jobs, even if they were well qualified. Some were compelled to choose between staying in the United States as second-class citizens and going to China, a country whose language and culture had, ironically, become alien to them on account of their attempted assimilation.

For the immigrant generation, there was only one choice: staking their future in China. China's modernization occupied their attention and energy because they attributed their inferior status in the United States to the impotence of China as a nation under Western domination. Reformers from opposing camps in China invariably found an eager audience and generous supporters among the Chinese in the United States. Among the political reformers who frequented Chinatowns across the United States to raise funds and recruit supporters were Kang Youwei, Liang Qichao, and Sun Yat-sen before the 1911 Revolution. During the Sino-Japanese War (1937–1941), several leaders of the ruling Kuomintang also toured the United States to mobilize Chinese American support; among them were General Cai Tingkai and Madame Chiang Kai-shek. The factional dispute between the pro-China and pro-Taiwan forces is very much a part of this political legacy. In essence, China's political factionalism became an integral part of Chinese American life.

Due in part to the efforts of the missionaries and political reformers, many churches and political parties were established, and sectarian schools and newspapers catering to the Chinese American community soon followed. Schools and newspapers became some of the most influential and enduring institutions in Chinese America. Together they played an important role in perpetuating the Chinese culture among the Chinese and in introducing Chinese Americans to ideas of modernity and nationalism.

Cuisine Chinese tea was a moderately popular beverage in eighteenth- and nineteenth-century America. Since the 1960s, Chinese cuisine has been an integral part of the American diet as well. Chinese restaurants are found in small towns and large cities across the United States. Key ingredients for preparing authentic Chinese dishes are now found in all chain supermarkets, and lessons in Chinese cooking are regular features on national television. Chinese takeout, catering, and chain restaurants have become commonplace in major cities, and Chinese *dim sum*, soups, stir-fries, and pastas can be found in cocktail lounges and exclusive clubs and resorts. Less popular today are such pre-1960 dishes as chop suey, chow mien, egg foo yung, and barbecue spareribs. In fact, many Americans have mastered the use of chopsticks and acquired the taste for sophisticated Chinese regional cuisines, such as Cantonese, Kejia (Hakka), Sichuan (Szechuan), Shangdong, Hunan, Mandarin (Beijing), Taiwan (Minnan), Chaozhou (Teo-Chiu), and Shanghai. American households now routinely use Chinese ingredients such as soy sauce, ginger, and hoisin sauce in their food; employ Chinese cooking techniques, such as stir-frying; and include Chinese cooking utensils, like the wok and the cleaver, in their kitchens.

Clothing Very few Chinese Americans (or Chinese, for that matter) now wear traditional Chinese clothing, which is generally characterized by brightly colored, embroidered silk shirts, pants, or dresses. On special occasions, some traditional costumes are worn. For example, on her wedding day, a bride might wear a Western wedding gown for the wedding ceremony and then change into a traditional Chinese wedding gown, called *qun kwa*, for the tea ceremony and banquet. In some traditional families, the elders sometimes wear traditional Chinese formal clothes to greet guests on Chinese New Year's Day. Young Chinese American women sometimes wear the tightly fitted *cengsam* (*chongsam*), or *qipao*, for formal parties or banquets. Occasionally, Chinese styles find their way into American high fashion and Hollywood movies.

Dances and Songs Chinese opera and folk songs are performed and sung in the Chinese American community. Cantonese opera, once very popular in Chinatown, is performed for older audiences, and small opera singing clubs are found in major Chinatowns in North America. Rarer is the

CHINESE PROVERBS

A great number of Chinese proverbs have been recorded throughout history, several of which have been adapted into American culture. Some examples of Chinese proverbs include:

Shui zhang chuan gao

When the tide rises, boats float higher

Tong chuang yi meng

Same bed, different dreams

Xie nong yu shui

Blood is thicker than water

Zao qi de niao er you chong chi

The early bird catches its prey

Shu neng sheng qiao

Practice makes perfect

Chen er da tie

Strike while the iron is hot

Hai na bai chuan

All rivers run into the sea

performance of Peking opera. Among the well-educated Chinese, concerts featuring Chinese folk and art songs are well attended and amateur groups singing this type of music can be found in most cities with significant Chinese American populations. Similarly, both classical and folk dances continue to find some following among Chinese Americans. The Chinese Folk Dance Association of San Francisco is one of several groups that promote this activity. Most American-born Chinese and younger new immigrants, however, prefer either American popular music or Cantonese and Mandarin popular music from China, Taiwan, and Hong Kong.

Holidays Most Chinese Americans today observe the major holidays of the Chinese lunar calendar (*yin li*). Today, Chinese calendars routinely provide both the solar (*yang li*) and lunar calendars, and Chinese daily newspapers provide both kinds of dates. The most important holiday is the Chinese New Year or the Spring Festival (*chun jie*), which is also a school holiday in San Francisco.

Family members get together for special feasts and celebrations. The Feast of the Dead (*qing ming* or *sao mu*), the fifteenth day of the third lunar month, is devoted to tidying tombs and worshiping ancestors. The Dragon-boat Festival (*duan wu* or *duan yang*), on the fifteenth day of the fifth lunar month, commemorates the death of renowned poet Qu Yuan, who threw himself into the River Milu Jiang in 277 BCE.

Usually a dragon-boat race is held and a special dumpling (*zong zi*) is served. For the August Moon Festival (*zhong jiu*), the ninth day of the eighth lunar month, family and friends gather to admire the moon and eat "moon cakes" (*yue bing*).

The founding of the People's Republic of China (*guo qing jie*), October 1, 1949, is observed by Chinese Americans with banquets and cultural performances in major cities in the United States. Likewise, the founding of the republic by Dr. Sun Yat-sen on October 10, 1911, is commemorated each year in Chinatowns by groups closely associated with the Nationalist government in Taiwan.

Health Care Issues and Practices Prewar housing and job discrimination forced the Chinese to live within American ghettos. Discrimination also denied Chinese Americans access to health care and other services. Most relied on traditional Chinese herbal medicine, and the community had to found its own Western hospital, Chinese Hospital in San Francisco, in the early twentieth century. By the time the postwar immigrants arrived in large numbers in the 1960s, Chinatowns were bursting at the seams, burdened with seemingly intractable health and mental health problems.

Chinatowns in San Francisco and New York City are among the most densely populated areas in the United States. Housing has always been substandard and overcrowded. Throughout the 1960s and 1970s, Chinatown in San Francisco had the dubious distinction of having the highest tuberculosis and suicide rates in the United States. High unemployment and underemployment rates exposed thousands of new immigrants to severe exploitation in sweatshops and restaurants. School dropouts, juvenile delinquency, and gang wars were symptoms of underlying social pathology.

However, health and mental health problems are not confined to the Chinatown ghettos. The overwhelming majority of Chinese Americans no longer

Confetti is blown into the air during the Chinese New year celebration in New York City's Chinatown. OOTE BOE 3 / ALAMY

live in historic Chinatowns, as mentioned above. While many of the health and mental health-related problems in Chinatown are class-based, many others, such as the language barrier, cultural and generational conflict, and attitudes toward illness and soliciting help, are peculiar to Chinese Americans regardless of their class position, education, and place of residence. Mental health service agencies, like the Richmond Maxi Center in the middle-class Richmond district of San Francisco, and the Asians for Community Involvement in the Silicon Valley of California, have been established to meet the needs of Chinese Americans and other Asian Americans. Today, both Chinese and Western medicines are widely used by Chinese Americans, although some use exclusively Chinese medicine while others use only Western medicine.

FAMILY AND COMMUNITY LIFE
Since most Chinese who immigrated before 1882 came as itinerant laborers to perform specific tasks, the Chinese population in the United States in the nineteenth century consisted of predominantly young men, either not yet married or married with their wives and children left in the villages in southern China. According to the 1890 census, there were 107,488 Chinese in the United States. Of these, 103,620, or 96.4 percent, were boys and men and only 3,868, or 3.6 percent, were girls and women. Among the male population, 26.1 percent were married, 69 percent single, and 4.9 percent were either widowed or divorced. The male-female ratio would not be balanced until 1970, and has since tipped toward women, with the 2011 American Community Survey reporting that 55 percent of Chinese Americans are female.

Today, most middle-class Chinese Americans place the highest priority on raising and maintaining the family: providing for the immediate members of the family (grandparents, parents, and children), acquiring an adequate and secure home for the family, and investing comparatively greater amounts of time and annual income in their children's education.

The uneven sex distribution in the early years of Chinese immigration gave rise to an image of Chinatown as a bachelor society, vividly captured in the pictures taken by Arnold Genthe in San Francisco before the 1905 earthquake and in the description by Liang Qichao during his 1903 travel to the United States. The abnormal conditions also contributed to widespread prostitution, gambling, and opium smoking, most of which were overseen by secret societies, known as *tongs*, often with the consent of both the Chinatown establishment and corrupt local

law-enforcement agencies. The struggle for control of these illicit businesses also gave rise to frequent intrigues, violence, and political corruption and to sensational press coverage of the so-called tong wars.

The exclusion and anti-miscegenation laws forced most Chinese in the United States to maintain their families across the Pacific. Only men in the privileged merchant class were able to bring over their wives and children. Under such circumstances, the Chinese population in the United States declined steadily, dipping as low as 61,639 in 1920 before it started to rise again. The Chinese American population therefore had to wait until after World War II for the emergence of an American-born political leadership. Normal family life for most Chinese Americans also did not begin until after World War II, when several thousand Chinese American GIs were eligible to bring their wives and children to America under the War Bride Act. While the reunification of Chinese American families after the war led to a brief period in which American-born Chinese Americans outnumbered those born in foreign countries, the massive influx of Chinese immigrants beginning in the 1970s once again reversed this ratio. Unlike the prewar immigrants, however, these new immigrants came to the United States with their families, and they came to stay permanently.

Nevertheless, it is wrong to assume that all Chinese Americans are living in happy, intact, successful families and raising obedient, motivated, and college-bound children. Traditional Chinese concepts of family and child-rearing, for both rich and poor, have undergone drastic changes in the United States due to job status, income levels, living arrangements, and neighborhood conditions, as well as the social and cultural environment of the United States. Chinese Americans face their share of family break-ups, domestic violence, school dropouts, drug addiction, gang activities, and other social problems. According to a 2008 study by the University of Maryland, "A Chinese American Portrait," the divorce rate among Chinese Americans is around half that of the general population, but some researchers suggest this is because immigrants from Asia, and particularly women, value family and a sense of community over personal fulfillment, making them more likely to remain in unhealthy relationships, even when there are instances of domestic abuse.

Education Today, most middle-class Chinese Americans place the highest priority on raising and maintaining the family: providing for the immediate members of the family (grandparents, parents, and children), acquiring an adequate and secure home for the family, and investing comparatively greater amounts of time and annual income in their children's education. Even among lower-income families with neither financial security nor decent housing, keeping the family intact and close and doing all they can to support their children are also priorities. This is why Chinese Americans continue to perform well in education across all income levels, even if the success rates among the poor are less impressive than those among the better off. Across the nation, Chinese American educational achievement is well known. In particular, Chinese Americans are disproportionally represented among the top research universities and the elite small liberal colleges. In graduate and professional schools, they are overrepresented in certain areas, but underrepresented in others. In addition to Chinese American students, there are thousands of Chinese foreign students from China, Taiwan, and Hong Kong.

EMPLOYMENT AND ECONOMIC CONDITIONS

Before the 1882 Chinese exclusion law, Chinese enjoyed relative autonomy in their employment choices. However, with the rise of anti-Chinese movements and the enactment of anti-Chinese laws, Chinese were effectively driven out of most jobs and businesses competitive with whites. Until World War II, Chinese were left with jobs in laundries, Chinese restaurants, sweatshops, gift shops, and grocery stores located in Chinatowns. Even those who were American-born and college educated were unable to find jobs commensurate with their training.

World War II was a turning point for Chinese Americans. Not only were they recruited into all branches of military service, they were also placed in defense-related industries. In spite of racial prejudice, young Chinese Americans excelled in science and technology and made substantial inroads into many new sectors of the labor market during the war. Two significant developments during this era changed the fortune of Chinese Americans. First, the rise of the military-industrial complex during the war created opportunities for Chinese Americans in defense-related industries. Around thirteen thousand Chinese Americans served in the military during the war, enough that entire units such as the 407th Air Service Squadron and the 987th Signal Company of the 14th Air Force's so-called Flying Tigers were made up entirely of Chinese Americans. Second, there was the arrival of many highly educated Chinese immigrants from China, Taiwan, and Hong Kong after the war, whose talents were immediately put to use in leading research centers and universities.

In general, the intellectual immigrants settled in middle-class suburbs near new industrial or research centers, such as Silicon Valley in Santa Clara County, California, and NASA Johnson Space Center outside of Houston, Texas. Likewise, pockets of affluent Chinese Americans can be found in such metropolitan areas as Seattle, Minneapolis, Chicago, Los Angeles, Pittsburgh, San Diego, and Dallas. Since the 1970s, some even used their talents to start their own businesses in the highly competitive high-tech industries. Among the best known are An Wang of Wang Laboratories, David Lee

A father and daughter celebrate the Year of the Dragon during Chinese New Year celebrations, 2012, in New York City's Chinatown. DAVID GROSSMAN / ALAMY

of Qume Corporation, Tom Yuen of AST, and Charles Wang of Computer Associates International. Many of the intellectual-immigrants also became leading scientists and top engineers in the United States, giving rise to the false impression that the prewar oppressed Chinese working class had finally pulled themselves up by their own bootstraps. This is the misleading "model minority" stereotype that the media originated and has fiercely maintained since the late 1960s. These highly celebrated intellectuals, in fact, have little politically, economically, or socially in common with the direct descendants of the prewar Chinese communities in big cities.

Among the post-1965 immigrants were also thousands who came to be reunited with their long-separated loved ones. Most of them settled in well-established Chinese American communities in San Francisco, New York, Boston, Chicago, Philadelphia, Oakland, and Los Angeles where they became the new urban working class. Many also became small entrepreneurs in neighborhoods throughout these cities, concentrating mostly in laundries, restaurants, and grocery stores. In fact, their presence in these three areas of small business has made them an integral part of the cityscape of American cities. Usually with little or no English, they pursued their "American dream" by working long hours, often with free or cheap labor from relatives.

The Chinese American population is, therefore, bifurcated between the poor (working class) and the middle class (professionals and small business owners). The interests of these two groups coincide with each other over such issues as racism and access to quality education, but most of the time they are at odds with each other. There is much debate over the China-Taiwan conflict, and, regarding housing and employment, their relations are frequently those of landlord-tenant and management-labor, typified by the chronic struggle over land use (e.g., the International Hotel in San Francisco's Chinatown) and working conditions in Chinatowns (e.g., the Chung Sai Sewing

Factory, also in San Francisco's Chinatown) since 1970. Nevertheless, as a whole, Chinese Americans remain among the highest-educated and highest-earning ethnic groups in America. The 2011 American Community Survey found the median household income of Chinese Americans to be $58,710, around $8,000 higher than the total U.S. population.

POLITICS AND GOVERNMENT

Unlike European immigrants and African Americans since the Civil War, Chinese immigrants were denied citizenship, systematically discriminated against, and disenfranchised until after World War II. Numerically far smaller than European Americans and African Americans, Chinese Americans posed no political threat to the entrenched power, even after they were granted the right of naturalization after the war. They were routinely denied, de jure and de facto, political and civil rights through biased hiring practices, routine discrimination based on persistent stereotypes, and a general disregard for their property rights through widespread gentrification of Chinatown districts. It was not until the late 1960s, under the militant leadership of younger Chinese Americans, that they began to mobilize for equal participation with the help of African Americans and in coalition with other Asian American groups.

Three key elements shaped the formation and development of the Chinese American community: racism, U.S.-China relations, and the interaction between these two forces. The intersection of American foreign policy and domestic racial politics compelled Chinese Americans to live under a unique structure of dual domination. They were racially segregated and forced to live under an apartheid system, and they were subject to the extraterritorial domination of the Chinese Nationalist government, condoned, if not encouraged at times, by the U.S. government. Chinese Americans were treated as aliens and confined to urban ghettos and governed by an elite merchant class legitimated by the U.S. government and reinforced by the omnipresent diplomatic representatives from China. Social institutions, lifestyles, and political factionalism were reproduced and institutionalized. Conflict over homeland partisan disputes—including the dispute between the reform and revolutionary parties at the beginning of the twentieth century and between the Nationalists led by Chiang Kai-shek and Communists led by Mao Tse-tung in China—kept the community deeply divided. Such divisions drained scarce financial resources and political energy from pressing issues within the community and left behind a legacy of preoccupation with motherland politics and deep political cleavage to this date. During the Cold War, the extraterritorial domination intensified, as military dictators in Taiwan, backed by the United States, extended their repression into the Chinese American community in an effort to ensure political loyalty and suppress political dissent.

The African American civil rights movement inspired and inaugurated a new era of ethnic pride and political consciousness. Joined by other Asian American groups, American-born, college-age Chinese rejected both the racist model of forced assimilation and the political and cultural domination of the Nationalist government in Taiwan. They also rejected second-class citizenship and the option of returning to Asia. Instead, they demanded liberation from the structure of dual domination. These college students and, later, young professionals contributed most significantly to raising the ethnic and political consciousness of Chinese Americans and helped achieve civil rights. Furthermore, they founded many social service agencies and professional, political, and cultural organizations throughout the United States. They also joined forces with other Asian American college students to push for the establishment of Asian American studies programs in major universities and colleges across the nation.

The politicization of Chinese Americans soon led to the founding of new civil rights and partisan political organizations. Most notable was the founding of Chinese for Affirmative Action (CAA) in San Francisco in 1969, a civil rights organization that has been at the forefront of all major issues—employment, education, media, politics, health, census, hate crime, etc.—affecting Chinese Americans across the nation. By the 1970s, two national organizations, the Organization of Chinese Americans (OCA) and the National Association of Chinese Americans (NACA), were formed in most major cities to serve, respectively, middle-class Chinese Americans and Chinese American intellectuals. Likewise, local partisan clubs and Chinese American Democrats and Republicans were organized to promote Chinese American participation in politics and government.

By the 1980s, some middle-class Chinese Americans began to take interest in local electoral politics. They have enjoyed modest success in races for less powerful positions, such as school boards and city councils. Among the notable political leaders to emerge were March Fong Eu, secretary of state of California; S. B. Woo, lieutenant governor of Delaware (1984–1988); Michael Woo of the Los Angeles City Council (1986–1990); and Thomas Hsieh and Mabel Teng of the San Francisco Board of Supervisors in 1988. In 2001 Elaine Chao became the first Chinese American to serve as a member of the cabinet when she was appointed by President George W. Bush. Gary Lock became the first Chinese American governor when he was elected by the state of Washington; he is currently the U.S. ambassador to China.

With increased interest in electoral politics came the demand for greater participation in other branches of government. In 1959 Delbert Wong became the first Chinese American to be appointed a municipal judge in Los Angeles. In 1966 Lim P. Lee was appointed postmaster of San Francisco, and Harry Low, a municipal judge. Low was later appointed to the Superior Court and the California Appellate Court. Also appointed to the municipal bench were Samuel Yee, Leonard Louie, Lillian Sing, and Julie Tang in San Francisco and Jack Bing Tso, James Sing Yip, and Ronald Lew in Los Angeles. Thomas Tang was appointed to the Ninth Circuit Court in 1977 and Elwood Lui to the federal district court in 1984.

Chinese Americans have been predominantly an urban population since the late nineteenth century. Their community has long been divided between the merchant elites and the working class, and the influx of both poor and affluent immigrants since the late 1960s has deepened the division in the community by class, nativity, dialect, and residential location, giving rise not to just conflicting classes and public images but also to conflicting visions in Chinese America. The sources of this open split can be traced to the changes in U.S. immigration laws and Cold War policies and to the arrival of diverse Chinese immigrants from China, Taiwan, Hong Kong, and Southeast Asian countries throughout the Cold War. The division has had serious political and social consequences as Chinese Americans from opposing camps seek political empowerment in cities with a deeply entrenched white ethnic power structure and emerging African American forces.

NOTABLE INDIVIDUALS

Literature Maxine Hong Kingston (1940–) and Amy Tan (1952–) have captured the imagination of the United States with their writings based in part on their personal experiences and stories told in their families. Kingston is best known for *The Woman Warrior* (1976), *Chinamen* (1977), and *Tripmaster Monkey* (1989), while Tan is known for *The Joy Luck Club* (1989) and *The Kitchen God's Wife* (1991). Gish Jen (1955–) is the author of four novels, including *Typical American*, and a collection of stories called *Who's Irish?*, that offer nuanced explorations of the experiences of Asian Americans. Other prominent Chinese American fiction writers include David Wong Louie (1954–), author of *Pangs of Love* and *The Barbarians Are Coming*, and Faye Myenne Ng (1956–), whose novels *Bone*) and *Steer Toward Rock* have been widely lauded. Equally successful in the world of Chinese-language readers are literary works written in Chinese by Chinese American writers such as Chen Ruoxi, Bai Xianyong, Yu Lihua, Liu Daren, and Nie Hualing, who are also widely read in Hong Kong, Taiwan, China, and Southeast Asia.

Science and Technology Chinese Americans who have received Nobel Prizes include.

Charles Kao (1933–), Chen-ning Yang (1922–), Daniel Tsui (1939–), and Steven Chu (1948–) in physics and Roger Tsien (1952–) and Yuan-tse Lee (1936–) in chemistry. In mathematics, Shiing-shen Chern (1911–2004), Sing-tung Yao (1949–), and Terence Tao (1975–) are ranked among the top in the world. In the biological sciences, the leading American researcher in superconductivity research is Paul Chu (1941–). In engineering, T. Y. Lin (1912–2003), structural engineer, received the Presidential Science Award in 1986. Others include Chang-Lin Tien (1935–2002), a mechanical engineer and chancellor of the University of California, Berkeley; Henry Yang (1940–), an aerospace engineer and the chancellor of the University of California, Santa Barbara; and Steven Chen (1978–), the leading researcher on the next generation of supercomputers. Among Chinese American women with national and international reputations in science is physicist Chien-Hsiung Wu (1912–1997).

In March 1997, Wen Ho Lee (1939–), an atomic scientist at the Los Alamos National Laboratory near Albuquerque, New Mexico, was arrested on suspicion of spying for China. Wen Ho Lee was fired for unspecified security violations, but in early May 1999, federal officials revealed that Wen Ho had transferred secret nuclear weapons computer programs from the Los Alamos computer system to his own desktop computer. Wen Ho denied the charges that he was a spy and claimed that he let no one see the nuclear weapons computer program. In a prepared statement issued on May 6, 1999, Wen Ho said he would "not be a scapegoat for alleged security problems at our country's nuclear laboratories" and denied that he ever gave classified information to unauthorized persons.

Theater David Henry Hwang (1957–) Genny Lim (1946–), and Frank Chin (1940–) have all made lasting contributions to the theater. Among the best-known plays of Hwang are *FOB*, *The Dance and the Railroad*, *Family Devotions*, and *M. Butterfly*. Lim is the author of the play *Paper Angels* and is also a poet and children's book author. Though perhaps best known as a controversial critic and champion of Asian American literature, Chin is also the author of numerous influential novels and plays, including *The Year of the Dragon*.

Film Director, producer, screenwriter, and editor Wayne Wang (1949–) has made a number of critically acclaimed and commercially successful movies, including *Chan Is Missing*, *Dim Sum*, *Eat a Bowl of Tea*, and *The Joy Luck Club*.

Music Saxophonist and composer Fred Ho is both a prominent figure in the American jazz scene and an activist for Asian American causes. Jon Jang (1954–) is a San Francisco-based composer who is perhaps best known for his *Chinese American Symphony*, a work that honors the Chinese laborers who built America's first transcontinental railroad.

Visual Arts Besides their enormous contributions to science and technology, many Chinese Americans also excel in art and literature. Maya Ying Lin (1959–) is already a legend in her own time. At twenty-one, while an architecture student at Yale University, she created the Vietnam Veterans Memorial in Washington, D.C., one of the most frequented national monuments. After this enormous success, she went on to design the Civil Rights Memorial in Atlanta, a giant outdoor sculpture commemorating the history of women at her alma mater, and a monumental sculpture at the New York Pennsylvania Railroad Station.

Just as impressive are the architectural wonders of I. M. Pei (1917–). Among his best known works are the East Wing of the National Art Gallery in Washington, D.C., the John F. Kennedy Library at Harvard University, the Boston Museum and the John Hancock Building in Boston, Dallas Symphony Hall, the modern addition to the Louvre in Paris, the Bank of China in Hong Kong, and the Xiangshan Hotel in Beijing.

Anna Sui (1955–), a native of Detroit, is a famous Chinese American fashion designer. Known for her stylistic versatility, Sui has dabbled in everything from 1960s fashion to formal evening wear.

MEDIA

PRINT

Chinese American Forum (CAF)

Founded in 1982, this quarterly magazine cultivates understanding among U.S. citizens of Chinese American cultural heritage.

C. C. Tien, President
P.O. Box 3034
Seattle, Washington 98114
Phone: (206) 523-4984
Email: cctien@juno.com
URL: http://caforumonline.org/

Chinese characters and their English translation.
ROBERTLAMPHOTO / SHUTTERSTOCK.COM

Sampan

The only bilingual newspaper in New England serving the Asian community.

Ling Mei Wong, Editor
87 Tyler Street
5th Floor
Boston, Massachusetts 02111
Phone: (617) 426-9492
Fax: (617) 482-2316
Email: editor@sampan.org
URL: www.sampan.org

Sing Tao Daily

Founded in Hong Kong in 1938, this newspaper opened its American office in San Francisco in 1975. The company also operates a popular Chinese language radio network.

Tim S. Lau, Vice President
5000 Shoreline Court
#300
South San Francisco, California 94080
Phone: (650) 808-8800
Fax: (650) 808-8801
URL: www.singtaousa.com

World Journal

Formerly Chinese Daily News, this Chinese-language daily newspaper as affiliated with the Taiwanese United Daily News.

Shihyaw Chen, Editor
1588 Corporate Center Drive
Monterey Park, California 91754
Phone: (213) 268-4982
Fax: (213) 265-3476
URL: www.worldjournal.com

RADIO

Multicultural Radio Broadcasting, Inc. (MRBI)

Founded in 1982, MRBI operates three AM stations in Los Angeles (KAZN-AM1300, KAHZ-AM1600 and KMRB-AM1430), two AM stations in New York (WZRC-AM1480 and WKDM-AM1380), and one AM station in San Francisco (KEST-AM1450) that produce original programming in Chinese (Mandarin and Cantonese) for the Chinese-American population in those cities.

27 William Street
11th Floor
New York, New York 10005
Phone: (212) 966-1059
Fax: (212) 966-9580
URL: www.mrbi.net

TELEVISION

Crossings TV

Operating in Sacramento, Fresno, and Stockton, California, as well as in New York, Crossings broadcasts programming in Chinese and other Asian languages.

2030 West El Camino Boulevard
Suite 263
Sacramento, California 95833-1868

Phone: (888) 901-5288
Fax: (888) 878-8936
Email: info@crossingstv.com
URL: www.crossingstv.com

LA 18

On air since 1977, LA 18 serves Southern California's culturally diverse, multilingual community, providing a unique assortment of news, sports, drama, and entertainment programs aired in thirteen different languages, including Chinese.

1990 South Bundy Drive
Suite 850
Los Angeles, California 90025
Phone: (310) 478-1818
Fax: (310) 479-8118
Email: info@la18.tv
URL: www.la18.tv

WMBC

Broadcasting in parts of New York and New Jersey, WMBC includes a variety of news, sports and entertainment from China, Korea, Latin America and India.

Mountain Broadcasting Corp
99 Clinton Road
West Caldwell, New Jersey 07006
Phone: (973) 852-0300
Fax: (973) 808-5516
Email: cc@wmbctv.com
URL: www.wmbctv.com

KTSF

KTSF, which has been serving the San Francisco Bay Area Asian community since 1976, provides quality news, information and entertainment programming and reaches over 1.4 million Chinese and other Asian Americans.

100 Valley Drive
Brisbane, California 94005
Phone: (415) 468-2626
Fax: (415) 467-7559
URL: www.ktsf.com

ORGANIZATIONS AND ASSOCIATIONS

Chinese American Citizens Alliance (CACA)

A national organization founded early in the twentieth century to fight for Chinese American rights, with chapters in different Chinatowns.

Collin Lai, President
1044 Stockton Street
San Francisco, California 94108
Phone: (415) 982-4618
Email: info@cacanational.org
URL: www.cacanational.org

Chinese Consolidated Benevolent Association (CCBA)

The most powerful Chinese American organization in America, the CCBA is largely considered the voice of the Chinese American community.

Ted Win Wong
843 Stockton Street

San Francisco, California 94108
Phone: (415) 982-6000
Fax: (415) 982-6010
Email: info@ccbausa.org
URL: www.ccbausa.org

Chinese for Affirmative Action (CAA)

The leading civil rights organization of Chinese in the United States.

Vincent Pan, Executive Director
17 Walter U. Lum Place
San Francisco, California 98108
Phone: (415) 274-6750
Email: info@caasf.org
URL: www.caasf.org

Organization of Chinese Americans (OCA)

A national organization committed to promoting the rights of Chinese Americans, with chapters throughout the United States and a lobbyist office in Washington, D.C. Publishes newsletter *OCA Image*.

Daphne Quok, Executive Director
1001 Connecticut Avenue NW
Suite 707
Washington, D.C. 20036
Phone: (202) 223-5500
Fax: 202-296-0540
Email: oca@ocanational.org
URL: www.ocanational.org

MUSEUMS AND RESEARCH CENTERS

Center for Chinese Studies (University of Michigan)

Promotes and supports research in social sciences and humanities relating to China, past and present, by faculty members, graduate students, and associates of the center.

Dr. Ernest P. Young, Director
1080 South University
Suite 3668
Ann Arbor, Michigan 48109-1106
Phone: (734) 764-6308
Fax: (734) 764-5540
Email: chinese.studies@umich.edu
URL: www.umich.edu/iinet/ccs/index.html

Chinese Culture Center of San Francisco

A community-based cultural and educational facility, this organization provides space for exhibits, performing arts, conferences, classrooms, and meetings.

Manni Liu, Acting Executive Director/Curator
750 Kearney Street
3rd Floor
San Francisco, California 94108
Phone: (415) 986-1822
Fax: (415) 986-2825
Email: info@ccc.org
URL: www.ccc.org

Chinese Historical Society of America

Devoted to the study of the Chinese people in the United States and the collection of their relics.

Ethnic and historical interests of the society are published in its bulletin.

Philip Choy, President
965 Clay Street
San Francisco, California 94108
Phone: (415) 391-1188
Fax: (415) 391-1150
Email: info@chsa.org
URL: www.chsa.org

Museum of Chinese in America (MOCA)

Founded in 1980 as the New York Chinatown History Project; adopted its present name in 1995. Strives "to reclaim, preserve, and broaden understanding about the diverse history of Chinese people in the Americas." Included is the most extensive collection of Chinese-language newspapers in the United States.

215 Centre Street
New York, New York 10013
Phone: (212) 619-4785
Email: info@mocanyc.org
URL: www.mocanyc.org

SOURCES FOR ADDITIONAL STUDY

Chang, Iris. *The Chinese in America: A Narrative History*. New York: Viking, 2003.

Kwong, Peter. *Chinatown, NY: Labor & Politics, 1930–1950*. New York: Monthly Review Press, 1979.

Lowen, James W. *The Mississippi Chinese: Between Black and White*. Cambridge, MA: Harvard University Press, 1971.

Ma, L. Eve Armentrout. *Revolutionaries, Monarchists, and Chinatowns: Chinese Politics in the Americas and the 1911 Revolution*. Honolulu: University of Hawaii Press, 1990.

McClain, Charles. *In Search of Equality: The Chinese Struggle Against Discrimination in Nineteenth-Century America*. Berkeley and Los Angeles: University of California Press, 1994.

Nee, Victor G., and Brett de Barry. *Longtime Californ': A Documentary Study of an American Chinatown*. New York: Pantheon Books, 1972.

Wong, Kevin Scott. *Americans First: Chinese Americans and the Second World War*. Cambridge, MA: Harvard University Press, 2005.

Wong, Kevin Scott, and Sucheng Chan, eds. *Claiming America: Constructing Chinese American Identities During the Exclusion Era*. Philadelphia: Temple University Press, 1998.

Yung, Judy, Gordon H. Chang, and Him Mark Lai, eds. *Chinese American Voices: From the Gold Rush to the Present*. Berkeley: University of California Press, 2006.

Zinzius, Birgit. *Chinese America: Stereotype and Reality*. New York: Peter Lang, 2005.

CHOCTAWS

D. L. Birchfield

OVERVIEW

Choctaws are Native Americans who traditionally lived in what today is part of the southeastern United States. Before 1820 Choctaw territory encompassed more than 23 million acres, primarily in present-day Mississippi, and extended into sections of present-day Alabama and Louisiana. A Choctaw legend traces the origin of the Choctaw to Nanih Waiya, an ancient earthwork mound located in east-central Mississippi near the town of Noxapter. (The name *Nanih Waiya* can be translated as "productive mound.") The etymology of the name *Choctaw* is uncertain. One theory is that it derives from the word *chahta*, meaning "flat head," and might be related to the practice once followed by the Choctaw of flattening the forehead of boy infants by means of a strapped board.

In the mid-eighteenth century the Choctaw population was estimated to be about 20,000. The Choctaw had come together as a people from three or more major independent groups sometime between the mid-sixteenth to the late seventeenth centuries. Although the Choctaw were an agricultural people, their economy also relied on trade.

Today Choctaws live primarily in the states of Oklahoma and Mississippi. In Oklahoma the Choctaw Nation encompasses ten and one-half counties in the southeastern part of the state, and in Mississippi the Choctaw live on several noncontiguous blocks—together larger than the state of Massachussetts—that are located primarily in east-central Mississippi. The Choctaw people ended up in Oklahoma because of a series of forced removals by the United States government from 1831 to 1834. About 11,500 Choctaw were removed to present-day Oklahoma, but an estimated 6,000 individuals remained in Mississippi. The primary populations of Choctaw today are descendants of these two groups.

According to the American Community Survey administered by the U.S. Census Bureau, 195,764 Choctaw citizens resided in the United States in 2010, a number comparable to the population of Little Rock, Arkansas. Of this number, about 127,000 have membership in the Choctaw Nation of Oklahoma, which has headquarters in Durant, Oklahoma. The population of the Mississippi Band of Choctaw Indians is estimated at around 10,000 people. Much of the Choctaw population maintains a distinctive identity through its affiliation with these two groups, but there are also Choctaw communities in Alabama, California, Arkansas, Louisiana, and Texas.

HISTORY OF THE PEOPLE

Early History According to one Choctaw legend about their origins, the first people to appear upon the earth emerged from deep beneath the earth's surface through a cave near the sacred mound Nanih Waiya. They draped themselves on bushes around the cave to dry themselves in the sunshine, and then moved far away. Many others followed the same pattern, making their homes closer and closer to the cave. Some of the last to emerge were the Choctaw's closest neighbors—the Cherokees, Creeks, and Natchez. Finally, the Choctaw emerged and established their homeland around Nanih Waiya. (Today, Nanih Waiya is a park owned and administered by the Mississippi Band of Choctaw Indians.)

Another Choctaw legend holds that the Choctaw migrated to the site of Nanih Waiya after a great long journey from the Northwest. During this migration, a sacred pole was planted in the ground every evening. In the morning the Choctaw would find the pole leaning in a direction that they would then follow for that day's journey. Finally, they awoke one morning to find the pole standing upright. According to the legend, they then built Nanih Waiya on that site and made their home there.

Archaeologists believe that Nanih Waiya was constructed as long ago as 400 BCE, but it is not known whether there is an ancestral connection between the Choctaw and extensive mound-building cultures that once flourished in North America. These cultures constructed approximately 100,000 mounds from the Great Lakes to the Gulf of Mexico, some of which are among the most colossal structures of antiquity. The base of the Great Temple Mound near Cahokia, Illinois, for example, covered an area three acres larger than that covered by the Great Pyramid of Egypt.

After the arrival of Europeans on the North American continent, the Choctaw were heavily influenced by their practices of trading. With the establishment of Louisiana by the French in 1700, the Choctaw were the pivotal Indian nation with whom the French had to maintain good relations for the security of the Louisiana colony. The French were helped immeasurably in this regard by the depredations of English slave raiders who operated out of the Carolinas and took thousands of Choctaw into slavery in the early eighteenth century.

Choctaw relations with other Indians in the region were greatly affected by the presence of the French. In the 1730s the French waged a war of extermination against the Natchez, close neighbors of the Choctaw. The surviving Natchez fled to the Chickasaws for protection, and the Choctaw were drawn into a war against the Chickasaws that would rage on and off until the French left Louisiana.

The Choctaw experienced a devastating civil war from 1747 to 1750. The Choctaw were divided between those who wanted to maintain trade relations exclusively with the French and those who wanted to enter into trade relations with the English. Along with the removal of the Choctaw to the west, the civil war ranks as one of the most catastrophic events in recorded Choctaw history.

After the French were expelled from North America in the 1760s, the Choctaw maintained relations with the British and Spanish, both of whom courted their allegiance. One result of the Choctaw civil war was that the Choctaw became very cautious, skilled diplomats at dealing with European colonial powers, an attribute of Choctaw political life that would carry over to dealings with the Americans.

In 1786, after the American Revolutionary War, the Choctaw entered into their first formal treaty with the United States—a treaty of peace and friendship. In the second treaty between the Choctaw and the U.S. government, in 1801, the Americans secured Choctaw permission to build a wagon road through the Choctaw Nation. Shortly afterward, Americans began appearing in Choctaw country in increasing numbers and demanding land by treaty, with a frequency that alarmed the Choctaw. In 1805, at the negotiations for the Treaty of Mount Dexter, the Americans began pressuring the Choctaw to accept President Thomas Jefferson's idea of removing themselves to new homes west of the Mississippi River.

Despite these pressures, the Choctaw maintained friendly relations with the United States. In 1811 the Choctaw expelled the Shawnee chief Tecumseh from their nation when he tried to enlist them in his Indian confederacy, and they fought against the Red Stick faction of the Creeks in the ensuing war between the United States and the Creeks, who had chosen to join Tecumseh's alliance. The Choctaw war chief Pushmataha led 800 Choctaw troops who became a part of General Andrew Jackson's army. Despite Choctaw loyalty, the United States demanded further land cessions in 1816.

Modern Era In a 1820 agreement called the Treaty of Doak's Stand, the Choctaw agreed to cede to the United States a large portion of their remaining land east of the Mississippi River for land west of the river, primarily in the western part of present-day Arkansas, but the Choctaw continued to live on their remaining ancestral lands. In 1830, to accommodate an ever-growing number of settlers, the U.S. government under Andrew Jackson passed the Indian Removal Act, which affected all the Native Americans in the southeastern United States. The federal government also set up a new treaty with the Choctaw that superseded previous treaties with the Choctaw. Known as the Treaty of Dancing Rabbit Creek, it ceded all the remaining land held by the Choctaw east of the Mississippi River for land in Indian Territory (in what is today the state of Oklahoma), and it established the general terms of the removal of the Choctaw to the West.

The Choctaw were the first Indians to be removed as a nation by the U.S. government to new land in the West. The removal was accomplished for the most part in three successive, brutal winter migrations during which 2,500 Choctaws died, many from exposure and starvation. The newly created Bureau of Indian Affairs was in charge of the removal in 1831. The government decided that the removal had been too costly, even though by the terms of the removal treaty the Choctaw were to pay the cost of removal out of profits from the sale of their lands in Mississippi. The U.S. Army was placed in charge of the 1832 and 1833 removals, and it cut costs by severely reducing both rations and blankets. When the Choctaw ran out of food and attempted to purchase supplies, the citizens of Arkansas reacted by raising the price of corn. By 1834, some 11,500 Choctaws had been removed to the West.

About 6,000 Choctaws remained in Mississippi. By the terms of Article 14 of the removal treaty, they were to be allowed to choose individual land holdings of 640 acres for each head of household, 320 acres for children over the age of ten, and 160 acres for younger children. However, only 69 Choctaw heads of households were allowed to register for land in Mississippi. Finding themselves dispossessed of everything they owned, they became squatters in their former land.

The Choctaw who survived the journey to Indian Territory soon recovered from the trauma of removal and established a republic that flourished for a generation. During this generation of peace and prosperity, the Choctaw Nation built a stable economy, established its own public-school system, governed itself under its own laws.

The Choctaw remained largely free from the encroachments of the advancing American frontier until they were caught between warring Americans factions and drawn into the American Civil War. At its outbreak, the Union removed its troops from Indian Territory, leaving the Choctaw defenseless and surrounded by Confederates. In addition, a small percentage of the population, predominantly wealthy mixed-blood Choctaw, owned slaves and grew cotton for the Southern market. Therefore, the Choctaw entered into formal diplomatic relations with the Confederacy, at which point the United States considered the Choctaw to be in rebellion.

In 1866, following the Union victory, the Choctaw were forced to sell a portion of their land holdings in Indian Territory, according to their final treaty with the United States. Under the treaty, the Choctaw also adopted a new constitution, which was patterned after the American form of government. The most profound effect of the treaty was its granting of a railroad right of way through their remaining land. Like the right of way for a wagon road through Choctaw lands in the early part of the century, the railroad right of way allowed Americans to flood into Choctaw land. By 1890 the Choctaw were outnumbered by Americans by more than three to one. The Americans did not have the right to own land, were not allowed representation within the Choctaw Nation, and were not allowed to send their children to the Choctaw public schools. However, they were required to pay taxes, which the Americans considered intolerable. Rather than move elsewhere, they clamored for Congress to abolish the Indian nations.

Congress, for its part, had already decided that the U.S. government no longer needed to enter into treaties with Indian nations and that it would legislate Indian affairs. Under the auspices of the Dawes Commission, the government spent three years attempting to pressure the Choctaw and other Indians into agreeing to allot their lands to individuals. Finally, under the threat that Congress would allot the lands for them, the Choctaw negotiated and signed the Atoka Agreement of 1897, which provided for the allotment of the tribal estate. In 1906, enrollment of tribal members for allotment was closed by the Congress, and in 1907 the Choctaw Nation was absorbed into the new state of Oklahoma.

For the Choctaw in Oklahoma, allotment proved to be disastrous. Within a generation, most of the allotted land passed from Choctaw ownership to white ownership, often by fraudulent means, and many Choctaw fell to an impoverished standard of living.

Meanwhile, the U.S. government had virtually ignored the Choctaw who had remained in Mississippi. Then, in 1908 and 1916, Congress commissioned studies on their condition. The Mississippi Choctaw had remained isolated, living on the margins of the dominant society for generations, and some had even moved to swamp land, where they lived as furtive refugees. Nevertheless, the Choctaw had retained their language and culture, and they were provided with a small reservation near Philadelphia, Mississippi.

During the tenure of President Franklin D. Roosevelt, the Indian Reorganization Act of 1934 was passed in an attempt to counter some of the negative effects of allotment. Although the outcome of reorganization resulted in a patchwork of Native American territory—based on the way that individual land owners held plots in a haphazard pattern across tribal territories—it did allow the U.S. government to purchase around 2 million acres of land that could be distributed to Native American tribes.

Not long after the passage of this act, however, the U.S. government shifted its approach and it sought to end the protective relationship it had with Native American tribes. The government removed federal assistance and funding that had been allocated to Native American tribes, and it began a policy of legally terminating tribes. Under this arrangement, members of tribes that were terminated would receive full U.S. citizenship. In addition, they would became subject to paying U.S. taxes and the U.S. government would gain control of natural resources that had been on the lands previously controlled by the Native American tribes.

The Choctaw were slated for termination through legislation that was passed by Congress in 1959. Many Choctaws vigorously protested termination, despite their chief's support of the process. By 1970 they succeeded in having the termination legislation repealed. The tribe then began efforts, which were eventually successful, to have its constitution from the 1860s recognized as a valid document. In 1984, after reorganizing the constitution, the Choctaw Nation of Oklahoma established its independent governance structure, which was based on that of the U.S. federal government. The Mississippi Band of Choctaw Indians adopted a similar structure.

After a period of economic difficulties, the Mississippi Band of Choctaw Indians has become financially successful, lowering an unemployment rate from 70 percent in 1997 to below 3 percent in 2007. The group is now one of the largest employers in Mississippi. The Choctaw Nation of Oklahoma has been similarly successful, as it has over 6,000 employees with seven casinos, as well as other industrial and production companies.

SETTLEMENT IN THE UNITED STATES

In the mid-eighteenth century the Choctaw were a well-established group in North America, with an estimated population of 20,000 people living in more than 100 agricultural centers. Choctaw territory encompassed more than 23 million acres in present-day Mississippi as well as portions of Alabama and Louisiana. In the first decades of the nineteenth century, the U.S. government pressured the Choctaw and other Native Americans in the southeastern United States to relocate west of the Mississippi River. In the early 1830s, following the U.S. Indian Removal Act and the Treaty of Dancing Rabbit Creek between the U.S. government and the Choctaw, the majority of the Choctaw who were living in Mississippi were relocated

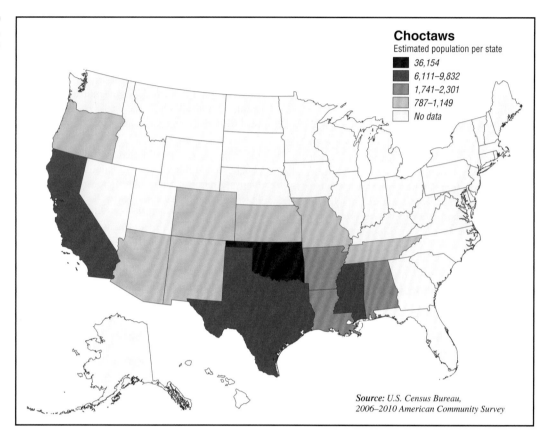

Choctaws
Estimated population per state

- 36,154
- 6,111–9,832
- 1,741–2,301
- 787–1,149
- No data

*Source: U.S. Census Bureau,
2006–2010 American Community Survey*

to lands in what later became the state of Oklahoma. By 1834, some 11,500 Choctaw had been removed to the west, but about 6,000 Choctaws remained in Mississippi.

Throughout the nineteenth century, some of the Choctaws remaining in Mississippi continued to move west to the Choctaw Nation established in Indian Territory (Oklahoma). In the early twentieth century, however, the Choctaw in Mississippi were granted their own land in the east-central part of the state. Today the Choctaw Nation is divided into separate governmental jurisdictions, each operating under its own constitution. The largest of these, which are formally recognized by the U.S. government, are the Choctaw Nation of Oklahoma, with a membership of about 127,000, and the Mississippi Band of Choctaw Indians, which a membership estimated at about 10,000. Choctaw communities also exist in Alabama, California, Arkansas, Louisiana, and Texas.

LANGUAGE

Linguists classify the Choctaw language as Muskogean, and they theorize that at some time in the past the Choctaw and other native peoples of the Southeast who speak Muskogean languages all formed part of the same group. The language of the Alabamas of the Muskogee Confederation (Creeks) is still identifiably Choctaw, although it is a distinctive dialect. The Chickasaw language is so similar to Choctaw, that linguists surmise that the separation of the two occurred relatively recently.

Language is also a key to gaining some understanding of how influential the Choctaw were among the native people of North America at the time of early European contact. Ancient trading paths radiated throughout the continent, facilitating commercial intercourse between greatly distant peoples. A pidgin version of the Choctaw language called Mobilian was used along many of the trading paths as the universal medium of trade communication among an assortment of diverse peoples. The trading paths were spread over a vast region that encompassed most of what is now generally referred to as the South and extended to other areas.

Attempts made by missionaries to preserve the Choctaw language contribute to the predominance of one dialect over others, especially among those Choctaw who were removed to the West. The missionaries used the Okla Falaya dialect of the Choctaw language to translate ancient myths of the Hebrews for hymns and other proselytizing materials, which in time made the Okla Falaya dialect the standard dialect of the Choctaw language among the Choctaw who were removed to the West. Within twenty years after the missionaries' arrival among the Choctaw, their printing activity had become feverish. In 1837 alone, Presbyterian minister Cyrus Byington published 576,000 pages of text in the Choctaw language. The effect was comparable to the way in which the printing activity of Thomas Caxton helped to make the dialect of London the standard dialect of the English language.

According to the American Community Survey administered by the U.S. Census Bureau, in the Choctaw Nation of Oklahoma, a majority of households speak English only. English is also the dominant language spoken in general. Other languages spoken include Spanish, other Indo-European languages, and Asian and Pacific Island languages. In the Choctaw population in general, 80 percent of households speak English exclusively, 12 percent also have some household members that speak another language, and 7 percent of households are made up of persons who all speak a language other than English. One percent of households is considered linguistically isolated: these households do not have a member over the age of fourteen who speaks only English or who speaks English "very well."

Attempts are made in schools to maintain usage of the Choctaw language. In the tribal schools, new personnel are provided with a class to help them become familiar with the language. In addition, the school system also offers programs that celebrate traditional Choctaw festivities and teachers are strongly encouraged to integrate Choctaw-specific content into their implementation of the curriculum.

Greetings and Popular Expressions Some common Choctaw phrases (written using "modern" orthography) include the following: *Chahta*—Choctaw; *Halito!*—Hello!; *Chi pisa la chike!*—See you later!; *Yakoki*—Thank you; *Chi hohchifo yat nanta?*—What is your name?; *Sa hohchifo yat …*—My name is …; *A*—Yes; *Kiyo*—No; *Ohmi*—Okay; *Ak akostinincho.*—I don't understand; *Ak ikháno.*—I don't know; *Chahta imanompa ish anompola hinla ho_?*—Do you speak Choctaw?; *Yammat nanta?*—What is that?

RELIGION

In terms of their celebrations of life, the Choctaw had a large ceremony—the Green Corn Festival, which would take place in the summer. A feast would begin the ceremony, followed by a general cleansing of both public spaces and private living areas. The tribes would then fast for a forty-eight-hour period, and during this period conflicts would be discussed in a social arena. At the conclusion of the period, a fire would be lit that was considered symbolic of a purifying cleanse. This fire would then be extinguished, and a tribal spiritual leader would light a new fire, at which time people donned their most beautiful apparel for eating and dancing.

CULTURE AND ASSIMILATION

During the early part of the twentieth century, Native Americans were treated as outsiders by the U.S. government, especially when established Indian nations or territories that had been legally set aside for Native Americans stood in the way of westward expansion and American "progress." This trend can be tracked through narratives such as that written by historian Angie Debo in the 1930s. She discusses the plight of Native Americans in *And Still the Waters Run: The Betrayal of Five Civilized Tribes* (1940). This book focuses on the treatment of Native Americans in Oklahoma in particular and details the fraudulent acquisition of Indian land by people then prominent in Oklahoma politics. Debo reported that the dispossession of Indian land allotments was often achieved under the guise of guardianship.

Over the course of much of the twentieth century, the trend of projecting and presenting Native Americans as being inferior citizens was perpetuated. For example, in common U.S. vernacular speech, Americans usually referred to Indians in the past tense and as being apart from contemporary American culture. For most of the twentieth century, the media in Oklahoma, for example, ignored Indians altogether, with the exception of an occasional piece deploring high rates of alcoholism among Indians or focusing on Indian dances as a means of attracting tourist dollars to the state.

The Indian Reorganization Act of 1934 granted Native Americans certain rights that they had previously been denied. During the mid-twentieth century, however, the federal government took steps that undermined the act. As a result of the belief that Native Americans could become more productive members of society if they were assimilated into U.S. society, the federal government began a long-term process of taking control of areas previously controlled by Native Americans. Ostensibly, Native Americans were granted full U.S. citizenship; however, these steps simultaneously terminated federal funds they had received in prior years.

The policy of terminating Native American tribes stretched from the 1940s until the 1960s. By the end of this period, however, there was heightened national awareness of the treatment of Native Americans. Increased levels of alcoholic abuse and domestic violence and neglect were present in many Native American communities, and many lacked access to health care, education, and basic survival necessities.

The Choctaw Nation had, in general, attempted to assimilate itself into mainstream American culture. Historically, the Choctaw had been a people who adopted practices of groups with whom they came into contact if they thought the practices might prove beneficial to their own lives and existence. Legislation to terminate the Choctaw tribe was passed in 1959, at the behest of the Choctaw chief Harry Belvin. Despite his support for termination, many Choctaw actively resisted the idea. Organizations such as the Choctaw Youth Movement formed a dynamic political movement designed to oppose the termination legislation, and the legislation was ultimately repealed in 1970 before termination took effect. The movement also sparked a sense of pride among the Choctaw.

Court rulings in the late 1980s allowed Indian nations to operate gambling facilities on tribal land. As Americans witnessed the new found prosperity of Indian nations, and many recognized the presence of Indian nations for the first time, the Indian nations have achieved a new visibility in American culture. Although the independent nations of the Mississippi Band of Choctaw Indians and the Choctaw Nation of Oklahoma have prospered financially, numerous infrastructural and institutional challenges remain in the twenty-first century, based on the decades during the majority of the twentieth century in which Native Americans lived under persecuted and marginalized conditions.

Traditions and Customs Observers have characterized the Choctaw attitude toward life as one that illustrates their belief that they do not exist for the benefit of any political, economic, military, or religious organization. The Choctaw also did not favor spectacular ceremonies, religious or otherwise, showing a nearly complete lack of public display, except in the area of oratory and diplomacy.

The Choctaw relished and excelled in public oratory, causing some observers to draw comparisons between the Choctaw communities and the small republics of Greek antiquity. When an occasion for public debate presented itself, a large brush arbor was constructed with a hole in the center of the roof. Whoever wanted to speak stood beneath the hole in the full heat of the Mississippi sun while the audience remained comfortably seated in the shade. The Choctaw said they could bear to listen as long as the speaker could bear to stand in the heat and speak.

Oratory skill provided an avenue to upward mobility in Choctaw society. Each district chief appointed a *tichou mingo* as the official spokesperson. The *tichou mingo* had a more visible presence in official life than did the chief. Choctaw chiefs were also skilled orators, however, and the war chief Pushmataha of the Okla Hannali was the most persuasive Choctaw public speaker of his generation. In open debate, Pushmataha persuaded the Choctaw not to join Tecumseh when Tecumseh visited their country seeking their enlistment in his pan-Indian alliance in 1811. The debate was witnessed and later recalled by John Pitchlynn, United States interpreter to the Choctaw.

Ball play, called *ishtaboli*, was traditionally an important social event in the life of the Choctaw. Men and women had teams, and when two villages met on the field of play, every item of any value in the villages was riding on the outcome. The object of the game was to sling a ball made of sewn skins from the webbed pocket at the end of a *kapucha* stick—a slender, stout stick made of hickory—and propel it so that it struck an upright plank at the end of the playing field, which was often a mile long or longer. There were dozens of players on each side, and there appeared to be no rules. Whatever means one might employ to stop the progress of the opponent toward the goal, including tackling, was allowed. The games demonstrated great skill at handling, throwing, and

At a an outdoor arena in Phoenix, a Choctaw man dances in a colorful costume with a large feather headdress for the benefit of tourists. BUDDY MAYS / CORBIS

passing a ball, but the rough game often resulted in serious injury or death, for which there was no punishment. Today a version of *ishtaboli*, called stickball, is still played by the Choctaw.

Customs and traditions like oratory and ball play as part of the Choctaw heritage continue to be discussed and even enacted in Choctaw schools and other arenas. Faculty are encouraged to become familiar with the Choctaw nation and culture, and in making new hires for schools, preference is given to applicants with some knowledge of the Choctaw heritage. Students can learn the Choctaw language at all levels of education, from kindergarten through the university level. Online classes are also offered for students interested as adults. Since about 1980 through the first decades of the twenty-first century, increased efforts have been made to resuscitate and preserve Choctaw cultural practices such as stickball. Native dances are also taught to the young, and the Choctaw Nation of Oklahoma in particular keeps a list of practicing Choctaw artists knowledgeable in traditions such as beadwork, basket making, and wood carving.

Cuisine Choctaw cuisine includes dishes that the Choctaw have traditionally prepared using ingredients generally based on foods that were indigenous to the regions in which the Choctaw lived. One notable traditional dish is *tamfula*, which is made from cornmeal, chicken broth, pinto beans, green chilies, turkey breast or other meat, onions, sweet peas, and sometimes hickory nuts. The dish is then typically prepared by boiling it for hours or even days. Traditional staples include maize, from which corn meal and corn bread is made; sunflower seeds, and various kinds of beans. *Banaha* Indian bread is made by wrapping cornmeal in corn shucks and boiling them. The diet of some groups has also traditionally included wild sweet potatoes and foods made from acorns and various types of berries. Many Choctaws enjoy fry bread, hunter's stew, wild onions with eggs, and polk salad greens.

Traditional Dress The traditional dress for Choctaws originally was dependent upon the types of garments that could be readily constructed from materials available to the Choctaw, such as buckskin or other animal hides. Women typically wore simple skirts and shirts that resembled modern blouses, and men wore breechcloths. When the weather was cooler, the men might also wear leggings insulated with animal fur. A shirt somewhat similar to women's blouse-like garments was also sometimes worn by men.

As the Choctaw were exposed to new materials through trade, they started constructing clothes from cotton. Women added shawls to their outfits when they needed extra warmth. By the early 1800s the Choctaw had adopted a style influenced by the clothing of arriving settlers. Choctaw women wore longer skirts and dresses that were flowing and unconstricting. They

HOMASSATUBBEE'S 1801 SPEECH

A brief speech by Homassatubbee, district chief of the Okla Tanap, was recorded by the Americans at the negotiations for the Treaty of Fort Adams in 1801:

> I understand our great father, General Washington, is dead, and that there is another beloved man appointed in his place, and that he is a well-wisher of us. Our old brothers, the Chickasaws, have granted a road from Cumberland as far south as our boundary. I grant a continuance of that road which may be straightened. But the old path is not to be thrown away entirely, and a new one made. We are informed by these three beloved men that our father, the President, has sent us a yearly present of which we know nothing. Another thing our father, the President, has promised, without our asking, is that he would send women among us to teach our women to spin and weave. These women may first go among our half-breeds. We wish the old boundary which separates us and the whites to be marked over. We came here sober, to do business, and wish to return sober and request therefore that the liquor we are informed our friends have provided for us may remain in the store.

added aprons and head scarf coverings as accessories. As manufactured clothing became more widely available, the Choctaw gradually started wearing these garments. In the twenty-first century, Choctaws follow general fashion trends and their clothing is essentially the same as that of mainstream Americans. For special ceremonies, however, they still wear handmade clothing (such as brightly colored and ruffled ceremonial dresses worn with decorative white aprons) and handmade accessories (such as earrings, necklaces, and ornamental combs).

Dances and Songs Traditional Choctaw festivities included many activities, especially dances. The early Choctaw also used dances to prepare for battle. During social dances, tribal musicians played traditional instruments such as the Choctaw drum and dance sticks. Generally, a song would be defined by the rhythm of a chant and the rise and fall of a chanter's voice. Frequently, chants were linked syllables used to carry a melody. Many songs communicated elements of Choctaw heritage, such as stories that were told and passed down through generations. Other songs were attached to specific symbolic rituals, such as the snake dance.

In general, dances emphasized participation rather than achieving some sort of refined performance, and they were considered to be a type of entertainment similar to ball games. Songs and dance reflect Choctaw pride and serve as a way to bring together a community. They also demonstrate the strong spirit of cooperation evident in Choctaw culture, as in the way Choctaw dance leaders interact with the dancers.

In the twenty-first century, many performing dance troupes in Mississippi and Oklahoma sustain and preserve knowledge and performance of these dances and songs, although the two groups differ somewhat in the way they perform and celebrate dances.

Holidays The premiere annual event of the Mississippi Choctaw is the Choctaw Indian Fair, a four-day event in July. Established in 1949, the fair draws more than 20,000 visitors each year and features the Stickball World Championship, national entertainers, and traditional Choctaw costumes and food. The fair continues to be held, and it is sponsored by the Mississippi Band of Choctaw Indians.

The largest annual celebration in the Oklahoma nation is the four-day Labor Day celebration at Tuskahoma, which dates from the early 1900s and now draws thousands of Choctaws each year. It includes a viewing of the tribal buffalo herd; softball, horseshoe, volleyball, and checkers tournaments; national entertainers; a mid-way carnival and exhibition halls featuring dozens of crafts booths; a parade; and the state-of-the-nation address by the principal chief. Several scholarship princess pageants are also held in association with this festival, which continued to prosper in the early decades of the twenty-first century.

In 2008 the Mississippi Band of Choctaw Indians was able to obtain the deed to the site of Nanih Waiya, the sacred mound that figures prominently in their legends of origin. The occasion is celebrated annually on the second Friday of August as Nanih Waiya Day, with festivities and traditional customs such as dancing and oration.

FAMILY AND COMMUNITY LIFE

Historically, the geographic divisions among Choctaw tribes were roughly decided according to the crests of watersheds. The villages of the Okla Falaya (Long People) lived along the headwaters of the Pearl River on the western side of the nation. On the eastern side of the nation, along the headwaters of the Noxubee River, lived the Okla Tanap (People of the Opposite Side). The villages of the Okla Hannali (The Six Town People) were along the headwaters of the Chickasawhay River at the southern side of the nation.

The Okla Falaya's relations with the Chickasaws, their nearest northern neighbors, were more congenial than those of other Choctaw divisions. Likewise, the Okla Tanap were generally on good terms with their eastern neighbors, the Muskhogean-speaking Alabamas of the Muskogee Confederation, and the Okla Hannali enjoyed frequent contact with the Indians around Mobile Bay. In addition, the Choctaw had chiefs within their nation who served as spokesmen and apologists to neighboring tribes. Called *fanni mingoes*, or squirrel chiefs, they provided individuals the opportunity to seek redress for some grievance or an injury caused by an outsider from the *fanni mingo*,

rather than seek revenge against the offending tribe. The *fanni mingo* held counsel with the tribe whose interests he represented and tried to resolve the matter to the satisfaction of all parties.

Tribal divisions of the Choctaw Nation operated with virtual independence. The republic was, in fact, a loose confederation. Within tribal divisions, villages also exercised a great deal of local autonomy. Individuals exercised such a large degree of personal freedom that the system bordered on anarchy. It was able to function successfully only because the Choctaw exercised remarkable restraint regarding encroachment upon the rights of others within the group.

As the emphases of the educational system in the Choctaw Nation of Oklahoma demonstrate, the time period since 1980 has witnessed a resurgence of interest in resuscitating Choctaw traditions. Opportunities to learn about and participate in practices and demonstrations of these cultural phenomena like stickballing, oral storytelling, and public speaking have been made much more widely available through both the schools and other access points (such as events held by the Choctaw Nation Cultural Services, including classes, presentations, and lectures). The Mississippi Band of Choctaw Indians also offer a number of opportunities for interested parties to participate in cultural happenings, including workshops, classes, personal training, and demonstrations.

Gender Roles Europeans and Americans universally failed to appreciate or report the powerful and predominant role of women in Choctaw traditional life. Choctaw culture is matrilineal and, in many respects, matriarchal. Choctaw males were conspicuous in their roles as warriors, and war chiefs exercised a good deal of authority in time of war and conducted the diplomatic business of the nation, whereas the traditional role of women was farming. Likening such practices to those of their own patriarchal models, European observers failed to appreciate that the real decision-making power in times of peace was found among the women within the nation. The Choctaw have adjusted to the expectations of U.S. society regarding gender roles in visible positions of leadership, but in Choctaw family and social life, and in many organizations, a mature female is found at the very center of the life of the group, whether visible to outsiders or not. In 2011 the Mississippi Band of Choctaw Indians elected its first woman tribal chief, Chief Phyliss J. Anderson.

EMPLOYMENT AND ECONOMIC CONDITIONS

The Mississippi Choctaw have brought industry to the reservation, to the extent that the unemployment rate has dropped from 70 percent in 1997 to less than 3 percent in 2007. These numbers can be linked to an increased interest in cultivating industrial endeavors over the past forty years. These efforts began with the construction of an industrial park in 1973, at the

Pearl River community. A division of General Motors Corporation established the Chata Wire Harness Enterprise, which assembles electrical components for automobiles. Shortly thereafter, the American Greeting Corporation's Choctaw Greeting Enterprise began production, and the Oxford Investment Company started manufacturing automobile radio speakers at the Choctaw Electronics Enterprise. These companies and others employed more than 1,000 Choctaw Indians on the reservation.

Even earlier than efforts to develop the industrial sector, the Mississippi Choctaw engaged in endeavors to increase construction on the reservation. In 1965 the Choctaw Housing Authority constructed the first of more than 200 modern homes on the reservation. In 1969 the Chata Development company, which builds and remodels homes, and constructs offices and buildings for the nation, was established. The Choctaw Health Center, a forty-three-bed hospital, opened in 1976. The tribe was the third largest employer in the state of Mississippi in the early twenty-first century. In 2012 it employed over 5,000 tribe members and non-Indian employees.

The larger community of Oklahoma Choctaw have built community centers and clinics in towns throughout the nation. The Choctaw Housing Authority has provided thousands of Choctaws with low-cost modern homes. The nation operates the historic Indian Hospital at Talihina, which it acquired from the Indian Health Service; it purchased the sprawling Arrowhead Resort on Lake Eufaula from the state of Oklahoma and operates it as a tourist and convention facility.

Tribal industries include the Choctaw Finishing Plant and the Choctaw Village Shopping Center in Idabel, and the Choctaw Travel Plaza in Durant.

The buildings and grounds at the historic Choctaw Council House at Tuskahoma, in the center of the nation, have been restored, and the stately three-story brick Council House has been converted into a museum and gift shop. The Choctaw Tribal Council holds its monthly meetings in the new, modern council chamber nearby. Also constructed on the grounds were a large, roofed, outdoor amphitheater, and softball fields for the tremendously popular fast-pitch softball tournaments. Exhibition buildings, a cafeteria, showers and toilets, campgrounds, and parking facilities have been added.

By far the greatest economic gain in the nation has been through the inauguration of high-stakes Indian bingo. Charter buses bring bingo players daily from as far away as Dallas, Texas, to the huge Choctaw Bingo Palace in Durantto. After the first decade of the twenty-first century, the Choctaw Nation was operating seven casinos, as well as a manufacturing business, a management services company, numerous travel plazas, smoke shops, a printing company, and a document archiving company. The Nation produces revenue in the hundreds of millions, and employs more than 6,000 tribal and non-tribal Oklahomans.

POLITICS AND GOVERNMENT

In 1945 the U.S. Secretary of the Interior granted the Choctaw formal federal recognition, approving a constitution and bylaws for the Mississippi Band of

Choctaw Indians. The constitution provided for the election of a tribal council, which then appointed a tribal chairman. The land that had been acquired for them became a reservation.

The reservation remains outside of the political and judicial jurisdiction of the state of Mississippi. A 1974 revision of the Choctaw Nation's constitution provides for the popular election of the chief to a four-year term. The Indian Reorganization Act of 1934 allowed the Choctaw in Oklahoma to elect an advisory council, and in 1948 they were allowed to elect their own principal chief. Impetus toward reorganizing the nation met another shift in federal policy in 1953, when the U.S. Congress enacted House Concurrent Resolution 108, under which the federal government sought to terminate its relationship with all Indian nations in the United States. The Indian Self-Determination and Education Assistance Act of 1975 finally allowed the Choctaw a measure of self-government within the state of Oklahoma.

In 1976, after extended efforts by the Choctaw to have the federal government recognize the 1866 constitution as a valid legal document, the Choctaw purchased the campus of the former Presbyterian College in Durant, Oklahoma, as their national capitol. In 1984 they adopted a revised version of the original constitution—their first since the constitution of 1866 had been abrogated in 1906 with the establishment of Oklahoma as a state. Designating themselves the Choctaw Nation of Oklahoma, they adopted a tribal council form of government led by a principal chief elected by popular vote of the entire nation and council members elected by popular vote of council districts.

Since the mid-1970s, the tribal estate has steadily increased, along with the nation's administrative activities, enabling the Oklahoma Choctaw to exercise more vestiges of sovereignty. A recent federal court ruling stated that the state of Oklahoma could no longer exercise police powers on Indian land within the state. As a result, the Choctaw Nation Police were organized. The Choctaw Nation and the state of Oklahoma signed a pact to cross-deputize all law enforcement officers of both governments for the welfare and protection of all citizens.

The Choctaw Nation continues to govern itself with a governmental structure modeled after that of the U.S. federal government. The executive branch is led by a chief and assistant chief; these persons are elected to four-year terms. The legislative branch consists of twelve members of a tribal council; these members all represent a geographic district. Judicially, the nation operates a Court of General Jurisdiction: this body adjudicates on tribal disputes in all counties of the Nation and includes an appellate division which consists of three members.

NOTABLE INDIVIDUALS

Academia Clara Sue Kidwell (1941–) was a professor at the University of California at Berkeley and then worked for the Museum of American History at the Smithsonian Institution. She coauthored the study *The Choctaws: A Critical Bibliography* in 1980.

Anna Lewis (1895–1961) was a historian of Choctaw descent who in 1930 became the first woman to receive a PhD from the University of Oklahoma. She pursued a teaching career at the Oklahoma College for Women, now the University of Science and Arts, in Chickasaha, Oklahoma. She dedicated many years to researching a biography of the influential nineteenth-century Choctaw leader Pushmataha, which was published in 1959 under the title *Chief Pushmataha, American Patriot*.

Devon Mihesuah (1957–) is a historian and professor at the University of Kansas. She received her PhD from Texas Christian University in 1989. Her publications include *Recovering Our Ancestors' Gardens: Indigenous Recipes and Guide to Diet and Fitness* (2005).

Michelene Pesantubbee (1953–) became a professor at the University of Iowa in 2003. She received a PhD in 1994 from the University of California, Santa Barbara and is the author of studies such as *Choctaw Women in a Chaotic World* (2005).

Muriell Wright (1889–1975) served for two decades as editor of the *Chronicles of Oklahoma*, the quarterly historical scholarly journal of the Oklahoma Historical Society. In 1959 she produced *A Guide to the Indian Tribes of Oklahoma*, which provides a summary of the history, culture, and contemporary status of the sixty-five Indian nations that were either original residents of or were removed to the area before Oklahoma became a state.

Art Linda Lomahaftewa (1947–) is an accomplished Hopi/Choctaw artist and art instructor. Her work, which reflects the spirituality and storytelling traditions of her background, has garnered numerous awards and exhibitions.

Phil Lucas (1942–2007) was a film producer, director, and writer who created realistic images of his people in an effort to combat stereotypes.

Gary White Deer (1950–) is an artist who is well known for his paintings, especially his portraits of Choctaw in traditional dress. He has been active in presenting Choctaw culture and has lectured widely and appeared in many documentaries concerning the Choctaw.

Journalism Len Green was the first editor of *Bishinik*, the official monthly publication of the Choctaw Nation of Oklahoma, which is mailed to every registered voter of the nation. Green was also managing editor of the *McCurtain Gazette* in Idabel, Oklahoma, for thirty years. Early issues of *Bishinik* contain his scholarly writings about Choctaw history and treaties. For the U.S. bicentennial celebration, Green published *200 Years Ago in the Red River Valley* (1976), a study of Choctaw country in the West two generations before the Choctaw moved there.

Scott Kayla Morrison (1951–2000) collaborated with LeAnn Howe on the investigative article "Sewage of Foreigners" (*Federal Bar Journal & Notes*, July 1992), a detailed exposé that focused on contract negotiations by the Mississippi Band of Choctaw Indians to allow toxic waste dumps on Choctaw lands in Mississippi. Morrison has worked as a legal-services attorney among the Choctaw in Mississippi and as director of the Native American Office of Jobs in the Environment. In 1993 *Oklahoma Today* named her in its "Who's Who in Indian Country" in recognition of her environmental work. Her short stories and essays have appeared in publications such as *The Four Directions: American Indian Literary Quarterly* and *Turtle Quarterly* and in the anthology *The Colour of Resistance* (1994).

Literature M. Cochise Anderson is an actor, playwright, musician, spoken-word artist, and educator. He has performed at the Open House Arts Festival at the Kennedy Center for the Performing Art and the National Museum of the American Indian in Washington, D.C. Anderson received a Bush Artist Fellowship for his solo performance piece "The Only Good Poet Is a Read Poet" and a Verve Spoken Word Grant for his solo piece "Methods of Mass Deception" (2010). His poetry has appeared in *World of Poetry Anthology* (1983) and in *Nitassinan Notre Terre* (1990).

Jim Barnes (1933–), poet and editor, was named the poet laureate of Oklahoma for 2009–2010. For over thirty years he served as the editor of *Chariton Review* at Northwest Missouri State University, Kirksville, Missouri. Barnes won the Oklahoma Book Award for his *The Sawdust War* (1993), a volume of poetry. Among Barnes's other verse collections are *American Book of the Dead* (1982), *A Season of Loss* (1985), *La Plata Cantata* (1989), *On a Wing of the Sun* (2001), and *Visiting Picasso* (2007).

Don L. Birchfield (1948–2012) was a professor of Native American studies at the University of Lethbridge. He was the editor of *The Encyclopedia of North American Indians* (1997). His writings include the novel *Black Silk Handkerchief: A Hom-Astubby Mystery* (2006) and the nonfiction work *How Choctaws Invented Civilization and Why Choctaws Will Conquer the World* (2007).

Roxy Gordon (1945–2000) was a writer who published more than 200 poems, articles, and short fiction in publications such as *Rolling Stone*, the *Village Voice*, the *Texas Observer*, and the *Dallas Morning News*. His fiction has appeared in a number of anthologies, including *Earth Power Coming* (1983; edited by Simon J. Ortiz). Among Gordon's poetry collections are *Unfinished Business* (1985), *West Texas Midcentury* (1988), and *Smaller Circles* (1990).

Beatrice Harrell's memoirs of her mother's experiences in the Choctaw boarding schools have appeared in such publications as *The Four Directions:*

American Indian Literary Quarterly. *How Thunder and Lightning Came to Be: A Choctaw Tale* (1995) is one of several books in which Harrell recounts traditional Choctaw stories.

LeAnne Howe (1951–) is a widely published poet, essayist, novelist, short story writer, and playwright. Her poetry has appeared in anthologies such as *Gatherings IV: The En'owkin Journal of First North American People* and *Studies in American Indian Literatures*; her short stories have appeared in many collections and in the anthology *Earth Song, Sky Spirit: Short Stories of the Contemporary Native American Experience* (1993). She later wrote *Evidence of Red: Poems and Prose* (2005) and the novels *Shell Shaker* (2001) and *Miko Kings: An Indian Baseball Story* (2007). With Roxy Gordon she coauthored the play *Indian Radio Days*.

Gary McLain's nonfiction works include *Keepers of the Fire* (1987), *Indian America* (1990), and *The Indian Way* (1991).

Louis Owens (1948–2002) was a novelist and coeditor of the American Indian Literature Series of the University of Oklahoma Press and an English professor at the University of New Mexico. He had also taught at the University of California at Santa Cruz. His novels include *Wolfsong* (1991), *The Sharpest Sight* (1992), and *Bone Game* (1994); Owens's *Other Destines: Understanding the American Indian Novel* (1992) is a critical study; and *I Hear the Train: Reflections, Inventions, Refractions* (2001) is an autobiographical work.

Ronald Burns Querry (1943–), a descendant of Okla Hannali Choctaw, has been an English professor at the University of Oklahoma as well as an editor of horse-industry magazines and a professional farrier (horseshoer). He is the author of *The Death of Bernadette Lefthand* (1993), which received both the Border Regional Library Association Regional Book Award and the Mountains and Plains Booksellers Association Award as one of the best novels published in 1993. Querry also edited *Growing Old at Willie Nelson's Picnic, and Other Sketches of Life in the Southwest* (1983) and authored an autobiography, *I See by My Get-Up (That I Am a Cowboy)* (1987).

Wallace Hampton Tucker became the first three-time winner in 1992 of the Best Play Prize of the Five Civilized Tribes Museum in Muscogee, Oklahoma, for his play *Fire on Bending Mountain*. Tucker also won the first two prizes awarded by the biennial competition in 1974 and in 1976.

MEDIA

PRINT

Bishinik

Official monthly publication of the Choctaw Nation of Oklahoma.

Jully Allen, Director
16 West Locust Street
Durant, Oklahoma 74701
Phone: (580) 924-4148
Email: bishinik@choctawnation.com
URL: www.choctawnation.com/news-room/
biskinik-newspaper-archive/

Choctaw Community News

Official monthly publication of the Mississippi Band of
Choctaw Indians.

Julie Kelsey, Editor
Communications Program
P.O. Box 6010
Philadelphia, Mississippi 39350
Phone: (601) 656-1992
URL: www.choctaw.org/media/ccn.html

ORGANIZATIONS AND ASSOCIATIONS

Choctaw Nation of Oklahoma

Chief Gregory E. Pyle
101 Industrial Road
Choctaw, Mississippi 39350
P.O. Box 1210
Durant, Oklahoma 74702-1210
Phone: (800) 522-6170
Fax: (580) 924-4148
Email: chief@choctawnation.com
URL: www.choctawnation.com

Mississippi Band of Choctaw Indians

Phone: (601) 656-5251
Email: info@choctaw.org
URL: www.choctaw.org

MUSEUMS AND RESEARCH CENTERS

Choctaw Historic Preservation Department

Ian Thompson, Director
P.O. Box 1210
Durant, Oklahoma 74702-1210
Phone: (580) 924-8280 ext. 2216
Email: ithompson@choctawnation.com
URL: ww.choctawnation.com/services/departments/
historic-preservation-department/

Choctaw Museum

Mississippi Band of Choctaw Indians

101 Industrial Road
Choctaw, Mississippi 39350
Phone: (601) 650-1685
URL: www.choctaw.org/culture/museum.html

Choctaw Language Department

Choctaw School

James Parrish
Phone: (580) 924-8280
Email: jparrish@choctawnation.com

SOURCES FOR ADDITIONAL STUDY

Akers, Donna L. *Culture and Customs of the Choctaw Indians.* Westport, CT: Greenwood Press, 2013.

DeRosier, Arthur H., Jr. *The Removal of the Choctaw Indians.* New York: Harper and Row, 1972.

Galloway, Patricia Kay. *Choctaw Genesis, 1500–1700.* Lincoln: University of Nebraska Press, 1998.

Haag, Marcia, and Henry Willis. *Choctaw Language and Culture: Chahta Anumpa.* Norman: University of Oklahoma Press, 2001.

Howard, James H., and Victoria L. Levine. *Choctaw Music & Dance.* Norman: University of Oklahoma Press, 1997.

Kidwell, Clara Sue Kidwell. *The Choctaws in Oklahoma: From Tribe to Nation, 1855–1970.* Oklahoma City: University of Oklahoma Press, 2008.

Lambert, Valerie. *Choctaw Nation: A Story of American Indian Resurgence.* Lincoln: University of Nebraska Press, 2007.

Mould, Tom. *Choctaw Tales.* Jackson: University Press of Mississippi, 2004.

O'Brien, Greg, ed. *Pre-removal Choctaw History: Exploring New Paths.* Norman: University of Oklahoma Press, 2008.

Pesantubbee, Michelene E. *Choctaw Women in a Chaotic World: The Clash of Cultures in the Colonial Southeast.* Albuquerque: University of New Mexico, 2005.

Swanton, John Reed. *Source Material for the Social and Ceremonial Life of the Choctaw Indians.* Tuscaloosa: University of Alabama Press, 1931.

Wells, Samuel J., and Roseanna Tubby, eds. *After Removal: The Choctaw in Mississippi.* Jackson: University Press of Mississippi, 1986.

COLOMBIAN AMERICANS

Pamela Sturner

OVERVIEW

Colombian Americans are immigrants or descendants of people from Colombia, a country in the northwest corner of South America. Colombia is bound by the Caribbean Sea to the north and the Pacific Ocean to the west and shares terrestrial borders with the countries of Venezuela, Brazil, Peru, Ecuador, and Panama. Colombia is the only country in South America with both Caribbean and Pacific coasts, and the country's Point Gallinas is the northernmost tip of the South American mainland. The central region of Colombia is home to most of its population and is dominated by the Andes Mountains, which form three ranges that run the length of the country. The eastern plains, or *llanos*, account for 60 percent of Colombia's territory and are sparsely populated, as are the coastal lowlands. To the southeast lie undeveloped tropical rainforests of the Amazon basin. With an area of 439,735 square miles (1,138,914 square kilometers), Colombia is about three times the size of the state of Montana.

According to the *CIA World Factbook*, Colombia's highly diverse population numbered 45.2 million in 2012 and was made up of at least 15 distinct cultural and regional groups. About 65 percent of the population lives in urban areas, including the country's four largest cities: Bogotá, Medellín, Cali, and Barranquilla. Major ethnic groups include descendants of Indians, who are concentrated in the Andes and were known as Amerindians; persons of solely European descent, who have traditionally held most of the country's wealth and power and account for less than 20 percent of the population; *costeños*, persons of mixed African, Indian, and Spanish descent living primarily on the coasts; and *mestizos*, or persons of Indian and Spanish descent, who account for about 58 percent of the population. Most Colombian Americans are Roman Catholic, but a small number are Protestant, Jewish, Muslim, Buddhist, or Hindu. After years of political and social unrest, Colombia's economic policies and promotion of free trade have fostered almost a decade of strong economic performance, according to the *CIA World Factbook*. However, Colombia's 10.8 percent unemployment rate in 2011 was one of the region's highest, and about one-third of the population reportedly still lives in poverty.

Colombians began to immigrate to the United States in notable numbers after World War I, and many of them settled in middle-class neighborhoods of New York City while working in professional fields such as nursing and accounting. Despite the introduction of more stringent immigration laws during the second half of the twentieth century, the population of Colombian Americans continued to grow, and by the 1960s and 1970s many skilled and semiskilled laborers had joined professionals among the new arrivals. Beginning in the 1980s, the escalating violence and political upheaval associated with Colombia's booming illegal narcotics industry spurred locals to emigrate in even larger numbers, and immigrants to the United States included both documented and undocumented persons as well as persons seeking political asylum. This trend persisted throughout the 1990s and early twenty-first century, because the country continued to be plagued by the effects of drug trafficking and clashes between governmental forces and guerrilla groups.

The 2010 U.S. Census reported 908,734 Colombians living in the United States, making them the largest South American immigrant group in country. Some estimates (which include undocumented arrivals) speculate that the actual population may exceed two million. Throughout their history in the United States, Colombian Americans have worked to create their own identity within the Hispanic population while also finding a place in mainstream American culture. Unfortunately, stereotypes linking them with drug trafficking and organized crime continue, despite the fact very few Colombian Americans engage in criminal activity. During the past two decades, overcrowding, the increasing cost of living, and safety issues have prompted many Colombian Americans to leave large urban areas for suburban areas, though large communities still exist in major U.S. cities such as Miami, New York City, Philadelphia, and Washington DC.

HISTORY OF THE PEOPLE

Early History Indigenous peoples such as the Muisca, Quimbaya, and Tairona likely built hunter-gatherer societies in present-day Colombia as early as 10,000 BCE. Because of its location at the northernmost tip of South America, historians believe that the land served as a natural corridor for nomadic tribes migrating between Mesoamerica, the Andes, and the Amazon, and their civilizations grew to occupy much of the Andean interior prior to the arrival of Europeans at the end of the fifteenth century. Christopher Columbus probably explored the mouth of the Orinoco River in 1498. Spanish explorer Alonso de Ojeda led another expedition in 1509, and in 1525 the first Spanish city (Santa Marta) was founded on the Caribbean coast. In 1536 the conquistador Gonzalo Jiménez de Quesada sailed up the Magdalena River in search of the mythical city of El Dorado and, after defeating the indigenous Chibcha people, founded Bogotá in 1538.

During the years of the Spanish Main, the Caribbean port city of Cartagena (founded in 1533) was a point of departure for shipments of gold and other minerals bound for Spain. The Spanish relied increasingly on the labor of slaves to maintain the expanding colony, and Colombia soon had one of the largest African populations on the continent. After 1740 the colony formed the center of New Granada, a territory that included the greater part of what is now Colombia, Panama, and Venezuela. A movement for independence from Spain began in 1810, and in 1812 the territory came under the direction of Venezuelan military and political leader Simón Bolívar. Bolívar waged a series of campaigns that ended with the surrender of the Spanish in 1819. He renamed the territory Greater Colombia. Political differences led Venezuela to secede in 1829, followed by Ecuador in 1830.

Modern Era The 1830s were marked by the rise of the Partido Conservador and the Partido Liberal as the most powerful rivals in national politics. Their struggles fueled unrest throughout the century and resulted in a civil war from 1899 to 1902 that left 100,000 dead and brought the Conservatives to power. In 1902 crisis beset the country again when the United States seized the part of the country where the Panama Canal was being built. After rejecting a treaty that would establish American control, the Colombian government sent troops to Panama. The ensuing clash with the United States and U.S.-supported local forces resulted in Colombia's defeat, and Panama was created as an independent country in 1903. In the following year, a dictatorial regime and ushered in more than four decades of peace in Colombia. However, hostilities between the Liberals and Conservatives led, beginning in 1948, to civil war and a decade of political unrest known as "La Violencia" (The Violence). Between 200,000 and 300,000 inhabitants were killed, and large portions of the population were displaced, with rural populations forced into larger urban centers. In 1958, after the military dictatorship (1953–1957) of Rojas Pinilla, Liberals and the dictatorship Conservatives formed a coalition government known as the National Front, and under its leadership the country began its recovery from the lengthy war.

Since the 1960s, attempts have been made to address long-standing social, political, and economic problems in Colombia. Under the presidency (1966–1970) of Carlos Lleras Restrepo, inflation slowed, the economy was diversified, and land reforms were instituted. After a period of gradual transition toward full democracy, the government of the National Front ended with the elections held in 1974. Extreme disparity between the wealthy and the poor contributed to widespread disillusionment that kindled a Marxist guerrilla movement dedicated to revolution. Social problems worsened as the birth rate rose and farmers displaced by new technology moved to the cities, where they found their skills inapplicable in an industrial economy. During the 1980s, producers of illegal drugs flourished, banded together in cartels, and threatened the country's political and social stability through campaigns of bombings, abductions, murders, and the assassinations of officials, judges, and newspaper editors. Undocumented immigration to the United States and Venezuela increased, and in the mid-1980s an era of steady economic growth came to a close as Colombia's economy stagnated under the weight of foreign debt.

In the face of an escalating social and political crisis, President Virgilio Barco Vargas launched a campaign in 1989 to suppress the illegal drug trade, which resulted in hundreds of arrests, the confiscation of property worth millions of dollars, and violent retaliations by the cartels. Several presidential candidates were assassinated before the election of 1990, but victory nonetheless went to César Gaviria Trujillo, a well-known opponent of the drug trade. During his first years in office, Gaviria sought to restore the population's faith in the government by pursuing an aggressive policy against the cartels, encouraging the formation of new political parties, and offering a role in national affairs to Indians and former guerrillas. Agreements reached with foreign creditors eased the burden of debt, allowing Colombia to achieve a trade surplus, and during the 1990s negotiations began for new trade arrangements with other countries.

The ratification of a new Colombian constitution in 1991 was hailed by human rights advocates for its reforms on political, ethnic, and gender issues. Unfortunately, political turmoil and the effects of the drug trade continued to haunt the nation in the 1990s, and Marxist revolutionary groups such as the Revolutionary Armed Forces of Colombia (FARC) and the National Liberation Army intensified campaigns of terror against the government, the military, the Roman Catholic Church, and civilians.

Although armed conflict with drug traffickers and rebel groups continued into the twenty-first century, sharp declines in the country's murder and kidnapping rates were reported from 2002 to 2010. Coinciding with the term of President Álvaro Uribe and with support from the United States, these improvements ushered in a period of increased stability, economic growth,

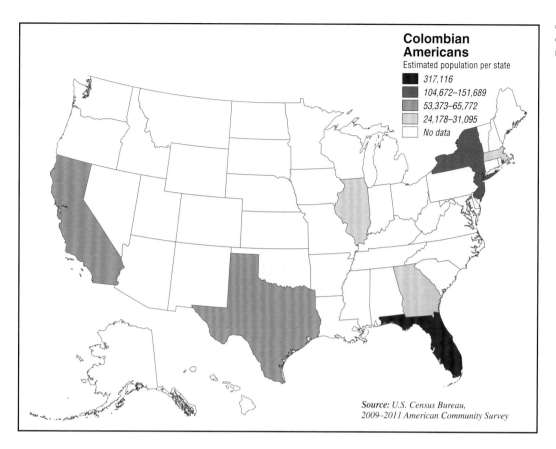

Colombian Americans
Estimated population per state
- 317,116
- 104,672–151,689
- 53,373–65,772
- 24,178–31,095
- No data

Source: U.S. Census Bureau, 2009–2011 American Community Survey

and tourism in Colombia. By 2012 the country had become South America's fourth-largest producer of petroleum, had served as a member of the UN Security Council, and was working to build better relationships with its neighbors and trade partners around the world.

SETTLEMENT IN THE UNITED STATES

The first Colombian immigrants were probably among the few South Americans who settled in the United States during the nineteenth century (the federal census did not specify the country of origin for South Americans until 1960). Little is known about these settlers, who maintained no ties with their native countries, and within a few generations identified themselves only as Americans. The first Colombian community formed when several hundred professionals, including nurses, accountants, laboratory technicians, pharmacists, and bilingual secretaries, moved to New York City after World War I. The population was augmented by students who stayed on in the United States after earning professional degrees. Most Colombian immigrants made their homes in Jackson Heights, a middle-class neighborhood in Queens (New York City) that was attractive for its proximity to employment in Manhattan and for its churches, comfortable houses, large yards, and fine schools. Known by residents as "El Chapinerito" (after Chapinero, a middle-class suburb of Bogotá), the neighborhood did not grow much until the 1940s, when New York City

and Venezuela surpassed Panama in popularity as destinations among Colombian emigrants.

The number of Colombians entering the United States each year increased only slightly until the early 1950s, when it rose from a few hundred to more than a thousand, owing in part to upheaval associated with the civil war of 1948. The rate did not decline with the restoration of civil order in Colombia. As a result of land reforms and the introduction of agricultural machinery during the 1960s, the population became concentrated in the metropolitan areas and a deep economic recession set in, forcing many Colombians to leave the country in search of work. The number that settled in the United States continued to grow rapidly; according to the annual reports of the Immigration and Naturalization Service, 116,444 Colombians entered the country between 1960 and 1977, the first large influx driven by purely economic reasons. These immigrants were far more racially and economically diverse than their predecessors, and with their admittance, skilled and semiskilled laborers gradually displaced professionals as the majority.

In the postwar years, Colombian Americans were among the groups at the center of a national political debate about immigration, which reached a peak when immigrants from Asia, Africa, and Latin America outnumbered those from Europe. Calls for stricter controls culminated in the Immigration Act of 1965, after which only 120,000 visas were to be reserved annually.

The law also sought to bar entry to all but the most needed and highly qualified workers, including professionals, technicians, and domestic servants. These measures presented a host of obstacles for Colombian Americans. The quota was so small relative to demand that families could wait 20 months for permission to be reunited. Pressure on the allotted visas was further exacerbated by unemployment and underemployment in Colombia, which escalated to between 20 and 25 percent by the mid-1970s. Patterns of settlement changed as a result of these conditions. In part because they had little hope of establishing legal residency, most Colombians who arrived after the mid-1960s planned to stay in the United States only temporarily. As a result, the rate of undocumented immigration soared: estimates of those living in the country without permanent residency status ranged from 250,000 to 350,000 in the mid-1970s. Discouraged by the law, some immigrants settled in Ecuador, which in 1973 had a Colombian population of 60,000.

Despite a succession of stringent immigration laws, the Colombian population in the United States continued to grow. New York remained the most popular destination. Those who could afford to do so moved to Jackson Heights, but other Colombian neighborhoods developed in nearby Corona, Elmhurst, Woodside, Rego Park, and Flushing. Smaller communities formed in Los Angeles, San Francisco, Houston, and Washington DC. During the 1970s, an enclave of a few thousand professionals developed on the North Side of Chicago. After the late 1970s, many Colombians chose to settle in Miami, which they found attractive for its climate, growing economy, and tradition of tolerance dating from the establishment of a Cuban community there. Initially they took up residence in Little Havana, the largest Cuban neighborhood, and many engaged in business related to the brisk trade between Miami and Latin America; a few worked in factories or as domestic servants. The area also became a haven for the wealthy, who moved there to receive medical care, send their children to school, and escape from social, economic, and political turmoil in Colombia. By 1987 Colombian Americans were one of the fastest-growing Latin American groups in Miami.

By the early 1990s overcrowding, crime, and the high cost of urban living led Colombian Americans to begin leaving metropolitan centers for the suburbs. This trend was perhaps first noticed in the coastal towns of Connecticut and New York, where, since the 1980s, many Colombian Americans and other Latin Americans have taken jobs in service industries left unfilled by the local population. A better choice of housing, which was much more affordable in these towns than in New York City, was also available. Enclaves in Connecticut (such as Stamford) and northern New Jersey (including Englewood, Victory Gardens, and the Bergenline Avenue district) grew during these years. Jacksonville and such suburbs as Kendall, Florida, attracted a growing number from Miami. Skokie, Evanston, Arlington Heights, and Park Ridge, Illinois, became fashionable alternatives to the North Side of Chicago. Nevertheless, the largest concentrations remained in Miami, New York City, and their environs: in 2008 there were 97,580 Colombian Americans in New York City (mainly in Queens) and in 2010 there were 114,701 in Dade County, Florida.

With other immigrants from developing countries, Colombian Americans faced serious obstacles to achieving success in the United States. As American society became more technologically advanced, much of the work traditionally performed by immigrants disappeared, leaving only dangerous, undesirable, poorly paid positions that offered no health care benefits and little promise for the future. Language was a definitive barrier against advancement, as most Colombian Americans lacked proficiency in English and the opportunity to gain it. Those living in cities often inherited abandoned neighborhoods, substandard schools, and a crumbling infrastructure. Perhaps the most pressing issue was the rising tide of hostility toward immigrants, especially Latin Americans and Asians, that swept the country on the heels of the economic recession during the late 1980s and early 1990s. After years of being virtually ignored by the larger society, Colombian Americans found themselves a target for American resentment over problems ranging from drug-related crime to a decline in the standard of living. According to the federal Census Bureau, 43,891 Colombians were admitted to the United States in 1990 and 1991, more than from any other South American country. They also accounted for the third-largest group of undocumented immigrants (after those from Mexico and Central America). The influx continued through the 1990s as guerrilla violence in Colombia escalated. Between 1992 and 1997, nearly 75,000 Colombians immigrated to the United States, with many settling in California. Such statistics figured prominently in debates about the effects of immigration, both legal and illegal, on the economy and even on society itself.

Colombian Americans were also subject to concern about the growth of the Latino population, which was perceived as a threat by those who considered immigrants, particularly the undocumented, an economic burden and resented Latinos' efforts to preserve their language and culture within American society. Such sentiments fueled a political backlash against immigrants that led to the passage of Proposition 187 by California voters in 1994. The law denied health care, education, and other services to undocumented immigrants. A federal appeals court ruled most of the measure unconstitutional and in 1999 the state decided not to appeal the ruling. In 1996 Congress enacted a law that denied welfare, nonemergency health care, and higher education benefits to undocumented aliens.

The large-scale emigration from Colombia in the last two decades of the twentieth century and the first decade of the twenty-first century is sometimes referred to as the Colombian "brain drain," since so many members of the country's educated middle and upper classes fled to escape intensifying tumult at home. During this period, the United States was the second-most popular destination for Colombian emigrants, trailing only Venezuela. Although Colombian officials said that the exodus peaked in 2000, the U.S. Department of Homeland Security reports that the number of Colombians immigrating to the United States remains steady. Each year from 2002 to 2005 an average of about 19,000 Colombians legally immigrated to the United States. The number swelled to about 43,000 in 2006 and subsequently declined gradually, with 22,635 immigrants in 2011.

LANGUAGE

In the United States, the majority of Colombian American households speak both English and Spanish: a 2010 report from the Pew Hispanic Center, a national nonpartisan research organization, showed that 59 percent of Colombians in the United States spoke English proficiently. For Colombian Americans, as for other immigrants, learning English is a compelling desire, because without advanced language skills they remain ineligible for most kinds of work. Spanish, however, continues to hold a vital role in Colombian American culture, as perhaps the surest means of preserving traditions. Colombians commonly consider themselves the stewards of the most elegant Spanish spoken in Latin America, and Colombian American professionals and other members of the upper classes worry about the deterioration of Colombian Spanish in U.S. cities, where it is subject to the influences of English and the Spanish of other countries. They tend to use formal address in more situations than other Latin Americans and to call only well-known acquaintances by their first names.

In 2010, 41 percent of Colombian Americans reported speaking English "less than very well," according to the Pew Center. These people often gravitate to Latin American networks, particularly in large cities, where there is little or no need to know English in either business or social life. Families sometimes rely on bilingual children for outside transactions. Many Colombian Americans consider Miami exceptionally hospitable, as Spanish is the second official language of government and is also used frequently in business and cultural affairs.

Together with the children of other immigrants, Colombian students are at the center of a debate about the future of bilingual education. Studies have shown that even after acquiring fairly advanced English skills, non-native speakers are unable to compete with their English-speaking classmates for several years. Some educators argue that bilingual programs are essential to help students of English as a second language build confidence and keep up with their peers. Their approach has aroused anger among Americans who believe that English should be the country's only language and consider wide use of other languages a threat to American culture.

RELIGION

Under Spanish rule, Roman Catholicism spread quickly throughout Colombia and displaced native religions. As a result, the majority of Colombian Americans continue to self-identify as Roman Catholics. Religious ceremonies are closely tied to important customs and traditions, such as *compadrazgo*, the establishment of kin networks through the choice of godparents. A child's godparents are usually the man and woman who acted as the best man and the maid of honor at the parents' wedding. The preservation of many such Latin American religious customs has been reinforced in recent years as parishes have added Spanish-language services in not only large cities but also a growing number of suburbs.

Although the church has historically been one of the few venues to offer a respite from the isolation and hostility encountered by immigrants entering American society, some churches were slow to respond to the needs of Latin American parishioners. For example, the Catholic Church in New York City was hesitant to accept Colombian Americans when they began to immigrate in notable numbers during the early to mid-twentieth century. Like other Latinos, Colombian Americans in Jackson Heights during the 1960s and 1970s were largely ignored by the local Catholic clergy, which was predominantly Irish and Italian and did not acknowledge the changing ethnicity of the neighborhood. Because few priests spoke Spanish, Latinos had difficulty obtaining information about services and programs offered by the church. Enrollment in parochial schools was a charged issue, as most parents initially failed to secure their children's enrollment because they were unaware of registration dates and the requirement to make donations at Sunday mass for a year before applying for admission.

In response to such problems, the diocese of Queens and Brooklyn sponsored the Instituto de Comunicación Internacional, a program for teaching Latin American culture and Spanish to the clergy. Some parishes sought to attract Hispanic congregants by offering masses that featured Latin American music. In Queens a few hundred Colombian Americans led by a Colombian priest established a church based on charismatic Catholicism. As of 2010, it was estimated that there were some 2,000 Hispanic churches in the New York–New Jersey metropolitan area.

CULTURE AND ASSIMILATION

Motivated by ethnic pride and a desire to circumvent legal, racial, and cultural obstacles encountered in living in the United States, Colombian Americans have traditionally maintained a distinct identity in the United States. According to the U.S. Census Bureau's 2010 American Community Survey, 65 percent of

A woman originally from Colombia chants during a rally on immigration reform in Washington, D.C. Immigrant rights organizations are advocating for comprehensive immigration reform. MARK WILSON / GETTY IMAGES

Colombians living in the United States were foreign born, compared to 37 percent of Hispanics and 13 percent of the U.S. population overall. Some new arrivals feel alienated from mainstream society, struggle with racial and economic discrimination, and seek to preserve their own culture by operating within Latin American social and economic networks as much as possible. However, many Colombian Americans also reject the notion of assuming a larger Latino identity, seeking instead to remain distinct from other Latin American groups. Because of Colombia's ethnically diverse population, which is derived from indigenous Amerindians, European immigrants, and African slaves, it is difficult to classify Colombian Americans ethnically.

In light of immigration laws that allow few to expect citizenship, many consider their stay in the United States temporary and retain strong ties to Colombia. However, Colombian Americans who are permanent residents tend to fare slightly better on average than many of their Hispanic peers. According to the Census Bureau, Colombian Americans overall have higher median incomes, higher homeownership rates, and higher education levels than other Hispanics in the United States. In addition, only 10 percent of Colombian Americans live in poverty, compared to 19.5 percent of Hispanics overall. Of the Colombian Americans who took part in the 2010 American Community Survey, 30 percent reported that they worked in management, professional, and related occupations, while another 24 percent were in sales and office support.

Since the 1970s the effort by Colombian Americans to be accepted in American society has been impeded by stereotypes associated with drug trafficking. Reports of a growing number of arrests for drug abuse and related activity in the United States during the 1980s and the escalating chaos in Colombia during that period fueled American fears that the violence and terrorism associated with drug cartels would spread to the United States. Sensationalism tinged much of the news reporting on these affairs, and since the mid-1980s stereotypes of ruthless drug lords supported by unlimited funds, sophisticated weapons, and armies of loyal thugs have captured the public's imagination. In the shadow of such characterizations, Colombian Americans found themselves objects of suspicion and experienced discrimination in housing and employment, even though by most estimates only a very small percentage engage in criminal activity.

Cuisine Traditional Colombian food varies from region to region and can be influenced by the country's many indigenous cultures as well as the European, African, Asian, and other South American groups that have settled there. Meat, stews, soups, bread, fresh fruit, and vegetables are a common part of most traditional Colombian diets. *Sancocho* is a popular stew that includes chicken, pork, or seafood in a broth with plantains, yucca, cilantro, corn, and potatoes. *Arepa* is a flatbread made from cornmeal or flour with many regional variations. *Tamales* (corn cakes) are also popular and boast many regional varieties. Traditional beverages include a chilled, blended drink made of milk, sugar, and a fruit known as *curuba*. Colombia is renowned for its coffee, which, along with petroleum, coal, and gold, is one of its main exports. In some areas of Colombia, roasted ants are consumed as part of traditional fare.

In Colombia's coastal regions, seafood and fresh fruit are plentiful. *Ceviche* (stew made from raw fish marinated in citrus juices and various spices), plantains, and *arepa* prepared with eggs or cheese are among the dishes commonly served along Colombia's Caribbean coast. Coconut is frequently used to flavor sauces or rice. In the mountainous Andean region near Bogotá, breakfast can consist of *changua*, a creamy soup made with milk and scallions; eggs are dropped into the mixture without breaking the yolks and it is often served with cilantro and bread.

Ajiaco, a hearty soup made with chicken, several varieties of potato, capers, herbs, avocado, and corn on the cob, is also popular for dinner. Beef and freshwater fish are popular in the eastern grasslands near the Venezuelan and Brazilian borders as well as in the Amazonian regions, and the meat is often barbecued on vertical spits over an open fire. In Colombia's central region, tamales are made from corn dough and filled with local vegetables, chicken, or pork. These tamales are called *tamales Tolimenses* after the centrally located area of Tolima.

When Colombian Americans consume traditional foods at home, their tastes may follow these regional norms. Generally speaking, the major staples of the traditional Colombian diet are also popular with Colombians in the United States. Common dishes include: various grilled meats, *arepas, sancocho, empanadas* (a stuffed pastry that is usually fried, not baked as Chilean or Argentine varieties are), *tamales, pandebono* (cheese bread), and *bandeja paisa* (a platter of assorted dishes, often including meat, rice, plantains, *arepa*, pudding, fruits, and vegetables). Colombian restaurants can be found in most major cities in the United State, ranging inexpensive cafes to fine-dining options. These restaurants offer a wide array of Colombian cuisine, but the most common features include *tamales, empanadas*, various meat dishes, *ceviche*, soups, and stews.

Holidays An important holiday for Colombian Americans is Colombian Independence Day on July 20 (celebrated on November 11 by immigrants from the Caribbean coast). The holiday is marked with traditional foods such as *tamales, chorizos* (fresh sausages), *empanadas*, Colombian coffee, *arepas*, and *obleas* (a confection made with two wafers and a layer of caramel in between). Colombian Americans also share in the celebration of other Latin American independence days and in cultural festivals held from time to time in major cities.

Dances and Songs Latin American dancing is a central activity at festivals and in local clubs. Since the late 1980s, the Colombian courtship dance known as *cumbia* has grown in popularity. Developed on the Caribbean coast by African slaves, it consists of intricate, restrained steps that reportedly trace the limits of the dancers' shackles. Colombian Americans keep the tradition of *cumbia* alive in the United States through dance and through a musical genre also called *cumbia*. The music, also developed by African slaves in Colombia, is in 2/4 time and performed with a button accordion, drums, maracas, and horns.

During the mid-twentieth century, Colombian music gained an international audience largely through the efforts of Antonio López Fuentes, who formed the first Colombian record company, Disco Fuentes, in 1934 and made well-received recordings of indigenous music using modern instrumentation. A music form related to *cumbia*, called *vallenato*, is still enjoyed in the United States and abroad and traditionally consists of vocals, an accordion, a cane scraper, a drum, and a curved flute. Versions of *vallenato* songs, put to rock instrumentation by Carlos Vives, have enjoyed tremendous success throughout the Americas. Colombian musicians tour the United States frequently, among them the accordionist Lisandro Meza and the bands such as Grupo Niche. Styles known as *porro* and *mapale* are performed to a lesser extent.

Health Issues Obtaining health care can pose a serious problem for many Colombian Americans. Those in poorly paid jobs rarely receive health benefits and cannot afford to pay for a health plan or leave their families long enough to receive treatment. In addition to these problems, undocumented immigrants are burdened with the fear that through the medical establishment their status might become known to the immigration authorities. As a result, many Colombian Americans have sought medical care only in emergencies or confined themselves to facilities available within Latin American networks.

Like other immigrants, Colombian Americans sometimes suffer from stress disorders associated with cultural adjustment. Few seek out mental health services, however, owing to long-standing taboos in Colombia against seeking help for mental illness. By the early 1990s, a few social service centers and programs catered to Latin Americans, and during the next two decades more and more health care providers began to follow suit. Today, most major cities in the United States offer bilingual medical services. Some of the first noteworthy facilities to offer support to Hispanics included La Familia in Marin County, California, and the Fordham Tremont Mental Health Center in New York City.

In 2012 *Hispanic Network Magazine* named the Mayo Clinic, Mount Sinai Medical Clinic, Johns Hopkins Hospital, and New York–Presbyterian University Hospital of Columbia and Cornell among the top hospitals for Hispanics in the United States. However, according to a 2008 survey by the Pew Hispanic Center, nearly one-fourth of all Hispanics in the United States are without health care. In 2012 multiple nationwide polls showed that a majority of Latinos approved of President Barack Obama's controversial plan for comprehensive nationwide health coverage.

FAMILY AND COMMUNITY LIFE

According to the Pew Hispanic Center, Colombian Americans are slightly more likely to be married than Hispanics overall. In 2010 the U.S. Census Bureau's American Community Survey showed that 47 percent of Colombian Americans were married, compared to 44 percent for Hispanics overall. Historically, a focal concern for Colombian immigrants has been to preserve the traditional family structure against pressures encountered in U.S. society. Families prefer to immigrate together but have increasingly been prevented from doing so by restrictive immigration laws. They are often forced to separate for months or even years while one member, usually a parent or an older child, finds work and establishes residency before sending for the rest of the family. Undocumented immigrants sometimes go for years without seeing their families, as they cannot return to the United States if they leave.

Family networks are the primary source of aid in both Colombia and the United States. Relatives, godparents, and friends already living in the United States are often the only source of support for immigrants. They provide not only money and housing but also advice about work, legal concerns, and cultural matters. Once they are financially independent, most immigrants from Colombia remit a large portion of their salaries to family that they have left behind. On several occasions they have also united in the wake of natural disasters in Colombia. They responded quickly in 1985, for example, to a volcanic eruption in the northern part of the country that killed more than 20,000 and destroyed untold property. Through nationwide campaigns, they mounted one of the world's largest relief efforts on behalf of the volcano victims. In addition, in the wake of severe flooding in Colombia during 2011, organizations such as the Colombian Consulate in Los Angeles, the Colombian American Rotary Club, and the Colombian Press hosted fund-raisers, organized benefits, and called upon the Latino community in the United States to help rebuild Colombian communities that had been affected.

Colombian American singer Jason Castro (1987–) signs CDs in Myrtle Beach, South Carolina, 2013. JOE QUINN / ALAMY

Gender Roles In Colombia, traditional values define the home. The husband is the wage earner and head of the house, while the wife sets the tone of the household and rarely holds outside employment. Children are taught to obey their parents and respect authority. In the United States, families sometimes discover mainstream American life undermines the traditional roles of individuals. Lacking access to well-paid jobs, nearly all rely on two incomes to meet living expenses and are forced to adjust to the entrance of women into the workforce. In earning their own salary for the first time, women gain a measure of independence virtually unknown in Colombia and they also have more opportunities for education. By contrast, men usually have more difficulty finding work and often take more responsibility for household chores than they do in Colombia. These changes sometimes tear families apart. Despite strong cultural prohibitions, immigrants divorce far more often than their counterparts in Colombia. In other cases, families are strengthened in uniting against such pressure and transmitting traditional values to their children.

Education Colombian Americans value education highly and often move to the United States for the chance to educate their children through high school and beyond, a privilege reserved in Colombia for the wealthy. Such ready access offers a crucial advantage to immigrants from the middle and lower classes, for whom an American academic degree represents an end to the cycle of limited education and poorly paid work that inhibits economic mobility in Colombia. Some parents are, nonetheless, disappointed by U.S. public schools; they consider the curriculum lacking and are disturbed by the informal tone of the classroom, the rate of delinquency among American students, and the wide availability of drugs. They usually look to Catholic schools for an environment that emphasizes values in keeping with their own and enroll their children as soon as they can afford to do so.

According to the U.S. Census Bureau, 32 percent of Colombian Americans aged 25 or older had obtained at least a bachelor's degree as of 2010, which was a much higher figure than the 13 percent of Hispanics overall. An additional 35 percent of Colombian Americans aged 25 or older had graduated from high school.

Social Networks Colombian social networks are extensive and difficult to categorize. Doctors' associations in New York City and Chicago were probably the first Colombian organizations in the United States, and other professional societies soon followed. Social clubs based on regional identity became another community institution. Colombian Americans also developed strong ties with other Latinos through more informal networks. To some extent they share a common culture through Spanish-language media, which provide news, entertainment, and music from Latin America unavailable elsewhere. Social events draw immigrants from throughout Latin America and

are often held at neighborhood restaurants and nightclubs. Soccer is also widely popular; many Colombian Americans take part in local games and also closely observe the fortunes of Latin American teams.

EMPLOYMENT AND ECONOMIC CONDITIONS

Colombian Americans move to the United States primarily to work. With the deterioration of the Colombian economy during the second half of the twentieth century, the rate of emigration increased as some sought to escape rising unemployment, underemployment, and inflation. In the United States many Colombian Americans pursued professional careers; took employment as laborers, factory workers, and domestic servants; and opened

> [In Colombia] my surroundings and the narrow-mindedness of the people always bothered me. In the United States, on the other hand, I could be myself without worrying that others would think ill of me and work at whatever was most profitable without having others think that it was degrading.
>
> Julia de Riano, cited in Ramiro Cardona Gutiérrez's *El éxodo de colombianos*, 1980.

small businesses, often catering to Latin Americans. In New York City, those who could afford to buy property did so as soon as possible. As immigration restrictions tightened, however, fewer Colombian Americans planned to remain permanently in the United States, and it became more common for them to seek to work only long enough to improve their financial status before returning to Colombia, where inflation made investment and saving nearly impossible. From the 1970s through the 1990s, plans for temporary settlement were common among professionals, who in the United States found opportunities unavailable in Colombia to use their skills, earn salaries commensurate with their education, and enhance their professional standing through advanced training. In the first years of the twenty-first century, Colombian Americans had one of the highest average incomes among Latinos. Many have prospered in business, especially in ventures in Miami related to trade with Latin America.

Work is the focus of Colombian households. While men usually find their earning power diminished in the United States, women have many more opportunities than in Colombia. Despite a long-standing tradition of *machismo*, their husbands offer little or no resistance to their wives' employment because their salaries are needed to repay sponsors, meet daily expenses, support family members who stayed behind, and save money toward children's education, trips to Colombia, and other costs. Husbands and wives often operate small businesses together, and many people hold more than one job.

POLITICS AND GOVERNMENT

Until the late 1990s most Colombian Americans devoted themselves primarily to politics of Colombia rather than of the United States, believing that they would not remain abroad long enough to have any impact on American politics. More recently, however, this attitude began to change in states where Colombian Americans boasted a significant population. Although many Colombian Americans continue to invest more of their attention and resources in the politics of their home country (and, as a result, have yet to harness the political force similar to Hispanic groups such Cubans and Mexican Americans) organizational efforts in the United States began to take shape during the early 2000s. According to a 2007 report from the *Miami Herald* newspaper, Colombian American communities in South Florida and elsewhere were beginning to flex some political muscle.

During the 1990s, Colombian American groups were organized to back two ultimately failed pieces of legislation aimed at granting thousands of undocumented Colombians the right to remain in the United States legally. In 2001, hundreds of Colombian Americans attended conferences in Atlanta and Houston hoping to set a national political agenda.

According to the *Herald*, Colombian Americans have elected state legislators in Florida, South Carolina, Minnesota, and Rhode Island. Former Florida governor Jeb Bush tapped a Colombian American as a Broward County court judge, and in 2009 the community of West Kendall, Florida, erected the Plaza de Colombia to commemorate Colombian American heritage. Colombian American Jorge E. Meneses was elected mayor of Hackensack, New Jersey, in 2011.

During the lead-up to the 2012 U.S. presidential election, incumbent Barack Obama began actively to court the Colombian American vote, hosting dozens of Colombian American business and community leaders at the White House for an Independence Day celebration on June 20. Although they do not yet constitute a powerful, cohesive voting bloc, the concentration of Colombian Americans in politically important swing states such as Florida could mean their political clout is on the rise.

Meanwhile, the Colombian government has begun to focus more resources on organizing and mobilizing its large expatriate community in the United States. By founding a group called Colombia Unites Us, it began sponsoring seminars for Colombian American leaders in cities such as Houston, New York, and Miami with the goal of promoting Colombian political and social issues abroad.

NOTABLE INDIVIDUALS

Business Perhaps the best-known Colombian in American business is the entrepreneur María Elena Ibanez (born in Barranquilla); after helping to manage her father's orchards as a child in 1973 she moved to Miami, where she earned a degree in computer science

and later formed International High-Tech Marketing, a firm that sells computer equipment in more than 100 developing countries. Andrés Mejia is one of the world's largest suppliers of Paso Fino horses, and he maintains stables in Miami and Colombia.

Literature The works of Nobel Prize winner Gabriel García Márquez (born in Aracata in 1928) were among the first from Latin America widely read by an English-speaking audience, and their critical acclaim stimulated interest in other Latin American artists. A number of Colombian writers living in the United States have also enjoyed success. Silvio Martínez Palau (born in Calí in 1954) moved to the United States in the late 1960s and published the play *The English-Only Restaurant*, a collection of short stories titled *Made in USA*, and the novel *Disneylandia*. The playwright Enrique Buenaventura (1925–2003) has had his work performed in several American cities; his best-known play, *¡Por mi madre que es verdad!* (*I Swear on My Mother's Grave*), is set in the southern Bronx. Among the works of New York writer and professor Alister Ramírez Márquez is *Mi vestido verde esmeralda* (2006), which was published in English as *My Emerald Green Dress* in 2010.

Medicine Pilar Bernal de Pheils, an assistant clinical professor of nursing at the University of California, San Francisco, has promoted educational exchange programs allowing Latin American nurses to study and teach in the United States.

Music Popular musicians of Colombian decent who have found success in the United States include pop singer Soraya (1969–2006), folk musician Jason Castro (1987–), reggaetón singer-songwriter Adassa (1987–), hardcore punk vocalist Freddy Cricien (1976–), rock musician Alex González (1969–), country signer Marty Stuart (1958–), rapper Tonedeff (1978–), and hip hop DJ Rob Swift.

Performing Arts The best-known Colombian American in the performing arts is actor and comedian John Leguizamo (born in Bogotá, 1965), who has written and performed one-man comedies based on his childhood in Jackson Heights, including *Spic-O-Rama* and *Mambo Mouth*. He also has appeared in the motion pictures *Die Hard II* and *Hangin' with the Homeboys*. The actor Wilmer Valderrama (1980–), who appeared on the television sitcom *That '70s Show* and in numerous films, is of Colombian and Venezuelan decent. Rosario Vargas helped to form the Aguijón II Theater Company, the first Spanish-language theater company in Chicago, and remains one of its artistic directors. Actress Alexa Vega (1988–) appeared in popular films such as the *Spy Kids* franchise, *Ghosts of Mississippi*, *The Glimmer Man*, and *Twister*. After hosting programs for the Spanish-language television network Univision in the late 1990s, actress Sofía Vergara (1972–) took roles in a number of television series on ABC, including

Hot Properties (2005) and *The Knights of Prosperity* (2007). In 2009 she was cast in a leading role in the popular series *Modern Family*. Also appearing in several films and on Broadway, Vergara had by 2012 become one of the highest-paid women in television in the United States.

The dancer Ricardo Bustamante made his debut as a soloist with the American Ballet Theater in June 1989. Standup comedian Greg Giraldo (1965–2010) was a regular on television specials that aired on the Comedy Central network, and he worked with other well-known comedians such as Colin Quinn and Lewis Black.

Sports Numerous Colombian American players have starred in U.S. Major League Soccer, including Fredy Montero, Carlos Valderrama, Carlos Llamosa, Juan Agudelo, Juan Pablo Ángel, and David Ferreira. Englewood, New Jersey, native Alejandro Bedoya played for the U.S. national soccer team beginning in 2010 and professionally for several notable club teams in Europe. Colombian American Scott Gomez (from Anchorage, Alaska) was a three-time all-star in the National Hockey League and won a pair of Stanley Cup championships while playing for the New Jersey Devils during the 1999–2000 and 2002–2003 seasons. Medellín native Lou Castro in 1902 became the

first Latin American player to play in Major League Baseball, paving the way for other Colombians to play baseball in the United States, including: Edgar Rentería, Orlando Cabrera, Jackie Gutierrez, and Julio Teheran. Several Colombians have also made names for themselves in auto racing, including Juan Pablo Montoya, who made the jump to NASCAR in the United States in 2007 after years of successful competition in Formula 1 racing.

Visual Arts The artist Fernando Botero (born in Medellín, 1932) has gained international renown for his paintings, drawings, and sculptures of rotund figures; after presenting his first solo exhibition of watercolors in Mexico City as a young man, he lived in New York City during the 1960s, where his painting *Mona Lisa, Age 12* was shown at the Museum of Modern Art. Although decried by members of the academy, his work was enthusiastically received by a wide audience. In 1994 the city of Chicago showed seventeen of his bronze sculptures in an outdoor exhibition. Another Colombian artist who has exhibited his work widely in the United States is Enrique Gran, who was born in Panama, spent his childhood in Cartagena (Colombia), and studied painting at the Art Students League in New York City from 1940 to 1943. María Fernanda Cardoso (1963–) is known for her haunting sculptures dealing with violence in Colombia. Los Angeles–based artist America Martin is known for exuberant and bold paintings, often of the human form. Her paintings have been shown in galleries across the United States.

ORGANIZATIONS AND ASSOCIATIONS

Colombian American Association (CAA)

Objectives are to facilitate commerce and trade between the Republic of Colombia and the United States and to foster and advance cultural relations and goodwill between the two countries.

Christian Murrle, President
641 Lexington Avenue
Suite 1430
New York, New York 10022
Phone: (212) 233-7776
Email: programs@andean-us.com

Colombian American Service Association (CASA)

Strives to develop the well-being and protect the rights of all immigrant families while providing them with the tools of self-sufficiency.

Carolina Freedman
10300 SW 72 Street
Suite 387
Miami, Florida 33173
Phone: (305) 463-7468
Fax: (305) 273-4385

Colombian American Coalition of Florida (CASA)

Seeks to empower Colombian Americans and foster civic engagement, advocacy, and cultural initiatives by working with local, state, and national organizations.

Jose L. Castillo, Chair
16275 SW 88 Street #163
Miami, Florida 33196
Email: jl@colombianamericancoalition.org
URL: www.colombianamericancoalition.org

Colombian American Cultural Society

Seeks to preserve the traditions of the Colombian community in Rhode Island through social and community events for the purpose of uniting Colombian Americans in the state.

Monica Cortez, Secretary
504 Weeden Street
Pawtucket, Rhode Island 02860
Phone: (401) 663-3924
URL: www.colcultura.com

SOURCES FOR ADDITIONAL STUDY

Antonio, Angel-Junguito. *A Cry of Innocence: in Defense of Colombians.* Plantation, FL: Distinctive Pub. Corp., 1993.

Birnabaum, Larry. "Colombia's Vallenato Up North," *Newsday*, August 24, 1994 (Nassau and Suffolk County edition), B7.

Booth, William. "Miami Auditions for Lead in Latin American Affairs; As Leaders Gather for Summit, America's Southern Trade Hub Tries to Shed Vice-Squad Image," *Washington Post*, December 9, 1994, A1.

Chaney, Elsa M. "Colombian Outpost in New York City." In *Awakening Minorities: Continuity and Change*, edited by John R. Howard. 2nd ed., 67–74. New Brunswick, NJ: Transaction Books, 1983.

Dockterman, Daniel. "Hispanics of Colombian Origin in the United States." *Pew Research Center*, May 26, 2011.

Feldman, Claudia. "It Is a Source of Irritation to Some, a Matter of Cultural Pride to Others. Either Way, It Is a Fact of Life in Houston: Spanish Spoken Here," *Houston Chronicle*, November 20, 1994, 1.

Garza, Melita Marie. "Census Puts Latinos in Bittersweet Light," *Chicago Tribune*, October 20, 1994, 1.

Woods, Casey. "U.S. Colombians Seek More Political Clout." *Miami Herald*, September 23, 2007.

CONGOLESE AMERICANS

Craig Beebe

OVERVIEW

Congolese Americans are immigrants or descendants of people from either of two southern African countries, the Democratic Republic of the Congo (DRC) and the Republic of the Congo (the Congo). Both are located in central Africa, along the Congo River, the world's ninth-longest river, which forms most of the border between the two countries. The Republic of the Congo lies to the west of the DRC and is bordered by the Atlantic Ocean and Gabon to its west and Cameroon and the Central African Republic to its north. The much-larger DRC is bordered by the Atlantic Ocean and the Republic of the Congo to its west; Zambia and Angola to its south; Uganda, Rwanda, Tanzania, and Burundi to its east; and South Sudan and the Central African Republic to its north. Much of the interior of both nations is forested; the DRC is home to the Congo rain forest, the world's second-largest after the Amazon. The DRC, Africa's second-largest nation and the world's eleventh largest, has an area of 905,355 square miles (2,345,409 square kilometers), about one-fourth the size of the United States; the Republic of the Congo, at 132,047 square miles (342,000 square kilometers), is slightly smaller than Montana.

A July 2012 estimate from the *CIA World Factbook* puts the DRC's population at about 74 million and the population of the Republic of the Congo at approximately 4.4 million. The people of both nations are at least half Christian, though the DRC is more so; about 25 percent of people in the Republic of the Congo practice animism—the belief that natural objects have souls or consciousness—and other indigenous African religions. About 10 percent of DRC residents practice animism or other indigenous religions, and another 10 percent are Muslim. The DRC has been scarred by decades of conflict, enduring a brutal dictatorship under Joseph Mobutu over three decades beginning in the 1960s, followed by extended conflict and political instability. Its economy is heavily dependent on mineral exports, though it has been slow to recover from decades of corruption and conflict. The relatively stable Republic of the Congo, which still experienced violent conflicts in the 1990s, was once one of Africa's largest petroleum producers, but this industry is declining.

Residents of the Congo region first came to American shores against their will during the transatlantic slave trade, which lasted from the early 1500s until the mid-nineteenth century. The west-central African region was one of the major sources of slaves. More recent immigration to the United States began in the mid-twentieth century, when poverty, violence, and war drove several million Congolese from the region, mostly to other African nations and Europe. Many Congolese Americans originally came to the United States for education, intending to return home, but were forced to stay due to deteriorating circumstances in the DRC and the Republic of the Congo. From the 1990s onward, most Congolese immigrants were war refugees from the DRC, many of them from the especially war-torn eastern part of the country.

The U.S. Census Bureau does not maintain estimates of the number of Congolese Americans; they are grouped together with other Americans of Sub-Saharan African origin. Some estimates suggest that the year 2010 alone saw more than 3,000 refugees from the DRC and therefore put the number of Congolese Americans somewhere between 60,000 and 200,000. Furthermore, no estimate exists of the number of African Americans who may be descendants of slaves from the region. According to the U.S. Census Bureau's American Community Survey estimates for 2006–2010, the states with the largest populations of Congolese Americans included Maryland, New York, North Carolina, and Texas.

HISTORY OF THE PEOPLE

Early History The Congo River network has been a site of human habitation, agriculture, and industry for several thousand years, sustaining a variety of ethnic groups amid the lush jungles and open plains of the Congo River and its tributaries. By 500 BCE, Bantu-speaking people had entered the Congo savannahs from the north, rapidly displacing the indigenous Pygmy people. Later migrations from Sudan and East Africa further diversified the ethnic milieu as a mixed economy developed throughout the region. The mouth of the Congo, named for the Kongo people who ruled it, became a significant trading site, particularly for slaves, and was claimed by the Portuguese empire in the fifteenth century CE. By the sixteenth century the Luba Empire had formed in what is now the southern DRC, maintaining military and economic control over a vast area of southern Africa with a wide-ranging trading network and developing a rich artistic and cultural identity. The Luba Empire declined in the late eighteenth century as slave raiders from the east weakened the state's power.

As the Luba Empire waned, European powers began to take more interest in the vast Congo region. Sir Henry Stanley Morton led the first European expedition to navigate the entire Congo River in the 1870s, on behalf of King Leopold II of Belgium. Leopold shrewdly played the other European powers off each other and was formally granted rights to own the Congo at the Conference of Berlin in 1885. Declaring the entire land that is now the DRC his private property and naming it the Congo Free State, his regime undertook major infrastructure projects, including a railway from the coast to the capital of Leopoldville (later renamed Kinshasa). At the same time Leopold began to exploit the resources of the land, particularly rubber, and the natives' labor in order to extract it. Slavery, brutal practices, and disease outbreaks brought serious misery to the Congolese people under Leopold's rule. Historian Adam Hoschild estimated in 1998 that about half the population (about 10 million, based on official Belgian census numbers from the time) of the Congo perished during the Free State period.

As these brutalities reached the attention of the international community through journalistic accounts and novels such as Joseph Conrad's *Heart of Darkness* (1899), the Belgian parliament took control of the rechristened Belgian Congo in 1908, with a promise to improve human conditions and foster development. It continued as such until 1960, with the colonial government opening new markets for copper and diamond mining, palm oil production, cotton, and later uranium. Although the colonial government brought considerable social progress to the region in the form of better health care, education, and water infrastructure, much of the nation's wealth was still being extracted with little benefit to its inhabitants, and the Congolese desire for full independence grew more pronounced in the years after World War II.

The Republic of the Congo, which had for many centuries been a major transatlantic shipping center for slaves, raw goods from the interior, and manufactured goods, came under French rule in 1880 as French Congo, later incorporated into French Equatorial Africa (AEF), with Brazzaville on the Congo River as its capital. While French rule was not as brutal as Leopold's, French policies also focused on extensive mineral extraction to be carried out by native people. After the Nazi occupation of France during World War II, Brazzaville became the symbolic capital of the French government-in-exile, and the nation's economy and stature benefited as a result. Following the war, the AEF was dissolved and the French began to take steps to grant full independence to the Republic of the Congo.

Modern History The DRC was granted independence from Belgium on June 30, 1960, just a month and a half before the Republic of the Congo was freed from French rule on August 15, 1960. Leopoldville was established as the capital of the DRC, while Brazzaville, just across the Congo River, became the capital of the Republic of the Congo.

Within a few months the DRC had fallen into a dispute over leadership. During the crisis the army chief of staff, Mobutu, acted with U.S. and Belgian backing to create a mutiny and took over the DRC's government in a coup. By 1965 he had a firm grip over the nation and in 1971 changed its name to Zaire. Mobutu ruled with an iron fist for several decades. He was largely supported by the U.S. government and other Western powers, as he was seen to be a road block to communism in the region. He established a one-party system, banned dissent, and created a cult of personality with his image on all currency and his portrait in most buildings. Corruption was also widespread; Mobutu himself reportedly stole as much as $4 billion dollars from the nation's coffers and from international assistance. He also engaged in Africanizing much of the country, renaming colonial cities and banning Western-style clothing.

After the fall of the Soviet Union in 1991, Mobutu began to face increasing pressure from within and outside the country to allow democratic reforms. Though on the surface he appeared to be open to such changes, his time in power was running out. In 1996 the Rwandan civil war and genocide spilled into Zaire as militias from the Hutu ethnic group entered the nation and military-occupied refugee camps. Reacting to this, Rwandan and Ugandan armies invaded the nation. Called the First Congo War, the fighting lasted until Mobutu fled into exile in May 1997.

Laurent-Désiré Kabila became president and immediately restored the old name of the Democratic Republic of the Congo. He also moved to consolidate power and expel foreign troops from the nation. Yet Rwanda and Uganda each created their own rebel movements within the country to remove Kabila and establish their own regimes. These militia attacked the DRC army in 1998, launching the Second Congo War. Angola, Zimbabwe, and Namibia also soon entered to defend the Kabila regime. Kabila was assassinated in 2001 and succeeded by his son, Joseph Kabila, who worked with the United Nations to initiate peace talks, resulting in a shared-power agreement that ended most of the armed conflict. Voters approved a new constitution at the end of 2005, and in July 2006 the nation held its elections. This led to street battles between supporters of Kabila and supporters of former rebel leader Jean-Pierre Bemba. A second round of elections swept Kabila firmly into power, and he was sworn in as president.

Conflict persists in the DRC, however, particularly in its eastern regions, where militias often fight with each other and the DRC army. Rwanda and other neighboring countries are accused of backing

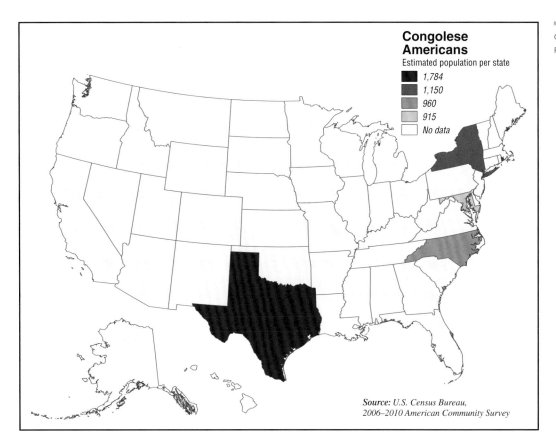

Congolese Americans
Estimated population per state

- 1,784
- 1,150
- 960
- 915
- No data

Source: U.S. Census Bureau, 2006–2010 American Community Survey

these militias as proxies, and the fighting has been brutal. Civilians have suffered immensely, with tens of thousands dying monthly from war, hunger, disease, and other humanitarian crises. Sexual violence is reported to be rampant, with as many as 200,000 women raped, and children have died in horrific numbers. As many as 400,000 citizens have fled as refugees, mostly to other African nations. Somewhere between three and six million DRC emigrants live abroad, with nearly three-quarters elsewhere in Africa and about 16 percent in Europe, particularly France. Another 2.5 million DRC citizens are internally displaced.

The Republic of the Congo has been more stable through its independence than its neighbor. After a succession of leaders in its first decade, a 1968 coup established Africa's first "people's republic" under a Marxist ideology. The nation aligned itself with the Soviet Union and depended on political repression and patronage to hold power. By the 1990s the Republic of the Congo had taken steps toward democratization and liberalization of its economy, with presidential elections held in 1992. These were interrupted, however, by a power struggle beginning in 1997 between the longtime socialist leader, Denis Sassou Nguesso, and the democratically elected president, Pascal Lissouba. A four-month war and Angolan invasion preserved Sassou's control. Disputed elections and a constitutional referendum followed, along with an

unsuccessful rebellion in the nation's south. Sassou was again named president in 2009 in an election that international observers said was marked by fraud and irregularities.

SETTLEMENT IN THE UNITED STATES
Although untold numbers of people (some studies report one in five people) in the Congo region were brought to North America via the transatlantic slave trade between the fifteenth and nineteenth centuries, modern Congolese immigration to the United States began shortly after the DRC and Republic of the Congo achieved independence in 1960. During this period many Congolese came to the United States for educational purposes—often on scholarships that had been created to help young Africans learn about government, education, health care, and other essential issues overseas—intending to return to their native countries to help with modernization.

But the increasingly violent civil strife in the Congo region led many of these once-temporary residents of the United States to stay. Some married Americans and began raising families; some left for other African nations or Europe. Many of these early immigrants were already well educated and were able to find work in academia or other professional fields. A number clustered around the Boston area and became connected with institutions such as

Harvard University and the Massachusetts Institute of Technology. These older waves and their children probably still make up most of the Congolese in the United States today. As the violence has grown in the Congo region, particularly in the DRC, many more recent immigrants from the region have been refugees or seekers of political asylum. However, the logistics and cost of making it to the United States, along with cultural and linguistic factors, have meant that most Congolese refugees immigrate to other African nations, France, and French-speaking cities in Canada.

The areas with the most Congolese Americans as of 2013 were Raleigh, North Carolina; Boston; Dallas; Los Angeles; the San Francisco Bay Area; New York; and Washington, D.C. Each of these had a minimum of 5,000 Congolese immigrants. Chicago also had a sizable Congolese American population. Several of these cities, including Raleigh, grew in importance in the 1980s and 1990s as destinations for Congolese after a few families were able to establish themselves, which then attracted more immigrants. Congolese immigrants in Boston are usually more educated and work for universities in the area. Washington, D.C., has a mix of diplomats and former Congolese government officials, many of whom worked with the Mobutu regime.

Some refugees find their way to relatively unexpected cities, including Syracuse, New York, which in 2012 claimed about 300 families, most of whom had arrived in the previous five years. Burlington, Vermont, is also a common destination for refugees. Nonprofits such as Catholic Relief Services, along with the U.S. Department of Homeland Security (DHS), have helped place Congolese in these and other less urban areas, where they are typically welcomed and have an easier time feeling a part of the community. For instance, Congolese Americans in Syracuse wrote and produced a play with Syracuse University titled *Cry for Peace*, which raised awareness of their journey. The play was performed in New York City in 2012.

Although estimates of the number of Congolese Americans vary widely, the annual arrivals to the United States remain quite small relative to the overall refugee population from the DRC. However, these numbers were larger toward the end of the first decade of the 2000s than in previous years. According to Department of Homeland Security statistics, from 2002 to 2005 the annual number of new permanent residents from the DRC was between 100 and 200; by the end of the decade, the number had risen to between 1,500 and 2,500 per year. Immigrants from the Republic of the Congo remained more constant at around 1,000 per year from 2006 to 2011. According to the DHS, refugees and asylum-seekers made up most of the new permanent residents in 2011. A much smaller number of immigrants from the Congo region become naturalized U.S. citizens each year, though these numbers also rose during the decade, from about

250 combined in 2002 to about 1,250 in 2011. Large numbers of Congolese Americans have settled in North Carolina, Texas, New York, and Maryland.

Since many Congolese in the United States are refugees, they may view their stay as temporary. They also face distinct challenges, including speaking a new language and living in environments quite unlike Congo. Some suffer from post-traumatic stress disorder, bipolar disorder, and other mental health problems due to previous trauma. This can contribute to difficulty in finding a community, housing, and employment in the United States. Fortunately, an informal network of Congolese exists throughout the nation for support, along with a number of organizations in various regions of the country. Some nonprofit groups refer to them as a forgotten group of immigrants and work actively to raise awareness about their needs and challenges.

LANGUAGE

More than 200 languages are spoken in the DRC and the Republic of the Congo, reflecting the cultural diversity of the region and the many peoples who live there. French is the official language of both countries and has been since colonial times. Most residents of both countries can speak at least some French, and it is an important common tongue that allows people of different ethnic groups to communicate. However, each country also recognizes several "national languages" spoken by large numbers of people in various regions. In the DRC these include Lingala, a Bantu language spread by missionaries that is now spoken by as many as ten million people through much of the north and in the capital region and remains the official language of the army; Kikongo, spoken in the southwest; Swahili, used in the east; and Tshiluba, spoken in south-central DRC. Kikongo was the language of many Congolese taken to the Americas during the slave trade, and some have argued that its influence can still be seen in the creole dialects of the Caribbean and the American South. The Republic of the Congo also recognizes Lingala as a national language, along with Kituba, which is similar to Kikongo.

Language is a particular difficulty for many recent Congolese arrivals to the United States. Very few speak English, and lacking significant concentrations of fellow Congolese Americans, they often must learn English quickly if they are to find work. Congolese American children born in the United States usually speak English fluently and often act as intermediaries or translators for their parents. Additionally, a number of Congolese Americans teach their children a native tongue at home, such as Lingala, and many are fluent in three or more languages.

RELIGION

European colonists and missionaries brought Christianity to the Congo region, and now it is by far the dominant faith among Congolese. In both the DRC and the Republic of the Congo, Catholicism is the largest Christian sect; as the official religion of colonial governments, it spread effectively throughout the region. Roughly half the population of each country is Catholic. Protestantism is also widespread, with missionaries gaining a foothold in the late nineteenth century. Today 35 to 40 percent of both countries' population is Protestant. The Church of Jesus Christ of Latter-day Saints (LDS) has been successful in the DRC since the arrival of Mormon missionaries in 1986, with about 30,000 adherents as of 2011, according to official LDS estimates. There are also several homegrown Christian sects that follow a specific leader or incorporate elements of traditional African religion into Christianity. Minorities practice Islam or animistic religions.

Religion is typically important to Congolese Americans, particularly refugees. For many Congolese Americans, church is not just a religious gathering but also a place to connect and build community. Many churches, including mainstream American denominations, work in the Congo region and help with the process of immigration and adaptation.

U.S. cities with the highest number of Congolese Americans are the most likely to have Congolese American churches. They typically feature pastors of Congolese descent and offer energetic services with a great deal of dancing, singing in Congolese languages, and vocal prayer. Often these Congolese churches use rented space in an existing American church—for instance, holding their service on a Sunday afternoon.

In some cases yet another immigrant group will use the church for its services in the evening. Sometimes Congolese Americans will combine with other African groups for church as well.

A smaller number of Congolese Americans are Catholic and attend Catholic services with other American groups. Thus, their worship experience is more Westernized than Catholic services in the Congo region. However, even these Catholics will sometimes attend a Protestant service at a Congolese American congregation in order to sing familiar songs from their homeland and participate in a familiar kind of worship.

CULTURE AND ASSIMILATION

Though they come from a variety of ethnic groups, speak many languages, and practice several religions, Congolese Americans are unified in their pride about the Congo. Since many of them are recent immigrants, they often find American culture quite different from their own and will seek to maintain traditional customs through immigrant associations and informal channels with fellow Congolese Americans. They seek opportunities to speak common languages, eat familiar food, and hear music from the homeland. At the same time, many are driven to succeed in American culture, and they often quickly pick up the ability to fit in with other Americans, learning the language and style of dress quickly, while maintaining long-held customs at home and with fellow Congolese Americans.

Hassan and Dawami Hadam moved to the United States, with their sons, as refugees from the Congo. MELANIE STETSON FREEMAN / THE CHRISTIAN SCIENCE MONITOR / GETTY IMAGES

MUAMBA NSUSU (CHICKEN SOUP)

Ingredients

1 3–4 chicken, cut into parts

1 large onion, chopped

palm oil

small can of tomato paste

½ cup natural peanut butter (made from only peanuts and salt)

dried chile pepper or cayenne pepper, to taste

Preparation

Fill a large pot with enough water for soup. Bring it to a boil. Add the chicken and simmer it until the meat is done and a broth is obtained, about 40 minutes. Skim foam or fat as it forms on the surface. When cooked, take the chicken from the broth and remove meat from the bones. Keep the broth at a low simmer.

While the chicken is simmering, gently sauté the onion in several tablespoons of palm oil until the onion is tender.

Combine 1 cup of the chicken broth with the peanut butter and tomato paste and stir until smooth.

Return the chicken meat and onions to the broth and add the peanut butter-tomato paste mixture. Stir and continue to simmer until the soup is thickened. Season to taste.

Serve with rice or fufu and more hot pepper to taste.

Traditions and Customs In addition to coming from two nations, Congolese Americans belong to a variety of ethnic groups with distinct customs, dress, and song. Many find it important to maintain the customs unique to their ethnic group while living in the United States, yet they also commonly identify as Congolese. As a whole they have strong national pride, even among second-generation Congolese Americans. They work for a strong sense of unity despite ethnic, religious, and linguistic differences.

Cuisine Congolese cuisine varies widely by region and ethnic group. An ingredient used by many Congolese ethnic groups is cassava. Though native to South America, cassava—also known as yuca or manioc—is common in much of Africa. It is a tuber and commonly provides the central starch for Congolese meals, often in a paste or mash called *fufu*. This can be eaten with a stew of meat or peanuts and vegetables. Also popular among Congolese are *lituma*, a mashed plantain dish, and *mikate*, a type of fried donut often dipped in peanut butter.

Popular meat dishes include a variety of preparations of goat and chicken, as well as smoked and fried fish (*mpiodi*). Congolese meals are often vegetarian—not for ethical or religious reasons but

because meat is too expensive for many in the DRC and the Republic of the Congo.

Most Congolese Americans continue to make traditional dishes in the United States, though many ingredients, such as traditional herbs and spices, are difficult to find, particularly in smaller cities. Many Congolese find American food too bland and feel there is not enough variety. Attendees of most Congolese American celebrations and festivals expect to be served traditional Congolese dishes; if certain ones are missing, guests will be disappointed.

To procure these ingredients, Congolese Americans in many cities have set up informal networks to import ingredients from the Congo. One individual will purchase the ingredients and then sell and distribute them to others in the local community. He or she will often alert the community via e-mail that the food is available. Similar trades and networks are maintained for goods such as clothing, music, and DVDs that are hard to find in the United States. In other cases Congolese Americans must adapt dishes using American ingredients. For instance, while palm oil is a common ingredient in the Congo, it is harder to find in the United States, so canola, peanut, or another oil must be used instead.

Since Congolese Americans are relatively scattered geographically and are a small ethnic group overall, few if any obviously Congolese restaurants exist in the United States. However, in some communities, including Pittsburgh, Pennsylvania, there are restaurants owned by Congolese Americans that serve some traditional dishes, though they are often marketed as simply African in order to attract a broader clientele. Other African restaurants owned by members of different ethnic groups will also sometimes serve Congolese dishes.

Traditional Dress Traditional Congolese dress typically features vibrant and colorful prints for both men and women, worn as long dresses for women and flowing suits for men. Patterns and colors often indicate something about a person's ethnicity, clan, or region. Because of the region's tropical climate, the cloth is usually very thin. In the DRC Mobutu's ideology of *authenticité* largely banned the wearing of Western-style clothing shortly after the country's independence, and men were forced to wear a simple suit known as an *abacost*. The bright traditional patterns of indigenous clothing were also strongly discouraged for many years but have crept back into fashion. Congolese Americans usually wear Western-style clothing to blend with American culture but don traditional colorful prints for events such as cultural festivals, holidays, and concerts or performances.

Dances and Songs The Congolese cultures are well known for their energetic dancing and drumming. Although styles vary between ethnic groups, the dancing symbolizes aspects of life and community and is often considered sacred. Other dances are considered more social and are improvised, with many dancers performing simultaneously.

Particularly important to the performance is the *ngoma* wooden drum, which is played by hand throughout southern and East Africa, often with many drummers playing complex rhythms at the same time. The drums look similar to congas but come in various sizes and shapes and are often carved from one log. In dancing performances *ngomas* are usually accompanied by other percussion instruments, including *nskalas*, rattles made from seed pods; *kisansis*, or thumb pianos; and the *ngongui*, a cowbell-type instrument.

Congolese dancing and drumming have grown increasingly popular in the United States in recent decades. Classes are taught in many major U.S. cities and at colleges and universities, often by Congolese refugees or immigrants. The Congolese have also continued to innovate in dance and have influenced many modern dance trends in Africa and the United States. The *soukous*, a style of dance music rooted in rumba, originated in the DRC in the 1940s and has remained popular throughout Africa. Another style, *kwassa kwassa*, has worked its way into American popular music in songs such as Vampire Weekend's 2007 hit "Cape Cod Kwassa Kwassa."

Congolese singing is also highly celebrated, with styles varying considerably between ethnic groups. One folk song that has risen to international popularity and is performed by choirs in the United States and other nations is the Kiluba-language "Banaha" (banana), originally sung as a marching song by soldiers. It features repetitive call-and-response lyrics and typically drums and other percussion instruments. Much of the indigenous music was suppressed in the DRC under Mobutu but has continued to be popular globally.

Holidays Recent immigrants to the United States from the Republic of the Congo and the DRC may celebrate their countries' Independence Days: August 15 and June 30, 1960, respectively. For the Republic of the Congo this day commemorates independence from France; the DRC holiday celebrates liberation from Belgian rule. In Africa the holidays are typically marked with parades, often including the military, as well as festivals and parties. Congolese Americans may celebrate with traditional song or dancing and dishes eaten with fellow Congolese immigrants.

Congolese Americans also observe major Christian holidays, with Christmas being an especially important holiday. In the DRC it is usually celebrated with festive singing and pageants performed at churches on Christmas Eve, often running late into the evening or even through the night. Gifts are less emphasized than in the United States.

FAMILY AND COMMUNITY LIFE

Family is very important in the DRC and the Republic of the Congo, and this strong sense of kinship also exists among Congolese Americans. All members of the family are responsible for each other's well-being, and each acts as a representative of the family in interactions with others. Some fraying of family bonds occurs upon immigration to the United States, especially as families are split up regionally or internationally. Furthermore, younger Congolese Americans typically do not find family ties to be as important. For instance, Congolese American children may not appreciate their parents' desire to know all about their friends' families before allowing a social engagement. Still, family bonds remain strong, and many Congolese Americans send significant sums of money back to Africa to support family members who have not immigrated. According to the International Fund for Agricultural Development, at least $1 billion is sent in remittances to the DRC and the Republic of the Congo each year by the global Congolese diaspora, representing a major part of the region's economy.

> *Congolese dancing and drumming have grown increasingly popular in the United States in recent decades. Classes are taught in many major U.S. cities and at colleges and universities, often by Congolese refugees or immigrants. The Congolese have also continued to innovate in dance and have influenced many modern dance trends in Africa and the United States.*

Extended family is very important to Congolese Americans, and many families are split between the two continents. Even Congolese Americans born in the United States will often have aunts, uncles, or cousins in Africa with whom they correspond or to whom they send remittances. Many traditions and attitudes toward gender, education, and work are passed down through families. Yet in the United States some Congolese Americans—particularly women—are beginning to challenge traditional attitudes and pursue new careers and lifestyles.

According to the U.S. State Department, the number of Congolese children adopted by American families has increased, from less than a dozen adoptions annually before 2008 to more than 130 in 2011, almost exclusively from the DRC. These families have access to classes, organizations, and local Congolese American communities to teach their children about Congolese traditions.

Gender Roles As a whole, Congolese culture is male dominated. However, as with other aspects of traditional life, Congolese Americans have varying attitudes toward gender depending on their ethnic group. For instance, before colonization the Bakongo people had a matriarchal system. To this day some Bakongo traditions related to weddings and other important

CRY FOR PEACE: VOICES FROM THE CONGO

Emmanuel Ndeze didn't find freedom as quickly as he thought he would when he escaped the Democratic Republic of the Congo. Instead, he spent twelve years in a Ugandan labor camp before he finally made it to Syracuse, New York, in 2008 with his wife, their two children, and his sister. Kambale Syaghuswa was trained to be a child soldier, but he, too, escaped and eventually made it to Syracuse, where he found work as a truck driver. On October 18, 2012, Ndeze, Syaghuswa, and three fellow Congolese Americans took the stage in New York City at La MaMa's Ellen Stewart Theatre to tell their stories. The play, *Cry for Peace: Voices from the Congo*, was produced by Ping Chong and Company and ran for two weeks, earning widespread praise from audience members and critics alike.

In Chong's production, the speakers, none of whom are trained actors, sit in a semicircle, reading their lines as series of photos depicting the Congo's breathtaking landscape and documenting its bloody history are projected on the screen behind them. Four of the five speakers experienced the atrocities they narrate. The fifth, Beatrice Neema, is a surrogate for a woman who could not bear the pain of telling her story but nevertheless wanted it shared.

The idea for the play started with Cyprien Mihigo, a Congolese American community activist and one of the play's speakers. In 2011 Mihigo brought Congolese refugees from several antagonistic tribes together to cowrite a play about the country's history. He gave a draft of the play to Kyle Bass, the dramaturge at Syracuse Stage, a local theater affiliated with Syracuse University. Bass asked Mihigo for permission to reshape the work into a documentary play that connected individual experience to the broader history of the Congo. Mihigo told Maureen Nolan of the *Syracuse Post Standard* that the goal of the play is to promote peace in the United States and in his native country, and that he hoped to one day stage the play in the Congo.

events cannot happen without the mother's approval. However, the majority of cultures are patriarchal. Under colonial and independent governments in Congo, men have generally held positions of power, received greater access to education, and filled most work positions, while women have been expected to be subservient and to raise children. These roles have changed somewhat for Congolese immigrants in the United States, perhaps due to the fact that there are more women than men in the Congolese American population.

Many Congolese American immigrants come to the United States and see things that were prohibited to them in Africa, whether this is women holding a high position in government or doing certain activities such as smoking in public. Inspired by this, a growing number of Congolese American women have sought higher education and as of 2013 have higher college attendance rates than men. This has created its own challenges, however, as many Congolese women want to marry Congolese men and are unable to find suitable partners to match their education and training. Some Congolese American groups are working to correct this imbalance.

Women in the Congolese American community have also created their own organizations for action and mobilization. One such group is the Diaspora Congolese Women Network, which is working to raise awareness about violence against women in the Congo.

Education Decades of war and neglect have taken a toll on the Congolese public school system. Facilities are often poor and overcrowded, books and materials are scarce, and instruction is inconsistent. Still more Congolese are unable to attend school due to conflict or poverty.

In the United States most Congolese American children attend public school, which is a vastly different experience, with free books, well-maintained facilities, sufficient teachers, and even buses to take students to and from school—all of which are rare in Africa. Relationships with teachers are also different; rather than showing extreme deference to teachers as in Africa, in the United States students are expected to interact with their teachers. Most Congolese Americans born in the United States have an easy time working through the primary and secondary educational system.

While most of these changes are positive for children's education, the transition can be difficult for recent arrivals from Africa, and many schools with large refugee populations have social workers to help with acculturation. Some schools receive sensitivity training to help children who have experienced trauma in Africa adjust to their lives in the United States. Stereotyping and bullying of recently arrived Congolese American children remain a problem in certain communities.

Courtship and Weddings Marriage is an important ritual among Congolese Americans, as it unites two families. Many families still practice dowry. Before a man can marry a woman, he must introduce himself to her family, who will ceremoniously list the dowry, or expected gifts that the groom and his family must provide for permission. These include money and goods, some of which then become part of the wedding ceremony and reception, which is usually paid for by the bride's family.

Many Congolese Americans practice three types of weddings: civil, religious, and cultural; these are sometimes mixed to varying extent. Religious wedding ceremonies are most likely to be Catholic or Protestant. The couple may bring their own choir or priest to match their traditions and customs, sometimes singing songs in their native language. Additionally, for the church service and reception, some ethnic groups have certain customary ceremonies, including dances, clothing, songs, stories, or food that must be part of the ceremony. When the newly married couple leave the ceremony, they typically are followed by a parade of guests in their cars, honking and waving to wish the couple well.

As important as tradition is, however, Congolese Americans have also adopted some American traditions, such as the bride wearing a white dress and the groom a tuxedo or suit.

EMPLOYMENT AND ECONOMIC CONDITIONS

Before the major refugee waves of the late twentieth and early twenty-first centuries, most Congolese immigrants arrived for educational reasons. Many earned advanced degrees and, after choosing to stay in the country, found professional work as professors, writers, doctors, researchers, or in other positions. More recent arrivals have tended to be refugees and, whatever their education and experience, have had to accept more menial employment. Many advocates worry that the relatively small number of Congolese Americans in the nation makes them less visible than other groups and thus more economically vulnerable.

According to the American Community Survey, in 2011 about 16 percent of working Congolese Americans held manufacturing jobs, and slightly more than 25 percent were employed in the service industry. Sales and office positions were also common, as were positions in education, health care, and social services. Some seek work with companies that have a Congolese American in a management position; this is true for some high-tech manufacturing positions in the Raleigh area and for a large food-distribution company in New York. Other Congolese Americans own or manage businesses such as convenience stores or hair salons, and still others work in the government sector.

Because many Congolese Americans support family members in the United States and in Africa, they work several jobs to earn enough to send remittances home. Others attend school in addition to working and are inspired by Congolese Americans who have achieved success in the United States.

POLITICS AND GOVERNMENT

Whether they regard their stay in the United States as permanent or not, many Congolese Americans remain interested in politics in their home countries, hoping for a peaceful resolution to continuing conflicts and a better health, prosperity, and quality of life for the Congolese people. Most still have numerous family members in Africa, so this concern is deeply personal.

To an increasing extent, Congolese Americans are participating in U.S. politics. Generally, Congolese Americans support candidates from the Democratic Party. Some have been working to elect a congressperson of Congolese descent; such efforts are particularly discussed in North Carolina. The election of Barack Obama as president in 2008 was an inspiring moment for many Congolese Americans. Many urge the U.S. government to take a more direct role in Africa by supporting democracy and development, assisting with the capture and prosecution of war criminals, and providing additional humanitarian aid.

NOTABLE INDIVIDUALS

Many African Americans who were enslaved may be of Congolese origin, since the region was such a significant source for the slave trade through the early nineteenth century. However, for many African American descendants of slaves, it is difficult or impossible to trace their Congolese heritage.

Government Thurgood Marshall (1908–1993) was the first African American justice of the U.S. Supreme Court. Born in Maryland, he was the great-grandson of a slave from what is now the DRC. After graduating from Lincoln University, he attended the Howard University School of Law, and in 1936 he began working with the National Association for the Advancement of Colored People (NAACP), for which he argued several significant civil rights cases before the Supreme Court. One of these cases, *Brown v. Board of Education* (1954), abolished segregation in the U.S. public education system. Marshall was made solicitor general by President Lyndon Johnson in 1965—he was the first African American to hold that position—before being appointed to the Supreme Court by Johnson two years later. Known as a liberal, his opinions on the court favored strong individual rights and civil rights. He resigned from the court in 1991.

Journalism Mvemba Dizolele (1963–) is a journalist who has researched and written extensively about relations between the United States and Africa. Born in the DRC, he came to the United States in 1988 and attended Southern Utah University before earning two master's degrees at the University of Chicago. He also served in the U.S. Marines. Dizolele has been honored as a Campbell Fellow and a Duignan Fellow at the Hoover Institution at Stanford University and has published articles in *Foreign Policy*, the *New York Times*, *Forbes*, and the *New Republic*, as well as providing commentary to numerous television and radio programs. He is fluent in seven languages, including Swahili, Kikongo, and Lingala, and blogs at www.dizolele.com.

Journalist Joy-Ann Reid has worked as a political commentator for television and radio news since 1998. In addition to her on-air work for stations such as MSNBC, CNBC, and Britain's Sky News, Reid has been the managing editor of TheGrio.com and a columnist for the *Miami Herald*. Born to a Congolese father and Guyanese mother, Reid attended Harvard University and was a 2003 Knight Center for Specialized Journalism fellow. In 2004 she became state deputy communications director for American Coming Together, a political action group focused on registering voters. In 2008 she served as a press aide for Barack Obama's presidential campaign. Reid blogs at *open salon* and *The Reid Report Blog*.

Literature Zamba Zembola (c. 1780–?) claimed to be the son of a Congolese king who went from the Congo to South Carolina as a free man in the early 1800s, only to be seized into slavery. He worked for forty years on a plantation before regaining his freedom and published a memoir, *The Life and Adventures of Zamba, an African Negro King, and His Experience of Slavery in South Carolina*, in 1847. The work captured the squalid and inhumane conditions endured by many American slaves and remains an important primary document for researchers today.

Philippe Wamba (1971–2002) was a memoirist and an editor who explored his Congolese roots in deeply personal works, including *Kinship: A Family's Journey in Africa and America* (1999), about his parents' origins and his childhood. Wamba's mother, an African American, met his father, a Congolese student, in the United States, and they raised him in Tanzania. After attending Harvard and Columbia University, Wamba died in a car accident in Kenya while doing research for another book.

Music Réjane Magloire (c. 1965–) is a vocalist and an actress. Born in the DRC, she grew up in New York, where she studied opera. She was well known for her role as Samantha on the children's television show *The Electric Company* in the 1970s. In the 1980s and 1990s she performed with the group Indeep, whose biggest hit was 1982's "Last Night a D.J. Saved My Life," and Technotronic, known for hits including "Pump Up the Jam." In 2005 she released a solo album, *Forbidden Opera*.

Sports Dikembe Mutumbo (1966–) was one of the top National Basketball Association players of the 1990s and 2000s, known especially for his defensive skills. Born in Kinshasa, he came to the United States to attend Georgetown University on a scholarship from the U.S. Agency for International Development. Though he spoke no English, he was recruited to play basketball and quickly became a star. He was drafted to the Denver Nuggets in 1991 and played for several teams before wrapping up his career with the Houston Rockets in 2009. He was named an all-star eight times during his career. Mutumbo has also been honored for humanitarian work in Africa and speaks nine languages.

MEDIA

As of 2013 Congolese Americans were too scattered and small a group to have created their own media sources in press or television. However, several radio programs that play African music feature Congolese music and culture in their programming.

RADIO

Africa Mix, KALW 91.7 FM

Each Thursday night from 9 p.m. until midnight, this public radio station in the San Francisco Bay Area plays a mix of African music, including Congolese popular music. Shows may also be streamed or downloaded online. The show is hosted by Emmanuel Nado and Edwin Okong'o.

Emmanuel Nado, Host and Edwin Okong'o, Host
500 Mansell Street
San Francisco, California 94134
Phone: (415) 841-4121
Fax: (415) 841-4125
Email: kalw@kalw.org
URL: www.kalw.org/programs/africa-mix

African Rhythms, WFSS 91.9 FM

Two hours of African music programming broadcast by a public radio station in Fayetteville, North Carolina, each Sunday from 6 to 8 p.m. The program may also be streamed online from the station's website.

Jimmy Miller, Music Director
1200 Murchison Road
Fayetteville, North Carolina 28301
Phone: (910) 672-2650
Fax: (910) 672-1964
Email: jmiller@uncfsu.edu
URL: www.wfss.org

Ambiance Congo, WRIR 97.3 FM

A show dedicated to Congolese popular music, hosted by David Noyes and broadcast on alternating Sundays from 3 to 5 p.m. by an independent radio station in Richmond, Virginia. The station also streams its broadcasts online, and podcasts may be downloaded.

David Noyes, Host
WRIR
P.O. Box 4787
Richmond, Virginia 23220
Phone: (804) 649-9737
Email: info@wrir.org
URL: http://wrir.org/index.php?/shows/program/ambiance_congo/

ORGANIZATIONS AND ASSOCIATIONS

Congolese Community of Arizona

Established in 2012, the Congolese Community of Arizona works to bring together Congolese immigrants and build a community despite ethnic differences, organize and provide humanitarian support for the Congo region, and motivate members of the Congolese community to become leaders and role models.

Phone: (602) 845-0402
Email: info@congolesecommunityofarizona.org
URL: www.congolesecommunityofarizona.org

Congolese Community of Chicago

The Congolese Community of Chicago's work is organized around two primary aims: assisting people of Congolese descent and educating them and other Americans about the culture of the Congo region. The organization is open to anyone of Congolese descent but also "to anyone interested in helping Congolese immigrants and refugees succeed." It also provides a speakers bureau and assists Chicago-area businesses with hiring and mentoring recent African immigrants.

Willy Mantua Butshidi
2069 West Roosevelt Road
Wheaton, Illinois 60187
Phone: (888) 809-9956
Email: info@congochicago.org
URL: www.congochicago.org

Friends of the Congo

Based in Washington, D.C., this global organization works for lasting peace and better living conditions in the Congo region of Africa. It seeks to raise awareness among non-Congolese people about the plight of the Congolese and also to organize Congolese Americans and other members of the diaspora to continue seeking justice in Africa.

Kambale Musavuli, Spokesperson
1629 K Street NW
Suite 300
Washington, D.C. 20006
Phone: (202) 584-6512
Fax: (775) 371-1064
Email: info@friendsofthecongo.org
URL: www.friendsofthecongo.org

INGA Association: Community of Congolese & Friends of Northern California

Originally founded through informal contacts among Congolese Americans in northern California, INGA's functions have expanded as the population of Congolese immigrants and refugees has grown. INGA is a community-based aid organization seeking to assist and develop a sense of community among Congolese Americans in Northern California, while also engaging in humanitarian projects and social action for the Congo region. It organizes large social gatherings and cultural events open to the public to educate non-Congolese about the nations' rich cultures.

5025 Hawkmount Way
San Ramon, California 94582
Phone: (650) 669-2832
Email: ingaleadership@yahoogroups.com
URL: www.ingaassociation.org

Leja Bulela

Created in 1993 in Detroit, this national organization is specifically concerned with living conditions in the DRC province of Kasai Oriental, where the Luba people live. The organization is composed mostly of people born in Kasai and first-generation Congolese Americans. It attempts to raise awareness about Luba culture and language (including to the children of immigrants) and to work to improve conditions for people still in the region. The organization sponsors an annual conference around these issues.

14781 Memorial Drive
Suite 1323
Houston, Texas 77079
Phone: (401) 874-5909
Email: info@aaysp.org
URL: www.lejabulela.org

MUSEUMS AND RESEARCH CENTERS

New Orleans African American Museum (NOAMM)

Located in the Tremé neighborhood of New Orleans, considered the oldest surviving black neighborhood in the United States, the NOAAM works to preserve African American heritage in Louisiana. It is well known for its "Louisiana-Congo: The Bertrand Donation" collection, illustrating links between traditional Congolese culture and Louisianan black culture.

Jonn E. Hankins, Executive Director
1418 Governor Nicholls Street
New Orleans, Louisiana 70116
Phone: (504) 566-1136
Fax: (504) 566-1137
Email: info@noamm.org
URL: www.noamm.org

Schomburg Center for Research in Black Culture

Part of the New York Public Library, the Schomburg Center catalogs, preserves, and provides access to information and resources about African American life and history, including that of Congolese Americans and other recent immigrant groups. The center offers programs, exhibits, and research assistance.

515 Malcolm X Boulevard
New York, New York 10037-1801
Phone: (212) 491-2200
URL: www.nypl.org/locations/schomburg

SOURCES FOR ADDITIONAL STUDY

Arthur, John A. *Invisible Sojourners: African Immigrant Diaspora in the United States.* Westport, CT: Praeger, 2000.

Crowe, Chris. *Thurgood Marshall: A Twentieth-Century Life.* New York: Viking, 2008.

Joworowski, Ken. "Survivors of Horrors, and Their Journey: 'Cry for Peace: Voices from the Congo,' at La MaMa." *New York Times*, October 19, 2012.

Montagne, Renee. "Update: Congolese Refugee Joshua Dimina." National Public Radio, December 23, 2005.

Mott, Tamar. *African Refugee Resettlement in the United States.* El Paso, TX: LFB Scholarly Publishers, 2009.

Wamba, Philippe. *Kinship: A Family's Journey in Africa and America.* New York: Dutton, 1999.

COSTA RICAN AMERICANS

Cida S. Chase

OVERVIEW

Costa Rican Americans are immigrants, or the descendants of immigrants, from the Central American nation of Costa Rica. Costa Rica is located in the southern end of Central America, bordered to the north by Nicaragua and to the south by Panama. Its terrain is rugged and divided from north to south by a central mountain range that separates the eastern and western coastal plains. Slightly smaller than the state of West Virginia, Costa Rica has an area of 19,652 square miles (51,032 square kilometers).

According to a December 2011 census conducted by the Instituto Nacional de Estadística y Censos (National Institute of Statistics and Census), the Costa Rican population was roughly 4.3 million. In 2008 the U.S. State Department—in its International Religious Freedom Report—cited a 2007 survey conducted at the University of Costa Rica when stating that 44.9 percent of Costa Ricans identify themselves as practicing Roman Catholics, 25.6 percent as nonpracticing Roman Catholics, 13.8 percent as evangelical Protestants, 11.3 percent as unaffiliated, and 4.3 percent declare "another religion." Methodist, Lutheran, Episcopal, Baptist, and other Protestant groups have the most significant memberships outside the Catholic Church, but Costa Rican membership in the Church of Jesus Christ of Latter-day Saints (Mormons) is growing rapidly, numbering 35,000 as of the 2007 survey. According to the Instituto's 2011 survey, 96 percent of the total population is of European ancestry, including *mestizos* (a Spanish word for Latin Americans of mixed European and native heritage), while roughly 2.5 percent of the population is of Native American descent and 1 percent of Afro-Caribbean heritage. Although the International Monetary Fund estimated Costa Rica's nominal gross domestic product at only $55 billion in 2011, the country consistently rates among the top Central and South American nations in the United Nations Development Programme's Human Development Index—ranking sixty-ninth in the world in 2011.

Because Costa Ricans reside in one of Latin America's most economically and politically stable states, they have not immigrated to the United States in significant waves. As such, it is difficult to pinpoint their earliest migrations. As with other Latin immigrant populations, however, Costa Ricans have tended to settle in major cities—the largest populations being in New York City and Los Angeles. Since the establishment of the modern Costa Rican democracy in 1949, Costa Rican immigrants to the United States have come mostly for higher education, research opportunities, or professional employment, often bringing their spouses and children with them. Into the twenty-first century, Costa Rica has consistently had one of the lowest rates of immigration to the United States among Latin American nations.

The 2010 U.S. Census placed the number of Americans of Costa Rican descent at 126,418—roughly equal to the total population of Hartford, Connecticut, or one-fifth the population of Boston. Costa Rican immigrants tend to assimilate into American society more quickly and easily than many other Latin American immigrant groups.

HISTORY OF THE PEOPLE

Early History Europeans first set foot in Costa Rica in 1502, when Christopher Columbus arrived during his fourth and last voyage to the New World. Formal settlement of the territory began in 1522, and for three hundred years the Spanish administered it under a military governor as part of the Captaincy General of Guatemala.

Costa Rica acquired its name when the Spanish, expecting to find an abundance of gold, named it *El Costa Rica*, "the Rich Coast." However, as there was little gold and few other valuable minerals in the area, the new settlers turned to agriculture for survival. Moreover, as the indigenous population was rather small, the Spanish were unable to establish an extensive forced-labor system. Consequently, Costa Rica developed differently from other Latin American nations. Its small landowners' modest standard of living, its people's ethnic and linguistic homogeneity, and its isolation from the large colonial centers of Mexico and South America produced a rather independent, individualist, agrarian society.

Costa Rica obtained its independence from Spain on September 15, 1821, without bloodshed, after joining other Central American provinces (most of whom had secured independence through armed conflict) in an 1821 joint declaration of independence from Spain. These newly created nations formed a confederation, which border disputes soon dissolved. Costa Rica acquired Guanacaste, its northernmost province, from Nicaragua after one of these border disputes. Since 1838, when it declared itself a sovereign nation, Costa Rica has enjoyed an independent existence, which it has zealously maintained. In 1856 the country was invaded by 240 filibusters, commanded by American lawyer and journalist William Walker, who had decided to conquer Central America on his own accord, declaring himself president of Nicaragua immediately upon landing. Costa Ricans promptly took up arms to defend their territory, and Juan Santamaría emerged as a Costa Rican national hero when he burned down the filibusters' headquarters in Santa Rosa.

Modern Era Costa Rica's egalitarian traditions have persisted throughout its history. Even though the introduction of banana and coffee plantations in the nineteenth century gave rise to a small oligarchy, Costa Rica has been able to maintain a strong middle class that sustains the nation's democratic ideals. The modern era of democracy in Costa Rica began after the elections of 1889, which are considered the first free elections in the country's history. This democratic tradition has experienced problems only twice: once in 1917–1918, when Federico Tinoco declared his government a dictatorship, and again in 1948, when a disputed election caused a civil war in which more than two thousand people lost their lives. After the civil war, a junta drafted a new constitution that guaranteed free elections with universal suffrage and abolished the national army. In 1948 José Figueres, who emerged as a hero during the civil war, became the first president under the new constitution.

The most prominent Costa Rican of the modern era is arguably Oscar Arias Sánchez, who was president of Costa Rica from 1986 to 1990, a significantly troublesome time in Central America, with unrest in El Salvador, Nicaragua, and Panama. Although Costa Rica enjoyed peace within its borders, it was not insulated from these regional conflicts. Instability in neighboring countries at this time impacted Costa Rica's tourism and foreign investment markets and brought a flood of refugees, particularly from Nicaragua and El Salvador.

In 1987 President Sánchez designed a regional peace plan—the Esquipulas Process—which became the basis for the peace agreement signed by the presidents of most of the other Central American nations. This peace plan brought about free and open elections in Nicaragua and the subsequent end of the civil war in that country. Sánchez's peace accomplishments in the region earned him the Nobel Peace Prize in 1987. He used the prize money to establish the Arias Foundation for Peace and Human Progress, which maintains three sources of funding: the Center for Human Progress, which funds programs for the advancement of women; the Center for Peace and Reconciliation, which works for Central American conflict resolution and prevention programs; and the Center for Philanthropy, which promotes the participation of nonprofit organizations in the building of just and peaceful Central American societies.

The nation saw its first hints of trouble in more than half a century when, in 2004, two former presidents—Rafael Ángel Calderón (1990–1994) and Miguel Ángel Rodríguez (1998–2002)—were incarcerated on charges of corruption while in office. Calderón was found guilty of accepting money from a Finnish financial firm in exchange for the promise of Costa Rican governmental contracts and was sentenced to five years in prison on October 5, 2009, forcing him to resign his candidacy in the 2010 presidential election. Rodríguez was found guilty of accepting money from a Taiwanese financial firm (it was unknown what promises were made in exchange) and sentenced to five years in prison on April 27, 2011, although an appeals court reversed that decision in December 2012.

SETTLEMENT IN THE UNITED STATES

Costa Ricans who have immigrated to and settled in the United States do not exhibit the same characteristics as many other Hispanic groups inasmuch as they did not have to flee their country as political or economic refugees. Consequently, there have never been significant waves of Costa Rican immigrants; nor, as U.S. immigration records show, have very many Costa Ricans tried to enter the country illegally.

Costa Ricans who did immigrate to the United States included those who had married Americans and raised their families in the United States, those who were hired to work in the United States after completing a degree at an American university, those who came seeking research opportunities that were not readily available at home, or those who believed they would find more success in various jobs and trades in the United States.

Fewer than 70,000 Costa Ricans are estimated to have immigrated to the United States since 1931. Hence, the number of Costa Rican immigrants has been increasing at an extremely slow rate, which is significantly different from the pattern of immigration to the United States from most other Central American countries. The only other countries in this region that show a consistently slow rate of immigration are Belize and Panama.

Costa Rican immigrants have tended to establish residence in California, Florida, Texas, and the New York City metropolitan area. These geographical preferences, evident in U.S. immigration statistics, are consistent with the results of the 2010 U.S. Census. The latter reports the largest concentration of Costa Rican Americans to be in the New York City area, including parts of Connecticut, New Jersey, and Long Island

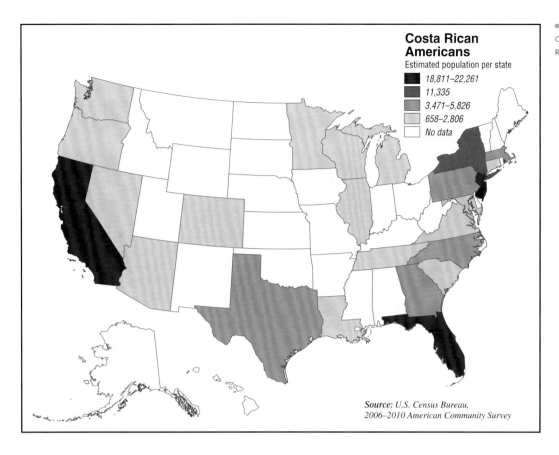

Costa Rican Americans
Estimated population per state
- 18,811–22,261
- 11,335
- 3,471–5,826
- 658–2,806
- No data

Source: U.S. Census Bureau,
2006–2010 American Community Survey

(27,394). The next-largest group is located along the southeastern coast of Florida in the Miami, Hialeah, and Fort Lauderdale areas (11,528). The third-largest group is in Los Angeles and its environs (11,371).

LANGUAGE

Costa Ricans are sometimes called *ticos* because they tend to append their own distinct suffix, "-tico," to create the diminutive form of a word as opposed to the traditional Spanish diminutive "-ito." For example, *chico* (meaning "small") in the traditional Spanish diminutive is *chiquito*, whereas Costa Ricans use the term *chiquitico*—both meaning "very small." The Costa Rican word *chirrisco* or *chirrisca* also means "very small," but many people, dissatisfied with conveying the idea of just "very small," add the suffix "-tico" or "-tica," making the word *chirrisquitico* or *chirrisquitica*—meaning "extremely small."

Distinguishing itself from standard Spanish even further, Costa Rican idiom exhibits a regional characteristic (common also in other Central American countries) known as *el voseo*, which is also found in the southern parts of South America. *El voseo* is the use of *vos* instead of *tú* as the familiar second-person singular form of address. Speakers adjust their verb tenses to agree with the form *vos*, as in "*Vos vivís en los Estados Unidos*" (You live in the United States)—rather than "*Tú vives en los Estados Unidos*," as is customary in most of the Spanish-speaking world. Although this form is more prominent in the

spoken language, increasingly more Costa Rican writers are using it as well. Costa Rican Americans are likely to drop the use of *el voseo* as they interact with Hispanics of other origins, and as they attempt to conform to the classroom standards of Spanish courses in the United States, which typically neglect this regional idiom.

Costa Rican Spanish is also marked by a softly pronounced double *r*, which means that the prominently trilled initial *r* or *rr* of the Spanish language is missing in the pronunciation of most Costa Ricans. Costa Ricans generally are nonetheless careful speakers of Spanish. They pronounce distinctly all the letters in the words and sound out a final "s," which is not always the case in the speech of other regions of Latin America, as well as of southern Spain.

As with many Latin American nations, indigenous languages have enriched Costa Rican Spanish with a number of distinctive words. Words ending in "-ate," "-te," and "-tle"—*zacate* (grass), *mecate* (rope), *chayote* (a type of squash), *quelite* (tender ends of the chayote vine), and *tepeizcuinte* or *tepeizcuitle* (paca, or spotted cavy, a rodent somewhat larger than a rabbit)—have entered the everyday speech of the people. Although this type of vocabulary is not as abundant in Costa Rica as it is in other Central American countries and Mexico, its presence in Costa Rica stands as a trace of the country's indigenous past.

Costa Rican immigrants to the United States often learn the English language early on, especially if they join a local church or have children in the public school system. For second and third generations, if both parents speak Spanish, the children are likely to be raised to be bilingual. However, if only one parent speaks Spanish, the children are more likely to grow up speaking only English.

Greetings and Popular Expressions *Jale*—Let's go; *Qué tiene?*—What's the matter?; *Si Dios quiere*—If God wills; *Ojalá*—If only; God grant; *Mae (or maje)*—Dude or man; *Una teja*—A hundred (of anything); *Cada muerte de obispo*—Literally, "every death of a bishop," roughly equivalent to "once in a blue moon"; *La dejó el tren*—Literally, "the train left her," said of a woman who has never married.

RELIGION

Roman Catholicism is the official, traditional, and dominant religion in Costa Rica. After the government, the Catholic Church is the most powerful institution in the country. Monsignor Sanabria, the archbishop of San José (Costa Rica's capital city) in the 1940s, organized and strengthened the modern church, guiding it toward social activism. His work promoted the foundation of church-oriented social organizations such as Catholic Action, the Young Catholic Workers, and a labor union called the Rerum Novarum (after an encyclical, or formal letter, of Pope Leo XIII on labor). This religious social orientation was weakened somewhat during the 1950s when the Partido Liberación Nacional (National Liberation Party), characterized by its conservatism, dominated the political arena and frowned on liberal social organizations.

Although they have great respect for the church, most Costa Ricans, especially those belonging to the middle class, maintain an independent, personal attitude toward church policies in regard to sensitive issues such as birth control and abortion. Political analyst Tom Barry, in his book *Costa Rica: A Country Guide*, describes this personal attitude, explaining that "Catholics in Costa Rica are eclectic believers, whose most fervent expressions of faith are evoked during Holy Week and at the baptism, marriage, or death of family members. Over 80 percent of Costa Rican Catholics do not attend mass regularly."

This characterization is equally true of Costa Rican immigrants to the United States, who tend to maintain the religious practices of their childhood. They look for a church in which they feel welcome, and if a church offers services in Spanish, they will worship with members of other Hispanic communities.

CULTURE AND ASSIMILATION

Due to a set of distinct historical realities—such as the absence of a war for independence or a prolonged revolutionary period—the politics of identity, race, and ethnicity play different roles in the lives of Costa Ricans, both in their home country and in the United States, than they do for other Latin American groups. Perhaps as a result of this dynamic, they seem to acculturate and assimilate more rapidly into mainstream American culture than do many of their Latin American counterparts.

They normally do not form communities, or *barrios*, as is often the case with Mexican Americans, Puerto Rican Americans, and other Central American immigrants. Instead, Costa Ricans tend to disappear into the English-speaking multitudes or form relationships with other Hispanics.

Traditions and Customs Costa Rica has a number of local traditions, many of which are religious. For example, during Holy Week *(Semana Santa)*, when Christians commemorate events leading up to Easter, the small towns hold processions. Also, every year on August 2, Costa Ricans take part in the *romería de la Virgen de los Angeles* (the pilgrimage of the Virgin of the Angels, the patron saint of Costa Rica), by making a 12.5-mile (20-kilometer) trip on foot from San José to Cartágo, where the Virgin's sanctuary is located.

Every year in the month of December the Costa Rican people enjoy the *fiestas cívicas* (civic celebrations), which are similar to state fairs in the United States. In addition to a wide variety of foods and the usual carnival rides and sideshows, there are simulated bullfights, in which youths try their luck "fighting" balloon-decorated *toros guacos* (mean bulls), by getting close enough to pull the bulls' tails or touch their rumps.

Although the majority of these traditions have not been translated to the United States, Costa Rican Americans try to maintain several other traditions. Such is the case with the *rosario del Niño*, wherein families prepare a special nativity scene for Christmas that does not display the Christ Child figure in the manger until December 25. The nativity scene remains in its place until January 6, Epiphany Day (the twelfth day of Christmas). After that date, families pray the rosary with a group of friends who bring over their small children. After the recitation of the rosary, the families have a party that includes ice cream and cake and, if available, Costa Rican foods.

Like many other Roman Catholics, Costa Ricans believe in calling upon Jesus and the saints for assistance when they are in need or in danger. Each saint is thought to have a special mission or to be able to satisfy a particular need. One would pray to Saint Anthony, for example, if something has been lost or misplaced.

Not all the Costa Rican popular beliefs are religious in nature, however. Costa Rican people are great believers in herbal medicine. Many of them know that gargling with a solution of boiled rue (a strong-scented plant) leaves will relieve a sore throat. Liquefied, strained raw eggplant is thought to lower cholesterol levels and to purify the blood. A popular cure for stomach discomfort is to drink liquid in which rhubarb or chamomile has been boiled. Costa Ricans also prepare a variety of herbal teas to soothe the nerves. Teas prepared with linden, orange, and lemon blossoms are thought to help those who drink them relax and and fall asleep at night.

Many Costa Ricans bring these customs and beliefs with them to the United States and continue to practice them, but often, as they assimilate into American society, they lose interest in these beliefs and cease practicing them. Consequently, second- and third-generation Costa Rican Americans may have minimal knowledge of such beliefs and practices.

Finally, Costa Rican Americans also celebrate all the American holidays, adopting American customs and typical holiday foods.

Traditional Dress If the opportunity arises, Costa Rican Americans share with others their native costumes by donning them at cultural festivals and community celebrations, which are typically free and open to the public. For women, such costume typically consists of a white peasant blouse decorated with embroidery or ribbon work and a colorful, ankle-length, full skirt. Men wear white peasant shirts and white pants. In addition, they frequently wear a colorful handkerchief around the neck and a straw hat. Both men and women wear sandals, and women braid colorful ribbons into their hair.

Cuisine Costa Rican cuisine is mild, free of hot and spicy sauces, and usually seasoned with herbs. Black pepper is used sparingly, but fresh cilantro, thyme, oregano, onion, garlic, pimiento, and tomato are fundamental ingredients in the preparation of meats, soups, and vegetable hashes. A variety of beef cuts, including tongue and kidney, are baked or simmered for long periods of time in herbal sauces until they are tender and flavorful. Chicken and pork are prepared in similar ways.

Complete daily meals in Costa Rica may include a meat dish, a vegetable hash, white rice, black or red beans, a lettuce and tomato salad, corn tortillas or crusty white bread, and a fresh-fruit drink. If the meal includes dessert, it is likely to be fruit; cakes, pastries, caramel flan, and ice cream are reserved for special occasions, holidays, or the afternoon tea. The traditional salad dressing is made of oil and vinegar, but mayonnaise is a favorite dressing for salads made of hearts of palm and fresh peas. Vegetable hashes, which include a small amount of beef, are made of cubed potatoes, chayote squash with fresh corn, and green plantains. Beef or vegetable soups are also popular in Costa Rica. Black bean soup topped with fresh herbs, a boiled egg, and white rice is a favorite side dish. Costa Ricans in the United States tend to adopt more typically American eating habits on a day-to-day basis—due in part to a limited availability (and thus high cost) of traditional Costa Rican ingredients—reserving traditional fare for large family gatherings, special celebrations (such as weddings and graduations), and holidays.

Holiday meals, both in Costa Rica and among Costa Rican Americans, often include tamales—corn-meal and mashed potatoes stuffed with meat, saffron rice, olives, a few garbanzo beans, green peas, pimientos, a wedge of boiled egg, and prunes or raisins. These tamales usually are 4-by-6-inch rectangles (10 by 15 centimeters) wrapped in banana leaves, each one a meal in itself. Holiday meals also often include a main dish of chicken and rice prepared with added vegetables and raisins. *Ensalada rusa* (Russian salad) is also a must at holiday meals. It consists of diced potatoes, fresh beets, and green peas all cooked separately then brought together in a mayonnaise dressing; sometimes diced hearts of palm are added as well.

Due to a set of distinct historical realities—such as the absence of a war for independence or a prolonged revolutionary period—the politics of identity, race, and ethnicity play different roles in the lives of Costa Ricans, both in their home country and in the United States, than they do for other Latin American groups.

Holidays Costa Ricans gather with friends and family for civic celebrations. It is customary to celebrate Independence Day (September 15) in Costa Rica with parades and school assemblies, although these celebrations are less common among Costa Ricans in the United States. Costa Rican Americans welcome the opportunity of celebrating with friends whether they are compatriots or people of other nationalities or ethnic backgrounds. They also join other Latin Americans in their celebrations, such as the Mexican American holiday Cinco de Mayo (May 5) and September 16, Mexican Independence Day.

Dances and Songs Like many Costa Rican folk dances, the Costa Rican national dance, the *punto guanacasteco*, comes from the province of Guanacaste. Couples wear traditional costumes and follow a melody played with a marimba (a sort of wooden xylophone) and several guitars. This dance, like other popular dances, portrays the courting traditions of the past. The male dancer always follows his female partner, and the latter, while smiling, pretends to elude him. The male dancer periodically stops the music by shouting "*Bomba!*" so that he may recite humorous praises, called *bombas*, to his lady. A traditional *bomba* goes as follows: "*Dicen que no me quieres / porque no tengo bigote / mañana me lo pondré / con plumas de zopilote.*" ("They say that you don't love me / because I

COSTA RICAN PROVERBS

Numerous Costa Rican proverbs come from Spanish culture and hence exist in many other Spanish-speaking countries also; however, there are some colorful sayings that seem to be typically Costa Rican or appear to be favored by Costa Ricans. These include the following:

En casa de herrero, cuchillo de palo.

> In the home of a blacksmith, a knife made of wood; meaning, roughly, that those too dedicated to their trade can often neglect their home lives.

A caballo regalado no se le busca colmillo.

> One does not look for the canine teeth on a gifted horse; similar in meaning to "Don't look a gift horse in the mouth."

A Dios rogando y con el mazo dando.

> To God, pleading, and with the pestle, giving; meaning, roughly, "Pray to God for help but work to improve your problems as well."

don't have a mustache / tomorrow I shall put one on / made out of buzzard feathers.")

Costa Rican folk songs are nostalgic, featuring ballad-like melodies. The lyrics praise the beauty of the country's women and of the landscape as they tell of the sorrows of love. While some Costa Rican communities in the United States, such as in New York City, host regular, sometimes weekly, traditional dance nights, Costa Rican Americans typically reserve the performance of traditional song and dance for community or school cultural festivities.

Health Care Issues and Practices There is no evidence of physical or mental health problems unique to either Costa Ricans or Costa Rican Americans. Costa Rica's government-sponsored health care system deserves much of the credit for the good health of Costa Ricans. Medical attention in that country is not only superior to that of most of Latin America but also surpasses the health services available in many communities in the United States. According to Barry, infant deaths are fewer than eighteen per thousand compared with seventy-nine per thousand in Guatemala. Moreover, life expectancy is seventy-four years for males and seventy-six for females—the highest in Central America.

During the 1980s, Costa Ricans were able to arrest the spread of illnesses brought into the country by the flood of Salvadoran and Nicaraguan refugees thanks to their health facilities and an effective method of disseminating information regarding health issues. Malaria and tuberculosis, which had been eradicated from the country years before, began to reappear with the arrival of refugees, but the immediate attention given to this issue brought an end to the problem.

Since Costa Rican immigrants customarily obey U.S. immigration laws, they usually have formal documentation of their good state of health upon entering the country. In 2011 the U.S. Census Bureau's American Community Survey reported that an estimated 27.4 percent of Costa Rican Americans were without health insurance coverage, compared to 15.2 percent for the U.S. population in general.

Death And Burial Rituals Holding a wake for deceased family and community members is an important custom among Costa Rican American families who have maintained their Roman Catholic traditions. They believe that the deceased must not be left alone while lying in state, and relatives and friends pray devoutly for his or her soul during the wake and thereafter. As is typical of any Roman Catholic wake, the deceased's family offers refreshments to visitors. After the funeral, the deceased's family and friends pray the rosary for nine evenings, offering refreshments after each night's prayers. Masses are said for the deceased's soul at the ninth day and also after the first month has passed. Relatives and friends also attend subsequent anniversary masses for the deceased.

FAMILY AND COMMUNITY LIFE

Costa Ricans generally have conservative family values and relationships. For many Costa Ricans, a family must have a father, a mother, and children. Like many other Hispanic groups, Costa Rican families tend to be patriarchal in nature, and extended family members also are accorded authority. The father is the head of the household, and the elder members of the extended family are both respected and obeyed.

A traditional Costa Rican home usually has the presence of another relative—such as a grandmother, grandfather, aunt, and/or uncle—who assists in the rearing of the children. However, as modern life has become more complicated for women, and it is sometimes not possible to keep an older relative in the home. As a result, residential homes and condominiums for the elderly and the retired are becoming fashionable in Costa Rica.

Costa Ricans are a gregarious people. They get together with their relatives and friends as often as possible. The weekend and holiday afternoon tea is one reason to get together and is an institution in Costa Rica. Extended family members and friends invite each other over for five o'clock tea in order to celebrate birthdays, anniversaries, and other special occasions. This afternoon tea, which constitutes almost a complete meal, including a main dish and a dessert, is also a favorite activity for wedding showers and class reunions. The afternoon tea has become a substitute for supper in modern Costa Rica, and occasionally, instead of taking place in the home, as is traditional, people may gather in a restaurant.

Gender Roles Like many Western cultures, particularly Christian ones, women have long played a subordinate role in Costa Rican family and community structures. Traditionally, they have been offered fewer academic and professional opportunities than have their male counterparts. As such, men have traditionally held more positions of prominence and have been responsible for family finances, while women have stayed home to raise children and keep house.

Among contemporary Costa Ricans and Costa Rican Americans alike, however, these dynamics have changed. Today, all areas of education and employment are open and acceptable for pursuit by all members of a family or community, and marriages are generally treated as partnerships, with each partner contributing equally to all aspects of family and community life.

Education Education has long been a priority in Costa Rica, and the country's policies closely resemble those of the United States or, indeed, any modern Western nation. An elementary-through-high-school education is compulsory, and pursuit of postsecondary education is widely encouraged. As a result, Costa Rican literacy rates are consistently among the highest in Latin America—94.9 percent as of 2011, according to the *CIA World Factbook*.

This tradition has carried over into the educational trends and practices of the Costa Rican American population. As the two nations' systems have long been nearly identical, there is little distinction between mainstream American and Costa Rican American education, save the possibility that Costa Rican Americans are more likely to earn a college degree. According to 2011 estimates from the U.S. Census Bureau's American Community Survey, only 19 percent of Costa Rican Americans attain less than a high school diploma, compared with roughly 14 percent in the general population. Of those that acquire at least a high school diploma, 26.4 percent go on to attain at least a bachelor's degree, compared with the significantly lower 17.7 percent of the general population. There also seems to be a high level of gender equality in this area, as male and female students attain a bachelor's degree or higher 25.2 and 27.5 percent of the time, respectively.

EMPLOYMENT AND ECONOMIC CONDITIONS

Political and economic stability, as well as high literacy and education levels, have led to unemployment rates consistently under 10 percent in Costa Rica— relatively low among Central American nations. Many Costa Ricans immigrate to the United States because they receive offers from American employers, not because they cannot find employment in

Costa Rica. As such, employment rates among Costa Rican Americans tend to surpass those of other Latin American immigrants and more closely resemble those of the general population. There is no distinctive pattern in the fields of employment for Costa Ricans in the United States. The U.S. Census Bureau's 2011 American Community Survey estimated that 20 percent of Costa Rican Americans were employed in education, health care, and social assistance; 13 percent in science, administrative work, and the professions; and roughly 9 percent each in retail and construction.

Perhaps the only distinctive employment statistic is one that defies American stereotypes of Spanish-speaking immigrants. Contrary to the common misperception of Central Americans as being employed primarily as farmworkers and manual laborers, the 2011 survey reported that only 0.4 percent of Costa Rican Americans were working in agriculture, forestry, fishing and hunting, and mining combined.

NOTABLE INDIVIDUALS

Literature Rima de Vallbona, born in 1931 in San José, Costa Rica, has taught Latin American literature and civilization at the University of St. Thomas in Houston, Texas, since 1964; her novels and short stories depict feminine characters who are trying to understand the world. *Mujeres y Agonías* (*Women and Grief*, 1982), *Mundo, Demonio y Mujer* (*World, Demon and Woman*, 1991) *Los Infiernos de la Mujer y Algo Más* (*Woman's Infernos and Something Else*, 1992) are three of her most acclaimed works.

Victoria Urbano (1926–1984) taught Spanish literature at Lamar University in Beaumont, Texas, from 1966 until her death in 1984; in addition to founding the *Asociación de Literatura Femenina Hispánica* (*Association of Hispanic Feminine Literature*) in the United States, Urbano published numerous short stories and poems; her *Los Nueve Círculos* (*The Nine Circles*, 1970) and *Exodos Incontables* (*Innumerable Exoduses*, 1982), published in Spain and Uruguay, are frequently studied in Spanish American centers.

Politics Sonia Chang-Díaz (1978–) is the daughter of astronaut Franklin Chang-Díaz. After serving as a public educator in Massachusetts for several years, in 2009 she became the first Hispanic woman elected to the state senate.

Science Franklin Chang-Díaz, born in San José, Costa Rica, in 1950, is a physical scientist. After graduating from the University of Connecticut in 1973 with a degree in mechanical engineering, he completed a doctorate in applied plasma physics from the Massachusetts Institute of Technology in 1977. At the University of Connecticut he helped design and construct high-energy atomic collision experiments, and as a graduate student he worked in the U.S.-controlled fusion program, doing intensive research in the design

Massachusetts State Senator Sonia Chang-Diaz's father, renowned scientist Franklin Chang-Díaz, emigrated from Costa Rica. PAT GREENHOUSE / THE BOSTON GLOBE VIA GETTY IMAGES

and operation of fusion reactors. After obtaining his doctorate, he joined the technical staff of the Draper Laboratory, working on the design and integration of control systems for fusion reactor concepts and experimental devices, and in 1979, he developed a concept to guide and target fuel pellets in an inertial fusion reactor chamber. Since then he has been working on the implementation of a new concept in rocket propulsion based on magnetically confined high-temperature plasmas. Chang-Díaz became an astronaut in August 1981 and continues to do research for the National Aeronautics and Space Administration (NASA).

Stage and Screen Harry Shum Jr. (1982–), born in Puerto Limón, Costa Rica, is an actor, dancer, choreographer, and singer. His parents are both Chinese: his mother from Hong Kong, his father from Guangzhou. Having been born in Costa Rica, however, his first language is Spanish. The family moved to California when he was six, and he became interested in dancing shortly thereafter. He is most recognized for his portrayal of Mike Chang on the popular Fox television musical drama *Glee* (2009), but has also appeared in the dance-themed movies *You Got Served* (2004), *Stomp the Yard* (2007), *Step Up 2: The Streets* (2008), and *Step Up 3D* (2010).

MEDIA

A.M. Costa Rica

Though based in San José, Costa Rica, this online newspaper has published stories of cultural, social, and political significance for the entire Costa Rican diaspora since August 2001. They publish exclusively in English and often report news and events involving both Costa Ricans in the United States and U.S. citizens in Costa Rica.

Email: editor@amcostarica.com
URL: www.amcostarica.com

ORGANIZATIONS AND ASSOCIATIONS

Costa Rican–American Chamber of Commerce (AMCHAM)

AMCHAM Costa Rica comprises over four hundred companies and thirteen hundred corporate representatives, with U.S. and Costa Rican membership being split nearly fifty-fifty. Through advocacy and community organizing efforts, they promote growth of binational businesses in agriculture, livestock, aquaculture, import/distribution, tourism, manufacturing, business services, construction, and the nonprofit sector.

Catherine Reuben, Executive Director
P.O. Box 025216
Miami, Florida 33102-5216
Email: chamber@amcham.co.cr
URL: www.amcham.co.cr

League of United Latin American Citizens (LULAC)

LULAC is composed of individual councils in thirty-three states and a national headquarters in Washington, D.C., all working to improve access to economic, educational, political, housing, health, and civil rights resources for the Hispanic population of the United States.

Brent A. Wilkes, LULAC National Executive Director
1133 Nineteenth Street NW
Suite 1000
Washington, D.C. 20036
Phone: (202) 833-6130
Fax: (202) 833-6135
URL: www.lulac.org

National Council of La Raza (NCLR)

The NCLR operates in forty-one states, Washington, D.C., and Puerto Rico, and is the largest national Hispanic civil rights and advocacy organization in the United States. According to its own mission statement, the NCLR "conducts applied research, policy analysis, and advocacy, providing a Latino perspective in five key areas—assets/investments, civil rights/immigration, education, employment and economic status, and health."

Janet Marguía, President and CEO
1126 Sixteenth Street NW
Suite 600
Washington, D.C. 20036-4845
Phone: (202) 785-1670
Fax: (202) 776-1792
Email: comments@nclr.org
URL: www.nclr.org

MUSEUMS AND RESEARCH CENTERS

Museum of Latin American Art (MOLAA)

The MOLAA, located in Long Beach, California, is the only museum in the United States dedicated exclusively to contemporary Latin American fine art. Included in its permanent collections are the works of Costa Rican and Costa Rican American artists such as Francisco

Amighetti (1907–1998), Leonel González (born 1962), Priscilla Monge (born 1968), and Cinthya Soto (born 1969).

Stuart A. Ashman, President and CEO
628 Alamitos Avenue
Long Beach, California 90802
Phone: (562) 437-1689
URL: www.molaa.org

SOURCES FOR ADDITIONAL STUDY

Barry, Tom. *Costa Rica: A Country Guide*. Albuquerque: Interhemisphere Education Resource Center, 1991.

Biesanz, Richard, Karen Zubris Biesanz, and Mavis Hiltunen Biesanz. *The Costa Ricans*. Englewood Cliffs, NJ: Prentice-Hall, 1982.

Gidal, Marc. "Contemporary 'Latin American' Composers of Art Music in the United States: Cosmopolitans Navigating Multiculturalism and Universalism," *Latin American Music Review* 31, no. 1 (2010): 40–78.

Mosby, Dorothy E. *Place, Language, and Identity in Afro-Costa Rican Literature*. Columbia: University of Missouri Press, 2003.

Rottenberg, Simon, ed. *Costa Rica and Uruguay*. Oxford: Oxford University Press, 1993.

Sandoval, García C. *Shattering Myths on Immigration and Emigration in Costa Rica*. Lanham, MD: Lexington Books, 2011.

Sawicki, Sandra. *Costa Rica in Pictures*. Minneapolis: Lerner Publications, 1987.

CREEKS

Chad Dundas

OVERVIEW

The Creek Indians are a coalition of indigenous peoples whose ancestors settled in the area that is now the southeastern United States possibly as early as 12,000 years ago. When Spanish explorers arrived in North America in the early 1500s, the Creeks occupied major portions of present-day Alabama and Georgia. They called themselves Muscogees or Muscogulges (alternatively spelled as Mvskoke or Muskogee), which identified them as people living on land that was wet or prone to flooding. English traders called those they first came across (the Kawitas tribe living on the lower Ocheese—now Ocmulgee—River) Ocheesee Creeks. The name Creeks was later extended to include all of the allied groups.

Exact estimates of the Creek population prior to the arrival of Europeans are difficult to obtain. According to author Richard L. Thornton's essay "Hierarchal Muskogean Societies from a Muskogee Perspective" (2004), archeological evidence suggests that the Creek civilization once contained not only vast numbers of people but also a robust and well-regulated voluntary workforce. Likely the descendants of prehistoric Mississippian cultures who erected extensive earthen mounds throughout valleys along the Mississippi River, the Muscogee Nation was a confederacy that welcomed new member tribes, even those of different linguistic and cultural backgrounds. Known for their sophisticated governmental and social structures, the Creeks maintained a tribal economy based on agriculture, homesteading, hunting, fishing, and contributing to communal efforts for the betterment of the tribe. Individual clans were assigned large tracts of farmland, but ownership of all lands remained with the tribe. Those who joined the nation blended their own traditions with the existing practices of the Creeks. Within a single town citizens might speak several languages and produce different styles of pottery or architecture while contributing to the collective economy. The standard of living might depend on a member's place within the tribe. Some elite families received special treatment, such as control over their own temple grounds and burial sites, but they were in the minority. Most Creeks, however, were common people who lived in scattered villages and on farmsteads.

Following the Indian Removal Act of 1830 and after ceding much of their former homeland to the U.S. government through various treaties, the Creeks were forcibly relocated in large numbers from Alabama and Georgia to Oklahoma. Many now work to retain their cultural identity. The tribal government actively seeks to assert the rights and responsibilities of a sovereign nation through the retention of existing tribal lands, acquisition of additional land, and improved access to places of significance to the tribe outside tribal lands.

The 2011 population of the Muscogee Creek Nation was listed as 70,982 (slightly more than the population of Santa Fe, New Mexico) on the official tribal website. The tribal government, headquartered in Okmulgee, Oklahoma, maintains more than 2,400 employees and operates with an annual budget of more than $100 million, maintaining facilities in eight administrative districts. For the most part Muscogee tribal members are fully integrated into the overall mainstream population of the United States. Oklahoma is the state with the highest concentration of Creeks, but Texas, Florida, Alabama, and California have significant populations as well.

HISTORY OF THE PEOPLE

Early History Historians believe the people who came to be known as the Creek Indians were mostly descended from the mound builders of the Mississippian culture, who constructed expansive and impressive earthen structures south of the Tennessee River in what would become the states of Georgia and Alabama. After establishing their permanent settlements in what is now the southeastern United States, Creeks separated into two groups: Settlements along the Coosa, Tallapoosa, and Alabama rivers became known as the Upper Towns, while communities along the Flint, Chattahoochee, and Ocmulgee rivers were called the Lower Towns. This partition was merely geographical at first, but as interaction with European colonists developed, the Lower Towns were more accessible to foreign influence. The Upper Towns tended to retain more traditional, political, and social characteristics.

The Creeks had contact with non-Indians as early as 1540, when Spanish explorer Hernando de Soto arrived with a party of explorers. Interaction with Europeans increased in the late 1600s when the English moved into South Carolina and the Spanish settled in Florida. The Creeks were reputed to be a hospitable people skilled in diplomacy. They traded actively with all of the European colonies, though they generally preferred to deal with the English, who offered a greater variety and better quality of goods, as well as lower prices and better credit terms than the Spanish or the French. In fact, the Creeks allied themselves militarily with the English in 1702, fighting in Queen Anne's War against the French and Spanish. When British general James Oglethorpe founded the colony of Georgia in 1733, he negotiated with Creek leaders to acquire the land. The following year a Creek delegation led by Chief Tomochichi traveled to England to see King George II and sign a treaty.

In 1770 European trader James Adair, who dealt with the Creeks for three decades, described them as the most powerful Indian nation known to the English. During the Revolutionary War, Creeks from the Upper Towns sided with the British and fought against the Americans, while Creeks from the Lower Towns stayed mostly neutral. After the war vanquished British forces included land belonging to the Creeks with territories they turned over to the newly independent United States. As the fledgling government of the United States began to encroach on Creek land, Chief Alexander McGillivray (also known as Hopoiłi Mikko; he was born to a Creek/French mother and a Scottish father) of the Upper Towns worked to create a national Creek identity and to oppose individual leaders who were selling land to the Americans.

McGillivray had served as a British military officer during the war and was regarded as a skilled diplomat. In 1790 he was among the indigenous leaders who signed the Treaty of New York, passing control of much of the Creeks' land to the United States in exchange for federal recognition of Creek sovereignty. As part of the treaty, McGillivray was commissioned as a brigadier general of the U.S. Army and used his annual salary of $1,200 to become a plantation owner in Alabama.

In 1789 newly elected President George Washington embarked on a plan to "civilize" the indigenous people of the United States by indoctrinating them in European-style culture. The Creeks were among the first tribes to be considered civilized as part of this program. In 1812, however, the Shawnee chief Tecumseh, whose mother was Creek, organized a rebellion against the U.S. government. The Creek Nation split over whether to join the uprising. Most of the Lower Creeks supported Tecumseh, whereas the Upper Creeks were evenly divided in their allegiance. The split resulted in a devastating conflict in which factions of Creeks fought against each other as well as against forces representing U.S. governmental interests.

Led by Red Eagle, the Creek rebels, called "Red Sticks," launched the Red Stick War, capturing Fort Mims near Mobile, Alabama, on August 30, 1813. An estimated 250 whites and assimilated mixed-blood Creeks died during the battle. In response, militias from Tennessee (led by Andrew Jackson), Georgia, and the Mississippi Territory launched attacks into Creek territories. In March of the following year, a

Chief Tomochichi and his Creek council meet in London with members of the British government. 1734. MARILYN ANGEL WYNN / UPPA / PHOTOSHOT

coalition of forces under Jackson crushed the Creeks at the Battle of Horseshoe Bend. Under the terms of the peace treaty signed in 1814, the tribe relinquished 22 million acres of land to the United States, including the town sites of some of the Upper Creeks who had fought alongside Jackson's forces against the rebels.

Jackson was elected president in 1824 and immediately pushed government policy on Indians in an even less hospitable direction. Some treaties signed with the tribe were obtained by fraudulent means, such as purposely negotiating with a nonrepresentative group of minor chiefs after being refused by the official delegation or forging the names of chiefs who refused to cooperate. In addition to gradually obtaining ownership of tens of millions of acres of Creek land, federal and state governments placed a succession of restrictions on the Indians. Alabama law, for example, prohibited an Indian from testifying against a white man. In *Indian Removal: The Emigration of the Five Civilized Tribes of Indians* (1932), Grant Foreman quotes a Creek delegation to the U.S. secretary of war in 1831: "We are made subject to laws we have no means of comprehending; we never know when we are doing right."

In 1830 Jackson signed the Indian Removal Act, which authorized the United States to negotiate with indigenous people for their remaining land holdings and to relocate them to designated areas west of the Mississippi River known as "Indian Territory." The treaty guaranteed the Creeks political autonomy and perpetual ownership of new homelands there in return for their remaining tribal lands in the East. It specified that each Creek could freely choose whether to remain in his homeland or move to the West. Those who decided to stay in the East could select homesteads on former tribal land. Land speculators eager to profit from the anticipated influx of white settlers devised a variety of ways to cheat the Indians out of their land, either by paying far less than its true value or by forging deeds. After a supposed Indian attack on a mail stage—for which a white man was later convicted—a brief civil war pitted Creeks who wanted to remain in the East against those who accepted the concept of relocation. The federal government finally ordered the forcible removal of all remaining Creeks in 1836.

Now known as the Trail of Tears, the forced relocation to Indian Territory in present-day east-central Oklahoma took a terrible toll on the Creeks, reducing their population from about 22,000 in the early 1830s to 13,500 by 1839. Emigrants were subjected to horrible conditions during the government-subsidized journeys. One group began their journey in December 1834, barefoot and scantily clothed; 26 percent of them died during the four-month journey. Leaders pushed onward as quickly as they could, not allowing the Indians to conduct funeral services to ensure the dead an afterlife and sometimes not even allowing the survivors to bury the dead. In July 1836 a party of 1,600 Creeks departed for the West with the warriors handcuffed and chained together for the entire journey.

Delegates from thirty-four tribes assemble in front of Creek Council House in Indian Territory (which later became the state of Oklahoma) in 1880. NATIONAL ARCHIVES AND RECORDS ADMINISTRATION

Upon arrival in Indian Territory, the Creeks and other tribes arriving at the same time faced opposition from Plains Indians, who would have to share diminished hunting grounds with 60,000 new residents. Although the Creeks were capable of defending themselves against attack, they took the lead in conducting negotiations between the immigrant tribes and the western indigenous people to establish peaceful coexistence. As they settled into their new homeland, the Creeks discovered that the U.S. government's promises of assistance went largely unfulfilled. Tools and farm implements did not come in time to build homes and plant crops. Weapons and ammunition did not arrive, so the men had to relearn bow-and-arrow hunting techniques. In order to maximize profits from their government contracts, food suppliers delivered partial shipments and rancid provisions. Especially during the first few years after relocation, annuity payments guaranteed by the treaty were made primarily in goods rather than in cash, and most of the items to be delivered were either useless to the Indians or were lost in shipment.

Despite these conditions, by the 1850s the Creek people had begun to achieve a relatively prosperous life in their new territory. By 1859 the Muscogee Nation had adopted a written constitution (later updated in 1867) that laid out a system of modern tribal government, including a principal chief, a judicial branch, and a bicameral legislature. Creeks also established a capital city on the Deep Fork of the Canadian River at Okmulgee, where they built a large stone council house that still stands at the center of town. In early 1861 the Southern states began seceding from the United States, prompting the American Civil War. The Creeks tried to remain neutral in the conflict but were drawn into hostilities by attacks on their people. Loyalties were once again divided. People from the original Lower Towns generally favored the retention of slavery and sided with the South, while the Upper Townspeople chose to abide by their treaties with the North. What ensued was another civil war within the Creek Nation. Further, in retribution for the failure of the entire tribe to support the Union, a postwar treaty with the U.S. government required the cession of 3.2 million acres, or about half of the Creek land in Indian Territory.

Modern Era Throughout the late 1800s and early 1900s, the U.S. government passed a number of laws aimed at dismantling tribal governments and the allotment of collectively held tribal lands. Acting on the recommendations of the Dawes Commission, Congress passed the Curtis Act in 1898, removing tribal lands from common ownership and distributing them among individual Indians for private ownership. In 1906 the U.S. government declared the Creek tribal government dissolved. Although these moves were meant to destroy the autonomy of tribal governments completely, the Creeks' system of self-rule never truly disappeared. During this period the Muscogee Nation maintained a principal chief and worked to preserve as much of its traditional culture as possible.

Federal policies dissolving tribal governments were reversed by the 1934 Wheeler-Howard Act, which encouraged tribal cultural and economic development. Two years later Congress passed the Oklahoma Indian Welfare Act, providing Indian tribes with a mechanism for incorporating. It also granted benefits such as a student loan program and a revolving fund to be used for extending credit to Indians. Despite these reforms, the Muscogees were unable to hold free and open tribal elections without the approval of the U.S. government until 1971. During the next decade tribal leadership established a new constitution, revitalized their national council, and began the process of reaffirming their sovereign rights. At Okmulgee a new tribal headquarters was built to house the offices of the national council and the tribal judiciary. By the 1990s the population of Creeks in the United States was 43,550, placing them tenth in size among Native American tribes. By 2011 the population had exceeded 70,000.

SETTLEMENT IN THE UNITED STATES

Long before the arrival of Europeans, some peoples belonging to the Mississippian cultures may have migrated to what would become the southeastern United States from environs west of the Mississippi River. The oral tradition of Creek Indians tells that their ancestors made a great journey toward the sunrise; traveled over large mountains called the "backbone of the world"; and finally crossed a wide, muddy river to conquer their new homeland. By the 1500s their civilization spanned the entire Southeast and boasted a sophisticated social structure and system of government.

Following the arrival of de Soto in 1540, Europeans began to encroach on Creek lands. This practice intensified after the United States won its

independence in the Revolutionary War. Georgia sold most of the Muscogee tribal lands within its borders to the U.S. government in the 1802 Compact. After the end of the Creek civil war, the tribes lost a total of about 21,750,000 acres in Georgia, Alabama, and Mississippi. By 1840 nearly all of the Creeks had been relocated to Indian Territory. A few, however, remained behind in Alabama, and a sizable population still lives there on the Poarch Creek Reservation. Today, members of the Muscogee Nation have settled throughout the southeastern United States, and affiliated tribes can be found in Oklahoma, Alabama, Louisiana, and Texas. The states with the highest population of Creeks are Alabama, California, Florida, Oklahoma, and Texas.

LANGUAGE

The Creeks spoke several related Muskogean languages, including Muscogee (Creek), Hichiti, Alabama, and Koasati, as well as the Yuchi linguistic isolate. There are references to other dialects early in Creek history, but they seem to have died out before or shortly after removal. In *Deerskins & Duffels: The Creek Indian Trade with Anglo-America, 1685–1815* (1993), Kathryn E. Braund asserts, "It was still the English who were forced to learn the melodious Muscogee tongue, for few Creeks expressed any willingness to adopt the harsh and strident tones of their new friends." Creeks who avoided relocation to Oklahoma tended to stop speaking the Muscogee language in order to avoid recognition and forced eviction.

In 1835, with the help of a Creek student named James Perryman, Presbyterian minister John Fleming created a phonetic alphabet for the Muscogee language. Fleming and Perryman published a book of hymns and a primer called *I stutsi in Naktsokv* (1835; The Child's Book). Another missionary published a Creek dictionary and grammar book in 1890.

By 1910, 72 percent of Creeks over the age of ten could speak English. Today, nearly all Creek adults speak English, but efforts are underway to preserve the Muskogean languages. Students at the College of the Muscogee Nation in Okmulgee can enroll in a Muskogean language certificate program. Language classes are also offered at the University of Oklahoma and in Oklahoma public schools in Tulsa, Holdenville, and Okmulgee.

Pronunciation and Common Words The language's vowels and their sounds are: "v" (as the vowel sound in), "a" (as in sod), "e" (as in tin), "o" (as in toad), "u" (as in put), and "i" (as in hate). Most consonants are pronounced as in English, except that "c" sounds like "ts" or "ch," while "r" is a lateral fricative, similar to the "th" sound but made on the side of the tongue..

Some of the basic words of the Creek language are *hes'ci* (hihs-jay)—"hello"; *henk'a* (hihn gah)—"yes"; *hek'us* (hihg oos)—"no"; and *mvto'* (muh doh)— "thank you."

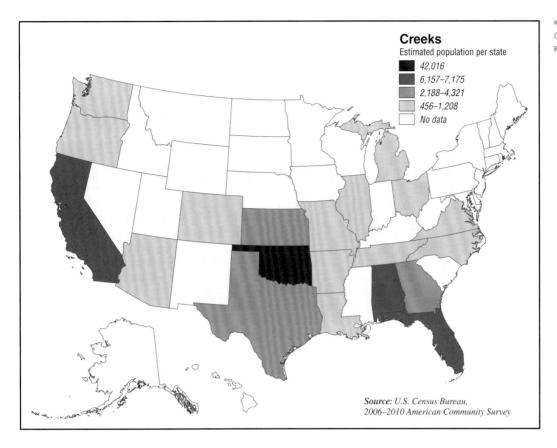

Creeks
Estimated population per state

- 42,016
- 6,157–7,175
- 2,188–4,321
- 456–1,208
- No data

Source: U.S. Census Bureau,
2006–2010 American Community Survey

RELIGION

The traditional Creek religion revered *Hesaketa Emesse*, Master of Breath, as the supreme being. He was believed to live in an upper realm that had the sky as its floor. The moon and the planets were seen as messengers to this deity. The Sun and Sacred Fire represented the Creator on Earth, and Thunder (the war god) and Grandmother Corn were also preeminent deities. The Green Corn Festival was the principal religious celebration. The Creeks recognized animal spirits. Prophets were called *owalas* and priests *heles-haya*.

Each Creek town kept certain sacred objects. The most famous were five copper and two brass plates held by the town of Tuckabatchee. The copper plates were oblong, with the largest being about 18 inches by 7 inches. The brass plates were circular, the larger being 18 inches in diameter, and one was stamped with the mark Æ. Although one legend indicated that the objects had been given them by the Shawnee, who may have obtained them from the Spanish, the plates were widely believed to have been bestowed on the Creeks by the Master of Breath.

Contact with European cultures brought a succession of missionaries to the Creek people. Gradually, many of them began to espouse Christianity, though most remained traditionalists until after their relocation to Oklahoma. Creeks continued to observe the Green Corn Festival, although those who had become Baptist or Methodist no longer participated

in the festival's customary ceremonial dancing. With this decrease in participation, the festival began to lose its former significance, and it deteriorated into little more than a wild party. Christianity became dominant among the Creeks after their removal to Oklahoma. Although some missionaries continued to work among the Creeks, most Creek churches were led by preachers who emerged from within the community. Today, the Creek Baptist Association operates churches that serve almost exclusively native members and offer services conducted in native languages. As Angie Debo describes in *The Road to Disappearance* (1940): "The Creeks had found in Christianity a means of expressing the strong community ties, the moral aspiration, the mystic communion with nature, the deep sense of reverence that had once been expressed by the native ceremonials."

CULTURE AND ASSIMILATION

Creeks traditionally welcomed outsiders in a spirit of equality. In fact, after their initial contact with Europeans, intermarriage between Creek women and foreign trading partners became common. This hastened assimilation and communication on both sides, as Creek wives acted as interpreters and taught their European husbands the language and customs of their people. Because they understood both the Indian and white cultures, many of the multiracial children of these marriages became tribal leaders as adults.

CREEK MYTHS

Although many Creek myths have been lost to history, some were documented by Frank G. Speck in 1904 and 1905. He reported that the myths described animal spirits in the sky world that were responsible for the earth's origin. Master of Breath, the Creek's supreme being, then placed his own innovations on creation, making the earth as it is now. Speck wrote in *Memoirs of the American Anthropological Association*, "The Creeks assert that they were made from the red earth of the old Creek Nation. The whites were made from the foam of the sea. That is why they think the Indian is firm, and the white man is restless and fickle."

After winning its independence from England in the late 1700s, the U.S. government considered Creeks to be among the so-called "Five Civilized Tribes," along with the Seminoles, Cherokees, Chickasaws, and Choctaws. The title derived from the fact that these tribes began to assimilate European ways from the earliest phases of contact. The Creeks eagerly traded deerskins for brightly colored cotton cloth and soon began using metal tools. Included among these tools were guns, which transformed their methods of hunting, making them increasingly reliant on continual trading. Although the acquisition of new goods improved parts of their lifestyle, it also eroded their traditional self-sufficiency.

Some Creeks voluntarily modified their way of life in response to interactions with white traders, but the U.S. government undertook an official effort to assimilate the tribes completely into white culture. White Americans in the eighteenth century had little appreciation for Indian cultures and assumed that the Indians would prefer white culture if they could be induced to learn about it. Many Creeks wanted to keep their culture intact, however. In 1937 University of Oklahoma professor Morris E. Opler wrote in an unpublished report that many people found it incongruous that Indians who belonged to one of the Five Civilized Tribes would want to retain any of their old ways. He further observed, "So far as the whites of Creek country (in Oklahoma) are concerned they have no intention of accepting the Creeks into the main stream of their social and political life."

With continued attacks on their lifestyle, many Creeks found ways to adapt traditional practices into their new societal surroundings. This effort included reestablishing their former towns after their relocation to Oklahoma in 1830. In their new homeland, Upper Creeks settled along the Deep Fork, North Canadian, and Canadian rivers, while the Lower Creeks located their towns farther to the north along the Arkansas and Verdigris rivers. The city of Tulsa evolved from a Creek relocation settlement built on sacred ashes brought from the old eastern town of Talsi.

Christian missionaries had worked among the Creeks since 1735, and by the time the tribe moved to Oklahoma, many Creeks already belonged to Baptist, Methodist, or Presbyterian churches. Under governmental pressure to abandon the tribal town structure, they simply shifted their community's center from the traditional town square to the church. Each congregation chose a preacher from among its members who would serve for life; it was a natural substitution for the town *micco*, or chief.

Since the first contact with whites, the Creeks have been subject to the same general prejudices that are directed at all Native Americans, including both the stereotype of the reserved, stoic Indian and that of the drunken Indian. The Creeks were not reticent, however; they respected impassioned public speakers, and lengthy oration was common at council meetings. The introduction of liquor and the ease with which it could be obtained after the arrival of Europeans caused both real damage to the Creek's society and prejudice against them. Traditionally, Creeks drank only water, *apuske* (made from cornmeal) and *osafke* (made from grits, *osafke kvmokse*, or sour *safke*, might be considered an intoxicant), and a variety of herbal decoctions employed for ritual purposes (mostly purification), collectively referred to as *ase* ("black drink") and considered as medicine. Having no tradition of social sanctions against drunkenness, many Indians imbibed freely, though the whites with whom they interacted also tended to get drunk. In *The Southern Indians and Benjamin Hawkins: 1796–1816* (1986), historian Florette Henri discusses the different perceptions of this activity:

> As a rule, it was Indian drinking that was stressed, and when both white and Indian drinking were mentioned, different terms were used for them. When Indians drank excessively, they were said to become noisy, rude, insolent, and violent; but when the garrison got drunk, gouging eyes and biting noses, Price [Hawkins's friend who managed a government trading post in Georgia] characterized the brawl as a 'drunken frolic.'

Like other Native American groups, the Creeks still encounter a mainstream U.S. culture that generally lacks understanding and appreciation for their values. Although many organizations of indigenous peoples are actively working to improve their living conditions, effects of the near-genocidal policies of the eighteenth and nineteenth centuries are still reflected in comparatively high statistical rates of poverty, suicide, and alcoholism and in high educational dropout rates among Native Americans. In 2012 a study by the U.S. Census Bureau recorded Native American poverty levels at 25.3 percent. According to the National Center for Educational Statistics, Native American students exhibited a dropout rate of nearly 50 percent in 2010, the highest of any ethnic group in the United States. Also troubling is a 2012 report from the National Center for

Disease Control, which notes that the suicide rate for Native Americans between fifteen and thirty-four years old is two and a half times higher than the national average, making suicide the second-leading cause of death for this age group among Indians.

Traditions and Customs As a confederacy of affiliated tribes, Creeks have long been noted for their sophisticated governmental and social structures. Their system may have developed from the need for safety: the Muscogee Nation formed to guard its members against other larger tribes of the region. The nation was constantly in flux, as various tribes either entered or abandoned the fold, so it required steady management by tribal leaders. Perhaps because of the shifting nature of their allegiances, the Creeks also developed a tradition of accepting and respecting other cultures.

In addition to the partitioning of the nation into Upper and Lower communities, the confederacy's fifty towns were divided into two categories based on descent. Each group was known as a moiety. Red towns (or war towns) took the lead in declaring and conducting war operations; councils addressing topics of diplomacy and foreign relations met in red towns. White towns (or peace towns) were cities of refuge; councils seeking to establish peace or enact laws governing internal affairs of the Creek Nation met in these towns. The moiety of each town was easily identifiable, as its color was painted on buildings and ceremonial articles and was used as body decoration by its people. There was an atmosphere of camaraderie among towns of the same moiety and definite rivalry between towns of opposite natures.

Annual spring floods provided the Creeks with favorable agricultural conditions, in turn allowing them to become less nomadic and more sedentary. They built permanent homes in thatched huts surrounding communal, ceremonial town squares called *pascova*. Creeks cultivated a variety of crops and gathered wild fruits, roots, and herbs. They were also skillful hunters, and over time they began raising cows, horses, and pigs as livestock. Each of these activities—hunting, gathering, and farming—was considered a communal task within the tribe.

The pascova was the heart of the Creek community and was used for warm-weather council meetings, dances, and rituals. The square was defined by four rectangular structures, each with one open side that faced inward. A ceremonial fire was kept burning in the center. Adjacent to the square were two other important facilities: the *chokofa*, or rotunda, and the chunkey yard. The chokofa was a circular structure about 40 feet in diameter that served as a meeting place for the town council during the winter. It was also used for social gatherings, during which the entire town could enjoy singing and dancing during inclement weather. The chunkey yard was a field 200 to 300 yards long that was recessed into the ground so that spectators could sit on the surrounding banks. The ball game played in the yard, resembling lacrosse, was an important part of Creek culture, offering recreation among town members or against a team

from a friendly town. Known as "brother to war," the game also provided a forum for settling disputes with unfriendly or enemy towns.

Even as whites attempted to indoctrinate Creeks into European-style culture, the Indians preserved many of their traditional customs, including the basic structure of communities. Today, the Muscogee Nation is proud of its traditional governmental and societal structures. Members are still affiliated with specific tribal towns that serve many of the same purposes as the original communities. The nation maintains sixteen separate ceremonial grounds for traditional cultural events, and the communities associated with these grounds, though they may act independently, remain part of the larger Creek Nation. The center of the Muscogee Nation's tribal complex in Okmulgee, Oklahoma, is constructed in the traditional mound style of the Mississippian culture, designed to honor the tradition and culture of the Creeks.

Cuisine Corn, beans, and squash were the staple crops of the Creeks. As early as 1000 BCE the Muscogee people began harvesting bottle gourds and squash to use both as a food source and as kitchen implements, fashioning water vessels, ladles, cups, and bowls from the skins of these vegetables. By 200 CE the Creeks were cultivating a variety of seed crops and within another five centuries had refined a process for growing modern domesticated corn and beans.

Two yearly varieties of early corn were eaten as they ripened, and a harvest of late corn was dried and stored for winter use as hominy. Each family compound contained a large wooden mortar and pestle used to process corn into meal or grits after it had been hulled by cooking with lye or mixing with ashes. The cornmeal was then cooked with lye and water, and the gruel was left to sour for two or three days. The resulting soup, called *sofkey*, was such a basic part of the diet that each household kept a bowlful at the door so visitors could partake as they entered. Corn was used in other ways as well: for example, cornmeal was mixed with burned shells of the field pea to make blue dumplings; and *apuske*, a drink, was made by sweetening a mixture of parched cornmeal and water. Sweet potatoes, pumpkins, peaches, and apples were eaten fresh or were dried for storage. The Creeks also commonly ate vegetable stews, either with or without meat. After relocation to Oklahoma, salt was extracted and processed from a natural creek-side deposit. Hickory nuts were used both as a cooking ingredient and as a source of oil. Bear fat was prized as a seasoning.

The most important meats in the Creek diet were deer, raccoon, wild turkey, and fish, supplemented by smaller game such as opossum and squirrel. Hogs, chickens, and cattle were adopted soon after the arrival of the Europeans and were all raised in abundance by the early eighteenth century. Beef, venison, and bison meat could be smoked for storage or cut into strips and dried. Meat and fish might be boiled or roasted. The Creeks employed several methods for catching fish, including netting, trapping, and spearing. During the summer the population of an entire town gathered at a favorable spot where a stream could be dammed or fenced to trap fish. Appropriate roots were prepared and thrown into the water to drug the fish, and as they floated to the surface, the men showed their marksmanship by shooting them with bows and arrows. The women then cooked *sofkey* and fried the fish for a feast.

Traditional Dress Traditional clothing for Creek men consisted of a breechcloth; deerskin leggings; a shirt; and, in winter, moccasins. Women wore shawls and skirts made of native textiles. Children generally went unclothed until puberty. During the winter additional warmth was provided by bearskins and buffalo hides. Both men and women wore their hair long. The men plucked their facial hair and also removed hair around their heads, leaving a long central lock that they braided with decorative feathers, shells, and strings. Sometimes they made turbans from strips of deerskin or cloth. The women, whose hair might reach to their calves, wound the turban about their head, fastening it with silver jewelry and adorning it with colorful streamers.

The men used extensive tattooing to decorate their trunks, arms, and legs. The indigo designs included natural objects, animals, abstract scrollwork, and even hunting and battle scenes. Both men and women employed body paint and wore earrings and other jewelry.

Trade with Europeans brought colorful woven fabrics to the Creek people. They quickly incorporated these into their customary fashions and began to decorate clothing and moccasins with trade beads. The women liked to wear clothing fashioned from calico and other printed cloth, and silk ribbons became popular hair ornaments. Creek women also bought the scrap threads of scarlet cloth that traders cleaned out of the bottoms of their packs; they boiled them to remove the dye, which they then added to berry juice and used to color other cloth.

Today, traditional dress is often worn during festivals and important cultural events on the Muscogee calendar. Although the Creeks themselves do not customarily hold powwow gatherings, many modern tribal members—some wearing traditional Muscogee dress—attend intertribal events held throughout the region.

Holidays The major annual holiday in the Creek calendar was the Green Corn Festival, which celebrated the beginning of the corn harvest in late July or early August. Depending on the size of the town, the festival typically lasted from four to eight days and involved a number of traditions, including dancing and moral lectures given by town leaders. To prepare for the festival, the entire town was cleaned and the square refurbished with fresh sand and

new mats for its buildings. Women made new clothing for their families, as well as new pottery and other household furnishings. Old clothing and furnishings, collected rubbish, and all remaining food supplies stored from the previous year were burned. When the fires in the town had been extinguished, a new fire was started in the square using the ancient method of rubbing sticks together. Each family carried some of this new fire home to relight their household fire.

The Green Corn Festival was also called the *busk*, especially among whites. The name was derived from the Creek word *apusketa* (or *boosketah*), meaning "a fast." The men cleansed themselves with ceremonial bathing and by fasting and drinking black drink in large volumes to induce vomiting. The beverage was also used on other occasions, but it was a central element of the Green Corn Festival. As time passed women were allowed to join in the festival dancing; by the late 1800s they also occasionally partook of the medicine. At the end of the festival, when spiritual appreciation had been given for the new crop, the people joined in a feast.

Inspired by the ripening of the new corn, the festival was a time of renewal and forgiveness. Drinking the medicine purged the body physically and purified it from sin. A general amnesty was conferred for all offenses committed in the past year, with the exception of murder. If a guilty person was able to hide between the time a crime was committed and the time of the Green Corn Festival, he or she could escape punishment entirely. The festival marked the beginning of a new year, and for this reason it became the official date for such events as marriages, divorces, and periods of mourning. It was also the occasion for young men's initiation rites.

Green corn ceremonies are still held today. The Muscogee Nation marks its Creek Festival during the month of June. The festival continues to include dancing, feasting, and fasting, though some of the more spiritual aspects of the celebration remain largely nonpublic.

Health Care Issues and Practices According to traditional Muscogee beliefs, illness was the result of an animal spirit or a conjurer placing a foreign substance in the victim's body. The *heles-haya* would affect a cure by concocting an suitable medicine from roots, herbs, and other natural substances. While brewing the potion, he would sing appropriate songs and blow into the mixture through a tube. The afflicted person would take the medicine internally and also apply it externally.

After establishing contact with the Europeans, the Creeks were affected by serious outbreaks of smallpox, measles, and other imported diseases; the number of fatalities went undocumented. During removal to Indian Territory, emigrating Creeks were subjected to difficult traveling conditions, including exposure to weather extremes. Overcrowded conditions on boats during portions of the journey, coupled with dietary changes and unclean drinking water from the Mississippi River, left the travelers vulnerable to illness. Maladies such as dysentery, diarrhea, and cholera contributed to the many casualties en route.

Health problems did not end with the Creeks' arrival in Indian Territory. Streams behaved differently in the West than they did in the East; unexpected flooding destroyed new homes and crops, while during dry spells the streams turned into breeding grounds for mosquitos, and many Creeks fell victim to malaria. During western winters periods of mild days alternated with sudden bouts of extremely cold weather; Creek shelters and clothing were inadequate for the climate, and many people perished from pneumonia. During the first year in Indian Territory, 3,500 Creeks died of disease or starvation.

The Muscogee Nation currently operates its own group of hospitals and treatment centers as part of its Division of Health, established in 1970. By 2013 it boasted a budget of $80 million and a system that included a hospital, six health centers, and nine community health programs. Among a wide array of services, the Muscogee health care centers offer pediatrics, family medicine, dentistry, emergency medical treatment, and physical therapy. Its community services include prevention programs for diabetes and tobacco use. Creeks experience a relatively high incidence of diabetes, which may be related to the poor economic conditions they have endured in modern times; alcoholism may also play a role.

FAMILY AND COMMUNITY LIFE

After their forced relocation to Indian Territory in the mid-1800s, Creeks attempted to preserve their traditional culture by rebuilding communities, known as *italwa*, in their new surroundings. This meant much more than simply erecting buildings. The substitution of the English word *town* dilutes the full meaning of *italwa*. An *italwa* had the autonomy of a Greek city-state and was the primary cultural unit of Creek society. Each town had its own traditions and its own versions of ceremonies, and the Creeks drew more of their identity from their town than from familial relationships. A child was considered a member of the town of his or her mother.

As populations grew, smaller settlements known as *talofa* were developed surrounding the larger towns. Creek society was based on a matrilineal clan system in which each person's identity was determined by the clan of his or her mother. Clan membership governed social interactions, with laws regulating everything from whom members could joke with to whom they could marry (marriage within one's clan was considered incest).

Gender Roles Within each clan most household jobs were communal and were differentiated according to gender. Men and older boys were largely charged with the tasks of hunting and fishing, while women and girls tended gardens and prepared most foods. A traditional Creek household was usually made up of a collection of several rectangular buildings. Each home site included a small garden plot in which the women of the family raised vegetables and tobacco. Shared work led the people to view food and property as belonging to the entire community.

One building in the community was provided for women's "retreats," used during menstruation as well as for a four-month period before and after childbirth. Following a birth, the father fasted for four days. Creek fathers were important to the family dynamic, but it was the mother's brother (or the mother's nearest blood relation) who served as the primary role model and disciplinarian for children. Raising children was principally his and the clan elders' responsibility. Babies spent their first year secured to cradle boards; boys were wrapped in cougar skins, while girls were covered with deerskins or bison hides. A daughter was called by a kinship term or named after an object or natural occurrence associated with her birth. A son was called by the name of his totem, such as bird or snake. At the age of puberty, a boy was initiated into adulthood in his town and

Two young women from Oklahoma's Muscogee (Creek) Nation search for artifacts in a sifting box during an archaeology project near Jacksonville, Georgia. 2006 AP PHOTO / ELLIOTT MINOR

was given a permanent name. His first name, which served as a surname, was that of his town or clan, while his second, or personal, name was descriptive of something about him or his personality.

In the event of the death a spouse, a widower was expected to mourn his wife for four months, during which time he would not bathe, wash his clothes, or comb his hair. The same mourning practices were required of a widow; she, however, was obligated to mourn for four years. The period of mourning for a widow could be decreased by the dead husband's clan if they so chose. After the mourning period, the widow often married a brother of her deceased husband.

In modern times Creek families have largely adopted mainstream American gender roles. Clan ties are still strong, however. According to the Muscogee Nation's official website, "The clan system adds structure to society by influencing marriage choices, personal friendships, and political and economic partnerships."

Education Traditionally, Creek girls learned the skills they would need as adults from their mothers and maternal aunts. Boys were instructed primarily by their maternal uncles, though they also felt their father's influence. Christian missionary schools established in 1822 were the first to formally educate Creeks in white American culture; a few earlier attempts at founding schools had been unsuccessful. By the late twentieth century, Creek students generally attended public schools, with a few attending boarding schools.

By 2013 the governmental body of the Muscogee Nation included an Office of Education and Training, which offers numerous programs aimed at helping Creeks reach their educational goals. The office facilitates programs directed at young children (Head Start), cultural and language preservation, and higher education as well as offering employment and training courses. The Oklahoma Institute of Technology, a branch of Oklahoma State University, is located in Okmulgee and also serves the Creek community in Oklahoma. In addition, the Poarch Creek Tribe in Alabama has an education department and offers on-the-job training through a Job Training Partnership Act (JTPA) program.

EMPLOYMENT AND ECONOMIC CONDITIONS

The early Creeks enjoyed a comfortable living based on agriculture and hunting. Their homeland was fertile, and game was plentiful. With the emergence of European contact, the focus of Creek hunting changed from subsistence to commercial. Trade expanded, and they began to sell not only venison, hides, and furs but also honey, beeswax, hickory nut oil, and other natural products. They also found markets for manufactured goods, including baskets, pottery, and decorated deerskins. As white settlers continued to move into Creek territory, the Indians were crowded into progressively smaller land areas. This process began in 1733 when the Creeks sold 2 million acres of land to the new colony of Georgia in order to pay debts to British traders.

An extensive series of other land cessions followed, and eventually the Creek economy collapsed. According to John K. Mahon's *Indians of the Lower South: Past and Present* (1975), in 1833 Lieutenant Colonel John Abert wrote to the U.S. Secretary of War that, during the previous three years, the Creek people had gone "from a general state of comparative plenty to that of unqualified wretchedness and want."

The Removal Treaty of 1832 gave land in Oklahoma to those Creeks who agreed to emigrate in exchange for their tribal lands in Alabama. To encourage the Indians to move westward, the government also promised a variety of benefits, including a cash payment of $210,000 (to be distributed according to tribal laws over a fifteen-year period), two blacksmith shops in the new territory, an educational annuity, and another cash payment of $100,000 to help the Creeks settle their debts and ease their economic hardship. In addition, each warrior would receive a rifle, ammunition, and a blanket; families' expenses would be paid during the migration and throughout their first year in the West.

At the time of Indian removal, a segment of the Creek people entered into an agreement with the government that enabled them to remain in the East. They were businesspeople who operated ferries, served as guides and interpreters, and raised cattle. Their descendants are the Poarch Creeks, whose tribal headquarters are located in Atmore, Alabama. During the early 1900s some Poarch Creeks began to work in the timber and turpentine industries. Others became tenant farmers or worked as hired farm laborers. Beginning in the 1930s the pulpwood industry became an important element in the Poarch Creek economy. Since the 1950s Poarch Creeks have worked in other nonagricultural jobs.

Some full-blooded Creeks still farm land in the area of Oklahoma that was settled by the Upper Creeks. The Muscogee Nation places a high priority on economic development, and it currently operates numerous tribal enterprises, including casinos in both Okmulgee and Tulsa, truck stops and travel plazas in numerous Oklahoma towns, construction businesses, technology and staffing services, and the Muscogee Document Imaging Company. Members of the Creek Indian tribe work throughout the state of Oklahoma, serving in a wide variety of occupations.

POLITICS AND GOVERNMENT

Throughout their history the Creeks governed themselves democratically. Each town elected a chief who served for life, though he could be recalled. Members of each town were informed about issues and participated actively in decision making. Town leaders met in daily council sessions, and when broader councils were called, each town sent several representatives to speak and vote on its behalf. Although there was no specific law that established a penalty for misrepresenting constituents, leaders who did so faced severe consequences; for example, after signing a 1783 treaty that ceded good hunting grounds to Georgia, a chief returned home to find his house burned and his crops destroyed.

Although Creek society was matrilineal, most tribal leadership positions were filled by men. Women did not vote, but they did enjoy full economic rights, including property ownership, and they exerted significant influence on decisions by discussing their opinions with the men of the town. Each town could also appoint a "Beloved Woman" who communicated with her counterparts in other towns. The roles of the Beloved Woman and perhaps other female leaders have been lost to history since European observers ignored them and omitted them from written accounts.

In the decades following their forced relocation to Oklahoma, the Creeks attempted to formalize their government. Opothle Yahola, a chief who led Creeks loyal to the United States during the Red Stick War and the Civil War, oversaw an effort to record Creek law into written form. A written constitution providing for elected tribal officers was adopted about 1859; in 1867 it was replaced with a new one modeled closely after the U.S. Constitution.

More than a century later, in 1974, the Muscogee Nation ratified a new written constitution, striving to stay true to the spirit of its original 1867 document. The formation of government laid out in the 1974 constitution still stands today: the Muscogee Nation is governed by an elected principal chief, a bicameral legislature, and a judicial branch. The Creek executive branch consists of a principal chief and a second chief, who are democratically elected to four-year terms and who are responsible for appointing an executive director and a chief of staff. This body oversees the daily operations of the tribe. The legislative branch is made up of a twenty-six-member national council, which is responsible for approving major legislation and writing the laws of the nation. The judicial branch consists of both district courts and a six-member supreme court. Much like the U.S. Supreme Court, the Muscogee court has final say in disagreements concerning the tribe's constitution and laws.

The 2,000 Poarch Creeks in Alabama are governed by an elected tribal council that selects a tribal chairman from among its nine members.

NOTABLE INDIVIDUALS

Listed below are some of the Creek people who have made notable contributions to American society as a whole. It is difficult to arrange their names by area of contribution, since some individuals attained prominence in several fields.

Art Acee Blue Eagle (1908–1959) was an acclaimed Creek painter. The painters Fred Beaver (1911–1980)

and Solomon McCombs (1913–1980) served with the U.S. Department of State as goodwill ambassadors, using their art as a means of bridging the communications gap around the world. Jerome Tiger (1941–1967), a painter and sculptor, was also a Golden Gloves boxer. His brother Johnny Tiger Jr. (1940–) is a master artist at the Five Civilized Tribes Museum. Joan Hill (1930–) is a Creek/Cherokee painter who has received numerous recognition awards, grants, and fellowships in the art world. She has done a series of paintings depicting the various treaties of the Five Civilized Tribes and another portraying the women of the tribes. Micah Wesley (1970–) is a contemporary mixed-media artist and disc jockey who lives in Norman, Oklahoma. Kenneth Johnson (1967–) is a metalsmith and artist who creates custom pieces and jewelry that celebrate Muscogee and mound-builder culture.

Academia Edwin Stanton Moore (1918–) was awarded the Department of the Interior Meritorious Service Medal upon retirement as the director of Indian Education in 1979. Moore attended Chilocco Indian School and Oklahoma A & M College, where he played football from 1938 to 1940. In 2010, at the age of ninety-two, he received a distinguished alumnus award from the Oklahoma State University Alumni Association. France Winddance Twine (1960–) is a professor of sociology at the University of California, Santa Barbara, and a documentary filmmaker. A noted ethnographer and feminist, Twine has published more than sixty articles, reviews, and books.

Activism Gale Thrower (1943–) received the Alabama Folk Life Heritage Award for her contributions to preserving her tribe's traditions and culture. Suzan Shown Harjo (1945–) is the president of the Morning Star Institute, a national organization based in Washington, D.C., that works to promote Native American rights. Harjo is also known as a poet, writer, lecturer, curator, and policy advocate.

Government Ernest Childers (1918–2005) was awarded the Congressional Medal of Honor for "exceptional leadership, initiative, calmness under fire, and conspicuous gallantry" on September 22, 1943, at Oliveto, Italy, while a soldier serving in World War II. John N. Reese (1923–1945) was posthumously awarded the Congressional Medal of Honor for "his gallant determination in the face of tremendous odds, aggressive fighting spirit, and extreme heroism at the cost of his life" on February 9, 1945, at Manila in the Philippine Islands, also while serving in World War II.

Literature Alexander (Alex) Lawrence Posey (1873–1908) was best known as a poet and prose writer. He was elected to the House of Warriors, the lower chamber of the Creek National Council, and he helped draft the constitution for the proposed State of Sequoia, a document on which the constitution for the state of Oklahoma was later based. As an educator he served as superintendent of two boarding schools and

Creek Indian and 2nd Lt. Ernest Childers receives the (Congressional) Medal of Honor from Lt. Gen Jacob L. Devers in 1944 for his valor in battle while serving in Italy during World War II. BETTMANN / CORBIS

Stage and Screen Will Sampson (1934–1987) acted in several motion pictures, including *One Flew over the Cuckoo's Nest* (1975), which won an Academy Award for Best Picture in 1976, and *The Outlaw Josie Wales* (1976). Gary Fife (1951–) is the producer and host of *National Native News*, which airs on more than 160 public radio stations around the country.

MEDIA

PRINT

Muscogee Nation News

The official publication of the Muscogee Nation, the newspaper is distributed twice monthly in English. Its estimated readership is 21,000.

Rebecca Landsberry
Department of Communications
P.O. Box 580
Okmulgee, Oklahoma 74447
Phone: (918) 732-7720
Fax: (918) 758-0824
Email: rlandsberry@muscogeenation-nsn.gov
URL: www.themuscogeecreeknation.com

Poarch Creek News

A monthly English-language publication of the Creek tribe in Alabama, the newspaper is available to tribal members for an annual fee.

Gayle Johnson, Media Specialist
5811 Jack Springs Road
Atmore, Alabama 36502
Phone: (205) 368-9136, ext. 2210
Email: gjohnson@pci-nsn.gov
URL: www.poarchcreekindians-nsn.gov

RADIO

Muscogee Radio, KOKL 1240 AM

Airing on Wednesdays at 9:30 a.m., the weekly radio program offers listeners the latest news concerning the Muscogee Nation. Previous broadcasts are available for download online.

Gerald Wofford
Department of Communications
P.O. Box 580
Okmulgee, Oklahoma 74447
Phone: (918) 732-7720
Fax: (918) 758-0824
URL: www.muscogeenation-nsn.gov/index.php/creek-history/language/205

ORGANIZATIONS AND ASSOCIATIONS

Muscogee (Creek) Nation

The official tribal government and organization of the Muscogee Creek Nation offers a variety of services for tribal members.

George Tiger, Principal Chief
Tribal Offices
P.O. Box 580

the Creek Orphan Asylum and as superintendent of public instruction for the Creek Nation of Oklahoma. Poet Louis (Littlecorn) Oliver (1904–1991) wrote *The Horned Snake* (1982); *Caught in a Willow Net: Poems and Stories* (1983); and *Chasers of the Sun: Creek Indian Thoughts, Poems, and Stories* (1990). Joy Harjo (1951–), winner of the Academy of American Poetry Award, has published several books of poetry, including *A Map to the Next World* (2000). Cynthia Leitich Smith (1967–) is a *New York Times* best-selling author of children's books, whose work centers on the everyday lives of modern Native Americans. From 2000 to 2013 she published twelve books as well as numerous short stories and essays.

Politics Enoch Kelly Haney (1940–), a Seminole and Muscogee tribal member and a former Oklahoma state senator, is nationally recognized for his political involvement and proactive stance for Native American rights. He is also an accomplished artist on canvas and in bronze and sculpted a 6,000-pound bronze statue of an American Indian warrior that was placed atop the Oklahoma State Capitol in 2002.

Sports Allie P. Reynolds (1917–1994) was a baseball pitcher with the Cleveland Indians from 1942 to 1946 and with the New York Yankees from 1947 to 1954. He had the best earned run average (ERA) in the American League in 1952 and 1954 and led the league in strikeouts and shutouts for two seasons. In 1951 he was named America's Professional Athlete of the Year. Jack Jacobs (1919–1974) played football for the University of Oklahoma from 1939 to 1942, then played professional football for fourteen years with several teams, including the Cleveland Rams, the Washington Redskins, and the Green Bay Packers.

Okmulgee, Oklahoma 74447
Phone: (800) 482-1979
Fax: (918) 758-0824
URL: www.muscogeenation-nsn.gov

Muscogee Nation Division of Health

Provides comprehensive health care coverage
and information for members of the
Muscogee Nation.

Seneca M. Smith, Director
1801 East Fourth Street
Okmulgee, Oklahoma 74447
Phone: (918) 756-4333
Email: seneca.smith@creekhealth.org
URL: http://creekhealth.org

Poarch Creek Indians

Descendants of the original Creek Nation, the Poarch
Creek Band were not removed to Oklahoma along
with other tribal members during the 1800s. They
continue to live in and around their reservation near
Poarch, Alabama.

Buford L. Rolin, Tribal Chairman
5811 Jack Springs Road
Atmore, Alabama 36502
Phone: (251) 368-9136, ext. 2202
Fax: (251) 368-4502
Email: mmartin@pci-nsn.gov
URL: www.poarchcreekindians.org

MUSEUMS AND RESEARCH CENTERS

Creek Council House Museum

A museum and library of tribal history.

David Anderson
106 West Sixth Street
Okmulgee, Oklahoma 74447
Phone: (918) 756-2324
Fax: (918) 758-1166
Email: creekmuseum@sbcglobal.net
URL: www.creekcouncilhouse.com

Five Civilized Tribes Museum

Displays Indian artifacts and artwork, with separate
sections devoted to each of the Five Civilized Tribes
(the Creek, Cherokee, Chickasaw, Choctaw, and
Seminole Nations).

Mary Robinson
1101 Honor Heights Drive
Muskogee, Oklahoma 74401
Phone: (918) 683-1701
Fax: (918) 683-3070
Email: 5tribesdirector@sbcglobal.net
URL: www.fivetribes.org

Poarch Creek Band of Indians Museum

A cultural center and library for the Eastern Creeks.

Amber Alvarez
5811 Jack Springs Road
Atmore, Alabama 36502
Phone: (251) 368-9136, ext. 2649
Email: asmith@pci-nsn.gov
URL: www.poarchcreekindians.org/westminster/
cultural_authority.html

SOURCES FOR ADDITIONAL STUDY

Braund, Kathryn E. Holland. *Deerskins & Duffels: The Creek Indian Trade with Anglo-America, 1685–1815.* Lincoln: University of Nebraska Press, 2008.

———. Tohopeka: *Rethinking the Creek War and the War of 1812.* Tuscaloosa: University of Alabama Press, 2012.

Gouge, Earnest. *Totkv Mocvse/New Fire: Creek Folktales.* Translated by Jack B. Martin, Margaret McKane Mauldin, and Juanita McGirt. Norman: University of Oklahoma Press, 2004.

Green, Michael D. *The Creeks.* New York: Chelsea House, 1990.

Hahn, Steven. *The Invention of the Creek Nation, 1670–1763.* Lincoln: University of Nebraska Press, 2004.

———. *The Life and Time of Mary Musgrove.* Gainesville: University Press of Florida, 2012.

Martin, Jack B., Margaret McKane Mauldin, Juanita McGirt. *A Grammar of Creek (Muskogee).* Lincoln: University of Nebraska Press; 2011.

Saunt, Claudio. *A New Order of Things: Property, Power, and the Transformation of the Creek Indians, 1733–1816.* New York: Cambridge University Press, 1999.

Swanton, John Reed. *Early History of the Creek Indians and Their Neighbors.* Gainesville: University Press of Florida, 1998.

Winn, William W. *The Old Beloved Path: Daily Life among the Indians of the Chattahoochee River Valley.* Columbus, GA: Columbus Museum, 1992.

CREOLES

Helen Bush Caver and Mary T. Williams

OVERVIEW

Unlike many other ethnic groups in the United States, Creoles do not constitute a group that immigrated from a specific country. Rather, Creoles are a self-identified group of various people of French, Spanish, and Portuguese descent who live in the coastal area of Louisiana, particularly in New Orleans. (In contrast, the word *creole* in Latin America, the Caribbean, and Africa is used to refer to distinct populations.) There is general scholarly agreement that the term *Creole* derives from the Portuguese word *crioulo*, which means "a person, especially a servant or a slave, born in the master's household." The word first came into common usage in the United States after the Louisiana Purchase in 1803. Louisianans of French and Spanish descent adopted the term to differentiate themselves from the Americans who were moving into the area in increasing numbers.

Although *Creole* remains a self-applied designation rather than an ethnic or racial distinction, since the early twentieth century most people who identify as Creole have been of African or mixed-race background. Frequently, the term *Creole* is restricted to mixed-race individuals who speak a Louisiana dialect of French. As a result, the terms *Creoles of color* and *black Creoles* are sometimes used to refer to Creoles. Creoles are distinguished from Cajuns, who are mostly whites who live in Louisiana and trace their ancestries to French-speaking exiles from Canada. These ethnic and linguistic designations are flexible, though, since self-identified Cajuns include people from many different backgrounds, and self-identified Creoles may share some of the same ancestors as the Cajuns. In addition, Thomas Klingler, an authority on Louisiana French dialects, has convincingly argued that the differences between Cajun French and Creole French are often based on the perceived racial identities of the speakers rather than on objective differences between dialects.

A single definition of *Creole* sufficed in the early days of European colonial expansion, but the term acquired different meanings as Creole populations established divergent social, political, and economic identities. Nevertheless, Creoles are, almost by definition, Catholic, and most are blue-collar workers. Determining the group's relative prosperity and patterns of economic activity are difficult to determine because of the indeterminacy of the population's makeup.

The origins of Louisiana's Creole population can be traced to the eighteenth century, when France controlled Louisiana and a diverse population of slaves, French merchants, and planters began to populate New Orleans and the surrounding area in growing numbers. Although the ancestries of many whites in Louisiana extend to these early Creoles, very few now use this term to describe themselves. During the time of the civil rights movement in the late 1950s through mid-1960s, many people in the state with African ancestry whose families had previously identified themselves as Creole began to describe themselves more commonly as black or African American. During the late twentieth and early twenty-first centuries, it again became more common for people of mixed race to describe themselves as Creole, particularly in the historically French-speaking regions of southwest Louisiana and of the Cane River area of north Louisiana. The New Orleans area has also had an increasing number of people who self-identify as Creoles in recent years.

No reliable estimate of the Creole population's size in the United States is available because of the unstable nature of the designation. In 2000 the U.S. Census included Creole as an option in the question about ancestry in the Public Use Microdata Sample. An estimated 5,065 people in Louisiana chose this option in that year. Among those who identified themselves to the Census as Creole, 37.2 percent gave their race as black; 25.3 percent gave their race as a combination of white, black, and American Indian; 13.5 percent gave "other race"; 10.2 percent gave "white and black"; 6.1 percent reported their race as white; 3.7 percent recorded "black and other race"; 3.6 percent identified as "white, black, and other race"; and 0.3 percent said that they were "white, Asian, and other race." Although the majority of Creoles live New Orleans and other parts of Louisiana, there are significant Creole communities in Texas, Chicago, and Los Angeles.

HISTORY OF THE PEOPLE

Early History In the seventeenth century, French explorers and settlers moved into the United States with their customs, language, and government. After

The Amand Broussard family home is preserved in Vermilionville, Louisiana as an excellent example of French Creole architecture and way of life in the late 1700s. CORBIS / DAVE G. HOUSER. REPRODUCED BY PERMISSION.

France ceded Louisiana to Spain in 1768, French language and customs continued to prevail. Persons of French or Spanish descent in New Orleans began referring to themselves as Creoles to set themselves apart from the Anglo Americans who began moving into the area after the Louisiana Purchase in 1803.

Louisiana Creoles of color were different and separate from other populations, both black and white, and in the nineteenth century they became part of an elite society, including leaders in business, agriculture, politics, and the arts. Nonetheless, as early as 1724 their legal status had been defined by the *Code Noir* (black code). According to Violet Harrington Bryan in *The Myth of New Orleans in Literature, Dialogues of Race and Gender*, they could own slaves, hold real estate, and be recognized in the courts, but they could not vote nor could they marry white persons, and they had to designate themselves as "f.m.c." or "f.w.c." ("free man of color" or "free woman of color") on all legal documents.

Many Creoles are descendants of French colonials who fled Saint-Domingue (Haiti) for North America's Gulf Coast when a slave insurrection in 1791 challenged French authority. According to Thomas Fiehrer's essay "From La Tortue to La Louisiane: An Unfathomed Legacy," Saint-Domingue had more than 450,000 black slaves, 40,000 to 45,000 whites, and 32,000 *gens-de-couleur libres*, who were neither white nor slaves. The slave revolt challenged French authority and, after defeating the expeditionary corps sent by French military commander Napoleon Bonaparte, the leaders of the slaves established an independent country named Haiti. Most whites were either massacred or fled, many with their slaves, as did many mulatto freemen.

When Toussaint L'Ouverture (1743–1803), a self-educated slave, took control of Saint-Domingue in 1801, some new exiles went directly to present-day Louisiana and some went to Cuba. Of those who went to Cuba, many went to New Orleans after 1803, when the United States purchased the Louisiana territory. By 1815 more than 11,000 refugees had settled in New Orleans, doubling the city's population of 1791. Some of the refugees moved on to areas outside New Orleans or traveled north along the Mississippi River.

Historically, white Creoles clung to their individualistic way of life, frowned upon intermarriage with Anglo Americans, refused to learn English, and were resentful and contemptuous of Protestants, whom they considered irreligious and wicked. Creoles generally succeeded in remaining separate in the rural sections, but they steadily lost ground in New Orleans. In 1803 there were seven Creoles to every Anglo American in New Orleans, but these figures dwindled to two to one by 1830.

Anglo Americans reacted to this disdain by disliking the Creoles with equal enthusiasm. Gradually New Orleans became not one city but two. Canal Street split them apart, dividing the old Creole city from the "uptown" section where the other Americans quickly settled. To cross Canal Street in either direction was to enter another world. These differences are still noticeable.

Living amid imported furniture, wines, books, and clothes, white Creoles were once immersed in a completely French atmosphere. Part of Creole social life has traditionally centered on the French Opera House; from 1859 to 1919 it was the place for sumptuous gatherings and glittering receptions. The interior, graced by curved balconies and open boxes of architectural beauty, seated 805 people. Creoles loved the music and delighted in attendance as the operas were great social and cultural affairs.

In "Ethnicity and Identity: Creoles of Colour in Louisiana" Dormon writes: "The American Civil War provided a major watershed in the continuity of Creole ethnohistory." The property of many Creoles was destroyed in the conflict. Then, after the conflict had ended, Creoles were denied their special legal status and were lumped together with former slaves as second-class citizens. While this led to a decline in economic and social standing, it strengthened the ethnic identity of Creoles, who bound together in an effort to maintain their distinctiveness from African Americans and resist the denigration of white racism.

Among the many persistent differences of opinion regarding Creole identity, the greatest controversy stems from the presence or absence of African ancestry. Charles Gayarre, in an 1886 lecture at Tulane University ("Creoles of History and Creoles of Romance," New Orleans: C. E. Hopkins, ca. 1886), and F. P. Poche, in a speech at the American Exposition in New Orleans (*New Orleans Daily Picayune*, February 8, 1886), both stated that Louisiana Creoles had "not a particle of African blood in their veins." In *A Few Words about the Creoles of Louisiana* (1892), Alcee Fortier repeated the same belief. These three men were probably the most prominent Creole intellectuals of the nineteenth century. Creole writers Lyle Saxon, Robert Tallant, and Edward Dreyer continued this argument in 1945 by saying, "No true Creole ever had colored blood."

According to Sister Dorothea Olga McCants, translator of Rodolphe Lucien Desdunes's *Our People and Our History* (1973), the free mixed-blood French speakers in New Orleans came to use the word *Creole* to describe themselves. The term *Creole of color* was used by these proud part-Latin people to set themselves apart from American blacks. These Haitian descendants were cultured, educated, and economically prosperous as musicians, artists, teachers, writers, and doctors. In "Louisiana's 'Creoles of Color,'" James H. Dormon states that the group was clearly recognized as special, productive, and worthy by the white community, citing an editorial in the *New Orleans Times Picayune* in 1859 that referred to them as "Creole colored people." Prior to the Civil War a three-caste system existed: white, black, and Creoles of color. After the Civil War and Reconstruction, however, the Creoles of color—who had been part of the free black population before the war—were merged into a two-caste system, black and white.

Modern Era As Jim Crow laws and segregation were institutionalized in Louisiana and throughout the South, Creoles and African Americans joined in the effort to resist the racist social and economic structure. According to Dormon, "As a generally better educated and more articulate group, Creoles naturally assumed the leadership roles in the fight against segregation, discrimination, and subordination, for themselves and for the 'Negro' population as a whole." When the civil rights movement emerged in the 1950s and 1960s, Creoles were divided as to whether or not they should or could maintain their ethnic distinctiveness while also maintaining solidarity with other black populations. To a large degree Creoles responded by maintaining their isolation in enclaves and through endogamy. However, some Creoles, especially the youth, joined the larger black-pride movement and moved away from their Creole identity.

In the late twentieth century the development of Creole identity was also influenced by the resurgence of Cajun identity in southern Louisiana. Cajuns, also known Acadians, are the descendants of French Canadians. Beginning in the 1970s the preservation and revitalization of Cajun culture was encouraged through the formation of festivals and organizations. These efforts were quite successful, and they led to similar efforts by non-Cajun Creoles. These efforts, too, were a success and led to the formation of various Creole cultural, linguistic, and educational organizations that helped to promote ethnic Creole pride and identification.

SETTLEMENT IN THE UNITED STATES

Creoles first settled in New Orleans and elsewhere along the Gulf Coast of Louisiana in the eighteenth century. They remained there, almost without exception, until after the American Civil War (1861–1865), which dramatically disrupted the economic, social, and political framework of the entire southern United States. In the postwar upheaval, that Creoles first began to move in significant numbers outside their traditional enclaves.

Although it is difficult to track the patterns of Creole migration because the group is not recognized as a distinct ethnicity, it is believed that most of these initial Creole migrants moved within the South, from rural areas of Louisiana to New Orleans and other nearby cities, especially in Texas. During World War I, as a result of growing demand for industrial labor, Creoles, like other white and nonwhite Southerners, began to move to northern cities in large numbers in search of work. Chicago, in particular, was a common destination for Creoles. World War II was another catalyst for Creole migration. Creole servicemen stationed on the West Coast began to see the economically thriving cities there as possible destinations for migration. After the war, Creoles began to move to these cities and to Los Angeles in particular.

In the early twenty-first century Creole migration was driven by the devastation wrought by Hurricanes Katrina and Rita in 2005. Those storms destroyed homes and infrastructure in many traditional Creole enclaves along the Gulf Coast and motivated many to leave the region, often for the established Creole communities of Texas, Los Angeles, and Chicago.

LANGUAGE

The original language community of the Creoles was composed of standard French and Louisiana Creole, which is based largely on French but also includes Spanish, Portuguese, African, and Native American elements and influences. French was the language of white Creoles; it should not be confused with Louisiana Creole. Morphologically and lexically, Louisiana Creole resembles Saint-Domingue Creole, although there is evidence that Louisiana Creole was well established by the time Saint-Domingue refugees arrived in Louisiana. For many years Louisiana Creole was predominantly a language of rural blacks in southern Louisiana. In the past Louisiana Creole was also spoken by whites, including impoverished whites who worked alongside black slaves as well as whites raised by black nannies.

French usage is no longer as widespread among Creoles as it once was. As Americans from other states began to settle in Louisiana in large numbers

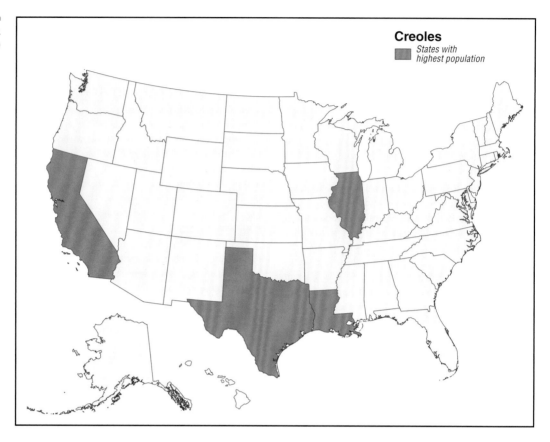

Creoles
States with highest population

after 1880, they became the dominant social group. As such, the local social groups were acculturated and became bilingual. Eventually the original language community of the Creoles—French and Louisiana Creole—began to be lost. Today Louisiana Creole is spoken mainly among elderly Creoles, primarily in rural areas.

An effort to combat the decline of Louisiana Creole and other regional forms of French took shape in the mid-1960s and continues in the early twenty-first century. Central to this effort is the Council for the Development of French in Louisiana. The group has been successful in its efforts to educate the public and has played a part in the ongoing revitalization of Creole identity and language in Louisiana.

Greetings and Popular Expressions The past sayings of the Creoles were unusual and colorful. According to Leonard V. Huber in "Reflections on the Colorful Customs of Latter-Day New Orleans Creoles," an ugly man with a protruding jaw and lower lip had *une gueule de benitier* (a mouth like a holy water font) and his face was *une figure de pomme cuite* (a face like a baked apple). A man who stayed around the house constantly was referred to as *un encadrement* (doorframe). The expression *pauvres diables* (poor devils) was applied to poor individuals. Anyone who bragged too much was called *un bableur* (a hot air shooter). A person with thin legs had *des jambes*

de manches-à-balais (broomstick legs). An amusing expression for a person who avoided work was that he had *les cotes en long* (vertical ribs). Additional Creole colloquialisms include *un tonnerre a la voile* (an unruly person), *menterie* (lie or story), *frou-frou* (giddy), and *homme de paille, pistolet de bois* (a man who is a bluff).

RELIGION

Roman Catholicism is strongly associated with Creoles. The French and Spanish cultures from which Creoles originate are so closely associated with Catholicism that some people assume that all Louisianans are Catholic and that all people in Louisiana are of French and/or Spanish ancestry. Records from churches in Mobile (Alabama), New Orleans, and other communities in the area indicate the presence of both black and white Creoles in church congregations very early in the eighteenth century.

After segregation of the Catholic Church in 1895, certain churches became identified with Creoles of color. In 1916 Corpus Christi Church opened in New Orleans's seventh ward, within walking distance of many Creoles of color. Other churches in the city, including St. Peter Claver, Epiphany, and Holy Redeemer, are also associated with black populations. Each church has a parish school run by the Blessed Sacrament Sisters. St. Louis Cathedral and St. Augustine's Church, also of New Orleans, are prominent in the larger Creole society, with women predominating in attendance. Today less than one-third of the people in Louisiana are Catholics, but the early dominance of Catholicism has left its mark on people of other denominations. In the southern part of the state, especially in New Orleans, place and street names are often associated with particular saints.

Traditionally central to the religious life of Creoles was devotion to the Virgin Mary, All Saints' Day (November 1), and the many activities associated with the observance of Lent and Holy Week, especially Mardi Gras, which occurs on the Tuesday immediately before the start of Lent. Other important religious figures are St. Jude (the patron saint of impossible cases), St. Peter (who opens the gates of heaven), and St. Anthony (who helps locate lost articles).

Traditionally, Holy Week was closely observed by Creoles, both as a religious celebration and as a time of customs and superstition. On Holy Thursday morning, housewives used to take pots from the stove and place them on the floor, making the sign of the cross when they heard the ringing of church bells. Also, nine varieties of greens were cooked—a concoction known as *gumbo shebes*. On Good Friday, Creoles visited churches on foot and in silence to bring good fortune. Among contemporary Creoles, the religious aspect has declined, but many of the customs remain intact.

CULTURE AND ASSIMILATION

Throughout its history, Creole culture has negotiated its complex relationship to mainstream American culture in various ways. Upon the U.S. annexation of Louisiana in 1803, Creoles were a radically distinct cultural group. In a predominantly English-speaking country they spoke French. In a country deeply divided between whites and blacks, Creoles were racially ambiguous, with a mix of European, African, and Native American genetic makeup.

Creoles sought to maintain this distinctiveness through various strategies. For one, they largely remained in traditional neighborhoods and enclaves in New Orleans and elsewhere in Louisiana. They were also largely endogamous—that is, they married almost exclusively within the community—and through the nineteenth century many marriages were arranged marriages. Creoles also maintained a communal commitment to middle-class pride in work and economic prosperity.

Although the Civil War devastated many Creole families and ended their legal distinctiveness from African Americans in Louisiana, Creoles "maintained their sense of identity and belonging, their basic group identity, as well as their conviction of their own superiority over the mass of the black population," according to Dormon in "Ethnicity and identity: Creoles of Colour in Louisiana." Over the course of the late nineteenth and twentieth century, as Jim Crow segregation took effect and the civil rights movement

emerged to combat racial disenfranchisement, the relationship between Creoles, African Americans, and white American culture continued to change. While many Creoles maintained their cultural distinctiveness, others began to identify increasingly with African American culture, which shared in the struggle to resist racial oppression.

After the end of the civil rights movement and through the early twenty-first century a movement to revitalize Creole culture emerged and grew. This movement has centered on language, cuisine, and music. While efforts to restore Creole identity have been somewhat successful, the assumption of a Creole identity is largely self-determined. Many young Creoles of color today live under pressure to identify themselves as African Americans. Some young white Creoles want to avoid being considered of mixed race. Therefore young black and white Creoles often choose an identity other than Creole.

Traditions and Customs Creole culture, as reflected in its traditions and customs, is a mixture of French, African, Caribbean, and Native American influences. Most Creoles are aware of and take great pride in the rich and distinct cultural history of their community. This pride manifests itself in the concerted effort to preserve the community's linguistic heritage as well as in the continued popularity of Creole food, music, and other traditions.

Creoles have a tradition of politeness in speech, especially when communicating with older adults. Traditional Creoles place a high value on taking the time to acknowledge and greet acquaintances. Today older Creoles complain that many younger Creoles do not adhere to these basic values. They complain that children walk past the homes of people they know without greeting acquaintances who are sitting on the porch or working on the lawn. Young males are particularly criticized for greeting others in a rushed and inarticulate manner.

A Creole woman sits with an infant on her lap, 1953. CORBIS / DAVE G. HOUSER. REPRODUCED BY PERMISSION.

Big Chief Walter Cook & the Creole Wild West Mardi Gras Indians perform during the New Orleans Jazz & Heritage Festival in New Orleans, Louisiana. AMY HARRIS / CORBIS

Cuisine Creole cooking is the distinguishing feature of Creole homes. It can be as subtle as oysters Rockefeller, as fragrantly explicit as a jambalaya, or as down-to-earth as a dish of red beans and rice. A Creole meal is a celebration, not just a means of addressing hunger pangs. Many of these dishes listed are features of African-influenced Louisiana—that is, Creoles of color and black Creoles.

The Europeans who settled in New Orleans found immense areas of inland waterways and estuaries alive with crayfish, shrimp, crab, and fish of many different varieties. Moreover, the swampland was full of game. The settlers used what they found and produced a cuisine based on good taste, experimentation, and spices. On the experimental side, it was in New Orleans that raw, hard liquor was transformed into the more sophisticated cocktail, and where the simple cup of coffee became *café Brulot*, a concoction spiced with cinnamon, cloves, and lemon peel and flambéed with cognac. The seasonings used are distinctive, but there is yet another essential ingredient—a heavy black iron skillet.

These ingredients formed the basis of the many-faceted family of gumbos. Gumbo is similar to a soup or a stew, yet too unique to be classified as one or the other. It starts with a base of highly seasoned roux (a cooked blend of fat and flour used as a thickening agent), scallions, and herbs including *filé* (the ground powder of the sassafras leaf, a native plant), which serves as a vehicle for oysters, crabs, shrimp, chicken, ham, various game, or combinations thereof. Oysters may be consumed raw (on the half-shell), sautéed and packed into hollowed-out French bread, or baked on the half-shell and served with various garnishes. Shrimp, crayfish, and crab are similarly starting points for the Creole cook who might have croquettes in mind, or a pie, an omelet, or a stew.

Dances and Songs Creoles are a festive people who enjoy music and dancing. In New Orleans during French rule, public balls were held twice weekly. After the Spanish took over, the practice continued. These balls were frequented by white Creoles, although wealthy Creoles of color may also have attended. Cotillions presented by numerous academies provided young ladies and gentlemen with the opportunity to display their skills in dancing quadrilles, valses (waltzes) *à un temps*, valses *à deux temps*, valses *à trois temps*, polkas, and *polazurkas*. Saturday night balls and dances were a universal institution in Creole country.

During the special festive season between New Year's and Mardi Gras, many brilliant balls were scheduled. Only the most respected families were asked to attend, with lists scrutinized by older members of the families to keep less prominent people away.

In addition to this upper-class tradition, Creole culture also produced a body of folk music that was sung in French and was influenced by French and African sources. In the nineteenth century the performance of Creole music centered on Congo Square in New Orleans. The Creole pianist and composer Louis Moreau Gottschalk (1829–1869) adapted and popularized this nascent Creole musical tradition. Late in the nineteenth century and early in the twentieth century, various musical styles, including those of the Creoles, combined in New Orleans to produce a new musical form known as jazz. One of the leading jazz innovators—and the self-proclaimed inventor of the genre—was the Creole Ferdinand Joseph Lementhe "Jelly Roll" Morton. Another important legacy of Creole musical tradition is zydeco, a genre that blends various Cajun, European, and American influences. In the early twenty-first century, music remains a vital aspect of Creole culture, with zydeco undergoing a resurgence beyond the traditional boundaries of Cajun communities.

Death and Burial Rituals In the past, when someone died, black-bordered announcements posted in the Creole section of town informed the public of the death and the time and place of the funeral. Usually the notices were placed in the neighborhood where the deceased had lived, but if the deceased was wealthy, notices would be placed all over the Vieux Carré (old quarter). These notices were also placed at St. Louis Cathedral on a death notice blackboard. Invitations were issued for the funeral, and funeral services were held in the home.

Today the Vieux Carré of New Orleans is a high-rent tourist area, and these customs are no longer followed. In New Orleans and some parts of lower Louisiana, Creoles and others still bury their dead in above-ground tombs.

The wearing of mourning was a rigorous requirement. The deceased's immediate family put on *grand deuil* (full mourning). During the six months of full mourning it was improper to wear jewelry or anything white or with colors. Men wore a black tie, black crepe band on the hat, and sometimes a black band on the arm. After six months the widow could wear black clothes edged with a white collar and cuffs. Slave or black Creole funeral processions often lasted an hour and covered a distance of less than six squares, or one-third mile. News of the deaths was received through the underground route by a system of telegraph chanting.

Cemeteries held an important place in Creole life. A family tomb received almost as much attention as a church. To not visit the family tomb on All Saints' Day (November 1) was unforgivable. Some well-known cemeteries include St. Louis Number

CREOLE PROVERBS

A collection of Creole proverbs can be found in several references. One of the best is from Lafcadio Hearn's *Gombo Zhebes: Little Dictionary of Creole Proverbs*. Proverbs include:

- The monkey smothers its young one by hugging it too much.

- Wait till the hare's in the pot before you talk.

- Today drunk with fun, tomorrow the paddle.

- If you see your neighbor's beard on fire, water your own.

- Shingles cover everything.

- When the oxen lift their tails in the air, look out for bad weather.

- Fair words buy horses on credit.

- A good cock crows in any henhouse.

- What you lose in the fire, you will find in the ashes.

- When one sleeps, one doesn't think about eating.

- He who takes a partner takes a master.

- The coward lives a long time.

- Conversation is the food of ears.

- It's only the shoes that know if the stockings have holes.

- The dog that yelps doesn't bite.

- Threatened war doesn't kill many soldiers.

- A burnt cat dreads fire.

- An empty sack cannot stand up.

- Good coffee and the Protestant religion were seldom if ever seen together.

- It takes four to prepare the perfect salad dressing—a miser to pour the vinegar, a spendthrift to add the olive oil, a wise man to sprinkle the salt and pepper, and a madcap to mix and stir the ingredients.

One, the oldest in Louisiana, and St. Louis Number Two. St. Roch Cemetery, which is noted for its shrine, was built by Father Peter Leonard Thevis in fulfillment of a vow to Saint Roch for protection of the congregation of Holy Trinity Church from the yellow fever epidemic of 1868. Cypress Grove, Greenwood, and Metairie cemeteries are among the most beautiful burial grounds in Louisiana. Large structures resembling churches with niches for lifelike marble statues of the saints may be found in Metairie Cemetery.

FAMILY AND COMMUNITY LIFE

Creoles are, to a large degree, defined by their place within the larger Creole community. Thus it is rare to find Creoles outside ethnic enclaves and neighborhoods, especially in New Orleans and the surrounding area. This trend was established, and has been maintained, by a tradition of endogamy that has knit a tightly woven community of Creoles from a diverse array of cultural, racial, and ethnic sources. One example of this form of community is that Creoles considered it a duty to take widowed cousins and orphaned children of kinspeople into their families. As a result, Creoles emphasize the need to maintain cultural and familial ties as a means of preserving the integrity of the community. This practice has become increasingly disrupted over the course of the twentieth and early twenty-first centuries by political, cultural, economic, and social change. Thus, while Creoles are still closely knit and tend to marry within the group, many are also moving into the greater community and assimilating.

Gender Roles Traditionally, men were the heads of Creole households, while women dedicated their lives to home and family. Unmarried women relatives (*tantes*) lived in many households. They provided a much-needed extra pair of hands in running the household and rearing the children. Women were also traditionally expected to be good hostesses and to entertain and feed guests.

While the custom of male dominance within the household has changed and diminished over time, Creoles typically maintain a patriarchal family structure. Men decide where the family will live and make financial decisions for the family, even as women increasingly enter the workforce. The maintenance of traditional roles is strongest among those Creoles who live in rural enclaves and weakest among those who have left Louisiana and the bonds of the Creole community.

Weddings In the old days Creoles married within their own class. The young man faced the scrutiny of older aunts and cousins, who were the guardians and authorities of family trees. The suitor had to ask a woman's father for his daughter's hand. The gift of a ring allowed them to be formally engaged. All meetings of young people were strictly chaperoned, even after the engagement. Weddings, usually held at the St. Louis Cathedral in New Orleans, were opulent affairs with Swiss Guards meeting the wedding guests and preceding them up the aisle. Behind the guests came the bride, accompanied by her father, and then the groom, escorting the bride's mother. The groom's parents followed, and then all the relatives of both bride and groom. A relative's absence was interpreted as a silent protest against the wedding. The bride's gown was handed down through generations or purchased in Paris to become an heirloom. Unlike today's weddings, there were no ring bearers, bridesmaids, matrons of honor, nor any floral decorations in the church. Ceremonies were held in the evenings. St. Louis Cathedral is still the place for New Orleans' Creole weddings, and many relatives still attend, though in fewer numbers.

Baptisms Baptisms usually took place when the child was about a month old. The godfather (*parrain*) and the godmother (*marraine*) were always relatives, usually from each side of the family. It was a decided honor to be asked to serve as a godparent. The *marraine* gave the infant a gift of a gold cross and chain, and the *parrain* offered either a silver cup or a silver knife and fork. The godfather also gave a gift to the godmother and paid for the celebration that followed the baptism. It was an expensive honor to be chosen *parrain*.

EMPLOYMENT AND ECONOMIC CONDITIONS

The image Creoles have of economic independence is rooted in the socioeconomic conditions of free people of color before the Civil War. Creoles of color were slave owners, land owners, and skilled laborers. Of the 1,834 free Negro heads of households in New Orleans in 1830, 752 owned at least one slave. New Orleans persons of color were far wealthier, more secure, and more established than blacks elsewhere in Louisiana.

Economic independence is highly valued in the colored Creole community. Being on welfare is a source of embarrassment, and many of those who receive government aid eventually drop out of the community. African Americans with steady jobs, respectable professions, or financial independence frequently marry into the community and become Creole, at least by association.

Creoles of color and black Creoles have been quick to adapt strategies that maintain their elite status throughout changing economic conditions. Most significant is the push to acquire higher education. Accelerated education has allowed Creoles to move into New Orleans's more prestigious neighborhoods, first to Gentilly, then to Pontchartrain Park, and more recently to New Orleans East.

POLITICS AND GOVERNMENT

When the Louisiana constitutional convention of 1811 met at New Orleans, twenty-six of its forty-three members were Creoles. During the first few years of statehood native Creoles were not particularly interested in national politics and the newly arrived Americans were far too busy securing an economic basis to seriously care much about political problems. Many Creoles were still suspicious of the American system and were prejudiced against it.

Until the election of 1834 the paramount issue in state elections was whether the candidate was Creole or Anglo American. Throughout this period many

English-speaking Americans believed that Creoles were opposed to development and progress, while the Creoles considered other Americans radical in their political ideas. Since then Creoles have actively participated in politics, and they have learned English to ease this process. In fact, Creoles of color have dominated New Orleans politics since the 1977 election of Ernest "Dutch" Morial as mayor. He was followed in office by Sidney Bartholemey and then by his son, Marc Morial, whose successor, Ray Nagin, was also of Creole descent. Although the Morials are a historic Creole of color family, they do not publicly identify themselves as such but instead as black or African American. Nagin also does not identify as Creole. It is difficult to say whether political figures in New Orleans from mixed-race Creole backgrounds now identify as African American for political reasons or because racial perceptions have changed

NOTABLE INDIVIDUALS

Chess In 1858 and 1859 Paul Morphy (1837–1884) was the unofficial but universally acknowledged chess champion of the world. Although he is little known outside chess circles, more than eighteen books have been written about Morphy and his chess strategies.

Literature Kate O'Flaherty Chopin (1851–1904) was born in St. Louis; her father was an Irish immigrant and her mother descended from an old French Creole family in Missouri. In 1870 she married Oscar Chopin, a native of Louisiana, and moved there; after her husband's death, she began to write. Chopin's best-known works deal with Creoles; she also wrote short stories for children in *The Youth's Companion*. *Bayou Folk* (1894) and *The Awakening* (1899) are her most popular works. Armand Lanusse (1812–1867) was perhaps the earliest Creole of color to write and publish poetry. Born in New Orleans to French Creole parents, he was a conscripted Confederate soldier during the Civil War. After the war he became the principal of the Catholic School for Indigent Orphans of Color, where he helped produce an anthology of Negro poetry, *Les Cenelles*.

Military Pierre Gustave Toutant Beauregard (1818–1893) is perhaps the best-known Louisiana Creole. He was born in New Orleans, educated in New York (which was unusual for the time), graduated from West Point Military Academy, and served with General Scott in the War with Mexico (1846). Beauregard was twice wounded in that conflict. He served as chief engineer in the draining of the site of New Orleans from 1858 to 1861. He was also a Confederate general in the Civil War and led the siege of Fort Sumter in 1861. After the Civil War Beauregard returned to New Orleans, where he later wrote three books on the Civil War. He was elected superintendent of West Point in 1869.

Music Louis Moreau Gottschalk (1829–1869) was a pianist and composer born in New Orleans. His mother, Aimée Marie de Brusle, was a Creole whose family had come from Saint-Domingue. Gottschalk went to Paris at age thirteen to study music. He became a great success in Europe at an early age and spent most of his time performing in concerts to support members of his family. His best-known compositions are "Last Hope," "Tremolo Etudes," and "Bamboula." Gottschalk is remembered as a true Creole, thinking and composing in French.

Ferdinand Joseph Lementhe "Jelly Roll" Morton (1885–1941), a jazz musician and composer born in New Orleans to Creole parents, was an important figure in the history and development of American jazz. As a child he was greatly influenced by performances at the French Opera House. Morton later played piano in Storyville's brothels; these, too, provided material for his compositions. His most popular works are "New Orleans Blues," "King Porter Stomp," and "Jelly Roll Blues."

In contemporary music, rapper Ice-T (1958–) is the son of a Creole woman. Drummer Sheila E. (1957–), best known for her work with pop artist Prince, also has a Creole mother. Pop singers Beyoncé Knowles (1981–) and Solange Knowles (1986–) are descendants of a Louisiana Creole grandmother.

Politics Former Secretary of State Condoleezza Rice (1954–) is of Creole descent on her father's side.

MEDIA

PRINT

Alexandria News Weekly

Founded in 1975, this general newspaper for the African American community contains frequent articles about Creoles.

Leon Coleman, Publisher
1746 East Mason Street
Alexandria, Louisiana 71301
Phone: (318) 443-7664
Fax: (318) 487-1827
Email: anwnews@bellsouth.net

Bayou Talk

A Cajun Creole newspaper founded in 1987.

Louis H. Metoyer, Publisher
Jo-Val, Inc.
Box 1344
West Covina, California 91793-1344
Email: louis@bayoutalk.com
URL: www.bayoutalk.com

Louisiana Weekly

Multicultural community newspaper published since 1925 that contains frequent articles about Creoles.

Edmund W. Lewis, Editor
2215 Pelopidas Street
New Orleans, Louisiana 70122
Phone: (504) 282-3705
Fax: (504) 282-3773
URL: www.louisianaweekly.com

Times of Acadiana

A weekly newspaper with Acadian/Creole emphasis.

> Kristin Askelson, Managing Editor
> P.O. Box 5310
> Lafayette, Louisiana 70502
> Phone: (337) 289-6300
> Fax: (337) 289-6443
> Email: timesedit@timesofacadiana.com
> URL: www.theadvertiser.com/section/ACADIANA/
> Times-of-Acadiana

RADIO

KANE Radio AM 1240

Louisiana radio station offering regional news
and zydeco music.

> Jeff Boggs, Director
> 800 South Lewis Street
> Suite 204-D
> New Iberia, Louisiana 70560
> Phone: (337) 365-3434
> Fax: (337) 365-3435
> Email: kane@kane1240.com
> URL: www.kane1240.com

ORGANIZATIONS AND ASSOCIATIONS

Creole American Genealogical Society (CAGS)

Formerly Creole Ethnic Association. Founded in 1983,
CAGS is a Creole organization that promotes Creole
American genealogical research. It provides family
trees and makes available to its members books and
archival material. Holds an annual convention.

> P. Fontaine, Executive Director
> P.O. Box 3215
> Church Street Station
> New York, New York 10008

Louisiana Creole Research Association

Founded in 2004, this nonprofit research association
provides assistance to the local Creole community
in researching genealogy and seeks to educate the
public about Creole history and culture.

> Dr. Elizabeth M. Rhodes, President
> P.O. Box 791845
> New Orleans, Louisiana 70179-1845
> Email: info@lacreole.org
> URL: www.lacreole.org

MUSEUMS AND RESEARCH CENTERS

Amistad Research Center

Independent, nonprofit research library, archive, and
museum established by the American Missionary
Association and six of its affiliated colleges. Collects
primary source materials pertaining to the history
and arts of American ethnic groups, including a
substantial collection regarding Creoles.

> Andrea G. Jefferson, President and Chair
> Tulane University

> 6823 St. Charles Avenue
> New Orleans, Louisiana 70118
> Phone: (504) 862-3222
> Fax: (504) 862-8961
> Email: amistad@mailhost.tcs.tulane.edu
> URL: www.amistadresearchcenter.org

Creole Institute at Indiana University

Specializes in linguistic research and educational training
for French-based Creoles from Haiti.

> Albert Valdman, Director
> Indiana University
> Ballantine 604
> Bloomington, Indiana 47405
> Phone: (812) 855-4988
> Fax: (812) 855-2386
> Email: creole@indiana.edu
> URL: www.indiana.edu/˜creole/

Louisiana Creole Heritage Center

An extension of Northwestern State University, this
research center houses histories of Louisiana
Creoles and other sources of research on Creole
history and culture.

> Janet Colson, Executive Director
> NSU Box 5675
> Natchitoches, Louisiana 71497
> Phone: (318) 357-6685
> Email: colsonj@nsula.edu
> URL: http://creole.nsula.edu

SOURCES FOR ADDITIONAL STUDY

Brasseaux, Carl A., Keith P. Fontenot, and Claude F.
Oubre. *Creoles of Color in the Bayou Country.* Jackson:
University Press of Mississippi, 1994.

Brasseaux, Carl A. *French, Cajun, Creole, Houma: A Primer
on Francophone Louisiana.* Baton Rouge: Louisiana
State University Press, 2005.

Bryan, Violet Harrington. *The Myth of New Orleans in
Literature: Dialogues of Race and Gender.* Knoxville:
University of Tennessee Press, 1993.

Dominguez, Virginia R. *White by Definition: Social
Classification in Creole Louisiana.* New Brunswick:
Rutgers University Press, 1986.

Dormon, James H., ed. *Creoles of Color of the Gulf South.*
Knoxville: University of Tennessee Press, 1996.

Gehman, Mary. *The Free People of Color of New Orleans:
An Introduction.* New Orleans: Margaret Media, Inc.,
1994.

Hirsch, Arnold R., and Joseph Logsdon, eds. *Creole New
Orleans: Race and Americanization.* Baton Rouge:
Louisiana State University Press, 1992.

Huber, Leonard V. "Reflections on the Colorful Customs
of Latter-day New Orleans Creoles," *Louisiana History*
21, no. 2 (1980): 223–35.

Jolivétte, Andrew. *Louisiana Creoles: Cultural Recovery and
Mixed-Race Native American Identity.* Lanham, MD:
Lexington Books, 2007.

Kein, Sybil. *Creole: The History and Legacy of Louisiana's
Free People of Color.* Baton Rouge: Louisiana State
University Press, 2000.

CROATIAN AMERICANS

Edward Ifković

OVERVIEW

Croatian Americans are immigrants or descendants of people from Croatia, which is now known as the Independent Republic of Croatia. Located on the Balkan Peninsula in southeastern Europe, Croatia is bordered by Bosnia-Herzegovina to the south, Italy to the west, Slovenia to the north and northwest, Hungary to the north and northeast, and Serbia to the east. The country, which runs along the Adriatic to Montenegro, has a distinctive elongated geography. Throughout much of the twentieth century, Croatia was one of five provinces that made up Yugoslavia, an amalgam of ethnicities and religions held together by dictatorship and economics. Occupying 21,829 square miles (56,538 square kilometers), Croatia is roughly the same size as West Virginia.

According to a 2011 census conducted by the Croatian Bureau of Statistics, Croatia had a population of approximately 4.3 million people. Roman Catholicism is the predominant religion, followed by Eastern Orthodox, Islam, and Protestantism. According to 2011 statistics from the World Bank, the gross national income per person was $13,850, compared to $47,310 per person in the United States. The economy is based on a mixture of industry, agriculture, forestry, fishing, and tourism. Recently the government has made a concerted effort to attract foreign investment, particularly in the area of scientific research. Incentives include customs benefits and changes to the tax structure (2006). The fledgling republic joined the European Union in July 2013.

Croatians began to arrive in the United States in the 1850s and found work as farmers, miners, saloonkeepers, grocers, tugboat operators, and restaurant owners; they settled primarily in the South and the West. From 1880 through 1914, a large number of Croatian peasants immigrated to the United States, but because statistics were so poorly kept, the exact number is not known. This wave of immigrants consisted of primarily illiterate, unskilled male laborers who left Croatia primarily for economic reasons. They came to the United States to make their fortunes and return home. During World War II and the rise of communist regimes in Eastern Europe, the majority of immigrants were political refugees and war orphans.

Croatians already in the United States found it difficult—and in some cases impossible—to leave, and they began to put down roots. Between the 1950s and 1960s, changes in U.S. immigration law facilitated more Croatian immigration. This new wave included many professionals seeking better educations, higher paying jobs, and increased opportunities for their children. They clashed with the Croatian Americans who had arrived four or five generations earlier.

Estimates of the number of Croatian Americans vary. Data from the Croatian Embassy estimated that there were approximately two million people of Croatian descent living in the United States as of 2012, but the U.S. Census Bureau's American Community Survey estimate for 2010 was 411,427. Areas with significant Croatian American populations include Pennsylvania, Illinois, and Ohio. California, New York, and Michigan also support sizable Croatian populations. The Croatian American community is notable for its civic engagement. Over the past 150 years, members of this group have formed hundreds of mutual-aid societies, as well as fraternal, cultural, and political organizations. Most groups are focused on Croatian Americans, but they are increasingly extending their outreach to American society as a whole.

HISTORY OF THE PEOPLE

Early History Croatia's long, turbulent history has been affected by the control exerted by several empires, including the Ottoman, Habsburg, and Venetian empires. During the fifth century BCE, nomadic Slavic tribes from beyond the Carpathian Mountains of Poland and Russia drifted down into the Balkans, pushing out the Romans. New religious ethnic identities evolved among these South Slavic people. The Croatians and Slovenians were strongly influenced by the Roman Catholic Church, and the Serbians, Montenegrins, and Macedonians by the Eastern Orthodox Church. The small independent countries of Slovenia and Croatia did not survive the Middle Ages. After a period of self-rule under King Tomislav and King Peter Kresimir IV, Croatia fell under the governance of Hungary in 1102.

During the fourteenth century, the Ottoman Turks began invading the Balkans. A powerful people, the Ottomans had gradually taken the region of Asia

Minor, now known as Turkey, from the Byzantines, who had controlled a great empire there since before the fall of Rome. By 1350 the Ottomans had begun their invasion of the Balkan Peninsula. After the legendary battle of Kosovo in 1389, Serbia fell under Turkish rule.

With the defeat of the Serbians, the Turks began to make inroads into Croatian territory. The Croatians turned to the Austrians for military support, but with the rise of the Austro-Hungarian Empire, the Croatians endured oppression on multiple fronts. For generations, the Croatians were used as a military buffer between Europe and the Turks. In 1573 Matija Gubec led an inspiring if disastrous rebellion against the Austrian nobles, but Austro-Hungarian control of the Croatians continued until 1918.

During the nineteenth century, Slavic nationalism grew in proportion to the decline of the Austro-Hungarian Empire. World War I erupted as a result of conflict between independent Serbia and the Austro-Hungarian Empire, and with the 1918 defeat of Austria-Hungary and its German allies, European geography was restructured.

U.S. President Woodrow Wilson advocated independence for various nationalities, and South Slavs seized the opportunity for freedom. The "Yugoslav idea" was a concept that began to take shape in the 1830s and 1840s, with proponents arguing for Slavic unification instead of continuing competition against one another as small, individual nations. Originally,

the Yugoslav idea was to unify the Slavic countries by adopting a common language and culture based on Serbian language and culture. After World War I, the architects of the newly created Yugoslavia took a more multicultural approach. The Serbo-Croatian Coalition issued a Declaration of Yugoslav Independence, and the Kingdom of Serbs, Croats, and Slovenes was formed on July 20, 1917, under the rule of Serbian Prince Alexander. Eight years later, Alexander changed the country's name to Yugoslavia.

Modern Era Internal dissension and ethnic rivalries persisted in the new Yugoslavia. Serbians conceived of the country as a Greater Serbia with a centralist government, whereas Federalist Croatians and Slovenians demanded that each republic have a strong voice in the government. When Stejpan Radic, the respected head of the Croat Peasant Party, was assassinated in parliament in 1928, the king dissolved parliament and made himself dictator. The king was himself assassinated by right-wing Croatian sympathizers in Marseilles, France, in 1934, and his cousin, Prince Paul, assumed control of the country.

On March 27, 1941, Yugoslavia (under fascist dictator Ante Pavic) signed a pact allying itself with Germany. When the Yugoslavian people revolted against this government action with the chant, "Better war than pact, better grave than slave," the military assumed control of the country and proclaimed young Peter II king. In retaliation, Adolf Hitler ordered an attack on Belgrade on April 6, 1941. After a bloody battle, the Nazis conquered Yugoslavia and set up a puppet government in Croatia. The fascist Ustashe eliminated thousands of Jews, Serbians, and unsympathetic Croatians. Underground resistance to the Germans included the Partisans, under the command of Croatian Communist Marshal Tito, and the Chetniks, who supported the monarchy in exile and who, some believe, later collaborated with the Germans.

The Partisans viewed the war as an opportunity to create a communist government in postwar Yugoslavia. Tito's forces wrested large sections of the country from German control, ultimately winning the support of Communists and non-Communists, including the Allies. When the war ended, the Socialist Party assumed control of the government and abolished the monarchy.

The 1945 Partisan massacre of thousands of Croatians alarmed the many Croatian Americans who wanted to support the new Titoist government. Despite such tactics, Tito used his personality and power to help placate ethnic and religious rivalries within Yugoslavia. Refusing to allow Yugoslavia to become a puppet of the Soviet Union, Tito asserted Yugoslav independence from Russian control in 1948, thus establishing Yugoslavia as one of the most liberal and progressive socialist countries of Eastern Europe. Upon Tito's death in 1980, Yugoslavia was ruled by a

A Croatian boy holds a scissors-like oyster rake, while standing on a bed of oyster shells in Olga, Louisiana, 1938. PHOTOGRAPH BY RUSSELL LEE. CORBIS. REPRODUCED BY PERMISSION.

collective state presidency and party presidium, which immediately suffered severe economic difficulties and saw the resurgence of nascent rivalries.

The breakdown of communism in Eastern Europe, most dramatically illustrated by the 1989 dismantling of the Berlin Wall, toppled a number of communist governments and affected still others, including Yugoslavia—where old rivalries and long-buried aspirations for independence resurfaced. Following the lead of Slovenia, Croatia challenged growing Serbian hegemony. In Yugoslavia's first postwar free elections, held in 1990, the Croatian Democratic Union (HDZ) ran on an anticommunist platform and won 205 of 356 seats in parliament.

Despite Croatia's first real independence in 1,000 years, many feared a rise in nationalistic fascism under the leadership of Franjo Tudjman, who viewed Greater Croatia as a means of countering Greater Serbia. Government corruption and censorship added to these fears and to overall dissatisfaction. On June 25, 1991, Croatia and Slovenia issued declarations of independence.

Although Croatia was recognized by the international community, including the European Community, its secession from Yugoslavia was not smooth. Yugoslav federal forces attacked Croatia, with long sieges of Dubrovnik, Vukovar, and other Croatian cities. The 1991 and 1992 seven-month war against the combined forces of the Yugoslav army and Serbian paramilitaries left thousands dead and many villages destroyed. The Serbians instituted policies of "ethnic cleansing" in Croatian villages and throughout Bosnia. With control of one-third of Croatian territory, the Serbians attacked ethnic Croatians in Bosnia and Croatia proper.

Intermittent "cease-fire" agreements in 1993 and 1994 did not stop hostilities, especially in the regions of Kraina and West Slavonia. In 1995, after Croatia recaptured these territories and relocated 300,000 Serbs to Serbia, the presidents of both countries signed the Dayton (Ohio) peace accord under the auspices of the United Nations.

SETTLEMENT IN THE UNITED STATES

By the time of the American Civil War, colonies of Croatians from a region of Croatia called Dalmatia had been established in Mississippi and Alabama. U.S. Census records of the 1850s and 1860s reveal hundreds of Dalmatian saloonkeepers, grocers, tugboat operators, and restaurant owners. By 1880 an estimated 20,000 Croatians lived in the United States, primarily in the South and the West. Not surprisingly, many fought on the side of the Confederacy during the Civil War, forming the Austrian Guards and two Slavonian rifle units.

Throughout the nineteenth century, Dalmatian sailors jumped ship at major American ports, especially at favored locations such as New Orleans. The former seamen found the oyster business a natural transition. Some, such as Luka Jurisich, who arrived in Bayou Creek,

Louisiana, from Duba, in 1855, are credited with building the trade in the region. Dalmatians also became early developers of oyster fisheries in Biloxi, Mississippi. Today, the huge fishing industry in these regions is heavily populated by descendants of the early Dalmatian settlers.

Many Dalmatians moved from New Orleans to ports in the West, establishing large colonies such as the one that grew in and around San Francisco. Some arrived as early as 1835, predating settlers from the eastern states. Although gold enticed many Croatians to move west, those who settled in California were captivated by the climate, which they likened to that of their sunny Adriatic homeland. Most made their living not from gold but by operating businesses. According to one study, more than fifty Dalmatian businesses occupied a single San Francisco street in the 1850s and 1860s.

In 1857 the Slavonic Illyrian Mutual and Benevolent Society was formed in San Francisco as the first Slavic charitable society of its kind in the United States. The society purchased land in 1861 for the first Croatian-Serbian cemetery in the United States. Vincent Gelcich, president of the Society in 1860, was a physician who served as a surgeon and colonel in the Union Army during the Civil War.

Perhaps the most important Dalmatian contribution to the United States was made in agriculture. Mateo Arnerich, a sailor from Brac, arrived in San Francisco in 1849, the year after gold was discovered at Sutter's Mill. One of the first Dalmatians to settle in the Santa Clara Valley, Arnerich bought land and established the vineyards that made his wealth. His two sons became lawyers, and one, a member of the state legislature, was the first Croatian to hold public office in the United States. In the 1870s Mark Rabasa introduced the apple industry to northern California. Another Dalmatian, Steve Mitrovich, imported the Dalmatian fig to Fresno and displayed the "Adriatic fig" at the Columbian Exposition in Chicago in 1893, winning first prize.

Due to Dalmatian success with growing and developing a superior quality of grapes, figs, plums, apples, and apricots in Pajaro Valley, the region was called New Dalmatia. Although the novelist Jack London feared "alien" control, he described the flourishing 12,000-acre apple paradise of the Dalmatians in his 1913 novel *Valley of the Moon*:

> Do you know what they call Pajaro Valley? New Dalmatia. We're being squeezed out. We Yankees thought we were smart. Well, the Dalmatians came along and showed they were smarter. …First, they worked at day labor in the fruit harvest. Next, they began, in a small way, buying the apples on the trees. The more money they made, the bigger became their deals. Pretty soon they were renting the orchards on long leases; and now they own the whole valley, and the last American will be gone.

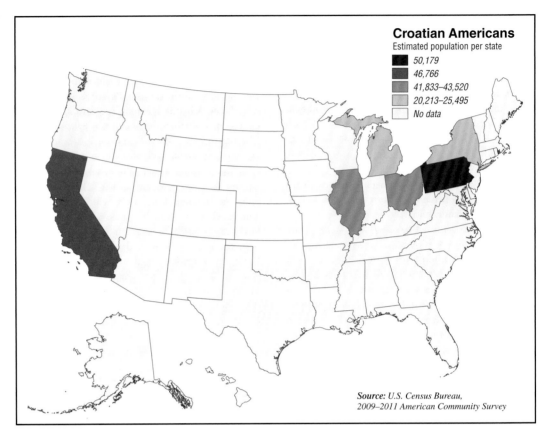

Croatian Americans
Estimated population per state

■ 50,179
■ 46,766
■ 41,833–43,520
■ 20,213–25,495
□ No data

*Source: U.S. Census Bureau,
2009–2011 American Community Survey*

The discovery of silver in the Nevada Territory in the late 1850s inspired the influx of Croatian settlers into towns such as Virginia City, Carson City, Austin, and Reno. These Slavs were commonly referred to as "Sclavonians" or "Slavonians." The successful Slavonian Gold and Silver Mining Company at Resse River, Nevada, was organized in 1863, but most settlers made their living in businesses that served miners. The largest food-provision house in Nevada in the 1860s was owned by Dalmatians, and Marco Medin, one of the first men to arrive in Nevada during the silver fever, grew rich in the fruit and saloon businesses.

The lives of Antonio Mazzanovich, Antonio Milatovich, and Captain John Dominus illustrate a more colorful side of Croatian history. Mazzanovich enlisted as a bugler in the U.S. 6th Cavalry when he was eleven years old and helped pursue the famous Apache Geronimo through the Southwest, which he recalled in his memoirs, *Trailing Geronimo* (1931). Milatovich sued the Republic of Mexico when a revolutionary change of government deprived him of more than one million acres of Mexican land he had acquired. He lost his fortune when the new government refused his claim on the basis of his Austrian citizenship. The Croatian captain John Dominus sailed to the United States in his own ship and subsequently settled in Hawaii, where he built a lavish mansion that

was later used as the official residence of the governor. Captain Dominus disappeared at sea while attempting to reach China. His son, John Owen Dominus, married the Hawaiian princess Lydia Kamekaha Kapaaka in 1862. She became Queen Liliuokalani, the last reigning queen of Hawaii, and Dominus served as her prince consort until his death in 1891.

From 1880 through 1914, Croatians and other eastern European peasants immigrated to the United States in large numbers. Fleeing from poverty brought on by changes in land inheritance laws, blight, and deteriorating farming-soil quality and spurred by growing population pressures, a young generation looked to the United States *trbuhom za kruhum* ("with belly after bread"). Because statistics were so poorly kept in general, and Slavs were so often lumped together or confused with other groups, it is not known how many Croatians entered the United States during this immigration wave, known as the Great Migration. In the 1930s Croatian historian Ivan Mladineo estimated that approximately one-half million Croatians were living in the United States at that time. During the Great Migration, most Croatians settled in already established immigrant communities in the industrial cities of Illinois, Indiana, Michigan, Ohio, and Pennsylvania. Many worked in coal mines and in the iron and steel mills.

The first wave of immigrants consisted of primarily illiterate, unskilled male laborers who came to the United States to make their fortunes and then return home. Many made frequent trips between the United States and eastern Europe and thus became known as "birds of passage." These men sent money to their villages, markedly improving the economic conditions of the Croatians who remained at home. In 1938 the *South Slav Herald* reported that two-thirds of the new homes built in Croatia during the previous thirty years had been built with American money.

According to the 1907 Immigration Commission survey, about 66 percent of Croatians who came to the United States ultimately returned home. The thousands who returned to Croatia took new ideas with them, including ideas about democracy. In 1906 Croatian writer Antun Matos wrote, "America is presently the most important factor in the creation of Croatian democracy."

Following World War II an unknown number of Croatians who feared reprisal for activities during the war sought refuge in the United States. Meanwhile, the rise to power of communist regimes in Yugoslavia and Eastern Europe meant that those who had immigrated to the United States with the hope of one day returning home could no longer do so. Of the 400,000 displaced people initially admitted into the United States, 18,000 were "Yugoslavs."

U.S. legislation such as the Refugee Relief Act of 1953 and the Refugee Escape Act of 1960, together with the demise of the quota system in 1965, facilitated more Croatian immigration. This new wave included many educated professionals. In "A Clash of Two Immigrant Generations," Bogdan Raditsa discusses the sharp contrast between the earlier, unskilled Croatian immigrants and their later counterparts, revealing the "bitterness that divides the Croatians who came here as displaced persons after 1945 from the Croatian American families established in this country for four or five decades."

The most recent large wave of migration occurred in response to the Yugoslav wars in the early 1990s, when political refugees left Croatia to escape the violence and joined migrant communities in other parts of the world, including the United States. According to the U.S. Census Bureau's American Community Survey, there were an estimated 411,427 Croatian Americans living in the United States in 2010.

Today, Pennsylvania has the largest Croatian American population of any state: approximately 50,000, according to the American Community Survey estimates for 2010. After Pennsylvania, the states with the largest numbers of Croatian Americans are California, Illinois, Ohio, New York, and Michigan. Croatians settlers in California found employment in fishing, farming, and mining. In San Francisco, Croatian Americans introduced new methods of drying fruits, packaging, and shipping.

LANGUAGE

The Croatian language spoken by early immigrants was largely dialect, identifiable by the region from which the immigrant came. The three primary dialects of Croatian are *cakavski*, from Dalmatia; *kajkavski*, from the far northwest near Zagreb; and two varieties of *stokavski*, the literary Croatian dialect. These dialects are often so different from each other that Croatians in the United States sometimes have difficulty understanding each other.

Writers such as Louis Adamic and Clement Mihanovich have pointed out the manner in which Croatians have added familiar endings to English words. Some linguists distinguish this as a "new" dialect. For example, the Croatian word for automobile is *kola*, and the Americanized Croatian word is *kara* (car); *novine* (paper) has become *papir*; *soba* (room) is now *rum*. This bastardization of the language has alarmed many purists. Consequently, Croatian American organizations such as clubs and churches offer weekend classes in Croatian language and culture for both children and adults.

Croatian and Serbian are, for the most part, the same language. Serbian, however, uses a Cyrillic alphabet, whereas Croatian uses a Latin alphabet. Until the breakup of Yugoslavia, the official language was Serbo-Croatian (*Srpskohrvatski*) or Croato-Serbian (*Hrvaskosrpski*). In the United States, many Croatians refuse to use the term "Serbo-Croatian," an issue that became less significant when Croatia gained independence. Several American colleges and universities teach Serbo-Croatian, including Stanford University, Yale University, and Northwestern University. According to the 1990 U.S. Census, about 9 percent of all Croatian Americans (about 45,000) declared Croatian as their mother tongue; presumably the remainder considered English as their main language. According to the American Community Survey for 2006–2010, about 16.2 percent of Croatian Americans (more than 60,000) spoke a language other than English at home.

Greetings and Popular Expressions Common Croatian expressions include the following (with pronunciation): *Dobro jutro* (dobro yootro)—Good morning; *Dobar dan* (dobahr dahn)—Good afternoon; *Dobro vecer* (dobro vehcheh)—Good evening; *Laku noc* (lahkoo noch)—Good night; *Zbogom* (zbogom)—Good-bye; *Kako stje* (kahko steh)—How are you?; *Hvala* (fahlah)—thank you; *sretan bozic* (srehtan bozich)—Merry Christmas.

RELIGION

A majority of Croatian Americans are Roman Catholics. The first U.S. Croatian parish was founded in 1895 in Allegheny City, Pennsylvania. Despite California's large Croatian population in the nineteenth century, a Croatian parish was not organized there until 1903. As late as 1912, there were still only twelve Croatian parishes and four parochial schools in the United States. The number doubled over the decade that followed, however many parochial school have closed since the 1970s as a result of the rise of a Croatian American middle class that left Croatian neighborhoods in cities to move to the suburbs. As of 2012, there are approximately thirty-five Croatian parishes in the United States. Today's Croatians are heavily disaffected with religion and with the clergy in particular.

Most of the small number of Protestant Croatians came from Slovakia and Slovenia. Croatian Muslims who emigrated to the United States mainly from Bosnia arrived after World War II and settled in Cleveland and Chicago.

CULTURE AND ASSIMILATION

Although events since the breakup of Yugoslavia in the early 1990s have made Croatia more visible internationally, Croatians are still mislabeled and subsumed into larger classifications such as Austrian-Hungarian or Yugoslavian. Croatians have also been the object of discrimination. During the period of the Great Migration, Croatians and other Slavs were often lumped together and assessed as an uninspired, stolid, sluggish people who were only useful as drudges and unskilled grunts.

The unskilled, often illiterate, early immigrants gave little thought to assimilation. They clustered together, often in cooperative boardinghouses called *društvo*, and worked at unskilled labor twelve to sixteen hours a day. In the process, they resisted acculturation. One Slavic commentator wrote, "My people do not live in America; they live underneath America. America goes on over their heads."

During and after World War I, when many Croatians who had planned to return to Europe could not, the number who became American citizens increased sharply. Organizations such as the Slovenian-Illyrian Mutual Charity Society (1857) in San Francisco and the Croatian Fraternal Union (1894) in Pittsburg were formed for the purpose of promoting Croatian culture, establishing lodges and clubs where Croatian Americans could socialize, and providing member benefits that ranged from insurance coverage to political organizing. These groups often encouraged members to apply for U.S. citizenship and assisted in the process. By 1919 a study showed that 60 to 65 percent of the immigrants had taken out naturalization papers. The Jugoslav Central organization—formed in Detroit in 1932 to promote unity among Slovenians, Serbians, and Croatians—had as one of its chief goals the encouragement of U.S. citizenship.

Traditions and Customs The rural concept of the godmother and godfather (*kum* and *kuma*) survived for some time in the United States. The parents of a newborn child selected family members, or friends considered part of the extended family (*zadruga*), to care for the child in the event that something happened to the parent and to take charge of the child's spiritual well-being, a responsibility that was taken seriously.

Cuisine Charcuterie, or cured meats, is one of the few categories of food traditional to all the regions. For the most part, traditional cuisine from Croatia differs depending upon whether it is from coastal or inland areas. The cuisine also differs among the nine major regions in Croatia. Croatian cuisine is sometimes referred to as a "cuisine of the region" because it has incorporated elements from the former Yugoslav regions as well as parts of neighboring European countries. Inland cuisine has influences from Hungary, Austria, and Turkey. Lard is the cooking fat of choice, and heavily used spices include black pepper, paprika, and garlic. A typical meal could include roasted lamb, stew, or goulash. Coastal cuisine has influences from Greece, Italy, and France. Olive oil is used instead of lard and heavily used spices include rosemary, sage, bay leaf, oregano, cinnamon, clove, and nutmeg, as well as lemon rind and orange rind. Coastal meals often include seafood and pasta.

Croatians are known to be coffee drinkers, a habit attributed to the influences of the Austro-Hungarian Empire and the country's proximity to the former Ottoman Empire. According to one source, 40 percent of the coffee houses on the San Francisco waterfront in 1875 were owned by Croatians. There are Viennese-style coffee houses throughout Croatia. In 2009 a Croatian coffee expert claimed that Croatians consume 22.5 tons of coffee per year and spend 2.25 million hours consuming it.

Today, Croatian restaurants can be found in major American cities such as Los Angeles, San Francisco, and Miami, and some of the Croatian American clubs offer cooking classes in addition to language classes for their members.

Traditional Dress Traditional Croatian dress (*narodna nosnja*) is distinguishable by its fine embroidery. Women wear a long linen shirt, often white, called a *kosulja*. The *kosulja* is covered by an overskirt called a *kotula*, a colored apron called an *anogrnjac* or *pregjaca*, and a shawl or a jacket worn over the shoulders called a *djaketa, paletun,* or *koret*. Women usually cover their heads with a kerchief. Croatian men wear wide slacks called *gace sirkoka* and white shirts topped with a colored vest or jacket called a *fermen* or *jacerma*. Their pants are often dark linen or wool, worn with high leather boots or kneesocks. Outer garments for men and women are embroidered in red or gold with geometric designs or images such as birds or flowers. Today, such costumes are only worn for ethnic festivals, religious holidays, weddings, or during traditional dance or musical performances.

Dances and Songs The popular *kolo* or circle dance is performed to the accompaniment of the tamburitza, a traditional stringed instrument that is similar to a mandolin. The tamburitza is a modern version of the one-stringed *gusle* used for centuries by the village poets. A tamburitza band performed at the White House during Theodore Roosevelt's presidency and in concert at Carnegie Hall in 1900. Today, Duquesne University supports tamburitza orchestras and festivals, and runs the Tamburitza School of Music—the only one of its kind in the United States.

Singing societies, which have also been popular, are patterned after an early group called Zora, which means "dawn." This group was founded in Chicago in 1903 to keep old folk songs and past experiences alive. Today, there are dozens of singing societies and tamburitza groups in the United States that gather at annual festivals in different parts of the country. Groups include the Novi Stari Tamburasi in California, the Gypsy Strings in Pennsylvania, and the Bajich Brothers from Kansas.

Holidays For Croatians food, tradition, and folk culture are interconnected, especially when it comes to holiday celebrations. In many Croatian households, the Christmas celebration begins on Christmas Eve with a meal of cod fish. On Christmas Day, *sarma* (cabbage and sauerkraut) and *orehnjaca* (nut cake) are traditional favorites.

St. Nicholas Day, Easter, and Independence Day are also important holidays to Croatians. On the eve of St. Nicholas Day, which is celebrated on December 6, children leave their boots on a windowsill so that St. Nicholas can fill them with small presents, including fruit and candy. Lamb and ham are central to Easter, a celebration of eating following a meatless Lent. *Pogaca* is an Easter bread that is braided and decorated with painted eggs. Independence from the former Yugoslav Federation, gained in 1991, is celebrated on June 25.

In Croatia, name days paid homage to the saint for whom you were named. As immigrants and later generations gradually adopted the American custom of celebrating birthdays, this traditional celebration disappeared.

Health Care Issues and Practices In the early days of settlement, Croatians relied on home health care. The local midwife, a Croatian woman, most often handled childbirth in the home. Because there were no labor compensation laws then, men injured on the job had no benefits for hospitalization. Folk remedies, the use of practiced "bonesetters," and treatments based on superstition (dropping hot coals in water to dispel headaches caused by the evil eye, for example) were often used in place of English-speaking doctors, and there was little involvement with the American medical establishment. However, those in cities who were involved with settlement houses—such as Hull House in Chicago—became conversant with doctors, health care, and such matters as ventilation and cleanliness.

FISH SOUP

Ingredients

1 2-pound whole fish, gutted and cleaned, with head intact.

¼ cup olive oil

½ pound carrots

1 celery root

2 parsley roots

1 small onion

2 cloves garlic

2 bay leaves

1 tablespoon peppercorns

salt

Preparation

Rinse the fish well and cut into portion-sized pieces. Retain the head.

In a soup pot, heat 2 tablespoons of oil and fry the onions until softened. Add the fish (with head), vegetables, garlic, bay leaves, and peppercorns. Cover with water and bring to a gentle boil. Reduce the heat and add the remaining olive oil. Simmer for a half hour.

After a half hour of cooking, remove fish pieces and vegetables. Strain broth with fine mesh sieve. Return the broth to the pot and season with salt and pepper. Place pieces of fish and vegetables in individual bowls and pour broth over.

Recipe courtesy of Missy Prusinski

Croatians were hesitant to accept welfare. In New York before World War I, one charity group reported that it had never had one application from a Croatian. There have been no studies done of mental health conditions among Croatian immigrants, and little research exists on their health care practices. Successive generations have adopted American ways for dealing with the medical community.

FAMILY AND COMMUNITY LIFE

Extended family has played an important role in Croatian culture. Multiple generations lived together, either sharing a house or living in very close proximity. Traditionally, after the wedding a young couple would move in with the groom's parents. The grandparents would help with childcare. Family provided a social network as well as a safety net. Even though living as a nuclear family has become more common in Croatia in the past few decades, people still tend to assume the care of elderly parents who can no longer care for themselves rather than sending them to nursing homes or other facilities. Religion (Roman Catholicism in most cases) also played an important role in family life. Parents raised their children with strict discipline and taught them to respect their elders.

Gender Roles Because the majority of early immigrants were single men, the saloon became their most important social institution. More than a place to drink, the Croatian saloon provided a place for men to exchange news about the Old Country, translate letters, and do banking.

As more and more men decided to settle in the United States, they sent for their wives and marriageable women. The traditional patriarchal Croatian family structure, which emphasized control and rigid discipline, remained a part of the early immigrant lifestyle. Coming from a preindustrial Roman Catholic peasant culture, the women were occupied with housekeeping and child rearing.

Men went into the workplace and, thus, the larger American society, and children went to American schools where they learned the language and mores, but women remained isolated in the home. Divorce was uncommon but did occur. In such cases, though both partners were ostracized by the larger community, the woman was treated more harshly.

Communal Croatian life and the tradition of taking in as many boarders as possible to earn money had socialized women to serve large numbers of people. Over time, women's subservient position in the United States changed, largely because they ran most of the boardinghouses and achieved some measure of economic security from doing so. As Croatian American women became more "Americanized," some men argued that once "a Croatian woman becomes Americanized and accepts the liberalization policy of American women … permissiveness with the children develops." Some Croatian women countered that because they bore fewer children and were free of the patriarchal restraints and demands of the Old Country, successive generations of mothers maintained better relationships with their children.

Education As the educational and economic lives of second- and third-generation Croatians improved, most left the Little Croatia ghettoes and the parochial schools where Croatian nuns taught in Croatian, and these communities began to die.

In response to the Yugoslav wars, Croatian Americans established an aid organization in California in 1989, the Croatian Scholarship Fund. The fund is a nonprofit organization devoted to developing leaders for Croatia by providing financial assistance to students of Croatian origin living in either Croatia or Bosnia-Herzegovina to attend university in Croatia. The Croatian American Association registered with the U.S. Congress to lobby on Croatian issues and rallied to support Croatia during the war in 1991. The group consists of American citizens and is a member-supported nongovernmental organization with regional chapters.

According to the American Community Survey estimates for 2006–2010, more than 50 percent of Croatian Americans over the age of twenty-five have at least some college education.

Relations with Other Americans Croatian interaction with Serbians and Slovenians grew out of a similarity of language and the fact that they often settled near one another. Croatians also interacted with other Slavic peoples who emigrated from Austria-Hungary, as well as with Germans, Italians, and Hungarians, with whom they shared the common bond of Roman Catholicism. Although immigrant men attend Catholic Mass with their Irish foremen, they had little social contact.

Alliances with Serbians were temporary and topical as old enmity persisted. There is a saying that "there is no putting history behind one's self in the Balkans; the battles one's ancestors fought are today's battles as well." Fights and flare-ups still erupt today.

Philanthropy Immigrants organized benevolent fraternal associations for protection in the event of on-the-job injury or unemployment. These included the Slavonian-Illyrian Mutual Charity Society, organized by Croatians and Serbians in San Francisco in 1857; the United Slavonian Benevolent Association, founded in New Orleans in 1874; and the Austrian Benevolent Society (later the First Croatian Benefit Society), established in New York in 1880, among others. Over the past 130 years, Croatian Americans have created hundreds of societies and fraternal, cultural, and political organizations. The groups have picnics and holiday parties, and celebrate saint days, dances, and banquets to promote unity among Croatian Americans.

An organization noted for its influence on Croatian American life is the Croatian Fraternal Union (CFU), established in Pittsburgh in 1894. The group's membership has grown from 300 to approximately 60,000 members worldwide, and its assets have grown from $43 to more than $400 million. The CFU has served the Croatian American community in a variety of ways, creating sports programs in the 1920s, organizing unions in the 1930s, providing scholarships starting in the 1950s, and sending humanitarian aid in the form of medicine and equipment to Croatia during its struggle for independence in the 1990s. In addition, the CFU sponsors tamburitza ensembles and festivals, dance groups, and cultural activities for its members. It also publishes a monthly magazine.

Croatian Americans have been quick to respond to crises in the immigrant community. They established an orphanage for the children of fellow immigrants who died during the flu epidemic of 1918–1919. After World War II, Croatian Americans operated an orphanage for Croatian children who lost parents in the war. During the 1991 Croatian war for independence, Croatian Americans rallied support for the motherland in the form of relief funds, supplies, and lobbying. In an effort to assist with rebuilding Croatia, groups in the United States offer college scholarships in Croatia to educate a new generation of leaders. Although the primary aim of these groups is to promote the well-being of Croatians and Croatian Americans, they increasingly extend their outreach to the American community as a whole, contributing to the American Cancer Society and other nonethnic philanthropic organizations.

EMPLOYMENT AND ECONOMIC CONDITIONS

Many companies paid immigrants' passage to the United States in return for a guaranteed period of servitude. Although this practice was outlawed in 1885, industrialists found ways around the law, and Croatians were sent to coke foundries, iron mines, lumber camps, and factories across the United States.

The traditional patriarchal Croatian family structure, which emphasized control and rigid discipline, remained a part of the early immigrant lifestyle and contributed to the Slavs' reputation as dependable and hardworking. Aside from arrests for drunkenness, there was little crime among the Croatians in the United States. A 1910 study revealed that Croatians in Pennsylvania were the lowest paid of the immigrant groups, and their unemployment rates the highest, with only 34 percent working as full-time, full-year employees. When Croatians arrived in industrialized American cities, manufacturers often coerced them into replacing striking workers. Uneducated and often unaware of the dynamics of American labor-management politics, the immigrants were happy to have jobs. Manufacturers were adept at pitting one ethnic group against another. Railroad magnate Jay Gould once declared: "I can hire one half of the working class to kill the other half."

By 1900 when labor unions were gaining power, Croatians and other Slavs played a role in establishing the viability of the United Mine Workers of America, which helped break the cycle of using immigrants as scabs and strikebreakers. In 1909 Anton Pavisic was a leader in a coal miners' strike at McKees Rocks, Pennsylvania, where more than 2,000 fellow Croatians followed him. The first miners' compensation law introduced into the Michigan legislature was the work of Anthony Lucas, a Croatian.

POLITICS AND GOVERNMENT

Politically, Croatian Americans have been torn between concern for Croatia and involvement in American democracy. Early immigrants were more preoccupied with the former, and this concern persisted for many generations. Croatian organizations formed in the United States campaigned for political goals abroad. These organizations ranged from conservative to radical.

During the years of the Great Migration, groups such as the National Croatian Society (NCS) and the Croatian League combated the tyrannical Austria-Hungary rule. In 1912 the Reverend Nikola Grskovíc founded the Croatian Alliance, calling for complete Croatian independence from the Habsburgs and advocating an alliance with the other South Slavs.

Influential South Slavic Americans, such as Serbian American Michael Pupin, worked on committees dedicated to the formation of the new nation of Yugoslavia after World War I. Michael Pupin and other high-profile South Slavs were joined by Reverend Grskovíc, Joseph Marohnić, and other leaders to create the South Slavic National Council of Chicago, with its main goal being the formation of Yugoslavia. When the Kingdom of Serbs, Croats, and Slovenes was realized in 1918, Croatian Americans were dissatisfied with the pan-Serbian centralist Yugoslav government and appealed in vain to the League of Nations for more encompassing ethnic representation.

During World War II, the Yugoslav Relief Committee was created to aid those living under a Nazi-installed puppet government in Croatia. After the war, American South Slavs—often under the guidance of high-profile leaders such as Slovenian American Louis Adamic—compelled the American government to lend its support to the partisan cause in Yugoslavia. Increasingly, Americans were supporting Tito and his partisan forces. At a 1943 meeting, the Congress of American Croatians advocated support of Tito, a momentous decision called for by the more than 700 affiliates of the Congress.

With the installation of communism in Yugoslavia by Tito after 1945, and rumors of mass killings of Croatians by Tito's command, many Croatians withdrew their support. The émigrés who came to the United States at that time included many radicals expelled from Yugoslavia.

Although interest in the homeland and its politics continues, the intensity of this interest has gradually diminished. Represented prominently in the Democratic Party, Croatian Americans have won local legislative seats, governorships, and positions in Congress. Active as voters and local campaigners, Croatians have become an integral part of American life. Croatian American Mark Begich, a Democrat, has served as the mayor of Anchorage and was elected in 2008 as the junior U.S. senator from Alaska. He is the son of former U.S. Congressman Nick Begich. Another Croatian American, John Kasish, was the governor for Ohio, and Dennis Kucinich began his

to raise funds for war relief, health care, and for political-action groups. The number of casualties alarmed many Croatian Americans, as did the wanton destruction of venerable old landmarks in Dubrovnik and elsewhere. Some organizations, such as the Croatian New Yorker Club, a group of business and professional people, organized a traveling exhibit of artwork done by Croatian and Bosnian children in refugee camps in Croatia to heighten awareness of the war there and to raise money to aid displaced children, many orphaned by the war.

NOTABLE INDIVIDUALS

Despite their small, low-profile population, Croatian Americans have made distinguished contributions to American literature, music, science, and business.

Academia Henry (Zucalo) Suzzallo (1873–1933) was born in San Jose, California, and earned degrees from Stanford University, Columbia, and the University of California. During World War I, he advised President Woodrow Wilson and was appointed to the War Labor Policy Board in 1918. Suzzallo assumed the presidency of the University of Washington in 1915, a position he held until 1926. During his tenure at Washington, Suzzallo helped increase enrollment, raise academic standards, and create new programs. In 1927 he became chair of the Carnegie Foundation for the Advancement of Teaching and served as president of the foundation until his death. His books (such as *Our Faith in Education*, 1924) are examples of the commitment he always felt to the children of the United States.

Other notable Croatian Americans include: historian Francis Preveden (1890–1959), who did comprehensive studies of Croatians; Ivo Banac (1947–), a professor of comparative literature at Yale University; and Clement S. Mihanovich (1913–1998), a St. Louis University sociologist. George Prpić (1920–2009) wrote extensively on Croatian culture in both the United States and Croatia.

Film, Television, and Theater Actor Peter Coe (Knego) (1919–2008) left a football career with the Detroit Lions to play "tough-guy" roles in numerous motion pictures. Silent screen star Laura La Plante (1934–1985) reached her peak during the 1920s. Walter Kray was one of the stars of the television series The Roaring Twenties. Slavko Vorkapic (1884–1976) acted throughout the 1920s and later became a director who worked with film montage and special effects. John Miljan (1892–1960) was in more than four hundred movies, playing lead opposite such actresses as Joan Crawford and Virginia Bruce. Gene Rayburn (1917–1999) was a television emcee. Michael Lah (1912–1995) worked for Walt Disney Studios and Metro-Goldwyn-Mayer, and she brought a new sensitivity and artistry to the animated cartoon. John Malkovich (1953–) is an Academy Award-nominated movie actor and director, known for his

Second-generation Croatian American Andrija Tokic works in his Nashville music studio, The Bomb Shelter. © ANDRIJA TOKIC.

political career as the mayor of Cleveland, served as a Democratic congressman from Ohio, and in 2004 was a Democratic candidate for U.S. president. Croatian American Mary Matalin was an assistant to President George W. Bush and subsequently worked as a political commentator.

Relations with Independent Croatia The majority of Croatian Americans have supported the newly independent Republic of Croatia. In fact, as the old Yugoslav federation began to crumble, Croatian Americans mounted letter-writing campaigns and fund-raising events to support the creation of a new government. In particular, when Germany recognized the new republic in 1990, many Croatian Americans wrote to the American government to do likewise. Since independence, there has been the on going war with old-guard Serbian nationalists, both in Croatia proper and from without. Croatian Americans have worked

roles in such films as *Dangerous Liaisons* (1988) and *Being John Malkovich* (1999).

Industry and Agriculture Marcus Nalley (Marko Narancic) (1890–1962) was a food-processing manufacturer. Nick Bez (Nikola Bezmalinović) (1895–1969) emigrated from the island of Brac in 1910 and eventually owned a fleet of salmon vessels, ultimately controlling much of the industry in Alaska. Paul Marinis (1893–1974), entrepreneur, was called "The King of Salmon" in the 1950s. John Slavich was owner of Del Monte Fruit Company. Nikola Sulentić was the inventor of the first valve-spring lifter.

In 1901 Anthony Lucas (Lučić) (1855–1921) became the first man to discover oil in Texas. In 1936 the American Institute of Mining and Metallurgical Engineering established the Anthony F. Lucas Medal, an award for "distinguished achievement and practice in finding and producing petroleum."

Journalism Vlaho S. Vlahović (1895–1969), a Dalmatian, edited the *Slavonic Monthly*. Bogdan Raditsa (1904–1993) worked as a columnist and journalist for many years.

Bill Kurtis (William Horton Kuretich) (1940–), born in Pensacola, Florida, is a television journalist and news anchor. He began with WIBW-TV (1966) in Topeka before moving to Chicago, where he worked for the CBS station WBBW-TV (1966–1982 and 1985–1996). From 1982 to 1985 he was a co-host of the *CBS Morning News*. In 1990 he founded his own production company and he worked on a variety of television documentaries and journalism series into the twenty-first century.

Literature Works such as Ivan Mladineo's *Zetva* (*Harvest*, 1932) remain inaccessible to the English-reading audience. The almanac (*kalendar*), filled with popular poetry and written in the ever-present decameter, was the wellspring for the start of a Croatian American literature. Zdravko Muzina, an influential journalist, started a Croatian-language newspaper in Pittsburgh, called *Hrvastko-Amerikanska Danica za Godinu*, in 1893. Josip Marohnić (1866–1921), "the founder of popular Croatian literature in America," published the first book of Croatian poetry in the United States, *Amerikanke*.

In 1937 Gabro Karabin published the autobiographical "Honorable Escape" in *Scribner's*. The tale of his psychological journey from the steel mills that were his home, the story promised a literary career that never materialized. Victor Vecki wrote *Threatening Shadows* (1931), the story of a Croatian American doctor in California. Antun Nizeteo's *Bez Povratka* (*Without Return*, 1957) and Nada Kestercanek-Vujica's *Short Stories*, 1959, were written in Croatian. The poet Boris Maruna, who lived in the United States, also wrote in Croatian. Joseph Hitrec, a Croatian whose works do not deal with Croatian experience, came to the United

States after years of travel, mostly in India. In 1946 he published *Ruler's Morning and Other Stories*, tales set in India. Other works by Hitrec include *Son of the Moon* (1948) and *Angel of Gaiety* (1951). George Vukelich (1927–1995) was a newspaper columnist, magazine writer, and an author of short stories and the novel *Fisherman's Beach* (1962). Edward Ifković wrote *Anna Marinkovich* (1980), the story of a Croatian immigrant family living on a farm in Connecticut during the Great Depression.

Music Milka Ternina (1863–1920), an operatic soprano, sang for nine seasons with the Metropolitan Opera Company in New York. She premiered in the United States in the opera *Tosca* with Enrico Caruso. Hailed by Italian conductor Arturo Toscanini as the "world's greatest artist," Ternina returned to Zagreb in 1906, where she discovered the young Zinka Milanov (1906–1989). Ternina coached Milanov for three years. Milanov made her Met debut in *Il Trovatore* in 1937 and for three decades remained as the Metropolitan's in-house coloratura. Violinist Louis Svecenski (1862–1926) studied in Zagreb and Vienna and in 1885 accepted a bid to become first violinist for the Boston Symphony Orchestra. He performed in the United States for thirty-three years. Guy Mitchell (1927–1999) was a popular recording artist in the 1950s and had his own television series in 1957. His recordings include "The Roving Kind," "Singing the Blues," and "My Heart Cries for You." Tony Butala (1938–) was one of the Lettermen, whose most famous recording was "Can't Take My Eyes Off of You."

Politics Rudolph G. Perpich (1928–1995), a dentist who began a career in politics in 1956, served two terms in the Minnesota state senate. Elected lieutenant governor in 1970, he became governor of Minnesota in 1976 when Governor Wendell Anderson resigned. Perpich was elected to two more terms in 1982 and 1986, making him the longest-serving governor of Minnesota.

Mike Stepovich (1919–), the first governor of the state of Alaska, had earlier helped establish a colony in Alaska. Nick Begich (1932–1972), of Alaska, was elected to the U.S. House of Representatives in 1970. His son Mark Begich (1962–) was elected U.S. senator from Alaska in 2009. Michael A. Bilandić (1923–2002) was elected mayor of Chicago in 1977 after the death of Richard J. Daley. Dennis J. Kucinich (1946–) served as mayor of Cleveland in the 1970s. From 1997 to 2013, he served as a U.S. representative (D–OH). In 2004 and 2008, he ran in the Democratic primary for the U.S. presidential election. He was hired by Fox News as a political commentator in 2013.

Sports Teodor Beg, a wrestler from Croatia, won eight gold medals during the 1910s for wrestling. Baseball players of Croatian descent include Walt Dropo (1923–2010) of the Baltimore Orioles, in the late 1940s through the 1950s; Joseph Beggs

CROATIAN AMERICAN NEWSPAPERS

Even though many Croatian immigrants were illiterate, newspapers in the "Little Croatias" of the United States assumed importance. They reported changes in American immigration law, carried employment opportunities, and kept up with major European events. The most popular newspaper among early immigrants was *Narodni List* (1898), published in New York by Frank Zotti, a colorful and controversial Croatian figure of the time. Zotti's tabloid featured gutsy topical reporting, melodramatic fiction, and popular peasant poetry. The Croatian Fraternal Union's *Zajednicar* (Unity) began in 1905 in Pittsburgh and is still published today with a circulation of 70,000.

(1910–1983) of the Cincinnati Reds, in the 1930s and 1940s; and Roger Maras (1934–1985) and Mickey Lolich (1940–), stars of the 1968 World Series. Joseph L. Kuharich (1917–1981) coached the Washington Redskins football team from 1954 to 1958 and in 1955 was named coach of the year. "Pistol" Pete Marovich (1947–1988) had a nationally publicized career with the New Orleans Jazz. Eleanor Laich was one of Olson's All-American Redheads touring basketball team in the late 1930s and early 1940s. Mike Karakas (1911–1992) played hockey for the Chicago Blackhawks, and Johnny Polich (1916–2001) played for the New York Rangers. Helen Crienkovich won the world diving championships in 1939. Fritzie Zivich was the world welterweight boxing champ in 1941.

Visual Arts Ivan Mestrović (1883–1962) showed his marble sculptures in one-man shows in Belgrade, Zagreb, and London, before establishing a studio in Paris in 1907. After World War I, he joined the art faculty of Syracuse University in New York and then taught at Notre Dame University, where he lived until his death. Mestrović's work demonstrated a consciousness of the suffering of people in Austria-Hungary. His work also shows the influence of Michelangelo, whose art he studied for four years in Rome. The first artist to hold a one-man exhibit at the Metropolitan Museum of Art in New York, Mestrović has left a legacy of works that can be found throughout the United States in churches, parks, and institutions that include Grant Park in Chicago and the Mayo Clinic in Minnesota.

The painter Vlaho Bukovac (1865–1963) studied art in Paris and worked in San Francisco. His home in his native Cavtat is now a museum. Another painter, Maksimiljan (Makso) Vanka (1889–1963), studied painting in Zabreb and Brussels. He came to the United States in 1934 with his American wife and attracted fame when he painted the towering frescoes for St. Nicholas Croatian Catholic Church in Millvale, Pennsylvania. Louis Adamić's novel *Cradle of Life* (1936) is based on Bukovac's life.

MEDIA

PRINT

Croatian Chronicle Network (CCN) in New York

An online news source written in English for and about Croatians living outside of Croatia.

P.O. Box 3360
Astoria, New York 11103
Email: info@croatianchronicle.com
URL: www.croatianchronicle.com

Croatian World Network (CROWN)

An online English-language network providing links to Croatian news, dating, travel information, language study, and more for the Croatian diaspora.

Nenad N. Bach, Editor in Chief
Email: letters@croatia.com
URL: www.croatia.org

Journal of Croatian Studies

Focuses on Croatian culture, literature, arts, music, sociology, economics, and government.

Jerome Jareb, Editor
Croatian Academy of America
P.O. Box 1767
New York, New York 10163-1767

RADIO

Croatian TV America

Provides programming available by subscription from fourteen Croatian TV stations and six radio stations for audiences in North America, including news, sports, popular TV shows, documentaries, and cartoons.

23811 Washington Avenue
Suite 110
Murrieta, California 92562
Phone: (888) 768-4788
Email: info@croatiantv-america.com
URL: www.croatiantv-america.com

WSBC 1240 FM Chicago

Billed as an ethnic radio station, it is operated by a nonprofit organization that offers the Croatian Radio Club on Saturdays from 1 to 2 p.m. The radio hour is broadcast in Croatian and plays Croatian music.

Mile Perkovic
7036 West Archer Avenue
Chicago, Illinois 60638
Phone: (773) 229-1555
Email: info@croradioclub.com
URL: www.croradioclub.com

ORGANIZATIONS AND ASSOCIATIONS

Croatian Academy of America (CAA)

Sponsors lectures for members and the public on Croatian literature, history, and culture. Also publishes the *Journal of Croatian Studies*.

Diane Gal, Executive Secretary
P.O. Box 1767
Grand Central Station
New York, New York 10163-1767
URL: www.croatianacademy.org

Croatian Fraternal Union of America (CFU)

Established in 1894, the CFU is a fraternal and life insurance organization concerned with Croatian American heritage preservation. More than just a financial organization, the CFU has been involved in the cultural, political, and social aspects of Croatian American life over the past century. There are fraternal lodges in many cities across the United States. Today their programs include scholarships for Croatians, humanitarian aid to those affected by the Croatian war for independence, annual cultural festivals, and folk music and dance festivals.

Bernard M. Luketich, President
100 Delaney Drive
Pittsburgh, Pennsylvania 15235
Phone: (412) 351-3909
Fax: (412) 823-1594
Email: info@croatianfraternalunion.org
URL: www.croatianfraternalunion.org

Croatian Genealogical Society (CGS)

Encourages Croatian genealogical and heraldic research. This organization is part of the Federation of Eastern European Family History Societies.

Adam S. Eterovich, Director
2527 San Carlos Avenue
San Carlos, California 94070
Phone: (415) 592-1190
Fax: (415) 592-1526

MUSEUMS AND RESEARCH CENTERS

Bernard M. Luketich Croatian Cultural Museum

This museum is housed at Croatian Fraternal Union of America headquarters and has on display a collection of Croatian folk costumes, works by Croatian artists, antique tamburitza instruments, and memorabilia from the organization.

Franjo Bertovic, Vice President/Member Services
100 Delaney Drive
Pittsburgh, Pennsylvania 15245
Phone: (412) 843-0380
Fax: (412) 823-1594
Email: info@croatianfraternalunion.org
URL: www.croatianfraternalunion.org

Croatian Heritage Museum and Library

Collects and exhibits artifacts, textiles, folk costumes, wood carvings, sculpture, leather works, and paintings.

Suzanne Jerin
34900 Lakeshore Boulevard
Eastlake, Ohio 44095
Phone: (440) 946-2044
Fax: (216) 991-3051
Email: croatianmuseum@sbcglobal.net
URL: www.croatianmuseum.com

SOURCES FOR ADDITIONAL STUDY

Eterovich, Francis H., and Christopher Spalatin, eds. *Croatia: Land, People, and Culture*. Toronto: University of Toronto Press, 1964.

Gorvorchin, Gerald G. *Americans from Yugoslavia*. Gainesville: University of Florida, 1961.

Preveden, Francis. *A History of the Croatian People*. New York: Philosophic, 1962.

Prpić, George. *The Croatian Immigrants in America*. New York: Philosophic, 1971.

Shapiro, Ellen. *The Croatian Americans*. New York: Chelsea House, 1989.

"South Slavic American Literature." In *Ethnic Perspectives in American Literature*, edited by Robert Di Pietro and Edward Ifković. New York: MLA, 1983.

CUBAN AMERICANS

Sean T. Buffington

OVERVIEW

Cuban Americans are immigrants (or descendants of immigrants) from the island nation of Cuba. Located on the northern rim of the Caribbean Sea, Cuba is the largest of the Greater Antilles islands. To Cuba's east is the island of Hispaniola, shared by Haiti and the Dominican Republic. Off the southeastern coast of Cuba lies Jamaica, and to the north is the state of Florida. The island is composed of rolling plains, with a few mountain ranges located in the southeast and the central regions. Although several rivers cut across Cuba's interior, the inland possesses only one large natural reservoir, the Laguna de Leche. In 1971 the Cuban government built the Zaza Reservoir, which is the largest inland water source in the country. Cuba's total land area is 42,426 square miles, which is slightly larger than the state of Tennessee.

According to a census conducted by the Cuban government, Cuba had a population of 11.2 million in 2010. In 2011 the World Bank estimated that the country's population was 11.3 million. Although the Cuban Constitution was amended in 1991 to define the nation as secular rather than atheist, approximately 40 to 45 percent of the population identify, at least nominally, as Roman Catholic. Many who call themselves Catholic practice Santería, a merging of traditions from Roman Catholicism and the Yoruba religion of West Africa. It is estimated that 5 percent of the population is affiliated with Protestant churches. Other religious groups include Greek Orthodox, Russian Orthodox, Jehovah's Witnesses, Muslims, Jews, Buddhists, Bahá'ís, and the Church of Jesus Christ of Latter-day Saints. The Cuban government maintains a series of restrictions on religious practices. However, since 1992 the restrictions have been eased, and the government now legally recognizes Catholics, Protestants, Jehovah's Witnesses, Muslims, and Jews. Additionally, the government works closely with the Cuban Council of Churches to monitor officially sanctioned religious practices. According to the United Nations 2010 Human Development Index, Cuba's economy and developmental potential are above the regional average of other Latin American and Caribbean countries. Cuba's socialist economy used to rely heavily upon the country's sugar, tobacco, and nickel enterprises; 75 percent of its GDP now comes

from the service sector, which is composed mostly of doctors and medical professionals. Since 2010 Cuba has encouraged some private sector growth, particularly in tourism.

Cubans began migrating to the United States in large numbers in the mid-nineteenth and early twentieth centuries, settling mostly in the lower Florida peninsula, where they engaged in tobacco manufacturing. A second wave occurred during the early to mid-twentieth century, with many seeking economic opportunities in the United States. Following the Cuban Revolution in 1959 that unseated Fulgencio Batista and placed Fidel Castro in power, hundreds of thousands of Cubans fled the communist country. The exodus continued throughout the next several decades, forcing the United States to continually revisit its immigration policy toward Cuba. In 1995 President Bill Clinton signed an agreement with the Cuban government to repatriate Cuban immigrants picked up at sea. In what was commonly known as the "Wet Feet, Dry Feet" policy, the Clinton administration agreed not to admit Cubans it found at sea but said it would continue to grant asylum and a chance for citizenship to Cubans who made it to shore. In 2008 the U.S. government began working with Mexico to curb the number of Cubans migrating to the United States by illegally crossing the Mexico-United States border.

The 2010 U.S. Census indicated that 1.8 million Cubans live in the United States, accounting for approximately 4 percent of the Hispanic American population. The majority of Cuban Americans live in Florida, particularly in Miami and the surrounding area, as a result of the state's proximity to the island. The largest population of Cuban Americans outside of Florida resides in the New York City metropolitan area.

HISTORY OF THE PEOPLE

Early History Cuba was colonized by the Spanish in 1511. Before colonization the island was inhabited by Ciboney and Taíno (or Arawak, as the Spanish named them) Indians. Shortly after colonization the native population was ravaged by disease, warfare, and enslavement, leading to their eventual extinction. In the sixteenth and seventeenth centuries, Spain lavished attention on its mainland colonies in the Americas but ignored its Caribbean colonies, including Cuba. By the end of the seventeenth century, Spain had begun to decline as a world power because of financial mismanagement, outmoded trade policies, and continued reliance on exhausted extractive industries. Cuba suffered during this period, as did all of Spain's colonies. In 1762 the British captured Havana and encouraged the cultivation of sugar cane, an industry that would dominate the economy of the area for centuries to come.

British rule of Cuba was short-lived, lasting only ten months before Spain resumed control. However, during this brief period North Americans had become buyers of Cuban goods, a factor that would contribute greatly to the prosperity of the island population. Meanwhile, the need for labor on sugar and tobacco plantations and for raising livestock (the island's first major industry) resulted in the growth of African slavery.

Trade increased in Cuba over the next sixty years, as did immigration from Europe and from other areas of Latin America. The introduction of the steam-powered sugar mill in 1819 hastened the expansion of the sugar industry. While the demand for African slaves grew, Spain signed a treaty with England agreeing to prohibit the slave trade after 1820. The number of slaves entering the area did decrease after that time, but the treaty was largely ignored. Several slave revolts took place over the next three decades, but all proved unsuccessful.

Cuba's political relationship with Spain during this period became increasingly antagonistic. The island's creoles—those of Spanish descent who had been born in Cuba and were chiefly wealthy landowners and powerful sugar planters—resented the control colonial administrators in Europe exercised over them in political and economic matters. Many of these landowners and planters were also concerned about the future of slavery on the island, wanting to protect their investment in slaves and their access to cheap African labor from zealous imperial reformers. At the same time, black slaves in Cuba and their liberal allies were interested in national independence and freedom for the island's slaves. There were three wars for independence: the Ten Years' War (1868–1878), the Little War (1879–1880), and the War of Independence (1895–1898). During the final war independence-minded black Cubans and white Cubans joined in a struggle against Spanish imperial forces. Their rebellion was cut short by the intervention of U.S. troops, who defeated the Spanish in the 1898 Spanish-American War and ruled Cuba for four years. Even after the end of its direct rule, however, the United States continued to exercise an extraordinary degree of influence over Cuba's politics and economy. The U.S. interventionist policy toward Cuba aroused the resentment of many Cubans, as did the irresponsible and tyrannical governance of the island by a succession of Cuban presidents.

Modern Era During the 1930s economic hardship and the dictatorship of Gerardo Machado led to another revolution. After the Revolt of the Sergeants (1933), led by Fulgencio Batista, the army succeeded in overthrowing Machado, who resigned and fled the country. Batista, backed by the United States, appointed himself chief of the armed forces and ruled Cuba through a series of hand-picked puppet presidents. He was elected president once (1940–1944) and in 1952 led a military coup that established him as dictator. Anger at the oppressive rule of Cuban leaders, many of them backed by the United States, exploded in the late 1950s, when a cross-class insurrection led by Fidel Castro launched an uprising against Batista's brutal dictatorship. Castro formed a socialist government after taking control of the island, turning to the Soviet Union for support in the polarized world of geopolitics during the Cold War. The relationship between Cuba and the United States has been cool at best since Castro's victory. In 1960 the United States enacted a partial commercial, economic, and financial embargo against Cuba, later strengthening it to a near-complete embargo in 1962. In January 1961 the United States broke diplomatic relations with Cuba. The 1961 Bay of Pigs invasion, an unsuccessful attempt by the U.S. government and Cuban exiles in the United States to overthrow Castro, was the first of many clashes between the two nations. Also noteworthy is the Cuban missile crisis of 1962, in which the United States successfully resisted an attempt by the Soviet Union to place nuclear weapons in Cuba.

During the 1970s and 1980s Castro's Cuba supported socialist revolutions throughout the world, particularly in Africa, with the Cuban military stationing troops in Angola and Ethiopia. In Cuba Castro used a heavy hand against dissidents, and many who opposed him were imprisoned, executed, or exiled. During the 1980s the Soviet Union experienced a series of financial crises and an extended period of political unrest that weakened the country. With the dissolution of the Soviet Union at the end of 1991, Cuba lost its most important trading partner and supporter.

The next decade brought immense challenges to the Cuban economy. Faced with a depleted oil supply and limited trading partners, Castro's Cuba fell into a deep economic depression, an era known as the "Special Period." During that time Cuba's infrastructure struggled and its people faced mass food and power shortages. The Cuban government sought to resurrect the country's economy through a variety of innovative methods, including mandated organic farming, permaculture, and mass transportation. Throughout the 1990s the economy continued to struggle, and although the United States provided some humanitarian aid, its economic embargo against Cuba continued to put additional strains on the island nation's fragile economy. In spite of the immense challenges that the country faced, the Cuban government found some respite by focusing on tourism, cash crops, mineral exports, and its public health care system, considered one of the most successful in the world.

After protests erupted in Havana in 1994, Castro responded by tightening his power. However, he also instituted a series of measures that promoted urban gardens to help remedy the country's food shortages and reduce food transportation costs. In 1998 Cuba entered into a lucrative partnership with Venezuela's newly elected socialist president, Hugo Chavez. In exchange for Cuba's medical and educational assistance, Venezuela agreed to enter into a variety of economic agreements with Cuba that alleviated Cuba's energy shortages. At the turn of the century, Cuba's economy had gotten a boost from the growth in tourism, and the government began to invest in rebuilding the country's infrastructure.

Throughout the country's economic instability, however, many Cubans had openly voiced their dissatisfaction with the government, leading to increased crackdowns and suppression of dissidents by the state. To maintain its legitimacy, Castro's government continually attempted to reinvent itself by allowing more foreign investors in the country, loosening some social restrictions, and investing in social services. Yet even as the government was attempting to stabilize the nation, thousands of Cubans continued to flee the island, leading to even greater government suppression.

In 2006 Fidel Castro fell ill and delegated all of his presidential duties to his brother Raúl Castro. Raúl served as temporary president of Cuba until he was officially elected in 2008. He then implemented a series of reforms, including removing restrictions on consumer goods such as electronics and releasing some state-owned land to independent farmers. Initially positioning himself as a reformer, Raúl Castro promised that he would institute a sweeping set of economic, social, and political changes that would rejuvenate the country. His reforms came slowly, leading many citizens and outside observers to question his ability to alleviate the country's problems within the confines of a one-party system.

SETTLEMENT IN THE UNITED STATES

Cubans have a long history of migrating to the United States, often for political reasons. Many Cubans, particularly cigar manufacturers, came during the clashes between Cuban nationals and the Spanish military known as the Ten Years' War (1868–1878). Yet the most significant Cuban migrations occurred in the second half of the twentieth century, with at least four distinct waves of Cuban immigration to the United States since 1959. Although many, if not most, Cuban migrants in the twentieth century were fleeing Cuba for political reasons, migrants in the early twenty-first century were more likely to have left the country because of its declining economic conditions.

Cuban refugees arrive in the United States in 1980. BETTMANN / CORBIS

The first of these four waves of Cuban migration began immediately after Castro's victory in 1959 and continued until the U.S. government strengthened its embargo against Cuba during the Cuban missile crisis in 1962. Supporters of Batista were the first to leave Cuba, but they moved to the Dominican Republic. They were later joined by Cubans who had not been prominent Batista allies but who nonetheless opposed Castro's socialist government. Before the U.S. government imposed its embargo, almost 250,000 Cubans had left Cuba for the United States.

The second notable wave of migration started in 1965 and continued through 1973. Cuba and the United States had agreed that Cubans with relatives residing in the United States could be legally transported from Cuba. The transportation of migrants began by boat from the northern port of Camarioca. After many migrants died in boat accidents, the transportation later continued by plane from the airstrip at Varadero. Almost 300,000 Cubans arrived in the United States during this period.

The third migration, known as the Mariel boatlift, occurred in 1980. It was precipitated by an incident in which five Cubans used a bus to crash through the gates of the Peruvian embassy in an attempt to gain political asylum. The Cuban guards stationed outside the embassy opened fire on the bus, and one of the guards was shot. When the Peruvian government refused to give up the five Cubans, Castro removed all guards from the entrance of the embassy, which was subsequently flooded by more than 14,000 Cubans seeking asylum. Finally the Cuban army was called in to cordon the area. Castro then announced that the Mariel port would be open to Cubans wishing to leave Cuba. More than 125,000 registered, but only 50 percent of them were allowed to emigrate. The ones that were denied were targeted as being disloyal to the Castro regime. Many of the people allowed to leave Cuba were hand-selected by the Cuban government and had not even registered; they also included prisoners and patients from mental institutions.

As economic conditions in Cuba continued to worsen after the fall of the Soviet Union, more and more people set out in makeshift boats from Cuba's shores in an attempt to make it to Florida. It was a criminal offense for anyone to leave the country without government permission, and anyone caught leaving was sentenced to several years in prison. The Cuban navy and air force patrolled the perimeter of the island, making escape difficult. As the numbers of people leaving in boats grew, the enforcement became stricter. In August 1994 the Cuban military shot at a boat filled with Cuban immigrants, causing a riot in Havana. Castro temporarily suspended the law that restricted immigration, and within days about 35, 000 Cubans headed for the United States by boat. U.S. president Bill Clinton initiated a policy of intercepting those migrants at sea and detaining them in tents at Guantanamo Bay, a policy that outraged many in the Cuban American community. In order to stop this mass exodus, the United States and Cuba signed an agreement that the United States would intercept the people at sea, but not the people who make it to U.S. soil. This policy was a revision of the 1966 Cuban Refugee Adjustment Act. The Cubans who are picked up at sea can request political asylum and are resettled in a third country. However, 95 percent of people picked up are sent back to Cuba. By 1996 the camps at Guantanamo Bay were closed and most of the Cuban immigrants residing in them were admitted to the United States. As part of the changes made to the Cuban Adjustment Act in 1994, the United States agreed to grant 20,000 visas a year to Cubans. However, each person is allowed to bring everyone listed on his or her ration card. Several family members can be on one ration card, which means that more than 20,000 Cubans each year immigrate to the United States.

These four waves of migration have brought substantial numbers of Cubans to the United States. Over the years, just as the migration "push factors" have changed, so has the composition of the migrant population. While the earliest migrants were typically from Cuba's highly educated and conservative middle and upper classes (those who had the most to lose from a socialist revolution), later migrants were generally poorer and less educated. Over the past several decades the Cuban American population has come to look more like the Cuban population as a whole and less like the highest socioeconomic stratum of that country.

According to the 2010 United States Census, nearly 1.8 million people of Cuban descent reside in the United States. Although there are sizable Cuban American communities in New York, New Jersey, and California—with those three states accounting for 23 percent of the Cuban American population—approximately 66 percent of Cuban Americans live in Florida. Florida is home to the most significant Cuban American political organizations, research centers, and cultural institutions, and Miami specifically is the center of the Cuban American community. The first Cubans to arrive in Florida settled in a section of Miami referred to by many as "Little Havana." Little Havana was originally the area west of downtown Miami, bounded by Seventh Street, Eighth Street, and Twelfth Avenue. However, the Cuban American population eventually spread beyond those initial boundaries, moving west, south, and north to west Miami, south Miami, Westchester, Sweetwater, and Hialeah.

Many Cuban immigrants moved even farther into the United States with the encouragement and assistance of the U.S. government. The Cuban Refugee Program, established by President John F. Kennedy's administration in 1961, provided assistance to Cuban migrants, enabling them to move out of southern Florida and into other areas of the United States. Almost 302,000 Cubans were resettled through the Cuban Refugee Program, although many subsequently returned to the Miami area.

For political reasons, returning to Cuba has not been an option for most Cuban Americans. Many early migrants expected Fidel Castro to be ousted quickly, allowing them to return to the country, but Castro retained his power for decades. In 2006 he passed the presidency on to his brother Raúl Castro, with whom he was politically aligned. Although there have been many prominent and powerful political organizations in the United States dedicated to ridding Cuba of its socialist government, recent surveys have shown that most Cuban Americans do not plan to return to Cuba permanently.

In 2009 U.S. president Barack Obama returned travel and remittance rules to pre-Bush levels because former president George W. Bush had not honored the Cuban Adjustment Act during his two terms. After decades of U.S. sanctions and trade embargoes, President Obama announced that his administration would remove all restrictions on Cuban Americans returning to Cuba to visit family members and on their remittances to family members still living in the island nation.

LANGUAGE

According to statistics compiled in 2010 by the Pew Research Center, 58.3 percent of Cuban Americans are proficient in English, while almost 70 percent of Cuban Americans speak a language other than English at home. Among Cuban Americans born abroad, 74.3 percent said that they speak Spanish better than English, though more than one-half of that same segment stated that they have some English ability.

These statistics do not capture the phenomenon of "Spanglish," a linguistic mixture of Spanish and English that is a common mode of verbal

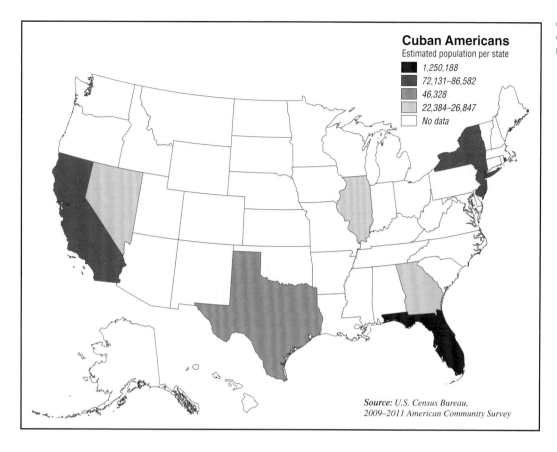

Cuban Americans
Estimated population per state

- 1,250,188
- 72,131–86,582
- 46,328
- 22,384–26,847
- No data

Source: U.S. Census Bureau, 2009–2011 American Community Survey

communication among Cuban Americans born in the United States. Many of them speak English at school and in other public domains but speak Spanish at home with relatives and neighbors. Younger Cuban Americans in particular often use Spanglish to talk with friends and acquaintances, incorporating English words, phrases, and syntactic units into Spanish grammatical structures. Facility with Spanglish, however, does not necessarily imply lack of facility with either English or Spanish, though a lack of facility with either language may characterize some Spanglish speakers.

RELIGION

Most people living in Cuba identify themselves as either Roman Catholic or as nonreligious. The large number of nonreligious people in Cuba is a consequence of the socialist government's stance toward religion, which is now more accepting than it was in the years immediately following the government's formation but nevertheless remains restrictive. In the United States, Cuban Americans are less likely to attend religious services than other Hispanic immigrant groups.

Information gathered in 2010 by the Pew Hispanic Research Center demonstrates that Americans of Cuban descent overwhelmingly identify themselves as Roman Catholic. That research showed that almost 80 percent of foreign-born Cuban Americans and 64 percent of those born in the United States are Catholic, while 14 percent of foreign-born

Cuban immigrants and 10 percent of U.S.-born Cuban Americans follow some form of Protestantism.

Among Protestant Cuban Americans living in Florida, most belong to mainline Protestant denominations, the most common being Baptist, Methodist, Presbyterian, Episcopalian, and Lutheran. However, there are increasing numbers of independent Cuban American church members, including Pentecostals, Jehovah's Witnesses, and Seventh-Day Adventists. This growth parallels the increasing popularity of charismatic, fundamentalist, and independent churches throughout Latin America and in the United States. Jewish Cuban Americans, while few, are also notable.

The Cuban religious tradition that has received the most publicity is Santería. Santería has been portrayed in movies and on television since the mid-1980s as a form of Afro-Caribbean black magic, similar to Haitian vodun, popularly known as voodoo. These largely negative and frequently inaccurate media portrayals have led to a public misunderstanding of the nature of Santería. The tradition is, like vodun, a synthesis of West African and Roman Catholic religious vocabularies, beliefs, and practices. *Santeros*, or adherents of Santería, seek the guidance, protection, and intervention in their lives of *orishas*, divine personages who trace their lineage both to Yoruba West African gods and Roman Catholic saints. The practice of Santería involves healing rituals, spirit possession, and animal sacrifice. This latter aspect of Santería

WHITE BEAN SOUP

Ingredients

1 pound small white beans

1½ pounds beef stew meat, cut into 1-inch cubes

3 small spanish chorizo sausages or ½ a large one, casing removed cut into rounds

1 green bell pepper, minced

1 onion, minced

½ head garlic, pressed with garlic press

1 pound winter squash, peeled, seeded, and cut into chunks (banana, kabucha, butternut, hubbard squash, etc.)

3 medium potatoes peeled cut into chunks

1 teaspoon salt, and more to taste

1 teaspoon ground cumin

extra-virgin olive oil or lard as needed

Preparation

Bring beans to a boil in enough water to cover them about 2–4 inches. After it comes to a rolling boil, add beef stew meat and season with 1 teaspoon salt. Cover and let boil until beans are tender at medium-low heat, about an hour.

When beans and beef are tender, heat olive oil or lard in a large pan over medium high. Begin the the sofrito by sautéeing the Spanish chorizo; when the oil turns reddish, add the onions and bell pepper and cook for about until translucent. Then add garlic and cook another 1–2 minutes until fragrant. Put the sofrito, squash, and potatoes into the pot of beans and beef, along with cumin and more salt if necessary. Return to a boil and cook together, uncovered, until the squash and potatoes are tender and soup has thickened.

caused controversy in the late 1980s when leaders of a Santería church challenged a Miami-area law prohibiting animal sacrifice. The U.S. Supreme Court later struck down the law as unconstitutional. In a similar case decided in 2009, the U.S. Supreme Court Fifth Circuit Court of Appeals found in favor of Jose Merced, a Santería priest who had been banned from performing goat sacrifices as part of his religious ceremonies, under the Texas Freedom of Religion statute.

In 1997, after an agreement between Fidel Castro and Pope John Paul II, Cuba recognized Christmas as a national holiday and eased some of its restrictions on religious practices in preparation for Pope John Paul II's 1998 visit to the country. Both Pope John Paul II in 1998 and Pope Benedict XVI in his 2012 visit to Cuba refused to meet with leaders of the Santería faith. In spite of the Vatican's dismissal of the religion, Cuba maintains its secular society while allowing the practice to continue.

CULTURE AND ASSIMILATION

The Cuban American community is well assimilated in the United States, but the challenges presented to Cuban immigrants serve as a reminder that Cuban Americans are not a monolithic community. Rather, they are quite diverse. The initial waves of migrants were comprised mostly of affluent and well-educated Cubans, allowing them to assimilate somewhat easily into the larger American culture. Since the 1990s, however, the population of Cuban immigrants has become more economically diverse. Cubans who come to the United States in search of jobs and economic prosperity have a more difficult time assimilating than financially stable Cubans who arrive in the country.

Older generations of Cuban Americans maintain many of the habits they held in their home country. For example, older men gather to play dominoes and participate in political debates. However, younger generations appear to have embraced the American way of life, generally participating in the vibrant nightlife of cities like Miami. By merging traditional dances with contemporary music, the "New Cubans" have found a way to negotiate the pressures of assimilation by retaining elements of their cultural heritage.

Most Cuban Americans attempt to maintain their traditional cultural beliefs and activities. According to a 2006 Susan Eckstein essay titled "Cuban Emigres and the American Dream," many Cuban Americans resist English-only movements and celebrate their Cuban heritage by forming Cuban-only social groups and starting Cuban businesses, professional associations, and humanitarian groups.

Cuisine Like many recent migrant groups, Cuban Americans enjoy both Cuban and American cuisines. Traditional Cuban food is the product of the mingling of Spanish and West African cuisines in the climate of the Caribbean. Pork and beef are the most common meats in the traditional Cuban diet. Rice, beans, and root vegetables usually accompany such dishes. The ingredients necessary for Cuban cooking are available in most major cities where there are significant Hispanic populations. Dishes commonly prepared in Cuban American homes include *arroz con pollo* (rice with chicken), a Cuban variation of the tamale, white-bean stew (such as *fabada*), and a panini-type sandwich known as a "Cuban." Many Cuban Americans, especially those raised in the United States, have easy access to a variety of American foods and tend to reserve traditional cooking for special occasions.

Traditional Dress As in much of Latin America and the Caribbean, the clothing commonly worn in Cuba is designed to be comfortable in a warm climate. Thus, the guayabera style of shirt is extremely popular. With various unconfirmed claims about its origins, including some who argue that it was invented in Cuba, *guayabera* shirts are loose, short-sleeved, collared shirts made of thin material. They can have either two or four pockets and have vertical pleats running along the front and back. When Cubans began immigrating to the United States in large numbers after the revolution, they brought the *guayabera* style with them. Today, it is popular not only among Cuban Americans but also, albeit to a lesser degree, among Americans at large. Though largely worn by men, *guayabera* shirts and even dresses are also designed for, and worn by, women.

Traditionally, Cuban girls wear an elaborate white ball gown and tiara for their *quinceanera*, a celebration of their fifteenth birthday and transition into womanhood. While Cuban Americans still celebrate this occasion, girls have more freedom in choosing their style of dress and often decline to wear the conventional style of gown.

Dances and Songs Cuba has a rich musical and dance tradition that emerged from the country's unique blend of Spanish, African, and indigenous influences. The result is a unique and diverse style of song and dance that had a profound influence on both Latin and American music. From such diverse sources as Spanish *flamenco* music and Yoruba religious songs emerged the *conga, rumba, mambo,* and *cha-cha-chá*. At the heart of Cuban dance music is a musical style called *son*, which emerged in the late nineteenth century and formed the foundation for many of the popular rhythms that followed. *Son* is structured from call-and-response vocals known as the *montuno*, a syncopated bass line, and a five-note pattern called the *clave* that is kept on a pair of sticks known. The *clave* was soon incorporated in a

new Cuban style: the salsa. Many of the dance styles based on the *son* found popularity in the United States, both within and outside Cuban American communities.

The connection between American and Cuban musical styles became tightly intertwined during the twentieth century. Jazz was heavily influenced by Cuban music, and, in turn, jazz music became popular and influential in Cuba in the 1910s and 1920s. Later in the century, beginning in the 1960s, American rock, funk, and dance styles were integrated with Cuban *son* rhythms to create new sounds on the island. More recently, rap and hip-hop merged with Cuban rhythms to form a new style known as *timba*.

Among Cuban Americans, Cuban music remains popular. Traditional groups are common throughout Cuban American communities and especially in Miami, where clubs featuring Cuban music and dance thrive in Little Havana and throughout the city. Interest in traditional Cuban culture, including its music and dance, has grown in recent years among the Cuban American population, as the community's connection to its homeland has grown increasingly remote and distant and young people have become more interested in connecting with their cultural roots. Miami is also a hotbed for the ongoing melding of American and Cuban musical traditions and dance styles. By merging traditional dances with contemporary music, the Cuban Americans have found a way to negotiate the pressures of assimilation by retaining elements of their cultural heritage.

Cuban American children march in the Calle Ocho Parade in Miami, Florida. JEFF GREENBERG / ALAMY

CUBAN PROVERBS

Sarna con gana no pica y si pica no mortifica.

A rash when desired doesn't itch, and if it itches, doesn't torment.

Si la cosa no tiene remedio, ¿por qué te preocupas? Y si tiene remedio, ¿por qué te preocupas?

If the situation cannot be remedied, why worry? And if it can be remedied, why worry?

No llores como mujer lo que no supiste defender como hombre.

Don't cry like a woman for what you could not defend like a man.

En el reino de los ciegos, el tuerto es rey.

In the kingdom of the blind, the one-eyed man is king.

Mono vestido de seda, mono sigue.

A monkey dressed in silk is still a monkey.

El hombre que no probó la adversidad es el más desdichado.

The man who never experienced adversity is the most unlucky of all.

El perro tiene cuatro patas y coge un solo camino.

The dog has four feet, but it takes only one path.

Holidays Like other Hispanic communities, Cuban Americans tend to observe traditional Roman Catholic holidays, such as Christmas and Easter. Cuban Americans may also celebrate Three Kings' Day (January 6), marking the day when the "three wise men" delivered gifts to Jesus Christ. Additionally, many Cubans celebrate All Saints' Day (November 1), commemorating those who have achieved sainthood, and All Souls' Day (November 2), sanctifying the souls that remain in purgatory. While celebration of the 1959 Cuban Revolution is a hotly contested issue among many Cuban Americans, many immigrants from Cuba observe Cuban Independence Day on May 20, celebrating the nation's independence from Spain.

Health Care Issues and Practices According to an article by Fernando S. Mendoza published in a 1991 issue of the *Journal of the American Medical Association* (*JAMA*), Cuban Americans are generally healthier than other Hispanic Americans but often less healthy than non-Hispanic white Americans. Several indicators demonstrate the overall health of Cuban Americans. The proportion of Cuban American babies with low birth weight is lower than the percentage of all infants in the United States with low birth weight and slightly higher than that of non-Hispanic white Americans. Similarly, the proportion of Cuban American infants born prematurely, while lower than the proportion of Mexican Americans or Puerto Ricans born early, is nonetheless higher than that of non-Hispanic white Americans.

In another article in the same issue of *JAMA*, the Council on Scientific Affairs described the relative position of Cuban Americans in other areas. If found that Cuban Americans are far more likely than non-Hispanic white Americans to be murdered or to commit suicide. Still, they are less likely to be murdered than black or Puerto Rican Americans and less likely to die in accidents than black, Puerto Rican, or Mexican Americans. The article also stated that when Cuban Americans seek treatment for injury or disease, they frequently must pay the entire cost of emergency care, since Cuban Americans as a group are more likely to be uninsured than the general U.S. population. Many Cuban Americans turn to the Santería tradition for health care, participating in Santería healing services and seeking the advice of Santería healers.

FAMILY AND COMMUNITY LIFE

The Cuban American family is different in significant ways from the Cuban family. The Cuban family is characterized by patriarchy, strong parental control over children's lives, and the importance of non-nuclear relationships for the nuclear family. In the United States these elements have become less characteristic among families of Cuban descent. For example, the Cuban tradition of selecting *compadres*, or godparents who maintain a close and quasiparental relationship with a child, has begun to decline among Cubans living in the United States. However, Cuban Americans have the lowest rates of teen pregnancy (23.5 percent) of any group in the United States, including non-Hispanic whites. This is may be due to a greater sense of obligation they feel toward their family to not get pregnant until married.

In 2010 about 52 percent of Cuban Americans over the age of eighteen were married, while almost 12 percent of U.S.-born Cuban Americans were divorced, compared with a 7 percent divorce rate among other Hispanic American communities. Cuban Americans born in the United States are less likely to have children than Cuban Americans born abroad. Finally, nearly 30 percent of married U.S.-born Cuban Americans are married to Anglo-Americans, compared to 3.6 percent of Cuban-born Americans.

Gender Roles Although women in Cuba are legally recognized as being equal with men, gender equity has not been achieved in practice. Because of the persistence of gender stereotypes and sexism, women are disproportionately burdened with housekeeping and caregiving responsibilities, despite also often working outside the home. The burden of such housework is, in important ways, greater in Cuba than in the United States, because Cubans have greatly reduced access to such common American conveniences as dishwashers, washing machines, microwaves, and frozen foods.

Cuban American women are more likely to have greater authority in the family than women still living in Cuba. This is in part attributable to the greater workforce participation of Cuban American women. These women, because they contribute to the household income and to the overall security and independence of the family, claim a greater share of authority and power within the household.

Education In Cuba a sixth-grade education is compulsory, and the literacy rate in 2010 was close to 100 percent. There is a strong emphasis on math and science in the country, and Cuba has become a center for preparing medical personnel, generating scores of young doctors. Cuban Americans are equally concerned about education, and their children are often well educated. The overwhelming majority (83 percent) of U.S.-born Cuban Americans have completed high school and some form of further education. In 2011 the National Center for Education Statistics found that more than 25 percent of U.S.-born Cuban Americans have gone to postsecondary schools, compared to less than 16 percent of U.S.-born Puerto Ricans and 10 percent of U.S.-born Mexican Americans.

More than any other Hispanic migrant group, Cuban Americans have shown a willingness and an ability to pay for private education for their children. Almost 47 percent of U.S.-born Cuban Americans have attended private schools. These numbers indicate that education is extremely important to Cuban Americans and that, more than any other Hispanic migrant group, they have the resources to pay for postsecondary schooling and private education.

Relations with Other Americans The first waves of Cuban immigrants entered the United States with the blessing of a president and a nation committed to combating communism. However, they endured severe discrimination when they arrived. In Miami in the early 1960s, it was common for businesses to hang signs that said "No Dogs, No Cubans." The movement of Cuban Americans beyond the Little Havana enclave of Miami was accompanied by a movement of non-Hispanic whites out of the areas into which Cuban Americans were moving.

There has also been long-standing antagonism between Cuban Americans and African Americans in Florida, especially as Cuban Americans have asserted themselves politically and economically in the Miami area, becoming the dominant ethnic community there. African American community leaders have

accused Cuban Americans of shutting them out of the political process and have even charged the powerful Cuban American Chamber of Commerce with blocking African Americans from making significant gains in the tourism industry. In 1991, according to an article by Nicole Lewis in *Black Enterprise*, black residents in one Florida community were so outraged by five Cuban American mayors' failure to officially welcome South African president Nelson Mandela that they initiated a boycott of all tourism-related businesses in the Miami area.

Most Cuban Americans report and perceive a nondiscriminatory relationship with white Americans. A survey of Hispanic Americans conducted from 1989 to 1990 showed that 82.2 percent of Cubans who were U.S. citizens said they had not personally experienced discrimination because of their national origin. Nonetheless, 47 percent of Cuban Americans surveyed said that they thought there was discrimination against Cuban Americans in general.

EMPLOYMENT AND ECONOMIC CONDITIONS
Cuban Americans enjoy slightly more economic security than other Hispanic groups in the United States. In 2006 the median family income of Cuban Americans was $38,000, which was $10,000 less than the median of overall family incomes in the United States but $2,000 more than the median of overall Hispanic American family incomes. Approximately 61 percent of Cuban Americans owned their own home, compared to 47 percent of other Hispanic American groups. Cuban Americans are also highly educated compared to other Hispanic migrant groups. Approximately 25 percent of the Cuban American population has completed college or college with some graduate schooling, compared to 12 percent of other Hispanic American groups. In other significant ways, too, Cuban Americans closely resemble the total

Sometimes I have dreams, and I see myself walking to my grandparents' house in Cuba. ...It brings back a lot of memories. The States is home. I have no qualms about it, but I'm still attracted to that little island, no matter how small it is. It's home. It's your people. You feel, if it's ever possible again, you'd like to reconstruct what was there. You want to be a part of it.

Ramón Fernández in 1961, cited in *American Mosaic: The Immigrant Experience in the Words of Those Who Lived It*, edited by Joan Morrison and Charlotte Fox Zabusky (New York: E. P. Dutton, 1980).

U.S. population. Two-parent households account for 78 percent of all Cuban American households, compared to 80 percent of all U.S. households. The average U.S. family has 3.19 members, while the average Cuban American family has 3.18 members.

Cuban Americans have traditionally maintained a higher employment rate than other Hispanic American groups. Cuban Americans, both foreign-born and U.S.-born, maintained an 11.2 percent unemployment rate in 2011. Their rates of unemployment are lower than those of Puerto Ricans and Mexican Americans, though somewhat higher than those of non-Hispanic white Americans. Almost 20 percent of employed Cuban Americans are professionals or managers. More than one-third of Cubans Americans are employed in technical, sales, or administrative support positions, compared to 15 percent of Anglo-Americans holding those positions.

Financially, Cuban Americans are nearly as well off as the average American. Their economic and employment profiles look very little like those of other recent Hispanic Caribbean immigrant groups (Puerto Ricans and Dominicans, for example). In the Miami area, the center of the Cuban American community, Cuban Americans are prominent in virtually every profession. The 2007 Survey of Business Owners found that Cuban Americans own 186,312 private companies in Florida, totaling $34.6 billion in sales. Manuel Viamonte's book *Cuban Exiles in Florida: Their Presence and Contribution* states that there are approximately 2,000 Cuban American medical doctors in the Miami area. Similarly, the Cuban Medical Association in Exile claims more than 3,000 members in the United States.

Cubans are widely regarded as a successful migrant group. They are reputed to be excellent and dedicated entrepreneurs who have been able to build profitable industries in the United States despite arriving in the country with almost nothing. Scholars report that more recent Cuban immigrants have been able to build upon the connections and resources of the established Cuban community in the United States. Many of the wealthiest Cuban American businesspeople built their businesses by catering to the Cuban community or by using their connections to it. Nonetheless, there are many exceptions to this portrait of the successful Cuban American. More than 33 percent of Cuban American households earn less than $20,000 per year. While this proportion is close to the proportion of Anglo-Americans in the same income category, it represents a large number of Cuban Americans who have not yet achieved the "American Dream" of security and prosperity.

POLITICS AND GOVERNMENT

Cuban Americans share many basic political values and a willingness to exercise their voting power to advance those values. Fully 78 percent of Cuban Americans registered to vote in 1989 and 1990, compared to 77.8 percent of non-Hispanic white Americans. Moreover, 67.2 percent of Cuban Americans reported that they voted in the 1988 presidential election, compared to 70.2 percent of Anglo-Americans, 49.3 percent of Mexican Americans, and 49.9 percent of Puerto Ricans. This trend continued into the late twentieth and early twenty-first centuries, with close to 70 percent of Cuban Americans reporting that they voted in the 1996, 2000, 2004, and 2008 presidential elections.

Cuban Americans are reputed to be politically conservative and to vote overwhelmingly for the Republican Party. Dario Moreno and Christopher L. Warren's 1992 essay in the *Harvard Journal of Hispanic Policy* explored this reputation by examining the voting patterns of Cuban Americans in the 1992 presidential election. Voting returns from Dade County, Florida, showed that 70 percent of Hispanic Americans in that county voted for President George H. W. Bush, a Republican. Another survey indicated that, of Cuban Americans who voted in 1988, almost 78 percent voted for Republican candidates. This trend continued throughout much of the 1990s and early 2000s, with approximately 80 percent of Cuban Americans voting Republican. In 2008, however, data showed that while older generations maintained their loyalty to the Republican Party, closer to 50 percent of Cuban Americans thirty years old or younger voted for the Democratic Party. During the 2012 presidential election, Democratic president Barack Obama received 47 percent of Cuban Americans votes, which is 10 percent more than he received in the during the 2008 election.

Owing at least in part to its large size, the Cuban American community has significant political influence in the United States. Some of the most powerful Cuban American political organizations are dedicated to shaping U.S. policy toward Cuba and—prior to the election of Raúl Castro as president in 2008—ridding Cuba of Fidel Castro. Perhaps the most important of these organizations is the Cuban American National Foundation (CANF), which was headed until 1997 by Jorge Mas Canosa, a wealthy and well-connected Miami businessman who participated in the 1961 Bay of Pigs invasion attempt. In 1993 CANF successfully lobbied against the Clinton administration's appointment of an Assistant Secretary of State for Inter-American Affairs whom it viewed as too sympathetic to the Cuban regime. CANF also pushed for the passage of the 1992 Cuban Democracy Act, which imposed further restrictions on trade with Cuba, and for the passage of the controversial Cuban Liberty and Democratic Solidarity Act of 1996 (the Helms-Burton Act). This law, which allowed the United States to impose sanctions on foreign companies that trade with Cuba, provoked intense resentment throughout the world and was challenged in the International Court of Justice. In addition to sponsoring research on Cuba, raising money for political purposes, and lobbying elected officials, CANF occasionally supports anti-Communist ventures outside the United States. Many regard the organization as representative of the Cuban American community. Some, however, have charged that the foundation tries to stifle dissent within the community.

After Mas's death in 1997, the role of CANF diminished. Growing numbers of Cuban Americans resent what they consider the organization's excesses, and, in opposition to the CANF position, prefer an end to the U.S. trade embargo against Cuba. Groups such as the Cuban Committee for Democracy, which advocate an end to the embargo, were given renewed support when Pope John Paul II denounced U.S. policy toward Cuba when he visited the island in 1998. The fact that President Bill Clinton softened restrictions on travel to Cuba and on donations of food and medicines to the country suggested to many that CANF's power to dictate U.S. policy toward Cuba had begun to wane during the late 1990s.

As diverse as the population it represents, CANF has pursued a variety of goals in the twenty-first century. The organization has repeatedly pushed for dialogue between its leaders and the Cuban government (excluding Fidel and Raúl Castro). In 2007 CANF released a report that challenged the policy of the George W. Bush administration to democratize Cuba, citing bureaucratic corruption and claiming that 80 percent of the money earmarked for Cuba had been spent in the United States by the organizations responsible for delivering the funds to Cuba. Although CANF continues to be a powerful organization, its waning influence among Cuban Americans illustrates the community's diversity and the inability of one organization to represent all its desires.

Cuban Americans have been elected to Congress, and they dominate the political arena in the Miami area. Consequently, candidates have courted Cuban Americans as a group in the past few presidential elections. Although Cuban immigrants have been known to vote predominantly for the Republican Party, change may lie in the community's political future. Some within the community have raised questions about the conservatism that has guided Cuban Americans since the 1960s. Canosa, a staunch Republican, gave some support to Bill Clinton in the 1992 campaign, and CANF donated $275,000 to the Democrat's coffers during that election cycle. Indeed, Clinton received more Hispanic support in the Miami area than any of his Democratic predecessors. More than 75 percent of Cuban Americans supported George W. Bush in 2000 and 2004, but only 64 percent supported John McCain in 2008. This slight shift did not necessarily translate to support for Barack Obama, however. Although 35 percent of Cuban Americans voted for Obama in the 2008 presidential election, a larger percentage of Cuban Americans voted for Bill Clinton in 1996.

Since they began immigrating to the United States, Cuban Americans have been greatly concerned with the political status of Cuba, and many remain committed to Cuba's political transformation. In their voting habits, Cuban Americans have been largely conservative, supporting candidates who take a hard line against Cuba. However, Cuban Americans are becoming less committed to the struggle against socialism in their home country—or, perhaps more accurately, the anti-Socialist, anti-Fidel Castro struggle is becoming less central to the Cuban American identity. A principal challenge facing the Cuban American community in the years ahead is a reconsideration of what it means to be Cuban American. What had once seemed like a politically united community is now divided on issues such as immigration, the U.S. embargo against Cuba, and the Cuban American commitment to politically conservative values.

These internal divisions may serve to strengthen the Cuban American community. Since his election in 2008, Raúl Castro has pushed for better relations with Cubans who have emigrated from the country. In an attempt to lure back some Cubans to the island, Raúl has enacted several policies that allow for the sale of private property under certain conditions and has loosened restrictions on foreign currency. Nevertheless, most Cuban Americans view Raúl Castro's promises of reform with skepticism, in part because he retained many of the high- and mid-level functionaries of Fidel Castro's government. When Raúl released fifty-two political prisoners in 2010, the Cuban government said that it continued to hold only one political prisoner. However, Amnesty International estimated that at least 167 political prisoners remained in Cuba, and Human Rights Watch and a number of Cuban exiles and nationals estimated that the count was far greater.

Cuban Americans are becoming less resistant to the idea of the U.S. government's pursuing talks with the Cuban government. Although much of the Cuban American community remains pessimistic about the changes that may occur in Cuba, some Cuban Americans are becoming more optimistic about the country's future and, according to a 2011 survey by the Pew Research Center, almost 45 percent of them say that they would consider returning to Cuba if a Democratic government took shape.

NOTABLE INDIVIDUALS

Academia Lydia Cabrera (1900–1991) was one of Cuba's most prominent scholars and writers. Cabrera was born in Havana and later lived in exile in Spain and Miami. She studied Afro-Cuban folklore and edited many collections of folk literature. She was also a prolific fiction writer.

Poet and art historian Ricardo Pau-Llosa was born in Havana in 1954 and moved to the United States in 1960, later becoming a naturalized citizen. He is an authority on contemporary Latin American art and has written texts for more than thirty exhibition catalogs. He has also published several collections of poetry.

Gustavo Pérez Firmat is an author, poet, and academic who writes in both Spanish and English. Born in Havana, he moved to the United States in 1960 and eventually became a naturalized citizen. He has been awarded numerous fellowships and taught at Duke

University before becoming a professor of literature at Columbia University.

Ruth Behar (1956–) is a prominent Cuban-born scholar who specializes in the Jewish-Cuban community. Ernesto Sosa (1940–) is a leading American philosopher. Gregory Rabassa (1922–) is a distinguished translator and literary historian.

Business Born in Havana, Roberto Goizueta (1931–1997) was the chief executive of the Coca-Cola Company. Jorge Mas Canosa (1939–1997) was a Miami businessman and chairman of the Cuban American National Foundation (CANF). Born in Cuba, Mas was also president of his own company, the Mas Group, and chair of the advisory board of Radio Martí, the U.S.-government-sponsored radio station that broadcasts to Cuba. Alvaro de Molina (1957–) served as chief financial officer of Bank of America Corporation and the chief executive officer of GMAC. Raul Fernandez (1967–) is one of the few minority owners in American professional sports and has served as co-owner of the Washington Capitals, Washington Wizards, and Washington Mystics.

Literature Cristina Garcia (1958–) is a journalist and a fiction writer who was born in Havana. She has served as a bureau chief and correspondent for *Time* magazine and was a National Book Award finalist for her book *Dreaming in Cuban*.

Oscar Hijuelos (1951–), a Cuban American born in New York City, won the Pulitzer Prize for Fiction in 1990 for *The Mambo Kings Play Songs of Love*, a novel that was later made into a movie of the same name. One of the leading voices in contemporary American literature, Hijuelos is the author of several novels and short stories that address his Cuban American heritage.

Reinaldo Arenas (1943–1990), who came to the United States in the Mariel boatlift in 1980, was considered one of the leading experimental writers in Cuba. Imprisoned by Fidel Castro for homosexuality and political dissent, Arenas wrote frankly about his erotic life, most notably in his posthumously published memoir, *Before Night Falls*. Arenas committed suicide in New York City in 1990 while in the last stages of AIDS.

Medicine Pedro José Greer Jr., born in 1956 in Miami to Cuban immigrants, has been nationally recognized for his contributions to medical care for the homeless. Greer founded the Camillus Health Concern in Miami and developed a medical-school course that focused on the specific medical needs of homeless persons. He has received numerous awards, including a MacArthur Fellowship in 1993, and has advised the federal government on health care reform. His book *Waking Up in America*, which details his work with the homeless, was published in 1999.

Isabel Pérez Farfante (1916–2009) was a Cuban-born zoologist specializing in the study of crustaceans. She became the first Cuban American woman to graduate from an American Ivy League school when she completed her PhD at Radcliffe College, which at the time was the coordinate college for Harvard University.

Albert Siu is the chairman of the Mount Sinai Medical Center in New York City and is one of the most respected practitioners in the field of geriatrics and palliative medicine.

Music The popular salsa musician Celia Cruz had a cameo role in the film *The Mambo Kings Play Songs of Love.*

Gloria Estefan (1958–), a Cuban-born singer and songwriter, enjoyed top-ten popularity when the song "Conga" propelled her band, Miami Sound Machine, to national prominence in 1985. Estefan went on to launch a successful solo career, selling more than 100 million albums worldwide.

Juan Croucier (1959–), Dave Lombardo (1965–), and Al Jourgenson (1958–) found success in American rock groups Ratt, Slayer, and Ministry, respectively.

Cuba-born Senen Reyes (1965–) and U.S.-born Louis Freese (1970–) were two of the primary members of hip-hop group Cypress Hill.

Politics Lincoln Diaz-Balart (1954–) is a Cuba-born Republican who has been representing Florida as a member of Congress since 1993. U.S. Senator Marco Antonio Rubio (1971–) is a Cuban American who previously served in the Florida House of Representatives, including two years as Speaker of the House.

Robert Menendez (1954–) is a Democratic member of the U.S. Senate, representing New Jersey. Born in New York City to Cuban immigrants, Menendez was also a member of the New Jersey State Assembly and served as mayor of Union City, New Jersey, from 1986 to 1993.

Ileana Ros-Lehtinen (1952–) is a Cuba-born Republican member of Congress from Florida. Born in Havana, Ros-Lehtinen became the first Hispanic woman to serve in Congress after being elected in 1989.

Born in Las Villas, Cuba, Xavier Suarez (1949–) was the first Cuba-born mayor of Miami, serving two separate terms in the 1980s and 1990s.

Bob Martinez (1934–) served as the first Hispanic governor of Florida from 1987 to 1991. In 1991 President George H. W. Bush appointed him director of the Office of National Drug Control Policy.

Sports Tony Oliva (1940–) is a former Major League Baseball (MLB) right fielder and designated hitter for the Minnesota Twins who won the American League batting title three times.

Tony Perez (1942–) was an MLB infielder, mostly with the Cincinnati Reds, and a seven-time National League all-star.

Cuban-born José Canseco (1964–) began playing for the MLB team the Oakland Athletics as an outfielder in 1985, and the following year he was proclaimed rookie of the year. In 1988 Canseco became the first player to have forty home runs and forty stolen bases in one year, though his career was later tarnished by his admitted steroid use.

Rafael Palmiero (1964–) was a perennial MLB all-star and slated to be a Hall of Famer until steroid allegations also tainted his legacy.

Stage and Screen Desi Arnaz (1917–1986) was an actor and musician who is perhaps best remembered for his role in the popular 1950s TV series *I Love Lucy*, which he helped create with his wife, Lucille Ball.

Cuban American dancer Fernando Bujones (1955–) danced with the American Ballet Theatre from 1974 to 1985.

Maria Conchita Alonso (1957–) is a Cuba-born singer and film actress. She has appeared in films such as *Moscow on the Hudson* and *House of the Spirits*, and was nominated for a Grammy Award for a solo album.

Andy Garcia (1956–), a Cuba-born television and film actor, has starred in such films as *The Untouchables*, *Internal Affairs*, *When a Man Loves a Woman*, *Ocean's Eleven*, and *The Godfather Part III*, for which he was nominated for an Oscar for best supporting actor.

Elizabeth Peña (1959–) is a television and movie actress. Born in New Jersey, she has appeared onstage and in such films as *Jacob's Ladder*, *Blue Steel*, *La Bamba*, and *The Waterdance*, as well as in the television series *Hill Street Blues* and *L.A. Law*.

Cameron Diaz (1972–) is a high-profile actress who has starred in blockbuster movies that include *There's Something About Mary*, *Being John Malkovich*, and *Gangs of New York*.

MEDIA

PRINT

Cuba Update

Reflects the aim of the Center for Cuban Studies, which is to disseminate accurate and up-to-date information about Cuba. Recurring features include editorials; book reviews; forums; a calendar of events; notices of publications issued by the center; and news about research, conferences, and exhibitions.

Sandra Levinson, Executive Director
Center for Cuban Studies
231 West 29th Street
Suite 401
New York, New York 10001
Phone: (212) 242-0559
Fax: (212) 242-1937
Email: cubanctr@igc.apc.org
URL: www.cubaupdate.org

Diario Las Américas

Although not strictly Cuban American, one of the principal forums for Cuban American expression since 1953. Its readership is around 70,000.

Alejandro Aguirre, Deputy Editor and Publisher
2900 Northwest 39th Street
Miami, Florida 33142
Phone: (305) 633-3341
Fax: (305) 635-7668

El Nuevo Herald

The Spanish-language subsidiary of the *Miami Herald*. Founded in 1976, it has a circulation of 120,000.

Manny Garcia, Executive Editor
One Herald Plaza
Miami, Florida 33132
Phone: (305) 376-3535
URL: www.elnuevoherald.com

El Nuevo Patria

Founded in 1959; has a circulation of 28,000.

Eladio Jose Armesto, Publisher
P.O. Box 350002
José Martí Station
Miami, Florida 33135
Phone: (305) 530-8787
Fax: (305) 577-8989
Email: enpnews@aol.com
URL: http://elnuevopatria.com

RADIO

WAQI-AM (710)

A Spanish-language news and talk station.

Tomas Regalado, News Director
2690 Coral Way
Miami, Florida 33145
Phone: (305) 445-4040
URL: www.waqi.com

WRHC-AM (1550)

Programs Spanish talk and news shows.

Tomas Regalado, Jr.
3330 Southwest 27th Avenue
2nd Floor
Miami, Florida 33135
Phone: (305) 541-3300
Fax: (305) 541-2013
URL: www.wrhc.com

TELEVISION

WLTV-Channel 23 (Univision) and WSCV-Channel 51 (Telemundo) are two of the most prominent Spanish-language television stations serving the Cuban American population in the Miami area and provide diverse programming created by Cuban American journalists and administrators.

WLTV-Channel 23 (Univision)

Alina Falcon, News Director
215000 Southwest 27th Street
Miramar, Florida 33027
9405 Northwest 41st Street
Miami, Florida 33178
Phone: (305) 471-3900
Fax: (305) 471-4160
URL: http://univision23.univision.com

WSCV-Channel 51 (Telemundo)

Phone: (305) 888-5151
Fax: (305) 888-9270
Email: info51@ypunto.com
URL: www.telemundo51.com

ORGANIZATIONS AND ASSOCIATIONS

Cuban-American Committee

Works to improve interaction between the United States and Cuba.

Alicia Torrez, Executive Director
733 15th Street NW
Suite 1020
Washington, D.C. 20005
Phone: (202) 667-6367

Cuban American National Council (CNC)

Aims to identify the socioeconomic needs of the Cuban population in the United States and to promote human services.

Sonia Lopez, President and CEO
1223 Southwest 4th Street
Miami, Florida 33135
Phone: (305) 642-3484
Fax: (305) 642-7463
Email: info@cnc.org
URL: http://www.cnc.org

Cuban American National Foundation (CANF)

Consists of Americans of Cuban descent and others with an interest in Cuban affairs. Serves as a grassroots lobbying organization promoting freedom and democracy in Cuba and worldwide.

Francisco Hernandez, President
1312 Southwest 27th Avenue
Miami, Florida 33145
Phone: (305) 592-7768
Fax: (305) 592-7889
Email: canfnet@icanect.net
URL: http://www.canf.org

National Association of Cuban American Women of the U.S.A.

Addresses current issues, concerns, and problems affecting Hispanic and minority women.

Siomara Sanchez-Guerra, President
308 38th Street
Union City, New Jersey 07087
Phone: (201) 271-9308
Fax: (201) 223-0035
Email: contactus@nacaw-us.org
URL: www.nacaw-us.org

MUSEUMS AND RESEARCH CENTERS

Center for Cuban Studies (CCS)

An organized collection of individuals and institutions that provide resource materials on Cuba to educational and cultural institutions. Sponsors film showings, lectures, and seminars; organizes tours of Cuba; sponsors art exhibits; and maintains a Cuban art collection with photographic archives, paintings, drawings, ceramics, and posters.

Sandra Levinson, Executive Director
231 West 29th Streat
Suite #401
New York, New York 10001
Phone: (212) 242-0559

Fax: (212) 242-1937
Email: cubanartspace@gmail.com
URL: www.cubanartspace.net/gallery/index.php

Cuban Research Institute

An integral unit of Florida International University, operates under the direction of the Latin American and Caribbean Center. Sponsors an annual teacher training workshop and a journalist workshop in addition to supporting and encouraging research on Cuba.

Jorge Duany, Director
Modesto A. Maidique Campus
Deuxième Maison, 363
11200 Southwest 8th Street
Miami, Florida 33199
Phone: (305) 348-1991
Fax: (305) 348-3593
Email: cri@fiu.edu

SOURCES FOR ADDITIONAL STUDY

Ackerman, Holly, and Juan M. Clark. *The Cuban Balseros: Voyage of Uncertainty*. Miami: Policy Center of the Cuban American National Council, 1995.

Álvarez-Borland, Isabel. *Cuban-American Literature and Art: Negotiating Identities*. Albany: State University of New York Press, 2009.

Boswell, Thomas D., and James R. Curtis. *The Cuban American Experience: Culture, Images, and Perspectives*. Totowa, New Jersey: Rowman and Allanheld, 1983.

De la Garza, Rodolfo O., et al. *Latino Voices: Mexican, Puerto Rican, and Cuban Perspectives on American Politics*. Boulder, Colorado: Westview Press, 1992.

González-Pando, Miguel. *The Cuban Americans*. Westport, CT: Greenwood Press, 1998.

Grenier, Guillermo J., and Lisandro Pérez. *The Legacy of Exile: Cubans in the United States*. Boston: Allyn and Bacon, 2003.

Herrera, Andrea O'Reilly, ed. *Cuba: Idea of a Nation Displaced*. Albany: State University of New York Press, 2007.

Ojito, Mirta A. *Finding Mañana: a Memoir of a Cuban Exodus*. New York: Penguin Press, 2005.

Pérez Firmat, Gustavo. *Life on the Hyphen: The Cuban-American Way*. Austin: University of Texas Press, 1994.

West-Durán, Alan, ed. *Cuba*. Detroit: Charles Scribner's Sons, 2012.

CYPRIOT AMERICANS

Olivia Miller

OVERVIEW

Cypriot Americans are immigrants or descendants of people from the Republic of Cyprus, an island country located at the eastern end of the Mediterranean. Cyprus lies north of Egypt, west of Syria, and south of Turkey. The island of Cyprus is partitioned, essentially along ethnic lines, with the southern part of the country under the control of the Greek government and the northern 37 percent of the land under the autonomous Turkish Cypriot administration, supported by the presence of Turkish troops. Cyprus is the third-largest island in the Mediterranean, after Sicily and Sardinia, measuring 3,572 square miles (9,251 square kilometers), relatively the same size as the state of Connecticut.

According to the 2011 census conducted by the Statistical Service of the Republic of Cyprus, the Greek-controlled portion of the island has a population of 839,000 people; however, the *CIA World Factbook* estimated in 2013 that the total population was closer to 1,155,403 people, including both the southern portion and the Turkish-controlled area of Northern Cyprus. The Greek Cypriot population constitutes approximately 77 percent of the island's population, while the remaining population is made up of 18 percent Turkish Cypriots and 5 percent Christian and Muslim minorities. Similar to the divisions of the ethnic population, Greek Cypriots belong to the Autocephalous Greek Orthodox Church of Cyprus, and Turkish Cypriots practice Sunni Islam. Minority groups, such as the Armenians, the Maronites, and the Latin populations, identify with the Greek Orthodox Church. In 2011 the United Nations (UN) ranked Cyprus at number 31 on its worldwide Human Development Index (HDI), a composite index that measures life expectancy, educational attainment, and income. Although Cyprus maintains a highly functioning, high-income economy with a strong tourist base, the island was not immune to the tumultuous banking crisis that swept through the European Union (EU) in 2012.

Cyprus reports that there was immigration to the United States as early as the 1930s, but there are no available data in the United States before 1955. The first major wave of Greek Cypriot immigrants (approximately 1,500 people) arrived in the United States during the late 1950s and early 1960s, times of political instability and socioeconomic insecurity on the island. Following the 1974 Turkish invasion of Cyprus, more Cypriots immigrated to the United States, a total of 8,343 between 1974 and 2004, according to the U.S. Office of Immigration Statistics.

The 2010 U.S. Census reported that 5,625 people of Cypriot ancestry were living in the United States. Around 36 percent of the population settled in the Northeast, primarily in Flemington, Brickton, and Wayside, New Jersey. Approximately 30 percent of Cypriot Americans live in the western United States, with large concentrations in San Diego and Los Angeles, California. Other states with significant populations of Cypriot Americans include New York, Pennsylvania, Florida, Maryland, and Illinois.

HISTORY OF THE PEOPLE

Early History Cypriot culture is one of the oldest in the Mediterranean region. The discovery of copper on the island in around 3000 BCE led to more frequent visits from traders, as well as invasions by more powerful neighbors. Cypriots were influenced by traders from the Minoan civilization, who developed a script for Cypriot commerce. By 2000 BCE, a distinctively Hellenic culture had developed on Cyprus.

The island was ruled successively by Assyrians, Egyptians, Persians, Greeks, and Romans. Beginning in 364 CE, Byzantium ruled Cyprus for 800 years, during which Cypriots suffered from three centuries of Arab wars. These wars led to the deaths of thousands of Cypriots and the destruction of Cypriot cities, which were never rebuilt. After Richard I of England (reigned 1189–1199) briefly possessed Cyprus during the Crusades, the island came under Frankish control in the late twelfth century. It was ceded to the Venetian Republic in 1489.

Cyprus was subsequently conquered by the Ottoman Turks in 1571. During this time, nearly 6,000 Turkish households were resettled into approximately 100 empty villages in the Mesaoria, Mazoto, and Paphos regions of Cyprus. The Ottomans allowed religious authorities in Cyprus to govern their own non-Muslim minorities, reinforcing the position of the Orthodox Church and the union of the ethnic Greek population.

Modern Era Most of the Turks who settled on the island during the three centuries of Ottoman rule remained after control of Cyprus was yielded to Great Britain in 1878. The British had been offered Cyprus three times (in 1833, 1841, and 1845) before accepting it in 1878 to prevent Russian expansion into the area. At the time of British arrival under the Cyprus Defense Alliance between Great Britain and the Ottoman Empire, approximately 95,000 Turkish Cypriots lived on the island. Many, however, moved to Turkey during the 1920s. The island was formally annexed by the United Kingdom in 1914, at the outbreak of World War I. It became a British colony in 1925.

After almost a century of British rule, Cyprus gained its independence in 1960 under the Treaty of Guarantee, which provided that Greece, Turkey, and Britain would ensure the independence and sovereignty of the Republic of Cyprus. Independence was spearheaded by the Greek Cypriot EOKA (*Ethniki Organosis Kyprion Agoniston*, or National Organization of Cypriot Fighters), a guerrilla group that pushed for political union with Greece. Archbishop Makarios, a charismatic religious and political leader, was elected president. Almost immediately the two communities disagreed over the implementation and interpretation of the constitution, and by December 1963 Turkish Cypriots ceased participation in the central government. Nearly 80 percent of the population, who were ethnically Greek, wanted *enosis*, or union with Greece. Ethnic Turks, however, who made up a little less than 20 percent of the population, wanted *haksim*, or partition from Greece. UN peacekeepers were deployed on the island in 1964 and remain there. Following another outbreak of intercommunal violence during 1967 and 1968, a Turkish Cypriot provisional administration was formed. Because of its strategic location and its impact on the national interests of Greece and Turkey, Cyprus has led North Atlantic Treaty Organization (NATO) allies close to war several times over its control.

Believing that Makarios had abandoned the idea of Cyprus uniting with Greece, the Athens military sponsored a coup led by extremist Greek Cypriots in July 1974. Citing the 1960 Treaty of Guarantee, Turkey intervened militarily to protect Turkish Cypriots, sending troops to take control of the northern portion of the island. Many Greek Cypriots fled south, while many Turkish Cypriots fled north. Some 30,000 Turkish mainland troops still occupy the northern part of the island, while 10,000 Greek Cypriot national guardsmen protect the south. Since then the country has been divided, with the government of Cyprus controlling the southern region and the Turkish Cypriot administration controlling the northern region.

In 1983 the Turkish Cypriot administration proclaimed itself the Turkish Republic of Northern Cyprus; it was recognized only by Turkey. UN peacekeeping forces maintain a buffer zone between the two sides. Except for occasional demonstrations or infrequent incidents between soldiers in the buffer zone, there were no violent conflicts between 1974 and 1995. However, in 1996 violent clashes led to the deaths of two demonstrators and escalated Greek-Turkish tensions. There remained little movement of citizens and essentially no trading of goods or services between the two parts of the island. Efforts to reunite the island under a federal structure continued, however, under the auspices of the UN, whose efforts focus on creating a bizonal, bicommunal state under a federated government. In 1999 the UN sponsored talks between the Greek and Turkish sides in an effort to secure a comprehensive settlement, known as the Annan Plan. Between 1999 and 2003, the UN spearheaded a series of negotiations in anticipation of Cyprus joining the EU, leading to a series of revisions to the Annan Plan. Known as Annan III, the 2003 version was presented to the Turkish Cypriot president Rauf Denktash and the newly elected Greek Cypriot president Tassos Papadopoulos. The effort dissolved, however, in March of that year when Denktash refused to put the measure to a referendum, citing his belief that the plan did not adequately account for the needs of the Turkish Cypriot people.

With the May 2004 date for Cyprus to join the EU looming, the involved parties pressured both the Greek and Turkish sides to resume negotiations. Portions of the militarized buffer zone were opened, allowing citizens of both parts of Cyprus to cross the border at open checkpoints. In 2003 Mehmet Ali Talat—running on a pro–Annan Plan platform—won election as prime minister of Northern Cyprus over the incumbent, Derviş Eroğlu. Similarly, Recep Tayyip Erdoğan had won election as prime minister of Turkey earlier that year and pushed toward negotiations that would open up relations between the two sides as well as respect the needs of Turkish Cyprus.

In early 2004 UN secretary-general Kofi Annan presented the revised plan, Annan IV, to both leaders. Following highly volatile and contentious negotiations, the plan was amended and revised, culminating in the final version, Annan V. In April 2004 simultaneous votes in Greek Cyprus and Turkish Cyprus were held to approve the stipulations of reunification under the Annan Plan. An overwhelming majority of Turkish Cypriots voted in favor of the plan; however, Greek Cypriots voted against it, claiming that the settlement would violate Cyprus's sovereignty because Turkey would maintain its troops in Cyprus while the Cyprus National Guard would be dissolved. Relationships between the two sides remained strained as Papadopoulos took a hardline approach to dealing with the Turkish minority. Continued negotiations stalled, and the two sides operated under separate, sovereign states. In 2008 Dimitris Christofias, candidate for the AKEL, the communist party of Cyprus, was elected president over the nationalist, right-wing candidate Ioannis Kasoulidis. Almost immediately Christofias opened up talks with Talat, and the wall that had separated the two parts of the country was demolished. In April 2008, Ledra Street, the centerpiece of the buffer zone and the main artery in the capital city of Nicosia, was reopened. Reunification talks, however, lost traction when nationalists gained a majority in the 2009 parliamentary elections.

Like much of the EU, Cyprus suffered through the economic crisis that erupted throughout the region and the world in 2008 and 2009. Because Cyprus relied heavily on the Greek economy, the country was immensely vulnerable when Greece was consumed by debt. By 2011 Cyprus's credit rating had been reduced to "junk status," and Cyprus was unable to borrow from international credit agencies. Rising debt levels forced many EU nations, including Cyprus, to look to third-party governments for assistance. In spite of their best efforts, many of the nations were forced to seek bailouts from Brussels. Poised to take control of the presidency of the EU in 2011, Cyprus, which many viewed as a microcosm of the financial crisis, was forced to borrow close to 10 billion euros (approximately $12 billion U.S.). In 2012 Talat and Christofias renewed negotiations to push for a reunification settlement, but many of the initial problems remained, with Greek Cypriots advocating for a bilateral agreement between the two communities.

SETTLEMENT IN THE UNITED STATES

There is no information available on immigration to the United States from Cyprus before 1955. The earliest Cypriot immigrants may have been a wave of Turkish Cypriots came to the United States between 1820 and 1860, likely fleeing religious or political persecution.

Most Cypriot Americans immigrated to the United States in order to escape a variety of economic, political, and military upheavals. In the early part of the twentieth century, Cypriots, like many of their European counterparts, immigrated to the United States looking for economic and social opportunities. Most of the immigrants came from rural areas that suffered through drought, particularly in 1932–1933. Settling primarily in the northeastern United States, Cypriots formed small communities and opened up coffeehouses. Cypriots maintained a steady flow of immigration into the 1930s, developing communities that were loosely associated with their village of origin. During the 1950s, Greek Cypriots pushed for independence

from British colonial rule. The violence escalated, and in the spring of 1955, the pro-nationalist group EOKA launched attacks against British military and police. For four years EOKA utilized guerrilla warfare tactics, targeting British interests and sympathizers. According to immigration statistics, 749 Greek Cypriots immigrated to the United States during this time.

The Republic of Cyprus was established in August 1960, but the new nation was rife with problems. EOKA had based its anticolonial campaign on a potential union with Greece. Turkish Cypriots resisted the move, and after negotiations the UN established a constitution that would protect the interests of both sides. Uncertainty over the newly formed government as well as over the stability of the nation led to a mass emigration between 1960 and 1963. Approximately 37,000 Cypriots fled the country. Most settled in Britain, and 720 are recorded as immigrating to the United States. The tenuous provisional government was undercut by increasing moments of civil unrest as intercommunal violence broke out in the latter part of the 1960s. Between 1964 and 1974, approximately 30,000 Cypriots fled the bloodshed, with just over 3,000 Cypriots immigrating to the United States. In 1974 the Cypriot National Guard overthrew President Makarios and replaced him with Nikos Sampson, a staunch Greek nationalist who championed anti-Turkish policies. In response, Turkey invaded Cyprus in July 1974, claiming that an invasion was the only means to protect the Turkish Cypriots from further violence. Following the Turkish invasion, 8,343 Cypriots immigrated to the United States between 1974 and 2004, according to the Office of Immigration Statistics.

Although many of the immigrants came from rural areas, Cypriots tended to settle in large urban communities. Cypriots in urban centers tended to find employment in the restaurant and service industries, while Cypriots who migrated to the Midwest sought agricultural jobs. Similar to other immigrant communities, as families progressed, broader opportunities were afforded to the younger generations. By the end of the twentieth century, over half of Cypriot immigrants were employed as professionals.

The 2010 U.S. Census reported that 5,625 Americans stated they were of Cypriot ancestry. Some Cypriots settled in the Midwest and along the West Coast, but the largest communities reside in New York, New Jersey, and Florida. Other states with significant numbers of Cypriot Americans are California, Pennsylvania, Maryland, and Illinois.

LANGUAGE

The three principal languages spoken in the Republic of Cyprus are Greek, Turkish, and English. Modern Greek contains twenty-four characters,

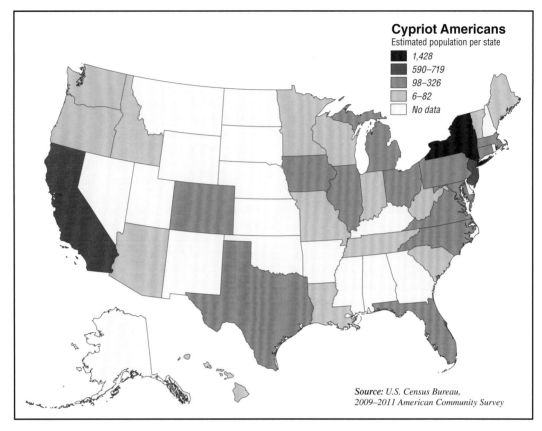

Cypriot Americans
Estimated population per state

- 1,428
- 590–719
- 98–326
- 6–82
- No data

*Source: U.S. Census Bureau,
2009–2011 American Community Survey*

with five vowels and four vowel sounds. It is written in Attic characters; their names, transliterations, and pronunciations are as follows:

> *Aa*—alpha/a (ah); *Bß*—beta/v (v); *Gg*—gamma/g (gh, y); *Dd*—delta/d, dh (th); *Ee*—epsilon/e (eh); *Zz*—zeta/z (z); *Hh*—eta/e (ee); *Qq*—theta/th (th); *Ii*—yiota/i (ee); *Kk*—kappa/k, c (k); *Ll*—lambda/l (l); *Mm*—mu/m (m); *Nn*—nee/n (n); *Xx*—kse/x (ks); *Oo*—omicron/o (oh); *Pp*—pee/p (p); *Rr*—rho/r (r); *Ss*—sigma/s (s); *Tt*—taf/t (t); *Uu*—ypsilon/y (ee); *Ff*—fee/ph (f); *Cc*—khee/h (ch [as in ach]); *Yy*—psee/ps (ps [as in lapse]); *Ww*—omega/o (oh).

For Greek Cypriots, the "b" sound of standard Greek is usually replaced with a "p," so that a Cypriot says "tapella" for "tabella," meaning sign or placard. The letter combination sigmi-iota (*s-i*) is pronounced as "sh." When *k* begins a word, it sounds more like "g," as in "good," and the letter *t* sounds more like "d," as in "dog."

Turkish is the official language of Northern Cyprus, but English is the standard second language for Cypriots in both ethnic communities. The Turkish dialect spoken by Turkish Cypriots is closely related to other dialects of Anatolia but is distinct from the

urban dialects of Istanbul, Ankara, and Zmir. Turkish Cypriots followed the reforms of Mustafa Kamal, a Turkish World War I hero who became known as "Ataturk," or "father of the Turks." Ataturk drove the Greeks out of Turkey and initiated many reforms, including replacing the Arabic alphabet with a modified Latin alphabet. The Turkish Cypriot community was the only Turkish minority in former Ottoman territories outside mainland Turkey to adopt these linguistic changes.

Turkish is part of the Ural-Altaic linguistic group. The alphabet consists of twenty-nine letters—twenty-one consonants and eight vowels. Six of these letters do not occur in the English alphabet. Turkish has no gender distinction, and there is no differentiation between he, she, and it. Several Turkish American organizations in the United States teach Turkish, but few second- and third-generation Turkish Americans speak the language.

Similar to many immigrant communities in the United States, both Greek and Turkish Cypriot Americans continue to speak their native tongue within the home. However, because both communities speak English as a second language, the transition between private and public language use is much more fluid for Cypriot Americans than it is for other immigrant groups. In the 2010 U.S. Census, close to 68 percent of respondents who spoke Greek in their homes in the New York City Metropolitan Area reported that they could speak English "very well." Statistical data for Turkish Cypriots is harder to discern, but anecdotal evidence suggests that Turkish Cypriots enjoy the same proficiency with English. Since the 1980s both communities have attempted to rejuvenate their traditional languages by enrolling their children in programs that teach Greek and Turkish.

Greetings and Popular Expressions For Greek Cypriots, *éla!* means "come here and speak to me," and *Pó-pó-pó!*—"You don't say!"—is an expression of dismay. The standard telephone response is *Embrós!* or *Léyeteh! Orísteh?* means "What can I do for you?" *Sigá sigá* means "Take your time and slow down." Other popular Greek expressions include *cronia polla* (pronounced "chrohnyah pohllah"), which means "many years/happy birthday"; and *kalh tuch* ("kahlee teechee"), which means "good year."

Common expressions among Turkish Cypriot Americans include the following: *Merhaba*, which means "hello"; *Gun aylin*, which means "good morning"; *Iyi Aksamlar*, which means "good evening"; *Bilmiyorum*, which means "I don't know"; *Bir dakika!* which means "wait a minute"; *Tesekkur ederim*, which means "thank you"; and *Na'pan*, a friendly "What are you doing?"

RELIGION

Most Greek Cypriots are Greek Orthodox Christians, followers of the Church of Cyprus, a tradition using the Greek liturgy and headed by a synod composed of bishops and an elected archbishop. Turkish Cypriots are Muslims and form the second-largest religious group. Ritual is the center of activity for the Orthodox Church. Seven sacraments are recognized: baptism in infancy, followed by confirmation with consecrated oil, penance, the Eucharist, matrimony, ordination, and unction in times of sickness or when near death. Many Greek Cypriot Americans are members of local Orthodox churches founded by Greek immigrants. The church has routinely functioned as a locus for social and political identity for Greek Cypriots, resulting in a generational space in which Greek Cypriots can identify simultaneously with both their homeland and their growing American community. Although overall church attendance has declined in the United States, close to 50 percent of Cypriots reported that they attend church on a regular basis, according to the 2010 estimates by the U.S. Census Bureau's American Community Survey.

Although 98 percent of Northern Cyprus's population are Muslims, the Turkish administration that controls the region does not impose Islam on the people. The few Greek Cypriots who live in Northern Cyprus are free to follow their Greek Orthodox faith. Turkish Cypriots are among the most secular of Islamic peoples, not abstaining from alcohol as standard Muslim teaching requires but following traditional Mediterranean drinking customs. Wedding ceremonies are civil rather than religious. Religious leaders have little influence on politics in Northern Cyprus, and religious instruction, while available in schools, is not obligatory. Although there is some fasting during the month of Ramadan, moderate attendance at the Friday prayers, and widespread observation of the Muslim holy days, few Turkish Cypriots are orthodox Muslims. Some Turkish Cypriot immigrants become more devoted Muslims after they settle in the United States, but most Turkish Cypriot Americans continue a less fervent adherence to Muslim beliefs.

CULTURE AND ASSIMILATION

Cypriot Americans are family-oriented and hardworking. Greek and Turkish Cypriots share many customs but maintain distinct identities based on religion, language, and close ties with Greece and Turkey. Greek Cypriots tend to settle where there are established Greek communities, and these surroundings help immigrants become accustomed to the new culture. Turkish Cypriot Americans often face a more difficult time adjusting, as many Americans have negatively stereotyped Turks as "Islamic terrorists." The earliest Turk immigrants settled in industrial cities and found factory work. A large part of the American Turkish community, however, returned to Turkey before the Depression during the 1930s. In the early twenty-first century, the Turkish American community is small and close-knit. Turkish Cypriot Americans tend to be more accepted among American Turks than among Greek Cypriot Americans.

Traditions and Customs The ancient Greek poets and playwrights frequently mention the early influences of Cyprus. Aphrodite, the Greek goddess of love and beauty, was said to have been born out of the sea foam on Cyprus's west coast. The most important temple to Aphrodite was built at Paphos in Cyprus, where the love goddess was worshiped for centuries. In his epics the *Iliad* and the *Odyssey*, the poet Homer mentions Aphrodite and a Cypriot king, Kinyras of Paphosin.

Greek Cypriots are proud of their Greek heritage. Greek Cypriot Americans continue strong church traditions, such as abstaining from meat, fish, or dairy products during the Lenten season. Easter is the most celebrated religious holiday for Greek Cypriot Americans. *Avgolemono* soup, made from eggs and lemons in chicken stock, is traditional Easter fare, as are *flaounes*, savory Easter cakes that contain a special Easter cheese, eggs, spices, and herbs, all wrapped in a yeast pastry.

Turkish Cypriots value a society in which roles are clearly defined. For example, they regard public service as a more prestigious (though low-paying) occupation than a successful business career. Turkish Cypriot Americans, though not strict Muslims, also often become a part of the Muslim community in the United States. Adjustments to American culture tend to be more difficult for them than for Greek Cypriot immigrants.

Cuisine The distinctive dishes created by Cypriots blend Greek traditions with influences from other countries, including Turkey, Armenia, Lebanon, Syria, Italy, France, and Britain. Cypriots cook with less oil than their Mediterranean neighbors, and their diet is healthy. A popular food is *halloumi*, the traditional white cheese of Cyprus, which has been produced on the island for centuries. It is a semihard cheese prepared from sheep's milk, with mint added to it. Halloumi is delicious when grilled or fried. Greek Cypriots enjoy traditional Greek foods, such as *baklava*, which is made from phyllo pastry, nuts, honey, and syrup.

Cypriots drink a lot of coffee, and the beverage is made in individual servings in small, long-handled pots called *mbrikia*. One heaped teaspoon of finely ground fresh coffee is added to a demitasse of cold water. Sugar is added before the coffee is heated. Cypriots order coffee *glykos* (sweet), *metrios* (medium sweet), or *sketos* (unsweetened). The *mbrikia* is heated on the stove, and when the sugar has dissolved, the coffee is allowed to come to a boil, forming a creamy froth, *kaimaki*, on top. As the froth turns in from the sides and the coffee begins to rise in the pot, it is removed from the heat, and a little is poured into each cup to distribute the froth. Cyprus coffee is strong and is always served with a glass of cold water. It contains no spices and leaves a little sediment in the bottom of the cup.

Turkish Cypriot cuisine owes its heritage to a mixture of Mediterranean, southern European, and Middle Eastern influences. Local dishes include *meze*, a specialty of Cyprus that consists of a large number of cold and hot hors d'oeuvres, such as salads, meats, vegetables, and fish dishes. It is eaten either as an appetizer or as a main course. Other typical dishes include *choban salatasi* (peasant-style salad), one of the most popular salads in Northern Cyprus. Ingredients include tomatoes, onions, green peppers, olives, cucumber, halloumi cheese, oregano, and olive oil. *Yalanci dolma* is vine leaves stuffed with rice, onions, and tomatoes. *Shish kebab* is marinated lamb, skewered and grilled over charcoal. *Musakka* consists of layers of mince, potatoes, and eggplant baked in the oven with cheese topping. *Cacik* is yogurt with cucumber and mint. *Ahtapot salatasi* is octopus salad.

Desserts and pastries from Turkish Cyprus include *ceviz macunu*, made from green walnuts in syrup; *lokum*, which is Turkish delight; *turunch macunu*, a delicacy made of bitter oranges in syrup; and *sucuk*, a traditional Cypriot sweet, made of thickened grape juice and almonds.

Northern Cyprus produces a small number of wines, the best known of which are *aphrodite* and *kantara*. Both wines are light and fruity and make good accompaniments to local dishes. The country also produces its own sherry, called *monarch*. A locally famous drink is the anise seed-based *raki*, and brandy sour is another favorite with the Turkish Cypriots.

Traditional Dress Traditional Cypriot clothing included simple cottons and silks with little variation from village to village. The outer garments were made from *alatzia*, a durable cotton cloth similar to ticking, usually with fine vertical or crossed stripes in deep red, blue, yellow, orange, or green on a white ground. Men's shirts and women's dresses for everyday wear were generally of blue alatzia with white stripes. Black was substituted for blue in the cloth used for the jackets of elderly men, while those of younger men were of standard red-striped *alatzia zibounisimi*. There were local variations for the festival costumes, which had a characteristic color combination and were named according to their source of origin, such as *marateftikes*, *morphitoudes*, *lapithkiotikes*, and *interalia*.

In medieval times Cyprus was known for its silk bridal chemises and undergarments. Though the fabric varied from region to region, the fine pure silk and the silk and cotton *taista* and *itaredes* of Nicosia and the towns of Lapithos and Karavas in Karpasia were impressive. Everyday chemises were made of white, hand-woven cottons. There were few distinct regional differences in the male costume of Cyprus, which generally was the densely pleated baggy trousers (*vra'ka*), the waistcoat (*yilekko*), and the jacket (*zibouni*). The Cypriot female costume consisted of an outer garment, a chemise, and distinctive long pantaloons fastened at the ankle. The *saya*, a kind of frock open at the front and sides, was common in most urban and rural regions of Cyprus until the nineteenth century. The *foustani*, a one-piece waisted and pleated dress, was the preferred overgarment in the rural areas of Cyprus well into the 1950s.

Dances and Songs The traditional Turkish folk dances of Cyprus vary significantly based on the dancers and musicians, the region of origin, and the theme. The names for dances also change with these variables. Many are known by the accompanying items, including wooden spoons, sword and shield, knife, and drinking glass. There are Turkish Cypriot folk dances, such as the circle, semicircle, one-lined, and double-lined. Few of these dances are performed solely by either men or women. Traditional Greek dances may be danced in a circle, in a straight line, or between couples.

Varieties of Greek Cypriot music include *dimotika*, *laika* (or *laïkó*), and *evropaika*. Dimotika are traditional rural folk songs often accompanied by a clarinet, a lute, a violin, a dulcimer, and a drum. Laika is an urban-style song popularized in the mid-twentieth century that may feature the *bouzouki*, a long-necked string instrument. *Evropaika* is Euro-style music set to Greek words that is popular with the older generations.

Holidays Greek Cypriots celebrate many Greek Orthodox holy days throughout the year in addition to Christmas, Easter, and New Year's Day. New Year's Day is known as St. Basil's Day in Cyprus. In celebration a special cake called *vasilopitta* is baked by each family, and when it is cut, the person who finds a coin in his slice is promised luck for the next year. Greek Cypriot Americans celebrate Cyprus Independence Day on October 1, and many celebrate Greek Independence Day on March 25, commemorating Greek independence from the Ottoman Empire in 1821. Turkish Cypriot Americans observe both civil and religious holidays. In addition, Turkish Americans began a unique holiday in 1984, celebrating Turkish American Day with a parade down New York's Fifth Avenue.

FAMILY AND COMMUNITY LIFE

The family is traditionally the most important institution in Greek Cypriot society. In villages people think of themselves primarily as members of families. Greek Cypriot households typically consist of a father, a mother, and their unmarried children. Traditionally, marriages are arranged, generally through the mediation of a matchmaker. When children marry, parents give them a portion of land, if available, along with money and household items. Even at the beginning of the 1990s, such economic considerations remained a decisive factor in marriage settlements. From 1985 to 1989, the country's annual marriage rate was the highest in Europe. On the other hand, the divorce rate among Greek Cypriots almost doubled between 1980 and 1988. The number of extramarital births, however, remains very low by European standards.

In the United States, Greek Cypriots have attempted to balance their traditional beliefs within the larger culture. American culture affords women the ability to break from patriarchal family structures while also contributing to the development of Greek American culture. The family continues to serve as a mechanism of historical memory, but it also has become a place in which families test their new identities against their traditional beliefs. Second and third generations of immigrants have been able to secure better education and employment opportunities, creating a larger tension between upholding traditional values with the demands of the larger culture.

Turkish Cypriots are also concerned with encouraging economic prosperity within their families. A major portion of household income goes to educating children, finding them suitable spouses, and helping them find good jobs. More than in most Western societies, Turkish Cypriots are conscious of their extended family. The nuclear or core traditional family might include not only the husband, the wife, and their unmarried children, but also a newly married son and his family and sometimes the mother's parents. The presence of the mother's parents in the core family is an important variation from the traditional Turkish family structure, in which the husband's parents live with the family.

CYPRIOT PROVERBS

Cypriots have many proverbs, including the following:

Abu binni grasin vereshe, methkia thkio fores.

> He who drinks wine on debt gets drunk twice.

Athkiaseros babas thafki je dus zondanus.

> A priest with time on his hands buries even the living.

Biamen belli j' irtamen arkobelli.

> We went as fools and came back as arch-fools.

Do galon horkon golauzin en theli.

> A good village needs no guide.

Enan shelionin en ferni din annixin.

> One swallow doesn't bring the spring.

I abandisi du bellu en i siobi.

> The response to a fool is silence.

I alithkia je do lain banda fkennun bubano.

> Truth and oil always rise above.

O fronimos eyinin du bellu ghaurin.

> The wise man became the fool's donkey.

Thkio yelun gadi xerun, enas yela bellos eni.

> Two who laugh know something; one who laughs is mad.

Zefkarin aderkaston, horafin sherisson.

> An ill-matched couple is a barren field.

As with virtually every immigrant group in the United States, traditional practices and values tend to decline with each succeeding generation. Particularly among Greek Cypriot Americans, but also among the Turkish Cypriots, each succeeding generation increasingly embraces the patterns and practices of the dominant American culture. Old-world practices and beliefs that are viewed as quaint fall into disuse, and traditional celebrations increasingly cluster around such events as baptisms, marriages, and religious holidays.

Education The Republic of Cyprus boasts a high level of education and a 99 percent literacy rate. For Greek Cypriots, pre-primary, primary, and secondary levels in academic and technical vocational high schools are free and mandatory. Higher education is available at specialized schools and at a university that opened in the early 1990s.

The majority of Cypriots who pursue higher education do so at Greek, Turkish, British, or American universities. Many Cypriots are educated at foreign universities, and the percentage of Cypriot students studying at the university level is among the highest in the world. During the 1970s and 1980s, an average of more than 10,000 Cypriots studied abroad annually, mostly in Greece and Britain. In the 1980s the United States became a major destination for Cypriot students going abroad, generally surpassing Britain. Studying abroad continued to be common into the early twenty-first century, with approximately 78.7 percent of Cypriot university students studying abroad in 2009. The number of women studying abroad increased during the 1970s and 1980s, from 24 percent in 1970 to 40 percent in 1987.

Gender Roles Modern Greek Cypriot American women are typically better educated than their mothers and are more likely to work outside the home. While the traditional domestic role is still an expectation, Greek Cypriot American women are more likely to balance the homemaking responsibilities with a professional occupation.

After World War II, Greek Cypriot women had greater access to education and increased their participation in the workforce. At the beginning of the twentieth century, the ratio of girls to boys enrolled in primary education was one to three. By 1943 about 80 percent of girls attended primary school. When elementary education was made mandatory in 1960, there were equal enrollment levels for boys and girls. By the 1980s girls made up 45 percent of those receiving secondary education. Only after the mid-1960s did women commonly leave Cyprus to receive

Cypriot American cinematographer Harris Savides (1957–2012) attends the Cinema Society and Details screening of *Milk* at the Landmark Sunshine Theater in 2008 in New York City. JIM SPELLMAN/WIREIMAGE/ GETTY IMAGES

higher education. In the 1980s women made up about 32 percent of those studying abroad. By 2006 more women than men studied abroad.

Cypriot women have long participated in the workforce, traditionally in agriculture. From 1960 to 1985, the women's share of the urban workforce rose from 22 percent to 41 percent, while their share of the rural workforce fell from 51 percent to 44.4 percent. Special protective legislation in 1985 provided women with marriage grants and maternity grants that paid them 75 percent of their insurable earnings. Occupational gender segregation persisted in Cyprus at the beginning of the twenty-first century.

Reflecting cultural imperatives, Turkish Cypriot women are bound by traditional rules to a greater extent than their Greek counterparts. Although most Cypriot women work outside the home, they were expected to fulfill the traditional domestic roles with little help from their husbands. Women with full-time jobs were pressured by the traditional standards of keeping a clean house and providing daily hot meals. In the 1990s Cypriot Muslim women were still burdened with the expectation of safeguarding the honor of the family by avoiding any social contact with men that could be construed to have a sexual content. Whatever their career or other outside responsibilities, a woman is expected to keep a "good home" and to raise children who are aware and proud of their heritage.

Courtship and Weddings In Greek Cypriot culture, an engagement is traditionally preceded by negotiations between parents, but parents do not force their children to accept arranged marriages. This once-universal practice is declining in Cyprus, however, and Cypriot Americans usually choose their mates without parental involvement.

For Turkish Cypriots, marriage and divorce are governed by law based on the Quran. Turkish law applies in all religious and family matters among Muslims and in marriages and engagements involving a non-Muslim woman. Marriage between a Muslim woman and a non-Muslim man is prohibited. Turkish Cypriots traditionally married someone from their own lineage, the descendants of a common ancestor connected through the male line. Turkish Cypriot Americans do not follow the custom of marriage within the lineage. Even in Cyprus, marriage within one's lineage became less common in the second half of the twentieth century.

In Greek Cyprus the most popular time for weddings is in the summer, and the whole village celebrates. *Resi*, a rich pilaf of lamb and wheat, is prepared, and special little shortbreads, *loukoumi*, are piled high for the guests. The sponsor at a Cypriot wedding, similar to an American best man or maid of honor, becomes a ceremonial relative. The male sponsor, *koumbaros*, or female sponsor, *koumbara*, is expected to pay for all of the wedding expenses, except the purchase of the rings. The sponsor usually becomes the godparent of the couple's first child, and sponsors are considered to be relatives, part of the extended family. Most weddings involve several sponsors.

Traditionally, the bridegroom provided the house, and the bride's family supplied the furniture and linens. These items constituted the dowry, the allocation of an equal portion of the parents' property to the children, male or female, at the time of marriage, rather than after the death of the parents. Until the 1950s this transfer of property at marriage was agreed to orally by the parties involved; more recently the so-called written dowry contract has been introduced. A formal agreement specifying the amount of property to be given to the couple, the dowry contract is signed by all parties and enforced by religious authorities. After World War II it became the bride's obligation to provide the house. Ownership of a house, given the scarcity of land (especially after the invasion of 1974) and the considerable expense of building, became a great advantage for a single woman seeking to marry. In the 1990s a working woman's income went primarily toward the construction of a house.

In rural Turkish Cypriot society, the wedding festivities traditionally lasted for several days. Modern Turkish Cypriot couples often do not rely on their parents to arrange a match. Although dating, as practiced in the United States, was not common even at the beginning of the twenty-first century, couples often met in small groups of friends. Once a couple decided to marry, both sets of parents were consulted. The families then arranged the engagement and marriage.

Turkish Cypriots adapted the Greek Cypriot tradition of the bride's family providing substantial assistance to the newlyweds. Turkish Cypriots modified it to include assistance from both families. Traditionally, the bride's family provided a house, some furniture, and money as part of their daughter's dowry. The bridegroom's family met the young couple's remaining housing needs. If the bride's family was unable to provide such assistance, the young couple lived with the bride's family until they saved enough money to set up a separate household. The bride brought to her new home the rest of her dowry, known as *cehiz*, which made the new family financially more secure. Turkish Cypriot Americans often provide their own housing, though families will send assistance where possible.

Baptisms For Greek Cypriot children, the naming of the child is done at baptism, not at birth. After a child has been baptized, his or her name day, meaning the day of the saint for whom he or she was named, is celebrated each year instead of his or her actual birthday or day of baptism.

The wedding sponsors, or *koumbari*, also act as godparents to the first child. The baptism ceremony

U.S.-CYPRUS RELATIONS

Relations between Cyprus and the United States were hindered by the 1974 assassination of U.S. Ambassador Roger Davies in Nicosia. The Nixon and Ford administrations became involved in refugee resettlement and peace talks during the 1974 crisis, and a more activist American policy was institutionalized. A special Cyprus coordinator position in the Department of State was established in 1981. The position was first held by Reginald Bartholomew (1981–1982) and later by Thomas Weston (1999–2004). In June 1997 the United States appointed Ambassador Richard C. Holbrooke as special presidential emissary for Cyprus. Efforts to stimulate discussion about confidence-building measures, intercommunal projects and cooperation, and new directions in the United States' annual aid program to Cyprus met with resistance from the republic's government. The republic looked to the U.S. Congress and the Greek American community to correct what they considered a pro-Turkish bias in U.S. policy.

Since the mid-1970s the United States has channeled millions of dollars in assistance to the two communities through the United Nations High Commissioner for Refugees and the Cyprus Red Cross. The United States provides funds annually to promote bicommunal projects and to finance U.S. scholarships for Greek and Turkish Cypriots. Successive U.S. administrations have viewed UN-led intercommunal negotiations as the best means to achieve a fair and permanent settlement in Cyprus. Beginning in 1999, the United States aided the UN secretary-general's efforts to settle the divisions in Cyprus. Following the Annan Plan, the Obama administration announced that it would continue to push for a single government that adequately represented both the Turkish and the Greek Cypriots. These efforts tend to be hampered by strong and continuing antagonism between the Greeks and Turks—an antagonism sharpened by the strife of the twentieth century as well as historic antipathy reaching back to the days of Ottoman rule.

of the Greek Orthodox Church is a special ceremony involving several steps. It begins at the narthex of the church, where the godparents speak for the child, renounce Satan, blow three times in the air, and spit three times on the floor. After the Nicene Creed is recited, the child's name is spoken for the first time. At the front of the church, the priest uses consecrated water to make the sign of the cross on various parts of the child, who is undressed. The godparents rub the child with olive oil, and the priest immerses the child in water three times before handing the child to the godparents, who wrap him in a new white sheet. Following baptism, the child is anointed with a special oil (*miron*) and dressed in new clothing. A candle is lit, and the priest and godparents hold the child while other children walk around in a dance signifying joy. Then scriptures are read, and Communion is given to the child. The parents will often sponsor a joyous celebration, including a lavish meal, after the ceremony.

white-collar professions. The expanding economy in the second half of the twentieth century allowed many Cypriots to obtain more sophisticated work than their parents had. Within one generation, a family could move from an agricultural background to urban professions in teaching, government, or small business. The traditional economy of subsistence agriculture and animal husbandry was replaced by a commercial economy, centered in expanding urban areas. The flight from agriculture reached a peak in 1974, when the best and most productive agricultural land fell under Turkish occupation. In 1960 some 40.3 percent of the economically active population were agricultural workers; in 1973 the figure was down to 33.6 percent. In 1988 government figures estimated that only 13.9 percent of the workforce earned a living from farming full-time.

POLITICS AND GOVERNMENT

Numerous Greek American political and social organizations have existed since the 1880s. Turkish American involvement in U.S. politics did not begin until the Turkish invasion of Cyprus in 1974 mobilized individuals seeking to counter the U.S. government's support for the Greeks. In the 1990s Cypriot American organizations for both Greek and Turk ethnic groups exerted lobbying influences aimed at seeking political advantage in Cyprus. Cypriot Americans remain involved in political issues of importance to Cyprus.

Greek Cypriot immigrants feel patriotic duties to both Cyprus and the United States. During both World Wars, Greek Cypriot Americans served in the U.S. armed forces and participated in assorted war fund drives. Cypriots were staunch supporters of the Allied cause in World War II, particularly after the invasion of Greece by Germany in 1940. The draft was not imposed on the colony, but during the war more than 30,000 Cypriot volunteers served in the British forces.

NOTABLE INDIVIDUALS

Academics Chrysostomos L. Nikias (1952–) is a Greek Cypriot American who was appointed president of the University of Southern California in 2010. Symeon C. Symeonides is a Cyprus-born Greek Cypriot American who began serving as dean of the Willamette Law School in 1999.

Government Charlie Crist (1956–), an American of Greek Cypriot heritage, served as governor of Florida from 2007 to 2011.

Sports Garo Yepremian (1944–), football placekicker from 1966 to 1981, was born in Larnaca, Cyprus. He played for the Miami Dolphins and led the National Football League in scoring in 1971.

Stage and Screen Hal Ozsan (1976–) is a British-born actor of Turkish Cypriot descent who moved to the United States in the 1990s; he is known primarily for his role in the television series *Dawson's Creek* but continued to appear in a variety of television shows, including *Californication, Beverly Hills, 90210,* and *Bones.*

EMPLOYMENT AND ECONOMIC CONDITIONS

Greek Cypriot Americans tend to be highly educated. Many are teachers and academics. Turkish Cypriot Americans are also highly educated and are often employed as physicians, scientists, and engineers. While many immigrants in the first half of the twentieth century were unskilled laborers who found employment in large industrial cities, subsequent immigrants were highly skilled professionals employed in virtually every field. Among Cypriot Americans, education is valued as a mark of status, but it also is viewed in very practical terms as the key to economic achievement. Children are expected to work hard and to do well in school. Cypriot American parents expect that their children will attain comparable or greater levels of success.

Education was a common way of rising in social status, and most Cypriots respect higher education and

ORGANIZATIONS AND ASSOCIATIONS

Panpaphian Association

This organization seeks to preserves Greek Cypriot culture and promote good relations between the United States and Cyprus. Among other activities, it sponsors an annual scholarship awards program.

Michael Hadjiloucas, President
48-02 25th Avenue
Suite 303
Astoria, New York 11103
Phone: (908) 227-5576
Email: mikehadjiloucas@verizon.net
URL: www.panpaphianusa.org

Cyprus Federation of America

An organization that works to maintain Greek Cypriot culture and to raise awareness about issues relating to Cyprus. It operates a youth program, the Cyprus Youth Association of America.

Despina Axiotakis
Phone: (201) 444-8237
Email: cyprusfederation@aol.com
URL: www.cyprusfederation.org

United Cypriots of Southern California, San Diego

John Vassiliades, President
8032 Bluebird Lane
La Palma, California 90623
Email: Johnvassil@Yahoo.com
URL: mysite.verizon.net/johnvassil/index.html

MUSEUMS AND RESEARCH CENTERS

Institute of Cypriot Studies

An integral unit of the State University of New York–Albany, the program encourages research and cultural activities related to Cyprus.

Matthew Griggs
Humanities 372
Albany, New York 12222
Phone: (518) 442-3982
Fax: (518) 442-4033
Email: mpgriggs@gmail.com

SOURCES FOR ADDITIONAL STUDY

Borowiec, Andrew. *Cyprus: A Troubled Island*. Westport, CT: Praeger, 2000.

Durrell, Lawrence. *Bitter Lemons*. With a new introduction by the author. New York: Marlowe, 1996.

Hannay, David. *Cyprus: The Search for a Solution*. London: I. B. Tauris, 2007.

Mallinson, William. *Cyprus: A Modern History*. London: I. B. Tauris, 2000.

Salih, Halil Ibrahim. *Cyprus: Ethnic Political Counterpoints*. Maryland: UP of America, 2004.

Streissguth, Tom. *Cyprus: Divided Island*. Minneapolis, MN: Lerner Publications, 1998.

Uslu, Nasuh. *The Turkish-American Relationship Between 1947 and 2003: The History of a Distinctive Relationship*. Hauppague, NY: Nova, 2006.

CZECH AMERICANS

Christine Molinari

OVERVIEW

Czech Americans are immigrants or descendants of people from the Czech Republic, a landlocked country located in central Europe that is bordered by Germany on the west, Austria on the south, Slovakia on the southeast, and Poland on the northeast. Bohemia, in the western part of the Czech Republic, consists of plains and plateaus surrounded by low mountains, and Moravia and southern Silesia in the east is hilly country. The Czech Republic sits astride historical European land routes, and its famous Moravian Gate serves as a corridor between the Northern European Plain and the Danube River. The Czech Republic, with historic Prague as its capital city, occupies a territory of 78,867 square miles, an area slightly smaller than South Carolina.

According to the Czech Statistical Office, the Czech Republic had an estimated population of 10,562,214 in 2011. The major ethnic groups are as follows: 9.6 million Czech, 200,000 Roma, 193,000 Slovak, 52,000 Polish, 40,000 Vietnamese, 39,000 German, 22,000 Ukrainian, and 11,000 Silesian. The Catholic Church in the Czech Republic has the largest following, with about 1.1 million believers; the Evangelical Church of the Czech Brethren has just under 52,000 members; and the Czechoslovak Hussite Church stands at 39,276 strong. More than 700,000 Czechs are spiritual but not active in organized religion, and about 3.6 million claim no religion. Because Czechs tend to be private about religious matters, nearly 4.8 million individuals chose not to provide an answer to the question on religion. The Czech Republic is a stable and prosperous market economy with a well-developed auto industry that accounts for 24 percent of Czech manufacturing. Its primary trading partner is Germany. The Czech Republic ranks forty-fifth in the world in total GDP, estimated at $285 billion by the *CIA World Factbook*.

Although there were reports of Czech settlers to the United States as early as 1600, the first notable immigration took place between 1865 and 1914, with more than half of immigrants settling in the states bordering the Great Lakes and nearly a quarter settling in the Great Plains in order to buy and work the affordable agricultural land. In the early twentieth century, many Czechs immigrated to the United

States as families rather than individually. Since 1930, Czech immigration to the United States has been relatively low. The number of immigrants increased slightly during the German occupation (1938-1945), the communist takeover (1948) of Czechoslovakia, and the Soviet-led invasion (1968) of the country. These immigrants were primarily Czech professionals, including scholars, artists, teachers, students, and journalists. On entering the United States, most individuals continued their professional careers and spoke out against both fascism and communism. Since the 1990s, young, single people have made up the majority of Czech immigrants to the United States.

According to the U.S. Census Bureau's American Community Survey estimates for 2009-2011, the number of Americans claiming Czech or Czechoslovakian ancestry was 1.85 million. Texas, Minnesota, Illinois, Wisconsin, and California had the largest Czech American populations. Although Nebraska has a small overall population in comparison to these other states, it has held the highest percentage of Czech Americans—around 5 percent—since 1890.

HISTORY OF THE PEOPLE

Early History The Boii—a Celtic tribe that inhabited the region as early as the fourth century BCE—were among the earliest settlers of Czech lands. Germanic tribes were also present around the first century CE. Between the fifth and seventh centuries, the Slavic ancestors of the Czechs arrived from the east and inhabited the region that subsequently became known as Bohemia. Although for a time assimilated into the neighboring kingdom of Great Moravia, Bohemia emerged as the stronger power and absorbed Moravia in the eleventh century. Under the Premyslids, its ruling dynasty, Bohemia became Christian in the ninth century and a member of the Holy Roman Empire in the eleventh century, led by the German kings but retaining its own monarchy. Two prominent rulers of the House of Premysl were Wenceslas the Holy (c. 907-929) and Otaker II (1253-1278), who extended Bohemia's territorial borders to the Adriatic. After the decline of the Premyslids, Bohemia was ruled for a time by the House of Luxembourg. The union of King John of Luxembourg with the Czech princess Elizabeth produced a son, Charles IV (1346-1378). As emperor of the Holy

Roman Empire, Charles IV established Bohemia as the center of the empire and made Prague its cultural center. He founded the University of Prague in 1348. In the fifteenth century the university became the center of a church reform movement led by Jan Hus (1369-1415), who was burned as a heretic in 1415. Divided between the followers of Hus—the Hussites—and the Catholics, the country was attacked by crusaders in 1420 and plunged into turmoil.

Through a dynastic union with the Jagiello family in Poland, the kings of Bohemia eventually became linked to the House of the Austrian Habsburgs, which ruled there from 1526 to 1918. Favoring monarchical control over the Protestant Reformation, the Habsburgs opposed the Bohemian estates, a struggle that resulted in the defeat of the Bohemian Protestant insurgents at the Battle of the White Mountain in 1620. Many thousands of noblemen were expelled from the country, and Bohemia was completely absorbed into the Habsburg Empire, with German becoming the primary language of instruction in the schools. However, a national awakening in the nineteenth century, culminating in the political protest movement of 1848, reestablished a sense of Czech identity. After the Austrian declaration of war on Serbia and Russia in 1914, the Czechs and Slovaks, in a struggle to establish a common republic, joined the side of the Allies. Under the leadership of Tomáš Garrigue Masaryk (1850-1937), Edvard Beneš (1884-1948), and Milan Rastislav Štefánik (1880-1919), they were able to persuade the Allied governments to dissolve the Habsburg Empire. On October 28, 1918, a revolutionary committee in Prague declared the establishment of the Czechoslovak Republic.

Modern Era In 1918 Tomáš Masaryk was elected the first president of the Czechoslovak Republic, a parliamentary democracy. He served in that position until 1935, when he was succeeded by his pupil Edvard Beneš. But after occupation by the invading forces of Adolph Hitler in 1939, the republic never completely regained autonomy. In the aftermath of World War II, the Soviet Union began to tighten its control over central Europe, and in February 1948 it staged a governmental crisis in Czechoslovakia that solidified communist control over the Czech government. A trend toward democratic liberalization in the 1960s culminated in the events of the Prague Spring in 1968, when a cultural revolution headed by reformer Alexander Dubcek was suppressed by the military intervention of the Soviet Union. Under Soviet leader Mikhail Gorbachev, a further period of liberalization began in the 1980s that led to the downfall of communism in 1989, when largely peaceful strikes and demonstrations in Prague swept aside the old regime in the "velvet revolution" and elevated dissident playwright Vaclav Havel to the presidency. After a brief coexistence in a federation with Slovakia, the Czech Republic became fully independent in 1992. This separation has been labeled "the velvet divorce."

In 1999 the Czech Republic was granted full membership of NATO and then joined the European Union in 2004. The country held the Presidency of the Council of the European Union from January 1 to June 30, 2009. The Czech Republic is a parliamentary representative democracy.

Despite the United States initially opposing the separation of Czechoslovakia in 1992, it recognized the Czech Republic and Slovakia as separate nations on January 1, 1993. Since then, U.S.-Czech relations have been strong economically, politically, and culturally.

SETTLEMENT IN THE UNITED STATES

Prior to the nineteenth century, few Czechs had immigrated to the United States, and evidence of their presence during the colonial and revolutionary periods is sketchy. Hermann Augustine (1605-1686), one of the founders of the Virginia tobacco trade and compiler of the first map of Maryland and Virginia, is thought to be the first Czech immigrant. In 1638 Czech Protestant exiles, who had set sail for America in the service of the Swedish army, assisted in the building of Fort Christina on a tributary of the Delaware River.

The first major immigration wave occurred in 1848 when the Czech "Forty Eighters" fled to the United States to escape political persecution by the Habsburgs. This year also saw the arrival of Vojta Náprstek, a radical free thinker and a vocal opponent of the Austrian government. He returned to his native land in 1857 as part of a general amnesty extended to political refugees and opened an American museum to acquaint European Czechs with America.

The earliest significant Czech colony in the United States was in New York, which by 1854 had about forty families. In Texas, the first Czech settlement was established at Catspring in 1847. In 1848 the Czechs settled alongside Germans, Irish, and Norwegians in Wisconsin, mainly in the counties of Adams, Kewaunee, Manitowok, Marathon, and Oconto, with the first major Czech farming town established at Caledonia, north of Racine. Other settlements followed in Iowa, Kansas, and Nebraska. The first Czech settlers to arrive in Chicago in 1852 settled in what is today the Lincoln Park area, assisting in local building by cutting trees and loading lumber. Minnesota Territory was populated by the first Czechs in 1855, whereas the Dakota Territory saw its first Czech settlements in 1870. Czech Americans also lent names to several U.S. towns and cities in which they settled, including New Prague and Litomysl in Minnesota, and Pilsens, Iowa, to name a few.

By the late 1850s there were an estimated 10,000 Czechs living in the United States. Chicago, tied to the eastern United States by rail and more readily accessible to the immigrants, became the most populous Czech settlement. By 1870 other cities with Czech concentrations included St. Louis, Cleveland, New York, and Milwaukee.

At the turn of the century, Czech immigrants were more likely to make the journey to the United States with their families. This marks a contrast with the immigration patterns of other ethnic groups, such as Germans, English, Poles, and Slovaks, who tended to come over individually, as exhibited by the high ratio of male to female immigrants in U.S. demographic statistics of the period. Moreover, in large families it was not uncommon for the head of the household to make more than one trip to the United States, bringing along one or more children each time. Many of those who immigrated in the late nineteenth century were of Moravian ancestry. One important characteristic of this group was their staunch adherence to the Catholic faith at a time when membership among Czech Americans was declining and a distinct anti-Catholic spirit prevailed.

By the turn of the century, a widening gap between the first and second generations was already in evidence. In 1900 there were 356,579 Czech Americans, 56 percent of whom had been born in the United States. Czech immigration slowed notably during World War I, and in the 1920s the number of Czechs entering the country was reduced by the temporary Emergency Quota Act, legislated by Congress in 1921, and the National Origins Act of 1924. Settlement patterns were also changing. Perhaps as a reflection of the growing trend toward urbanization in the United States, two-thirds of Czech Americans now lived in urban areas.

The next major immigration to the United States occurred during the German occupation of Czechoslovakia (1938–1945), when approximately 20,000 fled to the United States to escape Nazi persecution. About one-quarter of these individuals were professionals, including scholars and artists. Between 1946 and 1975, 27,048 Czechs immigrated to the United States. With the communist takeover in 1948, a large number of refugees, many of them students, teachers, journalists, and professional people, began pouring into the United States. This immigration was authorized by the Displaced Persons Act of 1948, which permitted the admission of refugees of communist countries. Financial support for these refugees was provided by the American Fund for Czechoslovak Refugees, established with the assistance of Eleanor Roosevelt.

In 1968 the relaxed atmosphere in Czechoslovakia under the Dubček regime was conducive to the immigration of hundreds of refugees to the United States. Many of them were middle-aged, skilled, and educated; consequently, they had little difficulty finding employment. This community of immigrants made significant contributions to American society but has

Czech American farmers sit on the front porch of their house in Wisconsin in 1937. RUSSELL LEE / CORBIS

been characterized more by its capacity for assimilation than by its ability to stimulate a resurgence in Czech American culture.

According to the 2000 U.S. Census, 1.7 million Americans reported themselves to be of Czech or Czechoslovakian ancestry, with more than half of these individuals residing in the Midwest. By 2011 that number had grown to 1.85 million (American Community Survey estimate for 2009-2011). The number of foreign-born Czechs in the United States has been steadily decreasing; in 2011 only 2.5 percent of Czech Americans were foreign-born.

LANGUAGE

Czech is a Slavic language with a declension system based on seven cases. The present orthographic system was introduced in the fourteenth century by religious reformer Jan Hus, who instituted a system of diacritical markings to eliminate consonant clusters. Thus, the consonants ž, š, č, ř, ň, ť, and d' stand for "sh," "ch," "rzh," "zh," "ny," "ty," and "dy," respectively. Czech is a phonetic language; every sound is pronounced as it is written, with the accent always on the first syllable.

Because of the differences between Czech and English—Czech is a Slavic language, whereas English is Germanic—the acquisition of English as a second language presents a challenge to Czech Americans. The U.S. public school system and Czech American benevolent organizations have provided systematic English-language instruction to assist Czech American immigrants in learning English. Numerous American colleges and universities also teach the Czech language, including Stanford University, Yale University, the University of Chicago, the University of Michigan, and Harvard University.

The early Czech communities created schools where their children could learn about Czech heritage,

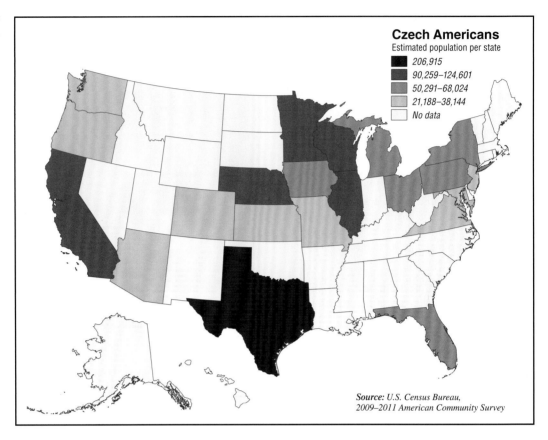

Czech Americans
Estimated population per state

- 206,915
- 90,259–124,601
- 50,291–68,024
- 21,188–38,144
- No data

*Source: U.S. Census Bureau,
2009–2011 American Community Survey*

and these schools usually offered courses in the Czech language. Czech was frequently spoken at home by first-generation immigrants. More recently, Czech organizations such as the Czech Heritage Society of Texas and the American Czech Educational Center in St. Louis, Missouri, have promoted the study of the Czech language.

Greetings and Popular Expressions Greetings and expressions include *dobre jitro*—good morning; *dobrý den*—good afternoon; *dobrou noc*—good night; *nazdar*—hello; *sbohem*—good-bye; *na shle-da-nou*—till we meet again; *prosim*—please; and *děkuji pěkne*—thank you very much. Other polite expressions are *Jak se mate?*—a polite form of How are you?, and *Jak se maš* (the familiar form); *Jak se jmenujete?*—What's your name? (polite form), and *Jak se jmenuješ* (familiar form); *Těší mne*—Nice to meet you; and *Dobre chutnani*—Enjoy your meal.

RELIGION

Many of the Czechs who immigrated to the United States were Roman Catholic when they arrived. But the Czech immigration movement is unique in that as many as 50 percent of Czechs immigrants broke their religious ties when they arrived in the United States. Their arrival in this country gave many Czechs an opportunity to sever their relationships with the Roman Catholic Church, an institution that was closely associated with the oppressive Habsburg

regime they had left behind. Some of them were influenced by movements that questioned all forms of religious dogma, such as the Progressives and Freethinkers.

The first Czech Roman Catholic church was established in St. Louis. According to Kenneth Miller in *The Czech-Slovaks in America*, the official almanac of the Czech Benedictines, called the *Katolik*, listed as many as 338 Roman Catholic parishes and related organizations in 1920. Traditionally, the Roman Catholic Church was strong in Texas, Wisconsin, Nebraska, and Minnesota, and had a greater following in rural than urban areas. Among urban centers, Chicago and St. Louis had the strongest Czech Roman Catholic following. The Roman Catholic Church maintained its following by establishing churches or mission stations, founding benevolent chapters, publishing Catholic periodicals, and opening schools, which included a Czech college and seminary: Illinois Benedictine College (formerly St. Procopius), located in Lisle, Illinois.

In the early part of the twentieth century, approximately 2 percent of Czechs living in the United States were Protestant. Czech Protestants typically affiliated with American denominations. Common affiliations were Presbyterian, Methodist, the Bohemian Moravian Brethren, and Congregational. The predominantly high number of Presbyterian adherents was due both to the perceived similarities between the Presbyterian

Church and the old-world Reformed Church and to early missionary efforts.

The Moravian Church was renewed in the eighteenth century. The renewed Moravian Church traced its origins back to the older *Unitas Fratrum* (Unity of Brethren) founded in 1457 in what is today the Czech Republic. The Moravians first came to America in 1735 in order to establish a community in Savannah, Georgia. This venture was unsuccessful; but in 1741 Moravian settlers purchased 500 acres of land in Bethlehem and, soon after, the 5,000-acre barony of Nazareth, both in Pennsylvania. The two communities Bethlehem and Nazareth were linked economically, and they spread the gospel to Native Americans. The Moravians soon built other communities, including Lititz and Hope. They established a number of schools; in keeping with the precepts of educator John Amos Comenius, who believed in equal education for women, the Moravians founded the first American preparatory school for girls in 1742.

CULTURE AND ASSIMILATION

The Czechs were uniquely suited to assimilate into American society. Although they lacked direct experience with democratic institutions, the first generation—many of whom left their homeland to escape the oppression of the Austrian Habsburgs—nevertheless brought with them a love of liberty and social equality. A relatively large proportion of nineteenth-century Czech immigrants were literate, a result of the educational policies of the Austrian regime, which made education compulsory to age fourteen throughout Bohemia and Moravia.

The years between 1914 and 1941 marked a turning point for the Czech community in two important ways. First, as a result of World War I, the Czech community became less isolated because of an increased desire to assimilate. This desire came about mainly because Czech Americans did not want to be viewed as sympathizers of the German Empire during the war. A growing trend toward Americanization could be seen particularly in the second and third generations, which were already moving out of the Czech communities and marrying into families with ethnic backgrounds that differed from their own. Second, perhaps partially in response to this trend, the Czech American community was becoming more protective of its traditions, emphasizing the study of Czech language and culture.

As relatively recent arrivals in the United States, the Czechs were forced to deal with prejudice as they established their homes in the midst of other immigrant communities. The self-sufficiency of Czech urban settlements, with their assemblage of Czech-owned banks, theaters, amusement halls, and shops, may have contributed to a perception of Czechs as clannish. Despite the immigrants' insistence that they be referred to as "Czechs," many Americans persisted in calling them by the pejorative "Bohunks" or by the less pejorative but equally unacceptable "Bohemians." When the Czechs began moving out of urban neighborhoods into the suburbs after World War II, their search for new homes was not always greeted with enthusiasm. Some efforts at community expansion were met with strong prejudice, as when a Czech real-estate developer attempting to purchase land in a Chicago suburb returned home to find a burning cross on his land.

To many early twentieth-century observers, the Czechs were a relatively successful immigrant community. They were perceived as law-abiding and family- and community-oriented citizens. Because they were dedicated to becoming fully Americanized, their assimilation into American culture was relatively smooth and complete.

Traditions and Customs Community festivals such as polka celebrations and *houby* (mushroom) hunting contests continue to play a prominent role in Czech American culture. Some traditions celebrated in the early days of immigration were centered on the church. At box-supper church fund-raisers, women baked their fanciest dinners and put them into boxes decorated with crepe paper, hearts, and ribbons to be auctioned off to the highest bidder.

Customs frequently were derived from old pagan traditions. On Palm Sunday, children created an effigy of *Smrt* (death), a life-size straw doll that might be dressed in rags and have a necklace of eggs. The straw woman, who symbolized the end of winter, was then cast into a river as the children sang a welcome to the beginning of spring. On New Year's Eve, young men would gather in circles and fire their rifles into the air three times, a practice known as "shooting the witches." These customs and others can still be seen at the annual Czech Festival in Yukon, Oklahoma, and are frequent subjects of discussion on Saturday nights at Czech Hall in Mustang, Oklahoma.

Czech superstitions were retained by many first generation immigrants in the United States. If not believed today, they are at least remembered by family members. The most prevalent of these include the following: a bird that flies into a house is an omen of death; a dream about a body of water means a death is soon to occur; rattles made by placing pebbles inside eggshells are given to children to drive away evil spirits; and a garnet that dims while worn on the body is thought to be a sign of melancholy. Superstitions often provide moral guidance; for example, a person who does not give Christmas presents will become impoverished.

Cuisine Czech American cooking boasts a range of savory meat dishes and rich, flavorful desserts that can be prepared with simple ingredients. Potatoes, mushrooms, and cabbage are the staples of Czech cooking. To make a potato strudel, flour was added to mashed potatoes to form a stiff dough, which was then sprinkled with cinnamon and melted goat's milk butter and baked in the oven. Mushrooms picked during

CZECH PROVERBS

Czech proverbs express popular wisdom on themes such as the family, labor, fortune, and benevolence. Common proverbs among Czech Americans in the United States include:

- Father and mother have taught us how to speak, and the world how to keep quiet.

- Too much wisdom does not produce courage.

- A pocketful of right needs a pocketful of gold.

- The poor are heaven's messengers.

- He who has daughters has a family, and he who has sons has strangers.

- If there were no children, there would be no tears.

- All the rivers do what they can for the sea.

- Better a lie that heals than a truth that wounds.

- As long as the language lives, the nation is not dead.

autumn field trips were brought home in bushels and set out in neat rows to dry. They were then turned into a sour mushroom soup that also contained sauerkraut juice and fried onions. Sauerkraut, made from boiled cabbage, could also be mixed with pork and rice to make a cabbage roll.

The best-known Czech American dessert is *kolače*. This is a round or square pastry most often filled with fruit such as prunes and apricots and rimmed with soft dough. American cities such as Montgomery, Minnesota; West, Texas; and Prague, Nebraska are well known for the production of this beloved Czech dessert. Traditional at Christmastime among Czech Americans is *vanočka*, a Christmas twist loaf flavored with mace, anise, and lemon and sprinkled with almonds and seedless raisins. It is common for Czech Americans to have baking contests during the holidays.

Traditional Dress Czech American traditional costumes were worn as everyday apparel in some parts of the country until the twentieth century, when they were worn only on ceremonial occasions. Women's billowy skirts, multicolored or solid, were topped by gold-trimmed black vests and blouses with full puffed sleeves that might be trimmed in gold or lace and embroidered with a floral geometric motif. Women's bright caps were worn flat on the

head and had flaps on either side. Men's trousers were of a solid hue but were often decorated according to individual taste. Men wore a black vest over a full embroidered shirt.

Bridal costumes were particularly ornate. The bride wore a crown covered with rosemary wreaths made by the groom; this crown might also be strewn with long, flowing ribbons. Her white vest was covered with light sea beads or with red, yellow, or green streamers. The groom wore a close-fitting blue or red vest and a plumed hat.

Dances and Songs Most Americans are familiar with the polka, but few of them know that it is a Czech courtship dance. The polka originated in the Czech land in the first half of the nineteenth century. Derived from the Czech word for "half," it is danced with a half step to music written in two-quarter time, with the accent on the first three eighth notes. Another popular Czech dance is the *beseda*, a collection of mazurkas, polkas, and waltzes arranged according to local tradition and performed at festivals.

Czech melodies, strongly western European in character, were usually composed to accompany dances. The *koledy*—ritual carols that were sung at Christmas, the New Year, and Easter—date back to the fourteenth and fifteenth centuries. A typical rustic band included a clarinet, violins, and the *dudy*, a shepherd's bagpipe that had a goat's head on top.

Founded in Houston, Texas, in 1932 by Joseph Drozda, the Czech Tamburash Orchestra was the only Czech orchestra in the United States at the time. They frequently performed not only classical works by Dvorak and Smetana, but also folk songs, waltzes, marches, and polkas that were very popular with Czech Americans. The tamburash—an instrument from the lute family—was part of the stringed instrument section of the orchestra.

Holidays For many Czech Americans, Christmas is an important holiday. It begins on December 24 with a Christmas dinner that is served in the early evening. *Rizek* (batter-fried pork or chicken) and potato salad are immensely popular contemporary Christmas Eve dishes. Sometimes extra place settings are left for deceased members of the family, who are said to be present in spirit. On Christmas Day, carp is a popular dish among contemporary Czech Americans. Christmas is often celebrated at church in an extended ceremony where the women and girls stand in front of the altar for the duration of the service. New Year's Eve (commonly called Saint Sylvester's in Czech) is celebrated at street festivals, with revelers spending much of the night singing and dancing. Also commemorated are Epiphany (January 6), to honor the journey of the Magi; Saint Valentine's Day; and Whitsunday, in remembrance of the Ascension.

Sprinkling Day was a popular holiday in the early twentieth century, but it is no longer practiced today.

According to custom, on the first Monday of Easter week, boys would go through the town spraying the girls with little homemade water spritzers; sometimes a boy would abduct a girl, and throw her into the river. The girl was required to show her gratitude for this treatment by baking the boy a home-cooked meal. Czech Americans also observe Saint Joseph's Day (March 19), a day honoring their national heritage.

Mother's Day, on the second Sunday of May, is an important holiday for Czech Americans. It is celebrated at church, at festivals, and at home. It is often marked by the wearing of red and white carnations grown especially for the occasion; a red carnation signifies that one's mother is living, whereas a white carnation indicates that she is deceased. The American Czech-Slovak Cultural Club in Miami, Florida, among other Czech American organizations, holds annual Mother's Day celebrations with traditional music, dance, and cuisine. The popularity of Mother's Day among Czech Americans is, in part, due to Czechs' rejection of Women's Day, a holiday that had been introduced to Czechoslovakia by the Soviets. Women's Day and its extravagant celebrations are still seen as symbols of the hated communist regime. Thus, many Czech Americans have adopted Mother's Day in its place.

Rogation Days—the Monday, Tuesday, and Wednesday before the Feast of the Ascension (which takes place the fortieth day after Easter Sunday)—are celebrated by Czech Americans in Iowa and Minnesota. After the mass, the congregation follows the priest through the fields, reciting the Litany of the Saints and praying for a good harvest.

Health Care Issues and Practices First-generation Czech immigrants, particularly in the early twentieth century, turned to home remedies to cure common ailments. A wedding ring tied around the neck of a child was believed to cure fever. Poultices made of bread and milk were used to heal cuts. Concern about scoliosis prompted Czech women to ensure that their babies had adequate calcium, and at one time it was mandatory for newborns to have their hips examined to see whether they would develop the disease. Czech Americans have always been very diet conscious. When fruits were in scarce supply in the winter, they served rosehip tea as well as sauerkraut, a rich source of vitamin C.

Czech Americans believe there is a strong connection between mental and physical well-being. Their commitment to physical fitness led to the establishment of the Sokol (Falcon) gymnastic organization, which strives to develop a person "perfect physically, spiritually, and morally, of a firm and noble character, whose word is irrevocable, like the law."

Death and Burial Rituals In the nineteenth and early twentieth centuries, death vigils were still held in the home, a custom brought over from Europe. The casket might be brought to the home by the undertaker, if the village were prosperous enough to have one; in some villages, the caskets were kept in the general store. Family members would take turns sitting by the side of the deceased, who was waked in the home for a period of days.

On the day of the funeral, the religious officiant came to pray over the coffin with the family. In some rural areas, as in central Texas, businesses might be closed one hour before a funeral. The town bells summoned the townsfolk to the service. After the procession to the cemetery, the family would gather around the grave and sing hymns while the earth was shoveled into the grave. In populous areas, the Czechs sometimes established their own national cemeteries; Bohemian National Cemetery in Chicago is one example.

After the funeral, the entire family–not just the surviving husband or wife–would observe a period of mourning, usually for several months. Widows observed the custom of wearing black; other family members, children included, were expected to preserve an atmosphere of deep solemnity, neither laughing nor indulging in games or amusement.

FAMILY AND COMMUNITY LIFE

The lifestyle of nineteenth-century Czech immigrants was determined by the region and community in which they settled. Those who came to New York in the 1860s lived in sparsely furnished rented quarters, and it was not uncommon to find two families sharing the same small apartment. Immigrants who came to Chicago in the early 1850s had trouble settling permanently; driven from place to place, they resided in makeshift housing until they could find permanent lodging. While the men loaded lumber to assist in the new building in the area, the women and children did the chores and went to the slaughterhouse, where they could obtain the poorer cuts of meat, often purchased on a cooperative plan.

Members of rural communities also endured hardships. Dwellings in Nebraska, Kansas, and Iowa were simple sod houses—no more than underground burrows. Immigrants to rural Wisconsin built log cabins and lived off meager provisions, in some cases subsisting on cornbread and on the "coffee" they made from ground roasted corn.

The accumulation of wealth by first-generation families made it easier for the second generation to purchase property. They began by building wood-frame homes and eventually saved enough money to build with brick. In the early twentieth century, an estimated 64 percent of Czech families living in Chicago owned their own dwellings, a high proportion for an immigrant community at that time. Children were sent to college and frequently went on to pursue professional vocations, such as law, education, or medicine.

Historically, the Czechs have been markedly active in community groups that have assisted immigrants and have promoted greater familiarity with Czech culture. In 1854 Czechs in Ripon, Wisconsin, formed the Czech-Slavonic Benevolent Society, the oldest continuous benevolent society in the United States, to provide insurance and aid to immigrants, as well as social services to the young, the elderly, and the poor. The Sokol (Falcon) gymnastic organization, established in St. Louis, Missouri, in 1865, continues to attract people of all ethnic backgrounds to its sponsored gymnastic meets.

Gender Roles Czech American women have played an exceptionally important role in community life, forming a number of active social and political organizations. As early as 1868, Czech women in Chicago founded an organization called Libuse. By 1930 approximately one-third of the membership of Czech American benevolent societies consisted of women. The National Council of Women in Exile, convened in 1948, provided assistance to Czech refugees. Although Czech women were prominent in their communities, the women's suffrage movement in the early twentieth century was viewed with either polite tolerance or outright scorn and had difficulty winning acceptance among Czech Americans. Today, Czech American women participate in organizations such as the American Czech Women's Club in Los Angeles, attend prominent universities, travel abroad, and hold jobs ranging from politics to education.

Education Czech Americans have placed great value on education. Of those who arrived in the United States, 96 percent could read and write, in contrast to the Slavic average of 66 percent. As soon as Czech immigrants settled in the United States, they found ways to educate their children. They established their own schools to teach children about their Czech heritage. In 1885 Oberlin College created a theological seminary for Protestant Czech Americans, and two years later the Czech Benedictines established the College of St. Procopius in Chicago. The Czech Freethinkers established the Slavic Linden, their most important school, which taught in the Czech language. By 1930, 21,000 Czech Americans attended 121 elementary schools founded by Czech Catholics. But due to the assimilation process, most Czech schools eventually shut down. In the twenty-first century, Czech is taught at many universities, including the University of Nebraska, and numerous organizations offer courses and programs that promote Czech heritage.

Courtship and Weddings Contemporary Czech American weddings do not generally follow traditional Czech customs, but a few traditions continue because they are relatively easy to perform. At the end of the wedding ceremony, guests throw peas at the departing couple. At the wedding reception, there is often the traditional breaking of plates by the bride and groom, after which the couple cleans up the broken bits with a broom. If they

work well together, it is said that the marriage will be a lucky one. Another tradition is tying together the bride's right hand with the groom's left. They proceed to feed each other a popular dumpling soup or a Czech goulash with one spoon. This demonstrates how well they cooperate and proves the importance of sharing life's burdens. At the peak of the wedding party, the bride is sometimes taken away and hidden by the friends of the groom. The groom must find her as soon as possible. This tradition emphasizes the bride's separation from her parents, her vulnerability, and groom's responsibility in protecting her. Simple traditions such as these have continued.

In the late nineteenth and early twentieth centuries, traditional Czech American weddings were announced by the groom's attendants, who would go from house to house extending the invitations. Food and drink were prepared days in advance. On the day of the wedding, the couple, their parents, and the bridal party would gather for the wedding breakfast. The groom was not allowed to see the bride in her gown until two o'clock in the afternoon, when a sponsor would present the bride and the parents to the groom, admonishing him to be kind, gentle, and worthy, and telling the bride to be moral, obedient, and submissive. After the wedding ceremony, as the guests proceeded to the feast, friends of the couple would stand along the path and tie a ribbon from one side to the other, requesting a donation. This gift was later presented to the couple or was sometimes given to the musicians as a gratuity. At the wedding feast, the bridesmaids would present the guests with sprigs of rosemary, a symbol of fidelity, and a collection would be taken up for the birth of the first child.

Baptisms Most Czechs entering the United States before 1880 identified themselves as Catholics, but by the late 1880s more than half had left the church and rejected Catholicism. Catholic Czech Americans follow the sacrament of baptism as specified in the catechism of the Catholic Church. Some Czech traditions have survived in relation to the birth of a child; for example, preparation for the birth of a child begins even before the wedding, when the bride-to-be knits clothing such as white bonnets, boots, jackets, and shawls—sometimes enough for a family of six children—which were then carefully arranged in neat, ribbon-tied bundles and set aside until the arrival of the firstborn. Following Catholic traditions, baptisms occur as early as a week after birth. It is not uncommon for Czech American Catholics to have baptismal parties, where the godfather recites a customary toast and the godmother presents the gifts. Godparents adhere to a pledge to safeguard the child in the event of the parents' death. Six weeks after the baptism, the baby is taken to the church, where the religious officiant joins with the parents at the altar to say prayers of thanksgiving for the baby's arrival and health.

Relations with Other Americans The earliest immigrants settled in proximity to ethnic groups for whom they had a strong affinity. In an important early study on Czech immigration (*The Czechs (Bohemians) in America*), Thomas Capek notes that many Czech settlements were located near German settlements (e.g., in St. Louis and Milwaukee) and observes that "the Czechs were drawn to the Germans by a similarity, if not identity, in customs and mode of life." By 1900, intermarriages with other nationalities were more common, most of them occurring with Germans, but also with Austrians, Hungarians, and Poles.

During World War II, Czech Americans participated in the national American Slav Congress, which convened in Detroit in 1940 and 1942. The war effort brought them closer to other Slavic ethnic groups, particularly to the Poles, an alliance that had its international parallel in a European concord of November 1940, when Czech and Polish refugees living in Europe agreed to establish friendly relations after the conclusion of the war.

The Czechs were a relatively successful immigrant group dedicated to becoming Americanized, thus assimilating into American society with ease and success. Despite assimilation, many Czech Americans of the twenty-first century belong to Czech American organizations and keep up on events occurring in the Czech Republic in order to preserve their Czech heritage.

Surnames On arrival, many Czechs Americanized their last names. Some last names were translated into English (for example, Jablečnik became Appleton, Krejči became Taylor, and Vlk became Wolf), whereas others were changed to American-sounding equivalents (for example, Červeny became Sweeney, and Maršálek became Marshall).

EMPLOYMENT AND ECONOMIC CONDITIONS

Many of the Czechs who immigrated to the United States in the late 1850s were farmers or laborers. Of the three classes of Czech peasants who lived in Europe—the *sedlák*, or upper-class farmer, who owned 25 to 100 acres and a farmhouse; the *chalupník*, or cottager, who owned 5 to 25 acres and a small cottage; and the *nadeníci*, or day laborer, who dwelt on the nobleman's estate or on the farm of the *sedlák* and owned no property—Czech immigrants to the United States most frequently derived from the middle, or cottager, class. This was probably because the *sedlák* had little to gain by leaving behind his rich farmland, whereas the *nadeníci* did not have the means to emigrate.

Settlers who came to the Midwest lived in log cabins; those on the plains resided in dugouts and sod houses. With no tools at their disposal, farmers were limited to hard manual labor. In the off season they focused on survival, migrating to the cities or to the lumber and mining camps to find what work they could.

Occasionally, Czechs specializing in a certain industry—such as the cigar-making industry in New York—had emigrated from a particular region, in this case, Kutna Horá, which was preeminent in the cigar trade. In the 1870s, 95 percent of the Czechs in New York were employed in the cigar-making industry. Working conditions were harsh and wages poor. Joseph Chada noted that it took the average Czech industrial laborer ten years to attain the economic status of the average American laborer. Many women and children were also employed in these factories.

Urban-dwellers were eager to purchase property. Community-minded and thrifty, the Czechs created the Building and Loan Association, an institution that became one of their most significant contributions to U.S. economic life. The Building and Loan Association, introduced in Chicago in 1873, was a small cooperative agency to which shareholders made minimal weekly contributions with an aim toward eventually purchasing a home. So successful were these agencies that during the Great Depression, when other banks were failing, Czech building and loan associations posted a total of $32 million in deposits, a substantial figure for that period.

By the first half of the twentieth century, Czech businesses were flourishing. Czech breweries (Pilsen and Budweiser are both derived from Czech place names) kept pace with the best German establishments. The Bulova watch company, a Czech enterprise, is an example of a successful, well-established Czech American business. And the character of the Czech labor force was changing as well. By the second generation, there was a greater proportion of salesmen, machinists, and white-collar laborers among Czech immigrants.

> The factories in the regions of Seventieth Street, New York, are filled with Bohemian women and girls employed in the making of cigars. … [They] dread going into the cigar factories. The hygiene is bad, the moral influences are not often the best, and the work is exhausting.
>
> Jane E. Robbins, "The Bohemian Women in New York," cited in *The Czechs in America, 1633-1977*, edited by Vera Laska (Dobbs Ferry, New York: Oceana Publications, 1978, p. 111).

Czech immigration to the United States in the twenty-first century has declined, in part because of the stable and prosperous market economy and democracy of the Czech Republic. Czech immigrants immigrate to the United States for reasons such as joining other family members. Many Czech immigrants are young, single people that seek new and different life experiences. They frequently pursue professional jobs, but because of their relative ease in the assimilation process, Czech Americans pursue every type of career.

POLITICS AND GOVERNMENT

The Czechs were relatively slow to take part in U.S. political life. By the 1880s, however, Czechs were playing an increasingly active role in government, both at the state and local levels. Most Czechs voted the Democratic ticket, in part because of the perception that the Democrats favored labor. Some Czechs ran successfully for high public office. Charles Jonáš served as senator of Wisconsin in 1883 and as governor of Wisconsin in 1890.

By the 1880s support had grown among Czech American labor for the socialist movement. But in the aftermath of the Haymarket Riot of 1886—a violent confrontation between labor protesters and police in Haymarket Square in Chicago, initially triggered by the crusade for the eight-hour work day—the movement was forced underground. With the emergence of the American Socialist Party, Czech Americans renewed their membership, many of them recruited by appeals in the ethnic press. By 1910, Czech American Socialists numbered approximately 10,000. They reduced their activities during World War I, however, as the concerns of nationalism began to loom over those of internationalism. And as the lifestyle of second- and third-generation Czech Americans improved, they became less concerned with the labor situation. By the 1920s the movement had all but come to a standstill.

The prospect of establishing Czech independence from Austria led Czech Americans to fervently support the Allied cause during World War I. Prior to the outbreak of the war, Czech Americans openly demonstrated their support for the Serbs and rallied for the establishment of an independent Czech homeland. The Czech National Alliance was established in Chicago to provide political and financial support to the Czech cause in Europe. Also characteristic of this period was the willingness of the Czech American community to band together with the Slovak American community to establish a common political framework that would unite Bohemia, Moravia, and Slovakia under a single government. On October 25, 1915, the Czechs and Slovaks met in Cleveland to agree on such a program. In April 1917, the Czechs succeeded in gaining the introduction of resolutions in Congress supporting the establishment of an independent European homeland.

Czech Americans also played an active role in supporting the cause of Czechoslovakia during World War II. During the Munich Crisis, Czechs organized a protest rally of 65,000 at Chicago Stadium. The war efforts of Czech Americans were coordinated primarily by the Czechoslovak National Council. In addition to publishing *News Flashes from Czechoslovakia*, with a circulation of 5,000 to 105,000, the council aided soldiers and refugees who participated in the Allied campaign. Czech Americans effectively used propaganda to direct world attention to the Nazi massacre of the village of Lidice.

After the Soviet takeover of Czechoslovakia, Czechs were admitted to the United States under the American Displaced Persons Act. The Czechoslovak National Council assisted these individuals in their struggle to regain their homeland, primarily through the publication of anticommunist propaganda. In addition to requesting that members of the Czech American community sign affidavits that would assist refugees in obtaining shelter and employment, the Council presented a memorandum to President Harry Truman on June 3, 1949, asking that the United States push for United Nations–sponsored free elections in Czechoslovakia.

Twenty-first century Czech Americans are well informed about the Czech Republic, and it is not uncommon for them to tour the country or even to visit distant relatives that still live there. Many Czech Americans participate in community centers and associations, finding these places of heritage preservation more important than political activity. This is, in part, due to the economic and political stability of the Czech Republic.

Military Service Czech Americans on the whole were opposed to slavery and therefore supported the North during the U.S. Civil War, serving at Chancellorsville, Fredericksburg, and Bull Run. Many of those living in the Confederacy (primarily in Texas) avoided conscription into the Southern army at enormous cost to their lives, hiding in the woods or swamps or serving as drivers on perilous journeys to Mexico.

Czech Americans in the First World War either served in the Czechoslovak army on the Western Front (if they were immigrants) or enlisted as draftees in the U.S. Army. Approximately 2,300 Czech immigrants served in European Czech contingents. During World War II Czech American loyalties were divided between providing active military service to their country and providing moral support to the Czech community in Europe, both duties that they fulfilled admirably. They also made a financial contribution to the war effort by investing substantially in war loans.

NOTABLE INDIVIDUALS

Academia Aleš Hrdlička (1869-1943), curator of the physical anthropology division at the Smithsonian Institution, developed the theory that Native Americans migrated to North America from Asia across the Bering land bridge; he also did extensive research on Neanderthal man. Francis Dvorník (1893-1975) was a noted Byzantine scholar affiliated with the Dumbarton Oaks Center for Byzantine Studies. Managed by Harvard University, the center is located in Washington, D.C.

Business Ray Kroc (1902-1984), founder of McDonald's restaurants, was a pioneer in the establishment of the fast-food industry. Francis Korbel (1830-1920), who entered the United States illegally to avoid an arrest warrant, purchased redwood forest in northern California and established the Korbel winery. Louis D. Brandeis (1856-1941) descended from a Jewish family that immigrated to the United States in 1849 and became the first Jewish Supreme Court justice (1916-1939). He helped draft the Czechoslovak Declaration of Independence, issued in 1918.

Journalism Charles Jonáš (1840-1896), who served in the Wisconsin state legislature, founded *Pokrok* (*Progress*), an anticlerical weekly. In 1869 Frank Kořízek (1820-1899) established the weekly *Slowan Amerikánský* in Iowa City. In 1860 Lev J. Palda (1847-1912), the founder of Czech American socialism, established the first Czech social-democratic or socialist newspaper, *Národní Noviny* (*National Newspaper*), in St. Louis, Missouri. Josephine Humpal-Zeman (1870-1906), an important figure in the women's suffrage movement, founded the *Ženské Listy* (*Woman's Gazette*) in 1894.

Literature René Wellek (1903-1995), a member of the Prague Linguistic Circle, settled in the United States in 1939, where he established the field of comparative literature at Yale University. Bartoš Bittner (1861-1912) was an essayist and political satirist. Paul Albieri (1861-1901) wrote stories of military life.

Peter Sis (1949–) is a writer and illustrator of children's books that have won such prestigious awards as the ALA Caldecott Honor, the *New York Times Book Review* for Best Illustrated Book of the Year, the Hans Christian Anderson Award, and the Boston Globe-Horn Book Award.

Nicholas Sparks (1965–) is a best-selling American novelist of Czech ancestry. Sparks has written novels such as *The Notebook* (1996), *Message in a Bottle* (1998), *A Walk to Remember* (1999), and *Dear John* (2007), each of which has been adapted into successful Hollywood films. He is a well-known philanthropist, providing scholarships in the Creative Writing Department at the University of Notre Dame and donating money to many charities.

Politics Madeleine Albright (1937–), who was born in Prague, was the first woman to serve as the United States secretary of state (1997-2001).

President George W. Bush (1946–) is of Czech ancestry on his mother's side. He was governor of Texas (1995-2000), and he served two terms (2001-2009) as the forty-third president of the United States.

Science and Technology Astronaut Eugene A. Cernan (1934–) was copilot on the Gemini 9 mission, lunar module pilot of the Apollo 10 mission, and spacecraft commander of Apollo 17. James Lovell (1928–) served on the Apollo 8 mission, the first crewed flight around the moon.

Biochemists Gerty Cori (1896-1957) and Carl Cori (1896-1984) won the 1946 Nobel Prize for Physiology or Medicine for their studies on sugar metabolism. Physician Joseph Goldberger (1874-1929) discovered a cure for pellagra, which he correctly attributed to diet deficiency, in contrast to the prevailing view that it was caused by infection. Frederick George Novy (1864-1957) made important contributions to the field of microbiology.

Sports George Halas (1895-1983) was founder and owner of the Chicago Bears football team. He was widely known as "Papa Bear." As head coach he led his team to seven championship seasons. Jack Root (1876-1963) became the first world champion lightweight boxer in 1903. Stan Musial (1920–) was an outstanding baseball hitter and outfielder with the St. Louis Cardinals who won seven batting championships. Martina Navratilova (1956–), born in Prague, dominated women's tennis in the 1970s and 1980s, winning the U.S. Open and Wimbledon numerous times and becoming only the fifth person in history to win the Grand Slam. Czechoslovakia-born Ivan Lendl (1960–) dominated men's tennis in the 1980s, winning the U.S. Open in 1985 and the Australian Open in 1989.

Nicole Bobek (1977–) is a popular figure skater who won the gold medal at the U.S. Championships and the bronze medal at the World Championships, both in 1995. Bobek had a role in the movie *All the King's Men* (2006) and has appeared in television commercials.

Stage and Screen Filmmaker Miloš Forman (1932–), who immigrated to the United States in 1969, won Academy Awards for best direction for *One Flew over the Cuckoo's Nest* (1975) and *Amadeus* (1984). His other films include *The People vs. Larry Flint* (1996) and *Goya's Ghosts* (2006).

Independent filmmaker Jim Jarmusch (1953–) is known for directing such critically acclaimed films as *Mystery Train* (1989), *Dead Man* (1995), *Ghost Dog: The Way of the Samurai* (1999), and *Broken Flowers* (2005).

Actress Kim Novak (1933–), who made her screen debut in 1954, starred in such films as Alfred Hitchcock's *Vertigo* (1958), *Pal Joey* (1957), and *Boys' Night Out* (1962).

Sissy Spacek (1949–) is known primarily as a film actress. She won the Academy Award for Best Actress in the film *Coal Miner's Daughter* (1980), in which she played the role of country singer Loretta Lynn. She has appeared in many other films, including *Carrie* (1976), *Missing* (1982), and *Crimes of the Heart* (1986).

John Kriza (1919-1975) was a ballet dancer who performed with the American Ballet Theater and the Chicago Opera Ballet.

Visual Arts Alphonse Mucha (1860-1939) was an Art Nouveau decorative artist recognized for his posters promoting actress Sarah Bernhardt.

Before a naturalization ceremony, a woman originally from the Czech Republic and her daughter look at a card printed with the Oath of Allegiance that she will take to become an American citizen. SYRACUSE NEWSPAPERS / D LASSMAN / THE IMAGE WORKS

MEDIA

PRINT

Hospodar

Prints general news, letters, and features on farm topics.

> Jan Vaculik, Editor
> P.O. Box 301
> West, Texas 76691
> Email: jan_vaculik@hotmail.com

Kosmas: Czechoslovak and Central European Journal

A biannual publication that focuses on Czech and Slavic Studies.

> Clinton Machann
> Texas A&M University
> Department of English
> 4227 Tamu
> College Station, Texas 77843-4227
> Email: cmachann@tamu.edu

Prague Post

Online newspaper written in English that features news on business, education, sports, opinion, and more.

> Stepanska1677/20
> Prague, Czech Republic 1 110 00
> Phone: +420 296 334 400

> Email: info@praguepost.com, office@ praguepost.com
> URL: www.praguepost.com

RADIO

Radio Prague

Produces an international online daily broadcast in numerous language that include English. Also provides news. music, and information on Czech American relations.

> URL: www.radio.cz/en

KMIL-AM (1330)

Broadcasts eight hours weekly in Czech, including a polka show.

> Joe Smitherman
> Drawer 832
> Cameron, Texas 76520
> Phone: (817) 697-6633
> Fax: (254) 697-6330
> Email: kmil@nstar.net
> URL: http://www.kmil.com

WCEV-AM (1450)

"Czechoslovak Sunday Radio Hour" in Chicago is a weekly one-hour broadcast in Czech.

> Diana Migala
> 5356 West Belmont Avenue
> Chicago, Illinois 60641-4103

Phone: (773) 282-6700
Fax: (773) 282-0123
Email: wcev@wcev1450.com
URL: www.wcev1450.com

ORGANIZATIONS AND ASSOCIATIONS

American Czech Association

Founded in 1940, the American Czech Association is dedicated to the preservation of Czech heritage. Includes Sokol activities.

William Zelenka
16332 Marilyn Drive
Grenada Hills, California 91344
Phone: (818) 360-6184
Email: wzelenka@earthlink.net

American Czech Educational Center

Founded in 1966, the American Czech Educational Center provides Czech language instruction, Sokol activities, and social events in addition to celebrating Czech festivals.

Donna Ohlman
4690 Lansdowne Avenue
St. Louis, Missouri 63116
Phone: (314) 752-8168
Email: czech_hall@yahoo.com

American Sokol Organization

Founded in 1865, ASEPCO is a physical fitness organization for children and adults of all ages, with 8,500 adult members and 8,000 gymnasts. It sponsors gymnastic meets and competitions, clinics, workshops, and schools; the organization also conducts educational activities and offers lectures and films.

American Sokol Organization

9126 Ogden Avenue
Brookfield, Illinois 60402
Phone: (708) 255-5397
Email: aso@american-sokol.org
URL: www.american-sokol.org

Czech Catholic Union (CCU)

Founded in 1879, the CCU is a Catholic fraternal benefit life insurance society that makes an annual donation to the Holy Family Cancer Home, bestows awards, participates in local civic and cultural events, and provides services for children.

Mary Ann Mahoney, President
5349 Dolloff Road
Cleveland, Ohio 44127
Phone: (216) 341-0444
Fax: (216) 341-0711
Email: insurance@czechccu.org
URL: www.czechccu.org

Czech Heritage Foundation

Foundation for individuals interested in Czechoslovak heritage and culture. Purpose is to foster interest in Czechoslovak culture, heritage, language, and the collection of artifacts of Czechoslovak origin, especially in the Cedar Rapids area.

Russell Novotny, President
P.O. Box 8476
Cedar Rapids, Iowa 52408
Phone: (319) 365-0868
Email: chfwebmaster@gmail.com
URL: www.czechheritagefoundation.com

Czechoslovak Genealogical Society International (CGSI)

Founded in 1988, CGSI supports research in Czechoslovakian culture and genealogy, hosts workshops, and maintains a research library. Publishes a quarterly newsletter, *Nase rodina* and a journal titled *Rocenka*.

Mark Bigaouette
P.O. Box 16225
St. Paul, Minnesota 55116-0225
Phone: (612) 595-7799
Email: cgsi@aol.com
URL: www.cgsi.org

The Czech Heritage Society of Texas

This is a non-profit organization founded in 1982. It has fifteen established chapters throughout the state of Texas and its library and archives are located in La Grange. The organization is committed to the preservation of Texas Czech heritage; this includes genealogy, history, music, costumes, food, and language.

P.O. Box 1027
La Grange, Texas 78945
Phone: (979) 968-5230
Email: webmaster@czechhertitage.org
URL: www.czechheritage.org

MUSEUMS AND RESEARCH CENTERS

Czechoslovak Heritage Museum

Founded in 1974, the museum is home to many artifacts that focus on the culture of the Czech Republic. Exhibits include costumes, paintings, garnets, and more. The library and archives offer a wealth of historical books and documents, including genealogies.

122 West 22nd Street
Oak Brook, Illinois 60523
Email: czechoslovakmuseum@gmail.com
URL: www.czechoslovakmuseum.com

Moravian Historical Society

Hosts guided tours through its collection of art and artifacts on the history of the Moravian Church. The museum also exhibits paintings by John Valentine Haidt, as well as early musical instruments.

Megan Van Ravenswaay
214 East Center Street
Nazareth, Pennsylvania 18064
Phone: (610) 759-5070
Email: info@moravianhistoricalsociety.org
URL: www.moravianhistoricalsociety.org

National Czech and Slovak Museum and Library

Located in the restored home of a Czech immigrant, this museum preserves national costumes, as well as porcelain ethnic dolls, handwork, wood-carved items, paintings, prints, maps, and farm tools. There is also a library with reference materials and oral history videotapes.

John Dusek
David Muhlena, Library Director
1400 Inspiration Place SW
Cedar Rapids, Iowa 52404
Phone: (319) 362-8500
Email: dmuhlena@ncsml.org
URL: ncsml.org

University of Nebraska at Lincoln

The Robitschek Czech Study Program provides scholarships for students in the Czech Republic to study at the University of Nebraska. The Czech Language Program offers numerous classes in the Czech language, which are taught by native speakers.

Office of Admissions
1410 Q Street
Lincoln, Nebraska 68588-0417
Phone: (800) 742-8800
Fax: (402) 472-0670
Email: admissions@unl.edu

The Western Fraternal Life Association

Established in 1897, the Western Fraternal Life Association houses a library and archives, and sponsors educational lectures on Czech language and culture.

Charles H. Vyskocil
1900 First Avenue NE
Cedar Rapids, Iowa 52402
Phone: (319) 363-2653
Email: info@wflains.org
URL: www.wflains.org

Wilber Czech Museum

Maintains a collection of dolls, dishes, murals, pictures, laces, costumes, and replicas of early homes and businesses.

Irma Ourecky, Chairman
102 West Third Street
Wilber, Nebraska 68465
Phone: (402) 821-2183
Email: wilburczechmuseum@gmail.com

SOURCES FOR ADDITIONAL STUDY

Čapek, Thomas. *The Čechs (Bohemians) in America*. Boston and New York: Houghton Mifflin, 1920.

Bicha, Karel. *The Czechs in Oklahoma*. Oklahoma City: University of Oklahoma Press, 1980.

Chada, Joseph. *The Czechs in the United States*. Chicago: SVU Press, 1981.

Dvornik, Francis. *Czech Contributions to the Growth of the United States*. Washington, D.C., 1961.

Habenicht, Jan. *History of Czechs in America*. St. Paul, MN: Czechoslovak Genealogical Society International, 1996.

Konecny, Lawrence, and Clinton Machann. *Perilous Voyages: Czech and English Immigrants to Texas in the 1870s*. College Station: Texas A&M University Press, 2004.

Laska, Vera. *The Czechs in America, 1633-1977*. Dobbs Ferry, NY: Oceana Publications, 1978.

Sabol, John, and Lisa Alzo. *Cleveland Czechs*. Mount Pleasant, SC: Arcadia Publishing, 2009.

Saxon-Ford, Stephanie. *The Czech-Americans*. Philadelphia: Chelsea House Publishers, 1998.

Sternstein, Malynne. *Czechs of Chicagoland*. Mount Pleasant, SC: Arcadia Publishing, 2008.

Writers' Program of the Work Projects Administration in the State of Minnesota. *The Bohemian Flats*. St. Paul: Minnesota Historical Society Press, 1986.

ANNOTATED BIBLIOGRAPHY

Acuña, Rodolfo, and Guadalupe Compean. *Voices of the U.S. Latino Experience*. Westport, CT: Greenwood Press, 2008. The history of Latinos in the United States derived from letters, memoirs, speeches, articles, essays, interviews, treaties, government reports, testimony, and more.

Aguirre, Adalberto. *Racial and Ethnic Diversity in America: A Reference Handbook*. Santa Barbara, CA: ABC-CLIO, 2003. Examines, through current and historical census data, the populations and social forces that contribute to the racial and ethnic diversity of the United States.

Alba, Richard D., and Victor Nee. *Remaking the American Mainstream: Assimilation and Contemporary Immigration*. Cambridge, MA: Harvard University Press, 2003. Demonstrates the importance of assimilation in American society by looking at language, socioeconomic attachments, residential patterns, and intermarriage.

Alba, Richard D., and Mary C. Waters. *Next Generation: Immigrant Youth in a Comparative Perspective*. New York: New York University, 2011. An examination of second-generation immigrant youth in the United States and Western Europe.

American Ethnic Writers. Rev. ed. Pasadena, CA: Salem Press, 2009. Compiles and describes the works of African American, Asian American, Jewish American, Hispanic/Latino, and Native American writers.

Anderson, Wanni W., and Robert G. Lee, eds. *Displacements and Diasporas: Asians in the Americas*. New Brunswick, NJ: Rutgers University Press, 2005. An interdisciplinary look at the experiences of Asians in North and South America and how they have been shaped by the social and political dynamics of the countries in which they have settled as well as by their countries of origin.

Angell, Carole S. *Celebrations around the World: A Multicultural Handbook*. Golden, CO: Fulcrum, 1996. A month-by-month look at festivals from around the world.

Anglim, Christopher. *Encyclopedia of Religion and the Law in America*. 2nd ed. Amenia, NY: Grey House, 2009. Covers topics from prayer in schools to holiday displays on public property; includes a description of major cases.

Atwood, Craig D., et al. *Handbook of Denominations in the United States*. 13th ed. Nashville: Abingdon Press, 2010. This frequently updated handbook serves as a guide to the many denominations that make up the American religious experience.

Axtell, Roger E. *Gestures: The Do's and Taboos of Body Language around the World*. Rev. ed. New York: Wiley, 1998. Lists, illustrates, and explains the meaning of gestures from eighty-two countries around the world.

Banks, James A., ed. *Encyclopedia of Diversity in Education*. Thousand Oaks, CA: SAGE, 2012. A guide to research and statistics, case studies, best practices, and policies.

———, ed. *Handbook of Research on Multicultural Education*. 2nd ed. San Francisco: Jossey-Bass, 2004. A guide to advances in the research of multicultural education.

———. *Teaching Strategies for Ethnic Studies*. 8th ed. Boston: Pearson/Allyn & Bacon, 2009. Examines the current and emerging theory, research, and scholarship in the fields of ethnic studies and multicultural education.

Barkan, Elliott Robert, ed. *Immigrants in American History: Arrival, Adaptation, and Integration*. Santa Barbara, CA: ABC-CLIO, 2013. Covers the arrival, adaptation, and integration of immigrants into American culture from the 1500s to 2010.

Barkley, Elizabeth F. *Crossroads: The Multicultural Roots of America's Popular Music*. 2nd ed. Upper Saddle River, NJ: Pearson Prentice Hall, 2007. A comparative exploration of the music of Native Americans, European Americans, African Americans, Latino Americans, and Asian Americans.

Bayor, Ronald H., ed. *The Columbia Documentary History of Race and Ethnicity in America*. New York: Columbia University Press, 2004. Seeks to shed light on the many ways in which immigration, racial histories, and ethnic histories have shaped contemporary American society.

———, ed. *Multicultural America: An Encyclopedia of the Newest Americans*. Santa Barbara. CA: Greenwood, 2011. Profiles fifty of the largest immigrant groups in the United States.

Benson, Sonia, ed. *The Hispanic American Almanac: A Reference Work on Hispanics in the United States*. 3rd ed. Detroit: Gale, 2003. Examines the history and culture of Hispanic Americans with coverage of events, biographies, and demographic information.

Berlin, Ira. *The Making of African America: The Four Great Migrations*. New York: Viking, 2010. Interprets the history of African Americans by examining the forced migration of slavery, the relocation of slaves to interior southern states, the migrations to the north, and the more recent arrival of immigrants from African and Caribbean nations.

Berzok, Linda Murray, ed. *Storied Dishes: What Our Family Recipes Tell Us about Who We Are and Where We've Been*. Santa Barbara, CA: Praeger, 2011. An exploration of family history through recipes.

Bird, Stephanie Rose. *Light, Bright, and Damned Near White: Biracial and Triracial Culture in America*. Westport, CT: Praeger, 2009. Explores the challenges for, and psychological issues of, people with ethnically mixed ancestry.

Blank, Carla. *Rediscovering America: The Making of Multicultural America, 1900–2000*. New York: Three Rivers Press, 2003. A retelling of American history through the contributions of women, African Americans, Asian Americans, Hispanic Americans, and Native Americans, immigrants, artists, "renegades, rebels, and rogues."

Bona, Mary Jo, and Irma Maini, eds. *Multiethnic Literature and Canon Debates*. Albany: State University of New York Press, 2006. Critiques the debate over the inclusion of multiethnic literature in the American literary canon.

Boosahda, Elizabeth. *Arab-American Faces and Voices: The Origins of an Immigrant Community*. Austin: University of Texas Press, 2003. Looking at the long history of Arab Americans in the United States, this book includes personal interviews, photographs, and historical documents.

Bowler, Shaun, and Gary M. Segura. *The Future Is Ours: Minority Politics, Political Behavior, and the Multiracial Era of American Politics*. Thousand Oaks, CA: SAGE, 2012. A data-based examination of whether and how minority citizens differ from members of the white majority in political participation.

Brettell, Caroline. *Constructing Borders/Crossing Boundaries: Race, Ethnicity, and Immigration*. Lanham, MD: Lexington Books, 2008. Essays on a diverse range of immigrant populations from past to present that look at the boundaries and borders created by the social construction of race and ethnicity.

Bronner, Simon J., ed. *Encyclopedia of American Folklife*. Armonk, NY: M. E. Sharpe, 2006. Looks at the oral and written literary traditions, songs, and stories that make up a community's identity.

Brooks, Christopher Antonio, ed. *The African American Almanac*. 11th ed. Farmington Hills, MI: Gale Cengage Learning, 2011. A continually updated work from Gale's series of multicultural reference sources. Provides chronology, biography, events, and demography.

Buenker, John D., and Lorman A. Ratner, eds. *Multiculturalism in the United States: A Comparative Guide to Acculturation and Ethnicity*. Rev. ed. Westport, CT: Greenwood Press, 2005. Discusses how American culture has affected immigrants as well as how it has been shaped by them.

Cannato, Vincent J. *American Passage: The History of Ellis Island*. New York: Harper, 2009. Tells the story of Ellis Island from 1892 to 1924 using a variety of primary sources.

Carlisle, Rodney P., general ed. *Multicultural America*. 7 vols. New York: Facts On File, 2011. Presents the social history, customs, and traditions of ethnic groups throughout American history.

Carter, Susan B., ed. *Historical Statistics of the United States: Earliest Times to the Present*. 5 vols. New York: Cambridge University Press, 2006. Provides a historical perspective on statistics about the U.S. population, economy, government, and international relations.

Cesari, Jocelyne, ed. *Encyclopedia of Islam in the United States*. Westport, CT: Greenwood Press, 2007. Based on primary documents, this encyclopedia provides historical context for the current state of the practice of Islam in the United States.

Chi, Sang, and Emily Moberg Robinson, eds. *Voices of the Asian American and Pacific Islander Experience*. Santa Barbara, CA: Greenwood, 2012. Explores the experiences, views, and politics of recent Asian immigrants, emphasizing the diversity of experiences and viewpoints of individuals within the different nationalities and generations. Based on primary documents.

Ciment, James, and John Radzilowski, eds. *American Immigration: An Encyclopedia of Political, Social, and Cultural Change*. 2nd ed. 4 vols. Armonk, NY: M. E. Sharpe, 2013. American immigration from historic and contemporary perspectives. Primary documents include laws and treaties, referenda, Supreme Court cases, historical articles, and letters from 1787 to 2013.

Cohen, Selma Jeanne, ed. *International Encyclopedia of Dance*. 6 vols. New York: Oxford University Press, 2004. The definitive reference book for dance, documenting all types and styles of dance from around the world and throughout history.

Condra, Jill, ed. *The Greenwood Encyclopedia of Clothing through World History*. 3 vols. Westport, CT: Greenwood Press, 2008. Examines the history of clothing from all corners of the globe from pre-history to modern times.

Coontz, Stephanie, ed. *American Families: A Multicultural Reader*. 2nd ed. New York: Routledge, 2008. Brings together articles that look at the ethnic and racial diversity within families.

Cullum, Linda, ed. *Contemporary American Ethnic Poets: Lives, Works, Sources*. Westport, CT: Greenwood Press, 2004. Presents the lives and works of seventy-five poets.

Cordry, Harold V. *The Multicultural Dictionary of Proverbs: Over 20,000 Adages from More than 120 Languages, Nationalities and Ethnic Groups*. Jefferson, NC: McFarland, 1997. Presents 1,300 headings arranged by nationality, with a focus on European cultures.

Daniels, Roger. *Coming to America: A History of Immigration and Ethnicity in American Life*. 2nd ed. New York: Perennial, 2002. An overview of immigration to the United States from the colonial era to the beginning of the twenty-first century.

Danilov, Victor J. *Ethnic Museums and Heritage Sites in the United States*. Jefferson, NC: McFarland, 2009. A directory of all ethnic heritage sites in the United States.

Danky, James P., and Wayne A. Wiegand, eds. *Print Culture in a Diverse America*. Urbana: University of Illinois Press, 1998. Examines the multicultural world of reading and readers in the United States.

Davis, Rocío G., ed. *The Transnationalism of American Culture: Literature, Film, and Music*. New York: Routledge, 2012. A study of the border-crossing aspects of literature, film, and music.

Dinnerstein, Leonard, and David M. Reimers. *Ethnic Americans: A History of Immigration*. 5th ed. New York: Columbia University Press, 2009. Chapters examine the history of immigration to the United States chronologically, from the fifteenth century to 2008.

Dinnerstein, Leonard, Roger L. Nichols, and David M. Reimers. *Natives and Strangers: A History of Ethnic Americans*. 5th ed. New York: Oxford University Press, 2010. Examines the history of American ethnic groups and their impact on the character and social fabric of the United States.

Dodge, Abigail Johnson. *Around the World Cookbook*. New York: DK Publishing, 2008. A children's cookbook with fifty step-by-step recipes for preparing ethnic cuisine.

Ellicott, Karen, ed. *Countries of the World and Their Leaders Yearbook 2014*. 2 vols. Detroit: Gale, 2014. U.S. Department of State reports looking at all social, political, legal, economic, and environmental aspects for selected countries of the world.

Fleegler, Robert L. *Ellis Island Nation: Immigration Policy and American Identity in the Twentieth Century*. Philadelphia: University of Pennsylvania Press, 2013. Uses World War II films, records of Senate subcommittee hearings, and anti-Communist propaganda to view the evolution in the debate over immigration in the United States.

Franco, Dean J. *Ethnic American Literature: Comparing Chicano, Jewish, and African American Writing*. Charlottesville: University of Virginia Press, 2006. Provides a comparative approach to American ethnic literature.

Frazier, John W., Eugene L. Tettey-Fio, and Norah F. Henry, eds. *Race, Ethnicity, and Place in a Changing America*. 2nd ed. Albany: State University of New York Press, 2011. Looks at how race and ethnicity affects all aspects of everyday life.

Fredrickson, George M. *Diverse Nations: Explorations in the History of Racial and Ethnic Pluralism*. Boulder, CO: Paradigm Publishers, 2008. A comparative exploration of slavery and race relations in the United States, Europe, South Africa, and Brazil.

Gillota, David. *Ethnic Humor in Multiethnic America*. New Brunswick, NJ: Rutgers University Press, 2013. Investigates the role of humor in the national conversation on race and ethnicity and the response of contemporary comedians to multiculturalism.

Gilton, Donna L. *Multicultural and Ethnic Children's Literature in the United States*. Lanham, MD: Scarecrow Press, 2007. The history of and contemporary trends in U.S. multicultural children's literature.

Glenn, Evelyn Nakano. *Unequal Freedom: How Race and Gender Shaped American Citizenship and Labor*. Cambridge, MA: Harvard University Press, 2002. A comparative look at the history of inequality and specifically how labor and citizenship have been defined, enforced, and challenged in the United States.

González, Alberto, et al., eds. *Our Voices: Essays in Culture, Ethnicity, and Communication*. 5th ed. New York: Oxford University Press, 2012. Short first-person accounts that examine the varieties of intercultural communication covering discourses of gender, race, and ethnicity.

Grant-Thomas, Andrew, and Gary Orfield, eds. *Twenty-First Century Color Lines: Multiracial Change in Contemporary America*. Philadelphia: Temple University Press, 2009. The result of work initiated by the Harvard Civil Rights Project, this book provides an overview of contemporary racial and ethnic conditions in the United States.

Graves, Joseph L., Jr. *The Race Myth: Why We Pretend Race Exists in America*. New York: Dutton, 2004. Writing from a scientific perspective, Graves posits that racial distinctions are in fact social inventions, not biological truths.

Greene, Victor R. *American Immigrant Leaders, 1800–1910: Marginality and Identity*. Baltimore: Johns Hopkins University Press, 1987. The history of immigration through the lives of those who led.

Handlin, Oscar. *The Uprooted: The Epic Story of the Great Migrations That Made the American People*. 2nd ed. Philadelphia: University of Pennsylvania Press, 2002. Looks specifically at European migration to the United States during the late nineteenth and early twentieth centuries.

Hoerder, Dirk, ed. *The Immigrant Labor Press in North America, 1840s–1970s: An Annotated Bibliography*. New York: Greenwood Press, 1987. A look at the European immigrant press in the United States.

Jackson, Kenneth T., ed. *The Encyclopedia of New York City*. New Haven, CT: Yale University Press; New York: New York Historical Society, 2010. Entries on every aspect of the life and culture of the population of New York City.

Johansen, Bruce E. *Native Americans Today: A Biographical Dictionary*. Santa Barbara, CA: Greenwood Press, 2010. Biographical profiles of Native Americans from the twentieth and twenty-first centuries.

Johnson, Michael. *Encyclopedia of Native Tribes of North America*. Richmond Hill, Ontario: Firefly Books, 2007. An illustrated encyclopedia that provides information on North America's Native American populations.

Koppelman, Kent L., ed. *Perspectives on Human Differences: Selected Readings on Diversity in America*. Boston: Allyn & Bacon, 2011. An anthology of essays and short stories that explores issues of human diversity from multiple perspectives.

Kukathas, Uma, ed. *Race and Ethnicity*. Farmington Hills, MI: Greenhaven Press, 2008. Reflections on racial and ethnic identity in the United States as represented through institutional classification and the media.

Kurian, George Thomas, and Barbara A. Chernow, eds. *Datapedia of the United States: American History in Numbers*. 4th ed. Lanham, MD: Bernan Press, 2007. Based on historical statistics of the United States and the annual Statistical Abstract of the United States, Datapedia provides statistics in twenty-three areas for the years 1790–2003 with demographic projections to 2050. Updated regularly.

Lee, Erika, and Judy Young. *Angel Island: Immigrant Gateway to America*. New York: Oxford University Press, 2010. A comprehensive history of the Angel Island Immigration Station in the San Francisco Bay.

Lippy, Charles H., and Peter W. Williams, eds. *Encyclopedia of Religion in America*. Washington, DC: CQ Press, 2010. Explores origins, development, influence, and interrelations of faiths practiced in North America.

Mason, Patrick L., ed. *Encyclopedia of Race and Racism*. 2nd ed. 4 vols. Detroit: Macmillan Reference USA, 2013. A survey of the anthropological, sociological, historical, economic, and scientific theories of race and racism in the modern era.

McDonald, Jason. *American Ethnic History: Themes and Perspectives*. New Brunswick, NJ: Rutgers University Press, 2007. Looks at the reasons different ethnic groups have come to the United States, their treatment and adaptations, and the aspects that together build a sense of ethnic identity.

Min, Pyong Gap, ed. *Encyclopedia of Racism in the United States*. 3 vols. Westport, CT: Greenwood Press, 2005. Seeks to provide an understanding of U.S. minority groups and their experiences with the dominant culture.

Morgan, George G. *How to Do Everything: Genealogy*. 3rd ed. New York: McGraw-Hill, 2012. A guide to genealogical research in the twenty-first century.

Morrison, Joan, and Charlotte Fox Zabusky. *American Mosaic: The Immigrant Experience in the Words of Those Who Lived It*. Pittsburgh, PA: University of Pittsburgh Press, 1993. First-person accounts of the experiences of immigrants from Europe, Asia, the Middle East, South America, and South Africa.

Nelson, Emmanuel S., ed. *The Greenwood Encyclopedia of Multiethnic American Literature*. 5 vols. Westport, CT: Greenwood Press, 2005. Entries on authors and literature from multiethnic America.

Nettl, Bruno, et al., eds. *Garland Encyclopedia of World Music*. 10 vols. with CDs. New York: Garland, 1998–2002. A comprehensive look at music around the world by region and country. Also available online through Alexander Street Press.

Neusner, Jacob, ed. *World Religions in America: An Introduction*. 4th ed. Louisville, KY: Westminster John Knox Press, 2009. Each chapter examines the religious beliefs and practices of a separate American immigrant group.

Nimer, Mohamed. *The North American Muslim Resource Guide: Muslim Community Life in the United States and Canada*. New York: Routledge, 2002. Presents the history and contemporary status of Muslim communities in the United States. Also provides a directory of organizations, schools, centers, publications, and more.

Norton, Donna E. *Multicultural Children's Literature: Through the Eyes of Many Children*. 2nd ed. Upper Saddle River, NJ: Pearson/Merrill Prentice Hall, 2005. Highlights outstanding multicultural literature for children and young adults.

Ochoa, George, and Carter Smith. *Atlas of Hispanic-American History*. Rev. ed. New York: Facts on File, 2009. Using text, maps, and illustrations, this volume looks at the history of Hispanic American cultures.

Olson, James Stuart, and Heather Olson Beal. *The Ethnic Dimension in American History*. 4th ed. Malden, MA: Wiley-Blackwell, 2010. A survey of the role that ethnicity has played in shaping the history of the United States.

Overmyer-Velázquez, Mark. *Latino America: A State-by-State Encyclopedia*. 2 vols. Westport, CT: Greenwood Press, 2008. A chronological account of the presence and contributions of Latinos in each state and the District of Columbia from the beginning of recorded American history to the present.

Parrillo, Vincent N. *Strangers to These Shores: Race and Ethnic Relations in the United States*. 10th ed. Boston: Allyn & Bacon, 2011. A frequently updated text on racial and ethnic relations in the United States that looks at the experiences of more than fifty racial, ethnic, and religious groups.

Pinder, Sherrow O., ed. *American Multicultural Studies: Diversity of Race, Ethnicity, Gender, and Sexuality*. Thousand Oaks, CA: SAGE, 2013. Provides an interdisciplinary view of multicultural studies in the United States that addresses current and continuing issues of race, gender, ethnicity, sexuality, cultural diversity, and education.

Queen, Edward L., et al., eds. *Encyclopedia of American Religious History*. 3rd ed. 3 vols. New York: Facts On File, 2009. Covers the social and cultural histories of religious practices in the United States.

Ramsey, Paul J., ed. *The Bilingual School in the United States: A Documentary History*. Charlotte, NC: Information Age Pub., 2012. A history of bilingual education in the United States from the nineteenth century forward.

Rappoport, Leon. *Punchlines: The Case for Racial, Ethnic, and Gender Humor*. Westport, CT: Praeger, 2005. Looks at ethnic, racial, and gender humor as an instrument of prejudice and as a defense against it.

Recinos, Harold J., ed. *Wading through Many Voices: Toward a Theology of Public Conversation*. Lanham, MD: Rowman & Littlefield, 2011. Examines Christian theology as expressed by different immigrant and minority groups in the United States as well as its impact and implications for public discourse.

Reimers, David M. *Other Immigrants: The Global Origins of the American People*. New York: New York University Press, 2005. Chronicles the history of black, Hispanic, and Asian immigrants to the American continent from the fifteenth century through World War II.

Rhodes, Leara. *The Ethnic Press: Shaping the American Dream*. New York: Peter Lang, 2010. Documents the history of immigrants in America through an examination of their newspapers and their impact on American culture.

Rose, Christine, and Kay Germain Ingalls. *The Complete Idiot's Guide to Genealogy*. 3rd ed. New York: Alpha, 2012. The how-tos of exploring personal heritage through genealogical practice.

Rudnick, Lois Palken, Judith E. Smith, and Rachel Lee Rubin, eds. *American Identities: An Introductory Textbook*. Malden, MA: Blackwell, 2006. A collection of critical essays and primary documents taken from American history, literature, memoir, and popular culture that focuses on American identities of ethnicity and gender from World War II to the present.

Rumbaut, Rubén G., and Alejandro Portes, eds. *Ethnicities: Children of Immigrants in America*. Berkeley: University of California Press, 2001. Draws on the Children of Immigrants Longitudinal Study to look at second-generation immigrant youth from families of Mexican, Cuban, Nicaraguan, Filipino, Vietnamese, Haitian, Jamaican, and West Indian origin.

Sadie, Stanley. *The New Grove Dictionary of Music and Musicians*. 29 vols. New York: Grove, 2001. A 29-volume encyclopedic look at music from all time periods and all countries covering folk music and folk instruments as well as the classical tradition. Updated by Oxford Music Online.

Shay, Anthony. *Choreographing Identities: Folk Dance, Ethnicity and Festival in the United States and Canada*. Jefferson, NC: McFarland, 2006. A look at the importance of dance in the representation of cultural identity.

Sherrow, Victoria. *Encyclopedia of Hair: A Cultural History*. Westport, CT: Greenwood Press, 2006. Everything about hair across cultures and throughout time.

Shinagawa, Larry Hijime, and Michael Jang. *Atlas of American Diversity*. Walnut Creek, CA: AltaMira Press, 1998. A visual exploration through maps and charts of the social, economic, and geographic state of an ethnically diverse United States.

Shorris, Earl. *Latinos: A Biography of the People*. New York: W. W. Norton, 1992. Looks at Latino history from the time of the Spanish conquest of North and South America.

Snodgrass, Mary Ellen. *World Clothing and Fashion: An Encyclopedia of History, Culture, and Social Influence*. Armonk, NY: M. E. Sharpe, 2013. Approaches fashion from a global, multicultural, social, and economic perspective, covering prehistory to the present time.

Spickard, Paul R., ed. *Race and Immigration in the United States: New Histories*. New York: Routledge, 2012. Each essay looks at a particular aspect of immigrant experience, drawing attention to the ways the experiences differ depending on country of origin.

Statistical Abstract of the United States. Washington, DC: U.S. Gov. Print. Off., 1878–2012. The *Statistical Abstract* was compiled and published annually by the U.S. Census Bureau through 2012; beginning in 2013 it was instead published digitally by ProQuest. Provides an annual update of statistics about the characteristics and conditions of most aspects of life in the United States. For the historical perspective see *Historical Statistics of the United States: Earliest Times to the Present*, edited by Susan B. Carter.

Stave, Bruce M. Salerno, John F. Sutherland, and Aldo Salerno. *From the Old Country: An Oral History of European Migration to America*. New York: Maxwell Macmillan International, 1994. A compilation of oral histories describing the experience of migration and all aspects of the transition to life in a new country.

Strobel, Christoph. *Daily Life of the New Americans: Immigration since 1965*. Santa Barbara, CA: Greenwood, 2010. A history of twentieth- and twenty-first-century American immigrants through first-person and biographical narratives.

Stuhr, Rebecca. *Autobiographies by Americans of Color 1980–1994: An Annotated Bibliography*. Troy, NY: Whitston, 1997.

Stuhr, Rebecca, and Deborah Stuhr Iwabuchi. *Autobiographies by Americans of Color, 1995–2000: An Annotated Bibliography*. Albany, NY: Whitston, 2003. These two works together provide a comprehensive bibliography with extensive annotations for autobiographical works and oral histories.

Takaki, Ronald T. *A Different Mirror: A History of Multicultural America*. Boston: Little, Brown, 1993.

———. *Double Victory: A Multicultural History of America in World War II*. Boston: Little, Brown, 2000.

———. *Strangers from a Different Shore: A History of Asian Americans*. Boston: Little, Brown, 1989. Ronald Takaki was a pioneer in the field of ethnic studies. His books were among the very first to carefully and comprehensively explore the history and contemporary experiences of immigrants who crossed the Pacific to North America.

Thernstrom, Abigail M., and Stephan Thernstrom, eds. *Beyond the Color Line: New Perspectives on Race and Ethnicity in America*. Stanford, CA: Hoover Institution Press, Stanford University, 2002. Examines social, political, and economic changes that have taken place within ethnic America and the persistence of attitudes that create conditions of inequality.

Thernstrom, Stephan, ed. *Harvard Encyclopedia of American Ethnic Groups*. Cambridge, MA: Belknap Press of Harvard University, 1980. Although this work has never been updated, it continues to serve as a foundational text on the history and makeup of the population of the United States.

Thompson, William N. *Native American Issues: A Reference Handbook*. 2nd ed. Santa Barbara, CA: ABC-CLIO, 2005. An assessment of the problems faced by Native Americans, both historically and in the twenty-first century.

Ueda, Reed, ed. *A Companion to American Immigration*. Malden, MA: Blackwell, 2006. Scholarly essays on a range of topics, including law, health, politics, prejudice and racism, housing, education, labor, internationalism, and transnationalism.

Upton, Dell, ed. *America's Architectural Roots: Ethnic Groups That Built America*. New York: Preservation Press, 1986. An illustrated overview of the ethnic derivations of American architecture.

U.S. Census Bureau. *2000 Census of Population and Housing: Population and Housing Unit Counts* and *Summary Social, Economic, and Housing Characteristics*. Washington, DC: U.S. Dept. of Commerce, Economics, and Statistics Administration, U.S. Census Bureau, 2003. Two separate publications from the United States decennial census providing demographic and economic statistics on all populations within the United States.

Verbrugge, Allen, ed. *Muslims in America*. Detroit: Greenhaven Press, 2005. Looks at different aspects of life for Muslims in the United States, including gender, family, college life, politics, and the repercussions of 9/11, with narratives of personal experiences.

Vigdor, Jacob L. *From Immigrants to Americans: The Rise and Fall of Fitting In*. Lanham, MD: Rowman & Littlefield, 2009. A view of the challenges of belonging in the United States, with chapters on economics, linguistics, citizenship, neighborhoods, and family.

Walch, Timothy, ed. *Immigrant America: European Ethnicity in the United States*. New York: Garland, 1994. Examines the experiences of European immigrants to specific regions of the United States.

Waldman, Carl. *Encyclopedia of Native American Tribes*. 3rd ed. New York: Facts On File, 2006. Covers more than 200 American Indian tribes of North America.

Walkowitz, Rebecca L., ed. *Immigrant Fictions: Contemporary Literature in an Age of Globalization*. Madison: University of Wisconsin Press, 2006. A look at contemporary literature by immigrant authors from China, Eastern Europe, and other countries. Includes interviews.

Webb, Lois Sinaiko, and Lindsay Grace Roten. *The Multicultural Cookbook for Students*. Rev. ed. Santa Barbara, CA: Greenwood Press, 2009. Recipes are arranged by region and country and are preceded by an account of the geography, history, and culinary traditions of their country of origin.

Weil, François. *Family Trees: A History of Genealogy in America*. Cambridge, MA: Harvard University Press, 2013. A history of the practice of genealogy from its early methodology to the use of the database Ancestry.com and DNA testing; from a preoccupation with social status to an acceptance and celebration of diverse ethnic heritage.

Welsch, Janice R., and J. Q. Adams. *Multicultural Films: A Reference Guide*. Westport, CT: Greenwood Press, 2005. Provides brief synopses and critiques of motion pictures that explore race and ethnicity.

Wertsman, Vladimir. *What's Cooking in Multicultural America: An Annotated Bibliographic Guide to Over Four Hundred Ethnic Cuisines*. Lanham, MD: Scarecrow Press, 1996. An annotated bibliography to cookbooks, covering the cuisines of more than four hundred ethnic groups from all continents.

Wills, Chuck. *Destination America*. New York: DK Pub., 2005. Through personal accounts, letters, diaries, photographs, statistics, maps, and charts, examines the reasons immigrants leave home to travel to the United States and the conditions of their lives once they arrive.

York, Sherry. *Ethnic Book Awards: A Directory of Multicultural Literature for Young Readers*. Worthington, OH: Linworth, 2005. Provides an alphabetical listing of titles winning various book awards, including the Coretta Scott King, Carter G. Woodson, and Tomás Rivera Mexican American Children's book awards.

PERIODICALS

African American Review (1992–). Terre Haute: Dept. of English, Indiana State University. Print and online. Continues *Black American Literature Forum* (1976–1991). History and criticism of African American literature.

Amerasia Journal (1971–). Los Angeles: University of California, Los Angeles; and Yale Asian American Students Association. Print and Online. An interdisciplinary journal studying all aspects of Asian American society, jointly published by the UCLA Asian American Studies Center and the Yale Asian American Students Association.

Callaloo (1976–). Baltimore, MD: Johns Hopkins University Press. Print and Online. An African diaspora literary journal founded at Southern University in Baton Rouge, Louisiana, and now sponsored by Texas A&M University and published by Johns Hopkins University Press.

Ethnic NewsWatch (1998–). ProQuest Information and Learning. Online. Newspaper articles from the ethnic American presses. Dates of coverage depend on arrangements with each particular newspaper. Searchable via keywords and broad ethnic group.

Ethnic Studies Review: The Journal of the National Association for Ethnic Studies (1996–). Tempe, AZ: National Association for Ethnic Studies. Print and Online. A multidisciplinary international journal devoted to the study of ethnicity, ethnic groups and their cultures, and intergroup relations. Preceded by *Explorations in Ethnic Studies*.

Hispanic American Historical Review (HAHR) (1918–). Durham, NC: Duke University Press. Print and Online. Covers Latin American history and culture.

International Migration Review: IMR (1966–). New York: Center for Migration Studies. Print and Online. A quarterly interdisciplinary, peer-reviewed journal created to encourage and facilitate the study of all aspects of international migration.

Journal of American Ethnic History (1981–). Champaign: University of Illinois Press. Print and Online. Addresses various aspects of American immigration and ethnic history, including history of emigration, ethnic and racial groups, Native Americans, immigration policies, and the processes of acculturation.

Journal of Intercultural Studies (1980–). Melbourne: River Seine Publications. Print and Online. Covers cultural studies, sociology, gender studies, political science, cultural geography, urban studies, race, and ethnic studies.

MELUS: Society for the Study of the Multi-Ethnic Literature of the United States (1974–). Storrs: University of Connecticut, Dept. of English. Provides interviews and reviews that explore and bring light to the multiethnic character of American literature.

Multicultural Education (1993–). San Francisco: Caddo Gap Press. An independent quarterly magazine featuring research on promising pedagogical practices in art, music, and literature.

Rebecca Stuhr